The Complete Encyclopedia
of
Television Programs

The Complete Encyclopedia
of
Television Programs
1947-1979

Vincent Terrace

South Brunswick and New York:
A. S. Barnes and Company
London: Thomas Yoseloff Ltd

FIRST PAPERBACK EDITION 1980

New material © 1979 by A.S. Barnes and Co., Inc.
© 1976 by A. S. Barnes and Co., Inc.

A. S. Barnes and Co., Inc.
Cranbury, New Jersey 08512

Thomas Yoseloff Ltd
Magdalen House
136-148 Tooley Street
London SE1 2TT, England

Library of Congress Cataloging in Publication Data

Terrace, Vincent, 1948-
    The complete encyclopedia of television programs.

    Includes index.
    1. Television programs—United States—Catalogs.
I.   Title
PN1992.3.U5146   1978   791.45'7   77-89651
ISBN 0-498-02488-1 (pbk)

For my parents

Printed in the United States of America

Preface

This revised edition of *The Complete Encyclopedia of Television Programs*, the total result of five years work, is just that, complete—every known entertainment program, no matter how obscure, from 1947 to 1979, has been included. There are now 221 photographs and almost 3,500 network and syndicated programs: adventure, animated cartoon, anthology, children's, comedy, crime, documentary, drama, educational (with entertainment value), game, human interest, mystery, pilot film series, science fiction, serial, sequencial special series, spy drama, talk-interview-discussion, TV movie series, variety, and western. Listings contain not only U.S. programs, but those imported for use by American TV stations as well.

The alphabetically arranged entries provide story line information, cast lists (character and performer), announcers, technical credits (music, producer, director, creator, choreographer), network or syndicated information, running dates, length of broadcast, sponsors (from 1947 to approximately 1954 when one sponsor handled an entire program), trivial information (such as street addresses and names of pets), program openings (those immortal words spoken by an announcer), and the number of first run episodes produced for a series. Also, in addition to the new photographs and information, the inclusion of an index now makes it easier to find the information you are seeking.

The Complete Encyclopedia of Television Programs is the complete world of television between covers—it's the only reference work that covers the medium's thirty-year entertainment history in depth. It's your personal, nostalgic guide to the almost 3,500 programs that evolved from and shaped more than a quarter of a century of television broadcasting.

Acknowledgments

Individuals:
Bob Elliott, Ray Goulding, Albert Stangler, Mary Stangler, Bart Polin, Tim Faracy, Phil Foley, James Robert Parish, Paula Patyk, Stu Grossman, Roy Bright, Alvin Marill, Jim Douglass, Keno Don Rosa, Kevin Schluter, Joel Tator, Stephen L. Eberly.

Special thanks to Robert J. Reed, Paul Perry, and David Strauss.

Organizations:
I.T.C. (Independent Television Corporation; and ATV Company); especially Arnold Friedman.
Hanna-Barbera Productions; especially John Michaeli.
Screen Gems (Columbia Pictures Television); especially Jerome Gottlieb.
Walt Disney Productions; especially, Rose Mussi, and Tom A. Jones.
A.S.C.A.P.; especially Lenore Terry.
The Television Information Office; especially Leslie Slocum.
B.M.I.; Hal Seeger Productions; Ken Snyder Enterprises; The New York Public Library at Lincoln Center; Emil Asher, Inc.; ABC-TV.

Photographs:
Independent Television Corporation: "The Adventurer"; "The Champions"; "Department S"; "The Julie Andrews Hour"; "My Partner the Ghost"; "The Persuaders"; "The Protectors"; "The Saint"; "Shirley's World"; "Thriller"; "U.F.O."
Hanna-Barbera Productions: "The Banana Splits Adventure Hour"; "The Flintstones"; "Help, It's the Hair Bear Bunch"; "Huckleberry Hound"; "The Jetsons"; "Moby Dick"; "Quick Draw McGraw"; "Samson and Goliath"; "Shazzan"; "Scooby-Doo, Where Are You?"; "Top Cat"; "Yogi Bear."
Screen Gems: "Bewitched"; "Camp Runamuck"; "Casey Jones"; "Circus Boy"; "The Donna Reed Show"; "The George Burns & Gracie Allen Show"; "Gidget"; "The Farmer's Daughter"; "Father Knows Best"; "Hazel"; "I Dream of Jeannie"; "The Interns"; "Love on a Rooftop"; "Mr. Deeds Goes to Town"; "The Monkees"; "The Partridge Family"; "Route 66"; "The Second Hundred Years"; "Tallahassee 7000"; "The Three Stooges"; "Tightrope"; "The Ugliest Girl in Town"; "The Wackiest Ship in the Army"; "Wild Bill Hickok"; "The Young Rebels."
Walt Disney Productions: "Davy Crockett"; "The Mickey Mouse Club"; "The Nine Lives Of Elfego Baca"; "The Swamp Fox"; "Texas John Slaughter"; "Zorro."
Joe Franklin: "The Joe Franklin Show."
Others: *Movie Star News;* The Memory Shop.

Author's Notes

Networks:

Domestic:

ABC: The American Broadcasting Company.
CBS: The Columbia Broadcasting System.
NBC: The National Broadcasting Company.
DuMont: The DuMont Network; defunct.
NET: National Educational Television.
PBS: The Public Broadcasting Service.

Foreign:

The B.B.C.: The British Broadcasting Corporation.
A.B.C.: Associated British Corporation.
C.B.C.: The Canadian Broadcasting Corporation.

Program exclusions: Religious, sport, news, and specials (excluding those broadcast as a series).
Syndicated. This is a term that indicates programs that are sold or rented to local stations. A network program is broadcast by a key station and picked up by affiliated member stations across the country on a specific day and time. A syndicated program is broadcast by a local station ac-cording to its particular needs and is seen only in its coverage area. There are two main types of syndication.

Type One: First Run Syndication. This indicates programs that are made specifically for sale to any station that wants to buy it. Because these programs do not appear on a network, a station will not appear in its write-up. These types of programs are indicated as follows (for example):

DUSTY'S TRAIL—30 minutes—Syndicated 1973.
MY PARTNER THE GHOST—60 minutes—Syndicated 1974.

Type Two: Off-Network Syndication. After programs have completed their network runs, some are placed into syndication—sold or rented to any station that wants to buy the reruns for airing at any time. These types of programs are listed as follows (for example):

THE DEPUTY—30 minutes—NBC—September 12, 1959 - September 16, 1961. Syndicated.

THE FLINTSTONES—30 minutes—ABC—September 30, 1960 - September 2, 1966. Syndicated.

When the term *syndicated* appears after a network program it indicates that these series have been placed into syndication.

Dates. Dates are based on what information was available. All first-run syndicated programs are listed by their first year of distribution only. It would be impossible to provide years of resyndication, because programs of this type are constantly being sold over and over again.

Length or Time (pertaining to programs under thirty-minutes duration). Programs in this category are cartoon series. The length listed for each is the original produced length. In cases where programs are only four or six minutes per episode, stations are permitted to run these back to back to fill fifteen-minute or half-hour time periods.

a

THE ABBOTT AND COSTELLO SHOW

Comedy. Background: Hollywood, California. The misadventures of comedians Bud Abbott and Lou Costello. Stories relate their attempts to acquire work and relieve monetary burdens.

The Abbott and Costello Show. Bud Abbott (top), and Lou Costello.

CAST

Bud Abbott	Himself
Lou Costello	Himself
Sidney Fields, their landlord, the owner of the Fields Rooming House	Himself
Hillary Brooke, Lou's girlfriend	Herself
Mike Kelly, the not-so-bright police officer	Gordon Jones
Stinky, Lou's friend	Joe Besser
Mr. Botchagalup, the entrepeneur	Joe Kirk
Mrs. Bronson, a tenant	Renie Riano
	Sarah Haden
Mrs. Crumcake, a neighbor	Alvia Allman
Lieutenant Smith, Mike's superior	Roy Walker
The unnamed tall, thin man who faints	Robert Cherry
Bingo the Chimp, Lou's pet chimpanzee	Himself

Stock performers: Joan Shawlee, Veda Ann Borg, Iris Adrian, Joe Sawyer, Gloria Henry, Joyce Compton, Bobby Barbar, George Chandler, Lucien Littlefield.

Music: Raoul Kraushaar.

Executive Producer: Pat Costello.

Producer: Alex Gottlieb, Jean Yarbrough.

Director: Jean Yarbrough.

Address of the Fields Rooming House: 214 Brookline Avenue.

THE ABBOTT AND COSTELLO SHOW—30 minutes—CBS—1952 1954. Syndicated. 52 episodes.

Animated Version:

THE ABBOTT AND COSTELLO SHOW—05 minutes—Syndicated 1966. A Hanna-Barbera production. 156 episodes.

Characters' Voices

Bud Abbott	Himself
Lou Costello	Stan Irwin

Music: Hoyt Curtin.

ABC ALBUM

Anthology. Adaptations of works by noted authors.

Host: Donald Cook.

Included.

Justice. The story of a young, impoverished wife who seeks help from the Legal Aid Society when she believes her husband is being blackmailed.

CAST
Lee Grant, Paul Douglas.

Hogan's Daughter. The story of an office girl who suddenly sees her slow, unimaginative boyfriend in a new light when she discovers lipstick on his collar.

CAST
Sheila Bond, Joshua Shelley.

Jamie. The story of the relationship between a lonely boy and an old man. The pilot film for the series of the same title.

CAST
Brandon DeWilde, Ernest Truex.

Mr. Glencannon Takes All. The story of Colin Glencannon and his attempts to win the trade of a whiskey manufacturer for his shipping company.

CAST
Robert Newton, Melville Cooper, Myron McCormick.

ABC ALBUM—30 minutes—ABC—April 12, 1953 - July 5, 1953. Also known as: "Plymouth Playhouse."

THE ABC COMEDY HOUR

See title: "The Kopycats."

THE ABC AFTERNOON PLAYBREAK

Anthology. Dramatic presentations.

Included:

Alone with Terror. The story of Susan Maroni, a police lieutenant's widow, who attempts to prove that her husband was not on the take at the time of his apparent suicide.

CAST
Susan Maroni: Juliet Mills; Marian Webb: Virginia Vincent; Leonard Walters: Colby Chester.

A Mask of Love. A biographer's ardent search for a deceased novelist's personal papers — a treasure now jealousy guarded by his last mistress.

CAST
Tina Bordereau: Barbara Barrie; John Connors: Harris Yulin; Juliana Bordereau: Cathleen Nesbitt; Mary Prest: Geraldine Brooks.

Last Bride of Salem. A young mother struggles to prevent demonic forces from possessing her husband and daughter.

CAST
Jennifer Clifton: Lois Nettleton; Matt Clifton: Bradford Dillman; Kelly Clifton: Joni Bick; Sebastian Mayhew: Paul Harding.

THE ABC AFTERNOON PLAYBREAK—90 minutes—ABC—October 30, 1973 - May 20, 1976. Broadcast monthly.

THE ABC AFTERSCHOOL SPECIAL

Anthology. Programs relating various aspects of the world to children.

Included:

My Dad Lives in a Downtown Hotel. The story centers on a young boy as he struggles to understand and accept his parents' separation.

CAST
Joe Grant: Beau Bridges; June Grant: Margaret Frye; Joey Grant: Ike Eisenmann.

The Runaways. The story of two runaways, a teenage girl and a street-smart boy, and their struggle for survival.

CAST
Cindy Britton: Belinda Balaski; Francis: Claudio Martinez; Louis Britton: Patricia Blair; John Turner: Anthony Eisley.

Alexander. The story of a retired clown and his undying love for children.

CAST
Alexander: Red Buttons; Sue: Jodie Foster; Raymond: Robbie Rist; Tom: Kerry MacLane.

Cyrano. An animated adaptation of Edmond Rostand's romantic tragedy. The story of soldier-poet, Cyrano de Bergerac.
Voices: Cyrano: Jose Ferrer; Roxanne: Joan Van Ark; Rogueneau: Kurt Kaszner.

THE ABC AFTERSCHOOL SPECIAL—60 minutes—ABC—Premiered: October 4, 1972. Broadcast on the first Wednesday of each month.

THE ABC MONDAY NIGHT COMEDY SPECIAL

Pilot Films. Proposed comedy series for the 1977-78 season.

Included:

Bumpers. Background: Detroit, Michigan. The would-be series that was to depict the life of a car assembly-line worker, showed, in the only filmed episode, his attempts to earn $600 to help put his wife through dental school.

CAST
David: Richard Masur; Roz: Stephanie Faracy; Murphy: Jack Riley.
Producer: David Davis, Charlotte Brown.
Director: James Burrows.
Music: The Brecker Brothers.

Great Day. The misadventures of a group of skid-row bums living at an inner-city mission in Los Angeles.

CAST
Peavy: Al Molinaro; Boomer: Guy Marks; Doc: Dub Taylor; Billy: Billy Barty.
Producer: Aaron Ruben.
Director: Peter Baldwin.

Stick Around. Set in the year 2055, the story follows the misadventures of a Space Age family.

CAST
Andy the robot: Andy Kaufman; Elaine Keefer: Nancy New; Vance Keefer: Fred McCarren; Backus: Cliff Norton.
Producer: Fred Freeman, Lawrence Cohen.
Director: Bill Hobin.

THE ABC MONDAY NIGHT COMEDY SPECIAL—30 minutes—ABC—Premiered: May 16, 1977.

THE ABC MONDAY NIGHT SPECIAL

Specials. Entertainment and news presentations.

Included:

Hollywood: The Dream Factory. The story of filmmaking featuring clips from MGM movies.
Narrator: Dick Cavett

The Robinson Crusoe Ice Spectacle. A musical variety hour set on ice.
Starring: Reg Park, Lorna Brown.

The Undersea World of Jacques Cousteau: The Forgotten Mermaids.
Narrator: Jacques Cousteau, Rod Serling.

In Search of the Lost World. An expedition's search for the artifacts and remnants of early man.
Narrator: E.G. Marshall.

THE ABC MONDAY NIGHT SPECIAL—60 minutes—ABC—January 10, 1972 - August 14, 1972.

THE ABC FRIDAY NIGHT MOVIE

Theatrical and made-for-television films. Listed are examples of the films produced especially for television. See "ABC Movies" for the additional network film series.

The New, Original Wonder Woman. The 1975 pilot film for the series. The story follows the adventures of the immortal super woman as she helps Steve Trevor foil a German plot to destroy a new American bomb site.

CAST
Wonder Woman: Lynda Carter; Steve Trevor: Lyle Waggoner; Queen Mother: Cloris Leachman; Marcia: Stella Stevens.

Hey, I'm Alive. A 1975 TV movie that re-creates the true story of two airplane crash victims who survived forty-nine days of winter in the Yukon before they were rescued.

CAST
Ralph Flores: Edward Asner; Helen Klaben: Sally Struthers.

Hustling (1975). The world of the prostitute—from street corners and bars to police vans and jail cells—as seen through the eyes of reporter Kate Morrison.

CAST
Kate Morrison: Lee Remick; Wanda: Jill Clayburgh; Dee Dee: Melanie Mayrun; Orin: Monte Markham.

THE ABC FRIDAY NIGHT MOVIE—90 minutes to 2 hours—ABC—Premiered: July 25, 1975.

THE ABC MOVIE OF THE WEEK
THE ABC TUESDAY MOVIE OF THE WEEK

Movies. Feature films produced especially for television.

Included:

Playmates. The story of two divorced men who make secret plays for each other's ex-wives.

CAST
Patti Holvey: Connie Stevens; Marshall Burnett: Alan Alda; Lois Burnett: Barbara Feldon; Kermit Holvey: Doug McClure.

Divorce His/Divorce Hers. The incidents, separate interests, and marital indifferences that destroy the marriage of a sophisticated couple.

CAST
Jane Reynolds: Elizabeth Taylor; Martin Reynolds: Richard Burton; Diane Proctor: Carrie Nye; Donald Trenton: Barry Foster.

The Sex Symbol. The rise and fall of Kelly Williams, a glamorous but neurotic Hollywood film star.

CAST
Kelly Williams: Connie Stevens; Agatha Murphy: Shelley Winters; Manny Foxe: Jack Carter; Grant O'Neal: Don Murray.

Two on a Bench. The efforts of a federal investigator to discover which of two people—a beautiful but far-out girl, or a handsome but square young man—is working for a spy.

CAST
Marcy Kramer: Patty Duke; Preston Albright: Ted Bessell; Brubaker: Andrew Duggan.

The Night Stalker. Background: Las Vegas. A newspaper reporter attempts to prove that the murders of several young women were committed by a vampire. Pilot film for the series "The Night Stalker."

CAST
Carl Kolchak: Darren McGavin; Gail Foster: Carol Lynley; Vincenzo: Simon Oakland; Vampire: Barry Atwater.

THE ABC MOVIE OF THE WEEK— 90 minutes—ABC—September 23, 1969 - September 2, 1975. Later titled: "The ABC Tuesday Movie of the Week."

THE ABC MOVIE OF THE WEEKEND
THE ABC WEDNESDAY MOVIE OF THE WEEK

Movies. Feature films produced especially for television.

Included:

If Tomorrow Comes. Background: California during World War Two. The tender story of the love between an American girl and a Japanese-American boy—a love overshadowed by the fear and hatreds of war.

CAST
Eileen Phillips: Patty Duke; David: Frank Liu; Frank Phillips: James Whitmore; Miss Cramer: Anne Baxter.

Every Man Needs One. The complications that ensue when a male chauvinist is forced to hire a beautiful militant women's liberationist.

CAST
Beth: Connie Stevens; David: Ken Berry; Nancy: Carol Wayne; Wally: Henry Gibson; Louise: Louise Sorel.

The Daughters of Joshua Cade. A fur trapper attempts to win a homesteading claim by recruiting three shady women to pose as his daughters.

CAST
Joshua Cade: Buddy Ebsen; Charity: Karen Valentine; Ada: Sandra Dee; Mae: Leslie Warren; Bitterfoot: Jack Elam.

Family Flight. The story of four people and their struggle for survival after their plane crash lands in the remote regions of Baja California.

CAST
Jason: Rod Taylor; Florence: Dina Merrill; Carol: Janet Margolin; David: Kristopher Tabori.

THE ABC MOVIE OF THE WEEK-END—90 minutes—ABC—September 18, 1971 - May 27, 1972. Returned, September 13, 1972 to September 3, 1975 as: "The ABC Wednesday Movie of the Week."

ABC MOVIES

Movies. Theatrical features.

Titles:

THE ABC SUNDAY NIGHT MOVIE —2 hours—ABC—Premiered: September 20, 1963.

THE ABC MONDAY NIGHT MOVIE —2 hours—ABC—Premiered: January 1970. (The mid-season replacement for "ABC Monday Night Football"; Movies air each season from January through September.)

THE ABC WEDNESDAY NIGHT MOVIE—2 hours—ABC—1968 - 1969.

THE ABC SATURDAY SUMMER MOVIE—2 hours—ABC—June 3, 1972 - August 26, 1972.

THE ABC SHORT STORY SPECIAL

Anthology. Adaptations of well-known short stories. Broadcast monthly.

Music: Ray Ellis.

Executive Producer: Allen Ducovny.

Producer: William Beaudine, Jr.

Director: Hollingsworth Morse, Arthur H. Nadel, Ezra Stone.

Included:

Valentine's Second Chance. The story of a reformed safecracker who risks exposing his former criminal past when he attempts to rescue a boy who's trapped in a locked bank vault.

CAST
Jimmy Valentine: Ken Berry; Ben Price: Greg Morris; Annabel Randall: Elizabeth Baur; Joe Randall: Sean Marshall.

The Haunted Trailer. The story concerns a college girl and her attempts, after purchasing a mobile home that is haunted by four elderly male ghosts seeking peace and quiet, to rid herself of them by finding them a house to haunt.

CAST
Sharon Adams: Lauren Tewes; Mickey Adams: Monie Ellis; Clifford Tredwell: Murray Matheson.

My Dear Uncle Sherlock. The story revolves around a child's efforts to apprehend the thief who stole a neighbor's dog.

CAST
Joey Trimble: Robbie Rist; Uncle George: Royal Dano; Esther Trimble: Inga Swenson; Hector Trimble: John Carter.

THE ABC SHORT STORY SPECIAL—30 minutes—ABC—Premiered: January 29, 1977.

ABC STAGE '67

Anthology. Original productions, both comedic and dramatic.

Included:

ABC Stage '67. Marilyn Monroe, the subject of the presentation, "The Legend of Marilyn Monroe."

The Legend of Marilyn Monroe. A documentary tracing the life of actress Marilyn Monroe from her childhood sorrows to her adult heartaches and death.

Narrator: John Houston.

The Confession. A detective attempts to discover the truth behind a girl's reported suicide.

CAST
Lt. Hammond: Arthur Kennedy; Carl: Brandon de Wilde; Bonnie: Katherine Houghton.

Olympus 7-000. Background: A New England College. The story of football coach Todd Bronson and his attempts to organize a professional team from a group of fumbling recruits.

CAST
Todd Bronson: Larry Blyden; Hermes: Donald O'Connor; Mary: Phyllis Newman; Dean Severance: Fred Clark; Featured: The New York Jets.
Music: Richard Adler.

On The Flip Side. The story of a young singer, Carlos O'Connor, and the effect on his life when he is saved from obscurity by a quartet of spirits, the Celestials.

CAST
Carlos: Rick Nelson; Angie: Joanie Sommers.

Music: Burt Bacharach.
Lyrics: Hal David.
Orchestra: Peter Matz.

ABC STAGE '67–60 minutes–ABC–September 14, 1966 - May 11, 1967. 28 programs.

THE ABC SUSPENSE MOVIE

Movies. Suspense features produced especially for television.

Included:
Runaway. The story centers on an engineer's desperate attempts to halt a brakeless train that is cascading down a mountain.

CAST
Holly Gibson: Ben Johnson; Ellen Staffo: Vera Miles; Nick Staffo: Ed Nelson; Carol Lerner: Darleen Carr.

The Alpha Caper. The planning and execution of a thirty million-dollar gold heist from six armored cars.

CAST
Mark Forbes: Henry Fonda; Mitch: Leonard Nimoy; Tudor: Larry Hagman; Hilda: Elena Verdugo.

Double Indemnity. The conspiracy of a woman and an insurance man to kill her husband and collect on his policy.

CAST
Walter Neff: Richard Crenna; Phyllis Dietrickson: Samantha Eggar; Barton Keyes: Lee J. Cobb; Lola Dietrickson: Kathleen Cody.

Live Again, Die Again. The story of a woman who is brought back to life after being frozen for thirty-four years.

CAST
Caroline: Donna Mills; Susie: Geraldine Page; Thomas Carmichael: Walter Pidgeon; Marcia: Vera Miles.

THE ABC SUSPENSE MOVIE–90 minutes–ABC–September 29, 1973 - August 31, 1974.

THE ABC TUESDAY NIGHT PILOT FILM

Pilot Films. Proposed comedy series for the 1976-1977 season.

Included:
Flatbush/Avenue J. The episode, set against the background of Brooklyn, New York, focuses on the misadventures of newlyweds Stanley and Frannie Rosello.

CAST
Stanley Rosello: Paul Sylvan; Frannie Rosello: Brooke Adams; Annie: Jamie Donnelly.
Music: Paul Jabara.
Executive Producer-Director: Martin Davidson.
Producer: Lee Miller.

Charo and the Sergeant. The story of a U.S. Marine Sergeant plagued by the antics of his beautiful but scatterbrained wife, Charo, a Spanish entertainer.

CAST
Charo: Charo Cugat; Her husband: Tom Lester; The Captain: Dick Van Patten.
Executive Producer: Aaron Ruben, John Rich.
Director: John Rich.

Rear Guard. Era: World War II. The antics of an American civil defense volunteer group.

CAST
Raskin: Lou Jacobi; Rosatti: Cliff Norton; Wayne: Eddie Foy, Jr.; Crawford: John McCook.

THE ABC TUESDAY NIGHT PILOT FILM–2 hours (4 half-hour pilots per program)–ABC–August 10, 1976 - August 24, 1976.

THE ABC WEEKEND SPECIAL

Anthology. Dramatizations geared to children. Includes first-run stories and repeats from "The ABC Afterschool Special" and "ABC Short Stories."

Included:

It Must Be Love 'Cause I Feel So Dumb. The story of Eric, a shy, thirteen-year-old boy, and his fruitless attempts to impress Lisa–the girl on whom he has a puppy love crush.

CAST
Eric: Alfred Lutter; Lisa: Vicki Dawson.

Trouble River. Set in the early days of the Pacific Northwest, the story follows the adventures of a teenager as he rafts his grandmother down a raging river to escape renegades.

CAST

Dewey: Michael LeClair; Grandmother: Nora Denney.

The Ransom of Red Chief. The story of two scalawags who kidnap a financier's son in an attempt to make a fast buck. The tables are turned, however, when they discover the boy, who calls himself Red Chief, is a little terror—and have to pay his parents to take him back.

CAST

Sam: Jack Elam; Billy: Strother Martin; Red Chief: Patrick J. Petersen.

THE ABC WEEKEND SPECIAL—30 minutes—ABC—Premiered: September 10, 1977. Broadcast on Saturday afternoons at 12 p.m., EST. Also known as "The Out-of-School Special."

ABC WIDE WORLD OF ENTERTAINMENT

Variety. Various entertainment programs occupying the ABC weeknight 11:30 P.M.-1:00 A.M. (E.S.T) time period.

Announcer: Fred Foy.

Included:
VARIETY:
The Dick Cavett Show (see title "Dick Cavett"). Aired one week each month.

Jack Paar Tonight (see title "Jack Parr"). Aired one week each month.

In Concert. Rock Music. Guests performing and hosting. Aired Friday evenings.

MYSTERY-SUSPENSE:
The Screaming Skull. The story of a woman who returns from the dead to avenge her death.

CAST

David McCallum, Carrie Nye.

Lady Killer. A suspense drama that details a man's carefully laid plot to murder his young wife.

CAST

The man: Robert Powell; his wife: Barbara Feldon; Toni: Linda Thorson.

This Child Is Mine. The custody battle between a child's natural and foster parents.

CAST

Elizabeth Thatcher: Rosemary Prinz; Shelley Carr: Robin Strasser; Judge: Marjorie Lord.

COMEDY:
Madhouse 90. Topical sketches performed by a cast of regulars:

CAST

J.J. Barry, Michael Bell, Tom Denver, Kay Dingle, Danny Flanigan.

Comedy News. A satirization of network news broadcasting.

CAST

Robert Klein, Stephanie Edwards, Mort Sahl, Dick Gregory, Bob and Ray, Kenneth Mars, Marian Mercer, Fannie Flagg.

Honeymoon Suite. Background: California, Room 300 of the plush Honeymoon suite of the Beverly Hills Hotel. Vignettes depicting brief incidents in the lives of newlywed couples.

CAST

Maggie, the housekeeper: Rose Marie; Charlie, the bellboy: Morey Amsterdam (also played by Henry Gibson); Duncan, the hotel manager: Richard Deacon.
Music: Jack Elliott, Allyn Ferguson.

ABC WIDE WORLD OF ENTERTAINMENT—90 minutes—ABC—January 8, 1973 - January 10, 1976.

ABE BURROWS ALMANAC

Satire.

Host: Abe Burrows.
Orchestra: Milton DeLugg.
Producer: Abe Burrows, Alan Dinehart.

ABE BURROWS ALMANAC—30 minutes—CBS 1950.

ABOUT FACES

Game. Competing: Specially selected studio audience members. The contestants are placed opposite each other and presented with clues concerning incidents in their past lives. The player first to correctly associate his relationship with the person opposite him, is the winner and receives a merchandise prize.

At home participation segment: "Place the Face." Viewers, chosen through a post card drawing, are telephoned and asked to identify the silhouette of a famous celebrity. If able, a merchandise prize is awarded.

Host: Ben Alexander.
Producer: Joe Landis.

ABOUT FACES—30 minutes—ABC—January 4, 1960 - June 30, 1961.

ACAPULCO

Adventure. Background: Acapulco. Dissatisfied with life in the States, Patrick Malone and Gregg Miles, Korean War veterans, retreat to Southern Mexico. Adopting the lifestyle of a beachcomber, they begin a search for an idyllic existence. Stories relate their experiences as they encounter and assist people in distress.

CAST

Patrick Malone	Ralph Taeger
Gregg Miles	James Coburn
Chloe, a nightclub hostess	Allison Hayes
Bobby Troup, the club owner	Himself
Mr. Carver, a retired criminal lawyer	Telly Savalas

Music: Bobby Troup.

ACAPULCO—30 minutes—NBC—February 27, 1961 - April 24, 1961. 8 episodes.

ACCIDENTAL FAMILY

Comedy. Jerry Webster, widower and Las Vegas nightclub entertainer, is awarded custody of his eight-year-old son, Sandy, providing that the boy not live in Vegas. Jerry, who owns a farm in the San Fernando Valley, relocates and encounters a problem when he finds he is unable to evict his tenants: Susannah Kramer, a young divorcee; her daughter, Tracy; and her uncle, Ben McGrath, an ex-vaudevillian. The situation is resolved by a decision to share the house — Jerry will reside there on weekends, and Susannah will care for Sandy and not pay rent.

The story of two mischievous children and the inevitable problems that befall an "Accidental Family."

CAST

Jerry Webster	Jerry Van Dyke
Susannah Kramer	Lois Nettleton
Sandy Webster	Teddy Quinn
Tracy Kramer	Susan Benjamin
Ben McGrath	Ben Blue
Marty, Jerry's manager	Larry D. Mann

ACCIDENTAL FAMILY—30 minutes

—NBC—September 15, 1967 - January 5, 1968. 16 episodes.

ACCUSED

Courtroom Drama. Based on actual case files.

CAST

Judge	Edgar Allan Jones, Jr.
Clerk	Jim Hodson
Bailiff	Tim Farrell
Reporter-Announcer	Violet Gilmore

ACCUSED—30 minutes—ABC—December 31, 1958 - September 30, 1959.

ACROBAT RANCH

Children. Circus variety acts are interspersed with game contests with children competing against one another for merchandise prizes.

Host: Jack Stillwill, as Uncle Jim.

Regulars: Billy Alberts (as Flying Flo) and Valerie Alberts (as Tumbling Tim).

Producer: Norman Heyne.

Sponsor: General Foods.

ACROBAT RANCH—30 minutes—ABC 1950.

ACROSS THE BOARD

Game. Two competing players. Object: To complete crossword puzzles from a series of picture and word clues.

Host: Ted Brown.

ACROSS THE BOARD—30 minutes—ABC—June 1, 1959 - October 9, 1959.

ACROSS THE SEVEN SEAS

Travel. Films depicting the people and customs of various countries around the world.

Host/Narrator: Jack Douglas.

ACROSS THE SEVEN SEAS—30 minutes—Syndicated 1962. 39 episodes.

ACTION AUTOGRAPHS

Variety. Basically, a fifteen-minute commercial for Bell and Howell motion-picture equipment. The program itself spotlights celebrities home-made films.

Host: Jack Brand.

Producer: Jack Brand, Marge Bishop.

Director: Tony Rizzo.

ACTION AUTOGRAPHS—15 minutes—ABC 1949.

ACTION IN THE AFTERNOON

Western. Background: The town of Huberie, Montana, during the 1890s. Stories depict the differences placed on values then as compared with those of the 1950s. Broadcast live from Suburban Philadelphia.

CAST

Jack Valentine, Mary Elaine Watts, Blake Ritter, Phil Sheridan, Creighton Stewart, Kris Keegan, Jack V. Harriss Forest.

Music: The Tommy Ferguson Trio.

ACTION IN THE AFTERNOON—30 minutes—CBS—February 9, 1953 - January 29, 1954.

ACTION TONIGHT

Anthology. Rebroadcasts of dramas that were originally aired via other filmed anthology programs.

Included:

The Woman On The Bus. Fleeing from two gunmen, a woman takes refuge with a family in a remote area. Suddenly, she realizes that she has jeopardized their lives. The story centers on her attempts to escape without causing any harm to her protectors.

CAST

Dorothy Green, Ross Elliott, Linda Sterling, Onslow Stevens.

My Son Is Gone. The story of a man who retreats to a world of self-pity when his son is killed in a hunting accident.

CAST

Dean Jagger, Fay Wray, Sammy Ogg.

The Enchanted. The owner of a roadhouse has acted as guardian to a girl since she was twelve years old intending to marry her when she grows up. The story revolves around the conflict that ensues when the girl, now a young woman, falls in love with a musician.

CAST

Anna Maria Alberghetti, Kurt Kasznar, John Ericson.

ACTION TONIGHT—30 minutes—NBC—July 15, 1957 - September 27, 1957.

ACT IT OUT

Game. A scene that can be described by a single word is performed on stage by a group of actors. When it is completed, a telephone call is placed to a home viewer. If the participant can state the word that explains the scene, he receives a prize.

Host: Bill Cullen.

Regulars: Patty Adair, Roc Rogers, Monte Banks, Jr., Leon Kay, Ed Casey.

ACT IT OUT—30 minutes—DuMont 1947.

ACTOR'S HOTEL

Musical Variety. Background: A small rural boarding house.

CAST

Carlo Corelli, the proprietor	William Edmunds
Uncle Antonio	Alan Dale

ACTOR'S HOTEL—30 minutes—ABC—September 25, 1951 - May 13, 1952.

ACTOR'S STUDIO

Anthology. Dramatizations based on stories by Hemingway, Steinbeck, and Saroyan. Varying casts and presentations.

Producer: Donald Davis, Hume Cronyn.

Director: Fred Carr, David Pressman, Ralph Warren.

ACTOR'S STUDIO—30 minutes—CBS 1949.

THE ADAMS CHRONICLES

Drama. A thirteen-part series that profiles four generations of a historic American family—the Adamses, a family that produced two U.S. Presidents and a Secretary of State.

CAST

John Quincy Adams	George Grizzard
	David Birney
	William Daniels
Abigail Adams	Kathryn Walker
	Tammy Heinz
	Leora Dana
Louisa Katherine Adams	Pamela Payton-Wright
Samuel Adams	W.B. Brydon
John Quincy Adams II	Steven Grover
	Mark Wentworth
	Nicholas Pryor
	Alan Carlsen
Molly Adams	Julia Barr
Abigail Adams II	Lisa Lucas
	Katherine Houghton
	Nancy Coleman

Charles Francis Adams II	J. C. Powell
	John Beal
	Philip Anglim
	Thomas A. Stewart
	Charles Siebert
George Washington Adams	Donald Ellis
Minnie Adams	Patricia Elliott
Thomas Adams	Tom V. V. Tommi

Narrator: Michael Tolan.

Music: John Morris.

Producer: Virginia Kassel, Robert Costello, Paul Bogart, Jack Benza.

Director: Paul Bogart, Anthony Page.

Creator: Virginia Kassel.

THE ADAMS CHRONICLES—60 minutes—PBS—January 20, 1976 - April 13, 1976.

ADAM'S RIB

Comedy. Background: Los Angeles, California. The story of the relationship between Assistant District Attorney Adam Bonner and his wife, Amanda, a lawyer with the firm of Kipple, Kipple, and Smith. Episodes relate Amanda's crusade for women's rights and the clash that ensues when she as the defense attorney and Adam as the prosecuting attorney are assigned to the same case. Adapted from the movie of the same title.

CAST

Adam Bonner (nickname: "Pinky")	Ken Howard
Amanda Bonner (nickname: "Pinkie")	Blythe Danner
Kip Kipple, Amanda's employer	Edward Winter
Grace Peterson, Amanda's secretary	Dena Dietrich
Roy Mendelsohn, Adam's partner	Ron Rifkin
Francis Donahue, the District Attorney	Norman Bartold

Music: Perry Botkin, Jr.

ADAM'S RIB—30 minutes—ABC—September 14, 1973 - December 28, 1973. 13 episodes.

ADAM-12

Crime Drama. Background: Los Angeles, California. After his partner is killed in a gun battle, patrol car (Adam-12) officer Pete Malloy, bitter and disillusioned, is teamed with an over-eager rookie, Jim Reed. Malloy feels responsible and is determined to keep his young partner safe and alive. Stories involve their assignments, their close teamwork, and police law enforcement procedures.

CAST

Officer Pete Malloy (Badge No. 2430)	Martin Milner
Officer Jim Reed (Badge No. 744)	Kent McCord
Sergeant MacDonald	William Boyett
Officer Ed Wells	Gary Crosby
Officer Woods	Fred Stromsoe
Officer Walters	William Stevens
Sgt. Jerry Miller	Jack Hogan
Jean Reed, Jim's wife	Mikki Jamison
Voice of the police radio dispatcher	Sharon Claridge

Music: Frank Comstock.

Music Supervision: Stanley Wilson.

Executive Producer: Jack Webb, Herman S. Saunders.

Producer: Tom Williams.

Director: Dennis Donnelly, Leo Gordon, Jack Webb, Hollingsworth Morse, James Neilson.

Creator: Jack Webb.

ADAM-12—30 minutes—NBC—September 21, 1968 - August 26, 1975. Syndicated. 174 episodes.

ADAMS OF EAGLE LAKE

Crime Drama. Background: The resort town of Eagle Lake. The story of Sheriff Sam Adams and his attempts to maintain law and order in a small, peaceful town.

CAST

Sheriff Sam Adams	Andy Griffith
Margaret Kelly, his assistant	Abby Dalton
Officer Jubal Hammond	Iggie Wolfington
Officer Jerry Troy	Nick Nolte

Music: Jerry Goldsmith.

Executive Producer: Richard O. Linke.

Producer: Walter Grauman, Charles Stewart.

Director: Walter Grauman, Lawrence Dobkin.

Sam's home address: 500 North Shore Road.

ADAMS OF EAGLE LAKE—60 minutes—ABC—August 23, 1975 - August 30, 1975. 2 episodes.

THE ADDAMS FAMILY

Comedy. Background: The macabre Addams's home on North Cemetery Ridge. The story of its eccentric residents, the Addams family — Gomez, a wealthy lawyer; his beautiful wife, Morticia; their children, Pugsley and Wednesday; and a variety of odd relatives. Living in their own funeral world and believing themselves normal, the family struggles to cope with the situations that foster their rejection by the outside world. Based on the characters created by Charles Addams.

CAST

Morticia Addams	Carolyn Jones
Gomez Addams	John Astin
Uncle Fester, Morticia's relative	Jackie Coogan
Lurch, the zombie-like butler	Ted Cassidy
Wednesday Addams	Lisa Loring
Pugsley Addams	Ken Weatherwax
Grandmama Addams, Gomez's mother	Blossom Rock
Ophelia Frump, Morticia's sister	Carolyn Jones
Cousin Itt, four feet tall, completely covered with blonde hair	Felix Silla
Mr. Briggs, the postman	Rolfe Sedan
Esther Frump, Morticia's mother	Margaret Hamilton
Thing, the family's servant, a human right hand	Itself
Arthur J. Henson, the Addamses' insurance agent	Parley Baer
Horace Beesley, Henson's assistant	Eddie Quillan
Mother Lurch	Ellen Corby

Addams Family pets: Kit Kat, a lion; Cleopatra, Morticia's African Strangler (a man-eating plant); Aristotle, Pugsley's octopus; Homer, Wednesday's Black Widow Spider.

Music: Vic Mizzy.

Executive Producer: David Levy.

Producer: Nat Perrin.

Director: Sidney Lanfield, Nat Perrin, Sidney Solkon, Jean Yarbrough, Sidney Miller, Jerry Hopper.

The Addams address: 000 Cemetery Lane

Wednesday's doll: Marie Antoinette (minus her head, of course).

THE ADDAMS FAMILY—30 minutes—ABC—September 18, 1964 - September 2, 1966. Syndicated. 64 episodes.

Animated Version: "The Addams Family."

The Addams's two-story home is converted into a camper, and the family leaves Cemetery Ridge on a motor tour of America. Stories relate their attempts to cope with the variety of con artists they encounter.

Characters: Gomez Addams, Morticia Addams, Uncle Fester, Lurch, Wednesday Addams, Pugsley Addams, Grandmama Addams, Thing.

Voices: Josh Albee, Janet Waldo, Jackie Coogan, Ted Cassidy, Cindy Henderson, Pat Harrington, Jr., Bob Holt, John Stephenson, Don Messick, Herb Vigran, Howard Caine, Lennie Weinrib.

Music: Hoyt Curtin.

THE ADDAMS FAMILY–30 minutes–NBC–Premiered: September 8, 1973 - August 30, 1975.

THE AD-LIBBERS

Game. Object: For a group of actors to ad-lib their way through story ideas that are submitted by home viewers. For each suggestion that is used, the sender receives a case of the sponsor's product.

Host: Peter Donald.

Regulars: Jack Lemmon, Charles Mendick, Patricia Hosley, Joe Silver, Cynthia Stone, Earl Hammond.

Producer-Director: Hal Perone.

THE AD-LIBBERS–30 minutes–CBS–August 3, 1951 - September 1, 1951.
Copy of a local New York program entitled "What Happens Now?" (WOR-TV, Ch. 9, 1949).

Host: Nelson Olmstead.

CAST
Ross Martin, Carol Omart, Larry Blyden, Cecily Burke, Joyce Gordon, Thorton DeCosta.
Announcer: Nelson Olmstead.

Music: Recorded.

THE ADMIRAL BROADWAY REVUE
See title: "Sid Caesar."

ADVENTURE

Educational. Set against the background of the American Museum of Natural History, the program stresses the accomplishments of outstanding men of science.

Host: Mike Wallace.

Reporter: Charles Collingwood.

ADVENTURE–30 minutes–CBS 1953.

ADVENTURE AT SCOTT ISLAND

See title: "Harbourmaster."

ADVENTURE CALLS

Adventure. Films depicting the exploits of various adventurers, e.g., mountain climbers, hunters, explorers.

Host-Narrator: Richard Simmons.

ADVENTURE CALLS–30 minutes–Syndicated 1966. 26 episodes.

THE ADVENTURER

Adventure. The exploits of United States Government Espionage Agent Gene Bradley, a multimillionaire businessman who adopts the guise of an international film star. Produced by I.T.C.

CAST
Gene Bradley	Gene Barry
Mr. Parminter, his contact, an agent posing as his producer	Barry Morse
Diane Mash, a contact	Catherine Schell
Gavin Jones, an agent posing as Bradley's accompanist, Wildman Jones	Garrick Hagon
Also (various roles)	Stuart Damon

Music: John Barry.

THE ADVENTURER–30 minutes–Syndicated 1972. 26 episodes.

THE ADVENTURERS

Adventure. The global exploits of newspapermen.

CAST
Newspaperman	Edward Meeks
Newspaperman	Yves Renier

THE ADVENTURERS–30 minutes–Syndicated 1966. European title: "The Globetrotters." 39 episodes.

ADVENTURES IN PARADISE

Adventure. Background: The South Pacific. The experiences of Adam Troy, skipper of the schooner *Tiki*.

CAST
Adam Troy	Gardner McKay

Clay Baker	James Holden
Oliver Kee	Weaver Levy
Chris Parker	Guy Stockwell
Renee	Linda Lawson
Kelly	Lani Kai
Lovey	Henry Slate
Penrose	George Tobias
Sondi	Sondi Sodsai
Inspector Bouchard	Marcel Hillaire

Music: Lionel Newman.

Producer: Dominick Dunne, Art Wallace, Richard Goldstone.

Creator: James Michener.

ADVENTURES IN PARADISE–60 minutes–ABC–October 5, 1959 - April 1, 1962. Syndicated. 94 episodes.

ADVENTURES IN RAINBOW COUNTRY

Life in Northern Canada as seen through the eyes of a teenager.

Starring: Lois Maxwell, Billy Williams, and Peter Garva. 30 minutes–Syndicated 1970.

THE ADVENTURES OF A JUNGLE BOY

Adventure. Background: Nairobi, Africa. The exploits of Boy, the young, orphaned survivor of an airplane crash, as he and Dr. Laurence, a research scientist, battle the sinister forces of evil.

CAST
Boy	Michael Carr Hartley
Dr. Laurence	Ronald Adam

THE ADVENTURES OF A JUNGLE BOY–30 minutes–Syndicated 1957.

THE ADVENTURES OF BLACK BEAUTY

Adventure. Background: England, 1877. Based on the classic children's story, *Black Beauty* by Anna Sewell. The love, devotion, and adventures shared by a young girl, Victoria Gordon, and her horse, Black Beauty. British produced.

CAST
Victoria Gordon	Judi Bowker
Dr. James Gordon, her father	William Lucas
Kevin Gordon, her brother	Roderick Shaw
Amy Winthrop, their housekeeper	Charlotte Mitchell

Music: Dennis King.

THE ADVENTURES OF BLACK BEAUTY–30 minutes–Syndicated 1972.

THE ADVENTURES OF CAPTAIN HARTZ

Adventure. Stories relating the sea adventures of Captain Hartz. Geared for young children.

CAST

Captain Hartz (the host and
    story teller)   Philip Lord
Also: Tony Mercern, Jerry Garvey.

Versions:

ABC—15 minutes—1953.
Syndicated—30 minutes—1955.

THE ADVENTURES OF CHAMPION

Western. Background: America's Southwest during the 1880s. The adventures of twelve-year-old Ricky North, and his stallion, Champion, a once-mighty leader of a herd of wild horses.

CAST

Ricky North   Barry Curtis
Sandy North, his uncle   Jim Bannon
Will Calhoun   Francis MacDonald

Ricky's German Shepherd: Rebel.

Music: Norman Luboff, Marilyn Keith.

THE ADVENTURES OF CHAMPION—30 minutes—CBS—October 7, 1955 - February 3, 1956. Syndicated. 26 episodes.

THE ADVENTURES OF FU MANCHU

Adventure. London, England. Dr. Fu Manchu, a respected Chinese physician, is awarded custody of Lia Elthram, a young Caucasian girl. Shortly after, during the Boxer Rebellion, his wife and son are inadvertently killed by Jack Petrie, a British officer. The doctor, who is unable to properly adjust to the circumstances, becomes deranged and vows to avenge the death of his family by destroying the Petrie family and the entire white race. He raises and teaches the young girl to share his hatred.

Retreating to Tibet, he establishes *SUBTLY,* his sinister organization of evil through which he provokes tension between East and West. Stories depict his attempts to achieve vengeance; and the efforts of Scotland Yard Inspector Sir Dennis Nayland Smith to thwart his plans.

CAST

Dr. Fu Manchu   Glenn Gordon
Lia Elthram   Laurette Luez
Sir Dennis

Nayland Smith   Lester Stevens
Dr. Jack Petrie   Clark Howat
Malik, the French
    detective   Lee Matthews
Karameneh, the
    slave girl   Carla Balenda
Also   John George

THE ADVENTURES OF FU MANCHU—30 minutes—Syndicated 1956.

Originally planned as a network (NBC) series in 1950, but sponsor disappointment in scripts fostered only a televised pilot film.

CAST

Fu Manchu: John Carradine; Nayland Smith: Sir Cedric Hardwicke.

THE ADVENTURES OF GULLIVER

Animated Cartoon. Era: The 18th century. Adapted from Jonathan Swift's classic novel, *Gulliver's Travels,* which told of the voyages of Lemuel Gulliver.

Believing his father is missing, Gary Gulliver sets sail to find him. Caught in a tropical storm, he and his dog, Bib, are shipwrecked on the island of Lilliput. Winning Lilliputian friendship by defeating a dreaded foe, Gary, assisted by the six-inch people, begins the search for his father. Stories relate his adventures and his attempts to overcome the foul deeds of the evil Captain Leech, who seeks to acquire Gulliver's treasure map.

Voices: Jerry Dexter, Allan Melvin, Don Messick, John Stephenson, Ginny Tyler, Herb Vigran.

Musical Direction: Ted Nichols.

Producer-Director: William Hanna, Joseph Barbera.

THE ADVENTURES OF GULLIVER—30 minutes—ABC—September 14, 1969 - September 5, 1970. Syndicated.

THE ADVENTURES OF HIRAM HOLLIDAY

Comedy. Correcting a story and averting a multi-million dollar libel suit, Hiram Holliday, a meek and mild-mannered newspaper proofreader, is awarded a one-year-round-the-world tour by his publisher. Stories depict his adventures as he stumbles upon and attempts to foil the dealings of unscrupulous characters.

CAST

Hiram Holliday   Wally Cox
Joel Smith, his friend and
    reporter sent along to

cover his activities   Ainslie Pryor

THE ADVENTURES OF HIRAM HOLLIDAY—30 minutes—NBC—October 3, 1956 - February 28, 1957. 26 episodes.

THE ADVENTURES OF JIM BOWIE

Adventure. Background: The territory from New Orleans to Texas in the era following the strife of the Louisiana Purchase. The exploits of frontiersman-pioneer Jim Bowie, as he crusades for and defends liberty.

Starring:
Scott Forbes as Jim Bowie (the inventor of the Bowie Knife).

Music: Ken Darby.

Producer: Louis F. Edelman, Lewis Foster.

THE ADVENTURES OF JIM BOWIE —30 minutes—ABC—September 7, 1956 - August 29, 1958. Syndicated. 78 episodes.

THE ADVENTURES OF JONNY QUEST

Animated Cartoon. The global expeditions of Dr. Benton Quest and his young son, Jonny, as they search for the unexplained answers to scientific mysteries.

Characters' Voices
Dr. Benton Quest   John Stephenson
Jonny Quest   Tim Matthieson
Roger "Race" Bannon,
    their bodyguard   Mike Road
Hadji, their traveling
    companion   Danny Bravo
Bandit, their dog   Don Messick
Music: Hoyt Curtin.

THE ADVENTURES OF JONNY QUEST—30 minutes. ABC—September 18, 1964 - September 9, 1965; CBS—September 9, 1967 - September 5, 1970; NBC—September 11, 1971 - September 2, 1972. Syndicated. 26 episodes.

THE ADVENTURES OF KIT CARSON

Western. Background: The Frontier during the 1880s. The exploits of Christopher "Kit" Carson, Frontiersman and Indian scout, and his Mexican sidekick, El Toro.

CAST

Kit Carson   Bill Williams
El Toro   Don Diamond

THE ADVENTURES OF KIT CARSON—30 minutes—Syndicated 1956. 104 episodes.

THE ADVENTURES OF MIGHTY APE GO-KU

A thirty-minute science fiction series about a talking monkey who becomes the leader of the poor people. Syndicated 1970. 39 films.

THE ADVENTURES OF OZZIE AND HARRIET

Comedy. Background: 822 Sycamore Road, Hillsdale, the residence of the Nelson family — Ozzie*; his wife, Harriet; and their children, Dave and Ricky. Stories relate the events that befall an American family—the good times and the bad.

*On television, Ozzie's occupation was never identified; on radio, he was, as in real life, a bandleader and Harriet, a vocalist. In the feature film HERE COME THE NELSONS, Ozzie is seen as an executive for the H. J. Bellows and Company Advertising Agency.

CAST

Ozzie Nelson	Himself
Harriet Hillard Nelson	Herself
Ricky Nelson	Himself
David Nelson	Himself
Kris Nelson, Ricky's wife	Herself
June Nelson, Dave's wife	Herself
Mr. Thornberry, a neighbor	Don DeFore
Joe Randolph, Ozzie's friend	Lyle Talbot
Clara Randolph, his wife	Mary Jane Croft
Darby, a friend	Parley Baer
Doc Williams, a friend	Frank Cady
Wally, Dave and Ricky's friend	Skip Young
Ginger, Wally's girlfriend	Charlene Salern
Melinda, a friend	Diane Sayer
Sally, Kris's friend	Kathy Davies
Miss Edwards, Dave and Ricky's secretary (establishing a law firm after college)	Connie Harper
Dean Hopkins, the college head	Ivan Bonar
Mr. Baxter, Ozzie's friend (early episodes)	Frank Cady
Herb Dunkel, Ozzie's friend	Joseph Kearns
Ralph Dobson, David's employer at the law firm	Francis DeSales
Don Kelley, Dobson's partner	Joe Flynn
Happy Hotpoint, the dancing elf in Hotpoint commercials (1955)	Mary Tyler Moore

Also: Barry Livingston, Kent Smith, James Stacy.

Announcer: Verne Smith.

Music: Basil Adlam.

Producer: Robert Angus, Bill Lewis, Ozzie Nelson, Leo Penn.

THE ADVENTURES OF OZZIE AND HARRIET—30 minutes—ABC—October 3, 1952 - September 3, 1966. Syndicated. 435 filmed episodes (200 are syndicated).

THE ADVENTURES OF POW WOW

Animated Cartoon. The story of Pow Wow, a young Indian boy, as he learns about life.

THE ADVENTURES OF POW WOW —05 minutes—NBC 1957.

THE ADVENTURES OF RIN TIN TIN

Adventure. Background: California during the 1880s. While on patrol, the 101st Cavalry discovers the survivors of an Apache Indian raid on a wagon train — a young boy, Rusty, and his dog, Rin Tin Tin. Brought back to Fort Apache, they are unofficially adopted by Lieutenant Rip Masters.

Fearing a general's forthcoming inspection will cause the boy and his dog to be banished from the fort, Masters places them in the care of Sergeant Biff O'Hara. In seeking a place to hide, they uncover and ultimately foil an Indian plot against the colonel's life. In gratitude the colonel grants Rusty the title of Corporal to ensure his and the dog's continued presence on the post in accordance with regulations.

The story of a young boy, Corporal Rusty, his dog, Rin Tin Tin, and their efforts to assist the cavalry in maintaining law and order.

CAST

Corporal Rusty	Lee Aaker
Lt. Rip Masters	James L. Brown
Sgt. Biff O'Hara	Joe Sawyer
Corporal Randy Boone	Rand Brooks
The Colonel	John Hoyt
Major Swanson	William Forest
Corporal Carson	Tommy Farrell
Corporal Clark	Hal Hopper

Music: Hal Hopper.

Producer: Herbert B. Leonard, Fred Briskin.

Director: Robert G. Walker, Lew Landers, Charles Gould, Earl Bellamy, Douglas Heyes, Fred Jackman.

Rin Tin Tin Owned and Trained By: Lee Duncan.

THE ADVENTURES OF RIN TIN TIN—30 minutes—ABC—October 15, 1954 - September 1958; ABC—September 28, 1959 - September 22, 1961. CBS—30 minutes—September 29, 1962 - September 19, 1964. Syndicated. 164 episodes. In 1975, the original stories were resyndicated in sepia tint and new opening and closing segments, filmed in color in Utah, were added. James Brown, re-creating his role of Lt. Masters, ap-peared to relate stories of Rusty and his dog to a group of children visiting the fort.

THE ADVENTURES OF ROBIN HOOD

Adventure. Background: England, 1191. When King Richard the Lion-Hearted sets forth for the Crusades in the Holy Land, he presents the regency of the kingdom to his trusted friend, Longchamps, and angers his brother, Prince John. While visiting Austria, Richard is seized by Prince John's cohort, Sir Leopold, and held captive in Vienna. Assuming control of Nottingham, the evil Norman, Prince John, heavily burdens the Saxons with taxes—pay or suffer cruel consequences.

Appalled by the Norman mistreatment of Saxons, Sir Robin of Locksley opposes Prince John and finds himself declared a wanted outlaw (Robin Hood). Retreating to the Gallows Oak in Sherwood Forest, he organizes a small band of free-born Englishmen (the Merry Men). Stories relate their attempts to usurp Prince John and restore the throne to its rightful king, Richard the Lion-Hearted.

CAST

Robin Hood	Richard Greene
Friar Tuck (Francis Tucker)	Alexander Gauge
Little John (John Little)	Archie Duncan
Maid Marian Fitzwater, a ward of King Arthur's court	Bernadette O'Farrell Patricia Driscoll
Prince John	Donald Pleasance Hubert Gregg
The Sheriff of Nottingham	Alan Wheatley
Sir Richard the Lion-Hearted	Ian Hunter
Lady Genevieve	Gillian Sterrett
Will Scarlet (Will of Winchester)	Paul Eddington

King Arthur   Peter Asher
Duncan, the
    Scotsman   Hugh McDermott
Music: Carl Sigman.

Producer: Sidney Cole, Hannah Weinstein.

THE ADVENTURES OF ROBIN HOOD—30 minutes—CBS—September 26, 1955 - September 22, 1958. Syndicated. 135 episodes.

THE ADVENTURES OF THE SEA HAWK

Adventure. Background: The Caribbean Islands. The research undertakings of the schooner *Sea Hawk,* a floating electronics lab.

CAST
Commander John Hawk John Howard
His aide, an atomic
    scientist   John Lee

THE ADVENTURES OF THE SEA HAWK—30 minutes—Syndicated 1958. 26 episodes.

THE ADVENTURES OF THE SEASPRAY

Adventure. Background: The South Pacific. The exploits of Australian writer John Wells, skipper of the eighty-three-foot sailing schooner *Seaspray,* as he searches for story material.

CAST
John Wells   Walter Brown
Mike Wells,
    his son   Gary Gray
Sue Wells,
    his daughter   Susanne Haworth
Noah Wells,
    his son   Rodney Pearlman
Willyum, their
    Fugian crewman Leoni Lesinawai

Producer: Roger Mirams for Pacific Films.

Director: Eddie Davis.

THE ADVENTURES OF THE SEASPRAY—30 minutes—Syndicated 1968. 32 episodes.

THE ADVENTURES OF SIR LANCELOT

Adventure. Background: Twelfth-century England. The exploits of Sir Lancelot du Lac, a Knight of King Arthur's Round Table, and the paramour of Queen Guinevere.

CAST
Sir Lancelot du Lac   William Russell

Queen Guinevere   Jane Hylton
Merlin the Magician   Cyril Smith
King Arthur   Ronald Leigh-Hunt
                            Bruce Seton
Squire Brian   Robert Scroggins
Music: Bruce Campbell, Alan Lomax.

Producer: Dallas Bowen, Hannah Weinstein.

THE ADVENTURES OF SIR LANCELOT—30 minutes—NBC—September 24, 1955 - June 29, 1957; ABC—October 1, 1957 - September 26, 1958. Syndicated. 30 episodes.

THE ADVENTURES OF SUPERMAN

Adventure. Faraway, in the outer reaches of space, there exists a planet known as Krypton, which is inhabited by superintelligent people. Suddenly, due to radioactive chain reactions, the planet begins to experience minor earthquakes. Jor-El, a leading scientist, approaches the Council of Scientists and states his belief that their world, which is being drawn closer to the sun, is doomed. Marked as a fool, Jor-El returns home and begins preparations to save his family, his wife, Lara, and their infant son, Kal-El, from the approaching disaster.

Shortly after, when completing only a miniature experimental rocket, the planet begins to explode. Because the ship cannot hold all three, Jor-El and Lara decide to save Kal-El. Wrapping him in red and blue blankets, Lara places him in the craft. Jor-El sets the controls and directs the ship to a planet he knows to be inhabited, Earth. Moments following its take-off, Krypton explodes and scatters billions of radioactively charged particles of Kryptonite, the only substance that is able to destroy Kal-El, into the universe.

Landing in Smallville, U.S.A., the space craft and its infant passenger are discovered by Eben and Martha Kent, a childless farm couple. Fearing that no one will ever believe their fantastic story, they adopt the baby as their own and name him Clark Kent.

As the years pass, each bestows evidence of his remarkable powers: "super strength, super breath and super speed; the ability to fly; X-ray, telescopic and microscopic vision. . . super memory, super hearing and super thinking."

Clark, now twenty-five years of age, is urged by his mother to use his great powers to benefit mankind. Shortly after Martha fashions an indestructible costume for him from the blankets that were originally wrapped around him, Clark moves to Metropolis, where he takes up residence at the

Standish Arms Hotel, Apartment 5-H. To conceal his true identity as Superman, he adopts the guise of mild-mannered Clark Kent. To learn of disasters immediately, and to be readily available to combat crime as Superman, he acquires a position as reporter for *The Daily Planet,* a crusading newspaper. Editor Perry White and reporters Lois Lane and Jimmy Olsen quickly become his friends.

Stories relate Clark's relentless battle against crime as the mysterious figure for justice, Superman.

The 1930s saw, through the efforts of Mort Weisinger, Forrest J. Ackerman, Jerry Siegel, and Joe Shuster, the emergence of the magazine *Science Fiction,* from which the first Superman evolved. In 1938, writer Siegel and artist Shuster introduced the character in D.C. Publications' *Action Comics.* Its instant success led to the evolvement of *Superman* magazine. Worldwide distribution was obtained through its purchase by the McClure Syndicate.

The first "live" Superman was the voice of Bud Collyer, heard over the Mutual Radio Network in the 1940s. (His was also the voice in the animated TV version.) An animated theatrical version, produced by Paramount Pictures, appeared in the late 1940s. A fifteen-episode serial was produced in 1948 by Columbia Pictures and featured Kirk Alyn as "The Man of Steel." In 1950, the first feature-length film, *Atom Man vs. Superman,* was produced by Columbia Pictures; and also starred Alyn. In 1951, Lippert Pictures introduced George Reeves as Earth's mightiest hero in *Superman and the Mole Men.* Reedited, it served as the video series pilot and became the only two-part episode.

Theatrical Cast:
Clark Kent/Superman: Kirk Alyn; Perry White: Pierre Watkin; Lois Lane: Noel Neill; Jimmy Olsen: Tommy Bond.

TV CAST
Clark Kent/Superman   George Reeves
Lois Lane   Phyllis Coates

                            Noel Neill
Perry White   John Hamilton
Jimmy Olsen   Jack Larson
Inspector Bill
    Henderson   Robert Shayne
Professor J.J. Pepperwinkle,
    a scientist   Phillips Tead
Sy Horton, a
    Mob leader   Herb Vigran
Ethel, the *Daily Planet*
    receptionist   Yvonne White
Jor-El, Clark's Krypton
    father   Ross Elliott

Lara, Clark's Krypton
   mother   Aline Towne
Eben Kent, Clark's
   Earth father   Tom Fadden
Martha Kent, Clark's
   Earth mother (a.k.a.
   Sara Kent)   Dina Nolan
Clark, as a boy   Stuart Randall

Producer: Whitney Ellsworth, Robert J. Maxwell, Bernard Luber.

Director: Harry Gerstad, George Reeves, Lew Landers, Bob Barnes, Tommy Carr, Phil Ford, Lee Scholem, Howard Bretherton.

Sponsor: Kellogg's cereals.

Program open:
Scene: Metropolis. Superman is seen flying above a crowd of people.
Voices: "It's a bird! It's a plane! It's Superman!"
Announcer: "Yes, it's Superman, strange visitor from another planet who came to Earth with powers and abilities far beyond those of mortal men. Superman, who can change the course of mighty rivers, bend steel in his bare hands; and who, disguised as Clark Kent, mild-mannered reporter for a great metropolitan newspaper, fights a never ending battle for truth, justice, and the American Way."

THE ADVENTURES OF SUPERMAN —30 minutes—Syndicated 1953. 104 episodes.

Animated Version:

The New Adventures of Superman— 30 minutes—CBS—September 10, 1966 - September 2, 1967.

Format: Two cartoons relating the adventures of Clark Kent and Lois Lane, and one relating the adventures of Superboy.

Characters' Voices
Clark Kent/Superman   Bud Collyer
Lois Lane   Joan Alexander
Narrator: Jackson Beck.

Program open:
Announcer: "Superman, rocketed to Earth as an infant when the distant planet Krypton exploded, and who, disguised as Clark Kent, mild-mannered reporter for *The Daily Planet,* fights a never ending battle for truth, justice and freedom with super powers far beyond those of ordinary mortals."

Also presented as a segment of the following programs:

The Superman-Aquaman Hour—Animated Cartoon—60 minutes—CBS—September 9, 1967 - September 7, 1968.

The Batman-Superman Hour—Animated Cartoon—60 minutes—CBS—September 14, 1968 -September 6, 1969.

The Super Friends—Animated Cartoon—55 minutes—ABC—Premiered: September 8, 1973.

THE ADVENTURES OF WILLIAM TELL

Adventure. Background: Fourteenth-century Switzerland. The efforts of William Tell, the leader of the Confederation of the Forest Cantons, to liberate his country from the rule of the tyrannical Austrian Empire Army. Based on the story by Johann von Schiller.

CAST
William Tell   Conrad Phillips
Walter Tell   Richard Rogers
Hedda   Jennifer Jayne
Gessler   Willoughby Goddard
The Bear   Nigel Green

THE ADVENTURES OF WILLIAM TELL—30 minutes—Syndicated 1957. 39 episodes.

ADVENTURE SHOWCASE

Anthology. Dramatic presentations.

Included:

Brock Callahan. The story of a private detective and his attempts to uncover the murderer of an interior decorator.

CAST
Brock Callahan: Ken Clark; Jan Bennett: Randy Stuart; Lt. Pascal: Richard Shannon.

Dr. Mike. The story concerns a doctor's attempts to save the life of a woman against the persistent attempts of the woman's husband to prevent him from performing the operation.

CAST
Dr. Mike Grant: Keith Andes; Dr. Talbert: Lewis Martin; Mary Barker: Mary Adams; Alex Bartos: Joe DeSantis; Anna Bartos: Greta Granstedt.

ADVENTURE SHOWCASE—30 minutes—CBS—August 11, 1959 - September 1, 1959. 4 programs.

ADVENTURE THEATRE

Anthology. British-produced suspense dramas.

Host: Paul Douglas.

Included:

Thirty Days To Die. Blaming his failure on a much-hated critic, a disappointed playwright seeks to disgrace him.

CAST
Sidney Marvel: Hubert Gregg; Harcourt Garrett: Laurence Naismith.

The Marriage Trap. Background: London, England. The grim police hunt for a modern-day Jack the Ripper.

CAST
Inspector Mathew: Maurice Denham; Dr. Ingram: Cameron Hull; Della: Jo Huntley-Wright.

The Missing Passenger. A man, dating two sisters, attempts to jilt both of them.

CAST
Patrick Barr.

ADVENTURE THEATRE—60 minutes—NBC—June 16, 1956 - September 1956. 10 episodes.

ADVENTURE THEATRE

Anthology. Rebroadcasts of dramas that were aired via "Playhouse of Stars." See title for information on the type of program that was presented.

ADVENTURE THEATRE—30 minutes—CBS—July 21, 1961 - September 22, 1961.

THE AFRICAN PATROL

Adventure. Background: Kenya, East Africa. The cases of the African Police Patrol, a unit of specially trained men organized to combat crime.

Starring:
John Bently as Inspector Derek, chief of the African Patrol.

THE AFRICAN PATROL—30 minutes—Syndicated 1957. 39 episodes.

THE AFTERNOON FILM FESTIVAL

Movies. Theatrical features.

Host: Don Gordon.

THE AFTERNOON FILM FESTI-VAL—90 minutes—ABC 1956.

THE AGE OF KINGS

History. Dramatizations based on eighty-six years of British history, beginning with the reign of Richard II. Based on the plays of William Shakespeare and performed by the British Broadcasting Repertory Company.

CAST

King Richard II	David Williams
Harry Percy (Hotshot)	Sean Connery
John of Gaunt	Edgar Wreford
Henry Bolingbroke	Thomas Fleming
Thomas Mowbray	Noel Johnson
Edmund Langley	Geoffrey Bayldon
The Duke of Aumerle	John Greenwood
Northumberland	George A. Cooper

THE AGE OF KINGS—Two hours—Syndicated 1961.

AIR POWER

Documentary. The history of aviation from its beginnings at Kitty Hawk to its progress with missiles in the 1950s.

Host-Narrator: Walter Cronkite.

Producer: Perry Wolff, James Faichney.

AIR POWER—30 minutes—CBS—November 11, 1956 - October 19, 1958. 26 episodes.

AIR TIME

Musical Variety. Presented by the U.S. Air Force Reserve.

Hosts: Vaughn Monroe, Merv Griffin.

Music: The Bobby Hackett Jazz Group; The Elliott Alexander Orchestra.

AIR TIME—30 minutes—ABC—1956-1957.

THE AL CAPP SHOW

Discussion. Discussions on various topical issues with guests whose opinions inevitably differ from those of the host.

Host: Al Capp.

THE AL CAPP SHOW—90 minutes—Syndicated 1971. 27 episodes.

THE ALAN BURKE SHOW

Discussion. Unusually strong conversations between the host, his guests, and members of the studio audience on topics infrequently discussed on television at that time (1966); e.g. sexchange operations, abortion, civil rights, underground movies.

Host: Alan Burke.

THE ALAN BURKE SHOW—2 hours—Syndicated 1966. Originally produced in New York as a ninety-minute program for Metromedia-owned stations. Daily thirty-minute syndicated title: "Dear Alan."

ALAN YOUNG

Listed: The television programs of comedian Alan Young.

The Alan Young Show—Comedy—30 minutes—CBS—April 6, 1950 - June 1953.

Host: Alan Young.

Regulars: Polly Bergen, Fran Warren, Joseph Kearns, Ben Wright, Connie Haines, David Alpert, Mabel Paige, Phillips Tead, Dawn Adams, Russell Gaige, The Rodney Bell Dancers (Jane Hollar, Jerry Antes, Tom Mahoney, Jean Mahoney).

Orchestra: Lud Gluskin.

Format: Two to three vignettes depicting the misadventures of Alan Young, a well-meaning, good-natured man. Segments are alternated with songs by popular vocalists.

The Alan Young Show—Musical Variety—60 minutes—Associated Redifussion Television from London (British produced and broadcast)—1958.

Host: Alan Young.

Regulars: Ellen Drew, Laurie Payne, Nion Yonson, Daniele Roma, The Young Lovelies, The Brisas de Mexico.

Orchestra: Billy Ternet.

Format: Various comedy sketches, musical numbers, and songs.

The Alan Young Show. Center: Alan Young. Left: Jan Hollar, Tom Mahoney (dancers). Right: Jerry Antes, Jean Mahoney (dancers).

Mr. Ed—Comedy—30 minutes—CBS—1961 - 1966. (See title).

ALARM

Drama. Background: California. The work of Paramedics, the men of the Los Angeles County Fire Department.

CAST

The Captain	Richard Arlen
Fireman	J. Pat O'Malley

ALARM—30 minutes—Syndicated 1954.

THE ALASKANS

Adventure. Background: Skagway, Alaska, 1898. Infatuated with Rocky Shaw, a beautiful saloon entertainer, a prospector reveals the location of a sled holding gold to her. Soon after, he is killed in a desperate attempt to retrieve it himself. When Miss Shaw learns of an expedition to the area, she persuades two prospectors, Reno McKee, a rugged cowpoke, and his fast-talking partner, Silky Harris, to let her join them. Her attempts to uncover the gold fail as an avalanche buries it beneath tons of snow. The three continue their journey and establish an operational base in Eagle City.

Stories relate the adventures of Rocky Shaw, Silky Harris, and Reno McKee as they search for gold in the beautiful but dangerous Ice Palace of the Northland.

CAST

Rocky Shaw	Dorothy Provine
Silky Harris	Roger Moore
Reno McKee	Jeff York
Nifty Cronin, a saloon owner and swindler	Ray Danton
Fantan	Frank DeKova

Music: Paul Sawtell.

Producer: William T. Orr.

THE ALASKANS—60 minutes—ABC—October 4, 1959 - September 25, 1960. Syndicated. 36 episodes.

ALCOA PREMIERE

Anthology. Dramatic presentations.

Host: Fred Astaire.

Producer: Richard Lewis.

Included:

Blues for a Hanging. When her boyfriend insists that he killed a man while he was drunk, a nightclub singer begins an investigation to discover the truth.

CAST

Connie Rankin: Janis Paige; Ted Miller: Fred Astaire; Theresa Summer: Lurene Tuttle.

The Town Budget. After the sheriff of a small town resigns, two fleeing criminals make the town their hideout. The story centers on the townspeople and their desperate attempts to acquire help.

CAST

Earl Sherwood: James Whitmore; Fran Sherwood: Marilyn Erskine; Jona: Timothy Carey.

The Boy Who Wasn't Wanted. A young boy attempts to regain the affections of his bickering parents.

CAST

Father: Dana Andrews; Mother: Marilyn Erskine; Son: Billy Mumy.

The Girl with a Glow. When a movie director sees a beautiful girl leave the Hollywood library, he realizes that she would be the perfect girl for the lead in his next picture. After his attempts to find her fail, he haunts the library in hopes she'll return.

CAST

Peter Bronson: John Forsythe; June Baker: Patricia Crowley.

ALCOA PREMIERE—60 minutes—ABC—October 11, 1961 - September 12, 1963.

ALCOA PRESENTS

See title: "One Step Beyond."

ALCOA THEATRE

Anthology. Dramatic presentations.
Music: Frank DeVol.

Included:

The Incorrigibles. The story of an elder con artist and his attempts to discourage a younger deliquent who wants to follow in his footsteps.

CAST

Harvey Otis: Paul Douglas; Steve: Danny Richards.

Show Wagon. A man attempts to prove himself innocent of a murder charge.

CAST

Steve Emerson: Luke Anthony; Phoebe Malloy: Connie Hines; Pop: Jack Albertson.

Eddie. The story of a hoodlum and his desperate struggle to raise one thousand dollars or face death at the hands of gangsters.

Starring: Mickey Rooney as Eddie.

ALCOA THEATRE—60 minutes—NBC—October 14, 1955 - September 30, 1957; 30 minutes—NBC—October 7, 1957 - September 1960.

THE ALDRICH FAMILY

Comedy. Background: The town of Centerville. The trials and tribulations of the Aldrich family: Sam, the district attorney; his wife, Alice; and their teenage children, Mary and Henry. Stories depict the problems that befall Henry, a young, inexperienced and trouble-prone high-school student who one day hopes to become a lawyer. Based on the characters created by Clifford Goldsmith.

CAST

Henry Aldrich	Bob Casey (1949)
	Richard Tyler (1950)
	Henry Gerard (1951)
	Bobby Ellis (1952-1953)
Sam Aldrich	House Jameson
Alice Aldrich	Lois Wilson
	Nancy Carroll
	Barbara Robbins
	Jean Muir
Mary Aldrich	June Dayton
	Mary Malone
Homer Brown, Henry's friend	Jackie Kelk
	Robert Barry
	Jackie Grimes

Also: Peter Griffith, Nancy Carroll.

Producer: Ed Duerr, Frank Papp, Ralph Warren, Lester Vail, Joe Scibetta.

Director: Frank Papp, Lester Vail.

Sponsor: General Foods; Campbell Soup Company.

THE ALDRICH FAMILY—30 minutes—NBC—October 2, 1949 - May 29, 1953.

Alfred Hitchcock Presents. Cara Williams, from the episode "Voodoo," is one of the many relatively unknown performers to appear at the time and later achieve success. Charles Bronson, Steve McQueen, and Patrick Macnee are other notable examples.

ALFRED HITCHCOCK PRESENTS
THE ALFRED HITCHCOCK HOUR

Anthology. Mystery and suspense presentations.

Host: Alfred Hitchcock.

Music: Frederick Herbert; Stanley Wilson; Lyn Murray.

Additional Music: Joseph E. Romero, Bernard Herrmann, Leonard Rosenman.

Executive Producer: Alfred Hitchcock.

Producer: Joan Harrison, Robert Douglas, Herbert Coleman, Norman Lloyd, Charles Russell.

Director: Paul Henried, Herschel Daugherty, Ida Lupino, Harvey Hart, Robert Douglas, John Brahm, Alf Kjellin, Joseph Newman, Robert Stevens, James Neilson, Boris Sagal, Gene Reynolds, Don Taylor.

Included:

Voodoo. Background: An oil-mining camp in the Amazon. A wife, who is in love with her husband's partner, pretends to be stricken with fever. Unaware of deceit and believing his wife's sanity is threatened, the husband arranges for a native servant to take her down river to a psychiatrist. Uncomprehending, he takes her to his people, "the best head shrinkers in the world." "I do what you tell," he says and returns her shrunken head to his master.

CAST

Marie Jensen: Cara Williams; Jeff Jensen: Nehemiah Persoff; Mike: Mark Richman.

DeMortius (Latin: About the Dead). Two friends visit the home of an aging college professor. When they believe that the professor found out about his unfaithful wife's activities and killed her, they devise an air-tight alibi for him. Taking advantage of the situation, the professor kills his beautiful young wife and buries her beneath the cellar floor. The closing narration states only one fact: that his act was discovered when he remarried.

CAST

Irene Rankin: Cara Williams; Professor Rankin: Robert Emhardt; Wally Long: Henry Jones.

Arthur. Arthur Williams, the owner of a chicken farm, is embittered after his fiancée jilts him to marry another. When a year later, she leaves her husband and returns to Arthur, he kills her. Although the police are suspicious, they are unable to find a body, prove a murder, or connect Arthur in any way.

Mr. Hitchcock, in the closing narrative, states that Arthur, who made his own chicken feed through the use of a large grinding machine, prepared a special mixture and added one extra ingredient — Helen. One of the very few episodes in which the criminal is undiscovered and unpunished.

CAST

Arthur Williams: Laurence Harvey; Helen: Hazel Court; Sgt. Farrell: Patrick Macnee.

ALFRED HITCHCOCK PRESENTS —30 minutes. CBS—October·2, 1955 - September 1960; NBC—September 13, 1960 - June 1962. Syndicated. 268 episodes.

THE ALFRED HITCHCOCK HOUR—60 minutes—NBC—September 1962 - May 10, 1965. Syndicated. 93 episodes.

ALIAS SMITH AND JONES

Western. Background: Kansas during the 1890s. After infamous bankrobbers Jed Kid Curry and Hannibal Heyes, the leaders of the Devil Hole gang, find themselves incapable of cracking the newly developed safes, they decide to "go straight." They seek amnesty from the Governor and hope to have their slates wiped clean.

The Governor's decision, which is related by their friend Sheriff Lom Trevors, is a granting of provisional amnesty. It will become a complete pardon within twelve months if they end their life of crime and prove themselves worthy. However, in the meantime, the decision remains a secret among them, the Sheriff, and the Governor.

They leave their gang and adopt the aliases Thaddeus Jones (Curry) and Joshua Smith (Heyes). Stories center on two of the West's most wanted men and their attempts to stray from the troublesome situations that could threaten the granting of their amnesty.

CAST

Jed Kid Curry/ Thaddeus Jones	Ben Murphy
Hannibal Heyes/ Joshua Smith	Peter Duel Roger Davis
Sheriff Lom Trevors	James Drury Mike Road
Harry Briscoe, a Batterman detective	J.D. Cannon

Acquaintances of Heyes and Curry:

Big Mac McCreedy, a wealthy rancher	Burl Ives
Clementine Hale	Sally Field
Silky O'Sullivan	Walter Brennan
Blackjack Jenny, a card shark	Ann Sothern
Georgette Sinclair	Michele Lee
Winford Fletcher, a real estate broker	Rudy Vallee

The Devil Hole Gang:

Wheat	Earl Holliman
Lobo	Read Morgan
Kyle	Dennis Fimple

Music: Billy Goldenberg.

ALIAS SMITH AND JONES—60 minutes—ABC—January 21, 1971 - January 13, 1973. 48 episodes.

ALICE

Comedy. Background: Phoenix, Arizona. The story of Alice Hyatt, aspiring singer and widowed mother, and her attempts to provide a decent life for herself and her twelve-year-old son, Tommy, while working as a waitress at Mel's Diner, a less than fashionable roadside café. Based on the film *Alice Doesn't Live Here Anymore.*

CAST

Alice Hyatt	Linda Lavin
Tommy Hyatt	Philip McKeon
Flo, the sexy, loud-mouthed waitress	Polly Holliday
Mel, the owner of the diner	Vic Tayback
Vera, the shy, clumsy waitress	Beth Howland
Andy, a customer, the cantankerous old man	Pat Cranshaw
Travis, a customer	Tom Mahoney

Music: David Shire.

Theme: "There's a New Girl in Town" by Alan and Marilyn Bergman; vocal by Linda Lavin.

Executive Producer: William P. D'Angelo, Ray Allen, Harvey Bullock, Thomas Kuhn.

Producer: Bruce Johnson.

Director: Bill Hobin, Bill Persky, Jim Drake, James Sheldon, Norman Abbott, William P. D'Angelo.

ALICE—30 minutes—CBS—Premiered: September 29, 1976.

THE ALICE PEARCE SHOW

Variety.

Hostess: Alice Pearce.

Pianist: Mark Lawrence.

THE ALICE PEARCE SHOW—15 minutes—ABC—January 28, 1949 - April 4, 1949.

ALL ABOUT FACES

Game. Two competing celebrity teams, composed of husband and wife or boy and girlfriend. Each team receives fifty dollars betting money. A previously filmed sequence involving people confronted with unexpected situations is played and stopped prior to its conclusion. After the teams wager any amount of their accumulated cash, they have to predict its outcome. The tape is played again and answers are revealed. Correct predictions add the bet amount to the player's score. A wrong answer deducts it. Winning teams, the highest cash scorers, donate their earnings to charity.

Host: Richard Hayes.

Candid film sequence cast: Glenna Jones, Ken Deas, Andy Kunkel.

Music: John Michael Hill.

Additional Music: Gordon Fleming.

Executive Producer: Dan Enright.

Producer: David B. Fein.

Studio Portions Director: Bill Burrows.

Film Portions Director: Dan Enright.

ALL ABOUT FACES—30 minutes— Syndicated 1971. 130 tapes.

ALL ABOUT MUSIC

Musical Variety. A three-week interim series.

Host: Milton Cross.

Week One: Calypso.

Guests: Johnny Banacuda, Helen Ferguson, Pearl Gonzalez, The Duke of Iron, the Trini Dancers, The Versatones.

Music: The King Carib Stud Band.

Week Two: American Folk.
Guests: Susan Reed, Jack Dabodoub, Buzz Miller, Rudy Tronto, Gomez Delappe, Bruce King, Bill Bradley, The Nelle Fisher Dancers.
Orchestra: Al Rickey.

Week Three: Jazz.

Guests: Lawrence Winters, The Nelle Fisher Dancers.

Orchestra: Paul Whiteman.

ALL ABOUT MUSIC—30 minutes— ABC—April 7, 1957 - April 21, 1957.

ALLEN LUDDEN'S GALLERY

Variety.

Host: Allen Ludden.

ALLEN LUDDEN'S GALLERY—90 minutes—Syndicated 1969.

ALL IN FUN

Variety. A two-week interim series.

First Week:
Host: Charles Applewhite.

Guests: The Fontaine Sisters, The

Step Brothers, Lou Marks, Al Fisher, Jim Jeffries.

Second Week:
Host: George DeWitt.

Guests: Johnny Mercer, Bill Hayes, Lou Fisher, Al Marks, The Goofers.

ALL IN FUN—30 minutes—CBS— April 2, 1955 - April 9, 1955.

ALL IN THE FAMILY

Comedy. Background: 704 Houser Street, Queens, New York, the residence of the Bunkers, a White Middle-Class Anglo-Saxon American family: Archie, a dock foreman for the Prendergast Tool and Dye Company, a prejudiced, uncouth, loud-mouthed, hardhat conservative who is unable to accept the aspects of a progressing world; Edith, his dim-witted, sensitive, and totally honest wife; Gloria, their married daughter, beautiful and completely independent; and Mike Stivic, Gloria's husband, an unemployed, idealistic college student, representative of the radical, outspoken youth of today. (In later episodes, after graduation, Mike acquires employment as a college instructor, and he and Gloria move into their own home, next door to the Bunkers.)

Through the events that befall and test the reactions of the Bunker and Stivic families, American television comedy was led out of infancy and into maturity. The series, which reveals the little traces of Archie Bunker that are within everyone, allows the viewer to laugh at his own flaws as it presents life as it is—rampant with bigotry and racism.

CAST

Archie Bunker	Carroll O'Connor
Edith Bunker ("Dingbat")	Jean Stapleton
Gloria Stivic	Sally Struthers
Mike Stivic ("Meathead")	Rob Reiner
Lionel Jefferson, their neighbor	Mike Evans
George Jefferson, Lionel's father	Sherman Hemsley
Louise Jefferson, Lionel's mother	Isabel Sanford
Henry Jefferson, Lionel's uncle	Mel Stewart
Irene Lorenzo, Archie's neighbor, his co-worker	Betty Garrett
Frank Lorenzo, Irene's	

husband	Vincent Gardenia
Bert Munson, Archie's friend, a cab-driver	Billy Halop
Tommy Kelsey, Archie's friend, the owner of Kelsey's Bar	Brendon Dillon Bob Hastings
Justin Quigley, a friend of the Bunkers	Burt Mustin
Jo Nelson, Justin's girlfriend	Ruth McDevitt
Stretch Cunningham, Archie's co-worker	James Cromwell
Barney Hefner, Archie's friend	Allan Melvin
Teresa Betancourt, the Bunker's boarder	Liz Torres

Music: Roger Kellaway.

Executive Producer: Norman Lear, Woody Kling, Hal Kanter, Mort Lachman.

Producer: Lou Derman, Brigit Jensen, John Rich.

Director: John Rich, Paul Bogart.

Archie's Lodge: The Kings of Queens.

ALL IN THE FAMILY—30 minutes— CBS—Premiered: January 12, 1971.

Based on the British series "Till Death Us Do Part." Starring Warren Mitchell, Pandy Nichols, Anthony Booth, and Una Stubbs in the story of a son-in-law who lives in his father-in-law's home.

ALL MY CHILDREN

Serial. Background: The community of Pine Valley. The dramatic story of the Tyler family. Episodes depict the incidents that befall and affect individual members.

CAST

Phoebe Tyler	Ruth Warrick
Amy Tyler	Rosemary Prinz
Ann Tyler	Diana de Vegh
	Beverly Owen
	Judith Barcroft
Paul Martin	Ken Rabat
	Bill Mooney
Mary Kennicott	Susan Blanchard
Kate Martin	Kay Campbell
	Christine Thomas
Ruth Brent	Mary Fickett
Jeff Martin	Christopher Wines
	Charles Frank
	Robert Perault
	James O'Sullivan

Dr. Charles Tyler	Hugh Franklin
Tara Martin	Karen Gorney
	Stephanie Braxton
	Nancy Frangione
Lois Sloane	Hilda Haynes
Mona Kane	Frances Heflin
Nick Davis	Larry Keith
Erica Kane	Susan Lucci
Lincoln Tyler	Paul DuMont
	Nick Pryor
	Peter White
Dr. Joseph Martin	Ray MacDonnell
Sydney Scott	Deborah Soloman
Charles Tyler II	Jack Stauffer
	Chris Hubbell
Kitty Shea	Francesca James
Jason Maxwell	Tom Rosqui
Edie Hoffman	Marilyn Chris
Bill Hoffman	Michael Shannon
Margo Flax	Eileen Letchworth
Clyde Wheeler	Kevin Conway
Philip Brent	Richard Hatch
	Nicholas Benedict
Dr. Hoffman	Peter Simon
Franklin Grant	John Danelle
Tad Gardiner	Matthew Anton
Ted Brent	Mark Dawson
Bobby Martin	Mike Bersell
Lois Sloane	Hilda Hayne
Nancy Grant	Avis MacArthur
	Lisa Wilkinson
Hal Short	Dan Hamilton
Claudette Montgomery	Paulette Breen
Little Philip	
Tyler	Ian Miller Washam
	Brian Lima
Dr. Marcus Polk	Norman Rose
Mark Dalton	Mark LaMura
Myrtle Lum	Eileen Herlie
David Thornton	Paul Gleason
Maureen Teller	Rosemary Murphy
Ellen Shepherd	Kathleen Noone
Danny Kennicott	Daren Kelly
Donna Beck	Francesca Poston
	Candice Earley
Brooke English	Elissa Leeds
	Julia Barr
Dr. Christina Karras	Robin Strasser
Dr. Frank Grant	John Danelle
Carolyn Murray	Pat Dixon
Benny Sago	Larry Fleischman

Music: Aeolus Productions.

ALL MY CHILDREN—30 minutes—ABC—January 5, 1970 - April 22, 1977. 60 minutes: Premiered: April 25, 1977.

ALL'S FAIR

Comedy. Background: Washington, D.C. A political satire that focuses on the unlikely relationship between Richard Barrington III, a forty-nine-year-old conservative newspaper columnist, and Charlotte "Charlie"

Drake, a beautiful twenty-three-year-old free-lance photographer.

CAST

Richard Barrington III	Richard Crenna
Charlotte "Charlie" Drake	Bernadette Peters
Al Brooks, Richard's assistant	J.A. Preston
Ginger Livingston, Charlie's roommate	Judy Kahan
Lucy Daniels, a CBS-TV newswriter; later Al's wife	Lee Chamberlain
Senator Wayne Joplin, Richard's adversary	Jack Dodson
Barbara Murray, Richard's agent	Salome Jens
Lenny Wolf, President Carter's joke writer; Ginger's romantic interest	Michael Keaton

Music: Jeff Barry.

Executive Producer: Rod Parker.

Producer: Bob Weiskopf, Bob Schiller, Michael Elias.

Director: Hal Cooper, Bob Claver.

ALL'S FAIR—30 minutes—CBS—Premiered: September 20, 1976.

ALL STAR ANYTHING GOES

Game. Two three- (or four-) member teams, each composed of celebrities from the entertainment world, compete in various outlandish contests—just for the fun of it.

Host: Bill Boggs.

Play-by-play Description: Jim Healy.

Score Girl: Judy Abercrombie.

Music: Recorded.

Exeutive Producer: Bob Banner.

Producer: Sam Riddle.

Director: Louis J. Horvitz.

ALL STAR ANYTHING GOES—30 minutes—Syndicated 1977.

THE ALL—STAR REVUE
THE FOUR—STAR REVUE

Variety. Varying program formats styled to the talents of its guest hosts.

Producer: Leo Morgan, Sidney Smith, Ezra Stone, Joseph Santley, Norman Zeno, Coby Ruskin.

Director: Gary Lockwood, Ezra Stone, Douglas Rogers, Coby Ruskin, Joseph Santley.

Included:

The Olsen and Johnson Show.

Hosts: Ole Olsen, Chick Johnson.

Guests: June Johnson, J. C. Olsen, John Melina, Marty May, The Dunhills.

Orchestra: Milton DeLugg.

The Jimmy Durante Show.

Host: Jimmy Durante.

Guests: Jules Buffano, Bob Crozier, Eddie Jackson, Phil Leeds, Helen Traibel, Candy Candito.

Orchestra: Roy Bargy; Jack Roth.

The Danny Thomas Show.

Host: Danny Thomas.

Guests: Kay Starr, Bunny Leubell, The Hurricaines.

Orchestra: Lou Bring.

The Victor Borge Show.

Host: Victor Borge.

Guests: Lauritz Melchior, Verna Zorina, June Hutton, Phil Leeds

The Martha Raye Show.

Hostess: Martha Raye.

Guest: Robert Cummings.

Orchestra: George Bassman.

The George Jessel Show.

Host: George Jessel.

Guests: Ray McDonald, Tony Martin, Dorothy Kirsten, The Skylarks.

The Ritz Brothers Show.

Hosts: The Ritz Brothers—Al, Jimmy, Harry.

Guests: Mimi Benzell, John Ireland, Bill Skipper.

Orchestra: Lou Bring.

The Ed Wynn Show.

Host: Ed Wynn.

Guests: Dinah Shore, Pat O'Brien, Ben Wrigley, Lucille Ball.

Also Hosting: Ezio Pinza, Jack Carson, Jane Froman, Herb Shriner, Phil Foster, Tallullah Bankhead.

Additional Orchestrations: Allan Roth.

THE FOUR—STAR REVUE (Original Title)—60 minutes—NBC—November 1, 1950 - May 16, 1951.

THE ALL—STAR REVUE (Retitled) —60 minutes—NBC—September 8, 1951 - April 18, 1953.

THE ALL—STAR SUMMER REVUE

Musical Variety. Summer replacement

for "The All-Star Revue."

Hosts: Carl Ballantine, Oliver Wakefield.
Regulars: Georgia Gibbs, The Paul Steffin Dancers, The Acromaniacs.
Orchestra: Dean Elliot.

THE ALL STAR SUMMER REVUE —60 minutes—NBC—June 28, 1952 - September 1952.

———ALL STAR THEATRE

An early 1950s syndicated anthology series that featured such performers as Marjorie Lord, Laraine Day, Robert Stack, and Natalie Wood. Space was left before the title to allow local stations to insert the sponsor's name.

ALL THAT GLITTERS

Comedy-Drama. An offbeat series that reverses the male-female roles to focus on a society wherein the women are the workers and the men the housekeepers and secretaries. Serial-type episodes relate the harried existences of the female executives of the Globatron Corporation, a large conglomerate.

CAST

Christina Stockwood, an executive	Lois Nettleton
Nancy Langston, an executive	Anita Gillette
L.W. Carruthers, the head of Globatron	Barbara Baxley
Andrea Martin, the lawyer	Louise Shaffer
Bert Stockwood, Christina's husband	Chuck McCann
Linda Murkland, the model	Linda Gray
Glen Langston, Nancy's husband	Wes Parker
Michael McFarland, a secretary	David Haskell
Dan Kincaid, a secretary	Gary Sandy
Joan Hamlyn, the theatrical agent	Jessica Walter
Smitty, an executive	Vanessa Brown
Jeremy, Christina and Bert's son	Marte Boyle Slout

Music: Alan and Marilyn Bergman.
Instrumentals: Shelly Mann.
Theme Vocal: Kenny Rankin.
Executive Producer: Stephanie Sills.
Producer: Viva Knight.
Director: Herbert Kenwith.
Developed by: Norman Lear.

ALL THAT GLITTERS—30 minutes—Syndicated 1977.

ALMOST ANYTHING GOES

Game. Three teams, each composed of six members and representing towns with a population of under 15,000, compete. The players, all of whom are amateurs, compete in a series of stunt contests. The team that scores highest at the end of the seventh game is the winner and receives the opportunity to compete in the national finals, which pits three of the highest scoring teams against each other. A trophy is awarded to the team that proves itself superior in the playoffs.

Hosts: Charlie Jones, Lynn Shakelford, Sam Riddle.
Field Interviewers: Dick Wittington, Regis Philbin.
Music: Recorded.
Executive Producer: Bob Banner, Beryl Vertue.
Producer: Jeff Harris, Robert Stigwood, Camilla Dunn.
Director: Mark Hemion, Kip Walton.

ALMOST ANYTHING GOES—60 minutes—ABC—July 31, 1975 - August 28, 1975; January 24, 1976 - May 9, 1976.

THE AL PEARCE SHOW

Variety.
Host: Al Pearce

THE AL PEARCE SHOW—30 minutes—CBS—July 10, 1952 - September 18, 1952.

ALUMNI FUN

Game. Two competing teams, each composed of three celebrity college alumni members. The host states a question. The player first to identify himself (through a buzzer signal) receives a chance to answer. If the response is correct, money is awarded. The winners, highest cash scorers, donate their earnings to their college alumni.

Host: Peter Lind Hayes, Clifton Fadiman.

ALUMNI FUN—30 minutes—CBS—January 20, 1963 - April 28, 1963; January 5, 1964 - April 5, 1964; January 10, 1965 - March 28, 1965; January 23, 1966 - May 1, 1966.

THE ALVIN SHOW

Animated Cartoon. The misadventures of songwriter Dave Seville, the manager of the Chipmonks (Alvin, Theodore, and Simon), a group of singing animals. Plots revolve around his reluctant involvement in their unpredictable antics.

Additional segments:
"The Adventures of Clyde Crashcup." The attempts of world famous inventor Clyde Crashcup to perfect his discoveries, e.g., the bed, the safety match, the wheel.

"Sinbad Jr." The adventures of sailor Sinbad Jr., and his parrot, Salty.

Characters' Voices

Dave Seville	Ross Bagdasarian
The Chipmonks	Ross Bagdasarian
Clyde Crashcup	Shepard Menken
Sinbad	Tim Matthieson
Salty	Mel Blanc

Additional voices: June Foray, Lee Patrick, Bill Lee, William Sanford, Res Dennis.
Music: Ross Bagdasarian.
Producer: Herbert Klynn.
Director: Rudy Lariva, Osmond Evans.

THE ALVIN SHOW—30 minutes—CBS—October 14, 1961 - September 12, 1962. Syndicated. 26 episodes.

A.M. AMERICA

News-Information. Broadcast from 7:00 a.m. - 9:00 a.m., E.S.T.
East Coast Hosts: Bill Beutel, Stephanie Edwards.
West Coast Hosts: Ralph Story, Melanie Noble.
Guest Hostess: Jessica Walter, Barbara Feldon, Lynn Redgrave, Rene Carpenter, Candice Bergen, Barbara Howar.
Newscaster: Peter Jennings.
Regulars: Roger Caras, Dr. Sonya Friedman, Dr. Tim Johnson.

Music: Recorded.

A.M. AMERICA—2 hours—ABC—January 6, 1975 - October 31, 1975. Revised as "Good Morning, America." See title.

THE AMATEUR HOUR

See title: "Ted Mack."

THE AMATEUR'S GUIDE TO LOVE

Game. A taped, prearranged romantic situation, which involves unsuspecting individuals, is played and stopped prior to its conclusion. Two of the subjects involved in the situation appear opposite a panel of three guest celebrities, "The Guidebook Experts." The celebrities first advise as to what the outcome of the situation should be, then predict the subjects' answers —whether or not they actively involved themselves in it. The tape is played to reveal the answers. If the celebrities have predicted correctly, the subject receives two hundred dollars; if not, he receives one hundred dollars.

Host: Gene Rayburn.

Announcer: Kenny Williams.

Appearing in candid sequences: Barbara Crosby; guests.

Music: Recorded.

THE AMATEUR'S GUIDE TO LOVE–30 minutes–CBS–March 27, 1972 - June 23, 1972. 65 tapes.

THE AMAZING DUNNINGER

See title: "Dunninger."

THE AMAZING CHAN AND THE CHAN CLAN

Animated Cartoon. The investigations of Charlie Chan, a Chinese detective who specializes in solving baffling crimes. Plots concern the intervention of his ten children and their meaningful, but disasterous efforts to assist him. A Hanna-Barbera production. Based on the famous movie character.

Characters' Voices

Charlie Chan	Keye Luke
Henry Chan	Bob Ito
Stanley Chan	Stephen Wong
	Lennie Weinrib
Suzie Chan	Virginia Ann Lee
	Cherylene Lee
Alan Chan	Brian Tochi
Anne Chan	Leslie Kumamota
	Jodie Foster
Tom Chan	Michael Takamoto
	John Gunn
Flip Chan	Jay Jay Jue
	Gene Andrusco
Nancy Chan	Debbie Jue
	Beverly Kushida
Mimi Chan	Leslie Kawai
	Cherylene Lee
Scooter Chan	Robin Toma
	Michael Morgan
Chu Chu, the clan dog	Don Messick

Additional voices: Lisa Gerritsen,

Hazel Shermit, Janet Waldo, Len Wood.

Music: Hoyt Curtin.

Producer-Director: William Hanna, Joseph Barbera.

THE·AMAZING CHAN AND THE CHAN CLAN–30 minutes–CBS–September 9, 1972 - September 22, 1974.

THE AMAZING MR. MALONE

Crime Drama. Background: Chicago. The investigations of John J. Malone, a light-hearted criminal attorney.

Starring:
Lee Tracy as John J. Malone.

Producer-Director: Edward Peterson, Edgar Peterson.

THE AMAZING MR. MALONE–30 minutes–ABC–August 27, 1951 September 24, 1952.

THE AMAZING THREE

Animated Cartoon. Background: Twenty-first century Earth. The exploits of three celestial beings, creatures who have adopted the identities of a horse, a dog, and a duck to protect themselves, and Earthling Kenny Carter, as they battle the sinister forces of evil.

THE AMAZING THREE–30 minutes –Syndicated 1967. 52 episodes.

THE AMAZING WORLD OF KRESKIN

Variety. Feats of mind reading, E.S.P., and sleight of hand.

Starring: Kreskin.

Host-Announcer: Bill Luxton.

Music: Recorded.

THE AMAZING WORLD OF KRESKIN–30 minutes–Syndicated 1972.

AMERICA

History. A thirteen-episode "personal history" of the United States. The country is explored through historical paintings and commentary from its founding to the twentieth century. Filmed by the B.B.C.

Host-Narrator: Alistair Cooke.

Music: Charles Chilton.

Episodes:
1. "The New Found Land." America's discovery.
2. "Home from Home." The seventeenth and eighteenth centuries.
3. "Making a Revolution." The American Revolution.
4. "Inventing a Nation." The American Constitution.
5. "Gone West." The Pioneers and the beginning of Western settlement.
6. "A Fireball in the Night." The Civil War.
7. "Domesticating a Wilderness." The taming of the West.
8. "Money on the Land." The development of American technology.
9. "The Huddled Masses." The influx of immigration.
10. "The Twenties." The songs, the sports, and the events of the twenties.
11. "The Arsenal." America's development and emergence as a military giant.
12. "Dixieland Jazz." A profile of the New England States.
13. "America Today." An analysis of American life.

AMERICA–60 minutes–NBC–November 14, 1972 - May 15, 1973. Syndicated.

AMERICA AFTER DARK

See title: "The Tonight Show."

AMERICAN ADVENTURE

Adventure. Films relating the experiences of various adventurers, e.g., mountain climbers, hunters, racers, etc.

Narrator: Gary Merrill.

Music: James Fagas.

AMERICAN ADVENTURE–30 minutes–Syndicated 1972.

AMERICAN BANDSTAND

Variety. Music and entertainment geared to teenagers.

Host: Dick Clark.

Original Hosts (when shown on WFIL-TV in Philadelphia): Ron Joseph, Lee Stewart (1952-1956;

Dick Clark became the host in 1956).

Announcers: Charlie O'Donnell, Dick Clark.

Original Theme: "The Bandstand Boogie," composed by Charles Albertine; performed by the Les Elgart Orchestra.

Current Theme: Opening performed by Joe Porter; closing by Barry Manilow.

Creator: Bob Horn, Lee Stewart.

Music: Recorded.

Featured: Performances by top music personalities; dancing contests, undiscovered professional talent.

Featured Segment: "Rate-A-Record." Selected studio audience members are asked to rate a record from a thirty-five to a ninety-eight.

AMERICAN BANDSTAND—60 minutes—ABC—Premiered: October 7, 1957. Originally boradcast as a local program in Philadelphia from 1952 to 1957 before becoming a network attraction.

AMERICAN LIFESTYLE

Documentary. The story of America's past, present, and future. Emphasis is placed on the men and women who had the greatest impact on the development of the country.

Host-Narrator: E.G. Marshall.

Music: Michael Shapiro.

AMERICAN LIFESTYLE—30 minutes—Syndicated 1972.

AMERICAN MUSICAL THEATRE

Music. Guests, discussions, and demonstrations on the various types of American music.

Host: Earl Wrightson.

Vocalists: Christine Spencer, Ralph Curtis.

Music: The CBS Orchestra, conducted by Alfredo Antonini.

AMERICAN MUSICAL THEATRE—30 minutes—CBS—1961-1965.

AMERICANS

Drama. Background: Virginia during the Civil War. The wartime activities of two brothers, both farmers and in conflict against each other: Ben Canfield, a Union loyalist, and Jeff Canfield, a Confederate loyalist.

CAST

Ben Canfield	Darryl Hickman
Jeff Canfield	Dick Davidson
Pa Canfield	John McIntire

AMERICANS—60 minutes—NBC—January 23, 1961 - September 11, 1961. 17 episodes.

AMERICAN SHORT STORY

Anthology. Dramatic adaptations of famous American short stories. The stories, nine of which are dramatized, trace, decade by decade, one hundred years of American experience.

Hostess: Coleen Dewhurst.

Music: Ed Bogas.

Executive Producer: Robert Geller.

Producer: Paul Gurain.

Director: Noel Black, Joan Micklin Silver.

Included:

Bernice Bobs Her Hair. F. Scott Fitzgerald's story of a shy young woman who struggles to become more popular.

CAST

Bernice: Shelley Duvall; Marjorie: Veronica Cartwright; Warren: Bud Cort; Mrs. Harvey: Polly Holliday.

I'm a Fool. Sherwood Anderson's story about a race car driver who pretends to be rich in an attempt to impress a beautiful woman.

CAST

Andy: Ron Howard; Lucy: Amy Irving; Burt: Santiago Gonzales.

AMERICAN SHORT STORY—90 and 60 minutes (depending on the story)—PBS—April 5, 1977 - May 10, 1977.

THE AMERICAN WEST

Travel. Tours of America's present-day frontier.

Host-Narrator: Jack Smith.

THE AMERICAN WEST—30 minutes—Syndicated 1966. 78 tapes.

AMERICA'S TOWN HALL MEETING

Interview.. Background: A simulated Town Hall.

Hosts: George V: Denny; John Daly.

Guests: Political figures.

AMERICA'S TOWN HALL MEETING—30 minutes—ABC—October 5, 1948 - July 6, 1952.

THE AMES BROTHERS SHOW

Musical Variety. The format follows that of a fan magazine wherein highlights of the Ames Brothers career is injected into each program.

Hosts: The Ames Brothers: Ed, Vic, Joe, and Gene.

Orchestra: Harry Geller.

THE AMES BROTHERS SHOW—15 minutes—Syndicated 1955.

The Amos and Andy Show. Left to right: Spencer Williams, Jr., Tim Moore, Alvin Childress.

THE AMOS AND ANDY SHOW

Comedy. Background: New York City. The story of three men: Andrew Halt Brown, the naive and dim-witted president of The Fresh Air Taxi Cab Company of America, Amos Jones, his level-headed partner, the cab driver, and George "Kingfish" Stevens, an inept con artist, the head of "The Mystic Knights of the Sea" fraternity.

Stories relate Andy's romantic involvements and efforts to stray from the paths of matrimony; and, finding Andy the perfect sucker, George's endless attempts to acquire money from the cab company, despite Amos's warnings and efforts to protect his investment and keep the company solvent. Adapted from the radio program created by Freeman Gosden and Charles Correll.

CAST

Andrew Halt Brown	Spencer Williams, Jr.
George "Kingfish" Stevens	Tim Moore
Amos Jones	Alvin Childress
Sapphire Stevens, George's wife	Ernestine Wade
Mama, Sapphire's mother	Amanda Randolph
Lightnin', the cab company janitor	Horace Stewart
Algonquin J. Calhoune, the inept lawyer	Johnny Lee
Ruby Jones, Amos's wife	Jane Adams
Arabella Jones, Amos and Ruby's daughter	Patty Marie Ellis
Madame Queen, Andy's former romantic interest	Lillian Randolph
The Old Maid Gribble Sisters (3)	Monnette Moore Zelda Cleaver Willa P. Curtis
Miss Genevieve Blue, the cab company secretary	Madaline Lee

Orchestra and Chorus: Jeff Alexander

Producer: James Fonda, Freeman Gosden, Charles Correll.

Director: Charles Barton.

Sponsor: Blatz Beer.

Program Open:

Announcer: "Out of the library of American Folklore, those treasured stories such as Huck Finn, Paul Bunyan, and Rip Van Winkle—which have brought us laughter and joy for generations—come the warm and lovable tales of Amos and Andy; created by Freeman Gosden and Charles Correll. Presented by the Blatz Brewing Company of Milwaukee, Wisconsin on behalf of Blatz dealers everywhere. Now enjoy Blatz, Milwaukee's finest beer."

THE AMOS AND ANDY SHOW—30 minutes—CBS—June 28, 1951 - June 11, 1953. Withdrawn from syndication in 1966. The first television series to feature an all-Negro cast. 78 episodes.

AMOS BURKE, SECRET AGENT

Mystery. The global investigations of Amos Burke, a former millionaire police captain turned United States government undercover agent. Stories depict his attempts to infiltrate crime organizations and expose high-ranking officials. A spin-off from "Burke's Law."

CAST

Amos Burke	Gene Barry
The Man, his superior	Carl Benton Reid

Music: Herschel Burke Gilbert.

AMOS BURKE, SECRET AGENT— 60 minutes—ABC—September 15, 1965 - January 12, 1966. Syndicated. 17 episodes.

AMY PRENTISS

See title: "NBC Sunday Mystery Movie," *Amy Prentiss* segment.

AN AMERICAN FAMILY

Documentary. A cinema-verité portrait of the Louds: husband, William; his wife, Patricia; and their children, Kevin, Lance, Michele, Delilah, and Grant—an American family residing at 35 Wood Dale Lane, Santa Barbara, California. Of the three hundred hours of film used to record their daily lives, only twelve aired, which were presented in segments over a three-month period.

Music: John Adams.

Producer-Director: Craig Gilbert.

AN AMERICAN FAMILY—PBS—60 minutes—January 10, 1973 - March 28, 1973.

THE ANDROS TARGETS

Crime Drama. Background: New York City. The story of Mike Andros, an investigative reporter for the *New York Forum,* a crusading newspaper.

CAST

Mike Andros	James Sutorius
Sandi Farrell, his assistant	Pamela Reed
Norman Kale, the city editor	Alan Mixon
Chet Reynolds, the managing editor	Roy Poole
The Metropolitan Editor	Jordan Charney
The National Editor	Ted Beniades
Judy, the *Forum* switchboard operator	Gwyn Gillis

Music: Bill Conti, Jerry Fielding, Morton Stevens, Patrick Williams.

Executive Producer: Bob Sweeney, Larry Rosen.

Producer: Edward H. Feldman.

Director: Bob Sweeney, Don Weis, Marc Daniels, Harry Falk, Seymour Robbie, Edward H. Feldman, Irving J. Moore.

Creator: Jerome Coopersmith.

THE ANDROS TARGETS—60 minutes—CBS—January 31, 1977 - May 16, 1977.

THE ANDY GRIFFITH SHOW

Comedy. Background: Mayberry, North Carolina. The story of the relationship between two friends: Sheriff Andy Taylor, widower, and his bachelor cousin, Deputy Barney Fife. Episodes depict Andy's attempts to raise his young son, Opie, and his and Barney's efforts to maintain law in a virtually crime-free town.

CAST

Andy Taylor	Andy Griffith
Barney Fife	Don Knotts
Opie Taylor	Ronny Howard
Bee Taylor, Andy's aunt	Frances Bavier
Ellie Walker, a druggist, Andy's first girlfriend	Elinor Donahue
Mary Simpson, the county nurse	Sue Ane Langdon Julie Adams
Irene Fairchild, the county nurse (later episodes)	Nina Shipman
Helen Crump, the fifth-grade school teacher, later Andy's wife	Aneta Corsaut
Thelma Lou, Barney's girlfriend	Betty Lynn
Otis Campbell, the town drunk	Hal Smith
Howard Sprague, the county clerk	Jack Dodson
Briscoe Darling, a hillbilly	Denver Pyle
Charlene Darling, his daughter	Margaret Ann Peterson
Briscoe Darling's Boys	The Dillard Brothers
Ernest T. Bass, a trouble-making hillbilly	Howard Morris
Gomer Pyle, the naive gas station attendant at Wally's Filling Station	Jim Nabors
Malcolm Merriweather, an Englishman, a friend	

of the Taylor's	Bernard Fox
Goober Pyle, Gomer's cousin	George Lindsey
Clara Edwards, Bee's friend	Hope Summers
Floyd Lawson, the barber	Howard McNair
Deputy Warren Ferguson, Barney's replacement	Jack Burns
Mayor Pike (early episodes)	Dick Elliot
Mayor Stoner (later episodes)	Parley Baer
Jim Lindsey, a friend of Andy's	James Best
Captain Barker, the State Police Chief	Ken Lynch
Emma Brand, the town hypochondriac	Cheerio Meredith
Sam Jones, the town councilman, a widower	Ken Berry
Millie Swanson, Sam's girlfriend	Arlene Golonka
Mike Jones, Sam's young son	Buddy Foster
Emmet Clark, the owner of the Fix-it-Shop	Paul Hartman
Skippy, a fun-loving girl from Raleigh, sweet on Barney	Joyce Jameson
Daphne, her girlfriend, sweet on Andy	Jean Carson
Martha Clark, Emmet's wife	Mary Lansing
Leon, the boy with the peanut butter sandwich	Clint Howard
Johnny Paul, Opie's friend	Richard Keith
Peggy McMillan, Andy's girlfriend (early episodes)	Joanna Moore
Mrs. Sprague, Howard's mother	Mabel Albertson

Music: Earle Hagen.

Executive Producer: Sheldon Leonard (in association with Danny Thomas Enterprises).

Producer: Aaron Ruben, Richard O. Linke, Bob Ross.

Director: Alan Rafkin, Coby Ruskin, Earl Bellamy, Bob Sweeney, Lee Philips, Richard Crenna.

Andy's Home Address: 14 Maple Street.

THE ANDY GRIFFITH SHOW—30 minutes—CBS—October 3, 1960 - September 16, 1968. 249 episodes. Syndicated. Also titled: "Andy of Mayberry." Spin-off series: "Mayberry R.F.D." See title.

ANDY OF MAYBERRY

See title: "The Andy Griffith Show."

ANDY'S GANG

Children's Variety. Music, songs, comedy, and stories set against the background of a clubhouse.

Original title: "The Buster Brown TV Show with Smilin' Ed McConnell and the Buster Brown Gang." Later titled: "Smilin' Ed McConnell and His Gang." In 1955, after the death of Mr. McConnell, Andy Devine became its host under the title, "Andy's Gang."

Characters: Squeaky the Mouse; Midnight the Tabby Cat; Froggie the Gremlin, a mischievous frog; Old Grandie, the talking piano.

Story segment: "Gunga, the East India Boy." Background: The village of Bakore. The adventures of Gunga and his friend Rama, young men who perform hazardous missions for their leader, the Maharajah.

CAST

Ed McConnell (Host)	Himself
Andy Devine (Host)	Himself
Gunga Ram	Nino Marcel
Rama	Vito Scotti
The Maharajah	Lou Krugman
Algernon Archibald Percival Shortfellow, the Poet	Alan Reed
The Teacher	Billy Gilbert
Buster Brown	Jerry Marin
The Sound of his dog. Tige	Bud Tollefson
Froggie the Gremlin	Ed McConnell Frank Ferrin
Voice of Midnight the cat	June Foray
Voice of Grandie	June Foray

Also: Joe Mazzuca, Peter Coo, Paul Cavanaugh, Billy Race

Announcer: Arch Presby.

Producer-Director: Frank Ferrin.

Sponsor: Buster Brown Shoes.

THE BUSTER BROWN TV SHOW WITH SMILIN' ED McCONNELL AND THE BUSTER BROWN GANG —30 minutes—NBC—September 23, 1950 - August 4, 1951.
SMILIN' ED McCONNELL AND HIS GANG—30 minutes. NBC—August 11, 1951 - August 15, 1953. ABC—August 22, 1953 - April 16, 1955. NBC—April 23, 1955 - August 13, 1955.
ANDY'S GANG—30 minutes—NBC— August 20, 1955 - September 1960.

ANDY WILLIAMS

Listed: The television programs of singer Andy Williams:

The Andy Williams-June Valli Show— Musical Variety—15 minutes — NBC—July 2, 1957 - September 5, 1957.

Host: Andy Williams.

Hostess: June Valli.

Orchestra: Alvy West.

The Chevy Showroom—Musical Variety—30 minutes—ABC—July 3, 1958 - September 25, 1958.

Host: Andy Williams.

Regulars: Dick Van Dyke, Jayne Turner, Gail Kuhr.

Music: The Bob Hamilton Trio.

The Andy Williams Show—Musical Variety—60 minutes—CBS—July 7, 1959 — September 22, 1959.

Host: Andy Williams.

Regulars: Michael Storm, The Peter Gennaro Dancers, The Dick Williams Singers.

Orchestra: Jack Kane.

The Andy Williams Show—Musical Variety—60 minutes—NBC—September 22, 1962 - September 3, 1967.

Host: Andy Williams.

Regulars: Randy Sparks and the New Christy Minstrels, The Osmond Brothers, The Good Time Singers, The George Wyle Singers, The James Starbuck Dancers, The Nick Castle Dancers.

Orchestra: Colin Romoff; Allyn Ferguson; Dave Grusin.

The Andy Williams Show—Musical Variety—60 minutes—NBC—September 20, 1969 - July 17, 1971.

Host: Andy Williams.

Regulars: Janos Prohaska (The Cookie-Seeking Bear), Irwin Corey, Charlie Callas, The Jaime Rogers Singers, The Earl Brown Dancers, The Archie Tayir Dancers.

Orchestra: Mike Post.

The Andy Williams Show—Musical Variety—30 minutes—Syndicated 1976.

Host: Andy Williams.

Regular: Wayland Flowers, a puppeteer.

Orchestra: George Wyle.

AN EVENING WITH ...

Variety. Background: A simulated nightclub atmosphere. Programs are tailored to the personalities of its guests.

Appearing: Julie London, Gretchen Wyler, Xavier Cougat, Pete Fountain, Marty Allen and Steve Rossi, The King Sisters, Louis Prima, Gene Pitney.

AN EVENING WITH. . .–30 minutes –Syndicated–1965-1967. 56 tapes.

ANGEL

Comedy. Background: Suburban New York. The trials and tribulations of young marrieds: John Smith, an architect; and his French wife, Angel. Stories depict Angel's difficulties as she struggles to cope with the bewildering American lifestyle.

CAST

Angel Smith	Annie Fargé
John Smith	Marshall Thompson
Susie, Angel's friend, a neighbor	Doris Singleton
George, Susie's husband	Don Keefer

ANGEL–30 minutes–CBS–October 6, 1960 - September 20, 1961. 33 episodes.

ANIMAL KINGDOM

Documentary. Wildlife films depicting the animal struggle for survival.

Host-Narrator: Bill Burrud.

ANIMAL KINGDOM–30 minutes– NBC–June 16, 1968 – September 1968. 38 episodes.

ANIMALS, ANIMALS, ANIMALS

Children. A magazine type of series that attempts to explain the relationship of animals to man in history, art, music, mythology, and literature.

Host: Hal Linden.

Voices for cartoon segments: Estelle Parsons, Mason Adams.

Singer: Lynn Kellogg.

Music: Michael Kamen.

Executive Producer: Lester Cooper.

Producer: Peter Weinberger.

ANIMALS, ANIMALS ANIMALS–

25 minutes–ABC–Premiered: September 12, 1976.

ANIMAL SECRETS

Documentary. Wildlife films depicting the animal struggle for survival.

Host-Narrator: Loren Eisley.

ANIMAL SECRETS–30 minutes– NBC–October 15, 1966 - April 8, 1967. 24 episodes.

ANIMAL WORLD

Documentary. Wildlife films depicting the animal struggle for survival.

Host-Narrator: Bill Burrud.

ANIMAL WORLD–30 minutes. CBS–May 8, 1969 - September 18, 1969; ABC–May 1970 - September 1970; CBS–July 11, 1971 - September 12, 1971. Syndicated.

ANNA AND THE KING

Comedy-Drama. Background: Siam, 1862. Anna Owens, a young widowed American school teacher, is hired to educate and introduce Western culture to the royal children of the King of Siam. His Majesty, the absolute Monarch, rules all but Anna. Independent and forthright, she is prompted to defy rules and customs, hoping to enlighten him to the principles of freedom and justice. Based on the movie of the same title.

CAST

The King of Siam	Yul Brynner
Anna Owens	Samantha Eggar
Prince Kralahome	Keye Luke
Louis Owens, Anna's son	Eric Shea
The Crown Prince Chulolongkorn	Brian Tochi
Lady Thiang, the King's head-wife	Lisa Lu
Princess Serana, the King's eldest daughter	Rosalind Chao
Child (unnamed), the King's daughter	Wendy Tochi
Kai-Lee Ling, the King's daughter	Tracy Lee

Music: Richard Shores.

ANNA AND THE KING–30 minutes –CBS–September 17, 1972 - December 31, 1972. 13 episodes.

ANNIE OAKLEY

Western. Background: The town of

Diablo during the 1860s. The exploits of Annie Oakley, woman rancher and expert sharpshooter, as she attempts to maintain law and order.

CAST

Annie Oakley	Gail Davis
Deputy Lofty Craig	Brad Johnson
Tagg Oakley, Annie's kid brother	Jimmy Hawkins
Annie's horse: Buttercup.	

ANNIE OAKLEY–30 minutes–ABC –1953-1958. 80 episodes. Syndicated.

THE ANNIVERSARY GAME

Game. Three husband-and-wife teams compete for merchandise prizes.

Rounds One and Two: One member of one team is subjected to a prearranged situation. The spouse is asked to predict the outcome. If correct, points are awarded. Each couple participates in turn, and each spouse has the opportunity to predict his or her partner's reaction.

Round Three: One stunt involving the three couples. The one player that remains wins points for his or her team.

Round Four: "The Lightning Fast Round." Couples are seated and asked general knowledge questions. The player first to sound a bell signal and be recognized receives a chance to answer. If correct, one point is awarded; incorrect, no penalty.

Winners are the highest scoring couple.

Host: Al Hamel.

Announcer: Dean Webber.

THE ANNIVERSARY GAME–30 minutes–Syndicated 1969. 26 tapes.

THE ANN SOTHERN SHOW

Comedy. Background: New York City. The misadventures of Katy O'Connor, the assistant manager of the fictitious Bartley House Hotel.

CAST

October 6, 1958 - March 2, 1959:

Katy O'Connor	Ann Sothern
Jason Maculey, the hotel manager	Ernest Truex
Flora Maculey, his wife	Reta Shaw
Olive Smith, Katy's secretary	Ann Tyrrell

Paul Martine, the bellboy ... Jacques Scott

Music: Thomas Adair.

CAST

March 9, 1959 - September 25, 1961:

Katy O'Connor ... Ann Sothern
James Devery, the hotel manager ... Don Porter
Olive Smith ... Ann Tyrrell
Dr. Delbert Gray, the hotel dentist ... Louis Nye
Woody, the bellboy ... Ken Berry
Oscar Pudney, Katy's nemesis ... Jesse White

Music: Thomas Adair.

THE ANN SOTHERN SHOW—30 minutes—CBS—October 6, 1958 - September 25, 1961. 93 episodes. Syndicated.

ANOTHER WORLD

Serial. Background: The town of Bay City. The dramatic story of two families, the Randolphs and the Matthews. Episodes relate the conflicts and tensions that arise from the interactions of the characters.

CAST

Jim Matthews ... John Beal, Leon Janney, Shepperd Strudwick, Hugh Marlowe
Mary Matthews ... Virginia Dwyer
Grandma Matthews ... Vera Allen
Alice Matthews ... Jacqueline Courtney
Pat Matthews ... Susan Trustman, Beverly Penberthy
Russ Matthews ... Joey Trent, Sam Groom, Robert Hover, David Bailey
Janet Matthews ... Liza Chapman
Liz Matthews ... Sara Cunningham, Nancy Wickwire, Irene Dailey
Bill Matthews ... Joe Gallison
Melissa Palmer ... Carol Roux
Ken Baxter ... William Prince
Tom Baxter ... Nicholas Pryor
Gerald Davis ... Walter Matthews
Helen Moore ... Muriel Williams
Dr. John Bradford ... John Crawford
Susan Matthews ... Fran Sharon, Lisa Cameron
John Randolph ... Michael M. Ryan
Lee Randolph ... Gaye Huston, Barbara Rodell
Danny Fargo ... Anthony Ponzini
Michael Dru ... Geoffrey Lumb
Wayne Addison ... Robert Milli
Walter Curtin ... Val Dufour
Cindy Clark ... Leonie Norton
Ted Clark ... Steve Bolster
Michael Bauer ... Garry Pillar
Alex Gregory ... James Congdon
Karen Gregory ... Ellen Watson
Dr. Ernest Gregory ... Mark Lenard
Peggy Harris ... Micki Grant
Mrs. Hastings ... Mona Burns
Flo Murray ... Marcella Martin
Hope Bauer ... Elissa Leeds
Cathryn Corniny ... Ann Sheridan
The Assistant District Attorney ... Billy Dee Williams, Alex Wipf
Lenore Moore ... Judith Barcroft, Susan Sullivan
Luella Watson ... Dorothy Blackburn
Dr. David Thornton ... Joseph Ponazecki, Colgate Salisbury
Ellen ... Irene Biendie, Gail Dixon
Andy Cummings ... Jim Secrest
Bernice Addison ... Janis Young
Chris Tyler ... Steve Harmon
Fred Douglas ... Charles Baxter
Ernie Downs ... Harry Bellaver
Dan Shearer ... John Cunningham
Barbara Shearer ... Christine Cameron
Jane Overstreet ... Frances Sternhagen
Belle Clark ... Janet Ward
Marianne Randolph ... Tracy Brown, Ariane Munker
Michael Randolph ... Christopher Corwin, Christopher J. Brown, Lionel Johnston
Rachel Davis ... Robin Strasser, Margaret Impert, Victoria Wyndham
Mark Venable ... Andrew Jarkowsky
Prof. Philip Lessner ... Ed Bryce
Mrs. McCrea ... Nancy Marchand
Raymond Scott ... James Preston
Dr. Philbin ... Charles Siebert
Jamie Matthews ... Aidan McNulty
Robert Delaney ... Nick Coster
Zack Richards ... Terry Alexander
Gil McGowen ... Dolph Sweet
Linda Metcalf ... Vera Moore
Gloria Metcalf ... Rosetta LeNoire
Ada Downs ... Constance Ford
Eliot Carrington ... James Douglas
Denis Carrington ... Mike Hammett
Iris Carrington ... Beverlee McKinsey
Louise Goddard ... Anne Meacham
Lahoma Vane ... Ann Wedgeworth
Dr. Paula McCrea ... Beverly Owen
Stephen Frame ... George Reinholt
Frank Chadwick ... Robert Kya-Hill
Tom Albini ... Pierrino Mascorino
Gil McGowen ... Charles Durning
Madge Murray ... Doris Belack
Lefty Burns ... Larry Keith
Walter Curtin, Jr. ... Scott Firestone, Denis McKiernan, Jason Gladstone
Janice Frame ... Victoria Thompson
Tim McGowen ... Christopher Allport
MacKenzie Corey ... Robert Emhardt, Douglas Watson
Sam Lucas ... Jordan Charney
Dr. Curt Landis ... Donald Madden
Olga Bellin ... Ann Fuller
Rachel Corey ... Victoria Wyndham
Jamie Frame ... Bobby Doran, William McMillan
Carole Lamont ... Jeanne Lange
David Gilchrist ... John Aprea, David Ackroyd
Vic Hastings ... John Considine
Neil Johnson ... John Getz
Angela Perrini ... Toni Kalem, Maeve Kinkead
Sally Spencer ... Cathy Greene
Beatrice Gordon ... Jacqueline Brookes
Chris Pierson ... Stephen Yates
Clarice Hobson ... Gail Brown
Loretta Simpson ... Elaine Kerr
Pam Sloane ... Karin Wolfe
Scott Bradley ... Michael Goodwin
Alice Frame ... Susan Harney
Roy Gordon ... Ted Shackelford, Gary Carpenter
Brian Bancroft ... Paul Stevens
Daryll Stevens ... Richard Dunne
Donna Beck ... Francesca Poston
Sharlene Matthews ... Laura Heineman
Burt McGowan ... William Russ
Sven Peterson ... Robert Blossom
Quentin Ames ... Peter Ratray
Helga Lindstrom ... Helen Stenborg
Regine Lindeman ... Barbara eda Young
Jeff Stone ... Dan Hamilton
Theresa Lamont ... Nancy Marchand
Tracy DeWitt ... Caroline McWilliams
Ken Palmer ... Kelly Monaghan, William Lyman
Barbara Weaver ... Kathryn Walker
Willis Frame ... John Fitzpatrick, Leon Russom
Keith Morrison ... Fred Beir
Rocky Olsen ... John Braden
Evan Webster ... Barry Jenner
Olive Gordon ... Jennifer Leak
Gwen Parrish ... Dorothy Lyman
Molly Ordway ... Rolonda Mendels

Also: Edmund Hashem, Elspeth Eric, Tom Ruger, Stephen Bolster, Bobby Doran, Jill Turnbull, Glenn Zachar, Tiberia Mitori.

Music: Chet Kingsbury.

Announcer: Bill Wolff.

Program Open:

Announcer: "We do not live in this world alone, but in a thousand other worlds. The events of our own lives represent only the surface, and in our minds and feelings we live in many other worlds."

ANOTHER WORLD—30 minutes—NBC—May 4, 1964 - January 3, 1975; 60 minutes: Premiered: January 6, 1975.

ANOTHER WORLD IN SOMERSET

See title: "Somerset."

ANSWER YES OR NO

Game. Contestants are presented with a situation dilemma and asked to secretly choose a yes or no card, indicating whether or not he would or would not become involved. A celebrity panel of four then predict the contestants' answers. Each correct guess awards that contestant a merchandise prize.

Host: Moss Hart.

Panelists: Arlene Francis, Jane Pickens, Peter Lind Hayes, Mary Healy.

ANSWER YES OR NO—30 minutes—NBC 1950.

ANYBODY CAN PLAY

Game. A panel of four contestants compete for points. They are seated opposite a guest who possesses a concealed object. By means of indirect questions the panelists have to identify the object. The highest point accumulators are the winners and receive merchandise prizes.

Host: George Fenneman.

Producer: John Guedel, Dolph Nelson.

ANYBODY CAN PLAY—30 minutes —ABC—July 6, 1958 - December 8, 1958.

ANYONE CAN WIN

Game. Players: A panel of four celebrities — three regulars and one guest. Object: to identify an anonymous celebrity-guest whose face is hidden behind a rubber mask of the Al Capp character, Hairless Joe. Each panelist is given an allotted time to ask questions and foster a guess. A preselected studio audience member is then asked to back one of the panelists. The mystery guest is revealed and the contestant receives a cash prize if his choice is correct.

Host: Al Capp.

Panelists: Patsy Kelly, Ilka Chase, Jimmy Dykes.

ANYONE CAN WIN—30 minutes—CBS 1950.

ANYTHING YOU CAN DO

Game. Two three member teams, men vs. women. Located above each team is a category board containing three physical and/or mental stunts. The men select from the women's side and vice versa. Each team must perform the activities within a specified time limit (usually 90 seconds). The team accumulating the least amount of overall time is declared the winner and receives merchandise prizes.

Hosts: Gene Wood; Don Harron.

Announcer: Bill Luxton.

ANYTHING YOU CAN DO—30 minutes—Syndicated 1971.

ANYWHERE, U.S.A.

Anthology. Stories depicting the overlooked and often neglected health problems of people.

CAST

Doctor	Edward Dowling
Doctor	Robert Preston

ANYWHERE, U.S.A—30 minutes—ABC—November 9, 1952 - December 14, 1952.

APARTMENT 3-C

Comedy. Background: 46 Perry Street, New York City, Apartment 3-C. The trials and tribulations of young marrieds: John Gay, a writer, and his scatterbrained wife, Barbara.

CAST

John Gay	Himself
Barbara Gay	Herself

APARTMENT 3-C—15 minutes—CBS —September 1949 - December 1949.

APPLE'S WAY

Drama. Background: The small town of Appleton, Iowa. The dreams, frustrations, and ambitions of the Apple family: George; his wife, Barbara; and their children, Paul, Cathy, Patricia, and Steven. Stories depict George's attempts to recapture for himself and his family the treasured memories of his childhood: "the wonders of streams and woods. . .the mystery of growing crops and days filled with adventure. . .with participation in good and comforting things."

CAST

George Apple	Ronny Cox
Barbara Apple	Lee McCain
Paul Apple	Vincent Van Patten
Cathy Apple	Pattie Cohoon
Patricia Apple	Franny Michel
	Kristy McNichol
Steven Apple	Eric Olsen
Aldon Apple, George's father	Malcolm Atterbury

Apple family pets: Dogs: Muffin, Sam and Bijou; snake: Ruby.

Music: Morton Stevens.

APPLE'S WAY—60 minutes—CBS— February 10, 1974 - January 12, 1975. 24 episodes.

APPOINTMENT WITH ADVENTURE

Anthology. Dramatizations based on the actual experiences of ordinary people in all walks of life.

Included:

Minus Three Thousand. Background: The Pyrenees Mountains between France and Spain. The story of two friends who decide to explore a cave; the conflict; one loves the other's wife.

CAST

Louis Jourdan, Claude Dauphin, Mala Powers.

Five In Judgement. A group of people are forced to remain in a roadside diner during a tornado. As they listen to the radio, a broadcast describes two men wanted for murder. The story depicts the desperation that arises when it is realized that two of their number resemble the description.

CAST

Paul Newman, Henry Hull, James Gregson, Jeff Harris.

The Fateful Pilgrimage. The story of an ex-G.I. who returns to the German village he helped capture during World War II to find the girl who nursed him back to health when he was wounded.

CAST

William Prince, Viveca Lindfors, Theodore Bikel.

APPOINTMENT WITH ADVENTURE—30 minutes—CBS—April 3, 1955 - March 25, 1956.

APPOINTMENT WITH LOVE

Anthology. Rebroadcasts of episodes that were originally aired via other filmed anthology programs. Dramatizations stressing the gentleness of life and the goodness of Nature.

Included:

Autumn Flames. The story of a wife who falls in love with another man after fourteen years of marriage.

CAST

Maria Palmer, Onslow Stevens.

Some Small Nobility. Believing her husband has only one year to live, a wife strives to make the year the happiest.

CAST

Joan Banks.

This Little Pig Cried. The story of a young couple's first marital spat.

CAST

Frances Rafferty, Robert Rockwell.

APPOINTMENT WITH LOVE—30 minutes—ABC—December 23, 1952 - September 25, 1953.

AQUAMAN

Animated Cartoon. Aquaman, born of an Atlantian mother and a human father (a lighthouse keeper), establishes himself as the ruler of the Seven Seas. He is capable of commanding all sea creatures through telepathic, radiating brain waves. Stories concern his battle against the sinister forces of evil as he attempts to protect the Kingdom of Atlantis.

Additional characters: Aqualad, his aide; Minnow, Storm, and Tadpole, their sea horses; and Tusky the walrus.

Voice characterizations: Marvin Miller.

AQUAMAN—07 minutes—Syndicated 1970. Originally broadcast as part of "The Superman-Aquaman Hour"—60 minutes—CBS—September 9, 1967 - September 7, 1968. 18 episodes.

THE AQUANAUTS

Adventure. Background: Honolulu, Hawaii. The cases of Drake Andrews, Larry Lahr, and Mike Madison, professional divers.

CAST

Drake Andrews	Keith Larsen
Larry Lahr	Jeremy Slate
Mike Madison	Ron Ely

Their boat: The *Atlantis.*

Music: Andre Previn.

Producer: Irwin Allen.

THE AQUANAUTS—60 minutes—CBS—September 14, 1960 - May 1961. 32 episodes.

ARCHER

Crime Drama. Background: Melrose, California. The investigations of private detective Lew Archer. Based on the character created by Ross Macdonald.

CAST

Lew Archer	Brian Keith
Lt. Barney Brighton	John P. Ryan

Music: Jerry Goldsmith.

ARCHER—60 minutes—NBC—January 30, 1975 - March 14, 1975. 7 episodes.

THE ARCHIE SHOW

Animated Cartoon. The misadventures of a group of high school students in the mythical town of Riverdale. Based on the comic "Archie," by Bob Montana.

Characters: Archie Andrews; Jughead Jones; Betty Cooper; Veronica Lodge; Reggie Mantle, Sabrina, the teenage witch; Hot Dog, the gang pet; Salem, Sabrina's cat; Mr. Weatherby, the school principal; Aunt Hilda and Cousin Ambrose, Sabrina's realtives; Big Ethel; Ophelia; Spencer; Harvey.

Voices: Jane Webb, Dallas McKennon, Howard Morris.

Music: George Blais, Jeff Michael.

Musical Supervision: Don Kirshner.

Producer: Lou Scheimer, Norm Prescott.

Director: Hal Sutherland.

Versions:

The Archie Show—30 minutes—CBS—September 14, 1968 - September 9, 1969.

Format: Two ten-minute sketches and a dance-of-the-week-selection.

The Archie Comedy Hour—60 minutes—CBS—September 13, 1969 -September 5, 1970.

Format: Various sketches and musical numbers.

Archie's Funhouse Featuring the Giant Joke Box—30 minutes—CBS—September 12, 1970 - September 4, 1971.

Format: Dances and comedy sketches centered around a "Giant Joke Box" (which resembles and operates like a juke box).

Archie's TV Funnies—30 minutes—CBS—September 11, 1971 - September 1, 1973.

Format: The Archie Gang, operators of a television station, present animated adaptations of eight comic strips: "Dick Tracy," "The Captain and the Kids," "Moon Mullins," "Smokey Stover," "Nancy and Sluggo," "Here Come the Dropouts," "Broom Hilda," "Emmy Lou."

Everything's Archie—30 minutes—CBS—September 8, 1973 - January 26, 1974.

Format: Various comedy sketches and musical numbers.

The U.S. of Archie—30 minutes—CBS —September 7, 1974 - September 5, 1976.

Format: Stories of the accomplishments of great Americans.

Note: All the Archie programs are syndicated under the title "The Archies." On May 18, 1977, ABC presented a live-action pilot film, titled "Archie," that failed to become a regular series.

CAST

Archie: Dennis Brown; Betty: Audrey Landers; Veronica: Hilary Thompson; Reggie: Mark Winkworth; Jughead: Darryl Murphy.

Producer: James Komack.

Director: Robert Scheerer.

Music: Stu Gardner.

ARE YOU POSITIVE?

Game. Celebrity panelists attempt to identify well known personalities from their baby pictures. The panelists, representing a home viewer who is selected by a postcard drawing, forfeit five dollars to that person if they are unable to identify the photograph.

Hosts: Bill Stern; Frank Coniff.

Panelists: Frank Frisch, Lefty Gomez (plus guests).

ARE YOU POSITIVE?—30 minutes—NBC 1952.

ARK II

Science Fiction Adventure. Era: Earth

in the year 2476. The Earth, fertile and rich for millions of years; suddenly, pollution and waste take their toll and a once-great civilization falls into ruin. Conventional civilization no longer exists; and only a handful of scientists remain to rebuild what has been destroyed. Their one major achievement: *Ark II*, a mobile storehouse of scientific knowledge manned by three young scientists: Jonah, Ruth, and Samuel. Stories relate their experiences as they set out to "bring the hope of the new future to mankind."

CAST

Jonah	Terry Lester
Ruth	Jean Marie Hon
Samuel	Jose Flores

Their Assistant: Adam, a chimpanzee.

Music: Yvette Blais, Jeff Michael.

Executive Producer: Norm Prescott, Lou Scheimer.

Producer: Dick Rosenbloom.

Director: Ted Post, Hollingsworth Morse.

ARK II—25 minutes—CBS—Premiered: September 11, 1976.

ARLENE DAHL'S BEAUTY SPOT

Women. Beauty and cosmetic tips.

Hostess: Arlene Dahl.

Music: Recorded.

ARLENE DAHL'S BEAUTY SPOT—05 minutes—ABC—September 27, 1965 - June 24, 1966.

ARLENE DAHL'S PLAYHOUSE

Anthology. Dramatic presentations.

Hostess: Arlene Dahl.

Included:

The Night Light at Vordens. The story of a possessive mother who attempts to dominate her daughter's life.
CAST
Craig Stevens, Jean Byron.

Death Has A System. A story of violence and retribution behind the scenes of a gambling casino.

CAST
Kim Spaulding, Sally Mansfield, Ian MacDonald.

The House Nobody Wanted. The fear

that confronts a wife when she begins to suspect that her husband is a murderer.

CAST
Marilyn Erskine, Craig Stevens.

Claire. The story of a woman who constantly neglects her family to further her career.

CAST
Marguerite Chapman, Marilyn Erskine.

ARLENE DAHL'S PLAYHOUSE—30 minutes—ABC—1953 - 1954.

THE ARLENE FRANCIS SHOW

Variety. Guests, interviews, music, and songs. Comments on books, movies, and current events.

Hostess: Arlene Francis.

Music: The Norman Paris Trio.

Producer: Alan Beaumont.

THE ARLENE FRANCIS SHOW—30 minutes—NBC—August 12, 1957 - February 21, 1958.

ARMCHAIR DETECTIVE

Game. Selected studio audience members compete. A criminal case is reenacted and stopped prior to the denouncement. The first player to solve the case, based on script clues, is the winner and receives a merchandise prize.

Host: John Milton Kennedy.

Assistants: Jerome Sheldon, Cy Kendall.

Producer: Mike Stokey.

ARMCHAIR DETECTIVE—30 minutes—CBS 1949.

THE ARMSTRONG CIRCLE THEATRE

Anthology. Dramatizations based on true incidents.

Producer: Robert Costello, Jacqueline Babbin, George Simpson, Selig Alkon.

Included:

Crisis On Tangier Island. The story centers on the efforts of a priest to

find a doctor who is willing to remain on a remote island.

CAST
Reverend Richel: Kent Smith; Mrs. Richel: Frances Reid; Sam Parker: Frank M. Thomas.

Assignment: Junkie's Alley. Background: Philadelphia. The story of the Narcotics Squad and their attempts to curtail the drug market through the use of police women.

CAST
Ann Rosen: Monica Lovett; Freddie: Addison Powell; Jimmy: James Congdon.

John Doe Number 154. The story of an amnesiac as he searches for his real identity.

CAST
George Applegate: John Napier; Mrs. Gentile: Ruth White; Dr. Kryslot: William Prince.

Have Jacket Will Travel. The story of three foreign children adopted by American families.

CAST
Gina: Patty Duke; Aristides Andros: Martin Brooks; Lewis Stidman: Don Briggs.

THE ARMSTRONG CIRCLE THEATRE—60 minutes—NBC—January 6, 1950 - June 25, 1957; CBS—October 2, 1957 - August 28, 1963.

ARNIE

Comedy. Background: Los Angeles, California. After twelve years as a dock boss for Continental Flange, Inc., Arnie Nuvo is promoted to the position of "New Head of Product Improvement." Stories concern Arnie's struggles as he attempts to adjust to the responsibilities of an executive position.

CAST

Arnie Nuvo	Herschel Bernardi
Lillian Nuvo, his wife	Sue Ane Langdon
Andréa Nuvo, their daughter	Stephanie Steele
Richard Nuvo, their son	Del Russell
Hamilton Majors, Jr., the company president	Roger Bowen
Julius, a friend of Arnie's	Tom Pedi

Neil Ogilvie, the plant
  supervisor   Herbert Voland
Fred Springer, the
  advertising head   Olan Soule
Felicia Farfas, Arnie's
  secretary   Elaine Shore
Randy Robinson, Arnie's
  neighbor, TV's
  "The Giddyap
  Gourmet."   Charles Nelson Reilly

ARNIE—30 minutes—CBS—September 19, 1970 - September 9, 1972. 48 episodes.

ARREST AND TRIAL

Crime Drama. Background: Los Angeles, California. A depiction of two aspects of justice: The Arrest — police apprehension methods; and the Trial — the courtroom hearing.

CAST
Sgt. Nick Anderson   Ben Gazzara
John Egan, the defense
  counselor   Chuck Connors
Pine   John Kerr
Jake   Joe Higgins
Miller   John Larch
Kirby   Roger Perry

Producer: Frank P. Rosenberg.

ARREST AND TRIAL—90 minutes—ABC—September 15, 1963 - September 13, 1964. 30 episodes. Syndicated.

AROUND THE WORLD IN 80 DAYS

Animated Cartoon. England, 1872. After Phileas Fogg and Balinda Maze are unable to be married because her uncle, Lord Maze, objects, Fogg accepts Lord Maze's challenge to travel around the world in eighty days to prove himself worthy of the girl. Believing him incapable of the feat, Lord Maze wagers twenty thousand pounds against him and hires, unbeknown to Fogg, the evil Mister Fix to foil the attempt and ensure his winning the bet.

After a letter granting them permission to leave is acquired from the queen, Fogg and his aide, Jean Paspepartout, depart in a traveling balloon. Episodes depict their attempts to overcome the foul deeds of Mister Fix and complete their journey within the allotted time. Adapted from the novel by Jules Verne.

Characters' Voices
Phileas Fogg   Alistair Duncan
Jean Passepartout   Ross Higgins

Mister Fix   Max Obistein

Additional Voices: Owen Weingott.

Music: John Sangster.

AROUND THE WORLD IN EIGHTY DAYS—30 minutes—NBC—September 9, 1972 - September 1, 1973. 16 episodes. Syndicated. Australian produced.

THE ART FORD SHOW

Musical Game. After a musical selection is played, the host asks a panel of three disc jockeys a related question. If panelists, who play for a home viewer selected by a postcard drawing, fail to answer correctly, they forfeit five dollars to that person.

Host: Art Ford.

Assistant: Arlene Cunningham.

Panelists: Freddie Robbins, Johnny Syme, Hal Moore.

Music: The Archie Koty Trio.

Producer: Ray Buffum.

THE ART FORD SHOW—30 minutes—NBC 1951.

ARTHUR GODFREY

Listed: The television programs of radio and television personality Arthur Godfrey.

Arthur Godfrey's Talent Scouts—Variety—30 minutes—CBS—December 6, 1948 - July 7, 1958. Showcased: Undiscovered professional talent.

Host: Arthur Godfrey.

Substitute Hosts: Joe E. Brown, Steve Allen, Guy Mitchell.

Vocalists: The Holidays.

Announcer: Tony Marvin.

Orchestra: Archie Bleyer.

Producer: Irving Mansfield, Jack Carney.

Director: Robert Stevens, Jack Carney.

Sponsor: Lipton Tea.

Arthur Godfrey and Friends—Musical Variety—60 minutes—CBS—January 12, 1949 - June 6, 1956.

Host: Arthur Godfrey.

Substitute Hosts: Robert Q. Lewis; Herb Shriner.

Regulars: Pat Boone, The McGuire Sisters (Christine, Phyllis, and Dorothy), Marion Marlowe,

Janette Davis, Julius LaRosa, Johnny Nash, Lu Ann Simms, Allen Case, Frank Parker, Bill Lawrence, Haleloke (Dancer), Carmel Quinn, Stan Noonan, The Chordettes (Janet Erlet, Dottie Schwartz, Jimmy Osborn, Carol Hagedorn), The Mariners (James Lewis, Nathaniel Dickerson, Martin Karl, Thomas Lockard).

Announcer: Tony Marvin.

Orchestra: Archie Bleyer; Neil Hefti.

Producer: Jack Carney.

Sponsor: Chesterfield Cigarettes; Pillsbury; Toni.

Arthur Godfrey and His Ukelele—Musical Variety—30 minutes—CBS—April 4, 1950 - June 30, 1950.

Host: Arthur Godfrey.

Announcer: Tony Marvin.

Orchestra: Archie Bleyer.

Producer: Mug Richardson.

Sponsor: Hi V Fruit Drinks.

Arthur Godfrey Time—Musical Variety—30 minutes—CBS—January 7, 1952 - April 24, 1959.

Host: Arthur Godfrey.

Announcer: Tony Marvin.

Orchestra: Archie Bleyer.

Producer: Larry Puck, Will Roland.

The Arthur Godfrey Show—Musical Variety—60 minutes—CBS—September 23, 1958 - February 24, 1959.

Host: Arthur Godfrey.

Regulars: Johnny Nash, Lani Nill.

Announcer: Tony Marvin.

Orchestra: Dick Hyman.

Producer: Margaret Richardson, Jack Carney.

Director: Paul Nickell.

1960-1961: The host of "Candid Camera." See title.
1969: The host of "Your All-American College Show." See title.

ARTHUR MURRAY'S DANCE PARTY

Variety. Dance instruction, dancing contests (judged by three guest celebrities), songs, and sketches.

Hostess: Kathryn Murray.

Regulars: Arthur Murray, Arnold Stang, Jack Norton, Teresa Brewer, Victor Borge, Joyce Bulifant, Lauritz Melchoir, Mary McCarthy, Bill and Cora Baird, Fran Warren, David Street, Jeri Gale, Mary Beth Hughes, Nelson Case, The Pastels, The Arthur Murray Dancers.

Choreographer: June Taylor.

Orchestra: Ray Carter; Emil Coleman.

Producer: Howard G. Barnes, Frederick Heider, West Hooker.

Director: Franklin Warren, Howard G. Barnes, Leslie Gorall, Eddie Nugent.

Sponsor: The Arthur Murray Dance Studios.

ARTHUR MURRAY'S DANCE PARTY—30 minutes. DuMont—October 15, 1950 - March 18, 1951; CBS—July 11, 1952 - August 29, 1952; NBC—June 1953 - September 1953; NBC—June 1954 - September 1954; NBC—July 1955 - September 1955; NBC—June 1956 - September 1956; NBC—April 9, 1957 - September 16, 1957; NBC—September 29, 1958 - September 6, 1960.

ART LINKLETTER

Listed: The television programs of radio and television personality Art Linkletter.

Program nature: Interviews, points of interest, discussions, music, and audience participation.

Life With Linkletter—Variety—30 minutes—ABC—October 6, 1950 - April 25, 1952.

Host: Art Linkletter.

Announcer: Jack Slattery.

Music: The Muzzy Marcellino Trio.

House Party—Variety—30 minutes—CBS—September 1, 1952 - September 5, 1969. Later titled "The Linkletter Show."

Host: Art Linkletter.

Announcer: Jack Slattery.

Music: The Muzzy Marcellino Trio.

People Are Funny—Comedy—30 minutes—NBC—1951-1961. 150 of 246 filmed episodes are syndicated.

Format: Selected people attempt to cope with unusual situations.

Host: Art Linkletter.

Announcer: Pat McGeehan.

The Art Linkletter Show—Variety—30 minutes—NBC—February 18, 1963 - September 23, 1963. Humorous glimpses (recorded on film) of everyday life. Game portion: Selected studio audience members are presented with various minor emergencies. Those best at solving them receive a merchandise prize.

Host: Art Linkletter.

Life With Linkletter—Variety—30 minutes—NBC—December 29, 1969 - September 25, 1970.

Host: Art Linkletter.

Co-Host: Jack Linkletter (his son).

ASPEN

Drama. Background: Aspen, Colorado. A three-part miniseries that follows the trial of Lee Bishop, an accused rapist-murderer.

CAST
Tom Keating	Sam Elliott
Gloria Osborne	Michelle Phillips
Lee Bishop	Perry King
Carl Osborne	Gene Barry
Kit Pepe	Jessica Harper
Alex Budde	Anthony Franciosa
Max Kendrick	Roger Davis
Owen Keating	John McIntire
Jon Osborne	Douglas Heyes, Jr.
Budd Townsend	Bo Hopkins
Angela Morelli	Debi Richter
Joseph Drummond	John Houseman
Horton Paine	Joseph Cotten
Abe Singer	George DiCenzo

Music: Tom Scott, Michael Melvoin.

Executive Producer: Michael Klein.

Producer: Jo Swerling, Jr.,

Director: Douglas Heyes.

ASPEN—6 hours (total)—NBC—November 5, 1977 - November 7, 1977.

THE ASPHALT JUNGLE

Crime Drama. Background: New York City. The investigations of the Metropolitan Squad, an elite team of plainclothes detectives designed to corrupt the workings of the underworld.

CAST
Matthew Gower, the Deputy Police Commissioner	Jack Warden
Captain Gus Honocheck	Arch Johnson
Sergeant Danny Miller	Bill Smith

THE ASPHALT JUNGLE—60 minutes—ABC—April 2, 1961 - September 29, 1961. Syndicated. 13 episodes.

ASSIGNMENT: DANGER

See title: "Martin Kane, Private Eye."

ASSIGNMENT: FOREIGN LEGION

Anthology. Dramatized: The role of the French Foreign Legion during the North African campaign of World War Two. Stories depict the events in the lives of its men and officers.

Starring: Merle Oberon as The Correspondent.

ASSIGNMENT: FOREIGN LEGION—30 minutes—CBS—September 15, 1957 - December 24, 1958. Syndicated. 24 episodes.

ASSIGNMENT: MANHUNT

Anthology. Dramatizations depicting the work of police law enforcement agencies in tracking down wanted criminals. Varying stories and casts.

Producer: Julian Claman.

Director: Dan Petrie.

ASSIGNMENT: MANHUNT—30 minutes—NBC—July 1951 - September 1951.

ASSIGNMENT: UNDERWATER

Adventure. Background: Florida. The story of Bill Greer, ex-marine, widower, professional diver, and his daughter, Patty, the operators of the charter boat, the *Lively Lady.* Episodes depict Bill's investigations into acquired cases.

CAST
Bill Greer	Bill Williams
Patty Greer	Diane Mountford

ASSIGNMENT: UNDERWATER—30 minutes—Syndicated 1960. 39 episodes.

ASSIGNMENT: VIENNA

See title: "The Men," *Assignment: Vienna,* segment.

AS THE WORLD TURNS

Serial. Background: Oakdale, U.S.A. Dramatic incidents in the lives of the Hughes and Lowell families.

CAST

Grandpa Hughes	Santos Ortega
Chris Hughes	Don McLaughlin
Nancy Hughes	Helen Wagner
Penny Hughes	Rosemary Prinz
	Phoebe Dorin
Lisa Miller	Eileen Fulton
Tom Hughes	Peter Link
	Peter Galman
	Paul O'Keefe
	David Colson
Bob Hughes	Don Hastings
	Bobby Alford
Hank Barton	Gary Sandy
Susan Stewart	Marie Masters
	Jada Rowland
Dr. Douglas Cassen	Nat Polen
Alma Miller	Ethel Rainey
Judge Lowell	William Johnstone
Ellen Lowell	Patricia Bruder
	Wendy Drew
Donald Hughes	Peter Brandon
	Martin West
Dr. John Dixon	Larry Bryggman
Julia Burke	Fran Carlon
Dan Stewart	John Reilly
	John Colenback
Jennifer Ryan	Geraldine Cort
	Gillian Spencer
Dawn Stewart	Jean Mazza
Carol Ann Stewart	Ariane Muenker
	Barbara Jean Ehrhardt
	Carol Ann Stewart
Betsy Stewart	Tiberia Mitri
	Susan Davids
	Simone Schacter
	Suzanne Davidson
Dr. Rick Ryan	Con Roche
Paul Stewart	Dean Santoro
	Stephen Mines
	Michael Hawkins
Charles Shea	Pip Sarser
	Roger Morgan
Sara Fuller	Gloria DeHaven
Jack Davis	Martin Sheen
Barbara Ryan	Donna Wandry
Grant Coleman	Konrad Matthaei
	James Douglas
Jay Stallings	Dennis Cooney
Kim Reynolds	Kathryn Hays
Marty	Don Scardino
Amy Hughes	Yah-Ling Sun
Carol Demming	Rita McLaughlin
Peggy Reagan	Lisa Cameron
Dr. Flynn	Sidney Walker
Simon Gilbey	Jerry Lacey
Meredith Harcourt	Nina Hart
Claire Shea	Anne Burr
	Nancy Wickwire
	Barbara Berjer
David Stewart	Henderson Forsythe
Dr. Michael Shea	Roy Schumann
Martha Wilson	Anna Minot
Carl Wilson	Martin Rudy
Dick Martin	Edward Kemmer
Roy McGuire	
(early role)	Konrad Matthaei
Jimmy McGuire	Michael Cody
Karen Adams	Doe Lang
Mrs. Brando	Ethel Everett
Alice	Jean McClintock
Sandy McGuire	Dagne Crane
	Barbara Rucker
Sally Graham	Kathleen Cody
Dr. Jerry Turner	James Earl Jones
Neil Wade	Michael Lipton
Franny Brennan	Toni Darnay
	Kelly Campbell
Wally Matthews	Charles Siebert
Jeff Baker	Mark Rydell
Bruce Elliott	James Pritchett
Elizabeth Talbot	Jane House
Edith Hughes	Ruth Warrick
Jim Lowell	Les Damon
Dr. Tim Cole	William Redfield
Betty Stewart	Pat Benoit
Mark Galloway	Anthony Herrera
Joyce Coleman	Barbara Rodell
Natalie Bannon	Judith Chapman
Kim Dickson	Patty McCormick
Holly Bauer	Ellen Barber
Ralph Mitchell	Keith Charles
Pat Holland	Melinda Peterson
Ellen Stewart	Pat Bruder
Frannie Hughes	Maura Gilligan
Ted Ellison	Joseph Christopher
Jay Stallings	Dennis Cooney
Anne Stewart	Martina Deignam
Laurie Keaton	Laurel Delmar
Emmy Stewart	Jenny Harris
Beau Spencer	Wayne Hudgins
Dee Stewart	Marcia McClain
Valerie Conway	Judith McConnell
Mary Ellison	Kelly Wood

Also: Joyce Van Patten, Teri Keane, Conrad Fowkes, Barbara Hayes.

Announcer: Dan McCulla.

Music: Charles Paul.

Additional Music: Mi-Voix.

Producer: Ted Corday, Allen Potter, Charles Fisher, William Howell.

Creator: Irna Phillips, Ted Corday.

AS THE WORLD TURNS—30 minutes—CBS—April 2, 1956 - November 28, 1975; 60 minutes: Premiered: December 1, 1975.

ASTRO BOY

Animated Cartoon. Background: Twenty-first-century Earth. After his wife and son are killed in an automobile accident, a scientist, Dr. Boynton, creates Astro Boy, and indestructible, super-powered robot for companionship. Episodes depict their and Dr. Elefun's battle against evil. Japanese produced.

ASTRO BOY—30 minutes—Syndicated 1963. 104 episodes.

THE AT HOME SHOW

Musical Variety.

Host: Earl Wrightson.

Music: The Norman Paris Trio.

Producer: Ward Byron, Franklin Heller.

Sponsor: Masland Carpets.

THE AT HOME SHOW—15 minutes—CBS 1950.

THE AT LIBERTY CLUB

Musical Variety.

Hostess: Jacqueline.

Regulars: Gordon Gaines, Shara DeVries.

Orchestra: D'Artega.

Producer-Director: Roger Muir.

THE AT LIBERTY CLUB—15 minutes—NBC 1948.

THE ATOM ANT/SECRET SQUIRREL SHOW

Animated Cartoon. The adventures of Atom Ant, the world's mightiest insect, and Secret Squirrel, the animal kingdom's most dauntless undercover agent. Episodes relate their battle against crime and corruption. Produced by Hanna-Barbera Productions.

Additional segments: "Precious the Dog"; "The Hillbilly Bears"; "Squiddly Diddly" (an octopus).

Characters' Voices

Atom Ant	Howard Morris
	Don Messick
Secret Squirrel	Mel Blanc
Morroco Mole	Paul Frees
Precious Pup	Don Messick
Granny Sweet	Janet Waldo
Squiddly Diddly	Paul Frees
Chief Winchley	John Stephenson

HILLBILLY BEARS:

Paw Rugg	Henry Corden
Maw Rugg	Jean Vander Pyl
Flora Rugg	Jean Vander Pyl
Shag Rugg	Don Messick

Music: Hoyt Curtin.

Musical Director: Ted Nichols.

Producer-Director: William Hanna, Joseph Barbera.

THE ATOM ANT/SECRET SQUIRREL SHOW—30 minutes—NBC—October 2, 1965 - September 7, 1968. Syndicated. 26 episodes.

THE ATOM SQUAD

Spy Drama. Background: New York City — the operational base of the Atom Squad, a secret government organization established to combat cosmic invaders and safeguard U.S. atomic secrets. Episodes depict their attempts to protect the western world from the sinister forces of evil.

CAST

Steve Elliot, the
    squad leader   Bob Hastings
His assistants   Bob Courtleigh
                        Bram Nossem

THE ATOM SQUAD—15 minutes—NBC 1953.

AUCTION AIRE

Game. The format permits both the studio and home audiences to bid for expensive merchandise items. Labels from Libby's food products are used as "money" and the person who bids highest (home viewers bid via the telephone) receives that particular item.

Host-Auctioneer: John Gregson.

Assistant: Rebel Randall.

Announcer: Glenn Riggs.

Producer: Paul Masterson, Ralph Nelson.

AUCTION AIRE—30 minutes—ABC—1949 - 1950.

AUDUBON WILDLIFE THEATRE

Documentary. Wildlife films depicting the animal struggle for survival.

Host: Bob Davidson.

Narrator: Robert C. Hermes.

Music: Ron Harrison.

AUDUBON WILDLIFE THEATRE—30 minutes—Syndicated 1971.

AUTHOR, AUTHOR

Panel Discussion. Critical analysis of authors' works.

Host: Marc Connelly.

Panel: Gilbert Seldes, Dorothy Fields, Charles Sherman, Robert Lattor; plus guests.

Producer: Phillip Messing, Phillip Schaefer.

Director: James Furness.

AUTHOR, AUTHOR—30 minutes—ABC 1951.

THE AVENGERS

Adventure. Distinguished by four formats. The background for each is London, England.

Format One: March 18, 1961 - March 1962.

The Avengers. Diana Rigg and Patrick Macnee.

A gangster mistakenly delivers heroin to the fiancée of Doctor David Keel. She is killed by the dope ring when they discover their error and fear she will identify the messenger. Embittered, Keel vows to avenge her death. Investigating, he meets Steed, a mysterious individual seeking to infiltrate and expose the ring. Through Steed's guidance, Keel penetrates the ring. Exposed, and about to be killed, Steed, assisted by the police, intervene and save him, but—and in a rare moment in television—the ring leader escapes undetected. Vowing to avenge crime, the two men team, and on an alternating basis, battle criminal elements.

An actors strike ended the series. When first introduced, Steed's full name and occupation were not revealed. No one knows for whom he works except that his cover is that of a dilettante man about town and a purveyor of old-world courtesy.

Format Two: September 1962 — September 1965.

Following settlement of the strike in May of 1962, series production resumed. In September of that year, the program returned to the air with a

The Avengers. Linda Thorson (Patrick Macnee's partner in later episodes.)

complete change in format. Stories now concern the investigations of two British Government Ministry Agents: the dashing and debonair John Steed, and his glamorous female assistant, a widow, Mrs. Catherine Gale.

Format Three: September 1965 - March 20, 1968.

Shortly after Mrs. Gale resigns, Steed meets and befriends the "lovely and delectable" Emma Peel, widow of a test pilot, when they are involved in a minor automobile accident. Emancipated and independently wealthy, she teams with Steed for the sheer love of adventure. Stories depict their investigations as they attempt to solve baffling crimes.

Format Four: March 20, 1968 - May 26, 1969.

Emma's husband Peter Peel, believed to have been killed in an airplane crash in the Amazon, is found alive and flown back to England. As Emma returns to him, Steed is teamed with a beautiful and shapely brunette, Ministry agent Tara King. Stories relate their attempts to avenge bizarre crimes perpetrated against the British Government.

CAST

John Steed   Patrick Macnee
Dr. David Keel   Ian Hendry
Mrs. Catherine Gale   Honor Blackman
Mrs. Emma Peel   Diana Rigg
Tara King   Linda Thorson
Mother (a man), Steed's
    invalid superior Patrick Newell

Rhonda, Mother's aide (a
    woman; a nonspeaking
    part)   Screen credit is not given

Steed's Other Partners:

Venus Smith (six episodes
during the Catherine
Gale era)   Julie Stevens
Also (three episodes during
the Catherine Gale
era)   Jon Rollason
Olga Volousby (one episode
during the Emma Peel
era)   Anna Quayle
Georganna Price Jones (one
episode during the
Emma Peel era)   Liz Fraser
Lady Diana Forbes Blakney
(one episode during the
Tara King era)   Jennifer Croxton
Jimmy Merlin (one episode
during the Tara
King era)   Peter Barksworth
Penelope Blaine (one
episode during the
Emma Peel era)   Valerie Van Ost

Steed's home address: Number Three
Stable Mews, City of London.
Tara's home address: Number Nine
Primrose Crescent, City of London.
Music: Johnny Dankworth; Laurie
Johnson; Howard Blake.

Producer: Leonard White, John Bryce,
Julian Wintle, Brian Clemens,
Albert Fennell.
Director: Charles Crichton, Don
Leaver, Richmond Harding,
Roger Jenkins, Cliff Owen, Peter
Sykes, Bill Bain, Gerry O'Hara,
Quentin Lawrence, John Hough,
Robert Day, Robert Fuest, Peter
Scott, James Hill, Don Sharp,
Leslie Norman, Ray Austen,
John Moxey, Robert Asher,
Peter DuFell, Roy Baker, Cyril
Frankel, Sidney Hayers, Gordon
Flemyng.

THE AVENGERS—60 minutes—
ABC—March 28, 1966 - September 1,
1966; January 20, 1967 - September
1, 1967; January 10, 1968 - September 15, 1969. Syndicated. 83 episodes. Premiered in London, ABC-TV
(Associated British Corporation) on
March 18, 1961. The episodes telecast
from 1961 to 1965 were never seen in
the U.S.

AWARD THEATRE

Anthology. Rebroadcasts of dramas
that were originally aired via "Alcoa
Theatre."

Included:

Hello, Charlie. The story of two safe-

crackers and their attempts to release
a little girl who is trapped in a locked
vault.

CAST
Tony Randall, John Dehner, Joe E.
Ross.

Shadow Of Evil. The story of an
ex-alcoholic who attempts to run for
governor.
CAST
Cliff Robertson.

Any Friend of Julie's. After the death
of a well-know playwright, a man tries
to prove that he was the ghostwriter
of all of his plays.
CAST
Leslie Neilson.

AWARD THEATRE—30 minutes—
Syndicated 1958. 78 episodes.

AWAY WE GO

Musical Variety. Songs, dances, and
comedy sketches.
Host: Buddy Greco, George Carlin.
Regulars: Buddy Rich, his band; The
Miriam Nelson Dancers.
Orchestra: Allyn Ferguson.

AWAY WE GO—60 minutes—CBS—
June 3, 1967 - September 2, 1967.

ℬ

BAA BAA BLACK SHEEP

Adventure. Background: The South
Pacific during World War II. The
exploits of Major Gregory "Pappy"
Boyington, a daring air ace and commander of the VMF 214 Black Sheep,
a squadron of misfit pilots who, once
awaiting court-martial, were fashioned
by Boyington into an often decorated,
but seldom disciplined fighter squadron.

CAST
Major Gregory "Pappy"
Boyington   Robert Conrad
General Moore, the
C.O.   Simon Oakland
Colonel Lard   Dana Elcar

The Black Sheep Squadron
Capt. James W.
Gutterman   James Whitmore, Jr.

Lt. Joseph E.
Wiley (T.J.)   Robert Ginty
Lt. Jerry Bragg   Dirk Blocker
Pvt. Larry Casey   W.K. Stratton
Lt. Robert
Anderson   John Larroquette
Lt. Donald French   Jeff MacKay
Lt. Robert Boyle   Jake Mitchell
Larry Manetti
Lt. Hutch   Joey Aresco
Sgt. Micklin, the
mechanic   Red West

Also:
T. Harachi, the
enemy pilot   Byron Chung
Narrator: Robert Conrad.
Pappy's Dog: Meatball.
Music: Mike Post and Pete Carpenter.
Executive Producer: Stephen J. Cannell.
Producer: Russ Mayberry, Alex
Beaton.
Director: John Peyser, Russ Mayberry, Jackie Cooper, Larry
Doheny, Ivan Dixon, Edward
Dein, Philip DeGuere.

BAA BAA BLACK SHEEP—60 minutes—NBC—Premiered: September 21,
1976.

THE BABY GAME

Game. Three husband-and-wife teams
compete in a game designed to test
their knowledge of childhood behavior. A specific situation that involves a child is explained. Players
then bet points and state what they
believe is the child's reaction to the
situation. A previously filmed sequence is shown and the results are
determined. Points are awarded if
players are correct; deducted if they
are wrong. Winners, the highest
scorers, receive merchandise prizes.
Host: Richard Hayes, "America's
favorite baby sitter."

THE BABY GAME—30 minutes—
ABC—December 4, 1967 - July 12,
1968.

BACHELOR FATHER

Comedy. Background: 1163 Rexford
Drive, Beverly Hills, California, the
residence of Bentley Gregg, a bachelor-attorney; his Chinese houseboy,
Peter Tong; and his orphaned thir-

teen-year-old niece, Kelly, who became his legal ward after her parents were killed in an automobile accident.

Stories relate Bentley's attempts to adjust to the responsibilities of life as a Bachelor Father.

Special note concerning the cast. Kelly's friend, Ginger, is distinguished by three last names:

1957-1958: Ginger Farrell. Her mother, Louise, is a widow.

1958-1960: Ginger Loomis. Catherine McLeod, who played her mother, was dropped, and Whit Bissel and Florence MacMichael were added as her parents, Bert and Amy Loomis. It should also be noted here that Whit Bissel, before portraying Ginger's father, played Steve Gibson, the father of a friend of Kelly's.

1960-1962: Ginger Mitchell. For unknown reasons, Whit Bissel and Florence MacMichael were dropped, and Del Moore and Evelyn Scott added as her parents, Cal and Adelaide Mitchell.

CAST

Bentley Gregg	John Forsythe
Kelly Gregg	Noreen Corcoran
Peter Tong	Sammee Tong
Howard Meechim, Kelly's boyfriend	Jimmy Boyd
Ginger Farrell	
Ginger Loomis	
Ginger Mitchell	Bernadette Winters
Louise Farrell	Catherine McLeod
Bert Loomis	Whit Bissel
Amy Loomis	Florence MacMichael
Cal Mitchell	Del Moore
Adelaide Mitchell	Evelyn Scott
Vickie, Bentley's first secretary	Alice Backes
Kitty Deveraux, Bentley's second secretary	Shirley Mitchell Jane Nigh
Kitty Marsh, Bentley's third secretary	Sue Ane Langdon
Connie, Bentley's fourth secretary	Sally Mansfield
Chuck Forest, Bentley's friend, a bandleader	Pat McCaffrie
Elaine Meechim, Howard's sister	Joan Vohs
Charles Burton, Bentley's friend	Karl Swenson
Gloria Gibson (later, Lila Gibson), Kelly's friend	Cheryl Holdridge
Steve Gibson, her father	Whit Bissel
Charlie Fong, Peter's conniving cousin	Victor Sen Yung
Grandpa Ling, Peter's relative, the world's "oldest juvenile delinquent"	Beal Wong

Harry, the delivery boy	Sid Melton
Frank Curtis, Bentley's neighbor	Harry Von Zell
Warren Dawson, Bentley's law partner	Aaron Kincaid
Blossom Lee, Peter's niece	Cherlyene Lee
Susie, Peter's romantic interest; employed in a supermarket	Frances Fong
Horace Dawson, Warren's father	David Lewis
Myrtle Dawson, Warren's mother	Sheila Bromley
Aunt Rose, Peter's relative	Beulah Quo

Also, various roles: Mary Tyler Moore, Donna Douglas, H.W. Gim, Benson Fong.

Gregg family dog: Jasper.

Music: Conrad Salinger; Johnny Williams.

Music Supervision: Stanley Wilson.

Producer: Everett Freeman, Harry Ackerman, Robert Sparks.

Director: Earl Bellamy, Abby Berlin, John Newland, Stanley Z. Cherry, Greg Garrison.

BACHELOR FATHER—30 minutes. CBS—September 15, 1957 - June 11, 1958. NBC—June 18, 1958 - September 19, 1961. ABC—October 3, 1961 - September 25, 1962. Syndicated. 157 episodes.

BACK THE FACT

Game. Contestants are interviewed by the host and asked personal background questions. Players can answer truthfully or bluff. If a false statement is believed to have been made, an off-stage voice interrupts the proceedings and asks the player to back the fact. If he is able, he presents the proof (e.g., a newspaper clipping) and wins a prize. However, should his bluff be called, he relinquishes his post to another player.

Host: Joey Adams.

Announcer-Offstage Voice: Carl Caruso.

Producer: Barry Enright, Fred W. Friendly.

BACK THE FACT—30 minutes—ABC 1955.

BADGE 714

See title: "Dragnet."

BAFFLE

Game. Two teams, each composed of a celebrity captain and a noncelebrity contestant. After one member of each team is placed in an individual soundproof booth, the sound is turned off in one. The other team plays the game. The outside player stands before a table containing large plastic letters which spell out a phrase. At six-second intervals, he places one letter at a time on a wall rack. The object is for his partner to correctly identify the phrase in the shortest amount of time. The sound is then turned on in the other booth and the other team plays the same phrase. The team accumulating the least amount of time each round receives the at-stakes merchandise prize. The team accumulating the least amount of time, in two out of three games is the overall winner. The noncelebrity contestant receives a chance at "The Solo Round."

First half. Object: the identification of ten words within thirty seconds. Parts of the words (e.g. PRT — Pretty; FRM — From) are displayed one at a time. Each correct identification awards the player fifty dollars and three seconds in the second half. *Second half.* Displayed: several letters of one word (e.g. MDY — Monday). The time a player has to identify it is determined by the number of words he correctly guesses in the first half. If the player correctly identifies the word he receives a new car.

Revised format: "All Star Baffle." Four celebrities play for selected studio audience members. The winning team's contestant receives a chance to play "The Solo Round."

Host: Dick Enberg.

Announcer: Kenny Williams.

Music: Mort Garson.

BAFFLE—30 minutes—NBC—March 26, 1973 - October 5, 1973. ALL STAR BAFFLE—30 minutes—NBC—October 8, 1973 - March 29, 1974.

BAGGY PANTS AND THE NITWITS

Animated Cartoon.

Segments:

Baggy Pants. The misadventures of a hobo cat that is reminiscent of Charlie Chaplin's famous tramp. Characters are nonspeaking.

The Nitwits. The story focuses on the misadventures of Tyrone, a retired super hero who forsakes retirement to assist the world in its battle against crime. His wife and assistant: Gladys. The characters "Tyrone" and "Gladys" first appeared on the series "Laugh-In."

Characters' Voices

Tyrone	Arte Johnson
Gladys	Ruth Buzzi

Music: Doug Goodwin, Steve DePatie.

Producer: David DePatie, Friz Freleng.

Director: Bob McKimson, Sid Marcus, Spencer Peel, Brad Case.

BAGGY PANTS AND THE NIT-WITS—30 minutes—NBC—Premiered: September 10, 1977.

BAILEY'S COMETS

Animated Cartoon. The saga of a global skating race and of the seventeen competing roller derby teams who are seeking the million-dollar first prize. Clues to the prize are presented through an endless trail of poetic rhymes; and episodes depict the attempts of one team, Bailey's Comets, to overcome the diabolical schemes of the other teams as they attempt to eliminate them from the competition.

Teams: Bailey's Comets; The Broomer Girls; The Roller Bears; The Doctor Jekyll/Hydes; The Hairy Madden Red Eyes; The Duster Busters; The Yo Ho Ho's; The Mystery Mob; The Rambling Rivits; The Cosmic Rays; The Roller Coasters; The Texas Flycats; The Stone Rollers; The Gusta Pastas; The Rock 'N' Rollers; The Black Hats; The Gargantuan Giants.

Bailey's Comets Team Members: Barnaby, Dee Dee, Bunny, Wheelie, Pudge, and Sarge.

Helicopter Reporters: Dooter Roo, the pilot; and Gabby, the race commentator.

Voices: Don Messick, Sarah Kennedy, Daws Butler, Jim Brigg, Karen Smith, Bob Halt, Kathy Gori, Frank Welker.

Music: Doug Goodwin. Score: Eric Rogers.

BAILEY'S COMETS—30 minutes—CBS—September 8, 1973 - January 26, 1974. 16 episodes.

The Bailey's of Balboa. Paul Ford.

THE BAILEYS OF BALBOA

Comedy. Background: Bailey's Landing, Balboa Beach, California. The story of the bickering relationship between two men: Sam Bailey, the captain of a noisy and decrepit character boat, the *Island Princess,* and his objecting neighbor, Cecil Wyntoon, the commodore of the high-class Balboa Yachting Club.

CAST

Sam Bailey	Paul Ford
Cecil Wyntoon	John Dehner
Barbara Bailey, Sam's daughter	Judy Carne
Jim Wyntoon, Cecil's son	Les Brown, Jr.
Buck Singleton, Sam's shipmate	Sterling Holloway

THE BAILEYS OF BALBOA—30 minutes—CBS—September 24, 1964 - March 29, 1965. 26 episodes.

BALANCE YOUR BUDGET

Game. Selected female members of the studio audience compete. Players first state the amount of money that is required to run their household for one year, then attempt to replenish it. The host reads a general-knowledge type of question. The player who is first to identify herself through a buzzer signal receives a chance to answer. If correct cash is scored. The winner, the highest scorer, receives the opportunity to compete again. Contestants end their play when they have balanced their budget or are defeated by another player.

Host: Bert Parks, "The keeper of the Horn of Plenty."

Assistant: Lynn Connor.

Producer: Louis Cowan.

Sponsor: Sealy Mattresses.

BALANCE YOUR BUDGET—30 minutes—CBS 1952.

BALL FOUR

Comedy. Background: Washington. A satirization of major league baseball as seen through the off-field antics of the Washington Americans, a disorganized baseball team. Based on the book *Ball Four* by Jim Bouton.

CAST

Jim Barton, the relief pitcher	Jim Bouton
Plunkett, the pitcher	Marco St. John
Benjamin "Rhino" Rhinelander, the catcher	Ben Davidson
Travis, the outfielder	Sam Wright
Walter Lopez, the utility man	Jaime Tirelli
Harold "Pinky" Pinkney, the coach	Bill McCutcheon
Cappy, the manager	Jack Somack
Westlake, the rookie	David-James Carroll
Birdman, the troublemaker	Lenny Schultz

Music: Harry Chapin.

Producer: Don Segall.

Director: Jay Sandrich, Nick Havoniga, Peter Lewis.

BALL FOUR—30 minutes—CBS—September 22, 1976 - October 27, 1976.

BANACEK

See title: "NBC Wednesday Mystery Movie," *Banacek* segment.

THE BANANA SPLITS ADVENTURE HOUR

Children. The misadventures of the

Banana Splits, four live-action animals: Fleegle, the dog; Drooper, the lion; Bingo, the gorilla; and Snorky, the runt elephant. A Hanna-Barbera production.

Characters' Voices

Fleegle	Paul Winchell
Bingo	Daws Butler
Drooper	Allan Melvin
Snorky	Don Messick

The Banana Splits Adventure Hour. Left to right: Drooper (seated), Bingo, Snorky, and Fleegle. *Courtesy Hanna-Barbera Productions.*

Cartoon segments:

The Three Musketeers

Character's Voices

D'Artagnan	Bruce Watson
Porthos	Barney Phillips
Aramis	Don Messick
Athos	Jonathan Harris
Tooly	Teddy Eccles
The Queen	Julie Bennett
Constance	Julie Bennett

The Arabian Knights

Characters' Voices

Bez	Henry Corden
Evil Vangore	Paul Frees
Raseem	Frank Gerstle
Princess Nidor	Shari Lewis
Turban	Jay North
Fariik	John Stephenson

The Hillbilly Bears

Characters' Voices

Paw Rugg	Henry Corden
Maw Rugg	Jean VanderPyl
Flora Rugg	Jean VanderPyl
Shagg Rugg	Don Messick

Film segments:

The Micro Venture. Life in the world of microscopic creatures.

Characters' Voices

Professor Carter	Don Messick
Jill Carter	Patsy Garrett
Mike Carter	Tommy Cook

Danger Island. The adventures of archeologist/explorer, Professor Irwin Hayden.

CAST

Professor Irwin Hayden	Frank Aletter
Leslie Hayden, his daughter	Ronnie Troup
Link Simmons, his assistant	Michael Vincent
Morgan, the castaway	Rockne Tarkington
Chongo	Kahana
Mu-Tan	Victor Eberg
Chu	Rodrigo Arrendondo

Music: Hoyt Curtin; Jack Eskrew.

THE BANANA SPLITS ADVENTURE HOUR—60 minutes—NBC—September 7, 1968 - September 5, 1970. Syndicated title: "Banana Splits and Friends." Official title: "Kellogg's of Battle Creek Presents the Banana Splits Adventure Hour."

BAND OF AMERICA

Musical Variety.

Host: Paul Lavalle.

Regulars: Ray Crisara, Ross Gorman, Chauncey Moorehouse.

Announcer: Ford Bond.

Music: The Green and White Quartet.

BAND OF AMERICA—30 minutes—NBC 1949.

BANDSTAND

Musical Variety.

Host: Bert Parks.

Music: The Tex Beneke Band.

BANDSTAND—30 minutes—NBC—July 30, 1956 - August 23, 1956. Also known as "NBC Bandstand."

THE BANG-SHANG LALAPALOOZA SHOW

Animated Cartoon. Background: The town of Riverdale. Newly animated adventures of the Archies (Archie, Betty, Veronica, Reggie, Jughead, and Hot Dog). See also "The Archie Show."

Voices: Jane Webb, Dallas McKennon, Don Messick, Howard Morris, John Erwin, Jose Flores.

Music: Yvette Blais, Jeff Michael.

Executive Producer: Norm Prescott, Lou Scheimer.

Producer: Don Christensen.

THE BANG-SHANG LALAPALOOZA SHOW—30 minutes—NBC—Premiered: November 19, 1977.

BANK ON THE STARS

Game. Two competing two member teams. Basis: The answering of questions drawn from the observation of film clips. Each correct response awards that team one point. The highest scoring team is declared the winner and receives fifty dollars for each point. The losing team's earnings correspond to what is obtained by dipping one hand into a barrel of silver dollars.

Hosts: Jack Paar; Jimmy Nelson.

Orchestra: Ivan Ditmars.

BANK ON THE STARS—30 minutes —CBS 1953.

BANYON

Crime Drama. Background: Los Angeles, California, 1937. The investigations of private detective Miles C. Banyon.

CAST

Miles C. Banyon	Robert Forster
Sgt. Peter McNeil, L.A.P.D.	Richard Jaeckel
Peggy Revere, a friend, the owner of the Revere Secretarial School	Joan Blondell
Abby Graham, a singer, a friend of Banyon's	Julie Gregg

Executive Producer: Quinn Martin.

BANYON—60 minutes—NBC—September 15, 1972 - January 12, 1973. 13 episodes.

THE BARBARA COLEMAN SHOW

See title: "Here's Barbara."

THE BARBARA McNAIR SHOW

The Barbara McNair Show. Left to right: Gordon MacRae, Barbara McNair, and Rich Little. © *Screen Gems.*

Musical Variety. Staged as an informal concert.

Hostess: Barbara McNair.

Assistant-Announcer: Ronald Long.

Music: The Coldridge Perkinson Quintet.

THE BARBARA McNAIR SHOW—60 minutes—Syndicated 1969. 52 tapes.

THE BARBARA STANWYCK THEATRE

Anthology. Dramatic presentations.

Hostess-Frequent Performer: Barbara Stanwyck.

Music: Earle Hagen.

Producer: Lou Edelman.

Director: Jacques Tourneur, Robert Florez, David Lowell Rich, Richard Whorf.

Included:

Ironback's Bride. A woman, married to a shiftless outlaw, struggles to prevent her son from following in his father's footsteps.

CAST
Ella Cahill: Barbara Stanwyck; Isaiah Richardson: Charles Bickford; Charlie Cahill: Gerald Mohr.

No One. A producer's attempts to convince the backer of a Broadway play to hire a talented but unknown actress for the lead.

CAST
Cara Lester: Barbara Stanwyck; Tracy Lane: Susan Oliver; Jack Harrison: Alan Hewitt.

House In Order. A woman, told she may have only a short time to live, struggles to regain the love of her husband and daughter.

CAST
Elizabeth Moury: Barbara Stanwyck; Susan Moury: Yvonne Craig; Bill Moury: Shepperd Strudwick.

Discreet Deception. A tale of the deceptive romance between a woman and her late husband's married brother.

CAST
Amelia Lambert: Barbara Stanwyck; Simon Lambert: Patric Knowles; Vivian Lambert: Virginia Gregg.

THE BARBARA STANWYCK THEATRE—30 minutes—NBC—September 19, 1960 - September 11, 1961. 36 episodes.

BARBARY COAST

Adventure. Background: San Francisco during the 1880s. The story of Jeff Cable, an undercover agent for the governor of California, and Cash Canover, his partner, the owner of Cash Canover's Golden Gate Casino. Episodes relate their attempts to apprehend lawbreakers on San Francisco's notorious Barbary Coast.

CAST
Jeff Cable	William Shatner
Cash Canover	Doug McClure
Moose, an employee of Canover's	Richard Kiel
Thumbs, an employee of Canover's	Dave Turner
Brandy, one of the dance girls	Francine York
Rusty, one of the dance girls	Brooke Mills
The Bartender	John Dennis
	Eddie Fontaine

Music: John Andrew Tartagla.

Executive Producer: Cy Chermak.

Director: Bill Bixby, Alex Grasshoff, Herb Wallerstein.

Creator: Douglas Heyes.

BARBARY COAST—60 minutes—ABC—September 8, 1975 - January 9, 1976.

BAREFOOT IN THE PARK

Comedy. Background: New York City. 49 West 10th Street, Manhattan, Apartment 5-B, the residence of the Bratters; Paul, an attorney with the firm of Kendricks, Kein, and Klein, and his wife, Corie. Episodes relate the struggles of a young couple as they attempt to survive the difficult first years of marriage. Based on the

Barefoot in the Park. Scoey Mitchlll (left) and Tracy Reed.

Broadway play and movie by Neil Simon.

CAST

Paul Bratter	Scoey Mitchlll
Corie Bratter	Tracy Reed
Honey Robinson, their friend, the owner of "Honey's Pool Hall"	Nipsey Russell
Mabel Bates, Corie's mother	Thelma Carpenter
Arthur Kendricks, Paul's employer	Harry Holcombe

Music: J. J. Johnson; Charles Fox.

BAREFOOT IN THE PARK—30 minutes—ABC—September 24, 1970 - January 14, 1971. 12 episodes.

BARETTA

Crime Drama. The investigations of Tony Baretta, an undercover police detective with the 53rd Precinct who has little respect for standard police procedures.

CAST

Tony Baretta	Robert Blake
Billy Truman, his friend, the house detective at the King Edward Hotel	Tom Ewell
Inspector Schiller	Dana Elcar
Lt. Hal Brubaker	Edward Grover
Rooster, Baretta's information man	Michael D. Roberts
Mimi Ames, Tony's girlfriend	Sharon Cintron
Detective Foley	John Ward
Fats, the overweight cop	Chino Williams

Little Moe, Tony's informant	Angelo Rosetti
Fred, Tony's pet cockatoo	Lala

Music: Dave Grusin; Tom Scott.

Theme Vocal: Sammy Davis, Jr.

Executive Producer: Bernard L. Kowalski, Anthony Spinner.

Producer: Charles E. Dismukes, Howie Horwitz, Jo Swerling, Jr., Robert Lewis, Robert Harris.

Director: Don Medford, Reza S. Badiyi, Vincent Sherman, Bernard L. Kowalski, John Ward, Chris Robinson, Bruce Kessler, Robert Dougals, Douglas Heyes, Burt Brickeroff.

Creator: Stephen J. Cannell.

BARETTA—60 minutes—ABC—Premiered: January 17, 1975.

THE BARKLEYS

Animated Cartoon. The main characters are. dogs who are modeled after the characters in "All in the Family." Episodes relate the life of Arnie Barkley, an outspoken, opinionated and loud-mouthed bus driver as he attempts to cope with life, understand his progressive children, and bridge the generation gap that exists between them.

Characters' Voices

Arnie Barkley	Henry Corden
Agnes Barkley, his wife	Joan Gerber
Terri Barkley, their daughter	Julie McWhirter
Chester Barkley, their son	Steve Lewis
Roger Barkely, their son	Gene Andrusco

Additional voices: Frank Welker, Bob Halt, Don Messick, Bob Frank, Michael Bell.

Music: Doug Goodwin; Score: Eric Rogers.

THE BARKLEYS—30 minutes—NBC—September 9, 1972 - September 1, 1973: 13 episodes.

BARNABY JONES

Crime Drama. Background: Los Angeles, California. The investigations of private detective Barnaby Jones. Tragically forced out of retirement by the murder of his partner-son, he

represents the new image in detectives—an older man with a quaint country charm and trigger wit.

CAST

Barnaby Jones	Buddy Ebsen
Betty Jones, his daughter-in-law-assistant	Lee Meriwether
Lieutenant Biddle, L.A.P.D.	John Carter

Barnaby Jones. Buddy Ebsen and Lee Meriwether.

J.R. Jones, Barnaby's cousin and legman	Mark Shera

Executive Producer: Quinn Martin.

Producer: Philip Saltzman.

Director: Leslie H. Martinson, Mel Damski, Walter Grauman, Michael Caffrey, Allen Reisner.

Music: Duante Tatro; Jerry Fielding; Jeff Alexander; John Elizade.

BARNABY JONES—60 minutes—CBS—Premiered: January 28, 1973.

BARNEY BLAKE, POLICE REPORTER

Crime Drama. Background: New York City. The investigations of police reporter Barney Blake as he seeks to ascertain the facts behind criminal cases.

Starring: Gene •O'Donnell as Barney Blake.

Producer: Wynn Wright.

Director: Dave Lewis, Garry Simpson.

BARNEY BLAKE, POLICE REPORTER—30 minutes—NBC 1948.

Barney Miller. Left to right: Jack Soo, Max Gail, Hal Linden, Steve Landesberg, Ron Carey, Ron Glass. *Courtesy of the Call-Chronicle Newspapers, Allentown, Pa.*

BARNEY MILLER

Comedy. Background: Greenwich Village in New York City. The trials and tribulations of Captain Barney Miller, the chief of detectives of the 12th police precinct.

CAST

Captain Barney Miller	Hal Linden
Elizabeth Miller, his wife	Barbara Barrie
Sergeant Chano	Gregory Sierra
Sergeant Phil Fish	Abe Vigoda
Sergeant Wojehowicz	Max Gail
Sergeant Nick Yemana	Jack Soo
Detective Ron Harris	Ron Glass
Police Inspector Frank Luger	James Gregory
Bernice Fish, Phil's wife	Florence Stanley
Detective Janet Wentworth	Linda Lavin
Detective Battista	June Gable
Detective Arthur Dietrich	Steve Landesberg
Detective Mike Lovaetti	Art Metrano
Officer Kogan	Milt Kogan
Officer Carl Levitt	Ron Carey
Rachel Miller, Barney's daughter	Anne Wyndham
David Miller, Barney's son	Michael Tessier

Music: Jack Elliott, Allyn Ferguson.
Executive Producer: Danny Arnold, Theodore J. Flicker.
Producer: Chris Hayward.
Director: Bruce Bilson, Alex March, Danny Arnold, Noam Pitlink, Dennis Steinmetz.

BARNEY MILLER—30 minutes—ABC—Premiered: January 23, 1975.

THE BARON

Mystery. Background: London, England. The story of John Mannering, a wealthy American antique dealer known as The Baron. Episodes depict his investigations into crimes associated with the art world.

CAST

John Mannering	Steve Forrest
Cordella, his assistant	Sue Lloyd
David Marlow, his assistant	Paul Ferris
Templeton Greene, a diplomatic service agent	Colin Greene

Music: Edwin Astley.
Producer: Monty Berman.

THE BARON—60 minutes—ABC—January 20, 1966 - July 14, 1966. Syndicated. 26 episodes.

BARRIER REEF

Adventure. Background: Australia. The explorations of the marine biologists assigned to investigate and study the Great Barrier Reef.

CAST

Captain Chet King	Joe James
Kip King	Ken James
Joe Francis	Richard Meikle
Steve Goba	Howard Hopkins
Tracy Dean	Rowena Wallace
Dr. Elizabeth Hanna	Ihab Nafa
Diana Parker	Elli MacLure
Elizabeth Grant	Sussana Brett
Ken	Peter Adams
Jack	George Assang
Professor Barnard	Peter Carver

Their ship: The *Endeavor,* a two-hundred-twenty-ton windjammer.

BARRIER REEF—30 minutes—NBC—September 11, 1971 - September 2, 1972. 39 episodes.

BATMAN

Adventure. Background: Gotham City. Inheriting a vast fortune after his parents are killed by a gangster, ten-year old Bruce Wayne vows to avenge their deaths by spending the rest of his life fighting crime.

Cared for by Alfred, the family butler, he works in total isolation and becomes a master scientist. Fourteen years later, after constructing the world's greatest crime lab beneath Wayne Manor, he adopts the guise of the mysterious caped crusader, "Batman," a figure designed to strike fear into the hearts of criminals.

Bruce Wayne adopts the orphaned, teenaged Dick Greyson after the tragic death of his parents in a circus high-wire act. Dick is taught to perfect his mental and physical skills, and adopts the guise of "Robin, The Boy Wonder." Joining Batman they form "The Dynamic Duo."

Several years later, when Police Commissioner Gordon's daughter, Barbara, returns home following her college graduation, she acquires employment in the Gotham City Library and adopts the guise of the mysterious "Batgirl." Though operating independently, she forms "The Terrific Trio" when working with Batman and Robin.

Stories relate their crusade against the sinister forces of evil.

Created by Bob Kane, "Batman" first appeared in *Detective Comics* in May 1939. In the Spring of 1940, *Batman Comics* evolved.

In the 1940s, Batman and Robin, through the voices of Stacy Harris and Ronald Liss, respectively, occasionally made guest appearances on the Mutual Radio Network program, "Superman."

The first fifteen-chapter serial, "Batman," produced by Columbia Pictures, was released to theatres in 1943.

In 1949, the final theatrical serial, "The New Adventures of Batman and Robin," produced by Columbia, appeared.

TV CAST

Bruce Wayne/Batman	Adam West
Dick Greyson/Robin	Burt Ward
Barbara Gordon/Batgirl	Yvonne Craig
Alfred, the Wayne family butler	Alan Napier
Commissioner Gordon	Neil Hamilton
Police Chief O'Hara	Stafford Repp
Harriet Cooper, Bruce's aunt	Madge Blake
Mayor John Lindseed	Byron Keith
Mrs. Lindseed	Jean Byron
Narrator	William Dozier

Criminals:

The Penguin	Burgess Meredith
Dawn Robbins, his aide	Leslie Parrish
Lola Lasagne	Ethel Merman
Gluten, her aide	Horace McMahon
The Joker	Cesar Romero

Batman. Left to right: Burgess Meredith (The Penguin), Cesar Romero (The Joker), Burt Ward (Robin), Adam West (Batman), Frank Gorshin (behind Batman, The Riddler), and Lee Meriwether (Catwoman).

Cornelia, his aide	
Venus, his aide	Kathy Kersh
The Riddler	Terry Moore
	Frank Gorshin
	John Astin
Molly, his aide	
	Jill Saint John
Anna Gram, his aide	
	Deanna Lund
The Archer	Art Carney
Maid Marilyn, his aide	
	Barbara Nichols
Crier Tuck, his aide	
	Doodles Weaver
The Catwoman	Julie Newmar
	Lee Ann Meriwether
	Eartha Kitt
Pussycat, her aide	Lesley Gore
Leo, her aide	Jock Mahoney
Lady Penelope Peasoup	Glynis Johns
Lord Marmaduke Ffogg	Rudy Vallee
Colonel Gumm	Roger C. Carmel
Pinky, his aide	Diane McBaine
The Black Widow	Tallulah Bankhead
Egghead	Vincent Price
Olga, his aide	Anne Baxter
Chicken, his aide	Edward Everett Horton
Dr. Cassandra	Ida Lupino
Cabala, her aide	Howard Duff
Falseface	Malachi Throne
Blaze, his aide	Myrna Fahey
The Sandman	Michael Rennie
The Puzzler	Maurice Evans
Rocket O'Rourke, his aide	Barbara Stuart

Sophie Starr	Kathleen Crowley
Eagle Eye, her aide	Harvey Lembeck
Chandell	Liberace
Jervis Tetch, the Mad Hatter	David Wayne
Mr. Freeze	George Sanders
	Eli Wallach
	Otto Preminger
Ma Parker	Shelley Winters
Clock King	Walter Slezak
The Minstrel	Van Johnson
The Siren	Joan Collins
Shame	Cliff Robertson
Marsha, Queen of Diamonds	Carolyn Jones
Louie the Lilac	Milton Berle
The Bookworm	Roddy McDowall
The Devil, his aide	Joan Crawford
Lydia, his aide	Francine York
King Tut	Victor Buono
Minerva	Zsa Zsa Gabor

Batman and Robin's car: The *Batmobile.*

Batgirl's mode of transportation: The *Batcycle.*

Music: Nelson Riddle; Billy May; Neil Hefti.

Executive Producer: William Dozier.

Producer: Howie Horwitz.

Director: Sam Strangis, Oscar Rudolph, Larry Peerce, George Waggner, James Clark, James Sheldon, Robert Butler, Norman Foster, Tom Gries, William Graham, Leslie H. Martinson, Richard Sarafian, Charles R. Rondeau.

Music Supervision: Lionel Newman.

BATMAN—30 minutes—ABC—January 12, 1966 - March 14, 1968. Syndicated. 120 episodes.

THE BATMAN/SUPERMAN HOUR

See individual titles: "The Adventures of Superman;" "Batman."

THE BATMAN/TARZAN ADVENTURE HOUR

See individual titles: "The New Adventures of Batman," and "Tarzan: Lord of the Jungle" for information.

BAT MASTERSON

Western. Background: The territory from Kansas to California during the 1880s. The exploits of William Bartley "Bat" Masterson, a wandering law enforcer. Legend associates him with several trademarks: a gold-tipped cane, a derby hat, and a custom built gun—items presented to him by the greatful citizens of Dodge City during his service as sheriff.

Starring: Gene Barry as Bat Masterson.

Announcer-Narrator: Bill Baldwin.

Producer: Andy White, Frank Pittman.

BAT MASTERSON—30 minutes—NBC—October 8, 1957 - September 21, 1961. Syndicated. 108 episodes.

BATTLELINE

Documentary. The key battles and campaigns of World War II are traced through film.

Host-Narrator: Jim Bishop.

BATTLELINE—30 minutes—Syndicated 1963. 39 episodes.

BATTLE OF THE AGES

Game. Two talent teams compete: The Show Business Veterans and The Youngsters. The teams compete in a series of talent contests designed to determine the better of the two. Winners, which are determined by off-stage judges, receive cash prizes.

Hosts: Morey Amsterdam; John Reed King.

Announcer: Norman Brokenshire.

Orchestra: Al Fennelli.

Producer: Norman Livingston.

Sponsor: Serutan Lotion.

BATTLE OF THE AGES—30 minutes—DuMont 1951; CBS 1952.

THE BEACHCOMBER

Adventure. Pressured by society, John Lackland, a wealthy merchandising executive, departs San Francisco and retreats to Amura, a tropical island paradise in the South Pacific. Adopting the life of a beachcomber, he searches for the true meaning of life and happiness. Episodes relate his struggles as he encounters and assists people in distress.

CAST

John Lackland	Cameron Mitchell
Captain Huckabee, his friend	Don Megowan
Andrew Crippen, the Commissioner	Sebastian Cabot

Music: Joseph Hooven.

THE BEACHCOMBER—30 minutes—Syndicated 1961. 39 episodes.

BEACON HILL

Serial. Background: Boston during the 1920s. Dramatic incidents in the lives of the Lassiters, a rich, powerful Irish-American family; and their servants, Irish immigrants, who live below them in a fashionable home on Louisburgh Square. Based on the British series, "Upstairs, Downstairs," which was broadcast in the United States via "Masterpiece Theatre." (See title.)

CAST
The Lassiter Family:

Benjamin Lassiter, an attorney	Stephen Elliott
Mary Lassiter, his wife	Nancy Marchand
Emily Bullock, their married daughter	DeAnn Mears
Trevor Bullock, Emily's husband	Roy Cooper
Betsy Bullock, their daughter	Linda Purl
Maude Palmer, Ben and Mary's married daughter	Maeve McGuire
Richard Palmer, Maude's husband	Edward Herrmann
Rosamond Lassiter, Ben and Mary's daughter	Kitty Winn
Fawn Lassiter, Ben and Mary's daughter	Kathryn Walker
Robert Lassiter, Ben and Mary's son	David Dukes

The Servants:

Mr. Hacker, the head butler	George Rose
Emmaline Hacker, his wife	Beatrice Straight
William Piper, the cook	Richard Ward
Brian Mallory, the chauffeur	Paul Rudd
Terence O'Hara, Mr. Hacker's assistant	David Rounds
Eleanor, a maid	Sydney Swire
Maureen, a maid	Susan Blanchard
Kate, a maid	Lisa Pelikan

Music: Marvin Hamlisch.

Executive Producer: Beryl Vertue.

Producer: Jacqueline Babbin.

Director: Fielder Cook, Peter Lewis, Jay Sandrich, Mel Ferber.

BEACON HILL—60 minutes—CBS—August 25, 1975 - November 4, 1975.

THE BEAGLES

Animated Cartoon. The misadventures of Stringer and Tubby, canines who comprise The Beagles, a Rock and Roll duo.

THE BEAGLES—30 minutes—CBS—September 10, 1966 - September 2, 1967. ABC—September 9, 1967 - September 7, 1968. Syndicated. 36 episodes.

BEANIE AND CECIL

Children. The global misadventures of a small boy, Beany; his pet sea serpent, Cecil; and Huffenpuff, the captain of their boat, the *Leakin' Lena.* Based on the characters created by Bob Clampett.

Versions:

Time For Beany—Puppet Adventure—15 minutes—Syndicated 1950.

Characters: Beany, Cecil, Captain Huffenpuff, Moon Mad Tiger, Jack Webfoot, Dizzy Lou and Hey You, the Double Feature Creature with the Stereophonic Sound, Marilyn Mongrel, Louie the Lone Shark.

Voices: Stan Freberg, Daws Butler, Jerry Colona.

The Beany and Cecil Show—Animated Cartoon—30 minutes—Syndicated 1961. Also broadcast on ABC—30 minutes—December 27, 1964 - October 23, 1966. 78 episodes.

Characters: Beany, Cecil, Captain Huffenpuff, Crowy the lookout, Dishonest John.

Voices: Daws Butler, Don Messick, Joan Gerber.

Music: Jack Roberts, Hoyt Curtin, Eddie Brandt, Melvyn Lenard.

BEARCATS!

Adventure. Background: the turbulent

Southwest, 1914. The experiences of free-lance troubleshooters Hank Brackett and Johnny Reach. Episodes depict their battle against the early breed of twentieth-century criminal.

CAST
Hank Brackett   Rod Taylor
Johnny Reach   Dennis Cole

BEARCATS!—60 minutes—CBS—September 16, 1971 - December 30, 1971. 13 episodes.

THE BEATLES

Animated Cartoon. The songs and misadventures of the famous Liverpool rock group, the Beatles.
Characters' Voices
John Lennon   Himself
Ringo Starr   Himself
George Harrison   Himself
Paul McCartney   Himself
Music: Recorded Beatle songs.

THE BEATLES—30 minutes—ABC—September 25, 1965 - September 7, 1969. Syndicated. 52 episodes.

BEAT THE CLOCK

Game. Contestants, usually married couples, attempt to perform stunts and beat the amount of time shown on a ticking sixty-second clock. Cash and/or merchandise prizes are awarded.

Versions:

CBS—30 minutes—March 23, 1950 - February 16, 1958.

Beat the Clock. Guest Sheila MacRae and host Jack Narz.

ABC—October 13, 1958 - September 26, 1962.
Host: Bud Collyer.
Assistant: Dolores Rosedale (Roxanne).

Syndicated—30 minutes—1969.
Hosts: Jack Narz; Gene Wood.
Assistants: Gail Sheldon, Betsy Hirst, Ellen Singer, Linda Somer, Diane Mead.
Announcers: Gene Wood; Dick Holenberg.
Music: Dick Hyman.

BEAT THE ODDS

Game. Two competing contestants. The game revolves around a large electronic spinning wheel which contains the first and last letters of numerous word possibilities and a point reclaimer, Mr. Whamie. After the host spins the wheel one player at a time presses a button and stops it. If two letters appear (e.g. S.....E) he must give a word corresponding to it (e.g. *SinglE*). Acceptable words earn the player ten points. However, should Mr. Whamie appear (the odds are four to one) the contestant loses his turn at play and any points he has accumulated. The only way a contestant can retain points is to freeze his score when he feels safe. When a score is frozen it cannot be affected by Mr. Whamie on that player's next turn. The player first to score one hundred points is the winner and he receives that amount in dollars.
Host: Johnny Gilbert.
Announcer: Bill Baldwin.

BEAT THE ODDS—30 minutes—Syndicated 1969.

THE BEAUTIFUL
PHYLLIS DILLER SHOW

Variety. Various comedy sketches satirizing world problems.
Hostess: Phyllis Diller.
Regulars: Norm Crosby, Rip Taylor, Dave Willock, Bob Jellison, Merryl Jay and the Curtin Calls, The Jack Regas Dancers.
Announcer: Norm Crosby.
Orchestra: Jack Elliott.

THE BEAUTIFUL PHYLLIS DILLER SHOW—60 minutes—NBC—September 15, 1968 - December 22, 1968. 13 tapes.

BEHIND CLOSED DOORS

Anthology Drama. Tales of international intrigue based on the files of Admiral Zacharies, a World War II Naval Intelligence Chief.
Host-Narrator (appearing as Commander Matson): Bruce Gordon.

BEHIND CLOSED DOORS—30 minutes—ABC—May 25, 1959 - September 20, 1960. 26 episodes.

BELIEVE IT OR NOT

Anthology. Dramatizations based on unusual but actual incidents compiled by Robert Ripley for his newspaper column, "Believe It Or Not."
Host: Robert Ripley.
Producer: Vic McLeod, Douglas Storer, Harry Herrmann.
Director: Harry Herrmann, Joe Cavalier.
Sponsor: Ballantine Beer.

BELIEVE IT OR NOT—30 minutes—NBC 1950.

THE BELL TELEPHONE HOUR

Music. A documentary style presentation wherein outstanding guests appear in distinguished programs devoted entirely to the music fields of opera, ballet, jazz, popular, and classical.
Music: The Bell Telephone Orchestra.
Conductor: Donald Voorhees.

THE BELL TELEPHONE HOUR—60 minutes—NBC—January 12, 1959 - June 1968.

BEN CASEY

Medical Drama. Background: County General Hospital. The victories and defeats of Ben Casey, a chief resident in neurosurgery.

CAST
Dr. Ben Casey   Vincent Edwards
Dr. David Zorba, his mentor,
  the neurosurgical
  chief   Sam Jaffe
Dr. Freeland, the neuro-

The Beautiful Phyllis Diller Show. Phyllis Diller.

surgical chief
(later episodes)   Franchot Tone
Dr. Maggie Graham,
Casey's romantic
interest   Bettye Ackerman
Nurse Willis   Jeanne Bates
Dr. Ted Hoffman   Harry Landers
Orderly Nick Kanavars   Nick Dennis
Dr. Terry McDaniel   Jim McMullan

Music: George Bassman.

Additional Music: Walter Scharf, Richard Sendry.

Executive Producer: John E. Pommer, Matthew Rapf.

Producer: Wilton Schiller, Jack Laird, James E. Mosher.

BEN CASEY—60 minutes—ABC—October 2, 1961 - March 21, 1966. Syndicated. 153 episodes.

BEN JERROD

Serial. Background: The town of Indian Hill. The dramatic story of two lawyers: John P. Abbott, a retired judge, the elder, set in his ways; and Ben Jerrod, his assistant, a Harvard-educated youth. Their first and only case: "The Janet Donelli Murder Trial." Episodes relate their defense of a woman who is accused of murdering her husband.

CAST
Ben Jerrod   Michael Ryan
John Abbott   Addison Richards

Janet Donelli   Regina Gleason
Jim O'Hara   Ken Scott
Engle, the coroner   William Phillips
The District Attorney   John Napier
Peter Morrison   Peter Hansen
Lieutenant Choates   Lyle Talbot
Lil   Martine Bartlett

BEN JERROD—30 minutes—NBC—April 1, 1963 - June 28, 1963.

THE BENNETS

Serial. Background: A small midwestern town. The dramatic story of attorney Wayne Bennet and his wife Nancy.

CAST
Wayne Bennet   Don Gibson
Nancy Bennet   Paula Houston

Also: Jerry Harvey, Roy Westfall, Sam Gray, Kay Westfall, Jim Andelin, Viola Berwick, Beverly Younger, Jack Lester, Sam Siegel.

THE BENNETS—15 minutes—NBC—July 6, 1953 - January 8, 1954.

THE BENNY RUBIN SHOW

Variety. The program features performances by guest artists, but deviates slightly from the normal presentation method (e.g. as on "The Ed Sullivan Show") in that the acts are interwoven around the antics of the series master of ceremonies, a bumbling talent agent.

Host: Benny Rubin (the talent agent).

His nine-year-old office boy: Vinnie Monte.

Regulars: Jackie Coogan, Edith Fellows, The Andrews Twins, Lois and Lillian Bernard.

Orchestra: Rex Maupin.

Producer: Jerry Rosen.

Director: Larry Schmah, Jr.

THE BENNY RUBIN SHOW—30 minutes—NBC 1949.

BEN VEREEN . . . COMIN' AT YA

Variety. Music, songs, dances, and comedy sketches.

Host: Ben Vereen.

Regulars: Arte Johnson, Avery Schreiber, Liz Torres, The Louis DaPron Dancers.

Ben's Dancing Partner: Lee Lund.

Orchestra: Jack Elliott, Allyn Ferguson.

Special Musical Material: Ray Charles.

Choreographer: Jerry Grimes.

Dance Numbers Staged By: Louis DaPron.

Producer: Jaime Rogers, Jean McAvoy.

Director: Peter Calabrese.

BEN VEREEN . . . COMIN' AT YA—60 minutes—NBC—August 7, 1975 - August 28, 1975.

BE OUR GUEST

Variety. The series spotlights the unknown or unusual talents of celebrities.

Host: George DeWitt; Keefe Brasselle.

Vocalist: Mary Ann Mobley.

Music: The Glenn Miller Orchestra conducted by Ray McKinley; The Bert Farber Orchestra.

BE OUR GUEST—60 minutes—CBS—January 27, 1960 - June 1, 1960.

BERT D'ANGELO/SUPERSTAR

Crime Drama. Background: San Francisco, California. The story of Bert D'Angelo, a tough, unorthodox police detective who constantly defies rules and regulations in an attempt to get his job done. Because of his impressive record of arrests and convictions, he has earned the nickname "Superstar."

CAST
Bert D'Angelo   Paul Sorvino
Det. Larry Lorenzo, his
    partner   Robert Pine
Capt. Jack Breen, their
    superior   Dennis Patrick
Music: Duante Tatro, Patrick Williams, John Elizade.

Executive Producer: Quinn Martin.

Producer: Mort Fine.

Director: David Friedkin, Virgil W. Vogel, Michael Caffrey, Harry Falk, Bill Bixby.

BERT D'ANGELO/SUPERSTAR—60 minutes—ABC—February 21, 1976 - April 10, 1976; May 29, 1976 - July 10, 1976.

THE BERT PARKS SHOW

Variety. Music, songs, guests, and interviews.

Host: Bert Parks.

Regulars: Betty Ann Grove; Bobby Sherwood; The Heathertones: Bix Brent, Marianne McCormick, Nancy Overton, Jean Swain, and Marray Scholmann.

Music: The Bobby Sherwood Quintet.

Producer: Sherman Marks, Mary Harris, Louis Cowan.

Director: Hal Gerson, Jr.

Sponsor: General Foods.

THE BERT PARKS SHOW—30 minutes—NBC—November 1, 1950 - January 11, 1952.

THE BEST IN MYSTERY

Anthology. Rebroadcasts of suspense dramas that were originally aired via other filmed anthology series.

Hostess: Polly Bergen.

Included:

Lost Kid. The story of a grandmother who uses every possible device to keep her juvenile deliquent grandson from embarking on an adult life of crime.

CAST
Elizabeth Patterson, Mary Field, Harry Harvey, Jr.

Death Makes A Pair. The story of a businessman who finds himself with gambling fever after becoming involved with an associate.

CAST
Lloyd Corrigan, Jay Novello, Margia Dean.

The Watchers And The Watched. The story of three people who set out on an evil mission: to drive someone out of his mind; the motive: robbery.

CAST
Fay Roope.

THE BEST IN MYSTERY—60 minutes—NBC—July 16, 1954 - September 3, 1954.

THE BEST IN MYSTERY

Drama. Background: San Francisco, California. The story of Willie Dante, former gambler turned owner of Dante's Inferno Nightclub. Episodes relate his struggles to overcome the situations that occur when his past reputation attracts unscrupulous characters. Originally broadcast as occasional episodes of "Four Star Playhouse."

CAST
Willie Dante   Dick Powell
Jackson, his aide   Alan Mowbray
Monte, his aide   Herb Vigran
Lieutenant Waldo,
    S.F.P.D.   Regis Toomey

THE BEST IN MYSTERY—60 minutes—NBC—July 13, 1956 - August 31, 1956.

THE BEST OF BROADWAY

Anthology. A monthly series that re-creates for television the best comedies, dramas, and musicals of the Broadway stage.

Orchestra: David Broekman.

Producer: Martin Manulis, Felix Jackson.

Director: Paul Nickell, Sidney Lumet, Franklin Schaffner.

Sponsor: Westinghouse.

Included:

The Royal Family. A comedy about the lives of America's first family of the theater, the Cavendishes.

CAST
Oscar Wolfe: Charles Coburn; Julie Cavendish: Claudette Colbert; Franny Cavendish: Helen Hayes; Tony Cavendish: Fredric March; Gwen Cavendish: Nancy Olson.

Stage Door. A drama that tells of the hopes and ambitions of would-be Broadway actresses.

CAST
Terry Randall: Diana Lynn; Jean Maitland: Rhonda Fleming; Kaye Hamilton: Peggy Ann Garner; Mrs. Orcutt: Elsa Lanchester; Judith Canfield: Nita Talbot.

Broadway. Set against the background of a speakeasy in 1926, the story follows the lives of a local gangster, his girl, and the Broadway Dick who enters their lives at the wrong moment.

CAST
Dan McCorn: Joseph Cotten; Steve Crandell: Keenan Wynn; Billie Moore: Piper Laurie.

THE BEST OF BROADWAY—60 minutes—CBS—September 15, 1954 - May 4, 1955. 9 live presentations.

THE BEST OF EVERYTHING

Serial. Background: New York City. The dramatic story of three young women: April Morrison, Linda Warren, and Kim Jordan, secretaries at Key Publishing. Episodes relate their experiences as they struggle to fulfill their lives.

CAST
April Morrison   Julie Mannix
Linda Warren   Patty McCormack
Violet Jordan   Geraldine Fitzgerald

Amanda Key	Gale Sondergaard
Ed Peronne	Vice Arnold
Ken Lamont	Barry Ford
Kim Jordan	Kathy Glass
Johnny Lomart	Stephen Grover
Randy Wilson	Ted La Platt

Also: M'el Dowd, Terry O'Sullivan, Jill Melody, Jane Alice Brandon.

THE BEST OF EVERYTHING—30 minutes—ABC—March 30, 1970 - September 24, 1970.

THE BEST OF GROUCHO

See title: "You Bet Your Life."

THE BEST OF ERNIE KOVACS

Comedy. A ten-part series that spotlights the genius of Ernie Kovacs through film and video tape clips from his various network series. See title "Ernie Kovacs" for a complete rundown on the Kovacs series.

Narration Host: Jack Lemmon.

Producer-Director: Dave Erdman.

THE BEST OF ERNIE KOVACS—30 minutes—PBS—April 14, 1977 - June 16, 1977.

THE BEST OF THE POST

Anthology. Dramatizations based on stories appearing in the *Saturday Evening Post.*

Included:

Treasury Agent. The story of treasury agents Don Kearns and Paul Corbin and their attempts to apprehend the infamous gangster Vince Lewis.

CAST
Michael Higgins, Richard Arlen, Joe Mell.

The Baron Loved His Wife. The story of a Viennese nobleman who attempts to trail a British agent despite the constant hindrance of his wife.

CAST
Peter Lorre, Ingrid Goride.

Frontier Correspondent. Background: The Old West. The story of an Eastern newspaper reporter as he attempts to take a picture of Jesse James.

CAST
Bert Douglas.

THE BEST OF THE POST—30 minutes—Syndicated 1959. 26 episodes.

BEST SELLERS

Anthology. Dramatizations of best-selling novels.
Best Sellers Theme: Elmer Bernstein.

Included:

Captains and the Kings. The story of Joseph Armagh, a strong-willed Irish immigrant, as he struggles for wealth. Based on the novel by Taylor Caldwell.

CAST
Joseph Armagh: Richard Jordan; Ed Healey: Charles Durning; Katherine Hennessey: Joanna Pettet; Martinique: Barbara Parkins; Mrs. Finch: Ann Sothern; Tom Hennessey: Vic Morrow; Harry Zeff: Harvey Jason; Sister Angela: Celeste Holm; Father Hale: John Carradine; Bernadette: Patty Duke Astin.

Executive Producer: Roy Huggins.
Producer: Jo Swerling, Jr.
Director: Douglas Heyes.
Music: Dana Kaproff.

Once An Eagle. Adapted from the novel by Anton Myrer, which chronicles the lives of two American soldiers from 1918 through W.W. II.

CAST
Sam Damon: Sam Elliott; Courtney Massengale: Cliff Potts; George Caldwell: Glenn Ford; Tommy Caldwell: Darleen Carr; Emily Massengale: Amy Irving; Marge Chrysler: Lynda Day George; Alvin Merrick: Clu Gulager; Ben Chrysler: Ben Hogan; Mrs. Damon: Kim Hunter; Joyce: Juliet Mills; Bert: Albert Salmi; Capt. Townsend: John Saxon; Gen. Bannerman: Barry Sullivan; Col. Avery: Forrest Tucker; Gen. Lane: William Windom.

Executive Producer: William Sackheim.
Producer: Peter Fischer.
Director: E.W. Swackhamer, Richard Michaels.
Music: Dana Kaproff.

Seventh Avenue. The story concerns a New York rags-to-riches climb in the garment industry. Based on the novel by Norman Bogner.

CAST
Jay Blackman: Steven Keats; Rhoda Blackman: Dori Brenner; Eva Meyers: Jane Seymour; Myrna Gold: Anne Archer; Joe Vitelli: Herschel Bernardi; Frank Topo: Richard Dimitri; Finkelstein: Jack Gilford; Morris: Michael Kellin; Harry Lee: Alan King; Douglas Fredericks: Ray Milland; Dave Shaw: Paul Sorvino; Gus Farber: Eli Wallach; John Meyers: William Windom; Moll: Gloria Grahame.

Executive Producer: Franklin Barton.
Producer: Richard Irving, Russ Mayberry.
Music: Nelson Riddle.

BEST SELLERS—60 minutes—NBC—September 30, 1976 - March 21, 1977.

THE BETTER SEX

Game. Two teams, the male and the female, each composed of six members, compete. One player, from one team (as determined by the flip of a coin) appears at the verbal attack post. A question is read by the host (or hostess, depending on which team is at the post) and a card, which contains two answers (one correct, the other a bluff), is given to the player. He or she then chooses one answer and states it. It is up to the opposing team to determine whether the answer is correct or incorrect. Each of the players is asked his (or her) opinion—to agree or disagree. When two opinions match, the correct answer is given. If the attack player fooled the opponents his (or her) team wins that round and two opposing players are defeated. If, however, the attack player failed to fool the opposing team, he, or she, as well as one other member of his or her team is defeated. The game continues in this manner until one team defeats the other by knocking out all its members. One thousand dollars is then divided between the winning teams members.

Host: Bill Anderson.
Hostess: Sarah Purcell.
Announcer: Gene Wood.
Music: Score Productions.
Executive Producer: Mark Goodson, Bill Todman.
Producer: Robert Sherman.

Director: Paul Alter.

THE BETTER SEX—30 minutes—ABC—Premiered: July 18, 1977.

THE BETTY CROCKER SHOW

Women. The format features Betty Crocker, the General Mills homemaking expert, demonstrating kitchen techniques and answering questions submitted by viewers.

Hostess: Betty Crocker [the actress portraying the role is not identified; however, when the series switched networks and became "The Betty Crocker Star Matinee" (which see), Adelaide Hawley was revealed to be portraying the part.]
Announcer: Win Elliott.

THE BETTY CROCKER SHOW—30 minutes—CBS—1950-1951.

THE BETTY CROCKER STAR MATINEE

Variety. Guests, interviews, and dramatic vignettes.
Hostess: Adelaide Hawley.
Announcer: Win Elliott.
Producer: Tom Hicks, Al Ward.
Sponsor: General Mills.

THE BETTY CROCKER STAR MATINEE—30 minutes—ABC—November 3, 1951 - April 26, 1952.

THE BETTY HUTTON SHOW

Comedy. Background: New York City. Goldie Appleby, manicurist, one-time vivacious show girl, accepts a dinner invitation from a customer, a lonely millionaire. His sudden death finds her the unaccountable beneficiary of his will — head of the Strickland Foundation, the executrix of his sixty-million-dollar Park Avenue estate, and guardian of his three orphaned children.

Episodes concern her struggles to adjust to new responsibilities, run the foundation, and care for and secure the affections of Patricia, Roy, and Nicky, the spendthrift Strickland children.

CAST

Goldie Appleby	Betty Hutton
Patricia Strickland	Gigi Perreau
Nicky Strickland	Richard Miles
Roy Strickland	Dennis Joel
Lorna, Goldie's friend	Joan Shawlee
Howard Seaton, the Strickland attorney	Tom Conway
Rosemary, the maid	Jean Carson
Hollister, the butler	Gavin Muir

THE BETTY HUTTON SHOW—30 minutes—CBS—October 1, 1959 - June 30, 1960. Also known as: "Goldie."

THE BETTY WHITE SHOW

Variety. Music, songs, guests, and interviews.

Versions:

NBC—30 minutes—1954.
Hostess: Betty White.
Announcer: Del Sharbutt.
Orchestra: Frank DeVol.

ABC—30 minutes — February 5, 1958 - April 30, 1958.

Hostess: Betty White.
Regulars: John Dehner, Chill Wills.
Orchestra: Frank DeVol.

THE BETTY WHITE SHOW

Comedy. Background: Los Angeles, California. A satirization of television as seen through the experiences of Joyce Whitman, a struggling, mediocre actress who stars in "Undercover Woman," a second-rate series that is directed by her estranged husband, John Elliott. The recurring story line concerns Joyce's attempts to reconcile herself with John even though he insists they can't live together.

CAST

Joyce Whitman	Betty White
John Elliott	John Hillerman
Mitzi Maloney, Joyce's friend	Georgia Engel
Fletcher Huff, the police chief in "Undercover Woman"	Barney Phillips
Hugo Muncy, Joyce's double for the show	Charles Cyphers
Doug Porterfield, the CBS liaison for the show	Alex Henteloff
Tracy Garrett, an actress on "Undercover Woman"	Caren Kaye
Lisa Vincent, same as Tracy, but for the pilot film	Carla Borelli

Music: Dick De Benedictis.
Executive Producer: Ed Weinberger, Stan Daniels.
Producer: Bob Ellison.
Creator: Ed Weinberger, Stan Daniels.

THE BETTY WHITE SHOW—30 minutes—CBS—Premiered: September 12, 1977.

BEULAH

Comedy. Background: New York City. The trials and tribulations of the Henderson family: Harry, an attorney; his wife, Alice; their son, Donnie; and their maid, Beulah, the irrepressible Queen of the Kitchen. Stories relate Beulah's attempts to solve arising household crises and the problems that are created by her unpredictable girlfriend, Oriole and her boyfriend, Bill Jackson, a fix-it-shop owner.

CAST

1950-1952:

Beulah	Ethel Waters
	Hattie McDaniel
Harry Henderson	William Post, Jr.
Alice Henderson	Ginger Jones
Donnie Henderson	Clifford Sales
Oriole	Butterfly McQueen
Bill Jackson	Percy "Bud" Harris

1952-1953:

Beulah	Louise Beavers
Harry Henderson	David Bruce
Alice Henderson	June Frazee
Donnie Henderson	Stuffy Singer
Oriole	Butterfly McQueen
Bill Jackson	Dooley Wilson

Music: Gordon Kibbee.
Producer: Roland Reed.
Director: Jean Yarbrough.
Sponsor: Procter & Gamble.

BEULAH—30 minutes—CBS—October 10, 1950 - September 22, 1953. Syndicated. Withdrawn.

THE BEVERLY HILLBILLIES

Comedy. Background: 518 Crestview Drive, Beverly Hills, California, the residence of the Clampett family: Jed, a widowed mountaineer; his beautiful and unmarried daughter, Elly May; his mother-in-law, Daisy "Granny" Moses; and his not-too-bright nephew,

Jethro Bodine — a simple backwoods family who became multimillionaires when oil was discovered on their property in the Ozark community of Sibly. Stories relate their struggles to adjust to the fast, sophisticated, modern life of the big city.

Jed, though content, longs for life as before. Granny, unable to practice her unlicensed mountain doctoring (Dr. Roy Clyburn has threatened to press charges), make her lye soap (the process pollutes the air), or find needed ingredients in the city stores (e.g., "possum innerds") is miserable and wants to return home.

Elly May, determined to prove herself superior to any man, is unable to find a steady beau, and prefers life with her countless "critters." Jethro, educated and graduated from the sixth grade, delights in the excitement of the big city and endlessly attempts to attract the opposite sex and "find...a sweetheart."

CAST

Jed Clampett	Buddy Ebsen
Daisy Moses (Granny)	Irene Ryan
Elly May Clampett	Donna Douglas
Jethro Bodine	Max Baer
Jethrene Bodine, his sister	Max Baer
Milburn Drysdale, the President of the Commerce Bank, which houses Jed's money	Raymond Bailey
Jane Hathaway, his secretary	Nancy Kulp
Margaret Drysdale, Milburn's wife, a woman determined to rid her life of her unsavory neighbors, the Clampetts	Harriet MacGibbon
Pearl Bodine, Jethro's mother	Bea Benaderet
John Brewster, the president of the O.K. Oil Company	Frank Wilcox
Isabel Brewster, his wife	Lisa Seagram
Lester Flatt, a friend of the Clampetts	Himself
Earl Scruggs, a friend of the Clampetts	Himself
Gladys Flatt, Lester's wife	Joi Lansing
Louise Scruggs, Earl's wife	Midge Ware
Homer Winch, a backwoods oldster, fond of Pearl (a widow)	Paul Winchell
Jasper DePew, Jethrene's boyfriend	Phil Gordon
Ravenscott, the Drysdale's butler	Arthur Gould Porter
Marie, the Drysdale's maid	Shirry Steffin
Dash Riprock (Homer Noodleman),	

a movie star, Elly May's beau	Larry Pennell
Mark Templeton, Elly May's beau (later episodes)	Roger Torrey
Homer Cratchit, the bank bookkeeper	Percy Helton
Elverna Bradshaw, Granny's nemesis	Elvia Allman
Sonny Drysdale, Milburn's son, in his 19th year in college	Louis Nye
Janet Trego, a bank secretary	Sharon Tate
Dr. Roy Clyburn, Granny's nemesis	Fred Clark
The Psychiatrist	Richard Deacon
Harry Chapman, a movie producer at Mammoth Studios	Milton Frome

Announcer: Bill Baldwin.

Music: Perry Botkin; Curt Massey.

Executive Producer: Al Simon.

Producer: Joseph DePew, Paul Henning, Mark Tuttle.

The Clampett Dog: Duke, a blood hound.

Note: Jethrene, who is played by Max Baer, is voiced by Linda Kaye Henning.

THE BEVERLY HILLBILLIES—30 minutes—CBS—September 26, 1962 - September 7, 1971. Syndicated.

BEWITCHED

Comedy. Background: 1164 Morning Glory Circle, West Port, Connecticut, the home of Darrin Stevens, a mortal and advertising executive with the Manhattan firm of McMann and Tate; and his wife, a beautiful witch, Samantha. Episodes relate Samantha's attempts to adopt the role of housewife, and Darrin's struggles to curtail and conceal his wife's powers and cope with his disapproving mother-in-law, Endora, who, when angered, delights in casting spells upon him.

CAST

Samantha Stevens	Elizabeth Montgomery
Serena, her beautiful, funloving cousin	Elizabeth Montgomery
Darrin Stevens	Dick York
	Dick Sargent
Endora	Agnes Moorehead
Larry Tate, Darrin's employer	David White
Louise Tate, his wife	Irene Vernon
	Kasey Rogers
Gladys Kravitz, the Stevens's nosey neighbor	Alice Pearce
	Sandra Gould

Bewitched. Left to right: Erin Murphy, Dick York, Elizabeth Montgomery, and Agnes Moorehead. © *Screen Gems.*

Abner Kravitz, her husband	George Tobias
Maurice, Samatha's father	Maurice Evans
Uncle Arthur, a warlock, Samantha's relative	Paul Lynde
Doctor Bombay, Samantha's family physician	Bernard Fox
Aunt Clara, an aging, bumbling witch	Marion Lorne
Tabitha Stevens, the Stevens daughter, a witch	Erin & Diane Murphy (identical twins)
Frank Stevens, Darrin's father	Robert F. Simon
	Roy Roberts
Phyllis Stevens, his wife	Mabel Albertson
Esmeralda, a shy witch	Alice Ghostley
Adam Stevens, the Stevens son, a warlock	David & Greg Lawrence (identical twins)
Betty, Darrin's secretary	Marcia Wallace
	Samantha Scott
	Jean Blake
Harriet Kravitz, Abner's sister	Mary Grace Canfield
Aunt Hagatha, Samantha's relative	Ysabel MacClosky
	Reta Shaw
Howard McMann, Larry's partner	Leon Ames
	Gilbert Roland
The drunk Darren meets at the bar	Dick Wilson
Margaret McMann, Howard's wife	Louise Sorel
The Apoticary, the old warlock	Bernie Kopell

Music: Warren Barker; Jimmie Haskell.

Executive Producer: Harry Ackerman.

Producer: William Froug, Danny Arnold, Jerry Davis.

Director: Ernest Losso, William Asher, Richard Michaels, Robert Rosenbaum, Jerry Davis.

Creator: Sol Saks.

BEWITCHED—30 minutes—ABC—September 17, 1964 - July 1, 1972. Syndicated. 306 episodes.

BICENTENNIAL MINUTES

History. A series of 732 sixty-second programs celebrating the birth of America. Personalities relate authenticated aspects of America's past — obscure or well-known incidents that occurred two hundred years prior to that particular evening's broadcast.

Appearing: Annette Funicello, Bernadette Peters, Walter Matthau, Celeste Holm, Nancy Malone, Pat O'Brien, Raymond Massey, Paul Newman, Roger Moore, Milton Berle, Bethel Leslie.

Executive Producer: Bob Markell.

Producer: Paul Wagner, Garreth Davis.

Creator: Louis Freedman.

BICENTENNIAL MINUTES—01 minute (12 hours total)—CBS—July 4, 1974 - July 4, 1976. Broadcast each evening at either 8:27 or 8:28 P.M., (E.S.T.) depending on whether the previous program is a half hour or an hour. On July 5, 1976, CBS decided to continue the series and began airing one-minute programs dealing with historic U.S. events two hundred years prior to that evening's broadcast. After 180 more such minutes, the series ended its run on December 31, 1976.

BIFF BAKER, U.S.A.

Adventure. Background: The Soviet Union. The cases of Biff and Louise Baker (man and wife) American export buyers secretly working for the United States Government. Stories relate their attempts to investigate the secrecy barriers behind Iron Curtain rule.

CAST
Biff Baker	Alan Hale, Jr.
Louise Baker	Randy Stuart

Producer: Alan Miller.

Sponsor: Lucky Strike Cigarettes.

BIFF BAKER, U.S.A.—30 minutes—CBS—1952-1953. 26 episodes.

THE BIG ATTACK

Anthology. Backgrounds: The European Front during World War Two, and Korea during the 1950s. True stories of Americans in combat. Dramas relate the lives of particular individuals on missions; the driving forces that enable a person to accomplish amazing feats of daring.

Narrator: The actual person featured in each episode.

Music: Bert Grund.

THE BIG ATTACK—30 minutes—Syndicated 1957. 39 episodes. Also known as "Citizen Soldier."

THE BIG BANDS

Musical Variety. Performances by the personalities of the Big Band Era.

Appearing: Tommy Dorsey, Count Basie, Glenn Miller, Harry James, Guy Lombardo, Buddy Rogers.

THE BIG BANDS—30 minutes—Syndicated 1965.

BIG EDDIE

Comedy. Background: New York City. The misadventures of Big Eddie Smith, a former gambler turned legitimate entrepreneur as the owner of the Big E Sports Arena. Created by Bill Persky and Sam Denoff.

CAST
Eddie Smith	Sheldon Leonard
Honey Smith, his wife	Sheree North
Ginger Smith, Eddie's granddaughter	Quinn Cummings
Monty "Bang Bang" Valentine, Eddie's cook	Billy Sands
Jessie Smith, Eddie's brother	Alan Oppenheimer
Raymond McKay, an employee of Eddie's	Ralph Wilcox

Music: Jack Elliott, Allyn Ferguson, Earle Hagen.

Executive Producers-Creators: Bill Persky, Sam Denoff.

Producer-Director: Hy Averback.

BIG EDDIE—30 minutes—CBS—August 23, 1975 - November 7, 1975.

THE BIGELOW SHOW

See title: "Paul Winchell and Jerry Mahoney."

THE BIGELOW THEATRE

Anthology. Dramatic presentations.

Producer: Frank Woodruff, Jerry Fairbanks.

Sponsor: Bigelow Products.

Included:

Papa Romani. The story of an immigrant who acquires his first telephone and of the complications that result from his friends and neighbors who seek to use it.

Starring: Chico Marx.

The Swan. The story of a society mother who attempts to marry her only daughter to the prince of a neighboring European kingdom.

Starring: Ferenc Molnar, Maria Riva.

Betrayal. The story of a middle-aged woman who becomes involved in a murder.

Starring: Nina Foch, Philip Reed.

THE BIGELOW THEATRE—30 minutes—CBS—December 10, 1950 - January 12, 1951.

THE BIG EVENT

Anthology. Special presentations.

Announcer: Don Stanley.

Included:

The First 50 Years. NBC's own celebration of its fifty years in broadcasting. A four and a half hour marathon of film clips and recordings to recall the TV and radio history of the network.

Hosts: Jack Albertson, Milton Berle, David Brinkley, Johnny Carson, John Chancellor, Angie Dickinson, Joe Garagiola, Bob Hope, Gene Kelly, Jerry Lewis, Dean Martin, Don Meredith, Gregory Peck, George C. Scott.

Narrator: Orson Welles.

Executive Producer: Greg Garrison.

The Hallmark Hall of Fame Presentation of Peter Pan. J.M. Barrie's story of the perennial youth Peter Pan and his adventures with the Darling children in Never-Never Land.

CAST

Peter Pan: Mia Farrow; Capt. Hook: Danny Kaye; Mrs. Darling: Virginia McKenna; Lily: Paula Kelly; Wendy: Briony McRoberts.

Narrator: Sir John Gielgud.

Music: Anthony Newley.

THE BIG EVENT—NBC—Premiered: September 26, 1976. Running times vary.

BIG FOOT AND WILD BOY

See title: "The Krofft Supershow II," *Big Foot and Wild Boy* segment.

BIG GAME

Game. Two competing contestants. Undertaken: the big African game hunt (played similar to "Battleships.") Each player sets three translucent animals on a board concealed from the other. The host asks a general knowledge question. The player first to identify himself through a buzzer signal receives a chance to answer. If the response is correct, he receives the opportunity to hunt his opponent's game. A position is called and marked on a peg board. If the number called indicates the spot on which one of his opponent's animals is located, a hit is called. The player continues calling numbers until a miss is indicated. When that occurs, the questions resume and the game follows as before. The player first to "shoot" his opponent's animals is the winner and receives a cash prize.

Host: Tom Kennedy.

BIG GAME—30 minutes—NBC—June 13, 1958 - September 12, 1958.

BIG HAWAII

Drama. Background: The Paradise Ranch in Ohana, Hawaii. The series focuses on the lives of Barrett Fears, a wealthy old-line rancher, and his son, Mitch, a determined, rebellious liberal.

CAST

Barrett Fears	John Dehner
Mitch Fears	Cliff Potts
Karen "Kete," Barrett's niece	Lucia Stralser
Oscar Kalahani, the ranch foreman	Bill Lucking
Lulu, the Fears's housekeeper	Elizabeth Smith
Anita Kalahani, Oscar's wife	Josie Oliver
Garfield, a ranch hand	Moe Keal
Kimo, Garfield's son	Remi Abellira

Music: Jack Elliott, Allyn Ferguson.

Executive Producer: Perry Lafferty.

Producer: William Wood, William Finnegan.

Director: Lawrence Doheny, Seymour Robbie, Harry Falk, Richard Michaels.

Creator: William Wood.

BIG HAWAII—60 minutes—NBC—September 21, 1977 - November 30, 1977. 7 episodes. Originally titled "The New Hawaiians," then "Big Island," "Danger In Paradise," and finally "Big Hawaii." The pilot, "Danger In Paradise," aired May 12, 1977.

BIG JOHN, LITTLE JOHN

Comedy. While vacationing in Florida, John Martin, science teacher at Madison Junior High School, and his family visit the Ponce De Leon National Park. Straying from his family, John finds a small spring—the supposed mythical fountain of youth sought by De Leon—and drinks from it. Some weeks later, the effects of the water become evident—it unpredictably keeps changing the middle-aged Big John into the twelve-year-old Little John, and vice versa. Stories depict his struggles to cope with the situations that occur as a result of the changes, and his attempts to discover the cure for the rejuvenation process.

CAST

Big John Martin	Herb Edelman
Little John Martin	Robbie Rist
Marjorie Martin, John's wife	Joyce Bulifant
Ricky Martin, their son	Mike Darnell
Miss Bertha Bottomly, the principal	Olive Dunbar

Big John's Students:

Valerie	Cari Anne Warder
Homer	Christoff St. John
Stanley	Stephen Cassidy

Music: Richard LaSalle.

Executive Producer: William P. D'Angelo, Harvey Bullock, Ray Allen, Sherwood Schwartz.

Producer: Lloyd J. Schwartz.

Director: Gordon Wiles, Wes Kenny, Ross Bowan.

BIG JOHN, LITTLE JOHN—30 minutes—NBC—Premiered: September 11, 1976.

THE BIG PARTY

Variety. An informal gathering of celebrities at a personality's home. An old piano is the center of attraction with the guests milling about, exchanging talk, and performing.

Included Parties:

Host: Rock Hudson. *Guests:* Tallulah Bankhead, Esther Williams, Mort Sahl, Sammy Davis, Jr.

Hostess: Greer Garson. *Guests:* Martha Raye, Sal Mineo, Walter Slezak, Mike Nichols, Elaine May, Peter Lind Hayes, Mary Healy.

Hostess: Irene Dunne. *Guests:* Gypsy Rose Lee, Jack Carter, Pearl Bailey.

Hostess: Eva Gabor. *Guests:* Carol Channing, Sir John Gielgud, The Benny Goodman Trio.

Commercial Spokeswoman: Barbara Britton.

Musical Director: Gordon Jenkins.

THE BIG PARTY—90 minutes—CBS—1959-1960.

THE BIG PAYOFF

Variety. A combination of music, songs, dances, and game contests. Players, selected studio audience members, compete for furs, trips, and clothing via general knowledge question and answer or stunt rounds.

Hosts: Bert Parks; Randy Merriman; Mort Lawrence; Robert Paige.

Hostesses: Bess Myerson; Betty Ann Grove (Sandy Grove); Denise Lor; Dori Anne Grey.

Music: The Burt Buhram Trio.

THE BIG PAYOFF—30 minutes—CBS—1952 - 1960.

THE BIG PICTURE

Documentary. The history and development of the United States Army.

Host: George Gunn.

Narrator: Leonard Graves.

Announcer: Captain Carl Zimmerman.

THE BIG PICTURE—30 minutes—Syndicated 1951.

THE BIG RECORD

Variety. The recording industry's top

entertainers perform the material that made them famous.

Hostess: Patti Paige.

Orchestra: Vic Schoen.

Producer: Lester Gottlieb, Lee Cooley, Jack Philbin.

THE BIG RECORD—60 minutes—CBS—September 18, 1957 - June 11, 1958.

THE BIG SHOWDOWN

Game. Three competing contestants. A playoff point is established (e.g., 8) and an accompanying money value (from twenty-five to five hundred dollars) appears. The host reads a toss-up question. The player who is first to identify himself by a light-buzzer signal receives a chance to answer. If correct, he receives one point and control of a board that contains six subjects, each worth points (1,2,3,4,5, or 6). After the player chooses a subject, the host reads an accompanying question. The player who is first to identify himself receives a chance to answer. If correct, the points are added to his score; if incorrect, no penalty, and a new toss-up round begins. The player who is first to score the playoff points exactly receives the money. Additional rounds follow the same format with the playoff point increased by seven each time, each with a different amount of money. The two highest scoring players then compete in "Final Show Down."

A category board, which contains three subjects, each distinguished by points (1,2, or 3) is displayed. The playoff point is established at seven. The player with the highest score from the previous round chooses one subject. The question is asked and the player who first identifies himself receives a chance to answer. If correct, he chooses the next category. The player who is first to score seven points is the winner, receives two hundred and fifty dollars, and the opportunity to win $10,000 in cash.

The player is escorted to a dice board. Two dice, which contain the word "Show" and "Down" on one side each are used. The player receives one roll. If he rolls "Show Down" he wins ten thousand dollars. If not, he receives thirty seconds to roll the dice. If "Show Down" appears, he receives five thousand dollars. If not, his original round earnings are won, and he returns to compete again.

Host: Jim Peck.

Announcer: Dan Daniels.

Music: Score Productions.

Jim Peck's Assistant: Heather Cunningham.

Producer: Don Lipp, Ron Greenberg.

Director: Dick Scheinder.

THE BIG SHOWDOWN—30 minutes—ABC—December 23, 1974 - July 4, 1975.

BIG STORY

Anthology. Dramatizations based on the journalistic achievements of newsmen. Reporters receive five hundred dollars for the use of their stories.

Hosts-Narrators: William Sloane; Ben Grauer; Burgess Meredith.

Orchestra: Wladimar Selinsky.

Additional Music: Milton Weinstein.

Producer: Bernard Prockter, Everett Rosenthal.

Director: Charles Skinner, Daphne Elliot.

Sponsor: American Tobacco Company.

Included:

Theory And Practice. A reporter attempts to find the murderer of a policeman.

Starring: Wesley Addy.

The Smell Of Death. A reporter attempts to free two youngsters who are being held hostage by a berserk gunman.

Starring: Peter Turgeon, Tom Carlin.

A Madman Is Loose. After two cab drivers are killed by a psycopathic killer who has an obsession for canaries, a reporter attempts to apprehend the murderer by exploiting his quirk.

Starring: Bernard Grant, Leonardo Cimino.

Nightmare. A reporter investigates the methods of treatment used by a psychiatrist in North Carolina.

Starring: Sara Seeger.

BIG STORY—30 minutes—NBC—September 6, 1949 - July 6, 1956. Syndicated.

THE BIG SURPRISE

Human Interest. People, chosen for a particular act of kindness, tell of their unselfish deeds. The program then unites the humanitarian with the recipient, and awards the former an item that he has wanted, but was unable to afford.

Host: Jack Barry.

THE BIG SURPRISE—30 minutes—NBC—October 8, 1955 - June 9, 1956.

THE BIG TOP

Variety. American and foreign circus acts, "the biggest circus show on the air."

Ringmaster: Jack Sterling.

Clowns: Ed McMahon, Chris Keegan.

Regulars: Circus Dan, the Muscle Man; Lott and Joe Anders; La Paloma.

Music: The Quaker City String Band; Joe Basile's Brass Kings.

Producer: Charles Vanda.

Director: Joseph Tinney, Jr.

Sponsor: The National Dairy Association.

THE BIG TOP—60 minutes—CBS—July 1, 1950 - September 21, 1957.

BIG TOWN

Crime Drama. Background: Big Town, U.S.A. The story of two Illustrated Press newspaper reporters: Steve Wilson, an intrepid crime reporter, and Lorelei Kilbourne, the society reporter. Episodes relate their attempts to acquire headline-making and newspaper-selling stories.

Special note. Episodes from 1950 to 1954 portrayed Wilson as the ex-managing editor of the paper, a man observing people and their problems. For the duration of the series, 1954 to 1956, Wilson is returned to the position of managing editor and becomes actively involved in investigations.

CAST

Steve Wilson	Patrick McVey (1950-1954)
	Mark Stevens (1954-1956)
Lorelei Kilbourne	Margaret Hayes (1950-1951)
	Mary K. Wells (1951)
	Jane Nigh (1951-1953)
	Beverly Tyler (1953)
	Trudy Wroe (1954)
	Julie Stevens (1954-1955)
Diane Walker, I.P. reporter	Doe Averdon (1955-1956)

Charlie Anderson, the city
editor   Barry Kelly
Lt. Tom Gregory   John Doucette

Music: Albert Glasser.

Producer: Lloyd Gross, Charles Robinson, Jack Gross.

Director: David Rich.

Sponsor: Lever Brothers.

BIG TOWN—30 minutes—NBC—October 5, 1950 - September 23, 1956. 169 episodes. Syndicated titles: "By Line—Steve Wilson"; "City Assignment"; "Crime Reporter"; "Headline Story"; and "Heart of the City."

THE BIG VALLEY

Western. Background: The San Joaquin Valley in Stockton, California, 1878. The saga of the close-knit Barkley family, cattle ranchers: Victoria, widow of Tom (killed by railroad officials in a stubborn defense of his independence), a woman of beauty and courage, a strong-willed matriarch; Jarrod, her eldest son, a lawyer; Nick, her second born, quick tempered and two fisted, the ranch foreman; Audra, her daughter, young, beautiful, proud, sensuous, and impulsive, a woman yet to be tamed by the love of a man; Heath, Tom's illegitimate son (born of an Indian maiden), a man who struggled, fought, and ultimately achieved his birthright—the name of Barkley—a man, troubled by the memories of a difficult childhood, still reaching out for the love that he never had; and Eugene, her youngest, shy and sensitive (dropped early in the series).

Stories depict the life, struggles, and loves of the Barkley's as they attempt to maintain and operate their thirty-thousand-acre cattle ranch in an era of violence and lawlessness.

CAST

Victoria Barkley   Barbara Stanwyck
Jarrod Barkley   Richard Long
Nick Barkley   Peter Breck
Heath Barkley   Lee Majors
Audra Barkley   Linda Evans
Eugene Barkley   Charles Briles
Silas, their servant Napoleon Whiting
Sheriff Steve Madden (also
    referred to as Fred
    Madden)   Douglas Kennedy
                    James Gavin
                    Mort Mills
Harry, the bartender Harry Swoger
Frequently cast, various
    roles   Gene Evans
                    James Gregory

The Big Valley. Left to right: Peter Breck, Barbara Stanwyck, and Richard Long.

Music: George Duning; Joseph Mullendore; Elmer Bernstein.

Executive Producer: Arthur Gardner, Arnold Laven, Jules Levy.

Producer: Lou Morheim.

Director: Virgil W. Vogel, Charles S. Dubin, Arnold Laven, Paul Henried, Richard Long, Bernard McEveety, Nicholas Webster, Lawrence Dobkin, Norman S. Powell.

Victoria's Horse: Misty Girl.

THE BIG VALLEY—60 minutes—ABC—September 15, 1965 - May 19, 1969. Syndicated. 112 episodes.

THE BIG WORLD OF LITTLE ATOM

An animated series that explores the mysteries of the planets as seen by Little Adam, a young boy. 06 minutes—Syndicated 1964.

BILKO

See title: "You'll Never Get Rich."

THE BILL ANDERSON SHOW

Musical Variety. Performances by Country and Western entertainers.

Host: Bill Anderson.

Regulars: Lou Brown, Jan Howard, Jimmy Gately, The Po' Boys.

THE BILL ANDERSON SHOW—30 minutes—Syndicated 1966. 39 tapes.

THE BILL COSBY SHOW

Comedy. Background: The mythical Richard Allen Holmes High School in Los Angeles, California. Stories depict the trials and tribulations of Chet Kincaid, its physical education instructor and athletic coach; a man who gives of himself to help others.

CAST

Chet Kincaid   Bill Cosby
Marsha Patterson, the
    school guidance
    counselor   Joyce Bulifant
Brian Kincaid, Chet's married
    brother, a garbage
    collector   Lee Weaver
Verna Kincaid, Brian's
    wife   Olga James
                    Dee Dee Young
Roger Kincaid, Brian's
    son   Donald Livingston
Rose Kincaid, Chet's
    mother   Lillian Randolph
                    Beah Richards
Mr. Kincaid, Chet's
    father   Fred Pinkard
Tom Bennett, the
    coach   Robert Rockwell

Music: Quincy Jones.

Executive Producer: William H. Cosby, Jr.

Producer: Marvin Miller.

Director: Bill Cosby, Ivan Dixon, Eliot Lewis, Jay Sandrich, Seymour Robbie, Luther James, Coby Ruskin.

Creator: William H. Cosby, Jr., Ed Weinberger, Michael Zager.

THE BILL COSBY SHOW—30 minutes—NBC—September 14, 1969 - August 31, 1971. Syndicated. 52 episodes.

THE BILL DANA SHOW

Comedy. Background: The Metropolitan Hotel in New York City. The struggles of José Jiménez, a bewildered Latin American. Episodes depict his attempt to tend guests, enhance regular establishment services, and adjust to the American way of life.

CAST

José Jiménez   Bill Dana
Byron Glick, the fumbling
    house detective Don Adams

Mr. Phillips, the hotel
    manager   Jonathan Harris
Susie, the hotel coffee
    shop waitress   Maggie Peterson
Eddie, Jose's co-
    worker   Gary Crosby
Mrs. Phillips   Amzie Strickland

Music: Earle Hagen.

The Bill Dana Show. Guest Virginia
Kennedy and star Bill Dana.

Producer: Danny Thomas, Howard
    Leeds.
THE BILL DANA SHOW—30 minutes—NBC—September 22, 1963 - January 17, 1965. Syndicated. 42 episodes.

THE BILL GOODWIN SHOW

Variety. Music, songs, guests, and in-
terviews.
Host: Bill Goodwin.
Vocalists: Eileen Barton, Roger Dann.
Music: The Joe Bushkin Trio.

Producer: Louis Cowan.
Sponsor: General Electric.

Featured: "The Nostalgia Game." In
    return for prizes, selected studio
    audience members reenact the
    incidents in their lives that were
    affected by popular songs.

THE BILL GOODWIN SHOW—30
minutes—NBC—September 11, 1951 -
March 27, 1952.

THE BILLY BEAN SHOW

Comedy. The series focuses on the
lighthearted romantic misadventures
of Billy Bean, a shy, clumsy soda jerk
at a corner drugstore as he attempts to
romance the daughter of his employer—a crusty old gentleman who disapproves of their relationship.

CAST

Billy Bean   Arnold Stang
The boss's
    daughter   Billie Lou Watt
The boss   Phillips Tead
Also: Harry Bellaver, Mort Stevens.
Producer: Jeffrey Hayden.
Director: Sean Dillon.

THE BILLY BEAN SHOW—30 minutes—ABC 1951.

BILLY BOONE AND
COUSIN KIBB

Children. A series of cartoon strips,
drawn by Cousin Kibb, that follows
the daring adventures of Billy Boone.
The cliffhanger-type of stories are
interspersed with parlor games for
children.
Host: Carroll Colby (as Cousin Kibb).
Assistant: Patty Milligan.
Producer: Judy Dupucy.
Director: Don Richardson.

BILLY BOONE AND COUSIN
KIBB—30 minutes—CBS 1950.

THE BILLY DANIELS SHOW

Musical Variety.
Host: Billy Daniels.
Featured: Jimmy Blaine.
Music: The Benny Payne Trio.

THE BILLY DANIELS SHOW—15
minutes—ABC—October 5, 1956 -
December 28, 1956.

BILLY ROSE'S PLAYBILL

Anthology. Dramatizations based on
stories appearing in the newspaper
column, "Pitching Horseshoes."
Host: Billy Rose.
Announcer: Frank Waldecker.
Producer: Jed Harris.
Sponsor: Hudson Paper Products.

BILLY ROSE'S PLAYBILL—30 minutes—NBC 1951.

THE BING CROSBY SHOW

Comedy. Background: Los Angeles,
California. The trials and tribulations
of the Collins family: Bing, a former
singer-musician turned building
engineer; his wife, Ellie; and their
children, Joyce (fifteen years of age)
and Janice (ten).

CAST

Bing Collins   Bing Crosby
Ellie Collins   Beverly Garland
Joyce Collins   Carol Faylen
Janice Collins   Diane Sherry
Willie Walters, their live-in
    handyman   Frank McHugh
Orchestra: John Scott Trotter.

THE BING CROSBY SHOW—30 minutes—ABC—September 14, 1964 -
June 14, 1965. 28 episodes.

BIOGRAPHY

Documentary. The lives of outstand-
ing figures of twentieth-century his-
tory are traced via newsreel footage,
stills, and interviews.
Host-Narrator: Mike Wallace.
Music: Jack Tillar.
Producer: Jack Haley, Jr.
Director: Allan Landsburg.

BIOGRAPHY—30 minutes—Syndicated 1962. 65 episodes.

The Bionic Woman. Lindsay Wagner.

THE BIONIC WOMAN

Adventure. Background: Ojai, California. When Jaime Sommers, the
beautiful girlfriend of Colonel Steve

Austin ("The Six Million Dollar Man"), is critically injured during a sky-diving accident, Oscar Goldman of the O.S.I. (Office of Scientific Intelligence) authorizes Dr. Rudy Wells to perform a bionic operation in an attempt to save her life. Jaime's body, however, rejects the artificial replacements (both legs, her right arm, and right ear), causing extreme pain and finally death.

Having experimented with cryogenic surgery and believing that he can bring Jaime back to life, Dr. Michael Marchetti (a member of Rudy's bionic surgery team) performs the extremely delicate and highly complicated operation that restores Jaime's life and her body's accepting the bionic limbs.

Relinquishing her career as a tennis pro, and taking up residence in the ranch home of her foster parents, Jim and Helen Elgin, Jaime adopts a new career as a schoolteacher at the Ventura Air Force Base—her cover as an agent for the O.S.I. Stories depict Jaime's assignments on behalf of the O.S.I. A spin-off from "The Six Million Dollar Man."

CAST

Jaime Sommers	Lindsay Wagner
Oscar Goldman	Richard Anderson
Dr. Rudy Wells	Martin E. Brooks
Jim Elgin	Ford Rainey
Helen Elgin	Martha Scott
Janet Callahan, Oscar's secretary	Jennifer Darling
Dr. Michael Marchetti	Richard Lenz
Andrew, one of Jaime's students	Robbie Rist
Mark, one of Jaime's students	Robbie Wolcott
Steve Austin (guest roles)	Lee Majors

Music: Jerry Fielding, Joe Harnell, J.J. Johnson, Luchi DeJesus.

Executive Producer: Kenneth Johnson.

Producer: Harve Bennett.

Director: Alan Levi, Barry Crane, Leo Penn, Mel Damski, Phil Bondelli, Kenneth Johnson, Alan Crosland.

THE BIONIC WOMAN—60 minutes—ABC—Premiered: January 14, 1976.

BIRDMAN

Animated Cartoon. An American, Ray Randall, is saved from a firey death by the goodness of the Egyptian Sun God, Ra. Bestowed with amazing powers, he becomes the crime-fighting Bird-

man and unites with the Galaxy Trio (Vapor Man, Galaxy Girl, and Meteor Man). Stories depict their battle against the sinister forces of evil. A Hanna-Barbera production.

Characters' Voices

Ray Randall (Birdman)	Keith Andes
Falcon 7	Don Messick
Birdboy	Dick Beals
Vapor Man	Don Messick
Galaxy Girl	Virginia Eiler
Meteor Man	Ted Cassidy

Music: Hoyt Curtin.

BIRDMAN—30 minutes—NBC—September 9, 1967 - September 14, 1968.

BIRTHDAY HOUSE

Children. Three children, each accompanied by two or three friends, celebrate their birthdays.

Host: Paul Tripp.

Assistants: Jan Leonakis, Kay Elhart.

Music: Kathryn Lande.

BIRTHDAY HOUSE—60 minutes—Syndicated 1963.

THE BLACK ROBE

Courtroom Drama. Reenactments based on actual metropolitan night-court cases. The program uses ordinary people as it mirrors the struggles of life.

Judge: Frankie Thomas, Sr.

THE BLACK ROBE—30 minutes—NBC 1949.

BLACK SADDLE

Western. Background: Latigo, New Mexico during the late 1860s. The cases of Clay Culhane, an ex-gunfighter turned circuit lawyer.

CAST

Clay Culhane	Peter Breck
Marshal Gib Scott	Russell Johnson
Nora Travis, the operator of the Marathon Hotel	Anna-Lisa

Music: Herschel Burke Gilbert.

Additional Music: Jerry Goldsmith, Arthur Morton.

Producer: Hal Hudson, Tony Ellis.

BLACK SADDLE—30 minutes—ABC—October 2, 1959 - September 28, 1960. 44 episodes.

THE BLACK SHEEP SQUADRON

Revised series title for "Baa Baa Black Sheep," which see for information.

BLACKSTONE MAGIC SPOTS

Variety. Short video sequences featuring magic tricks performed by Harry Blackstone.

Host: Harry Blackstone.

BLACKSTONE MAGIC SPOTS—03 minutes—Syndicated 1952. 39 episodes.

THE BLACK TULIP

See title: "Family Classics Theatre," *The Black Tulip* segment.

BLANK CHECK

Game. Of the six players that compete, one is designated as the check writer and the remaining five are the challengers. The check writer pulls a lever that reveals five numbers and secretly selects one. A question is read to the challengers and the player who is first to identify himself through a light signal receives a chance to answer. If correct, he receives the opportunity to guess the number chosen by the check writer. If he does not guess it, the number chosen by the check writer appears in the fourth digit of a four digit blank check. The check writer then selects another number and another question is asked to acquire another challenger. If the challenger fails to guess the number, it appears in the third digit. The object is for the check writer to fill in a four digit blank check. However, should the challenger guess the number, he defeats the check writer—who in turn loses the money—and becomes the new check writer. The six players compete for five days and the player who writes the single largest check is the grand winner and receives, in addition to the money, a new car.

Host: Art James.

Assistant: Judy Rich.

Announcer: Johnny Jacobs.

Music: Recorded.

Executive Producer: Jack Barry.

Producer: Mike Metzger.

Director: Marty Pasetta.

BLANK CHECK—25 minutes—NBC—January 6, 1975 - July 4, 1975.

BLANKETY BLANKS

Game. Four contestants compete. A

subject category is revealed along with six numbered but concealed clues to its identity. The host selects a blank computer type card from a spinning wheel and places it in an electronic machine that pinpoints one of the players and reveals an amount of money, from ten to one hundred dollars. This player selects a clue, which is revealed, and receives a chance to identify the subject. If he does, he wins the money; if not, another player is selected in the same manner (each player has an equal amount of cards). After each subject is guessed, that player receives the opportunity to double his money by attempting to answer the Blankety Blank—a nonsense riddle (e.g., "The hurricane that hit the pretzel factor was a real   "). If he can ("twister") he wins the money. The first player to score $2,000 is the winner.

Host: Bill Cullen.

Announcer: Bob Clayton.

Music: Recorded.

Producer: Bob Stewart.

BLANKETY BLANKS—30 minutes—ABC—April 21, 1975 - June 27, 1975.

BLANSKY'S BEAUTIES

Comedy. Background: The Oasis Hotel in Las Vegas, Nevada. The trials and tribulations of Nancy Blansky, seamstress, producer, and den mother to ten beautiful budding showgirls.

CAST

Nancy Blansky	Nancy Walker
Joey Delucca, her nephew	Eddie Mekka
Anthony Delucca, Joey's brother	Scott Baio
Studs, manager of the hotel for its never seen owner, Major Putnam	George Pentecost
Mr. Smith, Major Putnam's right-hand man	Not Credited
Arnold Takahashi, the owner of the coffee shop	Pat Morita

The Showgirls:

Bambi Benton	Caren Kaye
Ethel "Sunshine" Akalino	Lynda Goodfriend
Hillary Prentiss	Taaffee O'Connell
Misty Knight	Jill Owens
Arkansas Baits	Rhonda Bates
Bridget Muldoon	Elaine Bolton
Sylvia Silva	Antonette Yuskis
Jackie Outlaw	Gerri Reddick
Gladys "Cochise"	

Littlefeather	Shirley Kirkes
Lovey	Bond Gideon

Nancy's dog: Blackjack.

Music: Charles Fox, Jack Hayes.

Executive Producer: Garry Marshall, Edward K. Milkis, Thomas L. Miller.

Producer: Bruce Johnson, Nick Abdo, Tony Marshall.

Director: Garry Marshall, Jerry Paris, Alan Rafkin.

BLANSKY'S BEAUTIES—30 minutes—ABC—February 12, 1977 - April 30, 1977. Returned with two first-run episodes, aired as specials on June 6 and June 27, 1977.

BLESS THIS HOUSE

Comedy. Background: London, England. Events in the hectic lives of the Abbott family.

CAST

Sid Abbott, the husband	Sidney James
Jean Abbott, his wife	Diana Coupland
Sally Abbott, their daughter	Sally Geeson
Mike Abbott, their son	Robin Stewart
Betty, their neighbor	Patsy Rowlands

Music: Geoff Love.

Producer-Director: William Stewart.

BLESS THIS HOUSE—30 minutes—Syndicated 1977. Produced in England.

BLIND DATE

Game. Players: six men, representing two universities, and three women, leading Manhattan models. Two men are seated on one side of a wall and one female on the other. The males, the Hunters, telephone the girl, the Hunted, and attempt to talk her into accepting a date with him. On the basis of voice and specially prepared questions, she chooses the most impressive one. The couple receives an all-expense paid romantic evening, including an invitation to the Stork Club. Three such rounds are played per broadcast.

Hostess: Arlene Francis.

Host: Jan Murray.

Announcers: Walter Herlihy, Rex Marshall.

Orchestra: Glenn Osser.

Producer: Bernard L. Schubert, Richard Lewis.

Director: Fred Carr, Richard Lewis, Ed Nugent.

Sponsor: Esquire Shoe Polish.

BLIND DATE—30 minutes—ABC. May 9, 1949 - March 9, 1950; March 16, 1950 - June 8, 1950; June 7, 1952 - July 19, 1952; June 1953 - September 1953.

BLONDIE

Comedy. The trials and tribulations of the Bumstead family: Dagwood, an architect with the Dithers Construction Company; his wife, Blondie; and their children, Alexander and Cookie. Faced with an ever-present lack of financial resources, Blondie's ineffable sense of logic, and a tightwad boss, Julius C. Dithers, Dagwood, the simple-minded bumbler, struggles to cope with life and ease his monetary burdens. Based on the comic by Chic Young.

Versions:
NBC—30 minutes—January 4, 1954 - December 5, 1954; July 5, 1958 - October 4, 1958.

CAST

Blondie Bumstead	Pamela Britton
Blondie Bumstead (on radio and in features)	Penny Singleton
Dagwood Bumstead	Arthur Lake
Alexander Bumstead	Stuffy Singer
Cookie Bumstead	Ann Barnes
Julius C. Dithers	Florenz Ames
Cora Dithers, his wife	Lela Bliss-Hayden Elvia Allman
Eloise, Dithers's secretary	Pamela Duncan
Herb Woodley, Dagwood's neighbor	Hal Peary
Georgia Woodley, his wife	Lois Collier
Foghorn, Alexander's friend	George Winslow
Mr. Beasley, the postman	Lucien Littlefield

Bumstead family dog (both versions): Daisy, "the purebred mongrel."

CBS—30 minutes—September 26, 1968 - January 9, 1969.

CAST

Blondie Bumstead	Patricia Harty

Blondie (CBS 1968). Left to right: Peter Robbins, Will Hutchins, Patricia Harty, Pamelyn Ferdin, and Daisy.

Dagwood Bumstead	Will Hutchins
Alexander Bumstead	Peter Robbins
Cookie Bumstead	Pamelyn Ferdin
J.C. Dithers	Jim Backus
Cora Dithers	Henny Backus
Tootsie Woodley, the Bumstead neighbor	Bobbie Jordan

Music: Bernard Green.

THE BLUE ANGEL

Musical Variety. A revue set against the background of New York City's Blue Angel Supper Club.

Host: Orson Bean.

Songstress: Polly Bergen.

Music: The Norman Paris Trio.

THE BLUE ANGEL—30 minutes—CBS—July 6, 1954 - October 12, 1954.

THE BLUE ANGELS

Adventure. The experiences of Wilbur Scott, Hank Bertelli, Zeke Powers, and Cort Ryker, the pilots of the Blue Angels, a team of four precision U.S. Naval Jets.

CAST

Cdr. Arthur Richards	Dennis Cross
Lt. Russ MacDonald	Mike Galloway
Captain Wilbur Scott	Warner Jones
Pilot Hank Bertelli	Don Gordon
Pilot Zeke Powers	Robert Knapp
Pilot Cort Ryker	Ross Elliott

THE BLUE ANGELS—30 minutes—

Syndicated 1960. 39 episodes.

THE BLUE KNIGHT

Crime Drama. Background: Los Angeles, California. The exploits of William "Bumper" Morgan, a veteran cop-on-the-beat. Stories realistically detail the life of a policeman "whose beat is his world and whose people are his people." Based on the novel by Joseph Wambaugh.

CAST

William Morgan	George Kennedy
Sgt. Newman, his superior	Phillip Pine
Wimpy, his informant	John Steadman
Toby, his informant	Billy Benedict
Vera, Bumper's friend, the owner of a pawn shop	Aneta Corsaut
Carrie Williamson, Bumper's girlfriend	Barbara Rhoades

Music: Pete Rugolo; Henry Mancini; Robert Prince.

Executive Producer: Lee Rich.

Director: Gordon Hessler, Charles S. Dubin, Don McDougall, Paul Krasny, Daniel Haller, Alvin Ganzer.

Also in the cast: Leo, a seemingly unowned dog who plagues Bumper.

THE BLUE KNIGHT—60 minutes—CBS—December 17, 1975 - July 28, 1976; September 22, 1976 - October 20, 1976. Originally aired as a four-part movie that ran on NBC from November 13 to November 16, 1973 and that starred William Holden as Bumper Morgan.

BLUE LIGHT

Adventure Serial. Era: World War II. David March, foreign correspondent, the last remaining agent of Blue Light Control, an American organization of eighteen men designed to destroy the Nazi High Command, renounces his citizenship and poses as a traitor. His plan to accomplish its objectives takes effect when he joins the ranks of the German Command and is assigned to its intelligence division in Berlin.

Episodes detail his suicide mission as he attempts to destroy the Third Reich from within under the code name Blue Light.

CAST

| David March | Robert Goulet |
| Suzanne Duchard, his assistant | Christine Carere |

Music: Lalo Schifrin; Joseph Mullendore.

BLUE LIGHT—30 minutes—ABC—January 12, 1966 - August 31, 1966. 17 episodes.

BOB AND BETTY IN ADVENTURELAND

Animated Cartoon. The adventures of a boy and a girl as they travel throughout the world.

BOB AND BETTY IN ADVENTURELAND—05 minutes—Syndicated 1959.

BOB & CAROL & TED & ALICE

Comedy. Background: Los Angeles, California. The story of two families: Bob and Carol Sanders, a young, progressive couple in their late twenties; and their neighbors, Ted and Alice Henderson, an older, conservative couple in their thirties. Episodes relate the incidents and situations that test their reactions, their values, and their marriages. Based on the movie of the same title.

CAST

Bob Sanders, a film director	Robert Urich
Carol Sanders	Anne Archer
Ted Henderson, a lawyer	David Spielberg
Alice Henderson	Anita Gillette
Elizabeth Henderson, Ted and Alice's twelve-year-old daughter	Jodie Foster
Sean Sanders, Bob and Carol's six-year-old son	Bradley Savage

Music: Artie Butler.

BOB & CAROL & TED & ALICE—30 minutes—ABC—September 26, 1973 - November 7, 1973. 12 episodes.

BOB AND RAY

Listed: The television programs of comedians Bob Elliott and Ray Goulding.

The Bob and Ray Show—Satire—15 minutes—NBC—November 1951 - May 1952.

Hosts: Bob Elliott and Ray Goulding.

Regulars: Audrey Meadows, Bob Denton.

Announcer: Bob Denton.

Music: Paul Taubman.

Format: Two or three three-minute vignettes; and a four- to five-minute soap opera, "The Life and Loves of Linda Lovely."

The Bob and Ray Show—Satire—30 minutes—NBC—July 1952 - September 1952.

Hosts: Bob Elliott and Ray Goulding.

Featured: Cloris Leachman.

Announcer: Durwood Kirby.

Music: The Alvy West Band.

Club Embassy—Satire—15 minutes-NBC—1952-1953.

Starring: Bob Elliott and Ray Goulding.

Hostess: Julia Meade.

Featured: Audrey Meadows, Florian ZaBach.

The Bob and Ray Show—Satire—15 minutes—ABC—1953 - 1954.

Hosts: Bob Elliott and Ray Goulding.

Regulars: Marion B. Brash, Charles Wood.

Announcer: Charles Wood.

BOBBIE GENTRY'S HAPPINESS HOUR

Variety. Music, songs, dances, and comedy sketches.

Hostess: Bobbie Gentry.

Regulars: Valri Bromfield, Michael Greer, Earl Pomerantz.

Orchestra: Jack Elliott, Allyn Ferguson.

BOBBIE GENTRY'S HAPPINESS HOUR—60 minutes—CBS—June 5, 1974 - June 26, 1974.

THE BOBBY DARIN AMUSEMENT COMPANY

Variety. Music, songs, dances, and comedy sketches.

Host: Bobby Darin.

Regulars: Dick Bakalyan, Tony Amato, Steve Landesberg, Charlene Wong, Rip Taylor, Kathy Cahill, Sarah Frankboner, Dorrie

Thompson, Geoff Edwards, The Jimmy Joyce Singers.

Announcer: Roger Carroll.

Orchestra: Eddie Karam.

THE BOBBY DARIN AMUSEMENT COMPANY—60 minutes—NBC—July 27, 1972 - September 7, 1972. Returned as "The Bobby Darin Show" —60 minutes—NBC—January 19, 1973 - April 27, 1973.

THE BOBBY GOLDSBORO SHOW

Musical Variety.

Host: Bobby Goldsboro.

Featured: Calvin Calaveris, a frog muppet voiced by Peter Cullen.

Announcer: Peter Cullen.

Musical Director: Robert Montgomery.

THE BOBBY GOLDSBORO SHOW—30 minutes—Syndicated 1973.

THE BOBBY LORD SHOW

Musical Variety. Performances by Country and Western entertainers.

Host: Bobby Lord.

Music: The Jerry Byrd Band.

THE BOBBY LORD SHOW—30 minutes—Syndicated 1965. 52 tapes.

THE BOBBY VINTON SHOW

Variety. Music, songs, and comedy sketches.

Host: Bobby Vinton.

Regulars: Billy Van, Arte Johnson, Freeman King, Jack Duffy.

Orchestra: Jimmy Dale.

Vinton's Vocal Backing: The Peaches.

Producer: Allan Blye, Chris Bearde, Bud Granoff.

Director: Michael Steele.

THE BOBBY VINTON SHOW—30 minutes—Syndicated 1975. Produced in Canada.

THE BOB CRANE SHOW

Comedy. Background: Los Angeles, California. The story of Bob Wilcox, a

forty-two-year-old executive who quits his job as an insurance salesman to pursue a medical career.

CAST

Bob Wilcox	Bob Crane
Ellie Wilcox, his wife, a real estate saleswoman	Trisha Hart
Pam Wilcox, their daughter	Erica Petal
Ernest Busso, their landlord	Ronny Graham
Lyle Ingersoll, the dean of the City Medical School of University Hospital	Jack Fletcher
Marvin Sussman, a medical student	Todd Sussman
Jerry Mallory, a medical student	James Sutorius

Music: Mike Post and Pete Carpenter.

Producer: Martin Cohen, Norman S. Powell.

Director: Norman S. Powell, Buddy Tyne.

THE BOB CRANE SHOW—30 minutes—NBC—March 6, 1975 - June 19, 1975. 13 episodes.

BOB CROSBY

Listed: The television programs of singer-musician Bob Crosby.

The Bob Crosby Show—Musical Variety—60 minutes—CBS—1953 - 1954.

Host: Bob Crosby.

Regulars: Joan O'Brien, The Modernaires.

Announcer: Steve Dunne.

Music: Bob Crosby's Bob Cats.

The Bob Crosby Show—Musical Variety—60 minutes—NBC—June 14, 1958 - September 6, 1958.

Host: Bob Crosby.

Regulars: Gretchen Wyler, The Clay Warnick Singers, The Peter Gennaro Dancers.

Orchestra: Carl Hoff.

THE BOB CUMMINGS SHOW, LOVE THAT BOB

See title: "Love That Bob."

THE BOB CUMMINGS SHOW

Comedy. Background: California. The misadventures of bachelor-pilot Bob Carson. Stories relate his attempts to acquire charter flights and terminate his monetary burdens.

CAST

Bob Carson	Bob Cummings
Lionel, his side-kick	Murvyn Vye
Hank Geogerty, Bob's neighbor, a pretty teenage tomboy	Roberta Shore

Producer: Bob Finkel.

THE BOB CUMMINGS SHOW—30 minutes—CBS—October 5, 1961 - March 1, 1962. 22 episodes.

THE BOB HOPE CHRYSLER THEATRE

Anthology. Dramatic and comedic productions.

Host: Bob Hope.

Music: Johnny Williams.

Included:

The Enemy On The Beach. Era: World War II. The efforts of a team of demolition experts to disarm newly developed German mines.

'CAST

Robert Wagner, Sally Ann Howes, James Donald.

Corridor 400. A nightclub singer attempts to trap a narcotics kingpin for the F.B.I.

CAST

Suzanne Pleshette, Andrew Duggan, Joseph Campanella.

Murder In The First. The tense trial of a law student accused of murdering a married woman.

CAST

Janet Leigh (her dramatic TV debut), Bobby Darin, Lloyd Bochner.

The Reason Nobody Hardly Ever Seen A Fat Outlaw In The Old West Is As Follows. The saga of the Curly Kid as he attempts to make a name for himself.

CAST

The Curly Kid: Don Knotts; the Sheriff: Arthur Godfrey; his daughter: Mary Robin Reed.

Holloway's Daughters. The story of two teen-age girls and their attempts to assist their detective father on a jewel robbery case.

CAST

Robert Young, David Wayne, Brooke Bundy, Barbara Hershey.

THE BOB HOPE CHRYSLER THEATRE—60 minutes—NBC—October 4, 1963 - September 6, 1967. Preempted one week per month for presentation of "The Bob Hope Special." 114 episodes.

THE BOB HOPE SHOW

Variety. A basic format unchanged since Mr. Hope's radio programs: an opening monologue and various comedy sketches with his guest stars. Most notable of his presentations has been the yearly Christmas programs for American servicemen in remote regions of the world.

Host: Bob Hope.

Featured: The Nick Castle Dancers.

Announcer: Frank Barton.

Orchestra: Les Brown.

THE BOB HOPE SHOW—60 minutes—NBC—Premiered: October 12, 1952. Broadcast as a series of specials. Also titled: "Chrysler Presents a Bob Hope Special"; and "The Bob Hope Special."

BOB NEWHART

Listed: the television programs of comedian Bob Newhart.

The Bob Newhart Show—Variety—30 minutes—NBC—October 11, 1961 - June 13, 1962.

Host: Bob Newhart.

Announcer: Dan Sorkin.

Orchestra: Paul Weston.

The Entertainers—Variety—60 minutes—CBS—1964. See title.

The Bob Newhart Show—Comedy—30 minutes—CBS—Premiered: September 16, 1972.

Background: Chicago. The home and working life of psychologist Robert Hartley.

CAST

Robert Hartley (Bob)	Bob Newhart
Emily Hartley, his wife, a third-grade school teacher at Gorman Elementary School	Suzanne Pleshette
Howard Borden, their friend, a 747 navigator	Bill Daily
Jerry Robinson, their friend, an orthodontist	Peter Bonerz

The Bob Newhart Show. Left to right: Marcia Wallace, Bob Newhart, Peter Bonerz, Suzanne Pleshette, Bill Daily.

Carol Kester, Bob and Jerry's secretary	Marcia Wallace
Margaret Hoover, Emily's friend	Patricia Smith
Elliott Carlin, Bob's patient	Jack Riley
Mrs. Bakerman, Bob's patient	Florida Friebus
Michelle, Bob's patient	Renne Lippin
Mr. Peterson, Bob's patient	John Fiedler
Mr. Gianelli, Bob's patient	Noam Pitlik
Dr. Bernie Tupperman	Larry Gelman
Ellen Hartley, Bob's sister	Pat Finley
Howard Borden, Jr., Howard's son	Moosie Drier
Herb Hartley, Bob's father	Barnard Hughes
Martha Hartley, Bob's mother	Martha Scott
Cornelius "Junior" Harrison, Emily's father	John Randolph
Aggie Harrison, Emily's mother	Ann Rutherford
Cliff Murdock, Bob's friend	Tom Poston
Larry Bondaurant, Carol's boyfriend, later husband	Will MacKenzie
Edgar Vickers, Bob's patient	Lucien Scott

Music: Pat Williams.

Executive Producer: Jay Tarses, Tom Patchett, Michael Zinberg.

Director: Alan Myerson, John C. Chauley, Alan Rafkin, Michael Zinberg, Peter Bonerz.

THE BOB SMITH SHOW

Musical Variety.
Host: Bob Smith.
Music: Enoch Light and the Light Brigade Orchestra.
Producer: Edward Keene.
Director: Roger Muir.

THE BOB SMITH SHOW—30 minutes—NBC 1948.

BOLD JOURNEY

Travel. The filmed explorations of various adventures.
Hosts: John Stevenson; Jack Douglas.

BOLD JOURNEY—30 minutes—ABC —July 16, 1956 - August 31, 1959 (Stevenson); Syndicated 1958 (Douglas). 140 episodes.

THE BOLD ONES

Drama. The overall title for four rotating series: "The Doctors," "The Lawyers," "The Protectors" and "The Senator."

The Doctors. Background: Los Angeles, California, the Benjamin Craig Institute, a medical research center founded by Dr. Benjamin Craig, a renowned neurosurgeon. Stories depict the pioneering of his protégés, Dr. Paul Hunter, research head, and Dr. Ted Stuart, surgical chief, as they attempt to break the barriers of ignorance and fight disease.

CAST
Dr. Ben Craig	E.G. Marshall
Dr. Ted Stuart	John Saxon
Dr. Paul Hunter	David Hartman
Dr. Cohen	Robert Walden

Music: Richard Clements.

The Lawyers. Background: Los Angeles, California. The cases and courtroom defenses of attorney Walter Nichols and his protégés Brian and Neil Darrell, brothers.

CAST
Walter Nichols	Burl Ives
Brian Darrell	Joseph Campanella
Neil Darrell	James Farentino

The Protectors. Also called: "The Law Enforcers." Background: California. The story of the relationship between two men — Deputy Police Chief Sam Danforth, and District Attorney William Washburn. Episodes relate their attempts to maintain law and order in a city beset by urban crises.

CAST
Sam Danforth	Leslie Nielsen
William Washburn	Hari Rhodes

The Senator. Background: California. The life of Senator Hays Stowe, a progressive politician who attempts to meet and understand the needs and desires of the people he represents.

CAST
Hays Stowe	Hal Holbrook
Ellen Stowe, his wife	Sharon Acker
Norma Stowe, their daughter	Cindy Eilbacher
Jordan Boyle, his assistant	Michael Tolan

THE BOLD ONES—60 minutes—NBC —September 14, 1969 - January 9, 1973. Syndicated. 85 episodes.

BOLD VENTURE

Adventure. Summoned to the bedside of a dying friend, Duval, adventurer Slate Shannon agrees to become the legal guardian of his daughter, the beautiful Sailor Duval. Shannon, bored with his sophisticated life style, leaves the United States accompanied by Sailor, who is reluctant to abide by her father's wish. They retreat to Trinidad, where they purchase *The Bold Venture*, a hotel and boat. Episodes relate their varied island charters and attempts to assist the distressed. Based on the radio program of the same title.

CAST
Slate Shannon	Dane Clark
Sailor Duval	Joan Marshall

Slate's girl crew: Jerri Bender, Joyce Taylor, Barbara Wilson, Narda Onyx.

BOLD VENTURE—30 minutes—Syndicated 1959. 39 episodes.

BONANZA

Western. Era: The nineteenth century. The saga of the Cartwright family. Returning to New England after months at sea, First Mate Ben Cartwright and his fiancée, Elizabeth Stoddard, marry. Possessing a dream to settle in the West, but lacking the money, Ben settles down and establishes a ship chandler's business.

Shortly after giving birth to their son Adam, Elizabeth dies. Motivated by Elizabeth's desire for him to seek his dream, Ben journeys west and settles in Saint Joseph, Missouri where, after eight years, he marries a Swedish girl named Inger.

Still determined to establish a life in California, he organizes a wagon train. During the hazardous journey, Inger gives birth to a son named Eric Hoss after her father and brother Gunner.

Bonanza. Left to right: Pernell Roberts, Dan Blocker, Lorne Greene, and Michael Landon.

Shortly thereafter, during an Indian attack, Inger is killed. Abandoning his dream, Ben settles in Virginia City, Nevada, and establishes the Ponderosa Ranch in the Comstock Lode Country.

When a ranch hand, Jean DeMarné, is fatally injured after saving Ben's life, his last request prompts Ben to travel to New Orleans to inform his mother and his wife, Marie, of his demise. Speaking first to Mrs. DeMarné, then to Marie, Ben hears a troublesome story. He discovers that Marie was supposed to have had an affair with another man. Jean, believing the incident true, had fled his home in disgrace. Investigating further, Ben uncovers the fact that Mrs. DeMarne had arranged the incident to discredit Marie, who she felt was not worthy of her son.

Ultimately Ben and Marie marry. Shortly after the birth of their son, Joseph, Marie is killed when her horse steps in a chuckhole and throws her.

Stories relate the struggles of the Cartwright family as they attempt to maintain and operate their one-thousand-square-mile timberland ranch, the Ponderosa, in an era of violence and lawlessness. Building a reputation for fairness and honesty, they are admired and respected and often beseeched by those in distress to see that justice is done.

CAST

Ben Cartwright	Lorne Greene
Adam Cartwright	Pernell Roberts
Hoss (Eric) Cartwright	Dan Blocker
(Little) Joe Cartwright	Michael Landon
Hop Sing, their houseboy	Victor Sen Yung
Sheriff Roy Coffee	Ray Teal
Deputy Clem Poster	Bing Russell
Jamie Cartwright, the adopted son	Mitch Vogel
Mr. Canaday (Candy) the ranch foreman	David Canary
Griff King, a ranch hand	Tim Matheson
Dusty Rhodes, a ranch hand	Lou Frizzell
Elizabeth Stoddard (flashback; "Elizabeth, My Love")	Geraldine Brooks
Inger (flashback; "Inger, My Love")	Inga Swenson
Marie (flashback; "Marie, My Love")	Felicia Farr

Music: David Rose.

Additional Music: Harry Sukman, Raoul Kraushaar.

Producer: Richard Collins, David Dortort, Robert Blees.

Director: Don Richardson, Marc Daniels, Don McDougall, William F. Claxton, John Florea, Herbert Stark, Christian Nyby, Michael Landon, Leon Benson.

Creator: David Dortort.

Ben's horse: Buck.

Hoss's horse: Chub.

Little Joe's horse: Cochise.

BONANZA—60 minutes—NBC—September 12, 1959 - January 16, 1973. Syndicated. Rebroadcasts (NBC), under title: "Ponderosa"—May 12, 1972 - August 29, 1972. 440 episodes.

BONINO

Comedy. Background: New York City. Having spent little time with his family due to concert commitments, and feeling himself a stranger to his six children, Babbo Bonino impulsively decides to give up his operatic career and adopt the role of active father. Stories relate his attempts to raise his motherless children and solve the problems that he encounters.

CAST

Babbo Bonino	Ezio Pinza
Martha, his housekeeper	Mary Wickes
Rusty, his valet, confidant	Mike Kellin
Walter Rogers, his concert manager	David Opatoshu
Allentuck, the butler	Francis Butler
Andrew Bonino	Van Dyke Parks
Doris Bonino	Lenka Paterson
Edward Bonino	Conrad Janis
Terry Bonino	Chet Allen
Francesca Bonino	Gaye Huston
Carlo Bonino	Oliver Andes

Orchestra: Donald Voorhees.

Producer: Fred Coe.

BONINO—30 minutes—NBC—September 19, 1953 - December 26, 1953.

THE BONNIE PRUDDEN SHOW

Women. Exercises, guests, interviews, health, and nutritional tips.

Hostess: Bonnie Prudden

THE BONNIE PRUDDEN SHOW—30 minutes—Syndicated 1968. 65 episodes.

THE BONTEMPIS

Variety. The preparation of Italian meals; songs, guests, and interviews.

Hosts: Fedora and Pino Bontempi.

Pianist: Pino Bontempi.

THE BONTEMPIS—30 minutes—Syndicated 1952. Also called: "Breakfast Time" (1958) and "Continental Cookery" (1966).

BON VOYAGE

Game. Two contestants compete. Object: To identify geographical locations through stills and rhyming clues. The player with the most correct identifications is the winner and receives a trip to the place of his desire.

Host: John Weigel.

Producer: Alan Fishburn.

Director: Greg Garrison.

BON VOYAGE—30 minutes—ABC—April 24, 1949 - May 8, 1949. Also known as "Treasure Quest."

BOOTS AND SADDLES

Western. Background: Fort Lowell during the 1870s. The life and times of the American Fifth Cavalry.

CAST

Captain Shank Adams	Jack Pickard
Luke Cummings, the trail scout	Michael Hinn
Colonel Hays	Patrick McVey

BOOTS AND SADDLES—30 minutes —Syndicated 1957. 39 episodes.

BORN FREE

Adventure. Background: Kenya, East Africa. The experiences of Game Warden George Adamson and his wife and assistant, Joy. Derived from and continuing where the books and the films *BORN FREE* and *LIVING FREE* ended. A story of man-animal friendship as depicted through the Adamsons' raising, conditioning (to face the rigorous life of her native habitat), and releasing of a young lioness, Elsa. Emphasis is placed upon conservation in contemporary Africa.

CAST

George Adamson	Gary Collins
Joy Adamson	Diana Muldaur
Makedde, their senior scout	Hal Frederick
Nuru	Peter Lukoye
Kanini	Joseph de Graft

Music: Dick De Benedictis; Richard Shores.

BORN FREE—60 minutes—NBC—September 9, 1974 - December 30, 1974.

BOSS LADY

Comedy. Background: California. The story of Gwen F. Allen, owner and operator of the Hillendale Homes Construction Company. In the pre-Women's Lib era, Ms. Allen struggles to cope with and overcome abounding obstacles in a male-oriented field.

CAST

Gwen Allen	Lynn Bari
Jeff, her general manager	Nicholas Jay
Mr. Allen, her father	Glenn Langan
Gwen's brother	Charles Smith
Gwen's secretary	Lee Patrick
Gwen's attorney	Richard Gaines

Producer: Jack Wrather, Robert Mann.

Sponsor: Procter and Gamble.

BOSS LADY—30 minutes. Broadcast on both DuMont and NBC from July

1, 1952 to September 23, 1952. The series was again seen on DuMont the following year.

BOSTON BLACKIE

Mystery. Background: New York City. The investigations of Boston Blackie, one-time master thief turned private detective. Based on the minor character originally appearing in the novels by George Randolph Chester.

CAST

Boston Blackie	Kent Taylor
Mary Wesley, his girlfriend	Lois Collier
Inspector Faraday, N.Y.P.D.	Frank Orth

Music: Joseph Hooven.

BOSTON BLACKIE—30 minutes—NBC—1951-1953. 58 episodes. Syndicated.

BOURBON STREET BEAT

Mystery. Background: The French quarter of New Orleans, Louisiana. The investigations of private detectives Cal Calhoun and Rex Randolph.

CAST

Cal Calhoun	Andrew Duggan
Rex Randolph	Richard Long
Melody Lee Mercer, their secretary	Arlene Howell
Ken Madison, their junior assistant	Van Williams
The Baron	Eddie Cole

Music: Paul Sawtell.

Theme: Mack David and Jerry Livingston.

Producer: William T. Orr, Charles Hoffman.

BOURBON STREET BEAT—60 minutes—ABC—October 5, 1959 - September 26, 1960. Syndicated. 39 episodes.

BOWLING FOR DOLLARS

Game. The format, which is syndicated, varies slightly from market to market. Basically, it encompasses non-professional bowlers who strive to acquire two strikes in a row and break a jackpot for its cash award. Depending on the local station's financial resources, the jackpot also varies. In New York, for example, it begins at $500 and increases by $20 with each bowler's failure to break it.

Unlike the format, talent (host) and technical staff are supplied by each station on which the program airs. Radio personality Larry Kenny, for example, hosts in New York, while former "Dating Game" emcee Jim Lange hosts the Los Angeles version.

BOWLING FOR DOLLARS—30 minutes—Syndicated 1971.

BOZO THE CLOWN

Children. Set against the background of a circus big top, the program features game contests, "Bozo" cartoons, and sketches geared to children.

Basically, the entire program is produced by any local station that purchases the syndicated format from its creator-producer, Larry Harmon. Most often, the local station's announcer, to earn extra money, will become "Bozo the Clown" for that particular station.

The series idea, as described above, was first syndicated in 1959. In 1975, the "Bozo" program produced by a local Midwest TV station was syndicated nationally and is today, perhaps best representative of the series. Listed is the cast for this version:

Starring, as Bozo the Clown: Frank Avruch.

The Ring Master: Peter Barth.

Regulars: A. Del Grosso, Ruth Carlson, Ed Spinney.

Music: Recorded.

Producer: Larry Harmon.

BRACKEN'S WORLD

Drama. Background: Century Studios in Hollywood California. A behind-the-scene look at the world of film producing as seen through the eyes of studio head John Bracken, a man making and/or breaking careers. Filmed at 20th Century Fox Studios

CAST

John Bracken	Leslie Nielsen
Sylvia Caldwell, his executive secretary	Eleanor Parker
Kevin Grant, a producer	Peter Haskell
Marjorie Grant, his alcoholic wife	Madlyn Rhue
Laura Deane, head of the New Studio Talent School	Elizabeth Allen

THE YOUNG HOPEFULS:

Davey Evans	Dennis Cole
Tom Hutson	Stephen Oliver
Rachel Holt	Karen Jensen
Paulette Douglas	Linda Harrison
Diane Waring	Laraine Stephens

Also:

Anne Frazer, Bracken's secretary, later episodes	Bettye Ackerman
Bobby Jason, Kevin's assistant	William Tyler
Sally, the script girl	Marie Windsor
Mitch, Kevin's secretary	Kathleen Hughes
Mark Grant, Kevin's son	Gary Dubin
Grace Douglas, Paulette's mother	Jeanne Cooper
Millie, Sylvia's secretary	Sue Englund
Jim Carter, the studio gate guard	Lee Amber
Bernie, Kevin's assistant	Fred Sardoff
The Sound Mixer	Edward G. Robinson, Jr. Robert Shayne
Pat, the screening room projectionist	Billy Halop

Music: David Rose.

Additional Music: Jack Elliott, Robert Dranşin, Harry Geller, Lionel Newman, Warren Barker.

Theme: "Worlds" by Alan and Marilyn Bergman; sung by the Lettermen.

Executive Producer: Del Reisman.

Producer: George M. Lehr, Stanley Rubin, Robert Lewin.

Director: Gerald Mayer, Jack Erman, Herschel Daugherty, Paul Henried, Charles S. Dubin, Lee Philips, Gary Nelson, James Neilson, Allen Reisner, Robert Day.

Creator: Dorothy Kingsley.

BRACKEN'S WORLD—60 minutes—NBC—September 19, 1969 - January 1, 1971. Syndicated. 41 episodes.

THE BRADY BUNCH

Comedy. Background: Los Angeles, California. Architect Michael Brady, widower and the father of three sons, Greg, Peter, and Bobby, and Carol Martin widow, and the mother of three daughters, Marcia, Janice, and Cindy, marry and establish housekeeping on Clinton Avenue in the four-bedroom, two-bathroom Brady home. Aided by their housekeeper, Alice, Mike and Carol attempt to cope with the problems and chaos that

Bracken's World. Left to right: Karen Jansen, Linda Harrison, Laraine Stephens.

exist in trying to raise six children.

CAST

Carol Brady	Florence Henderson
Mike Brady	Robert Reed
Alice Nelson	Ann B. Davis
Marcia Brady	Maureen McCormick
Janice Brady.	Eve Plumb
Cindy Brady	Susan Olsen
Greg Brady	Barry Williams
Peter Brady	Christopher Knight
Bobby Brady	Michael Lookinland

The Brady Bunch. Bottom, left to right: Ann B. Davis, Florence Henderson, Michael Lookinland, Maureen McCormick. Top, left to right: Eve Plumb, Barry Williams, Susan Olsen, Robert Reed, Christopher Knight.

Oliver, Alice's nephew	Robbie Rist

Music: Frank DeVol.

Additional Music: Kenyon Hopkins.

Music Supervision: Leith Stevens.

Executive Producer: Sherwood Schwartz.

Producer: Howard Leeds, Lloyd Schwartz.

Director: Hal Cooper, Jerry London, Leslie Martinson, John Rich, Oscar Rudolph, Richard Michaels, Robert Reed.

Brady family dog: Tiger.

THE BRADY BUNCH—30 minutes—ABC—September 26, 1969 - August 30, 1974. ABC daytime rebroadcasts: June 30, 1975 - August 29, 1975. Syndicated. 117 episodes.

THE BRADY BUNCH HOUR

Variety. The format features the fictional Brady family in songs, dances, and comedy sketches.

CAST

Carol Brady, the mother	Florence Henderson
Mike Brady, the father	Robert Reed
Marcia Brady, their daughter	Maureen McCormick
Greg Brady, their son	Barry Williams
Jan Brady, their daughter	Geri Reischl
Peter Brady, their son	Chris Knight
Cindy Brady, their daughter	Susan Olsen
Bobby Brady, their son	Michael Lookinland

Alice Nelson, their housekeeper	Ann B. Davis

Regulars: The Krofft Dancers, The Water Follies.

Orchestra: George Wyle.

Executive Producer: Sid and Marty Krofft.

Producer: Lee Miller.

Director: Jack Regas.

THE BRADY BUNCH HOUR—60 minutes—ABC—January 23, 1977 - May 24, 1977.

THE BRADY KIDS

Animated Cartoon. A spin-off from "The Brady Bunch." The story of the Brady children: Marcia, Greg, Janice, Peter, Cindy, and Bobby, and their attempts to independently solve problems without help from the adult world.

Characters' Voices

Marcia Bardy	Maureen McCormick
Greg Brady	Barry Williams
Janice Brady	Eve Plumb
Peter Brady	Christopher Knight
Cindy Brady	Susan Olsen
Bobby Brady	Michael Lookinland

Additional Voices: Larry Storch, Jane Webb.

Background Music: Yvette Blais.

Executive Producer: Sherwood Schwartz.

Producer: Lou Scheimer, Norm Prescott.

Director: Hal Sutherland.

Brady Kids' dog: Moptop.

The Brady Kids pets: Marlon, the magical bird; and Ping and Pong, talking Panda Bears.

THE BRADY KIDS—30 minutes—ABC—September 9, 1972 - August 31, 1974.

BRAINS AND BRAWN

Game. Two competing teams, each composed of four contestants — the Brain, which includes a professional expert, vs. the Brawn, which encompasses a professional athlete. The Brain portion of the program is broadcast from the network's studios and involves the players' attempts to answer difficult questions. The Brawn portion, broadcast from a remote location, puts the contestants through a series of physical-dexterity contests. The segments, though different in concept, are equal in difficulty. Teams are judged and awarded prizes according to their ability to complete assigned tasks.

Hosts:
Fred Davis (the Brain portion).
Jack Lescoulie (the Brawn portion).

BRAINS AND BRAWN—30 minutes—NBC—September 13, 1958 - December 27, 1958.

BRANDED

Western. Background: Southwestern Wyoming, 1870s. During the Battle of Bitter Creek, Jason McCord, army captain, is knocked unconscious when Comanches attack his division. Awakening, he finds that the conflict has ended and that he is the lone survivor. His story, which is disbelieved by military brass, fosters a court-martial. Stripped of his rank and dishonorably discharged, he is branded a coward—"scorned as the one who ran."

Thinking and hoping that someone else may have survived the battle, McCord undertakes a trek to clear his name. Episodes relate his difficulties as he encounters the hatred of men in a country torn by war.

Starring: Chuck Connors as Jason McCord.

Music: Dominic Frontiere.

BRANDED—30 minutes—NBC—January 24, 1965 - September 4, 1966. Syndicated. 48 episodes.

BRAVE EAGLE

Western. Background: The early settlement days of the Old Frontier. The hardships of the American Indian as he struggles to safeguard his homeland from settlers is seen through the eyes of Brave Eagle, a young Cheyenne Chief, and his foster son, Keena.

CAST

Brave Eagle	Keith Larsen
Keena	Keena Nomleena
Morning Star, a Sioux maiden turned Cheyenne	Kim Winona
Smokey Joe, a half-breed	Bert Wheeler

BRAVE EAGLE—30 minutes—CBS—September 28, 1955 - February 15, 1956.

BRAVE STALLION

See title: "Fury."

BREAKFAST CLUB

See title: "Don McNeill's TV Club."

BREAKFAST IN HOLLYWOOD

Variety. Adapted from the radio program. Broadcast from the Sun Club of the Ambassador Hotel in Hollywood, California.

Host: Johnny Dugan.

Features: Audience participation contests; a guest hostess of the week; a tribute to the oldest lady in the audience; the traditional Good Neighbor Award.

BREAKFAST IN HOLLYWOOD—60 minutes—NBC 1954.

BREAKFAST PARTY

Variety. Music, songs, guests, and interviews.

Hosts: Mel Martin, Eileen Martin.

Featured: Larry Downing.

Music: The Bell Airs Trio.

BREAKFAST PARTY—30 minutes—NBC 1951.

BREAKING POINT

Drama. Background: Los Angeles, California. The work of two psychiatrists: Dr. Edward Raymer, director of York Hospital's Psychiatric Clinic, and Dr. McKinley Thompson, a resident psychiatrist. Episodes relate their attempts to assist the distressed—those reaching the breaking point of human emotion.

CAST

Dr. McKinley Thompson	Paul Richards
Dr. Edward Raymer	Eduard Franz

Music: David Raksin.

BREAKING POINT—60 minutes—ABC—September 16, 1963 - September 7, 1964. Syndicated. 30 episodes.

BREAK THE BANK

Game. Players are quizzed in a category of their choice. Each correct response earns cash, which increases with the difficulty of the question. Eight straight answers break the bank, and its cash amount is awarded to the player. Two misses in a row defeat the player and his funds are forfeited and added to the bank.

Hosts: Bert Parks; Bud Collyer.

Assistant: Janice Gilbert.

Announcer: Win Elliott.

Orchestra: Peter Van Steeden.

BREAK THE BANK—30 minutes—ABC—October 22, 1948 - September 23, 1949. NBC—October 5, 1949 - September 1, 1953.

Spin-off: **BREAK THE $250,000 BANK.**
Basically the same format, the change being to allow contestants to choose an expert to assist in the answering of questions.

Host: Bert Parks.

Announcer: Johnny Olsen.

Orchestra: Peter Van Steeden.

BREAK THE $250,000 BANK—NBC—1956 - 1958.

BREAK THE BANK

Game. Two contestants compete. Nine celebrity guests appear, each seated on the left side and top of a large board that contains twenty numbered boxes. Nine boxes contain three money amounts (three $100, three $200, and three $300); five are blank; one is wild card; and five contain money bags. One player selects a number and its content is revealed. If it is other than a blank (which costs a player his turn) or a money bag, two celebrities, represented by the particular box, are asked a question by the host. One answers truthfully, the other fibs. If the player selects the right celebrity in answering the question, he wins that box. He continues to pick and seeks to win by acquiring three boxes with the same money amounts. If the player chooses the wrong celebrity, the opponent receives the box and a turn at play. If three money bags are picked (questions need not be answered, but players forfeit their turn if they elect to keep it) the player breaks the bank, which begins at $5,000 and increases by $500 after each game until it is broken.

Host: Tom Kennedy.

Announcer: Johnny Jacobs, Ernie Anderson.

Music: Stu Levin.

Executive Producer: Jack Barry, Dan Enright.

Director: Richard S. Kline.

BREAK THE BANK—30 minutes—ABC—April 12, 1976 - July 23, 1976.

Syndicated Version: Follows the above format with larger money boxes—$100, $300, $500, and a $10,000 bank.

Host: Jack Barry.

Announcer: Ernie Anderson, Jack Barry.

Music: Stuart Zachary.

Executive Producer: Jack Barry, Dan Enright.

Director: Richard S. Kline.

BREAK THE BANK—30 minutes—Syndicated 1976.

BRENNER

Crime Drama. Background: New York City. The story of two policemen: Detective Lieutenant Roy Brenner, head of the Confidential Squad, a special crime-busting detective force, and his son, Patrolman Ernie Brenner.

CAST

Lt. Roy Brenner	Edward Binns
Officer Ernie Brenner	James Broderick
Captain Laney	Joseph Sullivan

BRENNER—30 minutes—CBS—June

6, 1959 - September 1959; June 19, 1961 - September 1961; June 7, 1962 - September 1962; May 10, 1964 - September 1964. 25 episodes.

THE BRIAN KEITH SHOW

See title: "The Little People."

BRIDE AND GROOM

Wedding Performances. Actual services performed in a chapel setting in New York City.

Hosts: Byron Palmer; Bob Paige; Phil Hanna; Frank Parker; John Nelson.

Orchestra: Paul Taubman.

Producer: John Reddy, John Nelson, John Masterson.

Director: John Masterson.

Sponsor: General Mills; the Hudson Paper Company.

BRIDE AND GROOM—30 minutes—CBS—1946 - 1958.

BRIDGET LOVES BERNIE

Comedy. Background: New York City. Bridget Fitzgerald, an elementary grade school teacher, and Bernie Steinberg, a struggling writer and cabdriver, marry. Religious and social differences are dramatized.

Bridget's parents, Walter and Amy Fitzgerald, are wealthy socialites. Walter is a staunch Irish-Catholic; Amy, pleasant and rather naive; and their son, Michael, a liberal, realistic priest.

Bernie's parents, Sam and Sophie Steinberg, are Jewish and own a delicatessen in lower Manhattan, where they live over the store, as do Bridget and Bernie. They are simple, unpretentious, and unsophisticated.

A rich Catholic girl and a poor Jewish boy attempt to overcome family opposition and bridge the ethnic gap existing in their lives.

CAST

Bridget Fitzgerald Steinberg	Meredith Baxter
Bernie Steinberg	David Birney
Walter Fitzgerald	David Doyle
Amy Fitzgerald	Audra Lindley
Sam Steinberg	Harold J. Stone
Sophie Steinberg	Bibi Osterwald
Moe Plotnic, Sophie's brother	Ned Glass
Father Michael Fitzgerald	Robert Sampson
Otis Foster, Bernie's friend	William Elliott
Charles, the Fitzgerald's Butler	Ivor Barry

Music: Jerry Fielding.

BRIDGET LOVES BERNIE—30 minutes—CBS—September 16, 1972 - September 8, 1973. 24 episodes.

A BRIGHTER DAY

Serial. Background: The small Midwestern town of New Hope. The dramatic story of Reverend Richard Dennis. Episodes depict the conflicts and tensions that arise from the interactions of the characters.

CAST

Reverend Richard Dennis	William Smith
	Blair Davies
Sandra Talbot	Gloria Hoye
Vince Adams	Forrest Compton
Mrs. Jarrett	Abby Lewis
Crystal Carpenter	Vivian Dorsett
Larry	Del Hughes
Randy	Larry Ward

Also: Patty Duke, Lois Nettleton, Hal Holbrook, Mary Lynn Beller, Jack Lemmon, Lori March, Joe Sirola, Mona Burns, June Dayton, Santos Ortega, Mary K. Wells, Bill Post, Sam Gray.

Producer: Allen Potter, Theresa Lewis, Leonard Blair, Mary Harris.

Sponsor: Procter and Gamble.

A BRIGHTER DAY—15 minutes—CBS—January 4, 1954 - September 28, 1962.

BRIGHT PROMISE

Serial. Background: Bancroft, a college community beset by contemporary crises. Stories dramatize the private and professional lives of its president, Thomas Boswell, his faculty, students, friends, and family.

CAST

Professor Thomas Boswell	Dana Andrews
Professor William Ferguson	Paul Lukather
Ann Boyd Jones	Coleen Gray
	Gail Kobe
Sylvia Bancroft	Regina Gleason
	Anne Jeffreys
Jennifer	Nancy Stevens

Chet	Gary Pillar
Red Wilson	Richard Eastham
Gypsy	Annette O'Toole
Bob Cocharan	Philip Carey
Jody Harper	Sherry Alberoni
Martha Ferguson	Susan Brown
Dr. Tracy Graham	Dabney Coleman
Dr. Brian Walsh	John Considine
Charles Diedrich	Anthony Eisley
David Lockhart	Tony Geary
Henry Pierce	David Lewis
Samantha Pudding	Cheryl Miller
Howard Jones	Mark Miller
Sandra Jones Pierce	Pamela Murphy
Stuart Pierce	Peter Ratray
Dr. Amanda Winninger	June Vincent
Isabel Jones	Lesley Woods
Clara	Ruth McDevitt
Sandy	Susan Darrow
Dean Pierce	Tod Andrews
Professor Townley	Nigal McKeard
Bert	Peter Hobbs
Alice	Synda Scott
Fay	Kimetha Laurie

BRIGHT PROMISE—30 minutes—NBC—September 29, 1969 - March 31, 1972.

BRINGING UP BUDDY

Comedy. Background: Los Angeles, California. The trials and tribulations of Buddy Flower, a bachelor investment broker. Stories concern his efforts to overcome the plotting of his meddlesome and spinster aunts, Iris and Violet, as they attempt to find him a wife.

CAST

Buddy Flower	Frank Aletter
Violet Flower	Enid Markey
Iris Flower	Doro Merande

Producer: Joe Connelly, Bob Mosher.

BRINGING UP BUDDY—30 minutes—CBS—October 10, 1960 - September 25, 1961. Syndicated. 34 episodes.

BROADSIDE

Comedy. Background: The South Pacific during World War II. New Caledonia, a tropical island paradise untouched by war and women, is chosen to be a United States Navy supply depot. Four beautiful WAVES, Lieutenant Anne Morgan and Privates Molly McGuire, Roberta Love, and Selma Kowalski, assigned to attend the motor pool, disrupt the island serenity and the life of its commander, Adrian. Unable to rescind

their orders, Adrian deviously attempts to rid the island of women by discrediting Anne and her WAVES. Determined not to be underminded by a man, the girls counterscheme, attempting to foil his efforts and remain on the island. A spin-off from "McHale's Navy."

CAST

Lt. Anne Morgan	Kathleen Nolan
Private Molly McGuire	Lois Roberts
Private Roberta Love	Joan Staley
Private Selma Kowalski	Sheila James
Commander Adrian	Edward Andrews
Lt. Maxwell Trotter, Anne's romantic interest	Dick Sargent
Marion Botnick, a male WAVE, by clerical error	Jimmy Boyd
Lieutenant Beasley, Adrian's aide	George Furth
Admiral Whitehead	Paul Byan
Nicky	Don Edmonds

Music: Axel Stordhal.

BROADSIDE—30 minutes—ABC—September 20, 1964 - September 5, 1965. 32 episodes.

BROADWAY GOES LATIN

Musical Variety. Latin arrangements for Broadway songs.

Host: Edmundo Ross.

Regulars: Margie Ravel, Hector de San Juan, Chi Chi Navaroo, The Arnoldo Dancers, The Ros Singers.

Orchestra: Edmundo Ross.

BROADWAY GOES LATIN—30 minutes—Syndicated 1962-1963.

BROADWAY OPEN HOUSE

Variety. Music, songs, dances, and comedy sketches. Network television's first late-night entertainment show. Broadcast from 11:00 PM-12:00 PM, E.S.T., Monday through Friday.

Hosts: Jerry Lester, Morey Amsterdam, Jack E. Leonard.

Regulars: Dagmar (real name: Virginia Ruth Egnor, known also as Jennie Lewis), Barbara Nichols (portraying Agathon), David Street, Ray Malone, Buddy Greco, Frank Gallop, Andy Roberts, Jane Harvey, The Eileen Barton Dancers, The Kirby Stone Quintet, The Mello-Larks.

Broadway Open House. Jennie Lewis (Dagmar).

Announcer: Wayne Howell.

Orchestra: Milton DeLugg.

Producer: Doug Coulter, Ray Buffum, Vic McLeod.

Director: Joe Cavalier, Jack Hein.

BROADWAY OPEN HOUSE—60 minutes—NBC—May 22, 1950 - August 24, 1951.

BROADWAY TO HOLLYWOOD

Variety. Music, songs, and dances.

Host: Bill Slater.

Regulars: Dorothy Claire, Jerry Wayne, Earl Barton.

Music: The Al Logan Trio.

Producer: Ted Hammerstein.

Sponsor: Tidewater Oil.

BROADWAY TO HOLLYWOOD—30 minutes—DuMont—1951 - 1953.

BROADWAY TO HOLLYWOOD HEADLINE

Variety.

Host: George Putnam.

Format: Headline resumes of world affairs, Hollywood gossip, celebrity interviews, and quizzes.

Quiz Segment: The Host telephones a viewer and asks him a question based on a news event. If the question is correctly answered, the player receives a prize.

BROADWAY TO HOLLYWOOD HEADLINE—30 minutes—DuMont 1949.

BROADWAY TV THEATRE

Anthology. Condensed versions of Broadway plays.

Included:

Adam and Eva. A comedy depicting the misadventures of the wealthy head of a spoiled family.

CAST
Hugh Riley, Katherine Bard.

The Acquitted. A reporter attempts to uncover the murderer of an aged, wealthy man.

CAST
Judith Evelyn, John Baragrey.

R.U.R. A depiction of the world of the future — a state in which robot slaves rebel against their human masters.

CAST
Dorothy Hart, Hugh Riley.

Smilin' Through. A feud between two families and its effect on their children who want to be married.

CAST
William Prince, Beverly Whitney, Wesley Addy.

Death Takes A Holiday. Death visits Earth in an attempt to discover why mortals fear him. During his sojourn, there is no death anywhere. Conflict occurs when he falls in love.

CAST
Nigel Green, Wendy Drew.

BROADWAY TV THEATRE—60 minutes—Syndicated 1952.

BROKEN ARROW

Western. Background: Tucson, Arizona, 1870s, the era of the Apache Wars — the Indian and White Man struggling over the possession of land.

Tom Jeffords, an army captain, is assigned to resolve the constant Indian attacks on mail carriers. He studies the ways of the Apache and tries to persuade officials to understand the plight of the Indian, not slaughter him. In his attempt to accomplish through talk what weapons cannot, he confronts Apache Chief Cochise. Mutual respect leads the Chief to guarantee the safety of the Pony Express riders through Apache Territory.

Army officials, seeking to open the territory to settlers, acquire through Jeffords efforts, a treaty with the Apache and a Broken Arrow — the Indian symbol of peace, friendship, and understanding. Appointed as an Indian Agent to the Apaches, Jeffords becomes the blood brother of Cochise.

Stories relate Jeffords fight against the blindly prejudiced attitudes toward the Apache in the Southwest, fully believing that the White Man is as guilty as the Indian in frontier outrages.

CAST
Tom Jeffords	John Lupton
Cochise	Michael Ansara
Marshal Stuart Randall	Russ Bender
The hotel clerk	Sam Flint
Duffield, Tom's friend	Tom Fadden
Geronimo, Cochise's enemy	Charles Horvath

Narrator: John Lupton.
Music: Stanley Wilson; Paul Sawtell; Ned Washington.
Music Supervision: Alec Compinsky.
Producer: Mel Epstein.
Director: Bernard L. Kowalski, Alvin Ganzer, Charles Haas, William Beaudine, Albert S. Rogell, Frank McDonald, Richard L. Bare, Joe Kane, Hollingsworth Morse, Ralph Murphy.

BROKEN ARROW—30 minutes—ABC—September 25, 1956 - September 18, 1960. Syndicated. 72 episodes.

BRONCO

Western. Background: The Texas Plains during the 1860s. The exploits of Bronco Layne, a wandering ex-Confederate army captain.
Starring: Ty Hardin as Bronco Layne.
Music: Paul Sawtell.
Producer: Arthur Silver, William T. Orr.

BRONCO—60 minutes—ABC—October 20, 1959 - September 20, 1960. Syndicated. 68 episodes.

BRONK

Crime Drama. Background: Ocean City, California. The investigations of Alex "Bronk" Bronkov, a police lieu-tenant operating under special assignment to the city's mayor, Pete Santori.

CAST
Lt. Alex Bronkov	Jack Palance
Pete Santori	Joseph Mascolo
Ellen Bronkov, Alex's daughter, crippled in an accident that killed his wife	Dina Ousley
Sgt. John Webster, Alex's partner	Tony King
Harry Mark, a former cop who operates the M and B Junk Yard, Alex's information man	Henry Beckman
Marci, Pete's secretary	Marcy Lafferty
Mrs. Moury, Ellen's nurse	Peggy Rea
Policewoman Harley	Sally Kirkland

Music: Lalo Schifrin; George Romanis; Robert Dransin.
Executive Producer: Carroll O'Connor (the creator) and Bruce Geller.
Producer: Leigh Vance.
Director: Stuart Hagmann, Richard Donner, John Peyser, Sutton Roley, Russ Mayberry, Corey Allen, Paul Krasny, Reza S. Badiyi, Allen Baron.
Bronk's Badge Number: 25.

BRONK—60 minutes—CBS—September 21, 1975 - July 18, 1976.

THE BROTHERS

Comedy. Background: San Francisco, California. Inexperienced and desperately in need of money, Harvey and Gilmore Box, brothers, pool their resources and purchase a photography studio. Stories relate their misadventures as they attempt to succeed in the business world.

CAST
Harvey Box	Gale Gordon
Gilmore Box	Bob Sweeney
Marilee Dorf, Gilmore's girlfriend	Nancy Hadley
Carl Dorf, her father	Oliver Blake
Barbara, Harvey's girlfriend	Barbara Billingsley
Captain Sam Box, the brothers' father, a retired sea captain	Howard McNair Frank Orth
Barrington Steel, a friend, a playboy	Robin Hughes

THE BROTHERS—30 minutes—CBS—October 4, 1956 - March 27, 1957. 26 episodes.

THE BROTHERS BRANNAGAN

Crime Drama. Background: Phoenix, Arizona. The investigations of private detectives Mike and Bob Brannagan, brothers.

CAST

Mike Brannagan	Steve Dunne
Bob Brannagan	Mark Roberts

THE BROTHERS BRANNAGAN—30 minutes—Syndicated 1960. 39 episodes.

THE BUCCANEERS

Adventure. Background: The Caribbean Colony of New Providence during the 1720s. The exploits of buccaneer Dan Tempest as he battles the injustices of Spanish rule.

CAST

Captain Dan Tempest	Robert Shaw
Lieutenant Beamish, his aide	Peter Hammond
Governor Woodes Rogers	Alec Clunes
Blackbeard, the pirate	Terrence Cooper
Gaff	Brian Rawlinson

Producer: Hannah Weinstein.

Tempest's ship: The *Sultana.*

THE BUCCANEERS—30 minutes—CBS—September 22, 1956 - September 14, 1957. 39 episodes. Syndicated. Also known as "Dan Tempest."

BUCK OWENS TV RANCH

Musical Variety. Performances by Country and Western artists.

Host: Buck Owens.

Regulars: Susan Raye, Merle Haggard, Kenni Huskey, Tommy Collins, Mayfi Nutter, Buddy Alan, The Stamp Quartet.

Music: The Buckaroos; The Bakersfield Brass.

BUCK OWENS TV RANCH—30 minutes—Syndicated 1968. 130 tapes.

BUCK ROGERS IN THE 25th CENTURY

Adventure. Pittsburg, 1919. A young United States Air Force veteran, Buck Rogers, begins surveying the lower levels of an abandoned mine. When the crumbling timbers give way, the roof from behind him caves in. Unable to escape, he is rendered unconscious by a peculiar gas that places him in a state of suspended animation.

As the Earth shifts, fresh air enters and awakens Buck. Emerging from the cave, he finds himself standing in the midst of a vast forest. Meeting Lieutenant Wilma Deering of the Space General's staff, he discovers that it is the year 2430 and the place is no longer Pittsburg, but Niagra, America's capitol. Stories depict Buck's attempts to aid Wilma and the scientific genius, Dr. Huer, in their battle against evil. Based on the comic strip and radio versions.

CAST

Buck Rogers	Kem Dibbs
Wilma Deering	Lou Prentis
Dr. Huer	Harry Sothern
Barney Wade	Harry Kingston

Also: Sanford Bickart, Robert Pastene.

Producer: Joe Cates, Babette Henry.
Director: Babette Henry.
Sponsor: Peter-Paul Candies.

BUCK ROGERS IN THE 25th CENTURY—30 minutes—ABC—April 15, 1950 - January 30, 1951.

BUCKAROO 500

Children. Variety set against the background of a Western ranch.
Host: Buck Weaver.

Animals: Pom Pom, the trained stallion; Dixie, "the world's smartest Doberman."

BUCKAROO 500—30 minutes—Syndicated 1963.

BUCKSKIN

Western. Background: Buckskin, Montana, 1880s. The story of Annie O'Connell, widow and owner and operator of the town hotel. Episodes relate her attempts to provide a decent life for herself and her son, Jody. Jody, seated atop a corral fence, plays his harmonica and narrates each story — stories of struggle in a lawless territory.

CAST

Annie O'Connell	Sallie Brophie
Jody O'Connell	Tommy Nolan
Sheriff Tom Sellers	Mike Road
Ben Newcomb, the school teacher	Michael Lipton

Music: Stanley Wilson; Mort Green.

BUCKSKIN—30 minutes—NBC—July 3, 1958 - September 25, 1958; NBC (rebroadcasts): July 11, 1965 - August 15, 1965. 39 episodes.

BUFFALO BILL, JR.

Western. Background: Wileyville, Texas, 1890s. The story of Buffalo Bill, Jr., and his sister, Calamity, orphans adopted by Judge Ben Wiley, the founder of the town. Appointed marshal, and aided by his sister Calamity, Bill attempts to maintain law and order.

CAST

Buffalo Bill, Jr.	Dick Jones
Calamity	Nancy Gilbert
Judge Ben Wiley	Harry Cheshire

BUFFALO BILL, JR.—30 minutes—Syndicated 1955. 40 episodes.

THE BUFFALO BILLY SHOW

Western Puppet Adventure. Era: The 19th century. The exploits of Buffalo Billy, a young seeker of adventure as he journeys West with a wagon train.

Characters: Buffalo Billy; Ima Hog, his aunt; Pop Gunn, an Indian fighter; Blunderhead, Billy's horse; Dilly, the armadillo.

Voices: Don Messick, Bob Clampett, Joan Gardiner.

Producer: Eric Jansen.
Director: Richard Goode.

THE BUFFALO BILLY SHOW—30 minutes—CBS 1950.

THE BUGALOOS

Comedy. Background: Tranquility Forest. The story of the Bugaloos, Harmony, Joy, Courage, and I.Q., human-formed singing insects, the protectors of the forest and its creatures. Episodes concern the evil Benita Bizarre's disasterous attempts to destroy their "disgusting goodness."

CAST

Benita Bizarre	Martha Raye
Joy	Caroline Ellis
Harmony	Wayne Laryea
Courage	John Philpott
I.Q.	John Mcindoe

Characters (The Sid and Marty Krofft Puppets): Sparky, the firefly; Flunky, Benita's chauffeur;

Tweeter and Woofer, Benita's aides.

Music: Charles Fox.

THE BUGALOOS—30 minutes—NBC—September 12, 1970 - September 2, 1972. 26 episodes.

THE BUGS BUNNY SHOW

Animated Cartoon. The antics of Bugs Bunny, a rabbit who excells in causing misery to others. Often depicted: The attempts of Elmer Fudd and Yosemitte Sam to shoot that "darned wabbit" and end his relentless pranks.

Additional Segments:

"Sylvester the Cat." A hungry cat attempts to catch a decent meal — Tweety Pie, the canary.

"The Road Runner." A hungry coyote's determined efforts to catch a decent meal — the Road Runner, an out-foxing bird.

Voice Characterizations: Mel Blanc.

Music: Carl Stalling; Milt Franklin; William Lava; John Celly.

THE BUGS BUNNY SHOW—30 minutes—ABC—October 11, 1960 - September 25, 1962.

THE BUGS BUNNY-ROAD RUNNER HOUR—60 minutes—CBS—September 14, 1968 - September 4, 1971.

THE BUGS BUNNY SHOW—30 minutes—CBS—September 11, 1971 - September 1, 1973.

THE BUGS BUNNY SHOW—30 minutes—ABC—September 8, 1973 - August 30, 1975.

THE BUICK CIRCUS HOUR

Variety. Music, songs, dances, and circus variety acts.

Host: Jimmy Durante.

Regulars: Dolores Gray, John Raitt.

Announcer: Frank Gallop.

Orchestra: Victor Young.

Producer: John C. Wilson.

Sponsor: Buick Automobiles.

THE BUICK CIRCUS HOUR—60

minutes—NBC—October 7, 1952 - June 16, 1953. Presented every fourth week in place of Milton Berle's "Texaco Star Theatre."

THE BULLWINKLE SHOW

See title: "Rocky and His Friends."

BURKE'S LAW

Mystery. Background: Los Angeles, California. The investigations of Amos Burke, multimillionaire police captain of the Metropolitan Homicide Squad.

CAST
Amos Burke	Gene Barry
Detective Tim Tillson	Gary Conway
Detective Sergeant Lester Hart	Regis Toomey
Henry, Burke's houseboy-chauffeur	Leon Lontoc

Burke's Law. Left to right: Gene Barry, Ellen O'Neal, Gary Conway.

Sergeant Ames, policewoman	Ellen O'Neal

Music: Herschel Burke Gilbert.

BURKE'S LAW—60 minutes—ABC—September 20, 1963 - August 31, 1965. Syndicated. Spin-off series: "Amos Burke, Secret Agent" (see title). 81 episodes.

BURNS AND ALLEN

See title: "The George Burns and Gracie Allen Show."

THE BURNS AND SCHREIBER COMEDY HOUR

Variety. Low-key, physical comedy.

Hosts: Jack Burns and Avery Schreiber.

Regulars: Teri Garr, Fred Willard, Pat Croft, Frank Leaks, Fred Welker.

Announcer: Dick Tufeld.

Orchestra: Jack Elliot, Allyn Ferguson.

THE BURNS AND SCHREIBER COMEDY HOUR—60 minutes—ABC—June 30, 1973 - September 1, 1973.

BUS STOP

Drama. Background: The Sherwood, combination bus depot and diner in Sunrise, Colorado. Real-life situations are played against mythical backgrounds as lost and troubled people attempt to overcome their difficulties.

CAST
Grace Sherwood, the proprietress	Marilyn Maxwell
Elma Gahringer, the waitress	Joan Freeman
Will Mayberry, the sheriff	Rhodes Reason
Glenn Wagner, the district attorney	Richard Anderson

Music: Frank DeVol.

BUS STOP—60 minutes—ABC—October 1, 1961 - March 25, 1962. Syndicated. 25 episodes.

BUSTING LOOSE

Comedy. Background: New York City. The misadventures of Lenny Markowitz, a twenty-four-year-old who decides to cut the apron strings. Stories concern his attempts to search for a career and independence while constantly finding his life hampered by his domineering parents.

CAST
Lenny Markowitz	Adam Arkin
Sam Markowitz, Lenny's father	Jack Kruschen
Pearl Markowitz, Lenny's mother	Pat Carroll
Melody Feebeck, Lenny's neighbor	Barbara Rhoades
Vinnie Mordabito, Lenny's friend	Greg Antonacci
Allan Simmonds, Lenny's friend	Stephen Nathan

Woody Warshaw, Lenny's
   friend   Paul Sylvan
Ralph Kabell, Lenny's
   employer, the
   owner of the
   Wear-Well Shoe
   Store   Paul B. Price
Raymond, Ralph's prize
   salesman   Ralph Wilcox
Lester Bellman, Lenny's
   friend   Danny Goldman
Music: Jack Elliott and Allyn Ferguson.

Executive Producer: Lowell Ganz,
Mark Rothman.

Producer: Lawrence Kasha.

Director: Howard Storm, James Burrows, Tony Mordente.

BUSTING LOOSE—30 minutes—
CBS—January 17, 1977 - May 9,
1977. Returned: Premiered: July 27,
1977.

BUTCH AND BILLY AND THEIR BANG BANG WESTERN MOVIES

Live Action-Animation. Cliff-hanger
type Western adventure serials reedited from "Bronco Billy" silent features. Cartoon, characters Billy Bang
Bang and his brother Butch host and
provide commentary.

CAST
Bronco Billy
Billy Bang Bang   Bob Cust
   (voiced by)   Steve Krieger
Butch Bang Bang
   (voiced by)   Danny Krieger

BUTCH AND BILLY AND THEIR
BANG BANG WESTERN
MOVIES—05 minutes—Syndicated
1961. 150 episodes.

BUTCH CASSIDY AND THE SUNDANCE KIDS

Animated Cartoon. The global investigations of Butch Cassidy and the
Sundance Kids (Stephanie, Wally,
Marilee, and Freddy), U.S. government agents who pose as a Rock
group under contract with the World
Wide Talent Agency, a front for an
international spy ring.

Gang dog: Elvis.

Voices: Cameron Arthur Clark, Henry
Corden, Ronnie Schell, Hans
Conried, Mickey Dolenz, Ross
Martin, Alan Oppenheimer, John
Stephenson, Virginia Gregg,
Pamela Peters, Frank Maxwell.

Music: Hoyt Curtin.

BUTCH CASSIDY AND THE SUN-
DANCE KIDS—30 minutes—NBC—
September 8, 1973 - August 31, 1974.
13 episodes.

BWANA MICHAEL OF AFRICA

Documentary. Films depicting animal
behavior and African tribal customs.

Host-Narrator: George Michael
(hunter and explorer).

BWANA MICHAEL OF AFRICA—30
minutes—Syndicated 1966. Also released as theatrical shorts.

BY CANDELIGHT

A thirty-minute musical variety series,
broadcast on DuMont in 1950, and
starring Tony Fontaine and Paula
Wray.

BY LINE—BETTY FURNESS

Variety. Music, songs, and celebrity
interviews.

Hostess: Betty Furness.

Regulars: Don Cherry, Hank Fost, Bill
Stern, David Ross.

Music: The Buddy Weed Trio.

Producer: Hal Davis, George Quint.

Director: Cort Steen.

BY LINE—BETTY FURNESS—30
minutes—ABC 1950.

BY LINE—STEVE WILSON

See title: "Big Town."

BY POPULAR DEMAND

Variety. Performances by undiscovered professional talent.

Host: Robert Alda.

Orchestra: Harry Sosnick.

Producer: Frank Satenstein.

Director: Herbert Sussan.

BY POPULAR DEMAND—30 min-
utes—CBS 1950.

C

CADE'S COUNTY

Modern Western. Background: The

Southwestern community of Madrid
County. The story of Sheriff Sam
Cade and his attempts to maintain law
and order in an area easily able to
become a lawless wasteland. The series
emphasizes relations with and acceptance of the Indian.

CAST
Sheriff Sam Cade   Glenn Ford
Deputy J.J. Jackson Edgar Buchanan
Deputy Arlo Pritchard Taylor Lacher
Deputy Rudy Davillo Victor Campos
Pete, a deputy   Peter Ford
Kitty Ann Sundown, the radio
   dispatcher   Sandra Ego
            Betty Ann Carr

Music: Henry Mancini.

CADE'S COUNTY—60 minutes—CBS
—September 19, 1971 - September 4,
1972. 24 episodes.

CAFE De PARIS

Musical Variety.

Hostess: Sylvie St. Clair.

Featured: Jacques Arbuschon.

Music: The Stan Free Trio.

CAFE De PARIS—15 minutes—Du-
Mont 1949.

CAFE DUBONNETT

Musical Variety.

Host: Andy Russell.

Hostess: Della Russell.

Music: The Cy Coleman Trio.

CAFE DUBONNETT—15 minutes—
ABC 1950.

CAIN'S HUNDRED

Crime Drama. The story of Nicholas
Cain, a former underworld attorney
who teams with the U.S. authorities in
an attempt to infiltrate the ranks of
organized crime and bring the nation's
top one hundred criminals to justice.

Starring: Mark Richman as Nicholas
Cain.

Music: Jerry Goldsmith; Morton
Stevens.

CAIN'S HUNDRED—60 minutes—
NBC—September 19, 1961 - September 10, 1962. Syndicated. 30 episodes.

THE CALIFORNIANS

Western. Background: San Francisco, California, 1851, during the era of its turbulent pioneering years. The story of two men, and their attempts to establish a system of law enforcement. Abandoning his original plan to seek gold, a settler, Dion Patrick, becomes a somewhat unofficial source of law and order. Following his departure, lawlessness once again prevails. Attempting to combat it, the citizens organize and hire Matt Wayne as their marshal. Episodes relate their experiences and the struggles of settlers as they attempt to establish a new life.

CAST
Dion Patrick	Adam Kennedy
Marshal Matt Wayne	Richard Coogan
Jack McGivern, the owner of the General Store	Sean McClory
Martha McGivern, his wife	Nan Leslie
R. Jeremy Pitt, a lawyer	Arthur Fleming
Wilma Fansler, a widow, the owner of the gambling house	Carol Matthews

THE CALIFORNIANS—30 minutes—NBC—September 24, 1957 - January 5, 1958 (Kennedy episodes); January 12, 1958 - September 1959 (Coogan episodes). Syndicated. 69 episodes.

CALLAN

Crime Drama. Background: London, England. The investigations of David Callan, a British Intelligence Agent. Produced by Thames TV of London.

Starring: Edward Woodward as David Callan.

Producer: Reginald Collin.

CALLAN—60 minutes—Syndicated 1976.

CALL MR. D

See title: "Richard Diamond, Private Detective."

CALL MY BLUFF

Game. Two competing teams each composed of three members — two studio-audience contestants and one celebrity captain. Object: to determine the correct definitions of obscure words. The Host presents a card to each member of one team. One card contains the correct meaning of the word to be guessed. Each player

states a definition, but two are bluffing. The opposing team must determine the purveyor of the truth.

Host: Bill Leyden.

CALL MY BLUFF—30 minutes—NBC—March 29, 1965 - September 24, 1965.

CALL OF THE WEST

Anthology. Rebroadcasts of Western dramas that were originally aired via "Death Valley Days."

Host: John Payne.

Music: Marlen Skiles.

CALL OF THE WEST—30 minutes—Syndicated 1969. 52 episodes.

CALL OF THE WILD

Documentary. Filmed accounts of wildlife behavior.

Host-Narrator: Arthur Jones.

CALL OF THE WILD—30 minutes—Syndicated 1970.

CALUCCI'S DEPARTMENT

Comedy. Background: New York City. The harassed life of Joe Calucci, a soft-hearted state unemployment office supervisor who constantly finds himself at odds with his position of authority as he attempts to curtail the antics of his staff of seven rude and raucous bureaucrats.

CAST
Joe Calucci	James Coco
Shirley Balukis, Joe's girlfriend, a pretty, but not-too-bright secretary	Candy Azzara
Ramon Gonzales, the assistant supervisor, Joe's protégé	Jose Perez
Oscar Cosgrove, the claims adjuster	Jack Fletcher
Elaine P. Fusco, a secretary	Peggy Pope
Jack Woods, an employee	Bill Lazarus
Mitzi Gordon, the telephone operator	Rosetta Lenore
Walter Frohler, an employee	Bernard Wexler
Mrs. Clairmont, the elderly claiment	Judith Lowry
Mrs. Calucci, Joe's mother	Vera Lockwood

The Priest	Philip Stirling

Music: Marvin Hamlisch.

CALUCCI'S DEPARTMENT—30 minutes—CBS—September 14, 1973 - December 28, 1973. 13 episodes.

CALVIN AND THE COLONEL

Animated Cartoon. Background: A big city up North. The misadventures of two backwoods Southern animals as they struggle to cope with life: Calvin, not-too-bright bear, and his friend, the Colonel, a cunning fox. Created by Freeman Gosden and Charles Correll. Based on their "Amos and Andy" characters.

Characters' Voices
The Colonel	Freeman Gosden
Calvin	Charles Correll
Maggie Bell, the Colonel's wife	Virginia Gregg
Sue, Maggie's sister	Beatrice Kay
Oliver Wendell Clutch, the lawyer (a weasel)	Paul Frees

Additional Voices: Frank Gerstle, Barney Phillips, Gloria Blondell.

CALVIN AND THE COLONEL—30 minutes—ABC—October 3, 1961 - November 7, 1961; January 27, 1962 - September 22, 1962. Syndicated. 26 episodes.

CAMEL CARAVAN

Alternate title for "The Vaughn Monroe Show" (which see) when broadcast on CBS from October 10, 1950 to July 3, 1951.

CAMEO THEATRE

Anthology. Rebroadcasts of dramas that were originally aired via "Matinee Theatre."

CAMEO THEATRE—60 minutes—Syndicated 1959. 26 episodes.

CAMERA THREE

Anthology. A program, unsponsored, reflecting the interests of the people producing it — "an experimental educational series, a market place of ideas from drama, literature, dance, music, and art."

Host: James Macandrew.

Included:

The Music Of A Different Drummer.
The life of author Henry David
Thoreau.

Edgar Allen Poe: Israfel. Geddeth
Smith, as Poe, discussing his life.

The World In 1984. A discussion with
guest Nigel Calder.

The Eagle, The Tiger, And The Fly. A
program depicting works of art in-
spired by these creatures.

A Salute To Stravinsky. *Orchestra:*
The New York Philharmonic, conducted by Pierre Boulet.

The Art Of The Animator. A demonstration, with guest Faith Hubley.

The Sorrow And The Pity. Excerpts
from the French film, with director
Marcel Ophails as guest.

CAMERA THREE—30 minutes—Pre-
miered: Local New York, WCBS-TV,
May 16, 1953; Network: CBS, 1956.
Original title: "It's Worth Knowing."

CAMOUFLAGE

Game. Two competing players. A
camouflaged cartoon drawing, containing a hidden object, is flashed on a
screen. Through correct responses during a series of general-knowledge question-answer rounds, players receive a
chance to trace the object. If they are
unable to guess it, a section of the
camouflage is removed. The game
continues until someone identifies the
object.

Host: Don Morrow.

Organist: Paul Taubman.

CAMOUFLAGE—30 minutes—ABC—
January 9, 1961 - November 16,
1962.

CAMP RUNAMUCK

Comedy. Background: Summer
camps, Runamuck for boys, and
Divine for girls. Runamuck is
slipshodly operated by Commander
Wivenhoe, a child hater, and his staff
of lamebrains: Spiffy, Pruett, Malden,
and Doc. Divine is impeccably main-
tained under the auspices of Counselor Mahalia May Gruenecker and her
beautiful assistant, Caprice
Yeudleman.
Stories relate Wivenhoe's attempts
to cope with his horde of detested

brats and the female manipulation of
his counselors into performing
burdensome tasks for Divine.

CAST

Commander Wivenhoe	Arch Johnson
Caprice Yeudleman	Nina Wayne
Mahalia May Gruenecker	Alice Nunn
Spiffy	Dave Ketchum
Pruett	Dave Madden
Malden	Mike Wagner
Doc	Leonard Stone
	Frank DeVol
Eulalia Divine, the camp	
owner	Hermione Baddeley

Music: Frank DeVol.

CAMP RUNAMUCK—30 minutes—
NBC—September 17, 1965 - September 2, 1966. 16 episodes.

CANDID CAMERA

Comedy. Ordinary people, suddenly
confronted with prearranged, ludicrous situations, are filmed by hidden
cameras and seen in the act of being
themselves. Based on the radio program "Candid Microphone."

First Version:
CANDID CAMERA—30 minutes.
ABC—December 5, 1948 - August 15,
1949; CBS—September 12, 1949 -
August 19, 1951; ABC—August 27,
1951 - August 22, 1956.

Host: Allen Funt.
Featured: Jerry Lester.
Announcer: Ken Roberts.

Second Version:
CANDID CAMERA—30 minutes—
CBS—October 2, 1960 - September 3,
1967.

Host: Allen Funt
Co-Hosts: Arthur Godfrey (October 2,
1960 - September 24, 1961);
Durwood Kirby (October 1,
1961 - September 4, 1966); Bess
Myerson (September 11, 1966 -
September 3, 1967).
Regulars: Marilyn Van De Bur, the
Candid Camera girl; Dorothy
Collins; Joey Faye; Betsy Palmer;
Al Kelly; Marge Green; Tom
O'Mally; Thelma Pellmige;
Fannie Flagg.
Music: Sid Ramin; Henri Rene.

Third Version: British—
CANDID CAMERA—30 minutes—
ABC-TV from Manchester—
1961-1967.

Host: Bob Monkhouse.
Co-Host: Jonathan Routt.

Fourth Version:
THE NEW CANDID CAMERA—30
minutes—Syndicated 1974.

Host: Allen Funt.
Announcer-Co-Host: John
Bartholomew Tucker.
Music: Recorded.

Fifth Version:

THE NEW CANDID CAMERA—30
minutes—Syndicated 1975.

Camp Runamuck. Left to right: Arch
Johnson, Dave Ketchum, and Leonard
Stone. © *Screen Gems.*

Host: Allen Funt.

Hostesses: Phyllis George (1975); Jo Ann Pflug (1976).

Regulars: Sheila Burnett, Fannie Flagg.

Music: Frank Grant.

CAN DO

Game. Object: For contestants to determine whether or not guest celebrities can perform certain stunts. After a series of indirect question-and-answer rounds between the contestant and the celebrity, the player is escorted to an isolation booth and given a limited amount of time to reach a decision. The guest is then asked if he is able to perform the stunt in question. If the contestant correctly guesses, he wins a cash prize.

Host: Robert Alda.

CAN DO–30 minutes–NBC–November 26, 1956 - December 31, 1956.

CANNON

Crime Drama. Background: Los Angeles, California. The investigations of Frank Cannon, a highly paid and overweight private detective.

Starring: William Conrad as Frank Cannon.

Music: John Parker; John Cannon.

Additional Music: George Romanis, Duante Tatro.

Executive Producer: Quinn Martin.

Producer: Anthony Spinner.

CANNON–60 minutes–CBS–September 14, 1971 - September 19, 1976. 96 episodes.

CANNONBALL

Adventure. Background: Various areas between the United States and Canada. The experiences of Mike "Cannonball" Malone and his partner, Jerry, drivers for the International Transport Trucking Company.

CAST
Mike "Cannonball" Malone Paul Birch
Jerry   William Campbell

CANNONBALL–30 minutes–Syndicated 1958. 39 episodes.

CAN YOU TOP THIS?

Game. Jokes, submitted by home viewers are relayed to the audience by the "Joke Teller." The response, zero to one hundred, is registered on a laugh meter. A panel of three then tries to beat the established score with other jokes in the same category.

The home viewer receives twenty-five dollars for his joke and an additional twenty-five dollars for each joke that registers a lesser response. The limit is one hundred dollars. Based on the radio program of the same title.

Versions:
ABC–30 minutes–October 3, 1950 - March 21, 1951.

Host: Ward Wilson.

Joke Teller: Senator Edward Ford.

Panel: Harry Hersfield, Joe Laurie, Jr., Peter Donald.

Syndicated – 30 minutes–1970.

Host: Wink Martindale.

Joke Tellers (alternating): Dick Gautier, Richard Dawson.

Regular Panelist: Morey Amsterdam (assisted by two guests per week).

THE CAPTAIN AND TENNILLE

Musical Variety.

Hosts: The Captain and Tennille (Toni Tennille and her husband, Daryl Dragon, the Captain).

Regulars: Dave Shelley, Damian London, Billy Barty, Melissa Tennille, Jerry Trent, Joan Lawrence, Milton Frome.

Featured: Toni and Daryl's bulldogs: Broderick and Elizabeth.

Orchestra: Lenny Stack.

Dance Music: Al Mello.

Choreography: Bob Thompson.

Executive Producer: Alan Bernard.

Producer: Bob Henry.

Director: Tony Charmoli.

THE CAPTAIN AND TENNILLE–60 minutes–ABC–September 20, 1976 - March 14, 1977.

CAPTAIN BILLY'S SHOWBOAT

Musical. Variety set against the background of an Ohio River showboat.

Host (appearing as Captain Billy Bryant): Ralph Dunne.

Regulars: Ralph Dumke, Johnny Downs, Bibi Osterwald, Juanita Hall, Betty Brewer, George Jason.

Orchestra: John Gart.

CAPTAIN BILLY'S SHOWBOAT–30 minutes–CBS 1948.

CAPTAIN DAVID GRIEF

Adventure. Background: The West Indies. The story of sloop captain David Grief, and his traveling companion, Anura. Episodes relate their search for adventure.

CAST
Captain David Grief   Maxwell Reed
Anura   Maureen Hingert

CAPTAIN DAVID GRIEF–30 minutes–Syndicated 1956. 39 episodes.

CAPTAIN GALLANT

See title: "Foreign Legionnaire."

CAPTAIN KANGAROO

Educational. Entertainment geared to preschool children. Background: The Treasure House. Various aspects of the adult world are explained to children through cartoons, stories, songs, and sketches.

CAST
Captain Kangaroo   Bob Keeshan
Mr. Green Jeans, his assistant   Lumpy Brannum
Debbie   Debbie Weems
Dennis   Cosmo Allegretti
Mr. Baxter   James E. Wall
Banana Man   A. Robbins
Also: Ann Leonardo, Bennye Gatteys, Dr. Joyce Brothers.

Vocalists: The Kangaroos (Beverly Hanshaw, Holly Mershon, Phil Casnoff, Terrence Emanuel).

Puppets: Mr. Moose, Bunny Rabbit, Miss Worm, Miss Frog.

Characters: Dancing Bear, Grandfather Clock.

Music: Recorded.

Producer: Peter Birch, Jon Stone, Robert Myhreim, Bob Claver, Dave Connell, Sam Gibbon, Al Hyslop, Jack Miller, Jim Hirschfield.

CAPTAIN KANGAROO–60 minutes–CBS–Premiered: October 3, 1955.

Based on a local New York Program, hosted by Bob Keeshan, entitled: "Tinker's Workshop." Spin-off: "Mister Mayor"—60 minutes—CBS—September 26, 1964 - September 1965. Bob Keeshan as an acting Mayor who relates various aspects of the world to children. Also cast: Jane Connell, Bill McCutcheon, and Cosmo Allegrette. Broadcast in place of the Saturday morning edition of "Captain Kangaroo."

CAPTAIN MIDNIGHT

Adventure. The story of a private citizen who devotes his life to fighting crime. Named "Captain Midnight" for his daring air tactics against the enemy during the war, Captain Albright commands the Secret Squadron, a U.S. government organization designed to combat evil. Assisted by Tut and Ickky, he battles the sinister forces threatening world security.

Based on the radio program of the same title. After the program was dropped by network television, its syndicated title became "Jet Jackson, Flying Commando." By voice-over dubbing, the name, Captain Midnight, was also changed to Jet Jackson. Ovaltine, the sponsor and owner, reserved the right to the original name.

CAST

Captain Midnight
 (Jet Jackson)   Richard Webb
Ichabod (Ickky) Mudd, his
 mechanic   Sid Melton
Tut, a scientist   Olan Soule
Chuck Ramsey, the Captain's
 ward   Renee Beard
Marcia Stanhope,
 a Secret Squadron
 agent   Jan Shepard

Captain Midnight's plane: The *Sky King.*

Music: Don Ferris.

CAPTAIN MIDNIGHT—30 minutes—CBS—September 4, 1954 - September 1958. 39 episodes.

CAPTAIN NICE

Comedy. Background: Big Town, U.S.A. Experimenting, Carter Nash, a mild-mannered police chemist, discovers Super Juice, a liquid, that when taken, transforms him into Captain Nice, a heroic crime fighter.

Secretly appearing as Captain Nice whenever the need arises, Nash fights an endless battle against the diabolical fiends of crime-ridden Big Town.

CAST

Carter Nash/Captain
 Nice   William Daniels
Mrs. Nash, his
 mother   Alice Ghostley
Police Sergeant Candy Kane,
 his girlfriend   Ann Prentiss
Police Chief Segal   William Zuckert
Mayor Finny   Liam Dunn
Mr. Nash, Carter's
 father   Byron Foulger

Music: Vic Mizzy.

CAPTAIN NICE—30 minutes—NBC—January 9, 1967 - September 4, 1967.

CAPTAIN SAFARI

Children. The fantasy-like adventures of Captain Safari, a jungle explorer whose expeditions unfold through his magic TV screen, which can view all the jungles of the world at the press of a button.

Starring: Randy Knight as Captain Safari.

His Sidekick: Sylvester, played by Zippy the chimp.

CAPTAIN SAFARI—30 minutes—CBS 1955. 15 episodes.

CAPTAIN SCARLET AND THE MYSTERONS

Marionette Adventure. Era: The twenty-first century. During an exploration of the planet Mars, the Mysterons, its inhabitants, misconstrue a visit by Spectrum, an international organization established to safeguard the world, as an unprovoked attack and declare a war of revenge on Earth.

Seeking a champion to their cause, the Mysterons contrive an automobile accident that claims the life of Spectrum Agent Captain Scarlet (named as all agents after the colors of the spectrum). Able to recreate any person or object after it has first been destroyed, the Mysterons restore his life. However, retaining his human force, as well as Mysteron characteristics, he fails to fulfill their expectations; instead, he becomes their indestructible enemy.

Episodes depict Spectrum's battle against the never-seen Mysterons' war of attrition. Filmed in Supermarionation. An I.T.C. presentation.

Characters' Voices

Captain Scarlet, Spectrum's chief
 operative   Francis Matthews
Colonel White, the commander of
 Spectrum   Donald Gray
Captain Grey, a Spectrum
 agent   Paul Maxwell
Captain Blue, a Spectrum
 agent   Ed Bishop
Captain Ochre, a Spectrum
 agent   Jeremy Wilkins
Captain Magenta, a Spectrum
 agent   Gary Files
Lieutenant Green, a
 Spectrum agent   Cy Grant
Doctor Fawn, the medical
 commander   Charles Tingwell
Symphony Angel, a Spectrum
 pilot   Janna Hill
Melody Angel, a Spectrum
 pilot   Sylvia Anderson
Rhapsody Angel, a Spectrum
 pilot   Liz Morgan
Harmony Angel, a Spectrum
 pilot   Lian-Shin
Destiny Angel, a Spectrum
 pilot   Liz Morgan
The Mysteron Voice   Donald Gray
The World President   Paul Maxwell

Additional characters:

Captain Black, a former Spectrum Agent, now the Mysteron Agent on Earth.

Music: Barry Gray.

Vocals: The Spectrum.

Producer: Reg Dunlap.

Director: Desmond Saunders.

Creator: Gerry and Sylvia Anderson.

CAPTAIN SCARLET AND THE MYSTERONS—30 minutes—Syndicated 1967. 26 episodes.

CAPTAIN VIDEO AND HIS VIDEO RANGERS

Adventure. Era: Earth, A.D. 2254. Background: A lab hidden deep in a mountain peak, the central headquarters of Captain Video, "The Guardian of the Safety of the World." Possessing amazing scientific genius and electronic weapons, he assists various world governments, and attempts to destroy persons dangerous to the safety and peace of the universe.

CAST

Captain Video
 (1949-1950)   Richard Coogan
Captain Video
 (1950-1956)   Al Hodge
The Video Ranger, a teen-
 ager (fifteen) the
 Captain hopes to one
 day carry on his vital
 work   Don Hastings
Dr. Pauli, an enemy
 seeking to secure the
 Captain's secrets   Hal Conklin

Dr. Tobor	Dave Ballard
Agent Carter	Nat Polen
Nargola	Ernest Borgnine

Also: Tony Randall, Jack Klugman.

Producer: Olga Druce, Frank Telford.

Sponsor: Johnson Candies; General Foods.

Program Open (one of several):

Announcer: "Captain Video! Master of space! Hero of science! Captain of the Video Rangers! Operating from his secret mountain headquarters on the planet Earth, Captain Video rallies men of good will everywhere. As he rockets from planet to planet, let us follow the champion of justice, truth, and freedom throughout the universe."

Captain Video's Rocket: The *Galaxey.*

Featured: Frequent Video Ranger messages; short, inspirational communications designed to instill viewers with the spirit of fair play, antidiscrimination, and the Golden Rule.

When first begun, "Captain Video and His Video Rangers-" was telecast as a continuing serial. In 1953, when it was titled "The Secret Files of Captain Video," it became a weekly adventure complete in itself. In 1956, the adventure format was dropped, and Al Hodge became the host of "Captain Video's Cartoons," a weekly presentation featuring the animated antics of "Betty Boop," voiced by Mae Questel. 1951 saw a fifteen-episode theatrical version, "Captain Video," starring Judd Holdren as the Captain.

CAPTAIN VIDEO AND HIS VIDEO RANGERS—30 minutes—DuMont—1949-1953. THE SECRET FILES OF CAPTAIN VIDEO—30 minutes—DuMont—1953-1956. CAPTAIN VIDEO'S CARTOONS—30 minutes—DuMont—1956.

CAPTAIN Z-RO

Adventure. Captain Z-Ro, the inventor of a time machine, establishes a day of crisis in the life of an individual. His young assistant, Jet, is placed in its chamber and transported to a past era. As the Captain controls his activities, the boy assists where possible and attempts to resolve encountered difficulties.

CAST

Captain Z-Ro	Roy Steffins
Jet	Bobby Trumbull

The Captain's Rocket Ship: ZX-99.

CAPTAIN Z-RO—15 minutes—Syndicated 1955. 26 episodes.

CAPTURE

Adventure. Films depicting the capture of wild animals.

Hosts-Narrators: Bill Wilson, Arthur Jones.

CAPTURE—30 minutes—Syndicated 1965. 39 episodes.

CAPTURED

Crime Drama. Retitled episodes of "Gangbusters."

Host-Narrator: Chester Morris.

Included:

Man From Mars. The story of a thief who dresses as a Martian to rob banks in broad daylight.
Starring: Bob Karnes, Eddie Marr.

Hogan-Yates. The story details the risks taken by a group of prisoners as they attempt to escape from jail.

Starring: Leonard Bill, Eddie Hyans.

Max Baroda. The story concerns the grim police hunt for a murderous gang of thieves.
Starring: John Seven.

CAPTURED—30 minutes—Syndicated 1954. 26 episodes.

THE CARA WILLIAMS SHOW

Comedy. Distinguished by two formats. The background for each is Los Angeles, California.

Format One:
The story of a young bride and groom who are employed by Fenwick Diversified Industries, Incorporated, a company that prohibits the employment of married couples. Cara Wilton, a beautiful, but scatterbrained file clerk, and Frank Bridges, the efficiency expert, resolve their problem by concealing their marriage. Episodes relate their struggles to keep their marriage a secret.

Format Two (five months following):
. Plagued by a constant fear of discovery, Cara and Frank reveal the fact of their marriage to Damon Burkhardt, the company manager. When discovering that Frank is to be discharged, Cara, whose complicated filing system makes her inexpendable,

The Cara Williams Show. Frank Aletter and Cara Williams.

questions the company's marriage policy and convinces Mr. Fenwick, the president, to alter the rule. Stories relate the home and working lives of young marrieds.

CAST

Cara Wilton (Bridges)	Cara Williams
Frank Bridges	Frank Aletter
Damon Burkhardt, Cara and Frank's employer	Paul Reed
Fletcher Kincaid, Cara and Frank's neighbor, a hip-talking jazz musician	Jack Sheldon
Mary Hamilmyer, Mr. Burkhardt's secretary	Jeanne Arnold
Mr. Fenwick, the company president	Edward Everett Horton

Music: Kenyon Hopkins.

THE CARA WILLIAMS SHOW—30 minutes—CBS—September 23, 1964 - September 10, 1965. 26 episodes.

CAR 54, WHERE ARE YOU?

Comedy. Background: The Bronx, the 53rd precinct on Tremont Avenue. The on-duty and off-duty lives of two fictitious New York policemen, Gunther Toody and Francis Muldoon, patrol car officers assigned to Car 54.

CAST

Gunther Toody	Joe E. Ross
Francis Muldoon	Fred Gwynne
Captain Martin Block	Paul Reed
Lucille Toody, Gunther's wife	Beatrice Pons
Patrolman Leo Schnauzer	Al Lewis
Sylvia Schnauzer, his wife	Charlotte Rae

Patrolman Ed
  Nicholson   Hank Garrett
Desk Sgt. Sol
  Abrams   Nathaniel Frey
Officer Rodrequez   Jack Healy
Officer O'Hara   Al Henderson
Officer Anderson   Nipsey Russell
Officer Steinmetz   Joe Warren
Officer Wallace   Fred O'Neal
Officer Murdock   Shelly Burton
Officer Nelson   Jim Gromley
Officer Reilly   Duke Farley
Officer Kissel   Bruce Kirby
Officer Antonnucci   Jerry Guardino
Mrs. Bronson, the Bronx
  troublemaker   Molly Picon
Mrs. Muldoon, Francis's
  mother   Ruth Masters
Peggy Muldoon, his
  sister   Helen Parker
Al, a friend of Toody and
  Muldoon   Carl Ballantine
Rose, his
  wife   Martha Greenhouse
Bonnie Kalsheim,
  Muldoon's occasional
  date   Alice Ghostley
Mrs. Block, the Captain's
  wife   Patricia Bright
Charlie, the drunk, a
  friend of Toody and
  Muldoon   Larry Storch

Theme: CAR 54, WHERE ARE YOU?

Words: Nat Hiken.

Music: John Strauss.

Copyright by Emil Ascher, Inc., Reprinted by permission.

There's a hold-up in the Bronx,
Brooklyn's broken out in fights.
There's a traffic jam in Harlem,
That's backed up to Jackson Heights.
There's a scout troop short a child,
Krushchev's due at Idlewild—
CAR 54, WHERE ARE YOU?

Music: John Strauss.

Announcer: Carl Caruso.

Producer: Nat Hiken.

Director: Nat Hiken, Stanley Prager.

CAR 54, WHERE ARE YOU?—30
minutes—NBC—September 17, 1961 -
September 8, 1963. Syndicated. 60
episodes.

CARIBE

Crime Drama. The cases of Ben Logan
and Mark Walters, Miami-based police
agents who handle special assignments
fighting crime in the Caribbean.

CAST

Lt. Ben Logan   Stacy Keach

Sgt. Mark Walters   Carl Franklin
Captain Rawlings   Robert Mandan

Music: John Elizade.

Additional Music: Nelson Riddle.

Executive Producer: Quinn Martin.

Producer: Anthony Spinner.

Director: Virgil W. Vogel.

Creator: Charles Peck, Jr.

CARIBE—60 minutes—ABC—February 17, 1975 - August 11, 1975. 18
episodes.

THE CARLTON FREDERICKS SHOW

Information. Nutrition and health
advice.

Host: Carlton Fredericks.

THE CARLTON FREDERICKS
SHOW—30 minutes—Syndicated
1967.

THE CARMEL MYERS SHOW

A fifteen-minute interview series with
hostess Carmel Myers. Broadcast on
ABC from June 19, 1951 to February
21, 1952.

CARNIVAL

Anthology. Rebroadcasts of dramas
that were originally aired via other
filmed anthology programs.

Included:

My Nephew Norville. The story of a
traveler from outer space who is befriended by an amateur inventor.
Starring: Harold Peary, Gil Stratton.

Old Mother Hubbard. The story of a
woman who resorts to desperate tactics to determine if her daughter's
employer can be trusted.
Starring: Ellen Corby.

My Rival Is A Fiddle. The story of a
school teacher and her struggles to
snatch the attentions of a man whose
love is his fiddle.
Starring: Hans Conried.

Never Trust A Redhead. The story of
a wealthy but spoiled girl and her
attempts to run her fiancé's life.
Starring: Sandra Dorn.

CARNIVAL—30 minutes—ABC—June
1953 - September 1953.

CAROL BURNETT AND FRIENDS

Comedy. A series of half-hour programs culled from Carol Burnett's
Saturday night CBS series. See title
"The Carol Burnett Show" for information.

CAROL BURNETT AND
FRIENDS—30 minutes—Syndicated
1977.

THE CAROL BURNETT SHOW

Variety. Music, comedy, songs, and
dances.

Hostess: Carol Burnett.

Regulars: Harvey Korman, Vicki
  Lawrence, Lyle Waggoner, the
  Ernest Flatt Dancers, Tim Conway, Dick Van Dyke, Shirley
  Kirkes, April Nevins, Vivian Bonnell, Don Crichton.

Announcer: Lyle Waggoner.

Orchestra: Harry Zimmerman; Peter
  Matz.

THE CAROL BURNETT SHOW—60
minutes—CBS—Premiered: September
11, 1967.

THE CAROL MANN CELEBRITY GOLF CHALLENGE

Game. Background: The Fountain
Valley Golf Course in St. Croix (U.S.
Virgin Islands). The format pits golf
pro Carol Mann against a celebrity
guest. A nine-hole match is played,
but due to time restrictions, only the
highlights are seen. The celebrity receives a check for $5,000 for participating.

Hostess: Carol Mann.

Announcer-Assistant: Bruce Roberts.

Music: Recorded.

Producer-Director: Roger Blaemiere.

THE CAROL MANN CELEBRITY
GOLF CHALLENGE—30 minutes—
Syndicated 1975.

THE CAROLYN GILBERT SHOW

A variety series, broadcast on ABC
from January 15, 1950 to October 6,
1950, and starring actress Carolyn
Gilbert.

CARTER COUNTRY

Comedy. Background: Clinton Corners, Georgia. The series focuses on the bickering relationship between Roy Mobey, a white, old-fashioned police chief, and Curtis Baker, an urbane black New York City trained police officer, his sergeant. (The series derives its title from the fact that Clinton Corners is just a "hoot 'n' a holler" from Plains, Georgia, the home of President Jimmy Carter.)

CAST

Chief Roy Mobey	Victor French
Sgt. Curtis Baker	Kene Holliday
Mayor Teddy Burnside	Richard Paul
Officer Jasper Clinton	Harvey Vernon
Officer Cloris Phebus	Barbara Cason
Officer Harley Puckett	Guich Koock
Lucille Banks, the mayor's secretary	Vernee Watson

Music: Pete Rugolo.
Executive Producer: Bud Yorkin, Saul Turteltaub, Bernie Orenstein.
Producer: Douglas Arango, Phil Doran.

CARTER COUNTRY—30 minutes—ABC—Premiered: September 15, 1977.

CARTOON THEATRE

Children. Line sketch drawings illustrating off-stage story telling.
Yarn Spinner: Jack Lucksinger.
Artist: Chuck Lucksinger.
Organist: Rosa Rio.

CARTOON THEATRE—30 minutes—ABC 1947.

CARTOON THEATRE

Cartoons. Paul Terry's animated creations: "Heckle and Jeckle," "Gandy Goose," "Dinky Duck," and "Little Roguefort."
Host: Dick Van Dyke.

CARTOON THEATRE—30 minutes—CBS—June 13, 1956 - September 1956.

CARTOONSVILLE

See title: "Paul Winchell and Jerry Mahoney."

CARTUNE-O

Game. The object is for contestants to guess the identity of song titles from clues drawn by a cartoonist. The game segments are interspersed with songs.
Host: Holland Engle; Lee Bennett.
Cartoonist: Arv Miller.
Regulars: Nancy Wright, Peggy Taylor, The Temptones.
Orchestra: Robert Trendler.

CARTUNE-O—60 minutes—DuMont 1950.

CASABLANCA

See title: "Warner Brothers Presents," *Casablanca* segment.

THE CASE OF THE DANGEROUS ROBIN

Mystery. The story of insurance investigators Robin Scott and Phyllis Collier. Episodes relate their attempts to expose "The Cheaters," people who defraud insurance companies with false claims.

CAST

Robin Scott	Rick Jason
Phyllis Collier	Jean Blake

Music: David Rose.

THE CASE OF THE DANGEROUS ROBIN—30 minutes—Syndicated 1961. 38 episodes.

THE CASES OF EDDIE DRAKE

Crime Drama. Background: New York City. The investigations of Eddie Drake, a private detective, and Dr. Karen Gayle, a psychologist who assists him to acquire information for a book she is compiling on criminal behavior.

CAST

Eddie Drake	Don Haggerty
Karen Gayle	Patricia Morrison

Producer: Harlan Thompson.

THE CASES OF EDDIE DRAKE—30 minutes—CBS 1949 (dropped after nine episodes); Syndicated 1952. 13 episodes.

CASEY JONES

Adventure. Background: Jackson, Tennessee, during the latter half of the nineteenth century. The saga of the famed 382 Engine, the Cannonball Express (Illinois Central Railroad) and its legendary engineer, Casey Jones.

CAST

Casey Jones	Alan Hale, Jr.
Alice Jones, his wife	Mary Lawrence

Casey Jones. Left to right: Eddy Waller, Paul Keast, Bobby Clark, (holding Cinders), Dub Taylor, Mary Lawrence, Pat Hogan, Alan Hale, Jr. © *Screen Gems.*

Casey Jones, Jr., their son	Bobby Clark
Red Rock, the Cannonball Conductor	Eddy Waller
Willie Sims, the Cannonball Fireman	Dub Taylor
Sam Peachpit, Casey's Indian friend	Pat Hogan
Mr. Carter, the businessman	Paul Keast

Jones family dog: Cinders.

CASEY JONES—30 minutes—Syndicated 1957. 32 episodes.

CASPER, THE FRIENDLY GHOST

Animated Cartoon. The story of Casper, a ghost who struggles to befriend humans and animals.
Characters: Casper; Wendy, the Good Witch; Spooky, the mischievous ghost; Poil, Casper's girlfriend; and the Ghostly Trio.
Voices are not given screen credit.
Music: Winston Sharples.

CASPER, THE FRIENDLY GHOST—6 minute, 30-second theatrical cartoons—Syndicated 1953. On October 5, 1963, ABC presented "The New Casper Cartoon Show," which consisted of new made-for-television episodes of Casper the Friendly Ghost, and which ran for thirty minutes on Saturday mornings until September 2, 1967.

THE CATTANOOGA CATS

Animated Cartoon. The misadventures of the Cattanooga Cats (Chessie, Kitty Jo, Scootz, Groovey, and Country), a feline Rock group. A Hanna-Barbera production.

Additional segments:

It's The Wolf. The story of Mildew, a wolf who is determined to catch a decent meal: Lambsy, the poor defenseless lamb. Savior of the lamb is Bristol Hound—"Bristol Hound's my name and saving sheep's my game."

Around The World In 79 Days. The adventures of Phineas Fogg, Jr. as he attempts to travel around the world in seventy-nine days. His aides: Jenny Trent and Happy; his enemies: Crumdon and Bumbler, who plot to thwart his efforts.

Auto Cat And Motor Mouse. The story of a cat who is determined to beat a mouse in a race.

Characters' Voices
Country	Bill Galloway
Groovey	Casey Kaseem
Scoots	Jim Begg
Kitty Jo	Julie Bennett
Chessie	Julie Bennett
Mildew Wolf	Paul Lynde
Lambsy	Daws Butler
Bristol Hound	Allan Melvin
Phineas Fogg, Jr.	Bruce Watson
Jenny Trent	Janet Waldo
Happy	Don Messick
Smerky	Don Messick
Crumdon	Daws Butler
Bumbler	Allan Melvin
Motor Mouse	Dick Curtis
Auto Cat	Marty Ingels

Music: Hoyt Curtin.

THE CATTANOOGA CATS—60 minutes—ABC—September 6, 1969 - September 5, 1970; 30 minutes—September 13, 1970 - September 4, 1971. 17 episodes.

CAVALCADE OF AMERICA

Anthology. Dramatizations based on past events. The struggles of outstanding individuals in the shaping of America.

Producer: Jack Denove, Jack Chertok.
Sponsor: DuPont.

Included:

Sunset At Appomattox. The events leading to and the men responsible for the ending of the Civil War.

CAST
William Johnstone, Henry Morgan.

Duel At The O.K. Corral. A recreation of the famed gunfight—the Earps against the outlaw Dalton Brothers.

CAST
Kenneth Tobey, Harry Morgan.

The Texas Ranger. The story of the hardships endured by the men of the Nation's oldest law enforcement agency, the Texas Rangers.

CAST
Jim Davis, William Tollman.

CAVALCADE OF AMERICA—60 minutes. NBC—October 1, 1952 - September 1953. ABC—September 29, 1953 - September 6, 1955. As "Cavalcade Theatre"—60 minutes—ABC—September 13, 1955 - September 14, 1956.

CAVALCADE OF BANDS

Musical Variety. The recreated sounds of the Big Band Era.

Host: Buddy Rogers.
Regulars: Marsha Van Dyke, The Mello-Larks, The Clark Brothers.
Orchestra: Weekly guest band leaders.
Producer: Milton Douglas, Charles Ross.
Director: Frank Bunetta.

CAVALCADE OF BANDS—60 minutes—DuMont 1951.

CAVALCADE OF STARS

Variety. Music, songs, dances, and comedy routines.

Host: Jack Carter.
Regulars: Joan Edwards, Larry Storch, The Fontaines, The Arnauts.

Orchestra: Sammy Spear.

CAVALCADE OF STARS—60 minutes—DuMont—1949-1950. Broadcast from January 7, 1950 - September 3, 1952, with Jackie Gleason as its host. See title: "Jackie Gleason."

THE C.B. BEARS

Animated Cartoon. A series of cartoons hosted by the C.B. Bears (Hustle, Boogie, and Bum), three crime-fighting, trouble-prone bears who receive their orders from a female named Charlie via a C.B. radio. A take-off on "Charlie's Angels."

Additional Segments:

Blast-off Buzzard and Crazy Legs. Set in a desert, the cartoon focuses on the attempts of a hungry buzzard to catch a decent meal—an out-foxing snake named Crazy Legs. A takeoff on "The Road Runner."

Heyyy, It's The King! The misadventures of a 1950s type hip-talking lion, the King, and his friends: Big H, the hippo; Clyde, the ape; Yukey Yuka, the mole; and Skids, the alligator. A takeoff on "Happy Days."

Posse Impossible. Background: The town of Saddle Sore. The exploits of an Old West sheriff and his three bumbling deputies.

Shake, Rattle, and Roll. The misadventures of three ghosts—Shake, Rattle, and Roll, as they attempt to run the Haunted Inn, a hotel for the unearthly.

Undercover Elephant. The cases of a fumbling U.S. Government agent named Undercover Elephant and his assistant Loud Mouse.

Voices: Sheldon Allman, Daws Butler, Henry Corden, Joe E. Ross, Paul Winchell, Joan Gerber, Vic Perrin, Lennie Weinrib, William Woodson, Pat Parris, Susan Silo.
Music: Hoyt Curtin, Paul DeKorte.
Executive Producer: William Hanna, Joseph Barbera.
Producer: Iwao Takamoto.
Director: Charles A. Nichols.

THE C.B. BEARS—60 minutes—NBC—Premiered: September 10, 1977.

THE CBS CHILDREN'S FILM FESTIVAL

Movies. International award-winning films for and about children.

Hostess: Fran Allison.

Puppets: Kukla, a bald-headed, round-nosed little man; and Ollie, the scatterbrained dragon.

Puppeteer: Burr Tillstrom.

THE CBS CHILDREN'S FILM FESTIVAL—60 minutes—CBS—Premiered: September 11, 1971. Previously, broadcast on CBS as a series of specials from 1966-1971.

THE CBS COMEDY PLAYHOUSE

Pilot Films. Proposed comedy series for the 1971-1972 season.

Included:

An Amateur's Guide To Love. A Candid Camera type of program featuring various filmed sequences involving ordinary people and their reactions to questions relating to love and courtship.

Host-Narrator: Joe Flynn.

Eddie. The story of Eddie Skinner, a conniving private patrolman who manipulates people and machines to benefit himself.

CAST

Eddie Skinner: Phil Silvers; Chief Pike: Fred Clark; Sylvia: Joanna Barnes; Callahan: Frank Faylen.

Elke. The story of a homely American who marries a beautiful German Countess.

CAST

Elke Sommer, Peter Bonerz, Paul Peterson, Debi Storm.

My Wives Jane. The story of actress Jane Franklin—a woman, married to a doctor, and who also portrays a doctor's wife on a TV serial.

CAST

Jane Franklin: Janet Leigh; Nat Franklin: Barry Nelson; Vic Semple: John Dehner.

Shepherd's Flock. The misadventures of an ex-football player turned priest.

CAST

Jack Shepherd: Kenneth Mars; Abby Scofield: Jill Jaress; Dr. Hewitt: Don Ameche.

THE CBS COMEDY PLAYHOUSE— 30 minutes—CBS—August 1, 1971 - September 5, 1971.

CBS MOVIES

Movies. Theatrical releases.

Titles:

THE CBS SUNDAY NIGHT MOVIE —2 hours—September 19, 1971 - August 27, 1972.

THE CBS THURSDAY NIGHT MOVIE—2 hours—September 16, 1965 - November 27, 1975.

THE CBS FRIDAY NIGHT MOVIE— 2 hours—September 17, 1965 - September 10, 1971. Returned: September 15, 1972.

THE CBS LATE MOVIE—Times approximate depending upon the feature: one hour, thirty-five minutes, to two hours, thirty minutes. Premiered: February 14, 1972.

THE CBS NEWCOMERS

Variety. Showcased: Undiscovered professional talent.

Host: Dave Garroway.

Regulars: Rodney Winfield, Joey Garya, Cynthia Clawson, David Arlen, Paul Perez, Rex Allen, Jr., Gay Perkins, Peggy Sears, The Good Humor Company, The Californians.

Orchestra: Nelson Riddle.

THE CBS NEWCOMERS—60 minutes —CBS—July 12, 1971 - September 6, 1971. 13 tapes.

THE CBS WEDNESDAY NIGHT MOVIE

Theatrical and made-for-television feature films. Listed are examples of the films produced especially for television. See "CBS Movies" for additional information on the network's film series.

Cage Without a Key (1975). The story of Valerie Smith, an innocent teenage girl who is mistakingly convicted of a murder and sent to a girls' penal institution. Her experiences are dramatized.

CAST

Valerie Smith: Susan Dey; Ben Holian: Michael Brandon; Joleen: Anne Bloom; Tommy: Jonelle Allen; Buddy: Sam Bottoms; Betty: Karen Carlson; Angel: Edith Diaz.

The Amazing Howard Hughes. A 1977 TV movie that traces the life and times of the mysterious billionaire.

CAST

Howard Hughes: Tommy Lee Jones; Dietrich Thomas: Ed Flanders; Katherine Hepburn: Tovah Feldshuh; Billie Dove: Lee Russell; Jane Russell: Marla Carlis.

Helter Skelter (1976). The film traces the trial of Charles Manson and three women accused of the bizarre 1969 Tate-La Bianca murders.

CAST

Vincent Bugliosi: George DiCenzo; Charles Manson: Steve Railsback; Susan Atkins: Nancy Wolfe; Linda: Marilyn Burns; Patricia: Christina Hart.

THE CBS WEDNESDAY NIGHT MOVIE—2 hours—CBS—July 21, 1976 - September 15, 1976; Returned— Premiered: November 11, 1976.

CELANESE THEATRE

Anthology. Dramatic presentations.

Producer: Burke Crotly, Alex Segal.

Director: Alex Segal.

Sponsor: The Celanese Corp.

Included:

Saturday's Children. The story revolves around the problems that befall a middle-class family.

Starring: Mickey Rooney.

I Am Still Alive. The story of a young author who becomes a hero on false pretenses.

Starring: Donald Woods, Judy Parrish, Jack Hartley.

Unfinished Business. The story of a man who is allowed to return to earth after his death to resume his normal existence.

Starring: Dane Clark, Ann Rutherford, Alan Mowbray.

CELANESE THEATRE—30 minutes—ABC 1951.

CELEBRITY BILLIARDS

Game. Famed hustler Minnesota Fats vs. a guest celebrity, the challenger. Various games of billiards are played. Celebrities donate their winnings to charity.

Host: Rudolph Wanderone, Jr. (Minnesota Fats).

CELEBRITY BILLIARDS—30 minutes—Syndicated 1967. 39 tapes.

CELEBRITY BOWLING

Game. Four celebrities, divided into two teams of two, play for selected studio audience members. A game based on a ten-frame score wherein the best ball doubles. Two alleys are used. The members of one team each stand on one lane. The player on Lane one bowls first. If a strike is not achieved (which would end the frame and score twenty points), his or her partner then bowls. If, again, a strike is not achieved, the player first to bowl receives a second chance. Taking one of the two lanes, he attempts to acquire the spare. Points are determined accordingly. The second team bowls in the same manner. Gifts are awarded to studio audience members according to team scores.

Host: Jed Allen.

Assistants: Bill Buneta; Bobby Cooper; Dave Davis.

Announcer: Jed Allen.

Music: Recorded.

CELEBRITY BOWLING—30 minutes —Syndicated 1971.

CELEBRITY CLUB

Variety. Music, songs, dances, and celebrity interviews.

Host: Ray Heatherton.

Hostess: Ellen Madison.

CELEBRITY CLUB—30 minutes— ABC 1956.

CELEBRITY CONCERTS

Musical Variety. Solo performances by celebrity guests.

Appearing: Tom Jones, Vikki Carr, Paul Williams, Anne Murray, Jack Jones.

Music: The Edmonton Orchestra, conducted by Lawrence Holloway and Johnnie Spencer.

Additional Orchestrations: Jimmie Haskell, Sid Feller, Bob Frank.

Executive Producer: Wendell Wilkes.

Producer: Gary Jones, Tommy Banks.

Director: Stanley Dorfman.

CELEBRITY CONCERTS—60 minutes—Syndicated 1976.

THE CELEBRITY GAME

Game. Nine celebrity guests, two competing players. The host reads a yes-or-no type question. The celebrities, by pressing a button, secretly lock in their answers. Contestants, in turn, select a guest and try to guess his or her answer. Each correct prediction awards a player a cash prize.

Host: Carl Reiner.

THE CELEBRITY GAME—30 minutes—CBS—April 5, 1964 - September 13, 1964. Returned: April 8, 1965 - September 9, 1965. 41 tapes.

CELEBRITY PLAYHOUSE

Anthology. Rebroadcasts of dramas that were originally aired via other filmed anthology programs.

CELEBRITY PLAYHOUSE—30 minutes—Syndicated 1956. 39 episodes.

CELEBRITY REVUE

Variety. A daily series featuring interviews with and performances by celebrities.

Hostess: Carole Taylor.

Host: Tommy Banks.

Orchestra: Tommy Banks.

Executive Producer: Jack Rhodes.

Producer: Tommy Banks, Gary Jones.

Director: Stanley Dorfman, Geoff Theobald.

CELEBRITY REVUE—60 minutes— Syndicated 1976.

CELEBRITY SWEEPSTAKES

Game. Players: Six celebrities; two contestants, who each receive twenty dollars betting money; and the studio audience.

Round One: The host asks a general knowledge question; the celebrities write their answers on a card which is electronically screened backstage; the studio audience, through electronic panels before them, vote for the celebrity each feels has the correct answer. When the odds for each celebrity are established, each contestant chooses a celebrity and bets a specified amount of money (twenty, ten, five, or two dollars). If correct, the player's amount is increased in accord with the displayed odds; if incorrect, the bet amount is deducted. Celebrities' answers are tabulated on a tote board.

Round Two: Same play as round one; however, the contestant may bet any amount of his accumulated money. If he guesses correctly, he may bet the amount won on another celebrity. If he is correct again, the cash is doubled; if incorrect, the amount bet is deducted.

Round Three: All or Nothing. The host asks a question; each contestant secretly chooses a celebrity, betting all or nothing on odds determined by the track record of the stars (number of questions missed). The contestants reveal their celebrity choices; the personalities one at a time reveal their answers. Cash is awarded according to the bet.

Host: Jim McKrell.

Announcer: Bill Armstrong.

Music: Stan Worth; Alan Thicke.

Regular Panelists: Carol Wayne, Joey Bishop, Buddy Hackett.

Executive Producer: Burt Sugarman.

Producer: Neil Marshall.

CELEBRITY SWEEPSTAKES—30 minutes—NBC—April 1, 1974 - October 10, 1976. Syndicated first run.

CELEBRITY TENNIS

Game. Background: The West Side Racquet Club in Los Angeles, California. Two competing teams, each composed of two celebrities. Played: A two set doubles match. Teams play for selected spectators who receive prizes according to the final score.

Host: Tony Trabert.

Assisting: Guest Celebrities.

Music: Recorded.

CELEBRITY TENNIS—30 minutes— Syndicated 1973.

CELEBRITY TIME

See title: "Conrad Nagel."

CENTER STAGE

Anthology. Rebroadcasts of dramas that were originally aired via other filmed anthology programs.

CENTER STAGE—30 minutes—ABC —June 1, 1954 - September 21, 1954.

CESAR'S WORLD

Documentary. The lives, work, and customs of people around the world.

Host—Narrator: Cesar Romero.

CESAR'S WORLD—30 minutes—Syndicated 1968.

CHAIN LETTER

Game. Two competing teams, each composed of a celebrity captain and a noncelebrity contestant. The host presents a category topic to the teams. One contestant has to respond with a word suitable to the subject. His or her celebrity partner then has to use the last letter of the word and name another word within the same category. Each player is afforded ten seconds in which to give another word, using his or her partner's word. Failure results in a broken chain and a loss of points. Winners are the highest point scorers.

Host: Jan Murray.

CHAIN LETTER—30 minutes—NBC —July 4, 1966 - October 14, 1966.

THE CHAMBER MUSIC SOCIETY OF LOWER BASIN STREET

Variety. Swing music dedicated to "The Three B'S—Barrelhouse, Boogie-Woogie, and the Blues." Adapted from the radio program of the same title.

Host: Orson Bean.

Vocalist: Martha Lou Harp.

Music: Henry Levine's Dixieland Octet.

THE CHAMBER MUSIC SOCIETY OF LOWER BASIN STREET—30 minutes—ABC—September 14, 1948 - September 22, 1951. NBC—30 minutes—June 15, 1952 - September 1952.

THE CHAMPIONS

Adventure. Background: Geneva, Switzerland—the headquarters of

The Champions. Left to right: Alexandra Bastedo, Stuart Damon, William Gaunt. *Courtesy Independent Television Corporation, an ATV Company.*

Nemesis, a powerful, top-secret organization handling sensitive, difficult international assignments.

Agents Sharron Macready, Craig Stirling, and Richard Barrett are assigned to obtain deadly bacteria specimens from Chinese scientists in Tibet. Their attempt to escape after acquiring the specimens triggers an alarm. Pursued by armed guards, the agents take off in an awaiting plane. The craft, struck by gun fire, crash lands in the forbidding Himalayas.

Found by an old man, the lifeless agents are taken to his world — a lost city inhabited by the survivors of an unknown race. There, they are healed and endowed with super powers — "their mental and physical capacities fused to computer efficiency; their sight, sense and hearing, raised to their highest, futuristic stage of mental and physical growth." Still unconscious, they are returned to the site of the crash.

Later, meeting the old man, Richard learns what has befallen them and promises that he and his friends will keep the secret of the lost city and use their gifts to benefit mankind.

Stories relate the exploits of Sharron Macready, Craig Stirling, and Richard Barrett, The Champions, as they, possessing unique powers, strive to ensure law, order, and justice throughout the world.

CAST
Sharron Macready Alexandra Bastedo

Craig Stirling, the American
    member of the British
    team   Stuart Damon
Richard Barrett   William Gaunt
W.L. Tremayne, the head
    of Nemesis, their
    superior   Anthony Nicholls
Music: Albert Elms; Edwin Astley.

THE CHAMPIONS—60 minutes—NBC—July 11, 1967 — September 12, 1967. Syndicated. An I.T.C. Presentation. 30 episodes (10 off-network; 20 first run).

CHANCE FOR ROMANCE

Human Interest. Three men or women seeking friendship are introduced to three members of the opposite sex with the intent being to spark a romance.

Host: John Cameron Swayze.

CHANCE FOR ROMANCE—30 minutes—ABC—October 13, 1958 - December 12, 1958.

CHANCE OF A LIFETIME

Variety. Showcased: Undiscovered professional talent. Winners, determined through the Old Gold Star Maker, which registers studio audience applause, receive one thousand dollars and a chance of a lifetime — possible discovery.

Hosts: Dennis James; John Reed King.

Regulars: Denise Darcel, Dick Collins, Russell Arms, Liza Palmer.

Orchestra: Bernie Leighton.

Organist: John Gart.

Producer: Robert Jennings.

Director: Charles Harrell, Lou Sposa.

Sponsor: Bendix Products; P. Lorillard.

CHANCE OF A LIFETIME—30 minutes—ABC 1952.

CHAN-ESE WAY

Cooking. The preparation and cooking of various Oriental meals.

Host: Titus Chan, a Hawaiian restaurateur.

CHAN-ESE WAY—30 minutes—PBS—June 4, 1973 - August 27, 1973.

CHANNING

Drama. Background: Channing University. Life in a mythical Midwestern coeducational college as seen through the eyes of Joseph Howe, English professor.

CAST
Joseph Howe	Jason Evers
Dean Fred Baker	Henry Jones

Producer: Jack Laird, Stanley Rubin Jack Guss.

CHANNING—60 minutes—ABC—September 18, 1963 - April 8, 1964. 26 episodes.

CHARADE QUIZ

Game. Charades, submitted by home viewers, are enacted by a stock company. A panel of three has to identify it within ninety seconds. If they are able to, the sender receives ten dollars. If unable, fifteen dollars is awarded.

Host: Bill Slater.

Panelists: Minna Bess Lewis, Herb Polesie, Bob Shepard.

Stock Company: Ellen Fenwick, Sandra Poe, Allan Frank, Richard Seff, Johnny Fester.

CHARADE QUIZ—30 minutes—DuMont 1948.

CHARGE ACCOUNT

Game. Two competing players. Object: To purchase expensive merchandise items through money earned on the program. Contestants choose a packet containing sixteen letters. The host reveals its contents to one player at a time. The players place letters into a block in a manner figured to make the most three and four letter words. Twenty-five dollars is awarded for each four letter word; ten for each three. The winner, the highest cash scorer, is permitted to purchase any previously displayed item. If he hasn't accumulated enough money, he is permitted to continue playing to seek the additional cash to purchase the item sought.

Host: Jan Murray.

Assistants: Maureen Arthur, Morgan Schmitter.

Announcer: Bill Wendell.

Orchestra: Milton DeLugg.

CHARGE ACCOUNT—30 minutes—NBC—September 5, 1960 - September 28, 1962. Also known as "The Jan Murray Show."

THE CHARLES BOYER THEATRE

Anthology. Dramatic presentations.

Host-Frequent Star: Charles Boyer.

Included:

Command. The story of a first mate on a merchant ship who yearns to command a ship of his own.

CAST
Charles Boyer, Richard Hale.

Magic Night. The story of a mild-mannered bookkeeper who embarks on a mad whirl to forget his sorrows.

CAST
Charles Boyer, Joyce Gates.

Wall Of Bamboo. The story of an American intelligence agent who attempts to end the reign of a derelict man who has risen to power in Red China.

CAST
Charles Boyer.

THE CHARLES BOYER THEATRE—30 minutes—Syndicated 1953.

CHARLIE CHAN

See titles: "The Amazing Chan and the Chan Clan"; and "The New Adventures of Charlie Chan."

THE CHARLIE CHAPLIN COMEDY THEATRE

Comedy. Reedited Charlie Chaplin silent films.

Starring: Charlie Chaplin.

Also Cast: Edna Purviance, Bud Jamison, Albert Austin, Leo White, Charles Insley.

THE CHARLIE CHAPLIN COMEDY THEATRE—30 minutes—Syndicated 1966. 26 episodes.

THE CHARLIE FARRELL SHOW

Comedy. Background: Palm Springs, California; the Racquet Club vacation resort for Hollywood personalities. The misadventures of its owner-operator, Charlie Farrell, a retired film actor.

CAST
Charlie Farrell	Himself
Dad Farrell	Charles Winninger
Sherman Hull, the director of the club	Richard Deacon
Rodney Farrell, Charlie's nephew	Jeff Silver
Mrs. Papernow, the housekeeper	Kathryn Card
The Chef	Leo Askin
Doris Mayfield, Charlie's girlfriend	Anna Lee
The newspaper editor	Marie Windsor

THE CHARLIE FARRELL SHOW—30 minutes—CBS—July 2, 1956 - September 24, 1956; August 1, 1960 - September 19, 1960. Syndicated.

CHARLIE'S ANGELS

Crime Drama. Background: Los Angeles, California. The exploits of Sabrina Duncan, Jill Munroe, and Kelly Garrett, three beautiful private detectives, former policewomen, now the employees of Charlie Townsend, the wealthy, never-seen head of Townsend Investigations.

CAST
Sabrina Duncan	Kate Jackson
Jill Munroe	Farrah Fawcett-Majors
Kelly Garrett	Jaclyn Smith
John Bosley, Charlie's attorney and representative for the girls	David Doyle
Kris Munroe, Jill's sister	Cheryl Ladd
Voice of Charlie Townsend	John Forsythe

Linda, the firm
   receptionist   Kim Basinger
                    Linda Oliver

Music: Jack Elliott, Allyn Ferguson.

Executive Producer: Aaron Spelling, Leonard Goldberg.

Producer: Rick Huskey, David Levinson, Barney Rosenzweig.

Director: John Moxey, Richard Lang, Allen Baron, Phil Bondelli, Richard Benedict, George McCowan, Daniel Haller, George Brooks, Cliff Boyle, Georg Stanford Brown.

Program Open:

Charlie: "Once upon a time, there were three girls who went to the police academy . . . and they were each assigned very hazardous duties . . . but I took them away from all that and now they work for me; my name is Charlie."

CHARLIE'S ANGELS—60 minutes—ABC—Premiered: September 22, 1976.

Charlie's Angels. Left to right: Jaclyn Smith, Kate Jackson, Farrah Fawcett-Majors.

Charlie's Angels: Second Season. Jaclyn Smith (left), Kate Jackson (center) and Cheryl Ladd (replaced Farrah Fawcett-Majors; see preceding photo). *Courtesy of the Call-Chronicle Newspapers, Allentown, Pa.*

CHARLIE WILD, PRIVATE DETECTIVE

Crime Drama. Background: New York City. The investigations of private detective Charlie Wild.

CAST

Charlie Wild   John McQuade
                Kevin O'Morrison
Effie Perrine, his
   secretary   Cloris Leachman

Producer: Carlo De'Angelo, Herbert Brodkin.

Director: Leonard Valenta.

Sponsor: Mogen-David wines

CHARLIE WILD, PRIVATE DETECTIVE—30 minutes—CBS—1951 1952.

CHARTER BOAT

See title: "Crunch and Des."

CHASE

Crime Drama. Background: Los Angeles, California. The investigations of Chase, a secret unit of undercover police agents designed to crack the cases that are unable to be broken by homicide, robbery, or burglary.

CAST

Captain Chase Reddick Mitchell Ryan
Sergeant Sam
   MacCray   Wayne Maunder
Officer Steve
   Baker   Michael Richardson
Officer Fred Sing   Brian Fong
Officer Norm Hamilton   Reid Smith
Inspector Frank Dawson Albert Reed
Officer Ed Rice   Gary Crosby
Officer Tom Wilson Graig Gardner

Music: Oliver Nelson.

CHASE—60 minutes—NBC—September 11, 1973 - September 4, 1974. 24 episodes.

THE CHEATERS

Mystery. Background: London, England. The cases of John Hunter, Eastern Insurance Company investigator, as he attempts to expose "The Cheaters," people who attempt to defraud insurance companies with false claims.

CAST

John Hunter   John Ireland
Walter Allen, his
   assistant   Robert Ayres

THE CHEATERS—30 minutes—Syndicated 1960. 39 episodes.

CHECKMATE

Mystery. Background: San Francisco, California. The investigations of Don Corey and Jed Sills, the owner-operators of Checkmate, Incorporated, a private detective organization.

CAST

Don Corey   Anthony George
Jed Sills   Doug McClure
Carl Hyatt, the firm's
   criminologist   Sebastian Cabot
Chris Devlin, a firm
   detective   Jack Betts

Music: Pete Rugolo; Johnny Williams; Morton Stevens.

CHECKMATE—60 minutes—CBS—September 10, 1959 - September 19, 1962. Syndicated. 70 episodes.

CHER

Variety. Music, songs, dances, and comedy sketches.

Hostess: Cher Bono.

Featured: The Tony Charmoli Dancers.

Orchestra: Jimmy Dale.

Additional Orchestrations: Jack Eskew.

Special Musical Material: Earl Brown, Billy Barnes.

Choreography: Anita Mann, Tony Charmoli.

Executive Producer: George Schlatter.

Director: Bill Davis, Art Fisher.

CHER—60 minutes—CBS—February 16, 1975 - January 4, 1976.

THE CHESTERFIELD SUPPER CLUB

See title: "Perry Como."

CHESTER THE PUP

Children. The adventures of Chester the puppy, told via off screen narration and on the air cartoon sketches.

Narrator: Art Whitefield.

Cartoonist: Sid Stone.

Producer: Frank Dyson.

Sponsor: Jason Candies.

CHESTER THE PUP—15 minutes—ABC 1950.

CHEVROLET ON BROADWAY

Musical Variety.
Host: Snooky Lanson.
Featured: The Mello-larks.
Announcer: Bill Wendell.
Orchestra: Hal Hasting.

CHEVROLET ON BROADWAY—15 minutes—NBC—June 1956 - September 1956.

CHEVROLET TELEVISION THEATRE

Anthology. Varying presentations, both comedic and dramatic.
Producer: Fred Coe, Vic McLeod, Owen Davis, Jr.
Director: Gordon Duff, Garry Simpson, Barry Bernard.
Sponsor: Chevrolet.

CHEVROLET TELEVISION THEATRE—30 minutes—NBC 1949. Broadcast in 1948 under the title: "Chevrolet on Broadway."

CHEVY MYSTERY SHOW

Anthology. Rebroadcasts of dramas that were originally aired via other filmed anthology programs.
Host: Walter Slezak.

Included:

Enough Rope. The story revolves around a psychiatrist who plots to murder his wife so he can marry his mistress.

CAST
Roy Flemming: Richard Carlson; Susan: Joan O'Brien; Claire: Barbara Stuart; Lt. Columbo: Bert Freed.

Dark Possession. The story concerns the turmoil faced by a woman who receives a series of poison pen letters accusing her of murdering her husband.

CAST
Charlotte: Diana Lynn; Emily: Anne Seymour; Ann: Marion Ross.

Dead Man's Walk. The story concerns an amnesiac's search for his identity.

CAST
Abel: Robert Culp; Karen: Abby Dalton; Lt. Spear: Bruce Gordon.

CHEVY MYSTERY SHOW—60 min-utes—NBC—May 29, 1960 - September 25, 1960.

THE CHEVY SHOW

Variety. Musical salutes to cities around the country.
Hosts: Janet Blair, John Raitt.
Orchestra: Harry Zimmerman.

THE CHEVY SHOW—60 minutes—NBC—June 7, 1959 - September 20, 1959.

THE CHEVY SHOWROOM

See title: "Andy Williams."

THE CHEVY SUMMER SHOW

Variety. Dinah Shore's summer replacement.
Host: John Raitt, Janet Blair.
Regulars: Edie Adams, Dan Rowan, Dick Martin, Dorothy Kirsten.
Orchestra: Harry Zimmerman.
Sponsor: Chevrolet.

THE CHEVY SUMMER SHOW—60 minutes—NBC—June 22, 1958 - September 28, 1958.

CHEYENNE

Western. Background: The Frontier during the 1860s. The exploits of frontier scout Cheyenne Bodie, a man of Indian descent and learned in both the ways of the White Man and the Cheyenne.
Starring: Clint Walker as Cheyenne Bodie.
Music: Stan Jones; William Lava; Paul Sawtell.
Producer: William T. Orr, Arthur Silver, Burt Dunne.
Note: During the 1958 - '59 season, at a time when Clint Walker was suspended for demanding a larger piece of the action, Warner Brothers, the producers, introduced Ty Hardin as Bronco Layne in an effort to keep Walker in line. Thus, for one year, the "Cheyenne" series starred Ty Hardin as Bronco Layne (from 9-23-58 to 9-8-59). Upon Walker's return in 1959, the "Cheyenne" series continued as did "Bronco," now under its own title (which see).

CHEYENNE—60 minutes—ABC—September 20, 1956 - August 30, 1963. Syndicated. Originally telecast as part of "Warner Brothers Presents." 107 episodes.

CHEZ PAREE REVUE

Musical Variety.
Host: Jim Dimitri.
Regulars: Joyce Sellers, Dave Dursten, The Meadowlarks.

Cheyenne. The original logo as appearing on the Warner Brothers series. Sketched: Clint Walker.

Orchestra: Cee Davidson.

CHEZ PAREE REVUE–30 minutes–
DuMont 1950.

CHICAGOLAND
MYSTERY PLAYERS

Crime Drama. Background: Chicago.
The investigations of police criminologist Jeffrey Hall. Episodes depict his
attempts to solve baffling, bizarre
murders.

CAST
Jeffrey Hall	Gordon Urquhart
Sergeant Holland, his	
assistant	Bob Smith

Also: Ros Twokey, Ervin Charone,
Valerie McEliory, Sidney Breese,
Ilka Diehl.

CHICAGOLAND MYSTERY PLAY-
ERS–30 minutes–DuMont (from
Chicago)–1949-1950. Previously
broadcast locally in Chicago on
WGN-TV from 1947-1949.

THE CHICAGO TEDDY BEARS

Comedy. Background: Chicago during
the 1920s. The clash between rival
nightclub owners Linc McCray and his
mobster cousin Big Nick Marr. Stories
concern Linc's efforts to thwart
Nick's plans to add his establishment
to his list of illegal speakeasies.

CAST
Linc McCray	Dean Jones
Big Nick Marr	Art Metrano
Uncle Latzi, Linc's	
partner	John Banner
Marvin, Linc's	
accountant	Marvin Kaplan
Nick's Mob:	
Duke	Mickey Shaughnessy
Dutch	Huntz Hall
Lefty	Jamie Farr
Julius	Mike Mazurki

THE CHICAGO TEDDY BEARS–30
minutes–CBS–September 17, 1971 -
December 17, 1971. 17 episodes.

CHICO AND THE MAN

Comedy. Background: East Los
Angeles. The story of two men: Ed
Brown, an honest but cynical one-
pump garage owner, and his partner,
Chico Rodriquez, a cheerful young
Chicano (Mexican-American) who fast
talked Ed into taking him on and
letting him live in an old truck parked

in the garage. Episodes depict their
continual bickering, as they, representing different cultures and the generation gap, struggle to survive the
inflation of the seventies.

CAST
Ed Brown	Jack Albertson
Chico Rodriquez	Freddie Prinze
Louie, the garbage	
man	Scatman Crothers
Mondo, Chico's friend	Isaac Ruiz
Rudy, Ed's	
friend	Rodolfo Hoyos
Mabel, the letter	
carrier	Bonnie Boland
Della Rogers, Ed's	
landlord	Della Reese
Reverent Bemis	Ronny Graham

Music: Jose Feliciano.

Executive Producer-Creator: James
Komack.

Producer: Hal Kanter, Michael Morris,
Alan Sacs.

Director: Peter Baldwin, Jack Donohue.

CHICO AND THE MAN–30 minutes
–NBC–Premiered: September 13,
1974.

THE CHICO MARX SHOW

See title: "The College Bowl."

CHILDHOOD

Anthology. A series of five British
dramas, each of which focuses on the
theme of childhood.

Hostess: Ingrid Bergman.

Music: Bill Evans.

Producer: Mike Newell.

Director: James Barbazon.

Included:

Easter Tells Such Dreadful Lies. The
story concerns a nine-year-old girl
who fantasizes that her father is having an affair with a woman other than
her mother.

CAST
Easter: Rosiland McCabe; Harry:
Simon Griffiths; Nancy: Rosemary
Martin.

Baa Baa Black Sheep. An adaptation of Rudyard Kipling's story about
a brother and sister who are left in the
care of an austere woman and her
weak-willed husband.

CAST
Punch: Max Harris; Auntie Rosa:
Eileen McCallum; Uncle Harry: Fred-
die Jones; Judy: Claudia Jessop.

CHILDHOOD–60 minutes–PBS–
February 16, 1977 - March 16, 1977.

THE CHILDREN'S CORNER

Children. Through puppet adventures,
manners, songs, and foreign phrases
are taught.

Puppeteers-Voices: Fred Rogers, Josie
Carey.

Characters: King Friday XIII, the wise
old owl; Daniel S. Tiger, the
tame beast; Henrietta, the cat;
and Grandpere, the skunk.

THE CHILDREN'S CORNER–30
minutes–NBC–August 20, 1955 -
September 10, 1955.

THE CHILDREN'S HOUR

Variety. Performances by child entertainment acts.

Host-Announcer: Ed Herlihy.

Producer: Alice Clements.

Director: Desmond Marquette.

THE CHILDREN'S HOUR–30 minutes–NBC 1949.

CHINA SMITH

Adventure. Background: The Orient.
The story of China Smith, an American soldier of fortune. Episodes depict
his battle against the forces of injustice.

Starring: Dan Duryea as China Smith.

Music: Melvyn Lenard.

CHINA SMITH–30 minutes–Syndicated 1952.

CHIPS

Crime Drama. Background: California.
The experiences of Jon Baker and
Francis "Ponch" Poncherello, mem-
bers of Chips, the California Highway
Patrol.

CAST
Officer Jon Baker	Larry Wilcox
Officer Francis	
Poncherello	Erik Estrada
Sgt. Joe Getraer	Robert Pine

Music: Mike Post, Pete Carpenter,
John Parker.

Music Theme: John Parker.

Music Supervision: Harry Lojewski.

Producer: Rick Rosner, Ric Randall.

Creator: Rick Rosner.

CHIPS—60 minutes—NBC—Premiered: September 15, 1977.

CHOOSE UP SIDES

Children's Game. Two competing teams, the Cowboy and the Space Ranger (later: the Bronco Buster and the Space Pilot). Object: For one team to out perform the other in game contests. Prizes are awarded with the success of completed stunts.

Hosts: Dean Miller (CBS); Gene Rayburn (NBC).

CHOOSE UP SIDES—30 minutes—CBS—1953-1954; 30 minutes—NBC—1954-1955.

CHOPPER ONE

Crime Drama. Background: California. The story of West California Police Department (W.C.P.D.) officers Gil Foley and Don Burdick, the helicopter pilots of Chopper One. Episodes depict their attempts to assist patrol-car officers.

CAST
Officer Don Burdick   Jim McMullan
Officer Gil Foley   Dirk Benedict
Captain Ted McKeegan   Ted Hartley
Mitch, the copter
  mechanic   Lou Frizzell

Music: Dominic Frontiere.

Executive Producer: Aaron Spelling, Leonard Spelling.

Producer: Ron Austin, James Buchanan.

CHOPPER ONE—30 minutes—ABC—January 17, 1974 - July 11, 1974. 13 episodes.

CHUCK ASHMAN'S AMERICAN FREEWAY

Talk-Variety.

Host: Chuck Ashman.

Showgirls: Jean Carol Lopez, Sue Darty (from the Casino de Paris Club in Las Vegas).

Announcer: Jay Stewart.

Orchestra: Earl Green.

CHUCK ASHMAN'S AMERICAN FREEWAY—90 minutes—Syndicated 1975.

THE CHUCKLE HEADS

Comedy. Reedited silent films of the 1920s.

Starring: Snub Pollard, Ben Turpin, Poodles Hannaford.

THE CHUCKLEHEADS—15 minutes—Syndicated 1963.

CIMARRON CITY

Western. Background: Cimarron City, Oklahoma during the 1880s. Events in the growth of the city as seen through the eyes of Matthew Rockford, its first citizen, then mayor, now a benevolent cattle baron.

CAST
Matthew
  Rockford   George Montgomery
Beth Purcell,
  the owner of
  the boarding
  house   Audrey Totter
Lane Temple, the town
  blacksmith   John Smith

Narrator: George Montgomery.

CIMARRON CITY—30 minutes—NBC—September 27, 1958 - September 26, 1959. Syndicated. 26 episodes.

CIMARRON STRIP

Western. Background: Cimarron City, Oklahoma during the 1880s. The story of United States Marshal Jim Crown and his attempts to settle the question of the Cimarron Strip—land over which a range war is pending between settlers and cattlemen.

CAST
Marshal Jim Crown   Stuart Whitman
Dulcey Coopersmith, the
  operator of the Hotel
  Coffee Shop   Jill Townsend
Francis Wilde, a
  photographer   Randy Boone
MacGregor, Crown's
  Deputy   Percy Herbert

CIMARRON STRIP—90 minutes—CBS—September 7, 1967 - September 19, 1968. Rebroadcasts (CBS): July 20, 1971 - September 7, 1971. 26 episodes.

CIRCLE

Musical Variety.

Host: Lonnie Sattin.

Hostess: Barbara McNair.

Orchestra: Richard Hayman; Richard Wess.

CIRCLE—30 minutes—Syndicated 1960-1961. Withdrawn.

CIRCLE OF FEAR

Anthology. Tales of the supernatural. A spin-off from "Ghost Story."

Music: Billy Goldenberg.

Included:

Death's Head. After a man is murdered by his wife and her lover, he returns as a moth to seek revenge.

CAST
Carol: Janet Leigh; Larry: Rory Calhoun; Steve: Gene Nelson.

Graveyard Shift. Background: Fillmore Studios, a one-time production center for horror films, now closed and for sale. A couple, Fred Colby, the studio guard, and his pregnant wife, Linda, are haunted by the spirits of varied celluloid fiends seeking immortality by possessing Linda's unborn child. The story relates Fred's attempts to save Linda and the child by burning the films.

CAST
Linda Colby: Patty Duke Astin; Fred Colby: John Astin; Johnny Horne: Joe Renteria; J.B. Fillmore: William Castle.

Legion Of Deamons. A clique of devil worshipers attempt to obtain a new member for the purposes of a sacrifice.

CAST
Beth: Shirley Knight Hopkins; Keith: John Cypher; Janet: Kathryn Hayes; Mary: Neva Patterson; Dana: Bridget Hanley.

Spare Parts. The story of a doctor who returns from the dead to seek revenge through the hands, eyes, and vocal chords donated to others.

CAST
Ellen Pritcherd: Susan Oliver; Dr. Stephen Crosley: Rick Lenz; Chuck: Christopher Connelly; Georgia Grant: Barbara Stuart.

CIRCLE OF FEAR—60 minutes—NBC—January 5, 1973 - June 22, 1973.

CIRCLE THEATRE

See title: "Armstrong Circle Theatre."

CIRCUS

Variety. Various European circus variety acts are showcased.

Host-Narrator: Bert Parks.

Music: Performed by the various circus orchestras.

CIRCUS—30 minutes—Syndicated 1971.

Circus Boy. Mickey Braddock as Corky, atop Bimbo the elephant. © *Screen Gems.*

CIRCUS BOY

Adventure. Background: The Frontier during the latter half of the nineteenth century. After purchasing a bankrupt circus, Big Tim Champion discovers and unofficially adopts Corky, an orphaned and homeless boy whose parents were killed in a tragic high-wire act. Stories concern the struggles endured by the traveling one-ring Champion Circus, and the adventures of Corky, water boy to Bimbo the elephant.

CAST
Big Tim Champion   Robert Lowery
Joey the Clown   Noah Beery, Jr.
Corky   Mickey Braddock
Pete, the canvassman   Guin "Big Boy" Williams
Circus Jack, Corky's
    friend   Andy Clyde
Producer: Norman Blackburn, Herbert B. Leonard.

CIRCUS BOY—30 minutes—NBC—September 23, 1956 - September 8, 1957; ABC—30 minutes—September 19, 1957 - September 11, 1958. Syndicated. 49 episodes.

THE CISCO KID

Western. Background: The territory of New Mexico during the 1890s. The exploits of "The Robin Hood of the Old West," The Cisco Kid and his partner, Pancho. The first television series to be filmed in color. Based on the character created by O'Henry.

CAST
The Cisco Kid   Duncan Renaldo
Pancho   Leo Carillo
Cisco's horse: Diablo.
Pancho's horse: Loco.
Music: Albert Glasser.
Program Open:
Announcer (under music): "Here's adventure . . . Here's romance . . . Here's O' Henry's famous Robin Hood of the Old West, the Cisco Kid" (music continues, then fades out).

THE CISCO KID—30 minutes—Syndicated 1951. 156 episodes.

CITIZEN SOLDIER

See title: "The Big Attack."

CITY ASSIGNMENT

See title: "Big Town."

CITY DETECTIVE

Crime Drama. Background: New York City. The investigations of Police Lieutenant Bart Grant.

Starring: Rod Cameron as Bart Grant.

CITY DETECTIVE—30 minutes—Syndicated 1953. 65 episodes.

CITY HOSPITAL

Drama. Background: New York's City Hospital. The infinite problems faced by a doctor in a large city.

Starring: Melville Ruick as Dr. Barton Crane.

Announcer: John Cannon.

Producer: Wendy Sanford, Walter Selden.

Sponsor: Carter Products.

CITY HOSPITAL—30 minutes—ABC—April 19, 1951 - November 3, 1951.

CITY OF ANGELS

Crime Drama. Background: Los Angeles, California during the 1930s. The investigations of Jake Axminster, a hard-boiled private detective. (The title is derived from the fact that at the time L.A. was one of the least corrupt cities.)

CAST
Jake Axminster   Wayne Rogers
Marsha, his friend,
    who operates an
    answering service for
    call girls   Elaine Joyce
Lieutenant Quint   Clifton James
Lester, Jake's
    informant   Timmie Rogers
Michael Brimm, Jake's
    attorney   Philip Sterling
Music: Nelson Riddle, Hal Mooney.
Executive Producer: Jo Swerling, Jr.
Producer: Roy Huggins.
Director: Don Medford, Sigmund Neufeld, Jr., Douglas Heyes, Robert Douglas, Barry Shear.
Creator: Stephen J. Cannell, Roy Huggins.

CITY OF ANGELS—60 minutes—NBC—February 3, 1976 - August 24, 1976.

CIVILIZATION

Documentary. The history of Western Man from the fall of the Roman Empire to the twentieth century.

Host-Narrator: Kenneth Clark.

Chapters:
1. "The Frozen World." An examination of the Dark Ages.
2. "The Great Thaw." A survey of the twelfth century.
3. "Romance and Reality." France and Italy during the Middle Ages.
4. "Man, The Measure of All Things." France during the Renaissance period (the fifteenth century).
5. "A World of Giants and Heroes." Sixteenth-century Italy.
6. "Protest and Communication." The effect of the Renaissance scholars.
7. "Grandeur and Obedience." Rome at the time of the Protestant Reformation.
8. "The Light of Experience." Seventeenth-century inventions.
9. "The Pursuit of Happiness." A study of the music of the eighteenth century.
10. "The Smile of Reason." The Enlightment period.
11. "The Worship of Nature." The

Romantic movement in eighteenth century France.
12. "The Fallacies of Hope." The Romantic movement during the nineteenth century.
13. "Heroic Materalism." A two-hundred-year survey of Europe since the Industrial Revolution.

CIVILZATION—60 minutes—PBS—October 3, 1971 - December 26, 1971.

CLASSIC THEATRE

Anthology. A series of British-produced period dramas.

Music: George Hall.

Producer: Cedric Messina.

Director: Michael Elliott.

Included:

Macbeth. William Shakespeare's story of an eleventh-century Scottish Nobleman who yearns to become the king.

CAST
Macbeth: Eric Porter; Lady Macbeth: Janet Suzman; Malcolm: John Alderton; Duncan: Michael Goodlife; Lady Macduff: Rowena Cooper.

Edward II. Christopher Marlowe's Elizabethan tragedy about a misfit king who ruled England from 1307 to 1327.

CAST
King Edward: Ian McKellen; Young Mortimer: Timothy West; Queen Isabella: Diane Fletcher.

She Stoops To Conquer. Oliver Goldsmith's 1773 comedy about a young gentleman whose timidity around upperclass women forces a genteel girl to resort to disguises to win his affections.

CAST
Kate Hardcastle: Juliet Mills; Mr. Hardcastle: Ralph Richardson; Marlow: Tom Courtenay.

CLASSIC THEATRE—2 hours—PBS—September 27, 1975 - December 20, 1975. 13 programs.

CLAUDIA: THE STORY OF A MARRIAGE

Comedy-Drama. Background: New York City. The trials and tribulations of the Naughtons: David, an architect, and his naive eighteen-year-old wife, Claudia. Stories depict Claudia's struggles to "cut the apron strings" that bind her to her mother and adjust to marriage.

CAST
Claudia Naughton	Joan McCracken
David Naughton	Hugh Riley
Mrs. Brown, Claudia's Mother	Margaret Wycherly

CLAUDIA: THE STORY OF A MARRIAGE—30 minutes—NBC—January 6, 1952 - March 30, 1952.

CLEAR HORIZON

Serial. Background: The Cape Canaveral Space Center in Florida. Stories dramatize the problems faced by the first Cape Canaveral astronauts and their courageous wives. Episodes focus on the experiences of Roy Selby, a Signal Corps officer, and his wife, Ann.

CAST
Roy Selby	Edward Kemmer
Ann Selby	Phyllis Avery
Nora	Lee Meriwether
The Newspaperman	Richard Coogan

Also: Jimmy Carter, Rusty Lane, Eve McVeagh, Ted Knight, Mary Jackson, Denise Alexander, Grace Albertson, Michael Cox.

CLEAR HORIZON—30 minutes—CBS—July 11, 1960 - March 10, 1961. Returned (CBS): March 8, 1962 - June 11, 1962.

THE CLIFF EDWARDS SHOW

Variety.

Host: Cliff Edwards.

Featured: Eddie Fellows.

Music: The Tony Mottola Trio.

Producer-Director: Franklin Heller.

THE CLIFF EDWARDS SHOW—15 minutes—CBS 1949.

THE CLIFFWOOD AVENUE KIDS

Comedy. The misadventures of a group of preteen children, members of the Cliffwood Avenue Club, as they stumble upon and seek to solve crimes.

CAST
Poindexter	Himself
Samwich	J. Brennan Smith
Melora	Melora Hardin
Jeremy	Jeremy Lawrence
Sheldon	Kristopher Marquis
Andre	Andre Broadin
Police Sgt. Pat O'Dennis	Dennis Patrick

Music: Recorded.

Producer-Director: Win Opie.

THE CLIFFWOOD AVENUE KIDS—30 minutes—Syndicated 1977.

CLIMAX

Anthology. Suspense presentations.

Host: William Lundigan.

Hostess: Mary Costa.

Producer: Eva Wolass, Bretaigne Windlust.

Included:

A Leaf Out of the Book. The story of two women: one successful, the other ambitious.

CAST
Diana Lynn, Sylvia Sidney.

The Box of Chocolates. A much hated newspaper columnist attempts to clear himself of a murder charge.

CAST
Robert Preston, Pat O'Brien, Vanessa Brown.

The Chinese Game. After playing a Chinese game that he purchased in a curio shop, a newspaper columnist sees himself murdering his wife for another woman. He believes that the vision is a bad case of imagination and forgets about it. The story concerns the conflict and terror that enters his life when several days later he meets the woman he envisioned.

CAST
Macdonald Carey, Rita Moreno, Constance Ford, Anna May Wong.

The 13th Chair. The story of a man who attempts to find the murderer of his friend through a seance.

CAST
Ethel Barrymore, Dennis O'Keefe.

CLIMAX—60 minutes—CBS—October 7, 1954 - June 26, 1958.

CLOAK OF MYSTERY

Anthology. Rebroadcasts of dramas that were originally aired via "The Alcoa Theatre" and . "The General Electric Theatre."

Included:

The Fugitive Eye. The story concerns a man's attempts to clear himself of a false murder charge.

CAST
Charlton Heston, Leo G. Carroll; Jennifer Raine.

Pattern Of Guilt. The story centers on a reporter as he attempts to uncover the murderer of several spinsters.

CAST
Ray Milland, Myron McCormick, Lucy Prentiss, Joanna Moore.

Villa Portofino. By incorporating her late husband's three best friends, a woman attempts to uncover the mysterious circumstances surrounding his death.

CAST
Janet Lake, Gene Blakely, Bobby Van.

CLOAK OF MYSTERY—60 minutes—NBC—May 11, 1965 - August 10, 1965.

THE CLOCK

Anthology. Stories of people who attempt to overcome sudden crises before time runs out. Based on the radio program of the same title.

Producer: William Spier, Herbert Swope, Jr., Lawrence Schwab, Jr., Ernest Walling.

Director: William Spier, Fred Coe, Herbert Swope, Jr.

Sponsor: Emerson; Rhodes Pharmical; Lever Brothers.

THE CLOCK—30 minutes—CBS 1949; 30 minutes—NBC 1950.

CLUB CELEBRITY

Musical Variety.
Hostess: Ginny Simms.
Regulars: Jill Richards, Greg Mitchell, Bette Bligh, The Tune Tailors.
Announcer: Harry Von Zell.
Orchestra: Dick Peterson.

CLUB CELEBRITY—30 minutes—NBC 1950.

CLUB EMBASSY

See title: "Bob and Ray."

CLUB OASIS

Variety. A bi-weekly series that takes viewers directly inside a nightclub for one-man shows (e.g., Van Johnson on 9-28-58; Kay Starr, 10-12-58; Jimmy Durante, 11-9-58; Dean Martin, 11-23-58). On June 7, 1958, it became the weekly Spike Jones "Club Oasis" Show. See title: "Spike Jones," *Club Oasis* segment for more information.

CLUB OASIS—30 minutes—NBC—September 28, 1957 - May 24, 1958.

CLUB 60

Musical Variety.
Hosts: Don Sherwood, Dennis James, Howard Miller.
Regulars: Mike Douglas, Nancy Wright, The Mello-Larks.
Orchestra: Joseph Gallicchio.

CLUB 60—60 minutes—NBC 1957.

THE CLUE CLUB

Animated Cartoon. The investigations of Pepper, Larry, Dotty, and D.D., four professional teenage detectives who comprise the Clue Club. Assisted by two talking, cowardly bloodhounds, Woofer and Wimper, they strive to solve baffling crimes.

Characters' Voices

Pepper	Patricia Stich
Larry	David Jolliffe
D.D.	Bob Hastings
Dotty	Tara Talboy
Woofer	Paul Winchell
Sheriff Bagley	John Stephenson

Additional Voices: Joan Gerber, Julie McWhirter, Janet Waldo, Vic Perrin, Virginia Gregg.

Music: Hoyt Curtin.

Executive Producer: William Hanna, Joseph Barbera.

Director: Charles A. Nichols.

THE CLUE CLUB—25 minutes—CBS—Premiered: August 14, 1976.

CLUTCH CARGO

Animated Cartoon. The adventures of world traveler Clutch Cargo, and his companions, Spinner, a young boy, and his dog, Paddlefoot.
Music: Paul Horn.

CLUTCH CARGO—05 minutes—Syndicated 1959. 260 episodes.

CODE R

Adventure. Background: Channel Island, a small, coastal community off Southern California, the headquarters of Emergency Services, a specialized organization combining police, fire, and ocean rescue departments into the Code R rescue forces. Stories dramatize the work of Walt Robinson, the police chief, Rick Wilson, the fire chief, and George Baker, the chief lifeguard, as they seek to protect their island community.

CAST
Walt Robinson	Tom Simcox
Rick Wilson	James Houghton
George Baker	Martin Kove
Suzy, the Emergency Services secretary	Susanne Reed
Ted Milbank, the deputy	Ben Davidson
Harry, the owner of the Lighthouse Bar	W.T. Zacha
Bobby Robinson, Walt's son	Robbie Rundle
Doctor Sutherland	Tom Williams
Barbara Robinson, Walt's wife	Joan Freeman

Music: Lee Holdridge.

Producer-Creator: Edwin Self.

Director: Richard Benedict, Bruce Kessler, George Fenady, Andrew McLaglen, Phil Bondelli, Leslie H. Martinson, Alf Kjellin.

CODE R—60 minutes—CBS—January 21, 1977 - June 10, 1977.

CODE THREE

Crime Drama. Background: Lo. Angeles County, California. The investigations of Assistant Sheriff Barrett into crimes designated Code Three (murder, robbery, kidnapping). Based on actual case files.

CAST
Sheriff Barrett	Richard Travis
Sgt. Murchison	Denver Pyle
Lt. Bill Hollis	Fred Wynn

Appearing: Eugene W. Bissculuce, the

Sheriff of Los Angeles County at the time of filming.

CODE THREE—30 minutes—Syndicated 1957. 39 episodes.

COKE TIME

See title: "Eddie Fisher."

THE COLGATE COMEDY HOUR

Variety. Programs tailored to the talents of its guest hosts.

Producer: Sam Fuller, Ernest D. Glucksman, Jack Hurdle, Manning Ostroff, Charles Friedman.

Director: Ernest D. Glucksman, Jack Hurdle, Charles Friedman.

Sponsor: Colgate.

Included:

The Eddie Cantor Show.
Host: Eddie Cantor.
Guests: Yma Sumac, Lew Hearn, Joseph Buloff, Jack Albertson, Howard Smith, Bob Sari, Fay MacKenzie, Tommy Wonder, Danny Daniells, Helen Wood, Janet Gayelord, Charlotte Fayni, Lou Wills, Val Buttegnat.
Orchestra: Al Goodman.

The Dean Martin, Jerry Lewis Show.
Hosts: Dean Martin, Jerry Lewis.
Guest: Rosemary Clooney.
Orchestra: Dick Stabile.

The Abbott And Costello Show.
Hosts: Bud Abbott, Lou Costello.
Guests: Sid Fields, Joe Kirk, Bobby Barbor, Joan Shawlee.
Orchestra: Al Goodman.

The Donald O'Connor Show.
Host: Donald O'Connor.
Guests: Ben Blue, Lisa Kirk, Sid Miller, Andy Clyde, Chester Conklin.
Orchestra: Al Goodman.

The Judy Canova Show.
Hostess: Judy Canova.
Guests: Cesar Romero, Zsa Zsa Gabor, Hans Conried, Liberace.
Orchestra: Charles Dent.

THE COLGATE COMEDY HOUR—60 minutes—NBC—September 10, 1950 - December 25, 1955. In May of 1967, NBC presented a revival, titled same, with: Edie Adams, Kay Ballard, Carl Reiner, Mel Brooks, Phyllis Diller, Nanette Fabray, Bob Newhart, Nipsey Russell, and Dan Rowan and Dick Martin.

COLGATE THEATRE

A series of anthology dramas broadcast on NBC in 1949. Produced by Melville Burke and Charles Russell.

COLGATE THEATRE

Anthology. Rebroadcasts of dramas that were originally aired via other filmed anthology programs.

COLGATE THEATRE—30 minutes—NBC 1958.

COLISEUM

Circus Variety Acts.
Hosting: Guest Personalities.
Performers: Guests (Show Business).
Orchestra: Bernie Green

COLISEUM—60 minutes—CBS—January 26, 1967 - June 1, 1967.

THE COLLEGE BOWL

Variety. Background: The campus soda fountain, "The College Bowl," of a small-town university. Programs spotlight the talent performances of its youthful clientele.

Host: The College Bowl Proprietor: Chico Marx.
Clientele: Andy Williams, Paula Huston, Jimmy Brock, Evelyn Ward, Tommy Morton, Lee Lindsey, Stanley Prager, Barbara Ruick, Joan Holloway, Kenny Buffert, Vickie Barrett.
Producer: Martin Gosch.
Director: Marshall Diskin.

THE COLLEGE BOWL—30 minutes—ABC—October 2, 1950 - March 26, 1951.

COLONEL BLEEP

Animated Cartoon. Era: The universe a million light years from the present. An evil scientist, Dr. Destructo, "the master criminal of the universe," escapes from the planet Pheutora, and retreats to the distant planet Pluto, where he establishes a base.

Colonel Bleep, of the Pheutora Police Department and his Space Deputies, Squeak the Puppet and Scratch the Caveman, are assigned to capture him. Episodes relate their attempts to protect the universe from his power-mad plan to conquer it. Characters are nonspeaking.

Colonel Bleep's ship: The *Wonder Rocket.*

COLONEL BLEEP—06 minutes—Syndicated 1957.

COLONEL FLACK

Comedy. The story of two men, modern-day Robin Hoods — Humphrey Flack, a retired colonel, and his companion, Uthas P. (Patsy) Garvey. With larceny in their minds and charity in their hearts, they travel throughout the world and, through imaginative deceptions, con the confidence men in their attempt to assist the needy.

CAST
Colonel Humphrey
  Flack   Alan Mowbray
Uthas P. Garvey   Frank Jenks
Versions:
DuMont (Live)—30 minutes—1953-1954.
Syndicated (Filmed)—30 minutes—1958.

Also titled: "Colonel Humphrey Flack;" "Fabulous Fraud;" "The Imposter."

COLONEL MARCH OF SCOTLAND YARD

Mystery. Background: London, England. The investigations of Colonel March, an intrepid one-eye (a black patch covers the left eye) British Inspector, the head of Department D-3, the Office of Queens Complaints of the New Scotland Yard. Stories depict his attempts to solve the sinister acts of deranged criminals.
Starring: Boris Karloff as Colonel March.

COLONEL MARCH OF SCOTLAND YARD—30 minutes—Syndicated 1957.

COLONEL STOOPNAGLE'S STOOP

Comedy. Background: The front porch of Colonel Lemuel Q. Stoopnagle's home. Basis: The exchange of conversation between he and those friends and neighbors who just happen to pass by.

CAST

Colonel Lemuel Q.
  Stoopnagle   F. Chase Taylor
Friends and neighbors: Dave Ballard, Richard Collier, Gregg Mason, Eda Heinemann.

Producer: Arthur Moore.

Director: Charles Polacheck.

COLONEL STOOPNAGLE'S STOOP –30 minutes–CBS 1948.

THE COLORFUL WORLD OF MUSIC

Children. Interpretations of musical masterpieces by the Podrecca Piccolli Theatre Marionettes.

THE COLORFUL WORLD OF MUSIC–05 minutes–Syndicated 1964.

COLT .45

Western. Background: The Frontier during the 1880s. The story of Chris Colt, a United States government agent who poses as a salesman for the Colt .45 Repeater. Episodes depict his attempts to ensure law and order.

CAST

Christopher Colt   Wayde Preston
Sam Colt, Jr. (replaced
  Preston)   Donald May

Music: Hal Hopper; Douglas Heyes; Paul Sawtell.

Producer: William T. Orr, Harry Tateleman, Roy Huggins, Cedric Francis, Joseph Hoffman.

COLT .45–30 minutes–ABC– October 18, 1957 - October 10, 1962. Syndicated. 67 episodes.

COLUMBO

See title: "NBC Mystery Movie," *Columbo* segment.

COMBAT

Drama. Background: Europe during

World War Two. The saga of the United States Infantry, Second Platoon, K Company, followed from its D-Day landing to victory one year after.

CAST

Lt. Gil Hanley   Rick Jason
Sgt. Chip Saunders   Vic Morrow
"Wildman" Kirby   Jack Hogan
Caje   Pierre Jalbert
Littlejohn   Dick Peabody
Nelson   Tom Lowell
Doc   Conlan Carter
                        Steve Rogers
Braddock   Shecky Greene
McCall   William Bryant

Music: Leonard Rosenman.

Producer: Robert Altman, Gene Levitt, William Self, Selig Seligman.

COMBAT–60 minutes–ABC– October 2, 1962 - August 29, 1967. Syndicated. 152 episodes.

COMBAT SERGEANT

Drama. Background: North Africa during its campaign of World War Two. Detailed: The Allied Forces battle against Rommel's Afrika Korps.

CAST

Sergeant Nelson   Michael Thomas
General Harrison   Cliff Clark
Corporal Murphy   Frank Marlowe
Corporal Harbin   Mara Corday

COMBAT SERGEANT–30 minutes– ABC–June 29, 1956 - September 1956. Syndicated.

THE COMEBACK STORY

Interview. The lives of one-time famous personalities are recalled. The program relates the incidents that ended an individual's career and his attempt to make a comeback. The past is related through interviews with frineds of the subject and filmed highlights of his career; the present through interviews with the subject.

Host: George Jessel.

THE COMEBACK STORY–30 minutes–ABC–October 2, 1953 - February 5, 1954.

COMEDY PLAYHOUSE

Anthology. Rebroadcasts of comedy episodes that were originally aired via other filmed anthology programs.

COMEDY PLAYHOUSE–30 minutes –ABC–June 1958 - September 1958.

COMEDY PREVIEW

Pilot Films. Proposed comedy series for the 1970-1971 season.

The telecast order of the only three episodes aired:

Prudence And The Chief. The story of a missionary as she attempts to establish a school on an Indian Reservation.

CAST

Sally Ann Howes, Rick Jason, Cathryn Givney.

Three For Tahiti. The misadventures of three young men as they attempt to establish a life in a Tahitian paradise.

CAST

Robert Hogan, Bob Einstein, Steve Franken.

The Murdocks And The McClays. The feud that erupts between two hillbilly families when their offspring fall in love and want to be married against parental objections.

CAST

Dub Taylor, Kathy Davis, Noah Beery, Jr., Judy Canova.

COMEDY PREVIEW–30 minutes– ABC–August 19, 1970 - September 2, 1970.

COMEDY SPOT

Pilot Films. Proposed comedy series for the 1960-1961 season.

Host: Art Gilmore.

Included:

Head Of The Family. Pilot film for "The Dick Van Dyke Show." When his son Richie feels that his father is a failure because he is only the head writer of a television show, Rob Petrie takes him to the office to show him that is is as important as his friends' fathers.

CAST

Rob Petrie: Carl Reiner; Laura Petrie: Barbara Britton; Richie Petrie: Gary Morgan; Buddy Sorrell: Morty Gunty; Sally Rogers: Sylvia Miles; Alan Sturdy (later to become Alan Brady): Jack Wakefield.

The Incredible Jewel Robbery. The misadventures of two inexperienced safecrackers.

CAST

Harry: Harpo Marx; Nick: Chico Marx.

Welcome To Washington. The misadventures of Elizabeth Harper, a newly elected congresswoman.

CAST

Elizabeth Harper: Claudette Colbert; Paul Harper: Leif Erickson.

Meet The Girls. The story of three girls: Maybelle "the shape" Perkins; Lacey "the face" Sinclair; and Charlotte "the brain" Dunning as they search for fame, fortune, and rich husbands.

CAST

Maybelle: Mamie Van Doren; Lacey: Gale Robbins; Charlotte: Virginia Field.

COMEDY SPOT—30 minutes—CBS—July 19, 1960 - September 20, 1960.

COMEDY SPOT

Pilot Films. Proposed comedy series for the 1962-1963 season.

Included:

For The Love Of Mike. The misadventures of Betty and Mike Stevens, young marrieds.

CAST

Betty Stevens: Shirley Jones; Mike Stevens: Burt Metcalfe.

Life With Virginia. The story of a young girl and her attempts to assist the distressed.

Starring: Candy Moore as Virginia.

The Soft Touch. The story of Ernestine McDougal, the beautiful, but slightly scatterbrained daughter of a loan-company owner. The episode relates her attempts to prove her intuition is better than collateral in determining the recipients of loans.

CAST

Ernestine McDougal: Marie Wilson; Mr. McDougal: Charlie Ruggles.

COMEDY SPOT—30 minutes—CBS—July 3, 1962 - September 18, 1962.

COMEDY SPOTLIGHT

Anthology. Rebroadcasts of comedy episodes that were originally aired via "The General Electric Theatre."

Included:

Miracle At The Opera. The story of a lonely, veteran music teacher who finds great pleasure in the company of his dog, Linda.

Starring: Ed Wynn.

A Blaze Of Glory. The story of a meek plumber who encounters various misadventures when he answers an emergency service call.

Starring: Lou Costello, Jonathan Harris, Lurene Tuttle, Joyce Jameson.

Platinum On The Rocks. The effect of a false robbery charge on an aging ex-vaudevillian comic.

CAST

George Burns, Fred Beir, Milton Frome.

COMEDY SPOTLIGHT—30 minutes—CBS—July 25, 1961 - September 19, 1961.

COMEDY THEATRE

Pilot Films. Proposed comedy series for the 1975 - 1976 season.

Included:

The Cheerleaders. The story concerns the experiences of three high school girls as they attempt to perform embarrasing antics to get into a sorority.

CAST

Snowy: Kathleen Cody; B.J.: Debbie Zipp; Beverly: Teresa Medaris; Margie: Mary Kay Place.

Music: Earle Hagen.

Producer: Jerome Zeitman.

Director: Richard Crenna.

The Bureau. The hectic exploits of a group of bumbling Federal investigators.

CAST

Peter Dovlin: Henry Gibson; Agent Browning: Richard Gilliland; Agent Katie Peterson: Barbara Rhoades.

Music: Peter Matz.

Producer: Gerald Abrahms.

Director: Hy Averback.

Ace. The misadventures of a not-too-bright private detective.

CAST

Edward Ace: Bob Dishy; Gloria Ross; Rae Allen; Mr. Mason: Dick Van Patten.

Music: Patrick Williams.

Producer: Larry White.

Director: Gary Nelson.

COMEDY THEATRE—30 minutes—NBC—July 26, 1976 - August 16, 1976. 4 episodes.

COMEDY TIME

Pilot Films. Proposed comedy series for the 1977-1978 season.

Included:

Daughters. The misadventures that befall a widower as he attempts to cope with his three daughters.

CAST

Dominick: Michael Constantine; Diane: Olivia Barash; Cookie: Judy Landers; Terry: Robin Graves; Aunt Rosa: Julie Bovasso.

Music: George Tipton.

Executive Producer: Paul Junger Witt, Tony Thomas.

Producer: Susan Harris.

Director: Bob Claver.

Look Out World. The story concerns the misadventures of four ambitious young men who work at the Hollywood Auto Bath, a car wash.

CAST

Cannonball: Michael Huddleston; Benny: Justin Lord; Delfi: Bart Braverman; Beau: Steve Doubet.

Music: Tom Scott.

Executive Producer: Perry Lafferty.

Producer: Richard Rosenbloom.

Director: Hy Averback.

The Natural Look. The episode concerns itself with the misadventures that befall the newlywed Harrisons—Bud, a doctor, and Edie, a cosmetics executive.

CAST

Bud Harrison: Bill Bixby; Edie Harrison: Barbara Feldon; Jane: Caren Kaye.

Music: Charles Fox.

Producer: Leonora Thuna.

Director: Robert Moore.

COMEDY TIME—30 minutes—NBC—

July 6, 1977 - July 27, 1977. 4 programs.

COMEDY TONIGHT

Comedy. Various sketches satirizing life.

Host: Robert Klein.

Regulars: Barbara Cason, Peter Boyle, Marty Barris, Bonnie Enten, Judy Graubart, Laura Greene, Jerry Lacey, Madeline Kahn, Lin Lipton, Macintyre Dixon.

COMEDY TONIGHT—60 minutes—CBS—July 5, 1970 - August 23, 1970.

COMMANDO CODY

Adventure. The exploits of Commando Cody, "Sky Marshall of the Universe." Episodes depict his battle against celestial, sinister forces of evil.

CAST

Commando Cody	Judd Holdren
Joan Albright, his assistant	Aline Towne
Ted Richards, his assistant	William Schallert
Retik, the commander of the moon	Greg Grey
Dr. Varney	Peter Brocco
Henderson	Craig Kelly

Producer: Franklin Adreon.

Director: Fred C. Brannon, Harry Keller, Franklin Adreon.

Note: Commando Cody's name: Jeff King.

COMMANDO CODY—30 minutes—NBC—July 16, 1955 - October 8, 1955. 12 episodes.

CONCENTRATION

Game. Two competing players. A large electronic board with thirty numbered, three-sided wedges is displayed on stage. The first player chooses two numbers. The wedges rotate and reveal prizes. If they match, the wedges rotate again and reveal two puzzle parts. The player is then permitted to guess what the puzzle will read (slogan, name, or place). If he is unable, he picks two more numbers.

If the numbers do not match, the wedges return to numbers and his opponent receives a chance.

The player first to identify the puzzle is the winner and receives the prizes accumulated on his side of the board.

Versions:

NBC—30 minutes—August 25, 1958 - March 23, 1973.

Hosts: Hugh Downs; Jack Barry; Art James; Bill Mazer; Ed McMahon; Bob Clayton.

Announcers: Wayne Howell; Art James; Bob Clayton.

Music: Milton DeLugg; Dick Hyman; Milton Kaye; Tony Columbia.

Syndicated—30 minutes—1973.

Host: Jack Narz.

Announcer: Johnny Olsen.

Music: Ed Kalehoff.

CONCERNING MISS MARLOWE

Serial. Background: New York City. The dramatic story of Margaret Marlowe, a middle-aged actress.

CAST

Margaret "Meg" Marlowe	Louise Albritton
Bill Cooke	John Raby
James Gavin	Efrem Zimbalist, Jr.
Marian Cahill	Elaine Rost
Linda Cabot	Sara Burton
Louise Gavin	Jane Seymour
Dot Clayton	Helen Shields
Harry Clayton	John Gibson
Cindy Clayton	Patti Bosworth
Tommy Clayton	Eddie Brian
Hugh Fraser	Lauren Gilbert
Ronald Blake	Bert Thorn
Kit Christie	Chris White
Mrs. McClure	Abby Lewis
Mr. McClure	John Seymour
Celia	Lois Bolton
Jean Guthrie	Barbara Townsend
Adorno	Monty Banks, Jr.
Bojalina	Ross Martin
Jenny	Katherine Raht
Mrs. Nana McClure	Lois Holmes
Mike Donovan	Byron Sanders
Paul Sims	Norman MacKaye
Lt. Hansen	Jim Boles
Bud Gowen	Douglas Taylor
John Moran	Philip Coolidge
Bernie Kanner	Stephen Chase
Mrs. Koester	Leora Thatcher
Lila	Muriel Berkson
The desk clerk	Carlos Montalban
Senor Zaragpza	Don Mayo

Producer: Tom McDermott.

Sponsor: Procter and Gamble.

CONCERNING MISS MARLOWE—15 minutes—CBS—July 5, 1954 - July 1, 1955.

CONFIDENTIAL FILE

Anthology. Dramatizations of newspaper headline stories.

Host-Narrator: Paul V. Coates.

CONFIDENTIAL FILE—30 minutes—Syndicated 1955.

CONFIDENTIAL FOR WOMEN

Serial. Dramatizations of problems faced by women.

Hostess-Narrator: Jane Wyatt.

Consultant: Dr. Theodore Rubin.

CONFIDENTIAL FOR WOMEN—30 minutes—ABC—March 28, 1966 - July 8, 1966.

CONFLICT

See title: "Warner Brothers Presents," *Conflict* segment.

CONGRESSIONAL INVESTIGATOR

Drama. Background: Washington, D.C. The story behind the fifth amendment is dramatized. Episodes depict the activities of a team of U.S. government investigators as they seek to uncover evidence for congressional hearings.

CAST

Investigator	Edward Stroll
Investigator	William Masters
Investigator	Stephen Roberts
Investigator	Marion Collier

CONGRESSIONAL INVESTIGATOR—30 minutes—Syndicated 1959. 39 episodes.

CONRAD NAGEL

Listed: the television programs of actor Conrad Nagel.

Silver Theatre—Anthology Drama--30 minutes—CBS 1948.

Host: Conrad Nagel.

Celebrity Time—Panel Discussion—30 minutes—CBS 1949.

Host: Conrad Nagel.

Panel: Kitty Carlisle, Kyle McDonnell, Herman Hickman, Joe Wilson.

The Conrad Nagel Show—Celebrity Interview—30 minutes—DuMont 1953.

Host: Conrad Nagel.

Hostess: Maxine Barrett.

The Conrad Nagel Theatre—Anthology Drama—30 minutes—DuMont 1955. Young talent discoveries appear with established performers.

Host: Conrad Nagel.

Where Were You?—Celebrity Interview—30 minutes—DuMont 1955. The past lives of celebrities are recalled through films and interviews.

Host: Conrad Nagel.

Tell Us More—Documentary—30 minutes—NBC 1963. See title.

CONTEST CARNIVAL

Children. Performances by aspiring circus performances.

Host: Phil Sheridan.

Regulars: Joanie Coale, Harry Levin, Gene Crane.

Producer: Charles Vanda.

Sponsor: Quaker Oats.

CONTEST CARNIVAL—30 minutes—NBC—January 3, 1954 - December 18, 1955.

THE CONTINENTAL

Women. Setting: A bachelor's apartment — a romantic, candlelit room; a table for two, and a dashing, suave, and sophisticated host. His conversation, directed to the fairer sex, relating humor, poetry, and philosophy, is the focal point of the program.

Host: Renzo Cesana, the Continental.

Music: The Tony Mottola Trio.

Featured: His meeting with couples having their first date.

Additional Music: Ivan Ditmars.

Note: In late 1952, some stations began airing a feminine version of "The Continental" geared to male viewers. Broadcast late at night, and lasting only five minutes, a seductive girl (in New York, for example, Gloria Parker), in a provocative negligee would seduce the male audience—to wish them a good night.

THE CONTINENTAL—30 minutes—ABC—October 11, 1952 - January 6, 1953.

CONTINENTAL SHOWCASE

Variety. Filmed in Munich and featuring the talent of performers throughout the world.

Host: Jim Backus.

Regulars: The Kessler Twins, The Hazy Osterwald Sextet, The Showcase Dancers.

Orchestra: Harry Segers.

CONTINENTAL SHOWCASE—60 minutes—CBS—June 11, 1966 - September 10, 1966.

CONVOY

Drama. Era: World War II. The saga of a convoy of two hundred heavily armed American ships slowly heading toward England. Episodes focus on the experiences of the men in charge: Dan Talbot, commander of the escort destroyer *DD181*, and Ben Foster, captain of the freighter *Flagship*.

CAST

Commander Dan Talbot	John Gavin
Captain Ben Foster	John Larch
Chief Officer Steve Kirkland	Linden Chiles
Lieutenant Ray Glasser	James McMullan
Lieutenant O'Connell	James Callahan

CONVOY—60 minutes—NBC—September 17, 1965 - December 10, 1965. 13 episodes.

COOL McCOOL

An animated cartoon series that deals with the exploits of Cool McCool, a secret agent who has waged a war on crime. 30 minutes—NBC—May 17, 1969 - August 30, 1969.

COOL MILLION

See title: "NBC Wednesday Mystery Movie," *Cool Million* segment.

THE COP AND THE KID

Comedy. Background: Los Angeles, California. The harassed life of Frank Murphy, a tough bachelor police officer with the 6th Division of the L.A.P.D., and the guardian of Lucas Adams, a streetwise youth.

CAST

Officer Frank Murphy	Charles Durning
Lucas Adams	Tierre Turner
Mary Goodhew, the social worker	Sharon Spelman
Mrs. Murphy, Frank's mother	Patsy Kelly
Sgt. Zimmerman, Frank's superior	William Preston

Music: Jerry Fielding; Joe Reisman.

Executive Producer-Creator: Jerry Davis.

Producer: Ben Joeleson, Art Baer.

Lucas's Dog: Killer.

THE COP AND THE KID—30 minutes—NBC—December 4, 1975 - March 4, 1976.

COPTER PATROL

See title: "The Whirlybirds."

THE CORAL JUNGLE

Documentary. Filmed studies of the world beneath the sea.

Host-Narrator: Leonard Nimoy.

Music: Tom Anthony.

Executive Producer: Jack Reilly.

Producer: Richard Perin.

Director: Ben Cropp.

THE CORAL JUNGLE—60 minutes—Syndicated 1976. 8 episodes.

THE CORNER BAR

Comedy. Distinguished by two formats.

Format One:
Background: New York City, 137 Amsterdam Avenue, Manhattan, the address of Grant's Toomb, a restaurant-bar. Stories relate the misadventures of Harry Grant, its owner-operator, as he becomes involved with and struggles to solve staff and clientele problems.

CAST

Harry Grant	Gabriel Dell
Meyer Shapiro, the waiter	Shimen Ruskin
Mary Ann, the waitress	Langhorne Scruggs
Phil Bracken, a client, a henpecked Wall Street executive	Bill Fiore
Peter Panama, a client, a male fashion	

designer   Vincent Schiavelli
Fred Costello, a client, an
   Irish-American cab
   driver   J.J. Barry
Joe, the cook   Joe Keyes

Music: Norman Paris.

THE CORNER BAR—30 minutes—
ABC—June 21, 1972 - August 23,
1972.

Format Two:
Background: New York City, 137
Amsterdam Avenue, Manhattan, the
address of The Corner Bar. The harassed life of its owner-operators, Frank
Flynn, the bartender, and his partner,
Mae, who inherited her share with her
husband's death. Episodes relate their
attempts to solve staff and clientele
problems.

CAST

Mae   Anne Meara
Frank Flynn   Eugene Roche
Meyer Shapiro, the
   waiter   Shimen Ruskin
Fred Costello, a client,·
   a cab driver   J.J. Barry
Phil Bracken, a client, a
   Wall Street
   executive   Bill Fiore
Donald Hooten, a client,
   an actor   Ron Carey

Music: Norman Paris.

THE CORNER BAR—30 minutes—
ABC—August 3, 1973 - September 7,
1973.

CORONADO 9

Crime Drama. Background: San
Diego, California's Coronado Penin-
sula. The investigations of Dan
Adams, a retired naval officer turned
private detective. (Coronado 9: his
telephone exchange).

Starring: Rod Cameron as Dan
   Adams.

CORONADO 9—30 minutes—Syndicated 1960. 39 episodes.

CORONATION STREET

Serial. Background: Weatherfield,
England, the Rovers Bar at Number
Eleven Coronation Street. Stories
dramatize the lives and problems of
the working class Britons who inhabit
it. Coronation Street, a low- and
middle- income neighborhood, is one
of many that developed shortly after
the Coronation of Edward VII in
1902.

CAST

Ena Sharples	Violet Carson
Minni Caldwell	Margot Bryant
Elsie Howard	Patricia Phoenix
Albert Tatlock	Jack Howarth
Ken Barlow	William Roache
Anne Walker	Doris Speed
Dennis Maxwell	William Lucas
Bobby Walker	Kenneth Farrington
Alf Roberts	Bryan Mosley
George Greenwood	Arthur Penlow
Peter Bromley	Jonathan Adams
Ray Langton	Neville Buswall
Hilda Ogden	Jean Alexander
Stan Ogden	Bernard Youens
Betty Turpin	Betty Driver
Arnold Sheppard	Julian Somers
Frank Bradley	Alan Browning
Tommy Deacon	Paddy Joyce
Dirty Dick	Talfryn Thomas
Francois Dubois	Francois Pacal
Lucille Hewit	Jennifer Moss
Irma Barlow	Sandra Gough
Eddie Duncan	Del Henney
Jerry Booth	Graham Haberfield
Ernest Bishop	Stephen Hancock
Janet	Judith Barker
Dave Robbins	Jon Rollason
Tim	Ray Barron
Lorna	Luan Peters
Vinnie	Irene Sutcliffe
Emily	Eileen Derbyshire
Dave Smith	Reginald Marsh
Yvonne Chappell	Alexandra Marshall
Maggie Clegy	Irene Sutcliffe
Len Fairclough	Peter Adamson
Deirdre Hunt	Anne Kirkbride
Jerry Booth	Graham Haberfield
Bet Lynch	Julie Goodyear
Ron Cooke	Eric Landen
Mavis Riley	Thelma Barlow
Gordon Clegg	Bill Kenwright
Vera Hopkins	Kathy Staff
Idris Hopkins	Kathy Jones
Rita Littlewood	Barbara Mullaney
Norma Ford	Diana Davies
George Farmer	Phil McCall
Sidney Wilson	John Barrard
Megan Hopkins	Jessie Evan

Music: Eric Spear.

CORONATION STREET—30 min-
utes—Syndicated (PBS Network)
1972. Import begun with episode
1,082. Premiered in London, 1960. A
Granada Television Production.

CORONET BLUE

Mystery. Background: New York
City. Shot and believed to be dead,
Michael Alden is thrown into the East
River. Regaining consciousness in a
hospital room, he discovers that he is
suffering from amnesia. Unaware of
who his attackers are, or the reason
for their attempt on his life, he
remembers only two words, "Coronet

Blue," the phrase that holds the key
to his past and is able to set him free.
   Released from the hospital, he begins his investigation and attempts to
discover the meaning of the phrase.
Unknown to him, he is followed by
his mysterious attackers who seek to
right their mistake if he should come
too close to discovering who he is.
"Coronet Blue, no other clue. . .and
so I go my lonely way. . .even to
myself a stranger, wondering who am
I."
   Originally scheduled for a fall run,
the series was shelved and aired as a
summer replacement for "The Carol
Burnett Show." Subsequently, an ending was never filmed.

CAST

Michael Alden   Frank Converse
Brother Anthony, a monk, his
   assistant   Brian Medford
Max, a friend   Joe Silver

Music: Laurence Rosenthal.

CORONET BLUE—60 minutes—CBS
—July 24, 1967 - September 14, 1967.

CORRIGAN'S RANCH

Variety. Performances by Country
and Western artists.

Host: Ray "Crash" Corrigan.

CORRIGAN'S RANCH—30 minutes
—ABC—July 15, 1950 - August 19,
1950.

COS

Variety. Monologues, music, songs,
comedy sketches.

Host: Bill Cosby.

Regulars: Pat Delaney, Willie Bobo,
   The Cos Company.

Orchestra: Stu Gardner.

Choreography: Kevin Carlisle.

Animation: John Wilson.

Producer: Chris Bearde.

Director: Jeff Margolis.

COS—60 minutes—ABC—September
19, 1976 - October 31, 1976.

COSMOPOLITAN THEATRE

Anthology. Dramatic presentations.

Producer: Sherman Marks, Albert
   McCleery, Louis Cowan.

Director: Sherman Marks, David Crandell, Albert McCleery.

COSMOPOLITAN THEATRE—60
minutes—DuMont 1951.

THE COUNT OF MONTE CRISTO

Adventure. Background: Eighteenth-century France. Falsely accused of bearing treasonable information, Edmond Dantes is convicted and sentenced to life imprisonment in the Chateau d'If. Learning of a buried treasure from his cellmate, he digs his way out, escapes, and retreats to the island of Monte Cristo. Uncovering the treasure, he establishes himself as a mysterious and powerful figure for justice. Stories relate his battle against the forces of corruption.

CAST

Edmond Dantes, the Count of Monte Cristo	George Dolenz
Princess Anne	Faith Domergue
Jacopo	Nick Cravat
Mario	Fortunio Bonanova
Minister Bonjean	Leslie Bradley

THE COUNT OF MONTE CRISTO—30 minutes—Syndicated 1955. 39 episodes.

COUNTERPOINT

Anthology. Rebroadcasts of dramas that were originally aired via "Fireside Theatre."

COUNTERPOINT—30 minutes—Syndicated 1952. 26 episodes.

COUNTERSPY

Spy Drama. The investigations of David Harding, a United States government counterintelligence agent. Stories depict his battle against secret enemy societies — organizations posing a threat to the security of the Free World.

Starring: Don Megowan as David Harding.

COUNTERSPY—30 minutes—Syndicated 1958. 39 episodes.

COUNTERTHRUST

Adventure. Background: The Far East. The exploits of American espionage agents as they battle the forces of Communism.

CAST

Agent	Tod Andrews
Agent	Diane Jergens
Agent	Victor Diaz

COUNTERTHRUST—30 minutes—Syndicated 1959. 13 episodes.

COUNTRY CARNIVAL

Variety. Performances by Country and Western entertainers.
Hosts: Billy Walker, Del Reeves.
Regulars: Jamey Ryan, Chase Webster.
Music: The Goodtime Charlies.

COUNTRY CARNIVAL—30 minutes—Syndicated 1960. 52 tapes.

COUNTRY CLUB

Variety. Performances by Country and Western entertainers.
Host: Hugh X. Lewis.

COUNTRY CLUB—30 minutes—Syndicated 1971.

COUNTRY MUSIC CAROUSEL

Variety. Performances by Country and Western entertainers.
Host: Slim Wilson.

COUNTRY MUSIC CAROUSEL—30 minutes—Syndicated 1967.

THE COUNTRY MUSIC HALL

Variety. Performances by Country and Western entertainers.
Host: Carl Smith.
Regulars: Tommy Warren, Jeannie Shepherd.

THE COUNTRY MUSIC HALL—30 minutes—Syndicated 1965. 26 tapes.

COUNTRY MUSIC JUBILEE

See title: "Jubilee U.S.A."

THE COUNTRY PLACE

Variety. Performances by Country and Western entertainers.
Hosts: Jim Ed Brown, Black Emmons.
Regulars: Crystal Gale, The Gema.
Music: The Sound Seventies.

THE COUNTRY PLACE—30 minutes—Syndicated 1969. 52 tapes.

COUNTRY STYLE

Variety. Performances by Country and Western entertainers.
Hostess: Peggy Anne Ellis.

Regulars: Gloria Dilworth, Emily Baines, Bob Austin, Pat Adair, The Folk Dancers.
Music: The Alvy West Band.

COUNTRY STYLE—60 minutes—DuMont 1950.

COUNTRY STYLE, U.S.A.

Variety. Performances by Country and Western entertainers.
Host: Charlie Applewhite.
COUNTRY STYLE, U.S.A.—15 minutes—Syndicated 1959.

COUNTY FAIR

Variety.
Host: Bert Parks.
Announcer: Kenny Williams.
Music: The Bill Gale Band.

COUNTY FAIR—30 minutes—NBC—September 22, 1958 - June 16, 1959.

A COUPLE OF JOES

Variety. Music, songs, and comedy sketches.
Hosts: Joe Rosenfield, Joe Bushkin.
Regulars: Joan Barton, Beryl Richard, Allyn Edwards, Morgan the Wonder Dog.
Announcer: Tom Shirley.
Music: The Joe Bushkin Trio.

A COUPLE OF JOES—55 minutes—ABC—August 12, 1949 - July 22, 1950.

COURAGEOUS CAT

Animated Cartoon. Background: Empire City. The investigations of Courageous Cat and Minute Mouse, masked crusaders for justice.
Characters: Courageous Cat; Minute Mouse; the Police Chief (a dog). Their base: The Cat Cave. Mode of transportation: The *Catmobile.* Weapon: The thousand-purpose Catgun.
Villains: The Frog; Harry (a gorilla); Rodney Rodent; The Black Cat; Professor Noodle Stroodle (the only human figure); Professor Shaggy Dog.
Music: Johnny Holiday.
Executive Producer: Sam Singer.

Producer: Marvin Woodward, Reuben Timmins.

Director: Sid Marcus, Marvin Woodward.

Creator: Bob Kane.

COURAGEOUS CAT—05 minutes—Syndicated 1961. 130 episodes.

COURT-MARTIAL

Drama. Background: London, England, during World War Two. The story of Captain David Young and Major Frank Whitaker, attorneys attached to the Judge Advocate General's Office. Episodes relate their defense of American military personnel.

CAST

Major Frank Whitaker	Peter Graves
Captain David Young	Bradford Dillman
Wendy, their secretary	Diene Clare
Sergeant MacCaskey, their aide	Kenneth J. Warren

COURT-MARTIAL—60 minutes—ABC—April 8, 1966 - September 2, 1966. 26 episodes.

THE COURT OF LAST RESORT

Crime Drama. Programs designed to help people falsely accused of committing crimes. Details of actual case histories are related through private detective Sam Larsen's investigations and criminal attorney Earl Stanley Gardener's courtroom defenses.

CAST

Earl Stanley Gardener	Paul Birch
Sam Larsen	Lyle Bettger

Producer: Elliott Lewis, Jules Goldstone.

THE COURT OF LAST RESORT—30 minutes—ABC—August 26, 1959 - February 24, 1960. 36 episodes.

THE COURTSHIP OF EDDIE'S FATHER

Comedy. Background: Los Angeles, California. The story of the relationship between widower Tom Corbett, the editor of *Tomorrow* magazine, and his six-year-old son, Eddie, trustworthy people who seek one and other in time of need, and strive for each other's happiness.

Eddie, believing his father's happiness depends upon a wife, indulges in

The Courtship of Eddie's Father. Left to right: Bill Bixby, Brandon Cruz, Miyoshi Umeki.

endless matchmaking attempts. Tom, the innocent victim, finds himself confronted by beautiful women and embarrassing situations.

CAST

Tom Corbett	Bill Bixby
Eddie Corbett	Brandon Cruz
Mrs. Livingston, their Japanese housekeeper	Miyoshi Umeki
Norman Tinker, the magazine's art editor	James Komack
Tina Rickles, Tom's secretary	Kristina Holland
Joey Kelly, Eddie's friend	Jodie Foster
Cissy Drummond, Tom's employer	Tippi Hedren
Etta, Tom's secretary (early episodes)	Karen Wolfe

Music: George Tipton; Nilsson.

Executive Producer: James Komack.

Producer: Ralph Riskin.

Director: Ralph Senesky, Alan Rafkin, Harry Falk, Hal Cooper, Randal Hood, Bill Bixby, James Komack, Luther James, Bob Sweeney.

THE COURTSHIP OF EDDIE'S FATHER—30 minutes—ABC—September 17, 1969 - June 14, 1972. Syndicated. 78 episodes.

COWBOY G-MEN

Western. Background: California during the 1880s. The investigations of cowhand Pat Gallagher and wrangler Stoney Crockett, United States government undercover agents. Episodes depict their attempts to insure law and order.

CAST

Pat Gallagher	Russell Hayden
Stoney Crockett	Jackie Coogan

COWBOY G-MEN—30 minutes—Syndicated 1952. 26 episodes.

COWBOY IN AFRICA

Adventure. Background: Kenya, East Africa. Wing Commander Hayes undertakes a plan to guarantee the survival of· wild beasts through their domestication on his wild-animal ranch. Assisted by champion rodeo rider Jim Sinclair, and a Navaho Indian, John Henry, he attempts to prove his theory that game ranching is Africa's best defense "against the ravages caused by unrestricted cattle grazing," against the objections of the Boer cattlemen who feel his plan is foolish.

Filmed on location and in California's Africa U.S.A.

CAST

Jim Sinclair	Chuck Connors
John Henry	Tom Nardini
Commander Hayes	Ronald Howard
Samson, a young native friend	Gerald B. Edwards

Music: Malcolm Arnold.

COWBOY IN AFRICA—60 minutes—ABC—September 11, 1967 - September 16, 1968. Syndicated. 26 episodes.

THE COWBOYS

Western. Background: The Longhorn Ranch in Spanish Wells, New Mexico, during the 1870s. Faced with unpaid bills, a possible loss of the ranch, and a four-hundred-mile trek to Dodge City with fifteen hundred head of cattle, owner Will Andersen is reluctantly forced to hire and train eleven children, aged nine to fifteen (seven became the series regulars).

On the journey, Will is killed by rustlers who steal the herd. The boys and a range cook, Mr. Nightlinger, pursue and kill the culprits.

Returning to the ranch three months after, the eight present the money to Kate, Will's widow, and express a desire to remain as ranch hands. Assured of their education by Mr. Nightlinger, she hires them. Stories relate their attempts to maintain a cattle ranch in a turbulent era. Adapted from the movie of the same title.

CAST

Mr. Nightlinger	Moses Gunn
Kate Andersen	Diana Douglas
Marshal Bill Winter	Jim Davis
Cimarron	A. Martinez

Slim	Robert Carradine
Homer	Kerry MacLane
Steve	Clint Howard
Weedy	Clay O'Brien
Jim	Sean Kelly
Hardy	Mitch Brown
Will Andersen (feature)	John Wayne

Music: Johnny Williams; Harry Sukman.

THE COWBOYS—30 minutes—ABC—February 6, 1974 - August 14, 1974. 13 episodes.

C.P.O. SHARKEY

Comedy. Background: A Navy recruit training center in San Diego, California. A satirical look at Naval life as seen through the experiences of Steve Sharkey, an acid-tongued, twenty-four-year veteran who has waged his own private war against the changes that constitute the new Navy.

CAST
C.P.O. (Chief Petty Officer) Steve Sharkey	Don Rickles
C.P.O. Robinson	Harrison Page
Captain Quinlan	Elizabeth Allen
Lt. Wipple	Jonathan Daly
Drill Sgt. Pruitt	Peter Isacksen
Recruit Sholnick	David Landsberg
Recruit Kowalski	Tom Ruben
Recruit Shimokawa	Evan Kim
Recruit Mignone	Barry Pearl
Recruit Rodriquez	Richard Beaucamp
Recruit Daniels	Jeff Hollis

Music: Peter Matz.

Executive Producer-Creator: Aaron Ruben.

Producer: Gene Marcione.

Director: Peter Baldwin.

C.P.O. SHARKEY—30 minutes—NBC—Premiered: December 1, 1976.

CRAFTS WITH KATY

Instruction. The preparation and making of interesting and fashionable home furnishings—items constructed from inexpensive Fantasy Film liquid plastic, wire, and assorted accessories.

Hostess/Instructress: Katy Dacus.

Music: Recorded.

CRAFTS WITH KATY—30 minutes—Syndicated 1971.

CRAIG KENNEDY, CRIMINOLOGIST

Crime Drama. Background: New York City. The investigations of criminologist Craig Kennedy, a master of scientific deduction. Episodes depict his attempts to solve gangland crimes.

Starring: Donald Woods as Craig Kennedy.

Producer: Adrian Weiss.

CRAIG KENNEDY, CRIMINOLOGIST—30 minutes—Syndicated 1952. 26 episodes.

CRANE

A twenty-six-episode adventure series, set in Morocco, with Patrick Allen as Crane, the owner of a boat and café. 60 minutes—Syndicated 1965.

CREATIVE COOKERY

Cooking. The preparation of meals, from the simplest American to the most elaborate foreign dishes.

Host: Francois Pope.

Assistant: Bob Pope.

CREATIVE COOKERY—60 minutes—CBS 1951; ABC—1953-1954.

CRIME AND PUNISHMENT

Interview. Interviews conducted from various federal penitentiaries.

Host: Clete Roberts.

Commentator: Robert A. McGee.

CRIME AND PUNISHMENT—30 minutes—Syndicated 1961.

CRIME DOES NOT PAY

Anthology. Dramatizations based on the files of state police departments.

CRIME DOES NOT PAY—30 minutes—Syndicated 1960.

CRIME PHOTOGRAPHER

Crime Drama. Background: New York City. The investigations of Casey, a press-photographer for the *Morning Express,* a crusading newspaper. Based on the stories by George Harmon Coxe.

CAST
Casey	Richard Carlyle Darren McGavin
Ann Williams, his girlfriend, a reporter	Jan Miner
Ethelbert, the bartender at the Blue Note Café	John Gibson
Captain Bill Logan, N.Y.P.D.	Bernard Lenrow

Announcer: Ken Roberts.

Music: Morton Gould.

The Blue Note Café Musicians: The Tony Mottola Trio.

Producer: Charles Russell, Martin Manulis.

Director: Sidney Lumet.

Sponsor: Toni; Arrid.

CRIME PHOTOGRAPHER—30 minutes—CBS—April 17, 1951 - June 19, 1952.

CRIME REPORTER

See title: "Big Town."

CRIMES OF PASSION

Crime Drama. Background: France. Dramatizations based on the files of the French criminal records of *crimes passionels* (crimes of passion). Stories begin with a crime being committed in an emotional moment of passion; a courtroom trial follows, and through the use of flashbacks as witnesses testify, the program attempts to determine whether the crime was premeditated or not.

CAST
The President of the Courts (Judge)	Anthony Newlands
Maitre Saval, the defense attorney	Daniel Moynihan
Maitre Lacan, the prosecuting attorney	John Phillips

Music: Derek Scott.

Producer: Ian Fordyce, Robert Cardona.

Director: Peter Moffatt, Peter Jeffries, Valerie Hanson, Robert Cardona, Gareth Davies.

CRIMES OF PASSION—60 minutes—Syndicated 1976.

CRIME SYNDICATED

Documentary. True crime exposés based on the Kefauver Committee files.

Host-Narrator: Rudolph Halley.

Producer: Jerry Danzig.

Director: John Peyser.

Sponsor: Schick.

CRIME SYNDICATED—30 minutes—CBS—1951-1952.

CRIME WITH FATHER

Crime Drama. Background: New York City. The investigations of a homicide bureau chief and his self-proclaimed assistant, his teen-age daughter.

CAST
Father	Rusty Lane
Daughter	Peggy Lobbin

Producer: Wilbur Stark.

Director: Charles S. Dubin.

CRIME WITH FATHER—30 minutes—ABC—October 5, 1951 - February 1, 1952.

CRISIS

Anthology. Rebroadcasts of dramas that were originally aired via "The Bob Hope Chrysler Theatre" and "Kraft Suspense Theatre."

CRISIS—60 minutes—Syndicated 1971.

CROSS CURRENT

See title: "Foreign Intrigue."

CROSSROADS

Anthology. Dramatizations based on the experiences of the men of the clergy.

Included:

The Riot. The ordeal of a priest who becomes the unwitting accomplice in a prison break.

CAST
Father O'Neal: Pat O'Brien; Daniels: Roy Roberts.

The Comeback. The true story of Lou Brissie, a pitcher who returned to major league baseball after sustaining injuries during World War II.

CAST
Rev. C. E. Stoney Jackson: Don DeFore; Lou Brissie: Chuck Connors; Whitey Martin: Grant Withers.

Johnakunga—Called John. Background: Wisconsin, 1883. The true story of Rev. John Stucker, a missionary who risked his life to befriend the hostile Winnebago Indians.

CAST
Rev. Stucker: Hugh Marlowe; Johnakunga: Pat Hogan.

CROSSROADS—30 minutes—ABC—October 7, 1953 - September 4, 1956. Syndicated.

THE CROSS WITS

Game. Two three-member teams compete, each composed of two celebrities and one noncelebrity captain. A large crossword board, which contains the names of persons, places, or things, is revealed. The captain selects a position (e.g., five down; eight across) for which the host reads the corresponding clue. On a rotational basis, the celebrities have to answer. If a celebrity is unable to answer within seven seconds, the captain receives a chance to supply the correct answer. If the correct answer is given, the word appears on the board and the team scores ten points for each filled space. Failure to figure out a clue ends that team's chance at play. The team that is first to identify the puzzle is the winner of that round and receives one hundred additional points. The team accumulating the highest score is the winner and the contestant receives an opportunity to play the Cross Fire Round. With a celebrity partner of his choice, the player must fill in a crossword puzzle within sixty seconds. Additional prizes are awarded if he is successful.

Host: Jack Clark.

Assistant: Geri Fiala.

Announcer: John Harlan, Jay Stewart.

Music: Ron Kaye, Buddy Kaye, Phillip Springer.

Executive Producer: Ralph Edwards.

Producer: Roy Horl, Bruce Belland.

Director: Richard Gottlieb, Jerry Payne.

THE CROSS WITS—30 minutes—Syndicated 1975.

CROWN THEATRE WITH GLORIA SWANSON

Anthology. Dramatic presentations.

Hostess-Frequent Performer: Gloria Swanson.

Included:

Uncle Harry. The story of a man who is overly generous with other people's property.

CAST
Edgar Buchannan, Elizabeth Fraser.

A Chair In The Boulevard. An enterprising young Frenchman believes he has found the mysterious Mlle. Guard, the woman on whose identity a French newspaper has pinned a large sum of cash. Romantic complications ensue when he attempts to turn her in.

CAST
Gloria Swanson, Claude Dauphin.

The Buzzer. So she can marry her fiancé who is transferring to another city, a young girl desperately attempts to get rid of her invalid mother.

CAST
Lorna Thayer, John Oliver.

CROWN THEATRE WITH GLORIA SWANSON—30 minutes—Syndicated 1953.

CRUNCH AND DES

Adventure. Background: The Bahamas. The story of Crunch Adams and his partner, Des, the owners and operators of the charter boat service, *Poseidon.*

CAST
Crunch Adams	Forrest Tucker
Des	Sandy Kenyon
Sari Adams, Crunch's sister	Joanne Bayes

CRUNCH AND DES—30 minutes—Syndicated 1955. Also titled: "Charter Boat" and "Deep Sea Adventures."

THE CRUSADER

Adventure. The story of Matt Anders, a crusading free-lance magazine writer. Episodes relate his battle against the global forces of oppression and treachery.

Starring: Brian Keith as Matt Anders.

Music: Edmund Wilson.

THE CRUSADER—30 minutes—CBS—October 7, 1955 - December 28, 1956. Syndicated. 52 episodes.

CRUSADER RABBIT

Animated Cartoon. The misadventures

of Crusader Rabbit and his friend, Rags the Tiger.

CRUSADER RABBIT—04 minutes (theatrical cartoons)—Syndicated 1949. 260 episodes.

CURIOSITY SHOP

Educational. Various aspects of the adult world are explained to children via sketches, cartoons, and films.

CAST
Gittel the Witch	Barbara Minkus
Pam	Pamelyn Ferdin
Gerard	John Levin
Ralph	Kerry MacLane
Cindy	Jerelyn Fields

Animated features: "Dennis The Menace"; "Big George"; "Miss Peach"; "B.C."; "Mr. Mum"; "The Bears."

Puppets: Oogle; Flip the Hippo; Eeek A. Mouse; Nostalgia the Elephant.

Voices: Mel Blanc, Bob Halt, Chuck Jones.

Orchestra: Dick Elliott.

CURIOSITY SHOP—60 minutes—ABC—September 11, 1971 - September 9, 1973.

CURT MASSEY TIME

Musical Variety.
Host: Curt Massey.
Co-Hostess: Martha Tilton.

CURT MASSEY TIME—15 minutes—CBS 1950.

CURTAIN CALL

Anthology. Dramatic presentations based on classical and contemporary short stories.

CURTAIN CALL—30 minutes—NBC—June 20, 1952 - September 26, 1952. Also known as "Pond's Theatre."

CUT

Game. An amateurish script, suggesting an object or theme, is performed by a group of actors. An operator places a random phone call. The viewer is asked to identify the suggested theme. If correct, he is awarded a prize and receives a chance at the jackpot — to identify the portrait of a celebrity on a rapidly spun wheel.
Host: Carl Caruso.
Music: The Al Logan Trio.

CUT—60 minutes—DuMont 1949.

CYBORG BIG "X"

Animated Cartoon. The story of Arika, a cyborg with the brain of a human and the body of a robot. Armed with a special magnetic pen, his sole weapon, he combats the criminal world.

CYBORG BIG "X"—30 minutes—Syndicated 1965. 59 episodes.

CYBORG: THE SIX MILLION DOLLAR MAN

See title: "The Six Million Dollar Man."

𝒟

THE D.A.

Crime Drama. Background: Los Angeles, California. The story of Paul Ryan, a district attorney who functions as both a detective and a prosecutor.

CAST
Paul Ryan	Robert Conrad
H.M. "Staff" Stafford, the Chief Deputy	Harry Morgan
Kathy Benson, the Deputy Public Defender	Julie Cobb
Bob Ramerez, Ryan's chief investigator	Ned Romero

Music: Frank Comstock.

THE D.A.—30 minutes—NBC—September 17, 1971 - January 7, 1972. 13 episodes.

THE D.A.'S MAN

Crime Drama. Background: New York City. The investigations of Shannon, a private detective working anonymously under the auspices of the district attorney.

CAST
Shannon	John Compton
Al Bonacorsi, his contact at the D.A.'s office	Ralph Manza

Music: Frank Comstock.

THE D.A.'s MAN—30 minutes—NBC—January 3, 1959 - August 29, 1959. Syndicated 1965. 26 episodes.

DAGMAR'S CANTEEN

Musical Variety. Background: A military camp. Performances by the men and women in the U.S. Armed Forces.
Hostess: Dagmar (Jennie Lewis).
Regulars: Ray Malone, Joey Faye.
Orchestra: Milton DeLugg.

DAGMAR'S CANTEEN—15 minutes—NBC 1952.

THE DAKOTAS

Western. Background: The Dakota Territory during the 1880s. The story of United States Marshal Frank Regan and his attempts to maintain law and order.

CAST
Marshal Frank Regan	Larry Ward
Deputy Del Stark	Chad Everett
Deputy J.D. Smith	Jack Elam
Deputy Vance Porter	Michael Green

Music: Frank Perkins.

THE DAKOTAS—60 minutes—ABC—January 7, 1963 - September 9, 1963. Syndicated. 19 episodes.

DAKTARI

Adventure. Background: The Wameru Game Preserve and Research Center in Africa. The struggles of Daktari (Swahili for "doctor") Marsh Tracy and his associates to protect the endangered wildlife and ensure its future existence.

CAST
Dr. Marsh Tracy	Marshall Thompson
Paula Tracy, his teenage daughter, studying to become a scientist	Cheryl Miller
District Game Warden Headley	Hadley Mattingley
Jack Dane, a zoologist	Yale Sommers
Bart Jason, a game hunter	Ross Hagen
Mike, a zoologist	Hari Rhodes
Jenny Jones, an orphan, Marsh's six-year old admirer	Erin Moran

Animals: Clarence, the cross-eyed lion; Judy, the chimp.

Music: Shelly Mann; Ruby Raksin; Harold Gelman.

DAKTARI—60 minutes—CBS—January 11, 1966 - January 15, 1969. Syndicated. 89 episodes.

DAMON RUNYON THEATRE

Anthology. Dramatizations set against the background of old New York. Tales, as penned by Damon Runyon, detailing the soft-hearted characters of the underworld.

Host: Donald Woods.

Included:

Teacher's Pet. A young school teacher struggles to run a recently inherited bookmaking empire.

CAST
Emilie: Fay Bainter; Tony Rose: Gene Evans; Bo Peep: Adele Jergens.

The Mink Doll. Inheriting a large sum of money, a chorus girl moves to Park Avenue and struggles to be accepted by society.

CAST
Sally Bracken: Dorothy Lamour; Harry Bracken: Wayne Morris; Frankie Farrell: Joe Besser.

A Light In France. Era: World War II France. The story of two fleeing U.S. criminals and their attempts to stray from trouble.

CAST
Thaddeus: Edward Everett Horton; Packy: Hugh O'Brian; Marie: Lita Mann.

It Comes Up Money. Plans for a new skyscraper are blocked by the owner of an antique store who refuses to sell. Desperate, construction officials plot to make the man change his mind.

CAST
Sylvester: Thomas Mitchell; Abigail: Frances Bavier; Joey: Wally Vernon; Pat: Jackie Loughery.

DAMON RUNYON THEATRE—30 minutes—CBS—April 16, 1955 - June 9, 1956. 39 episodes.

DAN AUGUST

Crime Drama. Background: Santa Luisa, California, a small, fictitious coastal community. The investigations of Detective Lieutenant Dan August, a man caught between the hatreds of the Establishment and his duty to protect.

CAST
Det. Lt. Dan August   Burt Reynolds
Sgt. Charles Wilentz   Norman Fell
Sgt. John Rivera   Ned Romero
Police Chief George
   Untermyer   Richard Anderson
Kathy Grant, the
   secretary   Ena Hartman
Music: Dave Grusin.

DAN AUGUST—60 minutes—ABC— September 23, 1970 - September 9, 1971. Rebroadcasts: CBS—April 23, 1973 - October 17, 1973. Returned: CBS (rebroadcasts): April 16, 1975 - June 25, 1975. 26 episodes.

DANCING PARTY

See title: "The Lawrence Welk Show."

DANGER

Anthology. The art of murder is explored through dramatization.

Host-Narrator: Dick Stark.

Producer: Martin Ritt, Charles Russell, William Dozier.

Included:

Murder On Tenth Street. The story of a young woman who overhears a murder plot, then desperately struggles to prevent it from happening.

CAST
Katherine Bard, John Baragrey.

The Face Of Fear. The story of a switchboard operator trapped by a dangerous mental patient in a deserted office building.

Starring: Lee Grant.

Pete River's Blues. The story of a jazz musician who befriends a society woman, then finds himself involved with murder.

CAST
Conrad Janis, Barbara Nichols.

DANGER—30 minutes—CBS— October 3, 1950 - December 21, 1955.

DANGER IS MY BUSINESS

Documentary. Films depicting the hazardous occupations of people.

Host-Narrator: Col. John D. Craig.

DANGER IS MY BUSINESS—30 minutes—Syndicated 1958. 39 episodes.

DANGER MAN

Adventure. The story of John Drake, a special investigator for the North Atlantic Treaty Organization (NATO). Episodes depict his attempts to solve situations jeapardizing its objectives.

Starring: Patrick McGoohan as John Drake.

Music: Edwin Astley.

DANGER MAN—30 minutes—CBS— April 5, 1961 - September 14, 1961. Syndicated. 39 episodes.

DANGEROUS ASSIGNMENT

Adventure. The cases of Steve Mitchell, an international troubleshooter who investigates and solves crimes on behalf of the United States government.

Starring: Brian Donlevy as Steve Mitchell.

DANGEROUS ASSIGNMENT—30 minutes—Syndicated 1952.

DANGER ZONE

Documentary. Films depicting the hazardous work of specialized professionalists (e.g., people involved in air rescues at sea; professional divers; sea fire fighters).

Host-Narrator: Pappy Boyington, Marine Corps Ace.

DANGER ZONE—30 minutes—Syndicated 1960.

DANIEL BOONE

Adventure. Background: Boonesborough, Kentucky, during the latter eighteenth century. The exploits of legendary frontiersman-pioneer Daniel Boone.

CAST
Daniel Boone   Fess Parker
Rebecca Boone, his
   wife   Patricia Blair
Jemima Boone, their
   daughter   Veronica Cartwright
Israel Boone, their
   son   Darby Hinton
Yadkin, Daniel's
   sidekick   Albert Salmi
Mingo, Daniel's Oxford-
   educated friend, a
   Cherokee Indian   Ed Ames

Cincinnatus, Daniel's
friend   Dallas McKennon
Josh Clements, a
backwoodsman   Jimmy Dean
Gabe Cooper, runaway slave,
Chief Canawahchaquaoo of
The Tuscarora
Indians   Roosevelt Grier

Daniel Boone. Fess Parker and Patricia Blair.

Music: Lionel Newman.

Additional Music: Harry Sukman, Alexander Courage, Herman Stein, Leith Stevens.

Executive Producer: Aaron Rosenberg.

Producer: George Sherman.

Director: George Marshall, Nathan Juran, Tony Leader, Gerd Oswald, George Sherman, Earl Bellamy, John Florea, Barry Shear.

DANIEL BOONE—60 minutes—NBC —September 24, 1964 - September 10, 1970. Syndicated. 165 episodes.

THE DANNY KAYE SHOW

Variety. Music, songs, dances, and comedy sketches.

Host: Danny Kaye.

Regulars: Harvey Korman, Vikki Carr, Joyce Van Patten, Laurie Ichino, Victoria Meyerink, The Johnny Mann Singers, The Earle Brown Singers, The Tony Charmoli Dancers.

Announcer: Berne Bennett.

Orchestra: Paul Weston.

THE DANNY KAYE SHOW—60 min-

utes—CBS—September 25, 1963 June 7, 1967. 96 tapes.

DANNY THE DRAGON

A comical science fiction series that centers around Danny, an unintentional visitor from outer space, and his adventures with the three children who befriend him. Starring Sally Thomsett, Jack Wild, Peter Butterworth, and Christopher Cooper. 17 minutes—Syndicated 1970. 10 films.

THE DANNY THOMAS HOUR

Anthology. Varying presentations: dramatic, musical and comedic.

Host-occasional performer: Danny Thomas.

Music: Earle Hagen.

Included:

The Wonderful World Of Burlesque. A musical variety hour reviving the world of burlesque.

CAST

Danny Thomas, Phil Silvers, Nanette Fabray, Cyd Charisse, Ernie Ford.

Make More Room For Daddy. A revision of the classic "Make Room for Daddy" series. Danny attempts to adjust to the prospect of losing a son when Rusty marries.

CAST

Danny Williams: Danny Thomas; Kathy Williams: Marjorie Lord; Rusty Williams: Rusty Hamer; Linda Williams: Angela Cartwright; Charlie Helper: Sid Melton.

The Royal Follies Of 1933. Variety depicting the music, comedy, and entertainment of 1933.

CAST

Danny Thomas, Hans Conried, Eve Arden, Shirley Jones, Gale Gordon.

Instant Money. A comedy detailing the ill-fated efforts of a man as he attempts to acquire money through gambling.

CAST

Danny Thomas, Don Adams, Sid Caesar, Abby Dalton, Richard Deacon.

THE DANNY THOMAS HOUR—60 minutes—NBC—September 11, 1967 - September 9, 1968. 26 episodes.

The Danny Thomas Show. Danny Thomas and Marjorie Lord.

THE DANNY THOMAS SHOW

See title: "Make Room for Daddy."

DAN RAVEN

Crime Drama. Background: California. The story of Dan Raven, a detective lieutenant with the Hollywood Sheriff's Office. Episodes depict his attempts to assist his clientele—show business personalities.

CAST

Det. Lt. Dan Raven   Skip Homeier
Sergeant Burke, his
assistant   Dan Barton
Perry Levitt, a
photographer   Quinn Redeker

DAN RAVEN—30 minutes—NBC— September 23, 1960 - January 6, 1961. 13 episodes.

DANTE

Drama. Background: San Francisco, California. The exploits of Willie Dante, reformed gambler owner of Dante's Inferno Nightclub. Stories depict his attempts to overcome the situations that occur when his past reputation attracts unscrupulous characters. Based on the character portrayed by Dick Powell on "Four Star Playhouse."

CAST

Willie Dante   Howard Duff
Stewart Styles, the club
maitre'd, a former
confidence man   Alan Mowbray
Biff, his right-hand
man   Tom D'Andrea

DANTE—30 minutes—NBC—October 3, 1960 - April 10, 1961. Syndicated. 26 episodes.

DAN TEMPEST

See title: "The Buccaneers."

DARK ADVENTURE

Anthology. Dramatizations of people trapped in uncertain situations as the result of emotional problems.

Included:

The Second Mrs. Sands. A mother attempts to acquire her foster son's inheritance.
Starring: Hillary Brooke.

Lady With Ideas. An actress attempts to acquire publicity by pretending to be a European star.

CAST
Pamela Britton, Gig Young.

Conqueror's Isle. A psychiatrist's probe into the story, related by a hospitalized soldier, of a mad scientist's plans to enslave the world.
Starring: Ray Montgomery.

DARK ADVENTURE—30 minutes—ABC—January 5, 1953 - July 6, 1953.

DARK OF NIGHT

Anthology. The first live suspense program to originate from locations outside a network's studios (DuMont in New York). Dramatizations set against the background of New York City.

DARK OF NIGHT—30 minutes—DuMont—1952-1953.

DARK SHADOWS

Serial. Background: Collinsport, a small fishing village in Maine. The story of Victoria Winters, a young woman who is hired as governess for ten-year-old David Collins. Episodes relate her involvement in the supernatural existences of the Collins family. The first daytime serial to present horror—vampires, werewolves, witches, and black magic—for its stories.

Dark Shadows. Jonathan Frid.

CAST

Elizabeth Collins Stoddard	Joan Bennett
Victoria Winters	Alexandra Moltke
Barnabas Collins	Jonathan Frid
Carolyn Stoddard	Nancy Barrett
Charity	Nancy Barrett
Roger Collins	Louis Edmonds
Edward Collins	Louis Edmonds
Dr. Julia Hoffman	Grayson Hall
Magda	Grayson Hall
Maggie Evans	Kathryn Leigh Scott
Joe Haskell	Joel Crothers
Angelique	Lara Parker
Cassandra	Lara Parker
Quentin Collins	David Selby
Willie Loomis	John Karlen
David Collins	David Henesy
Peter Bradford	Roger Davis
Sarah Collins	Sharon Smyth
Sam Evans	David Ford
Mrs. Johnson	Clarice Blackburn
Cyrus Longworth	Chris Pennock
Jeb Hawks	Chris Pennock
Burke Devlin	Anthony George
Daphne Harridge	Kate Jackson
Bruno	Michael Stroka
Amy	Denise Nickerson
Sabrina Stuart	Lisa Richards
Mrs. Collins	Diana Millay
Adam	Robert Rodan
Eve	Marie Wallace
Beth	Terry Crawford
King Johnny	Paul Richard
Hallie Stokes	Kathy Cody
Professor Elliot Stokes	Thayer David
Count Petofi	Thayer David
Reverend Trask	Jerry Lacy
Balberith, Prince of Darkness	Humbert A. Astredo
Alexander	David Jay
Rondell Drew	Gene Lindsey
Amanda Harris	Donna McKechnie
Olivia Corey	Donna McKechnie
Michael	Michael Maitland

Final Cast

During the course of the program's last year on the air, stories related incidents in the Collins family during the nineteenth century—one hundred years prior to the original twentieth-century setting. Through the use of black magic, characters were able to travel from the present to the past and observe the lives of their ancestors—people also involved with the supernatural.

Flora Collins	Joan Bennett
Barnabas Collins-Bramwell	Jonathan Frid
Julia H. Collins	Grayson Hall
Quentin Collins	David Selby
Letitia Faye	Nancy Barrett
Gabriel Collins	Chris Pennock
Carrie Stokes	Kathy Cody
Mordecai Grimes	Thayer David
Edith Collins	Terry Crawford
Valerie Collins	Lara Parker
Samantha Collins	Virginia Vestoff
Daniel Collins	Louis Edmonds
Tad Collins	David Henesy
Daphne Harridge	Kate Jackson
Desmond Collins	John Karlen
Morgan Collins	Keith Prentice
Gerald Stiles	James Storm
Reverend Trask	Jerry Lacy
Laszlo	Michael Stroka
Roxanne Drew	Donna Wandrey
Charles Dawson	Humbert A. Astredo
The Werewolf	Alex Stevens

Also: Don Briscoe, Alan Feinstein, Conrad Fowkes, Alan Yorke.
Music: Robert Cobert.

DARK SHADOWS—30 minutes—ABC—June 27, 1966 - April 2, 1971. Syndicated. 1000 tapes.

DASTARDLY AND MUTLEY IN THEIR FLYING MACHINES

Animated Cartoon. Era: World War One. The efforts of the evil Dick Dastardly, on orders from the General, to intercept the vital messages of the American Courier, Yankee Doodle Pigeon. His unsuccessful attempts are assisted by a fumbling, snickering dog, Mutley, and a group of misplaced misfits, The Flying Squadron (Klunk and Zilly). A Hanna-Barbera Production.

Characters' Voices

Dick Dastardly	Paul Winchell
Mutley	Don Messick
Klunk	Don Messick
Zilly	Don Messick
The General	Paul Winchell

Music: Hoyt Curtin.
Musical Director: Ted Nichols.

Producer-Director: William Hanna, Joseph Barbera.

DASTARDLY AND MUTLEY IN THEIR FLYING MACHINES–30 minutes–CBS–September 13, 1969 - September 3, 1971. Syndicated. 17 episodes.

DATE IN MANHATTAN

Game. The format features selected studio audience members competing in various question-and-answer and stunt contests for prizes.

Host: Lee Sullivan.

Announcer: Ed Herlihy.

Music: The Cy Coleman Trio.

DATE IN MANHATTAN–30 minutes–NBC 1950.

DATELINE: EUROPE

See title: "Foreign Intrigue."

DATELINE: HOLLYWOOD

Variety. Celebrity interviews and filmland news.

Hostesses: Joanna Barnes; Rona Barrett.

Appearing: Jayne Mansfield (her last television appearance), Patty Duke, Cornel Wilde, Dean Jones, Marlo Thomas, Efrem Zimbalist, Jr., Chad and Jeremy, Nick Adams, Victor Buono, Gloria Swanson, Bob Crane, Pat Wayne, Ann Baxter, Charles Bronson, Meredith MacRae, Bobby Vinton, Barbara Parkins, Louis Nye, Sherry Jackson, Werner Klemperer.

DATELINE: HOLLYWOOD–30 minutes–ABC–April 3, 1967 - September 29, 1967.

A DATE WITH THE ANGELS

Comedy. Background: Los Angeles, California. The trials and tribulations of young marrieds: Gus Angel, a bright and determined insurance salesman, and his attractive, level-headed wife, Vickie.

CAST

Vickie Angel	Betty White
Gus Angel	Bill Williams
George Clemson, their neighbor	Roy Engle
Wilma Clemson, his wife	Natalie Masters
George Neise, a friend	Karl Koening
Dottie Neise, his wife	Joan Banks
Adam Henshaw, Gus's employer	Russell Hicks
Mary Henshaw, his wife	Isobel Elsom
Mr. Finley, the Angels' crusty neighbor	Burt Mustin
Roger Finley, Mr. Finley's son	Richard Deacon
Murphy, a neighbor	Richard Reeves
Cassie Murphy, his wife	Maudie Prickett

Producer: Don Fedderson, Fred Henry.

A DATE WITH THE ANGELS–30 minutes–ABC–May 10, 1957 - January 29, 1958.

A DATE WITH JUDY

Comedy. Background: Santa Barbara, California. The misadventures of Judy Foster, an unpredictable teenage girl. Based on the radio program of the same title.

CAST

Judy Foster	Patricia Crowley
	Mary Lynn Beller
Melvyn Foster, her father, president of the Foster Canning Company	Judson Rees
	John Gibson
Dora Foster, her mother	Anna Lee
	Flora Campbell
Randolph Foster, her brother	Gene O'Donnell
	Peter Avramo
Oogie Pringle, Judy's boyfriend	Jimmie Sommers

Also: Patty Pope.

A DATE WITH JUDY–30 minutes–ABC–June 2, 1951 - September 30, 1953.

A DATE WITH LIFE

Serial. Background: The town of Bay City. Life in a small American town as seen through the eyes of Jim Bradley, the editor of the *Bay City News.*

CAST

Jim Bradley	Logan Field
His brother	Mark Roberts
Jennifer, the school teacher	June Dayton
David, her boyfriend	Dean Harens

Also: Dolores Sulton, Billy Redfield, Barbara Britton, Anthony Eisley, Irene Hubbon.

Organist: John Gart.

A DATE WITH LIFE–30 minutes–NBC–October 10, 1955 - June 29, 1956.

A DATE WITH REX

Variety. Celebrity interviews.

Host: Rex Marshall.

Hostess: Sondra Deel.

A DATE WITH REX–30 minutes–DuMont–1950 - 1951.

THE DATING GAME

Game. Three handsome young men vie for a date with a lovely young bachelorette. Seated on opposite sides of a stage-separating wall, she asks them specially prepared questions designed to reveal the romantic nature of each individual. By their answers, she chooses the one she would most like to have as her date. The program furnishes the couple an all-expenses-paid romantic date. Also played in reverse–three girls, one bachelor.

Host: Jim Lange.

Announcer: Johnny Jacobs.

Music: Frank Jaffe.

THE DATING GAME–30 minutes–ABC–October 6, 1966 - July 6, 1973.

DAVE ALLEN AT LARGE

Comedy. Sketches and blackouts satirizing life.

Host: Dave Allen, a British comedian.

Regulars: Jacqueline Clarke, Chris Serle, Ivan Burford, Ronnie Brody, Michael Sharwell-Martin.

Music: Recorded.

Producer: Peter Whitmore for B.B.C. TV.

DAVE ALLEN AT LARGE–60 minutes–Syndicated 1975.

DAVE AND CHARLEY

Comedy. The misadventures of a pair of cronies–Charley, a senile oldster, and Dave, his friend, an unemployed clerk.

CAST

Dave Willock	Dave Willock
Charley Weaver	Cliff Arquette

DAVE AND CHARLEY–15 minutes–NBC 1952.

DAVE ELMAN'S CURIOSITY SHOP

Discussion. Guests and discussions on hobbies.

Host: Dave Elman.

DAVE ELMAN'S CURIOSITY SHOP —30 minutes—Syndicated 1952.

DAVE GARROWAY

Listed: The television programs of Dave Garroway.

Garroway At Large—Variety—30 minutes—NBC—April 16, 1949 - June 24, 1951.

Host: Dave Garroway.

Regulars: Connie Russell, Jack Haskell, Betty Shetland, Aura Vainio, Cliff Norton, James Russell, Betty Chapel, The Songsmiths.

Announcer: Jack Haskell.

Orchestra: Joseph Gallechio.

The Today Show—Information—2 hours—NBC—1952-1962 (Dave Garroway's run as host). See title.

The Dave Garroway Show—Variety— 30 minutes—NBC—October 2, 1953 - June 25, 1954.

Host: Dave Garroway.

Regulars: Jack Haskell, Jill Corey, Cliff Norton, Shirley Hammer.

Announcer: Jack Haskell.

Orchestra: Skitch Henderson.

Wide Wide World—News (diverse views on topical issues)—90 minutes—NBC —October 16, 1955 - June 8, 1958.

Host: Dave Garroway.

Announcer: Bill Wendell.

Orchestra: David Broekman.

Garroway—Discussion and Variety— 60 minutes—Live from Boston—Syndicated 1969.

Host: Dave Garroway.

The CBS Newcomers—Variety—30 minutes—CBS—July 12, 1971 - September 6, 1971. See title.

THE DAVE KING SHOW

Musical Variety.

Host: Dave King, "The British Como."

Regulars: The Jerry Packer Singers, The Bill Foster Dancers.

Announcer: Ed Herlihy.

Orchestra: Vic Schoen.

THE DAVE KING SHOW—30 minutes—NBC—May 1958 - September 1958; May 26, 1959 - September 23, 1959. Summer replacement for "The Kraft Music Hall." Official title: "Kraft Music Hall Presents Dave King."

THE DAVID FROST REVUE

Satire. Sketches based on various topical issues (e.g., food, sex, health, money).

Host: David Frost.

Regulars: Jack Gilford, Marcia Rodd, George Irving, Lynne Lipton, Larry Moss, Jim Catusi, Cleavon Little.

THE DAVID FROST REVUE—30 minutes—Syndicated 1971. 26 tapes.

THE DAVID FROST SHOW

Discussion-Variety.

Host: David Frost.

Announcer: Wayne Howell.

Orchestra: Billy Taylor.

THE DAVID FROST SHOW—90 minutes—Syndicated 1969-1972.

THE DAVID NIVEN THEATRE

Anthology. Dramatic presentations.

Host—Occasional Performer: David Niven.

Included:

The Lady From Winnetka. Background: A Mediterranean island. Vacationing and meeting a handsome guide, a woman seeks the romance that is lacking in her marriage.

CAST

Ellen Baird: Joanne Dru; Tavo: Jacques Bergerac; Mr. Baird: Carleton G. Young.

Good Deed. A newspaper reporter attempts to arrange the surrender of a cop killer.

CAST

Gentry: Keefe Brasselle; Simms: James Best; Hazel: Virginia Grey.

Fortune's Folly. The story centers on the struggles of a man as he attempts to overcome gambling fever.

CAST

Hal Shattuck: Cameron Mitchell.

Portrait. Background: Germany, World War II. A group of American soldiers, taking refuge in a home, are intrigued by the portrait of a beautiful woman. Each envisions what she is really like.

CAST

Woman: Carolyn Jones; Max: Otto Woldis; Private Dennis: Bob Nichols; Private Menoti: Joseph Tuckel; Private Boland: James Best.

THE DAVID NIVEN THEATRE—30 minutes—NBC—April 7, 1959 - September 15, 1959. 13 episodes.

DAVID NIVEN'S WORLD

Adventure. Documentary-style presentations that showcase the adventurous activities of ordinary people.

Host-Narrator: David Niven.

Music: Recorded.

Executive Producer: John Fleming Hall.

Producer: Marianne Lamour, Jim DeKay.

Director: Jim DeKay.

DAVID NIVEN'S WORLD—30 minutes—Syndicated 1976.

THE DAVID STEINBERG SHOW

Variety. Various comedy sketches designed to satirize the world and its problems.

Host: David Steinberg.

Announcer: Bill Thompson.

Orchestra: Artie Butler.

Guests: Carol Wayne, Patty Duke, John Astin, Burns and Schreiber, Ed McMahon, Carly Simon.

THE DAVID STEINBERG SHOW—60 minutes—CBS—July 19, 1972 - August 16, 1972. 4 tapes.

THE DAVID SUSSKIND SHOW

Discussion. A roundtable discussion on various topical issues with appropriate guests.

Host: David Susskind.

Music: Recorded.

THE DAVID SUSSKIND SHOW—2 hours—Syndicated 1967. Original title: "Open End"—60 minutes—Syndicated—1958-1967.

DAVY AND GOLIATH

Animated Religious Cartoon. The adventures of a young boy, Davy Hanson, and his talking dog, Goliath. Stories depict Davy's attempts to relate the meaning of God's Word in the solving of everyday problems.

Characters: Davy Hanson; Goliath; John Hanson, Davy's father; Mary Hanson, Davy's mother; Alice Hanson, Davy's sister; Miss Lindsey, the school teacher; Pastor Miller; and Tom, Davy's friend.

Voices: Richard Belar, Hal Smith, Nancy Wible, Norma MacMillan.

Music: John Seely Associates.

DAVY AND GOLIATH—15 minutes —Syndicated 1963.

DAVY CROCKETT

Adventure. The life of legendary frontiersman-pioneer Davy Crockett. Originally broadcast via the "Disneyland," *Frontierland* series.

Titles:
Davy Crockett, Indian Fighter (12/15/54). Background: Tennessee, 1813, during the era of the Creek Indian Uprising, the slaughter of settlers by Indians seeking to protect their land. Joining a small band of volunteers, Davy and his friend, George Russell, attempt to keep officials posted on Indian activities and convince the chief of the Blackfeet, Red Stick, to end his war. Confronting and defeating Red Stick in a tomahawk battle, Davy convinces him to join the other chiefs in a peace treaty.

Davy Crockett Goes To Congress (1/26/55). Shortly after their return home, Davy and George seek land on which to settle. Attempting to file a claim, they encounter the wrath of a bigoted, self-imposed magistrate, Big Foot Mason. After learning of Mason's practices of selling Indian land to settlers, Davy opposes him and ends his reign. Seeking representation in Nashville, the settlers elect Davy as their state legislator. The episode depicts his experiences as an elected senator in Washington, D.C.

Davy Crockett At The Alamo

Davy Crockett. Left to right: Nick Cravat, Fess Parker, Buddy Ebsen, and Hans Conried. © *Walt Disney Productions.*

(2/23/55). Era: 1836, the beginning of the Western March. Learning of the Texas struggle for independence, Davy and George, assisted by friends Thimbelrig and Bustedluck, journey to the Alamo where two hundred men, under the command of Jim Bowie, have established a stronghold against thousands of Santa Anna's Mexican soldiers. The episode depicts the final defense before the Alamo is captured by Santa Anna.

Davy Crockett's Keelboat Race (11/16/55). Background: The Ohio and Mississippi Rivers during the 1830s. The story of the keelboat race between Davy Crockett, his partner, George Russell, and Mike Fink, "King of the River."

Davy Crockett And The River Pirates (12/14/55). Background: Illinois, during the 1830s. Davy, George, and Mike Fink attempt to end the reign of the Ohio River Cave-In-Rock Den of pirates.

CAST

Davy Crockett	Fess Parker
George Russell	Buddy Ebsen
Polly Crockett, Davy's wife	Helen Stanely
Billy Crockett, their son	Eugene Brindle
Johnny Crockett, their son	Ray Whiteside
Chief Red Stick	Pat Hogan
Thimbelrig	Hans Conried
Bustedluck	Nick Cravat
Jim Bowie	Kenneth Tobey
Mike Fink	Jeff York
Big Foot Mason	Mike Mazurki

Davy's Rifle: Betsy.

Music: George Bruns.

DAYDREAMING WITH LARAINE

Variety. Dramatic vignettes, interviews, music and current events.

Hostess: Laraine Day.

Vocalist: Ruth Woodner.

Music: The Bill Harrington Trio.

DAYDREAMING WITH LARAINE— 30 minutes—ABC—May 3, 1951 - July 5, 1951. Daily, as titled above; Saturday afternoons as: "The Laraine Day Show"—30 minutes—ABC—May 5, 1951 - July 28, 1951.

DAY IN COURT

Courtroom Drama. Reenactments of city and state criminal and civil hearings.

Judge: Edgar Allan Jones Jr.; William Gwinn.

DAY IN COURT—30 minutes—ABC October 13, 1958 - June 25, 1965.

DAYS OF OUR LIVES

Serial. "Like sands through the hour glass, so are the days of our lives. . . ." Background: Salem, Massachusetts. The life of Dr. Thomas Horton, Professor of Medicine at University Hospital; and his family. Stories relate the events that befall and alter their daily existences.

CAST

Dr. Thomas Horton	Macdonald Carey
Alice Horton	Frances Reid
Marie Horton	Marie Cheatham
Dr. Laura Spencer	Susan Flannery
	Kate Woodville
	Susan Oliver
	Rosemary Forsyth
Mickey Horton	John Clarke
Sandy Horton	Heather North
Dr. Thomas Horton, Jr.	John Lupton
Michael Horton	Alan Decker
	John Amour
	Dick DeCort
	Wesley Eure
Dr. William Horton	Edward Mallory
Craig Merritt	David McLean
David Banning	Jeffrey Williams
John Martin	Robert Brubaker
Helen Martin	K.T. Stevens
Susan Martin	Denise Alexander
Addie Olson	Patricia Huston
	Patricia Barry
Dr. Greg Peters	Peter Brown
Kim Douglas	Helen Funai
Doug Williams	Bill Hayes
Jim Phillips	Victor Holchak
Cliff Patterson	John Howard
Scott Banning	Robert Hogan
	Ryan Macdonald
	Mike Farrell
Linda Peterson	Margaret Mason
Julie Olson	Charla Doherty
	Kathy Dunn
	Susan Seaforth
	Cathy Ferrar
Rick	Myron Natwick
Phyllis Anderson	Nancy Wickwire
	Corinne Conley
Eric Peters	Stanley Kamel
Anne Peters	Jeanne Bates
Phil Peters	Herb Nelson
Mary Anderson	Brigid Bazlen
	Karen Wolfe
	Carla Borelli
Wilbur Austin	Arlund Schubert
Diane Hunter	Coleen Gray
Richard Hunter	Terry O'Sullivan
Susan Peters	Bennye Gatteys
Bob Anderson	Mark Tapscott
Don Craig	Jed Allen
Meg Hansen	Suzanne Rogers
Hank	Frederick Downs
Dr. Neil Curtis	Joe Gallison
Ben Olsen	Robert Knapp
Steve Olsen	Flip Mark
Jim Fisk	Burt Douglas
Tony Merritt	Dick Colla
	Ron Husmann
Letty Lowell	Ivy Bethune
Jeri Clayton	Kaye Stevens
Mrs. Jackson	Pauline Myers
Betty Worth	Jenny Sherman
Brooke Hamilton	Adrianne LaRussa
David Banning	Steve Guthrie
Mary Anderson	Barbara Stanger

Karl DuVal	Alejandro Rey
Cathy Craig	Dorrie Kavanough
	Jennifer Harmon
Amanda Peters	Mary Frann
Trish Clayton	Patty Weaver
Robert LeClair	Robert Clary
Dr. Marlene Evans	Deidre Hall
Helen Grant	Ketty Lester
Maggie Horton	Suzanne Rogers
Hope Williams	Natasha Ryan
Danny Grant	Hassan Shaheed
Sharon DuVal	Sally Stark
Rebecca LeClair	Brooke Bundy
Valerie Grant	Tina Andrews
Paul Grant	Lawrence Cook
Samantha Evans	Andrea Hall Lovell

Music: Tommy Boyce, Bobby Hart, Barry Mann, Charles Albertine.

DAYS OF OUR LIVES—30 minutes —NBC—Premiered: November 8. 1965.

DAYTIME

Celebrity Interview.

Hostess: Penny DuPont.

Special Events Correspondent: Brian Lamb.

Film Reviewer: Joan O'Neill.

Music: Ed Kalehoff.

Producer: Sunni Davis.

Producer-Director: Ernest Sauer.

DAYTIME—60 minutes—Syndicated 1976.

A DAY WITH DOODLES

Comedy. Short slapstick sketches relating the misadventures of Doodles Weaver, as he attempts to cope with life's endless problems. Starring, as himself and everyone else in the cast: Doodles Weaver.

A DAY WITH DOODLES—05 minutes—Syndicated 1965. 150 episodes.

DEADLINE

Anthology. Dramatizations depicting the work of newspapermen throughout the country.

Host-Narrator: Paul Stewart.

Music: Fred Howard.

Included:

Thesis For Murder. The story of a mentally disturbed student who develops the perfect crime.

CAST
Robert Morris, Tony Franke.

Exposure. A reporter attempts to expose a photography racket that is operating in his city.

CAST
Patricia Englund, Henrietta Moore.

Massacre. The story of a newspaper reporter as he attempts to trap a berserk killer.

CAST
William Johnstone.

DEADLINE—30 minutes—Syndicated 1959.

DEADLINE FOR ACTION

Adventure. The investigations of Dan Miller, Wire Service reporter for *Trans Globe News.* Episodes were originally aired via "Wire Service."

Starring: Dane Clark as Dan Miller.

DEADLINE FOR ACTION—60 minutes—ABC—February 8, 1959 - September 20, 1959.

DEALER'S CHOICE

Game. Three competing contestants. Basis: Various games based on gambling.

Round One. Any Pair Loses. Two cards are placed on a board. Each player bets up to ten chips as to whether the next card will make a pair. Deductions or accumulations depend on the failure or success of the bet.

Round Two. Wheel of Chance. The four card suits, each represented by different odds (from one to one, to eleven to one) are displayed on a large electronic spinning wheel. Players are permitted to choose one and wager up to twenty-five chips. The wheel is spun and chips are added or deducted accordingly.

Round Three. Blackjack. A contestant is chosen from the studio audience. The bet limit is fifty. Two cards are dealt to each player. Players are then permitted to either freeze their score or receive another card. The player closest to or hitting an exact twenty-one is the winner and receives the bet amount. The chip total of the losers is the amount awarded to the studio-audience contestant who is able to trade his chips for a merchandise prize.

The Last Chance Round. Dealer's Derby. Three horses, each represented by different odds (one to one; three to one; five to one) are displayed on a board. The odds are determined by the corresponding number of numbered ping pong balls contained in a large air machine. Players secretly wager a bet, risking any part of their chips. The machine is turned on and balls are ejected one at a time. Each ball moves the horse one furlong in a five furlong race. The player with the highest chip total is the winner and trades his chips for a merchandise prize.

Host: Bob Hastings; Jack Clark.

Assistant: Jane Nelson.

Announcer: Jim Thompson.

Music: John La Salle.

DEALER'S CHOICE—30 minutes—Syndicated 1974.

DEAN MARTIN PRESENTS MUSIC COUNTRY

Musical Variety. Newcomers and established singers perform against the background of various Tennessee locales.

Regularly appearing: Loretta Lynn, Donna Fargo, Mac Davis, Jerry Reed, Lynn Anderson, Tom T. Hall, Kris Kristofferson, Marty Robbins, Ray Stevens, Tammy Wynette, Doug Kershaw, Doug Dillard.

Music: Jonathan Lucas.

Music Supervision: Doug Gilmer.

Music Co-ordinator/Arranger: Ed Hubbard.

DEAN MARTIN PRESENTS MUSIC COUNTRY—60 minutes—NBC—July 26, 1973 - September 6, 1973.

DEAN MARTIN'S COMEDY WORLD

Variety. Performances by new comedy talent. Taped on locations throughout the United States and England.

Host: Jackie Cooper.

Locational Hosts: Barbara Feldon, Nipsey Russell.

Regularly appearing: Eric Morecomb, Ernie Wise, Lonnie Shorr, Rich Little, Jud Strunk, Don Rickles, Phyllis Diller, Jack Benny, Ruth Buzzi, The Committee, and acts

from the British television series, "Monty Python's Flying Circus."

DEAN MARTIN'S COMEDY WORLD—60 minutes—NBC—June 6, 1974 - August 8, 1974.

THE DEAN MARTIN SHOW

Variety. A varying format featuring comedy and song and dance performances.

Host: Dean Martin.

Regulars: Ken Lane, Kay Medford, Marian Mercer, Lou Jacoby, Tom Bosley, Inga Nielson, Dom DeLuise, Nipsey Russell, Rodney Dangerfield, The Golddiggers, The Ding-a-ling Sisters (Lynn Latham, Tara Leigh, Helen Funai, Jayne Kennedy), The Krofft Marionettes.

Announcer: Frank Barton.

Orchestra: Les Brown.

THE DEAN MARTIN SHOW—60 minutes—NBC—September 16, 1965 - May 24, 1974.

DEAR PHOEBE

Comedy. Background: California, the city office of a newspaper, the *Los Angeles Daily Blade.* The misadventures of Bill Hastings, an ex-college professor employed as Phoebe Goodheart, the male advice-to-the-lovelorn columnist. Stories relate the romantic rivalries that occur between he, seeking a reporter's position, and his girlfriend, Mickey Riley, the female sportswriter.

CAST
Bill Hastings (Phoebe
    Goodheart)   Peter Lawford
Mickey Riley   Marcia Henderson
Mr. Fosdick, the managing
    editor   Charles Lane
Humphrey, the copy
    boy   Josef Corey
Also   Jamie Farr

Producer: Alex Gottlieb.

Sponsor: Campbell Soup.

DEAR PHOEBE—30 minutes—NBC—September 10, 1954 - September 2, 1955. 39 episodes.

DEATH VALLEY DAYS

Western Anthology. Background: Various areas between Nevada and Cali-

fornia during the latter half of the nineteenth century. Dramatizations depicting the pioneers journeying West and their struggles in establishing a new homeland.

Hosts: Stanley Andrews, the Old Ranger (twelve years).
    Ronald Reagan (three years).
    Robert Taylor (two years).
    Dale Robertson (three years).

Music: Marlen Skiles.

Commercial Spokeswoman: Rosemary DeCamp.

Included:

Sequoia. The true story of the self-sacrificing Cherokee Indian who spent twelve years developing an alphabet for his people.

Starring: Lane Bradford.

California's First Schoolmarm. A school teacher attempts to assemble her first class in the ruins of an old mission.

Starring: Dorothy Granter.

A Woman's Rights. The story of the first woman judge; and her fight against corruption.

CAST
Bethel Leslie, Dan Harens.

A Calamity Named Jane. The story of the relationship between Calamity Jane and Wild Bill Hickok.

CAST
Fay Spain, Rhodes Reason.

The Lady Was An M.D. A woman struggles to establish a medical practice.

Starring: Yvonne DeCarlo.

DEATH VALLEY DAYS—30 minutes—Syndicated 1952. 600 episodes.

DEBBIE DRAKE'S DANCERCIZE

Weight-reducing exercise. Dance steps combined with exercise movement.

Hostess: Debbie Drake.
DEBBIE DRAKE'S DANCERCIZE—30 minutes—Syndicated 1968. Original title: "The Debbie Drake Show"—30 minutes—Syndicated 1961. 260 tapes.

THE DEBBIE REYNOLDS SHOW

Comedy. Background: 804 Devon

The Debbie Reynolds Show. Debbie Reynolds.

Lane, Los Angeles, California, the residence of Jim Thompson, sportswriter for the *Los Angeles Sun;* and his beautiful and unpredictable wife, Debbie, who yearns for a career as a newspaper feature writer. Reluctant to have two newspaper writers in the family, Jim wants her to remain as she is: "a loving and beautiful housewife devoting herself to making her lord and master happy." Stories depict Debbie's attempts to prove her abilities and achieve her goal; and Jim's struggles to discourage her.

CAST
Debbie Thompson — Debbie Reynolds
Jim Thompson — Don Chastain
Charlotte Landers, her married
    sister — Patricia Smith
Bob Landers, Charlotte's husband,
    an accountant — Tom Bosley
Bruce Landers, their son, publisher
    of a neighborhood gossip
    sheet — Bobby Riha
Mr. Crawford, Jim's
    employer — Herbert Rudley
Music: Tony Romeo.

THE DEBBIE REYNOLDS SHOW—30 minutes—NBC—September 16, 1969 - September 8, 1970. 17 episodes.

DECEMBER BRIDE

Comedy. Background: Los Angeles, California. The trials and tribulations of Ruth and Matt Henshaw, a couple married eight years; and the life and romantic misadventures of Lily Ruskin, Ruth's mother, a widow who lives with them.

CAST
Lily Ruskin — Spring Byington
Matt Henshaw — Dean Miller
Ruth Henshaw — Frances Rafferty
Hilda Crocker, Lily's
    friend — Verna Felton
Peter Porter, the
    Henshaw's nextdoor
    neighbor — Harry Morgan
Music: Wilbur Hatch.
Producer: Parke Levy, Frederick de Cordova.
Sponsor: General Foods.

DECEMBER BRIDE—30 minutes—CBS—October 4, 1954 - September 24, 1959. Syndicated. Spin-off series: "Pete and Gladys" (see title). 159 episodes.

DECISION

Pilot Films. Proposed programs for the 1958-1959 season.

Included:

The Virginian. Western. The Virginian's investigation into a series of mysterious events that have been plaguing a judge's attempts to build a railroad spur to his ranch. Unsold as a half-hour series. Remade, four years later, as a ninety-minute pilot, the series was sold to NBC.

CAST
The Virginian: James Drury; Judge: Robert Burton; Dora: Jeanette Nolan.

Fifty Beautiful Girls. Mystery. A chorus girl attempts to solve the murders of three dancehall girls.
Starring: Barbara Bel Geddes.

The Danger Game. Adventure. A U.S. government undercover agent, posing as a singer, attempts to protect an American scientist.
Starring: Ray Danton as Stagg.

The Tall Man. Western. Background: Clayton City. A special investigator attempts to apprehend a gang of outlaws who robbed a train and killed the expressman.

CAST
Col. T.J. Allan: Michael Rennie; Leslie Henderson: William Phillips; Dawson: Dean Stanton.

DECISION—30 minutes—NBC—July 6, 1958 - September 1958.

DECISION—THE CONFLICTS OF HARRY S. TRUMAN

Documentary. Detailed via film clips: The decisions and conflicts of former U.S. President, Harry S. Truman.

DECISION—THE CONFLICTS OF HARRY S. TRUMAN—30 minutes—Syndicated 1964. 26 episodes.

DECOY

Crime Drama. Background: New York City. The investigations of Casey Jones, a beautiful and daring police woman.
Starring: Beverly Garland as Casey Jones.
Producer: David Alexander.

DECOY—30 minutes—Syndicated 1957. Also known as "Police Woman Decoy." 39 episodes.

DEEP SEA ADVENTURES

See title: "Crunch and Des."

THE DEFENDERS

Crime Drama. Background: New York City. The investigations and courtroom defenses of trial lawyer Lawrence Preston, and his son, attorney Kenneth Preston.

CAST
Lawrence Preston — E.G. Marshall
Kenneth Preston — Robert Reed
Helen Davidson, their
    secretary — Polly Rowles
Joan Miller, the
    social worker — Joan Hackett
                Rosemary Forsyth

Music: Leonard Rosenman.
Announcer: Bob Bryce, Herbert Duncan.
Producer: Herbert Brodkin, Robert Maxwell, Kenneth Utt.

THE DEFENDERS—60 minutes—CBS—September 16, 1961 - September 9, 1965. Syndicated. 132 episodes.

DELLA

Variety. Music, guests and interviews.
Hostess: Della Reese.
Co-Host: Sandy Baron.

DELLA—60 minutes—Syndicated 1970. 130 tapes.

THE DELPHI BUREAU

See title: "The Men," *The Delphi Bureau* segment.

DELVECCHIO

Crime Drama. Background: Los Angeles, California. The story of Police Detective Dominick Delvecchio, a law-school graduate whose legal ambitions are hindered by the demands and pressures of his job. (Delvecchio works out of the Washington Heights division of the L.A.P.D.)

CAST

Sgt. Dominick Delvecchio (Badge No. 425)	Judd Hirsch
Det. Paul Shonski, his partner	Charles Haid
Lieutenant Macavan, their superior	Michael Conrad
Tomaso Delvecchio, Dom's father	Mario Gallo
Assistant D.A. Dorfman	George Wyner

Music: Billy Goldenberg, Richard Clements.

Executive Producer: William Sackheim.

Producer: Michael Rhodes.

Director: Jerry London, Lou Antonio, Ivan Nagy, Arnold Laven, Walter Doniger.

DELVECCHIO—60 minutes—CBS— September 9, 1976 - July 17, 1977.

DEMI-TASSE TALES

Anthology. Rebroadcasts of dramas that were originally aired via other filmed anthology series. Also featured: first-run airings of theatrical shorts of the 1930s and 1940s.

DEMI-TASSE TALES—30 minutes— CBS 1953.

THE DENNIS DAY SHOW

Variety. Music, comedy, songs and dances.
Sketch: Background: Hollywood, California. The misadventures of Dennis Day, a swinging young bachelor.

CAST

Dennis Day	Himself
Charley Weaver, the apartment-house super	Cliff Arquette
Susan, Dennis's young admirer	Jeri Lou James
Marion, Dennis's girlfriend	Carol Richards Lou Butler
Lavinia, the landlady	Minerva Urecal Ida Moore
Hal, Dennis's friend	Hal March

Also: Verna Felton, Katy Phillips.

Dancers: Tom and Jean Mahoney.

Orchestra: Charles "Bud" Dante.

Producer: Paul Henning, Stanley Shapiro.

Sponsor: R.C.A. Victor.

THE DENNIS DAY SHOW—30 minutes—NBC—February 8, 1952 - August 2, 1954. Also known as: "The R.C.A. Victor Show."

DENNIS JAMES CARNIVAL

Variety.

Host: Dennis James.

Regulars: Dagmar (Jennie Lewis), Victoria Rone, Leonardo and Zola.

Music: Lew White.

Producer-Director: Ralph Levy.

DENNIS JAMES CARNIVAL—30 minutes—CBS—October 3, 1948 - November 7, 1948.

THE DENNIS JAMES SHOW

Variety. Interviews, audience participation, and discussions.
Host: Dennis James.
Assistant: Julia Meade.
Producer: Aaron Steiner.
Director: Lou Sposa.

THE DENNIS JAMES SHOW—30 minutes—ABC—February 8, 1952 - August 2, 1954.

DENNIS THE MENACE

Comedy. Background: 627 Elm Street, Hillsdale, the residence of the Mitchell family: Henry, an engineer with Trask Engineering; his wife, Alice; and their son, Dennis, a very mischievous young boy. Stories depict Dennis's disastrous attempts to assist people he believes are in trouble.

CAST

Dennis Mitchell	Jay North
Henry Mitchell	Herbert Anderson
Alice Mitchell	Gloria Henry
George Wilson, neighbor, avid gardener and bird watcher	Joseph Kearns
Martha Wilson, his wife	Sylvia Field
John Wilson, his brother	Gale Gordon
Eloise Wilson, John's wife	Sara Seeger
Tommy Anderson, Dennis's friend	Billy Booth
Seymour, Dennis's friend	Robert John Pitman
Margaret Wade, Dennis's friend, "That dumb old girl"	Jeannie Russell
Sgt. Theodore Mooney, the neighborhood policeman	George Cisar
Mr. Quigley, supermarket owner	Willard Waterman
Mr. Finch, drugstore owner	Charles Lane
Joey MacDonald, Dennis's friend	Gil Smith
Esther Cathcart, Dennis's friend, a woman desperately seeking a husband	Mary Wickes
Mr. Dorfman, the postman	Robert B. Williams
James Trask, Henry's employer	Henry Norell
Mr. Timberlake, president, the National Birdwatchers Society	Byron Foulger
June Wilson, George's sister	Nancy Evans
Mr. Merivale, the florist	Will Wright
Mr. Hall, Henry's employer	J. Edward McKinley
Mayor Yates	Charles Watts
Mr. Krinkie, the newspaper editor	Charles Seel
Ned Matthews, Mr. Wilson's uncle	Edward Everett Horton
Georgianna, Mr. Wilson's niece	Elinor Donahue
Mrs. Mitchell, Henry's mother	Kathleen Mulqueen
Mrs. Lucy Elkins, Mr. Wilson's cat-loving neighbor	Irene Tedrow

George Wilson's Dog: Freemont.

Music: Irving Friedman.

Executive Producer: Harry Ackerman.

Producer: Winston O'Keefe, James Fonda.

Director: Charles Barton, William D.

Russell, Norman Abbott.

DENNIS THE MENACE—30 minutes
—CBS—October 4, 1959 - September
22, 1963. CBS (rebroadcasts): October
5, 1963 - September 25, 1965.
Syndicated. 146 episodes.

THE DENNIS O'KEEFE SHOW

Comedy. Background: Los Angeles,
California. The home and working life
of widowed newspaper columnist Hal
Towne. Stories focus on his struggles.
to raise his young son, Randy.

CAST
Hal Towne	Dennis O'Keefe
Randy Towne	Rickey Kelman
Sarge, their housekeeper	Hope Emerson
Karen Hadley	Eloise Hardt
Eliot	Eddie Ryder

THE DENNIS O'KEEFE SHOW—30
minutes—CBS—September 22, 1959 -
June 14, 1960.

Department S. Left to right: Peter
Wyngarde, Joel Fabiani, and Rosemary
Nicols. *Courtesy Independent Television
Corp.; an ATV Company.*

DEPARTMENT S

Mystery. Background: Paris, France —
the headquarters of Department S, a
special investigative branch of Interpol
that undertakes the task of resolving
the unsolved baffling crimes of any
law enforcement organization in the
world. Director: Sir Curtis Seretse;
operatives: Jason King, the successful
author of Mark Cain Mystery Novels;
Annabell Hurst, a pretty scientific-
minded young woman; and Stewart
Sullivan, the American member of the
British team. Stories relate their investigations with Jason solving each
case as if it were a plot for one of his
books.

CAST
Jason King	Peter Wyngarde
Annabell Hurst	Rosemary Nicols
Stewart Sullivan	Joel Fabiani
Sir Curtis Seretse	Dennis Alaba Peters

Music: Edwin Astley.
Producer: Monty Berman.
Director: John Gilling, Gil Taylor,
Leslie Norman, Cyril Frankel,
Roy Baker, Ray Austen, Paul
Dickson.
Creator: Monty Berman, Dennis
Spooner.

DEPARTMENT S—60 minutes—Syndicated 1971. 28 episodes.

THE DEPUTY

Western. Background: Silver City,
Arizona during the 1880s. The story
of U.S. Marshal Simon Fry and his
deputy, Clay McCord, and their
attempts to maintain law and order.

CAST
Marshal Simon Fry	Henry Fonda
Deputy Clay McCord	Allen Case
Fran McCord, Clay's sister	Betty Lou Keim
Sergeant Tasker, a U.S. Cavalry agent assigned to duty in Silver City	Read Morgan
Herk Lamson, the owner of the general store	Wallace Ford

Music: Jack Marshall.

THE DEPUTY—30 minutes—NBC—
September 12, 1959 - September 16,
1961. Syndicated. 78 episodes.

DEPUTY DAWG

Animated Cartoon. Background: Mississippi. The misadventures of Deputy
Dawg, a simple-minded lawman, as he
attempts to maintain law and order.

Additional characters: The nearsighted Vincent Van Gopher;
Muskie the Muskrat; Ty Coon,
the Raccoon; Pig Newton, the
hombre seeking to rob the corn
fields; and the Sheriff, Deputy
Dawg's superior, the only human
figure.

Voice of Deputy Dawg: Dayton Allen.

DEPUTY DAWG—30 minutes—Syndicated 1960. NBC—September 11,
1971 - September 2, 1972. 78 episodes.

DESILU PLAYHOUSE

Anthology. Dramatic presentations.

Host: Desi Arnaz.
Music: Wilbur Hatch.

Included:

Meeting At Apalachin. Background:
The small town of Apalachin, New
York. The conflicts and tensions that
arise from a gangland convention.

CAST
Midge Rospond: Cara Williams; Gino
Rospond: Cameron Mitchell; Joe
Rogarti: Jack Warden; Sol Raimondi:
Luther Adler.

Dr. Kate. After their mother is
wounded and their father arrested, a
country doctor attempts to care for a
deaf boy, aged six, and his hostile
ten-year-old sister.

CAST

Dr. Kate: Jane Wyman; Sally: Karen Lee; Buddy: Bobby Buntrock.

Trial At Devil's Canyon. A sheriff attempts to apprehend a band of outlaws who robbed an army payroll and killed the stage passengers.

CAST

El Jefe: Lee J. Cobb; Farnsworth: Barry Kelly; Colonel Simmons: Edward Platt; Rose: Carol Thurston; Doc: Paul Bryar.

Change Of Heart. A blind detective, aided by a seeing-eye dog, seeks to track down a murderer.

CAST

Duncan McLain: Robert Middleton; Dick Sprague: Dick Sargent; Bill Wood: Donald May.

DESILU PLAYHOUSE—60 minutes— CBS—October 13, 1958 - June 10, 1960. Syndicated. 48 episodes.

THE DES O'CONNOR SHOW

Variety. Songs, dances, music, and comedy sketches. Taped in London, England.

Host: Des O'Connor.
Regulars: Connie Stevens, Jack Douglas, The Bonnie Birds Plus Two, The New Faces, Charlie Callas, Joe Baker, The Paddy Stone Dancers, The Mike Sammes Singers.
Announcers: Paul Griffith (from London); Ed Herlihy (for the sponsor).
Orchestra: Jack Parnell.

THE DES O'CONNOR SHOW—60 minutes—NBC—June 1970 - September 1970; June 21, 1971 - September 1, 1971. Summer replacement for "The Kraft Music Hall."

DESTINY

Anthology. Dramatizations of fate's intervention in the lives of ordinary people. Rebroadcasts of episodes that were originally aired via other filmed anthology programs.

Host-Narrator: Francis C. Sullivan.

Included:

Killer's Pride. The story of a college student who joins a posse to track down a killer.

CAST

Fay Wray, John Kerr, Mae Clarke.

Doctors Of Pawnee Hill. The story of two brothers, doctors, and their attempts to maintain law and order in a small frontier town.

CAST

Lee Marvin, Kevin McCarthy, Margaret Hayes.

Foreign Wife. The story of a group of enemy agents who try to blackmail the Viennese wife of a U.S. army officer into obtaining secret documents.

CAST

Phyllis Kirk, Stephen McNally, Larry Dobkin.

DESTINY—30 minutes—CBS—July 5, 1957 - September 1957; July 25, 1958 - September 1958.

DESTRY

Western. Background: The Frontier, 1860s. Harrison Destry, the peace-loving son of rugged gunfighter Tom Destry, is framed and falsely accused of a robbery charge. Stories relate his attempts to find the man responsible and clear his name.

Starring: John Gavin as Harrison Destry.

DESTRY—60 minutes—ABC— February 14, 1964 - May 9, 1964. 13 episodes.

THE DETECTIVES

Crime Drama. Background: New York City. The assignments of an elite team of N.Y.P.D. plainclothes detectives.

CAST

Captain Matt Holbrook	Robert Taylor
Lt. Johnny Russo	Tige Andrews
Sgt. Steve Nelson	Adam West
Sgt. Chris Ballard	Mark Goddard
Lisa Bonay, a police reporter	Ursula Thiess
Lt. Lindstrom	Russ Thorson
Lt. Conway	Lee Farr

Music: Herschel Burke Gilbert.

THE DETECTIVES—30 minutes— ABC—October 16, 1959 - September 22, 1961. Syndicated. 60 minutes— ABC—September 29, 1961 - September 21, 1962. Syndicated.

THE DETECTIVE'S WIFE

Crime Drama. Background: New York City. The investigations of Adam Conway, a private detective whose assignments are complicated by the intervention of his meaningful but troubleprone wife, Connie.

CAST

Adam Conway	Donald Curtis
Connie Conway	Lynn Bari

THE DETECTIVE'S WIFE—30 minutes—CBS—July 7, 1950 - September 29, 1950.

DEVLIN

Animated Cartoon. The story of three orphans, Ernie, Tod, and Sandy Devlin, and their attempts to support themselves by performing as a motorcycle stunt team.

Voices: Norman Alden, Michael Bell, Philip Clarke, Don Diamond, Mickey Dolenz, Sarina Grant, Bob Hastings, David Jolliffe, Robie Lester, Stan Livingston, Derrell Maury, Barney Phillips, Michele Robinson, Fran Ryan, John Stephenson, John Tuell, Ginny Tyler, Don Weiss, Jesse White.

Music: Hoyt Curtin.

DEVLIN—30 minutes—ABC—September 7, 1974 - February 15, 1976.

DIAGNOSIS: UNKNOWN

Crime Drama. Background: New York City. The cases of pathologist Dr. Daniel Coffe. Stories relate his attempts to solve unusual crimes through the use of scientific technology.

CAST

Dr. Daniel Coffe	Patrick O'Neal
Doris Hudson, the lab technician	Phyllis Newman
Dr. Matilal, a visiting colleague from India	Cal Bellini
Link, an associate	Martin Houston
Lieutenant Ritter, N.Y.P.D.	Chester Morris

DIAGNOSIS: UNKNOWN—60 minutes—CBS—July 5, 1960 - September 20, 1960.

THE DIAHANN CARROLL SHOW

Musical Variety.

Hostess: Diahann Carroll.

Orchestra: H.B. Barnum.

Special Musical Material: Earl Brown.

Choreography: Carl Joblonski.

Producer: Dick DeLeon.

Director: Mike Warren.

THE DIAHANN CARROLL SHOW—60 minutes—CBS—August 14, 1976 - September 4, 1976. 4 tapes.

DIAL 999

Crime Drama. Background: London, England. The investigations of Inspector Michael Maguire, a Royal Canadian Mounted Policeman assigned to study British methods of crime detection at the New Scotland Yard. (999: The Scotland Yard emergency telephone number.)

Starring: Robert Beatty as Inspector Michael Maguire.

DIAL 999—30 minutes—Syndicated 1959. 39 episodes.

THE DIAMOND HEAD GAME

Game. An outdoor game show taped in Hawaii. Eight players compete, two at a time. Round One: A question is read to the players by the host. The player who is first to identify himself through a buzzer signal receives a chance to answer. If he is correct he scores one point. The first player to score two points is the winner. Rounds 2, 3, and 4 involve the remaining six contestants and are played in the same manner.

The four winners are now situated at the bottom of a three-step climb. A category topic is revealed (e.g., "Actresses in Movies"), and a pertinent list of names is revealed. Players, who have to rely on their memories after hearing the names only once, each have to relate one of the subjects. Failure to mention one that is on the list or repeating one that was already said defeats that player and a new round begins. The three remaining players then move up one step and compete in another round. The game continues until one player remains.

The champion is escorted to Diamond Head, a glass room that is contained in a stage-constructed volcano. Once inside, an air machine is activated, which blows thousands of U.S. currency bills and slips of paper containing merchandise prizes around the room. The player receives 15 seconds with which to gather the bills and stuff them into a treasure bag. Whatever bills and/or gift certificates the player has managed to collect (to a limit of ten) are his prizes.

Host: Bob Eubanks.

Assistant: Jane Nelson.

Announcer: Jim Thompson.

Music: Alan Thicke.

Executive Producer: Ed Fisher, Randall Frees.

Director: Terry Kyne.

THE DIAMOND HEAD GAME—30 minutes—Syndicated 1975.

DIANA

Comedy. Background: New York City. The trials and tribulations of Diana Smythe, a beautiful young divorcée newly arrived in Manhattan from London.

Stories depict her home life at 4 Sutton Place, Apartment 11-B, a bachelor flat that is owned by her brother, Roger, an anthropologist who is presently in Equador; her work as a fashion illustrator at Buckley's Department Store; and her attempts to reclaim the numerous keys given out by her brother to his friends, acquaintances, and drinking companions—people, who are unaware of his absence and seek to use his apartment at all hours.

Diana. Diana Rigg.

CAST

Diana Smythe	Diana Rigg
Norman Brodnik, the president of Buckley's Department Store	David Sheiner
Norma Brodnik, his wife, the merchandising department head	Barbara Barrie

Howard Tolbrook, the copywriter   Richard B. Shull
Marshall Tyler, the window dresser   Robert Moore
Holly Green, a friend of Diana's, a model   Carol Androsky
Jeff Harmon, a mystery writer, a friend of Diana's   Richard Mulligan
Smitty, the Sutton Place Bellboy   Liam Dunn
Diana's dog (Roger's Great Dane): Gulliver.

Music: Jerry Fielding.

DIANA—30 minutes—NBC—September 10, 1973 - January 7, 1974. 15 episodes.

DICK AND THE DUCHESS

Comedy. Background: London, England. The investigations of Dick Starrett, an insurance claims detective, and his wife and assistant, Jane, a British duchess. Situations are played comically.

CAST

Dick Starrett	Patrick O'Neal
Jane Starrett	Hazel Court
Inspector Stark, a Scotland Yard investigator	Michael Shepley
Peter Jamison, Dick's boss	Richard Wattis

DICK AND THE DUCHESS—30 minutes—CBS—September 28, 1957 - May 16, 1958.

DICK CAVETT

Listed: The television programs of Dick Cavett.

This Morning—Discussion-Variety—90 minutes—ABC—April 1, 1968 - January 24, 1969.

Host: Dick Cavett.

Announcer: Fred Foy.

Orchestra: Bobby Rosengarden.

The Dick Cavett Show—Discussion-Variety—60 minutes—ABC—May 26, 1969 - September 19, 1969.

Host: Dick Cavett.

Announcer: Fred Foy.

Orchestra: Bobby Rosengarden.

The Dick Cavett Show—Disscussion-Variety—90 minutes—ABC-December 12, 1969 - January 1, 1975.

Host: Dick Cavett.

Announcer: Fred Foy.

Orchestra: Bobby Rosengarden.

The Dick Cavett Show—Talk-Variety—60 minutes—CBS—August 16, 1975 - September 6, 1975.

Host: Dick Cavett.

Series Regular: Leigh French.

Orchestra: Stephen Lawrence.

DICK CLARK PRESENTS THE ROCK AND ROLL YEARS

Variety. A nostalgic backward glance into the music and personalities of the fifties, sixties, and seventies via live appearances, tape, film, and newsreel footage.

Host: Dick Clark.

Orchestra: Billy Strange.

DICK CLARK PRESENTS THE ROCK AND ROLL YEARS—30 minutes—ABC—November 28, 1973 - January 9, 1974.

THE DICK CLARK SATURDAY NIGHT BEECHNUT SHOW

Variety. Performances by the top Rock and Roll personalities.

Host: Dick Clark.

THE DICK CLARK SATURDAY NIGHT BEECHNUT SHOW—30 minutes—ABC—February 15, 1958 - September 1959.

DICK CLARK'S WORLD OF TALENT

Discussion-Variety. Discussions, with two professional guests, based on the merits of material performed by young hopefuls.

Host: Dick Clark.

Permanent Panelist: Jack E. Leonard.

DICK CLARK'S WORLD OF TALENT—30 minutes—ABC—September 27, 1959 - December 20, 1960.

THE DICK POWELL THEATRE

Anthology. Dramatic presentations.

Host-Occasional Performer: Dick Powell.

Hostess: June Allyson (Mrs. Powell). When Syndicated in 1966 under the title "Hollywood Showcase."

Music: Herschel Burke Gilbert; Joseph Mullendore; Hans Salter; Richard Shores.

Producer: Dick Powell, Aaron Spelling, Tom McDermott.

Included:

Days Of Glory. The story of a power struggle involving a Latin-American dictator and an army colonel.

CAST
Morell: Charles Boyer; Marta: Suzanne Pleshette; Volera: Lloyd Bochner.

Doyle Against The House. A Blackjack dealer, needing five thousand dollars for his daughter's operation, attempts to rig a game against his employer.

CAST
Eddie Doyle: Milton Berle; Chris: Jan Sterling; Victor: Ludwig Donath.

Killer In The House. A man, faced with a vicious threat, attempts to help his brother, an escaped convict, evade a police dragnet.

CAST
Sid Williams: Edmond O'Brien; Paul Williams: Earl Holliman.

Thunder In A Forgotten Town. Returning home after serving ten years in a Red Chinese prisoner-of-war camp, a man struggles to readjust to life.

CAST
Jackie Cooper, Susan Oliver, David Janssen, Dewey Martin.

THE DICK POWELL THEATRE—60 minutes—NBC—September 26, 1961 - September 17, 1963. Syndicated.

DICK POWELL'S ZANE GREY THEATRE

Western Anthology.

Host-Occasional Performer: Dick Powell, introducing the evening's drama, with interesting facts about the Old West.

Music: Herschel Burke Gilbert; Joseph Mullendore.

Included:

Welcome From A Stranger. Returning from the Civil War, a lawman struggles to adopt the changing methods of law enforcement.

CAST
Ben Sanderson: Dick Powell.

Seed of Evil. A woman attempts to avenge the death of her son.

CAST
Irene: Cara Williams; West: Raymond Massey; Lance: Charles Maxwell.

Fearful Courage. After her husband is killed by a gunman, a woman attempts to return home and readjust to life.

CAST
Louise Brandon: Ida Lupino; Jeb: James Whitmore.

The Setup. Seeking his property, two land barons force Mike Bagley to marry a girl. When the ceremony is completed, he is forced to sign a paper relinquishing the property to her. After a fist beating, Mike is urged to leave or face death by the gun. Returning years following, Mike attempts to regain his property.

CAST
Mary Ann: Phyllis Kirk; Mike Bagley: Steve Forrest.

Hang The Heart High. A woman, discontent with her marriage, attempts to persuade a gunfighter to kill her husband.

CAST
Regan Moore: Barbara Stanwyck; Dix Porter: David Janssen; Regan's husband: Paul Richards.

DICK POWELL'S ZANE GREY THEATRE—30 minutes—CBS—October 10, 1956 - September 19, 1962. Syndicated. 145 episodes.

DICK TRACY

Crime Drama. Background: New York City. The investigations of Dick Tracy, a dauntless plainclothes police detective, and his assistant, Sam Catchem.

CAST
Dick Tracy	Ralph Byrd
Sam Catchem	Joe Devlin
Police Chief Murphy	Dick Elliott

Producer: Dick Moore, Keith Kalmer.

DICK TRACY—30 minutes—ABC—September 11, 1950 - April 7, 1951.

On October 12, 1931, Dick Tracy, the brainchild of Chester Gould, made its first appearance in comic strip form. Originally, the strip, submitted to the *Chicago Tribune-New York News* Syndicate, was entitled "Plainclothes Tracy," but was changed when Joseph Patterson, publisher of the *News* ran them as "Dick Tracy," since all cops are called "Dicks."

The popularity of the comics fostered movie interest, and in 1937, the first filmed version appeared, Republic's fifteen-episode serial, *Dick Tracy*, starring Ralph Byrd as Tracy in hot pursuit of the evil Spider. Byrd played Tracy in all but two films. 1939 saw *Dick Tracy's G-Men*, with Tracy pitted against the International Spy, Zarnoff. Two years later, 1941, the final Dick Tracy serial appeared, *Dick Tracy vs. Crime Incorporated*, with Tracy in battle against the evil Ghost.

In 1945, R.K.O. Pictures starred Morgan Conway as Tracy in two of four full-length features, *Dick Tracy* and *Dick Tracy vs. Cueball*. Ralph Byrd replaced Morgan for the remaining two, *Dick Tracy's Dilemma* and *Dick Tracy Meets Gruesome*. 1950-1951 saw the half-hour filmed television series, "Dick Tracy."

On August 18, 1952, Ralph Byrd's death ended the legend of a live Dick Tracy.

In 1961, U.P.A. Pictures distributed a syndicated version, "The Dick Tracy Show," an animated series of five-minute films designed to include a local market host acting as the Chief.

Characters:
Law Enforcers: Dick Tracy; Hemlock Holmes; The Retouchables Squad; Joe Jitsu; Speedy Gonzolez; and Heap O'Calorie.
Criminals: Sketch Paree and the Mole; Prune Face and Itchy; Flattop and Bee Bee Eyes; Stooge Villa and Mumbles; The Brow and Oodles.
Voices: Everett Sloane (Tracy), Mel Blanc, Benny Rubin, Paul Frees.

Music: Carl Brandt.

Producer: Peter DeMet, Henry Saperstein.

The sixth and latest version became, again in animation, a part of "Archie's TV Funnies." See title: "The Archie Show."

THE DICK VAN DYKE SHOW

Comedy. Background: 485 Bonnie Meadow Road, New Rochelle, New York, the residence of the Petrie family; Rob, the head writer of "The Alan Brady Show"; his wife, Laura; and their son, Richie. Stories relate the incidents that befall and complicate his life, and the lives of his friends and family.

Recurring story line: incidents in the lives of Rob and Laura before and shortly after their marriage. Flashbacks are used and first show Rob Petrie, a sergeant in the U.S. Army, and Laura Meeker (also referred to as Laura Mean), a dancer in a U.S.O. show, meeting when the show arrives at the Camp Crowder Base in Joplin, Missouri.

Later episodes relate the comical escapades of their courtship, marriage, and struggles as newlyweds in Ohio. The final sequence of flashbacks focus on Rob's securing employment as the head writer for "The Alan Brady Show"; the Petries move from Ohio to New Rochelle; the birth of their son, Richie; and Rob's hectic first days as a comedy writer.

The Dick Van Dyke Show. Left to right: Mary Tyler Moore, Dick Van Dyke, and Larry Matthews.

CAST

Rob Petrie	Dick Van Dyke
Laura Petrie	Mary Tyler Moore
Buddy Sorrell, Rob's co-worker	Morey Amsterdam
Sally Rogers, Rob's co-worker	Rose Marie
Millie Helper, the Petrie's neighbor	Ann Morgan Guilbert
Jerry Helper, her husband, a dentist	Jerry Paris
Mel Cooley, the producer	Richard Deacon
Alan Brady, the neurotic star	Carl Reiner
Richie Petrie	Larry Matthews
Pickles Sorrell, Buddy's wife, former showgirl, Pickles Conway	Barbara Perry
	Joan Shawlee
Freddie Helper, Millie and Jerry's son	Peter Oliphant
	David Fresco
Sam Petrie, Rob's father	Will Wright

	Tom Tully
	J. Pat O'Malley
Clara Petrie, his wife	Carol Veazie
	Isabel Randolph
Ben Meehan, Laura's father	Carl Benton Reid
Mrs. Meehan, his wife	Geraldine Wall
Herman Glimcher, Sally's mother-dominated boy friend	Bill Idelson
Stacy Petrie, Rob's brother	Jerry Van Dyke
Sol Pomeroy, Rob's army buddy	Marty Ingels
	Allan Melvin
Mrs. Glimcher, Herman's mother	Elvia Allman
Edward Petrie, Rob's grandfather	Cyril Delevanti

Music: Earle Hagen.

Executive Producer: Carl Reiner, Sheldon Leonard.

Producer: Ronald Jacobs.

Director: Jerry Paris, Sheldon Leonard, Hal Cooper, Theodore J. Flicker, Lee Philips, John Rich, Howard Morris, Claudio Guzman, James Niver, Stanley Z. Cherry, Robert Butler, James Komack, Peter Baldwin.

Creator: Carl Reiner.

Sally's Cat: Mr. Henderson.

Note: The Petrie address is also known to be 148 Bonnie Meadow Road.

THE DICK VAN DYKE SHOW—30 minutes—CBS—October 3, 1961 - September 7, 1966. Syndicated. 158 episodes.

DINAH SHORE

Listed: The television programs of singer-actress Dinah Shore.

The Dinah Shore Chevy Show—Musical Variety—15 minutes—NBC—November, 1951 - July 12, 1956. Also called "The Dinah Shore Show."

Hostess: Dinah Shore.

Regulars: The Notables, The Skylarks.

Announcer: Art Baker.

Orchestra: Vic Schoen; Harry Zimmerman.

The Dinah Shore Show—Musical Variety—30 minutes—NBC—September 20, 1956 - July 18, 1957.

Hostess: Dinah Shore.

Featured: The Skylarks (Gilda

Dinah Shore. Dinah Shore.

Maiken, Jackie Joslin, Earl Brown, Joe Hamilton, George Becker).

Announcer: Art Baker.

Orchestra: Harry Zimmerman.

The Dinah Shore Show—Musical Variety—60 minutes—NBC—October 20, 1957 - June 1, 1962.

Hostess: Dinah Shore.

Featured: The Tony Charmoli Dancers.

Orchestra: Harry Zimmerman; David Rose; Frank DeVol.

Dinah's Place—Variety—30 minutes—NBC—August 3, 1970 - July 26, 1974.

Format: An informal gathering of guests, lively talk, fashion, cooking, songs, decorating ideas, health, and beauty tips.

Hostess: Dinah Shore.

Regulars: Jerry Baker, gardening; Carol Board, sewing; Carol Owen, nutrition; Mary Ann Ryan, shopping advice; David Horowitz, auto advice; Bill Toomey, health; Merle Ellis, food.

Frequently appearing: Karen Valentine, beauty tips and advice; Lyle Waggoner, home decorating.

Music: The John Rodby Group.

Dinah—Variety—90 and 60 minutes versions (depending on individual local stations)—Syndicated 1974.

Hostess: Dinah Shore.

Music: The John Rodby Group.

Dinah and Her New Best Friends—Variety—60 minutes—CBS—June 5, 1976 - July 31, 1976.

Hostess: Dinah Shore.

Regulars: Diana Canova, Leland Palmer, Mike Neun, Gary Mule Deer, Bruce Kimmel, Michael

Preminger, Avie Falana, Dee Dee Rescher.

Orchestra: Ian Bernard.

Special Musical Material: Norman Martin.

Choreography: Hugh Lampbert.

Executive Producer: Henry Jaffe.

Producer: Carolyn Raskin, Rita Scott.

Director: Jeff Margolis.

DINAH'S PLACE

See title: "Dinah Shore."

DING DONG SCHOOL

Educational. Preschool instruction. Art, finger painting, and games.

Hostess-Instructress: Dr. Frances Horwich (Miss Frances).

Organist: Helen Morton.

Versions:

NBC—60 minutes—November 24, 1952 - December 28, 1956.

Syndicated—30 minutes—1959.

DINNER DATE

Variety.

Host: Vincent Lopez.

Announcer: Warren Lee Russell, George Putnam.

Orchestra: Vincent Lopez.

Producer-Director: Harry Coleman.

DINNER DATE—15 minutes—DuMont 1950.

THE DIONE LUCAS SHOW

A musical variety series starring songstress Dione Lucas. Produced by Byron Paul and first broadcast by CBS in 1949.

DIRTY SALLY

Western Comedy. Era: The 1880s. Sally Fergus, a ragged, tough, gray-haired, redeye drinkin', tobacco chewin' collector of prairie junk, and Cyrus Pike, an ornery young outlaw, a former ex-gunfighter regarded as the son she never had, join forces and become traveling companions destined for the gold fields of California. Stories relate one aspect of their journey—their attempts to assist the distressed.

CAST
Sally Fergus   Jeanette Nolan
Cyrus Pike   Dack Rambo
Sally's mule: Worthless.

Music: John Parker.

DIRTY SALLY—30 minutes—CBS—January 11, 1974 - July 19, 1974. 13 episodes.

DISCO '77

Music. Performances by current recording personalities.

Announcer: Ron St. John.

Producer-Director: Steve Marcus.

DISCO '77—30 minutes—Syndicated 1977.

THE DISCOPHONIC SCENE

Musical Variety. Performances by Rock personalities.

Host: Jerry Blavat, "America's teen-age music idol."

THE DISCOPHONIC SCENE—60 minutes—Syndicated 1966.

DISCOVERY

Educational. Explored: Various cultures and events of the world. Purpose: To familiarize children with an appreciation of history through filmed observations.

Hosts: Virginia Gibson; Frank Buxton; Bill Owen.

DISCOVERY—30 minutes—ABC—September 8, 1963 - September 5, 1971.

DISNEYLAND

See title: "Walt Disney's Wonderful World of Color."

DIVER DAN

Children's Adventure. Live action with marionettes. "He walks among creatures of frightening features, that's where you'll find Diver Dan. . . ." Background: The Sargasso Sea. The exploits of Diver Dan, a fearless explorer. Stories relate his efforts to aid the good fish and protect their watery domain from the rule of the evil Baron—a barracuda who is bent on controlling life amid King Neptune's world.

Characters: Diver Dan; Miss Minerva, the Mermaid; Baron Barracuda; Trigger Fish, the Baron's striped accomplice; Finley Haddock; Skipper Kipper; Scout Fish, reminiscent of an Indian—complete with tomahawk and feather; Killer Squid; Saw Fish Sam; Goldie the Goldfish; Hermit the Crab; Georgie Porgy; Gill-Espie, the bongo beating beatnick fish.

DIVER DAN—07 minutes—Syndicated 1961.

DIVORCE COURT

Drama. Staged courtroom sessions of divorce hearings.

Judge: Voltaire Perkins.

Announcer/Commentator: Bill Walsh.

DIVORCE COURT—30 minutes—Syndicated 1957. 390 episodes.

DIVORCE HEARING

Drama. Staged courtroom sessions of divorce hearings.

Host: Dr. Paul Popenoe.

DIVORCE HEARING—30 minutes—Syndicated 1958. 39 episodes.

DOBIE GILLIS

See title: "The Many Loves of Dobie Gillis."

DOC

Comedy. Background: New York City. The trials and tribulations of Dr. Joe Bogert, a general practitioner who lives in a rundown neighborhood and strives to treat his patients like human beings.

CAST

Dr. Joe Bogert	Barnard Hughes
Annie Bogert, his wife	Elizabeth Wilson
Beatrice Tully, his nurse	Mary Wickes
Happy Miller, Joe's friend	Irwin Corey
Laurie Fenner, Joe's married daughter	Judy Kahan
Fred Fenner, Laurie's husband	John Harkins
Mr. Goldman, a patient of Doc's	Herbie Faye
Michael Fenner, Laurie and Fred's son	Moosie Drier

Music: Pat Williams.

Executive Producer: Ed Weinberger, Stan Daniels.

Producer: Paul Wayne.

Director: Joan Darling, Bob Claver.

DOC—30 minutes—CBS—September 13, 1975 - August 14, 1976.

Revised Format:

Background: The Westside Community Clinic in New York City. Events in the life of Dr. Joe Bogert, the medical director of a free clinic.

CAST

Dr. Joe Bogert	Barnard Hughes
Janet Scott ("Scotty"), the nurse	Audra Lindley
Teresa Ortega, the receptionist	Lisa Mordente
Stanley Moss, the director of the clinic	David Ogden Stiers
Dr. Woody Herman	Ray Vitte

Music: Dick De Benedictis.

Theme: Stan Daniels.

Executive Producer: Ed Weinberger, Stan Daniels.

Producer: Lawrence Marks.

Director: Howard Storm.

DOC—30 minutes—CBS—September 25, 1976 - October 30, 1976.

DOC CORKLE

Comedy. The misadventures of Doc Corkle, a neighborhood dentist.

CAST

Doc Corkle	Eddie Mayehoff
Pop Corkle	Chester Conklin
Doc's Daughter	Connie Marshall

Also: Arnold Stang, Hope Emerson.

DOC CORKLE—30 minutes—NBC—October 5, 1952 - October 26, 1952.

DOC ELLIOT

Medical Drama. Benjamin R. Elliot, M.D., rejecting a lack of personal involvement and caring, resigns his position on the staff of Bellevue Hospital, New York, and retreats to the backwoods of Southern Colorado. There, in the Alora Valley, he is the only available doctor. Armed with a medically equipped camper and a citizens' band radio, he attempts to treat the inhabitants, who are suspicious of modern medicine and modern medical technology. Slowly, he wins acceptance by them.

CAST

Dr. Benjamin Elliot	James Franciscus
Barney Weeks, the owner/ operator of the general store	Noah Beery, Jr.
Margaret "Mags" Brimble, Ben's landlady	Neva Patterson
Eldred McCoy, a bush pilot who assists Ben in emergencies	Bo Hopkins

Music: Earle Hagen.

DOC ELLIOT—60 minutes—ABC—October 10, 1973 - August 14, 1974. 15 episodes.

THE DOCTOR

Anthology. Dramatizations of people confronted with mentally disturbing situations.

Host-Narrator: Warner Anderson.

Included:

Song For A Banker. When his future son-in-law wants to invest heavily in a music publishing company, a banker seeks to prove it a fraud.

CAST

Roland Young, Henry Jones, Isobel Elsom.

Googan. The story of a baseball manager who is helped to improve his team by the advice of his son's imaginary friend.

CAST

Ernest Truex, Virginia Gilmore, Thomas Coley.

The World Of Nancy Clark. The story of a young girl who attempts to prevent the marriage of her governess.

CAST

Lydia Reed, Rosemary Harris.

THE DOCTOR—30 minutes—NBC—1952-1953. Syndicated title (1956): "The Visitor." 44 episodes.

DOCTOR CHRISTIAN

Medical Drama. Background: The town of Rivers End. After Dr. Paul Christian retires, his nephew, Dr. Mark Christian, assumes control of his practice. Stories relate the infinite problems faced by a doctor in a small town. Based on the radio program.

CAST

Dr. Mark Christian   Macdonald Carey
Dr. Paul Christian   Jean Hersholt
Nurses   Jan Shepard
                      Cynthia Baer
                      Kay Faylen

DOCTOR CHRISTIAN—30 minutes—Syndicated 1956. 39 episodes.

DOCTOR DOLITTLE

Animated Cartoon. The world travels of Dr. Dolittle, a veterinarian who possesses the ability to talk to and understand animals. Stories relate his attempts to overcome the evils of Sam Scurvy, a fiend bent on learning his secrets to control animals for purposes of world domain. Based on the stories by Hugh Lofting.

Additional characters: Tommy Stubbins, Dolittle's assistant; Dum Dum, his pet duck; Chee Chee, his pet monkey; and Cyclops and Featherhead, Scurvy's cohorts.

Voices: Lennie Weinrib, Hal Smith, Barbara Towers, Robert Holt.

Music: Arthur Leonardi, Doug Goodwin, Eric Rogers.

DOCTOR DOLITTLE—30 minutes—NBC—September 12, 1970 - September 2, 1972. Syndicated. 17 episodes.

DOCTOR FU MANCHU

See title: "The Adventures of Fu Manchu."

DOCTOR HUDSON'S SECRET JOURNAL

Medical Drama. Background: Center Hospital. The problems faced by Dr. Wayne Hudson, neurosurgeon, in the pioneering of new methods of treatment.

CAST

Dr. Wayne Hudson   John Howard
Nurses   Jean Howel
                    Frances Mercer

DOCTOR HUDSON'S SECRET JOURNAL—30 minutes—Syndicated 1955. 39 episodes.

DOCTOR IN THE HOUSE

Comedy. Background: Saint Swithin's Teaching Hospital in London, England. The struggles and misadventures of seven young medical students. In later episodes: Of young doctors seeking to establish a practice. Based on the "Doctor" books by Richard Gordon. Produced by London Weekend Television.

CAST

Michael Upton,
    intern   Barry Evans
Geoffrey Loftus, Professor
    of Surgery   Ernest Clark
Duncan Waring,
    intern   Robin Newdell
Paul Collier,
    intern   George Layton
Huw Evans, intern   Martin Shaw
Dick Stuart-Clark,
    intern   Geoffrey Davis
Danny Wholey,
    intern   Jonathan Lynn
Dave Briddock, intern
    and part-time
    photographer   Simon Cuff
Helga, his live-in
    model   Yvette Stengaard
The Dean   Ralph Michael
Mr. Upton, Michael's
    father   Peter Brathurst
Mrs. Loftus, the Professor's
    wife   Joan Benham
Valerie Loftus, their
    daughter   Lynn Dalby

Music: Recorded.

DOCTOR IN THE HOUSE—30 minutes—Syndicated 1971. 52 episodes.

DOCTOR I.Q.

Game. A contestant is chosen from the studio audience. Dr. I.Q., the mental banker, asks him a question. If he correctly answers it he receives twenty silver dollars, plus a chance to earn additional silver dollars via a continuation of the question-answer rounds. The contestant plays until he is defeated by an incorrect response.

Hosts (Dr. I.Q.s): James McLain; Jay Owen; Tom Kennedy.

Assistants: Mimi Walters, Kay Christopher, Tom Reddy, Ed Michaels, Art Fleming, George Ansboro.

DOCTOR I.Q.—30 minutes—ABC—November 4, 1953 - January 7, 1954; January 15, 1958 - March 23, 1959.

DOCTOR JOYCE BROTHERS

Listed: The television programs of psychologist Dr. Joyce Brothers.

Format: An informal look into the world of modern psychology; discussions on the problems confronting many in terms that are understandable to the layman.

Doctor Joyce Brothers. Dr. Joyce Brothers.

Dr. Joyce Brothers—Advice—30 minutes—Local New York (WRCA-TV)—1958.

Hostess: Dr. Joyce Brothers.

Consult Dr. Brothers—Advice—30 minutes—Syndicated 1961.

Hostess: Dr. Joyce Brothers.

Tell Me, Dr. Brothers—Advice—30 minutes—Syndicated 1964.

Hostess: Dr. Joyce Brothers.

Appointment With Dr. Brothers—Advice—05 minutes—Syndicated 1969.

Hostess: Dr. Joyce Brothers.

Living Easy—Variety—30 minutes—Syndicated 1973. Guests, interviews, fashion, cooking, decorating tips, music, and songs.

Hostess: Dr. Joyce Brothers.

Announcer: Mike Darrow.

Orchestra: Bernie Green.

DOCTOR KILDARE

Medical Drama. Background: Blair General Hospital. The experiences, struggles, defeats, and victories of a young intern (later resident physician), James Kildare.

CAST

Dr. James
  Kildare   Richard Chamberlain
Dr. Leonard Gillespie, his
  mentor   Raymond Massey
Nurse Zoe Lawton   Lee Kurtz
Mrs. Salt   Cynthia Stone
Dr. Gerson   Jud Taylor
Dr. Lowry   Steven Bell
Dr. Agurski   Eddie Ryder
Dr. Kapish   Ken Berry
Nurse Conant   Jo Helton

Doctor Kildare. Richard Chamberlain and Raymond Massey.

Music: Jerry Goldsmith; Pete Rugolo; Harry Sukman.

Producer: David Victor, Calvin Clements, Norman Felton, Herbert Hirschmann.

DOCTOR KILDARE—60 minutes—NBC—September 27, 1961 - September 9, 1965. 30 minutes—NBC—September 13, 1965 - August 29, 1966. Syndicated. 132 hour episodes; 58 half hour.

THE DOCTORS

Serial. Background: Hope Memorial Hospital. The conflicts and tensions, the working and personal lives of doctors and nurses. Originally, it was an anthology series dramatizing medical cases in thirty-minute segments. Nine months later, the program was revamped and became a serial.

Original Cast (Alternating Daily)
Dr. Jerry Chandler   Richard Roat

Dr. Elizabeth Hayes   Margot Moses
Dr. William Scott   Jack Gaynor
Rev. Samuel Shafter,
  the hospital
  chaplain   Fred J. Scollay

Serial Cast
Dr. Matt Powers   James Pritchett
Brock Hayden   Adam Kennedy
Dr. Maggie Fielding   Bethel Leslie
                    Kathleen Murray
                    Ann Williams
                    Lydia Bruce
Nora Hansen   Joan Alexander
Jackie   Louise Lasser
Mr. Fielding   Fred Stewart
Steve   Craig Huebing
Dr. Althea Davis   Elizabeth Hubbard
                    Virginia Vestoff
Kate   Ellen MacRae
Jessie   Joselyn Somers
Willard   Court Benson
Peter Bonds   Gerald S. O'Loughlin
Gloria   Nancy Berg
Nurse Kathy Ryker   Nancy Barrett
                    Holly Peters
Dr. Mike Powers   Peter Burnell
                    Armand Assante
                    John Shearin
Nurse Carolee
  Simpson   Carolee Campbell
Dr. Hank Iverson   Palmer Deane
Dr. Nick Bellini   Gerald Gordon
Martha Allen   Sally Gracie
Dr. John Morrison   Patrick Horgan
Dr. Vito McCray   Paul Itkin
Dr. Karen Werner   Laryssa Lauret
Dr. Steve Aldrich   David O'Brien
Ginny   Greta Rae
Emma Simpson   Katherine Squire
Toni Ferra   Anna Stuart
Dr. John Rice   Terry Kiser
Dr. Bill Winters   James Noble
Mrs. Winters   Ann Whiteside
Kate Harris   Denise Nickerson
Dr. Ann Latimer   Geraldine Court
Margo Stewart   Mary Denham
Dr. Alan Stewart   Gil Gerard
Eric Aldrich   Keith Blanchard
Lauri James   Marie Thomas
Dr. Gil Lawford   Dale Robinette
Nurse   Susan Adams
Kurt Van Olsen   Byron Sanders
Simon Gross   Luis Van Rooten
Nurse Brown   Dorothy Blackburn
Keith Wilson   Morgan Sterne
Penny Davis   Julia Duffy
Anna Ford   Zaida Coles
Ed Stark   Conrad Roberts
Dr. Simon Harris   Mel Winkler
Mr. Stark   P. Jay Sidney
Mrs. Stark   Clarissa Gaylor
Dr. Powers Son   Rex Thompson
                    Harry Packwood
                    Robert La Tourne
                    Peter Burnell
Ma Thatcher   Madeleine Sherwood
Pa Thatcher   John Cullum
Dr. George Mitchell   Staats Cotsworth
Nora Harper   Muriel Kirkland

Margaret Liggett   Jean Sullivan
Mrs. Murtrie   Ruth McDevitt
Judy Stratton   Joanna Pettet
Dr. Johnny McGill   Scott Graham
Billy Allison   Bobby Hennessey
                    David Elliott
Dr. DeSales   Thomas Connolloy
Greta Powers   Jennifer Houlton
                    Eileen Kearney
Shana Golan   Marta Heflin
Jody Lee Bronson   C.C. Courtney
Dr. Nancy Bennett   Nancy Donahue
Mona Aldrich   Meg Mundy
Liz Wilson   Pamela Toll
Theodora Rostand   Clarice Blackburn
Stacy Sommers   Leslie Ann Ray
Paul Sommers   Paul Carr
Toni Powers   Anna Stuart
Jason Aldrich   Glenn Corbett
John Morrison   Patrick Horgan
Kyle Wilson   Wayne Tippit
Carolee Aldrich   Jada Rowland
Nola Dancy   Kathryn Harrold
Eleanor Conrad   Lois Smith
Dr. McIntyre   Dino Narizzano
Wendy Conrad   Fannie Speiss
                    Kathleen Eckles
Andy Anderson   Lloyd Bremseth
Kate Bartock   Ellen McRae
Dave Davis   Karl Light
Faith Collins   Katherine Meskill
Virginia Dancy   Elizabeth Lawrence
Sarah Dancy   Antoinette Panneck
Lew Dancy   Frank Telfer
Greta Powers   Jennifer Houlton
                    Jennifer Reilly
Joan Dancy   Peggy Whilton
Jerry Dancy   Jonathan Hogan
M.J. Match   Lauren White
Also: Nancy Fox, Ed Kemmer, Katherine Meskill, Court Benson, Robert Gentry, Angus Duncan.
Music: John Geller.

THE DOCTORS—30 minutes—NBC—Premiered: April 1, 1963.

THE DOCTORS AND THE NURSES

See title: "The Nurses."

DOCTORS HOSPITAL

Medical Drama. Life in the neurological wing of Lowell Memorial Hospital as seen through the eyes of Jake Goodwin, the chief neurosurgeon.

CAST

Dr. Jake Goodwin   George Peppard
Dr. Norah Purcell   Zohra Lampert
Dr. Felipe Ortega   Victor Campos
Dr. Janos Varga   Albert Paulsen
Nurse Connie
  Kimbrough   Elisabeth Brooks
Hester Stanton, the
  admissions
  nurse   Adrian Ricard

Dr. Anson Brooks   James Almanzar
Dr. Paul Herman   John Larroquette
The Circulating
  Nurse   Susan Franklin
Nurse Forester   Barbara Darrow
Nurse Willson   Elaine Church

Music: Don Ellis.

Executive Producer: Matthew Rapf.

Producer: Jack Laird.

Director: Edward Abroms, Leo Penn, Vincent Sherman, Robert Abrams.

Creator: James E. Mosher.

DOCTORS HOSPITAL—60 minutes—NBC—Premiered: September 10, 1975.

DOCTOR'S HOUSE CALL

Medical Advice.

Host: Dr. James Fox, specialist in internal and occupational medicine.

DOCTOR'S HOUSE CALL—05 minutes—Syndicated 1965.

DOCTOR SIMON LOCKE

Medical Drama. Background: Dixon Mills, Canada. Andrew Sellers, an aging doctor unable to properly care for his patients, places an ad for assistance in the medical journal. Simon Locke, a young doctor disgusted with his lucrative but unrewarding city practice, responds. Stories relate their attempts to assist the people of a poor community.

CAST
Dr. Simon Locke   Sam Groom
Dr. Andrew Sellers   Jack Albertson
Nurse Louise Wynn   Nuala Fitzgerald
Police Chief Dan
  Palmer   Len Birman

Music: Score Productions.

DOCTOR SIMON LOCKE—30 minutes—Syndicated 1971. 39 episodes. Spin-off series: "Police Surgeon" (see title).

DOCTOR SHRINKER

See title: "The Krofft Supershow," *Dr. Shrinker* segment.

DOCTOR SPOCK

Discussion. Two sets of patients discuss topics relating to children.

Host: Dr. Benjamin Spock, pediatrician.

DOCTOR SPOCK—30 minutes—NBC 1955.

DOCTOR WHO

Science Fiction Serial. The adventures of Dr. Who, scientist, the inventor of Tardis (Time And Relative Dimension In Space), a time machine that is capable of transporting him to any time or any place in the past or future or to any planet in the endless heavens. Episodes relate his battle against the sinister forces of evil. Created by Terry Nation. Produced by the B.B.C. Theatrical versions, culled from the serial: *Dr. Who and the Daleks* (1965); and *Invasion Earth, 2150 A.D.* (1966).

CAST
Dr. Who   William Hartnell
    Peter Cushing
    Jon Pertwee
Jo, his
  assistant   Katy Manning
Barbara, his
  niece   Jennie Linden
Susan, his
  niece   Roberta Tovey
Louise, his
  niece   Jill Curzon
Ian, his bumbling
  assistant   Roy Castle
Tom Campbell, his
  assistant   Bernard Cribbins
The Master, his
  nemesis   Roger Delgado

Music: Bill McGiffie.

Musical Director: Malcolm Lockyer.

Electronic Music: Barry Gray.

Executive Producer: Joe Vegoda.

Producer: Max J. Rosenberg, Milton Subotsky.

Director: Gordon Flemyng, Anthony Waye.

DOCTOR WHO—30 minutes—Syndicated (U.S.) 1973. 45 episodes.

DODO—THE KID FROM OUTER SPACE

Animated Cartoon. Dodo, an inhabitant of the atomic planet Hena Hydo, and his pet, Compy, are dispatched to Earth to assist Professor Fingers with

his research. Stories relate their attempts to resolve scientific mysteries.

DODO—THE KID FROM OUTER SPACE—30 minutes—Syndicated 1967. 78 episodes.

DOG AND CAT

Crime Drama. Background: California. The cases of police undercover agents J.Z. Kane, "The Cat," a beautiful, hip Southern college graduate, and her partner, Jack Ramsey, "The Dog," a by-the-books fourteen-year veteran cop. (Dog and Cat refers to precinct slang for male and female police teams. J.Z. and Ramsey are with the 42nd division of the L.A.P.D.)

CAST
Officer J.Z.
  Kane   Kim Basinger
Sgt. Jack Ramsey   Lou Antonio
Lt. Art
  Kipling, their
  superior   Matt Clark

Music: Barry DeVorzon.

Executive Producer: Lawrence Gordon.

Producer: Robert Singer.

Director: Michael Preece, Stephen Stern, Paul Stanley, Robert Davis, Arnold Laven.

Creator: Walter Hill.

DOG AND CAT—60 minutes—ABC—March 5, 1977 - May 14, 1977.

DO IT YOURSELF

Home repairs and maintenance. Comical and serious treatment is given to do-it-yourself projects.

Hosts: Dave Willock, Cliff Arquette.

Assistants: Mary McAdoo, Steve Woolton.

DO IT YOURSELF—30 minutes—NBC—June 26, 1955 - September 18, 1955.

DOLLAR A SECOND

Game. A humiliating stunt is announced at the beginning of the program. A contestant, chosen from the studio audience, competes in a series of rapid-fire general knowledge question-answer rounds. The player receives one dollar a second for each second of correct responses. He continues upon his own discretion and stops when he feels safe. However, if the announcer should interrupt the proceedings, and the player has not stopped, he loses all his accumulated money. The player then receives a chance to earn money by performing the stunt that was announced at the beginning of the program.

A ticking clock is set to establish a specific amount of money. The contestant then performs the stunt. For each second that the clock ticks before the player completes the stunt, one dollar is deducted from the established amount. His final cash prize depends on his swiftness in performing the stunt.

Host: Jan Murray.

Assistants: Patricia White, Bernard Martin, Stuart Mann.

Announcers: Ken Roberts, Terry O'Sullivan.

Producer: Jess Kimmel, Mike Dutton, Dave Brown.

Sponsor: Mogen-David Wines.

DOLLAR A SECOND—30 minutes—DuMont—September 20, 1953 - September 1954; ABC—October 1, 1954 - August 31, 1956.

DOLLY

Musical Variety.
Hostess: Dolly Parton.
Orchestra: Jerry Whitehurst.
Executive Producer: Bill Graham, Reg Dunlap.
Director: Bill Turner.

DOLLY—30 minutes—Syndicated 1976.

Dolly. Dolly Parton.

THE DOM DeLUISE SHOW

Variety. Music, songs, and comedy sketches.

Host: Dom DeLuise.
Regulars: Peggy March, Carol Arthur, Paul Dooley, Dick Lynn, Bill McCutcheon, Marian Mercer, The Gentry Brothers, The June Taylor Dancers.
Announcer: Johnny Olsen.
Orchestra: Sammy Spear.

THE DOM DeLUISE SHOW—60 minutes—CBS—June 1968 - September 18, 1968.

THE DON ADAMS SCREEN TEST

Game. One contestant, chosen from three finalists, receives the opportunity to star in a screen test. The contestant is brought on stage where he meets his celebrity partner and views a scene from a film that he and his partner must reenact. The actors are then sent to makeup where they are permitted to study their scripts and review the film clip. After a commercial break, the outtakes (mistakes) of the contestant's screen test are seen. A second round, played in the same manner, but involving different contestants and a different film reenactment, follows. At the end of the second screen test, the final, edited versions of both tests are seen. A guest producer or director then selects the contestant he feels was best. His decision awards the amateur a part in a movie or television series.

Host-Director of the Screen Tests: Don Adams.
Announcer: Dick Tufeld.
Music: Hal Mooney.
Executive Producer-Creator: Don Adams.
Producer-Director: Marty Pasetta.

THE DON ADAMS SCREEN TEST—30 minutes—Syndicated 1975.

DONALD O'CONNOR

Listed: The television programs of actor Donald O'Connor.

The Donald O'Connor Show—Musical Variety—60 minutes—NBC—1951.

Host: Donald O'Connor.
Regulars: Sid Miller, Walter Catlett, The Unger Twins.
Orchestra: Al Goodman.

The Donald O'Connor Show—Musical Variety—30 minutes—NBC—October 9, 1954 - September 10, 1955.

The Donald O'Connor Show. Host Donald O'Connor and guest Shari Lewis.

Host: Donald O'Connor.
Regulars: Sid Miller, Regina Gleason, Jan Arvan, Joyce Smight, Laurette Luez, Nestor Paiva, Olan Soule, Chief Santini, Phil Garris, Fritz Fields, Joyce Holden, Marcia Moe, Eilene Janssen.
Orchestra: Al Goodman.

The Donald O'Connor Show—Talk-Variety—90 minutes—Syndicated 1968.

Host: Donald O'Connor.
Announcer: Joyce Jameson.
Orchestra: Alan Copeland.

THE DON AMECHE SHOW

See title: "Don's Musical Playhouse."

THE DON AMECHE THEATRE

Anthology. Rebroadcasts of dramas that were originally aired via other filmed anthology programs.
Host: Don Ameche.

Included:

Trapped. A wife and her money-hungry lover attempt to murder her shrewd husband.

CAST
Dan O'Herlihy, Jerry Hayas.

Across The Dust. Though feeling incapable, a frontier scout attempts to lead a wagon train to California.
Starring: Lloyd Nolan.

Hour Of Truth. A bullfighter attempts

to regain his reputation after a serious goring.

Starring: Ricardo Montalban.

THE DON AMECHE THEATRE—30 minutes—Syndicated 1958.

THE DON HO SHOW

Variety.

Host: Don Ho.

Executive Producer: Bob Banner.

Producer: Brad Lachman.

Director: Jack Regas, Johnny Todd, Jeff Margolis.

THE DON HO SHOW—30 minutes—ABC—October 25, 1976 - March 4, 1977.

DON KIRSHNER'S ROCK CONCERT

Variety. Performances by Rock personalities.

Host: Don Kirshner.

DON KIRSHNER'S ROCK CONCERT—90 minutes—Syndicated 1973.

THE DON KNOTTS SHOW

Variety. Various comedy sketches.

Host: Don Knotts.

Regulars: Elaine Joyce, John Dehner, Gary Burghoff, Eddy Carroll, Kenneth Mars, Mickey Deems, Frank Welker, Bob Williams, and his dog, Louis.

Announcer: Dick Tufeld.

Orchestra: Nick Perito.

THE DON KNOTTS SHOW—60 minutes—NBC—September 15, 1970 - July 6, 1971. 24 tapes.

DON McNEILL'S TV CLUB

Variety. Music, comedy, songs, and conversation. Broadcast from the Terrace Casino of the Hotel Motel in Chicago. Based on the radio program: "Breakfast Club."

Host: Don McNeill.

Regulars: Fran Allison (Aunt Fanny), Johnny Desmond, Sam Cowling, Eileen Parker, Patsy Lee, Cliff Peterson, Jack Owen.

Announcer: Ken Nordine.

Orchestra: Eddie Ballantine.

DON McNEILL'S TV CLUB—60 minutes—ABC—September 5, 1950 - December 19, 1951; February 22, 1954 - February 25, 1955.

DON MESSER'S JUBILEE

Musical Variety. Performances by Country and Western entertainers.

Host: Don Messer.

Regulars: Don Tremaine, Mary Osburne, Charlie Chamberlain.

DON MESSER'S JUBILEE—30 minutes—Syndicated 1960. 59 episodes. Produced in Canada.

THE DONNA REED SHOW

Comedy. Background: The town of Hilldale. The dreams, ambitions, and frustrations of the Stone family: Alex, a pediatrician; his wife, Donna; and their children, Mary and Jeff. Trisha, their unofficially adopted daughter, appears in later episodes. An orphan, she follows them home from a picnic. Through an arrangement with her uncle-guardian, she is permitted to remain with the Stones.

CAST

Donna Stone	Donna Reed
Alex Stone	Carl Betz
Mary Stone	Shelley Fabares

The Donna Reed Show. Bottom, left: Patty Peterson, Carl Betz. Top, left: Donna Reed, right: Paul Peterson. © *Screen Gems.*

Jeff Stone	Paul Peterson
Midge Kelsey, Donna's	

friend	Ann McCrea
Dr. David Kelsey, her husband	Bob Crane
Smitty, Jeff's friend	Darryl Richard
Herbie Bailey, Mary's boy-friend (early eipisodes)	Tommy Ivo
Scotty Simpson, Mary's boy-friend (later episodes)	Jerry Hawkins
Karen, Jeff's girl-friend	Janet Languard
Bibi, Jeff's girl-friend	Candy Moore
Susanna, Smitty's girl-friend	Sandy Descher
Trisha	Patty Peterson

Producer: Tony Owen, William Roberts.

THE DONNA REED SHOW—30 minutes—ABC—September 24, 1958 - September 3, 1966. Syndicated. 275 episodes.

DONNY AND MARIE

Musical Variety.

Hosts: Donny and Marie Osmond (brother and sister).

Regulars: Paul Lynde, Sharon Baird, Jim Connell, Patty Maloney, Van Snowden, Jimmy Osmond, The Osmond Brothers, The Ice Vanities.

Announcer: George Fenneman, George Benedict.

Orchestra: Tommy Oliver.

Special Musical Material: Earl Brown.

Choreography: Ron Poindexter.

Producer-Creator: Sid and Marty Krofft.

Director: Art Fisher.

DONNY AND MARIE—60 minutes—ABC—Premiered: January 23, 1976.

Donny and Marie. Marie Osmond (left) and Donny Osmond.

DON QUIXOTE

Adventure. Background: Seventeenth-century Spain. Believing himself to be the knight errant described in books of chivalry, Don Quixote, a gaunt country gentleman of La Mancha, teams with his friend, Sancho Panza, and undertakes a crusade to defend the oppressed, avenge the injured, and capture the heart of his beloved Dulcinea. Based on the novel by Cervantes.

CAST

Don Quixote	Josef Meinrad
Sancho Panza	Roger Carrel
Dulcinea	Maria Saavedra

DON QUIXOTE—30 minutes—Syndicated 1965. 13 episodes.

DON RICKLES

Listed: The television programs of insult comedian Don Rickles.

The Don Rickles Show—Variety—30 minutes—ABC—September 27, 1968 - January 31, 1969.

Format: Guests, interviews and comedy sketches.

Host: Don Rickles.

Announcer: Pat McCormick.

Orchestra: Vic Mizzy.

The Don Rickles Show—Comedy—30 minutes—CBS—January 14, 1972 - May 26, 1972.

Background: Great Neck, Long Island, New York, the residence of the Robinson family — Don, an account executive with the advertising firm of Kingston, Cohen, and Vanderpool; his wife, Barbara, and their daughter, Janie. Stories depict the harassed life of Don Robinson, a man at odds with all and struggling to survive the red tape and the mechanizations of a computerized society.

CAST

Don Robinson	Don Rickles
Barbara Robinson	Louise Sorel
Janie Robinson	Erin Moran
Tyler Benedict, Don's friend, neighbor, co-worker	Robert Hogan
Jean Benedict, his wife	Joyce Van Patten
Audrey, Don's secretary	Judy Cassmore
Conrad Musk, the agency's hip advertising man	Barry Gordon
Arthur Kingston, Don's employer	Edward Andrews
Mr. Vanderpool, Don's employer	Parley Baer

M. Emmet Walsh

DON'S MUSICAL PLAYHOUSE

Musical Comedy. Background: A summer theatre. The lives and struggles of the performers.

Host: Don Ameche.

Regulars: Dorothy Greener, Betty Brewer, The June Graham Dancers, The Don Craig Chorus, The Charles Faler Dancers, The Myer Rappaport Chorus.

Orchestra: Bernie Green.

Producer: Felix Jackson.

Director: Joe Scibetta.

DON'S MUSICAL PLAYHOUSE—30 minutes—ABC—July 5, 1951 - September 1951. Also known as "The Don Ameche Show."

DON'T CALL ME CHARLIE

Comedy. Background: Paris, France, a United States Army Veterinary post under the command of Colonel Charles Baker, a man who fraternizes with the troops, but detests being called "Charlie." Stories relate the misadventures of Private Judson McKay, a simple, backwoods Iowa veterinarian who refuses to let the sophistication of Europe or the attempts of his fellow officers change his square but innocent ways.

CAST

Private Judson McKay	Josh Peine
Colonel U. Charles Baker	John Hubbard
First Sergeant Wozniah	Cully Richard
Patricia Perry, the general's secretary	Linda Lawson
General Steele	Alan Napier
Corporal Lefkowitz	Arte Johnson
Selma Yassarian, a secretary	Louise Glenn
Madame Fatime, the landlady	Penny Santon

DON'T CALL ME CHARLIE—30 minutes—NBC—September 28, 1962 - January 25, 1963. 26 episodes.

THE DOODLES WEAVER SHOW

Variety. Music, songs, dances, and comedy sketches.

Host: Doodles Weaver.

Regulars: Lois Weaver (Mrs.), Rex Marshall, Peanuts Mann, Dick Dana, Mariam Colby.

Announcer: Rex Marshall.

Orchestra: Milton DeLugg.

Producer: Mort Werner.

Director: Warren Jacober.

THE DOODLES WEAVER SHOW—30 minutes—NBC—June 9, 1951 - September 1951.

DOORWAY TO DANGER

Adventure. The U.S. government's battle against international intrigue as seen through the secret missions of undercover agents.

CAST

John Randolph, the chief	Roland Winters
Agent Doug Carter	Stacy Harris

Announcer: Ernest Chapell.

DOORWAY TO DANGER—30 minutes—NBC—July 4, 1952 - October 1, 1953.

THE DOOR WITH NO NAME

Spy Drama. Background: Washington, D.C. Dramatizations based on the secret activities of The Door With No Name, an unidentified portal through which presumably pass the most intrepid of spies and spy fighters.

CAST

The Intelligence Chief	Mel Ruick
The Undercover Agent	Grant Richards

Narrator: Westbrook Van Voorhis.

Music: Charles Paul.

THE DOOR WITH NO NAME—30 minutes—NBC—July 6, 1951 - September 1951.

THE DORIS DAY SHOW

Comedy. Distinguished by four formats.

Format One: September 24, 1968 — September 16, 1969.

Background: Mill Valley, California. Dissatisfied with the congestion of the big city, Doris Martin, widow and mother of two children, relinquishes her career as a singer and returns to her father's ranch. Stories depict her attempts to raise her children, Billie and Toby, and her involvement in local community affairs.

The Doris Day Show. Doris Day.

Format Two: September 22, 1969 - September 7, 1970.

Feeling a need to assist with the growing expenses on the ranch, Doris acquires a job in San Francisco as the executive secretary to Michael Nicholson, the editor of *Today's World Magazine.* Episodes relate her home and working life.

Format Three: September 14, 1970 - September 6, 1971.

With occasional reporting assignments and difficulty commuting from country to city, Doris relocates and rents apartment 207 at 965 North Parkway over Pallucci's Italian Restaurant. Her children reside with her; and her father, Buck Webb, and his handyman, Leroy B. Simpson, continue to operate the ranch.

Format Four: September 13, 1971 - September 3, 1973.

A complete change in format and cast. Background: San Francisco, California. The working and romantic life of a beautiful young bachelorette, Doris Martin, General News Reporter for *Today's World Magazine.*

CAST
September 24, 1968 - September 6, 1971 (formats one, two, and three).

Doris Martin   Doris Day
Buck Webb   Denver Pyle
Billy Martin   Philip Brown
Toby Martin   Tod Starke
Leroy B. Simpson   James Hampton
Aggie, their housekeeper (early
  episodes)   Fran Ryan
Juanita, their housekeeper (later
  episodes)   Naomi Stevens
Michael Nicholson McLean Stevenson
Ron Harvey, the associate
  editor   Paul Smith
Myrna Gibbons, his
  secretary   Rose Marie

Willard Jarvis, Doris's
  perfectionist
  neighbor   Billy DeWolfe
Angie Pallucci, the owner of
  the restaurant; Doris's
  landlady   Kaye Ballard
Louie Pallucci, her
  husband   Bernie Kopell
Colonel Fairburn, the
  publisher of *Today's
  World Magazine* Edward Andrews
Ethel, Billy and Toby's baby-
  sitter   Carol Worthington
Duke Farentino, Doris' friend,
  a boxer   Larry Storch

Martin family sheep dog: Lord Nelson.

Music: Jimmie Haskel.

CAST
September 13, 1971 - September 4, 1972 (first year of format four).

Doris Martin (Miss)   Doris Day
Cyril Bennett, the editor of
  *Today's World
  Magazine*   John Dehner
Jackie Parker, his
  secretary   Jackie Joseph
Willard Jarvis   Billy DeWolfe
Angie Pallucci   Kaye Ballard
Louie Pallucci   Bernie Kopell
Dr. Peter Lawrence, Doris's
  romantic interest Peter Lawford

Music: Jimmie Haskell.

CAST
September 11, 1972 - September 3, 1973 (final year of format four).

Doris Martin (Miss)   Doris Day
Cyril Bennett   John Dehner
Jackie Parker   Jackie Joseph
Jonathan Rusk, Doris's romantic
  interest, a foreign
  correspondent   Patrick O'Neal
Detective Broder, San
  Francisco Police
  Department   Ken Lynch

Music: Jimmie Haskell.

THE DORIS DAY SHOW—30 minutes—CBS—September 24, 1968 - September 3, 1973. Syndicated. 128 episodes.

DOTTO

Game. Two competing contestants. Displayed on a large frame are fifty dots that, when connected, represent a famous person. The host states a general knowledge type of question. The player first to identify himself through a buzzer signal receives a chance to answer. If his answer is correct, a connection is made between two of the dots and he receives a chance to identify the drawing. If he is unable, the game continues. Correct identifications earn players large sums of cash. Contestants compete until defeated by another player.

Host: Jack Narz.

Announcer: Wayne Howell.

Producer: Ed Jurist.

DOTTO—30 minutes—CBS—January 6, 1958 - August 15, 1958. Prime time run: July 1, 1958 - August 26, 1958.

THE DOTTY MACK SHOW

Variety. Pantomimed renditions of hit recordings.

Hostess: Dotty Mack.

Regulars: Bob Braun, Colin Male.

Music: Recorded.

THE DOTTY MACK SHOW—15 minutes—ABC—August 31, 1953 - September 3, 1956.

DOUBLE DARE

Game. Two contestants, each placed in an isolation booth, compete. A clue to the identity of a person, place, or thing appears before each player. If one feels he can identify it, he presses a button that automatically seals his opponent in a sound-proof room. Should the player give a correct response, he receives $50 and a dare: to let his opponent see an additional clue for five seconds. If he takes the dare and his opponent fails to identify the object, he wins $100. The opponent is again isolated and the player is offered a double dare—to let his opponent see another clue for five seconds. Again, if he accepts it and the opponent fails to identify the object, he wins $200. However, should the opponent identify the object, the opponent wins $50. A player's rejection of a dare begins a new game. If, when buzzing in a player answers incorrectly, his opponent receives one free clue and a chance to identify the object in question. Six clues are played per game and the player first to score $500 is the winner.

Host: Alex Trebek.

Announcer: Johnny Olsen.

Music: Bert Eskander.

Executive Producer: Mark Goodson, Bill Todman.

Producer: Jonathan Goodson.

Director: Marc Breslow.

DOUBLE DARE—30 minutes—CBS—
December 13, 1976 - April 29, 1977.

DOUBLE EXPOSURE

Game. Two competing contestants. Object: The identification of a famous celebrity or event that is hidden under a jigsaw puzzle. Contestants, in turn, choose a puzzle piece that, when removed, reveals a picture part, and a varying amount of cash or a merchandise prize that is placed on his side of a board. If neither player is able to identify it, the game continues. The first player to correctly identify the photograph is the winner and receives the prizes that are on his side of the board.

Host: Steve Dunne.

DOUBLE EXPOSURE—30 minutes—CBS—March 13, 1961 - September 29, 1961.

THE DOUBLE LIFE OF HENRY PHYFE

Comedy. Background: Washington, D.C. Henry Wadsworth Phyfe, a mild-mannered accountant and the exact double of foreign spy, U-31, is recruited by Central Intelligence to replace the spy, who was killed by a hit-and-run before he was able to reveal vital secrets.

Stories relate Henry's reluctant and fumbling investigations as he struggles to carry out U-31's vital missions.

CAST

Henry Phyfe	Red Buttons
Sub Chief Hannahan	Fred Clark
Judy, Henry's girl-friend	Zeme North
Florence, Henry's land-lady	Marge Redmond
Hamble, Henry's employer	Parley Baer
Sandy, a C.I. Agent	Rob Kilgallen
Larry, a C.I. Agent	Ed Faulkner

Music: Vic Mizzy.

THE DOUBLE LIFE OF HENRY PHYFE—30 minutes—ABC—January 13, 1966 - September 1, 1966. 17 episodes.

DOUBLE OR NOTHING

Game. Five contestants, working as a team, start with a specific amount of money. The host questions each on various category topics. Players receive additional cash for each correct response. Incorrect responses deduct the "at stakes" amount from their total. With each correct response players option to either stop or continue and risk. If risking, they may double their money by correctly answering three questions. If they fail, the money is deducted from the team's score. Final cash earnings are divided equally.

Host: Bert Parks.

Assistant: Joan Meinch.

Announcer: Bob Williams.

Orchestra: Ivan Ditmars.

Producer: Walt Framer.

Sponsor: Campbell's

DOUBLE OR NOTHING—30 minutes—CBS 1952.

DOUGH RE MI

Game. Three competing players, who each receive two hundred dollars betting money. Object: To identify song titles after hearing only the first three notes. If players are unable, they bid for the next note. The highest bidder receives it, and a chance to identify the song title. If he correctly guesses the title, he receives the "at stakes" cash. If incorrect, the player is permitted to challenge the remaining players to guess it. If the tune still remains a mystery, bidding begins on the next note. Winners are the highest cash scorers.

Host: Gene Rayburn.

Producer: Hugh Branigan.

DOUGH RE MI—30 minutes—NBC—February 4, 1958 - December 30, 1960.

DOUGLAS FAIRBANKS JR. PRESENTS

Anthology. Dramatizations of people caught in unusual circumstances.

Host: Douglas Fairbanks, Jr.

Included:

The Refugee. Background: Berlin. A British officer attempts to discover which member of a group of refugees from the Eastern Zone is a Russian spy.

Starring: Dennis O'Dea.

Someone Outside. An artist attempts to avenge the death of his wife; his victim is the fiancée of the doctor who operated on her.

Starring: Maurice Kaufman.

The Man Who Wouldn't Escape. Background: South America. The brother of a ruthless dictator attempts to begin a resistance movement.

CAST
Karel Slephanek, Christopher Lee.

Second Wind. With their daughter about to have a baby, a married couple attempt to overcome their feeling of growing old.

CAST
Michael Shepley, Nora Swimburne.

DOUGLAS FAIRBANKS JR. PRESENTS—30 minutes—NBC—1953 - 1957. 117 episodes.

THE DOW HOUR OF GREAT MYSTERIES

Anthology. Dramatizations depicting the plight of people confronted with uncertain situations.

Host: Joseph N. Welch.

Included:

The Datchet Diamonds. The story of Cyril Paxton, a handsome British con artist who suddenly loses Lady Luck, his money, and his beautiful fiancée, Daisy, who has given up on him. The drama centers on the changes in his life when he picks up the wrong valise and discovers he is in possession of stolen gems—the Datchet Diamonds.

CAST
Cyril Paxton: Rex Harrison; Daisy Strong: Tammy Grimes; Laurence: Robert Fleming.

The Bat. The story concerns a series of mysterious events that occur in a country house that a woman has rented for the summer.

CAST
Helen Hayes, Jason Robards, Jr., Margaret Hamilton, Bethel Leslie, Martin Brooks, Shepperd Strudwick.

THE DOW HOUR OF GREAT MYSTERIES—60 minutes—NBC 1960. Broadcast as a series of specials.

DOWN YOU GO

Game. Four regular panelists compete. The moderator presents a cryptic clue representing a popular slogan, quotation, or phrase, which is indicated by a line of dashes, one per letter, on a large board. Players, informed of the mystery expression, receive one free guess. If the phrase is not identified, each panelist suggests a letter of the alphabet. If an incorrect letter is posed, that player is disqualified from that round and forfeits five dollars to the sender (home viewer) of the phrase.

Moderator: Dr. Bergen Evans.

Panelists: Robert Breer, Fran Coughlin, Toni Gilmar, Carmelita Pope.

Producer: Louis Cowan, Joseph Stuhl, Barry McKinley.

Sponsor: Old Golds; Toni; Carter Products.

DOWN YOU GO—30 minutes—ABC—September 16, 1953 - September 8, 1956.

DO YOU KNOW?

Educational Quiz. Geared to children. Basis: The testing of knowledge acquired through the reading of specific books. After the quiz segment, authors and guest experts discuss the books' contents with the children.

Host: Bob Maxwell.

DO YOU KNOW?—30 minutes—CBS—January 4, 1964 - April 25, 1964.

DO YOU TRUST YOUR WIFE? WHO DO YOU TRUST?

Game. Married couples, chosen for their unusual backgrounds, compete. The host asks each couple two sets of questions for a total of twelve hundred dollars. The husband may either answer them or trust his wife to do so. The couple correctly answering the most questions is the winner and receives the additional prize of one hundred dollars a week for a year. Couples compete until defeated, and, if successful long enough, can win one hundred dollars a week for life. Retitled one year following its premiere: "Who Do You Trust?"

Host ("Do You Trust Your Wife?"): Edgar Bergen.

Assistants (Dummies): Charlie McCarthy, Mortimer Snerd, Effie Klinger.

Announcer: Ed Reimers.

Orchestra: Frank DeVol.

Host ("Who Do You Trust?"): Johnny Carson; Woody Woodbury.

Announcer: Del Sharbutt; Ed McMahon.

DO YOU TRUST YOUR WIFE?—30 minutes—CBS—January 3, 1956 - March 26, 1957.
WHO DO YOU TRUST?—30 minutes—ABC—July 14, 1958 - December 23, 1963.

DRAGNET

Crime Drama. Background: Los Angeles, California. The assignments of Police Sergeant Joe Friday. A realistic approach to the battle against crime as undertaken by the Los Angeles Police Department. Based on actual case histories.

CAST

Det. Sgt. Joe Friday (Badge: 714)	Jack Webb
Partners:	
Detective Sergeant Ben Romero (1951)	Barton Yarborough
Sergeant Jacobs (1952)	Barney Philips
Officer Frank Smith (1952-1959)	Ben Alexander
Officer Bill Gannon (1967-1970)	Harry Morgan
Ann Baker, Joe's fiancée	Dorothy Abbott
Captain Mack	Byron Morrow
Captain Brown	Art Balinger

Narrator: Jack Webb.

Announcers: George Fenneman; Hal Gibney.

Music: Frank Comstock; Walter Schumann; Nathan S. Scott; Lynn Murray.

Program open:

Sgt. Friday: "This is the city, Los Angeles, California. I work here, I carry a badge."

Music: Dum De Dum Dum.

Announcer: "Ladies and gentlemen, the story you are about to see is true, the names have been changed to protect the innocent."

Program close: The results of the trials or hearings of the involved criminals are given.

DRAGNET—30 minutes—NBC—December 16, 1951 - September 6, 1959. Syndicated as "Badge 714." Returned: NBC—30 minutes—January 12, 1967 - September 10, 1970. Syndicated.

DRAW ME A LAUGH

Game. An artist draws a cartoon from an idea submitted by a home viewer. Simultaneously, the gag line, but not the cartoon idea, is given to a contestant who must, within a two minute time limit, draw a sketch. A panel of four studio audience members judge the funniest of the two drawings. If the contestant wins, he receives a prize.

Host: Walter Hurley.

Cartoonist: Mel Casson.

Producer: Milton Kirents.

Director: Howard Cordery.

DRAW ME A LAUGH—30 minutes—ABC—January 5, 1949 - February 5, 1949.

DRAW TO WIN

Game. Four regular panelists. Object: The identification of persons, names, objects, or slogans based on an artist's sketchings. If, within a specified time limit, the charade remains unidentified, the sender (home viewer) receives cash (twenty-five dollars, maximum).

Host: Henry Morgan.

Panelists: Abner Dean, Bill Halman, Eve Hunter, Sid Hoff.

DRAW TO WIN—30 minutes—CBS—April 22, 1952 - June 10, 1952.

DREAM GIRL OF '67

Beauty Contest. Single girls compete for the title of "Dream Girl of '67." Contestants, twenty per week, are judged on their beauty, charm, and talent.

Stages:
The Daily Dream Girl Competition. Four of the twenty girls are judged daily. Each day, Monday through Thursday, one is selected and crowned "Dream Girl of the Day."

The Weekly Dream Girl Competition. The four daily winners compete in the Friday judging. One is crowned "Dream Girl of the Week."

The Year End Competition. Weekly winners vie for the title of "Dream Girl of '67." Prizes: A trip around the world, a film contract, five thousand

Dream Girl of '67. Four contestants in the evening-gown competition and host Dick Stewart.

dollars in cash, and a new car.

Hosts: Dick Stewart; Wink Martindale; Paul Peterson.

Judges: Guest celebrities.

DREAM GIRL OF '67—30 minutes—ABC—December 19, 1966 - December 29, 1967.

DREAM HOUSE

Game. Three competing husband-and-wife couples vie for their dream house, worth up to forty thousand dollars, and built for them anywhere in the United States.

Rounds:
The Preliminary Round: One couple is to be eliminated. Basis: General knowledge question-answer rounds. The team first to identify themselves by sounding a buzzer receives a chance to answer. If correct, points are awarded. Winners are the two highest scoring couples.

The Championship Round: Rapid-fire question-answer rounds. Winners, the highest scoring couple, receive one room and the chance to compete again and earn additional rooms. Teams compete until defeated or until they furnish their dream house by winning seven straight games.

Host: Mike Darrow.

Announcer: Chet Gould.

Music: Recorded.

DREAM HOUSE—30 minutes—ABC—April 1, 1968 - January 2, 1970.

DROODLES

Game. Object: For a celebrity panel to identify droodles, nonsense drawings either submitted by home viewers or drawn by the host. Home viewers who stump the panel receive cash prizes.

Host: Roger Price.

Panelists: Denise Lor, the Looker; Carl Reiner, the Cut-up; Marc Connelly, the Thinker.

DROODLES—30 minutes—NBC—June 21, 1954 - September 1954.

DROOPY DOG

Animated Cartoon. The chaotic misadventures of a sad-sack canine named Droopy Dog.

Music: Scott Bradley.

Producer: William Hanna, Joseph Barbera.

Director: Tex Avery, Dick Lundy, Michael Lah.

DROOPY DOG—05 minutes—Syndicated 1977.

THE DUDLEY DO-RIGHT SHOW

Animated Cartoon. Era: The early twentieth century. Dudley Do-Right, a simple-minded and naive young man, departs from home for the movies. After three miserable hours, he realizes that he has fallen through an open manhole and is sitting in a sewer. Believing he is guilty of tresspassing, and with a proud family tradition, "a Do-Right must always do right," he turns himself into the North Alberta Mountie Camp in Canada—five hundred miles from his home.

Shocked when learning of his foul deed, Inspector Ray K. Fenwick is prompted to ask Dudley if he would consider becoming a Mountie. Noticing the string that is attached to the Inspector's pistol, Dudley becomes hooked, signs up, and ninety minutes later completes his training. Stories relate his attempts to apprehend Snively Whiplash, the most diabolical of fiends.

Characters' Voices
Dudley Do-Right   Bill Scott
Nell Fenwick, the Inspector's
   daughter   June Foray
Snively Whiplash   Hans Conried
Inspector Ray K.
   Fenwick   Paul Frees

Narrator: Paul Frees.
Dudley's horse: Steed.

Additional segments:

The Hunter. A beagle detective, The Hunter, dispatched by Officer Flim Flanagan, attempts to apprehend the cunning Fox.

The World Of Commander McBragg. The tall tales of a retired naval officer.

Tutor The Turtle. The story of Tutor, a turtle who becomes what he wishes through the magic of Mr. Wizard, the lizard.

Voices: Bill Conrad, Walter Tetley, Skip Craig, Barbara Baldwin.

Music: Sheldon Allman; Stan Worth.

Producer: Jay Ward, Bill Scott.

Note: The character voiced by Hans Conried is also known to be Snidely Whiplash; and Do-Right's horse is also known to be called Horse.

THE DUDLEY DO-RIGHT SHOW—30 minutes—ABC—April 27, 1969 - September 6, 1970. Syndicated.

DUFFY'S TAVERN

Comedy. Background: Duffy's

Tavern, a run-down restaurant-bar on Third Avenue in New York City. The misadventures and dealings of Archie, a con artist who operates and manages the tavern for the never-seen Mr. Duffy. Duffy's Tavern, "Where the elite meet to eat," and where, with a beer, the free lunch costs fifteen cents. Based on the radio program of the same title.

CAST

Archie, the manager   Ed Gardner
Clifton Finnegan, Archie's simple-minded friend   Alan Reed
Miss Duffy, Duffy's unmarried daughter, seeking a husband— "Nature's revenge on Peeping Toms"   Patte Chapman
Charley, the waiter   Jimmy Conlin

Orchestra: Peter Van Steeden.

DUFFY'S TAVERN—30 minutes— NBC—April 5, 1954 - September 1954.

THE DUKE

Comedy. Background: New York City. Believing himself meant for the finer things in life, prize fighter Duke Zenlee discovers a love of the arts and oil painting. Impulsively, he decides to quit the ring and with a friend, Claude Stroud, opens a night club. Stories depict his attempts to enjoy his newly adopted life style against the wishes of his former trainer, Johnny, who schemes to get him to return to the ring.

CAST

Duke Zenlee   Paul Gilbert
Johnny   Allen Jenkins
Gloria, Duke's girlfriend   Phyllis Coates
Claude Stroud   Rudy Cromwell

Orchestra: Lou Bring.

THE DUKE—30 minutes—NBC—July 2, 1954 - September 24, 1954.

THE DUMPLINGS

Comedy. Background: New York City. The trials and tribulations of Joe and Angela Dumpling, the married, overweight proprietors of the Dumplings Luncheonette, a sandwich bar on the ground floor of the Bristol Oil Company, a Manhattan business office.

CAST

Joe Dumpling   James Coco
Angela Dumpling   Geraldine Brooks
Frederick Steele, their landlord   George Furth
Stephanie, Angela's sister   Marcia Rodd
Charles Sweetzer, the vice-president of Bristol Oil   George S. Irving
Norah McKenna, Sweetzer's secretary   Jane Connell
Cully, the cashier   Mort Marshall

Music: Billy Goldenberg.

Theme Vocal: Steve Lawrence.

Executive Producers-Creators: Don Nicholl, Bernie West, Michael Ross.

Producer: George Sunga.

Director: Paul Bogart, Hal Cooper, Dennis Steinberg.

THE DUMPLINGS—30 minutes— NBC—January 28, 1976 - March 24, 1976.

DUNDEE AND THE CULHANE

Western. Background: The Frontier of the 1870s. The story of Dundee, a sophisticated adverse-to-violence, trail-riding British barrister; and the Culhane, his assistant, an apprentice lawyer, rugged and fast with his fists and guns. Episodes relate their self-proclaimed mission to establish law and order throughout the West.

CAST

Dundee   John Mills
The Culhane   Sean Garrison

DUNDEE AND THE CULHANE—60 minutes—CBS—September 6, 1967 - December 13, 1967. 13 episodes.

DUNNINGER

Listed: The television programs of mentalist Joseph Dunninger.

Format: Demonstrations of mind reading ability.

Dunninger And Winchell—Variety—30 minutes. NBC—October 14, 1948 - September 28, 1949; CBS—October 5, 1949 - December 28, 1949.

Hosts: Paul Winchell, Jerry Mahoney.

Starring: Joseph Dunninger.

The Dunninger Show—Variety—30 minutes—Syndicated 1953.

Host: John K.M. McCaffrey.

Starring: Joseph Dunninger.

Featured: Orson Bean.

The Amazing Dunninger—Variety—30 minutes—Syndicated 1968.

Host: Hank Stohl.

Starring: Joseph Dunninger.

THE DuPONT SHOW OF THE MONTH
THE DuPONT SHOW OF THE WEEK

Anthology. Dramatizations based on real-life incidents.

Producer: ("DuPont Show of the Month"): Audrey Geller, Paul Gregory, David Susskind, Richard Lewine, Ralph Nelson, Lewis Warren.

Producer: ("DuPont Show of the Week"): Julian Claman, John Aaron, Jacqueline Babbin, William Nichols, David Susskind, Jesse Zousmer, Eugene Burr, Jack Philbin, Louis Freedman.

Sponsor: The DuPont Corporation.

Included:

Windfall. After purchasing a nine-teenth-century day sink in an antique shop, Frank Foster finds ninety-two thousand dollars hidden in it. He and his wife struggle over the decision of what to do with the money.

CAST

Frank Foster: Eddie Albert; Emily Foster: Glynis Johns; Bob Foster: Murray Hamilton.

Holdup. The efforts of a bright accountant and a top flight safe cracker to pull a million dollar heist, the proceeds from an amusement park's holiday activities.

CAST

Charles Hamilton: Hans Conried; Max Von Ritter: Hal March; Rudy Schrieber: Gerald Hickes.

The Winslow Boy. Background: Osborne, England. A Defense counselor attempts to defend a boy falsely accused of forging a five shilling postal order.

CAST

Arthur Winslow: Frederic March; Grace Winslow: Florence Eldridge; Ronnie Winslow: Rex Thompson; Sir Robert Morton: Noel Willman.

The Shadowed Affair. A journalist probes into the mysterious relationship between a famed novelist and his wife.

CAST

Juliette Harben: Greer Garson; Hans Harben: Douglas Fairbanks; Jennifer Graham: Lois Nettleton.

THE DuPONT SHOW OF THE MONTH—90 minutes—CBS—September 29, 1957 - March 21, 1961. 42 programs.

THE DuPONT SHOW OF THE WEEK—60 minutes—NBC—September 17, 1961 - September 6, 1964. 90 programs.

DUSTY'S TRAIL

Western Comedy. Era: The 1880s. A wagon train, destined for California, begins its long, hazardous journey. Through the efforts of a dim-witted scout, a stage and a wagon are separated from the main body and lost. Stories relate the wagon master's efforts to safely deliver his passengers to the Promised Land.

CAST

Mr. Callahan, the wagon
  master   Forrest Tucker
Dusty, the trail
  scout   Bob Denver
Lulu, a beautiful young
  dancehall girl hoping
  to open a saloon in
  California   Jeannine Riley
Betsy, a beautiful young
  teacher hoping to establish a school in
  California   Lori Saunders
Carter Brookhaven, a wealthy
  banker   Ivor Francis
Daphne Brookhaven,
  his wife   Lynn Wood
Andy, a well-educated, resourceful
  pioneer   Bill Cort

Callahan's horse: Blarney.

Dusty's horse: Freckles.

Music: Sherwood Schwartz; Frank DeVol; Jack Plees.

DUSTY'S TRAIL—30 minutes—Syndicated 1973. 13 episodes.

DUSTY'S TREEHOUSE

Children. Puppets, films, and stories.

Host: Stu Rosen (as Dusty).

Puppet Characters: Maxine the Crow, Stanley Spider, Scooter Squirrel.

Puppet Movement and Voices: Tony Urbano and Company.

Music: Barbara Rottman.

Producer: Don Hall.

Director: Jim Johnson.

DUSTY'S TREEHOUSE—30 minutes—Syndicated 1973.

E

THE EARL WRIGHTSON SHOW

Musical Variety.

Host: Earl Wrightson.

Vocalist: Betty Jane Watson.

Music: The Buddy Weed Trio.

Producer: Gil Fates.

Director: Jean Heaton.

Sponsor: Masland Carpets.

THE EARL WRIGHTSON SHOW—15 minutes—ABC 1948.

EARN YOUR VACATION

Game. A question, "Where on earth would you like to go and why?" is posed to the studio audience. Those with the best responses are selected as contestants and receive the opportunity to win an all-expenses-paid vacation to their place of desire. The player selects a subject category and answers questions of ascending difficulty within four plateaus. Each plateau represents a segment of the vacation. A player is defeated if he incorrectly answers any part of the plateau.

Host: Johnny Carson.

Assistants: Jackie Loughery, Millie Sinclair.

EARN YOUR VACATION—30 minutes—CBS—May 23, 1954 - September 1954.

EARTH LAB

Educational. Contemporary views of the physical sciences; geared to children eight to fourteen years of age.

Instructor: Tex Trailer.

EARTH LAB—60 minutes—Syndicated 1971. 26 tapes.

EAST SIDE COMEDY

Movies. Background: New York City. The story of a group of lower East Side kids who just manage to stay on the right side of the law.

From 1937 to 1943, wherein thirty-six feature films and three twelve-chapter serials were released, the group has been billed as the Dead End Kids (Leo Gorcey, Huntz Hall, Billy Halop, Gabe Dell, Bobby Jordan, Bernard Punsley), the Little Tough Guys (Billy Halop, Gabe Dell, Huntz Hall, Bernard Punsley, Hally Chester, David Gorcey), and the East Side Kids (see Cast).

Between 1945 and 1956, forty-two Bowery Boys films were made (see Cast). 1956 to 1957 saw the final era, the six remaining Bowery Boys films (see Cast).

1946 to 1948 saw the appearance of another group, the Gas House Kids (Carl "Alfalfa" Switzer, Bennie Bartlett, Rudy Wissler, Tommy Bond) in a three-feature series that failed to re-create the style of the original.

Today, via television, the 1937 to 1957 parade of tough guys finds renewed life and popularity as local stations endlessly air their antics under such titles as "East Side Comedy" (New York); and "West Side Comedy" (Los Angeles).

CAST:
THE EAST SIDE KIDS

Ethelbert "Muggs"
  McGinnis   Leo Gorcey
Glimpy   Huntz Hall
Danny   Bobby Jordan
Scruno   Sunshine Sammy Morrison
Benny   Bennie Bartlett
     Billy Benedict
Skinny   Dave Durand
     Donald Haines
Stash   Stanley Clements
Skid   Gabe Dell
Sniffy   Jack Raymond
Sleepy   Bill Bates
Dave   Bobby Stone
Pee Wee   David Gorcey
Also: Hally Chester, Harris Berger, Frankie Burke, Donald Haines, Eddie Brian.

CAST:
THE BOWERY BOYS

Terrence Aloysius Mahoney
  (Slip)   Leo Gorcey
Horace DeBussy Jones
  (Sach)   Huntz Hall
Louis Xavier Dumbrowsky
  (Louie), the owner of
  Louie's Sweet
  Shop   Bernard Gorcey
Chuck Anderson   David Gorcey
Dave Marino   Gabe Dell

East Side Comedy. Huntz Hall and Leo Gorcey as Bowery Boys Sach and Slip.

Gabe Marino	Gabe Dell
Whitey	Billy Benedict
Bobby	Bobby Jordan
Butch	Bennie Bartlett

CAST:
NEW EPISODES 1956-1957

Duke Stanislaus Kovilesky	Stanley Clements
Horace DeBussy Jones	Huntz Hall
Chuck Anderson	David Gorcey
Blinkey	Eddie LeRoy
Myron	Jimmy Murphy
Mike Clancy, the owner of the Sweet Shop	Percy Helton
	Dick Elliott
Mrs. Kelly, the owner of the boarding house at which the boys reside	Queenie Smith

EAST SIDE KIDS

See title: "East Side Comedy."

EAST SIDE/WEST SIDE

Drama. Background: New York City. The role of social workers in coping with the aged, the poor, and the desperate of a large metropolis. Stories depict the problems and their handling as seen through the eyes of Neil Brock, a Manhattan social worker.

CAST

Neil Brock	George C. Scott
Fredia "Hecky" Hechlinger, the agency director	Elizabeth Wilson

Jane Foster, the office secretary	Cicely Tyson

Music: Kenyon Hopkins.

Producer: David Susskind, Don Kranze, Arnold Perl, Larry Arrick.

EAST SIDE/WEST SIDE—60 minutes —CBS—September 30, 1963 - September 14, 1964. 26 episodes.

EASY ACES

Comedy. Events in the lives of the Aces: Jane, the Dumb Dora type; and Goodman, her husband, the recipient of her unpredictable antics. Based on the radio program of the same title.

CAST

Goodman Ace	Himself
Jane Ace	Herself
Dorothy, Jane's friend	Betty Garde

Announcer: Ken Roberts.

Music: Morris Surdin.

Producer: Goodman Ace (for ZIV TV Films)

Director: Jeanne Harris.

Sponsor: Phillips Soups Company.

EASY ACES—30 minutes—DuMont— 1949-1950.

EASY CHAIR THEATRE

Anthology. Dramatic presentations.

EASY CHAIR THEATRE—30 minutes—DuMont 1952.

EASY DOES IT

Variety. A blend of music, songs, and nostalgia.

Host: Frankie Avalon.

Regulars: Annette Funicello, Tim Reed, Susan Nesbitt, Vic Glazer, The War Babies Comedy Troupe.

Orchestra: Vic Glazer.

Executive Producer: Dick Clark.

Producer: Bill Lee, Robert Arthur.

Director: John Moffitt.

EASY DOES IT—30 minutes—CBS— August 25, 1976 - September 15, 1976. 4 tapes.

ED ALLEN TIME

Exercise.

Host: Ed Allen.

Assisting: Alice, his "talking dog."

ED ALLEN TIME—30 minutes—Syndicated 1967. 250 shows.

THE EDDIE CANTOR COMEDY THEATRE

Variety. Music, songs, and comedy sketches.

Host: Eddie Cantor.

Regulars: Helen O'Connell, Billie Burke, Ralph Peters, Frank Jenks, Pierre Watkin.

Orchestra: Ray Anthony.

THE EDDIE CANTOR COMEDY THEATRE—30 minutes—Syndicated 1955.

THE EDDIE CONDON SHOW

Music. Performances by Jazz personalities.

Host: Eddie Condon.

Musicians: Billy Butterfield, Joe Bushkin, Sidney Becket, Pewee Russell.

THE EDDIE CONDON SHOW—30 minutes—NBC 1949.

EDDIE FISHER

Listed: The television programs of singer Eddie Fisher.

Coke Time—Musical Variety—15 minutes—NBC—April 29, 1953 - February 20, 1957.

Host: Eddie Fisher.

Regulars: Jaye P. Morgan, Don Ameche, Fred Robbins.

Orchestra: Axel Stordahl; Carl Hoff.

The Eddie Fisher Show—Musical Variety—60 minutes—NBC—October 1, 1957 - March 17, 1959 (on an alternating basis with "The George Gobel Show").

Host: Eddie Fisher.

Regulars: George Gobel (his permanent guest), Debbie Reynolds (an occasional guest), Erin O'Brien, The Johnny Mann Singers.

Orchestra: Buddy Bergman.

EDDY ARNOLD

Listed: The television programs of singer Eddy Arnold.

The Eddy Arnold Show—Country—Western Musical Variety—15 minutes—CBS—July 14, 1952 - September 1952.

Host: Eddy Arnold.

Featured: Chet Atkins.

Music: Paul Mitchell's Instrumental Quintet.

The Eddy Arnold Show—Country-Western Musical Variety—15 minutes—NBC 1953.

Host: Eddy Arnold.

Vocalists: The Dickens Sisters.

Music: An unidentified combo.

Eddy Arnold Time—Country-Western Musical Variety—30 minutes—NBC—April 20, 1956 - July 19, 1956.

Host: Eddy Arnold.

Regulars: Betty Johnson, The Gordonaires Quartet.

Orchestra: Russ Case.

THE EDGAR WALLACE MYSTERY THEATRE

Anthology. Mysteries as penned by author Edgar Wallace.

Included:

Ricochet. A woman attempts to clear herself of a false murder charge.

CAST
Richard Leech, Maxine Audley.

Man At The Carlton Tower. Police efforts to apprehend a notorious murderer/jewel thief.

CAST
Maxine Audley, Nigel Green, Lee Montague.

Locker Sixty-Nine. A detective attempts to find his employer's murderer.

CAST
Walter Brown.

Death Trap. A girl attempts to prove that her sister's recorded suicide was actually murder.

CAST
Mercy Haystead, Albert Lieven, Barbara Shelly.

THE EDGAR WALLACE MYSTERY THEATRE—60 minutes—Syndicated 1963. 39 episodes. Originally produced in England as theatrical releases.

THE EDGE OF NIGHT

Serial. Background: The turbulent Midwestern city of Monticello. Stories depict the lives of ordinary people driven by intense feeling and difficult circumstances. Emphasis is placed on crime detection methods and courtroom proceedings.

CAST

Mike Karr	John Larkin
	Lawrence Hugo
	Forrest Compton
Sarah Lane	Teal Ames
Nancy Pollock	Ann Flood
Grace O'Leary	Maxine Stuart
Jackie Lane	Don Hastings
Adam Drake	Donald May
Dr. Kevin Reed	Stanley Grover
Nicole Travis	Maeve McGuire
Cookie Christopher	Fran Sharon
Winston Grimsley	Walter Greza
Ed Gibson	Larry Hagman
Ron Christopher	Burt Douglas
Kate Sloane	Jan Farrand
Elly Jo Jamison	Dorothy Lyman
Phil Caprice	Ray MacDonnell
	Robert Webber
Ken Emerson	Alan Manson
Joe Pollock	Alan Nourse
	John Gibson
Tango	Lynn Ann Redgrave
Steve Prentiss	Conrad Fowkes
Dr. Katherine Lovell	Mary Fickett
Ruth Tuttle	Barbara Hayes
Ernie Hall	George Hall
Bart Fletcher	James Ray
Harry Constable	Dolph Sweet
Julie Jamison	Millette Alexander
Dr. Jim Fields	Alan Feinstein
Liz Hillyer	Alberta Grant
Frank Sloane	Sam Grey
Martha Marceau	Teri Keane
Bill Marceau	Alan Feinstein
	Carl Frank
	Mandel Kramer
Laurie Ann Karr	Emily Prager
Orin Hillyer	Lester Rawlins
Simon Jessep	Hugh Riley
Vic Lamont	Ted Tinling
Nurse Hubbell	Frances Beers
Trudy	Mary Hayden
Lobo Haines	Fred J. Scollay
Fred Burns	William Kiehl
Celia Burns	Carol Teitel
Corky	Joy Claussen
Doug Hastings	Hal Studer
Angela Morgan	Valerie French
Jack Berman	Ward Costello
Dr. Warner	Richard Buck
Jessica Webster	Rita Lloyd
Jason Everett	Barry Ford
Phoebe Smith	Renne Jarrett
	Johanna Leister
	Hedi Vaughn
Pamela Stuart	Irene Dailey
Geraldine Whitney	Lois Kibbee
Gordon Whitney	Allan Gifford
Senator Colin Whitney	Anthony Call
Tiffany Whitney	Lucy Martin
Dr. Charles Weldon	David Hooks
Keith Whitney	Bruce Martin
Rose Pollock	Kay Campbell
	Virginia Kaye
Louise Caprice	Mary K. Wells
	Lisa Howard
Tracy Carroll	Kendall March
Eric Morgan	John Lehve
Lennie Small	Mike Minor
Lee Pollock	Tony Roberts
Kevin Jameson	Dick Schoberg
	John Driver
John	George Hall
Laurie Lamont	Jeanne Ruskin
Lt. Luke Chandler	Herb Davis
D.A. Peter Quinn	George Petrie
Mr. Lamarti	James Gallery
Kaye Reynolds	Elizabeth Farley
Babs	Leslie Ray
Dr. Lacy	Brooks Rogers
Johnny Dallas	John LaGioa
Sam English	Edward Moore
Floyd	James Ray
Ben Travis	Cec Linder
Mr. LePage	William Post Jr.
Danny	Lou Criscuolo
Betty Jean Lane	Mary Moor
The Detective Sergeant	Ian Martin
The Police Department secretary	Maxine Stuart
Mattie Lane	Betty Garde
Harry Lane	Lauren Gilbert
Harry's wife	Sarah Burton
Harry's secretary	Mary Alice Moore
Andre Lazor	Val Dufor

Malcolm Thomas	Edward Kemmer
John Barnes	Barry Newman
Rick Oliver	Keith Charles
Laurie Ann Karr	Emily Prager
Gerry McGrath	Milee Taggart
The Police Captain's secretary	Teri Keane
Mrs. Thatcher	Billie Lou Watt
Laurie Dallas	Emily Prager
	Jeanne Ruskin
	Linda Cook
Mark Faraday	Bernie McInerney
Ansel Smith	Patrick Horgan
Ada Chandler	Billie Allen
Brandy Henderson	Dixie Carter
Noel Douglas	Dick Latessa
Tracy Dallas	Patricia Conwell
Quentin Henderson	Michael Stroka
Gerald Kincaid	Allen Mixon
Trudy	Mary Hayden
Beau Richardson	David Gale
Josie and Serena Faraday	Louise Shaffer
Draper Scott	Tony Craig
Nicole Drake	Maeve McGuire
Clay Jordan	Niles McMaster
Steve Guthrie	Denny Albee
Nadine Alexander	Dorothy Stinnette
Raven Alexander	Juanin Clay
Timmy Faraday	Doug McKeon
Tony Saxon	Louis Turenne
Claude Revenant	Scott McKay
Molly O'Connor	Helena Carroll
Logan Swift	Joe Lambie

Also: Janet Margolin, Barbara Sharma, Ruby Dee, Jan Miner, Martin Rudy, Ann Minot, Audra Lindley, Charles Baxter, David Ford, Carl Low, Kathleen Cody, Eva Marie Saint, Wesley Addy, Nancy Wickwire, Karen Thorsell, Ruth Mattheson, Kathleen Bracken, Peggy Allenby, Ronnie Welsch, Peter Kastner, Joan Harvey, Anthony Ponzini, Robert Dryden, Priscilla Gillette, Jeremy Slate, Sam Groom, Diana Van derVlis, Nancy Pinkerton.

Announcer: Hal Simms.

Early Announcers: Herbert Duncan, Harry Kramer.

Music: Paul Taubman.

Additional Music: Elliott Lawrence.

Musical Coordinator: Barbara Miller.

THE EDGE OF NIGHT—30 minutes CBS—April 2, 1956 - November 28, 1975. ABC—30 minutes—Premiered: December 1, 1975.

THE EDIE ADAMS SHOW

See title: "Here's Edie."

THE ED NELSON SHOW

See title: "The Morning Show."

THE ED SULLIVAN SHOW

Variety. Lavish, top-rated entertainment acts.

Host: Ed Sullivan.

Regulars: The Toastettes Chorus Line; The Hugh Lambert Dancers.

Commercial Spokeswoman: Julia Meade.

Announcer: Ralph Paul.

Orchestra: Ray Bloch.

Producer: Jack Meegan, Ed Sullivan, Bob Precht, Jack McGeehan, Stu Erwin, Jr., Ken Campbell, Marlo Lewis, John Wray, John Moffitt, Jacques Andre.

THE ED SULLIVAN SHOW—60 minutes—CBS—September 25, 1955 - June 6, 1971. Broadcast as "Toast of the Town"—60 minutes—CBS—June 20, 1948 - September 18, 1955.

ED WYNN

Listed: The television programs of comedian Ed Wynn.

The Ed Wynn Show—Variety—30 minutes—NBC—October 6, 1949 - July 4, 1950.

Host: Ed Wynn.

Regulars: Ben Wrigley, Edith Praf, The Hannaford Family, The Merriel Abbott Dancers.

Orchestra: Lud Gluskin.

Producer: Harlan Thompson.

Sponsor: Camel Cigarettes.

The Ed Wynn Show—Comedy—30 minutes—NBC—September 25, 1958 - January 1, 1959.

Background: A small Midwestern college town. The trials and tribulations of John Beamer, widower and retired businessman. Stories focus on his struggles to raise his orphaned granddaughters, Midge and Laurie.

CAST

John Beamer	Ed Wynn
Laurie Beamer	Jacklyn O'Donnell
Midge Beamer	Sherry Alberoni
Ernie Hinshaw, his friend, an attorney	Herb Vigran
Mayor Brandon	Clarence Straight

Producer: Garry Simpson.

THE EGG AND I

Comedy Serial. Background: New York State. The struggles of Bob and Betty MacDonald, the owners and operators of a run-down chicken farm. Based on the book by Betty MacDonald.

CAST

Betty MacDonald	Patricia Kirkland
Bob MacDonald	Frank Craven
Jed Simmons, their handyman	Grady Sutton
Ma Kettle, their neighbor	Doris Rich
Pa Kettle, her lazy husband	Frank Twedell

Producer: Montgomery Ford.

Director: Jack Gage.

THE EGG AND I—15 minutes—CBS—September 3, 1951 - August 1, 1952.

THE EIGHTH MAN

Animated Cartoon. Era: The twenty-first century. Background: Metro City, the headquarters of Metro International, the futuristic police force. After agent Peter Brady is killed attempting to apprehend Saucer Lip, the most wanted of criminals, Professor Genius embodies Brady's life force into that of Tobor the Eighth Man, an indestructible robot that appears in the image of the mild-mannered Brady. Stories relate Brady's battle, as Tobor, against evil and his attempts to apprehend his killer, Saucer Lip.

THE EIGHTH MAN—30 minutes—Syndicated 1965. 52 episodes.

EIGHT IS ENOUGH

Comedy-Drama. Background: Sacramento, California. Events in the day-to-day lives of the Bradford family: Tom, a newspaper columnist for the *Sacramento Register,* his wife Joan, and their eight children, aged from seven to twenty-three.

CAST

Tom Bradford	Dick Van Patten
Joan Bradford	Diana Hyland
Donna, Tom's secretary	Jennifer Darling
Dr. Walt Maxwell, Tom's friend	Michael Thoma

The Bradford Children:

Nancy Bradford	Kimberly Beck
	Dianne Kay
Elizabeth Bradford	Connie Newton

Mary Bradford	Lani O'Grady
David Bradford	Mark Hamill
	Grant Goodeve
Tommy Bradford	Chris English
Joannie Bradford	Lauri Walters
Nicholas Bradford	Adam Rich
Susan Bradford	Susan Richardson

Music: Fred Werner.

Executive Producer: Lee Rich, Philip Capice.

Producer: Robert L. Jacks.

Director: E.W. Swackhamer, David Moessinger, Reza S. Badiyi, Vincent McEveety, Harvey Laidman, Harry Harris.

EIGHT IS ENOUGH–60 minutes–ABC–March 15, 1977 - May 3, 1977. 8 episodes. Returned: Premiered: ABC–August 10, 1977.

87th PRECINCT

Crime Drama. Background: New York City. The grim day-to-day activities of plainclothes detectives, the men of Manhattan's 87th police precinct.

CAST

Detective	
Steve Carella	Robert Lansing
Teddy Carella, his deaf-mute	
wife	Gena Rowlands
Detective Bert Kling	Ron Harper
Detective Meyer Meyer	Norman Fell
Detective	
Roger Havilland	Gregory Walcott

Music: Morton Stevens.

87th PRECINCT–60 minutes–NBC–September 25, 1961 - September 10, 1962. Syndicated. 30 episodes.

ELECTRA WOMAN AND DYNA GIRL

See title: "The Krofft Supershow," *Electra Woman and Dyna Girl* segment.

THE ELECTRIC COMPANY

Educational. Second to fourth graders. Objectives: To enable slow readers to increase their speed and to reinforce skills. The specifics of whole words and complete sentences are presented through cartoons, sketches, and/or musical numbers.

Regulars: Judy Graubart, Skip Hinnant, Rita Moreno, Bill Cosby, Jimmy Boyd, Lee Chamberlain, Morgan Freeman. *The Short Circus* (child singers and dancers): Byan Johnson, June Angela, Todd Graff, Rodney Lewis, Janina Matthews, Greg Burge, Rejane Magloire.

Also: Luis Avalos, Hattie Winston.

Announcer: Ken Roberts.

Original Music Composed and Conducted by: Joe Raposo.

Musical Director: Gary William Friedman, Dave Connar.

Musical Coordinator: Danny Epstein.

Choreographer: Patricia Birch, Liz Thompson.

Producer: Andrew B. Ferguson, Jr.

Director: Henry Behar.

THE ELECTRIC COMPANY–30 minutes–PBS–Premiered: October 25, 1971.

THE ELEVENTH HOUR

Drama. Background: New York City. The work of psychiatrist Theodore Bassett, court alienist and advisor to the state board of correction, as he attempts to assist people overcome by the turmoil of human emotion.

CAST

Dr. Theodore Bassett	Wendell Corey
Dr. Paul Graham, his assistant,	
a clinical	
psychologist	Jack Ging
Dr. Richard Starke (replaced	
Bassett)	Ralph Bellamy

Music: Harry Sukman.

Producer: Sam Rolfe, Norman Felton, Irving Elman.

THE ELEVENTH HOUR–60 minutes–NBC–October 3, 1962 - September 9, 1964. Syndicated. 62 episodes.

ELGIN HOUR

Anthology. Dramatic presentations.

Producer: Herbert Brodkin.

Sponsor: Elgin Watches.

Included:

Crime In The Streets. Having grown up in a tough neighborhood, a social worker attempts to prevent two boys from facing a possible life of crime.

CAST

Ben Wagner: Robert Preston; Mrs. Dorne: Glenda Farrell; Frankie Dorn: John Cassavettes; Richard Dorn: Van Dyke Parks.

Days Of Grace. Discharged after twenty years service, an advertising executive attempts to reconstruct his life.

CAST

William L'Hommedieu: Franchot Tone; Madge L'Hommedieu: Peggy Conklin; Gloria L'Hommedieu: Nancy Malone.

Family Meeting. Never allowed a voice in family disputes, a young woman attempts to assert her opinion.

CAST

Father: Alan Bunce; Mother: Polly Rowles; Daughter: Kaye Margery; Lyman Poole: William Redfield.

ELGIN HOUR–60 minutes–NBC–October 6, 1954 - June 14, 1955.

ELLERY QUEEN

Crime Drama. Background: New York City. The investigations of Ellery Queen, a suave, cynical, rugged, and incorruptable gentleman detective and writer.

Versions:

Ellery Queen–30 minutes–DuMont–1950-1955.

CAST

Ellery Queen	Richard Hart
	Lee Bowman
	Hugh Marlowe
Inspector Richard Queen,	
his father, with the	
N.Y.P.D.	Florenz Ames
Nikki Porter, Ellery's	
secretary	Charlotte Keane

Producer: Norman Pincus, Irving Pincus.

Director: Donald Richardson.

Sponsor: Kaiser-Frazer Products.

The Further Adventures Of Ellery Queen–60 minutes–NBC–September 1958 - September 1959.

CAST

Ellery Queen	George Nader
	Lee Philips

Producer: Albert McCleery.

Ellery Queen–60 minutes–NBC–Premiered: September 11, 1975.

CAST

Ellery Queen	Jim Hutton
Inspector Richard	
Queen	David Wayne
Sergeant Velie, the	

inspector's assistant	Tom Reese
Frank Flannigan, a reporter on the *New York Gazette*	Ken Swofford
Simon Brimmer, a criminologist	John Hillerman
Grace, the inspector's secretary	Nina Roman
Vera, Frank's secretary	Maggie Nelson
Director of Simon's radio programs	John H. Lowler

Music: Elmer Bernstein, Hal Mooney.

Additional Music: Dana Kaproff.

Executive Producer: Richard Levinson, William Link.

Producer: Peter S. Fischer, Michael Rhodes.

Director: David Greene, Charles S. Dubin, Peter Hunt, Jack Arnold, James Sheldon, Seymour Robbie.

Ellery's home address: 212-A West 87th Street.

The format allows the viewer to match wits with Ellery Queen. The viewer sees the murder being committed, is told who the suspects are, and is presented with all the clues—none are withheld from him and nothing extra is given to Ellery. Before the last commercial, Ellery faces the camera and asks viewers to identify the murderer. After the commercial break, all the suspects are gathered and Ellery reveals the guilty party.

EMERGENCY!

Drama. Background: California. The work of the paramedics of Squad 51 of the Los Angeles County Fire Department Rescue Division.

CAST

Dr. Kelly Brackett	Robert Fuller
Dr. Joe Early	Bobby Troup
Nurse Dixie McCall	Julie London
Fireman Roy DeSoto	Kevin Tighe
Fireman John Gage	Randolph Mantooth
Fire Captain Henderson	Dick Hammer
Fire Captain Stanley	Michael Norell
Fireman Marco Lopez	Marco Lopez
Fireman Kelly	Tim Donnelly
Fireman Mike Woiski	Jack Kruschen
Nurse Carol Williams	Lillian Lehman
Fireman Stoker	Mike Stoker
Dr. Morton	Ron Pinkard
Squad 51 dog: Boots.	

Music: Nelson Riddle; Billy May.

Executive Producer: Jack Webb.

Producer: Edwin Self, R.A. Cinader.

Note: The paramedics work in conjunction with Rampart Hospital.

EMERGENCY!–60 minutes–NBC–Premiered: January 22, 1972.

EMERGENCY PLUS FOUR

Animated Cartoon. A spin-off from "Emergency." Assisted by four youngsters, Sally, Matt, Jason, and Randy (the "Plus Four"), John Gage and Roy DeSoto, paramedics with the Squad 51 Rescue Division of the Los Angeles County Fire Department, continue their work, rescuing people trapped in life-and-death situations.

Characters' Voices

Roy DeSoto	Kevin Tighe
John Gage	Randolph Mantooth
Sally	Sarah Kennedy
Matt	David Joliffe
Jason	Donald Fullilove
Randy	Peter Haas

Plus Four pets: Flash the dog; Bananas the monkey; Charlmayne the bird.

Music: The Sound Track Music Company.

Executive Producer: Fred Calvert, Michael Caffrey.

Director: Fred Calvert.

EMERGENCY PLUS FOUR–30 minutes–NBC–September 8, 1973 - September 4, 1976.

EMPIRE

Drama. Background: The one-half million acre Garrett Ranch in Santa Fe, New Mexico. Stories focus on the work of Jim Redigo, the foreman, as he struggles to solve difficulties within the Garrett empire.

CAST

Jim Redigo	Richard Egan
Lucia Garrett, the owner of the ranch	Anne Seymour
Connie Garrett, her daughter	Terry Moore
Tal Garrett, Lucia's son	Ryan O'Neal
Paul Moreno, a ranch hand	Charles Bronson
Chuck, a ranch hand	Warren Vanders

Producer: Frank Parson, William Sackheim.

EMPIRE–60 minutes–NBC–September 25, 1962 - September 17, 1963. ABC–60 minutes–March 22, 1964 - September 6, 1964. 32 episodes. Spin-off series: "Redigo" (see title).

ENCORE THEATRE

Anthology. Rebroadcasts of dramas that were originally aired via other filmed anthology programs.

Included:

The Silence. The story of an engineer who falls in love with another man's wife.

CAST

Carolyn Jones, Rod Cameron.

Exit Laughing. After he promises his wife he will take her to Honolulu for a vacation, a television comic discovers that his manager has arranged bookings for him that will interfere with his plans. The story relates his wife's efforts to see that he keeps his promise.

CAST

Pat O'Brien, Fay Wray, John Baragen.

The Boy With The Beautiful Mother. The story of a foreign boy who struggles to adjust to a new life after he is adopted by an American couple.

CAST

Jean Byron, Natalie Norwick, Peter Votrian.

ENCORE THEATRE–30 minutes–NBC–July 7, 1956 - September 1956.

ENCOUNTER

Anthology. Dramatizations featuring both American and Canadian performers.

ENCOUNTER–60 minutes (Simultaneous broadcast)–U.S.–ABC; Canada –CBC–October 5, 1958 - October 26, 1958.

END OF THE RAINBOW

Human Interest. The basis of the program, which travels to a different city each week, is to offer a preselected subject an opportunity to realize a lifetime ambition, regain a sound footing in business, or be provided with an unexpected opportunity for success.

Host: Art Baker; Bob Barker.

Creator-Producer: Ralph Edwards.

END OF THE RAINBOW—30 minutes—NBC—January 11, 1958 - February 15, 1958.

THE ENGELBERT HUMPERDINCK SHOW

Musical Variety.
Host: Engelbert Humperdinck (Arnold Dorsey).
Featured: The Irving Davies Dancers.
Orchestra: Jack Parnell.

THE ENGELBERT HUMPERDINCK SHOW—60 minutes—January 21, 1970 - September 19, 1970. Syndicated. 13 tapes.

The Engelbert Humperdinck Show. Engelbert Humperdinck.

ENSIGN O'TOOLE

Comedy. Background: The South Pacific. The misadventures of the men and officers of the U.S. Navy Destroyer USS *Appleby*. Stories focus on a bickering relationship between two men: Commander Homer Nelson, a man with a penchant for adhering to the rules, which has earned him the antagonism of the crew; and morale officer Ensign O'Toole, a man whose philosophy is to take life as it comes, worry about the present, and dream of the future. Knowledgeable in all fields, lazy in his approach to work, and unable to be found when needed, he has earned the respect of the crew. Because of his carefree attitude and influence on the crew, he struggles to solve the problems that arise when they follow his leadership.

CAST

Ensign O'Toole	Dean Jones
Captain Homer Nelson	Jay C. Flippen
Lt. Rex St. John	Jack Mullaney
Lt. Cdr. Virgil Stoner	Jack Albertson
Seaman Gabby	
Di Julio	Harvey Lembeck
Seaman Spicer	Beau Bridges
Seaman White	Bob Sorrells

Music: Frank Comstock.
Producer: Hy Averback, Bob Claver.

ENSIGN O'TOOLE—30 minutes—NBC—September 23, 1962 - September 15, 1963. Syndicated. 32 episodes.

THE ENTERTAINERS

Variety. Music, song, dance, and comedy presented in the style of a revue.
Hosts: Bob Newhart, Carol Burnett, Caterina Valente.
Repertoire Company: John Davidson, Tessie O'Shea, Art Buchwald, Jack Burns, Dom DeLuise, Tony Hendra, Nic Ullet, The Lee Hale Singers, The Ernie Flatt Dancers, The Peter Gennaro Dancers.
Orchestra: Harry Zimmerman.

THE ENTERTAINERS—60 minutes—CBS—September 25, 1964 - March 27, 1965. 26 episodes.

THE ERNEST TUBB SHOW

A thirty-minute country and western variety series, hosted by Ernest Tubb and first syndicated in 1967.

THE ERN WESTMORE SHOW

Women. Beauty tips and advice.
Host: Ern Westmore.
Regulars: Betty Westmore (Mrs.); Dick Hyde.

THE ERN WESTMORE SHOW—30 minutes—ABC—August 7, 1955 - September 11, 1955.

ERNIE KOVACS

Listed: The television programs of comedian Ernie Kovacs. Developing visual trickery, he was the first to make full use of television's potential through the skilled use of cameras and technical equipment.

Format: Split-second blackouts; pantomimed sketches; and satirizations on life.

Deadline For Dinner—Satire—30 minutes—DuMont—1950.

Host: Ernie Kovacs.

Kovacs On The Corner—Satire—60 minutes—NBC—January 7, 1951 - March 28, 1952.

Host: Ernie Kovacs.

Regulars: Edie Adams, his wife, Miss U.S. Television, 1950; Peter Boyle, the Irish cop on the beat.

Music: The Dave Appel Trio.

It's Time For Ernie—Satire—15 minutes—NBC—May 14, 1951 - June 29, 1951.

Host: Ernie Kovacs.

Regulars: Edie Adams, Hugh Price.

Orchestra: Harry Sosnick.

Ernie In Kovacsland—Satire—30 minutes—NBC—July 21, 1951 - August 24, 1951.

Host: Ernie Kovacs.

Regulars: Edie Adams, Hugh Price.

Kovacs Unlimited—Satire—60 minutes—Local New York

(WCBS-TV)—April 21, 1952 - December 26, 1952.

Host: Ernie Kovacs.

Regulars: Edie Adams, Andy McKay, Trig Lund, Peter Hanley.

Orchestra: Eddie Hatrak.

The Ernie Kovacs Show—Satire—30 minutes--NBC—December 12, 1955 - July 27, 1956.

Host: Ernie Kovacs.

Regulars: Edie Adams, Matt Dennis, Kenny Delmar, Harry Lascoe, Al Keith.

Music: The Hamilton Trio.

The Ernie Kovacs Show—Satire—30 minutes—ABC—1958-1959.

Host: Ernie Kovacs.

Featured: Edie Adams.

Orchestra: Harry Geller.

Take A Good Look—Game—30 minutes—ABC—1959 - 1960. See title.

The New Ernie Kovacs Show—Satire—30 minutes—ABC—1961-1962.

Host: Ernie Kovacs.

Regulars: Jolene Brand, Maggi Brown, Bobby Leuher, Joe Mikalos, Leonard Allstar, Alice Novice, Francis McHale, Bob Warren.

Executive Producer: Ernie Kovacs.

Producer: Milt Hoffman.

Director: Ernie Kovacs, Maury Orr, Ken Herman.

THE ERROL FLYNN THEATRE

Anthology. Dramatic presentations.

Host-Occasional performer: Errol Flynn.

Included:

The Girl In Blue Jeans. The romance that develops when an actor-producer catches a beautiful girl breaking into his home.

CAST

The girl: Glynis Johns; the producer: Herbert Lom.

The 100th Night Of Don Juan. The story concerns Don Juan's efforts to prove his love for a woman.

CAST

Don Juan: Errol Flynn; the woman: Jean Kent.

Rescued. After Lord Alston is wounded on the battlefields and held prisoner by one of Cromwell's officers, his friends attempt to rescue him.

CAST

Errol Flynn, Andrew Keir.

Out Of The Blue. A stewardess on a flight to London agrees to take care of an infant child. When the plane lands in Rome, the baby is kidnapped. The episode relates her struggles to find the baby.

Starring: Rosanna Rory.

The Duel. The story of the duel between an arrogant lord and his ward's sweetheart.

CAST

Errol Flynn, Ann Silvers.

THE ERROL FLYNN THEATRE—30 minutes—DuMont 1957.

ESCAPE

Anthology. Dramatizations depicting the fate of people caught in life and death situations. Tales designed "to free you from the four walls of today for a half-hour of high adventure." Based on the radio program of the same title.

Announcer: Jack McCoy, Elliott Lewis.

Music: Cy Feurer.

Producer-Director: Wyllis Cooper.

ESCAPE—30 minutes—CBS 1950.

ESCAPE

Anthology. True stories of people caught in life-and-death situations.

Narrator: Jack Webb.

Music: Frank Comstock.

Included:

(Episode untitled). Background: The South Pacific, World War II. The story of a U.S. submarine caught in enemy waters by a Japanese destroyer. Partially crippled by depth charges, the sub sinks to the bottom. Unable to resurface to recharge its batteries, the crew is caught in a deadly game of waiting—to suffocate below or be shelled above.

After five hours, and out of oxygen, the sub surfaces. The enemy is gone. "Had they gone because they were sure they had made a hit? Or had they run out of depth charges? The answer will never be known."

CAST

Captain Frank Wyatt: Ed Nelson; Mike Coles: Ron Hayes; Murphy: Dennis Rucker; Kurczak: Kip Niven.

(Episode untitled). Background: California. On a family picnic, the McGowan children (Matthew, age nine, and Kate, age six) stray from camp and wander into dangerous mountain lion country while chasing a butterfly. Unknowingly stalked by a cougar, Matthew and Kate constantly change their position, making it difficult for rescuers to locate them. Confronted by the cougar, Kate's screams alert the searchers who scare away the beast and rescue the children.

CAST

Larry McGowan: Glenn Corbett; Matthew McGowan: Lee H. Montgomery; Kate McGowan: Dana Laurita; Fran McGowan: Marion Ross.

(Episode untitled). Era: The Korean War. Shortly after the village of Myling is destroyed by bombings, leaving one survivor, a little girl, the patrol helicopter of congressional investigator Brian Collyer is hit by enemy fire and crash lands behind enemy lines. Blinded by the accident, Collyer begins his journey south toward American lines. Stopping to rest, he comes upon the little girl. Not able to communicate because of the language barrier, but sensing he will not hurt her, she leads him through enemy lines to an American camp. Although he had lost his sight on the battlefields of Korea, congressional investigator Brian Collyer found something important.

CAST

Brian Collyer: John Ericson; the Korean Girl: Charlene Wong.

ESCAPE—30 minutes—NBC—February 11, 1973 - April 1, 1973. Rebroadcasts: NBC—August 19, 1973 - September 9, 1973. 4 episodes.

E.S.P.

Variety. The sixth sense of extrasenory perception (E.S.P., the ability to predict the future) is tested. Two people, screened by psychiatrists, are placed in separate isolation booths. Various experiments are conducted to determine the possessor of the higher degree of E.S.P.

Host: Vincent Price.

Consultant: Carroll B. Nash, Director of Parapsychology at St. Joseph's College in Philadelphia.

E.S.P.–30 minutes–ABC–July 11, 1958 - August 1, 1958.

E.S.P.

Anthology. Stories of people endowed with extrasensory perception, the ability to predict the future.

Host: Vincent Price.

E.S.P.–30 minutes–ABC–August 7, 1958 - August 22, 1958.

ESPECIALLY FOR YOU

See title: "The Roberta Quinlan Show."

ESPER

A science fiction adventure about a jet-age young boy who combats evil throughout the universe. 30 minutes–Syndicated 1968. 26 films.

ESPIONAGE

Anthology. Dramatizations based on the activities of international undercover agents. Through documented accounts and actual newsreel footage, events are covered from the American Revolution to the Cold War. Filmed in Europe.

Included:

A Covenant With Death. The story of two Norwegian resistance fighters who are tried for the wartime slaying of an elderly couple.

CAST
Mangus Anderson: Bradford Dillman; Ivar Kolstrom: Don Borisenko.

A Camel To Ride. Background: Arabia. The story of Father James, a Catholic priest who, by leading demonstrations, attempts to end the nation's repressive regime.

CAST
Father James: Bill Travers; Bishara: Marne Maitland; Gebal: Roger Delgado.

The Incurable One. Era: The years following World War II. Having been trained as an espionage agent during the war, a Danish countess attempts to recapture the excitement of wartime life.

CAST
Celeste: Ingrid Thulin; Andrew Evans: Steven Hill.

Do You Remember Leo Winters? The story of a frogman who is incorporated by British Intelligence to observe suspicious waterfront activities.

CAST
Leo Winters: George A. Cooper; Davenport: Peter Madden; Jane Vesey: Rhoda Lewis; Frank Vesey: Victor Platt.

ESPIONAGE–60 minutes–NBC–October 2, 1963 - July 1964. Syndicated. 30 episodes.

ETHEL AND ALBERT

Comedy. Background: The small town of Sandy Harbor. The trials and tribulations of Ethel and Albert Arbuckle, a happily married couple.

CAST
Ethel Arbuckle   Peg Lynch
Albert Arbuckle   Alan Bunce
Aunt Eva   Margaret Hamilton
Also: Helen Ray, Harrison Dowd, Nelson Olmstead.

Announcer: Lee Gordon.

Producer: Thomas Leob, Walter Hart.

Sponsor: The Sunbeam Corporation.

ETHEL AND ALBERT–30 minutes –CBS–June 20, 1955 - September 26, 1955. ABC–30 minutes–October 4, 1955 - July 6, 1956.

THE ETHEL BARRYMORE THEATRE

Anthology. Dramatic presentations.

Hostess: Ethel Barrymore.

Included:

The Victim. A courtroom drama concerning the regeneration of a once-brilliant lawyer.

Starring: Edward Arnold.

Dear Miss Lovelace. The story of an advice-to-the-lovelorn columnist who becomes involved with gangsters.

Starring: Anita Louise.

The Duke. The story of a clever thief who must prove his innocence in a jewel robbery he did not commit.

Starring: K. T. Stevens.

Winter In Spring. The misadventures of an elderly man as he takes a job as a baby-sitter.

Starring: Charles Coburn.

THE ETHEL BARRYMORE THEATRE–30 minutes–DuMont 1956.

THE EVA GABOR SHOW

Variety. Guests, interviews, beauty tips, and advice.

Hostess: Eva Gabor.

THE EVA GABOR SHOW–15 minutes–ABC–November 10, 1950 - October 22, 1951.

THE EVE ARDEN SHOW

Comedy. Background: Los Angeles, California. The misadventures of Liza Hammond, mother, widow, and traveling lecturer, as she struggles to divide her time among work, home, and her twin daughters, Jenny and Mary.

CAST
Liza Hammond   Eve Arden
Jenny Hammond   Gail Stone
Mary Hammond   Karen Greene
George Howell,
  her agent   Allyn Joslyn
Nora, her housekeeper and
  baby-sitter   Frances Bavier

Producer: Brooks West, Edmund Hartmann.

THE EVE ARDEN SHOW–30 minutes–CBS–September 17, 1957 - March 26, 1958. 26 episodes.

EVENING AT POPS

Music. The presentation of all styles and forms of music.

Host: Arthur Fiedler.

Soloists: Guests.

Music: The Boston Pops Orchestra conducted by Fiedler.

Producer: William Costel.

Director: David Atwood.

EVENING AT POPS–60 minutes– PBS 1970.

THE EVERGLADES

Adventure. Background: Southern Florida. The investigations of Lincoln Vail, a law-enforcement officer with the Everglades County Patrol.

CAST

Lincoln Vail	Ron Hayes
Chief Anderson	Gordon Cosell

THE EVERGLADES—30 minutes—Syndicated 1961. 38 episodes.

EVERYTHING GOES

Variety. Music, songs, and celebrity interviews.

Host: Norm Crosby.

Regulars: Mike Darrow, Katherine McKenna.

Orchestra: Moe Kaufman.

EVERYTHING GOES—60 minutes—Syndicated 1974.

THE EVERLY BROTHERS SHOW

Musical Variety.

Hosts: Phil Everly, Don Everly.

Regulars: Ruth McDevitt (as Aunt Hattie), Joe Higgins, Dick Clair, Jenna McMahon.

Announcer: Mike Lawrence.

Orchestra: Jack Elliott, Allyn Ferguson.

THE EVERLY BROTHERS SHOW—60 minutes—ABC—July 8, 1970 - September 16, 1970. 13 tapes. Official title: "Johnny Cash Presents The Everly Brothers Show."

EVERYBODY'S TALKING

Game. Two competing contestants. A film sequence that features the man-in-the-street talking about a famous personality, place, or thing is played and stopped prior to the denouncement. Players, who receive only one guess per film sequence, are permitted to guess at any time during the film. If the subject is still unidentified when the film stops, a celebrity panel then provide clues to its identity. Players then have to each hazard a guess. The film is played to reveal the answer. Correct identifications award players points. The first player to score one hundred points is the winner and receives merchandise prizes.

Host: Lloyd Thaxton.

Music: Score Productions.

EVERYBODY'S TALKING—30 minutes—ABC—February 6, 1967 - October 25, 1968.

EVERYTHING'S RELATIVE

Game. Two four-member families compete, each composed of a father, a mother, and two children. The host places one member of one family in a specific situation, and asks the remaining members of that family to predict the individual's outcome. The individual is then asked to perform a stunt or answer a question. Correct predictions award one point. Each member of each family has to face an individual task. Winners are the highest point scorers.

Host: Jim Hutton.

EVERYTHING'S RELATIVE—30 minutes—Syndicated 1965.

EVIL TOUCH

Anthology. Dramatizations depicting the plight of people who, possessing the deadly seed of evil, are driven to frustration.

Host: Anthony Quayle.

Music: Laurie Lewis.

Included:

Dear Cora, I'm Going To Kill You. The story of a woman who plots the almost perfect murder of her husband.

CAST

Cora Blake: Carol Lynley; Harry Winston: Charles McCallum; Lt. Brennan: Dennis Clinton.

A Game Of Hearts. The story of a doctor who is haunted by the original owner of a heart he transplanted.

CAST

Doctor: Darren McGavin; Marshall: Colin Croft; Anne: Judi Far.

Marci. A woman attempts to prevent her hostile stepchild from destroying her life.

CAST

Elizabeth: Susan Strasberg; Marci: Elizabeth Crosby; John: Peter Gwynne.

Happy New Year, Aunt Carrie. The story of an invalid who witnesses a gangland murder and becomes the killer's next quarry.

Starring: Julie Harris.

Program closing: (Host) "This is Anthony Quayle reminding you that there is a touch of evil in all of us. Goodnight. Pleasant dreams."

EVIL TOUCH—30 minutes—Syndicated 1973. 26 episodes.

EXCLUSIVE

Anthology. Dramatizations based on the experiences of the members of the Overseas Press Club of America.

EXCLUSIVE—30 minutes—Syndicated 1960.

EXECUTIVE SUITE

Drama. Background: California. A behind-the-scenes look at the problems that befall members of the fictitious Cardway Corporation, a large industrial conglomerate.

CAST

Don Walling, the president of Cardway	Mitchell Ryan
Helen Walling, his wife	Sharon Acker
Brian Walling, their son	Leigh McCloskey
Stacey Walling, their daughter	Wendy Phillips
Howell Rutledge, the vice-president	Stephen Elliott
Mark Desmond, the head of consumer relations	Richard Cox
Yvonne Holland, Mark's mistress	Trisha Noble
Astrid Rutledge, Howell's wife	Gwyda DonHowe
Glory Dalessio, daughter of the plant manager	Joan Prather
Summer Johnson, Brian's girlfriend	Brenda Sykes
Tom Dalessio, Glory's father	Paul Lambert
Hilary Madison, the vice-president in charge of advertising	Madelyn Rhue
Anderson Galt, a member of the board	William Smithers
Harry Ragin, the labor manager	Carl Weintraub
Malcolm Gibson, a member of the board	Percy Rodrigues
Pearce Newberry, a board member	Byron Morrow
Maggie, Don's	

secretary	Marged Wakeley
Leona Galt, Anderson's wife	Patricia Smith
Marge Newberry, Pearce's wife	Maxine Stuart
Katie, Hilary's secretary	Abbe Kanter
Elly Gibson, Malcolm's wife	Paulene Myers
	Kim Hamilton
Sharon Cody, the head of the rival Capricorn International Corp.	Joanna Barnes
Nick Kaslow, an industrial spy	Scott Marlowe
B.J. Kaslow, Nick's son	Moosie Drier
Julie Solkin, Leona's friend	Geraldine Brooks
Bernie Solkin, Julie's husband	Norman Fell
David Valerio, Helen's drama coach	Ricardo Montalban
Walter Johnson, Summer's brother	Nat Jones
Bessy Johnson, Summer's grandmother	Hilda Haynes

Music: Billy Goldenberg, John Parker, Nelson Riddle, Bill Conti, Gerald Fried, Gil Millé.

Executive Producer: Norman Felton, Stanley Rubin, Rita Lakin.

Producer: Don Brinkley, Buck Houghton.

Director: Joseph Hardy, Charles S. Dubin, Joseph Pevney, Vincent Sherman, John Newland, Corey Allen.

EXECUTIVE SUITE—60 minutes—CBS—September 20, 1976 - February 11, 1977.

EXERCISE WITH GLORIA

Exercise. Acrobatics coupled with nutritional guidance.

Hostess: Gloria Roeder.

Assistants: Her six daughters.

EXERCISE WITH GLORIA—30 minutes—Syndicated 1964.

EXPEDITION

Documentary. Films depicting the hazardous expeditions of modern-day adventurers.

Host-Narrator: Colonel John D. Craig.

EXPEDITION—30 minutes—ABC—September 1960 - June 20, 1961. Syndicated. 41 episodes.

THE EXPERT

The series, produced in England and syndicated to the U.S. in 1970, features Marius Goring as a criminologist who encompasses scientific methods to solve crimes.

THE EXPLORERS

Documentary. Films depicting the exploits of modern-day adventurers.

Host-Narrator: Leslie Nielsen.

THE EXPLORERS—30 minutes—Syndicated 1972.

EXPLORING

Educational. Through films, songs, and sketches, various aspects of the adult world are explained to children.

Host: Dr. Albert Hibbs.

Regulars: The Ritts Puppets, The Gus Soloman Dancers.

Orchestra: Fred Karlin.

Producer: Edward Scherer.

Director: Lynwood King.

EXPLORING—60 minutes—NBC—October 13, 1962 - April 10, 1965.

EYE GUESS

Game. Two competing players. Tested: The ability to observe and memorize. The "Eye Guess" game board, which contains eight numbered answers, is revealed for eight seconds. At the end of the time, the answers are hidden by overlaying corresponding numbers. The host then questions the players, one at a time, by reading questions relating to the hidden answers. Each answer that is remembered by a player awards him a merchandise prize. The first player to score seven correct answers is the winner. The loser receives his choice of any prize that is on his side of the board. The winner, who receives all the prizes that are contained on his side of the board, is escorted to the "Eye Guess Risk Board." The board contains eight numbered squares, seven of which contain the word "Go;" the other "Stop." The player, who receives twenty-five dollars, chooses numbers randomly. Each "Go" that is picked doubles his cash. If "Stop" is selected he is defeated and loses all his cash. Winners compete until defeated.

Host: Bill Cullen.

Announcer: Don Pardo; Jack Clark.

Music: Recorded.

EYE GUESS—30 minutes—NBC—January 3, 1966 - September 26, 1969.

THE EYES HAVE IT

Game. The object is for a panel of experts to answer questions based on the showing of newsreel film clips.

Host: Douglas Edwards.

Producer: Fred Rosen, Steve Alexander.

Director: Ralph Levy.

THE EYES HAVE IT—30 minutes—CBS 1948.

EYE WITNESS

Anthology. Stories of people who witness accidents or crimes and come forward to testify.

Host-Narrator: Richard Carlson.

Included:

The Baby-Sitter. The story concerns a police search for a baby-sitter—the only witness to the murder of a young mother.

CAST
Evelyn Varden, Sallie Brophy, Jean Carson.

My Father's A Murderer. The story of a young girl who tries to convince her stepmother that her father murdered his first wife.

CAST
Janet Parker, Mary Stuart, Wesley Addy.

Statement Of The Accused. The story of an attorney who prosecutes a murderer on the testimony of an eyewitness.

CAST
Carl Schiller.

EYE WITNESS—30 minutes—NBC 1953.

EYE WITNESS TO HISTORY

Documentary. In-depth coverage of the single most important news story of the week.

Host: Charles Kuralt.

Narrator: Walter Cronkite.

EYE WITNESS TO HISTORY—30 minutes—CBS—September 30, 1960 - June 16, 1961.

F

FABULOUS FRAUD

See title: "Colonel Flack."

FACE THE FACTS

Game. A criminal case is redramatized and stopped prior to conclusion. Contestants, acting as judges, bet a specific amount of points and state a verdict. The film is played and correct predictions award the bet amount of points. Winners, highest scorers, receive merchandise prizes.

Host: Red Rowe.

FACE THE FACTS—30 minutes—CBS —March 13, 1961 - September 29, 1962.

THE FACE IS FAMILIAR

Game. Two competing teams each composed of one celebrity captain and one noncelebrity contestant. Object: The identification of famous personalities who are shown in scrambled photographs. The host states a question. The team first to identify themselves through a buzzer signal receive a chance to answer. If the response is correct, a picture piece is placed in its appropriate position and the team receives a chance to identify the person. The game continues until the photograph is identified.

Host: Jack Whitaker.

THE FACE IS FAMILIAR—30 minutes—CBS—May 7, 1966 - September 3, 1966.

FACE THE MUSIC

Musical Variety. An entertainment session featuring two singers who alternate on the performances of current tunes.

Hosts: Johnny Desmond, Shaye Cogan.
Music: The Tony Mottola Trio.

FACE THE MUSIC—15 minutes—CBS 1949.

FACE OF DANGER

Anthology. Rebroadcasts of dramas that were originally aired via other filmed anthology programs.

Included:

Midnight Kill. A lawyer attempts to find the gangster who is responsible for the death of a policeman.

CAST
James Whitmore, Carl Benton Reid, Phyllis Avery.

Strange Defense. A lawyer attempts to discover whether a woman accused of murder is his wife who supposedly died while she was overseas, or her twin sister.

CAST
David Brian, Constance Ford.

Weapon Of Courage. The story of a disabled war veteran who struggles to overcome the feeling that he is now useless.

CAST
Kevin McCarthy, Victor Jory, Maxine Cooper.

FACE OF DANGER—30 minutes— CBS—April 18, 1959 - May 30, 1959.

FACES AND PLACES

Travel. Filmed interviews; explorations of areas about the globe.
Hosts-Narrators: Don and Bettina Shaw.

FACES AND PLACES—30 minutes— Syndicated 1965. 26 episodes. Titled in 1967: "Travel with Don and Bettina."

FAIR EXCHANGE

Comedy. Background: New York City and London, England. Basic plot: Two families, American and British, exchange their teenage daughters for one year. Stories emphasize the girls' struggles to adjust to a foreign country and a new family; and the fathers' struggles to adjust to the temporary loss of their daughters.
American family: Eddie Walker, a World War II veteran; his wife, Dorothy; their son, Larry; and their daughter, Patty, who hopes to become an actress and wants to study at London's Royal Academy of Dramatic Arts.
British family: Tommy Finch, a

World War II veteran, a friend of Eddie's; his wife, Sybil; their son, Neville; and their daugher, Heather, who wants to acquaint herself with the American way of life.

CAST
Eddie Walker	Eddie Foy, Jr.
Dorothy Walker	Audrey Christie
Patty Walker	Lynn Loring
Larry Walker	Flip Mark
Tommy Finch	Victor Maddern
Sybil Finch	Diana Chesney
Heather Finch	Judy Carne
Neville Finch	Dennis Waterman
Willie Shorthouse, Tom's friend	Maurice Dallimore

Producer: Cy Howard, Edward H. Feldman.

FAIR EXCHANGE—60 minutes—CBS —September 21, 1962 - March 21, 1963. 30 minutes—CBS—March 28, 1963 - September 19, 1963. 14 one hour episodes; 13 half-hour. Filmed in both New York and London.

FAIRMEADOWS, U.S.A.

Serial. Background: The town of Fairmeadows. The trials and tribulations of an American family.

CAST
The father	Howard St. John
His wife	Ruth Matheson
Their twenty-one-year-old son	Tom Tyler
Their nineteen-year-old daughter	Hazel Dawn, Jr.
Their thirteen-year-old daughter	Mimi Stragin

Producer: Ezra McIntosh.
Director: Allan Rhone.
Note: The series is also known as "A House in the Garden."

FAIRMEADOWS, U.S.A.—30 minutes—NBC 1950.

FAIR WINDS TO ADVENTURE

Travel. Films exploring little-known areas of the world.
Host-Narrator: Dr. Frank Baxter.

FAIR WINDS TO ADVENTURE—30 minutes—Syndicated 1966. 39 episodes.

FAITH BALDWIN ROMANCE THEATRE

Anthology. Dramatizations depicting

the problems faced by people in their everyday lives.

Hostess: Faith Baldwin.

Producer: Jack Barry, Dan Enright, Geoffrey Jones.

Director: Charles Powers.

Included:

Henry's Harem. The story concerns the problems that face an efficiency expert when his wife, a writer, begins to make herself the heroine of each novel.

Starring: Paul Hartman.

Barry and the Beautiful Doll. The story revolves around a lawyer who gets involved with a baby doll client and her marriage-plotting parents.

Starring: John Carradine.

When We Are Married. The story of a gallivanting young man who completely upsets the smug lives of two straight-laced English families.

Starring: Roddy McDowall, Bramwell Fletcher, Fred Pozene, Isabel Elsom.

FAITH BALDWIN ROMANCE THEATRE—30 minutes—ABC—January 20, 1951 - October 20, 1951.

THE FALCON

Adventure. The story of Michael Waring, a United States government undercover agent know as the Falcon. Episodes depict his battle against the global forces of injustice.

Starring: Charles McGraw as Michael Waring, The Falcon.

THE FALCON—30 minutes—Syndicated 1955. 39 episodes. Also known as "Streets of Danger."

FAMILY

Drama. Background: Pasadena, California. Incidents in the complex day-to-day lives of the Lawrences, an American middle-income family of five.

CAST

Doug Lawrence, the father	James Broderick
Kate Lawrence, his wife	Sada Thompson
Nancy Maitland, their married daughter	Elayne Heilveil Meredith Baxter Birney

Jeff Maitland, Nancy's husband	John Rubinstein
Lititia "Buddy" Lawrence, Doug and Kate's daughter	Kristy McNichol
Willie Lawrence, Doug and Kate's son	Gary Frank
Mrs. Canfield, the housekeeper	Mary Grace Canfield
Elaine Hogan, the neighbor	Priscilla Morrill
Fred Hogan, her husband	William Putch
Salina, Willie's girlfriend	Season Hubley

Music: John Rubinstein, Pete Rugolo.

Music Supervision: Rocky Moriano.

Executive Producer: Aaron Spelling, Leonard Goldberg, Mike Nichols.

Producer: Carol Mackeand, Carroll Newman.

Director: Mark Rydell, Glenn Jordan, Rendil Kleiser, John Erman, Richard Kinon.

FAMILY—60 minutes—ABC—March 9, 1976 - April 13, 1976. Returned: Premiered—ABC—September 28, 1976.

FAMILY AFFAIR

Comedy-Drama. Background: New York City, 600 East 32nd Street, Manhattan. When his brother and sister-in-law are killed in an automobile accident, Bill Davis, the president of the Davis and Gaynor Construction

Family Affair. Back, left to right: Sebastian Cabot, Johnnie Whitaker, Brian Keith. Bottom, left to right: Kathy Garver, Anissa Jones.

Company, agrees to raise his brother's children rather than split them up among the relatives who don't want them.

Assisted by his gentleman's gentleman, Jiles French, he attempts to provide love and security to one teenager and two lonely, disillusioned children (Catherine, known as Cissy, and twins, Buffy and Jody).

Realistically presenting children's needs and feelings, and showing that adults are capable of making mistakes, "Family Affair" distinguishes itself from other family comedies by its heartwarming, sentimental, and at times sad stories.

CAST

Bill Davis	Brian Keith
Giles French	Sebastian Cabot
Cissy Davis	Kathy Garver
Jody Davis	Johnnie Whitaker
Buffy Davis	Anissa Jones
Miss Faversham, a friend of Jiles	Heather Angel
Nigel French, Jiles's brother	John Williams
Gregg Bartlett, Cissy's boyfriend	Gregg Fedderson
Sharon James, Cissy's girlfriend	Sherry Alberoni
Emily Turner, Bill's inept maid	Nancy Walker
Ted Gaynor, Bill's partner	Philip Ober John Hubbard
Miss Cummings, the twin's school teacher	Joan Vohs
Miss Lee, Bill's secretary	Betty Lynn
Scotty, the doorman	Karl Lucas

Music: Frank DeVol.

Additional Music: Jeff Alexander, Gerald Fried, Nathan Scott.

Music Supervision: Edwin T. Luckey.

Executive Producer: Don Fedderson.

Producer: Edmund Hartmann, Edmund Belion, Henry Garson, Fred Henry.

Director: William D. Russell, James Sheldon, Charles Barton.

Buffy's Doll: Mrs. Beasley.

FAMILY AFFAIR—30 minutes—CBS—September 12, 1966 - September 9, 1971. Syndicated. 114 episodes.

FAMILY CLASSICS THEATRE

Serial. The overall title for three television adaptations of literary masterpieces: *The Black Tulip; Ivanhoe; Little Women.*

The Black Tulip (serialized in six chapters). Background: Seventeenth-century Holland. Against disbelievers, Cornelius attempts to perfect his dream, a black tulip.

CAST

Cornelius	Simon Ward
Cornelius de Wit	John Phillips
Isaac	Wolfe Morris
Rosa	Tessa Wyatt
Dirk	John Cater

Ivanhoe (serialized in ten chapters). Background: England, 1194. Provoking Norman hatreds, Prince John usurps the throne from his brother, Richard the Lionhearted, while he is leading a Crusade to the Holy Land. Returning from the Crusades, a young Saxon knight, Ivanhoe, finds that he has been disowned by his father for taking part in them. The story describes in detail Ivanhoe's struggles to procure his country's crown for the rightful king, regain his inheritance, and win the hand of Lady Rowena. Based on the story by Sir Walter Scott.

CAST

Ivanhoe	Eric Flynn
Sir Brian de Bois-Guilbert, the Templar Knight	Anthony Bate
Lady Rowena	Clare Jenkins
Richard the Lionhearted	Bernard Horsfall
Prince John	Tim Preece
Preceptor	Eric Woofe
Rebecca	Vivian Brooks
Isaac	John Franklyn Robbins

Little Women (serialized in nine chapters). Background: New England 1860s. The joys and sorrows of four young women, the March Sisters—Beth, frail and sickly; Meg, pragmatic; Jo, an aspiring writer; and Amy, feminine and flirtatious. A detailed insight into nineteenth-century life. Based on the story by Louisa May Alcott.

CAST

Mrs. March (Marmie)	Stephanie Bidmead
Beth March	Sarah Craze
Meg March	Jo Rowbottom
Amy March	Janina Faye
Jo March	Angela Down
Aunt March	Jean Anderson
Laurie	Stephanie Turner
Professor Bhaer	Frederick Jaeger

FAMILY CLASSICS THEATRE—30 minutes—Syndicated 1971.

FAMILY FEUD

Game. Two five-member families compete. The heads of each family are first involved. A board, with various blank spaces, is revealed. A question, whose answers are based on a survey of one hundred people, is read by the host (e.g., "Name an expensive car"). The first player to sound a buzzer receives a chance to answer. If the answer made the survey, it appears on the board in its appropriate place and its cash amount (number of people who said it) is revealed and placed in the bank. If it is incorrect, or not the number one response, the opponent receives a chance to answer. Whichever team's player picked the highest answer receives the option to either pass or play the category. If they play (or pass) the object is for that team to build the money in the bank by filling in the remaining blank spaces. Success means they keep the money. However, if after three strikes (wrong answers) the family fails to fill in a blank, the opposing family can steal the money by correctly filling in the blank. Four questions are played, each involving different members of each family. The family that is first to score two hundred dollars is the winner.

Host: Richard Dawson.

Announcer: Gene Wood.

Music: Score Productions.

Executive Producer: Mark Goodson, Bill Todman.

Producer: Howard Flesher.

Director: Paul Alter.

THE FAMILY FEUD—30 minutes—ABC—Premiered: July 12, 1976.

FAMILY FEUD—P.M.

Game. A spin-off from the afternoon game show, "Family Feud", which see for format, cast, and credits.

FAMILY FEUD—P.M.—30 minutes—Syndicated 1977.

THE FAMILY GAME

Game. Three families compete, each composed of the father, the mother, and two children. Questions, which were asked of the children prior to the broadcast, are restated with their answers in mixed order. The parents of each team then have to match the correct answers with the children who said them. Each correct match awards that family one point. The winners, the highest point scorers, receive merchandise prizes.

Host: Bob Barker.

THE FAMILY GAME—30 minutes—ABC—June 19, 1967 - July 2, 1968.

THE FAMILY HOLVAK

Drama. Background: The small Southern town of Benfield during the Depression of the 1930s. The life of Reverend Tom Holvak as he struggles to feed his family and maintain the faith of his congregation.

CAST

Rev. Tom Holvak	Glenn Ford
Elizabeth Holvak, his wife	Julie Harris
Ramey Holvak, their son	Lance Kerwin
Julie Mae Holvak, their daughter	Elizabeth Cheshire
Jim Shanks, the police deputy	William McKinney
Chester Purdle, the owner of the general store	Ted Gehring
Ida, Chester's assistant	Cynthia Hayward

Music: Dick De Benedictis; Lee Holdridge; Hal Mooney.

Theme: "Look How Far We've Come," sung by Denny Brooks.

Producer: Roland Kibbee, Dean Hargrove, Richard Collins.

Director: Alf Kjellin, Corey Allen, Vincent Sherman, John Newland, Ralph Senesky.

THE FAMILY HOLVAK—60 minutes—NBC—September 7, 1975 - October 27, 1975.

THE FAMOUS ADVENTURES OF MR. MAGOO

Animated Cartoon. Video adaptations of legendary tales and figures of past history and literature.

Host-Story Teller-Star: Quincy Magoo (Voiced by Jim Backus).

Additional Voices: Marvin Miller, Howard Morris, Julie Bennett, Shepard Menkin, Joe Gardner, Paul Frees.

Music: Charles Brandt.

THE FAMOUS ADVENTURES OF MR. MAGOO—30 minutes—NBC—September 19, 1964 - August 21, 1965. Syndicated. 25 episodes.

FAMOUS CLASSIC TALES

Animated Cartoon. Adaptations of literary works. Produced in Australia.

Voices: Elizabeth Crosby, Barbara Frawley, Tim Elliot, Richard

Meikle, Ron Haddrick, Bob Frawley, Don Pascoe.

Music: Richard Bowden.

Included:

The Prince And The Pauper. Background: Sixteenth-century England. The story of the begger boy who changes places with his double, the Prince of Wales. Based on the novel by Mark Twain.

The Legend Of Robin Hood. The story of Robin Hood, who stole from the rich to give to the poor. Based on the minstrel ballads, which tell of his skill as an archer.

Twenty Thousand Leagues Under The Sea. Jules Verne's classic tale of the submarine *Nautilus* and its deranged scientist-captain, Nemo.

Swiss Family Robinson. The story of the Robinson family's struggle for survival after being shipwrecked on a deserted island. Based on the story by Robert Louis Stevenson.

FAMOUS CLASSIC TALES—60 minutes—CBS—September 23, 1973 - December 2, 1973.

FAMOUS GUESTS

A thirty-minute variety series, syndicated in 1954, with Tito Guizar hosting.

FAMOUS JURY TRIALS

Drama. Background: A simulated courtroom. A case, usually murder, is in progress when an episode begins. The on-the-spot battle between the prosecutor and the defense attorney is depicted. Both present their briefs and the incidents of actual cases are reenacted through flashbacks.

Versions:

Famous Jury Trials—30 minutes—DuMont 1949.

Prosecutor: Jim Bender.

Defense Attorney: Truman Smith.

Famous Jury Trials—30 minutes—Syndicated 1971.

CAST

Donnelly Rhodes, Allen Doremus, Tim Henry, Joanna Noyers, Cec Linder.

FANFARE

Anthology. Rebroadcasts of dramas that were originally aired via other filmed anthology programs.

Host: Richard Derr.

Included:

For Better Or For Worse. Unable to accept the fact that his former law partner is guilty of destroying evidence in a blackmail case, for which he was arrested, Jim Pierson, now governor, attempts to clear his name.

CAST

Jim Pierson: Mark Stevens.

The Break Off. Because of his ability to keep himself under control in adverse conditions, pilot Duke Cavannaugh is selected to test an experimental supersonic jet. The story focuses on the conflict that arises when tragedy affects his personal life hours before the scheduled test.

CAST

Duke Cavannaugh: Ralph Meeker; Jim Mitchell: Barry Atwater; Dr. Temple: Barney Phillips

Operation Snowball. A wife is suspected of having an affair with her husband's best friend. Innocent, the wife decides to remedy the situation and attempts to find her supposed lover a wife.

CAST

Virginia Mayo, Lee Goodman, Art Fleming, Chris White.

Seed From The End. The true story of the Holt family, people who have devoted their lives to helping Korean-American war orphans find foster homes in the U.S.

CAST

Dean Jagger, Virginia Christine, Donna Boyce.

FANFARE—30 minutes—CBS—June 1959 - September 1959.

FANFARE

Musical Variety.

Host: Al Hirt.

Featured: The Don McKayle Dancers.

Orchestra: Mort Lindsey.

FANFARE—60 minutes—CBS—June 1965 - September 11, 1965.

THE FANTASTIC FOUR

Animated Cartoon. When their rocket ship penetrates a strange radioactive belt that is encircling the Earth, four people acquire fantastic powers. Scientist Reed Richards acquires the ability to stretch like taffy; Sue Richards, his wife, possesses the ability to become invisible at will; Ben Grimm becomes "The Thing," a beast with the strength of a thousand men; and Johnny Storm, who acquires the ability to turn to fire, becomes "The Human Torch." Stories relate their battle against the sinister forces of evil. A Hanna-Barbera production.

Characters' Voices

Reed Richards	Gerald Mohr
Sue Richards	Jo Ann Pflug
Johnny Storm	Jack Flounders
Ben Grimm	Paul Frees

Music: Hoyt Curtin.

THE FANTASTIC FOUR—30 minutes—ABC—September 9, 1967 - March 15, 1970. 26 episodes.

THE FANTASTIC JOURNEY

Science Fiction Adventure. Hoping to further man's knowledge of the sea, a scientific party charters the ship *Yonda* and embarks on an expedition for the Caribbean. Shortly after leaving Coral Cove, Florida, the ship passes through the Bermuda Triangle and is engulfed by a billowing green cloud that shipwrecks them on a mysterious, uncharted island.

Several days later, after exploring the island, the survivors (Paul Jordan, Eve Costigan, Fred Walters, Jill Sands, and Scott Jordan) meet and ally themselves to Varian, a man from the twenty-third century who tells them that they have passed through a time warp and are in a seemingly endless land where the past, present, and future coexist. They also learn that other people from other times also exist on the island—people who pose a threat to their safety. Stories depict their adventures as they encounter the various life forms that exist on the island.

CAST

Varian	Jared Martin
Dr. Fred Walters	Carl Franklin
Jonathan Willaway, a rebel scientist from the 1960s, an ally	Roddy McDowall
Liana, an alien from the galaxy Aros, an ally	Katie Saylor
Dr. Paul Jordan	Scott Thomas
Scott Jordan, Paul's son	Ike Eisenmann
Dr. Eve Costigan	Susan Howard

Dr. Jill Sands   Karen Sommerville

Main Title Narration: Mike Road.

Liana's Cat: Selel.

Music: Robert Prince, Dick De Benedictis.

Executive Producer: Bruce Lansbury.

Producer: Leonard Katzman.

Director: Andrew McLaglen, Vincent McEveety, Barry Crane, Irving J. Moore, Virgil W. Vogel, Art Fisher, David Moessinger.

Program Open:

Narrator: "Lost in the Devil's Triangle, trapped in a dimension with beings from the future and from other worlds, a party of adventurers journeys through zones of time back to their own time. Varian, a man from the twenty-third century, possessing awesome powers; from 1977, Fred, a young doctor just out of medical school; Scott Jordan, the thirteen-year-old son of a famous scientist; Liana, daughter of an Atlantian father and an extraterrestrial mother; and Jonathan Willaway, a rebel scientist from the 1960s. Together they face the frightening unknown on The Fantastic Journey."

THE FANTASTIC JOURNEY—60 minutes—NBC—February 3, 1977 - April 21, 1977. Returned with one last episode on June 17, 1977.

FANTASTIC VOYAGE

Animated Cartoon. Background: C.M.D.F. (Combined Miniature Defense Force), a secret United States government organization possessing the ability to reduce people to microscopic size. Agents: Commander Jonathan Kidd; biologist Erica Stone; scientist Cosby Birdwell; and The Guru, "the master of mysterious powers." Reduced in size the team travels in the *Voyager,* a microscopic plane. Stories relate their battle against the unseen, unsuspecting enemies of the free world (criminal and germinal matter). Based on the movie of the same title.

Voices: Marvin Miller, Jane Webb, Ted Knight.

Music: Gordon Zahler.

Producer: Lou Scheimer, Norm Prescott.

Director: Hal Sutherland.

FANTASTIC VOYAGE—30 minutes —ABC—September 14, 1968 - September 5, 1970. Syndicated. 26 episodes.

FARADAY AND COMPANY

See title: "NBC Wednesday Mystery Movie," *Faraday and Company* segment.

FARAWAY HILL

Serial. Television's first dramatic serial. Background: New York. The story of a woman who, after the death of her husband, seeks an escape from the memories of their life together. The action is bridged by an off-stage voice talking to the lead and revealing her thoughts.

CAST

The Woman   Flora Campbell
Also: Ann Stell, Mel Brandt, Lorene Scott, Frederick Meyer, Melville Gilliart, Jacqueline Waite, Ben Low, Jack Holloran, Vivian King, Bill Gale, Eve Meagh, Julie Christy, Hal Studer, Barry Doig, Munia Gabler.

FARAWAY HILL—30 minutes— DuMont 1946.

FARMER ALFALFA

An animated cartoon series depicting the misadventures of an old farmer. 200 six-minute films. Syndicated. 1962.

THE FARMER'S DAUGHTER

Comedy. Background: 307 Marshall Road, Washington, D.C., the residence of the Morley family: Glen, widower and congressman; his mother, Agatha; and his children, Steven and Danny.

Seeking a government job teaching underprivileged children in the Congo, Katy Holstrum, a beautiful Minnesota farm girl, approaches Glen and requests his help and endorsement. His offer to assist her results in the unexpected delay of red tape and application approval.

Residing with the Morleys, she quickly wins over the affections of Steve and Danny. Impressed with her beauty, and ability to handle his sons, Glen offers her the position of governess, which she accepts.

Stories depict: the home and working life of a congressman; and the attempts of a Swedish country girl to adjust to both political and city life.

The Farmer's Daughter. Inger Stevens and William Windom. © *Screen Gems.*

Based on the movie, *The Farmer's Daughter,* which stars Loretta Young.

CAST

Katy Holstrum   Inger Stevens
Glen Morley   William Windom
Agatha Morley   Cathleen Nesbitt
Steven Morley   Mickey Sholdar
Danny Morley   Rory O'Brien
Chester Cooper, Glen's
    associate   Philip Coolidge
Senator Charles Ames, Glen's
    friend   David Lewis
Lars Holstrum, Katy's
    father   Walter Sande
Mama Holstrum, his
    wife   Alice Frost
Clemmy Hoyle, Katy's
    friend   Emmaline Henry
Margaret, Katy's
    friend   Nancy Rennick
                         Barbara Bostock
Charlotte, Katy's
    friend   Marilyn Lovell
Molly, Katy's
    friend   Shelly Morrison

Music: Dave Grusin.

Additional Music: George Duning.

Producer: Steve Gethers, Peter Kortner, Harry Ackerman.

THE FARMER'S DAUGHTER—30 minutes—ABC—September 20, 1963 - September 2, 1966. Syndicated. 101 episodes.

FAR OUT SPACE NUTS

Comedy. While loading food aboard a moon rocket at a NASA space center, ground crewmen Junior and Barney accidentally launch the ship and are propelled into the vast regions of outer space. Stories relate their misadventures on unknown planets and their attempts to return to Earth.

CAST

Junior	Bob Denver
Barney	Chuck McCann
Honk, their pet space creature	Patty Maloney
Lantana, their alien friend	Eve Bruce
Crakor, Lantana's robot	Stan Jenson

Music: Michael Lloyd.

Executive Producer: Sid and Marty Krofft.

Producer: Al Schwartz.

Director: Claudio Guzman, Wes Kenny.

Their spaceship: PXL 1236.

FAR OUT SPACE NUTS—25 minutes—CBS—Premiered: September 6, 1975.

FASHION

Women. Fashion previews. Guests and interviews.

Hostess: Arlene Francis.

FASHION—15 minutes—CBS 1951.

FASHION MAGIC

Women. Fashion previews. Guests and interviews.

Hostess: Ilka Chase.

Music: Provided by guests.

FASHION MAGIC—30 minutes—CBS 1950.

FASHION PREVIEW

Women. Fashion trends as reported by the designers themselves. Filmed in cooperation with the leading women's magazines.

FASHION PREVIEW—12 minutes—Syndicated 1951.

FASHION SHOW

Variety. Fashion previews coupled with music, songs, and interviews.

Hosts: Marilyn Day, Carl Reiner.

Regulars: Pamela O'Neill, Doris Lane, Patsy Davis, Elaine Joyce, Don Saxon.

FASHION SHOW—30 minutes—NBC 1949.

FAST DRAW

Game. Two competing teams of two, each composed of one celebrity captain and one noncelebrity contestant. The host presents one member of each team with a secret phrase (book, movie, or song). Players, one at a time, within a fifteen second time limit, have to draw cartoon charades to identify it. The teammate has to identify the charade. Winners, the team that identify the most charades, receive merchandise prizes.

Host: Johnny Gilbert.

Announcer: Fred Scott.

FAST DRAW—30 minutes - Syndicated 1968.

FAST GUNS

See title: "Stories of the Century."

FAT ALBERT AND THE COSBY KIDS

Animated Cartoon. Background: Nothern Philadelphia. The fond recollections of Bill Cosby's childhood buddies—Fat Albert, Rudy, Weird Harold, Edward, Mush Mouth, Donald, Bucky, and Russell (Bill's brother). Characters and situations are designed, through their acitvities, to educate and entertain children as to the meanings of topics in everyday life.

Host: Bill Cosby.

Voices: Bill Cosby, Keith Allen, Gerald Edwards, Pepe Brown, Jon Crawford, Lane Vaux.

Music: The Horta-Mahana Corporation.

Executive Producer: William H. Cosby, Jr.

Producer: Norm Prescott, Lou Scheimer.

FAT ALBERT AND THE COSBY KIDS—30 minutes—CBS—Premiered: September 9, 1972.

FATHER DEAR FATHER

Comedy. Background: 121 Hillsdown Avenue, London, England. The chaotic misadventures of Patrick Glover, a divorced thriller writer, as he attempts to understand his family: his beautiful teenage daughters, Anna and Karen, his ex-wife, Barbara, and his well-meaning housekeeper, Nanny.

CAST

Patrick Glover	Patrick Cargill
Karen Glover	Ann Holloway
Anna Glover	Natasha Pyne
Barbara	Urusla Howells
Nanny	Noel Dyson
Philip Glover, Patrick's brother	Donald Sinden
Georgie, Patrick's literary agent	Dawn Addams
Mrs. Glover, Patrick's mother	Joyce Carey
Bill, Barbara's husband	Tony Britton

The Glover's Dog: H.G.

Music: Gordon Franks.

Producer-Director: William Stewart.

FATHER DEAR FATHER—30 minutes—Syndicated 1977. Produced by Thames TV of London.

FATHER KNOWS BEST

Comedy. Background: 607 South Maple Street, Springfield. The dreams, ambitions and frustrations of the Anderson family: Jim, manager of the General Insurance Company; his wife Margaret; and their children, Betty, Bud, and Kathy. Stories tenderly mirror their lives. Based on the radio program of the same title.

CAST

Jim Anderson	Robert Young
Margaret Anderson	Jane Wyatt
Betty Anderson (Princess)	Elinor Donahue
Bud Anderson (James Anderson, Jr.)	Billy Gray
Kathy Anderson (Kitten)	Lauren Chapin
Miss Thomas, Jim's secretary	Sarah Selby
Claude Messner, Bud's friend	Jimmy Bates
Kippy Watkins, Bud's friend	Paul Wallace
Joyce Kendell, Bud's girlfriend	Roberta Shore
Ralph Little, Betty's boyfriend	Robert Chapman
Ed Davis, the Anderson's neighbor	Robert Foulk
Myrtle Davis, his wife	Vivi Jannis
Dottie Snow, Betty's	

Father Knows Best. Bottom, left to right: Billy Gray, Lauren Chapin, Elinor Donahue. Top, left: Jane Wyatt. Right: Robert Young. © Screen Gems.

friend	Yvonne Lime
Patty Davis, Kathy's friend	Tina Thompson
	Reba Waters
April Adams, Bud's girlfriend	Sue George
Burgess Vale, Kathy's boyfriend (early episodes)	Richard Eyer
Grover Adams, April's brother,, Kathy's boyfriend (later episodes)	Richard Eyer
Hubert Armstead, the high school principal	Sam Flint
Emily Vale, Margaret's friend	Lenore Kingston
Joe Phillips, Bud's friend	Peter Heisser

Music: Irving Friedman.

Announcer: Carl Caruso.

Producer: Eugene B. Rodney, Robert Young.

Director: William D. Russell, Peter Tewksbury.

FATHER KNOWS BEST—30 minutes. CBS—October 3, 1954 - March 27, 1955; NBC—August 31, 1955 - September 17, 1958; CBS—September 22, 1958 - September 17, 1962; ABC (rebroadcasts)—September 30, 1962 - February 3, 1967. Syndicated. 203 episodes.

On May 15, 1977, NBC presented a ninety-minute special, titled "The Father Knows Best Reunion," which reunited the original Anderson family for celebration of Jim and Margaret's thirty-fifth wedding anniversary. (Betty is a widow with two daughters, Jenny and Ellen; Bud, now a motorcycle racer, is married to Jean, and the father of a young son, Robbie; and Kathy, still single, is engaged to a man ten years her senior).

Additional Cast:

Jean Anderson: Susan Adams; Robbie Anderson: Christopher Gardner; Jenny: Cari Anne Warder; Ellen: Kyle Richards; Frank Carlson, Betty's romantic interest: Jim McMullan; Dr. Jason Harper, Kathy's fiancé: Hal England.

Music: George Duning.

Producer: Eugene B. Rodney.

Director: Marc Daniels.

FATHER OF THE BRIDE

Comedy. Background: 24 Maple Drive, Fairview Manor, Connecticut. The trials and tribulations of attorney Stanley Banks, the father of the bride from the first shock of his daughter, Kay, becoming engaged through the meeting of the families, the wedding preparations, the ceremony, and the first months of marriage. Also detailed are the struggles of the newlyweds, Kay and Buckley Dunston, from the first spats and the threats to go home to mother through their new roles as parents. Based on the movie of the same title.

CAST

Stanley Banks	Leon Ames
Ellie Banks, his wife	Ruth Warrick
Kay Banks (Dunston)	Myrna Fahey
Buckley Dunston	Burt Metcalfe
Tommy Banks, Kay's brother	Rickie Sorensen
Delilah, the Banks' housekeeper	Ruby Dandridge
Gloria Bellamy, Stanley's secretary	Shelly Ames
Herbert Dunston, Buckley's father	Ransom Sherman
Doris Dunston, Buckley's mother	Lurene Tuttle

FATHER OF THE BRIDE—30 minutes—CBS—September 29, 1961 - September 14, 1962. 34 episodes.

FAVORITE STORY

Anthology. Dramatizations based on stories selected by guests.

Host: Adolphe Menjou.

Included:

The Gold Bug. Adapted from the story by Edgar Allen Poe. The story of two Confederate soldiers who take up residence on a desolate island to brood over their impoverishment.

Starring: Neville Brand.

Canterville Ghost. Adapted from the story by Oscar Wilde. The story of a ghost who is doomed to haunt his family home because of a cowardly act in his past.

Starring: John Qualen.

Strange Valley. Adapted from the story by H. G. Wells. The story of an adventurer who finds himself in the strange valley of the blind.

Starring: Kenneth Tobey, Carla Balenda.

FAVORITE STORY—30 minutes—Syndicated 1952. 78 episodes.

FAWLTY TOWERS

Comedy. Background: England. The misadventures of Basil Fawlty, the rude and incompetent innkeeper of a hotel called Fawlty Towers.

CAST

Basil Fawlty	John Cleese
Sybil Fawlty, his wife	Prunella Scales
Polly Sherman, the waitress	Connie Booth
Manuel, the bellboy	Andrew Sachs
Major Gowen, a hotel guest	Ballard Berkeley

Music: Dennis Wilson.

Producer: John Davies.

Creator: John Cleese, Connie Booth.

FAWLTY TOWERS—30 minutes—Syndicated 1977. 6 episodes.

FAY

Comedy. Background: San Francisco, California. The joys, sorrows, and romantic misadventures of Fay Stuart, a middle-aged divorcée.

CAST

Fay Stuart, a legal secretary	Lee Grant
Jack Stuart, her philandering ex-husband	Joe Silver
Lillian, Fay's neighbor	Audra Lindley
Linda Baines, Fay's married daughter	Margaret Willock
Dr. Elliott Baines, Linda's husband	Stewart Moss
Danny Messina, Fay's employer, a crusading young lawyer	Bill Gerber
Al Cassidy, Danny's conservative partner	Norman Alden
Letty Gilmore, Al's secretary	Lillian Lehman

Music: George Tipton.

Theme Vocal: Jaye P. Morgan.

Executive Producer: Paul Junger Witt.

Producer: Jerry Mayer, Tony Thomas.

Director: Richard Kinon, James Burrows, Alan Arkin.

Creator: Susan Harris.

FAY—30 minutes—NBC—September 8, 1975 - October 23, 1975. Returned: NBC—May 12, 1976 - June 2, 1976. 8 episodes.

FAYE AND SKITCH

See title: "Faye Emerson."

FAYE EMERSON

Listed: The television programs of actress Faye Emerson.

Paris Cavalcade Of Fashion—Fashion Highlights—15 minutes—NBC—August 13, 1948 - December 16, 1948.

Narrator: Faye Emerson.

The Faye Emerson Show—Interview—15 minutes—CBS—October 4, 1949 - April 12, 1952.

Hostess: Faye Emerson.

Regulars: Mary Bennett, Kenneth Banghart.

Orchestra: Skitch Henderson.

Wonderful Town—Variety—30 minutes—CBS 1951.

Format: A U.S. city is selected and interviews are conducted with outstanding individuals.

Hostess: Faye Emerson.

Vocalists: The Don Large Chorus.

Orchestra: Skitch Henderson.

Strictly Skitch—Musical Variety-Interview—15 minutes—NBC—1952-1953. Broadcast on ABC as "Faye and Skitch"—15 minutes—1953-1954.

Hostess: Faye Emerson.

Co-Host: Skitch Henderson.

Music (NBC): The NBC Symphony Orchestra; ABC: Skitch Henderson Orchestra.

Of All Things—Musical Variety—30 minutes—CBS—July 23, 1956 - August 20, 1956.

Hostess: Faye Emerson.

Regulars: Ilehe Woods, Jack Haskell.

Announcer: Del Sharbutt.

Orchestra: Billy Clifton.

THE F.B.I.

Crime Drama. Case dramatizations based on the files of the Federal Bureau of Investigation.

CAST

Inspector Lewis Erskine	Efrem Zimbalist, Jr.
Arthur Ward, the assistant director	Philip Abbott
Jim Rhodes, Erskine's assistant	Stephen Brooks
Barbara Erskine, the Inspector's daughter	Lynn Loring
Agent Tom Colby	William Reynolds
Agent Chris Daniels	Shelly Novack
Agent Chet Randolph	Anthony Eisley

Narrator: Marvin Miller.

Music: Richard Markowitz; John

The F.B.I. Lynn Loring (center), Stephen Brooks, and Efrem Zimbalist, Jr.

Elizade.

Additional Music: Bronislau Kaper, Sidney Cutner, Dominic Frontiere, Duante Tatro.

Executive Producer: Quinn Martin.

Producer: Charles Lawton.

Director: Jesse Hibbs, William Hale, Robert Douglas, Christian Nyby.

THE F.B.I.—60 minutes—ABC—September 19, 1965 - September 1, 1974. Syndicated. 208 episodes.

F.D.R.

Documentary. The life and administration of former president Franklin D. Roosevelt is traced through newsreel footage.

Host-Narrator: Arthur Kennedy.

F.D.R.'s writings read by: Charlton Heston.

F.D.R.—30 minutes—ABC—January 8, 1965 - September 10, 1965. 27 episodes.

FEAR AND FANCY

Anthology. Dramatizations of people involved with supernatural happenings.

FEAR AND FANCY—30 minutes—ABC—May 13, 1953 - September 5, 1953.

FEARLESS FOSDICK

Children. The comic escapades of

Fearless Fosdick, creator-cartoonist Al Capp's hopeless comic-strip detective.

Voices and Puppets: The Mary Chase Marionette Company.

Producer: Charles Buggenheim.

FEARLESS FOSDICK—30 minutes—ABC 1952.

THE FEATHER AND FATHER GANG

Crime Drama. Background: Los Angeles, California. The cases of Toni "Feather" Danton, a beautiful attorney with the firm of Huffaker, Danton, and Binkwell, and her father, Harry Danton, her assistant, an ex-confidence man who incorporates his knowledge of the con game to outwit and apprehend criminals.

CAST

Toni Danton	Stefanie Powers
Harry Danton	Harold Gould
Lou, Harry's aid	Lewis Charles
Margo, Harry's aid	Joan Shawlee
Enzo, Harry's aid	Frank Delfino
Michael, Harry's aid	Monte Landis
J.C. Hadley, the Deputy D.A.	Edward Winter
Jesse, Toni's secretary	Jessica Rains
"Huff" Huffaker, Toni's partner	William H. Bassett
Binkwell, Toni's partner	Allen Williams

Music: George Romanis.

Producer: Robert Mintz, Bill Driskill.

Director: Seymour Robbie, Ernest Pintoff, Bruce Bilson, Jackie Cooper, Jerry London, Barry Shear.

Creator: Bill Driskill.

THE FEATHER AND FATHER GANG—60 minutes—ABC—March 7, 1977 - April 4, 1977; Returned: ABC—May 21, 1977 - August 6, 1977. The pilot film, titled "Feather and Father" aired December 6, 1976.

FEATHER YOUR NEST

Game. Various household furnishings are displayed on stage. Two couples select desired pieces. Within a specified time limit, one member of each team has to find a hidden feather in chosen articles. The questions contained by the feather are answered by the other teammate. Each correct answer awards the couple the represented merchandise.

Host: Bud Collyer.

Assistants: Lou Prentiss, Janis Carter, Jean Williams.

Producer: Jack Selden.

Sponsor: The Colgate-Palmolive Company.

FEATHER YOUR NEST—30 minutes—NBC—October 11, 1954 - July 27, 1956.

FEDERAL MEN

See title: "Treasury Men In Action."

FEELING GOOD

Educational. Background: A luncheonette called Mac's Place. Through the health problems and behavior of its residents, and through songs, sketches, animation, and documentary segments, tips on staying healthy are presented.

CAST

Mac, the proprietor	Rex Everhart
Rita, the waitress	Priscilla Lopez
Mrs. Stebbins, an elderly addict of gossip columns	Ethel Shutta
Jason, a young doctor	Joe Morton
Melba, Jason's wife	Marjorie Barnes
Hank, the owner of a sporting-goods store	Ben Slack

Host: Dick Cavett.

Regular: Bill Cosby.

Orchestra: Stephen Lawrence.

Executive Producer: Robert Benedict, Bill Kobin.

Producer: Albert Waller.

Director: John Desmond.

FEELING GOOD—60 minutes—PBS—November 20, 1974 - January 29, 1975.

FELICIANO

A thirty-minute variety series hosted by Jose Feliciano. Syndicated 1969.

FELIX THE CAT

Animated Cartoon. The story of Felix, a cat who possesses a magic black bag that can grant its owner any wish. Cliff-hanger-type episodes relate the ill-fated attempts of the Professor and his accomplices, Rock Bottom and Poindexter, to acquire the bag for the power it will afford them. Voices and music are not given screen credit.

Producer: Joseph Orilo.

Creator: Pat Sullivan.

FELIX THE CAT—04 minutes—Syndicated 1960. 260 episodes.

THE FELONY SQUAD

Crime Drama. Background: Los Angeles, California. The investigations of L.A.P.D. detectives Sam Stone and Jim Briggs.

CAST

Detective Sam Stone	Howard Duff
Detective Jim Briggs	Dennis Cole
Sergeant Dan Briggs, Jim's father	Ben Alexander
Captain Nye	Frank Maxwell
Captain Franks	Barney Phillips

THE FELONY SQUAD—30 minutes—ABC—September 12, 1966 - January 31, 1969. Syndicated. 73 episodes.

THE FEMININE TOUCH

See title: "The Little Show."

FERNWOOD 2-NIGHT

Satire. An intentionally appalling series that satirizes the TV talk show. Produced by the mythical Channel 6 in imaginary Fernwood, Ohio, the home of "Mary Hartman," the program literally presents the most grotesque people imaginable to be interviewed by an obnoxious, conceited host and his acid-tongued announcer. The summer replacement for "Mary Hartman, Mary Hartman."

Host: Martin Mull as Barth Gimble.

Announcer: Fred Willard as Jerry Hubbard.

Music: Frank DeVol (as Happy Kyne) and his Orchestra (the Mirth Makers).

Executive Producer: Louis J. Horvitz.

Producer: Alan Thicke.

Director: Howard Storm, Tony Csiki, Jim Drake, Louis J. Horvitz.

Creator: Norman Lear.

FERNWOOD 2-NIGHT—30 minutes—Syndicated 1977.

The Felony Squad. Left to right: Dennis Cole, Kevin Hagen (guest), Howard Duff.

CAST

Fibber McGee	Bob Sweeney
Molly McGee	Cathy Lewis
Mayor Charles La Trivia	Hal Peary
Roy Norris, Fibber's friend and neighbor	Paul Smith
Hazel Norris, his wife	Elizabeth Fraser
Doctor John Gamble, the town physician	Addison Richards
Teeny, the little girl next door	Barbara Beaird
Mrs. La Trivia, the mayor's wife	Dorothy Neumann
Mrs. Driscoll, Molly's mother	Reta Shaw
Fred Nitney, Fibber's neighbor	Jack Kirkwood

Producer: William Asher.

FIBBER McGEE AND MOLLY—30 minutes—NBC—September 15, 1959 - January 26, 1960. 26 episodes.

FESTIVAL OF FAMILY CLASSICS

Animated Cartoon. Video adaptations of classic fairy tales.

Voices: Carl Banas, Peg Dixon, Keith Hampshire, Len Birman, Peggi Loader, Donna Miller.

Music: Maury Laws.

Included:

Hiawatha. Henry Wadsworth Longfellow's story of the strength and courage of an Indian warrior.

Snow White And The Seven Dwarfs. An adaptation wherein the Seven Dwarfs attempt to save Snow White from her cruel stepmother.

Around The World In 80 Days. The story of Phineas Fogg, who attempts to travel around the world in eighty days.

20,000 Leagues Under The Sea. Jules Verne's classic tale of Captain Nemo as he journeys to the ocean's depths.

FESTIVAL OF FAMILY CLASSICS —30 minutes—Syndicated 1972.

FESTIVAL OF STARS

Anthology. Rebroadcasts of episodes of "The Loretta Young Theatre" that do not star Loretta Young.

Host: Jim Ameche.

Included:

Incident In Kawi. Background: Africa. The story of a big-game hunter who attempts to adjust to new responsibilities when he is put in charge of his recently orphaned nephew.

CAST
Don O'Herlihy, Vanessa Brown, Frederick Worlock.

My Uncles O'Moore. Era: The 1920s. When a schoolmarm is imported for the sole purpose of marriage to one of the O'Moore boys, she finds herself rejected because she is considered too frail for ranch life. The story concerns her efforts to prove her ability.

CAST ·
Teresa Wright.

The Wise One. The story of a prospector who seeks a legendary silver mine to help a needy tribe of Indians.

CAST
Stephen McNally, Joy Page.

FESTIVAL OF STARS—30 minutes —NBC—June 30, 1956 - September 1956; July 2, 1957 - September 1957.

FIBBER McGEE AND MOLLY

Comedy. Background: The town of Wistful Vista. The trials and tribulations of the McGees: Fibber, amateur inventor, the world's greatest liar; and his tolerant wife, Molly, who reside at 79 Wistful Vista. Based on the radio program of the same title.

54th STREET REVUE

Musical Variety. Background: The 54th Street Theatre in New York City.

CAST
Jack Sterling, Carl Reiner, Joey Faye, Joe Silver, Marilyn Day, Tommy Wonder, Jordan Bentley, Virginia Gorski, Mort Marshall, Billy Vine, Joan Diener, Russell Arms, Patricia Bright, Bambi Linn, Annabell Lyons, Count Reno, Jonathan Lucas, Jimmy Spitarny.

Music: Albert Selden.
Producer: Barry Wood.
Director: Ralph Levy.

54th STREET REVUE—60 minutes— CBS 1949.

50 GRAND SLAM

Game. Players, those with knowledge in at least one specific field, compete in mental or physical dexterity contests. Two players, who possess knowledge in the same field, compete at a time. Each contestant is placed in an isolation booth; the sound is turned off in one while the other player is asked questions. When finished, the sound is turned on in the other booth and the contestant is asked the same questions. The player who scores the most correct answers is the winner and receives $200 for reaching the first plateau. Seven additional plateaus remain, worth $500, $1,000, $2,000, $5,000, $10,000, $20,000, and

$50,000 each. The player's decision to quit or continue after any plateau determines his winnings. However, should he risk taking a certain plateau and fail to complete it, he is defeated and loses everything he has earned to that point.

Host: Tom Kennedy.

Announcer: John Harlan.

Music: Recorded.

Executive Producer: Ralph Andrews.

Director: Marty Pasetta.

50 GRAND SLAM—30 minutes—NBC—October 4, 1976 - December 31, 1976.

THE FIGHT FOR LIFE

Medical Discussion. Interviews between doctors and their patients who have made near-miraculous recoveries.

Hostess: Kathryn Crosby, R.N.

THE FIGHT FOR LIFE—30 minutes —Syndicated 1967.

THE FILES OF JEFFREY JONES

Crime Drama. Background: New York City. The confidential investigations of private detective Jeffrey Jones.

CAST

Jeffrey Jones   Don Haggerty
Michele "Mike" Malone, his
  girlfriend, a newspaper
  reporter   Gloria Henry

Producer: Lindsley Parsons.

THE FILES OF JEFFREY JONES—30 minutes—Syndicated 1955. 39 episodes.

FILM ODYSSEY

Movies. Foreign and American film classics.

Host: Charles Champlin, Movie critic for the *Los Angeles Times.*

FILM ODYSSEY—2 hours—PBS—January 15, 1972 - July 3, 1973.

FIREBALL FUN FOR ALL

Variety. Music, songs, and slapstick comedy.

Hosts: John "Ole" Olsen (tall and thin); Harold "Chic" Johnson (short and fat)—insult comics.

Regulars: Pat Donahue, Marty May, June Johnson, Bill Hays, The Lyn Duddy Singers.

Orchestra: Charles Sanford.

Choreographer: Bob Sidney.

Producer-Director: Edward F. Cline.

FIREBALL FUN FOR ALL—60 minutes—NBC—1949-1950.

FIREBALL XL-5

Marionette Adventure. Era: Twenty-first-century Earth. Background: Space City, the headquarters of the Galaxy Patrol, the futuristic police force. Stories relate its attempts to protect the planets of a united solar system from the sinister forces bent on destroying its truce. Filmed in Supermarionation.

Characters:
Colonel Steve Zodiac, the pilot of
  Fireball XL-5.
Venus, his co-pilot.
Commander Zero, the Space City con-
  troller.
Lieutenant 90, a Space Patrol pilot.
Professor Matic, the scientific genius.
Robert the Robot, the electronic
  brain.
Mr. and Mrs. Superspy, notorious
  villains of the universe.
The Briggs Brothers, saboteurs, ene-
  mies of Space City.

Voices: Paul Maxwell, Sylvia Anderson, David Graham, John Bluthal.

Music: Barry Gray.

FIREBALL XL-5—30 minutes—NBC —October 5, 1963 - September 25, 1965. Syndicated. 39 episodes.

FIREHOUSE

Drama. Background: California. The work of the men of Engine Company Number 23 of the Los Angeles County Fire Department.

CAST

Captain Spike Ryerson   James Drury
Hank Myers   Richard Jaeckel
Sonny Capito   Mike Delano
Cal Dakin   Bill Overton
Scotty Smith   Scott Smith
Billy Del Zel   Brad David

Music: Billy Goldenberg.

Executive Producer: Dick Berg.

Producer: Dick Collins.

FIREHOUSE—30 minutes—ABC—January 17, 1974 - August 1, 1974. 13 episodes.

FIRESIDE THEATRE

Anthology. Dramatic presentations.

Hosts: Gene Raymond; Jane Wyman (under title: "Jane Wyman's Fireside Theatre").

Producer: Frank Wisbar, William Asher, Peter Barry, Brewster Morgan, Jules Bricken, Albert McCleery.

Director: Larry Schwab, Albert McCleery.

Sponsor: Procter and Gamble.

Included:

I Cover Korea. Possessing vital enemy information acquired from a prisoner, war correspondent Wanda Brown must decide whether to release it to the press or inform United Nations officials.

CAST
Wanda Brown: Marguerite Chapman; Steve Trent: Donald Woods.

His Name Is Jason. The story of an illiterate wife who devotes her life to her educated but alcoholic husband.

CAST
Gertrude Michtal, John Warburton.

Grey Gardens. After escaping the bounds of his Oriental jailers, a secret service agent returns to his home in the South and struggles to find peace.

Starring: Arthur Franz.

We'll Never Have A Nickel. The story of the unknown force behind a successful producer.

CAST
Gerry Warren: Hayden Rorke; Eva: Ann Doran; Penny: Gloria Talbot; Ben Morris: Taylor Holmes.

Mirage. Fleeing from police, a circus roustabout finds refuge at the farmhouse of a former circus performer, now housewife. Without arousing his suspicions, she seeks a way to acquire help.

CAST
Marjorie Lord, Bill Henry.

FIRESIDE THEATRE—30 minutes—NBC—1949-1955. Syndicated.

FIRING LINE

Discussion. Public officials are interviewed on topical issues.

Host: William F. Buckley, Jr., conservative spokesman.

FIRING LINE—60 minutes—Syndicated 1971; PBS—60 minutes—May 26, 1971 - June 1976. Syndicated first run, 1976.

THE FIRST HUNDRED YEARS

Serial. Background: New York City. The dramatic story of young marrieds Chris and Connie Thayer.

CAST

Chris Thayer	Jimmy Lydon
Connie Thayer	Anne Sargent
	Olive Stacey
Mr. Thayer, Chris's father	Don Tobin
Mrs. Thayer, his wife	Valerie Cassort
Mr. Martin, Connie's father	Robert Armstrong
Mrs. Martin, his wife	Nana Bryant

Also: Nancy Malone, Larry Haines.

Announcer: Cy Harris.

Organist: Clark Morgan.

Producer: Hoyt Allen.

Director: Everett Gannon.

Sponsor: Procter and Gamble.

THE FIRST HUNDRED YEARS—15 minutes—CBS—December 4, 1950 - June 27, 1952.

FIRST LOVE

Serial. The dramatic story of young marrieds Laurie and Zachary James.

CAST

Laurie Kennedy James	Patricia Barry
Zachary James	Val DuFour
Quentin Andrews	Frederick Downs
Sam Morrison	Hal Currier
Peggy Gordon	Henrietta Moore
Phil Gordon	Joe Warren
Ruth Taylor	Scotty McGregor
Wallace Grant	Henry Stanton
Mike Kennedy	John Dutra
Judge Kennedy	Howard Smith
Priscilla Cummings	Rita Fredricks
Jim Taylor	Alan Stevenson
Chris	Frankie Thomas, Jr.
Amy	Rosemary Prinz
Packy	Ray Brown, Jr.
Chuck Gibson	Humphrey Davis
Wallace Grant	Richard Keith
Paul Kennedy	Mel Ruick
Doris Kennedy	Peg Allenby
Harriet	Shirley O'Hara
Blair	Harry Holcombe
Jennie	Barbara Myers
Matthew James	Paul McGrath
Jack Doyle	Court Benson
Leona	Nancy Pollock
Garth Brown	Eric Dressler
Diane	Patricia Wheel

Producer: Al Morrison.

Sponsor: Jergens.

FIRST LOVE—15 minutes—NBC—July 5, 1954 - December 30, 1955.

FIRST PERSON SINGULAR

Anthology. Dramatizations incorporating the subjective camera—a technique developed by Fred Coe for the feature film *Lady in the Lake* (1946). The television camera becomes the eyes of the characters; and unseen actor or actress provides the voice and sets the emotional tone.

Included:

I'd Rather Be a Squirrel. The story of a man who, when situations become difficult, retreats to a tree.

Starring: Wally Cox.

August Heat. A tale of the supernatural; a man envisions his own doom.

Starring: Francis L. Sullivan, Nelson Olmstead.

Tears Of My Sister. The story of a woman who is forced to marry a man she does not love. The problems of the marriage arranged by their families is seen through the eyes of the woman's younger sister.

Starring: Kim Stanley, Lenka Patterson.

One Night Stand. A young man attempts to prove to his depressed father that he is a success as a jazz-band leader.

Starring: James Dunn, Conrad Janis.

Comeback. An agent attempts to trick a fading, but once glamorous, actress into accepting a role she doesn't want.

Starring: Jessie Royce Landis, Jack Warden, Murray Hamilton, John Fletcher.

FIRST PERSON SINGULAR—30 minutes—NBC—June 1953 - September 1953. The subjective camera technique was also encompassed in "The Plainclothesman." (See title.)

FISH

Comedy. Background: Brooklyn, New York. On a leave of absence after thirty-eight years with the New York Police Department, Detective Phil Fish reluctantly abides by his wife, Bernice's, decision to care for five children—five streetwise delinquents assigned to him by the Social Services Center. Stories relate his attempts to cope with a new life-style and supervise his newly acquired family. A spin-off from "Barney Miller."

CAST

Phil Fish	Abe Vigoda
Bernice Fish	Florence Stanley
Charlie Harrison, the associate host parent (to help care for the kids)	Barry Gordon

The Children:

Diane Palanski	Sarah Natoli
Jilly	Denise Miller
Mike	Lenny Bari
Victor	John Cassisi
Loomis	Todd Bridges

Music: Jack Elliott, Allyn Ferguson.

Executive Producer: Danny Arnold.

Producer: Norman Barasch, Roy Kammerman.

Director: Mike Warren, Dennis Steinmetz.

FISH—30 minutes—ABC—Premiered: February 5, 1977.

THE FITZPATRICKS

Drama. Background: Flint, Michigan. Events in the lives of the Fitzpatricks, an Irish-Catholic family of six.

CAST

Mike Fitzpatrick, the father, a steelworker	Bert Kramer
Maggie Fitzpatrick, his wife	Mariclare Costello
Jack Fitzpatrick, their son	James Vincent McNichol
Maureen "Mo" Fitzpatrick, their daughter	Michele Tobin
Max Fitzpatrick, their son	Sean Marshall
Sean Fitzpatrick, their son	Clark Brandon
Kerry Gerardi, Jack's friend	Helen Hunt
R.J., Max's friend	Derek Wells

The Fitzpatricks' Dog: Detroit.

Music: John Rubinstein.

Executive Producer: Philip Mandelker.

Producer: John Cutts.

Creator: John Young.

THE FITZPATRICKS– 60 minutes–CBS–Premiered: September 5, 1977.

FIVE FINGERS

Mystery. Background: Europe. The story of United States counterintelligence agent Victor Sebastian. Episodes relate his attempts to infiltrate and inform authorities of the activities of Soviet espionage rings.

CAST
Victor Sebastian	David Hedison
Simone Genet, his assistant	Luciana Paluzzi

Music Composed By: David Raksin.

Music Conducted By: Lionel Newman.

Producer: Herbert Swope, Jr., Martin Manulis.

Director: Gerald Mayer, Montgomery Pittman.

FIVE FINGERS–60 minutes–NBC–October 3, 1959 - January 6, 1960. Syndicated. 16 episodes.

FIVE STAR COMEDY

Comedy. Geared to children and featuring the performances of five comedians.

Hosts for the five-week run of the series: Ben Blue; Jerry Colona; Ole Olsen and Chic Johnson; Senior Wences; Paul Winchell and Jerry Mahoney.

FIVE STAR COMEDY–30 minutes–ABC–May 18, 1957 - June 15, 1957.

FIVE STAR JUBILEE

Variety. Performances by Country and Western entertainers.

Rotating Hosts: Rex Allen, Snooky Lansen, Tex Ritter, Carl Smith, Jimmy Wakely.

Regulars: The Jubilaires, The Promenaders.

Announcer: Joe Slattery.

Music: Slim Wilson and the Jubilee Band.

FIVE STAR JUBILEE–60 minutes–NBC–March 17, 1961 - September 22, 1961.

FLAME IN THE WIND

See title: "A Time For Us."

FLASH GORDON

Adventure. Era: Twenty-first-century Earth. The exploits of Flash Gordon, the resourceful son of a famous scientist; Dale Arden, "the beautiful blonde always in distress"; and Dr. Alexis Zarkov, the scientific genius who invented Earth's first rocket ship. Stories relate their efforts to preserve peace in outer space.

TV CAST
Flash Gordon	Steve Holland
Dale Arden	Irene Champlin
Dr. Alexis Zarkov	Joseph Nash

FLASH GORDON–30 minutes–Syndicated 1953. 39 episodes.

Based on the comic strip by Alex Raymond, which appeared in 1934, three theatrical series were also produced: *Flash Gordon,* 1936; *Flash Gordon's Trip To Mars,* 1939; and *Flash Gordon Conquers the Universe,* 1940.

FLATT AND SCRUGGS

Musical Variety. Performances by Country and Western artists.

Hosts: Earl Flatt and Lester Scruggs (singer-musicians).

FLATT AND SCRUGGS–30 minutes –Syndicated 1966.

FLIGHT

Anthology. Dramatizations based on true stories from the files of the United States Air Force.

Host: Gen. George C. Kenney, USAF (Ret.)

FLIGHT–30 minutes–Syndicated 1958. 39 episodes.

THE FLINTSTONES

Animated Cartoon. The life style of the twentieth century is depicted in the Stone Age era of the one million forties, B.C. Background: The town of Bedrock, 345 Stone Cave Road, the residence of the Flintstones: Fred, a dino operator for the Slaterock Gravel Company; and his wife, Wilma. With their friends and neighbors, Barney and Betty Rubble, they struggle to make ends meet and enjoy a few luxuries.

Produced by William Hanna and Joseph Barbera, "The Flintstones" became television's first "adult cartoon," a situation comedy in animated form, wherein a Stone Age family is beset by problems similar to the protagonists in "The Honeymooners" (see title). Fred and Barney are the prototypes of Ralph and Norton; and Wilma and Betty are the prototypes of Alice and Trixie. Similarities include their struggles to better their lives, and their association with lodges–Ralph and Norton belong to The Raccoon Lodge; Fred and Barney to The Royal Order of Water Buffalos.

Characters' Voices
Fred Flintstone	Alan Reed
Wilma Flintstone	Jean VanderPyl
Barney Rubble	Mel Blanc
Betty Rubble	Bea Benaderet
	Gerry Johnson
Dino, the Flintstone pet dinosaur	Chips Spam
Pebbles Flintstone, Fred and Wilma's daughter	Jean VanderPyl
Bamm Bamm Rubble, Barney and Betty's son	Don Messick
Hoppy, the Rubble family pet	Don Messick
George Slate, Fred's employer	John Stephenson
Arnold, the newspaper boy	Don Messick
The Great Gazeoo, a space creature	Harvey Korman
Mrs. Flaghoople, Wilma's mother	Jean VanderPyl

Music: Hoyt Curtin; Ted Nichols.

Spin-Offs:

Pebbles And Bamm Bamm. The story of the teenage Flintstone and Rubble children, Pebbles and Bamm Bamm. Episodes revolve around their activities while attending Bedrock High School.

Characters' Voices
Pebbles Flintstone	Sally Struthers
Bamm Bamm Rubble	Jay North
Moonrock	Lennie Weinrib
Fabian	Carl Esser
Penny	Mitzi McCall
Cindy	Gay Hartwig
Wiggy	Gay Hartwig

Music: Hoyt Curtin.

The Flintstones Comedy Hour; The Flintstones Show. Continued events in the lives of the Flintstones and the Rubbles.

Characters' Voices

The Flintstones. Left to right: Fred Flintstone, Wilma Flintstone, Barney Rubble, Betty Rubble. *Courtesy Hanna-Barbera Productions.*

Fred Flintstone	Alan Reed
Barney Rubble	Mel Blanc
Wilma Flintstone	Jean VanderPyl
Betty Rubble	Gay Hartwig
Pebbles Flintstone	Mickey Stevens
Bamm Bamm Rubble	Jay North
Moonrock	Lennie Weinrib
Penny	Mitzi McCall
Fabian	Carl Esser
Schleprock	Don Messick
Wiggy	Gay Hartwig
Bronto	Lennie Weinrib
Zonk	Mel Blanc
Noodles	John Stephenson
Stub	Mel Blanc

Music: Hoyt Curtin.

THE FLINTSTONES—30 minutes—ABC—September 30, 1960 - September 2, 1966. Syndicated. Rebroadcasts, NBC: September 2, 1967 - September 5, 1970. Syndicated.

PEBBLES AND BAMM BAMM—30 minutes—CBS—September 11, 1971 - September 2, 1972.

THE FLINTSTONES COMEDY HOUR—60 minutes—CBS—September 9, 1972 - September 1, 1973.

THE FLINTSTONES SHOW—30 minutes—CBS—September 8, 1973 - January 26, 1974.

FLIPPER

Adventure. Background: Coral Key Park in Florida. The story of Porter Ricks, widower, the marine preserve ranger; his sons, Sandy and Bud; and their pet dolphin, Flipper, who assists them in patrolling and protecting the park.

CAST

Ranger Porter Ricks	Brian Kelly
Sandy Ricks	Luke Halpin
Bud Ricks	Tommy Norden
Ulla Norstrand, a research chemist	Ulla Stromstedt
Hap Gorman, a friend of the boys	Andy Devine
Flipper	Susie

Porter family pets: Pete the pelican; and Spray the dog.

Music: Henry Vars; Samuel Motlovsky.

FLIPPER—30 minutes—NBC—September 19, 1964 - May 14, 1967. Syndicated. 88 episodes.

THE FLIP WILSON SHOW

Variety. Various comedy sketches.

Host: Flip Wilson.

Dancers: The Flipettes: Marguerite DeLain, Ka Ron Brown, Jaki Morrison, Edwetta Little, Bhetty Waldron, Mary Vivian.

Orchestra: George Wyle.

THE FLIP WILSON SHOW—60 minutes—NBC—September 17, 1970 - June 27, 1974.

FLOOR SHOW

Music. Performances by jazz musicians.

Host: Eddie Condon, Carl Reiner.

Regulars: Wild Bill Davison, Cutty Cuttshall, Sidney Bechet, Joe Bushkin, Billy Butterfield, Peewee Russell.

Music: Eddie Condon's All Stars.

FLOOR SHOW—30 minutes—NBC 1949; CBS 1950).

THE FLORIAN ZaBACH SHOW

Musical Variety.

Host: Florian ZaBach (a violinist).

Vocalist: Leila Hyer.

Music: Performed by an unidentified orchestra.

Producer: Dick Kissinger, Syd Rubin.

Director: Rick Leighton.

THE FLORIAN ZaBACH SHOW—15 minutes—CBS—March 10, 1951 - June 9, 1951.

THE FLYING DOCTOR

Adventure. Background: Australia. The story of an American physician who, by using an airplane, struggles to serve those far removed from society —from the remote ranchers to the Bushmen.

CAST

Greg, the flying doctor	Richard Denning
Mary, his nurse	Jill Adams
Dr. Harrison	Peter Madden
Charley, the pilot	Alan White

THE FLYING DOCTOR—30 minutes—Syndicated 1959. 39 episodes.

THE FLYING NUN

Comedy. Impressed by her missionary aunt, Elsie Ethrington decides to devote her life to helping the less fortunate and joins a convent. Ordained as Sister Bertrille, she is assigned to the Convent San Tanco in San Juan, Puerto Rico.

Shortly after beginning her duties she discovers the ability to fly. The coronets, the headgear worn by the nuns of her order, possess sides that resemble wings; and San Juan is an area affected by trade winds. Weighing only ninety pounds, she is able to soar above the ground when caught by strong gales. Through the manipulation of her coronets she acquires some control over flight, but not all, and landings become difficult.

Youthful, exuberant, with a knack for finding trouble, and a sincere desire to do good, Sister Bertrille seeks to use her gift of flight to benefit her poor community.

CAST

Sister Bertrille (Elsie Ethrington)	Sally Field
Sister Jacqueline	Marge Redmond
The Reverend Mother Plaseato (Mother Superior)	Madeleine Sherwood
Carlos Ramirez, a playboy, the owner of the Casino Carlos, a discotheque	Alejandro Rey
Sister Ana	Linda Dangcil
Sister Sixto	Shelley Morrison
Sister Teresa	Naomi Stevens
Captain Fomento, the fumbling police supersleuth	Vito Scotti
Jennifer Ethrington, Elsie's sister	Elinor Donahue
Chief Galindo, Fomento's superior	Don Diamond Rodolfo Hoyos
Salazar, Fomento's underling	Mike Pataki

Music: Dominic Frontiere; Warren Barker; Harry Geller.

Executive Producer: Harry Ackerman.

Producer: William Sackheim, Ed Jurist.

Director: Jerry Bernstein, Murray Golden, Richard Michaels, Jerry London.

THE FLYING NUN—30 minutes—ABC—September 7, 1967 - September 11, 1969. Syndicated. 82 episodes.

FOLLOW THE LEADER

Game. Two three-minute sketches are enacted by the Hostess. Selected studio audience members have to re-enact the same situation. Those who achieve a performance as close to the original as possible receive a merchandise prize.

Hostess: Vera Vague.

FOLLOW THE LEADER—30 minutes—CBS—June 1953 - September 1953.

FOLLOW THE SUN

Adventure. Background: Honolulu, Hawaii. The experiences of free-lance magazine writers Ben Gregory and Paul Templin.

CAST

Ben Gregory	Barry Coe
Paul Templin	Brett Halsey
Eric Jason, the legman for their ship, the *Scuber*	Gary Lockwood
Katherine Ann Richards, their part-time secretary, a Honolulu University student	Gigi Perreau
Frank Roper, a lieutenant, Honolulu Police Department	Jay Sanin

Music: Sonny Burke.

FOLLOW THE SUN—60 minutes—ABC—September 17, 1961 - September 9, 1962. Syndicated. 30 episodes.

FOLLOW THAT MAN

See title: "Man Against Crime."

FOLLOW YOUR HEART

Serial. A girl's efforts to break set traditions in her wealthy family. Unhappily engaged to a man her mother has chosen for her, she struggles to gain the right to choose her own spouse outside her social scale.

CAST

Julie Fielding	Sallie Brophy
Her boy friend	Louis Hallister
Julie's mother	Nancy Sheridan

Also: Anne Seymour, Maxine Stuart.

FOLLOW YOUR HEART—15 minutes—NBC—1953-1954.

FOODINI THE GREAT

Marionettes. The misadventures of Foodini the magician and his assistant, Pinhead.

Hostess: Ellen Parker; Doris Brown.

Puppet Characters and Voices: Hope Bunin, Mory Bunin.

Producer-Director: Hope and Mory Bunin.

Sponsor: Bristol-Myers.

FOODINI THE GREAT—15 minutes —ABC—August 23, 1951 - November 17, 1951.

FOOTLIGHT THEATRE

Anthology. Dramatic presentations.

Included:

National Honeymoon. The story of a bride who drags her unwilling husband onto a national television show to reveal the details of their courtship in return for a houseful of furniture.

CAST

Diana Lynn, Dick Haymes, Alan Mowbray.

The Sum Of Seven. The story of a college professor who discovers that a student has stolen a copy of an exam.

CAST

Victor Jory.

The Time Of Day. The story of a socialite who falls in love with a man with a dubious past — a relationship that threatens her family with unfavorable publicity.

CAST

Peggy Ann Garner.

FOOTLIGHT THEATRE—30 minutes—CBS—July 4, 1952 - September 1952.

FOR ADULTS ONLY

Interview. Guests in informative discussions on topical issues.

Hostesses: Joyce Susskind, Barbara Howar.

Music: Recorded.

FOR ADULTS ONLY—30 minutes—Syndicated 1970. 17 tapes. Also known as "Joyce and Barbara: For Adults Only."

FOR BETTER OR WORSE

Serial. Dramatizations of marital difficulties. Based on actual case histories. Guests appear in stories that last from one to two weeks.

Host-Narrator: Dr. James A. Peterson, a marriage counselor and teacher at the University of Southern California.

Producer: John Guedel.

Director: Hal Cooper.

FOR BETTER OR WORSE—30 minutes—CBS—June 29, 1959 - June 24, 1960.

FORD FESTIVAL

Variety. Music, songs, dances, and comedy sketches.

Host: James Melton.

Orchestra: David Broekman.

Producer-Director: Charles Friedman.

Sponsor: The Ford Motor Company.

FORD FESTIVAL—60 minutes—NBC 1951.

FORD STAR JUBILEE

Variety. Entertainment specials.

Included:

The Judy Garland Show (9/24/55). Musical Variety. Miss Garland's television debut. Basically, a one-woman show featuring the songs associated with Judy's career.

Hostess: Judy Garland.

Guest: David Wayne.

Dancers: The Escorts.

Orchestra: Jack Catheart.

High Tor (3/10/56). A musical fantasy based on Maxwell Anderson's play.

Starring: Bing Crosby, Nancy Olson, and Julie Andrews (her television debut).

The Wizard Of Oz (11/3/56). The first television presentation of L. Frank Baum's story about a girl and her adventures in the fantasy land called Oz.

Starring: Judy Garland, Ray Bolger, Bert Lahr, Jack Haley.

FORD STAR JUBILEE—60 minutes to 2 hours (pending production)—CBS—September 24, 1955 - November 3, 1956.

FORD STAR REVUE

Variety. Music, songs, dances, and comedy routines.

Host: Jack Haley.

Regulars: Mindy Carson, The Continentals, The Mellow-Larks.

Orchestra: David Broekman.

Producer: Sylvia Friedlander.

Director: Dick Berger, Buzz Kulik.

Sponsor: The Ford Motor Company.

FORD STAR REVUE—60 minutes—NBC—July 6, 1950 - September 1950.

FORD STARTIME

Anthology. Musical, dramatic, and comedic productions.

Included:

The Rosalind Russell Show. A musical revue tracing the changes in show business.

Hostess: Rosalind Russell.

CAST

Polly Bergen, Maurice Chevalier, Eddie Foy, Jr., Eddie Hodges, Ernie Kovacs, Arthur O'Connell, Jack Paar, Kate Smith.

Orchestra: Harry Sosnick.

The Jazz Singer. Drama. A father attempts to persuade his son, who wants to become a comedian, to carry on the family tradition and become a cantor.

CAST

Joey Robbins: Jerry Lewis; Ginny Gibbons: Anna Maria Alberghetti; Sarah: Molly Picon; Cantor: Edward Franz.

Turn Of The Screw. Suspense Drama. An adaptation of the Henry James novel. A governess attempts to protect a young girl and her brother from a spirit who seeks to possess them.

CAST

Governess: Ingrid Bergman (her American television debut); Miles: Hayward Morse; Flora: Alexandra Wagner.

Music: David Amron.

The Dean Martin Show. Musical Variety.

Host: Dean Martin.

Guests: Frank Sinatra, Mickey Rooney.

Orchestra: David Rose.

George Burns In The Big Time. Variety. The music, song, dance, and comedy of vaudeville.

Host: George Burns.

Guests: Jack Benny, Eddie Cantor, George Jessel, Bobby Darin.

Orchestra: Jeff Alexander.

Merman On Broadway. Variety. A program tracing the highlights of Ethel Merman's Broadway career.

Hostess: Ethel Merman.

Guests: Tab Hunter, Fess Parker, Tom Poston, Bobby Sherwood.

Orchestra: Jack Kane.

FORD STARTIME—60 to 90 minutes (pending the production)—NBC—October 6, 1959 - May 31, 1960.

FORD THEATRE

Anthology. Dramatic presentations.

Producer: Garth Montgomery, Joseph Hoffman, Fletcher Markle, Irving Starr, Winston O'Keefe.

Sponsor: The Ford Motor Company.

Included:

A Touch Of Spring. The story of a summer romance between a married woman and a young bachelor.

CAST

Maria Clark: Irene Dunn; Bill Hannagin: Gene Barry.

Deception. A mother attempts to prepare a happy homecoming after learning that her son, once reported dead in Korea is alive.

CAST

Laura Blake: Sylvia Sidney; Paul Blake: John Howard.

Sunday Morn. Returning to his peaceful hometown, a former gunfighter struggles to adjust to a nonviolent life.

CAST

Mano: Brian Keith; Sally Carter: Marilyn Maxwell.

FORD THEATRE—30 and 60 minute versions—NBC—September 27, 1948 - September 26, 1956; ABC—October 3, 1956 - June 26, 1957.

FOREIGN INTRIGUE

Mystery-Adventure. Distinguished by three formats.

Format One (1951- 1953):
    Background: Paris. The experiences of Robert Cannon and Helen Davis, Foreign Correspondents for *Consolidated News.* Stories relate their attempts to infiltrate and expose espionage rings. Syndicated under the title: "Dateline: Europe."

CAST

Robert Cannon	Jerome Thor
Helen Davis	Sydna Scott

Music: Charles Norman; Ervin Drake.

Format Two (1953-1954):
    Background: Europe. The experiences of Michael Powers and Patricia Bennett, Foreign Correspondents for *Associated News.* Syndicated under the title: "Overseas Adventures."·

CAST

Michael Powers	James Daly

Patricia Bennett	Ann Preville
Their aide in Paris	Nikole Milinaire

Music: Charles Norman; Ervin Drake.

Format Three (1954-1955):
Background: Vienna. The story of Christopher Storm, a hotel owner who aides the distressed against the international underworld. Syndicated under the title: "Cross Current."

CAST

Christopher Storm	Gerald Mohr

Music: Charles Norman; Ervin Drake.

FOREIGN INTRIGUE—30 minutes—NBC—1951 - 1955. Episode numbers: "Cross Current" 39; "Dateline Europe" 78; "Overseas Adventures" 39. Also titled "Foreign Assignment."

FOREIGN LEGIONNAIRE

Adventure. Background: The French Foreign Legion headquarters in North Africa. The story of Captain Michael Gallant and his ward, Cuffy Sanders, the son of a slain officer. Episodes relate the struggles of men as they attempt to uphold the causes of freedom and justice.

CAST

Captain Michael Gallant	Buster Crabbe
Cuffy Sanders	Cullen Crabbe
First Class Private Fuzzy Knight	Fuzzy Knight
Sergeant DuVal	Gilles Queant
Carla, Fuzzy's girlfriend	Norma Eberhardt
The Colonel	Roger Trevielle

FOREIGN LEGIONNAIRE—30 minutes—NBC—February 13, 1955 - February 7, 1957; 30 minutes—ABC—June 6, 1960 - September 24, 1960; NBC—30 minutes—October 1, 1960 - September 21, 1963. Syndicated. Also known as "Captain Gallant" and "Captain Gallant of the Foreign Legion." 65 episodes.

THE FOREST RANGERS

Adventure. Background: The Canadian North Woods. Stories realistically relate the experiences of the members of the Junior Ranger Club, four boys and two girls, as they assist the forest rangers. Produced in Canada.

CAST

Ranger Keeley	Graydon Gould
Joe Two Rivers	Michael Zenon
Sergeant Scott	Gordon Pinsent
Chub	Ralph Endersby

Mike	Peter Tully
Steve	Don Mason
Peter	Rex Hagen
Kathy	Susan Conway
Denise	Barbara Pierce
Ted	George Allen

THE FOREST RANGERS—30 minutes—Syndicated 1965. 104 episodes.

FOREVER FERNWOOD

Satire. The revised series title for "Mary Hartman, Mary Hartman" without star Louise Lasser (Mary*). Set against the background of mythical Fernwood, Ohio, the story focuses on the chaotic existences in the lives of its townspeople.

CAST

Tom Hartman	Greg Mullavey
Loretta Haggers, Tom's neighbor	Mary Kay Place
Charlie Haggers, Loretta's husband	Graham Jarvis
Martha Schumway, Tom's mother-in-law	Dody Goodman
George Schumway, Martha's husband	Tab Hunter
Cathy Schumway, Martha's daughter	Debralee Scott
Heather Hartman, Tom's daughter	Claudia Lamb
Merle Jeeter, the mayor	Dabney Coleman
Wanda Jeeter, Merle's wife	Marian Mercer
Raymond Larkin, Martha's father	Victor Kilian
Eleanor Major, the young woman who attaches herself to Tom	Shelley Fabares
Mac Slattery, the truck driver	Dennis Burkley
Harmon Farinella, Loretta's admirer	Richard Hatch
Penny Major, Eleanor's sister	Judy Kahan

Music: Bobby Knight.

Executive Producer: Norman Lear.

Producer: Eugenie Ross-Leming, Brad Buckner.

Creator: Gail Parent, Ann Marcus, Jerry Adelman, Daniel Gregory Browne.

FOREVER FERNWOOD—30 minutes—Syndicated 1977.

*The closing episode of "Mary Hartman" found Mary leaving Tom to run off with her lover, Police Sgt. Dennis Foley.

FOR LOVE OR MONEY

Game. Three competing players. Each

states his preference for a visible prize or an unknown series of cash awards. The host begins the game with a series of question-answer rounds. The player first to identify himself through a buzzer signal receives a chance to answer. Correct answers award points; incorrect responses deduct points. Winners, the highest scorers, receive their previous selection.

Host: Bill Nimmo.

Producer: Walt Framer.

FOR LOVE OR MONEY—30 minutes—CBS—June 30, 1958 - February 6, 1959.

THE FORSYTE SAGA

Serial. The intrigues, loves, and financial dealings of the Forsyte family. Stories span over a half-century beginning in Victorian England. Produced by the B.B.C. Based on the novels by John Galsworthy.

CAST

Jo Forsyte	Kenneth More
Soames Forsyte	Eric Porter
Old Jolyon Forsyte	Joseph O'Connor
Irene	Nyree Dawn Porter
Monty	Terence Alexander
Mrs. Heron	Jenny Laird
Frances	Ursula Howells
June	June Barry
Bosinney	John Bennett
Swithin	George Woodbridge
Helen	Lana Morris
Winnifred	Margaret Tyzack
Annette	Dallia Penn
Val	Jonathan Burn
Fleur Forsyte	Susan Hampshire
Jon Forsyte	Martin Jarvis
Michael Mont	Nicholas Pennell
Holly	Suzanne Neve
Lord Charles Ferrar	Basil Dingnam
Sir Lawrence Mont	Cyril Lukham
Marjorie	Caroline Blakiston
Bicket	Terry Scully
Mac Gowan	John Phillips
Francis Wilmot	Hal Hamilton

Music: Marcus Dods.

Producer: Donald Wilson.

Director: David Giles.

Note: The series was the last major program to be filmed in black and white.

THE FORSYTE SAGA—60 minutes—NET—October 5, 1969 - April 4, 1970.

FOR THE PEOPLE

Drama. Background: New York. The work of Assistant District Attorney

David Koster as he attempts to prosecute all crimes within the state.

CAST

David Koster — William Shatner
Phyllis Koster, his
   wife — Jessica Walter
Anthony Celese, his
   superior — Howard DaSilva
Frank Malloy, a detective
   assigned to the D.A.'s
   office — Lonny Chapman

FOR THE PEOPLE—60 minutes—CBS—January 31, 1965 - May 9, 1965. 13 episodes.

FOR YOUR PLEASURE

Musical Variety.

Hostess: Kyle MacDonnell.

Featured: Jack and Jill.

Music: The Norman Paris Trio; The Earl Sheldon Orchestra.

Producer: Fred Coe.

Director: Richard Goode.

FOR YOUR PLEASURE—15 minutes—NBC 1948; 30 minutes—NBC 1949.

FOUR-IN-ONE

Drama. The overall title for four individual rotating series: "McCloud"; "Night Gallery"; "The Psychiatrist"; and "San Francisco International Airport."

McCloud. Background: New York City. The investigations of Sam McCloud, a deputy marshall from New Mexico who is assigned to Manhattan's twenty-seventh precinct to study crime-detection methods.

CAST

Sam McCloud — Dennis Weaver
Peter B. Clifford, the chief
   of detectives — J.D. Cannon
Sergeant Joe
   Broadhurst — Terry Carter
Chris Coughlin, Sam's romantic
   interest — Diana Muldaur

Music: Lee Holdridge.

Night Gallery. Supernatural tales of the horrifying confrontation between nightmare and reality.

Host: Rod Serling—Guide through a bizarre Night Gallery whose exhibits hold beneath their canvasses twisted tales of another dimension.

Music: Eddie Sauter.

Included (three examples listed):

THE DIARY. Background: Hollywood, California. A one-time glamorous actress seeks revenge when she is insulted by a vicious television reporter. She presents her with a diary that writes its own bizarre entries that come true. Seeking to escape the foreboding diary, the reporter enters a sanitarium. Revenge is achieved when the reporter goes insane.

CAST

Holly Schaefer, the reporter: Patty Duke; Carrie Crane, the actress: Virginia Mayo; Dr. Mill: David Wayne.

THE BIG SURPRISE. Three boys, walking home from school, are approached by a farmer and told they will find a surprise if they dig a four-foot hole on a certain piece of his property. Thinking to find buried treasure, they eagerly begin to dig. Two boys leave as the hour grows late, but the third perseveres. Tension mounts when he uncovers and opens a large box. The dim light reveals the farmer in the box—"Surprise!"

CAST

The Farmer: John Carradine.

PROFESSOR PEABODY'S LAST LECTURE. Background: A college classroom. Lecturing to his students on the ancient Gods, a professor begins to ridicule them. Suddenly the skies darken, the clouds grow black, and the heavens become angry. Unable to stand his insults any further the Gods transform him into a hideous fiend.

CAST

Professor Peabody: Carl Reiner.

The Psychiatrist. Background: Los Angeles, California. The story of James Whitman, a young psychiatrist who practices the new but controversial techniques of modern mental therapy.

CAST

Dr. James Whitman — Roy Thinnes
Dr. Bernard Altman, his friend, a
   psychiatrist — Luther Adler

San Francisco International Airport. Background: San Francisco, California. Dramatizations based on the problems that plague large airports.

CAST

Jim Conrad, the
   manager — Lloyd Bridges

Bob Hatten, the security
   chief — Clu Gulager
Suzie Conrad, Jim's
   daughter — Barbara Sigel
June, Jim's
   secretary — Barbara Werle

FOUR-IN-ONE—60 minutes—NBC—September 16, 1970 - September 8, 1971. Spin-offs: "McCloud"—90 minutes—NBC—Premiered: September 16, 1971 (as a part of the "NBC Sunday Mystery Movie"); "Rod Serling's Night Gallery"—60 minutes—NBC—September 15, 1971 - September 6, 1972; 30 minutes—NBC—September 17, 1972 - January 14, 1973. Rebroadcasts—30 minutes—NBC—May 13, 1973 - August 12, 1973. Syndicated. 24 episodes (6 of each).

FOUR JUST MEN

Adventure. Four men, friends during World War II, but having gone their separate ways since, are summoned together in England by the last request of their former commander. Tim Collier, American newspaper journalist; Ben Manfred, English private investigator; Ricco Poccari, Italian hotel owner; and Jeff Ryder, French attorney, form a union of Four Just Men who travel about the world and combat injustice. Stories relate their experiences on a rotational basis.

CAST

Tim Collier — Dan Dailey
Ben Manfred — Jack Hawkins
Ricco Poccari — Vittorio De Sica
Jeff Ryder — Richard Conte

FOUR JUST MEN—30 minutes—Syndicated 1957. 39 episodes.

FOUR STAR PLAYHOUSE

Anthology. Dramatic presentations. The title, "Four Star Playhouse," took its name from the four stars who created Four Star Studios and its first series, the aforementioned "Playhouse." They were: Dick Powell, Charles Boyer, Rosalind Russell, and Joel McCrea. As two later dropped out (Russell and McCrea), two joined (Ida Lupino and David Niven). By 1955, the four became three as Miss Lupino parted.

Included:

Village In The City. After he finds the body of a woman in his Greenwich Village apartment, a man attempts to find her murderer.

CAST

David Niven.

Lost Kid. A grandmother attempts to prevent her juvenile delinquent grandson from embarking on an adult life of crime.

CAST

Elizabeth Patterson, Mary Field, Harry Harvey, Jr.

Death Makes A Pair. The story centers on the struggles faced by a businessman as he attempts to overcome gambling fever.

CAST

Lloyd Corrigan, Jay Novello, Margia Dean.

The Watchers And The Watched. A suspense drama that details a woman's carefully laid plot to drive a man insane.

CAST

Faye Roope.

FOUR STAR PLAYHOUSE—60 minutes—CBS—September 25, 1952 - September 27, 1956.

THE FOUR-STAR REVUE

See title: "The All-Star Revue."

FOURSQUARE COURT

Interview. A panel of masked, paroled convicts discuss their past crimes and their present struggles for reformation.

Host: Norman Brokenshire.

FOURSQUARE COURT—30 minutes—ABC 1957.

FRACTURED FLICKERS

Comedy. A satirization of Hollywood's Golden Era. Silent films are seen with added synchronized, zany dialogue.

Host: Hans Conried.

Creator: Jay Ward.

Featured: Interviews with past and present celebrities.

FRACTURED FLICKERS—30 minutes—Syndicated 1963. 26 episodes.

FRACTURED PHRASES

Game. Selected studio-audience members compete. Slogans or song or book titles phonetically written are flashed on a screeen. The player first to identify himself through a buzzer signal receives a chance to answer. If correct, one point is awarded. Winners, the highest point scorers, receive merchandise prizes.

Host: Art James.

FRACTURED PHRASES—30 minutes—NBC—September 27, 1965 - December 31, 1965.

THE FRANCES LANGFORD-DON AMECHE SHOW

Variety. Songs, dances, musical numbers, guests, and interviews.

Host: Don Ameche.

Hostess: Frances Langford.

Orchestra: Tony Romano.

Producer: Ward Byron.

Director: Robert Massell.

Sketch: "The Couple Next Door" (Jack Lemmon, Cynthia Stone). A domestic comedy depicting the struggles that make up a marriage.

Features: Excerpts from Miss Langford's diary, *Purple Heart;* and a studio audience participation segment wherein selected members compete in a current-events question-answer session.

THE FRANCES LANGFORD-DON AMECHE SHOW—60 minutes—ABC—1951-1952.

FRANKENSTEIN JR. AND THE IMPOSSIBLES

Animated Cartoon. The exploits of Frankenstein Jr., a thirty-foot mechanical robot, and The Impossibles, Coil Man, Fluid Man, and Multi Man, United States government agents who pose as a Rock and Roll group. Stories depict their battle against the sinister forces of evil. A Hanna-Barbera production.

Characters' Voices

Frankenstein Jr.	Ted Cassidy
Buzz	Dick Beals
Father	John Stephenson
Multi Man	Don Messick
Fluid Man	Paul Frees
Coil Man	Hal Smith

Music: Hoyt Curtin.

Musical Director: Ted Nichols.

Producer-Director: William Hanna, Joseph Barbera.

FRANKENSTEIN JR. AND THE IMPOSSIBLES—30 minutes—CBS—September 10, 1966 - September 7, 1968.

THE FRANKIE CARLE SHOW

Musical Variety.

Host: Frankie Carle, pianist.

Musical Backing: Perry Botkin; The Carle Combo.

THE FRANKIE CARLE SHOW—15 minutes—NBC—August 7, 1956 - October 29, 1956.

FRANKIE LAINE

Listed: The television programs of singer Frankie Laine.

The Frankie Laine Show—Musical Variety—15 minutes—CBS—July 20, 1955 - September 7, 1955.

Host: Frankie Laine.

Regulars: Connie Harris, Jud Conlon, Jack Toegander, Mitchell Choirloy, The James Starbuch Dancers, The Rhythmaires.

Announcer: Tony Marvin.

Orchestra: Hank Sylvern; Jimmy Carroll.

Premiere Guests: Connie, Russell, Shirley MacLaine, Dick Van Dyke, Duke Ellington.

Frankie Laine Time—Musical Variety—30 minutes—CBS—July 1955 - September 1955; August 1956 - September 1956.

Host: Frankie Laine.

Featured: The Lyn Duddy Chorus.

Announcer: Tony Marvin.

Orchestra: Jimmy Carroll.

FRANK SINATRA

Listed: The television programs of singer-actor Frank Sinatra.

The Frank Sinatra Show—Musical Variety—30 minutes—CBS—October 7, 1950 - April 1, 1952.

Host: Frank Sinatra.

Regulars: Erin O'Brien, Ben Blue, The Blue Family, Sid Fields, The Whipoorwills.

Orchestra: Axel Stordahl.

The Frank Sinatra Show—Variety—30 minutes—ABC—October 18, 1957 - June 27, 1958. A series capitalizing on all of his talents, from acting to singing.

Host (and occasional performer in anthology productions): Frank Sinatra.

Orchestra: Nelson Riddle.

Included:

Face of Fear. A governess attempts to discover the reason for a young child's state of shock.

CAST

Christie Nolan: Glynis Johns; Paul Dupree: Michael Pate; Claude: Eugene Martin.

That Hogan Man. A cab driver struggles to raise his children after the death of his wife.

CAST

Hogan: Frank Sinatra; Marty Potter: Jesse White; Michele: Reba Waters; Gaby: Johnny Crawford; Miss Douglas: Susan Cummings.

Brownstone Incident. A wife attempts to convince her city-born husband to move to the suburbs.

CAST

Al Wesson: Frank Sinatra; Helen Wesson: Cloris Leachman.

A Gun In His Back. Dissatisfied with a police investigation, a cabbie attempts to locate his own stolen car.

CAST

Sam Hatter: Frank Sinatra; Grace Hatter: Patricia Crowley.

THE FREDDY MARTIN SHOW

Musical Variety.

Host: Freddy Martin.

Regulars: Merv Griffin, Murray Arnold, Judy Lynn.

Orchestra: Freddy Martin.

Producer: Perry Lafferty.

Sponsor: Hazel Bishop Cosmetics.

THE FREDDY MARTIN SHOW—30 minutes—NBC—July 12, 1951 - September 1951.

FRED FLINTSTONE AND FRIENDS

Animated Cartoon. The series features excerpts from the Hanna-Barbera cartoon series originally broadcast on the networks on Saturday mornings: "The Flintstones Show," "The Flintstones Hour," "Goober and the Ghost Chasers," "Jeannie," "Partridge Family: 2200 A.D.," "Pebbles and Bamm Bamm," and "Yogi's Gang." See individual titles for information.

Program Host: Fred Flintstone (voiced by Alan Reed).

Executive Producer: William Hanna, Joseph Barbera.

Producer: Iwao Takamoto.

Director: Charles A. Nichols.

FRED FLINTSTONE AND FRIENDS—30 minutes—Syndicated 1977.

FRED WARING

Listed: The television programs of bandleader Fred Waring.

The Fred Waring Show—Musical Variety—60 minutes—CBS—April 17, 1947 - May 30, 1954.

Host: Fred Waring.

Regulars: Jane Wilson, Stuart Churchill, Joe Marine, Joanne Wheatley, Daisey Bernier, Gordon Goodman, Keith and Sylvia Textor, Virginia and Livingston Gearhart, Bob Sands, Nadine Gae, Frances Wyatt, Suzanne Lovell, Hugh Brannum, Leonard Kranendonk, Joan Woodward, The Waring Glee Club, The Marc Breaux Dancers.

Announcer: Red Barber.

Orchestra: The Pennsylvanians, conducted by Waring.

The Fred Waring Show—Musical Variety—30 minutes—CBS—July 22, 1957 - September 6, 1957.

Host: Fred Waring.

Orchestra: The Pennsylvanians.

FREEDOM RINGS

Game. Selected female studio-audience members have to solve various homemaker problems that are enacted and complicated by a cast of regulars. Contestants, judged by the studio audience, receive prizes according to their satisfaction (applause). The title, "Freedom Rings," stresses the sponsor's theme of freedom from the drudgery of housework.

Host: John Beal.

Cast: Alice Ghostley, Ted Telles, Chuck Taylor, Malcolm Broderick, Jay Hitton.

Announcer: Vince Williams.

Orchestra: Ben Ludlow.

FREEDOM RINGS—30 minutes—CBS 1953.

THE FRENCH CHEF

Cooking. The preparation of gourmet meals.

Hostess: Julia Child.

Music: John Morris.

Producer: Ruth Lockwood.

Director: Russell Fortier, David Atwood.

THE FRENCH CHEF—30 minutes. NET—1963-1970; PBS—1970-1974.

THE FRIDAY COMEDY SPECIAL

Pilot Films. Proposed comedy series for the 1975-1976 season.

Included:

Love Nest. The story of two widowed senior citizens who live together in a Florida trailer court.

CAST

Ned: Charles Lane; Jenny: Florida Friebus; Dorothy: Dee Carroll; Dickie: Burt Mustin.

Wives. The story centers on the daily activities of five married women.

CAST

Connie: Penny Marshall; Mary: Candy Azzara; Doris: Phyllis Elizabeth Davis; Lillian: Jacque Lynn Colton; Miss Chin: Barbara Luna.

The Boys. The would-be series deals with the misadventures that befall two comedy writers who reassess their values after the death of an old friend.

CAST

Ed: Tim Conway; Herb: Herb Edelman; Cassie: Esther Sutherland; Vicki: Phyllis Elizabeth Davis.

THE FRIDAY COMEDY SPECIAL—30 minutes—CBS—March 14, 1975 - May 23, 1975.

FRIENDS AND LOVERS

Comedy. Background: Boston, Mass. The life, fantasies, and romantic misadventures of a young bachelor, Robert Dreyfuss, a bass violist with the Boston Symphony Orchestra.

CAST
Robert Dreyfuss	Paul Sand
Charlie Dreyfuss, his brother	Michael Pataki
Janis Dreyfuss, Charlie's wife	Penny Marshall
Fred Myerback, Robert's friend	Steve Landesberg
Jack Reardon, the orchestra manager	Dick Wesson
Mason Woodruff, the orchestra conductor	Craig Richard
Ben Dreyfuss, Robert's father	Jack Gilford
Marge Dreyfuss, Robert's mother	Jan Miner
Mrs. Cooper, the babysitter	Merie Earle

Music: Pat Williams.

FRIENDS AND LOVERS—30 minutes—CBS—September 14, 1974 - January 4, 1975. Original title: "Paul Sand in Friends and Lovers."

FROM A BIRD'S EYE VIEW

Comedy. Background: London, England. The misadventures of two International Airline stewardesses: Millie Grover, British, meddlesome, and scatterbrained; and Maggie Ralston, her partner, a level-headed American on loan from the U.S. to International's European division. Stories relate Millie's continual interference in people's affairs and her and Maggie's efforts to resolve the chaos before customer complaints reach the office of Clyde Beauchamp, the personnel director.

CAST
Millie Grover	Millicent Martin
Maggie Ralston	Pat Finley
Clyde Beachamp	Peter Jones
Bert Grover, Millie's uncle	Robert Cawdron
Miss Fosdyke, Beachamp's secretary	Noel Hood

Music: Frank Barber.

FROM A BIRD'S EYE VIEW—30 minutes—NBC—March 29, 1971 - August 16, 1971. 18 episodes.

FROM THESE ROOTS

Serial. Background: The town of Strathfield. The life and struggles of the Frasers: Ben, a widower, the sixty-five-year-old editor-owner of the *Strathfield Record;* Liz, his youngest daughter, a writer living in Washington, D.C., and engaged to journalist Bruce Crawford; Emily, his eldest daughter, happily married to her high-school sweetheart, Jim Benson, a mill foreman; and Ben Fraser, Jr., his son, who married the wealthy Rose Corelli and decided not to follow in his father's footsteps.

CAST
Ben Fraser Sr.	Joseph Macauley
Liz Fraser	Ann Flood
	Susan Brown
Bruce Crawford	David Sanders
Jim Benson	Henderson Forsythe
Ben Fraser, Jr.	Frank Marth
Dr. Buck Weaver	Tom Shirley
Podge	Freeman Hammond
Maggie Barker	Billie Lou Watt
Lyddy Benson	Sarah Hardy
Emily Fraser	Helen Shields
Rose Fraser	Julie Bovasso
David Allen	Bob Mandan
Laura Tompkins	Audra Lindley
Lynn	Barbara Berjer
Gloria	Millette Alexander
Tom Jennings	Craig Huebing

Also: John Calenbeck, Mae Munroe, Grant Code, Vera Allen, John Stewart, Herb Shields, Sarah Burton, Mary Alice Moore, Charles Egelston, Dan White, Gary Morgan, Sam Gray.

FROM THESE ROOTS—30 minutes—NBC—June 30, 1958 - December 29, 1961.

FRONTIER

Anthology. Western dramatizations based on actual newspaper files.

Host: Walter Coy.

Included:

Tomas And The Widow. The story of a widow who plans revenge against the man who killed her husband.

CAST
Tomas: Mike Connors; Shona: Laura Elliot; Gavin: Sean McClory.

Shame Of A Nation. Background: Denver, 1864. The court-martial trial of J. M. Chivington, a U.S. Cavalry colonel accused of the needless slaying of Indians.

CAST
Scott Forbes, George Keyman, Hayden Rorke, Barry Atwater.

In Nebraska. The beginning of settlement in what is now the city of Omaha.

CAST
Sallie Brophy, Jeff Morrow, Ken Tobey.

FRONTIER—30 minutes—NBC—September 25, 1955 - September 9, 1956.

FRONTIER CIRCUS

Drama. Background: The Frontier during the 1880s. The saga of the traveling one-ring T and T (Thompson and Travis) Combined Circus. Stories relate the struggles involved and the dangers braved in presenting a frontier circus.

CAST
Colonel Casey Thompson, the owner	Chill Wills
Ben Travis, his partner	John Derek
Tony Gentry, the trail scout	Richard Jaeckel

Music: Jeff Alexander

FRONTIER CIRCUS—60 minutes—CBS—October 5, 1961 - September 1962. Syndicated.

FRONTIER DOCTOR

Western. Background: Rising Springs, Arizona during the early 1900s. The role of a doctor during the early settlement days of the twentieth century is dramatized. Stories relate the experiences of Dr. Bill Baxter as he struggles to enforce neglected medical laws and assist pioneers.

Starring: Rex Allen as Dr. Bill Baxter.

FRONTIER DOCTOR—30 minutes—Syndicated 1958. 39 episodes. Also known as: "Man of the West" and "Unarmed."

FRONTIER JUDGE

Western. The exploits of John Cooper, a circuit-riding judge, as he attempts to bring law and order to the Frontier.

Starring: Leon Ames as Judge John Cooper.

FRONTIER JUDGE—30 minutes—Syndicated 1956.

FRONTIER JUSTICE

Anthology. Rebroadcasts of western dramas that were originally aired via "Dick Powell's Zane Grey Theatre."

Hosts: Lew Ayres; Melvyn Douglas.

Music: Herschel Burke Gilbert; Joseph Mullendore.

Included:

Legacy Of A Legend. The story of a drifter who claims to be a famous lawman.

CAST
Lee J. Cobb, John Dehner.

Black Creek Encounter. The story of a man who must face the challenge from a gunfighter or ignore it and shame himself in the eyes of his son.

CAST
Jim Morrison: Ernest Borgnine; Kelly: Norma Crane; Davey Harper: Jan Merlin; Billy Morrison: Billy Chapin.

Fearful Courage. The story of a woman who attempts to return to her husband—a gunfighter.

CAST
Ida Lupino, James Whitmore.

FRONTIER JUSTICE—30 minutes—CBS—June 1958 - September 1958; June 1959 - September 1959. 26 episodes.

FRONT PAGE DETECTIVE

Crime Drama. Background: New York City. The investigations of David Chase, a newspaper columnist and amateur sleuth—a man possessing an eye for beauty, a nose for news, and a sixth sense for danger.

CAST
David Chase — Edmund Lowe
The homicide detective — Frank Jenks
Also — Paula Drew
Producer: Riley Jackson, Jerry Fairbanks.
Director: Arnold Webster.

Program Open:

Announcer: "Presenting an unusual story of love and mystery on 'Front Page Detective' starring Mr. Edmund Lowe as the famed newspaper columnist and amateur detective, David Chase. And now for another thrilling adventure as we accompany David Chase and watch him match wits with those who would take the law into their own hands."

Program Close:

Announcer: "For another exciting mystery read *Front Page Detective* magazine. And tune in next week, same time, same station, for another thrilling episode of 'Front Page Detective' on television. You're invited to be with David Chase as he again unravels a case of mystery and intrigue on 'Front Page Detective.' "

FRONT PAGE DETECTIVE—30 minutes—ABC—1951-1953; DuMont 1953.

FRONT PAGE STORY

Anthology. Dramatizations depicting the 1950s front-page stories.
Host-Narrator: Paul Stewart.

Included:

The Cave. The story of Robert J. Billeter of the *Preston* (W. Va.) *Times* as he attempts to rescue two boys who are trapped in a cave.

CAST
Robert Billeter: Carlton Colyer.

Birthday Present. A father and son playing catch in the yard follow the ball under the porch and discover a woman's body. The story relates the police investigation into her mysterious death.

CAST
Wayne: David Brenner; Charles Linden: John McGovern.

Hit And Run. A driver flees from the scene of a fatal accident. Reporter Nye Beaman of the *Waterburn* (Conn.) *American* attempts to track down the driver.

CAST
Nye Beaman: Allen Nourse.

FRONT PAGE STORY—30 minutes—Syndicated 1959.

FRONT ROW CENTER

Musical Revue.
Starring: Hal Loman, Monica Moore, Phil Leeds, Joan Fields, Marian Bruce, Cass Franklin.
Host: Frank Fontaine.
Producer-Director: Fletcher Markle.

Director: Milton Douglas.

FRONT ROW CENTER—60 minutes—DuMont 1950.

FRONT ROW CENTER

Anthology. Adaptations of works by noted authors.
Host: Fletcher Markle.

Included:

Dark Victory. The story of Judith Traherne, a flighty woman who becomes a woman of courage when she discovers that she faces blindness and almost certain death.

CAST
Judith Traherne: Margaret Field; Dr. Steele: Kent Smith; Aldin Blaine: Kay Stewart.

Outward Bound. The story of several people who find themselves aboard a strange ship that is leaving the land of the living.

CAST
Tom Prior: Wilfred Knapp; Rev. Thompson: Alan Napier; Mrs. Cliveden-Banks: Isobel Elsom.

Tender Is The Night. The story of Dr. Dick Diver, a psychoanalyst who violates professional ethics by marrying his lovely and wealthy patient.

CAST
Dr. Diver: James Daly; Michele Warren: Mercedes McCambridge; Rosemary: Olive Sturgiss.

FRONT ROW CENTER—30 minutes—CBS—July 1, 1955 - September 21, 1955.

F TROOP

Comedy. In an unidentified Union camp during the closing months of the Civil War, Wilton Parmenter of the Quarter Masters Corps, a private in charge of officers' laundry, encounters an excess of pollin, sneezes, and blurts out what sounds like "CHARGE!" Troopers, on stand-by, are prompted into action—an action that foils Confederate objects and fosters a complete Union victory. Promoted to captain and awarded the Medal of Honor, Wilton Parmenter is assigned to command F Troop at Fort Courage.

Kansas, 1866. Arriving and assuming command, Captain Wilton Parmenter meets those he will become closely associated with: Sergeant

Morgan O'Rourke, the head of the illegal O'Rourke Enterprises—a business dealing in Indian souvenirs made by the friendly Hekawi (prounced: Ha-cow-we) Indians and the town saloon; Corporal Randolph Agarn, his vice president; Private Hannibal Shirley Dobbs, the inept company bugler; Trooper Duffy, survivor of the Alamo; and Trooper Vanderbuilt, the almost blind look-out.

Dismissing the troops, he meets and befirends the beautiful, marriage-minded Jane Angelica Thrift (Wrangler Jane), the proprietress of the fort general store and U.S. Post Office.

Stories relate the misadventures of Captain Wilton Parmenter, "The Scourge of the West," as he struggles to maintain the peace, adjust to frontier life, and escape the matrimonial plans of his girlfriend. Complicating matters are Sgt. O'Rourke and Cpl. Agarn, who constantly devise schemes to conceal and expand their illegal enterprises.

CAST

Sgt. Morgan O'Rourke	Forrest Tucker
Cpl. Randolph Agarn	Larry Storch
Capt. Wilton Parmenter	Ken Berry
Wrangler Jane	Melody Patterson
Wild Eagle, the Hekawi Chief	Frank DeKova
Pvt. Hannibal Dobbs	James Hampton
Private Duffy	Bob Steele
Crazy Cat, the Chief's aide	Don Diamond
Private Vanderbuilt	Joe Brooks
Private Hoffenmeuller, the German recruit, the man unable to speak English	John Mitchum
Papa Bear, an Hekawi Indian	Ben Frommer
Private Dudleson	Irving Bell
Roaring Chicken, the Hekawi Medicine Man	Edward Everett Horton
Major Duncan	James Gregory
Pete, the bartender	Benny Baker

Other Troopers (screen credit is not given): McIntosh, Ashby, Hightower, Swenson, Hogan, Stanley, Livingston, Holmes, Watson, Franklin, Gilbert, Sullivan, Lewis, Clark.

Music: William Lava; Richard LaSalle.

Executive Producer: William T. Orr, Hy Averback.

Producer: Norm Saunders.

Director: David Alexander, Leslie Goodwins, Gene Reynolds, Charles R. Rondeau, Gene Nelson, Hal March.

Jane's Horse: Pecos.

F TROOP—30 minutes—ABC—September 14, 1965 - September 7, 1967. Syndicated. 65 episodes.

THE FUGITIVE

Drama. Indiana, the home of Dr. Richard Kimble. Preparing for dinner, Richard and his wife, Helen, begin to discuss the prospect of adopting children. Unable to have her own children, Helen refuses to adopt any, feeling it would be living with a lie. Failing in an attempt to convince her otherwise, Richard leaves and drives to a nearby lake. Reviewing his actions and believing them a mistake, he returns to apologize.

Entering the driveway, the car headlights catch the figure of a one-armed man running from the house. Rushing inside, Kimble finds Helen, dead, the victim of a burgular whom she caught in the act. Unable to prove his innocence, he is arrested and later charged with murder.

Numerous attempts by police to find the mysterious one-armed man fail. A courtroom trial ends, and based on circumstantial evidence, Richard Kimble is sentenced to death.

Enroute to the state penitentiary, the train derails and Kimble escapes the bounds of Indiana Police Lieutenant Philip Gerard. Though free, he is relentlessly pursued by Gerard, the man who is determined to apprehend his escaped prisoner. Assuming numerous identities, Kimble involves himself in the lives of troubled people and assists where possible, hoping that one will lead him to the one-armed man and freedom.

After four years, Johnson, the one-armed man is apprehended. Certain the news will bring Kimble, Gerard releases the story to the press. As Gerard had anticipated, Kimble surrenders. However, as Kimble is being taken into custody, Johnson escapes. Pleading with his cold-hearted pursuer, Kimble is released and granted the opportunity to find Johnson. Investigating, Kimble tracks Johnson to a closed amusement park. Fighting on the ledge of a water tower, Johnson, who has Kimble pinned to the floor, admits killing Helen. In an extremely tense and dramatic moment, Gerard, who had been following Kimble, enters the park. Faced with a dilemma, whether to believe Kimble's story or not, Gerard decides in favor of Kimble. A bullet, fired from his rifle, strikes Johnson, whose final words clear Richard Kimble of all suspicions.

CAST

Richard Kimble	David Janssen
Lt. Philip Gerard	Barry Morse
Fred Johnson, the one-armed man	Bill Raisch
Helen Kimble (flashbacks)	Diane Brewster
Donna Kimble, Richard's sister	Jacqueline Scott

Narrator: William Conrad.

Music: Pete Rugolo.

Executive Producer: Quinn Martin.

Producer: Wilton Schiller.

Director: Don Medford, Gerald Mayer, Leo Penn, Robert Douglas, James Nielson, Barry Morse, John Meredyth Lucas, James Sheldon, Lewis Allen, Jesse Hibbs, Lawrence Dobkin.

Creator: Roy Huggins.

THE FUGITIVE—60 minutes—ABC—

The Fugitive. David Janssen.

F Troop. Left to right: Larry Storch, Forrest Tucker, Ken Berry, and Melody Patterson.

September 17, 1963 - August 29, 1967. Syndicated. 120 episodes.

FULL CIRCLE

Serial. The story of Gary Donovan, a footloose wanderer who remains in one place only long enough to earn the resources he needs to continue his travels. The only story line presented: Background: Maryland. Donovan's involvement with Lisa Crowder and the mystery surrounding the death of her first husband.

CAST

Gary Donovan	Robert Fortier
Lisa Crowder	Dyan Cannon
Dr. Kit Aldrich	Jean Byron
Beth Perce	Amzie Strickland
David Talton	Bill Lundmark
Virgil Denker	Michael Ross
Roy Pollard	Andrew Colman
The Deputy	Sam Edwards

Also: John McNamara.

FULL CIRCLE—30 minutes—CBS—June 27, 1960 - March 1, 1961.

FUN AND FORTUNE

Game. The contestant must identify, within four clues, a piece of merchandise hidden on stage behind the "Magic Curtain." Cash prizes are awarded based on the number of clues used: beginning with fifty dollars and diminishing with each successive clue.

Host: Jack Lescoulie.

Producer: James Saphier.

Sponsor: Kleenex.

FUN AND FORTUNE—30 minutes—ABC 1949.

THE FUN FACTORY

Variety. The series combines music, comedy, songs, and various game contests wherein studio audience members vie for cash and merchandise prizes.

Host: Bobby Van.

Regulars: Betty Thomas (as the housewife), Jane Nelson, Doug Steckler, Dick Blasucci, Deborah Harmon.

Model: Jane Nelson.

Announcer: Jim Thompson.

Orchestra: Stan Worth.

Executive Producer: Ed Fishman, Randall Freer.

Producer: David Fishman.

Director: Walter C. Miller, Tom

Trbouichi.

THE FUN FACTORY—30 minutes—NBC—June 14, 1976 - October 1, 1976.

FUN FOR MONEY

Alternate title for "Fun and Fortune," which see for information.

THE FUNKY PHANTOM

Animated Cartoon. East Muddlemore, New England, 1776, the era of the Revolutionary War. Pursued by Red Coats, Jonathan Muddlemore runs into a deserted mansion and hides in a large grandfather clock. The door locks and traps him.

Almost two hundred years later (1971), three teenagers, April, Skip, and Augie, caught in a thunderstorm, seek shelter in the deserted mansion. Seeing the clock and resetting it to its correct time, Muddlemore, the Spirit of '76, emerges. Teaming, the four travel about the country and crusade against the forces of evil.

Characters' Voices

Jonathan Muddlemore ("Musty")	Daws Butler
April Stewart	Tina Holland
Skip	Mickey Dolenz
Augie	Tommy Cook

Additional voices: Jerry Dexter, Julie Bennett.

The gang dog: Elmo.

Musty's cat: Boo.

Music: John Sangster.

THE FUNKY PHANTOM—30 minutes—ABC—September 11, 1971 - September 1, 1972.

FUNNY BONERS

Game. Children compete. The host states a question. The player first to identify himself through a buzzer signal receives a chance to answer. If the response is correct, he is awarded points; if incorrect, he pays the penalty by performing a stunt. Winners, the highest point scorers, receive merchandise prizes.

Host: Jimmy Weldon, ventriloquist.

His Dummy: Webster Webfoot the duck.

FUNNY BONERS—30 minutes—NBC November 20, 1954 - July 9, 1955.

THE FUNNY BUNNY

Children's Variety. Game contests and cartoons.

Host: Dick Noel.

Assistant: Dick West (costumed as The Funny Bunny).

THE FUNNY BUNNY—30 minutes—DuMont 1954.

FUNNY FACE

Comedy. Background: Los Angeles, California. The misadventures of Sandy Stockton, a student teacher enrolled at U.C.L.A. and a part-time actress employed by the Prescott Advertising Agency. Stories relate her attempts to divide her time between school and work.

CAST

Sandy Stockton	Sandy Duncan
Alice MacRaven, her friend	Valorie Armstrong
Pat Harwell, the landlord	Henry Beckman
Kate Harwell, his wife	Kathleen Freeman
Maggie Prescott, the advertising agency head	Nita Talbot

Music: Pat Williams.

FUNNY FACE—30 minutes—CBS—September 18, 1971 - December 11, 1971. 13 episodes.

THE FUNNY MANNS

Comedy. Reedited theatrical comedy shorts. Eight-minute segments are integrated with the antics of the Funny Manns and his relatives: Milk Mann, Mail Mann, Fire Mann, Police Mann, Rich Mann, etc.

Starring: Cliff Norton as The Funny Manns.

Featuring: Ben Turpin, the Keystone Kops, Harry Langdon.

THE FUNNY MANNS—30 minutes—Syndicated 1961. 130 episodes.

THE FUNNY SIDE

Satire. The funny side of everyday life as seen through the eyes of five couples—from money, to sex, to self improvement.

Host: Gene Kelly.

Couples:

The Blue Collar Couple: Warren Berlinger, Pat Finley.

The Sophisticated Couple: Jenna McMahon, Dick Clair.

The Young Couple: Michael Lembeck, Cindy Williams.

The Middle Class Black Couple: Teresa Graves, John Amos.

The Senior Citizen Couple: Burt Mustin, Queenie Smith.

THE FUNNY SIDE—60 minutes—NBC—September 14, 1971 - December 28, 1971. 13 tapes.

FUNNY YOU SHOULD ASK

Game. Before air time, five celebrity guests are asked specific questions. On stage, the host presents the same questions to three competing contestants and states their answers in ·mixed order. Object: For each player to pair the celebrity with what he or she said. Each correct match awards one point. Winners, the highest point scorers, receive merchandise prizes.

Host: Lloyd Thaxton.

Music: Score Productions.

FUNNY YOU SHOULD ASK—30 minutes—ABC—October 28, 1968 - September 5, 1969.

THE FURTHER ADVENTURES OF ELLERY QUEEN

See title: "Ellery Queen."

FURY

Adventure. Background: Capitol City. Engaging in a game of baseball, a group of boys accidentally break a window. Fearing punishment, they place the blame on Joey, an innocent youngster who is suspected of being a troublemaker. Witnessing the act, rancher Jim Newton clears the boy's name. Learning that Joey is an orphan, Jim takes him home to the Broken Wheel Ranch and begins adoption procedures.

In an effort to acquire the boy's affections, Jim presents him with Fury, a recently captured black stallion. Given a sense of responsibility, Joey finds home and love.

Stories concern an orphan boy's growth into manhood.

CAST

Jim Newton	Peter Graves
Joey Newton	Bobby Diamond

Pete, Jim's top hand	William Fawcett
Helen Watkins, the school teacher	Ann Robinson
Pee Wee, Joey's friend	Jimmy Baird
Packey Lambert, Joey's friend	Roger Mobley
Harriet Newton, Jim's sister	Nan Leslie
The sheriff	James Seay
The deputy sheriff	Guy Teague
Fury	Gypsy

Producer: Leon Fromkess, Irving Cummings.

Packy's Horse: Lucky.

Pee Wee Jenkins's Horse: Pokey.

FURY—30 minutes—NBC—October 15, 1955 - September 3, 1966. Syndicated. 114 episodes. Also known as "Brave Stallion."

FUTURE COP

Crime Drama. Background: Los Angeles, California. The cases of Joe Cleaver, Bill Bundy, and John "Kid" Haven, law enforcement officers with the L.A.P.D. Unknown to Bundy, Haven is an android rookie programmed to be the perfect cop, and has been secretly assigned to Cleaver for training in the field.

CAST

Officer Joe Cleaver	Ernest Borgnine
Officer Bill Bundy	John Amos
Officer John Haven	Michael Shannon
Captain Skaggs	Herbert Nelson
Dr. Tingley, Haven's creator	Irene Tsu
Peggy, the waitress at Hennessy's, the café frequented by the officers	Angela May

Music: J.J. Johnson.

Executive Producer: Anthony Wilson, Gary Damsker.

Producer: Everett Chambers.

Director: Robert Douglas, Earl Bellamy, Vincent McEveety.

FUTURE COP—60 minutes—ABC—March 5, 1977 - April 22, 1977. Returned with a final episode on August 6, 1977.

𝓰

THE GABBY HAYES SHOW

Children. Background: The Double Bar M Ranch. Tales of the American West.

Host-Story Teller: Gabby Hayes.

Regulars: Clifford Sales, Lee Graham, Robert Simon, Michael Strong, Irving Winter, Malcolm Keer.

Producer: Joe Clair, Roger Muir, Martin Stone.

Sponsor: Quaker Oats.

THE GABBY HAYES SHOW—30 minutes —ABC—May 12, 1956 - July 14, 1956. An earlier version of the series was first seen on NBC in 1950.

THE GALE STORM SHOW

Comedy. The misadventures of Susanna Pomeroy, the trouble-prone social director of the luxury liner, S.S. *Ocean Queen.*

CAST

Susanna Pomeroy	Gale Storm
Miss Nugent (Nugey), her friend, the beauty-salon operator	ZaSu Pitts
Captain Huxley, the ship's commander	Roy Roberts
Cedric, the cook-waiter	James Fairfax
Dr. Reynolds, the ship's physician	Rolfe Sedan

Music: Alan Bergman

THE GALE STORM SHOW—30 minutes—CBS—August 30, 1956 - April 11, 1959. ABC—30 minutes—April 13, 1959 - April 1962. Syndicated. Original title: "Oh! Susanna."

The Gale Storm Show. Gale Storm.

THE GALLANT MEN

Drama. Background: Salerno, Italy during the Italian Campaign of World

War II (1943). The story of Conley Wright, a foreign correspondent assigned to the 36th Infantry of the American fifth army. Scared and unsure of himself, he accompanies the squad on suicide missions and reports the experiences of men desperately struggling to end the war and return home.

CAST

Captain James Benedict	William Reynolds
Conley Wright	Robert McQueeny

THE SQUAD:

Gibson, the radio operator	Roger Davis
D'Angelo	Eddie Fontaine
McKenna	Richard X. Slattery
Hanson	Robert Cothie
Lucavich	Roland La Starza
Kimbro	Robert Ridgley

THE GALLANT MEN–60 minutes–ABC–September 1962 - September 14, 1963. Syndicated. 26 episodes.

THE GALLERY OF MADAME LIU TSONG

Drama. Distinguished by two formats.

Format One:

The Gallery Of Mme. Liu Tsong–30 minutes–DuMont 1951 - 1952.

The experiences of Madame Liu Tsong, the beautiful Chinese proprietress of an art gallery, as she ventures forth in search of treasured art objects.

Starring: Anna May Wong as Madame Liu Tsong.

Format Two:

Madame Liu Tsong–30 minutes–DuMont 1952.

The story of Madame Liu Tsong, a Chinese exporter, "a good girl against bad men. . . .A combination of the daughter of Fu Manchu, the daughter of Shanghai, and the daughter of the Dragon."

Starring: Anna May Wong as Madame Liu Tsong.

THE GALLOPING GOURMET

Cooking. The preparation and making of gourmet meals. Spiced with light humor.

Host: Graham Kerr, international culinary expert.

Assistants: Patricia Burgess, Wilemina Meerakker.

Music: Champ Champagne.

Producer: Treena Kerr.

Director: Marion Dunn.

Note: In 1975 a five-minute version of "The Galloping Gourmet" was syndicated under the title "Take Kerr."

THE GALLOPING GOURMET–30 minutes–Syndicated 1969. Produced in Canada.

GAMBIT

Game. Two married couples compete. Basis: Blackjack (twenty-one). The dealer, standing between the four seated players, opens a sealed deck of fifty-two oversized cards. The first card is revealed. The host then asks a general-knowledge question. The team first to sound a buzzer signal receives a chance to answer. If correct, they choose to keep or pass the exposed card to their opponents. Questions continue with each team seeking to score as close as possible to twenty-one without going over. Winning couples receive one hundred dollars per game and compete until defeated.

Existing rules: No ties. Should one team "freeze" their score, for example at twenty, the other team must beat it to win. An exact twenty-one in any combination of cards earns five hundred dollars.

Card values: Ace, one or ten points, depending on the situation; picture cards, ten points; other cards, face values.

Host: Wink Martindale.

Dealer: Elaine Stewart.

Announcer: Kenny Williams.

Music: Mort Garson.

GAMBIT–30 minutes–CBS–September 4, 1972 - December 10, 1976.

GAMBLE ON LOVE

Game. Three married couples compete. Each is interviewed and quizzed via "The Wheel of Fortune." One member of one team spins the wheel and the mate answers its specific category questions. The winning team, the couple correctly answering the most questions, receive a chance to win a mink stole via "The Cupid Question."

Hostess: Denise Darcell.

GAMBLE ON LOVE–30 minutes–DuMont–July 9, 1954 - September 1954.

THE GAME GAME

Game. Three guest celebrities who comprise the panel; and one non-celebrity contestant. Basis: A psychological examination that is conducted through one question (e.g., "Should you be single?") that contains five parts. Before the game begins the contestant predicts whether he will score higher or lower than the panel. The host states question one and reveals four possible answers. Players answer in turn. The host then reveals the answers, which are validated by the Southern Institute of Psychology. Each answer is designated by points–From five to twenty. Points are scored to each player according to his choice. The remaining four questions are played in the same manner. The contestant receives money according to his prediction–twenty-five dollars for each celebrity he beats; one hundred dollars if he beats all three.

Host: Jim McKrell.

Announcer: Johnny Jacobs.

Music: Frank Jaffe.

THE GAME GAME–30 minutes–Syndicated 1969. 190 tapes.

GANGBUSTERS

Anthology. True crime exposés. Based on the files of local, state and federal law enforcement agencies. Adapted from the radio program of the same title.

Hosts-Narrators: Guest police chiefs.

Creator-Writer: Phillips H. Lord.

Producer: Phillips H. Lord.

Sponsor: Chesterfield Cigarettes.

Included:

Tri State Gang. Police efforts to end a hijacking ring that is operating on Maryland highways.

Starring: Tim Garez, Michael Grainger.

Chinatown. A depiction of how the murders of two Chinese are solved from an insignificant strand of hair.

Starring: Harold Craig.

Gnatz-Franx. The story of a criminal who used hypnosis to commit robberies.

Starring: Lou Polan, Thomas Nello.

GANGBUSTERS—30 minutes—NBC —1951-1953. Syndicated title: "Captured."

THE GARLUND TOUCH

See title: "Mister Garlund."

GARRISON'S GORILLAS

Adventure. Background: Europe, World War II. A group of convicts from various federal penitentiaries is assembled in France under the command of Lt. Craig Garrison, U.S. Army: Casino, master thief; Goniff, expert pickpocket; Actor, master con-artist; and Chief, professional switchblade artist. Their assignment: to harass the Germans. Their reward: full pardons.

CAST	
Craig Garrison	Ron Harper
Casino	Rudy Solari
Actor	Cesare Danova
Goniff	Christopher Cary
Chief	Brendon Boone

Music: Leonard Rosenman.

GARRISON'S GORILLAS—60 minutes—ABC—September 5, 1967 - September 10, 1968. Syndicated. 26 episodes.

GARROWAY AT LARGE

See title: "Dave Garroway."

GARRY MOORE

Listed: The television programs of comedian Garry Moore.

The Garry Moore Show—Variety—30, 45, and 60 minute versions—CBS—October 16, 1950 - June 27, 1958.

Host: Garry Moore.

Regulars: Ken Carson, Denise Lor, Durwood Kirby, Hattie Colbert.

Announcer: Durwood Kirby.

Music: Hank Jones; The Howard Smith Quartet.

I've Got A Secret—Game—CBS—1952-1964 Garry's run as Host. (See title.)

The Garry Moore Show—Variety—60 minutes—CBS—September 30, 1958 - June 16, 1964.

Host: Garry Moore.

Regulars: Durwood Kirby, Ron Martin, Carol Burnett, Denise Lor, Dorothy Loudon, Ken Carson.

Announcer: Durwood Kirby.

Orchestra: Irwin Kostal; Howard Smith.

The Garry Moore Show—Variety—60 minutes—CBS—September 11, 1966 - January 29, 1967.

Host: Garry Moore.

Regulars: Durwood Kirby, Jackie Vernon, Carol Corbett, Pete Barbutti, John Byner, Ron Carey, Eddie Lawrence, Dick Davey, Patsey Elliott, The Bob Hamilton Dancers.

Announcer: Durwood Kirby.

Orchestra: Bernie Green.

To Tell The Truth—Game—30 minutes—Syndicated 1970. (See title.)

THE GAS HOUSE GANG

See title: "East Side Comedy."

THE GAY COED

Variety. Era: The 1920s. A musical comedy depicting the life of a college coed during America's most reckless, carefree era.

CAST	
The Coed	Sandra Barkin
Her romantic interest	Gary McHugh
The football star	Bernie Barrow
His girlfriend	Evelyn Bennett

Also: Chuck Tranum, Melvin Nodell.

THE GAY COED—25 minutes—DuMont 1947.

GAYELORD HAUSER

Women. Beauty tips, advice, and nutritional guidance.

Host: Gayelord Hauser, Ph.D.

Producer: Sherman Dryer.

Sponsor: Minute Maid.

GAYELORD HAUSER—15 minutes

—ABC—November 21, 1951 - April 25, 1952.

GAY NINETIES REVUE

Musical Variety. A revue set against the background of the 1890s.

Host: Joe Howard, Gus Van.

Regulars: Pat O'Mally, Lulu Bates, Loraine Fontaine, Romona Lang, The Townsmen Quartet.

Orchestra: Ray Bloch.

Producer: Tel Air Associates.

Director: Tom DeHuff.

GAY NINETIES REVUE—30 minutes—ABC—August 11, 1948 - January 12, 1949.

THE GEMINI MAN

Science Fiction Adventure. While attempting to recover a space capsule from the ocean, INTERSECT Agent Sam Casey is caught in an underwater explosion that, due to heavy radiation, effects his DNA molecular field structure and causes invisibility. By incorporating a sophisticated, subminiature DNA stabilizer in a nuclear-powered digital wristwatch, Dr. Abby Lawrence finds a means by which to control Casey's invisibility: when the three gold contacts on the base of the watch touch his skin, he remains visible; however, by pressing the stem of the watch, Sam can change the frequency and revert to invisibility for a limit of fifteen minutes a day; any longer and he will disintegrate. Stories depict Sam's assignments on behalf of INTERSECT (International Security Technics).

CAST	
Sam Casey	Ben Murphy
Dr. Abby	
Lawrence	Katherine Crawford
Leonard Driscoll, their	
superior	William Sylvester

Music: Lee Holdridge, Mark Snow.

Executive Producer: Harve Bennett.

Producer: Leslie Stevens, Frank Telford.

Director: Alan J. Levi, Michael Caffrey, Charles R. Rondeau.

THE GEMINI MAN—60 minutes—NBC—September 23, 1976 - October 28, 1976.

THE GENE AUTRY SHOW

Western. Background: The Melody

Ranch. The exploits of Gene Autry, a daring defender of range justice.

CAST

Gene Autry	Himself
Pat Buttram, his partner	Himself

Also: Gail Davis.

Producer: Armand Schaefer for Flying A Productions.

Sponsor: Wrigley.

Gene's horse: Champion.

THE GENE AUTRY SHOW—30 minutes—Syndicated 1950. 85 episodes.

THE GENERAL ELECTRIC COLLEGE BOWL

Game. "Match wits with the champions in America's favorite question and answer game, live from New York, The General Electric College Bowl." Competing are two four-member varsity scholar teams, representatives of two colleges. Basis: Difficult liberal arts questions. The game begins with the Toss Up Round. The host asks a question. The first team to sound a buzzer receives a chance to answer and earn points (five to ten, depending on the question) and the opportunity to increase their score twenty-five to thirty points via a four-part bonus question. The game continues with Toss Up Rounds and Bonus Questions. Winners are the highest point scorers. Prizes: first place—a $3,000 scholarship grant and the right to return to defend their title; the runner-up—a $1,000 grant.

Hosts: Allen Ludden (CBS); Robert Earle (NBC).

THE GENERAL ELECTRIC COLLEGE BOWL—30 minutes—CBS—January 4, 1959 - June 16, 1963; NBC—September 22, 1963 - June 14, 1970.

THE GENERAL ELECTRIC GUEST HOUSE

Panel Variety. Hollywood celebrities are interviewed and quizzed on various aspects of the entertainment industry.

Host: Durwood Kirby; Oscar Levant.

Producer: Frank Telford.

Director: Preston Wood.

Sponsor: General Electric.

THE GENERAL ELECTRIC GUEST HOUSE—60 minutes—CBS—July 1, 1951 - September 1951.

GENERAL ELECTRIC SUMMER ORIGINALS

Anthology. Original dramatic productions.

Included:

It's Sunny Again. A musical comedy depicting the struggles of a popular singer who can't get bookings.

Starring: Vivian Blaine, Jules Munshin.

The Unwilling Witness. The story of a man, the only witness to a murder, who refuses to give a defense counselor the information that might save his client.

Starring: Zachary Scott, Frances Rafferty.

The Green Parrot. Assigned to deliver a parrot named Cleopatra to the U.S. War Department, a representative of the French government struggles to complete his mission and protect the bird from foreign agents who seek it for the atomic secrets it carries in its head.

Starring: Claude Dauphin.

GENERAL ELECTRIC SUMMER ORIGINALS—30 minutes—ABC—July 3, 1956 - September 17, 1956.

THE GENERAL ELECTRIC THEATRE

Anthology. Original productions.

Host-Occasional Star: Ronald Reagen.

Music: Elmer Bernstein, Melvyn Lenard; Johnny Mandell.

Additional Music: Wilbur Hatch.

Announcer: Ken Carpenter.

Producer: Harry Tugend, William Morwood, Joseph Bantman, Stanley Rubin, William Frye, Mort Abrams.

Sponsor: General Electric.

Included:

The Girl With The Flaxen Hair. The story of a lonely, girl-shy accounting clerk who yearns for the company of a beautiful saleslady in the department store where he is employed.

Starring: Ray Bolger.

The Web Of Guilt. The story of a famous trial lawyer who suddenly finds himself forced to defend his own life.

Starring: Arthur Kennedy.

The Stone. The dramatic retelling of the biblical story of David, a young poet-shepherd and his encounter with the giant Goliath.

Starring: Tony Curtis.

Robbie And His Mary. The dramatic story of Scottish poet Robert Burns's first love, Mary Campbell.

Starring: Dan O'Herlihy, Pippa Scott.

Man On A Bicycle. Background: The French Riviera. A luxury-loving opportunist attempts to help a young French girl in her work with a group of orphans.

Starring: Fred Astaire.

THE GENERAL ELECTRIC THEATRE—30 and 60 minute versions—CBS—February 1, 1953 - September 1961. 200 episodes.

GENERAL ELECTRIC TRUE

Anthology. Dramatizations based on stories appearing in *True Magazine*.

Host-Narrator-Occasional Performer: Jack Webb.

Producer: Jack Webb, Michael Meshekoff.

Sponsor: General Electric.

Included:

U.X.B. (Unexploded bomb). Background: London, 1962. The attempts of the Suicide Squad to disarm a live and ticking bomb.

CAST

Major Arthur Hartly: Michael Evans; Lt. Keith Allison: David Frankham.

Code Name Christopher. Background: Norway, 1944. An American captain attempts to sabotage Nazi attempts in the production of heavy water, the essential ingredient of the atom bomb.

CAST

Captain John Burke: Jack Webb; Erik Lund: Gunner Hilstrom; Sigrid Lund: Anna-Lisa.

V-Victor Five. Background: New York City. An off-duty patrolman attempts to apprehend five wanted criminals.

CAST

John Egan: Karl Held; Jean Egan: Barbara Wilkins; Eddy: John Sebastian.

The Handmade Private. Whenever their superior, Lt. Bronner, is out tracking missing soldiers, Corporals Coogan and Bailey have the easy life. In order to get him off their backs, Coogan and Bailey invent an A.W.O.L. soldier. The story depicts the U.S. Army's actual global search to find a mythical soldier.

CAST

Cpl. Bailey: Jerry Van Dyke; Cpl. Coogan: Arte Johnson; Lt. Bronner: James Milhollin.

GENERAL ELECTRIC TRUE—30 minutes—CBS—September 30, 1962 - September 22, 1963. 33 episodes. Syndicated title: "True."

THE GENERAL FOODS SUMMER PLAYHOUSE

Pilot Films. Proposed comedy series for the 1965-1966 season.

Included:

Hello Dere. The misadventures of two television news reporters.

Starring: Marty Allen, Steve Rossi.

Young In Heart. The story of a newly hired Kappa Phi sorority housemother and her clash with the student president.

Starring: Barbara Bain, Mercedes McCambridge, Lou Foster.

Kibbie Hates Finch. The bickering relationship between two firemen, Kibbie and Finch, once friends until Kibbie was promoted to the position of Captain of Hook and Ladder Company 23.

CAST

Kibbie: Don Rickles; Finch: Lou Jacobi.

Take Him—He's All Yours. The story of an American travel-agency manager in England and her attempts to adjust to a new homeland.

Starring: Eve Arden, Cindy Carol, Jeremy Lloyd.

THE GENERAL FOODS SUMMER PLAYHOUSE—30 minutes—CBS—July 1965 - September 1965.

GENERAL HOSPITAL

Serial. Background: General Hospital. Intimate glimpses into the personal and professional lives of doctors and nurses.

CAST

Dr. Steve Hardy	John Beradino
Audrey March	Rachel Ames
Nurse Iris Fairchild	Peggy McCay
Brooke Clinton	Indus Arthur
Al Weeks	Tom Brown
Sharon Pinkham	Sharon DeBord
Carol Murray	Nancy Fisher
Howie Dawson	Ray Girardin
Lee Baldwin	Peter Hansen
Jane Dawson	Shelby Hiatt
Mrs. Dawson	Phyllis Hill
Dr. Peter Taylor	Craig Huebing
Eddie Weeks	Doug Lambert
Dr. Henry Pinkham	Peter Kilman
Nurse Jessie Brewer	Emily McLaughlin
Nurse Kendell Jones	Joan Tompkins
Dr. Thomas Baldwin	Paul Savior
Diana Maynard	Valerie Starrett
Nurse Lucille March	Lucille Wall
Peggy Mercer	K. T. Stevens
Angie Costello	Jana Taylor
Dr. Phil Brewer	Roy Thinnes
	Martin West
	Robert Hogan
Dr. Lyons	Martin Blaini
Randy	Mark Miller
Dr. Leslie Williams	Denise Alexander
Meg Bentley	Patricia Breslin
Mary Briggs	Anne Helm
Clampett	Robin Blake
Scotty	Tony Campo
Beverly Cleveland	Sue Bernard
Mrs. Nelson	Ann Morrison
The District Attorney	Ivan Bonar
Lieutenant Adams	Don Hammer
Denise Wilson	Julie Adams
Mrs. Bailey	Florence Lindstrom
Polly Prentice	Jennifer Billingsley
Nurse Linda Cooper	Linda Cooper
Augusta McLeod	Judith McConnell
Dr. James Hobart	James Sikking
Gordon Gray	Eric Server
Florence Gray	Ann Collings
Mr. Chamberlain	Ed Platt
Papa Costello	Ralph Manza
Marge	Mae Clark
Johnny	Butch Patrick
Dr. Miller (early role)	Ed Platt
Secretary	Iris Fairchild
Janie Dawson	Shelly Hiatt
Ling Wang	George Chiang
Mailin	Virginia Ann Lee
Ann Coheen	Virginia Grey
Dr. Joel Stratton	Rod McCarey
Owen Stratton	Joel Mareden
Kira Faulkner	Victoria Shaw
Wallace Baxter	Len Wayland
Heather Grant	Georganne LaPiere
Dr. Mark Dante	Michael DeLano
	Gerald Gordon
Sally Grimes	Jenny Sherman
Cameron Faulkner	Don Matheson
Chase Murdock	Ivan Bonner
Martha Taylor	Jennifer Peters
Dr. Rick Weber	Michael Gregory
Jeff Weber	Richard Dean Anderson
Dr. Adam Streeter	Brett Halsey
Teri Arnett	Bobbi Jordan
Dr. Monica Weber	Patsy Ryan
Mary Ellen Dante	Lee Warrick
Barbara Vining	Judy Lewis
Laura Vining	Stacey Baldwin

Musical Director: George Wright.

GENERAL HOSPITAL—30 minutes —ABC—April 1, 1963 - July 23, 1976; 45 minutes—ABC—Premiered: July 26, 1976.

THE GENERATION GAP

Game. The younger generation is pitted against the older. Intent: To discover how much each knows about the other; how wide or narrow the gap may be. The younger contestants answer questions regarding the past; the older, the present.

Two three-member teams compete. Basis: Six rounds composed of three generation questions directed to specific members of each team (twenty-five points for each correct response) and three cross-generation rapid-fire questions with both teams competing (ten additional points for each correct response). The first person to sound the buzzer is the only one permitted to answer. Ten points are deducted if incorrect. Winners are the highest point scorers. The points are transferred into dollars and each member of the winning team receives that amount; losing team members divide their earnings.

Hosts: Dennis Wholey; Jack Barry.

Announcer: Fred Foy.

Orchestra: Norman Paris.

THE GENERATION GAP—30 minutes—ABC—February 7, 1969 - May 23, 1969.

GENTLE BEN

Adventure. Exploring the Bear River Game Reserve, young Mark Wedloe stumbles upon a baby cub. Suddenly, confronted by its angry mother, he climbs to the safety of a tree. As the bear approaches her cub, she is killed by Fog Hanson, a hunter. Unaware of Mark's presence, Fog takes the cub.

The next day, Mark discovers the bear cub concealed in Fog's waterfront shack. Sneaking in to feed the cub, he befriends him and names him Ben.

Months later, when Mark overhears Fog talking about killing the bear, now fully grown, and selling the meat, he becomes desperate and takes the bear to the safety of the woods. As the afternoon hour grows late, Ellen, Mark's mother, begins to search for him. Finding Mark with the bear, she discovers its gentleness, but after learning of Mark's act, she demands that he take Ben back. That evening, Mark speaks to his father, Tom, and asks him to purchase the six hundred pound bear from Hanson.

After accepting the position of game warden in the Florida Everglades, Tom complies with Mark's desire and purchases Ben. Stories depict Tom's experiences as a game warden; and the adventures shared by a boy and his pet bear.

CAST

Tom Wedloe	Dennis Weaver
Ellen Wedloe	Beth Brickell
Mark Wedloe	Clint Howard
Boomhauer, a friend	Rance Howard
Willie, a friend	Angelo Rutherford
Ellen Wedloe (pilot episode)	Vera Miles
Fog Hanson (pilot episode)	Ralph Meeker

Music: Samuel Matlowsky, Harry Sukman.

Executive Producer: Andy White.

Producer: Ivan Tors, George Sherman.

Creator: Ivan Tors.

GENTLE BEN–30 minutes–CBS–September 10, 1967 - August 31 1969. Syndicated. 56 episodes.

THE GEORGE BURNS AND GRACIE ALLEN SHOW

Comedy. Background: 312 Maple Street, Beverly Hills, California, the residence of comedian George Burns, a tolerant man who accepts life as it comes; and his scatterbrained wife, comedienne Gracie Allen, a woman who possesses the talent to complicate situations that are seemingly uncomplicatable.

Stories relate the home lives and misadventures of a show business couple. George, who creates the program as it is being viewed, is the only person that is aware of a viewing audience. He interrupts the plots, comments, delivers monologues, and explains the situations that result due to Gracie's harebrained activities.

The series ended with Gracie's retirement from show business in 1958. With a revised format, George continued the series via "The George Burns Show" (see title).

The George Burns and Gracie Allen Show. Left to right: Bea Benaderet, Larry Keating, Gracie Allen, and George Burns. © *Screen Gems.*

CAST

George Burns	Himself
Gracie Allen	Herself
Harry Von Zell, George's Announcer	Himself
Ronnie Burns, George and Gracie's son	Himself
Blanche Morton, Gracie's friend and neighbor	Bea Benaderet
Harry Morton, Blanche's husband*	Hal March John Brown** Bob Sweeney Fred Clark Larry Keating
Ralph Grainger, Ronnie's friend	Robert Ellis
Bonnie Sue McAfee, Ronnie's girlfriend	Judi Meredith
Imogene Reynolds, Ralph's girlfriend	Carol Lee
Mr. Beasley, the mailman	Rolfe Sedan
Chester Vanderlip, the bank president	Grandon Rhodes
Lucille Vanderlip, his wife	Sarah Selby
Edie Westlip, the eleven-year-old president of the Ronnie Burns fan club	Anna Maria NaNasse
Clara Bagley, Gracie's friend	Irene Hervey
Joe Bagley, Clara's husband	Michael Waylen
Roger, Blanche's brother	King Donovan
Harry Morton, Sr.	Russell Hicks
Joey Bagley, Clara and Joe's son	Garry Marshall
Detective Soyer, the cop plagued by Gracie	James Flavan
Cuspert Jansen, the plumber	Howard McNair

Jansen's daughters: Judy Walker, Yvonne Lime, Darlene Albert, Mary Ellen Kay.

Also, various roles: Sandra Burns, Barbara Stuart, Jackie Loughery.

Announcers: Bill Goodwin (early, not syndicated episodes); Harry Von Zell.

Music: Mahlon Merrick.

Producer: Al Simon.

Producer-Director: Frederick de Cordova, Ralph Levy, Rod Amateau.

Sponsor: Carnation.

THE GEORGE BURNS AND GRACIE ALLEN SHOW–30 minutes –CBS–October 12, 1950 - September 22, 1958. Syndicated (years '52-'58). 239 filmed episodes.

THE GEORGE BURNS SHOW

Comedy. Background: Beverly Hills, California. The life of George Burns, a comedian-turned-theatrical-producer. Stories relate his attempts to overcome the chaotic situations that arise

*In early episodes a real estate salesman; a C.P.A. in later shows.

**For a short time in 1951; Brown was blacklisted for supposedly being a Communist.

from auditions, performer tantrums, his son, Ronnie's, romantic entanglements, the antics of his secretary, Blanche Morton, and the attempts of his anouncer, Harry Von Zell, to convince George that he is capable of any role asssignment.

CAST
George Burns	Himself
Ronnie Burns	Himself
Harry Von Zell	Himself
Blanche Morton	Bea Benaderet
Harry Morton, her husband, a C.P.A.	Larry Keating
Lily, the waitress	Barbara Stuart

Announcer: Harry Von Zell.

THE GEORGE BURNS SHOW—30 minutes—NBC—October 21, 1958 - April 5, 1959.

GEORGE GOBEL

Listed: The television programs of comedian George Gobel.

The George Gobel Show—Variety—60 minutes—NBC—October 2, 1954 - June 29, 1957.

Host: George Gobel.

Regulars: Jeff Donnell (as Alice, his wife in sketches), Peggy King.

Orchestra: John Scott Trotter.

The George Gobel Show—Variety—60 minutes—NBC—September 4, 1957 - March 10, 1959. On alternating basis with "The Eddie Fisher Show."

Host: George Gobel.

Regulars: Eddie Fisher, Phyllis Avery (as Alice), Peggy King, The Johnnie Mann Singers.

Orchestra: John Scott Trotter.

THE GEORGE HAMILTON IV SHOW

Musical Variety. Performances by Country and Western entertainers.

Host: George Hamilton IV.

Regulars: Mary Klick, Buck Ryan, Roy Clark, Clint Miller, Elton Britt, Jack French, Billy Gibson, Joe Williams, Joe Davis, Jan Crockett, Smitty Irvin, The Country Lads.

Music: Alec Houston and The Texas Wildcats.

THE GEORGE HAMILTON IV SHOW—60 minutes—ABC—April 13, 1959 - May 29, 1959.

GEORGE JESSEL'S SHOW BUSINESS

Variety. Testimonial dinners honoring personalities of the entertainment world. Celebrity friends, seated about a banquet table, roast the honored guests.

Host: George Jessel, Toastmaster General.

Versions:

GEORGE JESSEL'S SHOW BUSINESS—60 minutes—ABC—1953-1954.

GEORGE JESSEL'S SHOW BUSINESS—60 minutes—Syndicated 1958.

HERE COME THE STARS—60 minutes—Syndicated 1968.

GEORGE OF THE JUNGLE

Animated Cartoon. Background: The Imgwee Gwee Valley in Africa. The exploits of George, the king of the jungle, a tree-crashing-prone, simpleminded klutz who aids people in distress.

Additional characters: Friends—Bella and Ursula, native girls; Ape, his overgrown gorilla; Shep, his elephant; Seymour, the man-eating plant; Wiggy, the rhino. Enemies—Tiger and Weavel, fiends out to foil George's mission of good.

Additional Segments:

Super Chicken. The story of Henry Cabot Henhouse III, a mild-mannered scientist who discovers Super Sauce, a liquid that when taken transforms him into the daring crime fighter Super Chicken. Episodes relate his battle against the forces of evil. He is assisted by Fred, the rooster.

Tom Slick. The misadventures of Tom Slick, a simple-minded racing car driver.

His aide: Marigold; his car: *The Thunderbolt Grease Slapper.*

Voices: Bill Scott, June Foray, Paul Frees, Bill Conrad, Walter Tetley, Skip Craig, Barbara Baldwin.

Music: Sheldon Allman, Stan Worth.

Producer: Jay Ward, Bill Scott.

Note: The Character Fred, in the "Super Chicken" segment is also known to be a lion.

GEORGE OF THE JUNGLE—30 minutes—ABC—September 9, 1967 - September 6, 1970.

THE GEORGE RAFT CASEBOOK

See title: "I'm the Law."

THE GEORGE SANDERS MYSTERY THEATRE

Anthology. Mystery presentations.

Host-Occasional Performer: George Sanders.

Included:

The Call. Plagued by mysterious phone calls in the night, a nurse attempts to uncover the caller's identity.

CAST
Ann: Toni Gerry; Lewis: James Gavin; Tom: Adam Williams.

Last Will And Testament. An amnesiac, told he resembles a missing heir, joins forces with a couple in attempt to claim the inheritance. The deal is to divide the money; his plan, however, is to kill the man and marry the woman.

CAST
George Cook: Robert Horton; Milo Davenport: Herb Butterfield; Felice: Dolores Dinlon.

Man In The Elevator. A married couple, planning to spend the weekend in the country, are about to leave when the wife remembers that she left her watch in the apartment. The husband returns for it. While he is in the elevator, she removes the fuse, trapping him between floors. The story concerns his frantic efforts to escape.

CAST
Don Haggerty, Dorothy Green.

THE GEORGE SANDERS MYSTERY THEATRE—30 minutes—NBC—June 22, 1957 - September 1957.

GEORGIA GIBBS MILLION RECORD SHOW

Variety. The presentation of songs that have sold over a million copies.

Hostess: Georgia Gibbs.

Orchestra: Eddie Safronski.

GEORGIA GIBBS MILLION RECORD SHOW—30 minutes—NBC—July 1, 1957 - September 1957.

GERALD McBOING-BOING

Animated Cartoon. The misadventures of a young boy, Gerald McCloy, who speaks in sound effects ("Boing! Boing!") rather than words.

Additional characters: The Twirlinger Twins; Dusty of the Circus.

Featured segments: "Meet the Inventor"; "Meet the Artist"; "Legends of Americans in the World."

Off-screen commentator and interpreter of Gerald's sounds: Bill Goodwin.

Voices: Marvin Miller.

Music: Ernest Gold.

GERALD McBOING-BOING—30 minutes—CBS (U.P.A. Theatrical Shorts) —December 16, 1956 - October 3, 1958.

GET CHRISTIE LOVE!

Crime Drama. Background: Los Angeles, California. The investigations of Christie Love, an undercover police agent who encompasses beauty, charm, wit, and an understanding of human nature as her weapons. Working for the L.A.P.D., she is assigned to a special investigative division consisting of eight men and two women. Hating to wear a uniform, she uses various disguises and is determined not to be hindered by procedures.

CAST

Christie Love	Teresa Graves
Lt. Matthew Reardon	Charles Cioffi
Captain Arthur P. Ryan	Jack Kelly
Lt. Steve Belmont	Dennis Rucker
Lt. Joe Caruso	Andy Romano
Officer Pete Gallagher	Michael Pataki

Music: Luchi de Jesus; Jack Elliott, Allyn Ferguson.

Executive Producer: David L. Wolper.

Producer: Paul Mason.

Developed for television by: Peter Nelson, George Kirgo.

Christie's Badge Number: 7332.

GET CHRISTIE LOVE!—60 minutes —ABC—September 11, 1974 - July 18, 1975. 22 episodes.

GET IT TOGETHER

Musical Variety. Performances by Rock personalities.

Hosts: Sam Riddle, Cass Elliott.

Announcer: Sam Riddle.

Music: Recorded.

GET IT TOGETHER—30 minutes—ABC—January 3, 1970 - September 6, 1970.

GET THE MESSAGE

Game. Two competing teams, each composed of three members—two celebrities and one studio audience contestant. The host presents an expression to the celebrities (title, name, place, or slogan). Contestants have to identify it through word-association clues. The first to acquire three identifications is the winner and receives one hundred dollars and the chance to compete again.

Hosts: Frank Buxton; Robert Q. Lewis.

GET THE MESSAGE—30 minutes—ABC—March 30, 1964 - December 25, 1964.

GET SMART

Comedy. Background: 123 Main Street, Washington, D.C., the headquarters of C.O.N.T.R.O.L., an international spy organization dedicated to destroying the diabolical objectives of K.A.O.S., an international organization of evil.

Stories relate the investigations of two C.O.N.T.R.O.L. agents: Maxwell Smart, Secret Agent 86, a bumbling klutz; and his partner, Agent 99, a beautiful, level-headed woman.

Max and The Chief, to protect their identities in the presence of 99's mother, adopt the guises of Maxwell Smart, a salesman for the Pontiac Greeting Card Company and the Chief, Howard Clark, his employer. Unaware of her daughter's activities as a spy, 99's mother believes she is The Chief's secretary.

CAST

Maxwell Smart	Don Adams
Agent 99 (real name not revealed)	Barbara Feldon
Thaddeus, The Chief	Edward Platt
Conrad Siegfried, the head of K.A.O.S.	Bernie Kopell
Larrabee, a C.O.N.T.R.O.L. agent	Robert Karvelas
C.O.N.T.R.O.L. Agent 44	Victor French
Admiral Harold Harmon Hargrade, the former C.O.N.T.R.O.L. Chief	William Schallert
Dr. Steele, head of C.O.N.T.R.O.L.'s lab, located in a burlesque theatre	Ellen Weston
Hymie, a C.O.N.T.R.O.L. robot	Dick Gautier
Charlie Watkins, a beautiful and shapely blonde C.O.N.T.R.O.L. agent (supposedly a man in disguise)	Angelique
Professor Windish, a C.O.N.T.R.O.L. scientist	Robert Cornthwaite
Charlson, a C.O.N.T.R.O.L. scientist	Stacy Keach
Dr. Bascomb, the head of C.O.N.T.R.O.L.'s crime lab	George Ives
Starker, Siegfried's aide	King Moody
99's mother	Jane Dulo
C.O.N.T.R.O.L. Agent 13	David Ketchum
Harry Hoo, the oriental detective	Joey Forman

C.O.N.T.R.O.L.'s dog agent: Fang (Agent K-13).

Music: Irving Szathmary.

Executive Producer: Leonard B. Stern.

Producer: Jess Oppenheimer, Jay Sandrich, Bert Nodella, Arnie Rosen.

Director: James Komack, David Alexander, Norman Abbott, Sidney Miller, Reza S. Badiyi, Bruce Bilson, Paul Bogart, Gary Nelson, Richard Donner, Earl Bellamy, Murray Golden, Joshua Shelley, Frank McDonald.

Creator: Mel Brooks, Buck Henry.

Get Smart. Don Adams and Barbara Feldon.

GET SMART—30 minutes—NBC—

September 18, 1965 - September 13, 1969. CBS—September 26, 1969 - September 11, 1970. Syndicated. 138 episodes.

GETTING TOGETHER

Comedy. Background: Los Angeles, California. The misadventures of composer Bobby Conway and lyricist Lionel Poindexter, songwriters anxiously awaiting success.

CAST

Bobby Conway	Bobby Sherman
Lionel Poindexter	Wes Stern
Jenny Conway, Bobby's sister	Susan Neher
Rita Simon, their landlady, a beautician	Pat Carroll
Rudy Colcheck, a police officer, Rita's boyfriend	Jack Burns

Music: Hugo Montenegro.

GETTING TOGETHER—30 minutes —ABC—September 18, 1971 - January 8, 1972. 15 episodes.

GHOST

Game. Distinguished by two formats.

Format One:
Four regular competing players. Words are supplied by home viewers. The host states the number of letters contained in a particular word. Players, one at a time, state a letter. If a correct letter is guessed, it appears in its appropriate place on a board. The object is for players to spell the word without supplying the last letter. If the last letter is given before the word is known, the sender receives fifty dollars. If the word is guessed before the last letter appears, the sender receives twenty-five dollars.

Format Two:
Three competing players. The host states the amount of letters contained in a word. Players, in turn, contribute letters to its formation. For each letter that is correct, beyond the first three, money is awarded. However, should a player supply the last letter he is disqualified. The player first to identify the word is the winner of that round. Players compete until defeated.

Host: Dr. Bergen Evans.

Panelist (format one): Robert Pallock, Shirley Stern, Gail Compton, Hope Ryder.

GHOST—30 minutes—NBC—July 27, 1952 - September 1952. Also known as "Super Ghost."

THE GHOST AND MRS. MUIR

Comedy. Background: Schooner Bay, New England. Determined to reconstruct her life after the death of her husband, free-lance magazine writer Carolyn Muir moves into Gull Cottage, a cottage haunted by the spirit of its nineteenth-century owner, Captain Daniel Gregg. Having passed away before he was able to complete his plans for its development, he is determined to maintain his privacy and continue with his original goal.

Stories relate Carolyn's efforts to make Gull Cottage her home despite the protests of the Captain.

CAST

Carolyn Muir	Hope Lange
Captain Daniel Gregg	Edward Mulhare
Jonathan Muir, her son	Harlen Carraher
Candy Muir, her daughter	Kellie Flanagan
Martha Grant, the housekeeper	Reta Shaw
Claymore Gregg, the Captain's nephew	Charles Nelson Reilly
Peevy, Martha's boyfriend	Guy Raymond
Noorie Coolidge, the owner of the town lobster house	Dabbs Greer

Muir family dog: Scruffy.

Music: Dave Grusin; Warren Barker.

Executive Producer: David Gerber.

Producer: Howard Leeds, Gene Reynolds, Stanley Rubin.

Director: Lee Philips, Gene Reynolds, John Erman, David Alexander, Ida Lupino, Hollingsworth Morse, Oscar Rudolph, Sherman Marks, Gary Nelson.

THE GHOST AND MRS. MUIR—30 minutes—NBC—September 21, 1968 - September 6, 1969. ABC—30 minutes —September 18, 1969 - September 18, 1970. Syndicated. 50 episodes.

THE GHOST BUSTERS

Comedy. The comic escapades of Kong and Spencer, Ghost Busters, and their assistant, Tracy, a gorilla, as they battle and attempt to dematerialize

The Ghost And Mrs. Muir. Hope Lange.

the ghosts of legendary fiends (e.g., Frankenstein's Monster, Dracula, the Mummy, the Werewolf, etc.).

CAST

Kong	Forrest Tucker
Eddie Spencer	Larry Storch
Tracy	Bob Burns

Music: Yvette Blais, Jeff Michael, The Horta-Mahana Corporation.

Producer: Norman Abbott.

Director: Norman Abbott, Larry Peerce.

THE GHOST BUSTERS—25 minutes —CBS—September 6, 1975 - September 4, 1976.

THE GHOST SQUAD

Crime Drama. Background: London, England. The cases of the Ghost Squad, a special police unit designed to corrupt the inner workings of the underworld. Produced in England.

CAST

Sir Andrew Wilson, the director of the Ghost Squad	Sir Donald Wolfit
His first assistant	Angela Brown
Nick Craig, his assistant	Michael Quinn

Music: Philip Green.

THE GHOST SQUAD—60 minutes— Syndicated 1960.

GHOST STORY

Anthology. Suspense dramas relating the plight of people suddenly confronted with supernatural occurrences.

Host: Sebastian Cabot, appearing as Winston Essex, a mysterious psychic gentleman who introduces stories.

Music: Billy Goldenberg.

Included:

At The Cradle Foot. A glimpse into the world of the future when a man envisions, in 1992, the murder of his daughter.

CAST
Paul: James Franciscus; Karen: Elizabeth Ashley; Emily, as a girl: Lori Busk; Emily, as a woman: Lisa James.

The Summer House. Alone in their summer home, Martha Alcot is caught in a world between nightmare and reality when she envisions her husband murdering her by pushing her into an open well in the celler. That evening, her husband lures her to the celler; and, in the attempt to murder her, he himself is killed when he falls into the well.

CAST
Martha Alcott: Carolyn Jones; Andrew Alcott: Steve Forrest; Charlie Pender: William Windom.

Alter Ego. Wishing to have a playmate, a bedridden student's dream becomes a reality when an exact double appears. However, he destroys everything he likes. The story concerns his teacher's efforts to return it from whence it came

CAST
Miss Gideon: Helen Hayes; Robert: Michael James Wixted.

The Dead We Leave Behind. The story of Elliot Brent, a man unable to control events in his life—tragic events that are forecast by his television set.

CAST
Elliot Brent: Jason Robards; Joann Brent: Stella Stevens.

GHOST STORY—60 minutes—NBC— September 15, 1972 - December 29, 1972. Spin-off series: "Circle of Fear." (See title.)

THE GIANT STEP

Game. Three youngsters, seven to seventeen years of age, compete. After selecting a subject category, contestants answer questions increasing in difficulty on each plateau they reach. Players vie for the top prize, a college education, which is earned by retaining the championship for a specified number of weeks.

Host: Bert Parks.

Orchestra: Jerry Bresler.

THE GIANT STEP—30 minutes— NBC—November 7, 1956 - May 29, 1957.

GIBBSVILLE

Drama. Background: Gibbsville, a Pennsylvania mining town, during the 1940s. The series, based on John O'Hara's short stories, depicts events in the lives of its citizens as seen through the eyes of Ray Whitehead, reporter for the *Gibbsville Courier,* the town newspaper, a one-time prestegious foreign correspondent whose career and reputation have been destroyed by alcohol.

CAST
Ray Whitehead	Gig Young
Jim Malloy, Ray's friend, a reporter	John Savage
Dr. Michael Malloy, Jim's father	Biff McGuire
Mrs. Malloy, Jim's mother	Peggy McCay
Pell, the city editor	Bert Remsen
Lefty, the bartender	Frank Campanella

Music: Leonard Rosenman, Jack Elliott, Allyn Ferguson.

Executive Producer: David Gerber.

Producer: John Furia, Jr.

Director: Alexander Singer, Harry Harris, Alf Kjellin, Gene Levitt, Marc Daniels.

Program Open:

Ray: "When I walk through the streets of Gibbsville, I see a small but growing town, a busy town with its roots deep in the coal-mined earth. But behind the closed doors and drawn curtains are the secret lives of its people. The lives of the wealthy and the poor, filled with ambition and need, love and hate, sorrow and private wars, and the dreams that make men go on. Behind the closed doors of Gibbsville lies the truth about this town, about any town. The real stories waiting to be told."

GIBBSVILLE—60 minutes—NBC—November 11, 1976 - December 30, 1976.

GIDEON, C.I.D.

Crime Drama. Background: London, England. The investigations of Commander George Gideon, the Chief Inspector of the Criminal Investigation Division (C.I.D.) of Scotland Yard.

Starring: John Gregson as Commander George Gideon.

GIDEON, C.I.D.—60 minutes—Syndicated 1966. 26 episodes. Also known as "Gideon's Way."

GIDGET

Comedy. Background: Santa Monica, California. Swimming and befelled by a cramp, fifteen-and-a-half-year-old Frances Lawrence is rescued by surfer Jeff Matthews, called Moon Doogie by other surfers. Nicknamed "Gidget,"* she befriends Jeff and discovers a new life: the world of surfing.

Stories relate her experiences as she and her friends become actively involved in the exciting world of surfing. Based on the movie, *Gidget,* which stars Sandra Dee.

CAST
Frances "Gidget" Lawrence	Sally Field
Russell Lawrence, her father, a widower, an English Professor	Don Porter
Anne, her married sister	Betty Conner
John, Anne's husband, a psychiatrist	Peter Deuel

*According to the movie, a reference to height for a girl who is approximately five feet two; not tall, yet not a midget.

Gidget. Don Porter and Sally Field. © *Screen Gems.*

Jeff Mathews	Steven Miles

Gidget's Friends:

Larue	Lynette Winter
Treasure	Beverly Adams
Becky	Heather North
Sally	Bridget Hanley
Mel	Ron Rifkin
Betty	Barbara Hershey
Ken	Tim Rooney
Ellen	Pam McMyler
Randy	Rickie Sorensen
Siddo	Mike Nader

Music: Howard Greenfield; Jack Keller.

GIDGET—30 minutes—ABC—September 15, 1965 - September 1, 1966. Syndicated. 32 episodes.

GIGANTOR

Animated Cartoon. Era: Twenty-first-century Earth. The battle against interplanetary evil as depicted through the activities of Gigantor, an indestructible robot; his twelve-year-old master, Jimmy Sparks; and police inspector Blooper.

Music: Lou Singer.

GIGANTOR—30 minutes—Syndicated 1966. 52 episodes. Produced in Japan.

GILLIGAN'S ISLAND

Comedy. Background: An uncharted island in the South Pacific. Shipwrecked after a tropical storm at sea, the seven members of the sight-seeing charter boat, the S.S. *Minnow,* develop a community after all attempts to contact the outside world fail. Stories relate their struggle for survival, and their endless attempts to be rescued despite their constant foiling by the bumbling actions of the first-mate, Gilligan.

CAST

Jonas Grumby, the skipper	Alan Hale, Jr.
Gilligan, the first-mate	Bob Denver
Ginger Grant, a beautiful movie actress	Tina Louise
Thurston Howell III, a multimillionaire	Jim Backus
Lovey Howell III, his wife	Natalie Schafer
Mary Ann Summers, a pretty general store clerk	

from Kansas	Dawn Wells
Roy Hinkley, the professor, a brilliant research scientist	Russell Johnson

Music: Sherwood Schwartz; Johnny Williams; Herschel Burke Gilbert; Lyn Murray; Gerald Fried; Morton Stevens.

Executive Producer: William Froug, Sherwood Schwartz.

Producer: Jack Arnold, Robert L. Rosen.

Director: Charles Norton, William D'Arcy, Stanley Z. Cherry, Ida Lupino, George M. Cahan, Jack Arnold, Jerry Hopper, John Rich, Tony Leader, David McDearmon, Hal Cooper, John Murray, Leslie Goodwins.

Creator: Sherwood Schwartz.

GILLIGAN'S ISLAND—30 minutes—CBS—September 26, 1964 - September 3, 1967. Syndicated. 98 episodes. Spin-off series: "The New Adventures of Gilligan." (see title).

GIRL ABOUT TOWN

Variety. Interviews and entertainment performances set against the background of a staged dress rehearsal.

Hostess: Kyle MacDonnell.

Announcer: Johnny Downs.

Music: The Norman Paris Trio.

Producer: Fred Coe, Craig Allen.

Sponsor: Bates Fabrics; Sanka Coffee.

GIRL ABOUT TOWN—20 minutes—NBC—April 15, 1948 - January 19, 1949.

THE GIRL FROM U.N.C.L.E.

Adventure. Background: New York City. A dry-cleaning establishment, Del Florias Taylor Shop, is the front for the headquarters of U.N.C.L.E.—the United Network Command for Law Enforcement—an international organization responsible for the welfare of peoples and nations against the subversive objectives of THRUSH, an international organization bent on world domination.

Stories relate the investigations of April Dancer and Mark Slate, U.N.C.L.E. agents battling the global forces of crime and corruption as influenced by THRUSH. A spin-off from "The Man From U.N.C.L.E." (See title.)

CAST

April Dancer	Stefanie Powers
Mark Slate	Noel Harrison
Alexander Waverly, the head of U.N.C.L.E.	Leo G. Carroll
Randy Kovacs, an U.N.C.L.E. Agent	Randy Kirby

Music: Jerry Goldsmith.

Additional Music: Dave Grusin, Jack Marshall, Richard Shores.

Music Supervision: Al Mack.

Executive Producer: Norman Felton.

Producer: Douglas Benton, Mark Hodges, George Lear, Barry Shear.

Director: John Brahm, Mitchell Lesian, Barry Shear.

Note: In the pilot film, titled "The Moonglow Affair," which was aired on "The Man From U.N.C.L.E.," Mary Ann Mobley portrayed April, and Norman Fell, Mark.

THE GIRL FROM U.N.C.L.E.—60 minutes—NBC—September 13, 1966 - September 5, 1967. Syndicated. 24 episodes.

The Girl From U.N.C.L.E. Stefanie Powers and Noel Harrison.

THE GIRL IN MY LIFE

Testimonial. Recognition of that "special girl in everyone's life" who has been kind, unselfish, and undemanding. The format unites or reunites the recipient of the good deed with the woman who performed it. Gifts are presented to that special girl.

Host: Fred Holliday.

Announcer: John Harlen; Bob Warren.

Music: Ed Kaleoff.

THE GIRL IN MY LIFE—30 minutes —ABC—July 9, 1973 - December 20, 1974.

GIRL TALK

Discussion. Setting: A living room. Guests, mainly women, discuss their thoughts, fears, joys, sorrows, aspirations, and confessions.

Versions:

Girl Talk—30 minutes—DuMont 1955.
Hostess: Wendy Barrie.

Girl Talk—30 minutes—Syndicated 1962-1970.
Hostesses: Virginia Graham; Gloria DeHaven; Betsy Palmer.

In 1969, contract difficulties forced Miss Graham to leave the program. Gloria DeHaven was hired to replace her, but a heavy schedule, including her own New York program, "Prize Movie," forced her to relinquish hosting duties. Betsy Palmer replaced her and continued with the series until it ended in September of 1970.

THE GIRL WITH SOMETHING EXTRA

Comedy. Background: Los Angeles, California. The trials and tribulations of young marrieds: John Burton, an attorney with the firm of Metcalf, Klein, and Associates; and his wife, Sally, who possesses E.S.P. and is able to preceive his every thought. Stories relate John's attempts to cope with the situations that develop when Sally inadvertently meddles into his private thoughts.

CAST

Sally Burton	Sally Field
John Burton	John Davidson
Jerry Burton, John's brother, a bachelor musician	Jack Sheldon
Anne, Sally's friend, operates a variety shop, "The Store"	Zohra Lampert
Owen Metcalf, John's employer	Henry Jones
Angela, John's secretary	Stephanie Edwards
Stewart Klein, John's employer	William Windom

Music: Dave Grusin.

THE GIRL WITH SOMETHING EXTRA—30 minutes—NBC—September 14, 1973 - May 24, 1974. 22 episodes.

THE GISELE MacKENZIE SHOW

Musical Variety.
Hostess: Gisele MacKenzie.
Vocalists: The Double Daters.
Producer: Jack Benny, Charles Isaacs.
Orchestra: Axel Stordahl.

THE GISELE MacKENZIE SHOW— 30 minutes—NBC—September 28, 1957 - March 29, 1958.

GIVE-N-TAKE

Game. Four female contestants, seated in a circle surrounding a large electronic spinning arrow, each receive an expensive merchandise gift, the value of which is not stated. Another prize is revealed and a question is read to the ladies. The player who is first to identify herself through a buzzer signal receives a chance to answer. If she is correct, she presses a button to slowly stop the arrow. If it pinpoints her or stops on a Give-N-Take box (which separate the players) she receives the prize; if the arrow pinpoints another player, that player receives it. The player who is selected by the arrow can either keep or pass the prize. The object is for players not to exceed $5,000 in merchandise cash value, but to come as close as possible to that amount to win. Players are not made aware of their cash totals and work blindly on keeping or passing items. Six prizes are played per game and the player who comes closest to the game's limit is the winner and receives the prizes she has accumulated.

Host: Jim Lange.
Models: Jane Nelson, Judy Rich.
Announcer: Johnny Jacobs.
Music: Stan Worth.
Executive Producer: William Carruthers.
Producer: Joel Stein.
Director: John Dorsey.

GIVE-N-TAKE—30 minutes—CBS— September 8, 1975 - December 10, 1976.

GLADYS KNIGHT AND THE PIPS

Variety. Music, songs, dances, and comedy sketches.

Hostess: Gladys Knight.
Co-Hosts: The Pips, her backup trio: Edward Patten, William Guest, and Merald "Bubba" Knight (Gladys's brother).

Orchestra: George Wyle.
Additional Orchestrations: Sid Feller.
Choreography: Tony Charmoli.
Producer: Bob Henry.
Director: Tony Charmoli.

GLADYS KNIGHT AND THE PIPS— 60 minutes—NBC—July 10, 1975 - July 31, 1975.

GLAMOUR GIRL

Women. A woman, selected from the studio audience, is given a complete fashion and beauty treatment.

Hosts: Harry Babbitt; Jack McCoy.

GLAMOUR GIRL—30 minutes— NBC—July 6, 1953 - January 14, 1954.

GLAMOUR-GO-ROUND

Women. Beauty tips and advice.
Hostess: Ilka Chase.
Announcer: Durwood Kirby.
Music: Billy Nalle.

GLAMOUR-GO-ROUND—15 minutes—CBS 1950.

THE GLEN CAMPBELL GOODTIME HOUR

Variety. Music, songs, and comedy set against a Country and Western atmosphere.

Host: Glen Campbell.
Regulars: Jerry Reed, Eddie Mayehoff, Larry McNeely, R.G. Brown, John Hartford, Pat Paulsen, Mel Tillis, The Mike Curb Congregation.
Announcer: Roger Carroll.
Orchestra: Marty Paich.

THE GLEN CAMPBELL GOODTIME HOUR—60 minutes—CBS—June 23, 1968 - September 8, 1968. Returned: CBS—60 minutes—January 22, 1969 - June 13, 1972.

GLENCANNON

Adventure. Background: Various Caribbean Islands. The experiences of Colin Glencannon, the skipper of the freighter, *Inchcliffe Castle*. Based on the stories by Guy Gilpatrick.

Starring: Thomas Mitchell as Colin Glencannon.

GLENCANNON–30 minutes–Syndicated 1958. 39 episodes.

GLENN MILLER TIME

Musical Variety. A recreation of the Glenn Miller sound.

Hosts: Ray McKinley, drummer, and Johnny Desmond, singer–both members of the Miller orchestra.

Regulars: Patty Clark, The Castle Sisters.

Music: The Glenn Miller Orchestra.

GLENN MILLER TIME–60 minutes –CBS–July 10, 1961 - September 11, 1961.

THE GLENN REEVES SHOW

Musical Variety. Performances by Country and Western artists.

Host: Glenn Reeves.

Music: The Glenn Reeves Band.

THE GLENN REEVES SHOW–30 minutes–Syndicated 1966.

GLOBAL ZOBEL

Travel. Various aspects of countries around the world.

Host-Narrator: Myron Zobel, photographer.

GLOBAL ZOBEL–30 minutes–Syndicated 1961. 27 episodes.

THE GLORIA DeHAVEN SHOW

Musical Variety.

Hostess: Gloria DeHaven.

Featured: Bobby Hackett.

Orchestra: Tony Mottola.

THE GLORIA DeHAVEN SHOW–15 minutes–ABC–October 9, 1953 - January 25, 1954.

THE GLORIA SWANSON SHOW

See title: "Crown Theatre with Gloria Swanson."

GLYNIS

Comedy. Background: San Diego, California. The misadventures of Glynis Granville, mystery-story authoress and amateur sleuth. Episodes detail her investigations as she attempts to solve crimes to acquire story material.

CAST
Glynis Granville	Glynis Johns
Keith Granville, her husband, an attorney	Keith Andes
Chick Rogers, her consultant, a retired policeman	George Mathews

Producer: Jess Oppenheimer, Edward H. Feldman.

Glynis. Glynis Johns.

GLYNIS–30 minutes–CBS–September 25, 1963 - December 18, 1963. Rebroadcasts: CBS–July 19, 1965 - September 6, 1965. 13 episodes.

THE GO GO GOPHERS

Animated Cartoon. Background: Gopher Gulch, 1860s. The efforts of two Indians (who resemble gophers), the double talking Ruffled Feather, and his interpreter, Running Board, to safeguard their domain from army colonel Kit Coyote as he attempts to rid the West of Indians.

THE GO GO GOPHERS–24 minutes –CBS–September 14, 1968 - September 6, 1969. Syndicated. 24 episodes.

GO LUCKY

Game. Two competing contestants. A group of performers enact a common phrase through charades. Players have to identify it within a two-minute time limit. The most correct identifications award a player a one-hundred-dollar bond. A fifty-dollar bond is awarded to the runner-up.

Host: Jan Murray.

Producer: Herb Morris.

Director: Jerome Schnurr.

GO LUCKY–30 minutes–CBS–July 15, 1951 - September 2, 1951.

GOING MY WAY

Comedy-Drama. Background: New York City. Father Charles O'Mally, a young Catholic Priest with progressive ideas, is assigned to Saint Dominic's Parrish and its conservative pastor, the aging Father Fitzgibbons. Stories relate his struggles to assist the needy, modernize the church, and reform its stubborn pastor. Based on the movie of the same title.

CAST
Father Charles O'Mally	Gene Kelly
Father Fitzgibbons	Leo G. Carroll
Tom Colwell, the community center director	Dick York
Mrs. Featherstone	Nydia Westman

Music: Leo Shuken.

GOING MY WAY–60 minutes–ABC –October 3, 1962 - September 11, 1963. 39 episodes.

THE GOLDBERGS

Comedy. Background: 1030 East Tremont Avenue, Bronx, New York, Apartment 3-B. Rent: $78.00 per month. Occupants: The Goldbergs– Molly, Jake, Rosalie, Sammy, and Uncle David. The trials and tribulations of a poor Jewish family who are guided through their difficult times by a warm, compassionate, and understanding woman. Molly is the typical mother trying to raise her children and run her home; the "yenta" talking through the window to her neighbor ("Yoo-hoo, Mrs. Bloom!"); the philosopher who has a theory and a solution for all problems. Based on the radio program.

Revised format. After twenty-five years, Molly uproots her family and moves from the Bronx to the mythical town of Haverville, U.S.A. Stories mirror the lives of the Goldbergs.

CAST
Molly Goldberg	Gertrude Berg

Jake Goldberg	Philip Loeb
	Harold J. Stone
	Robert H. Harris
Rosalie Goldberg	Arlene McQuade
Sammy Goldberg	Larry Robinson
	Tom Taylor
Uncle David	Eli Mintz
Mrs. Bloom	Olga Fabian

Also: Betty Walker, Dora Weissman, Henry Sharp.

Producer: Worthington Miner.

Director: Walter Hart.

Creator-Writer: Gertrude Berg.

Sponsor: General Foods.

THE GOLDBERGS—30 minutes—CBS—January 17, 1949 - September 25, 1953. Revised version: 30 minutes—Syndicated 1955.

THE GOLDDIGGERS

Variety. Music, songs, dances, and comedy sketches. The Golddiggers are a group of beautiful and talented young ladies, between eighteen and twenty-two years of age, assembled by producer Gregg Garrison through open auditions.

The Golddiggers: Michelle Della Fave, Rosetta Cox, Lucy Codham, Paula Cinko, Peggy Hansen, Nancy Bonetti, Susan Lund, Barbara Sanders, Patricia Mickey, Francie Mendenhall, Loyita Chapel, Lee Crawford, Jimmie Cannon, Tanya Della Fave, Nancy Reichert, Janice Whitby, Jackie Chidsey, Liz Kelley, Karen Cavenaugh, Rebecca Jones.

Programs:

Dean Martin Presents The Golddiggers—Musical Variety—60 minutes—NBC—July 1968 - September 12, 1968.

Hosts: Frank Sinatra, Jr., Joey Heatherton.

Regulars: Paul Lynde, Barbara Heller, Stanley Myron Handleman, Stu Gilliam, The Times Square Two, Avery Schrieber, Skiles and Henderson, Gail Martin.

Orchestra: Les Brown.

Dean Martin Presents The Golddiggers—Musical Variety—60 minutes—NBC—July 17, 1969 - September 11, 1969. The program features the music, comedy, song, and dance of the 1930s and 40s.

Hosts: Gail Martin, Paul Lynde, Lou Rawls.

Regulars: Stanley Myron Handleman, Tommy Tune, Albert Brooks, Danny Lockin, Darleen Carr, Fiore and Eldridge, Allison McKay, Joyce Ames.

Orchestra: Les Brown.

The Golddiggers In London—Musical Variety—60 minutes—NBC—July 1970 - September 10, 1970.

Host: Charles Nelson Reilly.

Regulars: Marty Feldman, Tommy Tune, Julian Chagrin.

Orchestra: Jack Parnell.

The Golddiggers—Variety—30 minutes—Syndicated 1971.

Hosts: Male Guests of the week: Van Johnson, Glenn Ford, Doug McClure, Rosey Grier, Buddy Hackett, Dom DeLuise, Steve Allen, John Davidson, Hugh O'Brian, Martin Milner.

Regulars: Larry Storch, Alice Ghostley, Charles Nelson Reilly, Jackie Vernon, Lonnie Shorr, Barbara Heller, Don Rice, Jennifer Buriner.

Orchestra: Van Alexander.

GOLDEN WINDOWS

Serial. Juliet Goodwin, a singer, leaves her home in Maine and struggles to further her career in New York City. Her actions are opposed by her boyfriend, Tom Anderson, and her foster father who has always sheltered her.

CAST

Juliet Goodwin	Leila Martin
Tom Anderson	Herbert Patterson
John Brandon	Grant Sullivan
Charles Goodwin	Eric Dressler
Mrs. Brandon	Harriet McGibbon
Hazel	Barbara Cook
Ellen	Monica Lovett
Margo	Naomi Ryerton
Anne	Sonny Adams
Carl Brown	Walter Kinsella
Ed Clifton	John Dutra
Paul Anderson	Philip Pine
Ellen Stockwell	Millicent Brewer
Fred Stanton	Jamie Smith
Anne d'Autremont	Jane Talbert
Ed Clifton	Kevin O'Morrison
Tilman	Mike Tolin
Jane	Vicki Cummings

Producer: Thomas Riley.

Sponsor: Procter and Gamble.

GOLDEN WINDOWS—15 minutes—NBC—July 5, 1954 - September 28, 1954.

GOLDEN VOYAGE

Travel. Filmed explorations, narrated by the traveler, to areas about the globe.

Host: Jack Douglas.

GOLDEN VOYAGE—30 minutes—Syndicated 1968. Before being syndicated, the program was produced and aired in Los Angeles for eleven years.

GOLDIE

See title: "The Betty Hutton Show."

GOLF FOR SWINGERS

Game. Background: The Talabasses Park Country Club in Southern California. Involved: Two guest celebrities; host, Lee Trevino; and several condensed versions of golf, "a stroke play match over three par four holes." By the flip of a coin, one player tees off. He may either hit the ball by himself or incorporate Lee, who may hit two shots for each celebrity on each hole. After four holes are played, the winning celebrity receives a check for one thousand dollars, which he donates to the charity of his choice.

Host: Lee Trevino.

Music: Recorded.

GOLF FOR SWINGERS—30 minutes—Syndicated 1972.

GOMER PYLE, U.S.M.C.

Comedy. Background: Camp Henderson, a marine base in Los Angeles, California. The life of Gomer Pyle, a simple-minded and naive private with the Second Platoon, B Company. Stories depict the chaos that ensues when he unconsciously diverges from the set rules of the system and complicates matters; and the efforts of his superior, Sergeant Vincent Carter, a man constantly plagued by Pyle's antics, to resolve the situations.

A spin-off from "The Andy Griffith Show," wherein Gomer Pyle was depicted as a gas-station attendant before he decided to join the marines.

CAST

Private Gomer Pyle	Jim Nabors
Sgt. Vincent Carter	Frank Sutton
Private Duke Slatter	Ronnie Schell
Private Frankie Lombardi	Ted Bessell
Bunny, Carter's	

girlfriend   Barbara Stuart
Sgt. Charles Hacker   Allan Melvin
Lou Anne Poovie, a friend
  of Gomer's, a singer at
  the Blue Bird
  Cafe   Elizabeth MacRae
Corporal Charles Boyle,
  Carter's aide   Roy Stuart
Colonel Edward Gray,
  the Commanding
  officer   Forrest Compton
Private Hummel   William Christopher
Anderson   Craig Huebing

Music: Earle Hagen.

GOMER PYLE, U.S.M.C.—30 minutes—CBS—September 25, 1964 - September 19, 1969. Daytime rebroadcasts: (CBS) September 8, 1969 - March 22, 1972. Syndicated. 230 episodes.

THE GONG SHOW

Variety. Three celebrity guest judges rate the performances of undiscovered talent. If, after forty-five seconds, a judge feels that an act is not worthy of continuing, he hits a large gong and the act is discontinued. Acts that are permitted to perform are rated by the judges on a number basis from one to ten. The highest scoring act is the winner and receives a trophy and a check for $516.32.

Host: Chuck Barris.

Assistant: Sivi Aberg.

Regular Panelists: Jaye P. Morgan, Arte Johnson, Jamie Farr.

Announcer: Johnny Jacobs.

Music: Milton DeLugg ("and his band with a thug").

Occasional substitute for Sivi Aberg: Stella Barris.

Executive Producer: Chuck Barris, Chris Bearde.

Director: John Dorsey, Terry Kyne.

THE GONG SHOW—25, then 30 minutes—NBC—Premiered: June 14, 1976.

Syndicated Version: Follows the same format with the prize money being $712.05.

Host: Gary Owens; Chuck Barris.

Assistant: Sivi Aberg.

Announcer: Johnny Jacobs.

Music: Milton DeLugg.

Executive Producer: Chuck Barris, Chris Bearde.

Director: John Dorsey.

THE GONG SHOW—30 minutes—Syndicated 1976.

GOOBER AND THE GHOST CHASERS

Animated Cartoon. Background: Los Angeles, California. The investigations of Ted, Tina, and Gillie, the staff members of *Ghost Chasers* magazine. Assisted by Goober, a dog who is able to become invisible when he is scared, they incorporate scientific evaluation in their attempt to expose the frauds who perpetrate ghostly occurrences.

Characters' Voices
Goober   Paul Winchell
Ted   Jerry Dexter
Tina   Jo Anne Harris
Gillie   Ronnie Schell
Additional voices: Alan Diehard Jr., Alan Oppenheimer.

Music: Hoyt Curtin.

Executive Producer: William Hanna, Joseph Barbera.

Director: Charles A. Nichols.

GOOBER AND THE GHOST CHASERS—30 minutes—ABC—September 8, 1973 - August 31, 1975. 17 episodes.

GOOD COMPANY

Interview. Celebrities are interviewed in their homes via remote pickup. The format follows that of "Person to Person." Cameras are placed in the homes and the host, seated in the studio, conducts the interview.

Host: F. Lee Bailey, attorney.

Music: Recorded.

GOOD COMPANY—30 minutes—ABC—September 7, 1967 - December 21, 1967.

GOOD DAY!

Talk-Interview. Produced in Boston.

Host: John Willis.

Hostess: Janet Langhart.

Music: Dave Witney.

GOOD DAY!—30 minutes—Syndicated 1976.

THE GOOD GUYS

Comedy. Background: Los Angeles,

California. Seeking to better their lives, Bert Gramus and Rufus Butterworth, life-long friends, pool their resources and purchase a diner. Assisted by Claudia, Bert's wife, they attempt to run "Bert's Place" and live the "good life."

CAST
Rufus Butterworth   Bob Denver
Bert Gramus   Herb Edelman
Claudia Gramus   Joyce Van Patten
Big Tom, Rufus's
  friend, a truck
  driver   Alan Hale
Gertie, Tom's girl-
  friend   Toni Gilman
Hal, a friend   George Furth

Music: Jerry Fielding.

THE GOOD GUYS—30 minutes—CBS—September 25, 1968 - January 23, 1970. 42 episodes.

The Good Guys. Left to right: Herb Edelman, Joyce Van Patten, Bob Denver.

GOOD HEAVENS

Anthology. The series, which presents a different comedy story and cast each week, features Mr. Angel, a celestial messenger whose function on Earth is to fulfill fantasies by granting deserving people one wish.

Starring: Carl Reiner as Mr. Angel.

Music: Pat Williams.

Executive Producer: Carl Reiner.

Producer: Mel Swope, Austin and Irma Kalish.

Director: Carl Reiner, John Erman, Peter Bonerz, Mel Swope, James Sheldon.

Creator: Bernard Slade.

Included:

Everything Money Can't Buy. Doris, a pretty but lonely young waitress, offers her seat on a bus to an elderly man. Observing this, Mr. Angel later appears to her and rewards her with one wish. She chooses and is granted the opportunity to meet "Mr. Right." Complications ensue when her boyfriend becomes jealous and decides to do something about it—prove his love for her.

CAST

Doris: Brenda Vaccaro; Chris Livingston: Bert Convy; Ernie: Peter Bonerz; Ethel: Kristina Holland.

Take Me Out to the Ball Game. When a father-to-be complies with his pregnant wife's desires and goes out late at night to get her tapioca pudding, English muffins, and celery, Mr. Angel rewards him with his dream of a lifetime: the chance to become a professional baseball player.

CAST

Luke Edwards: Rob Reiner; Peggy Edwards: Penny Marshall; Andy Reed: Shelly Novak.

See Jane Run. When the owner of an exclusive boutique refers a customer of limited resources to a less expensive dress shop, Mr. Angel rewards her kind deed by granting her one wish. Her wish: to find her long-lost twin sister.

CAST

Julia and Jane Grey: Florence Henderson; Dick: Edward Winter; Gary Lawrence: George Maharis.

GOOD HEAVENS—30 minutes—ABC—February 29, 1976 - June 24, 1976.

THE GOODIES

Comedy. Background: England. The chaotic misadventures of The Goodies, three men who will do anything at anytime as they attempt to succeed in the business world.

CAST

Graeme Garden	Himself
Tim Brooke-Taylor	Himself
Bill Oddie	Himself

Regulars: Patricia Hayes, Michael Aspel, Milton Reid.

Music: Bill Oddie, Michael Gibbs.

Producer: John Howard Davis.

Director: Jim Franklin.

THE GOODIES—30 minutes—Syndicated 1976.

THE GOOD LIFE

Comedy. Albert and Jane Miller, plagued by life's endless problems and expenses—a home in the process of repair, a broken car, numerous unpaid bills—seek a better life. An idea of how occurs to Al when their car breaks down in the country and they are befriended by a butler. After seeing the mansion and the style in which he lives, Al thinks "maybe there is a better way."

Donning the guise of a butler, and convincing Jane to pose as a cook, the Millers answer an ad for experienced help at the thirty-two room mansion of Charles Dutton, the head of Dutton Industries. They are invited to spend the night in the servant's quarters while they ponder their decision. Jane is hesitant but Al convinces her that they "can fake it." Their fate is sealed when Al quits his job as a stockbroker and sells their house.

Previously overhearing their discussion through an open intercom button, Nick Dutton, Charles's son by his third wife, promises to keep their secret and assist with the masquerade. Stories relate the Miller's struggles to maintain their cover, attend household duties, and enjoy "The Good Life."

CAST

Albert Miller	Larry Hagman
Jane Miller	Donna Mills
Charles Dutton	David Wayne
Grace Dutton, Charles's sister	Hermione Baddeley
Nick Dutton	Danny Goldman

Music: Sacha Distel.

THE GOOD LIFE—30 minutes—NBC—September 18, 1971 - January 8, 1972. 15 episodes.

GOOD MORNING, AMERICA

News-Information. A spin-off from "A.M. America." Broadcast from 7:00 a.m.-9:00 a.m., E.S.T.

Hosts: David Hartman, Nancy Dussault.

Hostess: Sandra Hill (replaced Nancy Dussault).

Regulars: Rona Barrett, Jonathan Winters, John Lindsay, Geraldo Rivera, Jack Anderson, Erma Bombeck, Nena and George O'Neill.

Newscasters: Steve Bell, Margaret Osmer.

Music Theme: Marvin Hamlisch.

GOOD MORNING, AMERICA—2 hours—ABC—Premiered: November 3, 1975.

GOOD MORNING WORLD

Comedy. Background: Los Angeles, California. The home and working lives of disc jockeys Dave Lewis, married, shy, and retiring, and Larry Clark, a swinging young bachelor, the hosts of "The Lewis and Clark Show," a radio program aired from 6-10 A.M.

CAST

Dave Lewis	Joby Baker
Larry Clark	Ronnie Schell
Linda Lewis, Dave's wife	Julie Parrish
Roland B. Hutton, Jr., the station manager	Billy DeWolfe
Sandy, the Lewis's gossipy neighbor	Goldie Hawn

GOOD MORNING WORLD—30 minutes—CBS—September 5, 1967 - September 17, 1968. 26 episodes.

GOOD TIMES

Comedy. Background: A housing project in Chicago. The struggles of the poor black Evans family in rough times when jobs are scarce.

CAST

James Evans, the husband	John Amos
Florida Evans, his wife	Esther Rolle
James Evans, Jr. their oldest son	Jimmie Walker
Thelma Evans, their teenage daughter	BernNadette Stanis
Michael Evans, their son	Ralph Carter
Willona, their friend and neighbor	Ja'net DuBois
Monty, a friend	Stymie Beard

Music: Marilyn Bergman, Alan Bergman, Dave Grusin.

Executive Producer: Norman Lear, Allan Manings.

Producer: George Sunga, Bernie West, Don Nicholl, Austin and Irma Kalish.

Director: Herbert Kenwith, Jack Shea, Gerren Keith.

Creator: Eric Monte, Mike Evans.

The Evans Address: 963 North Gilbert.

GOOD TIMES—30 minutes—CBS—Premiered: February 8, 1974.

GOODYEAR PLAYHOUSE

See title: "Philco Television Playhouse."

THE GOODYEAR SUMMERTIME REVUE

Musical Variety. Summer replacement for "The Paul Whiteman Revue."

Host: Earl Wrightson.

Regulars: Maureen Cannon, The Ray Porter Chorus.

Orchestra: Glenn Osser.

Producer: Richard Eckler, William H. Brown, Jr.

Director: William H. Brown, Jr.

Sponsor: Goodyear Products.

THE GOODYEAR SUMMERTIME REVUE—30 minutes—ABC—July 1951 - August 1951.

GOODYEAR THEATRE

Anthology. Rebroadcasts of dramas that were originally aired via "The General Electric Theatre."

Included:

You Should Meet My Sister. Adapted from the movie *My Sister Eileen.* Leaving their home in Ohio, sisters Ruth and Eileen Sherwood arrive in New York to further their careers. While Ruth pursues her career as a writer, the city's eligible males pursue would-be actress Eileen.

CAST
Elaine Stritch, Anne Helm, Joey Forman.

Squeeze Play. A truck driver attempts to prove that he is not guilty of an accident caused by a speeding white car with only one headlight.

CAST
Dick Shannon, William Campbell.

Marked Down For Connie. The story of Connie Peters, a salesgirl who decides to drum up extra business for the department store by advertising cut-rate cuckoo clocks.

CAST
Elinor Donahue, Tony Travis, Howard McNair.

GOODYEAR THEATRE—30 minutes—NBC—July 1960 - September 1960.

THE GORDON MacRAE SHOW

Musical Variety.

Host: Gordon MacRae.

Vocalists: The Cheerleaders.

Orchestra: Van Alexander.

THE GORDON MacRAE SHOW—60 minutes—NBC—March 5, 1956, - August 27, 1956.

THE GOURMET

Cooking. The preparation and cooking of gourmet meals.

Host: David Wade—"The Rembrandt of the Kitchen, the Edison of the cookbook. . . ."

Announcer: Jack Harrison.

Music: Recorded.

THE GOURMET—30 minutes—Syndicated 1969.

THE GOURMET CLUB

Cooking. Step-by-step methods in the preparation of gourmet meals.

Hostess: Dione Lucas.

Assisting: Guest celebrities.

THE GOURMET CLUB—30 minutes—Syndicated 1958.

GO—U.S.A.

Anthology. Dramatizations based on legendary folk heroes and heroines.

Music: Robert Maxwell.

Producer: George Heinemann, Chris Schwartz, Langbourne Rust.

Director: J. Philip Miller.

Included:

River Raft. The story of a poor family and their attempts to begin a new life in Kentucky.

CAST
Ruth Baxter: Lenke Peterson; Mark Baxter: David Dean; Sarah Baxter: Susan Jayne Jacoby; Grace Baxter: Susan Lawrence.

Deborah Sampson. The story of a girl who, disguised as a boy, enlists in the Confederate army.

CAST
Deborah Sampson: Maggi Low; Mrs. Sampson: Ruth Hunt.

Frostbite. The story of a veteran soldier and a raw recruit and their attempts to haul a cannon from Albany, N.Y. to Boston to aide General George Washington.

CAST
Amos: Mike Kellin; Tom: Daniel Tamm.

GO—U.S.A.—30 minutes—NBC—September 6, 1975 - September 4, 1976.

GOVERNMENT STORY

Documentary. The history and operation of the U.S. Federal Government is detailed through films and interviews.

Narrators: E. G. Marshall, Paul Long.

Music: Recorded.

GOVERNMENT STORY—30 minutes—Syndicated 1969.

THE GOVERNOR AND J.J.

Comedy. Background: A small, unidentified Midwestern state. The story of its governor, William Drinkwater, a widower, and his twenty-three-year-old daughter, his first lady, Jennifer Jo (J.J.), the curator of the local children's zoo, a woman who possesses the uncanny knack for getting him into and out of political hot water.

CAST
Governor William Drinkwater	Dan Dailey
Jennifer Jo Drinkwater	Julie Sommars
George Callison, the governor's press secretary	James Callahan
Maggie McCloud, the governor's secretary	Neva Patterson
Sara, the housekeeper	Nora Marlowe

Music: Jerry Fielding.

THE GOVERNOR AND J.J.—30 minutes—CBS—September 23, 1969 - January 6, 1971. Rebroadcasts: CBS—June 1, 1972 - August 11, 1972. 39 episodes.

GRADY

Comedy. Background: 636 Carlyle Street, Santa Monica, California, the residence of the Marshall family: parents Ellie and Hal, their children Laurie and Hayward, and Ellie's father, Grady Wilson. Stories relate Grady's misadventures, living with his family. A spin-off from "Sanford and Son."

CAST

Grady Wilson	Whitman Mayo
Ellie Marshall	Carol Cole
Hal Marshall	Joe Morton
Laurie Marshall	Rosanne Katon
Haywood Marshall	Haywood Nelson
Mr. Pratt, the landlord	Jack Fletcher

Music: John Addison.

Executive Producer: Saul Turteltaub, Bernie Orenstein.

Producer: Jerry Ross.

Director: Gerren Keith.

GRADY—30 minutes—NBC—December 4, 1975 - March 4, 1976.

THE GRAND JURY

Crime Drama. Case dramatizations based on the files of the Los Angeles Grand Jury. Episodes depict the work of Harry Driscoll, an ex-F.B.I. agent, and his partner John Kennedy, Grand Jury investigators.

CAST

Harry Driscoll	Lyle Bettger
John Kennedy	Harold J. Stone
Grand Jury investigator	Richard Travis
Grand Jury investigator	Douglas Dumbrille

Program Open; Announcer: "The forework of liberty, protecting the inalienable rights of free people, serving unstintingly and without prejudice to maintain the laws of our land, the Grand Jury."

THE GRAND JURY—30 minutes—Syndicated 1958. 39 episodes.

THE GRAND OLE OPRY

Musical Variety. Performances by Country and Western entertainers.

Host: Red Foley.

Regulars: Judy Lynn, Les Paul and Mary Ford, Hank Snow, Chet Atkins, Minnie Pearl, Ernest Tubb, Jimmy Dickens, Goldie Hull, Cal Smith, Lonzo and Oscar, The Lovin' Brothers, The Grand Ole Opry Square Dancers.

THE GRAND OLE OPRY—60 minutes—ABC—October 15, 1955 - September 15, 1956.

THE GRAY GHOST

Adventure. Background: Virginia during the Civil War, 1860s. In a desperate attempt to infiltrate the Confederacy, the Union army recruits a woman spy. However, she becomes a double agent when she reveals their plans to Confederate Major John Singleton Mosby.

Returning, she is exposed, apprehended, and sentenced to death by the Union. Learning of her fate, Mosby affects a dramatic raid on the Union camp and rescues her. He is proclaimed their enemy—The Gray Ghost.

Episodes depict Mosby's daring and cunning raids against the Union army in the hopes of fostering a Confederate victory.

CAST

Major John Mosby	Tod Andrews
Lieutenant Saint Clair	Phil Chambridge

THE GRAY GHOST—30 minutes—Syndicated 1957. 39 episodes.

GREAT ADVENTURE

Anthology. Dramatizations of events that shaped America's past.

Narrator: Van Heflin.

Included:

The Testing Of Sam Houston. The early years of his life from his days as lieutenant under Andrew Jackson through the start of his political life.

CAST

Sam Houston: Robert Culp; Andrew Jackson: Victor Jory.

Six Wagons To Sea. Background: California. Using a horse-drawn wagon, a raisin grower attempts to deliver his crop to San Francisco against railroad objections.

CAST

Misok Bedrozian: Lee Marvin; Mercer: Gene Lyons; Elissa: Ellen Madison.

The Story Of Nathan Hale. Era: The American Revolution. The events leading to the conviction and hanging of Nathan Hale, found guilty of spying.

CAST

Nathan Hale: Jeremy Slate; Jenny: Nancy Malone.

GREAT ADVENTURE—60 minutes—CBS—September 23, 1963 - May 8, 1964. 26 episodes.

GREAT ADVENTURE

Travel. Films exploring various areas around the world.

Host-Narrator: Jim Dooley.

GREAT ADVENTURE—60 minutes—Syndicated 1972.

GREAT ADVENTURES

Travel. Films exploring various areas around the world.

Host-Narrator: Ray Forrest.

GREAT ADVENTURES—30 minutes—Syndicated 1958. Canadian title: "Adventure Theatre."

THE GREAT AMERICAN DREAM MACHINE

Satire. A television magazine format designed "to make significant statements about the good and bad trends in our society." A satirization of everyday life from true love, to politics, to purchasing a frozen dinner at the supermarket.

Semiregulars: Marshall Efron, Ken Shapiro, Chevy Chase, Lee Meredith, Nicholas Van Hoffman, Andrew Rooney, Robert Townsend.

THE GREAT AMERICAN DREAM MACHINE—60 minutes—PBS—October 6, 1971 - February 9, 1972.

GREAT BANDS

Music: The re-created sound of the Big Band Era.

Host: Paul Whiteman, the Dean of American Music.

Appearing, with their orchestras: Xavier Cugat, Gene Krupa, Johnny Long, Ralph Marterie, Buddy Rogers, Percy Faith.

GREAT BANDS—60 minutes—CBS June 23, 1955 - September 24, 1955.

THE GREATEST GIFT

Serial. The dramatic story of a woman

doctor, who, after serving as a nurse in Korea, returns home to assume control of her late uncle's practice. Ultimately, she must decide whether to remain there or fulfill her desire for a large, city practice.

CAST

Dr. Eve Allen	Ann Burr
Dr. Phil Stone	Philip Foster
Lee Connor	Marion Russell
Peter Blake	Henry Barnard
Sam Drake	Josef Draper
Mrs. Blake	Helen Warren
Johnny Ryan	Peter Avramo
Capt. Jameson	Marvin Stephens
John Leeds	Henry Hamilton
	Winston Ross
Jim Hanson	Jack Klugman
Mrs. Eddy	Jean Mann
Nicky Randall	Bill Mason
	Arny Freeman
Joe	Hugh Thomas
Stubby	Lee Saunders
Emily	Joanna Ross
Judge Parker	Bob Allen
Fran Allen	Janet Ward
Virginia Deering	Mary Finney
Ned Blackman	Ward Costello
Arthur	Frank Maxwell
Dick Steele	Woody Parker
Martha	Doris Rich
Lillian	Mary K. Wells
Harriet	Anne Meara
Harold Matthews	Martin Balsam
Martin Beal	Allen Stevenson

Creator: Adrian Samish.

THE GREATEST GIFT—15 minutes —NBC—August 30, 1954 - September 28, 1954.

THE GREATEST MAN ON EARTH

Game. Tested: Male superiority. Five men compete for the title "The Greatest Man." Each contestant is nominated by five women who assist him in various stunts and question-answer rounds. One couple is eliminated in each round. Winners are the last remaining couple.

Host: Ted Brown.

Assistant: Pat Conway.

THE GREATEST MAN ON EARTH —30 minutes—ABC—December 3, 1952 - December 31, 1952.

THE GREATEST SHOW ON EARTH

Drama. Background: The Ringling Brothers Barnum and Bailey Circus. Stories dramatize the problems of the circus performers, and the struggles endured in presenting "The Greatest Show on Earth."

CAST

Johnny Slate, the working boss	Jack Palance
Otto King, the business manager	Stu Erwin

Music: Jeff Alexander.

THE GREATEST SHOW ON EARTH —60 minutes—ABC—September 17, 1963 - September 8, 1964. Syndicated. 30 episodes.

GREAT GHOST TALES

Anthology. Mystery and suspense presentations.

Host: Frank Gallop.

Included:

William Wilson. The story of a man plagued by his exact double— a man out to kill him.

CAST

William Wilson: Robert Duval; Whispers: Peter Brandon.

Lucy. The story of an actress who discovers a strange talent—what she wishes for comes true.

CAST

Lucy Morrison: Lee Grant. Also: Kevin McCarthy.

Shredni Vashtar. The tale of a young boy, Conradin, and his pet ferret, Shredni Vashtar.

Starring: Richard Thomas as Conradin.

GREAT GHOST TALES—30 minutes —NBC—July 6, 1961 - September 1961.

THE GREAT GILDERSLEEVE

Comedy. Background: The town of Summerfield, 217 Elm Street, the residence of Throckmorton P. "The Great" Gildersleeve, the water commissioner, and his wards, his orphaned niece and nephew, Marjorie and Leroy Forrestor. Stories relate the home, working, and romantic life of the bachelor uncle of two children. Based on the radio program of the same title.

CAST

Throckmorton P. Gildersleeve (Gildy)	Willard Waterman
Marjorie Forrestor	Stephanie Griffin
Leroy Forrestor	Ronald Keith
Leila Ransom, Gildersleeve's former girlfriend, a Southern belle eagerly awaiting his marriage proposal	Shirley Mitchell
Lois, Gildersleeve's girl-friend	Doris Singleton
Birdie Lee Coggins, the Gildersleeve house-keeper	Lillian Randolph
Judge Hooker, Gildy's nemesis	Earle Ross
Peavey, the druggist	Forrest Lewis

Music: Jack Meakin.

THE GREAT GILDERSLEEVE—30 minutes—NBC—1955 - 1956. 39 episodes.

THE GREAT GRAPE APE SHOW

Animated Cartoon. The misadventures of a forty-foot purple gorilla (the Grape Ape) and his friend Beegle Beagle, the fast-talking dog.

Voices: Lennie Weinrib, Henry Corden, Bob Holt, Paul Winchell, Joan Gerber, Alan Oppenheimer, Don Messick, Daws Butler, Marty Ingels.

Music: Hoyt Curtin, Paul DeKorte.

Executive Producer: William Hanna, Joseph Barbera.

Producer: Iwao Takamoto.

Director: Charles A. Nichols.

THE GREAT GRAPE APE SHOW— 30 minutes—ABC—Premiered: September 11, 1977.

THE GREAT MOVIE COWBOYS

Movies. A television revival featuring the rarely broadcast western theatrical films of the 1930s and 40s.

Host: Roy Rogers.

Featured Film Performers: Tex Ritter, Roy Rogers, Dale Evans, John Wayne, Gene Autry, Bob Steele, Gabby Hayes.

Music: Recorded open and close.

Producer: Tele Scene, Inc.

Director (of Roy Rogers segment): Bruce Fox.

THE GREAT MOVIE COWBOYS—60 minutes—Syndicated 1977. Originally conceived under the title "Cowboy Classics."

THE GREAT TALENT HUNT

See title: "Henry Morgan."

THE GREAT WAR

Documentary. A filmed history of British and American participation in the Second World War.

Host-Narrator: Sir Michael Redgrave.

THE GREAT WAR—30 minutes—Syndicated 1964.

GREEN ACRES

Comedy. Yearning to be a farmer all his life, attorney Oliver Wendell Douglas purchases, sight unseen, the 160-acre Haney farm in Hooterville. Much to the objections of his glamorous and sophisticated wife, Lisa, they relinquish their life of luxury in New York City, and retreat to a shabby, broken-down, unfurnished nightmare—Oliver's Green Acres dream.

Agreeing only to try farm life for six months, Lisa has a change of heart after discovering that their cow, Elinor, and chicken, Alice will be destroyed when they leave. Stories relate the struggles of two city slickers as they attempt to cope with the numerous trials and tribulations of farming and country living.

CAST

Oliver Douglas	Eddie Albert
Lisa Douglas	Eva Gabor
Eb Dawson, their handyman	Tom Lester
Mr. Haney, a conniving salesman	Pat Buttram
Hank Kimball, the agricultural representative	Alvy Moore
Fred Ziffel, a pig farmer	Hank Patterson
Doris Ziffel, his wife	Fran Ryan Barbara Pepper
Sam Drucker, the general store owner	Frank Cady
Newt Kiley, a farmer	Kay E. Kuter
Alf Monroe, a carpenter hired by Oliver to repair their house	Sid Melton
Ralph Monroe, his partner (his sister)	Mary Grace Canfield
Joe Carson, the Shady Rest Hotel Manager	Edgar Buchanan
Unis Douglas, Oliver's mother	Eleanor Audley
Darlene, Eb's girl-friend	Judy McConnell
Brian Williams, Oliver's partner in his Hooterville law office	Rick Lenz
Mr. Wheeler, Darlene's father	Robert Foulk
Roy Trendell, a farmer (early episodes)	Robert Foulk
Sarah, the telephone operator	Merie Earle
Lori Baker, the girl who spent the summer with the Douglases	Victoria Meyerink

Also: Arnold the Pig, Fred Ziffel's intelligent pet pig, the animal considerd to be his son.

Music: Vic Mizzy.

Music Supervision: Dave Kahn.

Executive Producer: Paul Henning.

Producer-Creator: Jay Sommers.

Director: Richard L. Bare (the entire series, except for one episode that was directed by Ralph Levy).

GREEN ACRES—30 minutes—CBS—September 15, 1965 - September 7, 1971. Syndicated. 170 episodes.

THE GREEN HORNET

Adventure. Background: Washington, D.C. Building the *Daily Sentinel* into America's greatest publication, editor Dan Reid turns over the management of the paper to his playboy bachelor son, Britt, hoping the responsibility will mature him, and hires an ex-cop, Mike Axford to secretly watch over Britt's activities.

Instilled with his father's goal, Britt, like his great-grand-uncle, John Reid (the Lone Ranger), undertakes a crusade to protect the rights and lives of decent citizens. Adopting the guise of the Green Hornet (the symbol of the insect that is the most deadly when aroused) he establishes a base in an abandoned building, and reveals his true identity to only three people— Kato, his Oriental houseboy; Frank Scanlon, the district attorney; and his secretary, Lenore Case.

Considered criminal and wanted by police, the Green Hornet and Kato avenge crimes as semifugitives rather than as a law-enforcement organization, always disappearing before authorities take over. Based on the radio program of the same title.

CAST

Britt Reid/The Green Hornet	Van Williams
Kato	Bruce Lee
Lenore Case (Casey)	Wende Wagner

The Green Hornet. Left to right: Bruce Lee, Beth Brickell (guest), Van Williams.

Frank Scanlon	Walter Brooke
Mike Axford	Lloyd Gough
The D.A.'s secretary	Sheila Leighton

The Hornet's mode of transportation: The *Black Beauty*.

Announcer: Gary Owens.

Music: Billy May.

THE GREEN HORNET—30 minutes—ABC—September 9, 1966 - July 14, 1967. Syndicated. 26 episodes.

GRIFF

Crime Drama. Background: Los Angeles, California. The investigations of Wade "Griff" Griffin, a former police captain turned private detective.

CAST

Wade Griffin	Lorne Greene
Mike Murdoch, his partner	Ben Murphy
Gracie Newcombe, their secretary	Patricia Stich
Police Captain Barney Marcus	Vic Tayback

Music: Elliot Kaplan; Mike Post, Pete Carpenter.

GRIFF—60 minutes—ABC—September 29, 1973 — January 4, 1974. 12 episodes.

GRINDL

Comedy. Background: New York City. The misadventures of Grindl, a maid with the Foster Employment Agency. Stories depict her attempts to successfully complete her assigned duties.

CAST

Grindl   Imogene Coca
Anson Foster, her
    employer   James.Millhollin

GRINDL—30 minutes—NBC—September 15, 1963 - September 13, 1964. 32 episodes.

THE GROOVIE GOOLIES

Animated Cartoon. Background: Horrible Hall, an ancient, spider-web-covered castle. The antics of its residents, the Groovie Goolies, practical-joke playing, musically inclined creatures who resemble celluloid monsters of the 1930s and 40s.

Characters: Frankenstein, Dracula, the Mummy, the Werewolf, Bella, the female Vampire, the two-headed Dr. Jekyll and Mr. Hyde, witches, warlocks, and walking and talking skeletons.

Voices: Larry Storch, Don Messick, Howard Morris, Jane Webb, Dallas McKennon, John Erwin.

Music: The Horta-Mahana Corporation.

THE GROOVIE GOOLIES—30 minutes—CBS—September 12, 1971 - September 17, 1972.

THE GROUCHO SHOW

See title: "You Bet Your Life."

GRUEN THEATRE

Anthology. Varying presentations, including drama, comedy, and fantasy.

Producer: Leon Fromkess for Revue Productions.

Director: Richard Irving.

Sponsor: Gruen Watches.

GRUEN THEATRE—30 minutes—ABC 1951.

GUESS AGAIN

Game. Three competing contestants are assisted by three guest celebrities. A skit is performed on a stage by a repertoire company. Contestants, through its clues, have to answer questions related to it.

Host: Mike Wallace.

Repertory Company: Joey Faye, Mandy Kaye, Bobbie Martin.

Producer: Al Span.

Director: Jerry Schnurr.

GUESS AGAIN—30 minutes—CBS 1951.

GUESS WHAT?

Game. Four celebrity panelists compete. The host relates short quotations or statements that refer to a famous person, place, or thing. Panelists, who are permitted to ask "yes" or "no" type questions, have to identify the subject within an allotted time limit. A cash prize, which is donated to charity, is awarded for each correct identification.

Host: Dick Kollmar.

Panelists: Virginia Peine, Quenton Reynolds, Mark Hanna, Cliff Norton, Audrey Christie, Lisa Fenaday.

GUESS WHAT?—30 minutes—Dumont—July 8, 1952 - September 1952.

GUESS WHAT HAPPENED?

Game. Object: For a panel to discover via question-answer probe rounds the stories behind their guests—people involved in unusual news stories.

Hosts: John Cameron Swayze; Ben Grauer.

Panelists: Neva Patterson, Roger Price, H. Allen Smith, Maureen Stapleton, Frank Gallop, Jack Norton.

GUESS WHAT HAPPENED?—30 minutes—NBC 1952.

A GUEST IN YOUR HOUSE

Variety.

Host: Edgar Guest.

Assistant: Rachel Stevenson.

Guitar Accompaniment: Paul Arnold.

A GUEST IN YOUR HOUSE—15 minutes—NBC 1951.

GUEST SHOT

Interview. Films revealing little-known aspects of Hollywood celebrities.

Hosts—Interviewers: Army Archard,

Vernon Scott, Earl Wilson, Joe Hyams, Hank Grant, Dan Jenkins.

Appearing: Jayne Mansfield, demonstrating her physical fitness program; Tina Louise, doing gymnastics; Rod Cameron, sailing his forty-two-foot Ketch; Jeffrey Hunter, skiing; Mamie Van Doren, motorcycling; Fess Parker, playing polo; Monique Van Vooren, ice skating; Robert Horton, flying; Fabian Forte, lion hunting.

GUEST SHOT—30 minutes—two fifteen minute segments—Syndicated 1962. Withdrawn.

GUESTWARD HO

Comedy. Dissatisfied with life in New York, advertising executive Bill Hootin purchases Guestward Ho, a dude ranch in New Mexico. Stories relate the attempts of he and his family—his wife, Babs, and their son, Brook—to adjust to new responsibilities and acquire paying customers.

Guestward Ho. Left to right: Mark Miller, J. Carroll Naish, Joanne Dru, Earl Hodgins.

CAST

Bill Hootin   Mark Miller
Babs Hootin   Joanne Dru
Brook Hootin   Flip Mark
Chief Hawkeye, the owner
    of the local trading post;
    an Indian on a campaign to
    win back the American
    continent for his
    people   J. Carrol Naish
Lonesome, their
    wrangler   Earl Hodgins
Pink Cloud, Hawkeye's
    assistant   Jolene Brand

Rocky, a friend   Tony Montenaro

GUESTWARD HO–30 minutes–ABC–September 29, 1960 - September 21, 1961. Syndicated. 38 episodes.

THE GUIDING LIGHT

Serial. Background: The town of Springfield. The dramatic story of the Bauer family. Episodes relate the conflicts and tensions that arise from the interactions of the characters.

CAST

Papa Bauer	Theo Goetz
Dr. Edward Bauer	Martin Hulswit
	Robert Gentry
Michael	Glenn Walker
	Michael Allen
	Garry Pillar
	Bob Pickering
	Don Stewart
Meta Roberts	Ellen Demming
Mark Holden	Whitfield Connor
Anne Benedict	Joan Gray
Dr. Paul Fletcher	Bernard Grant
Susan Carver	Judy Lewis
Leslie Jackson	Barbara Rodell
	Lynne Adams
Bertha Bauer	Charita Bauer
Don Peters	Paul Gallantyne
Dick	James Lypton
Kathy	Susan Douglas
Joe Roberts	Herb Nelson
George Hayes	Philip Sterling
Jane Hayes	Chase Crosley
Tracy Delmar	Victoria Wyndham
Dianah Buckley	Courtney Sherman
Kit Vested	Nancie Addison
Dr. Sara McIntyre	Millette Alexander
	Patricia Roe
Barbara Norris	Barbara Berjer
Deborah Mehren	Olivia Cole
Holly Norris	Lynn Deerfield
	Maureen Garrett
Peter Wexler	Michael Durrell
Charlotte Waring	Melinda Fee
David Vested	Dan Hamilton
Marion Conway	Kate Harrington
Hope Bauer	Elissa Leeds
	Robin Matson
Janet Mason	Caroline McWilliams
Peggy Dillman Fletcher	Fran Myers
Ken Norris	Roger Newman
Linell Conway	Christine Pickles
Stanley Norris	William Smithers
Dr. Stephen Jackson	Stefan Schnabel
Karen Martin	Tudi Wiggins
Roger Thorpe	Mike Zaslow
Dr. Joe Werner	Ed Zimmerman
	Anthony Call
Ellen Mason	Jeanne Arnold
Gil Mehren	David Pendleton
Flip Malone	Paul Carpinelli
Mrs. Herbert	Rosetta LeNoire
Baby Fred Fletcher	Albert Zungalo III
Baby Billy Fletcher	James Long

Adam Thorpe	Robert Milli
Marie Wallace Grant	Lynne Rogers
Dr. John Fletcher	Don Scardino
	Erik Howell
Betty Eiler	Madeline Sherwood
Charles Eiler	Graham Jarvis
Captain Jim Swanson	Lee Richardson
Dr. Bruce Banning	Barnard Hughes
	Les Damon
	Sideny Walker
	Bill Roerick
Bill Bauer	Lyle Surdow
	Ed Bryce
Dr. Jim Frazier	James Earl Jones
Martha Frazier	Cecily Tyson
	Ruby Dee
Claudia Dillman	Grace Matthews
Ann Fletcher	Elizabeth Hubbard
Alex Bowden	Ernest Graves
	Tom Klunis
Helene Benedict	Kay Campbell
Sir Clayton Olds	Myles Easton
Karl	Richard Morse
Victoria Ballinger	Carol Teitel
Lincoln Yates	Peter MacLean
Trudy Bauer	Actress Unknown
Dr. Wilson Frost	Jack Bels
Robin Holden	Zina Bethune
	Gillian Spencer
Tom Baldwin	Don Chastain
Viola Stapleton	Sudie Bond
	Kate Wilkinson
Peggy Thorpe	Fran Myers
Ken Norris	Roger Newman
Johnny Fletcher	Don Scardino
	Erik Howell
Dr. Steve Jackson	Stefan Schnabel
Pam Chandler	Maureen Silliman
Billie Fletcher	Shane Nickerson
Dr. Tim Ryan	Jordan Clarke
T.J. Werner	T.J. Hargrave
Andrew Norris	Barney McFadden
Chad Richards	Everett McGill
Ben McFarren	Stephen Yates
Eve Stapleton	Janet Grey
Justin Marlen	Tom O'Rourke
Rita Stapleton	Lenore Kasdorf
Maureen Mooney	Anne Jeffreys

Also: Betty Lou Gerson, Jone Allison, Willard Waterman, Ned LeFeore, Sandy Dennis, Adelaide Klein, Joseph Campanella, Diana Hyland, Ethel Everett, Charles Baxter, Carl Low, Anthony Call, Eric Howell, Sydney Walker, Kathryn Hays.

Announcer: Hal Simms.

Music: Charles Paul.

Additional Music: Mi-Viox.

Creator: Irna Phillips.

THE GUIDING LIGHT–15 and 30 minute versions--CBS–Premiered: June 30, 1952.

GULF PLAYHOUSE

Anthology. Dramatic presentations.

Producer: Frank Telford.

Sponsor: The Gulf Oil Corporation.

GULF PLAYHOUSE–30 minutes–NBC 1952.

GUMBY

Children. Background: Scotty McKee's Fun Shop. The misadventures of a boy, Gumby, and his horse, Pokey–animated clay figures.

Host (portraying Scotty McKee): Bob Nicholson.

GUMBY–30 minutes–NBC–March 23, 1957 - November 16, 1957. 66 five minute episodes, which are syndicated.

GUNSLINGER

Western. Background: Fort Scott in Los Flores, New Mexico, 1860s. The story of Cord, a United States Cavalry undercover agent who poses as a gunslinger. Episodes depict his attempts to apprehend criminals wanted by the army.

CAST

Cord	Tony Young
Captain Zachary Scott, the Commanding Officer	Preston Foster
Amber Hollister, Cord's romantic interest	Midge Ware
Pico McGuire, an undercover agent	Charles Gray
Billy Urchin, an undercover agent	Dee Pollock
Murdock, an undercover agent	John Pickard

Music: Dimitri Tiomkin.

GUNSLINGER–60 minutes–CBS–February 9, 1961 - September 5, 1961. 12 episodes.

THE GUNS OF WILL SONNETT

Western. Background: Wyoming during the 1880s. The travels of ex-cavalry scout Will Sonnett and his twenty-year-old grandson, Jeff, as they seek to find James Sonnett, Jeff's father, a wanted gunman and killer who deserted his family during the 1860s.

CAST

Will Sonnett	Walter Brennan

Jeff Sonnett	Dack Rambo
James Sonnett	Jason Evers

THE GUNS OF WILL SONNETT—30 minutes—ABC—September 8, 1967 - September 15, 1969. Syndicated. 50 episodes.

GUNSMOKE

Western. Background: Dodge City, Kansas during the 1880s. A realistic and tensely dramatic series that focuses on the lives and experiences of five people: Matt Dillon, a dauntless and fearless United States Marshal; Kitty Russell, proprietress of the Longbranch Saloon, a woman with a heart of gold and eyes for Matt; Chester Goode, Matt's deputy, a man who walks with a limp and "brews a mean pot of coffee" (half-hour episodes); Galen Adams, the kindly and dedicated physician; and Festus Haggen, the comic relief, Matt's unkempt, hillbilly deputy (hour episodes).

CAST

Marshal Matt Dillon	James Arness
Kitty Russell	Amanda Blake
Dr. Galen Adams (Doc)	Milburn Stone
Chester Goode	Dennis Weaver
Festus Haggen	Ken Curtis
Newly O'Brien, the gunsmith	Buck Taylor
Sam, the Longbranch bartender	Glenn Strange
	Robert Brubaker
Quint Asper, the blacksmith	Burt Reynolds

Gunsmoke. Left to right: James Arness, Burt Reynolds, Milburn Stone, Amanda Blake, Ken Curtis.

Nathan Burke, the freight agent	Ted Jordan
Hank Patterson, the stableman	Hank Patterson
Thad Greenwood, a friend of Matt's	Roger Ewing
Mr. Jones, the general-store owner	Dabbs Greer
Barney, the telegraph operator	Charles Seel
Ma Smalley, the owner of the Dodge City Boarding House	Sarah Selby
Mr. Bodkin, the town banker	Roy Roberts
Howie, the hotel clerk	Howard Culver
Percy Crump, the town undertaker	John Harper
Lathrop, the store-keeper	Woody Chambliss
Halligan, a friend of Matt's	Charles Wagenheim
Ed O'Connor, a rancher	Tod Brown
Louis Pheeters, the town drunk	James Nusser
Dr. John Chapman	Pat Hingle
Miss Hannah, the owner of the saloon after Kitty	Fran Ryan

Matt's horse: Marshal.

Festus's mule: Ruth.

Music: Richard Shores; John Parker.

Additional Music: Jerrold Immel.

Executive Producer: John Mantley.

Producer: Norman MacDonnell, Philip Leacock, Edgar Peterson.

Announcer: George Walsh.

GUNSMOKE—30 and 60 minute versions—CBS—September 10, 1955 - September 1, 1975. Syndicated. 233 half-hour episodes; 400 hour. Half-hour episodes are also known as "Marshal Dillon."

GUY LOMBARDO

Listed: The television programs of orchestra leader Guy Lombardo.

Guy Lombardo And His Royal Canadians—Musical Variety—30 minutes—Syndicated—1954 - 1956.

Host: Guy Lombardo.

Regulars: Lebert Lombardo, Carmen Lombardo, Victor Lombardo, Kenny Gardner, Bill Flannigan, Toni Arden.

Orchestra: The Royal Canadians.

Guy Lombardo's Diamond Jubilee—Musical Variety—CBS 1956.

Host: Guy Lombardo.

Regulars: Lebert Lombardo, Carmen Lombardo, Victor Lombardo.

Orchestra: The Royal Canadians.

Featured Segment: "The Song of Your Life." Letters sent in by home viewers describe how certain songs influenced their lives. The authors of selected songs receive one thousand dollars, appear on stage, and, as an off-stage voice reads the letter, the song is played in the background.

A New Year's Eve Party With Guy Lombardo—Annually—90 minutes. Stations vary, broadcast both by networks and on a syndicated basis. Guy, his Royal Canadians Orchestra, and guests ring out the old and welcome in the new. Began on radio in 1930.

THE GUY MITCHELL SHOW

Musical Variety.

Host: Guy Mitchell.

Regulars: The Guy Mitchell Singers, The Ted Cappy Dancers.

Orchestra: Van Alexander.

THE GUY MITCHELL SHOW—30 minutes—NBC—October 7, 1957 - January 13, 1958.

GYPSY ROSE LEE

Listed: The television programs of actress Gypsy Rose Lee.

The Gypsy Rose Lee Show—Talk-Variety—90 minutes—Syndicated 1958.

Hostess: Gypsy Rose Lee.

Regulars: Earl Wrightson, Stan Freeman, Mary Ellen Terry.

Gypsy—Talk-Variety—30 minutes—Syndicated 1966.

Hostess: Gypsy Rose Lee.

Music: Recorded.

ℋ

HAGGIS BAGGIS

Game. Four competing contestants. Object: The identification of concealed photographs. Contestants, one at a time, pick a category from a large board. The host reads a related question that, if correctly answered, will enable the player to see a small portion of the photograph. Winners are the players with the most number of correct identifications. With the runner-up, he receives a choice of one of two sets of prizes: The Haggis (Luxury) or the Baggis (Utility). The champion secretly locks in his choice; the runner-up chooses verbally. If his choice matches he loses and receives nothing; if he selects the other, he receives the prizes.

Hosts (afternoon version): Fred Robbins; Bert Parks.

Hosts (evening version): Jack Linkletter; Dennis James.

Assistant: Lillian Naud.

HAGGIS BAGGIS—30 minutes—NBC. Evening version: June 20, 1958 - September 20, 1958; Afternoon (daily): June 30, 1958 - June 19, 1959.

HAIL THE CHAMP

Game. Six children chosen from the studio audience compete in various original athletic stunts. The winners are crowned "Champ of the Week" and receive accompanying prizes.

Hosts: Herb Allen; Howard Roberts.

Assistants: Angel Casey; Jim Andelin.

HAIL THE CHAMP—30 minutes—ABC—September 22, 1951 - June 13, 1953.

HALF-HOUR THEATRE

Anthology. Dramatic presentations.

Included:

The Housekeeper. The story of a psychiatrist who believes that he has found a cure for neurotics.

CAST
Albert Dekker, Dorothy Adams.

Foo Young. A Chinese detective attempts to clear an innocent man accused of murder.

CAST
Richard Loo, Ed Gargan, Iris Adrian.

When The Devil Is Sick. The story of a man who believes he has only a short time to live and resolves to reform.

CAST
Larry Blake, Dorothy Adams.

HALF-HOUR THEATRE—30 minutes—ABC—June 19, 1953 - September 25, 1953.

HALF THE GEORGE KIRBY COMEDY HOUR

Variety. Sketches coupled with music and songs.

Host: George Kirby.

Regulars: Connie Martin, Jack Duffy, Julie Amato, Steve Martin, Joey Hollingsworth, The Walter Painter Dancers.

Orchestra: Hank Marr.

HALF THE GEORGE KIRBY COMEDY HOUR—30 minutes—Syndicated 1972.

THE HALLMARK HALL OF FAME

Anthology. Classical and serious dramas, period plays, and musical adaptations.

Hostess-Performer-Narrator (early years): Sarah Churchill.

Frequently Cast: Julie Harris, Dame Judith Anderson, Maurice Evans.

Included:

The Country Girl. The story of three people: Frank Elgin, a matinee idol drowning in self pity and alcohol; Georgie, his long-suffering wife; and Bernie Dodd, an ambitious film director.

CAST
Frank Elgin: Jason Robards; Georgie Elgin: Shirley Knight Hopkins; Bernie Dodd: George Grizzard.

The Littlest Angel. A musical adaptation of Charles Tazewell's Christmas story about a boy's attempts to adjust to heaven.

CAST
Michael: Johnnie Whitaker; Patience: Fred Gwynne; God: E.G. Marshall; Gabriel: Cab Calloway; Angel of Peace: John McGiver; Flying Mistress: Connie Stevens.

Brief Encounter. Noel Coward's play about two married strangers who meet by chance and fall in love.

CAST
Anna Jesson: Sophia Loren (her American TV debut); Alec Harvey: Richard Burton; Mrs. Gaines: Rosemary Leach.

Give Us Barabbas. A period drama that explores the reason for Pontius Pilate's decision to free the thief, Barabbas, and crucify Jesus Christ. The story also explains the evaluation of Barabbas "from a cold criminal to a man of awakening conscience."

CAST
Barabbas: James Daly; Pontius Pilate: Dennis King; Mara: Kim Hunter.

THE HALLMARK HALL OF FAME —90 minutes to 2 hours (depending on the production)—NBC—Premiered: December 24, 1951.

THE HALLS OF IVY

Comedy. Background: Number One Faculty Row of Ivy College in Ivy, U.S.A., the residence of Professor William Todhunter Hall, the president, and his wife, Vicky. Stories relate the incidents that befall a mythical college, its students, and its faculty.

CAST
Dr. William Todhunter Hall	Ronald Colman
Vicky Hall, a former stage performer, Victoria Cromwell	Benita Hume
Alice, their housekeeper	Mary Wickes
Clarence Wellman, the Chairman of the Board of Ivy College	Herb Butterfield
Mrs. Wellman, his wife	Sarah Selby
Professor Warren	Arthur Q. Bryan

Music: Les Baxter.

Producer: William Frye.

Sponsor: The National Biscuit Company (Nabisco).

THE HALLS OF IVY—30 minutes—CBS—October 19, 1954 - September 19, 1955. 26 episodes.

HANDLE WITH CARE

Anthology. Dramatization disclosing the problems encountered by the United States Postal Service in its handling of the mails. Stories relate the cases of postal investigators who attempt to curtail the misuse of mail.

HANDLE WITH CARE—30 minutes —ABC—October 7, 1954 - December 30, 1954. Original title: "The Mail Story."

HANDS OF DESTINY

Anthology. Dramatizations depicting the plight of people caught in a web of supernatural intrigue.

HANDS OF DESTINY—30 minutes—DuMont—1949-1951. Also titled: "Hands of Murder" and "Hands of Mystery."

HANK

Comedy. Background: Western State University. The story of Hank Dearborn, an enterprising young businessman who is determined to obtain the college education that he was denied when his parents were killed in an automobile accident and he was forced to quit high school and care for his younger sister, Tina.

Supporting himself by operating several campus concessions, he attends classes unregistered and under various aliases, struggling to achieve a long-awaited dream.

CAST

Hank Dearborn	Dick Kallman
Tina Dearborn	Katie Sweet
Doris Royal, his girl-friend	Linda Foster
Dr. Lewis Royal, her father, the registrar	Howard St. John
Professor McKillup	Lloyd Corrigan
Coach Weiss	Dabbs Greer
Franny, Tina's baby sitter	Kelly Jean Peters
Miss Mittleman, an instructress	Dorothy Neumann
Ralph, Hank's friend	Don Washbrook
Kim, a friend	Judy Parker
Loretta, a friend	Margaret Blye
Arlene Atwater, the social worker	Lisa Gaye
Mrs. Weiss, the coach's wife	Sheila Bromley

Music: Frank Perkins.

HANK—30 minutes—NBC—September 17, 1965 - September 2, 1966. 26 episodes.

THE HANK LADD SHOW

Variety.

Host: Hank Ladd.

Regulars: Antoinette Gilkey, Bob Dickson.

THE HANK LADD SHOW—30 minutes—NBC 1949.

THE HANK McCUNE SHOW

Comedy. The misadventures of Hank McCune, a kind-hearted bumbler who seeks but inevitably fails to achieve success.

CAST

Hank McCune	Himself
Lester, his friend	Hanley Stafford

Also: Sara Berner, Arthur Q. Bryan, Larry Keating.

Announcer: Larry Keating.

Producer: Dick Farrell, Hank McCune.

Director: Charles Maxwell.

Sponsor: Peter Paul Candies.

THE HANK McCUNE SHOW—30 minutes—NBC—1949 - 1950. Syndicated. Withdrawn.

HANS CHRISTIAN ANDERSON

Anthology. Dramatizations based on the magical kingdom of fantasy created by Hans Christian Anderson, a cobbler and spinner of stories.

Wee Willie Winkie. The story of a poor girl who, in an attempt to buy food, seeks to find the man who buys dreams.

The Emperors New Clothes. The story concerns an emperor whose vanity bankrupts his courts.

The Wild Swans. The story concerns a stepmother who casts a spell over a beautiful princess.

HANS CHRISTIAN ANDERSON—30 minutes—DuMont 1955.

HAPPENING '68

Musical Variety. Performances by Rock personalities.

Hosts: Paul Revere, Mark Lindsay.

Regulars: Freddie Welles, Keith Allison, The Raiders.

Features: The weekly band contest; undiscovered professional talent.

Music: The Raiders; Recorded.

HAPPENING '68—30 minutes—ABC—January 6, 1968 - September 20, 1969.

HAPPY

Comedy. Background: The Desert Palm Hotel in Palm Springs, California. The story of Sally and Chris Day, the owners and operators. As they struggle to successfully operate the hotel, their infant son, Christopher Hapgood (Happy) Day, observes and, through the voice-over technique, comments on their activities.

CAST

Sally Day	Yvonne Lime
Chris Day	Ronnie Burns
Christopher Hapgood Day	David Born
	Steven Born
Charley Dooley, Sally's uncle	Lloyd Corrigan
Clara Mason, the woman out to change Charley's bachelor status	Doris Packer

HAPPY—30 minutes—NBC—June 6, 1960 - September 2, 1960; Also: NBC—January 13, 1961 - September 8, 1961. Syndicated. 26 episodes.

HAPPY DAYS

Variety. The music, dance, song, and comedy of the 1930s and 40s.

Host: Louis Nye.

Regulars: Chuck McCann, Laara Lacey, Julie McWhirter, Clive Clerk, Bob Elliott, Ray Goulding, Alan Copeland, The Happy Days Singers, The Wisa D'Orso Dancers.

Orchestra: Jack Elliott.

HAPPY DAYS—60 minutes—CBS—June 1970 - September 10, 1970. 13 episodes.

HAPPY DAYS

Comedy. Background: Milwaukee, Wisconsin. Era: The latter 1950s (1956). Life in the nostalgic Eisenhower era as seen through the eyes of Richie Cunningham, a shy, naive teenager, and his friend, the wordly wise Warren "Potsie" Weber, Jefferson High School students.

CAST

Richie Cunningham	Ron Howard
Potsie Weber	Anson Williams
Howard Cunningham, Richie's father, the owner of a hardware store	Tom Bosley
Marion Cunningham, Richie's mother	Marion Ross
Chuck Cunningham, Richie's oldest brother	Gavan O'Herlihy
	Randolph Roberts
Joanie Cunningham, Richie's sister	Erin Moran

Happy Days. Left to right: Donny Most, Henry Winkler, Anson Williams, Ron Howard.

Arthur Fonzerelli (Fonzie),
   a friend, the respected,
   know-it-all drop-out; a
   mechanic at Otto's Auto
   Orphanage   Henry Winkler
Ralph Malph, Richie's
   friend   Donny Most
Marsha Simms, a waitress
   at Arnolds, the after-
   school hangout   Beatrice Colen
Trudy, a friend   Tita Bell
Gloria, Richie's girl-
   friend   Linda Purl
Wendy, a waitress at
   Arnolds   Misty Rowe
Moose, a friend   Ralph Greenberg
Arnold, the owner
   of the drive-in
   restaurant   Pat Morita
Al Delvecchio, the
   owner in later
   episodes   Al Molinaro
Laverne DaFazio, a
   friend of
   Fonzie's   Penny Marshall
Shirley Feeney, her
   friend   Cindy Williams
Spike, Fonzie's delinquent
   nephew   Danny Butch
Bag, a
   friend   Neil J. Schwartz
Bill "Sticks"
   Downey, Jr., a
   friend of
   Fonzie's   John Anthony Bailey
Pinky Tuscadero, Fonzie's
   love interest   Roz Kelly
Mickey Malph, Ralph's
   father   Alan Oppenheimer
                 Jack Dodson
Lola, one of Pinky's
   Pinkettes   Kelly Sanders
Tina, a Pinkette   Doris Hess

Background Music: Pete King;
   Recordings of the fifties.
Additional Music: Frank Comstock.
Executive Producer: Garry Marshall,
   Thomas L. Miller, Edward Milkis.

Producer: Tony Marshall, Jerry Paris,
   William S. Bickley.
Director: Jerry Paris, Frank Buxton,
   James Tayne, Mel Ferber, Don
   Weis, Herb Wallerstine, Art
   Fisher.
Note: Beginning with the September
   1977 episodes, Richie, Potsie,
   and Ralph, were students in the
   University of Wisconsin.

HAPPY DAYS—30 minutes—ABC—
Premiered: January 15, 1974.

HARBOR COMMAND

Crime Drama. Dramatizations based on incidents in the lives of the men of the U.S. Harbor Police Command. Stories relate the work of Ralph Baxter, a harbor police chief.

Starring: Wendell Corey as Captain Ralph Baxter.

HARBOR COMMAND—30 minutes—Syndicated 1957. 39 episodes.

HARBOURMASTER

Adventure. Background: Scott Island, Cape Ann, Massachusetts. The story of David Scott, the captain of the *Blue Chip II.* Episodes relate his attempts to curtail coastal crime in a small New England community.

CAST
Captain David
   Scott   Barry Sullivan
Jeff Kitredge, his
   partner   Paul Burke
Anna Morrison, a
   friend   Nina Wilcox
Professor Wheeler Murray Matheson
Captain Dan, a retired naval
   officer   Mike Keene
Danny Morrison, Anna's
   son   Evan Elliot
Producer: Jon Epstein, Leon Benson,
   Eddie Davis, Henry Kessler.

HARBOURMASTER—30 minutes—CBS—September 26, 1957 - December 26, 1957. 26 episodes. Syndicated title: "Adventures at Scott Island."

THE HARDY BOYS

Animated Cartoon. The global adventures of The Hardy Boys, a Rock and Roll group. Based on the mystery stories by Franklin W. Dixon.

Characters: Joe Hardy, Frank Hardy

(brothers), Wanda Kay Breckenridge, Pete, and Chubby.
Voices: Dallas McKennon, Jane Webb, Byron Kane.
Vocals: The real-life Rock group, The Hardy Boys.
Music: Gordon Zahler.

THE HARDY BOYS—30 minutes—ABC—September 6, 1969 - September 4, 1970. Syndicated. 26 episodes.

THE HARDY BOYS/ NANCY DREW MYSTERIES

See individual titles, "The Hardy Boys Mysteries" and "The Nancy Drew Mysteries" for information.

THE HARDY BOYS MYSTERIES

Mystery. Background: The town of Bayport. Based on the stories by Franklin W. Dixon, the series follows the intriguing investigations of juvenile detectives Frank and Joe Hardy, the sometimes mischievous sons of world-famous detective Fenton Hardy. Alternates with "The Nancy Drew Mysteries."

CAST
Frank Hardy   Parker Stevenson
Joe Hardy   Shaun Cassidy
Fenton Hardy   Edmund Gilbert
Gertrude Hardy, Fenton's
   sister   Edith Atwater
Calley Shaw, Fenton's
   secretary   Lisa Eilbacher
Music: Stu Phillips, Glen A. Larson.
Executive Producer: Glen A. Larson.
Producer: Joyce Brotman, B.W. Sandefur.
Director: Fernando Lamas, Stuart Margolin, Roland Satlof.

THE HARDY BOYS MYSTERIES—60 minutes—ABC—Premiered: January 30, 1977.

THE HARLEM GLOBETROTTERS

Animated Cartoon. The comedy adventures of the Harlem Globetrotters, basketball magicians who use their talents both on the court and off to help good defeat evil. A Hanna-Barbera production.

Characters' Voices
Meadowlark Lemon Scatman Crothers
Freddie "Curly" Neal   Stu Gilliam
Gip   Richard Elkins
Bobby Joe Mason Eddie Anderson
Geese   Johnny Williams
Pablo   Robert Do Qui

Granny   Nancy Wible

Music: Hoyt Curtin.

THE HARLEM GLOBETROTTERS

–30 minutes—CBS—September 12, 1970 - May 13, 1973. 26 episodes.

THE HARLEM GLOBETROTTERS POPCORN MACHINE

Children's Variety. Varied musical numbers and comedy sketches designed to relate social messages (e.g., good behavior, good manners).

Starring: The Harlem Globetrotters (a basketball team comprising: Meadowlark Lemon, Curley, Geese, Tex, Bobby Jo, Marques, John, Theodis, and Nate).

Regulars: Avery Schreiber (as Mr. Evil), Rodney Allen Rippy.

Orchestra: Jack Elliott, Allyn Ferguson.

THE HARLEM GLOBETROTTERS POPCORN MACHINE—25 minutes—CBS—September 7, 1974 - August 30, 1975.

HARRIGAN AND SON

Comedy. Background: New York City, the law firm of Harrigan and Harrigan. The story of James Harrigan, Senior, its founder, a conservative attorney who insists on the human angle in defending clients; and his son, James Harrigan, Junior, a recent Harvard graduate who disagrees with him and believes in defending clients strictly according to the book. Episodes depict the clash that ensues

Harrigan and Son. Left to right: Georgine Darcy, Pat O'Brien, Roger Perry.

as each attempts to prove his theory correct.

CAST

James Harrigan, Sr.	Pat O'Brien
James Harrigan, Jr.	Roger Perry
Gypsy, the elder's glamorous secretary	Georgine Darcy
Miss Claridge, the younger's sedate secretary	Helen Kleeb

HARRIGAN AND SON—30 minutes—ABC—October 14, 1960 - September 29, 1961. Syndicated. 34 episodes.

HARRIS AGAINST THE WORLD

See title: "Ninety Bristol Court," *Harris Against the World* segment.

HARRY O

Crime Drama. Background: San Diego, California. The investigations of private detective Harry Orwell, an ex-cop who was forced to retire when shot in the back and disabled. (The background in later episodes is Los Angeles, California.)

CAST

Harry Orwell	David Janssen
Detective Lt. Manuel (Manny) Quinn, S.D.P.D. (San Diego-based episodes)	Henry Darrow
Lt. K.C. Trench, L.A.P.D. (Los Angeles-based episodes)	Anthony Zerbe
Betsy, Harry's neighbor (Los Angeles-based episodes)	Katherine Baumann
Sue, Harry's neighbor (L.A. episodes)	Farrah Fawcett-Majors
Detective Don Roberts	Paul Tully
Lester Hodges, the criminologist	Les Lannom

Music: Kim Richmond; Billy Goldenberg.

Executive Producer: Jerry Thorpe.

Producer: Robert E. Thompson, Robert Dozier, Buck Houghton, Alex Beaton.

Director: Richard Lang, Jerry Thorpe, Joe Manduke.

Creator: Howard Rodman.

Harry's Address: 1101 Coast Road.

HARRY O—60 minutes—ABC—Premiered: September 12, 1974.

HARRY'S GIRLS

Comedy. Background: Europe. The romantic misadventures of Harry's

Harry's Girls. Dawn Nickerson (left), Diahn Williams (center), Larry Blyden (behind Diahn), Susan Silo (right).

Girls, a vaudeville type song-and-dance act that is touring the Continent.

CAST

Harry Burns, the manager	Larry Blyden
The Troup:	
Lois	Dawn Nickerson
Rusty	Susan Silo
Terry	Diahn Williams

HARRY'S GIRLS—30 minutes—NBC—September 13, 1963 - January 3, 1964. 15 episodes.

THE HARTMANS

Comedy. Background: Suburban New York. The trials and tribulations of Paul and Grace Hartman.

CAST

Paul Hartman	Himself
Grace Hartman	Herself
The brother-in-law	Loring Smith
The handyman	Harold Stone

Producer: Harry Herrimann.

Director: Jack Balch.

THE HARTMANS—30 minutes—NBC 1949.

THE HATHAWAYS

Comedy. Background: Los Angeles, California. The trials and tribulations of the Hathaways: Walter, a real-estate salesman, and his wife, Elinor, the manager-ower of three theatrical chimpanzees: Enoch, Charlie, and Candy.

CAST

Walter Hathaway	Jack Weston
Elinor Hathaway	Peggy Cass
Jerry Roper, the chimps' agent	Harvey Lembeck
Enoch, Candy, and Charlie	The Marquis Chimps
Mrs. Allison, the housekeeper	Mary Grace Canfield

THE HATHAWAYS—30 minutes— ABC—October 8, 1961 - August 3, 1962. 26 episodes.

HAVE A HEART

Game. Four competing contestants who comprise two teams of two. The host reads a general-knowledge type of question. The player who is first to identify himself through a buzzer signal receives a chance to answer. If correct, cash is scored. Winners, the highest scoring teams, donate their earnings to home-town charities.

Host: John Reed King.

HAVE A HEART—30 minutes— DuMont 1955.

HAVE GUN—WILL TRAVEL

Western. Background: San Francisco during the 1870s. The story of Paladin, a former army officer turned professional gunman who hires his guns and experience to people who are unable to protect themselves. Operating from the Hotel Carlton, he is distinguished by two trademarks: a black leather holster that bears the symbol of a Paladin, the white chess knight; and a calling card that reads: "Have Gun—Will Travel. Wire Paladin, San Francisco."

CAST

Paladin	Richard Boone
Hey Boy, his servant	Kam Tong
Hey Girl, his servant	Lisa Lu
Mr. McGunnis, the hotel manager	Olan Soulé

Music: Leith Stevens; Jeff Alexander; Fred Steiner; Wilbur Hatch; Bernard Herrmann; Rene Garriguenc; Jerry Goldsmith; Lud Gluskin; Lucien Moraweck.

Theme: "The Ballad of Paladin" sung by Johnny Western.

Producer: Frank Pierson, Don Ingalls, Robert Sparks.

Paladin's Gun: A Colt 45 single action with a seven-and-one-half-inch barrel.

HAVE GUN—WILL TRAVEL—30 minutes—CBS—September 14, 1957 - September 21, 1963. Syndicated. 156 episodes.

HAWAIIAN EYE

Mystery. Background: Honolulu, Hawaii. The investigations of Tom Lopaka, Tracy Steele, and Gregg MacKenzie, the owner-operators of Hawaiian Eye, a private detective organization. Assisted by Cricket Blake, a beautiful singer at the Hawaiian Village Hotel, they strive to eliminate the sources of trouble that invade a tropical paradise.

CAST

Cricket Blake	Connie Stevens
Tracy Steele	Anthony Eisley
Tom Lopaka	Robert Conrad
Gregg MacKenzie	Grant Williams
Kim, the taxicab driver	Poncie Ponce
Philip Barton, the hotel social director	Troy Donahue
Monk	Doug Mosam
Quon	Mel Prestidge

Music, Miss Stevens's accompaniment: The exotic sounds of Arthur Lyman.

Music, background: Frank Perkins, Paul Sawtell.

Theme: Mack David, Jerry Livingston.

Producer: William T. Orr, Charles Hoffman, Stanley Niss, Ed Jurist.

HAWAIIAN EYE—60 minutes—ABC —October 7, 1959 - September 10, 1963. Syndicated. 134 episodes.

Hawaiian Eye. Connie Stevens. Background: The Arthur Lyman Band.

HAWAII CALLS

Music. The music, song, and dance of Hawaii as performed by various artists.

Host-Narrator: Webley Edwards.

HAWAII CALLS—30 minutes—Syndicated 1966. 26 episodes.

HAWAII FIVE-O

Crime Drama. Background: Honolulu, Hawaii. The cases of Steve McGarrett, a plainclothes detective with Hawaii Five-O, a special computerized branch of the Hawaiian Police Force (based in the Lolani Palace, the fictitious headquarters of the Hawaiian government.)

CAST

Detective Steve McGarrett	Jack Lord
Detective Danny Williams	James MacArthur
Detective Chin Ho Kelly	Kam Fong
Detective Kono	Zulu
The governor	Richard Denning
Detective Ben Kokua	Al Harrington
Detective Che Fong	Harry Endo
Doc, the medical examiner	Al Eben
May, a secretary	Maggi Parker
Jenny, a secretary	Peggy Ryan
	Patricia Barne
The attorney general	Morgan White Glenn Cannon
Wo Fat, a wanted criminal	Khigh Dhiegh

Music: Morton Stevens; Pete Rugolo.

Additional Music: Bruce Broughton, Don B. Ray.

Executive Producer: Philip Leacock, Bob Sweeney.

Producer: Douglas Greene, David Finnegan, Richard Newton, Stanley Kallis, William O'Brien.

Director: Ernest Pintoff, Philip Leacock, Jack Lord, Joe Manduke, Bruce Bilson, Michael O'Herlihy, Douglas Greene.

Creator: Leonard Freeman.

HAWAII FIVE-O—60 minutes—CBS— Premiered: September 26, 1968.

HAWK

Crime Drama. Background: New York City. The investigations of John Hawk, a plainclothes detective with the Manhattan district attorney's special detective squad—an elite team designed to corrupt the workings of gangland. Part Iroquois Indian and a prowler of the night, Hawk excels in solving crimes perpetrated by those who find darkenss their specialty.

CAST

John Hawk	Burt Reynolds
Det. Dan Carter, his assistant	Wayne Grice
Sam Crown, Hawk's informant	John Marley
Murray Slacken, the assistant D.A.	Bruce Glover
Ed Gorten, Hawk's superior	Leon Janney

Music: Nelson Riddle, Kenyon Hopkins.

Musical Consultant: Don Kirshner.

Executive Producer: Hubbell Robinson.

Producer: Paul Bogart.

Director: Paul Henried, Burt Reynolds, Leonard Horn, Richard Benedict, Sam Wanamaker, Tom Donovan.

Creator: Allan Sloane.

HAWK–60 minutes–ABC–September 15, 1966 - December 29, 1966. Returned–NBC (rebroadcasts)–April 21, 1976 - August 11, 1976. 17 episodes.

HAWKEYE AND THE LAST OF THE MOHICANS

Adventure. Background: New York State, 1750s. The founding and growth of America as seen through the adventures of Nat Cutler, also known as Hawkeye and the Long Rifle, and Chingachgook, his blood brother, the Last of the Mohicans—fur traders and frontier scouts who assist the pioneers in settling and the army in its battle against the constant Huron uprisings.

CAST

Hawkeye	John Hart
Chingachgook	Lon Chaney, Jr.

HAWKEYE AND THE LAST OF THE MOHICANS–30 minutes–Syndicated 1957. 39 episodes.

HAWKINS

Crime Drama. Background: West Virginia. The cases and courtroom defenses of Billy Jim Hawkins, a shrewd, common-sense criminal attorney.

CAST

Billy Jim Hawkins	James Stewart

R. J. Hawkins, his cousin, his investigative assistant	Strother Martin

Music: George Duning; George Romanos.

HAWKINS–90 minutes–CBS–October 2, 1973 - September 3, 1974.

HAWKINS FALLS, POPULATION 6200

Serial. Background: The town of Hawkins Falls. Personality sketches of life in a small American town as seen through the eyes of Clate Weathers, the newspaper editor.

CAST

Clate Weathers (The Narrator)	Frank Dane

Also: Sam Gray, Arthur Peterson, Norm Sottschalk, Alice Dinsen, Jean Mowry, Viola Berwick, Les Spears, Hope Summers, Alma DuBus, Anozia Kukaki, Mary Frances Desmond, Bill Snary, Bernadene Flynn, Win Strackle, Jim Bannon.

Producer: Ben Park.

Director: Dave Brown, Ben Park.

Sponsor: Lever Brothers.

HAWKINS FALLS, POPULATION 6200–15 minutes–NBC–1950-1952.

HAYES AND HENDERSON

See title: "Oldsmobile Music Theatre."

HAZEL

Comedy. Distinguished by two formats.

Format One:
Background: 123 Marshall Road, Hydsberg, New York, the residence of the Baxter family: George, an attorney with the firm of Butterworth, Hatch, and Noell; his wife, Dorothy; their son, Harold; and their maid, Hazel Burke. Stories depict Hazel's misadventures as she attempts to solve arising crises, both household and legal, which result from meddling in George's business affairs.

Format Two:
Background: 325 Sycamore Street, Hydsberg, New York, the residence of

Hazel. Michael Callan (guest) and Shirley Booth. © *Screen Gems.*

Steve Baxter, George's younger brother, a real-estate salesman; his wife, Barbara; and their daughter, Susie. Transferred to the Middle East on business, George and Dorothy relocate and leave Harold in the care of Steve and Barbara to prevent interference to his education. Hazel becomes their maid and stories follow the original format, with Steve plagued by Hazel's intervention in his business affairs.

Based on the cartoon character appearing in the *Saturday Evening Post.*

CAST
1961-1965 (format one):

Hazel Burke	Shirley Booth
George Baxter	Don DeFore
Dorothy Baxter	Whitney Blake
Harold Baxter	Bobby Buntrock
Harriet Johnson, the helpless next-door neighbor	Norma Varden
Herbert Johnson, her husband, an interpreter of dead languages, a rich investor who had cornered the market on whale bones (427 tons)	Donald Foster
Rosie Hamicker, Hazel's friend, a maid	Maudie Prickett
Harvey Griffin, President of Griffin Enterprises, a client of George's	Howard Smith
Deirdre Thompson, George's sister	Cathy Lewis
Harry Thompson, her husband	Robert P. Lieb
Nancy Thompson, their daughter	Davey Davison
Eddie Burke, Hazel's nephew	John Washbrook
Barney Hatfield, the mailman	Robert B. Williams
Mitch Brady, the owner of the Checkerboard Cab	

Company, Hazel's friend	Dub Taylor
Stan Blake, the Baxter's neighbor	John Newton
Linda Blake, his daugher	Brenda Scott
Mavis Blake, his daughter	Judy Erwin
Don Blake, his son	Paul Engle
Miss Scott, George's secretary	Molly Dodd
Gus Jenkins, Hazel's boyfriend	Patrick McVey
Clara, a maid, a friend of Hazel's	Alice Backus
Miss Sharp, Mr. Griffin's secretary	Mary Scott

Baxter family dog: Smiley.

Music: Van Alexander.

1965-1966 (format two).

Hazel Burke	Shirley Booth
Steve Baxter, head of the Baxter Realty Company	Ray Fulmore
Barbara Baxter	Lynn Borden
Susie Baxter, their daughter	Julia Benjamin
Harold Baxter	Bobby Buntrock
Mona Williams, Barbara's friend	Mala Powers
Fred Williams, her husband	Charles Bateman
Jeff Williams, their son	Pat Cardi
Millie Ballard, Steve's part-time secretary	Ann Jillian
Deirdre Thompson	Cathy Lewis
Harry Thompson	Robert P. Lieb
Bill Fox, Steve's salesman	Lawrence Haddon
Ted Drake, Millie's boyfriend	Harvey Grant
Gus Jenkins	Patrick McVey

Music: Van Alexander; Howard Blake; Charles Albertine.

Music Supervision: Ed Forsyth.

Executive Producer: Harry Ackerman.

Producer: James Fonda.

Director: William D. Russell, Charles Barton, E.W. Swackhamer, Hal Cooper.

Creator: Ted Key.

HAZEL—30 minutes—NBC—September 28, 1961 - September 6, 1965. CBS—30 minutes—September 10, 1965 - September 5, 1966. Syndicated. 154 episodes.

THE HAZEL SCOTT SHOW

Musical Variety.

Hostess: Hazel Scott.

Announcer: Gloria Lucas.

Music: Hazel Scott (pianist).

THE HAZEL SCOTT SHOW—15 minutes—DuMont 1950.

HEADLINE STORY

See title: "Big Town."

HEADMASTER

Comedy-Drama. Background: Concord, a small, private, coeducational high school in California. A tender portrayal of student-teacher relationships and their problems; both scholastic and personal, as seen through the eyes of Andy Thompson, the headmaster.

CAST

Andy Thompson	Andy Griffith
Margaret Thompson, his wife	Claudette Nevins
Jerry Brownell, the athletic coach	Jerry Van Dyke
Mr. Purdy, the school custodian	Parker Fennelly
Judy, Andy's student helper	Lani O'Grady

Music: Dick Williams.

HEADMASTER—30 minutes—CBS—September 18, 1970 - January 1, 1971. Rebroadcasts: CBS—June 25, 1971 - September 10, 1971. 13 episodes.

HE AND SHE

Comedy. Background: New York City. The trials and tribulations of the Hollisters: Richard, a cartoonist, the creator of the comic-strip-turned-television-series, "Jetman"; and his wife, Paula, a beautiful, but scatterbrained traveler's-company aide. Stories depict Dick's struggles to survive Paula's meaningful but misguided attempts to assist others; the pressures of work and the complications of a computerized society.

CAST

Richard Hollister	Richard Benjamin
Paula Hollister	Paula Prentiss
Oscar North, the egotistical star of "Jetman"	Jack Cassidy
Andrew Humble, the building's not-so-handyman	Hamilton Camp
Harry, their friend, a fireman	Kenneth Mars
Norman Nugent, Dick's employer	Harold Gould
Murray Mouse, Dick's	
Accountant	Alan Oppenheimer

HE AND SHE—30 minutes—CBS—September 6, 1967 - September 18, 1968. Rebroadcasts, CBS—June 1970 - September 1970. 26 episodes.

HEART OF THE CITY

See title: "Big Town."

HEAVEN FOR BETSY

Comedy. Background: New York. The struggles that make up a marriage as depicted through the activities of newlyweds Peter and Betsy Bell.

CAST

Peter Bell	Jack Lemmon
Betsy Bell	Cynthia Stone

HEAVEN FOR BETSY—15 minutes—CBS—1952-1953.

HEAVENS TO BETSY

Comedy. Background: New York City. The struggles of two young Broadway hopefuls seeking a career in show business.

CAST

Betsy	Elizabeth Cote
Her friend	Mary Best
The cabdriver	Russell Nype
Their landlord	Nick Dennis

HEAVENS TO BETSY—30 minutes—NBC 1949.

THE HECKLE AND JECKLE SHOW

Animated Cartoon. The misadventures of Heckle and Jeckle, mischievous, talking magpies.

Additional segments: "Andy Pandy"; "Dinky Duck"; "Little Roquefort"; and "The Teddy Bears."

Voice characterizations: Paul Frees.

Music: Paul A. Scheib.

THE HECKLE AND JECKLE SHOW—30 minutes. Syndicated 1955; CBS—1956 - 1957; CBS—September 1965 - September 3, 1966; NBC—September 6, 1969 - September 7, 1971.

HEC RAMSEY

See title: "NBC Sunday Mystery Movie, *Hec Ramsey* segment."

THE HECTOR HEATHCOTE SHOW

Animated Cartoon. The misadventures of Hector Heathcote, a scientist who has invented the means by which to travel back through history. Stories relate his intrusion into the major events which have shaped the world.

Voice Characterizations: John Myhers.

Music: Phil Schieb.

Producer: Bill Weiss.

Director: Dave Tendlar.

Hector's dog: Winston.

THE HECTOR HEATHCOTE SHOW —30 minutes—NBC—October 1963 - September 1964.

HEE HAW

Variety. Performances by Country and Western artists coupled with short skits and running gags played against the Nashville Sound.

Hosts: Buck Owens, Roy Clark.

Regulars: Archie Campbell, Grandpa Jones, Sheb Wooley, The Hagers, Gordie Tapp, Jeannine Riley, Stringbean, Don Harron, Susan Raye, Cathy Baker, Jennifer Bishop, Lulu Roman, Zella Lehr, Gunilla Hutton, Lisa Todd, Minnie Pearl, Alvin "Junior" Samples, Claude Phelps, Jimmy Riddle, Don Rich, Ann Randall, Misty Rowe, Nancy Baker, Mary Ann Gordon, The Buckaroos, The Inspiration, Beauregard the Wonder Dog, John Henry Faulk, Barbi Benton, Buck Trent, Kenny Price, Don Gibson, Sue Thompson, George Lindsey, Jimmy Little, The Nashville Addition.

Musical Direction: George Richey.

HEE HAW—60 minutes—CBS—June 15, 1969 - July 13, 1971. Syndicated.

THE HELEN O'CONNELL SHOW

Musical Variety.

Hostess: Helen O'Connell.

THE HELEN O'CONNELL SHOW— 15 minutes—NBC—May 29, 1957 - September 1957.

THE HELEN REDDY SHOW

Musical Variety. A format tailored to the talents of guests.

Hostess: Helen Reddy.

Featured: The Jaime Rogers Dancers.

Orchestra: Nelson Riddle.

THE HELEN REDDY SHOW—60 minutes—NBC—June 28, 1973, - August 16, 1973.

HELP! IT'S THE HAIR BEAR BUNCH

Animated Cartoon. Background: Cave Block Number 9 at the Wonderland Zoo, the residence of the Hair Bear Bunch: Hair, Square, and Bubi. Stories relate their misadventures as they attempt to improve living conditions. A Hanna-Barbera production.

Characters' Voices

Hair Bear	Daws Butler
Bubi Bear	Paul Winchell
Square Bear	Bill Calloway
Mr. Peevley, the zoo-keeper	John Stephenson
Botch, his assistant	Joe E. Ross

Additional voices: Hal Smith, Jeannine Brown, Joan Gerber, Vic Perrin, Janet Waldo, Lennie Weinrib.

Music: Hoyt Curtin.

HELP! IT'S THE HAIR BEAR BUNCH—30 minutes—CBS—September 11, 1971 - September 2, 1972.

HENNESSEY

Comedy. Background: San Diego, California. The misadventures of Lieutenant Charles J. "Chick" Hennessey, a doctor assigned to the San Diego Naval base.

CAST

Lt. Chick Hennessey	Jackie Cooper
Nurse Martha Hale, his romantic interest	Abby Dalton
William Hale, Martha's father	Harry Holcombe
Lt. Dan Wagner	Herb Ellis
Pulaski	Frank Gorshin
Harvey Spencer Blair III, a dentist waiting out a million-dollar inheritance	James Komack
Chief Corpsman Max Bronsky	Henry Kulky
Captain Shafer	Roscoe Karns
Commander Wilker	Steve Roberts
Dr. King	Robert Gist
Chief Branman	Ted Fish

Music: Sonny Burke.

Producer: Jackie Cooper, Don McGuire.

HENNESSEY—30 minutes—CBS— October 4, 1959 - September 17, 1962. Syndicated. 96 episodes.

HENNY AND ROCKY

Variety. Music, songs, and comedy

HAIR BEAR   SQUARE BEAR   BUBI BEAR

Help! It's the Hair Bear Bunch. The Hair Bear Bunch. *Courtesy Hanna-Barbera Productions.*

sketches. Presented following the ABC network fights.

Hosts: Henny Youngman, Rocky Graziano.

Vocalist: Marion Colby.

Music: The Jazz Combo of Bobby Hackett, trumpeter; Morrey Feld, drummer; Buddy Weed, pianist; Peanuts Hucko, clarinetist.

HENNY AND ROCKY—15 minutes (approximately)—ABC—June 1, 1955 - September 1955.

HENRY FONDA PRESENTS THE STAR AND THE STORY

Anthology. Dramatizations of stories selected by guests.

Host: Henry Fonda.

Included:

Another Harvest. The honest young wife of a fugitive crook attempts to pay off his creditors.

CAST
Ruth Warrick, Philip Reed.

Malaya Incident. Background: Malaya. A plantation owner attempts to supply rubber to the free world against armed Red guerrillas.

CAST
Ann Sheridan, Richard Egan.

Call Me Irving. The story of a meek and mild-mannered actor who dons the guise of a vicious killer in order to land a part in a play.

CAST
Johnny Johnston, Jean Byron.

Valley Of The Shadows. Defying the gang that is terrorizing his town, a storekeeper attempts to end their reign by helping an enemy of the gang leader.

CAST
Dabbs Greer, Jeff York.

HENRY FONDA PRESENTS THE STAR AND THE STORY—30 minutes—Syndicated 1954. 39 episodes. Also known as: "Star and Story."

HENRY MORGAN

Listed: The television programs of comedian Henry Morgan.

On The Corner—Variety—30 minutes—ABC—April 18, 1948 - May 16, 1948.

Host: Henry Morgan.

Regulars: George Guest, Virginia Austin, Roy Davis, The Clark Sisters.

Henry Morgan's Talent Hunt—Satire—30 minutes—NBC 1951.

Format: Unusual talent acts and performers are presented.

Host: Henry Morgan.

Regulars: Arnold Stang, Dorothy Jarnac, Dorothy Claire, Art Carney, Kaye Ballard.

Here's Morgan—Satire—30 minutes—ABC 1953. Syndicated in 1959 under the title: "Henry Morgan and Company."

Format: Unusual talent acts are presented.

Host: Henry Morgan.

A Man's World—Discussion—30 minutes—DuMont 1955.

Format: Discussions on topics of interest primarily to men.

Host: Henry Morgan.

Music: The Three Bars.

HERB SHRINER TIME

Variety. Music, songs, and comedy sketches.

Host: Herb Shriner.

Regulars: Lenka Peterson, Peggy Allenby, Biff McGuire, Eda Heineman, Joseph Sweeny, Paul Huber.

Orchestra: Milton DeLugg; Bernie Greene.

Producer: Melvyn Ferber, Jack Mosman, Ashmead Scott.

Director: Ashmead Scott.

HERB SHRINER TIME—30 minutes—CBS—November 7, 1949 - February 4, 1950.

THE HERCULOIDS

Animated Cartoon. Background: Futuristic space. The story of the Herculoids, animals as strong as they are invincible, whose function is to protect their king, Zandor, and the inhabitants of their peaceful and utopian planet from creatures from other galaxies. A Hanna-Barbera Production.

Characters' Voices

Zandor	Mike Road
Tarra	Virginia Gregg
Zok, the lazor dragon	Mike Road
Dorno, the ten-legged rhinoceros	Teddy Eccles
Gloop, a shapeless blob	Don Messick
Gleep, a shapeless blob	Don Messick
Igoo, a come-to-life rock	Mike Road

Music: Hoyt Curtin.

Musical Director: Ted Nichols.

Producer-Director: William Hanna, Joseph Barbera.

THE HERCULOIDS—30 minutes—CBS—September 9, 1967 - September 6, 1969. 26 episodes.

HERE COMES THE BRIDE

Wedding performances. Actual ceremonies performed on TV.

Host: John Weigel.

Vocalist: Richard Paige.

Organist: Adele Scott.

HERE COMES THE BRIDE—30 minutes—DuMont 1951.

HERE COMES THE GRUMP

Animated Cartoon. A magic fantasy land is put under the Curse of Gloom by the evil Grump. Unaffected, Princess Dawn is the kingdom's lone savior. A young boy, Terry, and his dog, Bib, are magically transported from America to her domain. Informing Terry of the situation, she also tells him about the Land of a Thousand Caves. In the Cave of Whispering Orchids, the Grump has hidden the Crystal Key, which, if found, will lift the dreaded curse. Boarding a balloon car, Terry and the Princess begin their search. Stories depict their adventures and the Grump's efforts, traveling aboard his fumbling Jolly Green Dragon, to thwart their attempts and keep secret the location of the Cave of Whispering Orchids.

HERE COMES THE GRUMP—30 minutes—NBC—September 6, 1969 - September 4, 1971. 17 episodes.

HERE COME THE BRIDES

Adventure. Background: Seattle,

Washington, 1870, the dreary, and muddy logging camp of the Bolt brothers, Jason, Joshua, and Jeremy. Populated by men, with the exception of a few dancehall girls, the love-and-affection-starved loggers threaten to walk out. Agreeing to meet their demands and provide women, Jason begins preparations for a journey to New England. Faced with a lack of resources, he is approached by Aaron Stemple, the sawmill owner, who offers him a proposition. The agreement: in return for his financial backing, Jason must recruit one hundred respectable and marriageable women and keep them in Seattle for one full year. If, however, he should fail, he must forfeit Bridal Veil Mountain, the legacy left to the Bolts by their parents.

With the help of Captain Fred Clancy, one hundred women, mostly Civil War widows, are transported from Massachusetts to Washington. Episodes depict the adjustment of refined city women to rugged pioneer life and men.

CAST

Jason Bolt	Robert Brown
Joshua Bolt	David Soul
Jeremy Bolt	Bobby Sherman
Lottie Hatfield, the owner	
of the saloon	Joan Blondell
Candy Pruitt, Jeremy's romantic	
interest	Bridget Hanley
Aaron Stemple	Mark Lenard
Captain R. Fred	
Clancy	Henry Beckman
Corky Sam McGee,	
the Swede, the camp	
foreman	Bo Svenson
Biddie Gloom, one	
of the brides	Susan Tolsky
Miss Essie, the school	
teacher	Mitzi Hoag
Ben Jenkins, a	
logger	Hoke Howell
Molly Pruitt, Candy's	
sister	Patti Coohan
Christopher Pruitt, her	
brother	Eric Chase

Music: Warren Barker, Hugo Montenegro.

HERE COME THE BRIDES—60 minutes—ABC—September 25, 1968 - September 18, 1970. Syndicated. 52 episodes.

HERE COME THE DOUBLE DECKERS

Comedy. Background: A junkyard in England where a double-decker London bus is parked and reconstructed into the clubhouse of seven young children—Scooper, Spring, Billie, Brains, Doughnut, Sticks, and Tiger. Stories relate their misadventures and attempts to solve problems without help from the adult world.

CAST

Scooper	Peter Firth
Spring	Brinsley Forde
Billie	Gillian Bailey
Brains	Michael Auderson
Doughnut	Douglas Simmonds
Sticks	Bruce Clark
Tiger	Debbie Russ
Albert, their adult	
friend	Melvyn Hayes

HERE COME THE DOUBLE DECKERS—30 minutes—ABC—September 12, 1970 - September 3, 1972. 17 episodes. British produced.

HERE COME THE STARS

Testimonial dinners honoring guests. See title: "George Jessel's Show Business."

HERE'S BARBARA

Interview. Fashion, politics, and people—"an insider's look at Washington society."

Hostess: Barbara Coleman.

Music: Recorded.

HERE'S BARBARA—30 minutes—Syndicated 1969. Also known as: "The Barbara Coleman Show."

HERE'S EDIE

Variety. Music, songs, and comedy sketches.

Hostess: Edie Adams.

Orchestra: Peter Matz.

Producer: David Oppenheimer, John Bradford, Barry Shear.

HERE'S EDIE—30 minutes—ABC—September 26, 1963 - March 19, 1964.

HERE'S HOLLYWOOD

Interview. Intimate aspects of celebrities lives are revealed through in-person interviews.

Host: Dean Miller.

Hostess: Joanne Jordan.

Producer: Jess Oppenheimer, Pier Oppenheimer.

Director: Gene Law, Van B. Fox.

HERE'S HOLLYWOOD—30 minutes—NBC—September 20, 1961 - December 28, 1962.

HERE'S LUCY

Comedy. Background: 4863 Valley Lawn Drive, Los Angeles, California, the residence of Lucille Carter, widow, the nosey, overzealous secretary to Harrison Otis Carter, her brother-in-law, the owner of the Unique Employment Agency—"Unusual Jobs For Unusual People." Stories depict: her home life with her children, Kim and Craig; and her office life wherein she plagues Harry with her scatterbrained antics.

CAST

Lucille Carter	Lucille Ball
Harrison Otis Carter	
(Harry)	Gale Gordon
Kim Carter	Lucie Arnaz
Craig Carter	Desi Arnaz, Jr.
Mary Jane Lewis, Lucy's	
friend	Mary Jane Croft

Music: Marl Young.

Executive Producer: Gary Morton.

Producer: Cleo Smith.

Director: Herbert Kenwith, Danny Dayton, Jack Donohue, Jack Baker, Jack Carter, Ross Martin, Coby Ruskin.

HERE'S LUCY—30 minutes—CBS—September 23, 1968 - September 2, 1974. 144 episodes.

HERE WE GO AGAIN

Comedy. Background: Encino, California. A story of love, divorce, and remarriage.

Richard Evans, an easy-going architect, and his bossy and formidably efficient wife, Judy, the editor of *Screen World* magazine, terminate their relationship after seventeen years. They have one son, Jeff.

Jerry Standish, a philandering ex-quarterback for the Los Angeles Rams, now the owner of the Polynesia Paradise Cafe, and his wife Susan, end their marriage of ten years due to his endless romantic involvements. They have two children, Cindy and Jan.

Seeking information concerning the development of a research center for underprivileged children, Susan and Richard meet, fall in love, marry, and establish housekeeping in the Standish

Here We Go Again. Nita Talbot.

home. Jerry Standish maintains a bachelor apartment one block away; and Judy Evans and Jeff live one-half mile away.

Episodes relate the struggles of newlyweds to find serenity in a neighborhood where they are plagued by the constant intrusion of their former spouses.

CAST

Richard Evans	Larry Hagman
Susan Evans (Standish)	Diane Baker
Judy Evans	Nita Talbot
Jerry Standish	Dick Gautier
Jeff Evans	Chris Beaumont
Cindy Evans (Standish)	Leslie Graves
Jan Evans (Standish)	Kim Richards

Music: Al DeLory.

Producer: Bob Kaufman.

HERE WE GO AGAIN—30 minutes—ABC—January 20, 1973 - June 23, 1974. 13 episodes.

THE HERO

Comedy. Background: Hollywood, California. The home and working life of Sam Garrett, a bumbling klutz who portrays a fearless and dauntless law enforcer on the fictitious television series, "Jed Clayton, U.S. Marshall." Episodes depict his attempts to conceal his real life from his fans.

CAST

Sam Garrett	Richard Mulligan
Ruth Garrett, his wife	Mariette Hartley
Paul Garrett, their son	Bobby Horan
Fred Gilman, their neighbor	Victor French
Burton Gilman, his son	Joe Baio

THE HERO—30 minutes—NBC—September 8, 1966 - January 5, 1967. 16 episodes.

HE SAID, SHE SAID

Game. Four celebrity couples compete, playing for selected married couples from the studio audience. The husbands are before camera and the wives are isolated backstage in a soundproof room. The host reveals a topic. The men have to state a personal association that will hopefully trigger a response from the individual's wife, to recognize it as what "He Said."

The wives are aired and seen through four monitors that are built into the set and placed before their mates. The topic is restated and one answer is revealed. The first to recognize the answer sounds a buzzer. If she matches her husband, she receives points. The second round is played in the same manner. Rounds three and four are reversed. He has to recognize what "She Said."

Points. Each couple begins with one hundred. Matching answers add twenty-five; misses deduct ten. The highest-scoring team earns their selected studio audience couple two hundred and fifty dollars and a seven-day vacation at a Holiday Inn.

Host: Joe Garagiola.

Announcer: Johnny Olsen.

Music: Score Productions.

HE SAID, SHE SAID—30 minutes—Syndicated 1969.

HEY, JEANNIE!

Comedy. Background: New York City. The story of Jeannie MacLennan, a young lass newly arrived in the States from Scotland. Stories depict her misadventures as she struggles to adjust to the American way of life.

CAST

Jeannie MacLennan	Jeannie Carson
Al Murray, her guardian, a cab driver	Allen Jenkins
Liz Murray, his sister	Jane Dulo

Producer: Charles Isaacs.

HEY, JEANNIE!—30 minutes—CBS—September 8, 1956 - May 4, 1957. Rebroadcasts: ABC—June 30, 1960 - September 22, 1960. 32 episodes.

HEY, LANDLORD!

Comedy. Background: New York City. The misadventures of bachelors Woodrow "Woody" Banner, an aspiring writer; and Chuck Hookstratten, an aspiring comedian, the landlords of a ten-room apartment house in Manhattan.

CAST

Woody Banner	Will Hutchins
Chuck Hookstratten	Sandy Baron
Jack Ellenhorn, a tenant, a photographer	Michael Constantine
Timothy, a glamorous upstairs tenant	Pamela Rodgers
Kyoko, her roommate	Miko Mayama
Mrs. Henderson, a tenant	Ann Morgan Guilbert
Mrs. Teckler, a tenant	Kathryn Minner
Bonnie Banner, Woody's sister	Sally Field
Lloyd Banner, Woody's father	Tom Tully
Marcy Banner, Woody's mother	Ann Doran
Leon Hookstratten, Chuck's father	Joseph Leon
Fanny Hookstratten, Chuck's mother	Naomi Stevens

HEY, LANDLORD!—30 minutes—NBC—September 11, 1966 - May 14, 1967. Syndicated. 17 episodes.

Hey, Landlord! Will Hutchins (left) and Sandy Baron. Episode: "From Out of the Past Come Thundering Hoofbeats."

HEY MULLIGAN

Comedy. Background: Los Angeles, California. The misadventures of Mickey Mulligan, a page at the fictitious International Broadcasting Company. Undecided about his future, he attends the Academy of Dramatic

Arts and by taking various part-time jobs, he struggles to discover his goal in life.

CAST

Mickey Mulligan   Mickey Rooney
Mrs. Mulligan, his mother,
    a former burlesque
    star   Claire Carleton
Mr. Mulligan, his father,
    a policeman attached to
    the 23rd precinct Regis Toomey
Patricia, his girlfriend,
    a secretary at
    I.B.C.   Carla Balenda
Freddie, his friend   Joey Forman
Mr. Brown, his
    employer   John Hubbard
Mickey's drama
    instructor   Alan Mowbray
Also   Pauline Drake
                       Fred E. Sherman

Producer: Joseph Santley.

Director: Richard Quine.

Sponsor: Green Giant; Pillsbury.

HEY MULLIGAN—30 minutes—NBC —August 28, 1954 - June 4, 1955. 39 episodes. Also known as: "The Mickey Rooney Show."

HI MOM

Information. Advice and entertainment tailored to young mothers.

Hosts: Shari Lewis (1957-1959), ventriloquist. Puppets: Lamb Chop, Hush Puppy, and Charlie Horse. Johnny Andrews, Paul and Mary Ritts (1959).

Cooking authority: Josephine McCarthy.

Medical advice: Jane Palmer, R.N.

Features: Guests, stories, and films concerning children.

HI MOM—60 minutes—NBC—September 15, 1957 - March 20, 1959.

HIDDEN FACES

Serial. The dramatic story of Arthur Adams, a lawyer in a small, Midwestern town. Emphasis is placed on the methods incorporated to solve crimes.

CAST

Arthur Adams   Conrad Fowkes
Mimi Jaffe   Rita Gam
Also: Louise Shaffer, Stephen Joyce, Mark Curran, Roy Scheider, Gretchen Walther, Tony LoBianco, Joe Daly.

HIDDEN FACES—30 minutes—NBC —December 30, 1968 - June 30, 1969.

HIGH ADVENTURE WITH LOWELL THOMAS

Travel. The people and the customs of lands untouched by civilization.

Host: Lowell Thomas.

HIGH ADVENTURE WITH LOWELL THOMAS—60 minutes—CBS—November 12, 1957 - May 28, 1958 (7 specials); Syndicated—60 minutes— 1960 (11 episodes).

HIGH AND WILD

Travel. Filmed hunting and fishing adventures.

Host: Don Hobart.

Music: George Wasch.

HIGH AND WILD—30 minutes—Syndicated 1968. 78 episodes.

THE HIGH CHAPARRAL

Western. Background: Tucson, Arizona during the 1870s. The saga of the Cannon family as they struggle to maintain and operate the High Chaparral Ranch in an era of violence and lawlessness.

CAST

John Cannon   Leif Erickson
Buck Cannon, his
    brother   Cameron Mitchell
Victoria Sebastian Cannon,
    John's wife   Linda Cristal
Billy Blue Cannon, John's
    son, by a former mar-
    riage   Mark Slade
Don Sebastian, a Mexican
    land baron, the owner of
    the Montoya Ranch Frank Silvera
Manolito Sebastian, Don's
    son   Henry Darrow
Ranch Hands:
Sam, the forman   Don Collier
Ted Reno   Ted Markland
Pedro   Roberto Contreras
Wind   Rudy Ramos
Joe   Bob Hoy
Vasquero   Rodolfo Acosta

Music: Harry Sukman.

THE HIGH CHAPARRAL—60 minutes—NBC—September 10, 1967 - September 10, 1971. Syndicated. 96 episodes.

HIGH FINANCE

Game. Contestants, selected from various cities across the country, are quizzed on news items that appear in their local papers. Question-and-answer rounds, consisting of three levels, are played one per week. The winner of the first round, the highest cash scorer, receives the choice of either keeping his accumulated earnings or returning and attempting to earn additional cash in level two. If he succeeds again he may choose as before—keep his earnings or attempt level three. At this level the player may win his secret desire (up to $35,000 value), but he stands the chance of losing everything won previously if he fails.

Host: Dennis James.

Announcers: Jay Simms; Jack Gregson.

Producer: Peter Arnell.

HIGH FINANCE—30 minutes—CBS— July 7, 1956 - December 15, 1956.

HIGH LOW

Game. Object: For a contestant to challenge a panel of three experts by offering to answer one or more parts of questions containing several segments. The challenge: the player has to match the panelist claiming to have the most answers (High) or the one with the fewest (Low). If he matches the High expert, his five hundred dollars betting money is tripled; if he matches Low, his money is doubled. Failure to match either High or Low results in the loss of everything and a new challenger is introduced.

Host: Jack Barry.

HIGH LOW—30 minutes—NBC—1957 - 1958.

HIGH ROAD

Travel. Films exploring the people and the customs of distant lands.

Host-Narrator: John Gunther.

HIGH ROAD—30 minutes—Syndicated 1959. Also known as "John Gunther's High Road."

HIGH ROAD TO ADVENTURE

Travel. Films exploring the people and customs of various countries around the world.

Hosts-Narrators: Bill Burrud; Bob Stevenson.

HIGH ROAD TO ADVENTURE—30 minutes—Syndicated 1964.

HIGH ROAD TO DANGER

Documentary. Films relating the exploits of men who challenge Nature.

Host-Narrator: Steve Brodie.

HIGH ROAD TO DANGER—30 minutes—Syndicated 1957.

HIGH ROLLERS

Game. Two competing contestants. The host reads a general-knowledge type of question. The player first to identify himself through a light signal receives a chance to answer. If correct, he receives control of two dice. He is permitted to either pass or keep the roll. The dice are rolled by a girl and, according to the number that appears, he is permitted to select any combination of numbers that total the rolled number from a large number board (top line: 6,7,8,9,; bottom line: 1,2,3,4,5). Each number contains a prize that is placed on his side of the board. The remaining numbers, as they appear on the board, are the only active numbers. Any inactive numbers that are rolled automatically disqualify the player that acquires them. Winners are determined by the roll of the dice and receive the prizes that are accumulated on their side of the board.

Host: Alex Trebek.

Assistants (rolling the dice): Ruta Lee; Linda Kaye Henning.

Substitute Dice Rollers: Dawn Wells, Nanette Fabray, Suzanne Sommers, Leslie Uggams.

Announcer: Kenny Williams.

Music: Stan Worth.

Executive Producer: Merrill Heatter, Bob Quigley.

Producer: Robert Noah.

Director: Jerome Shaw.

HIGH ROLLERS—30 minutes—NBC —July 1, 1974 - June 11, 1976. Syndicated Version: Follows the same format with prizes being increased in value. All credits are the same with the exception of the Dice Roller, who is Elaine Stewart. 30 minutes—Syndicated 1975.

HIGH TENSION

Anthology. Dramatic ventures into the world of the possible but improbable.

HIGH TENSION—30 minutes—Syndicated 1953.

HIGHWAY PATROL

Crime Drama. Dramatizations based on the experiences of Highway Patrol officers in all forty-eight states (at the time of filming).

CAST

Dan Matthews, chief
of the Highway
Patrol   Broderick Crawford
Sergeant Williams, his
assistant   William Boyett

Music: Richard Llewelyn.

Program Open:

Announcer: "Whenever the laws of any state are broken, a duly authorized organization swings into action. It may be called the State Police, State Troopers, militia, the Rangers, or the Highway Patrol. These are the stories of the men whose training, skill, and courage have enforced and preserved our state laws."

HIGHWAY PATROL—30 minutes—Syndicated 1956. 156 episodes.

THE HILARIOUS HOUSE OF FRIGHTENSTEIN

Children. Background: The castle of Frightenstein in Transylvania. The series, which is composed of comedy sketches, songs, blackouts, and music, revolves around Count Frightenstein, his servant Igor, and their attempts to bring to life Bruce, an "out of order" Frankenstein type of monster.

Host: Vincent Price.

CAST

Count Frightenstein	Billy Van
Igor	Rais Fishka
Dr. Pet Vet	Billy Van
The Librarian	Billy Van
Gruselda, the cook	Billy Van

Regulars: Professor Julius Sumner Miller, Joe Torby, Guy Big.

Music: Recorded.

Producer-Director-Creator-Writer: Rife Markowitz.

THE HILARIOUS HOUSE OF FRIGHTENSTEIN—30 minutes—Syndicated 1975.

HIPPODROME

Variety. Showcased: European circus acts.

Hosts: Weekly guests including Allen Sherman, Woody Allen, Tony Randall, Eddie Albert, Merv Griffin.

Orchestra: Peter Knight.

HIPPODROME—60 minutes—CBS— July 5, 1966 - September 6, 1966.

HIRAM HOLLIDAY

See title: "The Adventures of Hiram Holliday."

THE HIS AND HER OF IT

Discussion-Variety. A topical-issues discussion revealing the male and female points of view—the His and Her of It.

Hosts: Geoff and Suzanne Edwards.

Premiere guests: Dick and Linda Smothers.

THE HIS AND HER OF IT—90 minutes—Syndicated 1969.

HIS HONOR, HOMER BELL

Comedy. Background: Spring City. The trials and tribulations of Homer Bell, the understanding and respected Justice of the Peace.

CAST

Homer Bell	Gene Lockhart
Cassandra "Casey" Bell	Mary Lee Dearing
Maude, their housekeeper	Jane Moutrie

HIS HONOR, HOMER BELL—30 minutes—Syndicated 1956. 39 episodes.

HIT SPOT

Musical Variety.

Host: Gene Fields, Vic Hyde.

Regulars: Peggy Taylor, The TuTones Vocal Group.

Music: The Four Notes.

HIT SPOT—30 minutes—NBC—1950 - 1951.

HOBBY LOBBY

Variety. People and their usual or unusual hobbies are showcased. Celebrities appear to lobby their hobbies.

Host: Cliff Arquette, portraying Mount Idy hillbilly Charlie Weaver.

Announcer: Tom Reddy.

Orchestra: John Gart.

Premiere guest: Maureen O'Hara.

HOBBY LOBBY—30 minutes—ABC— September 30, 1959 - April 23, 1960.

HOBBIES IN ACTION

Variety. People and their usual or unusual hobbies are showcased.

Host: Steve Booth.

HOBBIES IN ACTION—30 minutes— Syndicated 1958. 26 episodes.

HOGAN'S HEROES

Comedy. Background: Stalag 13, a German prisoner-of-war camp officially run by the naive and inept Colonel Wilhelm Klink and his obese, bumbling assistant, Sergeant Hans Schultz. Unofficially, events and camp life are manipulated by Colonel Robert Hogan, U.S. Army Air Corps, senior officer in the camp.

Assisted by inmates LeBeau, Newkirk, Carter, Kinchloe, and Baker, Hogan, under the code name Papa Bear, conducts vital missions for the Allies. Through phone taps, underground escape routes, radio contacts, and custom tailoring, the prisoners' assist Allied fugitives and secure top-secret information for their superiors.

CAST

Col. Robert Hogan	Bob Crane
Col. Wilhelm Klink	Werner Klemperer
Sgt. Hans Schultz	John Banner
Louis LeBeau, the French corporal	Robert Clary
Peter Newkirk, the English corporal	Richard Dawson
Andrew Carter, the American sergeant	Larry Hovis
Helga, the Commandant's secretary (early episodes)	Cynthia Lynn
Hilda, the Commandant's secretary (later episodes)	Sigrid Valdis
Colonel Crittendon, Hogan's nemesis, the Commandant of Stalag 16	Bernard Fox

Marya, the beautiful Russian spy	Nita Talbot
Major Hockstedder, the Gestapo commander	Howard Caine
Sgt. Richard Baker	Kenneth Washington
Cpl. James Kinchloe	Ivan Dixon
Gen. Alfred Burkhalter, the Luftwaffe Officer in charge of prison camps	Leon Askin
Gertrude Linkmier, Alfred's sister*	Kathleen Freeman

Music: Jerry Fielding.

Additional Music: Fred Steiner.

Music Supervision: Richard Berres.

Producer: Edward H. Feldman.

Director: Robert Butler, Gene Reynolds, Howard Morris.

*Her husband, Otto, is reported to be missing in Russia. Alfred is thus trying to marry her off to Klink.

HOGAN'S HEROES—30 minutes— CBS—September 17, 1965 - July 4, 1971. Syndicated. 168 episodes.

HOLD 'ER NEWT

Children. Background: The town of Figg Center. The series, which incorporates puppets, deals with the fanciful misadventures that befall Newt, the owner-operator of a country general store.

Puppet Voices: Don Tennant.

HOLD 'ER NEWT—15 minutes—ABC 1950.

HOLD IT PLEASE

Game. A telephone call is placed at random to a viewer. If he is able to correctly answer a question, he is awarded a prize and receives a chance at the jackpot, which consists of valuable merchandise prizes. To win he must identify the portrait of a celebrity that is located on a spinning wheel.

Host: Gil Fates.

Regulars: Cloris Leachman, Bill McGraw, Mort Marshall, Evelyn Ward.

Orchestra: Max Showalter.

HOLD IT PLEASE—30 minutes—CBS 1949.

HOLD THAT CAMERA

Game. Two competing contestants—a studio player and a home participant. The viewer, whose voice is amplified over the telephone, directs the studio player through a series of shenanigans. The player who performs the stunt in the least amount of time receives prizes for himself and the home viewer.

Host: Jimmy Blaine.

Orchestra: Ving Merlin.

Producer: West Hooker.

Sponsor: Esquire Shoe Polish.

HOLD THAT CAMERA—30 minutes —DuMont 1951.

HOLIDAY HOTEL

Variety. Background: New York City. Entertainment performances set against the background of the Pelican Room of the fashionable but fictitious Holiday Hotel on Fifth Avenue.

Hosts (the hotel managers for the unseen Mr. Holiday): Edward Everett Horton; Don Ameche.

Regulars: Betty Brewer, Dorothy Greener, Lenore Longergan, The June Graman Dancers, The Don Craig Chorus.

Orchestra: Bernie Green.

Producer: Monte Proser.

Director; Preston Wood.

Sponsor: Packard Automobiles.

HOLIDAY HOTEL—30 minutes— ABC—July 12, 1951 - October 4, 1951.

HOLIDAY LODGE

Comedy. Background: The plush Holiday Lodge Hotel in Upper New York State. The misadventures of social directors Johnny Miller and Frank Boone. Stories depict their efforts to provide interesting entertainment despite an encounter with ever-present obstacles.

CAST

Johnny Miller	Johnny Wayne
Frank Boone	Frank Shuster
J. W. Harrington, the hotel manager	Justice Watson
Dorothy Johnson, the hotel receptionist	Maureen Arthur
Woodrow, the bellboy and general handyman	Charles Smith

HOLIDAY LODGE—30 minutes— CBS—June 25, 1961 - October 8, 1961. 13 episodes.

HOLLYWOOD A GO GO

Musical Variety. Performances by Rock personalities.

Host: Sam Riddle.

Regulars: The Sinners, The Gazzarri Dancers.

Music: Recorded.

HOLLYWOOD A GO GO—60 minutes—Syndicated 1965.

HOLLYWOOD AND THE STARS

Documentary. The behind-the-scenes story of Hollywood—its stars and its celluloid accomplishments.

Host-Narrator: Joseph Cotten.

Music: Jack Tiller.

Producer: David L. Wolper, Jack Mulcahy, Jack Haley, Jr.

HOLLYWOOD AND THE STARS— 30 minutes—NBC—September 30, 1963 - September 28, 1964. Syndicated. 31 episodes.

HOLLYWOOD BACKSTAGE

Variety. A behind-the-scenes report on Hollywood, showcasing the people, the parties, and the premieres.

Host: John Willis.

Music: Recorded.

HOLLYWOOD BACKSTAGE—30 minutes—Syndicated 1965.

THE HOLLYWOOD CONNECTION

Game. Two noncelebrity contestants compete. One player, by a flip of coin decision, begins and selects either the top or bottom row of celebrity panel of three. The host reads a question that involves the celebrities in a hypothetical situation. Two answers are revealed and the celebrities secretly select one. The contestant then has to predict how each celebrity answered by choosing one of the available answers. The celebrities then reveal their answers and each correct prediction (connection) awards the player one point. The remaining player competes in the same manner with the remaining celebrities.

Rounds two and three follow the same basic format with points doubled then tripled. The player with the highest score is the winner and receives merchandise prizes.

Host: Jim Lange.

Announcer: Jay Stewart.

Producer: Jack Barry, Dan Enright.

THE HOLLYWOOD CONNECTION—30 minutes—Syndicated 1977.

HOLLYWOOD FILM THEATRE

Movies. Theatrical releases.

HOLLYWOOD FILM THEATRE—90 minutes—ABC 1957.

HOLLYWOOD JR. CIRCUS

Circus Variety Acts.

Ringmaster: Paul Barnes.

Regulars: George Cesar, Max Bronstein, Marie Louise, Bill Hughes, The Hanneford Family, Boffo the Clown, Zero the Candyman, Blackie the Talking Crow.

Orchestra: Bruce Chase.

HOLLYWOOD JR. CIRCUS—30 minutes—ABC—1951.

HOLLYWOOD OFF BEAT

Crime Drama. Background: Hollywood, California. The story of private detective Steve Randall, an unjustly disbarred attorney who seeks to find those responsible for framing him and regain his right to practice law.

Starring: Melvyn Douglas as Steve Randall.

Producer: Marlon Parsonett, Lester Lewis.

HOLLYWOOD OFF BEAT—30 minutes—ABC—May 24, 1953 - August 11, 1953. Also: ABC—August 7, 1955 - September 11, 1955. 13 episodes.

HOLLYWOOD OPENING NIGHT

Anthology. Comedy and drama presentations. The first anthology series to originate from the West Coast.

Producer: Bill Corrigan.

Director: Richard Irving.

Sponsor: Parson Pharmacal.

Included:

Let George Do It. A personal-service-bureau operator attempts to help a young chemist learn the art of wooing.

Starring: Ann Sothern.

Terrible Tempered Tolliver. The comic tale of a baseball umpire who never reverses decisions. Feature version: *Kill the Umpire.*

Starring: William Bendix.

Quite A Viking. A tomboy's reaction to her first kiss.

Starring: Ann Harding, James Dunn.

30 Days. The story concerns a brilliant lawyer and his attempts to clear an innocent man.

Starring: Edward Arnold, Robert Stack.

Hope Chest. To win the affections of a pretty girl, an interior decorator helps her find a job.

Starring: Macdonald Carey.

The Housekeeper. A psychiatrist attempts to rectify a mistake made in the diagnosis of an important case.

Starring: Albert Dekker.

HOLLYWOOD OPENING NIGHT— 60 minutes—ABC 1952.

THE HOLLYWOOD PALACE

Variety. Music, songs, dances, and comedy sketches set against the background of the Hollywood Palace Theatre. Guest artists perform.

Hosting: Weekly Guests.

Regulars: Raquel Welch (The Hollywood Palace Card Holder), The Ray Charles Singers, The Buddy Schawb Dancers.

Announcer: Dick Tufeld.

Orchestra: Mitchell Ayres.

THE HOLLYWOOD PALACE—60 minutes—ABC—January 4, 1964 - February 7, 1970.

HOLLYWOOD SCREEN TEST

Anthology. Dramatic productions. Young theatrical hopefuls appear with established performers.

Host: Neil Hamilton.

Hostess: Betty Furness.

Assistant: Martha Wayne.

Announcer: Ted Campbell.

Producer: Lester Lewis.

Sponsor: Ironite.

HOLLYWOOD SCREEN TEST—30 minutes—ABC—August 15, 1948 - September 26, 1949.

HOLLYWOOD SHOWCASE

See title: "The Dick Powell Theatre."

THE HOLLYWOOD SQUARES

Game. Two competing contestants—Player X and Player O. Nine guest celebrities each occupy a square on a huge Tic-Tac-Toe board. Object: To win two out of three Tic-Tac-Toe games.

The first player begins by choosing one celebrity who is then asked a question by the host. The player must determine whether the answer given is correct or a bluff, i.e., agree or disagree. If the player is correct, the appropriate letter is lit on the board; incorrect, the opponent receives the square. Exception: Should the square complete a Tic-Tac-Toe game for the opponent, he does not receive it. Players have to earn essential squares by themselves. Winners, those acquiring three squares in a row, up and down or diagonally, receive two hundred dollars. Two wins earns the championship. Players compete until defeated or until reaching the game limit of ten at which time he wins two thousand dollars and a new car.

One game per show is a jackpot round. If the player chooses "The Secret Square" (one of the squares designated before the game but unknown to the players or the celebrities), a special question is asked. If the player is correct in agreeing or disagreeing with the celebrity, he receives valuable merchandise prizes.

Host: Peter Marshall.

Announcer: Kenny Williams.

Music: Recorded.

Regulars Wally Cox, Cliff Arquette as Charlie Weaver, Paul Lynde, Rose Marie, Karen Valentine; George Gobel.

Executive Producer: Merrill Heatter, Bob Quigley.

Producer: Jay Redack.

Director: Jerome Shaw.

Note: The British version of "The Hollywood Squares" is titled "The Celebrity Squares" with host Bob Monkhouse.

THE HOLLYWOOD SQUARES—30 minutes—NBC—Premiered: October 17, 1966.

HOLLYWOOD'S TALKING

Game. Involved: Three competing contestants and approximately fifteen Hollywood celebrities. A video tape, divided into three cash segments ($150, $100, and $50) is played, showing celebrities expressing their opinions on people, places, or things. Contestants have to determine exactly what's being talked about. A press on a button automatically stops the tape. If the player guesses correctly, he receives cash according to the amount of tape run; if incorrect, he is disqualified from that particular round.

The first player to score two hundred and fifty dollars is the winner and receives a chance to earn additional cash via "The Bonus Round." The format follows the same as the game. Five short subjects are discussed. The player must identify as many as possible within a sixty-second time limit. Each correct identification earns cash equal to the amount won in the preceeding game. Players compete until defeated.

Host: Geoff Edwards.

Announcer: Johnny Jacobs.

Music: Recorded.

HOLLYWOOD'S TALKING—30 minutes—CBS—March 26, 1973 - June 23, 1973.

HOLLYWOOD TALENT SCOUTS

Variety. Performances by undiscovered professional talent presented by celebrity guests.

Versions:

CBS—60 minutes—August 1, 1960 - September 26, 1960.

Host: Sam Levenson.

Orchestra: Harry Sosnick.

CBS—60 minutes—July 3, 1962 - September 1962.

Host: Jim Backus.

Orchestra: Harry Sosnick.

CBS—60 minutes—July 2, 1963 - September 17, 1963.

Host: Merv Griffin.

Orchestra: Harry Sosnick.

CBS—60 minutes—June 12, 1965 - September 6, 1965.

Host: Art Linkletter.

Orchestra: Harry Zimmerman.

CBS—60 minutes—December 20, 1965 - September 5, 1966.

Host: Art Linkletter.

Orchestra: Harry Zimmerman.

Also known as "Celebrity Talent Scouts."

HOLLYWOOD TELEVISION THEATRE

Anthology. Original dramatic productions.

Included:

Lemonade. On a country road, two middle-aged women selling lemonade recall times past and what might have been if things had been different.

CAST
Mabel: Martha Scott; Edith: Eileen Herlie.

The Typists. The lives of two losers—a spinster and self-pitying married man.

CAST
Anne Jackson, Eli Wallach.

The Plot To Overthrow Christmas. A television adaptation of Norman Corwin's radio play about the devil's plot to kill Santa Claus.

CAST
Devil: John McIntire; Nero: Karl Swenson; Santa Claus: Allen Reed, Sr.; Simon Legree: Parley Baer; Lucrezia Borgia: Jeanette Nolan.

Awake And Sing. Background: The Bronx, New York 1930s. A Jewish family struggles to survive the Depression.

CAST
Walter Matthau, Ruth Storey, Felicia Farr, Robert Lipton.

Birdbath. The story of a young woman who seeks help after committing a murder.

CAST
Velma Sparrow: Patty Duke; Frankie Basta: James Farentino.

HOLLYWOOD TELEVISION THEATRE—60 minutes—PBS—Premiered: October 7, 1971. Originally broadcast as a series of monthly specials from 1970-1971 before becoming a weekly series.

HOLLYWOOD TODAY

Interview. A behind-the-scenes look at Hollywood during the mid-1950s.

Hostess: Sheila Graham.

HOLLYWOOD TODAY—30 minutes—NBC 1955.

HOLMES AND YOYO

Comedy. Background: Los Angeles, California. The cases of Alexander Holmes, a not-too-bright police officer, and his partner, Gregory "Yoyo" Yoyonovich, a robot, a top-secret, not-yet-perfected human-shaped computer designed to combat evil.

CAST
Sgt. Alexander Holmes	Richard B. Shull
Sgt. Gregory "Yoyo" Yoyonovich	John Schuck
Captain Harry Sedford	Bruce Kirby
Police Woman Maxine Moon	Andrea Howard
Chief Dwight Buchanan	Ben Hammer
Dr. Babcock, Yoyo's creator	Larry Hovis

Music: Leonard Rosenman, Dick Halligan.

Executive Producer: Leonard B. Stern.

Producer: Arne Sultan.

Director: Leonard B. Stern, Jack Arnold, Reza S. Badiyi, John Astin, Richard Kinon.

Creator: Jack Sher, Lee Hewitt.

HOLMES AND YOYO—30 minutes—ABC—September 25, 1976 - December 11, 1976.

HOME

Information-Variety. A woman's television magazine of the air.

Hostess, Leisure Activities Editor, Shopping Guide Expert: Arlene Francis.

Decorating Editor: Sydney Smith.

Women's Interest, Fashion and Beauty Editor: Eve Hunter.

Food Editor: Poppy Cannon.

Fix-It-Shop and Home Gardening Editor: Will Peiglebeck.

Children's Problem Editor: Rose Frangblau.

Special Projects Editor: Estelle Parsons.

Variety Editor (Vocalist): Johnny Johnston.

Music Editors: The Norman Paris Trio.

Announcer: Hugh Downs.

Producer: Dick Linkroum.

HOME—60 minutes—NBC (Daily)—March 1, 1954 - August 9, 1957.

HOMEMAKERS' EXCHANGE

Women. Cooking, decorating, household tips, and shopping advice.

Hostess: Louise Leslie.

HOMEMAKERS' EXCHANGE—30 minutes—CBS 1950.

HOMICIDE

Crime Drama. Background: Australia. The life and problems faced by detectives attached to the Melbourne Police Force.

CAST
Inspector Connolly	John Fegan
Det. Sgt. Bronson	Terry McDermott
Detective Frazer	Lex Mitchell
Det. Sgt. McKay	Leonard Teale
Detective Hudson	Les Dayman
Det. Peter Barnes	George Mallaby
Detective Costello	Lionel Long
Inspector Fox	Alwyn Kurts
Detective Patterson	Norman Yemm
Detective Delaney	Mike Preston
Detective Redford	Gary Day
Inspector Lawson	Charles Tingwell
Detective Kelly	John Stanton
Det. Harry White	Don Barker
Detective Deegan	Dennis Grosvenor

HOMICIDE—60 minutes—Produced in Australia by Crawford Productions from October 1964 to July 1976. 78 episodes are syndicated to the U.S.

HOMICIDE SQUAD

See title: "Mark Saber."

HONDO

Western. Background: The Arizona Territory, 1869. The exploits of Hondo Lane, a United States Army troubleshooter. Episodes relate his attempts to resolve the bloodthirsty conflict between settlers and Apache Indians over the possession of land.

CAST
Hondo Lane	Ralph Taeger
Buffalo Baker	Noah Beery, Jr.
Angie Daw, a settler, the woman Hondo saved from her murdering husband	Kathie Brown
Johnny Daw, her son	Buddy Foster
Apache Chief Vittoro	Michael Pate
Captain Richards, Hondo's superior	Gary Clarke
Hondo's dog: Sam.	

HONDO—60 minutes—ABC—September 8, 1967 - December 29, 1967. 17 episodes.

HONESTLY, CELESTE!

Comedy. Background: Manhattan. The misadventures of Celeste Anders, a college teacher from Minnesota as she struggles to acquire journalism experience through her job as a reporter for the *New York Express.*

CAST
Celeste Anders	Celeste Holm
Mr. Wallace, the editor	Geoffrey Lumb
Bob Wallace, his son	Scott McKay
Marty, her friend, a cab driver	Mike Kellin
Mr. Wallace's secretary	Mary Finny
The Obit Editor	Henry Jones
Also	Fred Worlock

Producer: Joseph Scibetta.

Sponsor: Bristol-Myers.

HONESTLY, CELESTE!—30 minutes—CBS—October 10, 1954 - December 12, 1954.

THE HONEYMOONERS

Comedy. Era: The 1950s. Background: 328 Chauncey Street, Bensonhurst, Brooklyn, New York, the apartment residences of the Kramdens and the Nortons, people, fifteen years after the Depression, still struggling to make ends meet, save some money, and move into larger, more modern apartments.

Meeting while working for the WPA, Ralph Kramden and Alice Gibson married following his acquiring employment as a bus driver with the Gotham Bus Company.

Ed Norton, a sewer worker for the New York City Department of Water Works, and his wife, Trixie, live above the Kramdens.

Stories depict the sincere attempts of two men to better their lives and the ensuing frustrations when their schemes to strike it rich inevitably backfire.

The success of "The Honeymooners" stems not only from its

sensitive portrayal of the struggles that make up a marriage in difficult times, but from the verbal interactions of the characters. Ralph, loud mouthed, impulsive and quick tempered; Alice, logical and tolerant, a constant source of his aggravation when she questions many of his ventures; Ed, calm and sensitive, representing Ralph's complement; and Trixie, undemanding and seemingly content, a woman who is totally devoted to Ed.

CAST

Ralph Kramden	Jackie Gleason
Alice Kramden	Audrey Meadows
Ed Norton	Art Carney
Trixie Norton	Joyce Randolph

Additional characters (not given screen credit): Mrs. Gibson, Alice's mother; Mrs. Manicotti, a tenant; Mr. Marshall, Ralph's employer; Mr. Johnson, the landlord; Morris Fink, the Grand High Exalted Ruler of the Raccoon Lodge, Ralph and Norton's fraternity; Mr. Monahan, the president of the bus company.

Announcer: Jack Lescoulie.

Orchestra: Sammy Spear.

Also, various roles: Frank Marth, George Petrie.

Executive Producer: Jack Philbin.

Producer: Jack Hurdle.

Director: Frank Satenstein.

Note: Ralph drives the Madison Avenue bus; the Kramden address is also known to be 728 Chauncey St.; and Norton is also known to be associated with The Sanitation Department and The Sewer Dept.

THE HONEYMOONERS—30 minutes—CBS—October 1, 1955 - September 22, 1956. Syndicated. 39 episodes.
History: "The Honeymooners" first appeared as a short segment on "Cavalcade of Stars" (DuMont 1950, wherein Pert Kelton portrayed Alice). After switching to CBS the following year, the series, titled "The Jackie Gleason Show" continued the *Honeymooners* segment. From 1955-1956 a weekly thirty-minute series, "The Honeymooners," was filmed at the Park Sheraton Hotel on the DuMont Electronicam System.* The series,

The Honeymooners. Left to right: Jackie Gleason, Art Carney, Audrey Meadows, Joyce Randolph.

failing to establish itself on its own, continued via short segments of "The Jackie Gleason Show" (CBS, 1956-1959).

After an absence of seven years, new episodes in the lives of the Kramdens and the Nortons appeared, first in short fifteen-minute segments, then later as full sixty-minute musical productions, also aired via "The Jackie Gleason Show" (CBS, 1966-1970).

On February 2, 1976, ABC aired a sixty-minute special titled "The Honeymooners Second Honeymoon." With Jackie Gleason (Ralph), Audrey Meadows (Alice), Art Carney (Norton), and Jane Kean (Trixie), the special celebrated the Kramden's twenty-fifth wedding anniversary.

In January of 1977, thirteen of the one-hour "Honeymooners" episodes were placed into syndication.

CAST (New Version)

Ralph Kramden	Jackie Gleason
Alice Kramden	Sheila MacRae
Ed Norton	Art Carney
Trixie Norton	Jane Kean

Featured: The June Taylor Dancers.

Announcer: Johnny Olsen.

Orchestra: Sammy Spear.

Executive Producer: Jack Philbin.

Producer: Ronald Wayne.

Director: Frank Bunetta.

THE HONEYMOON GAME

Game. Six engaged couples compete in contests of skill and knowledge.

Segments:

The Qualifying Round. Three couples at a time compete; two are to be eliminated. Basis: The identification of persons, places, objects, occupations, or actions. The host states a category (e.g., "A Living Woman") and proceeds to ask the women related questions which serve as clues

(e.g., "What is her profession?"). If the woman answers correctly, her partner receives a chance to identify the subject of the category, and thus score one point. If incorrect, a second clue is given. Six clues are given for each identification. Four segments are played, two of which are in reverse (clues are given to the men while the ladies have to identify subjects). Winners are the four highest-scoring couples.

The Semi-Final Round. Four couples, two at a time, compete, two to be defeated. Each team has before them a lever, which when pulled activates a large spinning wheel. The wheel contains three glass windows that reveal three celebrity-picture categories (e.g. Jaye P. Morgan representing show business; Don Drysdale representing sports). Five guest celebrities are present. Each team receives a chance to activate the wheel. One player of that team then chooses one window. The corresponding guest asks a question. If it is correctly answered, the team receives one point.

If a celebrity appears in two windows, the point value is doubled. If in three, it is tripled. Ten points wins the round. Should the word "Bonus" appear with any picture, the question, if correctly answered, earns one extra point; if it appears three times, on one spin, the round is automatically won. Off-stage couples compete in the same manner.

The Final Round. Two couples. The levers are pulled and players in turn answer the category questions that appear. The highest scoring team is the winner and receives their point value in dollars.

Grand Finale. The winning couple has the chance to win merchandise prizes and an all-expense-paid honeymoon. The spinning wheel, containing prizes, is incorporated. One member is permitted to pull the lever. The wheel, when stopping, pinpoints three prizes. The couple, if not satisfied, receives another chance to activate the spinning wheel. If still not pleased, they are allowed a final third spin and must keep what then appears.

As their gifts are established, three windows are revealed, each containing a honeymoon varying in luxury and elegance. The couple, aften ten seconds, select and receive the honeymoon of their choice.

Host: Jim McKrell.

Announcer: Harry Blackstone, Jr.

Music: Recorded.

THE HONEYMOON GAME—90 minutes—Syndicated 1971.

THE HONEYMOON RACE

Game. Three newlywed couples compete. Background: The Hollywood Mall Shopping Center in Hollywood, Florida. Basis: A scavenger hunt. A specific amount of time is established. Players, who each receive a series of clues, have to find the items that they represent. The couple who find the most items are the winners and receive these articles as their prize.

Host: Bill Malone.

THE HONEYMOON RACE—30 minutes—ABC—July 20, 1967 - April 1, 1968.

HONEY WEST

Mystery. Background: Los Angeles, California. The investigations of Honey West, owner and operator of H. West and Company, a private detective organization. Stories relate her attempts to solve crimes through advanced scientific technology.

CAST
Honey West	Anne Francis
Sam Bolt, her partner	John Ericson
Meg West, Honey's aunt	Irene Hervey

Honey's pet ocelot: Bruce.

Music: Joseph Mullendore.

HONEY WEST—30 minutes—ABC—September 17, 1965 - September 2, 1966. Syndicated. 30 episodes.

Honey West. Anne Francis, "Television's loveliest private detective."

HONG KONG

Adventure. Background: Hong Kong. The experiences of Glenn Evans, an American foreign correspondent assigned to cover the Cold War.

CAST
Glenn Evans	Rod Taylor
Neil Campbell, the police chief	Lloyd Bochner
Tully, the owner of the Golden Dragon Nightclub	Jack Kruschen
Ching Mei, a cocktail waitress	Mai Tai Sing
Fong, Evans's houseboy (1960)	Harold Fong
Ling, Evans's houseboy (1961)	Gerald Jann

Music: Lionel Newman.

HONG KONG—60 minutes—ABC—October 28, 1960 - September 27, 1961. Syndicated. 26 episodes.

HONG KONG PHOOEY

Animated Cartoon. The story of Henry, a meek police station janitor who possesses the ability to transform himself into the disaster prone Hong Kong Phooey, "America's secret weapon against crime." Episodes relate his fumbling attempts to solve baffling acts of criminal injustice. A Hanna-Barbera Production.

Characters' Voices
Henry/Hong Kong Phooey	Scatman Crothers
Sergeant Flint	Joe E. Ross
Rosemary, the switchboard operator	Jean VanderPyl

Additional Voices: Richard Dawson, Ron Feinberg, Kathy Gori, Casey Kaseem, Jay Lawrence, Peter Leeds, Allan Melvin, Don Messick, Alan Oppenheimer, Bob Ridgley, Fran Ryan, Hal Smith, Lee Vines, Franklin Welker, Janet Waldo, Paul Winchell, Lennie Weinrib.

Music: Hoyt Curtin.

Executive Producer: William Hanna, Joseph Barbera.

Director: Charles A. Nichols.

Henry's pet cat: Spot.

Hong Kong's car: The *Phooeymobile.*

HONG KONG PHOOEY—30 minutes—ABC—September 7, 1974 - September 4, 1976.

HOOTENANNY

Musical Variety. Performances by Folk singers. Filmed on college campuses throughout the country.

Host: Jack Linkletter.

Featured: Glenn Yarbrough of The Limeliters.

Music: The Chad Mitchell Trio.

HOOTENANNY—60 minutes—ABC—April 6, 1963 - September 21, 1963.

HOPALONG CASSIDY

Western. Background: The Bar 20 Ranch in Crescent City. The exploits of Hopalong Cassidy, a daring defender of range justice.

CAST
Hopalong Cassidy (Hoppy)	William Boyd
Red Connors, his partner	Edgar Buchanan

Hoppy's horse: Topper.

Producer: William Boyd, Toby Anguist.

Sponsor: General Foods.

HOPALONG CASSIDY—30 minutes—Syndicated 1948. 99 episodes.

In 1935 producer Harry Sherman bought the screen rights to Clarence E. Mulford's *Hopalong Cassidy* stories. Offered a chance to star in the first film, William Boyd accepted, but refused to play the part of the ranch foreman. His insistance awarded him the role of Cassidy. As written, Cassidy was originally an illiterate, "tabacco-chewin', hard-drinkin', ableswearin' son of the Old West who got his nickname because of a limp." However, when the first film, *Hop-a-Long Cassidy*, was released by Paramount, Boyd dropped everything that the original literary character had possessed, including the limp, with an explanation, in the second film, that the wound had healed.

Between 1935 and 1948, sixty-six Hopalong Cassidy films were made. A half-hour television series appeared in 1948; and a thirty-minute radio series, starring William Boyd, appeared on Mutual in 1949.

HOPPITY HOOPER

Animated Cartoon. The comic escapades of three talking animals: Hoppity Hooper, the frog; Uncle

Waldo, the fox; and Fillmore, the bear.

Characters' Voices

Hoppity Hooper	Chris Allen
Uncle Waldo	Hans Conried
Fillmore	Bill Scott
The Narrator	Paul Frees

HOPPITY HOOPER—30 minutes—Syndicated 1962. Also known as: "Uncle Waldo."

THE HORACE HEIDT SHOW

Musical Variety. Performances by undiscovered professional talent.

Host: Horace Heidt.

Announcer: Bud Collyer.

Orchestra: Horace Heidt.

Producer: Glenn Miller, Ralph Branton.

Director: Basil Wrangle.

Sponsor: Philip Morris Cigarettes.

THE HORACE HEIDT SHOW—30 minutes—CBS 1950.

HOT DOG

Educational. Filmed explorations of the technological mysteries surrounding the making of everyday items, e.g., footballs, rope, bricks, pencils, hot dogs, blue jeans, felt tip pens, baseballs, plywood, license plates, the canning of sardines, cuckoo clocks, and paper.

Regulars: Jonathan Winters, Woody Allen, Jo Anne Worley (tackling chosen subjects in a comical fashion).

Music: The Youngbloods.

HOT DOG—30 minutes—NBC—September 12, 1970 - September 4, 1971. 26 episodes.

HOTEL BROADWAY

Musical Variety.

Hostess: Jerri Blanchard.

Regulars: Avon Long, Rose and Rana, The Striders.

Music: The Harry Ranch Sextet.

Producer-Director: Harvey Marlowe.

HOTEL BROADWAY—30 minutes—DuMont 1949.

HOTEL COSMOPOLITAN

Serial. Background: The Cosmopoli-

tan Hotel in New York City. Dramatizations based on incidents in the lives of people frequenting the hotel as seen through the eyes of television actor Donald Woods.

CAST

Donald Woods	Himself
The House Detective	Henderson Forsythe

Also: Dinnie Smith, John Holmes, Wesley Larr, Walter Brooke, Tom Shirley.

Producer: Roy Windsor.

HOTEL COSMOPOLITAN—15 minutes—CBS—August 19, 1957 - April 11, 1958.

HOTEL de PAREE

Western. Background: George Town, Colorado, 1870s. The saga of the West's most colorful gathering place, the Hotel de Paree, and its legendary proprietor, a gunslinger turned law enforcer (upon his release from prison), the Sundance Kid.

CAST

Sundance (distinguished by a black Stetson with a hatband of polished silver discs)	Earl Holliman
Annette Devereaux, the hotel operator	Jeanette Nolan
Monique Devereaux, her niece	Judi Meredith
Aaron Donager, a friend	Strother Martin

Sundance's dog: Useless.

Producer: Stanley Rubin.

Note: Sundance's gun: A Colt .45

Hotel de Paree. Left to right: Peggy Joyce (guest), Earl Holliman (Sundance), and Kathleen Hughes (guest). Episode: "The Only Wheel in Town."

single action with a five-and-one-half-inch barrel.

HOTEL de PAREE—30 minutes—CBS—October 2, 1959 - September 23, 1960. 33 episodes.

HOT L BALTIMORE

Comedy. Background: Baltimore, Maryland. Life in the seedy Hotel Baltimore (the E in the neon sign has burned out) as seen through the activities of the eleven people who live like a family in the decaying establishment. Based on the Broadway play of the same title.

CAST

Bill Lewis, the desk clerk	James Cromwell
Suzy Madaraket, a prostitute	Jeannie Linero
April Green, a prostitute	Conchata Ferrell
Clifford Ainsley, the hotel manager	Richard Masur
Winthrop Morse, the cantankerous old man	Stan Gottlieb
Charles Bingham, the young philosopher	Al Freeman, Jr.
Jackie, a young, unemployed woman	Robin Wilson
Millie, the waitress	Gloria LeRoy
George, a homosexual	Lee Bergere
Gordon, a homosexual	Henry Calvert
Mrs. Esmee Belotti, the mother of the never-seen psychotic youngster, Moose	Charlotte Rae

Music: Marvin Hamlisch.

Executive Producer: Rod Parker.

Producer: Norman Lear.

Director: Bob LaHendro.

HOT L BALTIMORE—30 minutes—ABC—January 24, 1975 - June 13, 1975. 13 episodes.

HOT LINE

Discussion. Two guests and panelists discuss topical issues.

Host: Gore Vidal.

Panelists: Dorothy Killgallen, David Susskind.

HOT LINE—90 minutes—Syndicated 1964.

HOT SEAT

Game. Two husband-and-wife teams play, but compete one at a time. One member is placed in the Hot Seat, a skin-response machine that measures emotional reactions when two electrodes are attached to the fingers. As the sound is turned off in the booth, the other member is asked a question (e.g., "What does [name of wife] think of herself as a woman? Does she think she is healthy and wholesome or sexy and seductive?"). In this case, the husband chooses the response he feels will register highest on the machine. The sound is turned on in the booth and the wife is asked to respond negatively (e.g., "No, I'm not like that") to the question she will hear. Each response is registered, and if the higher score matches the response her husband selected they receive $100 (in round two, $200; round three, $400). The other couple competes in the same manner. Winners are the highest scorers.

Host: Jim Peck.

Announcer: Kenny Williams.

Music: Stan Worth.

Executive Producer: Merrill Heatter, Bob Quigley.

Producer: Bob Synes.

Director: Jerome Shaw.

HOT SEAT—30 minutes—ABC—July 12, 1976 - October 22, 1976.

HOT WHEELS

Animated Cartoon. Background: Metro City. The experiences of responsible young teenage drivers, members of the Hot Wheels automobile racing car club. Intent: To establish and explain, through the recklessness of rival gangs, the dangers of racing; and to advocate automotive safety.

Characters:
The Hot Wheels Club: Jack Wheeler, its organizer, owner of the Wheeler Motors Garage; Janet Martin, Skip Frasier, Bud Stuart, Mickey, Tag, Art, and Kip.
Rival Racing Car Clubs: Dexter Carter and His Demons; Stuff Haley and His Bombers.

Music: Jack Fascinato.

HOT WHEELS—30 minutes—ABC—September 6, 1969 - September 4, 1971. 26 episodes.

THE HOUNDCATS

Animated Cartoon. Background: The Western United States. The investigations of the Houndcats, bumbling government cat and dog agents organized to combat evil. A spin-off from "Mission: Impossible."

Characters' Voices
Studs, the leader — Daws Butler
Muscle Mut, the strong dog — Aldo Ray
Rhubarb, the inventor — Arte Johnson
Puddy Puss, the cat of-a-thousand faces — Joe Besser
Ding Dog, the dare devil — Stu Gilliam

Their car: Sparkplug.

Music: Doug Goodwin.

THE HOUNDCATS—30 minutes—NBC—September 9, 1972 - September 1, 1973. 26 episodes.

THE HOUR GLASS

Anthology. Dramatizations of people confronted with sudden, unexpected situtations.

Included:

One Night With You. The romantic story of an Italian teenager's chance meeting with a girl in a railroad station.

CAST
Giulio: Nino Martine; Mary: Patricia Roc.

Turn The Key Softly. Three women, released from prison, attempt to readjust to the outside world.

CAST
Monica: Yvonne Mitchell; Stella: Joan Collins; Joan: Dorothy Alison.

Another Shore. The story of a young man who believes that if he rescues an elderly man or woman he will receive a substantial sum of money as a reward, which will enable him to travel to a South Seas island. The episode relates his attempts to find someone in distress.

CAST
Gulliver Shields: Robert Beatly; Jennifer: Morra Lister; Alastair: Stanley Holloway.

THE HOUR GLASS—60 minutes—ABC—December 3, 1952 - September 30, 1953. Also: ABC—June 21, 1956 - September 1956.

HOUR OF STARS

Anthology. Rebroadcasts of dramas that were originally aired via "The Twentieth Century Fox Hour."

Host: John Conte.

Included:

The People Against McQuade. A soldier attempts to clear himself of a false homicide charge.

CAST
Tab Hunter, James Garner.

Men Against Speed. A female photographer tries to bring her two bickering brothers together again.

CAST
Mona Freeman, Farley Granger.

The Magic Brew. In his attempt to fleece the citizens, a medicine show huckster runs a contest for the "most popular girl in town."

CAST
Jim Backus, Fay Spain, Will Hutchins.

Deadlock. A father tries to hide the fact that he's a wanted criminal from his young daughter.

CAST
Charles McGraw.

HOUR OF STARS—60 minutes—Syndicated 1958.

HOUSE IN THE GARDEN

See title: "Fairmeadows, U.S.A."

THE HOUSE ON HIGH STREET

Serial. Background: Los Angeles, California. The cases of defense attorney John Collier. Based on actual records from the Domestic Relations Court. The series, which involves people in trouble with the law, is episodic, with stories running from three to five installments.

CAST
John Collier — Philip Abbott
Judge James Gehrig — Himself
Dr. Harris B. Peck — Himself

THE HOUSE ON HIGH STREET—30 minutes—NBC—September 29, 1959 - February 5, 1960.

HOUSE PARTY

See title: "Art Linkletter."

THE HOWARD MILLER SHOW

Musical Variety.
Host: Howard Miller.
Regulars: Mike Douglas, Barbara
   Becker, The Mello-Larks, The
   Art Van Damme Quintet.
Orchestra: Joseph Gallicchia.

THE HOWARD MILLER SHOW—30
minutes—CBS 1957.

HOW DO YOU RATE

Game. Selected studio-audience members compete. Tested: Hidden aptitudes. Players compete in rounds designed to test intelligence and reasoning power. The first to successfully complete the problems (mathematics, observation, logic, mechanics, etc.) is the winner and receives merchandise prizes.

Host: Tom Reddy.

HOW DO YOU RATE—30 minutes—
CBS—March 3, 1958 - June 26, 1958.

HOWDY DOODY

Children. Early history: Doodyville, Texas. On December 27, 1941, the wife of a ranch hand named Doody gave birth to twins, boys named Howdy and Double. The years swiftly passed and the boys enjoyed growing up on the ranch where their parents' earned a living by performing chores for the owner.

At the age of six, their rich uncle, Doody, died and bequeathed Howdy and Double a small plot of land in New York City. (Striking oil near Doodyville, the citizens named the town after him. Traveling east before the twins were born, he had always regretted the fact that he had never returned to see them).

Howdy cherished a dream of operating a circus. Double wished to remain in Texas. When NBC offered to purchase the land to construct a television studio, Mr. Doody arranged the deal to provide for Howdy to have his circus. NBC built the circus grounds, surrounded it with TV cameras and appointed Buffalo Bob Smith as Howdy's guardian.

After a tearful farewell, Howdy departed Texas for New York. Arriving and befriending Buffalo Bob, the

Howdy Doody. Bob Smith and Howdy Doody.

two began their television show in 1947.

Set against the background of Doodyville, and surrounded by "The Peanut Gallery" (children) the program depicts the efforts of a circus troupe to perform against the wishes of Phineas T. Bluster, an old man opposed to people having fun.

Characters:
Buffalo Bob Smith, an
   adventurer dressed in a
   pioneer costume, supposedly
   descended from Buffalo
   Bill   Bob Smith
Clarabell Hornblow, a highly
   skilled clown hired by
   Howdy when no other circus
   would stand for his constant
   playing of practical jokes.
   He remains silent and "speaks"
   through his honking of a "Yes"
   or "No" horn   Bob Keeshan
                              Bob Nicholson
                              Lou Anderson
The Story Princess   Alene Dalton
Tim Tremble   Don Knotts
Chief Thunderthud, a descendent
   of Chief Bungathud (a
   supposed founder of
   Doodyville), a friend
   of Phineas T.
   Bluster's   Bill Lecornec
Princess Summer-Fall-Winter-
   Spring   Judy Tyler
Lowell Thomas, Jr., the traveling
   lecturer   Himself
Additional Characters: Doctor Sing-a-
   Song; Grandpa Doody.

Puppets:
Howdy Doody (voiced by Bob
   Smith), a red-haired, freckle-
   faced (72 freckles), blue-eyed
   boy with an enormous grin who
   dresses in dungarees, a plaid
   work shirt, and a large bandana.
Phineas T. Bluster (voiced by Dayton
   Allen), the terror of Doodyville.
   Seventy years of age and as spry
   as a pup. An old man who is

forever undermining Bob and Howdy and causing trouble.
Dr. Jose Bluster, Phineas's twin brother, the opposite in character and not very bright, living most of his life in South America. He sides with Howdy and Bob against Phineas.
Double Doody, Howdy's twin brother.
Heidi Doody, Howdy's cousin.
Ugly Sam, Doodyville's wrestler, always trying to win a bout.
Lanky Lou, a talkative cowboy until someone asked him a question at which time he clammed up.
Trigger Happy, a notorious bad man.
Spin Platter, the disc jockey.
The Flubadub, the main circus attraction—a creature with a dog's ears, a duck's head, cat's whiskers, a giraffe's neck, a raccoon's tale, an elephant's memory, and a feather-covered body who craves meatballs and spaghetti.
Inspector John, the chief of police, a top-notch investigator.
Captain Scuttlebut, an old sea captain whose boat is docked in Doodyville Harbor.
The Bloop, an invisible, but sometimes visible creature.
Dilly Dally, a nervous chap who is able to wiggle his ears.
Sandy McTavish, a visitor from Scotland who is in Doodyville trying to build a factory.
Andy Handy, the business tycoon.
Doc Ditto, an old toymaker.
Sandra, the witch.

Voices: Bob Smith, Dayton Allen, Allen Swift, Herb Vigran.

Puppeteers: Rhoda Mann, Lee Carney.

Music: Edward Kean.

Narrator of the silent film segment: Dayton Allen.

Producer: Martin Stone, Roger Muir.

Sponsor: Tootsie Roll, Wonderbread, Hostess, Unique Toys.

HOWDY DOODY—60 and 30 minute versions—NBC—Decmeber 27, 1947 - September 24, 1960. 2,543 performances. Original title: "Puppet Playhouse."

HOW'S YOUR MOTHER-IN-LAW

Game. Object: For three guest celebrities, acting as lawyers for the defense, to judge, through a series of question and answer rounds on behavior, which of three contestants are the best mothers-in-law. Prizes are awarded to the winner.

Host: Wink Martindale.

HOW'S YOUR MOTHER-IN-LAW—
30 minutes—ABC—October 2, 1967 - March 1, 1968.

HOW THE WEST WAS WON

Western. Era: The mid-1860s. The saga of a Virginia homesteading family on the Great Plains. A three-part miniseries.

CAST
Zeb Macahan, the rugged mountain man — James Arness
Kate Macahan, a widow, Zeb's sister — Eva Marie Saint
Laura Macahan, Kate's daughter — Kathryn Holcomb
Jessie Macahan, Kate's daughter — Vicki Schrech
Luke Macahan, Kate's son — Bruce Boxleitner
Josh Macahan, Kate's son — William Kirby Cullen

Narrator: William Conrad.

Music: Jerrold Immel.

Executive Producer: John Mantley.

Producer: Jeffrey Hayden, John. G. Stephens.

Director: Burt Kennedy, Daniel Mann.

HOW THE WEST WAS WON—60 minutes— ABC—February 6, 1977 - February 14, 1977.

HOW TO

Discussion. A person with a problem is brought on stage. The host and panelists then attempt to resolve the difficulties.

Host: Roger Price.

Panelists: Anita Martell, Leonard Stern, Stapley Adams.

Announcer: Bob Lemond.

Producer: Richard Linkroum, Larry Berns.

Director: Richard Linkroum.

HOW TO—30 minutes—CBS 1951.

HOW TO MARRY A MILLIONAIRE

Comedy. Background: New York City. The story of three beautiful career girls: Loco Jones, a model; Michele (Mike) Page, a secretary; and Greta Lindquist, a secretary— bachelorettes sharing a Manhattan apartment and each desiring to marry a millionaire. Episodes depict their individual pursuits and attempts to secure a dream. Based on the movie of the same title.

CAST
Loco Jones — Barbara Eden
Michele (Mike) Page — Merry Anders
Greta Lindquist — Lori Nelson
Gwen Laurel (replaced Greta) — Lisa Gaye
Jessie, the elevator operator — Jimmy Cross

HOW TO MARRY A MILLIONAIRE —30 minutes—Syndicated 1958. 52 episodes.

HOW TO SURVIVE A MARRIAGE

Serial. Background: Los Angeles, California. The series, which is aimed primarily at young marrieds and divorcées, dramatizes the problems of marriage, divorce, separation, and readjustment.

CAST
Dr. Julie Franklin — Rosemary Prinz
Monica Courtland — Joan Copeland
Sandra Henderson — Lynn Lowry
Maria McGhee — Lauren White
Chris Kirby — Jennifer Harmon
Rachel Bachman — Elissa Leeds
David Bachman — Allan Miller
Fran Bachman — Fran Brill
Joan Willis — Tricia O'Neil
Lori Ann Kirby — Suzanne Davidson
 — Cathy Greene
 — Lori Lowe
Terry Courtland — Peter Brandon
Dr. Max Cooper — James Shannon
Dr. Tony DeAngelo — George Webles
Neil Abbott — George Shannon
Dr. Brady — Don Keyes
Larry Kirby — Michael Landrum
Dr. Charles Maynard — Paul Vincent
Jerry Nelson — Dino Narizzano
Joshua T. Browne (J. B.) — F. Murray Abraham
Johnny McGhee — Armand Assante
Dr. Robert Monday — Gene Bua
Susan Pritchett — Veleka Gray
Peter Willis — Steve Elmore
 — Berkeley Harris
Moe Bachman — Albert Ottenheimer
Greg Bachman — Richie Schectman
Lt. Bowling — Al Fann

Music: Score Productions.

Music Supervision: Sybil Weinberger.

Orchestrations: William Goldstein.

HOW TO SURVIVE A MARRIAGE— 30 minutes—NBC—January 7, 1974 - April 17, 1975.

H. R. PUFNSTUF

Children's Adventure. Playing near the edge of a river, Jimmy and his talking gold flute, Freddie, board a boat that suddenly materializes. As it drifts out to sea, the evil Miss Witchiepoo, seeking Freddie, the world's only talking flute, for her collection, casts a spell and makes the boat vanish.

Swimming to the shore of Living Island, they are rescued by its mayor, H.R. Pufnstuf.

Taken to the home of Dr. Blinkey, they learn about Judy the Frog, the only creature knowing the secret of the way off the island through the Secret Path of Escape.

Finding Judy, they are led to the path—and unknowingly followed by Miss Witchiepoo. Casting a spell, she makes it vanish and is angered when Jimmy refuses to trade the path for Freddie.

Overshadowed by the schemes of the evil Miss Witchiepoo, Jimmy and Freddie, assisted by the inhabitants of Living Island, struggle to find the secret of the way home to their world and safety.

CAST
Jimmy — Jack Wild
Miss Witchiepoo — Billie Hayes

Also: Joan Gerber, Felix Silla, Jerry Landon, John Linton, Angelo Rosetti, Hommy Stewart, Buddy Douglas.

Characters (The Sid and Marty Krofft Puppets): H.R. Pufnstuf; Judy the Frog; Dr. Blinkey; Cling and Clang, friends of the Mayor's; Dumb, Stupid, Orville and Seymoure, the Witch's aides; Grandfather Clock; Ludicrous Lion; The Four Winds (North, East, South, and West).

Vocals: The Pufnstuf.

Orchestra: Glen Paige, Jr.

H.R. PUFNSTUF—30 minutes—NBC —September 6, 1969 - September 4, 1971. ABC—September 9, 1972 - September 1, 1973. 17 episodes.

THE HUCKLEBERRY HOUND SHOW

Animated Cartoon. The misadventures of Huckleberry Hound, a slow-thinking and slow-talking animal who tackles various occupations in his struggle to discover his goal in life. A Hanna-Barbera production.

Additional Segments:
"Pixie and Dixie." The misadventures of two mischievous mice.
"Mr. Jinks." The story of a cantankerous cat.

The Huckleberry Hound Show. Huckleberry Hound. *Courtesy Hanna-Barbera Productions.*

"Hokey Wolf." The life of a mischievous wolf.

Characters' Voices
Huckleberry Hound	Daws Butler
Pixie	Don Messick
Dixie	Don Messick
Mr. Jinks	Daws Butler
Hokey Wolf	Daws Butler
Ding	Doug Young

Music Supervision: Hoyt Curtin.

THE HUCKLEBERRY HOUND SHOW—30 minutes—Syndicated 1958. 195 episodes.

THE HUDSON BROTHERS

Listed: The television programs of the Hudson Brothers.

The Hudson Brothers Show—Variety —60 minutes—CBS—July 31, 1974 - August 28, 1974.

Format: Various sketches, spoofs, and musical numbers.
Hosts: The Hudson Brothers: Bill, Mark, and Brett.
Regulars: Stephanie Edwards, Ronne Graham, Gary Owens, Ron Hull, The Jimmie Rogers Dancers.
Announcer: Gary Owens.
Orchestra: Jack Eskrew.
Special Musical Material: Earl Brown.

The Hudson Brothers Razzle Dazzle Comedy Show—Children's Variety— 25 minutes—CBS—September 7, 1974 - April 17, 1977.

Format: Varied songs, sketches, and musical numbers designed to convey value-related messages.
Hosts: Bill, Brett, and Mark Hudson.
Regulars: Billy Van, Peter Cullen, Ted Zeigler, Murray Langston, Rod Hull, Scott Fisher.
Announcer: Peter Cullen.
Orchestra: Jimmy Dale.

HUDSON'S BAY

Barry Nelson in a thirty-minute adventure series that details the exploits of fur trappers at Hudson's Bay, Canada, in the 1800s. Syndicated 1959; 39 films.

HULLABALOO

Variety. A weekly excursion into the world of Rock music.

Hosts: Guests of the week.
Regulars: Sheila Forbes, Lada Edmonds, Jr. (the caged Go Go Dancer), The Hullabaloo Dancers, The David Winters Dancers.
Orchestra: Peter Matz.

HULLABALOO—60 and 30 minute versions—NBC—January 12, 1965 - August 29, 1966. 16 one-hour tapes; 28 half-hour tapes.

THE HUMAN JUNGLE

Drama. Background: London, England. The work of psychiatrist Roger Corder. Stories depict his attempts to assist people overcome by the turmoil of human emotion.
Starring: Herbert Lom as Dr. Roger Corder.

THE HUMAN JUNGLE—60 minutes —Syndicated 1964. 26 episodes.

THE HUNTER

Adventure. The exploits of Bart Adams, a United States government undercover agent known as The Hunter. Adopting the guise of a wealthy American playboy, he attempts to corrupt the forces of communism in the Western world.
Starring: Barry Nelson as Bart Adams.
Producer: Edward J. Montagne.
Sponsor: Camel Cigarettes.

THE HUNTER—30 minutes—CBS —July 3, 1952 - September 24, 1952.

HUNTER

Adventure. Background: Southeast Asia. The exploits of John Hunter, a top operative of C.O.S.M.I.C. (the Office of Security and Military Intelligence), a British government organization. Unassisted by law enforcement officials, he and his partner, Eve Halliday, battle the sinister elements of C.U.C.W., an enemy organization bent on dominating the world.

CAST
John Hunter	Tony Ward
Eve Halliday	Fernande Glyn
Undercover Chief Blake	Nigel Lovell
Kragg, C.U.C.W.'s chief killer	Gerald Kennedy
Smith, the scheming representative for C.U.C.W.	Ronald Morse
Gil Martin, a C.O.S.M.I.C. agent	Rod Millinar

Note: C.U.C.W. is The Council for the Unification of the Communist World.

HUNTER—60 minutes—Syndicated 1968. 26 episodes.

Hullabaloo. The Hullabaloo Dancers.

HUNTER

Adventure. The cases of James Hunter and Marty Shaw, his beautiful assistant, U.S. Government Special Intelligence agents covering the world of contemporary espionage. (In his free time, Hunter operates a book shop in Santa Barbara; Marty is a model.)

CAST
James Hunter   James Franciscus
Marty Shaw   Linda Evans
Harold Baker, their
  superior   Ralph Bellamy

Music: Richard Shores.
Executive Producer: Lee Rich, Philip Capice.
Producer: Christopher Morgan.
Director: Gerald Mayer, Bruce Bilson, Harry Harris, Barry Crane, Gary Nelson.
Creator: William Blinn.

HUNTER—60 minutes—CBS—February 18, 1977 - May 27, 1977.

HURDY GURDY

Variety. The music, song, and dance of the Gay 90s era.
Host: Pete Lofthouse.
Regulars: Barbara Kelly, The Sportsmen, The Hurdy Gurdy Girls.
Music: The Second Story Men.

HURDY GURDY—30 minutes—Syndicated 1967. 26 tapes.

THE HY GARDNER SHOW

Discussion-Interview.
Host: Hy Gardner, newspaper columnist.

THE HY GARDNER SHOW—90 minutes—Syndicated 1965.

9

I AM THE GREATEST: THE ADVENTURES OF MUHAMMAD ALI

Animated Cartoon. The exploits of heavyweight boxing champion Muhammad Ali, who, as a modern day Robin Hood, helps good defeat evil.
Voice of Muhammad Ali: Muhammad Ali.
Music: Charles Blaker.
Executive Producer: Fred Calvert.
Producer: Janis Diamond.
Director: Fred Calvert.

I AM THE GREATEST: THE ADVENTURES OF MUHAMMAD ALI—30 minutes—NBC—Premiered: September 10, 1977.

THE IAN TYSON SHOW

Variety. Performances by U.S. and Canadian Folk and Country and Western entertainers.

Host: Ian Tyson.
Featured: Sylvia Tyson (Mrs.)
Music: The Great Speckled Bird.

THE IAN TYSON SHOW—30 minutes—Syndicated 1970. 90 tapes. Also known as: "Nashville Now."

THE ICE PALACE

Variety. Entertainment acts set against the background of a mythical Ice Palace.
Hosts: Weekly Guests (for its eight program run): Roger Miller, The Lennon Sisters (Peggy, Janet, Dianne, and Kathy), Leslie Uggams, Jack Jones, Vickki Carr, Johnny Mathis, John Davidson, Dean Jones.
Regulars (skating personalities): Tim Wood, Linda Carbonetto, Billy Chappell, Gisela Head, Don Knight, Tim Noyers, Roy Powers, Sandy Parker, The Bob Turk Ice Dancers.
Orchestra: Alan Copeland.
Executive Producer: Peter Engel.
Producer: Perry Cross.
Director: John Moffitt.

THE ICE PALACE—60 minutes—CBS —May 23, 1971 - July 25, 1971.

ICHABOD AND ME

Comedy. Background: Phippsboro, a small New England community. Discontent with life in New York, Bob Major, widower, businessman, quits his job and purchases the *Phippsboro Bulletin,* the town newspaper. Becoming the editor, and assisted by Ichabod Adams, the former owner, now the traffic commissioner, he struggles to learn the ropes and publish a weekly newspaper.

CAST
Bob Major   Robert Sterling
Ichabod Adams   George Chandler
Abby Adams, his
  daughter   Christine White
Benjie Major, Bob's
  son   Jimmy Mathers
Aunt Lavinnia, Bob's house-
  keeper   Reta Shaw
Jonathan, a
  friend   Jimmy Hawkins
Colby, a friend   Forrest Lewis
Martin, a friend   Guy Raymond
Olaf, a friend   Bert Mustin

Music: Pete Rugolo.

ICHABOD AND ME—30 minutes—

CBS–September 26, 1961 - September 18, 1962. 36 episodes.

I COVER TIMES SQUARE

Crime Drama. Background: New York City. The investigations of Johnny Warren, a crusading Broadway newspaper columnist. His beat is the out-of-town newsstand on Second Avenue in Times Square.

Starring: Harold Huber as Johnny Warren.

Music: Ethel Stevens.

Producer: Harold Huber.

Director: Murray Bennett.

Sponsor: Seeman Brothers.

I COVER TIMES SQUARE–30 minutes–ABC 1951.

THE IDA LUPINO THEATRE

Anthology. Dramatic presentations.

Hostess-Star: Ida Lupino.

Included:

With All My Heart. A tender drama revealing the feelings of an overweight woman as she watches the man she has loved since childhood marry another woman.

Starring: Ida Lupino, Walter Coy.

Woman Afraid. The story of a woman who is constantly spoiled by her husband's affections.

Starring: Ida Lupino.

The Case Of Emily Cameron. The story of a man who devotes his life to caring for his bedridden wife.

Starring: Ida Lupino, Scott Forbes.

Eddie's Place. The story of a beautiful parolee who jeopardizes her chances of reform when she becomes involved in a murder.

Starring: Ida Lupino.

THE IDA LUPINO THEATRE–30 minutes–Syndicated 1956.

I'D LIKE TO SEE

Documentary. Highlights of past historic events are shown through film clips.

Host-Narrator: Ray Morgan.

Producer: Bernard Karlen.

Sponsor: Procter and Gamble.

I'D LIKE TO SEE–15 minutes–NBC 1948.

IDENTIFY

A game show, hosted by Bob Elson, wherein a panel of sports experts answer questions asked of them by the emcee. First broadcast on ABC for 15 minutes in 1949.

I DREAM OF JEANNIE

Comedy. Early history: Jeannie was born in Baghdad, Iraq, April 1, 64 B.C. When she reached the age of marriage, her hand was sought by the Blue Djin, the most powerful and the most feared of all genies. When she refused his proposal, he became enraged; and in retribution turned her into a genie, placed her in a bottle, and sentenced her to a life of loneliness on a desert island.

The centuries passed and the girl in the bottle remained unaffected by time.

The 20th century. Saturday, September 18, 1965. Captain Tony Nelson, an astronaut on a flight from the NASA Space Center, Cape Kennedy, Cocoa Beach, Florida, crash lands on a desert island in the South Pacific. Seeking material with which to make an S.O.S. signal, he finds a strange green bottle. Upon opening it, pink smoke emerges and materializes into a beautiful girl dressed as a harem dancer – a genie.

"Thou may ask anything of thy slave, Master," she informs him; and with her hands crossed over her chest and a blink of her eyes, she proceeds to provide a rescue helicopter for him. Realizing the problems her presence and powers will cause him at NASA,

I Dream of Jeannie. Larry Hagman and Barbara Eden. © *Screen Gems.*

he sets her free, despite her desire to remain with him. Blinking herself back into smoke, and into her bottle, she places herself in Tony's survival kit without his knowledge.

Returning home, 1020 Palm Drive, and discovering Jeannie, Tony, realizing that she is determined to remain, makes her promise to conceal her presence, curtail her powers, and grant him no special treasures. Though reluctant she agrees, but secretly vows to always ensure his safety.

Accidentally stumbling upon Tony's secret, astronaut Roger Healey, his friend, becomes the only other person to know of Jeannie's existence. Caught in a web of mysterious, inexplicable situations that result from Jeannie's magic, he and Tony become the fascination of Dr. Alfred Bellows, a NASA psychiatrist who observes, records, and ponders their activities, determined to uncover the cause.

Stories depict the attempts of a jealous genie to protect her master from harm and from the influx of feminine admirers; and a master's efforts to control and conceal the presence of a beautiful, fun-loving genie.

CAST

Jeannie	Barbara Eden
Jeannie II, her sister, a genie who wanted Tony for herself, but lost	Barbara Eden
Captain Anthony Nelson (Tony), later promoted to major	Larry Hagman
Captain Roger Healey, later promoted to major	Bill Daily
Dr. Alfred Bellows	Hayden Rorke
Amanda Bellows, his wife	Emmaline Henry
General Martin Peterson	Barton MacLane
General Winfield Schaffer	Vinton Hayworth
Hadji, the Master of all genies	Abraham Sofaer
Habib, Jeannie's sister's master	Ted Cassidy
Various roles, including The Blue Djin	Michael Ansara

Jeannie's dog, a genie: Gin Gin.

Music: Hugo Montenegro; Richard Wess; Buddy Kaye.

Producer: Sidney Sheldon, Claudio Guzman.

Director: E.W. Swackhamer, Bruce Kessler, Gene Nelson, Hal Cooper, Claudio Guzman, Alan Rafkin, Joseph Goodson, Michael Ansara.

Creator: Sidney Sheldon.

I DREAM OF JEANNIE—30 minutes—NBC—September 18, 1965 - September 8, 1970. Syndicated. 139 episodes. Spin-off series: "Jeannie" (see title).

IF YOU HAD A MILLION

See title: "The Millionaire."

THE IGOR CASSINI SHOW

Interview. Artists, businessmen, and scientists are interviewed via the "Person to Person" format (cameras are placed in the homes; and via remote pickup, the host, seated in the studio, conducts the interview).

Host: Igor Cassini.

THE IGOR CASSINI SHOW—30 minutes—DuMont 1953.

I LED THREE LIVES

Drama. The story of Herbert Philbrick, the man who led three lives—private citizen, undercover agent, and F.B.I. counterspy. Episodes depict his life as a counterspy and his attempts to infiltrate the American Communist Party and inform U.S. government officials of the Red military movement.

CAST
Herbert Philbrick | Richard Carlson
Ann Philbrick, his wife | Virginia Steffan
The F.B.I. agent | John Beradino

I LED THREE LIVES—30 minutes—Syndicated 1953. 117 episodes.

I'LL BET

Game. Two married couples compete. A question is asked of one team member via telephone (to prevent other players from hearing it). He or she then silently bets points—twenty-five to one hundred—as to whether or not his partner "Can" or "Can't" answer it. The host then reads the question aloud. The partner's answer determines the score. If it is in accord with the prediction, the team wins the points; if incorrect, their opponents receive the points. Winners, the highest point scorers, receive merchandise prizes.

Host: Jack Narz.

I'LL BET—30 minutes—NBC—March 29, 1965 - September 24, 1965. Revised as "It's Your Bet" (which see).

I'LL BUY THAT

Game. Contestants, chosen from the studio audience, are assisted by four celebrity panelists. Object: The identification of articles submitted by home viewers and that are up for sale. The celebrities ask questions of the host regarding the article's identity. Each question raises the purchase price from five dollars to a limit of one hundred dollars. Players then receive a chance to identify the article. If one is successful, he receives the established purchase price of the article and the chance to possibly triple it by answering three questions. If the player fails to correctly respond to all three, the article becomes his parting prize.

Host: Mike Wallace.

Panelists: Vanessa Brown, Hans Conried, Robin Chandler, Albert Mooreland.

Commercial Spokeswoman: Robin Chandler.

Producer: Peter Arnell.

Sponsor: Seeman Brothers.

I'LL BUY THAT—30 minutes—CBS—June 19, 1953 - June 25, 1954.

THE ILONA MASSEY SHOW

Musical Variety. Background: A Continental supper club atmosphere.

Hostess: Ilona Massey.

Music: The Irving Fields Trio.

THE ILONA MASSEY SHOW—30 minutes—DuMont—1954-1955.

I LOVE LUCY

Comedy. Background: 623 East 68th Street, New York City, Apartment 3-B, the residence of Ricky Ricardo, an orchestra leader at the Tropicanna Club (later episodes, The Ricky Ricardo Babalu Club) and his wife Lucy. Stories depict the basic, most often copied premise: a husband plagued by the antics of his well-meaning, but scatterbrained wife. In this case, by a wife who longs for a career in show business, but encounters the objections of a husband who sees her as his housewife, not as an entertainer. Mirroring the trials and tribulations of marriage, "I Love

Lucy" has become a television classic.

CAST
Lucy Ricardo | Lucille Ball
Ricky Ricardo | Desi Arnaz
Fred Mertz, their friend, the landlord | William Frawley
Ethel Mertz, his wife | Vivian Vance
Little Ricky Ricardo, Lucy and Ricky's son | The Mayer Twins Richard Keith
Betty Ramsey, their neighbor (Connecticut-based episodes) | Mary Jane Croft
Ralph Ramsey, her husband | Frank Nelson
Mrs. Trumbull, the Ricardos' neighbor | Elizabeth Patterson
Jerry, Ricky's agent | Jerry Hausner
Mrs. McGillicuddy, Lucy's mother | Catherine Card
Carolyn Appleby | Doris Singleton
Charlie Appleby, Carolyn's husband | Hy Averback

Music: Wilbur Hatch, conducting the Desi Arnaz Orchestra.

Music Composed By: Elliot Daniel.

Announcer: Johnny Jacobs.

Executive Producer: Desi Arnaz.

Producer: Jess Oppenheimer.

Director: Marc Daniels, William Asher.

Sponsor: Philip Morris Cigarettes.

Note for the Little Ricky Credit: The baby to whom Lucy gave birth on January 19, 1953, was played by James John Gouzer; Richard Lee Simmons played the role on April 20, 1953, followed by the Mayer Twins and finally Richard Keith (who is now known as Keith Thibodeaux).

I LOVE LUCY—30 minutes—CBS—October 15, 1951 - September 1956. Prime time rebroadcasts: CBS—October 15, 1951 - June 24, 1957. CBS Rebroadcasts: 1957 - 1967. Syndicated. 179 filmed episodes.

Spin-offs:

The Lucille Ball-Desi Arnaz Show—60 minutes—CBS—November 6, 1957 - September 1958. Also titled: "The Luci-Desi Comedy Hour." Syndicated.

Continued events in the lives of Ricky and Lucy Ricardo, and their friends Fred (now Ricky's band manager) and Ethel Mertz.

Lucy In Connecticut—30 minutes—CBS—July 3, 1960 - September 25, 1960.

Retitled episodes of "I Love Lucy" wherein Ricky and Lucy purchase a home in Westport, Connecticut, and, with their boarders, Fred and Ethel Mertz, struggle to find a life of peace and quiet, despite Lucy's constant knack for finding trouble.

I MARRIED JOAN

Comedy. Background: Los Angeles, California. The trials and tribulations of the Stevens: Bradley, a sophisticated domestic-relations court judge; and his well-meaning but scatterbrained wife, Joan.

CAST

Joan Stevens	Joan Davis
Judge Bradley Stevens	Jim Backus
Charlie, their neighbor	Hal Smith
Mabel, his wife	Geraldine Carr
Janet Tobin, Joan's friend	Sheila Bromley
Kerwin Tobin, her husband	Dan Tobin
Mildred Webster, Joan's friend	Sandra Gould
Beverly Grossman, Joan's sister	Beverly Wills
Alan Grossman, her husband	Himself
Helen, Joan's friend	Mary Jane Croft

Producer: Dick Mack, J. Wolfson.

Sponsor: General Electric.

The Davises' Address: 345 Laurel Drive.

Program Open:

Song: "I Married Joan, what a girl, what a whirl, what a life. Oh, I Married Joan, what a mind, love is blind, what a wife . . . ."

Announcer: "The Joan Davis Show—'I Married Joan'—America's favorite comedy show; starring America's queen of comedy, Joan Davis as Mrs. Joan Stevens . . . and featuring Jim Backus as Judge Bradley Stevens."

I MARRIED JOAN—30 minutes— NBC—October 15, 1952 - April 6, 1955. Rebroadcasts: NBC—May 5, 1956 - March 9, 1957. Syndicated. 98 episodes.

I'M DICKENS. . .HE'S FENSTER

Comedy. Background: Los Angeles, California. The misadventures of car-

penters Harry Dickens, married and henpecked; and Arch Fenster, a swinging young bachelor.

CAST

Harry Dickens	John Astin
Arch Fenster	Marty Ingels
Kate Dickens, Harry's wife	Emmaline Henry
Mr. Bannister, their employer	Frank DeVol
Mel Warshaw, a friend and co-worker	Dave Ketchum
Mulligan, a friend and co-worker	Henry Beckman

Music: Frank DeVol; Irving Szathmary.

I'M DICKENS. . .HE'S FENSTER— 30 minutes—ABC—September 28, 1962 - September 13, 1963. Syndicated. 32 episodes.

THE IMMORTAL

Adventure. Seriously injured when his plane passes through an electrical turbulence area, aged and dying billionaire Jordan Braddock, the owner of Braddock Industries, is given a transfusion of Type O blood donated earlier by Ben Richards, an employee in the automotive division. Shortly after, Braddock miraculously recovers, feeling and looking younger.

Baffled, Dr. Matthew Pearce conducts tests and discovers that Richards, through a freak of nature is immortal, possessing a rare blood type that grants him immunity to old age and disease. Further tests reveal that Braddock's rejuvenation is only temporary; and that to sustain it, periodic transfusions are necessary. Ben, who is advised to leave with his fiancée, Sylvia Cartwright, and begin life anew elsewhere—to get away from the greedy who will seek a second or third lifetime—refuses, and chooses to remain and work with researchers until they discover a means by which to duplicate his blood.

Hoping to secure financial backing, Richards approaches Braddock. However, Braddock, who is obsessed with the idea of a new life, kidnaps Richards and imprisons him.

Discovering that as infants Ben and his brother Jason were separated after his parent's death, Braddock, who believes that Jason may also possess the same blood antibodies, begins a search for him.

Assisted by Braddock's wife, Janet, who opposes her husband's obsession, Richards escapes from the Braddock mansion. Angered, Jordan orders his apprehension.

After months of separation, Ben arranges a reunion with Sylvia. Though careful in her preparations to leave, she is followed by Braddock's men. Shortly after he and Sylvia meet, Braddock's men close in. In the ensuing chase and struggle, Sylvia is shot and critically injured.

Saved by a transfusion of his blood, Ben reluctantly leaves Sylvia. Driven by a constant thought that sooner or later Braddock will die and he and Sylvia will have their life together, he struggles to live free. "Sylvia, I love you. . .I'll always think about you. Even if Braddock wasn't after me, there would be others by now. . . .It's only a matter of time before other people find out. Dr. Pearce was right, I've got to run far and fast. While I'm doing it, I'm going to try to find my brother. Wherever he is, he's got to be warned. Warned that Braddock is looking for him, ready to throw him in a cage and drain him dry. Whatever happens to me finally, Sylvia, wherever I go, I want you to know I'm gonna miss you. I'm gonna miss you for as long as I live."

CAST

Ben Richards	Christopher George
Jordan Braddock	Barry Sullivan
Sylvia Cartwright	Carol Lynley
Fletcher, Braddock's right-hand man	Don Knight
Janet Braddock	Jessica Walter
Dr. Matthew Pearce	Ralph Bellamy
Jason Richards	Michael Strong

Music: Dominic Frontiere; Leith Stevens.

THE IMMORTAL—60 minutes—ABC —September 24, 1970 - September 8, 1971. 13 episodes.

THE IMOGENE COCA SHOW

Variety. Various comedy sketches.

Hostess: Imogene Coca.

Regulars: Billy DeWolfe, Ruth Donnelly, Hal March, David Burns, Bibi Osterwald.

Orchestra: George Bassman.

THE IMOGENE COCA SHOW—60 minutes—NBC—October 2, 1954 - June 25, 1955.

THE IMPOSTER

See Title: "Colonel Flack."

I'M THE LAW

Crime Drama. Background: New York City. The investigations of Lieutenant George Kirby, a plainclothes police detective. Stories relate his attempts to infiltrate and corrupt the ranks of organized crime.

Starring: George Raft as Lt. George Kirby.

I'M THE LAW—30 minutes—Syndicated 1953. Also known as "The George Raft Casebook."

THE INA RAY HUTTON SHOW

Musical Variety. Female guests (a nomen-allowed policy) coupled with a bevy of beautiful hostesses.

Hostess: Ina Ray Hutton.

Regulars: Dee Dee Ball, Helen Smith, Margaret Rinker, Janice Davis, Harriet Blackburn, Judy Var Buer, Mickey Anderson, Evie Howeth, Helen Wooley, Lois Cronen, Peggy Fairbanks, Helen Hammond, Zoe Ann Willy.

Announcer: Diane Brewster.

Music: The shapely Ina Ray Hutton All-Girl Orchestra.

THE INA RAY HUTTON SHOW—30 minutes—NBC—July 4, 1956 - August 31, 1956.

INCH HIGH PRIVATE EYE

Animated Cartoon. The investigations of Inch High, the world's smallest man, a master detective employed by the Finkerton Organization.

Characters:
Inch High; Laurie, his niece; Gator, his aide, a master of a thousand faces; Braveheart, his coward dog; Mr. Finkerton, Inch High's employer; Mrs. Finkerton his wife.

Inch High's car: The *Hugemobile.*

Voices: Lennie Weinrib, Ted Knight, Kathy Gori, Don Messick, Jamie Farr, John Stephenson, Allan Oppenheimer, Janet Waldo, Vic Perrin.

Music: Hoyt Curtin.

INCH HIGH PRIVATE EYE—30 minutes—NBC—September 8, 1973 - August 31, 1974. 13 episodes.

IN COMMON

Game. Three specially selected contestants who have never met, but who each have something in common, compete. Each has three minutes to question the other and determine the common denominator. Merchandise prizes are awarded to successful players.

Host: Ralph Story.

IN COMMON—30 minutes—CBS 1954.

INDIVIDUALLY YOURS

A women's program, with hostess Celeste Carlyle, featuring fashion tips and previews of new designs. Broadcast for 15 minutes on DuMont in 1950.

INFORMATION PLEASE

Game. Three panelists, assisted by guests, attempt to answer questions submitted by home viewers. Prizes are awarded to those which stump the experts, the Brain Panel.

Host: Clifton Fadiman.

Brain Panel: Franklin P. Adams, Oscar Levant, John Kiernan.

INFORMATION PLEASE—30 minutes—CBS—June 29, 1952 - September 1952.

THE INFORMER

Crime Drama. Background: London, England. The activities of Alexander Lambert, a disbarred barrister who has become a police informer.

CAST
Alexander Lambert   Ian Hendry
Also: Jean Marsh, Heather Sears.

THE INFORMER—43 minutes—Syndicated 1965. 8 episodes.

IN THE MORGAN MANNER

Musical Variety.
Host: Russ Morgan.
Orchestra: Russ Morgan.

IN THE MORGAN MANNER—30 minutes—ABC 1950.

THE INNER FLAME

See title: "Portia Faces Life."

THE INNER SANCTUM

Anthology. Mystery presentations. Tales of people confronted with sudden, perilous situations.

Host: Paul McGrath (as the unseen, only heard, Raymond).

Included:

The Third Fate The story of a young woman plagued by nightmares of a psychopathic killer.

CAST
Louise Horton, Donald Woods.

Family Skeleton. After discovering a skeleton in the basement of a home owned by a wealthy family, two moving men attempt blackmail.

CAST
Murray Hamilton, Edward Binns, Steve Elliot.

The Yellow Parakeet. Two confidence men attempt to dupe a lonely old man into stealing money for them.

CAST
Ernest Truex.

INNER SANCTUM—30 minutes—Syndicated 1954. 39 episodes. Based on the radio program of the same title.

IN THE NEWS

Children's Documentary. Newsreel presentations designed to acquaint young audiences with national and world events and people making headlines.

Narrator: Christopher Glen.

IN THE NEWS—02 minutes, 30 seconds—CBS—Premiered: September 12, 1970. Presented four minutes to the hour throughout the network's Saturday morning cartoon schedule.

IN SEARCH OF . . .

Documentary. A series that attempts to explain and provide answers for some of the mysteries that surround us in our everyday lives (e.g., ghosts, U.F.O.s, myths, monsters, and lost civilizations).

Host-Narrator: Leonard Nimoy.

Music: Laurin Rinder, Mike Lewis.

Executive Producer: Alan Landsburg.

Producer: Robert Lang, Deborah Blum, Alex Pomansanof.

Director: H.G. Stark.

IN SEARCH OF . . . —30 minutes—
Syndicated 1976.

INSIDE DETECTIVE

See title: "Rocky King, Detective."

INSIDE N.B.C.

Documentary. A behind-the-scenes
look into the past, the present, and
future of the National Broadcasting
Company. Features: visits to program
rehearsals, interviews, and previews of
forthcoming events.
Host: Bill Cullen.

INSIDE N.B.C.—15 minutes—NBC—
December 12, 1955 - June 1, 1956.

INSIDE U.S.A.

Variety. Music, songs, guests, and in-
terviews.
Hosts: Peter Lind Hayes, Mary Healy.
Regulars: Sheila Bond, Marian Colby.
Orchestra: Jay Blacton.

INSIDE U.S.A.—30 minutes—CBS
1949.

INSIDE U.S.A. WITH CHEVROLET

See title: "Inside U.S.A."

THE INSPECTOR

A thirty-nine-episode series, set in
England, that focuses on the crime-
solving exploits of a Scotland Yard
Police Inspector (played by Louis
Hayward) and his German Shepherd
dog, Iyan. Syndicated 1966.

INSPECTOR FABIAN
OF SCOTLAND YARD

Crime Drama. Background: England.
The investigations of Inspector Robert
Fabian, the Superintendant of Detec-
tives of the New Scotland Yard.
Stories stress the use of scientific
evaluation and modern techniques in
solving crimes.
Starring: Bruce Seton as Inspector
Robert Fabian.

INSPECTOR FABIAN OF SCOT-
LAND YARD—30 minutes—NBC
1955.

INSPECTOR MARK SABER

See title: "Mark Saber."

INTERLUDE

Anthology. Dramatic presentations.

Included:

Myrt And Marge. A video adaptation
of the 1930s radio classic. The story
of a stage-struck woman in New York.

CAST
Franklin Pangborn, Lyle Talbot.

Sadie And Sally. Background: New
York City. The misadventures of two
beautiful young career girls.

CAST
Sadie: Joi Lansing; Sally: Lois Hall.

Battsford's Beanery. A restaurant
owner attempts to prevent gangsters
from establishing a gambling conces-
sion in his establishment.

CAST
Joe Sawyer.

INTERLUDE—30 minutes—ABC
1953.

THE INTERNATIONAL ANIMATION FESTIVAL

Animated Cartoon. A thirteen-week
series comprised of award-winning car-
toons from around the world.
Hostess: Jean Marsh.
Music: Greig McRitchie.
Executive Producer: Zev Putterman.
Producer: Sheldon Renan.
Director (of Miss Marsh's segments):
James Scalem.

THE INTERNATIONAL ANIMA-
TION FESTIVAL—30 minutes—
PBS—April 7, 1975 - June 30, 1975.

INTERNATIONAL DETECTIVE

Crime Drama. The global investiga-
tions of Ken Franklin, a private detec-
tive for the William J. Burns Detective
Agency. Based on actual clientele
files.
Starring: Arthur Fleming as Ken
Franklin.
Music: Sidney Shaw, Leroy Holmes.

INTERNATIONAL DETECTIVE—30
minutes—Syndicated 1959. 39 episodes.

INTERNATIONAL PERFORMANCE

Variety. International entertainment
programs, opera, ballet, and concert,
performed especially for television.
English subtitles are incorporated
where appropriate.
Host: Robert Merrill.

Included:

Les Brigands. Italy, nineteenth century. The efforts of bandits, mas-
querading as royal escorts, to rob the
coffers of the Duke of Mantua.

CAST
Falsacappa: Dominique Tirmont;
Fiorella: Elaine Manchet; Duke of
Mantua: Andre Mallabera; Princess of
Granada: Nicole Fallien.

La Sylphide. The story of a young
Scottish nobleman's love for a cap-
tured woodland sprite. Enacted by the
Paris Opera Ballet.

CAST
La Sylphide: Ghislaine Thesmar;
James: Michael Denard; Effie:
Laurence Nerval.

Salome. The biblical story of Salome,
the daughter of Herod, and her lust
for and the ultimate destruction of
John the Baptist.

CAST
Salome: Ludmilla Tcherina; Herod:
Michael Auclaire; John the Baptist:
Jean Paul Zehnocker.

INTERNATIONAL PERFORM-
ANCE—60 minutes—PBS—October 5,
1972 - January 10, 1973.

INTERNATIONAL PLAYHOUSE

Anthology. Internationally produced
dramas.

INTERNATIONAL PLAYHOUSE—
30 minutes—Syndicated 1953.

INTERNATIONAL SHOWTIME

Variety. Highlights of various European circuses.
Host-Interpreter: Don Ameche.
Music: Performed by the various
circus orchestras.

Producer: Pat Pleven, Phil Levin, Joe Cates, Larry White.

INTERNATIONAL SHOWTIME—60 minutes—NBC—September 15, 1961 - September 10, 1965. 144 tapes.

THE INTERNS

Medical Drama. Background: New North Hospital in Los Angeles, California. The personal and professional lives of interns Greg Pettit, Lydia Thorpe, Pooch Hardin, Sam Marsh, and Cal Barrin.

CAST
Dr. Peter Goldstone, the interns' supervisor	Broderick Crawford
Dr. Pooch Hardin	Christopher Stone
Dr. Lydia Thorpe	Sandra Smith
Dr. Sam Marsh	Mike Farrell
Dr. Greg Pettit	Stephen Brooks
Dr. Cal Barrin	Hal Frederick
Bobbe Marsh, Sam's wife	Elaine Giftos
Dr. Jacoby	Skip Homeier

THE INTERNS—60 minutes—CBS—September 18, 1970 - September 10, 1971. 24 episodes.

INTERPOL CALLING

Crime Drama. The cases of Paul Duval, a chief inspector for Interpol, the International Police Organization formed by sixty-three member nations; the most complex and powerful law enforcement agency in the world.

Starring: Charles Korvin as Chief Inspector Paul Duval.

Producer: J. Arthur Rank.

INTERPOL CALLING—30 minutes—Syndicated 1961.

THE INVADERS

Adventure. Driving home on a deserted country road, architect David Vincent witnesses the landing of a craft from another galaxy. Its inhabitants, aliens who appear in human form and who plan to make the Earth their world, fail in their initial attempt to destroy Vincent. Witnessing the destruction of a young alien couple before his eyes (disintegrating in a glowing light) and learning of their one flaw, a crooked finger on the right hand, he becomes their mortal enemy.

Stories depict Vincent's lone attempts to thwart alien objectives

The Interns. Left to right: Hal Frederick, Sandra Smith, Stephen Brooks, Mike Farrell, and Christopher Stone. © *Screen Gems.*

and convince a disbelieving world "that the nightmare has already begun."

CAST
David Vincent	Roy Thinnes
Edgar Scoville, his one believer and assistant	Kent Smith

Music: Dominic Frontiere.

THE INVADERS—60 minutes—ABC—January 10, 1967 - September 17, 1968. Syndicated. 43 episodes.

THE INVESTIGATOR

Crime Drama. Background: New York City. The investigations of private detective Jeff Prior.

CAST
Jeff Prior	Lonny Chapman
Lloyd Prior, his father, a retired newspaper reporter; his occasional assistant	Howard St. John

THE INVESTIGATOR—30 minutes—NBC—June 30, 1958 - September 1958. 13 episodes.

THE INVESTIGATORS

Crime Drama. Background: New York City. The cases of crime specialists Steve Banks and Russ Andrews, highly paid and highly skilled private insurance investigators.

CAST
Steve Banks	James Philbrook
Russ Andrews	James Franciscus
Maggie Peters, their assistant	Mary Murphy
Bill Davis, their assistant	Al Austin
June Polly, their secretary	June Kenny

THE INVESTIGATORS—60 minutes—CBS—September 21, 1961 - December 28, 1961. 13 episodes.

THE INVISIBLE MAN

Adventure. Background: London, England. Experimenting with the problems of optical density (the refraction of light), Peter Brady, a young British scientist, is exposed to a leaking conductor and rendered invisible when the gasses mix with the oxygen.

Learning of his plight, the Ministry considers him a national menace (fearing panic to result if the existence of an invisible man is known) and imprison him.

When a rival experimentor fails to secure Brady's formula for invisibility, the Ministry is convinced otherwise and permits Brady to continue with his research.

Lacking the knowledge to become visible, Brady agrees to use his great advantage to assist the British government and undertakes hazardous missions throughout the world. Continuing his experiments, he struggles to discover the unknown formula into the realm of reality. Based on the stories by H. G. Wells.

CAST

Peter Brady, the Invisible Man	?*
Diane Brady, his sister	Lisa Daniely
Sally Brady, his niece	Deborah Walting
Sir Charles, the Cabinet Minister	Ernest Clark

*Though seen and heard, the actor's name has been withheld by the series producer, Ralph Smart, for reasons that are purely his own. One can only assume that perhaps it is to create the illusion of authenticity.

THE INVISIBLE MAN—30 minutes—Syndicated 1958. 26 episodes.

THE INVISIBLE MAN

Science Fiction Adventure. Background: Los Angeles, California. While working on a formula to transfer matter from one place to another through the use of lazer beams, Daniel Weston, a scientist employed by the KLAE Corporation, a research center that undertakes government contracts, injects himself with a newly developed serum that renders him invisible. When he discovers that his serum is to be used for military purposes, he destroys the process and his only means by which to become visible. By wearing a special plastic face mask and hands developed by a friend, Weston appears as he did before the experiment. Stories detail Weston's investigations into highly dangerous national and international assignments on behalf of the KLAE Corporation. Based on the story by H.G. Wells.

CAST

Daniel Weston	David McCallum
Kate Weston, his wife	Melinda Fee
Walter Carlson, his employer	Craig Stevens

Music: Henry Mancini; Pete Rugolo.

Additional Music: Richard Clements, Hal Mooney.

Executive Producer: Harve Bennett.

Producer: Leslie Stevens, Steve Bocho, Robert F. O'Neil.

Director: Robert Lewis, Alan J. Levi, Sigmund Neufeld, Jr., Leslie Stevens.

THE INVISIBLE MAN—60 minutes—NBC—September 8, 1975 - January 9, 1976. 13 episodes.

INVITATION TO MURDER

Anthology. Dramatizations of stories penned by mystery writer Edgar Wallace. Later titled, with additional episodes, "The Edgar Wallace Mystery Theatre." (See title.)

INVITATION TO MURDER—60 minutes—Syndicated 1962. 13 episodes.

I REMEMBER MAMA

Comedy-Drama. Background: San Francisco, California, 1910. The story of the Hansons, parents Marta and Lars, and their children, Katrin, Dagmar, and Nels, a Norwegian family living busily in a large American city. Events in their lives are seen through the sentimental eyes of Katrin, the older daughter, an aspiring writer who records their daily activities in her diary. Episodes focus on Mama, warm, wise, compassionate, and loving, the guiding light through their difficult times. Based on the book, *Mama's Bank Account,* by Kathryn Forbes.

CAST

Marta Hanson (Mama)	Peggy Wood
Lars Hanson (Papa), a carpenter	Judson Laire
Katrin Hanson	Rosemary Rice
Dagmar Hanson	Iris Mann Robin Morgan Toni Campbell
Nels Hanson	Dick Van Patten
Jenny, Mama's older sister	Ruth Gates
Trina, Mama's younger sister	Alice Frost
Uncle Gunnar	Carl Frank
T.R. Ryan	Kevin Coughlin
Also: Abby Lewis.	

Music: Billy Nalle.

Producer: Carol Irwin, Ralph Nelson, Donald Richardson.

Director: Ralph Nelson.

Sponsor: General Foods.

Note: The Hanson address is also known to be.118 Steiner Street; and the series itself was also called "Mama."

Program open:

Katrin: "I remember the big white house on Elm Street, and my little sister Dagmar, and my big brother Nels, and Papa. But most of all, I Remember Mama."

I REMEMBER MAMA—30 minutes—CBS—July 1, 1949 - March 17, 1957.

IRON HORSE

Western. Background: Wyoming during the 1870s. Ben Calhoun, a rugged gentleman cowboy, wins a near-bankrupt railroad in a poker game. Assuming control, he attempts to acquire customers, pay off overanxious creditors, replenish a lacking fund, and establish a successful operation.

CAST

Ben Calhoun	Dale Robertson
Dave Tarrant, his assistant	Gary Collins
Barnabas Rogers, his assistant	Bob Random
Nils Torvald, his assistant	Roger Torrey
Julie, the freight line operator	Ellen McRae

Ben's horse: Hannibal.

Ben's pet raccoon: Ulysses.

IRON HORSE—60 minutes—ABC—September 12, 1966 - January 6, 1968. 47 episodes.

IRONSIDE

Crime Drama. Background: San Francisco, California. Vacationing, Robert T. Ironside, San Francisco Police Chief, is shot by a would-be assassin. The bullet, shattering a spinal nerve junction, causes permanent paralysis.

Determined to continue his life, and his crusade against crime, he is appointed the special consultant to the San Francisco Police Department and is assigned a staff of crime fighters: Detective Sergeant Ed Brown and Policewoman Eve Whitfield (later replaced by Policewoman Fran Belding); and Mark Sanger, an ex-con who later becomes a lawyer, is "his legs" and general helper.

Stories depict their case investigations.

CAST

Chief Robert Ironside	Raymond Burr
Policewoman Eve Whitfield	Barbara Anderson
Det. Sgt. Ed Brown	Don Galloway
Mark Sanger	Don Mitchell
Policewoman Fran Belding	Elizabeth Baur
Diana Sanger, Mark's wife	Jane Pringle
The police commissioner	Gene Lyons

Music: Marty Paich; Oliver Nelson.

Executive Producer: Joel Rogosin, Cy Chermak.

Producer: Norman Jolley, Frank Price, Douglas Benton.

Director: Russ Mayberry, Don McDougall, Daniel Haller, Boris Sagal, Tony Leader, Allen Reisner, Don Weis, Abner Biberman, Dick Colla.

Creator: Collier Young.

IRONSIDE—60 minutes—NBC—September 14, 1967 - January 16, 1975. 120 episodes. Syndicated title: "The Raymond Burr Show."

I SEARCH FOR ADVENTURE

Documentary. Films depicting man's quest for adventure.

Host-Narrator: Jack Douglas.

I SEARCH FOR ADVENTURE—30 minutes—Syndicated 1954.

ISIS

Adventure. Early history: Background: Ancient Egypt. Presented with a magic amulet by the Royal Sorcerer, the queen and her descendants were endowed by the power of Isis (the Egyptian goddess of Fertility) and received the ability to soar, the power of the animals, and control over the elements of earth, sea, and sky.

Three thousand years later, Andrea Thomas, a young high school science teacher on an expedition, uncovers the lost amulet and becomes heir to the secrets and powers of Isis.

Series background: The town of Lockspur. Stories relate Andrea's battle against crime as the mysterious Isis, "dedicated foe of evil, defender of the weak, and champion of truth and justice." (When holding the amulet, which she wears as a necklace, and speaking the words, "Oh mighty Isis," Andrea becomes Isis.)

CAST
Andrea Thomas/ Isis	JoAnna Cameron
Rick Mason, Andrea's friend, a teacher	Brian Cutler
Cindy Lee, Andrea's friend, a student at Lockspur High School	Joanna Pang
Dr. Barnes,	

Isis. JoAnna Cameron.

the head of the science department	Albert Reed
Renee Carroll, a student	Ronalda Douglas

Andrea's pet crow: Tut.

Music: Yvette Blais, Jeff Michael.

Executive Producer: Lou Scheimer, Norm Prescott, Dick Rosenbloom.

Producer: Arthur H. Nadel.

Director: Hollingsworth Morse, Arnold Laven, Earl Bellamy, Arthur H. Nadel.

Note: The background is also known to be Larkspur, a town in California.

ISIS—25 minutes—CBS—Premiered: September 6, 1975.

THE ISLANDERS

Adventure. Background: The West Indies. The experiences of Sandy Wade and Zack Malloy, the pilots of the *Islander,* a two-man, one-plane airline based in the Spice Islands.

CAST
Zack Malloy	James Philbrook
Sandy Wade	William Reynolds
Whilhelmina "Steamboat Willie" Vandeveer, the business manager	Diane Brewster
Naja, a friend	Daria Massey
Shipwreck Callahan, a friend	Roy Wright

THE ISLANDERS—60 minutes—ABC—October 2, 1960 - January 1961. Syndicated. 24 episodes.

ISLANDS IN THE SUN

Travel. Visits to various tropical islands via the sailing ship *Islanda.*

Host-Narrator: Bill Burrud.

Assistant: Minzie the Mermaid.

The Islanders. James Philbrook (left), William Reynolds, Diane Brewster (right), and Daria Massey.

ISLANDS IN THE SUN—30 minutes—Syndicated 1969. 26 episodes.

I SPY

Anthology. Tales of intrigue and espionage spanning the 16th to 20th centuries.

Host-Story Teller: Raymond Massey, appearing as Anton, the spy master.

Included:

The Amateur. The story of a girl who becomes a spy for General Stonewall Jackson when Union troops take over her father's hotel.

Starring: Mary Linn Beller.

The Baby Spy. The story of an eight-year-old boy who unknowingly does spying for the Japanese at Pearl Harbor years before World War II.

Starring: Jacques Aubochan, Richie Andrusco, Abby Lewis.

Betrayal At West Point. The events that led Benedict Arnold to betray his country.

Starring: Otto Hulett, Louis Edmonds.

I SPY—30 minutes—Syndicated 1956. 39 episodes.

I SPY

Spy Drama. The investigations of U.S.

government undercover agents Kelly Robinson and Alexander Scott. Kelly, under the guise of an international tennis champion, and Scott, as his trainer-masseur, battle the destructive counterforces of democracy throughout the world.

CAST

Kelly Robinson	Robert Culp
Alexander Scott (Scotty)	Bill Cosby

Music: Earle Hagen; Carl Brandt.

I SPY—60 minutes—NBC—September 15, 1965 - September 9, 1968. Syndicated. 82 episodes.

IT COULD BE YOU

Game. Contestants selected from the studio audience compete by performing stunts. Winners receive a prize that they had always wanted (stated before the game begins), but could never afford to purchase. Featured: Friend and family reunions.

Host: Bill Leyden.

Announcer: Wendell Niles.

IT COULD BE YOU—30 minutes—NBC. Nightime: July 2, 1958 - September 17, 1958; December 11, 1958 - March 12, 1959. Daytime: June 7, 1961 - September 27, 1961.

IT HAPPENS IN SPAIN

Crime Drama. Background: Spain. The investigations of Joe Jones, a private detective who assists distressed American tourists.

CAST

Joe Jones	Scott McKay
Tina, his secretary	Elena Barra

IT HAPPENS IN SPAIN—30 minutes —Syndicated 1958.

IT PAYS TO BE IGNORANT

Comedy Game. Involved: Three regular panelists and two contestants. Each player, in turn, picks a question from "The Dunce Cap" and reads it aloud (e.g., "From what state do we get Hawaiian canned pineapple?"). The panelists provide comic answers while evading the correct response. Object: For the contestant, if at all possible, to get a word in and extract the right answer. Prizes are awarded accordingly—basically for attempting to face the panel.

Host: Tom Howard.

Panelists: Harry McNaughton, George Shelton, Lulu McConnell.

Announcer: Dick Stark.

Vocalists: The Townsmen Quartet.

Orchestra: Ray Morgan.

IT PAYS TO BE IGNORANT—30 minutes—CBS—June 6, 1949 - April 28, 1950. Based on the radio program of the same title.

In 1973, a thirty-minute syndicated version of the series appeared with Joe Flynn, Jo Anne Worley, Charles Nelson Reilly, and Bobby Baxter.

IT PAYS TO BE MARRIED

Interview-Quiz. Interview segment: Married couples converse with the host and relate their marital difficulties and how they overcame them. Quiz Segment: The host reads a general-knowledge question. The couple who are first to identify themselves through a buzzer signal, receive a chance to answer. If correct, points are scored. Winners, the highest point scorers, receive three hundred and fifty dollars.

Host: Bill Goodwin.

Announcer: Jay Stewart.

IT PAYS TO BE MARRIED—30 minutes—NBC—July 4, 1955 - October 28, 1955.

IT'S ABOUT TIME

Game. Competing: Selected studio-audience members. Through clues provided by the host, contestants have to identify incidents from the past. Highest scorers (most correct responses) receive merchandise prizes.

Host: Dr. Bergen Evans.

IT'S ABOUT TIME—30 minutes—ABC 1954.

IT'S ABOUT TIME

Comedy. Distinguished by two formats.

Format One:

A rocket, launched from the NASA Space Center in Florida, penetrates a turbulence area and breaks the time barrier. Crash landing in a swamp, its astronauts, Mac and Hector, escape unharmed.

Exploring the surrounding area, they discover and rescue a young boy, Breer, trapped on a ledge. Through him they discover they have landed in the Prehistoric Era. Befriending his family, his father, Gronk, his mother, Shad, and his sister, Mlor, the astronauts, through their strange dress, customs, and inventions, are believed by others to be evil spirits and ordered killed by the Cave Boss. Relating the story of Breer's rescue, Gronk persuades the Cave Boss to spare their lives. Stories relate the astronauts attempts to adjust to a past era and locate copper to repair their disabled spacecraft.

Format Two (five months later):

Discovering a copper mine, Mac and Hector repair the rocket. However, the Cave Boss, uneasy over the astronauts presence, orders them and Gronk and his family destroyed for aiding evil spirits. Learning of their plans, Mac and Hector prepare for blast off. The Cave Family, with no where else to turn, sneak aboard the craft.

Rebreaking the time barrier and landing in present day Los Angeles, California, the Cave Family is concealed in Mac's apartment. Stories relate the Cave Family's attempts to master the ways of modern society; and Mac and Hector's efforts to conceal their presence from NASA officials.

CAST

Mac	Frank Aletter
Hector	Jack Mullaney
Gronk	Joe E. Ross
Shad	Imogene Coca
Mlor	Mary Grace
Breer	Pat Cardi
The Cave Boss	Cliff Norton
Clon, the Boss's aide	Mike Mazurki
Mrs. Boss	Kathleen Freeman
Dr. Hamilton	Jan Arvan
General Tyler	Alan DeWitt

Music: Sherwood Schwartz; Gerald Fried; George Wyle.

IT'S ABOUT TIME—30 minutes—CBS—September 11, 1966 - September 3, 1967. 26 episodes.

IT'S A BUSINESS

Variety. Background: New York City during the 1900s. A musical comedy revolving around the operating difficulties of the Broadway Music Publishing Company. Stories depict the lives of song pluggers in an era when the performer visited the publisher to find material.

CAST

Song Plugger	Bob Haymes
Song Plugger	Leo de Lyon
The Secretary	Dorothy Loudon

IT'S A BUSINESS—30 minutes—DuMont—March 26, 1952 - May 27, 1952.

IT'S A GREAT LIFE

Comedy. Background: Hollywood, California. Recently discharged from the service, ex-G.I.s Denny David and Steve Connors answer an ad for a furnished room at the Morgan Boarding House. Renting the room, they meet and befriend Uncle Earl, the unemployed and conniving brother of its owner, Amy Morgan. A saga of three men plagued by financial matters and their harebrained attempts to terminate monetary burdens.

CAST

Denny David	Michael O'Shea
Steve Connors	William Bishop
Uncle Earl	James Dunn
Amy Morgan (widow)	Frances Bavier
Katy Morgan, her daughter	Barbara Bales

Music: David Rose.

Producer: Ray Singer, Dick Chevillat.

Sponsor: Chrysler-Plymouth.

IT'S A GREAT LIFE—30 minutes—NBC—September 7, 1954 - June 3, 1956. Syndicated. 78 episodes.

IT'S A HIT

Children. A game show format wherein two teams of children, aged seven to fourteen, compete for prizes in a question-and-answer session based on subjects the contestants are studying in school.

Host: Happy Felton.

IT'S A HIT—30 minutes—ABC—June 1, 1957 - September 21, 1957.

IT'S ALWAYS JAN

Comedy. Background: New York City. The home and working lives of three career girls: Janis Stewart, widow, nightclub entertainer, and hopeful Broadway actress; Valerie Malone, a shapely blonde model; and Patricia Murphy, a secretary with a heart of gold—women sharing a Man-hattan apartment. Stories depict Jan's attempts to raise her ten-year-old-daughter, Josie, and provide for her a life without the hardships of her own.

CAST

Janis Stewart	Janis Paige
Valerie Malone	Merry Anders
Patricia Murphy	Patricia Bright
Josie Stewart	Jeri Lou James
Stanley Schrieber, the delivery boy	Arch Johnson
Harry Cooper, Jan's agent	Sid Melton

IT'S ALWAYS JAN—30 minutes—CBS—September 10, 1955 - September 1, 1956.

It's Alway's Jan. Left to right: Merry Anders, Janis Paige, and Patricia Bright.

IT'S A MAN'S WORLD

Comedy. Background: Cordella, an Ohio river town. The story of three young men, Tom Tom DeWitt, Vern Hodges, and Wes Macauley, college students residing in a houseboat docked at the water's edge. Recently orphaned when their parents were killed in an automobile accident, Wes's younger brother, Howie, also lives with them. Episodes relate their experiences as they attempt to cope with life and prove it to be a man's world.

CAST

Wes Macauley	Glenn Corbett
Tom Tom DeWitt	Ted Bessell
Vern Hodges	Randy Boone
Howie Macauley	Michael Burns
Nora	Ann Schuyler
Irene	Jan Norris
Scott	Harry Harvey
Mrs. Dodson	Kate Murtagh
Alma Jean	Jeannie Cashell
Mrs. Meredith	Mary Adams

IT'S A MAN'S WORLD—60 minutes—NBC—September 17, 1962 - January 28, 1963. 19 episodes.

IT'S ANYBODY'S GUESS

Game. Two contestants compete and appear opposite a panel of five studio-audience members. A question is read to the panel (e.g., "Name something sold door-to-door"); an answer, chosen by the program, appears for all to see except the panelists. One contestant, chosen by a flip of a coin, has to predict whether or not the panel will come up with the same response ("Girl Scout cookies"). Each panelist then receives a chance to answer the question. Depending on the results, one point is scored: for the contestant at play if he is correct; for his opponent if he predicted incorrectly. Contestants now alternate turns and the first player to score five points is the winner.

Host: Monty Hall.

Announcer: Jay Stewart.

Music: Recorded.

Executive Producer: Stefan Hatos, Monty Hall, Stu Billet.

Producer: Steve Feke.

Director: Joe Behar.

IT'S ANYBODY'S GUESS—30 minutes—NBC—Premiered: June 13, 1977.

IT'S MAGIC

Children. Performances by guest magicians.

Host: Paul Tripp.

Orchestra: Hank Sylvern.

IT'S MAGIC—30 minutes—CBS—July 31, 1955 - September 1955.

IT'S NEWS TO ME

Game. Involved: Five celebrity panelists and two competing contestants, each of whom receive thirty dollars starting money. The panelists are presented with a prop or picture relating to a news event. Four of the celebrities give false identifications of the object; the fifth states the actual newsworthiness. Contestants, vying for additional cash (ten dollars per round) have to determine which one is telling the truth. One round per game involves a dramatic reenactment of a news event with the game continuing in the same manner.

Hosts: John Daly; Walter Cronkite; Quincy Howe.

Panelists: Nina Foch, Quenton Reynolds, John Henry Faulk, Constance Bennett, Anna Lee.

Performing Reenactments: Frank Wayne.

Producer: Mark Goodson, Bill Todman.

Sponsor: General Foods.

IT'S NEWS TO ME—30 minutes—CBS—1951 - 1955.

IT'S A WONDERFUL WORLD

Travel-Documentary. Films depicting specific customs and life styles of various countries throughout the world.

Host: John Cameron Swayze.

IT'S A WONDERFUL WORLD—30 minutes—Syndicated 1963. 39 episodes.

IT'S HAPPENING

The daily title for "Happening '68" (which see), which ran on ABC from July 15, 1968 to October 15, 1968.

IT'S YOUR BET

Game. Two celebrity couples play for studio-audience members. A small, movable wall is placed between each player. One partner is asked a question via telephone to prevent the other from hearing it. He then bets points (twenty-five to one hundred) as to whether his partner "Can," or "Can't" correctly answer it. The host then reads the question aloud. If the answer corresponds with the prediction, the team is awarded the points; if it does not, the points are awarded to their opponents. Winners: The first team scoring three hundred. The participating studio-audience members receive merchandise prizes.

Hosts, in order: Hal March; Tom Kennedy; Dick Gautier; Lyle Waggoner.

Announcer: John Harlan.

Music: Recorded.

IT'S YOUR BET—30 minutes—Syndicated 1969. 494 tapes.

IT'S YOUR MOVE

Game. Four competing contestants comprising two teams of two. One team member acts out a charade; the other must guess it in a specified time limit. The amount of time is determined through bidding—both teams bid for the charade. The team bidding the lowest time limit receives it. If they are successful, they receive merchandise prizes.

Host: Jim Perry.

IT'S YOUR MOVE—30 minutes—Syndicated 1967. 65 tapes.

IT TAKES A THIEF

Adventure. Through an arrangement with S.I.A. Chief Noah Bain, Alexander Mundy, a sophisticated and cunning cat burgular, is granted a pardon from prison when he agrees to become a spy for the United States government. Posing as an international playboy, he attempts to perform necessary but highly dangerous feats of thievery through the use of his unique skills.

CAST

Alexander Mundy	Robert Wagner
Noah Bain	Malachi Throne
Alister Mundy, Alex's father, a master thief	Fred Astaire
S.I.A. Agent Dover Chuck Brown, the beautiful, but kooky thief who complicates Al's	John Russell
assignments	Susan Saint James
Wally Powers, Al's superior, later episodes	Edward Binns

Music: Benny Golson; Ralph Ferraro.

Executive Producer: Frank Price, Gordon Oliver, Jack Arnold.

Producer: Winston Miller, Paul Mason, Gene L. Coon, Mort Zarcoff.

Director: Don Weis, Jack Arnold, Gerd Oswald, Roland Kibbee, Barry Shear, Michael Caffrey, Lee H. Katzin, Tony Leader.

IT TAKES A THIEF—60 minutes—ABC—January 9, 1968 - September 9, 1969. Syndicated. 65 episodes.

IT TAKES TWO

Game. Three competing celebrity couples. The host asks a question (e.g., "What was the total distance in feet of the Wright Brothers first flight at Kitty Hawk?"). Players, who are seated on revolving platforms, are separated. They then write their answers on a card. The platforms return and the responses are revealed. Team totals, excluding fractions, are automatically calculated. The announcer, stationed in the studio audience, selects someone who then chooses the couple he believes has come closest to the correct figure. If correct, the contestant receives an expensive merchandise prize; if incorrect, a less expensive gift is awarded.

It Takes a Thief. Robert Wagner and Malachi Throne.

Host: Vince Scully.

Announcer: John Harlan.

IT TAKES TWO—30 minutes—NBC—March 31, 1969 - August 1, 1970.

IT WAS A VERY GOOD YEAR

Variety. The past is recalled through film—the music, fads, sports, politics, movies, radio, and television programs, and the sensational and tragic moments of the years 1918 through 1968.

Host-Narrator: Mel Tormé.

IT WAS A VERY GOOD YEAR—30 minutes—ABC—May 10, 1971 - August 30, 1971. 13 episodes.

IVANHOE

Adventure. Background: England during the 1190s. The exploits of Ivanhoe, a young Saxon knight, as he battles the forces of injustice. Based on the character created by Sir Walter Scott.

CAST
Ivanhoe	Roger Moore
The Monk, his aide	Robert Brown
King Richard	Bruce Seton
Sir Maverick	Paul Whitsun

Music: Edwin Astley.

IVANHOE—30 minutes—Syndicated 1957. 39 episodes. British produced.

IVAN THE TERRIBLE

Comedy. Background: Moscow, Russia. The trials and tribulations of Ivan Petrovsky, headwaiter at the Hotel Metropole and head of a family of nine who live in a three-and-one-half-room apartment. Stories stress his attempts to solve family-related problems.

CAST
Ivan Petrovsky	Lou Jacobi
Olga Petrovsky, his wife	Maria Karnilova
Vladimir, Olga's ex-husband	Phil Leeds
Tationa, Olga's mother	Despo
Sonia Petrovsky, Ivan's daughter	Caroline Kava
Sascha Petrovsky, Ivan's son	Matthew Barry
Nikolai Petrovsky, Ivan's son	Alan Cauldwell
Sventlana Petrovsky, Nikolai's wife	Nana Tucker
Raoul Sanchez, the Cuban exchange student	Manuel Martinez
Federov, the government official	Christopher Hewell
Mr. Yoshanka, Ivan's employer	Joseph Leon

Music: Joe Raposo.

Executive Producer: Alan King.

Producer: Rupert Hitzig.

Director: Peter H. Hunt.

IVAN THE TERRIBLE—30 minutes—CBS—August 21, 1976 - September 18, 1976.

I'VE GOT A SECRET

Game. Through question-and-answer probe rounds, celebrity panelists have to guess the secret of a guest contestant. Contestants receive both cash and merchandise prizes.

Versions:

CBS—30 minutes—June 26, 1952 - September 3, 1967.

Hosts: Garry Moore; Steve Allen.

Regular Panelists: Jayne Meadows, Bill Cullen, Henry Morgan, Betsy Palmer, Faye Emerson, Steve Allen.

Announcers: John Cannon; Johnny Olsen.

Syndicated—30 minutes—1972.

Host: Steve Allen.

Regular Panelists: Pat Carroll, Richard Dawson, Nanette Fabray, Gene Rayburn, Anita Gilette, Henry Morgan, Jayne Meadows.

Announcer: Johnny Olsen.

CBS—30 minutes—June 15, 1976 - July 6, 1976.

Host: Bill Cullen.

Panelists: Henry Morgan, Elaine Joyce, Phyllis George, Richard Dawson, Pat Collins.

Announcer: Johnny Olsen.

Music: Norman Paris.

I'VE GOT NEWS FOR YOU

See title: "Jack Paar."

J

JABBERJAW

Animated Cartoon. Era: Earth in the year 2000. The adventures of the Neptunes, a teenage Rock group. Assisted by Jabberjaw, a fifteen-foot pet white shark who plays drums, they attempt to solve bizarre underwater crimes—the deeds of evil villains who seek to control the ocean floor.

Characters, who comprise the Neptunes: Jabberjaw, Biff, Shelley, Bubbles, and Clam Head.

Voices: Tommy Cook, Barry Gordon, Gay Hartwig, Casey Kaseem, Keye Luke, Julie McWhirter, Frank Welker, Don Messick, Vic Perrin, Janet Waldo, John Stephenson.

Music: Hoyt Curtain, Paul DeKorte.

Executive Producer: William Hanna, Joseph Barbera.

Director: Charles A. Nichols.

JABBERJAW—25 minutes—ABC—Premiered: September 11, 1976.

THE JACK BENNY PROGRAM

Variety. A situation comedy series focusing on the home and working life of comedian Jack Benny.

CAST
Jack Benny	Himself
Mary Livingston, his wife	Herself
Rochester, Jack's valet	Eddie Anderson
Dennis Day, Jack's vocalist	Himself
Don Wilson, Jack's announcer	Himself
Professor LeBlanc, Jack's violin teacher	Mel Blanc
Harlow Wilson, Don's awkward son	Dale White
Lois Wilson, Don's wife	Lois Corbett
Schlepperman	Sam Hearn

Also: Joyce Jameson, Benny Rubin, Beverly Hills, Frank Nelson, Joe Besser, Barbara Nichols, Barbara Pepper.

Vocalists: Dennis Day; The Sportsman Quartet.

Announcer: Don Wilson.

Orchestra: Mahlon Merrick.

Producer: Hilliard Marks, Seymour Berns, Ralph Levy, Frederick de Cordova, Irving Fein.

Director: Richard Linkroum, Ralph Levy, Frederick de Cordova.

Sponsor: Lucky Strike; Jello; Allstate Insurance.

THE JACK BENNY PROGRAM—30

minutes—CBS—October 29, 1950 - September 15, 1964. Syndicated. NBC—30 minutes—September 25, 1964 - September 10, 1965. 304 CBS episodes; 39 NBC episodes.

THE JACK CARSON SHOW

Variety. Music, songs, dances, and comedy sketches.

Host: Jack Carson.

Regulars: Don Ameche, Connie Towers, Kitty Kallen, Donald Richards, Peggy Ryan, Ray McDonald, The Asia Boys.

Announcers: Ed Peck; Bud Heistand.

Orchestra: Harry Sosnick; Vic Schoen.

THE JACK CARSON SHOW—60 and 30 minute versions—NBC—1950-1955.

JACK CARTER AND COMPANY

Variety. Music, songs, and comedy sketches.

Host: Jack Carter.

Regulars: Elaine Stritch, Rowena Rollin, Sonny King, Jack Albertson, Paul Castle.

JACK CARTER AND COMPANY—30 minutes—ABC—April 5, 1949 - April 21, 1949.

JACKIE GLEASON

Listed: The television programs of comedian Jackie Gleason.

The Life Of Riley—Comedy—30 minutes—DuMont—October 4, 1949 - March 28, 1950. See title.

Cavalcade Of Stars—The Jackie Gleason Show—Variety—60 minutes—DuMont—January 7, 1950 - September 13, 1952.

Host: Jackie Gleason.

Regulars: Art Carney, Pert Kelton, Audrey Meadows, Patricia Morrison, Zomah Cunningham, Joyce Randolph, The June Taylor Dancers.

Announcer: Jack Lescoulie.

Orchestra: Ray Bloch.

Characters portrayed by Jackie: Joe the Bartender—monologue with the unseen Mr. Dunahee about Crazy Guggenhiemer, Moriarty the undertaker, Duddy Duddleson, and Bookshelf Robinson; Charlie Barton the loudmouth; The Poor Soul, the well-meaning lad in an uphill battle with life;

Reginald Van Gleason III, the playboy philosopher; Fenwick Babbitt, the man out for revenge against people who annoy him; Rudy, the helpless repairman; Pedro, the Mexican; Father and Son; Rum Dum, the drunk; Stanley R. Sogg.

Format: Songs, dances, and comedy sketches.

Sketch: "The Honeymooners"—the trials and tribulations of Ralph (Jackie) and Alice (Pert Kelton) Kramden (See title).

The Jackie Gleason Show—Variety—60 minutes—CBS—September 20, 1952 - June 18, 1955. "Cavalcade Of Stars" retitled after a network switch. Format/performers, same.

The Honeymooners—Comedy—30 minutes—CBS—1955-1956. (see title.)

The Jackie Gleason Show—Variety—60 minutes—CBS—September 29, 1956 - June 22, 1957; 30 minutes—October 3, 1958 - January 2, 1961.

Host: Jackie Gleason.

Regulars: Art Carney, Audrey Meadows, Joyce Randolph, George Petrie, Buddy Hackett, The Gleason Girls, The June Taylor Dancers, The Lyn Diddy Singers.

Announcer: Jack Lescoulie.

Orchestra: Ray Bloch.

You're In The Picture—Game—30 minutes—CBS—January 20, 1961-March 24, 1961 (see title.)

Jackie Gleason And His American Scene Magazine—Variety—60 minutes—CBS—September 29, 1962 - June 4, 1966. Sketches based on topics drawn from newspapers and weekly journals.

Host: Jackie Gleason.

Regulars: Frank Fontaine (Crazy), Sid Fields, Alice Ghostley, Sue Ane Langdon, Jan Crockett, Helen Curtis, Barbara Heller (as Christine Clam, who introduces the segments), Peter Gladke, Patricia Wilson, Phil Burns, Elizabeth Allen (the "Away We Go" girl), The Glea Girls, The June Taylor Dancers.

Announcer: Johnny Olsen.

Orchestra: Sammy Spear.

The Jackie Gleason Show—Variety—60 minutes—CBS—September 17, 1966 - September 12, 1970. Taped in Miami Beach, Florida.

Host: Jackie Gleason.

Regulars: Art Carney (as Ed Norton), Sheila MacRae (Alice Kramden), Jane Kean (Trixie Norton), and Jackie as Ralph Kramden in the rebirth of "The Honeymooners"; Lanita Kent, Jami Henderson, Andrea Duda, Carlos Bas, The Glea Girls, The June Taylor Dancers.

Announcer: Johnny Olsen.

Orchestra: Sammy Spear.

THE JACK La LANNE SHOW

Exercise. The benefits of daily systematic exercise coupled with nutritional guidance.

Host-Instructor: Jack La Lanne, physical fitness expert.

Assistant: Elaine La Lanne (Mrs.)

Dogs: Happy and Walter.

THE JACK La LANNE SHOW—30 minutes—Syndicated—1951-1960; 1961-1965; 1966-1970.

JACK PAAR

Listed: The programs of comedian Jack Paar.

I've Got News For You—Game—30 minutes—NBC—July 28, 1952 - September 26, 1952.

Host: Jack Paar.

Format: Three competing players answer questions based on articles appearing in newspapers.

Bank On The Stars—Game—30 minutes—CBS—1953. (See title.)

The Jack Paar Show—Variety—30 minutes—CBS—November 11, 1953 - May 24, 1956.

Host: Jack Paar.

Regulars: Edie Adams, Richard Hayes, Martha Wright, Betty Clooney, Johnny Desmond, Jose Melis.

Announcer: Hal Simms.

Orchestra: Pupi Campo.

The Morning Show—Variety—CBS—1954. (See title.)

The Jack Paar Show—Variety—30 minutes—CBS—August 16, 1954 - July 1, 1955.

Host: Jack Paar.

Regulars: Edie Adams, Jack Haskell.

Announcer: Jack Haskell.

Orchestra: Jose Melis.

The Tonight Show—Variety—105 minutes—NBC—July 29, 1957 - April 30, 1962 (Jack's run as host). (See title.)

The Jack Paar Show—Variety—60 minutes—NBC—September 21, 1962 - September 10, 1965.

Host: Jack Paar.

Orchestra: Jose Melis.

Jack Paar Tonight—Variety—90 minutes—ABC—January 8, 1973 - November 16, 1973. Broadcast as part of "The ABC Wide World of Entertainment" series. Seen five times each month.

Host: Jack Paar.

Co-Host: Peggy Cass.

Announcer: Peggy Cass.

Orchestra: Charles Randolph Grean.

JACKPOT

Game. Sixteen contestants, competing for one week, vie for the opportunity to win up to $50,000 in cash. Each player possesses a different riddle, one the "Jackpot Riddle," worth from five to two hundred dollars. A target number (e.g., five hundred) is established and becomes the cash amount for the jackpot. One player, designated as "The Expert" calls on other players one at a time. The chosen player states the cash value of his riddle, then reads it. The money is calculated on a board; if the player solves it, he remains; if he fails to solve it, he trades places with the person who stumped him. Each riddle that is solved increases the money in the jackpot, but two plateaus have to be overcome before a player can win it. First, the jackpot amount has to be equaled or surpassed by answering riddles; and secondly, only by selecting the person possessing the "Jackpot Riddle" and correctly answering it. If successful, the expert and the player divide the money and a new game begins. If unsuccessful, the game still ends, but players do not receive anything. Should the "Jackpot Riddle" be selected before the target number is equaled, it is voided until the amount is reached. After the "Jackpot Riddle" has been selected, it can be answered at any time as determined by the expert who will either increase the money in the jackpot by continuing to answer riddles or stop when feeling safe and attempt to answer it. "The Super Jackpot." After the target number is established (e.g., five-hundred) a multiplication figure from five to fifty is established (e.g., ten). If the expert matches the target number

exactly through riddles, or if the last three digits of the jackpot match the target number, he receives a chance to answer the "Super Jackpot Riddle," which is possessed by the host. If it is correctly answered, the expert receives the money that figures when the target number is multiplied by the random multiplication figure (e.g., $5000).

Host: Geoff Edwards.

Announcer: Don Pardo.

Music: Recorded.

Executive Producer: Bob Stewart.

Producer: Bruce Burmester.

JACKPOT—30 minutes—NBC—January 7, 1974 - September 26, 1975.

THE JACKSON FIVE

Animated Cartoon. The misadventures of the Jackson Five, a Motown rock group.

Voices: The Jackson Five (brothers): Tito, Jackie, Michael, Marion, Jermaine.

Additional voices: Paul Frees, Edmund Silvers, Joe Cooper.

Background Music: Maury Laws.

Producer: Arthur Rankin, Jr., Jules Bass.

Director: Robert Balser.

THE JACKSON FIVE—30 minutes—ABC—September 11, 1971 - September 1, 1973.

THE JACKSONS

Musical Variety.

Hosts: The Jackson Five.

Regulars: Jim Samuels, Marty Cohen, The Jackson Sisters.

Orchestra: Rick Wilkins.

Choreography: Anita Mann.

Executive Producer: Joe Jackson, Richard Arons.

Producer: Bill Davis, Anne Hogan, Bonnie Burns.

Director: Bill Davis.

THE JACKSONS—30 minutes—CBS—June 16, 1976 - July 7, 1976; January 26, 1977 - March 9, 1977.

JACK THE RIPPER

Mystery. A six-part series that recreates three terrifying months in

British history—August 31, 1888 to November 9, 1888—a time wherein five women met death in Whitechapel, London, at the hands of the famed, but mysterious, still unapprehended murderer, Jack the Ripper. Through the modern-day investigations of Scotland Yard detectives Barlow and Watt, new evidence is presented in an attempt to uncover the identity of history's most notorious criminal.

Host: Sebastian Cabot.

Music: Bill Southgate.

CAST
Detective John
  Barlow   Alan Stratford-Johns
Detective Watt   Frank Windsor

JACK THE RIPPER—60 minutes—Syndicated 1974.

THE JACQUELINE SUSANN SHOW

Women. Fashion previews, guests, and interviews.

Hostess: Jacqueline Susann.

Announcer: John McNight.

THE JACQUELINE SUSANN SHOW—30 minutes—DuMont 1951; 30 minutes—ABC 1953.

JACQUES FRAY'S MUSIC ROOM

Musical Variety.

Host: Jacques Fray.

Regulars: Bess Myerson, Jeri Nagle, Conrad Thibault, Bob Calder, Joan Francis, Russell & Aura, Fredo Gordoni.

Orchestra: Charles Stark.

JACQUES FRAY'S MUSIC ROOM—30 minutes—ABC 1949.

JAMBO

Adventure. Stories of African wildlife.

Host-Storyteller: Marshall Thompson.

Assistant: Judy the Chimp.

JAMBO—30 minutes—NBC—September 6, 1969 - September 4, 1971. 51 episodes.

JAMBOREE

Musical Variety.

Hostess: Gloria Van.

Regulars: Danny O'Neill, Jane Brockman, Bud Tygett, Jimmy McPartland, Dick Edwards,

"Woo Woo" Stevens, Paula Raye, John Dolie.

Orchestra: Julian Stockdale.

JAMBOREE–60 minutes–DuMont 1950.

JAMES AT 15

Drama. Background: Boston. A realistic approach to the problems faced by today's teenagers as seen through the experiences of James Hunter, a student at Bunker Hill High School.

CAST
James Hunter	Lance Kerwin
Paul Hunter, his father	Linden Chiles
Joan Hunter, his mother	Lynn Carlin
Sandy Hunter, his younger sister	Kim Richards
Kathy Hunter, his older sister	Deirdre Berthrong
Marlene Mahoney, James's friend	Susan Myers
Ludwig "Sly" Hazeltine, James's friend	David Hubbard

Music: Jimmie Haskell.

Theme Vocal: Lee Montgomery.

Executive Producer: Martin Manulis, Joseph Hardy.

Producer: Ernest Losso.

Director: Joseph Hardy, James Sheldon.

Creator: Dan Wakefield.

JAMES AT 15–60 minutes–NBC– Premiered: October 27, 1977.

JAMES BEARD

Women. The preparation of gourmet meals; fashion, decorating ideas, and related subjects of interest to housewives.

Host: James Beard, gourmet, chef, cookbook author.

JAMES BEARD–30 minutes–Syndicated 1963. 130 tapes.

JAMES GARNER AS NICHOLS

See title: "Nichols."

JAMIE

Comedy. The story of Jamieson John Francis McHummer (Jamie), an orphan who comes to live with his relatives (his grandfather, Cousin Liz, and Aunt Laurie) after the death of his parents. The focal point of the series is the relationship between a young boy (Jamie) and an old man (his grandfather).

CAST
Jamie McHummer	Brandon De Wilde
Grandpa McHummer	Ernest Truex
Liz McHummer	Kathleen Nolan
Laurie McHummer	Polly Rowles
Annie Moakum, Laurie's assistant in her catering business	Alice Pearce

Music: Jacques Press.

JAMIE–30 minutes–ABC–September 28, 1953 - October 4, 1954. The pilot was broadcast as part of "ABC Album" shown April 26, 1953.

THE JAN MURRAY SHOW

Variety. Presented following the NBC network fights.

Host: Jan Murray.

Regulars: Tina Louise, Fletcher Peck, The Novelettes.

THE JAN MURRAY SHOW–15 minutes (approx.)–NBC 1955.

JANE FROMAN'S U.S.A. CANTEEN

Variety. Entertainment set against the background of an armed-services canteen. Performances by men and women in military service.

Hostess: Jane Froman, "The girl with a song in her heart."

Featured: The Peter Birch Dancers.

Announcer: Allyn Edwards.

Orchestra: Alfredo Antonini; Hank Sylvern.

JANE FROMAN'S U.S.A. CANTEEN –15 minutes–CBS–October 18, 1952 - July 2, 1953. As "The Jane Froman Show"–15 minutes–CBS–September 1, 1953 - June 23, 1955.

THE JANE PICKENS SHOW

Musical Variety.

Hostess: Jane Pickens.

Featured: The Vikings.

THE JANE PICKENS SHOW–15 minutes–ABC–January 31, 1954 - April 11, 1954.

JANET DEAN, REGISTERED NURSE

Drama. Background: New York City. The cases of Janet Dean, a private-duty nurse. Incorporating applied psychology, she seeks the facts behind patients' problems and attempts to attribute most illnesses as psychosomatic.

Starring: Ella Raines as Janet Dean.

JANET DEAN, REGISTERED NURSE–30 minutes–Syndicated 1954.

JANE WYMAN'S SUMMER PLAYHOUSE

Anthology. Rebroadcasts of dramas that were originally aired via "The Jane Wyman Theatre."

Hostess: Jane Wyman.

JANE WYMAN'S SUMMER PLAYHOUSE–30 minutes–CBS–June 1957 - September 1957.

THE JANE WYMAN THEATRE

Anthology. Tense, highly dramatic presentations.

Hostess: Jane Wyman.

Music: Melvyn Lenard.

Included:

Helpmate. A wife attempts to help her detective husband solve a case.

CAST
Janet Blaine: Imogene Coca; Henry Blaine: Dabbs Greer; Dino: Vincent Barnett.

The Girl On The Drum. The difficulties that arise from a respectable married businessman's involvement with a nightclub dancer.

CAST
Guy Whitman: Jack Kelly; Lonita: Lita Baron; Kenneth Neville: Carleton G. Young.

The Black Road. The effect of a black-sheep member on his family.

CAST
David Ederly: Robert Horton; Jenny: Judith Ames; Mrs. Ederly: Dorothy Adams.

A Place On The Bay. Dissatisfied with life on a houseboat, a wife attempts to convince her husband, an author, that the atmosphere is not necessary for writing best-selling novels.

CAST

Hal Robertson: Gene Barry; Laura Robertson: Gloria Talbot.

THE JANE WYMAN THEATRE—30

minutes—NBC—August 28, 1956 - June 25, 1957; Rebroadcasts (NBC): June 30, 1963 - September 8, 1963. ABC Version: A daily series of film drama rebroadcasts hosted by Jane Wyman. 30 minutes—January 2, 1962 - September 6, 1963.

THE JAYE P. MORGAN SHOW

Musical Variety.

Hostess: Jaye P. Morgan.

Regulars: The Morgan Brothers (Dick, Bob, Charlie, and Duke—Jaye's real-life brothers).

Orchestra: Joel Herron.

THE JAYE P. MORGAN SHOW—15 minutes—NBC—June 13, 1956 - September 1956. The Summer replacement for "Eddie Fisher's Coke Time."

The Jaye P. Morgan Show. Jaye P. Morgan.

JAZZ ALLEY

Music. The Jazz music of Chicago during the 1920s coupled with interviews and representative guests.

Host: Art Hodes.

Music: The Hodes Combo.

JAZZ ALLEY—30 minutes—NET—September 3, 1969 - October 9, 1969.

JAZZ SCENE, U.S.A.

A thirty-minute variety series that was first syndicated in 1962.

THE JEAN ARTHUR SHOW

Comedy. Background: Los Angeles, California. The investigations and courtroom defenses of a mother-and-son legal team, Patricia and Paul Marshall (Marshall & Marshall, attorneys at law).

CAST

Patricia Marshall (a widow)	Jean Arthur
Paul Marshall	Ron Harper
Mr. Morton	Leonard Stone
Richie Wells, a reformed hood	Richard Conte

Music: Johnny Keating.

THE JEAN ARTHUR SHOW—30 minutes—CBS—September 12, 1966 - December 12, 1966. 12 episodes.

THE JEAN CARROLL SHOW

See title: "Take It from Me."

Jeannie. Jeannie (bottom right). In motorcycle: Henry (above wheel), Babu (back), and Corey. © *Hanna-Barbera Productions.*

JEANNIE

Animated Cartoon. A spin-off from "I Dream of Jeannie." Background: Center City. Surfing, Corey Anders, a high school senior, is overcome by a wave that washes him upon the shore and exposes a bottle that was buried in the sand. Upon opening it, a beautiful young genie, named Jeannie, and her friend, an inept apprentice genie, Babu, emerge and become his slaves.

Stories depict Corey's attempts to conceal their presence and live the normal life of a teenager; and Jeannie's efforts to adjust to life in the 1970s and to protect Corey from the wiles of other girls.

Unlike Barbara Eden's portrayal of Jeannie ("I Dream of Jeannie"), whose powers are evoked by crossing her hands over her chest and blinking her eyes, the animated Jeannie's powers are in her pony tail.

Additional characters: Henry Glopp, Corey's friend, the only other person aware of Jeannie's presence; S. Melvin Fathinggale, a friend; Mrs. Anders, Corey's mother; Hadji, the master of all genies.

Characters' Voices

Jeannie	Julie McWhirter
Corey	Marc Hammil
Henry	Bob Hastings
Babu	Joe Besser

Additional Voices: Tommy Cook, Don Messick, Ginny Tyler, Julie Bennett, Sherry Alberoni.

Music: Hoyt Curtin, Paul DeKorte.

Executive Producer: William Hanna, Joseph Barbera.

Director: Charles A. Nichols.

Corey's address: 636 North Beach Street

JEANNIE—30 minutes—CBS—September 8, 1973 - August 30, 1975.

Jefferson Drum. Karen Steele (guest), star Jeff Richards.

JEFFERSON DRUM

Western, Background: The ruthless, lawless gold-mining town of Jubilee during the 1850s. The story of Jefferson Drum, widower, an embittered newspaper publisher struggling to establish peace through the power of the press.

CAST

Jefferson Drum	Jeff Richards
Joey Drum, his son	Eugene Martin
Lucius Coin, his type-	
setter	Cyril Delevanti
Big Ed, a	
friend	Robert J. Stevenson

JEFFERSON DRUM—30 minutes—NBC—April 25, 1958 - April 23, 1959. 26 episodes. Original title: "The Pen and the Quill."

THE JEFFERSONS

Comedy. Background: A fashionable East Side apartment in Manhattan. The trials and tribulations of the Jefferson family: George, the snobbish, pompous, and wealthy owner of several dry cleaning establishments; Louise, his tolerant, long-suffering wife; and Lionel, their twenty-two-year-old son. A spin-off from "All in the Family."

CAST

George Jefferson	Sherman Hemsley
Louise Jefferson	Isabel Sanford
Lionel Jefferson	Mike Evans
	Damon Evans
Tom Willis, their	
neighbor	Franklin Cover
Helen Willis, his	
wife	Roxie Roker
Jenny Willis, their	
daughter	Berlinda Tolbert
Harry Bentley,	
the Jefferson's	
neighbor	Paul Benedict
Mrs. Jefferson, George's	
mother	Zara Cully
Florence, the Jefferson's	
maid	Marla Gibbs

Music: Jeff Berry, Ja'net DuBois.

Executive Producer: George Sunga.

Producer: Michael Ross, Bernie West, Don Nicholl.

Director: Jack Shea.

THE JEFFERSONS—30 minutes—CBS—Premiered: January 17, 1975.

JEFF'S COLLIE

See title: "Lassie."

JENNIE: LADY RANDOLPH CHURCHILL

Biography. A seven-part series that dramatizes the life of Winston Churchill's American mother, Lady Randolph Churchill (nee Jeannie Jerome, 1854-1921).

CAST

Lady Randolph	
Churchill	Lee Remick
Lord Randolph	
Churchill	Ronald Pickup
Mr. Jerome	Dan O'Herlihy
Mrs. Jerome	Helen Horton
Leonie	Barbara Parkins
Clara	Linda Lilies
Duke of	
Marlborough	Rachel Kempson
Prince of Wales	Thorley Walters
Montie Porch	Charles Kay
Sir Henry James	John Barley
George Cornwallis-	
West	Christopher Cazenove
Bertha	Barbara Laurenson

Music Theme: Andre Previn.

Music Score: Tom McCall.

Executive Producer: Stella Richman.

Producer: Andrew Brown.

Director: James Cellan Jones.

JENNIE: LADY RANDOLPH CHURCHILL—60 minutes—PBS—October 8, 1975 - November 19 1975.

JEOPARDY

Game. Three competing players, a champion and two challengers. Object: To supply questions to given answers. A large board is revealed containing six subject categories (e.g., Say When, Television, Presidents, Movies, Alphabet, The Color Blue, Opera). Each one has five answers with monetary values increasing as the questions increase in difficulty. The champion chooses a subject and an amount. The host then states the answer as it is revealed on the board (e.g., Subject, Movies: "A musical spoof of the old West starring Doris Day."). The first player to sound his buzzer receives the chance to supply the question ("What is *Calamity Jane?*"). If correct, he earns its cash value; if incorrect, the amount is deducted. The person with the last correct answer chooses the next category and amount.

Round One: Single Jeopardy. Question values of ten, twenty, thirty, forty, and fifty dollars.

Round Two: Double Jeopardy. Cash values double from twenty to one hundred dollars.

Round Three: Final Jeopardy. One category topic is stated. Players are permitted to wager any amount of their accumulated earnings. The answer is stated and each player is allotted thirty seconds to write down the question. The players' questions are revealed and cash is added or deducted accordingly. Winners are the highest cash scorers.

Bonus: The Daily Double. Round one contains one Daily Double hidden somewhere on the board; round two features two. When a Daily double sign appears, the player may wager any or all of his earnings. The answer is given; and only the one player may answer. Cash is added or deducted accordingly.

Host: Art Fleming.

Announcer: Don Pardo.

Music: Recorded.

Producer: Bob Rubin.

Director: Jeff Goldstein.

JEOPARDY—30 minutes—NBC—April 30, 1964 - January 3, 1975.

JERICHO

Adventure. Background: Europe during World War II. The exploits of three Allied agents: Franklin Sheppard, American, Nicholas Gage, Englishman, and Jean-Gatson André, Frenchman. Stories relate their attempts to infiltrate enemy lines and sabotage and discredit the Germans. (Jericho is the code name under which they operate.)

CAST

Franklin Sheppard	Don Francs
Nicholas Gage	John Leyton
Jean-Gaston André	Marino Maśe

JERICHO—60 minutes—CBS—September 15, 1966 - January 1967. 16 episodes. Also known as: "Code Name Jericho.'

THE JERRY COLONNA SHOW

Variety. Music, songs, and comedy sketches.

Host: Jerry Colonna.

Regulars: Barbara Ruick, Gordon Polk, Frankie Laine, Arthur Duncan, Isobel Randolph, Louis Colonna.

Announcer: Del Sharbutt.

Orchestra: The Cookie Fairchild Band.

THE JERRY COLONNA SHOW—30 minutes—ABC—May 28, 1951 - September 1951.

THE JERRY LESTER SHOW

Variety. Music, songs, and comedy sketches.

Host: Jerry Lester.

Regulars: Nancy Walker, Betty George, Bobby Sherwood, Lorenzo Fuller, Leon Belasco, Kathy Callin, Ellie Russell.

Orchestra: Buddy Weed.

THE JERRY LESTER SHOW—60 minutes—Syndicated 1953.

JERRY LEWIS

Listed: The television programs of comedian Jerry Lewis.

The Jerry Lewis Show—Talk-Variety—2 hours—ABC—September 21, 1963 - December 22, 1963.

Format: Guests, conversation, and entertainment acts.

Host: Jerry Lewis.

Announcer: Del Moore.

Orchestra: Lou Brown.

The Jerry Lewis Show—Variety—60 minutes—NBC—September 12, 1967 - May 26, 1969.

Format: Music, songs, and comedy sketches.

Host: Jerry Lewis.

Regulars: Bob Harvey, Debbie Macomber, The Osmond Brothers, The George Wyle Singers, The Nick Castle Dancers.

Orchestra: Lou Brown.

Will The Real Jerry Lewis Please Sit Down—Animated Cartoon—30 minutes—ABC—September 12, 1970 - September 2, 1972. (See title.)

The Jerry Lewis Labor Day Telethon. A twenty-four-hour fund-raising telethon for muscular dystrophy. What started twelve years ago as a small local telethon is now a national event that raised over sixteen million dollars Labor Day 1974.

THE JERRY REED WHEN YOU'RE HOT, YOU'RE HOT HOUR

Variety. Music, songs, and comedy sketches played against a Country and Western background.

Host: Jerry Reed.

Regulars: Cal Wilson, Spencer Quinn, Merie Earle, John Twomey, Norman Alexander, The Lou Regas Dancers.

Announcer: Bill Thompson.

Orchestra: George Wyle.

THE JERRY REED WHEN YOU'RE HOT, YOU'RE HOT HOUR—60 minutes—CBS—June 20, 1972 - July 25, 1972.

JERRY VISITS

Interview. Hollywood celebrities open their homes to television cameras and reveal their dreams, their ambitions, and aspects of their private and public lives.

Host: Jerry Dunphy, Los Angeles newsman.

Music: Joseph Byrd Productions.

Producer: Jerry Dunphy.

Director: Ervin Zavada.

JERRY VISITS—30 minutes—Syndicated 1971.

JET JACKSON, FLYING COMMANDO

See title: "Captain Midnight."

THE JETSONS

Animated Cartoon. Background: Twenty-first-century Earth. The trials and tribulations of the Jetsons, an ultramodern family: George, an employee of Spacely Space Sprockets; his wife Jane; and their children, Judy and Elroy. A Hanna-Barbera production.

Characters' Voices

George Jetson	George O'Hanlon
Jane Jetson	Penny Singleton
Judy Jetson	Janet Waldo
Elroy Jetson	Daws Butler
Mr. Spacely, George's employer	Mel Blanc
Astro, the Jeston family dog	Don Messick
Rosie, the Jetson electronic maid	Jean VanderPyl

The Jetsons. The Jetson family (left to right): Elroy, Jane, George, and Judy. *Courtesy Hanna-Barbera Productions.*

Additional Voices: Shepard Menkin, Howard Morris.

Music: Hoyt Curtin.

THE JETSONS—30 minutes. ABC—September 1962 - September 1964; CBS—September 4, 1965 - September 3, 1966; NBC—September 10, 1966 - September 2, 1967; CBS—September 13, 1969 - September 5, 1970; NBC—September 11, 1971 - September 1, 1975. 24 episodes.

JIGSAW

See title: "The Men," *Jigsaw* segment.

JIGSAW JOHN

Crime Drama. Background: Los Angeles, California. The cases of John St. John, nicknamed Jigsaw John by his colleagues, an L.A.P.D. homicide detective whose best weapon is his talent for figuring people and solving complex crimes.

CAST

John St. John	Jack Warden
Maggi Hearn, his girlfriend	Pippa Scott
Sam Donner, John's partner	Alan Feinstein

Music: Pete Rugolo.

Producer: Ronald Austin, James David Buchanan.

Director: Harry Falk, Reza S. Badiyi, Charles S. Dubin, Paul Krasny, Charles R. Rondeau.

JIGSAW JOHN—60 minutes—NBC—February 2, 1976 - April 13, 1976; May 31, 1976 - September 13, 1976.

THE JIM BACKUS SHOW— HOT OFF THE WIRE

Comedy. The misadventures of John Michael O'Toole, editor-reporter of the *Headline Press Service,* a newspaper in financial trouble. Episodes depict his efforts to dodge creditors, acquire major stories, and improve circulation to obtain needed resources.

CAST

John Michael O'Toole	Jim Backus
Dora, his assistant	Nita Talbot
Sidney, the office boy	Bobs Watson

THE JIM BACKUS SHOW—HOT OFF THE WIRE—30 minutes—Syndicated 1960. 39 episodes.

JIMMIE RODGERS

Listed: The television programs of singer Jimmie Rodgers.

The Jimmie Rodgers Show—Musical Variety—30 minutes—NBC—March 31, 1959 - September 7, 1959.

Host: Jimmie Rodgers.

Regulars: Connie Francis, The Kirby Stone Four, The Clay Warnick Singers.

Orchestra: Buddy Morrow.

The Jimmie Rodgers Show—Musical Variety—60 minutes—CBS—June 16, 1969 - September 8, 1969.

Host: Jimmie Rodgers.

Regulars: Vicki Lawrence, Lyle Waggoner, Nancy Austin, Don Crichton, Bill Fanning, The Burgundy Street Singers.

Announcer: Lyle Waggoner.

Orchestra: Harry Zimmerman.

JIMMY DEAN

Listed: The television programs of singer Jimmy Dean.

The Jimmy Dean Show—Country-Western Musical Variety—CBS. 60 minutes—April 8, 1957 - November 23, 1957; 45 minutes—June 1957 - August 1958; 30 minutes—September 15, 1958 - January 26, 1959.

Host: Jimmy Dean.

Regulars: Jeri Miyazaki, Mary Kluck, Joan Crockett, Jo Davis, Herbie Jones, The Double Daters, The Country Lads, The Noteworthies, Alec Houston's Wildcats.

The Jimmy Dean Show. Left to right: Guest Jaye P. Morgan, host Jimmy Dean, and guest Jane Morgan.

Orchestra: Joel Herron.

The Jimmy Dean Show—Country-Western Musical Variety—60 minutes—ABC—September 19, 1963 - April 1, 1966.

Host: Jimmy Dean.

Regulars: Molly Bee; Rowlf, the hound dog muppet; The Grass Roots Band; The Doerr Hutchinson Dancers, The Chuck Cassey Singers.

Orchestra: Peter Matz; Al Pellegrini; Don Sebesky.

The Jimmy Dean Show—Country-Western Musical Variety—30 minutes—Syndicated 1974.

Host: Jimmy Dean.

Vocalists: The Imperials.

JIMMY DURANTE

Listed: The television programs of comedian Jimmy Durante.

The Buick Circus Hour—Variety—60 minutes—NBC—October 7, 1952 - June 6, 1953. (See title.)

The Texaco Star Theatre—Comedy-Variety—60 minutes—NBC—October 2, 1954 - September 24, 1955.

Host: Jimmy Durante.

Regulars: Eddie Jackson, Jack Roth, Jules Buffano, The Durante Girls.

Orchestra: Allen Roth; Roy Bargy.

The Jimmy Durante Show—Variety—30 minutes—CBS—June 1957 - September 1957. Featured: Kinescope highlights of "Star Theatre."

Host: Jimmy Durante.

Regulars: Eddie Jackson, Jack Roth, Jules Buffano.

Orchestra: Roy Bargy.

Jimmy Durante Presents The Lennon Sisters Hour—Musical Variety—60 minutes—ABC—September 26, 1969 - July 4, 1970. (See title.)

JIMMY DURANTE PRESENTS THE LENNON SISTERS HOUR

Variety. Music, songs, dances, and comedy sketches.

Jimmy Durante Presents the Lennon Sisters Hour. The Lennon Sisters: (left to right) Dianne, Kathy, Peggy, and Janet.

Host: Jimmy Durante.

Hostesses: The Lennon Sisters, Dianne, Peggy, Kathy, and Janet.

Regulars: Edna O'Dell, Bernie Kukoff.

Announcers: Charlie O'Donnell; Jay Stewart.

Orchestra: George Wyle.

JIMMY DURANTE PRESENTS THE LENNON SISTERS HOUR—60 minutes—ABC—September 26, 1969 - July 4, 1970. 26 tapes.

JIMMY HUGHES, ROOKIE COP

Crime. Drama. Background: New York City. Returning home from service in Korea, and learning that his father, a policeman, has been killed in the performance of duty, Jimmy

Hughes joins the force in an attempt to apprehend the slayers. Learning to serve for reasons other than revenge and finding that teamwork and concern for others are more important than individual action or motivation, he is presented with his father's badge.

Stories concern the life and problems faced by Jimmy Hughes, a rookie cop.

CAST

Jimmy Hughes	Billy Redfield
His sister	Wendy Drew
Inspector Ferguson	Rusty Lane

JIMMY HUGHES, ROOKIE COP—30 minutes—DuMont—May 8, 1953 - July 3, 1953.

THE JIMMY STEWART SHOW

Comedy. Background: 35 Hillview Drive, Easy Valley, California, the residence of three generations of Howards: James K., an anthropology professor at Josiah Kessel College; Martha, his wife of thirty years; Teddy, their eight-year-old son; Peter Jacob (P.J.), their twenty-nine year old married son, a construction engineer; his wife, Wendy; and their eight-year-old son, Jake.

Stories depict the home and working life of James Howard, and the problems that ensue when generations clash.

CAST

James Howard	Jimmy Stewart
Martha Howard	Julie Adams
P.J. Howard	Jonathan Daly
Wendy Howard	Ellen Geer
Teddy Howard	Dennis Larson
Jake Howard	Kirby Furlong
Luther Quince, a wealthy friend, the Chemistry Professor	John McGiver

Music: Van Alexander.

THE JIMMY STEWART SHOW—30 minutes—NBC—September 19, 1971 - September 3, 1972. 26 episodes.

THE JIM NABORS HOUR

Variety. Music, songs, dances, and comedy sketches.

Host: Jim Nabors.

Regulars: Frank Sutton, Ronnie Schell, Karen Morrow, The Tony Mordente Dancers, The Nabors Kids.

Orchestra: Paul Weston.

THE JIM NABORS HOUR—60 minutes—CBS—September 25, 1969 - May 20, 1971. 52 tapes.

THE JIM STAFFORD SHOW

Variety. Music, songs, dances, and comedy sketches.

Host: Jim Stafford.

Regulars: Valerie Curtin, Richard Stahl, Phil MacKenzie, Deborah Allen, Jeannie Sheffield, Tom Byner.

Announcers: Dick Tufeld; Bill Thompson.

Orchestra: Eddie Karam.

Choreography: Carl Jablonski.

Producer: Rick Eustis, Al Rogers.

THE JIM STAFFORD SHOW—60 minutes—ABC—July 30, 1975 - September 3, 1975.

JOANNE CARSON'S V.I.P.'s

Variety. Guests, interviews, cooking and household hints.

Hostess: Joanne Carson.

Announcer: Hugh Douger.

Music: Recorded.

JOANNE CARSON'S V.I.P.'s—30 minutes—Syndicated 1972.

JOE AND MABEL

Comedy. Background: New York City. The story of two young lovers: Joe Spartan, a cab driver who feels he is not ready to take on the responsibilities of marriage, and Mabel Spooner, a manicurist who yearns to become his wife. Episodes depict her attempts to change his mind by demonstrating her wifely interests; and Joe's attempts to avoid the paths of matrimony and retain a single life.

CAST

Joe Spartan	Larry Blyden
Mabel Spooner	Nita Talbot
Mrs. Spooner, Mabel's mother	Luella Gear
Sherman Spooner, Mabel's younger brother	Michael Mann
Mike, Joe's friend, a cabbie	Norman Field

JOE AND MABEL—30 minutes—CBS—September 20, 1955 - September 25, 1956.

JOE AND SONS

Comedy. Background: Erie, Pennsylvania. The trials and tribulations of widower Joe Vitale, a sheet metal worker, as he struggles to raise his teenage sons, Mark and Nick.

CAST

Joe Vitale	Richard Castellano
Mark Vitale	Barry Miller
Nick Vitale	Jimmy Baio
Gus, Joe's wise-cracking friend	Jerry Stiller
Josephine, Joe's sister	Florence Stanley
Estelle, Joe's neighbor, a cocktail waitress	Bobbi Jordan

Music: David Shire.

Executive Producer: Douglas S. Cramer.

Producer: Bernie Kickoff, Jeff Harris.

Director: Peter Baldwin.

Creator: Robert Illes, James Stein.

Note: The background changed to Hoboken, New Jersey, shortly after the premiere.

JOE AND SONS—30 minutes—CBS—September 9, 1975 - January 13, 1976.

THE JOE DIMAGGIO SHOW

Children. Set against the background of a clubhouse, the format features baseball's Joe DiMaggio chatting with youngsters, answering their questions, and interviewing guest stars.

Host: Joe DiMaggio.

The Club House Manager: Jack Barry.

Announcer: Ted Brown.

Producer: Jack Barry, Dan Enright.

Sponsor: Lionel Electric Trains.

THE JOE DIMAGGIO SHOW—15 minutes—NBC 1950.

JOE FORRESTER

Crime Drama. Background: An unidentified American City. The story of Joe Forrester, a veteran policeman who rejects a desk job and chooses to remain in uniform to walk his old beat—a rundown neighborhood that he now wants to build up again.

CAST

Officer Joe Forrester	Lloyd Bridges

Sgt. Bernie Vincent,
his superior   Eddie Egan
Georgia Cameron, Joe's
girlfriend, a
cocktail lounge
hostess   Patricia Crowley
Jolene, Joe's
informant   Dwan Smith

Music: Richard Markowitz; Robert Dransin.

Executive Producer: David Gerber.

Producer: Mark Rodgers, James H. Brown.

Director: Alf Kjellin, Alexander Singer, Jerry London, Barry Shear, Alexander March, Alvin Ganzer.

Creator: Mark Rodgers.

Joe's badge number: 147.

JOE FORRESTER—60 minutes—NBC—Premiered: September 9, 1975.

THE JOE FRANKLIN SHOW

Variety. Interviews with show business personalities; undiscovered professional talent; and films—the trip down memory lane—rarely or never before seen on television.

Basically, aired locally in New York; certain tribute programs (e.g., Louis Armstrong), are syndicated.

Host: Joe Franklin.

Appearing: Marilyn Monroe, George

Jessel, Ruta Lee, Bobby Darin, Hugh O'Brian, Connie Stevens, Ray Anthony, Kay Stevens, Tony Sandler, Ralph Young, Bill Cosby, Woody Allen, Flip Wilson.

Music: Recorded (theme: "12th Street Rag").

THE JOE FRANKLIN SHOW—Various running times, but most often 60 minutes—WABC-TV (Ch. 7); WOR-TV—1954 - Present.

THE JOE NAMATH SHOW

Interview. Interviews with sports and show-business personalities.

Host: Joe Namath.

Co-Host: Dick Schaap.

Announcer-Assistant: Louisa Moritz.

Music: Recorded.

Artist: LeRoy Neiman (sketches guests).

THE JOE NAMATH SHOW—30 minutes—Syndicated 1969.

THE JOE PALOOKA STORY

Comedy-Drama. Background: New York City. The fictitious story of heavyweight boxer Joe Palooka, a clean living, moral champ ignorant of gambling, fixed fights, blonde sirens, and nightclubs. Based on the character created by Ham Fisher.

CAST
Joe Palooka   Joe Kirkwood, Jr.
Ann Howe, his girl-
friend   Cathy Downs
Knobby Walsh, his
manager   Luis Van Rooten
          Sid Tomack
Humphrey Pennyworth, Joe's
trainer   Maxie Rosenbloom

THE JOE PALOOKA STORY—30 minutes—Syndicated 1954.

THE JOE PYNE SHOW

Discussion. A controversial-issues debate.

Host: Joe Pyne.

Music: Recorded.

THE JOE PYNE SHOW—2 hours—Syndicated 1966.

JOEY AND DAD

Variety. Music, songs, dances, and comedy sketches.

Hostess: Joey Heatherton.

Host: Ray Heatherton (her father).

Regulars: Pat Paulsen, Henny Youngman, Pat Proft, Bob Einstein, Nick Nicholas.

Announcer: Peter Cullen; Roger Carroll.

Orchestra: Lex de Azevedo.

Special Musical Material: David Black.

Choreographer: Joe Tremaine.

Producer: Allan Blye, Bob Einstein.

Director: Mark Warren.

JOEY AND DAD—60 minutes—CBS—July 6, 1975 - July 27, 1975.

JOEY BISHOP

Listed: The television programs of comedian Joey Bishop.

The Joey Bishop Show—Comedy—30 minutes—NBC—September 20, 1961 - June 20, 1962. Pilot aired via "The Danny Thomas Show."

Background: Hollywood, California. The life of Joey Barnes, a trouble-prone public-relations man with the advertising firm of Wellington, Willoughby, and Jones.

CAST
Joey Barnes   Joey Bishop
Stella Barnes, his stage-struck
sister   Marlo Thomas

The Joe Franklin Show. Guest George Jessel (left) and host Joe Franklin. *Courtesy of Joe Franklin.*

Mrs. Barnes, his widowed mother	Madge Blake
Larry Barnes, his younger brother	Warren Berlinger
Betty Barnes, his older sister	Virginia Vincent
Frank, his brother-in-law	Joe Flynn
Barbara, Joey's girl-friend	Nancy Hadley
J.R. Willoughby, Joey's employer	John Briggs
Peggy, J.R.'s secretary	Jackie Russell

Music: Earle Hagen.

The Joey Bishop Show—Comedy—30 minutes. NBC—September 15, 1962 - September 20, 1964. CBS—September 27, 1964 - September 7, 1965.

Background: New York City. The home and working life of nightclub comedian Joey Barnes.

CAST

Joey Barnes	Joey Bishop
Ellie Barnes, his wife	Abby Dalton
Jillson, the land-lord	Joe Besser
Freddie, Joey's manager	Guy Marks
Larry, Joey's writer	Corbett Monica
Hilda, the Barnes's baby's nurse	Mary Treen
Dr. Nolan, the baby's doctor	Joey Forman
Joey Barnes, Jr., Joey and Ellie's son	Matthew David Smith

Music: Earle Hagen.

The Joey Bishop Show—Talk-Variety—90 minutes—ABC—April 17, 1967 - December 20, 1969.

Host: Joey Bishop.

Announcer: Regis Philbin.

Orchestra: Johnny Mann.

THE JOHN BYNER COMEDY HOUR

Variety. Music, songs, and comedy sketches.

Host: John Byner.

Regulars: Patty Deutsch, Linda Sublette, R. G. Brown, Gary Miller, Dennis Flannigan, The Lori Regas Dancers.

Announcer: Bill Thompson.

Orchestra: Ray Charles.

THE JOHN BYNER COMEDY HOUR—60 minutes—CBS—August 1, 1972 - August 29, 1972.

JOHN CONTE'S LITTLE SHOW

See title: "The Little Show."

THE JOHN DAVIDSON SHOW

Variety. Music, songs, dances, and comedy sketches.

Host: John Davidson.

Regulars: Rich Little, Mireille Mathieu (French songstress), Amy McDonald (comedienne).

Orchestra: Jack Parnell.

THE JOHN DAVIDSON SHOW—60 minutes—ABC—May 30, 1969 - September 12, 1969. Produced in England.

THE JOHN DAVIDSON SHOW

Variety.

Host: John Davidson.

Regular and Announcer: Pete Barbutti.

Orchestra: Lenny Stack.

Choreographer: Ron Poindexter.

Executive Producer: Dick Clark, Oliver Bernard.

Producer: Bill Lee.

Director: Barry Glazer.

THE JOHN DAVIDSON SHOW—60 minutes—NBC—May 24, 1976 - June 14, 1976.

THE JOHN FORSYTHE SHOW

Comedy. Background: The Foster School for Girls in California. The trials and tribulations of John Foster, its headmaster, a former U.S. Air Force major who inherited the school from its founder, his late aunt. Stories relate his struggles as he attempts to adjust to new responsibilities and solve the problems that stem from one hundred and twenty teenage girls.

CAST

John Foster	John Forsythe
Sergeant Edward Robbins, an Air Force friend, his assistant	Guy Marks
Miss Culver, the principal	Elsa Lanchester
Miss Wilson, the physical education instructress	Ann B. Davis
Joanna	Peggy Lipton
Marcia	Page Forsythe
Kathy	Darleen Carr
Pamela	Pamelyn Ferdin
Janice	Sara Ballantine
Susan	Tracy Stratford
Norma Jean	Brook Forsythe

THE JOHN FORSYTHE SHOW—30 minutes—NBC—September 13, 1965 - August 29, 1966. 30 episodes.

JOHN GARY

Listed: The television programs of singer John Gary.

The John Gary Show—Musical Variety—60 minutes—CBS—June 22, 1966 - September 7, 1966.

Host: John Gary.

Regulars: The Jimmy Joyce Singers, The Jack Regas Dancers.

Orchestra: Mitchell Ayres.

The John Gary Show—Variety—60 minutes—Syndicated 1968.

Host: John Gary.

Orchestra: Sammy Spear.

JOHN GUNTHER'S HIGH ROAD

See title: "High Road."

JOHNNY CARSON

Listed: The television programs of comedian Johnny Carson.

Carson's Cellar—Variety—30 minutes. —Local Los Angeles (KNXT-TV, Ch. 2)—1953.

Host: Johnny Carson.

Music: The New Yorkers.

Earn Your Vacation—Game—30 minutes—CBS—1954. (See title.)

The Johnny Carson Show—Satire—30 minutes—CBS—1954.

Host: Johnny Carson.

Regulars: Barbara Ruick, Virginia Gibson, Jana Ekelund.

Orchestra: Lud Gluskin.

The Johnny Carson Daytime Show—Variety—30 minutes—CBS—1955.

Host: Johnny Carson.

Regulars: Laurie Carroll, Jill Corey, Glenn Turnbull.

Music: Cal Gooden's Six Piece Combo.

Format: Studio-audience interviews; offbeat guests; casual humor; and spoofs of television programs and commercials.

Who Do You Trust?—Game—30 minutes—ABC—1958. (See title: "Do You Trust Your Wife?").

The Tonight Show—Variety—90 minutes—NBC—1962. (See title.)

JOHNNY CASH AND FRIENDS

Musical Variety.

Host: Johnny Cash.

Regulars: June Carter Cash, Steve Martin, Jim Varney, Howard Mann, The B.C. and M. Choir.

Orchestra: Bill Walker.

Executive Producer: Joseph Cates.

Producer: Chet Hagen, Walter C. Miller.

Director: Walter C. Miller.

JOHNNY CASH AND FRIENDS—60 minutes—CBS—August 29, 1976 - September 19, 1976. 4 tapes.

The Johnny Cash Show. Johnny Cash and June Carter.

THE JOHNNY CASH SHOW

Musical Variety. Taped at the Nashville Grand Ole Opry.

Host: Johnny Cash.

Regulars: June Carter, The Carter Family, Carl Perkins, The Statler Brothers, The Tennessee Three.

Announcer: Mike Lawrence.

Music: The Nashville Orchestra, conducted by Billy Walker.

THE JOHNNY CASH SHOW—60 minutes—ABC—June 7, 1969 - September 6, 1969; 60 minutes—ABC—January 21, 1970 - May 21, 1971. 39 tapes.

JOHNNY CYPHER IN DIMENSION ZERO

Animated Cartoon. Experimenting, a scientist, Johnny Cypher, discovers Dimension Zero, the ability to travel through time and space. Using its power, he attempts to combat the sinister forces of evil.

JOHNNY CYPHER IN DIMENSION ZERO—06 minutes—Syndicated 1967.

THE JOHNNY DUGAN SHOW

Musical Variety.

Host: Johnny Dugan.

Vocalist: Barbara Logan.

THE JOHNNY DUGAN SHOW—30 minutes—DuMont 1952.

THE JOHNNY JOHNSTON SHOW

Musical Variety.

Host: Johnny Johnston.

Vocalist: Rosemary Clooney.

THE JOHNNY JOHNSTON SHOW—45 minutes—CBS 1951.

JOHNNY JUPITER

Fantasy. Distinguished by two storyline formats.

Format One:
    Background: The Frisbee General Store. Ernest P. Duckweather, clerk and amateur inventor, accidentally discovers interplanetary television and contacts the people of Jupiter. Stories relate the life-styles of Earth people as seen through the eyes of the inhabitants of another planet.

Format Two:
    Ernest P. Duckweather, a milquetoastish television station janitor, dreams of becoming a video producer. One day, after hours, he sneaks into the control room and, while playing producer, he accidentally discovers interplanetary television when he views and talks to the people of Jupiter. Befriending Johnny Jupiter, he relates information about life on Earth.

CAST
Ernest P. Duckweather   Wright King
Mr. Frisbee, the store
  owner   Vaughn Taylor
                         Cliff Hall
Also   Gilbert Mack

Characters (puppets): Johnny Jupiter; B-12; Reject the Robot; Katherine; Mr. Frisley; Dynamo.

JOHNNY JUPITER—30 minutes—DuMont—March 21, 1953 - May 29, 1954. 39 episodes.

JOHNNY MANN'S STAND UP AND CHEER

Variety. A program presenting America in a musical revue.

Host: Johnny Mann.

The Johnny Mann Singers: Marty McCall, Diane Bellis, Richard Brettiger, Thurl Ravenscroft (voice of Kellogg's Tony the Tiger), Mike Redman, Merry Vernon, Sharalle Beard, Errol Horne, Rob Stevens, Lyn Dolin, Steve Sweetland, Barbara Harris, Pat Corbett, Cathy Cahill, Tony Quinn, Freeman Celmente, Erroll Rorigwynne, Ken Prymus, Marcia Darcangelo.

Orchestra: Johnny Mann.

Music Co-ordinator: Paul Suter.

Musical Conductor: Dave Pell.

JOHNNY MANN'S STAND UP AND CHEER—30 minutes—Syndicated 1971.

JOHNNY MIDNIGHT

Crime Drama. Background: New York City. The investigations of Johnny Midnight, an actor turned private detective.

CAST
Johnny Midnight   Edmond O'Brien
Sergeant Sam Olivera,
    N.Y.P.D.   Arthur Batanides
Lieutenant Geller,
    N.Y.P.D.   Barney Phillips
Aki, Johnny's house-
    boy   Yuki Shemoda
Music: Joe Bushkin; Stanley Wilson.

JOHNNY MIDNIGHT—30 minutes—Syndicated 1960. 39 episodes.

JOHNNY OLSEN'S RUMPUS ROOM

Variety. Music, songs, dances, comedy

sketches, and audience participation. Game segment: Selected studio audience members compete for merchandise prizes by performing various stunts.

Host: Johnny Olsen.

Regulars: Kay Armen, Hal McIntyre, Gene Kirby.

Music: The Buddy Weed Trio; The Hank D'Amico Orchestra.

JOHNNY OLSEN'S RUMPUS ROOM –30 minutes–ABC 1946.

JOHNNY RINGO

Western. Background: Velardi, Arizona, 1870s. The story of Johnny Ringo, an ex-gunfighter turned law enforcer, and his deputy, Cully Charlcey, and their attempts to maintain law and order.

CAST
Johnny Ringo	Don Durant
Cully "Kid Adonas" Charlcey	Mark Goddard
Cason "Case" Thomas, the owner of the general store	Terrence DeMarney
Laura Thomas, his daughter	Karen Sharpe

Music: Herschel Burke Gilbert; Rudy Schrager.

JOHNNY RINGO–30 minutes–CBS –October 1, 1959 - September 29, 1960. Syndicated. 38 episodes.

Johnny Ringo. Left to right: Karen Sharpe, Don Durant, and Mona Freeman (guest).

JOHNNY SOKKO AND HIS FLYING ROBOT

Science Fiction Adventure. Background: Tokyo, Japan, during the 21st century. Secretly landing on Earth, aliens from another planet kidnap Dr. Lucas Gardion, a brilliant Earth scientist, and force him to construct Giant Robot–an indestructible mechanical machine that they plan to use to destroy Earth. Meanwhile, a prehistoric-type creature, brought to Earth by the aliens, escapes and attacks a Japanese ship. Two people, Johnny Sokko, a young boy, and Jerry Mono, an agent for Unicorn, an international defense organization, escape to a nearby uncharted island–the alien's base–where they are captured and imprisoned. Managing to escape from their cell, they meet Dr. Gardion, who tells them about the robot and what the aliens plan to do. They also learn that the robot will obey the first voice it will hear and that it is complete except for an atomic charge to activate its circuits. Just then, as the aliens attack the lab, Dr. Gardion detonates the atomic bomb he planted in the robot to destroy it. However, instead of destroying it, the bomb supplies the necessary power to activate it. Amid the ensuing confusion, Johnny finds the wristwatch-type control device and speaks to the robot. He becomes its master. With the help of Giant Robot (as Johnny calls it) Johnny and Jerry escape and return to Tokyo, where Johnny is sworn in as a Unicorn agent and Giant Robot becomes Earth's most valuable defense weapon. Stories depict Unicorn's battle against sinister, alien invaders.

CAST
Johnny Sokko, Agent 7	Mitsundbu Kaneko
Jerry Mono, Agent 43	Akjo Ito

Additional characters (screen credit is not given): Commander Azuma, the head of Unicorn; Nichole, Agent U-5; Marne, a Unicorn agent; Agent U-3; Agent U-6; and Guillotine, an enemy of Unicorn, the being bent on destroying the world.

Producer: Salvatore Billitera.

Director: Manuel San Fernando.

JOHNNY SOKKO AND HIS FLYING ROBOT–30 minutes–Syndicated 1968. 26 episodes.

JOHNNY STACCATO

Crime Drama. Background: New York City. The investigations of Johnny Staccato, a jazz musician turned private detective.

CAST
Johnny Staccato	John Cassavetes
Waldo, his friend, the owner of a Greenwich Village café, his hangout	Eduardo Ciannelli

Music: Elmer Bernstein.

JOHNNY STACCATO–30 minutes– NBC–September 10, 1959 - March 24, 1960. ABC (rebroadcasts): March 27, 1960 - September 25, 1960. Syndicated. 27 episodes. Also known as "Staccato."

THE JOKER'S WILD

Game. Two competing contestants. Displayed on stage is a large slot machine that contains five category topics. Contestants, in turn, pull levers to activate the machine, and then answer appropriate questions for varying cash prizes.

Values:
Each time the machine stops, three categories are revealed and players choose one to answer. If three separate topics appear, each is a single and worth $50. If two of the same topics appear, it is a pair and worth $100 if chosen and correctly answered. Should a triple appear (the same category across the board) the question has to be taken and is worth $150.

Also contained within the categories are Jokers. If one Joker appears with two singles, it (the Joker) is wild and allows the contestant to make a pair with any one category topic. If two Jokers and one single appears, it then becomes a triple. Should three Jokers appear, the game is automatically won.

Winners are the contestants first to score five hundred dollars. Players then decide whether to continue or depart. If continuing, he vies for the "Joker's Jackpot," worth up to $25,000 by winning four straight games. Should he fail to win the four games, all his money is forfeited and added to the jackpot, which begins at $2,500, to a maximum of $25,000.

Host: Jack Barry.

Announcer: Johnny Jacobs.

Music: Recorded.

Producer: Burt Sugarman, Jack Barry, Dan Enright.

Director: Richard Kline.

THE JOKER'S WILD–30 minutes– CBS–September 4, 1972 - October 31, 1975. Syndicated.

JONATHAN WINTERS

Listed: The television programs of comedian Jonathan Winters.

Here's The Show—Variety—30 minutes—NBC—July 9, 1955 - September 24, 1955.

Host: Jonathan Winters; Ransom Sherman.

Regulars: Stephanie Antie, Tommy Knox, Kay O'Grady, Ted Carpenter Singers, The Double Daters.

Orchestra: John Scott Trotter.

The Jonathan Winters Show—Variety—15 minutes—NBC—October 2, 1956 - June 25, 1957.

Host: Jonathan Winters.

Regulars: The Platters.

Orchestra: Eddie Shfronski.

Characters (portrayed by Jonathan): Elwood P. Suggins, Brooks Bixford, Baby Elizabeth, Granny Hopps.

The Jonathan Winters Show—Variety—60 minutes—CBS—December 27, 1967 - May 1969.

Host: Jonathan Winters.

Regulars: Dick Curtis, Paul Lynde, Alice Ghostley, Cliff Arquette, Pamela Rodgers, Abby Dalton, Debi Storm, Diane Davis, Georgene Barnes, Jerry Reneau, The Establishment, The Wisa D'Orso Dancers, The Andre Tayer Dancers.

Announcer: Bern Bennett.

Orchestra: Paul Weston.

Characters portrayed by Jonathan: Chester Hunihugger, Maynard Tetlinger, Maudie Frickett, Winslow G. Flydipper, Elwood P. Suggins, Lance Loveguard.

Hot Dog—Educational—30 minutes—NBC—September 12, 1971 - September 4, 1972. (See title.)

The Wacky World Of Jonathan Winters—Comedy—30 minutes—Syndicated 1972.

Host: Jonathan Winters.

Regulars: Marian Mercer, Mary Gregory, Ronnie Graham, The Soul Sisters.

Orchestra: Van Alexander.

Premiere Guest: Debbie Reynolds.

Format: Utilizes Jonathan's greatest gift—his ability to create on the spot. Cast regulars and guests appear in unrehearsed skits.

THE JOSEPH COTTEN SHOW

See title: "On Trial."

JOSEPHINE McCARTHY

Cooking. The preparation of foreign and American meals.

Hostess: Josephine McCarthy.

Assistant-Host-Announcer: Bob Kennedy.

JOSEPHINE McCARTHY—15 minutes—NBC 1953.

JOSEPH SCHILDKRAUT PRESENTS

Anthology. Dramatic productions.

Host-Occasional Performer: Joseph Schildkraut, stage and screen personality.

JOSEPH SCHILDKRAUT—30 minutes—DuMont—1953-1954.

JOSIE AND THE PUSSYCATS

Animated Cartoon. The global misadventures of Josie and the Pussycats, an all-girl Rock group. A Hanna-Barbera production.

Characters' Voices

Josie, the group leader	Janet Waldo
Melody, the drummer, the beautiful-but-dumb-blonde type	Jackie Joseph
Valerie, the guitarist	Barbara Pariot
Alan, a friend	Jerry Dexter
Alexander Cabot, the group manager	Casey Kaseem
Alexandra Cabot, his sister, in love with Alan, scheming to get his attention away from Josie	Sherry Alberoni
Sebastian, their pet cat	Don Messick

Vocals: The real life Rock group, Josie and the Pussycats: Cathy Douglas (Josie); Patricia Holloway (Valerie); Cherie Moore (Melody).

Music: Hoyt Curtin.

JOSIE AND THE PUSSYCATS—30 minutes—CBS—September 12, 1970 – September 2, 1972. Retitled: "Josie and the Pussycats in Outer Space." 26 episodes.

JOSIE AND THE PUSSYCATS IN OUTER SPACE

Animated Cartoon. The Rock group Josie and the Pussycats are posing for publicity pictures atop a space craft at NASA. Alexandra, standing to the side and unable to be seen clearly, walks forward and accidentally knocks the others off balance. As they fall backward into the open capsule hatch, Alexandra's arm hits and activates the blast-off mechanism, sending the craft and its passengers into the far reaches of outer space. Descending upon unexplored planetoids, they encounter and battle the sinister forces of evil. A Hanna-Barbera Production.

Characters' Voices

Josie	Janet Waldo
Melody	Jackie Joseph
Valerie	Barbara Pariot
Alan	Jerry Dexter
Alexandra Cabot	Sherry Alberoni
Alexander Cabot	Casey Kaseem
Sebastian	Don Messick
Bleep, their mascot, a space creature befriended by Melody on the planet Zelcor	Don Messick

Vocals: The Rock group, Josie and the Pussycats: Cathy Douglas, Patricia Holloway, Cherie Moore.

Music: Hoyt Curtin.

JOSIE AND THE PUSSYCATS IN OUTER SPACE—30 minutes—CBS—September 9, 1972 – January 26, 1974. 26 episodes.

THE JO STAFFORD SHOW

Musical Variety.

Hostess: Jo Stafford.

Vocalists: The Starlighters.

Orchestra: Paul Weston.

THE JO STAFFORD SHOW—15 minutes—CBS 1954.

JOURNEY THROUGH LIFE

Interview. Married couples relate anecdotes drawn from their personal experiences.

Host: Tom Reddy.

JOURNEY THROUGH LIFE—30 minutes—ABC 1954.

JOURNEY TO ADVENTURE

See title: "World Adventures."

JOURNEY TO THE CENTER OF THE EARTH

Animated Cartoon. Uncovering the long-lost trail of Arnie Saccnuson, a lone explorer who made a descent to the earth's center, but died with its secret when breaking his leg, Professor Oliver Lindenbrook organizes an expedition. With his niece Cindy, student Alec Hewit, a guide Lars, and his pet duck Gertrude, Professor Lindenbrook begins a journey to the center of the earth.

Unbeknownst to them, the evil Count Saccnuson, the last living descendent of the once-noble family, follows them. Possessing a power-mad scheme to claim the earth's core for his own sinister purposes, he instructs his servant, Torg, to set off an explosion. However, when detonated, the blast seals the entrance and traps them all.

Stories relate their adventures as they struggle to find the secret of the way back to the earth's surface. Based on the novel by Jules Verne.

Characters' Voices

Oliver Lindenbrook	Ted Knight
Alec Hewit (a.k.a. Alec McEwen)	Pat Harrington
Cindy Lindenbrook	Jane Webb
Lars	Pat Harrington
Count Saccnuson	Ted Knight
Torg	Pat Harrington

Music: Gordon Zahler.

Producer: Norm Prescott, Lou Scheimer.

Director: Hal Sutherland.

JOURNEY TO THE CENTER OF THE EARTH—30 minutes—ABC—September 9, 1967 - September 6, 1969. Syndicated. 17 episodes.

JOURNEY TO THE UNKNOWN

Anthology. Mystery and suspense stories. Tales of the slender thread between nightmare and reality.

Music: Norman Kaye, David Lindup.

Included:

The Madison Equation. An insurance investigator attempts to prove that a woman murdered her husband by programming a computer to destroy him.

CAST
Inga Madison: Barbara Bel Geddes; Adam Frost: Jack Hedley; Barbara Rossiter: Sue Lloyd.

The Last Visitor. Plagued by the shadowy figure of a man, a girl seeks to uncover its sinister presence.

CAST
Barbara: Patty Duke; Mrs. Walker: Kay Walsh.

Girl In My Dreams. The story of a girl who possesses the ability to predict people's deaths through dreams.

CAST
Greg Richards: Michael Callan; Carrie Clark: Zena Walker.

JOURNEY TO THE UNKNOWN—60 minutes—ABC—September 26, 1968 - January 30, 1969. 17 episodes. Produced in England.

JOYCE AND BARBARA: FOR ADULTS ONLY

See title: "For Adults Only."

THE JOYCE DAVIDSON SHOW

Interview. Discussions with celebrity and noncelebrity guests.

Hostess: Joyce Davidson.

Music: Recorded open and close.

Producer: Sandra Faire.

THE JOYCE DAVIDSON SHOW—30 minutes—Syndicated 1975.

JUBILEE U.S.A.

Musical Variety. Performances by Country and Western entertainers.

Host: Red Foley.

Regulars: Wanda Jackson; Bobby Lord and His Timberjack Trio; Leroy Van Dyke; Uncle Cyp and Aunt Sap Brasfield; Marvin Rainwater; Suzi Arden; Slim Wilson and His Jubilee Band; The Promenaders; Chuck Bowers; The Marksman; Bill Wimberly and His Country Rhythm Boys.

Featured: "The Junior Jubilee." Performances by young hopefuls (e.g., Brenda Lee).

JUBILEE U.S.A.—60 minutes—ABC—January 22, 1955 - November 21, 1961. Also known as: "Ozark Jubilee" and "Country Music Jubilee."

JUDD, FOR THE DEFENSE

Drama. Background: Texas. The cases and courtroom defenses of attorneys Clinton Judd and his partner Ben Caldwell.

CAST
Clinton Judd	Carl Betz
Ben Caldwell	Stephen Young

Music: Harry Geller; Lionel Newman.

Additional Music: George Duning, Alexander Courage, Leith Stevens.

Executive Producer: Paul Monash.

Judd, For the Defense. Carl Betz and Stephen Young.

Producer: Howard Gast, Charles Russell.

Director: William Hale, Alexander March, Boris Sagal, Leo Penn.

JUDD, FOR THE DEFENSE—60 minutes—ABC—September 8, 1967 - September 19, 1969. Syndicated. 50 episodes.

JUDGE FOR YOURSELF

Game. Six players, three studio-audience members and three guest celebrities. Object: To rate the performances of undiscovered professional acts. Cash prizes are awarded to the laymen panelists whose ratings correspond with those of the celebrities.

Hosts: Fred Allen; Dennis James.

Announcer: Dennis James.

Orchestra: Milton DeLugg.

Producer: Mark Goodson, Bill Todman.

Sponsor: Old Gold Cigarettes.

JUDGE FOR YOURSELF—30 minutes—NBC—August 18, 1953 - May 11, 1954.

JUDGE ROY BEAN

Western. Background: Langtry, Texas during the 1870s. The story of Judge Roy Bean (self-appointed), a storekeeper, and his attempts to maintain law and order in "America's most lawless region."

CAST

Judge Roy Bean — Edgar Buchanan
Jeff Taggard, his deputy — Jack Beutel
Letty Bean, the Judge's niece — Jackie Loughery
Steve, a Texas Ranger — Russell Hayden

Program open:

Announcer: "During the 1870s, the wildest spot in the United States was the desolate region west of the Pecos River, an area virtually beyond the reach of the authorities. The railroads, then pushing their way West, attracted the most vicious characters in the country. It was said that civilization and law stopped at the east bank of the Pecos. It took one man, a lone storekeeper who was sick of the lawlessness, to change all this. His name was Judge Roy Bean."

JUDGE ROY BEAN—30 minutes—Syndicated 1956. 39 episodes.

JUDO BOY

The story of a boy who uses Judo to battle evil. 30 minutes—Syndicated. 1969.

THE JUDY GARLAND SHOW

Musical Variety.

Hostess: Judy Garland.

Featured: Jerry Van Dyke (supposedly teaching her the ropes of television production).

Special Musical Material: Mel Tormé.

Orchestra: Mort Lindsey.

Premiere Guest: Mickey Rooney.

Executive Producer: Bill Coloeran.

Producer: Gary Smith, Norman Jewison, Bill Hobin, George Schlatter, Johnny Bradford.

Director: Dean Whitmore.

THE JUDY GARLAND SHOW—60 minutes—CBS—September 29, 1963 - March 29, 1964. 26 episodes.

THE JUDY LYNN SHOW

Musical Variety. Performances by Country and Western entertainers.

Hostess: Judy Lynn.

Music: The eight-piece all-male Judy Lynn Band.

THE JUDY LYNN SHOW—30 minutes—Syndicated 1969. 52 tapes.

JUDY SPLINTERS

Children. The series spotlights the talents and antics of Judy Splinters, a wooden female dummy controlled by Shirley Dinsdale. The recurring story line has Judy trying to get Shirley married off.

Hostess-Ventriloquist: Shirley Dinsdale.

Dummy, her alter ego: Judy Splinters.

Producer: Norman Felton, Roger Muir.

Director: Al Howard.

JUDY SPLINTERS—15 minutes—NBC 1949.

JULIA

Comedy. Background: Los Angeles, California. The story of Julia Baker, widow, a registered nurse with the Inner Aero-Space Center (an industrial health office). Episodes relate her struggles as she attempts to readjust to life after the death of her husband (an Air Force captain killed in Vietnam) and raise her young son, Corey.

CAST

Julia Baker — Diahann Carroll
Dr. Morton Chegley, Julia's employer — Lloyd Nolan
Corey Baker — Marc Copage
Earl J. Waggedorn, Corey's friend — Michael Link
Marie Waggedorn, his mother — Betty Beaird
Earl Waggedorn, her husband — Hank Brandt
Hannah Yarby, the head nurse — Lurene Tuttle
Carol Deering, Julia's part-time mother's helper — Alison Mills
Sol Cooper, Julia's landlord — Ned Glass
Mrs. Deering, Carol's mother — Virginia Capers
Ted Neuman, Julia's boyfriend — Don Marshall
Paul Carter, Julia's boyfriend — Chuck Wood, Paul Winfield
Steve Bruce, Julia's boyfriend, a student lawyer — Fred Williamson
Roberta, Corey's baby sitter — Jenear Hines
Lou, Julia's uncle, an exvaudevillian — Eugene Jackson
Melba Chegley, Morton's wife — Mary Wickes
Mrs. Bennett, a tenant in Julia's building — Jeff Donnell

Music: Van Alexander.

JULIA—30 minutes—NBC—September 17, 1968 - May 25, 1971. 86 episodes.

THE JULIE ANDREWS HOUR

Variety. Music, songs, dances, and comedy sketches.

Hostess: Julie Andrews.

Regulars: Rich Little, Alice Ghostley, The Tony Charmoli Dancers, The Dick Williams Singers.

Announcer: Dick Tufeld.

Orchestra: Nelson Riddle.

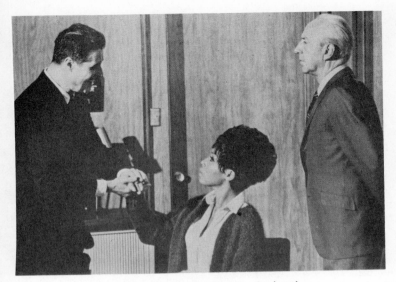

Julia. Left to right: Don Ameche (guest), Diahann Carroll, Lloyd Nolan. Episode: "The Grass Is Sometimes Greener."

Special Musical Material: Dick Williams.

Choreographer: Tony Charmoli.

Producer: Nick Vanoff.

Director: Bill Davis.

THE JULIE ANDREWS HOUR—60 minutes—ABC—September 13, 1972 - April 28, 1973.

JULIUS La ROSA

Listed: The television programs of singer Julius La Rosa.

The Julius La Rosa Show—Musical

The Julie Andrews Hour. Julie Andrews. *Courtesy Independent Television Corporation; an ATV Company.*

Variety—15 minutes—NBC—June 27, 1955 - September 22, 1955.

Host: Julius La Rosa.

Regulars: The Debutones—all-girl quartet—Sherry Ostrus, Connie Desmond, Bix Brent, Irene Carroll.

Orchestra: Russ Case.

The Julius La Rosa Show—Musical Variety—60 minutes—NBC—July 14, 1956 - August 4, 1956.

Host: Julius La Rosa.

Regulars: George De Witt, The Mariners, The Spellbinders, The Four Evans (Dancers).

Orchestra: Mitchell Ayres.

Perry Como Presents The Julius La Rosa Show—Musical Variety—60 minutes—NBC—June 15, 1957 — September 1957.

Host: Julius La Rosa.

Regulars: Steve Ashton, Lou Cosler, The Louis Da Pron Dancers, The Artie Malvin Chorus.

Orchestra: Mitchell Ayres.

THE JUNE ALLYSON THEATRE

Anthology. Dramatic presentations.

Hostess-Occasional Performer: June Allyson.

Music: Herschel Burke Gilbert; Hans Salter.

Included:

The Opening Door. A mother, lacking finances, attempts to enroll her mentally retarded daughter into a special school.

CAST
Dr. Gina Kerstas: Irene Dunne; Falk: Harry Townes.

The Tender Shoot. Kay Neilson, a successful young novelist, and Gary Stevens, a struggling young writer, meet. Infatuated with her, he reveals his ideas for a novel, unaware of her plan to use them as her own.

CAST
Kay Neilson: Ginger Rogers; Gary Stevens: Paul Carr; Jamie Bowers: Jan Norris.

Love Is A Headache. A young girl, infatuated with a young singer, attempts to impress him.

CAST
Ellie: Denise Alexander; Tony: Akim Tamiroff.

Child Lost. A nurse attempts to locate a missing child.

CAST
Nurse Vivian Wadron: June Allyson; Sgt. Lederman: Steve Brodie; Wim Wegless: Ronny Howard; Mrs. Wegless: Kathleen Mulqueen.

A Summer's Ending. The story of a summer romance involving a couple married, but not to each other.

CAST
Sharon Foster: June Allyson; Paul Martin: Dick Powell.

THE JUNE ALLYSON THEATRE—30 minutes—CBS—September 1959 — September 1961.

THE JUNE HAVOC SHOW

Interview.

Hostess: June Havoc.

Guests: Show-business personalities.

Music: Recorded.

THE JUNE HAVOC SHOW—60 minutes—Syndicated 1964.

JUNGLE BOY

See title: "The Adventures of a Jungle Boy."

JUNGLE JIM

Adventure. Background: Nairobi, Africa. The experiences of jungle guide Jungle Jim. Based on the character created by Alex Raymond.

CAST
Jungle Jim   Johnny Weissmuller
Skipper, his son   Martin Huston
Kaseem, his Hindu
  servant   Norman Fredric
Jim's chimpanzee: Tamba.
Skipper's dog: Trader.
Producer: Harold Greene.

Director: Don McDougall.

JUNGLE JIM—30 minutes—Syndicated 1955. 26 episodes.

JUNIOR ALMOST ANYTHING GOES

Game. A spin-off from "Almost Anything Goes." Geared for children, the series features three four-member teams competing in outrageous outdoor games for prizes.

Host: Soupy Sales.

Commentator: Eddie Alexander.

Music: The Junior High School Band.

Executive Producer: Bob Banner, Beryl Vertue.

Producer-Director: Kip Walton.

JUNIOR ALMOST ANYTHING GOES—25 minutes—ABC—Premiered: September 11, 1976.

JUNIOR HIGH JINKS

Children. Puppets, sketches, and film shorts.

Host: Warren Wright.

His Puppet: Willie the Worm.

JUNIOR HIGH JINKS—15 minutes—CBS 1952.

JUNIOR RODEO

Children. Western variety acts.

Host: Bob Atcher.

JUNIOR RODEO—30 minutes—ABC—January 15, 1952 – February 27, 1952.

Just for Laughs: The Barbara Eden Show. Barbara Eden.

JUST FOR LAUGHS

Pilot Films. Proposed comedy series for the 1974-1975 season. The complete series:

Ernie, Madge, and Artie. The story of a middle-aged newlywed couple who are plagued by the ghost of the bride's first husband.

CAST
Madge: Cloris Leachman; Ernie: Frank Sutton; Artie: Dick Van Patten; Blanche: Susan Sennett.

The Life And Times of Captain Barney Miller. The story of a compassionate policeman.

CAST
Barney Miller: Hal Linden; Elizabeth Miller: Abby Dalton; Rachel Miller: Anne Wyndham.

Ann In Blue. The story of Ann Neal, the head of a four-woman police unit.

CAST
Ann Neal: Penny Fuller; Bea Russo: Mary Elaine Monte; Elizabeth Jensen: Maybeth Hart; Jessie Waters: Hattie Winston.

The Barbara Eden Show. The story of a beautiful toy designer whose father wants to keep her under wraps and away from male suitors. Scheduled but never aired.

Starring: Barbara Eden.

JUST FOR LAUGHS—30 minutes—ABC—August 8, 1974 - August 29, 1974.

JUSTICE

Drama. Background: New York City.

The investigations of Richard Adam and Jason Tyler, attorneys for the Legal Aide Society. Based on official files.

CAST
Richard Adam   Dane Clark
                      William Prince
Jason Tyler   Gary Merrill
Narrator: Westbrook Van Voorhis.

JUSTICE—30 minutes—NBC—1952 - 1955.

JUVENILE JURY

Children's Panel. "Out of the mouths of babes oft time come gems." (The host's closing words). A panel of five children give their opinion as to the solving of or coping with a problem sent in by a home viewer or presented by an in-person guest.

Host-Announcer: Jack Barry.

Panelists, including: Patricia Bruder, Angela Bell, Jeff Silver, Veronique DeAllo, Paul Jackson, Ricky Cordell, Sean Masterson, Monique Althouse, Jeff Philips, Steve Andrews, Glena Sargent, Bobby Hull, Christine Hare, Wayne Chestnut, Paul Lazott, Curtis Helm, Neil Buller, Melanie Freeman, Joe Ward, Michele Fogel, Douglas Stewart.

Music: Joe Diamond.

VERSIONS:
NBC—30 minutes—April 3, 1947 - October 3, 1953.
CBS—30 minutes—October 11, 1953 - September 14, 1954.
NBC—30 minutes—January 2, 1955 - March 27, 1955.
Syndicated—30 minutes—1971.

K

THE KAISER ALUMINUM HOUR

Anthology. Dramatic presentations.

Included:

A Fragile Affair. Switzerland, World War II. The wife of a bitter delicatessen owner attempts to provide comfort and happiness to young soldiers.

CAST
Cristoff: Eli Wallach; Mary Cristoff: Gaby Rogers; Pip: Woodrow Parfrey.

Man On A White Horse. The story of an elderly sheriff who fears he's lost his ability to maintain law and order.

CAST

Sheriff Adam Griffith: James Barton; Dan Royal: Barton MacLane.

Army Game. A reluctant college draftee attempts to seek a psychiatric discharge.

CAST

Danny: Paul Newman; Berman: Edward Andrews; Manken: Philip Abbott.

THE KAISER ALUMINUM HOUR— 60 minutes—NBC—July 3, 1956 - June 18, 1957. Alternates with "The Armstrong Circle Theatre."

THE KALLIKAKS

Comedy. Background: California. The story of the Kallikaks, a poor Appalachian family, the owners-operators of a gas station, as they struggle for a better life.

CAST

Jasper T. Kallikak, Sr.	David Huddleston
Venus Kallikak, his wife	Edie McClurg
Bobbi Lou Kallikak, their daughter	Bonnie Ebsen
Jasper T. Kallikak, Jr., their son	Patrick J. Petersen
Oscar, Jasper's mechanic	Peter Palmer

Music: Tom Wells.

Theme Vocal: Roy Clark.

Executive Producer: Stanley Ralph Ross.

Producer: George Yanok.

Director: Dennis Steinmetz, Bob LaHendro, Ron Kantor.

Creator: Roger Price, Stanley Ralph Ross.

THE KALLIKAKS—30 minutes— NBC—August 3, 1977 - August 31, 1977. 5 episodes.

KAREN

See title: "Ninety Bristol Court," *Karen* segment.

KAREN

Comedy. Background: Washington,

Karen. Karen Valentine.

D.C. The trials and tribulations of Karen Angelo, a young idealist staff worker for Open America, a Capitol Hill citizens' lobby.

CAST

Karen Angelo	Karen Valentine
Dale W. Bush, the founder of Open America	Denver Pyle Charles Lane
Dena Madison, a staff worker at Open America	Dena Dietrich
Cissy Peterson, Karen's roommate	Aldine King
Adam Cooperman, a staff worker at Open America	Will Seltzer
Jerry Siegle, a tenant in Karen's rooming house	Oliver Clark
Cheryl Siegle, Jerry's wife	Alix Elias
Senator Bob Hartford, Karen's friend	Edward Winter
Ernie, Karen's friend	Joseph Stone

Music: Benny Golson.

Executive Producer-Director: Gene Reynolds.

Producer: Burt Metcalfe.

Creator: Gene Reynolds, Carl Kleinschmidt, Larry Gelbart.

Karen's Address: 1460 Cambridge Street in Jamestown, Washington, D.C.

KAREN—30 minutes—ABC—January 30, 1975 - June 19, 1975. 13 episodes.

THE KAREN VALENTINE SHOW

See title: "Karen."

KATE McSHANE

Drama. Background: California. The cases and courtroom defenses of Kate McShane, an uninhibited and unorthodox Irish-American lawyer.

CAST

Kate McShane	Anne Meara
Pat McShane, her father, an excop who is now her investigator	Sean McClory
Ed McShane, her brother, a Jesuit priest and professor of law	Charles Haid
Julie, her secretary	Rachel Malkin

Music: Charles Bernstein.

Executive Producer: E. Jack Neuman.

Producer: Robert Foster, Robert Stampler.

Director: Robert Scheerner, Jack Shea, David E. Friedkin, Corey Allen, John Peyser, Bill Bixby.

KATE McSHANE—60 minutes—CBS —September 10, 1975 - November 12, 1975.

KATE SMITH

Listed: The television programs of singer Kate Smith.

The Kate Smith Hour—Variety—60 minutes—NBC—September 25, 1950 - June 18, 1954.

Format: Music, songs, dances, sketches, cooking, guests, interviews, fashion, panel discussions, and news.

Hostess: Kate Smith.

Regulars: Jeff Clark, Jimmy Nelson (Ventriloquist; his dummy: Danny O'Day), Peggy Ryan, Ray MacDonald, Evalyn Tyner, Richard and Flora Stuart, Fran Barber, Billy Mills, Robert Maxwell, Claire Frim, Virginia McCurdy, Diane Carol, Peg Lynch, Alan Bunce, Charlie Ruggles, Ruth Mattheson, Glenn Walker, Hal Le Roy, Adolph Dehm, Barry Wood, Dorothy Day, The McGuire Sisters, Louren Gilbert, Tim Taylor, Monica Lovett, Mimi Stongin, James Vickery, Arlene Dalton, The Showtimers, The John Butler Ballet Group, The Jack Allison Singers.

Announcer: Andre Baruch.

Orchestra: Jack Miller.

Featured Segments:
"Ethel And Albert." A domestic comedy starring Peg Lynch and Alan Bunce. (See Title.)
"The World Of Mr. Sweeny." A comedy starring Charlie Ruggles and Glenn Walker. (See title.)
"The Talent Showcase." Performances by young hopefuls.
"The House in the Garden." A drama of life in a small town.

The Kate Smith Evening Hour—Musical Variety—60 minutes—NBC—1951-1952.
Hostess: Kate Smith.
Regulars: Ted Collins, Paul Lukas, Susan Douglas, Ann Thomas, Kay Thompson, The Williams Brothers, The Stuart Morgan Dancers, The John Butler Dancers, The Jack Allison Singers.
Announcer: Bob Warren.
Orchestra: Harry Sosnick.

The Kate Smith Show—Musical Variety—30 minutes—CBS—January 25, 1960 - July 18, 1960.
Hostess: Kate Smith.
Featured: The Harry Simeone Chorale.
Orchestra: Neal Hefti; Bill Stegmeyer.

THE KATHI NORRIS SHOW

A variety series, first broadcast in 1952, and starring Kathi Norris.

KAY KYSER'S KOLLEGE OF MUSICAL KNOWLEDGE

Variety-Quiz. Musical numbers are interspersed with a quiz segment situated against a college format. Contestants compete in tests of musical questions divided into midterms and final exams. The professor (host) leads the orchestra in a selection that the player must identify. If he is correct, a cash prize is awarded; if he is unable to answer, the song title is relayed by the studio audience (students).
Hosts: Kay Kyser, The Old Professor; Tennessee Ernie Ford (after Mr. Kyser's retirement in 1954).
Regulars: Mike Douglas, Sylvia Michaels, Diana Sinclair, Liza Palmer, Sue Bennett, Ish Kabbible (the comic relief, a member of Kay's band, on sax), Kenny Spaulding, The Honeydreamers, The Cheerleaders (Donna Brown, Maureen Cassidy, Spring Mitchell).
Announcer: Verne Smith (The Dean).

Orchestra: Carl Hoff; Kay Kyser; Frank DeVol.
Producer: Perry Lafferty.
Director: Earl Ebi, Buzz Kulik.
Sponsor: Ford Motor Company.

KAY KYSER'S KOLLEGE OF MUSICAL KNOWLEDGE—30 minutes—NBC—1949 - 1955.

THE KAY STARR SHOW

Musical Variety.
Hostess: Kay Starr.
Orchestra: Pete King.

THE KAY STARR SHOW—30 minutes—NBC 1957.

THE KEANE BROTHERS SHOW

Variety.
Hosts: John and Tom Keane.
Regulars: Jimmy Caesar, The Anita Mann Dancers.
Orchestra: Alan Copeland.
Executive Producer: Pierre Cossette.
Producer: Buz Kohan.
Director: Tony Charmoli.
Choreographer: Anita Mann.

THE KEANE BROTHERS SHOW—30 minutes—CBS—August 12, 1977 - September 2, 1977. 4 tapes.

THE KEEFE BRASSELLE SHOW

Musical Variety.
Host: Keefe Brasselle.
Regulars: Rocky Graziano, Ann B. Davis, Noelle Adam, The Style Sisters, The Bill Foster Dancers.
Orchestra: Charles Sanford.

THE KEEFE BRASSELLE SHOW—60 minutes—CBS—June 25, 1963 - September 17, 1963.

KEEP IT IN THE FAMILY

Game. Two families, each composed of five members, the father, mother, and three children, compete. General-knowledge questions are asked of each member of each family, beginning with the youngest. Each correct response earns points. Winners, the highest point scorers, receive merchandise gifts.

Hosts: Bill Nimmo; Keefe Brasselle.
Announcer: Johnny Olsen.

KEEP IT IN THE FAMILY—30 minutes—ABC—October 12, 1957 - February 8, 1958.

KEEP ON TRUCKIN'

Comedy. A potpourri of broad comedy sketches and freewheeling spoofs and blackouts.
Starring: Fred Travalena, Larry Ragland, Richard Lee Sung, Rhonda Bates, Gailard Sartain, Marion Ramsey, Franklyn Ajaye, Kathryn Bauman, Jennine Burnier, Dee Dee Kahn, Rilo, Charles Flascher, Welland Flowers, Jack Riley.
Musical Director: Marvin Larlaird.
Choreographer: Charlene Painter.
Producer: John Aylesworth.
Director: Tony Mordente.

KEEP ON TRUCKIN'—60 minutes—ABC—July 12, 1975 - August 2, 1975.

KEEP TALKING

Game. Four celebrity players compete (three regulars and one guest), composing two teams of two. One member on each team receives a secret phrase that he then must work into an ad-libbed conversation. A bell sounds the end of the round. Opponents then have to identify the concealed phrase. If successful, they receive points. Winners are the highest point scorers. Prizes are awarded to home and studio-audience members represented by the celebrities.
Hosts: Monty Hall (CBS); Merv Griffin (ABC).
Regular Panelists: Ilka Chase, Joey Bishop, Danny Dayton, Morey Amsterdam, Paul Winchell, Peggy Cass, Pat Carroll.

KEEP TALKING—30 minutes. CBS—July 8, 1958 - September 22, 1959; ABC—September 29, 1959 - May 3, 1960.

THE KELLY MONTEITH SHOW

Variety.
Host: Kelly Monteith.
Regulars: Nellie Bellflower, Harry Corden.
Orchestra: Dick De Benedictis.

Producer: Ed Simmons, Robert Wright.

Director: Dave Powers.

THE KELLY MONTEITH SHOW—30 minutes—CBS—June 16, 1976 - July 7, 1976. 4 tapes.

THE KEN BERRY WOW SHOW

Variety. A nostalgic look at yesterday through music, song, dance, and comedy. The thirties, forties, fifties, and sixties are re-created through sketch, animation, and imaginative effects.

Host: Ken Berry.

Regulars: Laara Lacey, Billy Van, Steve Martin, Carl Gotlieb, Teri Garr, Barbara Joyce, Don Ray, Cheryl Stufflemoore, The New Seekers, The Jaime Rogers Dancers.

Orchestra: Jimmy Dale.

Premiere Guests: Patty Duke, John Astin, The Lennon Sisters, Dr. Joyce Brothers, Monty Hall, Don Knotts, Dick Clark, Cass Elliott.

THE KEN BERRY WOW SHOW—60 minutes—ABC—July 15, 1972 - August 12, 1972.

THE KEN MURRAY SHOW

Variety. Blackouts, music, songs, dances, dramatic skits, and novelty acts.

Host: Ken Murray.

Regulars: Laurie Anders, Darla Jean Hood, Joe Besser, Annie Skelton, Betty Lou Walters, Art Lund, Jack Marshall, Richard Webb, Johnny Johnston, Anita Gordon, Herbert Marshall, Joan Shea, Lillian Farmer, Cathy Hild, Tommy Labriola (as Oswald), The Ken Murray Chorus, The Ken Murray Dancers, The Glamour Lovelies.

Announcer: Nelson Chase.

Orchestra: David Broekman; Jane Bergmeler.

Producer: Howard Reilly, Ken Murray, Frank Salem.

Director: Frank Satenstein, Herbert Sussan.

Sponsor: Anheuser-Busch.

THE KEN MURRAY SHOW—60 minutes—CBS—1948 - 1953.

KEN MURRAY'S HOLLYWOOD

Variety. Home movies of celebrities. Presented as a fill-in when an NBC network movie ended early.

Host-Narrator-Photographer: Ken . Murray.

KEN MURRAY'S HOLLYWOOD—10 minutes (approx.)—NBC—1964-1967.

Kentucky Jones. Dennis Weaver.

KENTUCKY JONES

Drama. Background: The Jones Ranch in California, a forty-acre spread owned by Kenneth (Kentucky) Yarborough Jones, a widowed professional horse trainer turned veterinarian.

Several weeks following the death of his wife, Jones receives notice informing him of the arrival of the Chinese orphan he and his wife had planned to adopt. Feeling himself no longer qualified to raise the child, he tries to halt the adoption but is unsuccessful and soon finds himself the foster father of a ten-year old boy, Dwight Eisenhower Wong (Ike).

Stories depict the efforts of Kentucky Jones and his partner, Seldom Jackson, to raise a young refugee; and Ike's attempts to secure the affections of his foster father.

CAST

Kentucky Jones	Dennis Weaver
Seldom Jackson, a former jockey who rarely brought in a winner	Harry Morgan
Dwight Eisenhower Wong (Ike)	Rickey Der
Annie Ng, a friend of Ike's	Cherylene Lee
Thomas Wong, a friend	Keye Luke

Music: Vic Mizzy.

KENTUCKY JONES—30 minutes—NBC—September 19, 1964 - September 11, 1965. 26 episodes.

KEY CLUB PLAYHOUSE

Anthology. Rebroadcasts of dramas that were originally aired via "Ford Theatre."

Included:

Bet The Queen. A gambler wins two tickets on the last boat to leave Fort Benton before the river freezes. The story relates the efforts of the wife of the man who lost the tickets to retrieve them.

CAST

Rory Calhoun, Gale Robbins, Donald Curtis.

A Past Remembered. Attending his twentieth-year college reunion, a middle-aged man discovers that he is the only one who is not a financial success. The story relates his attempts to acquire a job through one of his classmates by pretending to be a successful businessman.

CAST

William Bendix, Lyle Talbot, Joan Banks.

Passage to Yesterday. The story of an American captain and a British army nurse who meet and fall in love during the London Blitz of World War II.

CAST

Joanne Dru, Guy Madison, James Fairfax.

KEY CLUB PLAYHOUSE—30 minutes—ABC—June 1956 - September 1956; May 1957 - September 1957.

KEYHOLE

Documentary. Films showcasing the unusual occupations or experiences of people.

Host-Narrator: Jack Douglas.

KEYHOLE—30 minutes—Syndicated 1962. 38 episodes.

KHAN!

Crime Drama. Background: San Francisco's Chinatown. The investigations of Khan, a Chinese private detective.

CAST

Khan	Khigh Dhiegh
Ann Khan, his daughter	Irene Yah-Ling Sun
Kim Khan, his son	Evan Kim
Lt. Gubbins, S.F.P.D.	Vic Tayback

Music: Morton Stevens; Bruce Broughton.

Producer: Laurence Heath, Joseph Henry.

Director: Ivan Dixon, Bill Derwin.

Creator: Chet Gould.

Note: "Khan!" is the only television series in which the star refused billing.

KHAN!—60 minutes—CBS—February 7, 1975 - February 28, 1975. 4 episodes.

KID GLOVES

Children. Two contestants. Format: A series of three thirty-second boxing bouts that follow the rules of the professionals. Between rounds (thirty seconds), question and answer sessions are conducted with audience members by John Da Groza, the Pennsylvania Boxing Commissioner.

Host (presenting the blow-by-blow commentary): Bill Sears.

Referee: Frank Goodman.

KID GLOVES—30 minutes—CBS 1951.

KID POWER

Animated Cartoon. Background: The Rainbow Club—an anywhere club in an anywhere city or town. The story of its members, all children, who are struggling to save the environment and better the world. Object: To show kids of different ethnic backgrounds sharing thoughts on prejudice, teamwork, and responsibility.

Characters: Wellington, Oliver, Nipper, Diz, Connie, Jerry, Albert, Ralph, Sybil; Polly, Wellington's parrot; General Lee, Nipper's dog; and Tom, Ralph's cat.

Voices: John Gardiner, Jay Silverheels, Jr., Allan Melvin, Michele Johnson, Charles Kennedy, Jr., Carey Wong, Jeff Thomas, Gregg Thomas, Gary Shiparo.

Music: Perry Botkin, Jr.

KID POWER—30 minutes—ABC—September 16, 1972 - September 1, 1974.

KIDS AND COMPANY

Variety. The series features performances by child entertainers with the object being for the studio audience to judge one performer the best. The winner is crowned "Kid of the Week" and receives prizes.

Host: Johnny Olsen.

Assistant: Ham Fisher.

Organist: Al Greiner.

Producer: Wyatt-Schuebell Productions.

Sponsor: International Shoe Company.

KIDS AND COMPANY—30 minutes—DuMont 1951.

THE KIDS FROM C.A.P.E.R.

Comedy. Background: The town of Northeast Southwestern. The escapades of P.T., Bugs, Doomsday, and Doc, four teenage boys who comprise the Kids from C.A.P.E.R., a special crime-fighting unit of the local 927th police precinct. (C.A.P.E.R.: The Civilian Authority for the Protection of Everybody, Regardless.)

CAST

P.T.	Steve Bonino
Bugs	Cosie Costa
Doomsday	Biff Warren
Doc	John Lansing
Sergeant Vinton	Robert Emhardt
Mr. Clintsinger, the reporter	Robert Lussier

Music: Wally Gold, Jay Siegel.

Musical Supervision: Don Kirshner.

Executive Producer: Alan Landsburg, Don Kirshner.

Producer: Stanley Z. Cherry.

Director: Roger Duchowny, Stanley Z. Cherry.

THE KIDS FROM C.A.P.E.R.—30 minutes—NBC—September 11, 1976 - November 20, 1976. Returned: Premiered: April 16, 1977.

KID TALK

Discussion. Four child panelists and two guest celebrities discuss topical issues.

Host: Bill Adler.

Panelists: Mona Tera (age seven), Andy Yamamoto (ten), Nellie Henderson (twelve), Alan Winston (twelve).

Announcer: Johnny Olsen.

Music: Recorded.

KID TALK—30 minutes—Syndicated 1972.

KIMBA, THE WHITE LION

Animated Cartoon. Early history: Egypt, four thousand years ago. Squandering the country's wealth, the evil Pharoah, King Tut Tut, causes the kingdom to lose its prosperity. In an attempt to curtail the king's spending, Fradies, the King's Minister, develops a special wisdom formula that he feeds to his pet, a rare white lion. Sending the animal into the village, the people believe it to be the Spirit of the Sphinx, and follow its leadership. The lion teaches them economy and the development of strong bodies and minds. As Egypt prospers once again, the king extends good will to all African tribes.

Overwhelmed by the performance of one such tribe, the Kickapeels, the king offers them any treasure in his kingdom. The leader chooses and receives the white lion.

Returning to Africa, the Kickapeels are blessed with prosperity as the white lion becomes their king. Thus, generation after generation, the white lion has been in rule of Africa.

Africa, 1960s. Caesar, the ruler, old and dying, bestows upon his son Kimba, the rare white lion, the sacred throne. Stories relate Kimba's struggles to safeguard his homeland from evil.

Additional characters: Dan'l Baboon, Samson, Pauley Cracker, Tadpole, Roger Ranger, Kitty, King Speckle Rex, and Claw, an enemy determined to foil Kimba's plans.

Voice of Kimba: Billie Lou Watt.

Music: Bernie Baum, Bill Grant, Florence Kaye.

KIMBA, THE WHITE LION—30 minutes—Syndicated 1966. 52 episodes. Produced in Japan.

THE KING FAMILY

Listed: The television programs of the King Family.

The King Family Show—Variety—60 minutes—ABC—January 23, 1965 - January 8, 1966.

Orchestra: Mitchell Ayres; Ralph Carmichael; Alvino Rey.

The King Family Show—Variety—30 minutes—ABC—March 12, 1969 - September 10, 1969.

Orchestra: Alvino Rey.

The original eight members of the King Family: William King, Karlton King, Alyce King (married name: Alyce Clark), Luise King (married name: Luise Rey), Donna King (married name: Donna Conklin), Maxine King (married name: Maxine Thomas), Yvonne King (married name: Yvonne Birch), Marilyn King (married name: Marilyn Larsen).

The thirty-six-member King family at the time of their first series:

William King. Wife: Phyllis. Three children: Steve, Della, and Jonathan.

Karlton King. Two children: William (wife: Barbara; children: Tammy and Todd), Don (wife: Cheryl Crawley; children: Don and Ray).

Alyce Clark. Husband: Bob Clark (first married to Sydney de Azevedo, deceased); two children: Lex (married; children: Linda, Julie, and Carrie), and Cameron.

Luise Rey. Husband: Alvino Rey; two children: Liza and Robi.

Donna Conkling. Husband: James Conkling; four children: Candice (husband: Robert Wilson; children: Kristen and Brook), Jamie, Alexander (Xan), and Chris.

Maxine Thomas. Husband: La Varn Thomas; one child: Thomas (wife: Donna; one child: Carolyn, husband: Bill Brennan).

Yvonne Birch. Husband: Bill Birch (first married to Buddy Cole, deceased); two children: Tina Cole (husband: Volney Howard; parents of Volney IV), Cathy Birch (husband: Jim Greene).

Marilyn Larsen. Husband: Kent Larsen. Three children: Jennifer, Lloyd, and Susannah.

KING FEATURES TRILOGY

Animated Cartoon. An adaptation of three King Features comic strips: "Barney Google"; "Beetle Bailey"; and "Krazy Kat."

Voices: Howard Morris, Penny Phillips, Allan Melvin, Paul Frees.

Music: Winston Sharples.

Barney Google. The misadventures of Barney Google, a simple-minded hillbilly.

Additional characters: Snuffy Smith, his friend; Louisa May Smith, Snuffy's wife; Jughead Smith, Snuffy's nephew; and Clem Cutplug, a feuding enemy.

Beetle Bailey. Background: Camp Swampy. The trials and tribulations of Beetle Bailey, a dim-witted private.

Additional characters: Sergeant Snorkel; General Halftrack.

Krazy Kat. The misadventures of the love-sick Krazy Kat.

Additional characters: Offissa Pup; Ignatz Mouse.

KING FEATURES TRILOGY—05 minutes (each cartoon)—Syndicated 1963. 150 episodes.

KING KONG

Animated Cartoon. Background: The remote prehistoric island of Mondo in the Java Sea. After Professor Bond, an American scientist, establishes a research base, his young son Bobby, discovers and befriends the sixty-foot-tall gorilla, King Kong, a creature the professor believes is intelligent and an important clue in the study of anthropology. Stories relate the struggles of the professor, his children, Bobby and Susan, and Kong, as they battle the evil influences of Dr. Who, a power-mad scientist who seeks Kong for his own diabolical plan to control the world. Very loosely based on the film classic.

Also presented:

TOM OF T.H.U.M.B. Background: The secret U.S. government offices of T.H.U.M.B. (Tiny Humans Underground Military Bureau). The investigations of agents Tom and his Oriental assistant, Swinging Jack.

Music: Maury Laws.

KING KONG—30 minutes—ABC—September 10, 1966 - August 31, 1969. 78 episodes.

KING LEONARDO

Animated Cartoon. Background: Bongoland, a mythical African kingdom ruled by King Leonardo, a lion, and his assistant, the real power behind the throne, Odie Calognie. Stories depict their battle against the evil influences of Itchy Brother and Biggy Rat.

Additional Segments:

Tutor the Turtle. The story of a turtle who becomes whatever he wishes through the magic of Mr. Wizard, the lizard.

The Hunter. The story concerns a beagle detective's attempts to apprehend the cunning Fox.

Characters' Voices

King Leonardo	Jackson Beck
Biggy Rat	Jackson Beck
Odie Cologne	Allen Swift
Tutor	Allen Swift
Mr. Wizard	Sandy Becker
The Hunter	Kenny Delmar

Producer: Treadwell Covington, Peter Piech.

KING LEONARDO—30 minutes—NBC—October 15, 1960 - September 1963. 38 episodes. Syndicated title: "The King and Odie."

KING OF DIAMONDS

Adventure. The cases of John King, an investigator for the diamond industry.

CAST

John King	Broderick Crawford
Casey O'Brien, his assistant	Ray Hamilton

Music: Frank Ortega.

KING OF DIAMONDS—30 minutes—Syndicated 1961.

KING OF KENSINGTON

Comedy. Background: The city of Kensington in Toronto, Canada. Events in the lives of the Kings: Larry, the owner of King's Variety Store; his attractive, level-headed wife, Cathy; and Gladys, Larry's mother.

CAST

Larry King	Al Waxman
Cathy King	Fiona Reid
Gladys King	Helene Winston
Nestor Best, Larry's friend	Ardon Bess
Duke Zaro, Larry's friend	Bob Vinci
Max, Larry's friend	John J. Dee
Rosa Zaro, Duke's wife	Vivian Reis

Max's dog: Mary Theresa.

Music: Bob McMillin.

Theme Vocal: Bob Francis.

Executive Producer: Perry Rosemond.

Producer: Jack Humphrey, Louis Del Grande.

Director: Herb Roland, Garry Plaxton, Stan Jacobson, Sheldon Larry.

KING OF KENSINGTON–30 minutes–Syndicated 1977.

KING'S CROSSROADS

Film Shorts.

Host-Narrator: Carl King.

KING'S CROSSROADS–60 minutes –ABC–October 10, 1951 - July 20, 1952.

KING'S ROW

See title: "Warner Brothers Presents," *King's Row* segment.

THE KINGDOM OF THE SEA

Documentary. Films exploring the seas and oceans of the world.

Host-Narrator: Robert J. Stevenson.

THE KINGDOM OF THE SEA–30 minutes–Syndicated 1957. 41 episodes.

KINGSTON: CONFIDENTIAL

Crime Drama. Background: California. The story of R.B. Kingston, chief reporter and editor-in-chief of the Frazier News Group, an influential organization of newspapers and TV stations.

CAST

R.B. Kingston	Raymond Burr
Tony Marino, a reporter	Art Hindle
Beth Kelly, a reporter	Pamela Hensley
Jessica Frazier, the chairperson of the board of Frazier	Nancy Olson

Music: Pete Rugolo, Henry Mancini, Richard Shores.

Executive Producer: David Victor.

Producer: James Hirsch, Don Ingalls, Joe L. Cramer, Don Nicholl.

Director: Richard Moder, Harvey Laidman, Don Weis, Michael Caffrey, Don McDougall.

KINGSTON: CONFIDENTIAL–60 minutes–NBC–March 23, 1977 - August 10, 1977.

KIT CARSON

See title: "The Adventures of Kit Carson."

KITTY FOYLE

Serial. The dramatic story of Kitty Foyle, a teenage girl "just discovering life."

CAST

Kitty Foyle	Kathleen Murray
Edward Foyle	Bob Hastings
Pop Foyle	Ralph Dunn
Molly Scharf	Judy Lewis
Molly Scharf, as a girl	Patty Duke
Wyn Stafford	Billy Redfield
Kenneth	Jan Merlin
Rosie Rittenhouse	Les Damon
Oliva Strafford	Valerie Cassart
Stacylea	Marie Worsham
Mac	Lany Robinson
Ma Balla	Casey Allen
Myrtle	Mae Barnes
Carter Hamilton	Martin Newman
Joe Gaines	Arnold Robinson
Flip	Conrad Fowkes
Sophie	Kay Medford
George Harvey	Karl Webber

KITTY FOYLE–30 minutes–NBC– January 13, 1958 - June 27, 1958.

THE KITTY WELLS/JOHNNY WRIGHT FAMILY SHOW

Musical Variety. Performances by Country and Western artists.

Hosts: Kitty Wells, Johnny Wright.

Regulars: Carol Sue Wright, Bobby Wright, Bill Phillips, Rudy Wright.

THE KITTY WELLS/JOHNNY WRIGHT FAMILY SHOW–30 minutes–Syndicated 1969. 39 tapes.

KLONDIKE

Adventure. Background: Alaska during the 1890s. Stories dramatize the struggles of Kathy O'Hara as she attempts to maintain an honest hotel in a lawless territory; and the exploits of adventurer Mike Holliday as he struggles to find gold in the beautiful but dangerous Ice Palace of the Northland.

CAST

Kathy O'Hara	Mari Blanchard
Mike Holliday	Ralph Taeger
Jeff Durain, a con artist	James Coburn
Goldie, his assistant	Joi Lansing

Music: Vic Mizzy.

KLONDIKE–30 minutes–NBC– October 10, 1960 - February 13, 1961. 18 episodes.

KLONDIKE KAT

Animated Cartoon. The misadventures of Klondike Kat, an incompetent police feline who, on orders from the chief, Major Minor, struggles to apprehend the notorious rodent Savoir Faire.

KLONDIKE KAT–05 minutes–Syndicated 1965. 26 episodes.

KNOCKOUT

Game. Three noncelebrity contestants compete. The object is for players to earn eight letters and spell the word Knockout. Four items (e.g., Peach, Apple, Mustard, and Pizza) appear on a large board, one at a time. The first player to sound a buzzer signal receives the opportunity to identify the item that is out of place (Mustard in the given example). If he is correct, he scores one letter and receives a chance to earn an additional letter by identifying the common denominator for all three items (Pies, in this case) or two extra letters by challenging one of his opponents to identify the denominator. If he chooses to answer for himself and is correct he scores the extra letter; if the challenge is made and the opponent fails to identify the denominator, then the player scores the two additional letters; however, if the opponent guesses it, then he scores the extra letters. The first player to spell Knockout is the winner and receives merchandise prizes.

Host: Arte Johnson.

Announcer: Jay Stewart.

Producer: Ralph Edwards.

KNOCKOUT–30 minutes–NBC–Premiered: October 3, 1977.

KOBB'S CORNER

Musical Variety. Background: The Shufflebottom General Store, a southern business establishment that sponsors a musical-comedy get-together on Wednesday evenings.

Hostess: Hope Emerson (as the General Store owner).

Regulars: Jo Hurt, Stan Fritter, Jimmy Allen, Joan Nobles, The Korn Kobblers.

Producer: Barry Wood.

Director: Kingman T. Moore.

KOBB'S CORNER—30 minutes CBS 1948.

KODAK REQUEST PERFORMANCE

Anthology. Rebroadcasts of dramas that were originally aired via other filmed anthology programs.
Included:
Afraid To Live. Background: The Fiji Islands. The effect of an old man's wisdom and contentment on a wealthy young woman.

CAST
Dorothy Malone, Charles Drake.

Girl In Flight. Background: A small French town. A lawyer attempts to free a woman accused of murder.

CAST
Joan Leslie, Tom Drake, Hugo Haas.

Sgt. Sullivan Speaking. The son of a widow attempts to match his mother with a police sergeant.

CAST
William Bendix, Joan Blondell, William Fawcett, Sarah Selby, June Kenny, Jon Provost.

Trouble With Youth. Tale of a middle-aged theatrical producer who attempts to recapture his youth through the association of a young woman.

CAST
Paul Douglas, Constance Moore, Lucy Marlow, June Vincent.

KODAK REQUEST PERFORMANCE—30 minutes—NBC—April 13, 1955 - September 28, 1955.

KODIAK

Crime Drama. Background: Alaska. The cases of Cal "Kodiak" McKay, a member of the Alaska State Police Patrol. (McKay is named "Kodiak" by the natives after a great bear that roams the area.)

CAST
Cal "Kodiak" McKay   Clint Walker
Abraham Lincoln Imhook, his
    assistant   Abner Biberman
Mandy, the radio
    dispatcher   Maggie Blye
Music: Morton Stevens.

KODIAK—30 minutes—ABC—Sep-tember 13, 1974 - October 11, 1974. 4 episodes.

KOJAK

Crime Drama. Background: New York City. The investigations of Lieutenant Theo Kojak, a plainclothes detective with the Manhattan South Precinct. One of the more realistic police dramas dealing with current and some-times controversial topics and crimes.

CAST
Lt. Theo Kojak   Telly Savalas
Frank McNeil, Chief of
    Detectives   Dan Frazer
Lt. Bobby Crocker   Kevin Dobson
Detective Stavros   Demosthenes
Detective Rizzo   Vince Conti
Detective Saperstein   Mark Russell
Music: Billy Goldenberg; Kim Richmond; John Cacavas.
Executive Producer: Matthew Rapf.
Producer: James MacAdams, Jack Laird.
Director: Sigmund Neufeld, Jr., David Friedkin, Jerry London, Daniel Haller, Richard Donner, Paul Stanley, Allen Reisner, Nicholas Sagaria, Charles S. Dubin, Ernest Pintoff, Telly Savalas, Russ May-berry, Joel Olinsky, Edward Abroms.
Creator: Abby Mann.
Note: Demosthenes (Det. Stavros) is now known as George Savalas (Telly's brother).

KOJAK—60 minutes—CBS—Pre-miered: October 24, 1973.

KOLCHAK: THE NIGHT STALKER

See title: "The Night Stalker."

THE KOPYKATS

Variety. Songs, dances, and comedy sketches featuring impersonations of show-business personalities.
Hosts: Weekly Guests: Tony Curtis, Raymond Burr, Debbie Reynolds, Robert Young, Steve Lawrence, Ed Sullivan.
The Kopykats: Rich Little, Marilyn Michaels, Frank Gorshin, George Kirby, Charlie Callas, Joe Baker, Fred Travalena.
Featured: The Norman Maen Dancers.
Orchestra: Jack Parnell.

THE KOPYKATS—60 minutes—ABC

(Rebroadcasts)—June 21, 1972 - August 10, 1972. Originally broadcast as part of the "The ABC Comedy Hour"—60 minutes—ABC—January 12, 1972 - April 5, 1972. Syndicated. First appeared as two one-hour seg-ments of "The Kraft Music Hall," "The Kopykats," and "The Kopykats Copy TV."

KORG: 70,000 B.C.

Adventure. Background: Earth, 70,000 B.C. The struggle for survival in a primitive world as seen through the experiences of a Neanderthal fam-ily. Based on assumptions and theories drawn from artifacts.

CAST
Korg   Jim Malinda
Bok   Bill Ewing
Mara   Naomi Pollack
Tane   Christopher Man
Tor   Charles Morted
Ree   Janelle Pransky
Narrator: Burgess Meredith.
Music: Hoyt Curtin.
Executive Producers: William Hanna, Joseph Barbera.
Director: Christian Nyby.

KORG: 70,000 B.C.—30 minutes—ABC—September 7, 1974 - August 31, 1975. 24 episodes.

THE KRAFT MUSIC HALL

Versions:

The Kraft Music Hall—Musical Variety—30 minutes—NBC—October 8, 1958 - June 9, 1962.
Hosts: Milton Berle; Perry Como; Dave King.
Regulars: Ken Carpenter, The Bill Foster Dancers, The Jerry Packer Singers.
Announcer: Ed Herlihy.
Orchestra: Billy May.

The Kraft Music Hall— Musical Variety—60 minutes—NBC—Sep-tember 13, 1967 - September 8, 1971. Varying format; different presenta-tions weekly.
Hosts: Weekly guests, including Don Rickles, Wayne Newton, Mitzi Gaynor, Jack Jones, Alan King, Debbie Reynolds, Don Knotts, Herb Alpert, Roy Rogers & Dale Evans, Mike Douglas, Rock Hudson, Eddie Arnold.
Regulars: The Peter Gennaro Dancers,

The Michael Bennett Dancers.

Announcer: Ed Herlihy.

Orchestra: Peter Matz.

The Kraft Summer Music Hall—Musical Variety—60 minutes—NBC—June 1966 - September 1966.

Host: John Davidson.

Regulars: The Five King Cousins, The Lively Set, Jackie and Gayle.

Announcer: Ed Herlihy.

Orchestra: Jimmie Haskell.

The Kraft Summer Music Hall—Musical Variety—60 minutes—NBC—June 11, 1969 - September 10, 1969. Taped in London.

Hosts: Tony Sandler, Ralph Young, Judy Carne.

Featured: The Paddy Stone Dancers.

Announcer: Paul Griffith.

Orchestra: Jack Parnell.

THE KRAFT MYSTERY THEATRE

Anthology. Suspense presentations. Produced in England.

Host: Frank Gallop.

Included:

The Professionals. Posing as detectives, four criminals attempt a million-dollar bank robbery.

CAST
William Lucas, Andrew Faulds, Colette Wilde.

Account Rendered. Police efforts to apprehend a woman's murderer.

CAST
Honor Blackman, Griffith Jones, Ursula Howlls.

The House On Rue Rivera. A detective attempts to clear his name after finding himself the prime suspect in a woman's death.

CAST
Jayne Mansfield, Diana Trask, John Erickson.

THE KRAFT MYSTERY THEATRE —60 minutes—NBC—June 14, 1961 - September 27, 1961; June 13, 1962 - September 26, 1962; June 19, 1963 - September 25, 1963.

THE KRAFT SUMMER MUSIC HALL

See title: "The Kraft Music Hall."

THE KRAFT SUSPENSE THEATRE

Anthology. Mystery and suspense presentations.

Included:

That Time In Havana. A woman teams with a reporter to locate her husband who supposedly is in possession of a million dollars.

CAST
Mike Taggart: Steve Forrest; Ann Palmer: Dana Wynter; Conrad Easter: Victor Jory; Captain Santos: Frank Silvera.

The Trains Of Silence. After investing time and money in a friend's multimillion-dollar project, a tycoon attempts to uncover the secret behind it.

CAST
Fred Girard: Jeffrey Hunter; Lee Anne Wickheimer: Tippi Hedren; Mark Wilton: Warren Stevens.

Leviathan Five. Four scientists and a guard are trapped by an underground lab explosion. Air is calculated to last until rescue—but for only four. The episode depicts the desperate struggle for life before rescue arrives.

CAST
Dr. Walter Taylor: Arthur Kennedy; Dr. Nat Kaufman: Harold J. Stone; Dr. Adam Winters: Andrew Duggan; Dr. Eduardo Lenzi: John Van Dreelen; Arthur Jensen: Frank Maxwell.

The Case Against Paul Ryker. Pilot film for the series "Court-Martial." A captain's defense of a sergeant accused of treason.

CAST
David Young: Bradford Dillman; Maj. Frank Whitaker: Peter Graves; Paul Ryker: Lee Marvin; Ann Ryker: Vera Miles.

THE KRAFT SUSPENSE THEATRE —60 minutes—NBC—October 10, 1963 - September 9, 1965. 53 episodes. Syndicated title: "Suspense Theatre."

THE KRAFT TELEVISION THEATRE

Anthology. Dramatic and comedic productions adapted from the stories of famous writers and featuring Broadway veterans and unknown performers. Television's first hour-long anthology program to be broadcast to the Midwest over the coaxial cable (1949).

Producer: David Alexander, Dick Dunlap, Maury Holland, Stanley Quinn, Harry Herrmann.

Sponsor: Kraft.

Included:

My Son The Doctor. The widow of a European doctor comes to the U.S. to fulfill a powerful wish that her two sons should be trained as doctors.

CAST
Seymour: Martin Newman; Joe: Woodrow Parfrey; Professor: Hans Schumann.

A Child Is Born. An adaptation of Stephen Vincent Benet's blank verse Christmas play. The story of the arrival of Mary and the infant Jesus as seen through the eyes of the innkeeper and his wife.

CAST
Innkeeper: Harry Townes; Innkeeper's wife: Mildred Dunnock; Joseph: Alan Shayne; Mary: Nancy Marchand.

Death Takes A Holiday. Death attempts to learn why mortals fear him by visiting Earth.

CAST
Death: Joseph Wisemann; The Baron: Malcolm Lee Beggs; The Duke: Stiano Broggiotti; The Princess: Lydia Clair.

Professor Jones And The Missing Link. Comedy. The complications that ensue when a professor, a fish specialist, about to be married is recruited to head a secret ichthyologist mission to discover the missing link between fish and mammal.

CAST
Prof. Jones: Roger Price; Cecil: Bill Palfrey; Elizabeth: Eva Leonard-Boyne.

THE KRAFT TELEVISION THEATRE—60 minutes—NBC—May 7, 1947 - October 1, 1958. For four months it also appeared on ABC with a different first-run drama than the one telecast on NBC. ABC—60 minutes—October 15, 1953 - February 11, 1954.

THE KROFFT SUPERSHOW

Children. The overall title for three

series: "Dr. Shrinker," "Electra Woman and Dyna Girl," and "Wonderbug."

Segment Hosts: Kaptain Kool (Michael Lembeck) and the Kongs (Debby Clinger, Louise Duart, Bert Sommer, Micky McMeel), a Rock group.

Series Executive Producer: Sid and Marty Krofft.

Director (of the Kaptain Kool segment): Art Fisher.

Dr. Shrinker. Captured by Dr. Shrinker, a mad scientist, after their plane crashes on a remote island—the doctor's headquarters—three teenagers, B.J., Brad, and Gordie are held prisoner and used as guinea pigs for his diabolical invention: a machine that is capable of reducing the size of objects. Reduced to a height of six inches, B.J., Brad, and Gordie escape and establish a base in the woods. Stories concern Dr. Shrinker's efforts to recapture his escaped prisoners (the shrinkees) and the attempts of B.J., Brad, and Gordie to regain their normal height and escape from the island.

CAST

Dr. Shrinker	Jay Robinson
Hugo, his assistant	Billy Barty
B.J.	Susan Lawrence
Brad	Ted Eccles
Gordie	Jeff McKay

Music: Jimmie Haskell.

Producer-Director: Jack Regas.

Director: Bill Hobin, Bob Lally.

Electra Woman and Dyna Girl. The exploits of Laurie and Judy, reporters for *Newsmaker Magazine*, who, through the electronic abilities of Crimescope, an amazing computer complex, become Electra Woman and Dyna Girl, daring crime fighters. Stories detail their battle against diabolical villains.

CAST

Laurie/Electra Woman	Deidre Hall
Judy/Dyna Girl	Judy Strangis
Frank Heflin, the head of Crimescope	Norman Alden
The Pharoah, a villain	Peter Mark Richman
The Spider Lady, an enemy	Tiffany Bolling
The Sorcerer, an enemy	Michael Constantine
Miss Dazzle, the Sorcerer's aid	Susan Lanier
The Empress of Evil	Claudette Nevins
Lucriza, her aid	Jacqueline Hyde
Ali Baba, an enemy	Malachi Throne

Narrator: Marvin Miller.

Music: Jimmie Haskell.

Producer-Director: Walter Miller.

Wonderbug. Background: California. Seeking a used car, three teenagers, Susan, Barry, and C.C., find, in a junkyard, Schlep Car, a conglomeration of several wrecked cars. However, when pretty Susan places what turns out to be a magic horn on Schlep Car, it becomes Wonderbug, an automobile that is capable of performing fantastic feats. Stories detail the group's battle against evil.

CAST

Susan	Carol Anne Seflinger
Barry Buntrock	David Levy
C.C.	John Anthony Bailey
Voice of Wonderbug	Frank Welker

Music: Jimmie Haskell.

Producer: Al Schwartz.

Director: Art Fisher, Bob LaHendro.

THE KROFFT SUPERSHOW—55 minutes—ABC—Premiered: September 11, 1976.

THE KROFFT SUPERSHOW II

Children. The overall title for three miniseries: "Big Foot and Wild Boy," "Magic Mongo," and "Wonderbug." A revised version of the previous title.

Segment Hosts: The Rock Group, Kaptain Kool and the Kongs (Michael Lembeck, Debby Clinger, Louise Duart, Bert Sommer).

Series Executive Producer: Sid and Marty Krofft.

Director (of the Kaptain Kool segments: Jack Regas.

Big Foot and Wild Boy. Background: The Northwestern United States. The story concerns itself with the crime-fighting exploits of the legendary man-beast Big Foot and his foundling, Wild Boy—the child who was lost in the wilderness and raised by Big Foot.

CAST

Big Foot	Ray Young
Wild Boy	Joseph Butcher
Suzie, their friend	Monica Ramirez

Music: Michael Melvoin.

Producer: Arthur E. McLaird.

Director: Gordon Wiles.

Creator: Joe Ruby, Ken Spears.

Magic Mongo. The comedy concerns itself with the misadventures of three teenagers—Laraine, Christy, and Donald, and their mischievous genie, Magic Mongo, whom Donald found trapped in a bottle on the beach and released.

CAST

Magic Mongo	Lennie Weinrib
Laraine	Helaine Lembeck
Christy	Robin Dearden
Donald	Paul Hinckley
Ace, the hoodlike beach bully	Bart Braverman

Music: Michael Melvoin.

Producer: Jack Regas.

Director: Bill Foster, Jack Regas.

Creator: Joe Ruby, Ken Spears.

Wonderbug. See previous title, "Wonderbug" segment.

THE KROFFT SUPERSHOW II—55 minutes—ABC—Premiered: September 10, 1977.

THE KUDA BUX SHOW

Variety. Demonstrations depicting the powers of mind reading.

Host: Kuda Bux, Indian Mystic.

Featured: Janet Tyler.

Announcer: Rex Marshall.

Producer: Roger Bowman.

Director: Franklin Dyson.

Sponsor: Mason Candy.

THE KUDA BUX SHOW—30 minutes —CBS 1950.

KUKLA, FRAN, AND OLLIE

Children's Fantasy. Background: The Kuklapolitan Theatre puppet stage. The antics of its inhabitants, the Kuklapolitans.

Characters: Kukla, the bald-headed, round-nosed little man; Ollie, his friend, a scatterbrained dragon (distinguished by one large tooth on the upper part of his mouth); Beulah the Witch; Madam Ooglepuss; Colonel Crockie; Cecil Bill; Dolores Dragon; Mercedes Rabbit; Fletcher Rabbit.

Hostess: Fran Allison, the "straight man," conversing with the puppets and involved in their antics.

Puppeteer-Voices: Burr Tillstrom.

Versions:

Kukla, Fran, and Ollie. Burr Tillstrom (top, with puppets Kukla, left; and Ollie, right) and Fran Allison.

Kukla, Fran, And Ollie—15 minutes. Premiered locally in Chicago, WBKB-TV: October 13, 1947. Premiered on the Midwest network: November 29, 1948. Became national via NBC: November 12, 1949 - June 13, 1954. ABC—September 6, 1954 - August 30, 1957.

Regulars: Carolyn Gilbert, Casear Giovannini.

Announcer: Hugh Downs.

Orchestra: Jack Fascinato; Billy Goldenberg; Caesar Giovannini.

Burr Tillstrom's Kukla, Fran, And Ollie—05 minutes—NBC 1961.

Kukla, Fran, And Ollie—30 minutes—NET—1969-1970; PBS—1970-1971.

Kukla, Fran, and Ollie—30 minutes—Syndicated. 1975.

Hostess: Fran Allison.

Producer: Burr Tillstrom, Martin Tahse.

KUNG FU

Drama. Background: China (flashbacks) and the American Frontier during the 1870s. The story of Kwai Chang Caine, a Shaolin priest who wanders across the Frontier during the early days of social injustice and discrimination searching for an unknown brother.

Early history: Background: The Who Nun Province in China. An orphan, and not of full Chinese blood (a Chinese mother and an American father), Caine is accepted into the Temple of Shaolin to study the art of Kung Fu, the medieval Chinese science of disciplined combat developed by Taoist and Buddhist monks. Instructed, he learns of the knowledge of the inner strength, a disciplining of the mind and body to remove conflict from within one's self and "discover a harmony of body and mind in accord with the flow of the universe."

Still a young boy, he befriends one of the Masters, Po, his mentor, the old blind man who nicknames him "Grasshopper." One day, while speaking with Master Po, Caine learns of his great ambition to make a pilgrimage to the Forbidden City.

Completing his training, Caine leaves the temple with the final words of Master Teh: "Remember. The wise man walks always with his head bowed, humble, like the dust."

Recalling Master Po's dream, and desiring to help him celebrate it, Caine meets the old man on the Road to the Temple of Heaven. As they journey, the body guards of the Royal Nephew pass, pushing people aside. One is tripped by the old man. A ruckus ensues and Master Po is shot. At the request of his mentor, Caine picks up a spear and kills the Royal Nephew. Before he dies, Master Po warns his favorite pupil to leave China and begin life elsewhere.

The Emperor dispatches men to seek Caine; and the Chinese Legation circulate posters—"Wanted for murder, Kwai Chang Caine. $10,000 alive; $5,000 dead."

Though seen taking the life of another in the pilot film, the series depicts Caine as humble, just, and wise, with a profound respect for human life.

Episodes depict his search, his battle against injustice, and his remembrances back to his days of training (seen via flashbacks) while a student in China. Situations he encounters parallel those of the past; and through the use of flashbacks, the viewer learns of Caine's strict training and of the wisdom of his Masters as he disciplines himself to face circumstances as a respected Shaolin priest.

Unique in its approach, the photography adds power to the drama, and through slow motion, heightens and enhances the strength and discipline of the young priest.

CAST

Kwai Chang Caine   David Carradine
Master Po (flashbacks)   Keye Luke
Master Kan (flashbacks)   Philip Ahn
Master Teh (flashbacks) John Leoning
Caine, as a boy
  (flashbacks)   Radames Pera
Also, various character roles: Beulah Quo, James Hong, Benson Fong, Victor Sen Yung, David Chow.

Music: Jim Helms.

KUNG FU—60 minutes—ABC—October 14, 1972 - June 27, 1975. 72 episodes.

L

LADIES BEFORE GENTLEMEN

Discussion-Game. Six male panelists (five regulars and one guest) and one female celebrity guest discuss various topical issues. The program encompasses the format of a game, without prizes, wherein the female must successfully defend the woman's point of view to maintain her position on a pedestal. If she should fail, she loses her position and the argument is scored in favor of men; should she successfully defend it, the argument is scored in favor of women.

Host: Ken Roberts.

Panelists: Harvey Stone, Dick Joseph, Fred Robbins, Robert Sylvester, John Kullers.

Premiere Guests: Cara Williams, Steve Allen.

LADIES BEFORE GENTLEMEN—30 minutes—ABC 1951.

LADIES BE SEATED

Game. Various members of the studio audience, which comprises the fairer sex, compete in various contests (stunts, games, quizzes) for merchandise prizes.

Host: Tom Moore.

Assistant: Phil Patton.

Announcer: George Ansbro.

Music: The Buddy Weed Trio.

Producer: Phil Patton, Tom Moore.

Director: Greg Garrison.

LADIES BE SEATED—30 minutes—ABC 1949. In 1955, a daily, syndicated version of the series appeared wherein host Don Russell presented an hour of films.

LADIES' CHOICE

Variety. Performances by undiscovered professional talent acts that are presented by women talent scouts. Home participation segment: "The Quick Identity Quiz." An unrecognizable photograph, accompanied by a hint or a jingle, is flashed on the screen. A random telephone call is placed by the host and if the viewer can identify it, he wins merchandise prizes. If unsuccessful, he is awarded a watch.

Host: Johnny Dugan.

LADIES' CHOICE—30 minutes—NBC—June 8, 1953 - September 1953.

LANCELOT LINK, SECRET CHIMP

Comedy. The investigations of Lancelot Link, a fumbling counterespionage agent for A.P.E., the Agency to Prevent Evil, an international organization dedicated to fighting the evils of C.H.U.M.P. (Criminal Headquarters For Underground Master Plan), an international organization bent on world domination. Characters are enacted by chimpanzees with voice-over dubbing.

Characters:
Lancelot Link, an A.P.E. agent.
Commander Darwin, the head of A.P.E.
Marta Hari, Link's assistant.
Baron Von Butcher, the commander of C.H.U.M.P.
Creato, his assistant.

LANCELOT LINK, SECRET CHIMP—60 minutes—ABC—September 12, 1970 - September 4, 1971; 30 minutes—ABC—September 11, 1971 - September 2, 1972. 26 episodes.

LANCER

Western. Background: The Lancer Ranch in California's San Joaquin Valley, 1870. The story of three men: Murdoch Lancer, widower, the ranch owner, and his two sons, born of different mothers, Scott Lancer (son of an Irish lass), and Johnny Madrid Lancer (son of a Mexican woman), and their attempts to maintain a one-hundred-thousand-acre cattle and timberland ranch in an era of lawlessness. Episodes depict the rivalry that exists between Scott and Johnny and their mutual dislike of their father.

CAST
Murdoch Lancer	Andrew Duggan
Scott Lancer	Wayne Maunder
Johnny Madrid Lancer	James Stacy
Teresa O'Brien, Murdoch's ward, the daughter of his first foreman	Elizabeth Baur
Jelly Hoskins, the ranch foreman	Paul Brinegar

Lancer. Andrew Duggan.

Music: Joseph Mullendore; Lionel Newman.

LANCER—60 minutes—CBS—September 24, 1968 - September 8, 1970. Rebroadcasts: CBS—May 27, 1971 - September 9, 1971. 51 episodes. Syndicated.

LAND OF THE GIANTS

Science Fiction. Era: 1983. Enroute from New York to London, the *Spinthrift*, suborbital flight 612, penetrates a solar turbulence area and is violently thrust into the rages of a fierce storm. The plane, as if a magnet, is pulled farther into it, and in a blinding flash of light, passes through the atmospheric disturbance.

The experience, damaging the plane, forces the captain to land it.

Situated in a dense forest near the inoperable craft, the three crew members and four passengers discover themselves marooned in an unknown world—a land of human giants.

As their presence becomes known, they are branded fugitives, "The Little People." A reward is offered for their capture; and death is the penalty to assist them.

Stories depict their struggle for survival, and their attempts to secure the precious metals needed to repair the craft and hopefully return to Earth.

CAST
Steve Burton, the captain	Gary Conway
Dan Erickson, the co-pilot	Don Marshall
Betty Hamilton, the stewardess	Heather Young
Valerie Scott, a beautiful heiress	Deanna Lund
Alexander Fitzhugh, a master thief	Kurt Kasznar
Mark Wilson, an industrial tycoon	Don Matheson
Barry Lockridge, an orphaned child	Stefan Arngrim
S.I.B. Inspector Kobick, the giant seeking the little people	Kevin Hagen

Barry's dog: Chipper.
Music: Lionel Newman.

LAND OF THE GIANTS—60 minutes—ABC—September 22, 1968 - September 6, 1970. 51 episodes. Syndicated.

Land of the Giants. Left to right: Deanna Lund, Stephan Arngrim, and Kurt Kasznar. Episode: "The Deadly Pawn."

LAND OF THE LOST

Science Fiction Adventure. While exploring the Colorado River on a raft, Rick Marshall, a forest ranger, and his children, Will and Holly, are caught in a time vortex and transported to a mysterious, forbidding world called The Land of the Lost—a world of prehistoric creatures forgotten by time.

Stories, during the first season, depict the Marshall family's struggles for survival and their attempts to find the secret of the way back to their time. During the program's second season on the air, with the introduction of the character Enik, a Sleestak, a tall, lizard-like creature who fell through a time doorway and is now in his future, it is learned that the Land of the Lost was built by Enik's ancestors—a once peaceful people who are now savages. Desperate to return to his own time, to prevent his people from becoming the savages they are, he discovers that the Land of the Lost is a closed universe and that the only way to escape is through a time doorway contained in the Pylon—a mysterious, magical device that controls the Land of the Lost. With this added knowledge, both the Marshalls and Enik seek to unravel the secret of the Pylon. (It should be noted that, although Enik is a friend of the Marshalls, the other Sleestak are not and pose a constant danger to their survival.)

The third season still brought additional changes: While experimenting with a Pylon, Rick Marshall activates the time doorway and is swept back into his own time; however, since the Land of the Lost is a closed universe, for each being that leaves it, one must take his place.

Having begun a search to find his missing brother Rick, Jack Marshall is suddenly caught in a mysterious time vortex and, as Rick is freed, Jack is transported to the Land of the Lost, where he meets with Will and Holly and learns what has happened. Stories concern the Marshall family's attempts to escape from the Land of the Lost.

CAST
Rick Marshall	Wesley Eure
Jack Marshall	Ron Harper
Holly Marshall	Kathy Coleman
Will Marshall	Spencer Milligan
Enik	Walker Edmiston
Chaka, the monkey-boy, a member of the Palcus tribe	Philip Paley
Sa, the monkey-girl	Sharon Baird
Ta, the Palcus leader	Scott Fullerton
Malak, an enemy of the Marshalls	Richard Kiel

Zarn, a creature of glowing light also lost in time (portrayed by)	Van Snowden
Zarn (voiced by)	Marvin Miller
The Sleestak Leader	Jon Locke

Sleestak: Jack Tingley, Joe Giamalva, Scotty McKay, Mike Weston, Bill Boyd, Cleveland Porter.

Music: Jimmie Haskell, Linda Laurie, Michael Lloyd.

Executive Producer: Sid and Marty Krofft.

Producer: Jon Kubichan.

Director: Bob Lally, Joe Scanlon, Rick Bennewitz, Dennis Steinmetz, Gordon Wiles.

LAND OF THE LOST—30 minutes—NBC—Premiered: September 7, 1974.

LANIGAN'S RABBI

See title: "NBC Mystery Movie," *Lanigan's Rabbi* segment.

THE LANNY ROSS SHOW

Musical Variety.

Host: Lanny Ross.

Regulars: Sandra Gahle, Martha Logan.

Orchestra: Harry Simeone.

THE LANNY ROSS SHOW—30 minutes—NBC 1948. Also known as "The Swift Show."

THE LARAINE DAY SHOW

See title: "Daydreaming with Laraine."

LARAMIE

Western. Background: Laramie, Wyoming, 1880s. Events in the shaping of Wyoming as seen through the eyes of two friends, Slim Sherman and Jess Harper, ranchers operating a swing station, a combination ranch and stage depot for the Great Overland Mail Stage Lines.

CAST
Slim Sherman	John Smith
Jess Harper	Robert Fuller
Jonesy, their ranchhand/ cook	Hoagy Carmichael
Andy Sherman, Slim's kid brother	Robert Crawford, Jr.
Mike, their young ward, survivor of an Indian raid	Dennis Holmes

Daisy Cooper, their housekeeper, caring for	
Mike	Spring Byington
Sheriff Douglas	Roy Barcroft

Music: Cyril Mockridge; Hans Salter; Richard Sendry.

LARAMIE—60 minutes—NBC—September 15, 1959 - September 17, 1963. 124 episodes. Syndicated.

LAREDO

Western. Background: Laredo, Texas, 1880s. The investigations of three bickering Texas Rangers, Reese Bennett, Joe Riley, and Chad Cooper.

CAST
Reese Bennett	Neville Brand
Chad Cooper	Peter Brown
Joe Riley	William Smith
Captain Parmalee	Philip Carey
Ranger Erik Hunter	Robert Wolders
Ranger Cotton Buckmeister	Claude Akins

Music: Russell Garcia; Stanley Wilson.

LAREDO—60 minutes—NBC—September 16, 1965 - September 8, 1967. 56 episodes. Syndicated.

THE LARRY KANE SHOW

Variety. Performances by and interviews with Rock personalities.

Host: Larry Kane.

Music: Recorded.

THE LARRY KANE SHOW—60 minutes—Syndicated 1971.

THE LARRY STORCH SHOW

Variety. Music, songs, dances, and comedy sketches.

Host: Larry Storch.

Regulars: Milton Frome, Mildred Hughes, Tomi Romer, Georgianna Johnson, Russell Hicks, Ethel Owen, The June Taylor Dancers and Singers.

Announcer: Jack Lescoulie.

Orchestra: Sammy Spear; Ray Bloch.

THE LARRY STORCH SHOW—60 minutes—CBS—September 14, 1952 - September 2, 1953. Originally broadcast under the title: "Cavalcade of Stars"—60 minutes—DuMont—July 4, 1952 - September 6, 1952.

THE LAS VEGAS SHOW

Variety. Entertainment performances set against the background of various Las Vegas night clubs.

Host: Bill Dana.

Regulars: Danny Meehan, Ann Elder, Pete Barbutti, Jo Anne Worley, Cully Richards.

Musical Director: Jack Sheldon.

THE LAS VEGAS SHOW—90 minutes—Syndicated 1967.

LASSIE

Adventure. Distinguished by seven formats.

Format One:

Jeff's Collie (Syndicated title)—30 minutes—CBS—September 1954 - September 1957.

Background: The Miller farm in Calverton. After the death of a neighbor, eleven-year-old Jeff Miller inherits Lassie, a beautiful collie. Stories depict the world of love and adventure shared by a boy and his dog.

CAST

Jeff Miller	Tommy Rettig
Ellen Miller, his mother, a widow	Jan Clayton
George Miller (Gramps), Jeff's grandfather	George Cleveland
Sylvester "Porkey" Brockway, Jeff's friend	Donald Keeler
Sheriff Clay Horton	Richard Garland
Dr. Peter Wilson, the veterinarian (early episodes)	Arthur Space
Dr. Frank Weaver, the veterinarian (later episodes)	Arthur Space
Dr. Stuart, the Miller family physician	Dayton Lummis
Matt Brockway, Porkey's father	Paul Maxey
Jenny, the telephone operator	Florence Lake

Porkey's dog: Pokey.

Music: Raoul Kraushaar.

Producer: Sheldon Leonard, Robert Maxwell, Dusty Bruce.

Director: Philip Ford, Lesley Selander, Sheldon Leonard.

Executive Producer: Jack Wrather.

Format Two:

Timmy And Lassie (Syndicated title)—30 minutes—CBS—September 1957 - September 1964.

Background: Calverton. Shortly after Gramps's death, a seven-year-old boy, Timmy, runs away from an orphanage. Found by Lassie, he is taken to the Miller farm and given a temporary home. Unable to properly run the farm, Ellen sells it to Paul and Ruth Martin, a childless couple who later adopt Timmy. Unable to take Lassie to the city with them, Jeff leaves her to care for her new master, Timmy. Stories depict the adventures of a boy and his dog.

CAST

Timmy Martin	Jon Provost
Ruth Martin	Cloris Leachman
	June Lockhart
Paul Martin	Jon Shepodd
	Hugh Riley
Petrie Martin, Timmy's uncle	George Chandler
Boomer Bates, Timmy's friend	Todd Ferrell
Dr. Frank Weaver	Arthur Space
Sheriff Harry Miller	Robert Foulk
Cully, Timmy's friend	Andy Clyde

Boomer's dog: Mike.

Music: Sid Sidney; Nathan Scott.

Executive Producer: Jack Wrather.

Producer: Robert Golden, Bonita Granville Wrather, William Beaudine, Jr, Rudy Abel.

Sponsor: Campbell's.

Format Three:

Lassie—30 minutes—CBS—September 1964 - September 1968.

Background: Calverton. The need for American farmers overseas prompts Paul to sell the farm and move to Australia. Unable to take Lassie because of quarantine laws, she is left in the care of an elderly friend, Cully.

Shortly after, Cully is stricken by a heart attack. Sensing the situation, Lassie brings help in the form of Corey Stuart, a forest ranger. Recovering, but unable to properly care for Lassie, Cully presents her to Corey. Bound to a new master, Lassie assists Corey, protecting the forests and aiding both animals and humans in distress.

CAST

Ranger Corey Stuart	Robert Bray
Ranger Scott Turner	Jed Allan
Ranger Bob Erickson	Jack DeMave
Kirby Newman, Corey's assistant	John Archer

Music: Nathan Scott.

Executive Producer: Jack Wrather.

Producer: Bonita Granville Wrather, Robert Golden, William Beaudine, Jr.

Director: Dick Moder, William Beaudine, Robert Sparr, Jack B. Hively, James B. Clark, Ray English, Christian Nyby, Paul Nickell.

Format Four:

Lassie—30 minutes—CBS—September 1968 - September 1971.

Background: Various California locales. No longer bound to a human master, Lassie roams and assists those she finds in distress, both human and animal.

Starring: Lassie.

Music: Nathan Scott.

Format Five:

Lassie—30 minutes—Syndicated 1971.

The story and cast are the same as Format Four.

Format Six:

Lassie—30 minutes—Syndicated 1972.

Background: The Holden ranch in California State. Though still somewhat of a wanderer, Lassie finds a temporary home at the ranch of Keith Holden. Stories depict her adventures in and around the ranch.

CAST

Keith Holden	Larry Pennell
Dale Mitchell	Larry Wilcox
Ron Holden	Skip Burton
Lucy Baker, the deaf girl, a neighbor	Pamelyn Ferdin
Mike Holden	Joshua Albee
Sue Lampbert, the veterinarian	Sherry Boucher

Music: Nathan Scott.

Format Seven:

Lassie's Rescue Rangers—Animated Cartoon—30 minutes—ABC—September 8, 1973 - August 30, 1975.

Background: A ranger station in the Rocky Mountains. Commanding the Rescue Force, an all-animal rescue crew, Lassie and her human masters, the Turner family, struggle to protect the environment and save lives.

Characters: Lassie; Ben Turner, the head ranger; Laura Turner, his wife; Susan and Jackie Turner, their children; Ranger Jean Fox; Toothless, the mountain lion; Robbie, the raccoon; Musty, the skunk.

Voices: Ted Knight, Jane Webb, Keith Alexander, Lane Scheimer, Lassie.

Music: Yvette Blais, Jeff Michael.

LAST OF THE WILD

Documentary. Wildlife films depicting the struggle for survival.

Host-Narrator: Lorne Greene.

Music: Bill Loose, Jack Tiller.

LAST OF THE WILD—30 minutes—Syndicated 1974.

THE LAST WORD

Discussion. Discussions on vagaries of the English language.

Host: Dr. Bergen Evans.

Panel: June Havoc, Arthur Knight, John Mason Brown.

THE LAST WORD—30 minutes—CBS —1958 - 1959.

THE LATE FALL, EARLY SUMMER BERT CONVY SHOW

Variety. Music, songs, and comedy sketches.

Host: Bert Convy.

Regulars: Lenny Schultz (as Lennie, the Bionic Chicken), Sallie Janes, Donna Ponterotto, Henry Polic II, Marty Barris, The Tyvana Light Opera and Pottery Company.

Bert's Girls (Dancers): Susie Guest, Shirley Kirkes, Judy Pierce, Darcel Wynne.

Announcer: Donna Ponterotto.

Orchestra: Perry Botkin.

Choreographer: Dee Dee Wood.

Executive Producer: Sam Denoff.

Director: Bill Hobin.

THE LATE FALL, EARLY SUMMER BERT CONVY SHOW—30 minutes—CBS—August 25, 1976 - September 15, 1976. 4 tapes.

LAUGH-IN

Variety. A satirization of the contemporary scene through music, song, dance, and comedy sketches.

Hosts: Dan Rowan, Dick Martin.

Regulars: Goldie Hawn, Judy Carne, Pamela Rodgers, Teresa Graves, Arte Johnson, Byron Gilliam, Jeremy Lloyd, Dennis Allen, Barbara Sharma, Ann Elder, Harvey Jason, Richard Dawson, Jo Anne Worley, Alan Sues, Henry Gibson, Betty Ann Carr, Patty Deutsch, Sarah Kennedy, Brian Bressler, Donna Jean

Laugh-In. Goldie Hawn.

Young, Jud Strunk, Dave Madden, Ruth Buzzi, Lily Tomlin, Chelsea Brown, Johnny Brown, Larry Hovis, Nancy Phillips, Pigmeat Markham, Charlie Brill, Mitzi McCall, Willie Tyler (his dummy: Lester), Todd Bass, Dick Wittington, Muriel Landers, Elaine Beckett, Moosie Drier, The Beautiful Downtown Beauties (Janice Whitby, Rosetta Cox, Joy Robiero, Adele Yoshioka, Kyra Carlton, Meredith Bernhart—six girls who sing, dance, lead cheers, and introduce guests), Eileen Brennan, Roddy Maude- Roxby.

Announcer: Gary Owens.

Musical Director: Ian Bernard.

Producer: George Schlatter, Paul Keyes.

LAUGH-IN—60 minutes—NBC—January 22, 1968 - May 7, 1973. 124 tapes. Pilot presented as a special on: September 9, 1967 (NBC). Also known as: "Rowan and Martin's Laugh-In." Spin-off: "Letters To Laugh-In" (see title).

LAUGH-IN

Satire. A revival of the old series (see previous title) featuring a cast of virtual unknowns in comedic nonsense satirizing everyday life.

Starring: June Gable, Ed Bluestone, Wayland Flowers, Ben Powers, Bill Rafferty, Michael Sklar, Robin Williams Toad (Antoinette Attell), Nancy Bleiweiss, Kim Braden, Lennie Schultz, Hack Harrell, April Tatro.

Orchestra: Tommy Oliver.

Special Musical Material: Billy Barnes.

Producer: George Schlatter.

Director: Don Mischer.

Choreographer: Dee Dee Wood.

LAUGH-IN—60 minutes—NBC—Premiered: September 5, 1977. Broadcast as a series of monthly specials.

LAUGH LINE

Game. Object: For a celebrity panel to supply comic captions for cartoons that are presented in tableau form. The winners are determined by studio-audience applause, and contestants, represented by celebrities, receive prizes accordingly.

Host: Dick Van Dyke.

Panelists: Dorothy Loudon, Mike Nichols, Elaine May, Orson Bean.

LAUGH LINE—30 minutes—NBC—April 16, 1959 - June 11, 1959.

LAUGHS FOR SALE

Comedy. Guest comics perform material (sketches, monologues, or routines) submitted by fledgling comedy writers. After the performance the material is evaluated and offered for sale. Interested parties are able to purchase the material by contacting the program's producers.

Host: Hal March.

LAUGHS FOR SALE—30 minutes—ABC—October 20, 1963 - December 22, 1963.

LAUREL AND HARDY

Slapstick Comedy. Reedited theatrical shorts and features. The story of Stan Laurel and Oliver Hardy, two men struggling to cope with life.

CAST

Stan Laurel	Himself
Oliver Hardy	Himself

Titles: Local market choice, (e.g. "Laurel and Hardy"; "The Laurel and Hardy Show"; "The Laurel and Hardy Comedy Hour"; "Laurel, Hardy and Chuck"—New York, with Chuck McCann hosting).

Running times: Local—from 15 minutes to 90 minutes.

Films were first syndicated in 1948.

Spin-off: "The Laurel and Hardy Cartoon Show"—05 minutes—Syndicated 1966.

Characters' Voices

Stan Laurel	John MacGeorge
Oliver Hardy	Larry Harmon

Laverne and Shirley. Cindy Williams (left) and Penny Marshall.

LAVERNE AND SHIRLEY

Comedy. Background: Milwaukee, Wisconsin during the latter 1950s. The chaotic misadventures of Laverne DeFazio, a realist, and Shirley Feeney, a romantic, working girls who room together (at 730 Hampton Street, Apt. A) and work together in the bottle-capping division of the Shotz Brewery. A spin-off from "Happy Days."

CAST
Laverne DeFazio — Penny Marshall
Shirley Feeney — Cindy Williams
Lenny Kosnoski, their
    friend — Michael McKean
Andrew "Squiggy" Squiman,
    their friend — David L. Lander
Carmine Raguso, "The Big
    Ragoo," a dance instructor,
    their friend — Eddie Mekka
Frank DeFazio, Laverne's
    father, the owner of
    the Pizza Bowl, a
    combination pizzeria/
    bowling alley — Phil Foster
Edna Babbish, the
    landlady — Betty Garrett
"Big" Rosie Greenbaum,
    Laverne's nemesis — Carol Ita White
Mary, the waitress at
    the Pizza Bowl — Frances Peach

Music: Charles Fox, Richard Clements.

Executive Producer: Garry Marshall, Thomas L. Miller, Edward K. Milkis.

Producer: Mark Rothman, Lowell Ganz, Monica Johnson, Eric Cohen, Tony Marshall, Thomas L. Milkis.

Director: Garry Marshall, Alan Myerson, Jay Sandrich, James Burrows, Howard Storm, Michael Kidd, Dennis Klein, John Thomas Lennox.

Shirley's good luck charm: Boo Boo Kitty, a stuffed, cloth cat.

LAVERNE AND SHIRLEY–30 minutes–ABC–Premiered: January 27, 1976.

THE LAW AND MISTER JONES

Drama. Background: New York City. The cases and courtroom defenses of Abraham Lincoln Jones, an honest but tough criminal attorney.

CAST
Abraham Lincoln
    Jones — James Whitmore
Marsha Spear, his
    secretary — Janet DeGore
C.E. Carruthers, his
    law clerk — Colan Carter
Thomas Jones, his
    father — Russ Brown

Music: Herschel Burke Gilbert; Hans Salter.

THE LAW AND MISTER JONES–30 minutes–ABC–October 7, 1960 - September 22, 1961; April 10, 1962 - October 4, 1962. 45 episodes. Syndicated.

LAWBREAKER

Crime Drama. Dramatizations based on actual criminal cases. Filmed at scenes of occurences with the individuals involved.

Host-Commentator: Lee Marvin.

LAWBREAKER–30 minutes–Syndicated 1963. 32 episodes.

THE LAW ENFORCERS

See title: "The Bold Ones," *The Protectors* segment.

THE LAWLESS YEARS

Crime Drama. Background: New York City. The investigations of Barney Ruditsky, a plainclothes police detective. Stories depict his attempts to infiltrate the rackets and expose the racketeers.

CAST
Barney Ruditsky — James Gregory
Max, his assistant — Robert Karnes

THE LAWLESS YEARS–30 minutes–NBC–April 16, 1959 - September 22, 1961. 52 episodes.

LAWMAN

Western. Background: Laramie, Wyoming, 1870s. The story of Marshal Dan Troop and his deputy, Johnny McKay, and their attempts to maintain law and order.

CAST
Marshal Dan Troop — John Russell
Deputy Johnny McKay — Peter Brown
Lilly Merrill, the
    owner of the Birdcage
    Saloon — Peggie Castle
Jake, the bartender — Dan Sheridan
Dru Lemp, the owner
    of the Blue Bonnet
    Café — Bek Nelson
Julie Tate, the editor
    of the town newspaper,
    the *Laramie
    Weekly* — Barbara Lang

Music: Paul Sawtell; Frank Perkins.

LAWMAN–30 minutes–ABC–October 5, 1958 - October 9, 1962. Syndicated. 156 episodes.

THE LAW OF THE PLAINSMAN

Western. Early history: The Arizona territory during the 1870s. During a battle between the White Man and the Apache, a fourteen-year-old brave encounters a wounded army captain. About to scalp him, but unable when the captain shows no signs of fear, the brave assists him by acquiring help. Befriending the boy, the captain names him Sam Buckhart. Two years following, after the captain is killed in an Indian ambush, Sam inherits his money, a vast wealth that enables him to attend Harvard College as once did the captain. Graduating and desiring to help his people, he is commissioned as a United States Marshal.

Series background: The territory of New Mexico during the 1880s. Stories depict Buckhart's exploits as he patrols the area, attempting to apprehend wanted offenders and establish the long-sought road to peace between his people and the White Man.

CAST
Sam Buckhart — Michael Ansara
Billy Lordan, his
    assistant — Robert Harland

Music: Leonard Rosenman; Herschel Burke Gilbert.

THE LAW OF THE PLAINSMAN–30 minutes. NBC–October 1, 1959 - September 25, 1962; ABC–July 2, 1962 - September 17, 1962. 30 episodes.

Syndicated. Original title: "Tales of the Plainsman."

THE LAWRENCE WELK SHOW

Variety. Music, songs, and dances presented in Champagne style.

Host: Lawrence Welk.

Champagne Ladies: Alice Lon; Norma Zimmer.

Regulars: The Lennon Sisters (Dianne, Peggy, Kathy, and Janet), Dick Dale, Brian Siebman, Gail Farrell, Larry Dean, Sandi Jensen, Joe Fenny, Jim Roberts, Bob Lido, Mary Lou Metzgar, Buddy Merrill, Barbara Boylan, Bobby Burgess, Jack Imel, Larry Hooper, Art DePew, Bob Havens, Pete Fourtain, Bob Ralston, Frank Scott, Jerry Burke, Joe Livoti, Myron Floren, Jo Ann Castle, Neil Levang, Natalie Nevins, Arthur Duncan, Cissy King, Clay Hart, Lynn Anderson, Salli Flynn, Steve Smith, Andra Willis, Paula Stewart, Tanya Falan, Barney Liddel, Charlie Parlato, Kenny Trimble, Charlotte Harris, Ralna English, Guy Hovis, Peanuts Hucko, Aladdin, Rocky Rockwell, The Blenders, The Hotsy Totsy Boys, The Symanski Sisters, Clay Hart, Sally Finn, Nancy Sullivan, Tom Neatherland, Ken Delo, Bob Smale, Joe Feeney, Henry Cuesta.

Announcer: Bob Orrin.

Music: The Champagne Orchestra under the direction of Lawrence Welk; Lawrence Welk's Little Orchestra (1958-1959) composing ten children: Allen Imback, Joe Bellis, Warren Luening, Cubby O'Brien, Tom Owens, Mike Quatro, Brian Siebman, Bowen "Bo" Wagner, Jeff Woodruff, Pee Wee Spitelers.

Musical Director: George Cates.

Producer: Sam Lutz, James Hobson, Ed Sobel.

Director: James Hobson.

Note: Episodes broadcast after the ABC run in 1971 are syndicated first run.

THE LAWRENCE WELK SHOW—60 minutes—ABC—July 2, 1955 - September 3, 1971. Syndicated. Original title: "The Dodge Dancing Party." Spin-offs: "Top Tunes, New Talent"—60 minutes—ABC—October 8, 1956 - June 2, 1958; "The Plymouth Show Starring Lawrence Welk"—60 minutes—ABC—September 10, 1958 - June 3, 1959.

THE LAWYERS

See title: "The Bold Ones," *The Lawyers* segment.

LEARN TO DRAW

Art Instruction. Step-by-step video classes using methods of an exclusive program designed to improve, stimulate, or create an individual's art ability. Viewers participate via inexpensive "Learn To Draw" kits.

Host-Instructor: John Gnagy.

LEARN TO DRAW—30 minutes—Syndicated 1950.

LEAVE IT TO BEAVER

Comedy. Background: 211 Pine Street, Mayfield, the residence of the Cleaver family: Ward, an accountant; his wife, June; and their children, Wally and Theodore (Beaver). Stories relate the experiences of two brothers, Wally and Beaver Cleaver.

CAST

Ward Cleaver	Hugh Beaumont
June Cleaver	Barbara Billingsley
Wally Cleaver	Tony Dow
Theodore "Beaver" Cleaver	Jerry Mathers
Eddie Haskell, Wally's friend	Ken Osmond
Clarence "Lumpy" Rutherford, Wally's friend	Frank Bank
Julie Foster, Wally's girlfriend	Cheryl Holdridge
Larry Mondello, Beaver's friend	Rusty Stevens
Gilbert, Beaver's friend	Stephen Talbot
Whitey Witney, Beaver's friend	Stanley Fafara
Fred Rutherford, Lumpy's father, Wards' employer	Richard Deacon
Gwen Rutherford, his wife	Majel Barrett
Violet Rutherford, his daughter	Veronica Cartwright
Miss Landers, Beaver's teacher	Sue Randall
Mrs. Rayburn, the school principal	Doris Packer
Gus, the fire chief	Burt Mustin
Judy Hessler, the girl who delights in annoying Beaver and his friends	Jeri Vale
Mrs. Mondello, Larry's mother	Madge Blake
Benjie, Beaver's friend	Joey Scott
Miss Canfield, Beaver's teacher	Diane Brewster
Geraldine Rutherford, Fred's wife in early episodes	Helen Parrish
Violet Rutherford, Fred's daughter in early episodes	Wendy Winkelman
Harrison "Tuey" Brown, Beaver's friend (early episodes)	Stanley "Tiger" Fafara
Mrs. Brown, Tuey's mother	Katherine Warren
Richard, Wally's friend	Richard Correll
Chester Anderson, Wally's friend	Buddy Hart
Mr. Anderson, Chester's father	Francis DeSales
Martha, June's aunt	Madge Kennedy
Uncle Billy, Ward's uncle	Edgar Buchanan
Agnes Haskell, Eddie's mother	Ann Doran
George Haskell, Eddie's father	Karl Swenson
Also, Various roles	Carol Sydes

Music: Michael F. Johnson; Melvyn Lenard.

LEAVE IT TO BEAVER—30 minutes. CBS—October 11, 1957 - September 26, 1958. ABC—October 3, 1958 - September 12, 1963. 234 episodes. Syndicated.

LEAVE IT TO LARRY

Comedy. The misadventures of Larry, a fumbling, good-natured shoe clerk.

CAST

Larry	Eddie Albert
His wife	Katherine Bard
His father-in-law and employer	Ed Begley
Also: Olive Templeton, Bradley Huston, Gene Lee, Patsy Bruder.	

LEAVE IT TO LARRY—30 minutes—CBS—October 14, 1952 - December 23, 1952.

LEAVE IT TO THE GIRLS

Discussion. Three female panelists and one male defendant discuss topical issues.

Moderator: Maggie McNellis, Eddie Dunn.

Panelists (most readily identified with the program): Robin Chandler, Faye Emerson, Eloise McElone, Florence Pritchett, Binnie Barnes, Eva Gabor, Peggy Ann Garner.

Producer: Martha Roundtree.

Sponsor: Riggio Tabacco; Ex-Lax.

LEAVE IT TO THE GIRLS—30 minutes. NBC—August 21, 1947 - December 30, 1951; ABC—October 3, 1953 - March 27, 1954.

THE LEFT OVER REVUE

Musical Variety. A one-month replacement for the cancelled "Broadway Open House."

Host: Wayne Howell.

Vocalist: Vera Massey.

Orchestra: Milton DeLugg.

THE LEFT OVER REVUE—60 minutes—NBC—August 1951 - September 1951.

THE LEGEND OF CUSTER

Adventure. Background: Kansas, 1870s. Found guilty of dereliction of duty, Major General George Armstrong Custer, U.S. Cavalry, is reduced in rank (to Lt. Col.) and sent to Fort Hays where he is put in charge of the Seventh Labor batallion.

Refusing to be treated as a work detail, Custer trains his men, and after months of endurance, his Company C is recognized as The Fighting Seventh.

Stories depict Custer's exploits in Indian affairs; and his personal conflict with Crazy Horse, the Sioux Indian Chief.

CAST

Colonel George Armstrong Custer	Wayne Maunder
Joe Miller, the trail scout	Slim Pickens

The Legend of Custer. Wayne Maunder.

Sergeant James Bustard, an ex-Confederate, a member of the Seventh	Peter Palmer
Captain Myles Keogh	Grant Woods
General Terry, the commanding officer	Robert F. Simon
Crazy Horse	Michael Dante

Music: Lionel Newman.

Additional Music: Richard Markowitz, Joseph Mullendore, Leith Stevens.

Executive Producer: David Weisbar.

Producer: Frank Glicksman.

THE LEGEND OF CUSTER—60 minutes—ABC—September 6, 1967 - December 26, 1967. 17 episodes.

THE LEGEND OF JESSE JAMES

Western. Background: Saint Joseph, Missouri, 1860s. The story of outlaws Frank and Jesse James, hard working farmers, who were forced into a life of crime after railroad officials killed their mother when she refused to sell them her land. Avenging their mother's death, they strike and rob the Great Western Railroad and attempt to return rightful property to the survivors of innocent victims.

CAST

Jesse James	Chris Jones
Frank James	Allen Case
Sheriff Sam Corbett	Robert J. Wilke
Mrs. James (first episode)	Ann Doran

Music: Joseph Hooven.

THE LEGEND OF JESSE JAMES—30 minutes—ABC—September 13, 1965 - September 5, 1966. 26 episodes.

LEO CARILLO'S DUDE RANCH

A musical variety series, first broadcast on DuMont in 1951, and starring Leo Carillo.

THE LES CRANE SHOW

Discussion. Discussions on controversial issues.

Host: Les Crane.

Orchestra: Don Trenner.

THE LES CRANE SHOW—90 minutes—ABC—November 9, 1964 - March 1, 1965.

LESLIE THE SHREVE

A children's series featuring songs, stories, and visits to areas around the country.

Hostess: Leslie Shreve.

30 minutes—Syndicated 1976.

THE LES PAUL AND MARY FORD SHOW

Musical Variety. A quick opening, two songs, one commercial, and a short closing.

Hosts: Les Paul and Mary Ford.

THE LES PAUL AND MARY FORD SHOW—05 minutes—Syndicated 1954.

THE LESLIE UGGAMS SHOW

Variety. Music, songs, dances, and comedy sketches.

Hostess: Leslie Uggams.

Regulars: Lillian Hayman, Johnny Brown, Allison Mills, Lincoln Kilpatrick, The Donald McKayle Dancers, The Howard Roberts Singers.

Announcer: Roger Carroll.

Orchestra: Nelson Riddle.

THE LESLIE UGGAMS SHOW—60 minutes—CBS—September 28, 1969 - December 21, 1969. 13 tapes.

LET'S DANCE

Dance Music. Broadcast from both New York City and Chicago. New York City portion (from the Terrace Room of the Hotel New Yorker):

Host: Ralph Mooney.

Celebrity Table Hostess: Martha Wright.

Dancers: Bud and Cece Robinson.

Orchestra: Ralph Flanagan.

Chicago segment (from the Aragon Ballroom):

Host: Art Mooney.

Celebrity Table Hostess: Fran Allison.

Orchestra: Art Mooney.

LET'S DANCE—60 minutes—ABC—September 18, 1954 - October 16, 1954.

LET'S GO GO

Musical Variety. Performances by Rock personalities.

Host: Sam Riddle.

Music: Recorded.

LET'S GO GO—30 minutes—Syndicated 1965.

LET'S HAVE FUN

Variety.

Host: Hank Grant.

Vocalists: Elaine Neblett, Kyle Kimbrough.

Accordionist: Reno Tondelli.

LET'S HAVE FUN—55 minutes—DuMont 1951.

LET'S MAKE A DEAL

Audience Participation. Ten of forty previously selected studio-audience members vie for the opportunity to trade their home-made articles for cash and/or valuable merchandise prizes. The host selects a player and offers him his first deal—unknown cash or merchandise for what he's brought. After the deal is made, the player is asked to trade what he's just won for a chance at something better—usually what lies behind a curtain on stage. If the player is undecided, the host then tempts him by offering him money not to trade. Usually the outcome of this trade determines what the player will receive—anything from five thousand dollars in cash, to a color television set, to a zonk (a nonsense prize). Though trades vary greatly in presentation, the basic format is the offer, the counteroffer, and the final offer—all designed to test greed.

Program end: "The Big Deal of the Day." The two highest-scoring contestants (cash value) are permitted to make one last trade—their prizes for the choice of one of three doors—one of which beholds cash and/or merchandise valued to as high as $15,000.

Host: Monty Hall, "Television's Big Dealer."

Announcer-Assistant: Jay Stewart.

Model: Carol Merrill.

Music: Ivan Ditmars.

LET'S MAKE A DEAL—30 minutes—NBC—December 30, 1964 - December 27, 1968. ABC—December 30, 1968 - July 9, 1976. Evening run (ABC)—February 7, 1969 - August 30, 1971.

LET'S PLAY POST OFFICE

Game. Three competing contestants. Involved: Fictitious letters that could have been written by celebrities or figures of past history. The host reveals one line of content at a time (e.g., "I traveled down a river with Robert Mitchum."). The player first to associate the content with the author (Marilyn Monroe; from the film *The River of No Return*), sounds a buzzer. If he is correct, one point is scored. Winners, the highest point scorers, receive merchandise prizes.

Host: Don Morrow.

LET'S PLAY POST OFFICE—30 minutes—NBC—September 27, 1965 - July 1, 1966.

LET'S SING OUT

A thirty-minute variety series, with Oscar Brand as host, that was first syndicated in 1965.

LET'S TAKE A TRIP

Educational. Through visits to places of interest various aspects of the adult world are related to children.

Host: Sonny Fox.

Assistants: Ginger McManus, Brian Flanegan.

Producer: Roger Englander, James Calligan, Selig Alkon.

LET'S TAKE A TRIP—30 minutes—CBS—March 17, 1955 - February 23, 1958.

LET'S TAKE SIDES

Panel Discussion. Discussions on topical issues.

Moderator: Nina Foch.

Panelists: Maria Riva, Bob Considine.

Opposing Issues Representative: Guests.

LET'S TAKE SIDES—30 minutes—NBC—1953 - 1954.

A LETTER TO LEE GRAHAM

Discussion. Psychology-based discussions and advice presented in a manner that is understandable to the layman.

Host: Lee Graham.

A LETTER TO LEE GRAHAM—15 minutes—ABC—September 15, 1952 - May 22, 1953.

A LETTER TO LORETTA

Anthology. Responsive dramatizations based on problems expressed in fan letters to Miss Young.

Hostess-Frequent Performer: Loretta Young.

Announcer: Bob Wilson.

Music: Harry Lubin.

Producer: Matthew Rapf.

Sponsor: Procter and Gamble.

Included:

Kid Stuff. The story of a woman who constantly devotes her time to her young daughter after her husband's death.

CAST
Amanda Carrington: Loretta Young; Steve Baxter: George Nader; Natalie Carrington: Noreen Corcoran.

The Pearl. The tragedy that results when a Japanese fisherman tries to conceal a large pearl. Based on the story by John Steinbeck.

CAST
Kiku: Loretta Young; Kiyoshi: Teru Shimanda.

Thanksgiving on Beaver Run. Three youths rob a freight office. Escaping in a stolen car, they discover a crippled boy in the back seat. After two of the thieves flee, fearing apprehension, the third attempts to return the boy to his mother.

CAST
Betty Taylor: Loretta Young; Joe: William Campbell; Phill: Dick Foran; Billy Taylor: Hugh Corcoran; Art: John Smith.

A LETTER TO LORETTA—30 minutes—NBC—September 20, 1953 - June 27, 1954.

LETTERS TO LAUGH-IN

Comedy Game. A spin-off from "Laugh-In." Four joke tellers (guest celebrities) relate jokes submitted to "Laugh-In" by home viewers. Jokes are rated by a panel of ten selected studio audience members from a plus one hundred to a minus one hundred. The winner of the week's highest scoring joke receives merchandise prizes; the joke scoring the lowest awards its sender "seven action-packed days in beautiful downtown Burbank."

Host: Gary Owens.

Announcer: Gary Owens.

LETTERS TO LAUGH-IN—30 minutes—NBC—September 29, 1969 - March 3, 1970.

THE LIAR'S CLUB

Game. Two competing contestants. A panel of four liars (celebrities) are handed an unusual but real item and then proceed to describe in detail what its purpose is. Three falsify its actual purpose; one relates the truth. Object: For the player to discover which one is telling the truth on the basis of their descriptions. Correct guesses award one point. Winners, the highest scorers, receive one hundred dollars.

Host: Rod Serling, "President of the Liar's Club."

Resident Liar: Betty White; guests represent other liars.

Announcer: Jim Isaics.

THE LIAR'S CLUB—30 minutes—Syndicated 1969. Withdrawn.

THE LIAR'S CLUB

Game. Four players compete. Each of the four celebrity guests who appear describe an unusual, but real item. Three falsify its purpose, one relates the truth. Players, who each receive $100, bet any part of it they wish on the celebrity whom they feel is telling the truth. Incorrect guesses cost the player the bet amount deducted from his score; correct guesses add the money in accord with the established odds (Round one: 1 to 1; round two, 2 to 1; round 3, 5 to 1; round 4, 10 to 1). Winners are the highest scorers.

Host: Bill Armstrong; Allen Ludden.

Resident Liar: Larry Hovis.

Announcer: Joe Sider; Bill Beary

Music: Recorded.

Executive Producer: Larry Hovis.

Producer: Bill Yageman.

Director: Dick McDonoughe

THE LIAR'S CLUB—30 minutes—Syndicated 1976.

LIBERACE

Listed: The television programs of pianist Wladziu Valentino Liberace.

The Liberace Show—Musical Variety—15 minutes—Local Los Angeles—1951.

Host: Liberace.

Orchestra: George Liberace (his brother).

The Liberace Show—Musical Variety—15 minutes—NBC—July 1, 1952 - September 1952.

Host: Liberace.

Orchestra: George Liberace.

The Liberace Show—Musical Variety—30 minutes—Syndicated—1953-1955.

Host: Liberace.

Orchestra: George Liberace.

The Liberace Show—Musical Variety—30 minutes—ABC—October 13, 1958 - April 10, 1959.

Host: Liberace.

Regulars: Marilyn Lovell, Dick Roman, Erin O'Brien, Darias (a Bongo expert).

Announcer: Steve Dunn.

Orchestra: Gordon Robinson.

Liberace—Musical Variety—55 minutes—Granada TV From Manchester (British)—1960.

Host: Liberace.

Regulars: Janet Medlin, Ballet Ticanar.

Music: The Grandlers Orchestra.

The Liberace Show—Musical Variety—60 minutes—CBS—July 15, 1969 - September 16, 1969. Produced in England.

Host: Liberace.

Regulars: Georgina Moon, Richard Wattis, The Irving Davies Dancers.

Orchestra: Jack Parnell.

THE LID'S OFF

See title: "Art Linkletter."

LIDSVILLE

Children's Adventure. Intrigued by a magician's performance, a young boy,

Mark, remains behind as the theatre empties. Alone, he picks up the magician's hat, which suddenly begins to grow. Unable to hold it, he places it on the floor. Climbing on its brim, and attempting to look inside, he loses his balance and falls into it and reappears in Lidsville, the land of living hats.

Considered to be a spy, Mark is captured by the hats of Whoo Doo, an evil magician. Refusing to believe Mark's story, Whoo Doo summons his genie, Weenie, and commands her to imprison him. Speaking with Weenie, Mark learns of her dislike for Whoo Doo, and of his controlling power over her by possessing her magic ring. Offering to help her escape from Whoo Doo, and promising to take her back to America with him, Mark is released from his cell by Weenie. Spotting the magic ring on a table, Mark grabs it and commands Weenie to take them to safety. Instantly they are transported to the village of the good hats.

Acquiring the assistance of the good hats, Mark and Weenie struggle to find the secret of the way back to his world against the desires of Whoo Doo who seeks to regain his prisoner, his genie, and the magic ring.

CAST

Mark	Butch Patrick
Whoo Doo	Charles Nelson Reilly
Weenie the Genie	Billie Hayes

Also: Sharon Baird, Joy Campbell, Jerry Marling, Angelo Rosetti, Van Snowden, Hommy Stewart, Felix Silla, Buddy Douglas, The Hermine Midgets.

Characters: The Sid and Marty Krofft Puppets.

Orchestra: Charles Fox.

LIDSVILLE—30 minutes—ABC—September 11, 1971 - September 1, 1973; NBC—September 8, 1973 - August 31, 1974. 17 episodes.

THE LIEUTENANT

Drama. Background: The Camp Pendleton Marine Base in Oceanside, California. The personal and professional lives of three officers: Captain Raymond Rambridge; Second Lieutenant William Rice; and Lieutenant Samwell Panosian.

CAST

Lt. William Rice	Gary Lockwood
Cpt. Raymond Rambridge	Robert Vaughn
Lt. Samwell Panosian	Steve Franken
Lilly, the captain's	

secretary   Carmen Phillips

Music: Jeff Alexander.

Producer: Gene Roddenberry, Norman Felton.

THE LIEUTENANT—60 minutes—NBC—September 14, 1963 - September 12, 1964. 29 episodes. Syndicated.

THE LIFE AND LEGEND OF WYATT EARP

Western. Background: Dodge City, Kansas (early episodes); and Tombstone, Arizona (later episodes), during the 1870s. The story of Sheriff Wyatt Earp and his attempts to maintain law and order. Based on fact and fiction for its documentation of life in both Dodge City and Tombstone.

CAST

Wyatt Earp	Hugh O'Brian
Doctor Goodfellow	Damian O'Flynn
Bat Masterson	Alan Dinehart III
John Behan, the man out to smash Wyatt's legal power	Steve Brodie
Clanton, Behan's aide	Trevor Bardette
Doc Holliday, Wyatt's friend	Myron Healey / Douglas Fowley
Morgan Earp, Wyatt's brother	Dirk London
Virgil Earp, Wyatt's brother	John Anderson
Ned Buntline, Wyatt's friend, the man who designed his guns, the Buntline Special, in 1876—a Colt .45 with a twelve-inch barrel	Lloyd Corrigan
Kate Holliday, Doc's daughter	Carole Stone
Marsh Murdock	Don Haggerty
Dr. Fabrique (before his role of Holliday)	Douglas Fowley
Abbie Crandall	Gloria Talbot
Ben Thompson	Denver Pyle
Mayor Clum (Tombstone)	Stacy Harris
Shotgunn Gibbs, Wyatt's chief deputy	Morgan Woodward
Mayor Kelly (Dodge City)	Ralph Sanford / Paul Brinegar
Nellie Cashman, the owner of the saloon	Randy Stuart
Judge Spicer	James Seay
Old Man Clanton, leader of the notorious Clanton gang	Trevor Bardette
Emma Clanton, his wife	Carol Thurston
Phin Clanton, their son	Steve Rowland

Music: H. Adamson, H. Warren.

Producer: Robert Sisk, Louis F. Edelman.

THE LIFE AND LEGEND OF WYATT EARP—30 minutes—ABC—September 6, 1955 - September 26, 1961. 266 episodes. Syndicated.

THE LIFE AND TIMES OF GRIZZLY ADAMS

Adventure. Era: The 1850s. Falsely accused of a crime* he did not commit, James Adams flees to the wilderness where, establishing a new life as mountain man Grizzly Adams, he becomes a friend to all living creatures. Stories concern his adventures in the wilderness. Based on the 1974 feature film of the same title.

CAST

James "Grizzly" Adams	Dan Haggerty
Mad Jack, a mountain man, his friend	Denver Pyle
Nakuma, Grizzly's Indian blood brother	Don Shanks

Narrator: Denver Pyle.

Music: Bob Summers.

Music Supervision: Don Perry.

Executive Producer: Charles E. Sellier, Jr.

Producer: Art Stolnitz.

Director: James L. Conway, Sharron Miller, Jack Hively, Richard Friberg.

Grizzly's pet Bear: Ben (played by Bozo).

Mad Jack's mule: Number 7.

THE LIFE AND TIMES OF GRIZZLY ADAMS—60 minutes—NBC—Premiered: February 9, 1977.

*According to the film, a murder that occured near his home, but of which he is innocent.

LIFE BEGINS AT EIGHTY

Discussion. A panel of five senior citizens answer questions, either submitted by home viewers or presented by guests, relating to the problems of life.

Host: Jack Barry.

Producer: Jack Barry, Dan Enright, Fred W. Friendly.

Director: Douglas Rodgers, Charles Powers.

Sponsor: Arnold Bakeries.

LIFE BEGINS AT EIGHTY—30 min-

utes. NBC—January 13, 1950 - August 25, 1950; ABC—October 3, 1950 - March 24, 1952; ABC —July 31, 1955 - February 25, 1956.

THE LIFE OF LEONARDO da VINCI

Historical Biography. Five dramatic episodes recounting the life of Florentine artist Leonardo da Vinci (1452-1519). Based on facts drawn from his surviving journals.

CAST

Leonardo da Vinci	Philippe Leroy
Leonardo da Vinci (as a boy)	Alberto Fiorini
Leonardo da Vinci (as a young man)	Arduino Paolini

Narrator: Giulio Bosetti.

Host (PBS version): Ben Gazzara.

THE LIFE OF LEONARDO da VINCI—60 minutes—CBS—August 13, 1972 - September 10, 1972; PBS—60 minutes—November 20, 1974 - December 18, 1974. Produced by Italy's RAI-TV.

THE LIFE OF RILEY

Comedy. Background: 1313 Blue View Terrace, Los Angeles, California, the residence of the Riley family: Chester, a riveter with Stevenson Aircraft and Associates; his wife, Peggy; and their children, Babs and Junior. Stories relate the trials and tribulations of a not-too-bright husband and his family.

Versons:

The Life Of Riley—30 minutes—DuMont—October 4, 1949 - March 28, 1950. 26 episodes.

CAST

Chester A. Riley	Jackie Gleason
Peggy Riley	Rosemary DeCamp
Babs Riley	Gloria Winters
Chester Riley, Jr. (Junior)	Lanny Rees
Jim Gillis, Riley's neighbor	Sid Tomack
Digby "Digger" O'Dell, the mortician	John Brown
Waldo Binny, Riley's friend	Bob Jellison
Honeybee Gillis, Jim's wife	Maxine Semon
Egbert Gillis, Jim and Honeybee's son	George McDonald
Carl Stevenson, Riley's employer	Bill Green / Emory Parnell

Millie, Stevenson's
  secretary   Mary Treen

Music: Lou Kosloff.

Producer: Irving Brecher.

Director: Leslie Goodwins, Herbert I.
  Leeds.

Sponsor: Pabst Blue Ribbon Beer.

The Life Of Riley—30 minutes—NBC
—January 2, 1953 - August 22, 1958.
91 episodes. Syndicated.

CAST

Chester A. Riley   William Bendix
Peggy Riley   Marjorie Reynolds
Babs Riley   Lugene Sanders
Chester Riley, Jr.   Wesley Morgan
Jim Gillis   Tom D'Andrea
Honeybee Gillis, Jim's
  wife   Gloria Blondell
Don Marshall, Babs's
  boyfriend   Martin Milner
Carl Stevenson, Riley's
  employer   Douglas Dumbrille
Waldo Binny, Riley's
  friend   Sterling Holloway
Millicent, Waldo's
  girlfriend   Stanja Lowe
Otto Schmidlap, Riley's
  friend   Henry Kulky
Calvin Dudley, Riley's
  neighbor   George O'Hanlon
Belle Dudley, Calvin's
  wife   Florence Sundstrom
Cissy Riley, Chester's
  sister   Mary Jane Croft
Anne Riley, Chester's
  sister   Larraine Bendix
Moose, Junior's
  friend   Denny Miller
Hawkins, the plant
  manager   Emory Parnell

Music: Jerry Fielding.

Producer: Tom McKnight.

Director: Abby Berlin.

Sponsor: Gulf Oil.

Note: George O'Hanlon replaced
  Tom D'Andrea temporarily in
  the role of Gillis during 1955.
  Also, on the Bendix version of
  the series, the plant is also
  known to be Cunningham and
  Thomas Aircraft.

LIFE WITH BUSTER KEATON

Comedy. Reedited movie shorts of the
1930s and 40s. The misadventures of
Buster Keaton, a man struggling to
cope with life's numerous problems.

Starring: Buster Keaton.

LIFE WITH BUSTER KEATON—30
minutes—Syndicated 1952.

LIFE WITH ELIZABETH

Comedy. Background: San Francisco,
California. The story of Elizabeth and
Alvin White, newlyweds struggling to
survive the difficult first years of
marriage.

CAST

Elizabeth White   Betty White
Alvin White   Del Moore
Chloe, their neighbor   Jack Narz

LIFE WITH ELIZABETH—30 minutes—DuMont—1953 - 1955.

LIFE WITH THE ERWINS

See title: "Trouble With Father."

LIFE WITH FATHER

Comedy. Background: New York City
during the turn of the twentieth century. West 48th Street, Manhattan,
the residence of the Day family:
Clarence, a Wall Street banker; his
wife, Vinnie; and their children,
Clarence, Jr., John, Harlan, and
Whitney. Stories relate the struggles of
a middle-class American family who
are plagued by the stubborness of a
father who refuses to accept the progress attributed to a changing world.

CAST

Clarence Day, Sr.   Leon Ames
Vinnie Day   Lurene Tuttle
Clarence Day, Jr.   Steve Terrell
                        Ralph Reed
Whitney Day   Ronald Keith
John Day   Freddie Leiston
                        Malcolm Cossell
Harlan Day   Harvey Grant
The Irish Maid   Marion Ross

Announcer: Bob Lemond.

Orchestra: Lud Gluskin.

Producer: Fletcher Markle.

LIFE WITH FATHER—30 minutes—
CBS—November 22, 1953 - July 5,
1955. 26 episodes. Syndicated.

LIFE WITH LINKLETTER

See title: "Art Linkletter."

LIFE WITH LUIGI

Comedy. Background: 221 North
Holstead Street, Chicago, the resi-
dence and business address of Luigi
Basco, antique dealer, an immigrant

brought to Chicago from Italy by his
friend Pasquale, the owner of
Pasquale's Spaghetti Palace.

Stories relate Luigi's attempts to
adjust to a new homeland and his
struggles to evade Pasquale's endless
attempts to marry him to his overweight daughter, Rosa.

CAST

Luigi Basco   J. Carroll Naish
                        Vito Scotti
Pasquale   Alan Reed
                        Thomas Gomez
Rosa   Jody Gilbert
                        Muriel Landers
Miss Spaulding, Luigi's
  night-school teacher
  (English)   Mary Shipp
Schultz, Luigi's friend,
  the owner of a
  delicatessen   Sig Rumin
Horowitz, Luigi's
  friend   Joe Forte
Olson, Luigi's
  friend   Ken Peters

Music: Lud Gluskin.

Producer: Mac Benoff, Calvin Kuhl.

Sponsor: General Foods.

LIFE WITH LUIGI—30 minutes—
CBS—September 22, 1952 - June 11,
1953. Based on the same titled radio
program.

LIFE WITH SNARKY PARKER

Western Puppet Adventure. Background: The town of Hot Rock,
1850s. The story of Deputy Sheriff
Snarky Parker, and his attempts to
maintain law and order.

Characters (The Bill Burrud Puppets):
Snarky Parker
Blackie McGoo, a notorious outlaw
Cuda Barra, a sultry siren
Heatcliff, Snarky's talking horse
Miss Butterball, the schoolmarm
Slugger, the Hot Rock Café piano
  player
Noose Nolan, a reformed, but evil
  desperado
Fluffy Webster, his partner

LIFE WITH SNARKY PARKER—15
minutes—CBS 1950.

LIGHTS, CAMERA, ACTION

Variety. Performances by undiscovered professional talent. Winners
are determined by studio-audience
applause.

Host: Walter Wolfe King.

LIGHTS, CAMERA, ACTION—30
minutes—NBC 1949.

LIGHTS OUT

Anthology. Mystery and suspense presentations.

Host: Frank Gallop.

Announcer: Jack LaRue.

Music: Fred Howard.

Producer: Herbert Swope, Jr., Ernie Walling.

Director: William Corrigan.

Sponsor: Admiral.

Included:

The Upstairs Floor. Tale of the mystery surrounding a locked door on the second floor of a home.
Starring: Josephine Hull, John Forsythe.

A Love Came To Professor Gilder. The story of a bitter college professor who is haunted by the love of a spirit.
Starring: Arnold Moss.

Ann Adams Begot. Touring France, three modern-day people fall from a cliff and are captured by a Neanderthal man. The story relates their attempts to escape.
Starring: Kent Smith.

Sisters Of Shadow. A tale of the mystery surrounding two sisters.
Starring: William Eythe, Elinar Randal.

LIGHTS OUT—30 minutes—NBC—July 19, 1949 - September 29, 1952. Based on the radio program of the same title.

LILLI PALMER

Listed: The television programs of actress Lilli Palmer.

The Lilli Palmer Show—Celebrity Interview—30 minutes—ABC—April 1, 1953 - July 11, 1953.

Hostess: Lilli Palmer.

The Lilli Palmer Theatre—Anthology Drama—30 minutes—Syndicated 1955.

Hostess: Lilli Palmer.

Producer: Charles Keble.

Director: Bruce Anderson.

Included:

THE DOOR. Adapted from the story by Robert Louis Stevenson. Losing his way, a young man walks through a door and into a trap set for someone else.

CAST
Sam Wanamaker, Renee Asherson.

THE TRIUMPHANT. A woman struggles to return to freedom after she is acquitted of murder.

CAST
Margaret Leighton, Eleanor Summerfield.

DOWN FROM THE STARS. A small-town girl comes to New York and rents an apartment formerly occupied by an astronomer. Her life becomes hectic when his friends, unaware that he has left, disturb her at all hours of the night.

CAST
Diana Lynn, Lamont Johnson.

THE LINE-UP

Crime Drama. Background: San Francisco, California. The investigations of Inspector Matt Grebb and Lieutenant Ben Guthrie, plainclothes detectives with the San Francisco police department.

CAST
Lieutenant Ben Guthrie	Warner Anderson
Inspector Matt Grebb	Tom Tully
Sandy McAllister, policewoman	Rachel Ames
Officer Pete Larkin	Skip Ward
Inspector Dan Delaney	William Leslie
Inspector Charlie Summers	Tod Burton
Inspector Fred Asher	Marshall Reed
Also, various parts	Ruta Lee

Announcer: Art Gilmore.

Music: Eddie Dunsteder; Mischa Bakaleinkoff; Jerry Goldsmith.

THE LINE-UP—60 and 30 minute versions—CBS—October 1, 1954 - January 20, 1960. 183 half-hour episodes; 18 one-hour episodes. Syndicated title: "San Francisco Beat."

LINUS THE LIONHEARTED

Animated Cartoon. Background: Africa. The misadventures of Linus the Lionhearted, the gentle ruler of animals.

Additional characters: Sugar Bear; Loveable Truly, the postman; Royal Raccoon; So Hi, the Chinese boy; and Billi Bird. Characters first appeared on the Post cereal boxes Animal Crackers and Sugar Crisp.

Characters' Voices
Linus	Sheldon Leonard
Danny Kangaroo	Carl Reiner
The Mockingbird	Ed Graham
The Giant	Jonathan Winters
Sugar Bear	Sterling Holloway

Producer: Ed Graham.

LINUS THE LIONHEARTED—30 minutes. CBS—September 26, 1964 - September 3, 1966; ABC—September 25, 1966 - September 7, 1969. 39 episodes.

LIPPY THE LION

Animated Cartoon. The misadventures of Lippy the lion. A Hanna-Barbera production.

Characters' Voices
Lippy the Lion	Daws Butler
Hardy Har Har	Mel Blanc

Music: Hoyt Curtin.

LIPPY THE LION—05 minutes—Syndicated 1962. 52 episodes.

LITTLE HOUSE ON THE PRAIRIE

Drama. Background: The town of Walnut Grove in Plumb Creek, Minnesota during the 1870s. The struggles of the pioneering Ingalls family: Charles, the father; his wife, Caroline; and their children, Laura, Mary, and Carrie. Their experiences as homesteaders in the vastly unsettled regions of the Southwestern Frontier are viewed through the sentimental eyes of Laura, the second-born daughter. Based on the *Little House* books by Laura Ingalls Wilder.

CAST
Charles Ingalls	Michael Landon
Caroline Ingalls	Karen Grassle
Laura Ingalls	Melissa Gilbert
Mary Ingalls	Melissa Sue Anderson
Carrie Ingalls	Lindsay and Sidney Green Bush (twins)
Nels Oleson, the owner of the general store	Richard Bull
Harriet Oleson, his wife	Katherine MacGregor
Willie Oleson, their	

son Jonathan Gilbert
Nellie Oleson, their
daughter Alison Arngrim
Mr. Hanson, the
owner of the lumber
mill Karl Swenson
Miss Beadle, the school
teacher Charlotte Stewart
The Reverend Mr.
Alden Dabbs Greer
Dr. Baker Kevin Hagen
Isaiah Edwards, a friend
of the Ingalls
family Victor French
Cristy Kennedy, a friend
of Laura's Tracie Savage
Sandy Kennedy, a
friend of
Laura's Robert Hoffman
Grace Edwards, Isaiah's
wife Bonnie Bartlett
John Edwards, their
adopted son Radames Pera
Carl Edwards, their adopted
son Brian Part
Aliscia Edwards, their adopted
daughter Kyle Richards
Ebenezer Sprague, the
banker Ted Gehring
Jonathan Garvey, a
farmer-woodsman Merlin Olsen

Ingalls family dog: Jack.

Music: David Rose.

Executive Producer: Michael Landon.

Producer: John Hawkins, B.F. Sandefur.

Director: Michael Landon, Victor
French, William F. Claxton.

LITTLE HOUSE ON THE PRAIRIE
—60 minutes—NBC—Premiered: September 11, 1974.

LITTLE JOE

An animated cartoon series that focuses on the adventures of Little Joe,
an insect, and his friend Buzz, the bee.
39 six minute, thirty second films;
Syndicated 1968.

THE LITTLE PEOPLE

Comedy. Background: Kahala,
Hawaii. The trials and tribulations of
doctors Sean Jamison and his
daughter, Anne Jamison, pedia-
tricians.

CAST

Dr. Sean Jamison Brian Keith
Dr. Anne Jamison Shelley Fabares
Puni, their secretary-
nurse Victoria Young
Ronnie Collins, Sean's

general helper Michael Gray
Alfred Landis, the terror
of the island, the boy
who delights in annoying
Sean and his pa-
tients Stephen Hague
Officer Moe O'Shaughnessy,
Puni's cousin Moe Keal
Stewart, Alfred's
friend Sean Tyler Hall
Dr. Spencer Chaffey, the
allergist Roger Bowen
Mrs. Millar Gruber,
the owner of Sean's
clinic Nancy Kulp

Sean's parrot: Sam.

Music: Jerry Fielding; Artie Butler.

THE LITTLE PEOPLE—30 minutes—
NBC—September 15, 1972 - September 7, 1973. As "The Brian Keith
Show"—30 minutes—NBC—September
21, 1973 - August 30, 1974. 48
episodes.

THE LITTLE RASCALS

Children. Reedited theatrical comedy
shorts. The misadventures of a group
of children who, set free in a world of
troubled times, the late 1920s, 30s,
and 40s, struggle to solve problems
without help from the adult population.

CAST

Alfalfa Carl Switzer
Spanky George Emmett McFarland
Darla Darla Jean Hood
Porky Porky Lee
Butch Tommy Bond
Buckwheat Billy Thomas
Mary Ann Mary Ann Jackson
Chubby Chubby Chaney
Stymie Stymie Beard
Scott Scott Hastings
Dickie Dickie Moore
Wheezer Bobby Hutchins
Farina Allen Hoskins
Jackie Jackie Cooper
Waldo Dearwood Kaye
Mickey Mickey Gubitosi
Woim Sidney Kibrick
Mirianne Mirianne Edwards
Junior Gary Jasgar
Joe Joe Cobb
The Schoolteacher Mary Kornman
June Marlowe
Rosena Lawrence
Dorothy Dorothy De Borba
Also: J.R. Smith, Peggy Eames, Jean
Darling, Harry Spear, Scooter
Lowry, Janet Burston, Robert
"Froggy" McLaughlin, Baby
Patsy May, Shirley Jean Rickert,
Eugene Jackson, John Beradino,
Nanette Fabray, Sherwood Bai-

The Little Rascals. Left to right: Spanky,
Buckwheat, Porky, Alfalfa, and Darla.

ley, Rickie Van Daisen, Jackie
Condon, Ernie "Sunshine Sammy" Morrison, Johnny Downs.

The Gang dog: Petie.

Producer: Hal Roach.

Director: Nat Watt, Robert McGowan,
Gus Meins, Gordon Douglas,
Anthony Mack, Fred Newmeyer.

Note: Mickey Gubitosi, who plays
Mickey, is now known as Robert
Blake.

THE LITTLE RASCALS—20 minutes
—Syndicated 1955. Also known as:
"Our Gang Comedy" and "The Ter-
rible Ten" (silent version).

THE LITTLE REVUE

Musical Variety.

Host: Bill Sherry.

Vocalist: Gloria Van.

Orchestra: Rex Maupin.

THE LITTLE REVUE—15 minutes—
ABC 1949.

THE LITTLE SHOW

Musical Variety.

Host: John Conte.

Regulars: Marguerite Hamilton, The
Three Beaus and the Peep
Quartet.

Music: The Tony Mottola Trio.

Producer: Robert Smith.

Sponsor: Stokley-Van Camp Foods.

THE LITTLE SHOW—15 minutes—
ABC—April 5, 1953 - June 19, 1953.
Also known as "John Conte's Little
Show." Broadcast under the title
"The Feminine Touch"—15 minutes
—ABC—June 18, 1951 - August 17,
1951.

LITTLE WOMEN

See title: "Family Classics Theatre'"
Little Women segment.

THE LITTLEST HOBO

Adventure. Background: Canada. The story of London, a masterless German Shepherd dog who aids people in distress.

Music: Douglas Lackey.

Producer: Darrell and Stuart McGowan.

THE LITTLEST HOBO—30 minutes —Syndicated 1964. 57 episodes.

LIVING EASY

See title: "Doctor Joyce Brothers."

LIVE LIKE A MILLIONAIRE

Game. Children present their talented parents who vie for cash and/or merchandise prizes. Winners are determined via studio-audience applause.

Host: John Nelson.

Assistant: Connie Clawson.

Announcer: Jack McCoy.

Orchestra: Ivan Ditmars.

Producer: John Masterson, John Reddy, John Nelson.

Sponsor: Grove Labs; General Mills.

LIVE LIKE A MILLIONAIRE—30 minutes—ABC—October 18, 1952 - April 11, 1953.

THE LIVELY ONES

Variety. Music, song, and dance set against offbeat electronic background locations.

Host: Vic Damone.

Regulars: Joan Staley (as Tiger), Shirley Yelm (Charley), Gloria Neil (Melvin), Quinn O'Hara (Smitty); The Earl Brown Dancers.

Orchestra: Jerry Fielding.

THE LIVELY ONES—30 minutes— NBC—July 26, 1962 - September 13, 1962; NBC—July 25, 1963 - September 12, 1963. 13 tapes.

THE LIVING CAMERA

Documentary. Candid, unscripted film studies of people. The cinema verité method (a hand-held camera and portable sound equipment) is used to present the viewer with a sense of actual participation.

THE LIVING CAMERA—60 minutes —Syndicated 1964.

THE LLOYD BRIDGES SHOW

Anthology. Dramatic presentations recounting the stories of free-lance journalist Adam Sheppard.

Host-Adam Sheppard: Lloyd Bridges.

Producer: Aaron Spelling, Everett Chambers.

Included:

Wheresoever I Enter. A doctor attempts to rescue several people who are trapped in a coal-mine disaster.

CAST
Demetrois: Harry Guardino; Aristos: Michael Constantine; Doctor: Nick Alekos.

Mr. Pennington's Machine. Background: Hong Kong. Appalled by squalid living conditions, an American tourist attempts to expose the powerful racketeers who are responsible.

CAST
Bruce Pennington/Adam Sheppard: Lloyd Bridges; Ellen Pennington: Betty Garrett; Li: H.T. Tsiang; Quan: James Hong.

Just Married. After a Model A car, with the inscription, "Just Married" on its side, is pulled from a lake, Adam envisions himself as a gangster during the 1930s.

CAST
Brad/Adam: Lloyd Bridges; Cathy: Carolyn Jones; Doc: Edgar Buchanan.

To Walk With The Stars. Overshadowed by the fear of losing his life as his father did in a plane crash, a young man struggles to become a stunt pilot.

CAST
Adam Sheppard/Bill Wade: Lloyd Bridges; Carol Wade: Dolores Michaels; Dave Melkin: Jeff Bridges; Mrs. Melkin: Virginia Vincent.

THE LLOYD BRIDGES SHOW—30

minutes—CBS—September 11, 1962 September 3, 1963. 34 episodes.

LLOYD BRIDGES WATER WORLD

Instruction-Travel. Boating safety, marine-band radio use, and excursions to various tropical islands. Produced with the cooperation of the U.S. Coast Guard.

Host-Narrator: Lloyd Bridges.

Announcer: Commodore Harold B. Haney.

Music: Marty Gould.

LLOYD BRIDGES WATER WORLD —30 minutes—Syndicated 1972.

THE LLOYD THAXTON SHOW

Musical Variety. Performances by the sixties' top Rock personalities.

Host: Lloyd Thaxton.

Regulars: Lynn Marta, Mike Storm.

Music: Recorded.

THE LLOYD THAXTON SHOW—60 minutes—Syndicated 1964.

LOCK UP

Crime Drama. Background: Philadelphia. The cases and courtroom defenses of Herbert L. Maris, an attorney who defends unjustly accused people.

Starring: Macdonald Carey as Herbert L. Maris.

LOCK UP—30 minutes—Syndicated 1959. 78 episodes.

LOGAN'S RUN

Science Fiction Adventure. Era: Earth in the year 2319. Following an atomic holocaust that has ravaged the world, the remaining segment of civilization establishes itself in the City of Domes, a programmed society wherein no one over the age thirty is permitted to live. At precisely that age, each individual goes willingly, into carousel for the ceremony of the Great Sleep, where they are led to believe that their life will be renewed; in reality, however, they are exterminated. Those individuals who challenge to circumvent this tradition are labled Runners and become the prey of the Sandmen, whose duty it is to pursue and destroy them.

Runners, it is learned, are seeking Sanctuary, a supposed haven where all are free to live beyond age thirty. Having never seen anyone being reborn after entering the carousel, Logan, a Sandman, begins to question the ceremony. When he follows a male Runner to Quadrant Four, he meets Jessica, a girl Runner who aides those seeking Sanctuary. Jessica confirms Logan's doubts—telling him that the carousel means death—and convinces him that there is a Sanctuary. However, before he is able to do anything, Francis, another Sandman, appears and orders Logan to destroy the Runners. Logan's hesitation prompts Francis to kill the male; as he is about to kill Jessica, Logan knocks him unconscious. Now, a traitor, Logan becomes a Runner and joins forces with Jessica in an attempt to find Sanctuary.

Concerned about Logan's escape, the Council of Elders, who run the City of Domes (a.k.a. Dome City), assign Francis the task of returning Logan and Jessica so they be used as an example and testify that there is no Sanctuary. Told that the carousel is a myth, Francis learns that it is necessary because the city can only support a limited amount of people. Promised a seat on the council, Francis begins his assignment.

The series follows the adventures of Logan and Jessica as they seek to find Sanctuary—before Francis finds and captures them.

CAST

Logan 5	Gregory Harrison
Jessica 6	Heather Menzies
Francis 7	Randy Powell
Rem, the android*	Donald Moffat
Morgan, an elder leader	Morgan Woodward
Jonathan, an elder leader	Wright King
Martin, an elder leader	E.J. Andre
Benjamin, Francis's assistant	Stan Stratton

Music: Laurence Rosenthal.

Music Supervision: Harry Lojewski.

*An android with humanlike qualities who abandoned his robot-run world to join forces with Logan and Jessica.

Executive Producer: Ivan Goff, Ben Roberts.

Producer: Leonard Katzman.

LOGAN'S RUN—60 minutes—CBS—Premiered: September 16, 1977. Based on the film of the same title.

THE LOHMAN AND BARKLEY SHOW

A sixty minute variety series hosted by Al Lohman and Roger Barkley. 60 minutes—Syndicated 1976.

LOIS AND LOOEY

A fifteen minute, animated series about the adventures of a young girl and boy. Broadcast on ABC from October 16, 1950 to February 12, 1951.

THE LONDON PALLADIUM

Variety. Entertainment acts set against the background of the London Palladium Music Hall.

Hosts: Weekly guests, both British and American.

Vocalists: The Mike Sammes Singers.

Orchestra: Jack Parnell.

THE LONDON PALLADIUM—60 minutes—NBC—May 1966 - August 1966. Broadcast as a series of six specials.

THE LONER

Western. Era: The 1860s. The story of William Colton, a disillusioned Civil War officer who, one month after Appomattox, resigns his Union commission and heads West to search for the meaning of life. Aiding people he finds in distress, he struggles to overcome the bitterness and hatreds of men in a country torn by war.

Starring: Lloyd Bridges as William Colton.

Program opening:
Announcer: "In the aftermath of the blood-letting called the Civil War, thousands of ruthless, restless, searching men traveled West. Such a man is William Colton. Like the others he carried a blanket roll, a proficient gun, and a dedication to a new chapter in American history, the opening of the West."

THE LONER—30 minutes—CBS—September 18, 1965 - April 30, 1966. 26 episodes.

THE LONE RANGER

Western. Background: Texas, nineteenth century. Trailing the notorious Butch Cavendish Hole in the Wall Gang, a group of six Texas Rangers stop as they approach the canyon passage to Bryant's Gap. Their scout, who is secretly working for Butch, returns and informs Captain Dan Reid that the passage is clear. Riding in, the Rangers are led into a trap and downed by the Cavendish gang. Believing all are dead, the gang rides off.

Later that afternoon, Tonto, a Potawatomie Indian riding through the valley hunting for animals, discovers the lone survivor of the attack—the captain's brother, John Reid.

Upon regaining consciousness sometime later, Reid learns of his fate and recalls Tonto, the Indian he befriended as a child. (When still a young Brave, Tonto's village was raided by renegade Indians who killed his family and left him for dead. A young John Reid found Tonto and nursed him back to health. It was at this time that Tonto called Reid "Kemo Sabe"—translated as both "Trusted Scout" and "Faithful Friend.")

Bryant's Gap, a canyon about fifty yards wide, is bound by cliffs and scattered below with rocks broken by countless years of wind and storm. Near its western side, a small patch of grassland holds six mounds of earth—each marked by a crudely constructed cross—Captain Dan Reid, Jim Bates, Jack Stacey, Joe Brent, and Ben Cooper. The sixth cross bears the name of John Reid—placed there by Tonto to convince Cavendish that all the Rangers had been killed, to conceal the fact that one Texas Ranger had lived to avenge the others—the Lone Ranger.

At Tonto's suggestion, Reid fashions a mask from the black cloth of his borther's vest. Posing as an outlaw, Reid tracks down and apprehends the Cavendish gang—some of

The Lone Ranger. Left to right: Jay Silverheels, Silver (the Lone Ranger's horse), and Clayton Moore.

whom are imprisoned, others hanged.

Bearing the trademark of the silver bullet—a precious metal that constantly reminds him to shoot sparingly and to always remember the high cost of human life—the Lone Ranger and Tonto cut a trail of law and order across seven states, forcing "the powers of darkness into the blinding light of justice."

Disguises used by Reid to assist without arousing suspicion: The Old Timer; Professor Horatio Tucker, the smooth-talking medicine man; Don Pedro O'Sullivan, the Swede; and Jose, the Mexican Bandit.

CAST

John Reid, the Lone Ranger	John Hart
	Clayton Moore
Tonto	Jay Silverheels
Dan Reid, the Ranger's nephew	Chuck Courtney
Butch Cavendish (anniversary episode)	Glenn Strange
Father Paul, the Padre at the San Brado Mission, the Ranger's friend	David Leonard
Jim Blaine, the old miner who works the Ranger's silver mine	Ralph Littlefield
Dan Reid, the Ranger's brother (flashbacks)	Tristim Coffin

Also, various outlaw roles: Ben Weldon.

The Lone Ranger's Horse: Silver.

Tonto's Paint Horse: Scout.

Dan Reid's Horse: Victor.

Announcer: Fred Foy.

Program opening:

Announcer: "A fiery horse with the speed of light, a cloud of dust and a hearty hi-yo Silver! The Lone Ranger! With his faithful Indian companion, Tonto, the daring and resourceful masked rider of the plains led the fight for law and order in the early West. Return with us now to those thrilling days of yesteryear, the Lone Ranger rides Again!"

Additional Announcing: Gerald Mohr (during 1949).

Music: Elias Alfriede, Ralph Cushman.

Producer: Sherman Harris, George W. Trendle, Jack Chertok, Harry Pope.

Director: William Thiele, Charles Livingston, Paul Landers, John Morse, Oscar Rudolph, Earl Bellamy, George B. Seitz, Jr.

Creator: George W. Trendle.

Sponsor: General Mills.

THE LONE RANGER—30 minutes—ABC—September 15, 1949 - September 18, 1960; September 28, 1960 – September 20, 1961; June 11, 1965 - September 4, 1965. 221 episodes. Syndicated.

Animated Version:

THE LONE RANGER—30 minutes—CBS—September 10, 1966 - September 6, 1969. 26 episodes.

Voice Characterizations: Marvin Miller.

Executive Producer: Arthur Jacobs.

Producer: Herbert Klein.

THE LONE WOLF

Adventure. The story of Michael Lanyard, a private detective known as the Lone Wolf. Episodes relate his experiences as he crusades against the global forces of tyranny and injustice.

Starring: Louis Hayward as Michael Lanyard.

THE LONE WOLF—30 minutes—Syndicated 1954. 39 episodes. Also known as: "Streets of Danger."

THE LONG HOT SUMMER

Drama. Background: Frenchman's Bend, Mississippi. Returning home after a long absence, Ben Quick discovers that his father has died; the town is controlled by Will Varner; and he is considered trash. Befriending Clara Varner, Will's daughter, Ben decides to remain and rework the Quick farm, now a wasteland, unattended for years.

Approaching Will Varner, he finds that his request for a loan from the Varner bank has been denied. Will, distraught by his beautiful but spoiled daughter's attraction to the handsome drifter, hopes the refusal will discourage him.

Determined to remain, Ben reapproaches Varner, and, after agreeing to leave Clara alone, he is granted the money for his farm. Discovering her father's actions, Clara becomes angered, and, defying him, sets her goal to acquire Ben's love.

Stories depict the conflicts and tensions that exist between Ben Quick and Will Varner as Ben struggles to rebuild his life and prove himself worthy of Clara. Adapted from the movie of the same title.

CAST

Will Varner (a widower)	Edmond O'Brien
	Dan O'Herlihy
Ben Quick	Roy Thinnes
Clara Varner	Nancy Malone
Eula Varner, Will's younger daughter	Lana Wood
Jody Varner, Will's son	Paul Geary
Minnie, the owner of the town hotel; Will's romantic interest	Ruth Roman
Duane Galloway	John Kerr
Lucas Taney	Warren Kemmerling
Harve Anders	Paul Bryar
Agnes	Josie Lloyd
Shad Taney	Mike Zaslow
Sam Ruddabow	William Mims
Mitch Taney	Brian Cutler
Dr. Talicott	Jimmy Hayes
Amy	Anne Helm
Susan	Tisha Sterling
Dr. Clark	Jason Wingreen
Atkinson	Phil Chambers
Chamberlain	Harold Gould
Curley	Wayne Rogers
John Wesley Johnson	Zalman King

Music: Alex North, Sammy Cahn.

Music Supervision: Lionel Newman.

THE LONG HOT SUMMER—60 minutes—ABC—September 16, 1965 - July 3, 1966. 26 episodes.

LONG JOHN SILVER

Adventure. Background: The British-possessed island of Porto Bello, eighteenth century. The exploits of Long John Silver, pirate, as he defends the Crown against warring marauders and battles the Spanish for the acquisition of land.

CAST

Long John Silver	Robert Newton
Jim Hawkins, his ward	Kit Taylor
Purity Pinker, the pub owner, Long John's romantic interest	Connie Gilchrist
Governor Strong	Harvey Adams
Silver's Crew:	
Mendoza	Lloyd Berrell
Patch	Grant Taylor
Israel Hands	Rodney Taylor
Billy Bowledge	Henry Gilbert

LONG JOHN SILVER—30 minutes—Syndicated 1956. 26 episodes. Original title: "The Adventures of Long John Silver."

LONGSTREET

Crime Drama. Background: New Orleans, Louisiana. Returning home, Michael Longstreet, an insurance investigator, and his wife Ingrid, find a gift wrapped bottle of champagne in the courtyard. Believing it to be from Mike's employer, Duke Paige, Ingrid opens it. The bottle explodes, killing Ingrid and blinding Mike.

Enrolling in a clinic for the blind, he is taught to use his other senses to their best advantage. Assisted by Pax, a white German Shepherd seeing-eye dog, Mike investigates and uncovers Ingrid's killers as members of a circus, jewel thieves who, having read about Longstreet's expertise in solving cases, decided to eliminate him before attempting their next crime.

Determined not to be hindered by blindness, Mike continues in his capacity as an investigator. Stories depict his attempts to solve baffling crimes perpetrated against the Great Pacific Casualty Company.

CAST

Michael Longstreet	James Franciscus
Nikki Bell, his braille teacher	Martine Beswick Marlyn Mason
Duke Paige	Peter Mark Richman
Li Tsung, Mike's self-defense instructor	Bruce Lee
Mrs. Kingston, Mike's housekeeper	Ann Doran
Ingrid Longstreet (pilot; flashbacks)	Judy Jones

Music: Billy Goldenberg; Robert Dransin.

LONGSTREET—60 minutes—ABC—September 16, 1971 - August 10, 1972. 24 episodes.

LOOK YOUR BEST

Women. Beauty tips and advice.

Host: Richard Willis.

LOOK YOUR BEST—30 minutes—CBS 1950.

THE LORENZO AND HENRIETTA MUSIC SHOW

Variety. Music, songs, sketches, and interviews.

Hosts: Lorenzo and Henrietta Music (husband and wife).

Regulars: Samantha Harper, Dave Willock, Bob Gibson, Erick Darling, Bella Bruck, Sandy Hellberg, Murphy Dunne.

Announcer: Dave Willock.

Orchestra: Jack Eskew.

Executive Producer: Lorenzo Music.

Producer: Albert Simon.

Director: Bob Lally.

THE LORENZO AND HENRIETTA MUSIC SHOW—60 minutes—Syndicated 1976.

THE LORETTA YOUNG SHOW

Comedy. Background: Connecticut, the residence of Christine Massey, children's story book authoress, widow, and mother of seven children. Hoping to secure a position as a writer for *Manhattan* magazine, Christine submits a story to its New York offices. Granted an interview, she meets its editor, Paul Belzer, who offers to hire her providing she upgrade her material to accommodate the sophisticated publication. Her decision to comply prompts him to request her presence for dinner to discuss matters. She accepts. Following the format of a serial, succeeding episodes depict their falling in love, marrying, and establishing housekeeping in Connecticut. Following their marriage, stories relate the trials and tribulations of the nine-member Belzer family.

CAST

Christine Massey (Belzer)	Loretta Young
Paul Belzer	James Philbrook
The Children:	
Vickie Massey (Belzer)	Beverly Washburn
Maria Massey (Belzer)	Tracy Statford
Marnie Massey (Belzer)	Celia Kaye
Judy Massey (Belzer)	Sandra Descher
Dack Massey (Belzer)	Dack Rambo
Dirk Massey (Belzer)	Dirk Rambo
Binkie Massey (Belzer)	Carol Sydes

Music: Harry Lubin.

THE LORETTA YOUNG SHOW—30 minutes—CBS—September 24, 1962 - March 18, 1963.

THE LORETTA YOUNG THEATRE

Anthology. Dramatic and comedic productions. Miss Loretta Young, attired in a lovely evening gown, enters through double doors and introduces the evening's presentation. At its conclusion, she reappears and quotes, in accord with the presentation, proverbs from the Bible.

Hostess-Frequent Performer: Loretta Young.

Regularly Cast: John Newland, Beverly Washburn.

Music: Harry Lubin.

Included:

Blizzard. A newspaperman and his wife struggle to seek help after they are stranded by a blizzard.

CAST

George Ellsworth: Stephen McNally; Verna Ellsworth: Patricia Crowley.

A Greater Strength. Released from a communist prison camp, a woman struggles to readjust to life.

CAST

Jean Kennedy: Loretta Young; Mother Superior: Mae Clark; Marie Crane: Ann Morrison; Melissa: Cheryl Callaway.

The Choice. A woman attempts to rehabilitate her alcoholic husband.

CAST

Isobel: Loretta Young; Charles: Richard Ney; Austin: George Nader.

Emergency In 114. Seriously injured in an accident, a young boy is rushed into surgery. The story depicts the tense waiting-room torment of his parents.

CAST

Lucy Anderson: Loretta Young; Wayne Anderson: Alf Kjellin; Davy Anderson: Larry Adare; Dr. Goodman: Ted de Corsia.

THE LORETTA YOUNG THEATRE—30 minutes—NBC—August 29, 1954 - September 10, 1961. 225 episodes. Syndicated.

LOST IN SPACE

Adventure. Era: 1997. As the planet Earth becomes critical due to overpopulation, the Robinson family is selected from more than two million volunteers to begin the conquest of space. Believing that the star Alpha Centauri contains a similar atmosphere, scientists construct the Jupiter II, an electronically sophisticated rocket ship that will initiate man's thrust into space.

Critical, and determined to beat the United States to Alpha Centauri, an enemy nation resorts to sabotage. Sneaking aboard the Jupiter II, Colonel Zachary Smith reprograms the environmental control robot to destroy the ship eight hours after take-off.

As countdown preparations continue, the Robinson family, representing a unique balance of scientific advancement, emotional stability, and pioneer resourcefulness, board the craft. Entering the freezing chambers, where they are to spend the five-and-a-half-year voyage frozen in the state of suspended animation, systems are activated and all hatches are secured— trapping Smith inside the ship.

The Jupiter II is launched. Penetrating a meteor shower, the craft, unable to escape because of Smith's extra weight, is damaged. Entering the freezing chambers, Smith releases the pilot, geologist Major Donald West. Unaware that Smith is an enemy, West revives the Robinsons—John, an astrophysicist; his wife, Maureen, a biochemist; and their children, Judy, Penny, and Will.

With blast-off time nearing eight hours, Smith attempts, but fails to reprogram the robot. Its rampage is stopped, but only after it seriously damages the ship. Completely thrown off course, and unable to maintain orbit, the ship crash lands on an unknown planet, which becomes a temporary home and enables them to repair the ship.

Stories depict their struggle for survival and John Robinson's attempts to continue with the original goal and find Alpha Sentori despite Smith's endless attempts to thwart his efforts and return to Earth.

CAST

John Robinson	Guy Williams
Maureen Robinson	June Lockhart
Donald West	Mark Goddard
Zachary Smith	Jonathan Harris
Judy Robinson	Marta Kristen
Penny Robinson	Angela Cartwright
Will Robinson	Billy Mumy
The Robot	Bob May

Music: Johnny Williams; Lionel Newman; Herman Stein.

Additional Music: Gerald Fried, Alexander Courage.

Creator-Producer: Irwin Allen.

Director: Dick Moder, Sobey Martin, Don Richardson, Harry Harris, Ezra Stone, Jerry Juran, Justis Addiss, Robert Douglas, Seymour Robbie, Irving Moore, Sutton Roley.

LOST IN SPACE—60 minutes—CBS— September 15, 1965 - September 11, 1968. 83 episodes. Syndicated.

THE LOST SAUCER

Comedy. Exploring the universe, androids Fi and Fum, from the planet ZR-3 in the year 2369, penetrate a time wrap and land on present-day Earth. Anxious to make friends, they invite two Earthlings, a young boy, Jerry, and his babysitter, Alice, aboard their space ship (shaped like a flying saucer). Suddenly, as curious people begin to crowd around the alien craft, Fum becomes scared and activates the launch mechanism, sending the ship back into space where they become lost in time. Stories concern their adventures on strange, futuristic worlds and Fi and Fum's attempts to return their unwitting passengers to Earth in the year 1975.

CAST

Fi	Ruth Buzzi
Fum	Jim Nabors
Alice	Alice Playten
Jerry	Jarrod Johnson
The Dorse, Fi and Fum's pet (half horse, half dog)	Larry Larson

Music: Michael Lloyd.

Producer: Sid and Marty Krofft.

Director: Jack Regas, Dick Darley.

THE LOST SAUCER—30 minutes— ABC—September 6, 1975 - September 4, 1976.

LOTSA LUCK

Comedy. Background: Brooklyn, New York. The trials and tribulations of Stanley Belmont, a clerk in the Lost and Found Department of the New York City Bus Lines (N.Y.B.L.). Thirty-eight and single, he is the mainstay of an aggravating family—a loving but fretful mother, Iris Belmont, widow; an obnoxious, unkempt, and unemployed brother-in-law, Arthur Swann, his constant source of nervous tension; and a cry-baby sister, Arthur's wife, Olive Swann. Based on the London television series "On the Buses."

CAST

Stanley Belmont	Dom DeLuise
Iris Belmont	Kathleen Freeman
Arthur Swann	Wynn Irwin
Olive Swann	Beverly Sanders
Bummy Fitzer, their neighbor, a bus driver on the Q-5 route	Jack Knight

Music: Jack Elliott, Allyn Ferguson.

LOTSA LUCK—30 minutes—NBC— September 10, 1973 - May 24, 1974.

LOU GRANT

Drama. Background: Los Angeles, California. The experiences of Lou Grant, city editor of the *Los Angeles Tribune,* the second largest newspaper in the city. Can be considered a spin-off from "The Mary Tyler Moore Show" in so much as the title character evolved from said program. Following his dismissal from the Minneapolis TV station at which he worked, Lou relocates to L.A. where, after looking up an old newspaper friend, he acquires the job of city editor. (Originally, the paper had been called the *City Tribune.*)

CAST

Lou Grant	Edward Asner
Charlie Hume, the managing editor	Mason Adams
Margaret Pynchon, the publisher	Nancy Marchand
Carla Mardigian, a reporter	Rebecca Balding
Joe Rossi, a reporter	Robert Walden
"Animal," a reporter-photographer	Daryl Anderson
Art Donovan, Lou's assistant	Jack Bannon

Margaret's dog: Barney.

Music: Patrick Williams.

Executive Producer-Creator: Allan Burns, James L. Brooks, Gene Reynolds.

Lost in Space. Left to right: Angela Cartwright, Mark Goddard, Marta Kristen, the Robot, Jonathan Harris, June Lockhart, Guy Williams (behind June), and Billy Mumy.

Producer: Gene Reynolds.

Director: Richard Crenna, Jackie Cooper, Gene Reynolds, Charles S. Dubin.

LOU GRANT—60 minutes—CBS— Premiered: September 20, 1977.

LOVE, AMERICAN STYLE

Anthology. Comedy vignettes tackling the world's oldest subject, love. Segments are interspersed with blackouts.

Blackout Segment Regulars: Tracey Reed, James Hampton, Buzz Cooper, Mary Grover, Stuart Margolin, Bill Callaway, Barbara Minkus, Lynne Marta, Bernie Kopell, Phyllis Elizabeth Davis, Jaki DeMar, Richard Williams.

Music: Charles Fox.

Executive Producer: Ray Allen, Harvey Bullock, Jim Parker, Arnold Margolin.

Producer: Bill Idelson, Harvey Miller, Bruce Bilson, Alan Rafkin, William P. D'Angelo, Charles B. Fitzsimmons, Stuart Margolin, Donald Boyle.

Director: Bruce Bilson, Arnold Margolin, Howard Morris, Ken Johnson, William F. Claxton, Leslie Martinson, Jack Arnold, Richard Michaels, Charles R. Rondeau, Coby Ruskin, Oscar Rudolph, Allen Baron, Herbert Kenwith, Gary Nelson, Harry Harris, Jerry London, Sam Strangis, Frank Buxton.

Included:

Love And The Legal Agreement. The complications that ensue when a husband and wife agree to separate—but to continue living in the same house.

CAST

Louise: Connie Stevens; Darien: Bill Bixby.

Love And The Happy Days. A nostalgic backward glance at life in the 1950s. The pilot film for the series "Happy Days."

CAST

Richard Cunningham: Ron Howard; Potsie Weber: Anson Williams.

Love And The Girlish Groom. A girl struggles to hide the fact of her marriage to a female impersonator from her parents.

CAST

Marie Wilson, Kristina Holland, Peter Kastner, Vincent Gardenia.

Love And The Practical Joker. A man struggles to end his irritating habit of playing practical jokes to win the heart of the girl he loves.

CAST

Vera Evans: E.J. Peaker; Bill: Larry Storch.

LOVE, AMERICAN STYLE—60 and 30 minute versions—ABC—September 22, 1969 - January 11, 1974. Daytime rebroadcasts: ABC—30 minutes—June 28, 1971 - May 3, 1974. 65 programs.

LOVE AND MARRIAGE

Comedy. Background: The Harris Music Publishing Company in Los Angeles, California. The story of Bill Harris, widower, the owner of the bankrupt Tin Pan Alley firm; and his married daughter, Pat Baker, who, by acquiring Rock and Roll songs and personalities, struggles to save the family business.

CAST

Bill Harris	William Demarest
Pat Baker	Jeanne Bal
Steve Baker, her husband, an attorney	Murray Hamilton
Susan Baker, their daughter	Susan Reilly
Jenny Baker, their daughter	Jeannie Lynn
Stubby Wilson, the firm's song plugger	Stubby Kaye
Sophie, the firm secretary	Kay Armen

Music (Scored and conducted, as credited): MSI.

LOVE AND MARRIAGE—30 minutes—NBC—September 21, 1959 - January 25, 1960. 26 episodes.

THE LOVE BOAT

Comedy. Setting: The luxury liner *Pacific Princess,* nicknamed the Love Boat by her crew. Basically, a series of vignettes about floundering romances that occur during the ship's cruises.

CAST

Captain Merrill Stubing	Gavin MacLeod
Julie McCoy, the cruise director	Lauren Tewes
Dr. Adam Bricker, the ship's physician	Bernie Kopell
Burl "Gopher" Smith, the Yeoman Purser	Fred Grandy
Isaac Washington, the bartender	Ted Lange

Music: Charles Fox, Artie Kane, George Tipton.

Theme Vocal, "The Love Boat": Jack Jones.

Executive Producer: Aaron Spelling, Douglas S. Cramer.

Producer: Henry Colman, Gordon Farr, Lynne Farr.

Director: Richard Kinon, Stuart Margolin, Alan Rafkin.

THE LOVE BOAT—60 minutes— ABC—Premiered: September 24, 1977. Pilot aired May 5, 1977.

LOVE IS A MANY SPLENDORED THING

Serial. Background: San Francisco, California. The dramatic story of three families: The Chernaks, the Donnellys, and the Garrisons. Episodes depict the struggles of young people; and the problems of interracial love and marriage.

CAST

Betsy Chernak	Andrea Marcovicci
Mark Elliott	David Birney
	Michael Hawkins
	Vincent Cannon
	Tom Fuccello
Laura Elliott	Donna Mills
	Veleka Gray
	Barbara Stanger
Iris Garrison	Leslie Charleson
	Bibi Besch
Sara Hanley	Sasha Van Scherler
	Martha Greenhouse
Dr. Peter Chernak	Vincent Baggaetta
Ricky Donnelly	Shawn Campbell
Lily Chernak	Diana Douglas
Senator Al Preston	Don Gantry
Helen Donnelly	Gloria Hoye
Celia	Abagail Kellogg
Will Donnelly	Judson Laire
Doug Preston	Sean Lindsey
Spence Garrison	Edward Power
Joe Taylor	Leon Russom
Angel Chernak	Suzie Kay Stone
Tom Donnelly	Albert Stratton
Marion Hiller	Constance Towers
Mrs. Taylor	Betty Miller
Nichole Chernak	Andrea Grossman
Dr. Hiller	Stephen Joyce
	Peter White
Maria	Judy Safran
Dr. Chernak	Michael Glaser
Andy Hurley	Russ Thacker
Rusty Jackson	Greg Brown
Judd Washington	Thurman Scott
Rocco Fiore	Carmine Stipo
Jean	Jane Manning
Audrey Hurley	Salome Jens
Tommy Hale	Christopher Papes
Dr. Ellis	Robert Drew
Roger	David Jay
Mia	Nancy Hsuek

Amos Crump	Jack Somack
Donna Patrick (early episodes)	Barbara Stanger

Announcer: Lee Jordan.

Music: Eddie Layton.

LOVE IS A MANY SPLENDORED THING—30 minutes—CBS—September 18, 1967 - March 23, 1973.

LOVE OF LIFE

Serial. Original story line, 1951-1961. Background: The town of Barrowsville, Anywhere, U.S.A. The dramatic story of two sisters, Vanessa Dale and Meg Dale Harper. Episodes contrast their lifestyles and moral outlooks.

Revised story line, 1961-Present. Background: Rosehill, New York. Dramatic incidents in the lives of marrieds Vanessa and Bruce Sterling.

CAST

Vanessa Dale Sterling	Peggy McCay
	Bonnie Bartlett
	Audrey Peters
Meg Dale Harper	Jean McBride
	Tudi Wiggins
Bruce Sterling	Ron Tomme
Charles Harper	Paul Potter
Beanie Harper	Dennis Parnell
	Christopher Reeves
Paul Raven	Richard Coogan
	Robert Burr
Ellie Hughes	Hildy Parks
Mrs. Rivers	Marie Kennery
Bill Prentiss	Gene Bua
Judith Cole	Marsha Mason
	Virginia Robinson
Sandy Porter	Bonnie Bedelea
Arden Dellacorte	Geraldine Brooks
Candy Lowe	Susan Hubly
	Nancy MacKay
Dr. Leader	Shelley Blanc
Stacy Corby	Cindy Grover
Sarah Dale	Jane Rose
	Joanna Roos
Alex Caldwell	Charles White
Barbara Latimer	Zina Bethune
Hank Latimer	David Stambaugh
Vivian Carlson	Helen Dumas
Henry Carlson	Jack Stamberger
Diana Lamont	Diane Rousseau
Tess Krakauer	Toni Bull Bua
Jamie Rollins	Ray Wise
Sally Rollins	Catherine Bacon
Dan Phillips	Drew Snyder
Kate Swanson	Sally Stark
Link Morrison	John Gabriel
Jeannette DuBois	Loretta Allen
Todd	Rod Gibbons
Josh Bendarik	Brian Brownlee
Helen Hunt	Polly Rowles
Mrs. Swanson	Jane Hoffman
Gerry Brayley	Julia Duffy
Dr. Joseph Corelli	Tony LoBianco
	Michael Glaser
Jason Ferris	Robert Alda
John Prentiss	John O'Hare
	Andrew Tolan
	Trip Randall
Mrs. Bendarik	Lois Smith
Mr. Bendarik	Edward Grover
Link Porter	Gene Pellegrini
Tammy Porter	Ann Loring
Baby Johnny	Oren Jay
	Raymond Cass
Miguel	Raul Julia
Josh	Rick Losey
Baby Debbie	Mary Elizabeth Haring
Charles Lamont	John W. Moore
	Stan Watt
Atan Sterling	Dennis Cooney
Rick Latimer	Jerry Lacy
	Edward Moore
	Paul Savior
Mrs. Phillips	Nancy Marchand
	Beatrice Straight
Beatrice Swanson	Jane Hoffman
Jeff Hart	Charles Baxter
Caroline Aleata	Deborah Courtney
	Roxanne Gregory
Betsy Crawford	Elizabeth Kemp
Paul Waterman	Michael Fairman
Howie Howells	Ed Crowley
Dr. Ted Chandler	Keith Charles
David Hart	Brian Farrell
Mrs. Porter	Joan Copeland
Evans Baker	Ronald Long
Sharon Ferris	Eileen Letchworth
	Margo Flax
John Randolph	Byron Sanders
Tom Craythorne	Lauren Gilbert
Link Morrison	John Gabriel
Sarah Sprague	Zoe Connell
Julie Morano	Jessica Walter
Bob Mackey	Richard Cox
Walter Morgan	Richard McKensie
Phil Waterman	Michael Fairman
Jack Andrews	Donald Symington
Sally Bridgeman	Cathy Bacon
Clair Bridgeman	Renee Rory
Richard Rollins	Larry Weber
Dr. Kreisinger	Leon B. Stevens
Will Dale	Ed Jerome
Hal Craig	Steven Gethers
Ben Harper	Chris Reeve
	Chandeler Hill Harben
Ian Russell	Michael Allinson
Boby Mackay	Richard Cox
Betty Harper	Elizabeth Kemp
Edouard Aleata	John Aniston
Carrie Lovell	Peg Murray
Linda Crawford	Romola Robb Allrud
James Crawford	Kenneth McMillan
David Hart	Brian Farrell
Hank Latimer	David Stambough
	David Carlton
Felicia Fleming	Pamela Lincoln
Vivian Carlson	Helene Dumas
Henry Carlson	Jack Stamberger
Mia Marriott	Veleka Gray
Andrew Marriott	Richard Higgs
Will Dale	Ed Jerome
Sarah Dale	Jane Rose
Dr. Joe Cusack	Peter Brouwer

Also: Carl Betz, Jan Miner, David Ford, Carl Low, Clarice Blackburn, Conrad Fowkes, Alfred Markim, Joe Allen, Jr.

Narrator: Charles Mountain.

Announcer: Don Hancock; Ken Roberts.

Organist: John Gart.

Music: Carey Gold

LOVE OF LIFE—15 and 30 minute versions—CBS—Premiered: September 9, 1951.

LOVE ON A ROOFTOP

Comedy. Background: 1400 McDoogal Street, San Francisco, California, the residence (a rooftop apartment) of Dave Willis, an apprentice architect earning $85.37 a week; and his wife, Julie, an art student, the daughter of a wealthy car salesman who relinquished her world of luxury for Dave.

Stories depict: The struggles of young marrieds; and Dave's attempts to prove to Fred Hammond, Julie's father (bitter over his daughter's brashness and Dave's inability to properly support her), that he is capable of providing a decent life for Julie.

CAST

Julie Willis	Judy Carne
Dave Willis	Peter Deuel
Stan Parker, their friend and neighbor	Rich Little
Carol Parker, his wife	Barbara Bostock
Fred Hammond	Herbert Voland
Phyllis Hammond, Fred's wife	Edith Atwater

Music: Warren Barker.

LOVE ON A ROOFTOP—30 minutes—ABC—September 6, 1966 - January 6, 1967. Rebroadcasts: ABC—May 19, 1971 - August 8, 1971. 30 episodes.

LOVERS AND FRIENDS

Serial. Background: The town of Point Clare, a Chicago Suburb. The dramatic story of two families: the affluent Cushings; and their middle-class neighbors, the Saxtons.

CAST

Peter Cushing	Ron Rondell
Edith Cushing	Nancy Marchand
Eleanor Kimball	Flora Plumb
Connie Ferguson	Susan Foster
Megan Cushing	Patricia Estrin
Barbara Manners	Karen Phillipp

Love on a Rooftop. Left to right: Herb Voland, Judy Carne, Peter Deuel, Edith Atwater. © *Screen Gems.*

Amy Gifford   Christine Jones
Marlow   Daniel Heyes
Josie Saxton   Patricia Englund
Rhett Saxton   Bob Purvey
                           David Ramsey
George Kimball   Stephen Joyce
Jason Saxton   Richard Backus
Amy Gifford   Christine Jones
Sophia Slocum   Margaret Barker
Tessa Saxton   Vicki Dawson
Austin Cushing   Rob Arrants
Lester Saxton   John Heffernan
Bentley Saxton   David Abbott
Laurie Brewster   Dianne Harper

Music: Score Productions.

Executive Producer: Paul Rauch.

Producer: John Wendell, Harriet Goldstein.

Director: Peter Levin.

Creator: Harding Lemay.

LOVERS AND FRIENDS—30 minutes—NBC—January 3, 1977 - May 6, 1977.

LOVES ME, LOVES ME NOT

Comedy. Background: California. The romantic escapades of Jane Benson, a pretty, but undecisive grammar school teacher; and Dick Phillips, a klutz newspaper reporter—people who meet, fall in love, and struggle to make it through the travails of a latter 1970s romance.

CAST

Jane Benson   Susan Dey
Dick Phillips   Kenneth Gilman
Tom, Dick's
    friend   Art Metrano
Sue, Jane's
    friend   Udana Power
                       Phyllis Glick

Music: George Tipton.

Music Supervision: Lionel Newman.

Executive Producer: Paul Junger Witt, Tony Thomas.

Producer: Susan Harris, Ernest Losso.

Director: Jay Sandrich, Richard Kinon, Noam Pitlik.

LOVES ME, LOVES ME NOT—30 minutes—CBS—March 20, 1977 - April 27, 1977. 6 episodes.

LOVE STORY

Anthology. Dramas emphasizing the goodness in nature and the kindness in man.

Included:

Norma Loves Mike. The story of a newlywed couple's first fight.

CAST

Betty Lou Holland, Penny Fiske, Rusty Lane.

Timmy. A couple attempt to end their son's constant habit of running away from home.

CAST

James Gregory.

The Matchmaker. A lady matchmaker attempts to find a bride for a middle-aged sea captain.

CAST

Murray Mathieson.

Wedding Dress. Preparing a wedding gown for a client, a spinster seamstress envisions her own wedding.

CAST

Patricia Collinge, Paul McGrath.

LOVE STORY—30 minutes—DuMont 1954.

LOVE STORY

Interview-Quiz. Married or engaged couples are first interviewed, then, after relating personal experiences, they compete in a general-knowledge question-answer session wherein the highest scoring couple (most correct answers) receive an expense-paid two-week honeymoon in Paris.

Host: Jack Smith.

Assistant: Pat Meckle.

LOVE STORY—30 minutes—CBS—1955 - 1956.

LOVE STORY

Anthology. Adult and contemporary variations on the theme of love.

Music: Peter Matz; David Shire.

Theme: Francis Lai.

Included:

Love Came Laughing. The tender affair between a lonely young man and a pregnant girl.

CAST

Gary Stone: Michael Brandon; Alice Hartman: Bonnie Bedelia; Marge Stone: Eileen Hackett.

The Roller Coaster Stops Here. The affair between a married man and a nonconformist girl.

CAST

Neil Kaplan: Don Murray; Farrell Edwards: Barbara Seagull; Elaine Kaplan: Louise Lasser.

Beginners Luck. A college girl struggles to discover the difference between true love and sexual attraction.

CAST

Leonie: Janet Leigh; Barbara: Jan Smither; Scott: Kurt Russell; Mr. Jones: William Schallert.

Mirabelle's Summer. The story of a woman caught between her love for her energetic fiancé and her increasing attachment to a man crippled in an accident.

CAST

Mirabelle Terhune: Pamela Franklin; David Ross: David Huffman; Frank Randolph: Martin Sheen.

LOVE STORY—60 minutes—NBC—October 3, 1973 - January 2, 1974.

LOVE THAT BOB

Comedy. Background: Hollywood, California. The romantic misadventures of Bob Collins, a suave and sophisticated bachelor-photographer.

CAST

Bob Collins	Bob Cummings
Margaret MacDonald, his widowed sister	Rosemary DeCamp
Chuck MacDonald, her son	Dwayne Hickman
Charmaine Schultz ("Schultzy"), Bob's secretary-assistant	Ann B. Davis
Harvey Helm, Bob's friend	King Donovan
Ruth Helm, Harvey's wife	Mary Lawrence
Shirley Swanson, the beautiful blonde model determined to marry Bob	Joi Lansing
Paul Fonda, Margaret's romantic interest	Lyle Talbot
Francine Williams, Chuck's girlfriend	Diane Jergens
Joe DePew, Chuck's friend	Robert Ellis
Jimmy Lloyd, Chuck's friend	Jeff Silver
Pamela Livingston, Bob's friend, a bird-watcher	Nancy Kulp
Frank Crenshaw, Schultzy's friend	Dick Wesson
Josh Collins (Grandpa), Bob's father, a semi-retired photographer	Bob Cummings

The Models: Tammy Marihugh, Donna Foster, Gloria Marshall, Julie Bennett, Penny Edwards, Jean Moorhead, Katherine Hughes, Barbara Wilson, Lisa Davis, Carole Conn, Shirley Boone, Carole Le Vegue, Jeanne Vaughn, Jan Harrison, June Kirby, Leigh Snowden, Patricia Blake, Jeanne Evans, Patricia Murlin, Gloria Robertson, Valerie Allen, Kathy Marlowe, Elaine Edwards, Rose Beaumont, Sylvia Lewis, Marjorie Tenny, Gloria Marshall, Suzanne Alexander, Barbara Long.

Also: Rose Marie.

Announcer: Bill Baldwin.

Music: Gene LeGrande, Mahlon Merrick.

LOVE THAT BOB—30 minutes. NBC—January 2, 1954 - September 28, 1955; CBS—October 5, 1955 - June 1957; NBC—September 22, 1957 - July 14, 1959; ABC—October 12, 1959 - December 1, 1961. 173 episodes. Syndicated.

LOVE THAT JILL

Comedy. Background: New York City. The story of Jill Johnson and Jack Gibson, the rival heads of all-female modeling agencies. Through account snaring and publicity and model stealing, their individual attempts to become the number one agency in Manhattan leads to an unforeseen love that neither is willing to admit or give into under the normal circumstances. Business matters aside, each devises elaborate schemes to acquire the other's company.

CAST

Jill Johnson	Anne Jeffreys
Jack Gibson	Robert Sterling
Pearl, Jack's secretary	Betty Lynn
Richard, Jill's secretary	Jimmy Lydon
Monte, a friend	Henry Kulky
Peaches, Jill's model	Kay Elhardt
Ginger, Jill's top model	Barbara Nichols

LOVE THAT JILL—30 minutes—ABC—January 20, 1958 - April 28, 1958. 13 episodes.

LOVE THY NEIGHBOR

Comedy. Background: The Sherwood Forest Estates in San Fernando, California. Residing at 327 North Robin Hood Road are the Wilsons—Charlie, a shop steward at Turner Electronics, and his wife Peggy—a middle class white couple. Living next door are the Bruces—Ferguson, the efficiency expert at Turner Electronics, and his wife Jackie—a black couple who made the radical move into a white neighborhood. Dramatizing racial prejudices, stories depict the attempts of neighbors to adjust to each other. Based on the British series of the same title.

CAST

Peggy Wilson	Joyce Bulifant
Charlie Wilson	Ron Masak
Jackie Bruce	Janet MacLachlan
Ferguson Bruce	Harrison Page
Murray Bronson, a factory employee	Milt Kamen
Harry Mulligan, a factory employee	Herbie Faye
Louie Gordon, a factory employee	Louis Gus

Music: Pete Rugolo.

Theme lyric: Arthur Julian; vocal: Soloman Burke.

LOVE THY NEIGHBOR—30 minutes—ABC—June 15, 1973 - September 19, 1973. 12 episodes.

British Version: "Love Thy Neighbour." Background: London, England. Basically the same format as the American version: the story of a white couple, Eddie and Joan, and their neighbors, Bill and Barbie, a black couple who move into a white neighbourhood.

Cast: Eddie: Jack Smethurst; Joan: Kate Williams; Bill: Rudolph Walker; Barbie: Nina Baden-Semper.

Producer-Director: Stuart Allen.

LUCAN

Drama. While stalking game in Northern Minnesota during the summer of 1967, a group of hunters stumble across a strange creature—a ten-year-old boy who eats, sleeps, howls, and hunts like a wolf. Captured by scientists and named Lucan, all attempts to discover how he came to be there or whom his parents were fail. Brought to a research center and taught the ways of modern man, the boy survives and adapts. Now, ten years later, educated and free, he roams the country searching for his natural parents. His adventures, as he seeks his quest—helping people he finds in distress along the way—are dramatized.

Starring: Kevin Brophy as Lucan.

Music: Fred Karlin.

Executive Producer: Barry Lowen.

Producer: Harold Gast.

Creator: Michael Zagar.

LUCAN—60 minutes—ABC—Premiered: September 12, 1977. Broadcast on an irregular basis throughout the 1977-1978 season.

LUCAS TANNER

Drama. Background: Harry S. Truman Memorial High School in Webster Groves, Missouri. A realistic portrayal of student-teacher relationships and problems as seen through the eyes of Lucas Tanner, widower, English teacher.

CAST

Lucas Tanner	David Hartman
Margaret Blumenthal, the principal	Rosemary Murphy
Glendon Farrell, Tanner's young friend, his neighbor	Robbie Rist
Jaytee Druman, the school disc jockey	Alan Abelew
Cindy Damin, a student	Trish Soodik
Terry, a student	Kimberly Beck
Wally, a student	Michael Dwight-Smith
John Hamilton, the principal (later episodes)	John Randolph

Tanner's dog: Bridget (originally: O'Casey).

Music: David Shire.

Executive Producer: David Victor.

Producer: Charles S. Dubin, Jay Benson.

Director: Jay Benson, Alexander Singer, Leo Penn.

LUCAS TANNER—60 minutes—NBC —September 11, 1974 - August 20, 1975. 24 episodes.

THE LUCI-DESI COMEDY HOUR

See title: "I Love Lucy."

THE LUCILLE BALL-DESI ARNAZ SHOW

See title: "I Love Lucy."

LUCKY LETTERS

Game. The object is for contestants to unscramble words from clues given through musical, visual means, or by verse.

Host: Frankie Masters.

Regulars: Phyllis Myles and the West Twins.

LUCKY LETTERS—30 minutes—NBC 1950.

LUCKY PARTNERS

Game. Two competing contestants. Players and studio-audience members are each handed a sheet of paper with the word L U C K Y spelled on one side. Stage players, who possess their own dollar bills, write the last five digits of one bill under the letters of L U C K Y. The studio audience members who match the stage players join them and compete for merchandise prizes via general-knowledge question-and-answer rounds. Winners are the players who answer the most questions correctly.

Host: Carl Cordell.

LUCKY PARTNERS—30 minutes— NBC—June 30, 1958 - August 22, 1958.

LUCKY PUP

Children. Background: Toyland. The series focuses on the lighthearted misadventures that befall the members (puppet characters) of the Kindness Club.

Hostess: Doris Brown.

Puppet Characters and Voices: Hope and Morey Bunin.

Producer: Lloyd Gross, Clarence Schimmel.

LUCKY PUP—15 minutes—CBS 1949; 15 minutes—NBC 1950.

THE LUCKY STRIKE THEATRE

See title: "Robert Montgomery Presents."

LUCY IN CONNECTICUT

See title: "I Love Lucy."

THE LUCY SHOW

Comedy. Distinguished by two formats.

Format One—October 1, 1961 - June 1965.

Background: 132 Post Road, Danfield, Connecticut, the residence of Lucy Carmichael, widow, and mother of two children, Chris and Jerry; and her boarders, Vivian

The Lucy Show. Left to right: Ralph Hart, Vivian Vance, Lucille Ball, Jimmy Garrett, Candy Moore.

Bagley, a divorcée, and her son, Sherman. The story of two women, Lucy and Viv, and their harebrained attempts to acquire money.

CAST

Lucy Carmichael	Lucille Ball
Vivian Bagley	Vivian Vance
Theodore J. Mooney, the president of the Danfield First National Bank	Gale Gordon
Chris Carmichael	Candy Moore
Jerry Carmichael	Jimmy Garrett
Sherman Bagley	Ralph Hart
Mr. Barnsdahl, the bank president (before Mooney)	Charles Lane
Harry, Lucy's friend	Dick Martin

Music: Wilbur Hatch.

Format Two—September 13, 1965 - September 16, 1968.

Background: 708 Gower Street, San Francisco, California, the residence of Lucy Carmichael, secretary to Theodore J. Mooney, Vice President of the Westland Bank. Stories depict the trials and tribulations of a banker plagued by the antics of his scatterbrained secretary.

CAST

Lucy Carmichael	Lucille Ball
Theodore J. Mooney	Gale Gordon
Mary Jane Lewis, Lucy's friend, a secretary employed at Mammoth Studios	Mary Jane Croft
Harrison Cheever, the president of the bank	Roy Roberts

Music: Wilbur Hatch.

THE LUCY SHOW—30 minutes—CBS —October 1, 1961 - September 16, 1968. 198 episodes. Syndicated.

LUM AND ABNER

Comedy. Background: The Jot 'Em Down General Store in Pine Ridge, Arkansas. The misadventures of its owner-operators Lum Edwards and Abner Peabody.

CAST
Lum Edwards   Chester Lauck
Abner Peabody   Norris Goff

Announcer: Wendell Niles.

Orchestra: Opie Cates.

LUM AND ABNER—30 minutes—CBS 1949. Based on the radio program of the same title.

THE LUX VIDEO THEATRE

Anthology. Dramatic presentations. Based on its predecessor, "The Lux Radio Theatre."

Hosts: Ken Carpenter; Otto Kruger; James Mason; Gordon MacRae.

Music: Milton Weinstein.

Producer: Calvin Kuhl.

Director: Frederick Cook, Fielder Cour.

Sponsor: Lever Brothers.

Included:

One Foot In Heaven. The problems and responsibilities facing a minister in a small town.

Starring: Paul Kelly.

The Browning Version. The affair between the wife of a professor in a boys school and a young faculty member.

CAST
Andrew Crooker: Herbert Marshall; Mrs. Harris: Judith Evelyn: Taplow: Christopher Cook.

An Act Of Murder. After his wife is told that she has only a short time to live, a judge struggles to make her last days happy.

CAST
Cathy Cook: Ann Harding; Judge Cook: Thomas Mitchell.

THE LUX VIDEO THEATRE—30 minutes—NBC—1951 - 1954; 60 minutes—NBC—August 27, 1954 - September 12, 1957.

ℳ

McCLOUD

See title: "Four-In-One," *McCloud* segment.

McCOY

See title: "NBC Sunday Mystery Movie," *McCoy* segment.

MAC DAVIS

Listed: The television programs of singer-composer Mac Davis.

The Mac Davis Show—Musical Variety—60 minutes—NBC—July 11, 1974 - August 29, 1974.

Host: Mac Davis.

Orchestra: George Wyle.

Additional Orchestration: Sid Feller.

The Mac Davis Show—Musical Variety—60 minutes—NBC—December 19, 1974 - May 22, 1975.

Host: Mac Davis.

Regulars: Kay Dingle, Bo Koprel, The Tony Modente Dancers.

Orchestra: Mike Post.

Special Musical Material: Billy Barnes, Earl Brown.

The Mac Davis Show—Musical Variety—60 minutes—NBC—March 18, 1976 - June 17, 1976.

Host: Mac Davis.

Regulars: Shields and Yarnell, The Strutts, Ron Silver.

Orchestra: Tom Bahler, Mike Post.

Choreographer: Jim Bates.

Executive Producer: Gary Smith, Dwight Hemion.

Producer: Mike Post, Steve Binder, Nancy Henson.

Director: Steve Binder, Jim Cox.

McDUFF, THE TALKING DOG

Comedy. Background: The town of Peach Blossom. The comic misadventures of Calvin Campbell, a young, trouble-prone veterinarian. His escapades are helped and hindered by McDuff, the ghost of a sheep dog who appears and speaks only to him.

CAST
Dr. Calvin Campbell   Walter Willson

Amos Ferguson, his
  neighbor   Gordon Jump
Squeaky, Amos's
  nephew   Johnnie Collins III
Mrs. Osgood, Calvin's
  housekeeper   Monty Margetts
Kimmy Campbell, Calvin's
  sister   Michelle Stacy
McDuff's Voice   Jack Lester

Music: Richard LaSalle.

Executive Producer: William P. D'Angelo, Ray Allen, Harvey Bullock.

Producer: Victor Paul.

Director: Gordon Wiles, James Sheldon, William P. D'Angelo.

McDUFF, THE TALKING DOG—30 minutes—NBC—September 11, 1976 - November 20, 1976.

McHALE'S NAVY

Comedy. Distinguished by two formats.

Format One: September 11, 1962 - September 7, 1965.
  Background: The South Pacific; the island of Taratupa during World War II. The bickering relationship between Lieutenant Quinton McHale, the commander of Squadron 19 and P.T. Boat 73; and Captain Wallace B. Binghamton, the commanding officer who feels that his life is plagued by McHale and his crew of pirates who have turned the island into "the Las Vegas of the Pacific."
  Determined to enjoy the serenity the war provides from his nagging wife, Binghamton endlessly—but fruitlessly—schemes to expose McHale's illegal gambling activities, which he hopes will lead to a court-martial and transfer.

Format Two: September 14, 1965 - August 30, 1966.
  Background: Voltafiore, a small town in Southern Italy, 1944, where McHale, his Squadron 19, and Captain Binghamton are transferred to assist in the European theatre of war. Stories follow the previous format: Binghamton's determined efforts to rid his life of McHale.

CAST
Lt. Cdr. Quinton
  McHale   Ernest Borgnine
Captain Wallace B.
  Binghamton ("Old Lead
  Bottom")   Joe Flynn

McHale's Crew (8):

Ensign Charles Parker	Tim Conway
Seaman Lester Gruber	Carl Ballantine
Seaman Harrison "Tinker" Bell	Billy Sands
Seaman Willy Moss	John Wright
Seaman Happy Haines	Gavin MacLeod
Seaman Virgil Farrell	Edson Stroll
Quarter Master Christopher	Gary Vinson
Fuji Kobiaji, an unreported prisoner of war captured by McHale; now their chief cook and bottle washer	Yoshio Yoda
Lt. Elroy Carpenter, Binghamton's aide	Bob Hastings
Molly Turner, the chief nurse (format 1)	Jane Dulo
Admiral Bruce Rogers (format 1)	Roy Roberts
Admiral Benson (format 1)	Bill Quinn
Chief Tali Urulu, the native chief, a witch doctor and con-artist (format 1)	Jacques Aubuchon
Colonel Harrington (format 2)	Henry Beckman
General Bronson (format 2)	Simon Scott
Mario Lugatto, the mayor of Voltafiore (format 2)	Jay Novello
Dino, the mayor's aide (format 2)	Dick Wilson
Mama Rosa Giovanni, the restaurant owner (format 2)	Peggy Mondo
Lt. Gloria Winters, Christopher's girl-friend, then wife (format 2)	Cindy Robbins

Music: Axel Stordahl.

Producer: Edward J. Montagne.

Note: Seaman Virgil Farrell is also known as Virgil Edwards; and Col. Harrington is also known as Col. Harrigan.

McHALE'S NAVY–30 minutes–ABC–September 11, 1962 - August 30, 1966. 138 episodes. Syndicated.

MACK AND MYER FOR HIRE

Comedy. The misadventures of Mack and Myer, bumbling craftsmen struggling to succeed in the business world.

CAST

Mack	Mickey Deems
Myer	Joey Faye

MACK AND MYER FOR HIRE–15 minutes–Syndicated 1963. 200 episodes.

McKEEVER AND THE COLONEL

Comedy. Background: The Westfield Military Academy for boys. Stories depict the antics of Gary McKeever, a mischievous cadet; and the attempts of Harvey Blackwell, the school's commander, to discipline the boy.

CAST

Colonel Harvey Blackwell	Allyn Joslyn
Cadet Gary McKeever	Scott Lane
Sergeant Barnes, the Colonel's aide	Jackie Coogan
Miss Warner, the school dietician	Elizabeth Fraser
Tubby, a cadet	Keith Taylor
Monk, a cadet	Johnny Eimen

McKEEVER AND THE COLONEL–30 minutes–ABC–September 23, 1962–September 1963. 26 episodes. Syndicated.

MacKENZIE'S RAIDERS

Western. Background: Texas, 1870s. Organizing a small group of raiders, Colonel Ranald S. MacKenzie, an undercover agent with the U.S. Fourth Cavalry, attempts to end the reign of terror begun by marauding Mexican renegades.

CAST

Col. Ranald S. MacKenzie	Richard Carlson

The Raiders: Louis Jean Heydt, Morris Ankrum, Brett King, Jim Bridges, Charles Boax, Kenneth Alton.

MacKENZIE'S RAIDERS–30 minutes–Syndicated 1958. 39 episodes.

THE McLEAN STEVENSON SHOW

Comedy. Background: Evanston, Illinois. The misadventures of Mac Ferguson, a hardware store owner, as he struggles to cope with life, both at work and at home.

CAST

Mac Ferguson	McLean Stevenson
Peggy Ferguson, his wife	Barbara Stuart
Janet, their divorced daughter	Ayn Ruymen
Chris Ferguson, their son	Steve Nevil
Muriel, Peggy's mother	Madge West
David, Janet's son	David Hollander
Jason, Janet's son	Jason Whitney

Music: Paul Williams.

Executive Producer: Monty Hall.

Producer: Arnold Margolin, Don Van Atta.

Director: Alan Myerson, Bill Hobin.

THE McLEAN STEVENSON SHOW –30 minutes–NBC–December 1, 1976 - March 9, 1977.

McMILLAN

See title: "NBC Sunday Mystery Movie," *McMillan* segment.

McMILLAN AND WIFE

See title: "NBC Mystery Movie," *McMillan and Wife* segment.

McNAUGHTON'S DAUGHTER

Crime Drama. Background: Los Angeles, California. The cases and courtroom prosecutions of Laurie McNaughton, trial lawyer and Deputy District Attorney.

CAST

Laurie McNaughton	Susan Clark
Lou Farragut, her investigator	James Callahan
Charles Quintero, the D.A.	Ricardo Montalban

Music: George Romanis.

Music Supervision: Hal Mooney.

Executive Producer: David Victor.

Producer: Harold Gast.

Director: Daniel Haller, Gene Nelson, Jack Arnold.

McNAUGHTON'S DAUGHTER–60 minutes–NBC–March 24, 1976 - April 7, 1976. 3 episodes.

MADE IN AMERICA

Game. Involved: A celebrity panel of three, and self-made millionaire guests. Through a series of question-and-answer probe rounds with guests, panelists have to establish their identities.

Host: Bob Maxwell.

Panelists: Jan Sterling, Don Murray, Walter Slezak.

MADE IN AMERICA—30 minutes—CBS—April 5, 1964 - September 6, 1965.

MADIGAN

See title: "NBC Wednesday Mystery Movie," *Madigan* segment.

MAGGIE AND THE BEAUTIFUL MACHINE

Health-Exercise. Exercises and health tips designed to improve the body machine.

Hostess: Maggie Lettvin.

Assistants: Five noncelebrity guests.

Music: Recorded.

MAGGIE AND THE BEAUTIFUL MACHINE—30 minutes—PBS—1972-1974.

THE MAGGIE McNELLIS SHOW

Women. Celebrity interviews, human interest accounts, nightclub reviews, fashion previews, and gossip.

Hostess: Maggi McNellis.

THE MAGGI McNELLIS SHOW—30 minutes—ABC—July 3, 1952 - September 1952.

THE MAGIC CLOWN

Children. Games, songs, and magic performed against a circus background.

Host: Zovella, the Magic Clown (conducting the entire show by himself).

THE MAGIC CLOWN—15 minutes NBC—1949-1954.

THE MAGIC COTTAGE

Children. Stories, songs, fairy tales, games, and art instruction set against the background of a school classroom.

Hostess: Pat Meikle.

Substitute Host: Hal Cooper.

Assistant: Robert Wilkinson.

THE MAGIC COTTAGE—30 minutes —DuMont—1949-1953.

THE MAGIC GARDEN

Children. Background: The Magic Garden, a small, forestlike area where the make believe becomes real. With hostesses Carole and Paula, and through the antics of puppets Sherlock Squirrel and Flap the bird, stories, songs and related entertainment, geared for children, is charmingly and amusingly presented.

CAST

Carole	Carole Demas
Paula	Paula Janis
Sherlock	Cary Antebi
Flap	Cary Antebi

Music: Alton Alexander, George Kayatta, Alexander Demas.

Producer-Director: Irv Jarvis, Joseph L. Hall.

THE MAGIC GARDEN—30 minutes —Syndicated 1974. Originally produced as a local program by WPIX-TV in New York.

THE MAGICIAN

Adventure. Background: Hollywood, California. The story of Anthony Blake, the world's greatest magician. Incorporating the wizardry of his craft, he attempts to assist people in distress—people who are seeking escape, but who are unable to turn to police for help.

CAST

Anthony Blake (referred to as Anthony Dorian in the pilot film)	Bill Bixby
Max Pomeroy, a newspaper columnist, his contact	Keene Curtis
Jerry Anderson, the pilot of Blake's Boeing 737, the *Spirit*	Jim Watkins
Dennis Pomeroy, Max's son	Tod Crespi
Dominick, the owner of the Magic Castle Club	Joseph Sirola

Announcer: Bill Baldwin.

Music: Pat Williams.

THE MAGICIAN—60 minutes—NBC —October 2, 1973 - May 20, 1974. 24 episodes.

THE MAGIC LADY

Children. Songs, fairy tales, guests, and magic performances.

CAST

The Magic Queen	Geraldine Larsen
Boko, her pixie helper	Jerry Maren

THE MAGIC LADY—30 minutes— Syndicated 1951. 13 episodes.

THE MAGIC LAND OF ALLAKAZAM

Children. Background: The magical kingdom of Allakazam. Mythical adventures detailing illusionist Mark Wilson's battle against evil.

CAST

Mark Wilson	Himself
Nani Darnell, his wife	Herself
Mike Wilson, their son	Himself
Rebo the Clown	Bev Bergeson
The King of Allakazam	Bob Towner
Perriwinkle	Chuck Barnes

Puppets: Basil the Bunny; Doris the Dove; Bernard the Rabbit.

Producer: Jack Wipper, Mark Wilson Dan Whitman.

THE MAGIC LAND OF ALLAKA-ZAM—30 minutes. CBS—October 1, 1960 - September 1962; ABC—September 29, 1962 - September 28, 1963; ABC—April 25, 1964 - September 1964. 39 episodes.

MAGIC MIDWAY

Circus Variety Acts.

Ringmaster: Claude Kirchener.

Regulars: Bonnie Lee, a baton twirling champion; Bill "Boom Boom" Bailey; Phil "Coo Coo" Kiley; Douglas "Mr. Pocus" Anderson.

Music: The Jazz Band of Lou Stern and the Circus Seven.

MAGIC MIDWAY—30 minutes—NBC —September 22, 1962 - March 16, 1963. 26 episodes.

MAGIC MONGO

See title: "The Krofft Supershow II," *Magic Mongo* segment.

THE MAGIC OF MARK WILSON

Variety. A half-hour series that spotlights the talents of magician Mark Wilson.

Host: Mark Wilson.

Regulars: Nani Darnell, Greg Wilson.

Music: Frank Ortega.

Producer-Director: Herb Waterson.

THE MAGIC OF MARK WILSON—30 minutes—Syndicated 1977.

THE MAGIC RANCH

Children. Performances by guest magicians.

Host: Don Alan.

Producer: George Anderson.

THE MAGIC RANCH—30 minutes—ABC—September 30, 1961 - December 17, 1961. Syndicated.

THE MAGIC VAULT

Anthology. Dramatizations depicting the plight of people suddenly caught in unusual happenings.

THE MAGIC VAULT—30 minutes—Syndicated 1952. 104 episodes.

THE MAGILLA GORILLA SHOW

Animated Cartoon. Background: Los Angeles, California. The misadventures of Magilla, a mischievous, fun-loving gorilla, the permanent resident at Mr. Peebles Pet Shop. A Hanna-Barbera production.

Additional characters: Mr. Peebles, the pet shop owner; and Ogee, the little girl who longs to have Magilla as her own pet.

Additional segment: "Ricochet Rabbit." Plagued by the antics of his three fumbling deputies, Punkin' Puss, Mush Mouse, and Droop-a-Long, Sheriff Ricochet Rabbit attempts to maintain law and order.

Characters' Voices

Magilla Gorilla	Allan Melvin
Mr. Peebles	Howard Morris
Ogee	Jean VanderPyl
Punkin' Puss	Allan Melvin
Mush Mouse	Howard Morris
Ricochet Rabbit	Don Messick
Droop-a-Long	Mel Blanc

Music Supervision: Hoyt Curtin.

THE MAGILLA GORILLA SHOW—30 minutes—Syndicated 1964. 58 episodes.

MAGNAVOX THEATRE

Anthology. Dramatic presentations.

Producer: Garth Montgomery.

Director: Carl Beier.

Sponsor: Magnavox.

MAGNAVOX THEATRE—60 minutes—CBS 1950.

THE MAGNIFICENT MARBLE MACHINE

Game. Two teams, each composed of one celebrity and one noncelebrity contestant, compete. A question is read and, via electronics, the clue word appears on a board with a line of dashes to indicate the amount of letters contained in the answer. Contestants are first to play and the one who first sounds a buzzer signal receives a chance to answer. If correct, one point is scored; if not, the opponent receives a chance to answer. The celebrities next receive a chance at play. The team that is first to score four points is the winner and receives the opportunity to play the Magnificent Marble Machine, a huge, electronic pinball machine. The team receives two minutes at play and each time a bumper is hit five hundred points is scored and a prize is won. If the player reaches a goal of 15,000 points he receives the opportunity to play the gold money ball wherein, within one minute of play, each bumper that is hit earns $500. Players compete until defeated.

Host: Art James.

Announcer: Johnny Gilbert.

Music: Mort Garson; Score Productions.

Executive Producer: Merrill Heatter, Bob Quigley.

Producer: Robert Noah.

THE MAGNIFICENT MARBLE MACHINE—30 minutes—NBC—July 7, 1975 - June 11, 1976.

THE MAGNIFICENT SIX AND A HALF

Comedy. Background: England. The misadventures of seven children, six boys (the Magnificent Six) and a young girl (the Half). Produced in England.

CAST

Steve	Len Jones
Whizz	Michael Auderson
Dumbo	Ian Ellis
Toby	Brinsley Forde
Stodger	Lionel Hawkes
Pee Wee	Kim Tallmadge
Liz	Suzanne Togni

THE MAGNIFICENT SIX AND A HALF—18 minutes (approx.)—Syndicated 1970. 12 episodes.

THE MAIL STORY

See title: "Handle with Care."

MAIN CHANCE

Drama. Background: London, England. The cases and courtroom defenses of David Main, Barrister. Produced in England.

Starring: John Stride as David Main.

MAIN CHANCE—60 minutes—Syndicated 1970. 13 episodes.

MAJOR ADAMS, TRAILMASTER

See title: "Wagon Train."

MAJOR DELL CONWAY OF THE FLYING TIGERS

Adventure. Background: Los Angeles, California. The exploits of Major Dell Conway, the chief pilot of the Flying Tigers Airline. Stories depict his investigations into cases on behalf of G-2, American Military Intelligence.

Starring: Ed Peck as Major Dell Conway.

Producer: General Genovese.

Sponsor: Johnson Candy.

MAJOR DELL CONWAY OF THE FLYING TIGERS—30 minutes—DuMont 1951.

MAKE A FACE

Game. Three competing players. Each player sits before three revolving wheels that contain pictures of celebrities cut into puzzle parts. Within specified time limits, players have to assemble and identify the personalities. Each correct identification awards points. Winners, the highest scorers, receive merchandise prizes.

Host: Bob Clayton.

Assistant: Rita Mueller.

Producer: Art Baer, Herbert Gottlieb.

Director: Lloyd Gross.

MAKE A FACE—30 minutes—ABC—October 2, 1961 - March 30, 1962. Also: ABC—September 29, 1962 - December 22, 1962.

MAKE A WISH

Educational. Children six to eleven years of age. Through animation, films, songs, and sketches, the differences between fantasy and the real world are explained.

Host: Tom Chapin.

Orchestra: Bernie Green.

MAKE A WISH—30 minutes—ABC—Premiered: September 12, 1971.

MAKE THE CONNECTION

Game. Involved: Two specially selected contestants and a celebrity panel of four. Through question-and-answer rounds with the contestants, celebrities have to determine when, where, why, and how their paths have crossed with the laymen players. Prizes are awarded to the contestants if the panel fails to uncover the relationship.

Host: Jim McKay.

Panelists: Gloria DeHaven, Betty White, Eddie Bracken, Gene Klavan.

MAKE THE CONNECTION—30 minutes—NBC—July 7, 1955 - September 29, 1955.

MAKE ME LAUGH

Game. Contestants, one at a time, stand opposite three guest comics. The comics then provoke and attempt to make the contestants laugh. Object: For the contestant to remain straight-faced. Rounds are divided into one minute segments with the contestant receiving one dollar per second until he laughs.

Host: Robert Q. Lewis.

Assistant: Renny Peterson.

MAKE ME LAUGH—30 minutes—ABC—March 20, 1958 - June 12, 1958.

MAKE MINE MUSIC

Musical Variety.

Hostess: Carole Coleman.

Regulars: Larry Douglas, Bill Skipper.

Music: The Tony Mottola Trio.

MAKE MINE MUSIC—30 minutes—CBS 1948.

MAKE ROOM FOR DADDY

Comedy. Distinguished by two formats.

Format One: 1953-1957.
   Background: 505 East 50th Street, New York, Apartment 542, the residence of the Williams family: Danny, a nightclub entertainer at the Copa Club; his wife, Margaret; and their children, Terry and Rusty. Stories depict the home and working life of Danny Williams, a man whose career often leaves him with little time to spend with his beloved family.

CAST
Danny Williams	Danny Thomas
Margaret Williams	Jean Hagen
Teresa Williams (Terry)	Sherry Jackson
Russell Williams (Rusty)	Rusty Hamer
Louise, their maid	Amanda Randolph
Jesse Leeds, Danny's agent	Jesse White
Elizabeth Margaret O'Neal (Liz), Danny's press agent	Mary Wickes
Ben Lessy, Danny's piano player	Himself
Frank Jenks, Danny's taylor	Himself
Phil Arnold, Danny's agent (later episodes)	Horace McMahon
Charlie Helper, the owner of the Copa Club	Sid Melton

Williams family dog, a terrier: Laddie.

Music: Herbert Spencer, Earle Hagen.

Format Two: 1957-1964.
   Background: Same. Shortly after Margaret's death (the cause is not stated), Rusty contracts the measles. Hiring Kathleen O'Hara, a beautiful registered nurse, widow, and mother of a young daughter,* to care for Rusty, Danny and she fall in love and marry one year following. Stories relate the trials and tribulations of the Williams family.

CAST
Danny Williams	Danny Thomas
Kathy Williams (also referred to by the maiden name, Kathleen Daly)	Marjorie Lord
Terry Williams	Sherry Jackson Penny Parker
Rusty Williams	Rusty Hamer
Patty Williams (O'Hara)	Lelani Sorenson
Linda Williams	Angela Cartwright
Louise, their maid	Amanda Randolph
Elizabeth Margaret O'Neal	Mary Wickes
Charlie Helper	Sid Melton
Bunny Helper, Charlie's wife	Pat Carroll
Phil Arnold, Danny's agent	Sheldon Leonard
Uncle Tonoose, the head of the Williams family	Hans Conried
Pat Hannegan, a night club comedian, Terry's boyfriend; later her husband (1960)	Pat Harrington, Jr.
Harry Ruby, Danny's song writer	Himself
Gina Minelli, an Italian exchange student residing with the Williamses	Annette Funicello
Piccola Pupa, a young Italian singer discovered by Danny	Herself
Buck, Gina's boyfriend	Richard Tyler
José Jiménez, the elevator operator	Bill Dana
Alfie, a Copa Club waiter	Bernard Fox
Mr. Heckendorn, the building superintendant	Gale Gordon
Mr. Svenson, the building janitor	John Qualen
Mr. Daly, Kathy's father	William Demarest

Music: Herbert Spencer, Earle Hagen.

MAKE ROOM FOR DADDY—30 minutes—ABC—September 29, 1953 - July 17, 1957. CBS (as "The Danny Thomas Show")—30 minutes—October 7, 1957 - September 14, 1964. 336 episodes. Spin-off series: "Make Room for Granddaddy," See title.

*When first introduced in 1957, her name was Patty. When the series switched to another network, the original actress was replaced and the character name changed to Linda.

MAKE ROOM FOR GRANDDADDY

Comedy. To bridge the six-year gap between "Make Room for Daddy" and "Make Room for Granddaddy," two specials were aired:

"Make More Room for Daddy," NBC, 1967. Completing his college education, Rusty enlists in the army, where he meets, falls in love with, and marries Susan MacAdams, a colonel's daughter.

And, "Make Room for Granddaddy," CBS, 9/14/69. Discharged from the service, Rusty enrolls in medical school. Expecting their first child, he and Susan set up housekeeping away from the family nest.

The following background information provides the basis for the finished product: "Make Room for Granddaddy," ABC, 9/23/70.

Danny and Kathy are in Europe on a show-business engagement; Linda is residing at a boarding school in Connecticut to prevent any interference to her education; Rusty and Susan are struggling newlyweds; and Terry, the mother of a six-year-old son, Michael, is preparing to join her husband, Bill Johnson, a serviceman who is stationed in Japan. Michael is to stay with Bill's parents until he and Terry settle and find a house.

For reasons which are not explained, Terry is now married to Bill Johnson, not Pat Hannegan, as in the original series.

The Series:

Background: 505 East 50th Street, Manhattan, Apartment 781. Returning home after their European engagement, and welcomed by the family, Danny and Kathy discover Terry's plans. Wanting Michael to remain with them, Danny persuades Terry to let him stay with them for several days and let him decide where he'll be the happiest. Danny and Kathy cater to his every whim, and Michael chooses to remain with them. Stories relate the trials and tribulations of the individual members of the Williams family.

CAST

Danny Williams	Danny Thomas
Kathy Williams	Marjorie Lord
Linda Williams	Angela Cartwright
Rusty Williams	Rusty Hamer
Charlie Helper	Sid Melton
Michael Johnson	Michael Hughes
Rosey Robbins, Danny's accompanist	Rosey Grier
Uncle Tonoose	Hans Conried
Susan Williams	Jana Taylor
Terry Johnson	Penny Parker
Henry, the elevator operator	Stanley Myron Handleman

Music: Earle Hagen.

MAKE ROOM FOR GRANDDADDY—30 minutes—ABC—September 23, 1970 - September 2, 1971. 24 episodes.

MAKE YOUR OWN KIND OF MUSIC

Variety. Musical numbers interspersed with comedy sketches.

Hosts: Karen and Richard Carpenter (brother and sister).

Regulars: Al Hirt, Mark Lindsay, The New Doodletown Pipers, Patchett and Tarses (comics).

Orchestra: Allyn Ferguson, Jack Elliott.

MAKE YOUR OWN KIND OF MUSIC—60 minutes—NBC—July 20, 1971 - September 7, 1971. 8 tapes.

MALIBU RUN

Adventure. A spin-off from "The Aquanauts." Background: Malibu Beach in Southern California. The cases of diving instructors and part-time private investigators Larry Lahr and Mike Madison.

CAST

Larry Lahr	Jeremy Slate
Mike Madison	Ron Ely
Chaplan	Charles Thompson

Music: Andre Previn.

MALIBU RUN—60 minutes—CBS—May 21, 1961 - September 27, 1961.

MALIBU U.

Musical Variety. Background: Malibu U., a mythical college based on the beach of Southern California. Performances by the sixties' top music personalities.

Host (the Dean): Ricky Nelson.

President of the Student Body: Robbie Porter.

Featured: The Bob Banas Dancers, The Malibuties (bikini clad girls).

Music: Recorded and/or provided by guests.

MALIBU U.—30 minutes—ABC—July 2, 1967 - September 1, 1967.

MAMA

See title: "I Remember Mama."

MAMA ROSA

A serial drama that depicts the trials and tribulations of an Italian-American family. Broadcast on ABC from April 23, 1950 to June 15, 1950. The series, which was broadcast live in California and seen on kinescope in other areas of the country, was the first series to originate on the West Coast, where it began as a local show on KFI-TV in 1948.

THE MAN AGAINST CRIME

Crime Drama. Background: New York City. The investigations of Mike Barnett, an unarmed private detective.

CAST

Mike Barnett	Ralph Bellamy Frank Lovejoy
Pat Barnett, his brother	Robert Preston
Ralph Bellamy's stand-in:	Art Fleming.

Producer: Edward J. Montagne, Paul Nickell.

Director: Paul Nickell.

Sponsor: Camel Cigarettes.

THE MAN AGAINST CRIME—30 minutes—CBS—October 4, 1949 - October 2, 1953. 82 episodes. Syndicated title: "Follow That Man."

THE MAN AND THE CHALLENGE

Adventure. The story of Glenn Barton, a United States government research scientist assigned to test the limits of human endurance.

Starring: George Nader as Glenn Barton.

THE MAN AND THE CHALLENGE—30 minutes—NBC—September 12, 1959 - September 3, 1960. Syndicated. 36 episodes.

THE MAN AND THE CITY

Drama. Background: A turbulent Southwestern metropolis, the unidentified fictional equivalent of Albuquerque, New Mexico. The story of Thomas Jefferson Alcala, its mayor, a man who strays from the offices of city hall, mixes with the people, and struggles to solve their problems.

CAST

Thomas Alcala	Anthony Quinn

Andy Hays, his
 assistant   Mike Farrell
Marian Crane, his
 secretary   Mala Powers
Josefina, his house-
 keeper   Carmen Zapata

THE MAN AND THE CITY—60 minutes—ABC—September 15, 1971 - January 5, 1972. 13 episodes.

MAN BEHIND THE BADGE

Anthology. Crime dramatizations based on official law-enforcement records.

Host-Narrator: Charles Bickford.

Producer: Jerry Robertson, Bernard Prockter.

Sponsor: Bristol-Myers.

MAN BEHIND THE BADGE—30 minutes—Syndicated 1954.

A Man Called Shenandoah. Robert Horton and guest star Beverly Garland.

A MAN CALLED SHENANDOAH

Western. Era: The 1860s. A man, for unknown reasons, is shot and left to die on the Prairie. He is later found by two bounty hunters who bring him back to town where they hope to collect a reward in the event that he's wanted. Kate, a saloon girl, cares for him and nurses him back to health. Regaining consciousness, he finds himself a man without a memory—unaware of whom or what he was. Through Kate's assistance, he escapes his captors' bounds. The series follows the trail of an amnesiac—A Man Called Shenandoah—seeking an identity and a home.

CAST
Shenandoah   Robert Horton
Kate (first episode) Beverly Garland

Music: George Stroll, Robert Van Eps.

A MAN CALLED SHENANDOAH—30 minutes—ABC—September 13, 1965 - September 5, 1966. 34 episodes.

THE MAN CALLED X

Spy Drama. The investigations of Ken Thurston; an American intelligence agent who operates under the code name X.

Starring: Barry Sullivan as Ken Thurston.

THE MAN CALLED X—30 minutes—Syndicated 1956. 39 episodes.

THE MANCINI GENERATION

Musical Variety.

Host: Henry Mancini.

Music: The forty-piece Mancini Orchestra.

Additional Orchestrations: Alan Copeland.

Featured segment: "The Film Spot." Original celluloid sequences for Mancini compositions.

THE MANCINI GENERATION—30 minutes—Syndicated 1972.

THE M AND M CANDY CARNIVAL

Variety. Background: A carnival. Performances by undiscovered professional talent. Winners, determined by a judge, receive a twenty-five-dollar savings bond and a week's pro-booking at the Hamid Steel Pier in Atlantic City, New Jersey.

Ringmaster: Barry Cossell.

Judge: George Hammond.

Clowns: Don Lenox, Bill Bailey.

Orchestra: Gene Crane.

THE M AND M CANDY CARNIVAL —30 minutes—CBS 1952.

MANDRAKE THE MAGICIAN

Adventure. Early history: During the twelfth century, wizards carried on the secrets of ancient Egypt and the magic of ancient China. Sweeping the western world, the hordes of Genghis Khan destroyed the wizards and their lore. The few who managed to escape established the College of Magic in a Tibetan valley wherein the lore was preserved. Once a decade, one youth is selected from thousands of applicants and taught the ancient secrets.

The twentieth century. Brought to the college by his father, a former graduate who has only a few months to live, Mandrake is taught the ancient secrets by Theron, the Master of Magic.

Ten years later, Mandrake becomes greater than his masters, and, upon his release from the college, he teams with his servant, Lothar. Stories depict their crusade against evil. Based on the stories by Lee Falk and Phil Davis.

CAST
Mandrake the Magician   Coe Norton
Lothar   Woody Strode

MANDRAKE THE MAGICIAN—30 minutes—Syndicated 1954. Withdrawn.

THE MAN FROM ATLANTIS

Science Fiction Adventure. Background: California. A storm, deep in the Pacific Ocean, unearths the sole survivor of the fabled lost kingdom of Atlantis and brings it to shore. As it nears death from a malody that science cannot cure, Elizabeth Merrill, a naval doctor with the foundation for oceanic research, returns it to the sea and saves its life. Though the government permits the 'Atlantian, named Mark Harris by Elizabeth, to return to his former existence, Mark decides to remain with the foundation—to help us further our knowledge of the sea—and to gain his own knowledge about us. Stories detail Mark's work on behalf of the foundation.

CAST
Mark Harris   Patrick Duffy
Dr. Elizabeth
 Merrill   Belinda Montgomery
Dr. Miller Simon, Elizabeth's
 associate   Kenneth Tigar
Ginny Mendoza, the sec-
 retary-receptionist at
 the foundation Annette Cardona
C.W. Crawford, the head
 of the foundation   Alan Fudge

Executive Producer: Herbert F. Solow.

Producer: Robert Lewin.

Director: Marc Daniels, Reza S. Badiyi, Lee H. Katzin, Charles S. Dubin.

Music: Fred Karlin.

THE MAN FROM ATLANTIS—60 minutes—NBC—Premiered: September 1977. Previously seen as a series of specials on 3/4/77, 4/22/77; and 5/17/77.

THE MAN FROM BLACKHAWK

Western. Era: the 1870s. The cases of Sam Logan, a special investigator for the Blackhawk Insurance Company.

Starring: Robert Rockwell as Sam Logan.

THE MAN FROM BLACKHAWK—30 minutes—ABC—October 9, 1959 - September 24, 1960. 37 episodes. Syndicated.

THE MAN FROM INTERPOL

Crime Drama. The investigations of Tony Smith, a New Scotland Yard inspector assigned to active duty with the International Police Force (Interpol).

CAST
Tony Smith	Richard Wyler
The Superintendant	John Longden

Music: Tony Crombie.

THE MAN FROM INTERPOL—30 minutes—NBC—January 23, 1960- October 22, 1960. 39 episodes.

THE MAN FROM U.N.C.L.E.

Adventure. Background: New York City. A dry cleaning establishment, Del Florias Taylor Shop, is the secret headquarters of U.N.C.L.E., the United Network Command for Law Enforcement, an international organization responsible for the welfare of peoples and nations against the evils of THRUSH, a secret international organization bent on world domain.

Stories relate the investigations of Napoleon Solo and his partner, Illya Kuryakin, U.N.C.L.E. agents battling the forces of global crime and corruption as influenced by THRUSH.

CAST
Napoleon Solo	Robert Vaughn
Illya Kuryakin	David McCallum
Alexander Waverly, the head of U.N.C.L.E.	Leo G. Carroll
Del Floria, the owner of the taylor shop	Mario Siletti
Heather, an U.N.C.L.E.	

The Man From U.N.C.L.E. Left to right: Robert Vaughn, David McCallum, Leo G. Carroll.

agent	May Heatherly
U.N.C.L.E. Girls	Julie Ann Johnson
	Sharon Hillyer

Music: Jerry Goldsmith; Lalo Schifrin; Leith Stevens.

Additional Music: Gerald Fried, Morton Stevens.

Executive Producer: Norman Felton.

Producer: Sam Rolfe, Anthony Spinner, Boris Ingster.

Director: Daniel Hallenback, Boris Sagal, John Newland, Don Medford.

Creator: Norman Felton, Sam Rolfe.

THE MAN FROM U.N.C.L.E.—60 minutes—NBC—September 22, 1964 - January 15, 1968. 104 episodes. Syndicated. Spin-off series: "The Girl from U.N.C.L.E." (see title).

MANHATTAN HONEYMOON

Interview-Quiz. Three engaged or married couples are first interviewed, then, after relating experiences, they compete in a series of general-knowledge question-and-answer rounds. Each correct answer scores one point. Winners, the highest scorers, receive an all-expense-paid honeymoon in New York.

Hostess: Neva Patterson.

MANHATTAN HONEYMOON—30 minutes—ABC—February 22, 1954 - April 21, 1954.

MANHATTAN SHOWCASE

Variety. Performances by undiscovered professional talent.

Host: Johnny Downs.

Assistant: Helen Gallagher.

Music: The Tony Mottola Trio.

MANHATTAN SHOWCASE—15 minutes—CBS 1949.

THE MANHATTAN TRANSFER

Variety. A nostalgic series that recalls the music, song, and dance of the 1930s and 40s.

Hosts: The Manhattan Transfer, a flashy vocal quartet comprised of Laurel Masse, Janis Seigel, Alan Paul, and Tim Hauser.

Orchestra: Ira Newborn.

Executive Producer: Aaron Russo.

Producer: Bernard Rothman, Jack Wohl.

Director: Ron Field.

THE MANHATTAN TRANSFER—60 minutes—CBS—August 10, 1975 - August 31, 1975.

MANHUNT

Crime Drama. Background: San Diego, California. The investigations of Lieutenant Howard Finucane and his partner, police reporter Ben Andrews, into gangland-associated crimes.

CAST
Lt. Howard Finucane	Victor Jory
Ben Andrews	Patrick McVey

MANHUNT—30 minutes—Syndicated 1959. 78 episodes.

THE MANHUNTER

Crime Drama. Background: Cleary County, Idaho, during the Public Enemy days of the Depression era (1934). The cases of Dave Barrett, farmer, an amateur crimefighter who assists law-enforcement officials by tracking down wanted criminals for their offered rewards.

CAST
Dave Barrett	Ken Howard
Lizabeth Barrett, his sister	Hilary Thompson
James Barrett, his father	Ford Rainey
Mary Barrett, his mother	Claudia Bryar

Sheriff Paul Tate   Robert Hogan
Music: Duante Tatro.

THE MANHUNTER—60 minutes—CBS—September 11, 1974 - April 10, 1975. 24 episodes.

MAN IN A SUITCASE

Adventure. Background: London, England. The investigations of John McGill, a former American intelligence agent turned private detective. Produced in England.

Starring: Richard Bradford as John McGill.

Music: Albert Elms.

MAN IN A SUITCASE—60 minutes—ABC—May 3, 1968 - September 20, 1968. 28 episodes. Syndicated.

MANNIX

Crime Drama. Distinguished by two formats.

Format One:

Background: Los Angeles, California. The cases of Joe Mannix, an investigator for Intertect, a computerized private detective organization. Stories depict the conflict that exists between Mannix, a loner who constantly defies rules and regulations and is opposed to computerized detection; and Lou Wickersham, his superior, who believes in the scientific approach to solving crimes and is opposed to Joe's continual use of unorthodox methods of handling cases.

CAST
Joe Mannix   Michael Connors
Lou Wickersham   Joseph Campanella
Music: Lalo Schifrin.

MANNIX—60 minutes—CBS—September 7, 1967 - August 31, 1968.

Format Two:

The investigations of Joe Mannix, a private detective operating independently from his home in Los Angeles.

CAST
Joe Mannix   Michael Connors
Peggy Fair, his
  secretary   Gail Fisher
Lt. Arthur Malcolm,
  L.A.P.D.   Ward Wood
Lt. George Kramer Lawrence Linville
Lt. Adams Tobias   Robert Reed
Lt. Daniel Ives   Jack Ging
Toby Fair, Peggy's

son   Mark Stewart

Music: Lalo Schifrin; Kenyon Hopkins.

Producer: Ivan Goff, Ben Roberts.

Director: Sutton Roley, Fernando Lamas, Barry Crane, Don Taylor, Harry Harvey, Jr., Gerald Mayer, Allen Reisner, Seymour Robbie, Lee H. Katzin, Murray Golden, Arnold Laven, Paul Krasny.

Mannix's Address: 17 Paseo Verde.

MANNIX—60 minutes—CBS—September 21, 1968 - August 27, 1975. 194 episodes.

MAN OF THE WEST

See title: "Frontier Doctor."

MAN OF THE WORLD

Mystery. The assignments of Michael Strait, an international photo-journalist.

Starring: Craig Stevens as Michael Strait.

MAN OF THE WORLD—60 minutes —Syndicated 1962. 20 episodes.

A MAN'S WORLD

See title: "Henry Morgan."

MANTRAP

Discussion. One male guest, representing a topic of current interest, appears and sits opposite a panel of three women. Both sides first state their opinions, then debate the issue.

Host: Al Hamel.

Regular Panelists: Meredith MacRae, Phyllis Kirk, Jaye P. Morgan, Carol Wayne, Selma Diamond.

Music: Recorded.

MANTRAP—30 minutes—Syndicated 1971.

THE MAN WHO NEVER WAS

Spy Drama. Background: Europe. Pursued by East German police, who uncovered his identity, Peter Murphy, American espionage agent, wanders onto the grounds of an estate, the

scene of a society party. Straying from the house, multimillionaire Mark Wainwright—Murphy's exact double—is mistaken for Peter by the police and killed. Walking toward Wainwright, Murphy is mistaken for Mark by the Wainwright chauffeur and told of an impending meeting. Following through with the charade, he is driven to the Wainwright residence.

First meeting Peter, Eva, Marks's beautiful wife, is unaware that he is an imposter. Attending a meeting wherein Roger Berry, Mark's ambitious half-brother, is to assume control of Eva's family corporation, she becomes aware of a difference when Peter refuses to sign the transfer papers. Leaving the Berry residence, Eva questions the stranger posing as her husband. Unable to reveal his true identity, he tells her about Mark and asks her to continue posing as his wife. Mystified, but needing Mark Wainwright alive to save her family corporation, she agrees.

The body of Mark Wainwright is prepared as Peter Murphy, convincing East German officials that Peter Murphy is dead.

Posing as Mark Wainwright, agent Peter Murphy continues in his capacity as a spy and, assisted by Eva Wainwright, undertakes hazardous missions for the U.S. Government.

CAST
Peter Murphy/Mark
  Wainwright   Robert Lansing
Eva Wainwright   Dana Wynter
Jack Forbes, Murphy's
  superior   Murray Hamilton
Roger Berry   Alex Devion
Music: Lionel Newman.

THE MAN WHO NEVER WAS—30 minutes—ABC—September 7, 1966 - December 29, 1966. 18 episodes.

MAN WITH A CAMERA

Crime Drama. Background: New York City. The investigations of Mike Kovac, a free-lance photo-journalist who acquires material by assisting police and solving crimes perpetrated against insurance companies.

CAST
Mike Kovac   Charles Bronson
Lt. Donovan   James Flavin
Producer: Don Sharpe, Warren Lewis, A.E. Houghton.

MAN WITH A CAMERA—30 minutes

–ABC–October 10, 1958 - January 29, 1960. 29 episodes. Syndicated.

MAN WITHOUT A GUN

Western. Background: Yellowstone, Dakota, during the 1870s. The story of newspaper editor Adam MacLean and his attempts to establish peace through the power of the press.

CAST

Adam MacLean	Rex Reason
Marshal Frank Tallman	Mort Mills

MAN WITHOUT A GUN–30 minutes –Syndicated 1958.

MANY HAPPY RETURNS

Comedy. Background: Los Angeles, California. The misadventures of widower Walter Burnley, the manager of the complaint department of Krockmeyer's Department Store. Plagued by a misplaced staff and a boss who refuses to hear of the word *return*, Burnley struggles to resolve complaints in a way that will please both the customer and his employer.

CAST

Walter Burnley	John McGiver
Joan Randall, his married daughter	Elinor Donahue
Bob Randall, her husband	Mark Goddard
Laurie Randal, their daughter	Andrea Sacino
Lynn Hall, a staff member	Elena Verdugo
Joe Foley, a staff member	Richard Collier
Wilma Fritter, a staff member	Jesslyn Fax
J. L. Fox, the store manager, Burnley's employer	Jerome Cowan
Owen Sharp, the store owner	Russell Collins

Many Happy Returns. Elena Verdugo and John McGiver.

MANY HAPPY RETURNS–30 minutes–CBS–September 21, 1964 - April 12, 1965. 26 episodes

THE MANY LOVES OF DOBIE GILLIS

Comedy. The saga of a young man's indecision about life.

Formats:

September 29, 1959 - September 12, 1961:

Background: Central City, 285 Norwood Street, the business location of the Gillis Grocery Store, and the residence of the Gillis family: Herbert, the owner; his wife, Winnie; and their son, Dobie. Stories relate: Dobie's continual thoughts about the future; his running battle with his father over the prospect of acquiring work; his relationship with his Beatnick friend, his "good buddy," Maynard G. Krebs; and his endless romantic heartaches, most of which center around Thalia Menninger, a beautiful, greedy, self-centered young woman who struggles to improve Dobie and find him the job that will enable him to make "oodles and oodles of money" though not for her, the last hope her family has, but for her family—a sixty-year-old father with a kidney condition, a mother who isn't getting any younger, a sister who married a loafer, and a brother who is becoming a public charge.

September 26, 1961 - September 18, 1962:
Dobie and Maynard's experiences as army privates.

September 26, 1962 - September 18, 1963:

Completing their military service, and still undecided about life, Dobie and Maynard enroll in college. Stories depict, in addition to Dobie's romantic misadventures, his and Maynard's struggles to find their place in life.

CAST

Dobie Gillis	Dwayne Hickman
Maynard G. Krebs	Bob Denver
Thalia Menninger	Tuesday Weld
Herbert T. Gillis	Frank Faylen
Winifred Gillis (Winnie)	Florida Friebus
Zelda Gilroy, the girl who schemes to win Dobie's love	Sheila James
Chatsworth Osborne, Jr., a rich, spoiled friend	Steve Franken
Clarissa Osborne, Chatsworth's	

mother	Doris Packer
Leander Pomfritt*	Herbert Anderson William Schallert
Ruth Adams**	Jean Byron
Imogene Burkhart***	Jean Byron
Davey Gillis, Dobie's brother	Darryl Hickman
Duncan Gillis, Dobie's cousin	Bob Diamond
Virgil T. Gillis, Dobie's cousin	Roy Hemphill
Jerome Krebs, Maynard's cousin	Michael J. Pollard
Charlie Wong, the owner of the ice cream parlor, the after school hangout	James Yagi John Lee
Milton Armitage, Dobie's rival for Thalia	Warren Beatty
Clarice Armitage, Milton's mother (early format 1)	Doris Packer
Riff Ryan, a friend, the record shop owner	Tommy Farrell
Maude Pomfritt, Leander's wife	Joyce Van Patten
Trembly, the Osborne butler	David Bond
The Osborne Chauffeur	Angelo DeMeo
Dean Magruder, the head of S. Peter Pryor Jr. College, the university attended by Dobie and Maynard	Raymond Bailey
Lt. Meriwether, Dobie's commanding officer	Richard Claire
Blossom Kenny, a member of the school board	Marjorie Bennett

Also: Diana Millay, Ronny Howard, Jack Albertson, Jo Anne Worley.

Music: Lionel Newman.

Executive Producer: Martin Manulis.

Producer: Joel Kane, Guy Scarpitta.

Director: David Davis, Thomas Montgomery, Ralph Murphy, Stanley Z. Cherry, Guy Scarpitta, Rod Amateau.

Creator: Max Shulman.

Note: On May 10, 1977, CBS presented an unsold pilot entitled, "Whatever Happened To Dobie Gillis?" which reunited the original cast after 14 years. Dobie, now forty years old and married to Zelda, is a partner with his father in an expanded Gillis Grocery Store, and the father of his own teenage son, Georgie (played by

*In format one, the high school English teacher; in format 3, a college instructor.
**In format one, the math teacher.
***In format three, the college anthropology instructor.

The Many Loves of Dobie Gillis. Left to right: Frank Faylen, Dwayne Hickman, Bob Denver.

Stephen Paul). Maynard, now an entrepreneur, returned to help Dobie celebrate his 40th birthday.

Credits: Music: Randy Newman.

Executive Producer: George Komack.

Producer: Michael Manheim.

Director: James Komack.

THE MANY LOVES OF DOBIE GILLIS—30 minutes—CBS—September 29, 1959 - September 18, 1963. 147 episodes. Syndicated. Also known as "Dobie Gillis."

MARCH OF TIME THROUGH THE YEARS

History. Background: A projection room. Screenings of old March of Time newsreels with the added commentary of guests.

Host: John Daly.

MARCH OF TIME THROUGH THE YEARS—30 minutes—ABC—October 1, 1952 - December 11, 1952.

MARCUS WELBY, M.D.

Medical Drama. Background: Santa Monica, California. The story of doctors Marcus Welby, a general practitioner, and his young assistant, Steven Kiley, who attempt to treat people as individuals in an age of specialized medicine and uncaring doctors.

CAST

Marcus Welby	Robert Young
Steven Kiley	James Brolin
Consuelo Lopez, their nurse	Elena Verdugo
Myra Sherwood, widow, Welby's romantic interest	Anne Baxter
Nurse Kathleen Faverty	Sharon Gless
Janet Blake, Kiley's romantic interest (married on 10/21/75)	Pamela Hensley

Music: Leonard Rosenman.

Executive Producer: David Victor.

Producer: David J. O'Connell.

Director: Leo Penn, Jon Epstein, Hollingsworth Morse, Arnold Laven, Jerry London, David Alexander, Nicholas Cosalano, Bruce Kessler.

MARCUS WELBY, M.D.—60 minutes—ABC—September 23, 1969 - May 11, 1976. Syndicated. 172 episodes. Also known as "Robert Young, Family Doctor."

THE MARGE AND GOWER CHAMPION SHOW

Comedy. The misadventures of Marge and Gower Champion, husband and wife professional dancers, as they attempt to establish and live a life apart from the hectic demands of show business.

CAST

Marge Champion	Herself
Gower Champion	Himself
Marge's father, their agent and business manager	Jack Whiting
Cozy, a friend of theirs, a drummer	Buddy Rich
Amanda	Peg La Centra
Miss Weatherly	Barbara Perry

Music: Alan Bergman.

THE MARGE AND GOWER CHAMPION SHOW—30 minutes—CBS—March 31, 1957 - June 9, 1957.

MARGE AND JEFF

Comedy. Background: New York City. The misadventures of Marge and Jeff Green, newlyweds struggling to survive the difficult first years of marriage.

CAST

Marge Green	Marge Green
Jeff Green	Jeff Cain
Family dog: Paisley, a cocker spaniel.	

MARGE AND JEFF—15 minutes—DuMont—1953 - 1954.

MARGIE

Comedy. Background: the small New England town of Madison during the 1920s. The experiences of Margie Clayton, a pretty, delightful, and resourceful high-school girl; a carbonated teenager with an unquenchable thirst for life and an uncontrollable penchant for trouble.

CAST

Margie Clayton	Cynthia Pepper
Harvey Clayton, her father, a bank vice president	Dave Willock
Nora Clayton, her mother	Wesley Thackitt
Cornell Clayton, her brother	Johnny Bangert
Phoebe Clayton, her sophisticated aunt	Hollis Irving
Heywood Botts, Margie's boyfriend	Tommy Ivo
Maybell Jackson, Margie's girlfriend	Penny Parker
Johnny Green, a friend	Richard Gering
Mr. Jackson, Maybell's father	Herb Ellis
Mrs. Jackson, his wife	Marine Stuart

MARGIE—30 minutes—ABC—October 12, 1961 - August 31, 1962. 26 episodes. Syndicated.

THE MARILYN McCOO AND BILLY DAVIS, JR. SHOW

Variety. Music, songs, and comedy sketches.

Hosts: Marilyn McCoo and Billy Davis, Jr.

Regulars: Lewis Arquette, Tim Reid, Jay Leno.

Orchestra: John Myles.

Special Musical Material: Phil Moore.

Executive Producer: Dick Broder.

Producer: Ann Elder, Ed Scharlach.

Director: Gerren Keith.

Choreographer: Ron Poindexter.

THE MARILYN McCOO AND BILLY DAVIS, JR. SHOW—30 minutes—CBS—June 15, 1977 - July 20, 1977. 6 tapes.

MARINE BOY

Animated Cartoon. Era: Twenty-first-century Earth. The investigations of Marine Boy, an agent for the Ocean Patrol, an international defense organization established beneath the sea. Produced in Japan.

Characters:
Marine Boy
Splasher, his pet dolphin
Professor Fumble
Mr. Beacon
Dr. Mariner, Marine Boy's father, the head of the Ocean Patrol
Corrie, a member of the Ocean Patrol
Piper, a member of the Ocean Patrol
Voltan, a member of the Ocean Patrol

Voices: Jack Grimes, Caroline Owens, Jack Cortes.

Music: Norman Gould.

Theme: Ernest Gold.

Executive Producer: Stanley Jaffee.

MARINE BOY—30 minutes—Syndicated. 1966. 78 episodes.

MARKHAM

Crime Drama. Background: Los Angeles, California. The investigations and courtroom defenses of Roy Markham, a wealthy attorney.

CAST

Roy Markham	Ray Milland
John Riggs, his employer	Simon Scott

Music: Stanley Wilson.

Narrator: Ray Milland.

Producer: Joe Sistiam, Warren Duff.

MARKHAM—30 minutes—CBS—May 2, 1959 - September 29, 1960. 60 episodes.

MARK SABER

Crime Drama. Distinguished by two formats.

Format One, American:

The Mark Saber Mystery Theatre—30 minutes—ABC—September 1951 - September 1954. Syndicated title: "Homicide Squad."

Background: New York City. The invesitgations of Mark Saber, a plainclothes detective with the Homicide Division of the New York Police Department.

CAST

Mark Saber	Tom Conway
Sgt. Tim Maloney, his assistant	James Burke

Producer: J. Donald Wilson, Roland Reed.

Director: Eugene Forde.

Sponsor: Sterling Drug Company.

Format Two, British:

Saber Of London—30 minutes—NBC—October 13, 1957 - September 1959. Syndicated title: "Uncovered."

Background: London, England. The investigations of Mark Saber, the one-armed Chief Inspector of Scotland Yard.

CAST

Mark Saber	Donald Gray

His Assistants:
Barney O'Keefe	Michael Balfour
Stephanie Ames	Diane Decker
Peter Paulson	Neil McCallum
Bob Page	Robert Arden
Eddie Wells	Garry Thorne
Inspector Parker	Colin Tapley

Producer: Edward Donziger, Harry Donziger, Harry Lee.

MARLO AND THE MAGIC MOVIE MACHINE

Children. Background: The sub-sub basement of the L. Dullo Computer Company in New York City. The series revolves around Marlo Higgins, a struggling computer operator who was banished to the basement by his employer, Leo Dullo. Here, by day, he continues working, making his dull job exciting by secretly perfecting the L. Dullo Computer. After working hours, he opens a secret doorway and activates his invention—the Magic Movie Machine, a computer that can display a wide variety of historic films and video-tape material, and can also talk, tell jokes, and relate funny stories. Acting as a disc jockey, Marlo and his Magic Movie Machine present films, stories, jokes, and other related entertainment for children.

Starring: Laurie Faso as Marlo Higgins.

Voice of the Movie Machine: Mert Hoplin.

Music: Pete Dino; Score Productions.

Executive Producer: Sanford H. Fisher.

Producer: Ted Field.

Director: George Jason, Lynwood King.

MARLO AND THE MAGIC MOVIE MACHINE—60 minutes—CBS Owned and Operated Stations—Premiered: April 3, 1977.

THE MARRIAGE

Comedy-Drama. Background: New York City. The life of the close-knit Marriott family: Ben, an attorney; his wife, Liz; and their children, Emily and Peter.

CAST

Ben Marriott	Hume Cronyn
Liz Marriott	Jessica Tandy
Emily Marriott	Susan Strasberg
Peter Marriott	Malcolm Brodrick
Bobby Logan, Emily's boy friend	William Redfield

THE MARRIAGE—30 minutes—NBC—July 1, 1954 - August 19, 1954.

MARSHAL DILLON

See title: "Gunsmoke."

THE MARTHA RAYE SHOW

Variety. Music, songs; dances, and slapstick comedy sketches.

Hostess: Martha Raye.

Her Comedy Foil: Rocky Graziano.

Featured: The Martha Raye Dancers.

Orchestra: Carl Hoff.

THE MARTHA RAYE SHOW—60 minutes—NBC—December 26, 1953 - May 29, 1956.

THE MARTHA WRIGHT SHOW

Musical Variety.
Hostess: Martha Wright.
Vocalists: The Norman Paris Chorus.
Orchestra: Bobby Hackett.

THE MARTHA WRIGHT SHOW—15 minutes—ABC 1954.

MARTIN KANE

Crime Drama. Distinguished by two formats.

Format One:

Martin Kane, Private Eye—30 minutes—NBC—September 11, 1949 - September 1953.

Background: New York City. The investigations of Martin Kane, a private detective who achieves his desired results through determination and force of character.

CAST
Martin Kane (1949-1951)	William Gargan
Martin Kane (1951-1952)	Lloyd Nolan
Martin Kane (1952-1953)	Lee Tracy
Happy McMann, his aide	Walter Kinsella
Sergeant Ross, N.Y.P.D.	Nicholas Saunders
The Police Captain	Frank M. Thomas
Lt. Gray	King Calder

Music: Charles Paul.
Announcer: Fred Uttal.
Producer: Frank Burns, Edward C. Kahan, Ed Sutherland.
Sponsor: U.S. Tobacco.
Format Two:

The New Adventures Of Martin Kane—30 minutes—NBC—September 1953 - June 17, 1954. Syndicated title: "Assignment: Danger."
Background: Europe. The cases of Martin Kane, an American private detective who assists various international police departments.

Starring: Mark Stevens as Martin Kane.
Music: Charles Paul.
Announcer: Fred Uttal.
Producer: Frank Burns.

Sponsor: U.S. Tobacco.

THE MARTY FELDMAN COMEDY MACHINE

Comedy. A blend of contemporary humor with that of the Max Sennett era type of slapstick comedy.

Starring: Marty Feldman, British comedian.

Regulars: Barbara Feldon, Orson Welles, Spike Milligan, Fred Smoot, Leonard Schultz, Thelma Houston, Fred Roman.

Music: Recorded.

THE MARTY FELDMAN COMEDY MACHINE—30 minutes—ABC—April 12, 1972 - August 23, 1972. Taped in London. American audiences were first introduced to Marty Feldman via "Dean Martin Presents the Gold-diggers." Marty's previous series (British; BBC-1; BBC-2): "Marty"; "Marty on the Telly in England"; and "The Frost Report."

THE MARVEL SUPER HEROES

Animated adaptations of five *Marvel* comic book characters: "Captain America," "The Incredible Hulk," "Iron Man," "Mighty Thor," and "Sub Mariner." 195 six minute, 30 second films. Syndicated 1965.

THE MARY HARTLINE SHOW

Children. Music, songs, and games.
Hostess: Mary Hartline ("Queen of the Super Circus.")
Music: Chet Robel.

THE MARY HARTLINE SHOW—30 minutes—ABC—February 12, 1951 - June 15, 1951.

MARY HARTMAN, MARY HARTMAN

Serial. Background: 343 Bratner Avenue in the Woodland Hills section of mythical Fernwood, Ohio. The series, which satirizes life, focuses on the endless frustrations of Mary Hartman, a typical middle-aged housewife and mother.

CAST
Mary Hartman	Louise Lasser
Tom Hartman, her husband	Greg Mullavey
Cathy Schumway, Mary's sister	Debralee Scott
Loretta Haggers, Mary's neighbor	Mary Kay Place

Mary Hartman, Mary Hartman. Front row left to right: Claudia Lamb, Philip Bruns, Debralee Scott. Back row left to right: Greg Mullavey, Dody Goodman, Louise Lasser, and Victor Kilian.

- Charlie Haggers, Loretta's husband	Graham Jarvis
George Schumway, Mary's father	Philip Bruns
Martha Schumway, Mary's mother	Dody Goodman
Raymond Larkin, Mary's grandfather	Victor Kilian
Police Sgt. Dennis Foley	Bruce Solomon
Heather Hartman, Mary's daughter	Claudia Lamb
Mae Olinski, the bookkeeper at the auto plant	Salome Jens
Roberta Walashak, the social worker	Samantha Harper
Clete Meizenheimer, the TV reporter	Michael Lembeck
Dr. Ferman	Oliver Clark
Mona McKenzie, the sexy sex therapist	Sallie Janes
Tiny, an employee at the auto plant	Hugh Gilian
Merle Jeeter, the mayor	Dabney Coleman
Wanda Jeeter, his wife	Marian Mercer
Jimmy Joe Jeeter, Merle's son	Sparky Marcus
Mac Slattery, the truck driver	Dennis Burkley
Lila, the Jeeter's sexy maid	Marjorie Battles
Tex, an auto plant employee	Sid Haig
Vernon Bales, the plant manager	David Byrd
Dewey Johnson, the janitor	Richard Ward
Garth Gimble, the Hartman's neighbor	Martin Mull
Pat Gimble, his	

wife   Susan Browning
Barth Gimble, Garth's
   twin brother   Martin Mull
Annie "Tippytoes" Wylie,
   the lesbian   Gloria DeHaven
Garth Gimble, Jr.,
   Garth's son   Eric Shea
Muriel Haggers,
   Charlie's evil
   ex-wife   L. C. Downey
Detective Johnson   Ron Feinberg
Steve Fletcher, the
   deaf-mute, Cathy's
   boyfriend   Ed Begley, Jr.
Howie Freeze, Cathy's
   boyfriend   Sid Weisman
The Capri Lounge
   Bartender   Robert Stoneman
Betty McCullogh,
   the Hartman's
   neighbor   Vivian Blaine
Voice in the opening
   calling "Mary
   Hartman, Mary
   Hartman"   Dody Goodman

Also: Reva Rose (as Blanche Fedders),
Norman Alden (Leroy Fedders),
Sudi Bond (Fannie); Billy Beck
(Lt. Trask), Larry Haddon (Ed),
Beeson Carroll (Howard), John
Fink (Brian Adams) Andra Akers
(Christine Adams), Matthew La
Borteaux (Big Foot's child).

Guests: Dr. Joyce Brothers, Dinah
Shore, Gore Vidal, David Susskind, Merv Griffin.

Music: Earle Hagen.

Music Supervision: Bobby Knight.

Executive Producer: Norman Lear.

Producer: Lew Gallo, Vivi Knight,
Perry Krauss, Eugenie Ross-
Leming, Brad Buckner.

Director: Joan Darling, Jim Drake,
Mack Bing, Art Wolff, Bob Lally,
Nessa Hyams, Giovanni Nigro,
Harlene Kim Friedman, Jack Hel-
ler, Dennis Klein, Hal Alexander.

Creator: Gail Parent, Ann Marcus,
Jerry Adelman, Daniel Gregory
Browne.

MARY HARTMAN, MARY HART-
MAN—30 minutes—Syndicated 1976.

MARY KAY AND JOHNNY

Comedy. Background: Greenwich
Village, New York. The marital misadventures of Mary Kay and Johnny
Stearns, television's first domestic
couple. Based on their actual experiences.

CAST
Mary Kay Stearns   Herself

Johnny Stearns   Himself
Announcer: Jim Stevenson.
Producer: Ernest Walling.
Director: Garry Simpson, Joe Cava-
lier.
Sponsor: Whiteball.

MARY KAY AND JOHNNY—30 minutes—NBC—1947 - 1950.

THE MARY MARGARET McBRIDE SHOW

Celebrity Interview.
Hostess: Mary Margaret McBride.
Announcer-Assistant: Vincent Con-
nolly.
Producer: Stella Karn, George Foley.
Director: Garry Simpson.

THE MARY MARGARET McBRIDE
SHOW—30 minutes—NBC 1948.

The Mary Tyler Moore Show. Mary Tyler
Moore.

THE MARY TYLER MOORE SHOW

Comedy. Background: Minneapolis-St.
Paul, Minnesota. The misadventures,
joys, sorrows, and romantic heartaches of Mary Richards, a beautiful
young bachelorette.
   Stories depict: her home life at 119
North Weatherly, Apartment D, with
her friends, Rhoda Morganstern, the
upstairs tenant, an interior decorator
at Hempel's Department Store; and
Phyllis Lindstrom, a busybody, the

owner of the building; and her
working life in the newsroom at
WJM-TV Channel 12, where, as the
associate producer of "The Six
O'Clock News" program, she struggles
to function in the man's world of an
irascible producer, Lou Grant; a soft-
hearted newswriter, Murray Slaughter;
and a naricissistic anchorman, Ted
Baxter.

CAST
Mary Richards   Mary Tyler Moore
Rhoda Morganstern   Valerie Harper
Lou Grant   Edward Asner
Ted Baxter   Ted Knight
Murray Slaughter   Gavin MacLeod
Phyllis Lindstrom   Cloris Leachman
Bess Lindstrom, Phyllis's
   daughter   Lisa Gerritsen
Gordon Howard (Gordie),
   the station weather-
   man   John Amos
Ida Morganstern, Rhoda's
   mother   Nancy Walker
Martin Morganstern, Rhoda's
   father   Harold Gould
Georgette Franklin,
   Ted's romantic
   interest   Georgia Engel
Sue Anne Nevins, the host
   of Channel 12's
   "Happy Homemaker
   Show"   Betty White
Dotty Richards, Mary's
   mother   Nanette Fabray
Walter Reed Richards,
   Mary's father, a retired
   doctor   Bill Quinn
Marie Slaughter, Murray's
   wife   Joyce Bulifant
Pete, a newsteam staff
   member   Benjamin Chuley
Edie Grant, Lou's ex-
   wife   Priscilla Morrill
Andy Rivers, Mary's occasional
   date   John Gabriel
Charlene McGuire, Lou's
   girlfriend   Sheree North
David Baxter, Ted and
   Georgette's adopted
   son   Robbie Rist
The Bartender at the Happy
   Hour Bar   Peter Hobbs
                   Chuck Bergansky
Howard Gordon, Edie's second
   husband   Brad Trumbull
Janey, Lou and Edie's
   daughter   Nora Heflin

Music: Pat Williams.

Theme vocal: "Love Is All Around,"
Sonny Curtis.

Executive Producer: James L. Brooks,
Allan Burns.

Producer: Stan Daniels, Ed Weinberger.

Director: Jay Sandrich, Marjorie Mullen, James Burrows, Harry Mastrogeorge, Mel Ferber, Doug Rogers.

Creator: James L. Brooks, Allan Burns.

Note: In later episodes Mary is promoted to producer of the news show; Ted and Georgette married on November 8, 1975.

THE MARY TYLER MOORE SHOW —30 minutes—CBS—Premiered: September 19, 1970. Spin-off series: "Rhoda" (see title).

M*A*S*H

Comedy. Background: The 4077th M*A*S*H (Mobile Army Surgical Hospital) in Korea, 1950. The story of how medical men retain their sanity amid the insanity of war and their humanity in the face of dehumanization. Episodes focus on the antics of two skilled surgeons: Captain Benjamin Franklin "Hawkeye" Pierce, and Captain "Trapper" John McIntyre, reluctant draftees determined to make the best of the miserable conditions that exist. Though constantly breaking rules and regulations, defying their superior officers, pursuing nurses, and plaguing the life of Major Frank Burns, the saving of human life is uppermost in their thoughts—thoughts coupled with the realization that the war and the killing will all one day end. Situations are played to the limits of television permissiveness. Based on the movie of the same title.

CAST

Captain Benjamin Franklin Pierce (Hawkeye)	Alan Alda
Captain John McIntyre (Trapper John)	Wayne Rogers
Lt. Col. Henry Blake, the soft-hearted commanding officer	McLean Stevenson
Major Margaret Houlihan (Hot Lips), the head nurse	Loretta Swit
Corporal Radar O'Reilly, Henry's aide, possesses E.S.P.	Gary Burghoff
Major Frank Burns, Margaret's romantic interest	Larry Linville
Father John Mulcahy, the company priest	George Morgan William Christopher
Lieutenant Maggie Dish, a nurse	Karen Philipp
Spearchucker Jones, a doctor	Timothy Brown
Lieutenant Ginger Ballis, a	

nurse	Odessa Cleveland
Corporal Maxwell Klinger the man who, dressing as a woman, seeks a psycho discharge	Jamie Farr
Ho-John, Hawkeye's Korean houseboy	Patrick Adiarte
Ugly John, the anesthetist	John Orchard
General Hamilton Hammond, the chief medical officer	G. Wood
Lieutenant Leslie Scorch, a nurse	Linda Meiklejohn
Lieutenant Jones, a nurse	Barbara Brownell
Nurse Louise Anderson	Kelly Jean Peters
Nurse Maggie Cutler	Marcia Strassman Lynette Mettey
General Brandon Clayton	Herbert Voland
The cook	Joseph Perry
Mr. Kwang, the bartender in the officers club	Leland Sung
Colonel Sherman Potter, replaced Col. Blake	Harry Morgan
Captain B. J. Hunnicutt, replaced Trapper John	Mike Farrell
Colonel Flagg, the hard-nosed CIA Agent	Edward Winter
Major Sidney Freedman, the compassionate psychiatrist	Allan Arbus
Nurse Bigelow	Enid Kent
Nurse Abel	Judy Farrell
Major Donald Penobscott, Margaret's romantic interest (married 3/15/77)	Beeson Carroll

Music: Johnny Mandell; Lionel Newman; Duante Tatro.

Executive Producer: Larry Gelbart, Gene Reynolds.

Producer: Alan Katz, Don Reo.

Director: Alan Alda, Hy Averback, Jackie Cooper, Gene Reynolds, Harry Morgan, Burt Metcalfe, Joan Darling, William Jurgenson, George Tyne.

M*A*S*H—30 minutes—CBS—Premiered: September 17, 1972.

THE MASK

Mystery. Background: New York City. The investigations and courtroom defenses of Walter and Peter Guilfoyle, brothers, attorneys.

Walter Guilfoyle	Gary Merrill
Peter Guilfoyle	William Prince

THE MASK—60 minutes—ABC—January 10, 1954 - April 28, 1954. Television's first hour-long mystery series. Broadcast live on Sunday evenings, and rebroadcast (kinescope) on Tuesday and Wednesday evenings.

MASLAND AT HOME

Musical Variety.

Host: Earl Wrightson.

Music: The Norman Paris Trio.

Producer: Franklin Heller.

Sponsor: Masland Carpets.

MASLAND AT HOME—15 minutes—ABC—March 30, 1951 - May 22, 1951.

MASQUERADE

Anthology. Improvisational adaptations of folk tales.

CAST

Avery Schreiber, Barbara Sharma, Alice Playten, Bill Hinnant, Barbara Minkus, Seth Allen, Jacques Lynn Colton, Louise Lasser, J. J. Barry, Abraham Sobaloff, Phil Burns, Sudie Bond, Barbara Tracy.

Included: "The Emperor's New Clothes"; "The Legend of Sleepy Hallow"; "The Pied Piper of Hamelin"; "The Man Who Stole His Beard"; "Czar of the Sea"; "The Man With the Secret Smile"; "The Elephant's Child"; "The Green Fairy"; "Jack and the Beanstalk."

MASQUERADE—30 minutes—PBS—October 5, 1971 - December 28, 1971.

MASQUERADE PARTY

Game. Distinguished by two formats.

Format One:
Masquerade Party—30 minutes. NBC—July 14, 1952 - August 25, 1952; CBS—June 22, 1953 - September 13, 1954; ABC— September 29, 1954 - December 15, 1956; CBS—August 4, 1958 - September 15, 1958. CBS—November 2, 1959 - January 18, 1960.

Object: For five celebrity panelists to identify elaborately disguised guest personalities. Each panelist is permitted to ask five questions of the guest. Each second of questioning scores one dollar to a maximum of three hundred dollars. At the end of five minute segments, or at any time in between, panelists may hazard to guess the identity of the guest. Whether correct or incorrect, the money that is established is donated to charity.

Hosts: Bud Collyer; Eddie Bracken; Peter Donald; Bert Parks; Robert Q. Lewis; Douglas Edwards.

Panelists: Phil Silvers, Ilka Chase, Adele Jergens, Peter Donald, Madge Evans, Buff Cobb, John Young, Ogden Nash, Johnny Johnston, Betsy Palmer, Frank Palmer, Jonathan Winters, Jinx Falkenberg, Pat Carroll, Faye Emerson, Gloria DeHaven, Audrey Meadows, Sam Levinson, Lee Bowman.

Announcer: Don Morrow, William T. Lazar.

Format Two:

Masquerade Party—30 minutes—Syndicated 1974.

Follows the basis of the first format with the following changes: Three celebrity panelists who are permitted to ask only three questions of guests; and a studio audience participation segment that replaces the money segment of the first version. After the panel's questioning, two selected studio-audience members appear on stage and state who they believe the mystery guest is. The disguise is removed, and the player who is correct, if any, receives a merchandise prize.

Host: Richard Dawson.

Panelists: Bill Bixby, Lee Meriwether, Nipsey Russell.

Announcer: Jay Stewart.

Music: Sheldon Allman.

MASTERPIECE PLAYHOUSE

Anthology. Dramatizations based on the plays of William Shakespeare, Oscar Wilde, Richard Sheridan, and Anton Chekov.

Producer: Curtis Canfield, Albert McCleery.

Director: William Corrigan, Albert McCleery.

MASTERPIECE PLAYHOUSE—60 minutes—NBC 1950.

MASTERPIECE THEATRE

Anthology. A series of British produced serials.

Host: Alistair Cooke.

Included:

Clouds of Witness. Background: London, England. The investigations of Lord Peter Wimsey, a British sleuth, into the murder of his sister's fiancé. A five-part adaptation of the Dorothy Sayers story.

CAST

Lord Peter Wimsey	Ian Carmichael
Lady Mary Wimsey	Rachel Herbert
Bunter	Glyn Houston
Parker	Mark Eden
The Duke of Denver	David Langton
Denis Cathcart	Anthony Ainley
Cynthia	Kate O'Mara
Rachel	Petronella Ford

Cousin Bette. Background: Paris, 19th century. Bette Fisher, a spinster "embittered by her poor relation status in the influential Hulot family," amuses herself by housing an artist protégé, Steinbeck. Suddenly, bitterness and resentment is triggered when he is stolen from her and married by her cousin. The story relates her demand for and attempts to achieve revenge. A five-part adaptation of the Honore de Balzac novel.

CAST

Bette Fisher	Margaret Tyzack
Valerie Marneffe	Helen Mirren
Steinbeck	Colin Baker
Hector	Thorley Walters
Hortense	Harriett Harper
Adeline	Ursula Howells
Johann Fischer	Robert Speight
Marie	Sally James
Marneffe	Oscar Quitak
Crevel	John Bryans
Henri Montes	Edward De Souza

Elizabeth R. Background: Sixteenth-century England. A six-part chronicling of the reign of Elizabeth, the daughter of Henry VIII, as the Queen of England (1558-1603).

CAST

Elizabeth	Glenda Jackson
Cecil	Ronald Hines
Mary, Queen of Scots	Vivian Pickles
The Bishop	Esmond Knight
Dudley Leicester	Robert Hardy
Kat	Rachel Kempson
Alencon	Michael Williams
King Philip	Peter Jeffrey
Sir Francis Drake	John Woodvine
The Duke of Medina	Gordon Gostelow
Sir Walter Raleigh	Nicholas Selby
Elizabeth Vernon	Sonia Fraser
Lady Leicester	Angela Thorne
Earl of Essex	Robin Ellis

The First Churchills. Background: England during the Restoration period. The life and times of John Churchill, the first Duke of Malborough. A twelve-part dramatization.

CAST

John Churchill	John Neville
Sarah Jennings	Susan Hampshire
Charles II	James Villiers
Duke of York	John Westbrook
Duchess of Cleveland	Morra Redmond
Manmouth	James Kerry
Sidney Godolphin	John Standing
Lawrence Hyde	John Ringham
Rochester	Graham Armitage
Princess	Lisa Daniely
Margaret Godolphin	Holly Wilson
Princess Anne	Margaret Tyzack
Prince of Orange	Alan Rowe
Bishop Compton	George Merritt

Poldark. Background: Europe during the 1700s. A sixteen-part romantic adventure, based on four novels by Winston Graham, that focuses on the life of Ross Poldark, a dashing war veteran, in the period immediately following the Revolution.

CAST

Ross Poldark	Robin Ellis
Elizabeth	Jill Townsend
Demelza	Angharad Rees
Verity	Norma Streader
Zacky	Forbes Collins

Upstairs, Downstairs. Background: Edwardian England. A depiction of life in a fashionable London townhouse; the interactions of a family, the Bellamys, living upstairs; and, forming their own family, their servants, who live downstairs. A fifteen-part dramatization.

CAST

Richard Bellamy	David Langton
James Bellamy	Simon Williams
Hazel Bellamy	Meg-Wynn Owen
Virginia Bellamy	Hannah Gordon
Rose, the maid	Jean Marsh
Hudson, the butler	Gordon Jackson
Mrs. Bridges	Angela Baddeley
Alfred the footman	George Innes
Edward the footman	Christopher Beeny
Daisy, the maid	Jacqueline Tong
Sarah	Pauline Collins
Watkins	John Alderton
Emily	Evin Crowley
Lady Marjorie	Rachel Gurney
Lil	Angela Brown
Georgina Worsley	Leslie-Anne Down

Music: Alexander Faris.

Producer: John Hawkesworth.

Creator: Jean Marsh, Eileen Atkens.

The Bellamy's Address: 165 Eaton Place.

Vanity Fair. Depicted: The life of an amoral adventuress, Becky Sharp, "a female Napoleon determined to claw her way up in the world by fair means or foul." Charted: Her progress through the nineteenth century. A five-part adaptation of the William Thackeray novel.

CAST

Becky Sharp	Susan Hampshire
Amelia Sedley	Marilyn Taylerson
Joseph Sedley	John Moffatt
Sir Pitt Crawley	Michael Rothwell
Fawdon Crawley	Dyson Lovell
Miss Crawley	Barbara Couper
George Osborne	Roy Marsden
Dobbin	Bryan Marshall
Pauline	Consuela Burke

MASTERPIECE THEATRE—60 minutes—PBS—Premiered: January 10, 1971.

THE MATCH GAME

Game. Distinguished by two formats.

Format One:

THE MATCH GAME—30 minutes—NBC—December 31, 1962 - September 20, 1969.

Two teams compete, each composed of three members—one celebrity captain and two noncelebrity contestants. The host reads an incomplete sentence (e.g., "Tarzan said to Jane, why don't you BLANK your hair"). Players than fill in the blank with the word or words each feels will best complete the thought. Answers are revealed and if two players match by using the same word, twenty-five points is scored. If the celebrity matches the two players, fifty points is scored. The team first to score one hundred points is the winner. Points are transferred to cash and the team receives a chance to earn additional money via "The Studio Audience Match."

Questions, asked of one hundred members of a studio audience weeks ago, are restated. After players verbally state their answers, the studio-audience responses are revealed. Each match awards the team fifty dollars.

Host: Gene Rayburn.

Announcer: Johnny Olsen.

Music: Recorded.

Format Two:

MATCH GAME '73/'74—30 minutes—CBS—Premiered: June 25, 1973.

Two competing contestants, the champion and the challenger. The challenger selects one of two questions, A or B, which the host then reads to a panel of six celebrity guests (e.g. "George didn't like his first BLANK"). Panelists than fill in the blank with the word or words that each feels will best complete the thought. The players verbally reveal their responses. Panelists, one at a time, reveal their answers, and each match awards the player one point. The champion receives the remaining question and the game is played in the same manner. Two such rounds are played and the highest scoring player is the winner and receives one hundred dollars and a chance to play "The Super Match."

First half of "The Super Match." One word (e.g., "Fat BLANK") is revealed on a game board. Below it are three cash amount responses: $100, $250, and $500. The player chooses three celebrities who each state a word with which to fill in the blank. The player is permitted to choose any of their answers or use his own. If the answer he uses matches one of the cash amounts, he receives the chance to win ten times that amount in the second half.

Second half. The player selects one celebrity to whom the host reads a question that requires a blank to be filled in. The player verbally states his answer; if he matches the celebrity's written answer, he receives ten times the amount he won in the first half.

Players compete until defeated.

Host: Gene Rayburn.

Announcer: Johnny Olsen.

Regular Panelists: Brett Somers, Richard Dawson.

Music: Score Productions.

Syndicated Version: "Match Game P.M." Basically the same as version two with the only difference being that contestants can win up to $10,000 in the Super Match. All credits are the same. 30 minutes—Syndicated 1975.

MATCHES 'N' MATES

Married couples compete in a game wherein they have to match hidden answers with concealed questions.

Host: Art James.

30 minutes—Syndicated 1967.

MATINEE IN NEW YORK

Variety. Music, songs, and celebrity interviews.

Game portion: Selected studio-audience members compete in question-and-answer rounds. Winners, the highest scorers, receive a merchandise prize.

Game Emcees: Bill Cullen, Bill Goodwin.

Interview Host: Ted Collins.

Announcer: Andre Baruch.

Orchestra: Jack Millet.

MATINEE IN NEW YORK—60 minutes—NBC—June 9, 1952 - August 1952.

MATINEE THEATRE

Anthology. Dramatic presentations broadcast live from Burbank each weekday afternoon.

Host: John Conte.

Producer: Albert McCleery.

Included:

Beyond A Reasonable Doubt. The story concerns a school teacher and his efforts to clear himself of a false murder charge.

CAST
Cara Williams, De Forest Kelley, Charlie Evans.

Springfield Incident. The story concerns Abraham Lincoln's efforts to clear two brothers accused of murder

CAST
Tom Tryon, Ann Harding, Marshall Thompson, Alan Hale.

Fortune's Child. A café owner attempts to solve a custody battle over a girl.

Starring: Charles McGraw.

Mail Order Bride. A doctor attempts to assist a man who discovers his mail-order bride is quite older than he expected.

Starring: Jack Kelly.

MATINEE THEATRE—60 minutes—NBC—October 31, 1955 - June 27, 1958.

THE MATT DENNIS SHOW

Musical Variety.

Host: Matt Dennis, pianist.

Musical Backing: Trigger Albert (bass), Mundell Lowell (guitar), Jimmy Campbell (drums).

THE MATT DENNIS SHOW—15 minutes—NBC—June 27, 1955 - August 29, 1955.

MATT HELM

Crime Drama. Background: California. The investigations of Matt Helm, a dashing government intelligence agent turned private detective.

CAST
Matt Helm — Tony Franciosa
Miss Kronski, his
  lawyer and romantic
  interest — Laraine Stephens
Lt. Hanrahan — Gene Evans
Ethel, Matt's telephone
  answering service
  girl — Jeff Donnell
Music: Morton Stevens; Jerrold Emil; John Parker.
Producer: Ken Pettus, Charles B. Fitzsimmons.
Director: Earl Bellamy, Richard Benedict, Don Weis, John Newland.

MATT HELM—60 minutes—ABC—September 20, 1975 - November 3, 1975.

MATT LINCOLN

Drama. Background: Los Angeles, California. The cases of Matt Lincoln, a psychiatrist who practices preventive psychiatry and struggles to assist people in early stages of emotional distress to prevent the need for further, more complicated treatment.

CAST
Matt Lincoln — Vince Edwards
His Assistants:
Tag — Chelsea Brown
Jimmy — Felton Perry
Kevin — Michael Larrain
Ann — June Harding
Music: Oliver Nelson.

MATT LINCOLN—60 minutes—ABC—September 24, 1970 - January 14, 1971. 13 episodes.

MATTY'S FUNDAY FUNNIES

Animated Cartoon. The overall title for a series of Harvey Films theatrical cartoons: "Casper, the Friendly Ghost," about a ghost who seeks only to make friends; "Baby Huey," the story of a mischievous, overgrown baby duck; and "Little Audrey," a mischievous little girl.
Series Animated Hosts: Matty and Sisterbelle.

MATTY'S FUNDAY FUNNIES—30 minutes—ABC—October 11, 1959 - December 31, 1961. From January 6, 1962 to September 22, 1962, the series featured the adventures of "Beany and Cecil," about a boy and his pet sea serpent.

MAUDE

Comedy. Background: 39 Crenshaw Street, Tuckahoe, New York, the residence of the Findlays: Walter, the owner of "Findlay's Friendly Appliances" store; his wife, Maude; her divorced daughter, Carol; and Carol's eight-year-old son, Philip. The story of Maude Findlay, out-spoken and liberal, a woman who, married for the fourth time, struggles to solve the incidents that creep in, disrupt, and threaten to destroy her attempts to achieve a lasting relationship with Walter. A spin-off from "All in the Family," wherein the character of Maude, Edith's cousin, appeared several times.

CAST
Maude Findlay — Beatrice Arthur
Walter Findlay — Bill Macy
Carol Trener — Adrienne Barbeau
Philip Trener — Brian Morris
Arthur Harmon, their
  neighbor, a
  doctor — Conrad Bain
Vivian Harmon, Arthur's
  wife — Rue McClanahan
Florida Evans, the Findlay
  maid (early
  episodes) — Esther Rolle
Mrs. Naugatuck, the
  Findlay maid (later
  episodes) — Hermione Baddeley
Chris, Carol's fiancé, a
  pediatrician — Fred Grandy
Henry Evans, Florida's
  husband — John Amos

Maude. Left to right: Adrienne Barbeau, Beatrice Arthur, Bill Macy, Esther Rolle.

Sam, the bartender — Jan Arvan
Fred, the bar-
  tender — Fred Zuckert
Bert Beasley, Mrs. Nell
  Naugatuck's husband (married
  11/22/76) — J. Pat O'Malley
Victoria Butterfield, the
  Findlay's housekeeper
  (after Nell
  Naugatuck) — Marlene Warfield
Music: Alan Bergman, Marilyn Bergman, Dave Grusin.
Executive Producer: Norman Lear, Rod Parker.
Producer: Bob Weiskopf, Bob Schiller.
Creator: Norman Lear.
Director: Hal Cooper.

MAUDE—30 minutes—CBS—Premiered: September 12, 1972. Spin-off series: "Good Times" (see title).

MAURICE WOODRUFF PREDICTS

Variety. Predictions coupled with celebrity interviews.
Host: Maurice Woodruff.
Co-Hosts-Announcers: Robert Q. Lewis; Vidal Sasson.

MAURICE WOODRUFF PREDICTS—60 minutes—Syndicated 1969.

MAVERICK

Western. Background: The Frontier, 1880s. The exploits of Bret and Bart Maverick, brothers, self-centered, unconventional, and untrustworthy gentlemen gamblers. Seeking rich prey, they roam throughout the West, and more often than not, assist people they find in distress.

Though considered a western adventure, "Maverick" is actually a spoof of westerns, wherein the less-than-honorable intentions of the Mavericks are meant to satirize the square Western Code and the square-headed lawmen.

CAST
Bret Maverick — James Garner
Bart Maverick — Jack Kelly
Beau Maverick, their British
  cousin — Roger Moore
Samantha Crawford,
  a friend, a con-
  artist — Diane Brewster
Dandy Jim Buckley,
  a con artist
  friend — Efrem Zimbalist, Jr.
Beauregard "Pappy" Maverick,
  their father — James Garner
Gentleman Jack

Maverick. The original logo appearing on the Warner Brothers series.

Darby   Richard Long

Music: David Buttolph.

MAVERICK—60 minutes—ABC—September 22, 1957 - July 8, 1962. Syndicated. 124 episodes.

MAX LIEBMAN PRESENTS

Variety. A series of lavish monthly specials.

Regulars: Gale Sherwood, Bambi Linn, Rod Alexander, David Atkinson, The Bil and Cora Baird Marionettes.

Orchestra: Charles Sanford.

Producer: Max Liebman, Bill Hobin.

Sponsor: Oldsmobile.

Included:

Satins and Spurs. A romantic comedy about a rodeo queen who falls in love with a magazine reporter.

CAST
Cindy: Betty Hutton; Tex: Guy Raymond; Dirk: John Wheeler; Tony: Kevin McCarthy; Ursula: Neva Patterson.

A Connecticut Yankee. The story of a modern day groom-to-be who is sent back in time to the days of King Arthur. Based on the Rodgers and Hart musical.

CAST
Martin Barrett: Eddie Albert; Sandy: Janet Blair; King Arthur: Boris Karloff; Sir Kay: John Conte.

Heidi. A musical adaptation of Johanna Spyri's classic story about a lovable Swiss orphan named Heidi.

CAST
Heidi: Jeannie Carson; Peter: Wally Cox; Grandfather: Richard Eastham; Frau Rottenmeier: Elsa Lanchester; Karla Sesseman: Natalie Wood.

MAX LIEBMAN PRESENTS—90 minutes—NBC. September 12, 1954 - June 4, 1955 (11 shows); October 1, 1955 - June 9, 1956 (11 shows).

MAYA

Adventure. Background: India. Terry Bowen, an American boy from Montana, arrives in Bombay to join his father, great white hunter Hugh Bowen. At the American Counsel, he discovers that his father is missing and is believed to have been killed by the man eating tiger of Karkata while on a safari. Believing that no animal can kill his father, he escapes from the local authorities who want to send him back to America, and begins a search to find him.

Journeying to Karkata, he meets Raji, an Indian boy who was left alone in the world when a flood destroyed his village, and his pet elephant, Maya. When it was claimed that Maya did not legally belong to Raji, and that she was to be shipped to the desert for a lifetime of labor, he and Maya ran

away, and now, a fugitive, he is wanted by police for stealing the elephant.

Fourteen and homeless, the two boys join forces: Raji to help Terry find his father; and Terry to help Raji return Maya to the land of her birth and freedom.

Resourceful and determined, the two boys struggle to maintain their independence and complete their self imposed missions.

CAST
Terry Bowen   Jay North
Raji   Sajid Khan

Narrator: Marvin Miller.

Music: Hans Salter.

MAYA—60 minutes—NBC—September 16, 1967 - February 11, 1968. 18 episodes.

MAYBERRY R.F.D.

Comedy. Background: Mayberry, North Carolina. The simple pleasures and trying times of Sam Jones, a full-time farmer and a part-time city councilman. A spin-off from "The Andy Griffith Show."

CAST
Sam Jones, a
widower   Ken Berry
Mike Jones, his
son   Buddy Foster
Millie Swanson, Sam's
romantic interest   Arlene Golonka
Goober Pyle,
the gas-station
attendant   George Lindsey
Bee Taylor, Sam's
housekeeper   Frances Bavier
Howard Sprague, the county
clerk   Jack Dodson
Emmet Clark, the fix-it-shop
owner   Paul Hartman
Ralph, Mike's
friend   Richard Steele
Aunt Alice, Sam's
housekeeper (later
episodes)   Alice Ghostley
Arnold, Mike's
friend   Sheldon Collins
Martha Clark, Emmet's
wife   Mary Lansing

Music: Earle Hagen.

Executive Producer: Andy Griffith, Richard O. Linke.

Producer: Bob Ross.

MAYBERRY R.F.D.—30 minutes—CBS—September 23, 1968 - September 6, 1971. 78 episodes. Syndicated.

MAYOR OF HOLLYWOOD

Variety. Interviews with and performances by celebrity guests.

Host: Walter O'Keefe.

Announcer: Lou Crosby.

Orchestra: Irvine Orton.

MAYOR OF HOLLYWOOD—30 minutes—NBC—July 9, 1952 - September 18, 1952.

MAYOR OF THE TOWN

Comedy. Background: The town of Springdale. The home and working life of Thomas Russell, the first citizen, now mayor.

CAST

Mayor Thomas Russell	Thomas Mitchell
Minnie, his secretary	Jean Byron
Butch Russell, his nephew	David Saber
Marilly, his housekeeper	Kathleen Freeman
Joe Ainsley, his nemesis	Tudor Owen
Also	Eve Miller

Music: Albert Glasser.

MAYOR OF THE TOWN—30 minutes—Syndicated 1954. 39 episodes.

ME AND THE CHIMP

Comedy. Background: San Pascal, California. Escaping from an Air Force research center, a chimpanzee takes refuge in a drainpipe near a playground, where he is found by two children, Scott and Kitty Reynolds.

Bringing the chimp home, the children encounter the objections of their father, Dr. Mike Reynolds, a dentist who feels that the chimp (named Buttons after his continual habit of pressing buttons) dislikes him. Demanding that Buttons must go, Mike is approached by his wife, Liz, who persuades him to devote time to Buttons—to get to know and love him as she and the children do.

Stories concern Mike's struggles to adjust to the prospect of having a chimpanzee around the house.

CAST

Mike Reynolds	Ted Bessell
Liz Reynolds	Anita Gillette
Kitty Reynolds	Kami Cotler
Scott Reynolds	Scott Kolden
Buttons	Jackie

ME AND THE CHIMP—30 minutes—CBS—January 13, 1972 - May 18, 1972. 13 episodes.

MEDALLION THEATRE

A series of thirty-minute anthology dramas first broadcast by CBS in 1953.

Producer: Leonard Valenta, Mort Abrams.

MEDIC

Medical Dramatizations. Authentic and sophisticated approaches to medical problems and practices. Filmed at various Los Angeles hospitals. Varying casts and stories.

Host-Narrator: Richard Boone, appearing as Dr. Konrad Styner.

Theme: Blue Star.

Music: Victor Young.

Executive Producer: Worthington Miner.

Producer: Frank LaTourette.

Director: Ted Post, George Cahan.

Creator: James Mosher.

Program Open:

Dr. Styner: "My name is Konrad Styner. I'm a doctor of medicine. Tonight's story has the title [name of episode]. Guardian of birth, healer of the sick, comforter of the aged. To the profession of medicine, to the men and women who labor in its cause, this story is dedicated."

Included:

Someday We'll Laugh. The trials and tribulations of a general practitioner.

CAST
Eddie Firestone, Whitney Blake, Jack Tesler.

To The Great A Most Seldom Gift. The story of a successful businessman who struggles to hide the fact of an ulcer.

CAST
Harry Townes, June Vincent, Pat Knudson.

The Good Samaritan. When a woman is injured in an automobile accident and suffers partial paralysis, her husband believes it is Dr. Styner's fault and brings a malpractice suit against him. The story depicts the hospital board hearing.

CAST
Richard Boone, Helen Mack, Paul Newland, Andrew Duggan.

MEDIC—30 minutes—NBC—September 13, 1954 - August 27, 1956. Syndicated. 59 episodes.

MEDICAL CENTER

Medical Drama. Background: The University Medical Center in Los Angeles, California. The story of two doctors: Paul Lochner, the administrative surgeon, the wiser and older, established in his ways; and Joe Gannon, the professor of surgery, the younger, gifted, and progressive. Adult and technically accurate, episodes depict the problems that face doctors in a large city hospital.

CAST

Dr. Paul Lochner	James Daly
Dr. Joe Gannon	Chad Everett
Nurse Chambers	Jayne Meadows
Dr. Bartlett	Corinne Comacho
Nurse Holmby	Barbara Baldavin
Nurse Courtland	Chris Huston
Nurse Higby	Catherine Ferrar
Nurse Murphy	Jane Dulo
Nurse Wilcox	Audrey Totter

Music: George Romanis; Lalo Schifrin; John Parker.

MEDICAL CENTER—60 minutes—CBS—September 24, 1969 - September 6, 1976. Syndicated. 144 episodes.

MEDICAL STORY

Anthology. Dramatizations stressing an open, human approach to the problems of medicine as seen through the eyes of the doctor rather than the patient.

Creators: David Gerber, Abby Mann.

Music: Richard Shores; Jerry Goldsmith.

Executive Producer: David Gerber, Abby Mann.

Producer: Christopher Morgan.

Director: Paul Wendkos, Garry Nelson.

Included:

Million Dollar Baby. The story of Alma Geary, a blind woman who brings a malpractice suit against the doctor who delivered her prematurely twenty-two years before, claiming that his improper use of pure oxygen caused her loss of sight.

CAST

Dr. Amos Winkler: John Forsythe; Liz Winkler: Geraldine Brooks; Alma Geary: Catherine Burns.

Us Against the World. The story focuses on the problems faced by three female surgeons in a busy hospital.

CAST

Sunny: Meredith Baxter Birney; Audrey: Donna Mills; Hope: Christine Belford; Kim: Linda Purl.

MEDICAL STORY—60 minutes—NBC—Premiered: September 4, 1975.

MEET BETTY FURNESS

Women. Guests, interviews, and topics of special interest to housewives.

Hostess: Betty Furness.

Regulars: Don Cherry, Hank Ford, Bill Stern, David Ross.

Music: The Buddy Weed Trio.

MEET BETTY FURNESS—15 minutes—NBC 1953.

MEET CORLISS ARCHER

Comedy. The misadventures of Corliss Archer, a pretty, unpredictable teenage girl. Based on the radio program of the same title.

Versions:

Meet Corliss Archer—30 minutes—CBS—1951 - 1952 (Live.)

CAST

Corliss Archer	Lugene Sanders
Harry Archer, her father, an insurance salesman	Fred Sheldon
Janet Archer, his wife	Frieda Inescort
Dexter Franklin, Corliss's boyfriend	Bobby Ellis

Announcer: John Heistand.

Producer: Helen Mack.

Director: Alan Dinehard.

Meet Corliss Archer—30 minutes—CBS—1954 - 1955. (Filmed.)

CAST

Corliss Archer	Ann Baker
Harry Archer	John Eldridge
Janet Archer	Mary Bain
Dexter Franklin	Bobby Ellis

Music: Felix Mills.

Narrator-Producer: Hy Averback.

MEETING OF THE MINDS

See title: "Steve Allen."

MEET McGRAW

Crime Drama. The investigations of McGraw, a roving private detective, "a professional busy-body who wanders from state to state minding other people's business."

Starring: Frank Lovejoy as McGraw (unidentified by a first name).

MEET McGRAW—30 minutes—NBC —July 2, 1957 - June 24, 1958; ABC—November 23, 1958 - October 9, 1959. Syndicated.

MEET ME AT THE ZOO

Educational. Background: The Philadelphia Zoo. Curators discuss and relate aspects of various exhibits.

Host: Freeman Shelly.

MEET ME AT THE ZOO—30 minutes—CBS 1953.

MEET MILLIE

Comedy. Background: New York City. The trials and tribulations of Millie Bronson, a secretary who is secretly in love with her employer's son, Johnny Boone. Stories depict her mother's attempts to spark a romance between the two.

CAST

Millie Bronson	Elena Verdugo
Mrs. Bronson, her mother, a widow	Florence Halop
Johnny Boone	Ross Ford
Alfred Prinzmetal, a friend	Marvin Kaplan
J.R. Boone Sr., her employer	Earl Ross
Mrs. Boone, his wife	Isabel Randloph
Mr. Weems, a friend, the owner of a ranch in Texas	Harry Cheshire

Announcer: Bob Lemond.

Music: Irving Miller.

Producer: Frank Galen.

Meet Millie. Florence Halop and Elena Verdugo.

MEET MILLIE—30 minutes—CBS—October 25, 1952 - February 28, 1956.

MEET MR. McNUTLEY

See title: "The Ray Milland Show."

MEET THE PRESS

In-depth News Interview.

Hosts: Martha Rountree, Ned Brooks, Lawrence E. Spivak.

Press Representatives: Four guests.

MEET THE PRESS—30 minutes—NBC—Premiered: November 20, 1947.

MEET YOUR COVER GIRL

Interview. Fashion models appear and discuss various aspects of their careers, including background and home life.

Hostess: Robin Chandler.

Producer: Stanley Poss.

Director: Herbert Sussan.

MEET YOUR COVER GIRL—30 minutes—CBS 1949.

MEET YOUR MATCH

Game. One preselected contestant chooses one person from the studio audience as his opponent. A general-knowledge question-and-answer session is conducted wherein each correct response awards cash. If one player fails to correctly answer a question, he is defeated, and the opponent, the winner, receives the money he has accumulated and the privilege to choose another player with whom to match wits.

Host: Jan Murray.

MEET YOUR MATCH—30 minutes—NBC—August 25, 1952 - September 1, 1952.

THE MELBA MOORE-CLIFTON DAVIS SHOW

Variety. Music, song, dance, and comedy set against the background of a Manhattan brownstone.

Hosts: Melba Moore, Clifton Davis.

Regulars: Ron Carey, Timmie Rogers, Dick Libertini, Liz Torres.

Announcer: Johnny Olsen.

Orchestra: Charles H. Coleman.

THE MELBA MOORE-CLIFTON DAVIS SHOW—60 minutes—CBS—June 7, 1972 - July 5, 1972.

MELODY, HARMONY, RHYTHM

Musical Variety.

Host: Lynne Barrett.

Dancers: Dula & Lorenski.

Music: The Tony DiSimone Trio.

MELODY, HARMONY, RHYTHM—30 minutes—NBC 1948. CBS—15 minutes—1950.

MELODY STREET

Musical Variety. An informal stroll down Tin Pan Alley.

Host: Elliott Lawrence.

Music: The Tony Mottola Trio.

MELODY STREET—30 minutes—DuMont—1953 - 1954.

MELODY TOUR

Musical Variety. Staged tours of the world via music.

Host: Stan Freeman.

Regulars: Norman Scott, Nancy Kenyon, Jane Remes, Peter Gladhe, Nellie Fisher, Robert Rounsville, Jonathan Lucas.

Orchestra: Harry Sosnick.

MELODY TOUR—30 minutes—ABC—July 8, 1954 - September 30, 1954.

THE MEL TORMÉ SHOW

Musical Variety.

Host: Mel Tormé, "The Velvet Fog."

Regulars: Peggy King, Ellen Martin, Kaye Ballard, The Mello-Larks.

Music: The Red Norvo Trio; The Terry Gibbs Quintet.

Producer: Bob Bach.

Director: Lloyd Gross.

THE MEL TORMÉ SHOW—30 minutes—CBS—1951 - 1952.

THE MEMORY GAME

Game. Five competing female contestants, each of whom begin with fifty dollars. Each is presented with a packet of five questions and given twenty-five seconds to study them. At the end of the time, the questions are taken back and the host asks one player a question. If she cannot answer it, she is permitted to pass it to any other player by calling her number (1,2,3,4, or 5). The player who correctly answers the question receives five dollars; if a player cannot correctly answer it, five dollars is deducted. The player last to correctly answer a question becomes the player to receive the next question.

Round Two: Questions are marked by a one- to ten-second time limit. The game follows in the same manner, but if a player is caught by a buzzer when asked or passing a question, she has to answer it. Question values and deductions are ten dollars.

Final Round: Involves the champion, the highest scoring player. After she wages any amount of her accumulated earnings, the host asks her one question. If she correctly answers it, she receives the wagered amount; if she is unable, the amount is deducted.

Host: Joe Garagiola.

Announcer: Johnny Olsen.

THE MEMORY GAME—30 minutes—NBC—February 15, 1971 - July 30, 1971.

THE MEN

Mystery-Adventure. The overall title for three rotating series: "Assignment: Vienna," "The Delphi Bureau," and "Jigsaw."

Assignment: Vienna. Background: Vienna, Austria. The cases of Jake Webster, a United States government undercover agent who poses as the bartender-owner of Jake's Bar and Grill.

CAST

Jake Webster	Robert Conrad
Major Bernard Caldwell, his contact	Charles Cioffi
Inspector Hoffman	Anton Diffring

Music: Dave Grusin; John Parker.

The Delphi Bureau. Background: Washington, D.C. The Delphi Bureau is a top-secret intelligence agency responsible only to the President of the United States. Offices and staff are nonexistent and its purpose is to protect national security. Glenn Garth Gregory, a research specialist with a photographic memory, is its chief operative; and Sybil Van Loween, a beautiful but mysterious Washington society hostess, is his contact. Stories depict Gregory's investigations.

CAST

Glenn Garth Gregory	Laurence Luckinbill
Sybil Van Loween	Celeste Holm Anne Jeffreys

Music: Frank DeVol; Harper McKay.

Jigsaw. Background: The State Missing Persons Bureau in Sacramento, California. The investigations of Lieutenant Detective Frank Dain, its one-man operative who possesses a genius for solving complicated, clueless mysteries.

Starring: James Wainwright as Lt. Frank Dain.

Music: Harper McKay.

THE MEN—60 minutes—ABC—September 21, 1972 - September 1, 1973. 24 episodes.

MEN AT LAW

Crime Drama. Background: The Neighborhood Legal Services offices in Century City, downtown Los Angeles, California. The cases of David Hansen, Deborah Sullivan, and Gabriel Kay, lawyers who defend indigent clients. Emphasis is placed on courtroom proceedings. A spin-off from "The Storefront Lawyers."

CAST

David Hansen	Robert Foxworth
Deborah Sullivan	Sheila Larken
Gabriel Kay	David Arken
Attorney Devlin McNeil	Gerald S. O'Loughlin

Kathy, their
secretary   Nancy Jeris

MEN AT LAW—60 minutes—CBS—
January 20, 1971 - September 1,
1971. 13 episodes.

MEN IN CRISES

Documentary. Films recalling the vital
decisions of men whose leadership has
shaped twentieth-century history.
Narrator: Edmond O'Brien.

MEN IN CRISES—30 minutes—Syndicated 1954. 32 episodes.

THE MEN FROM SHILOH

See title: "The Virginian."

MEN INTO SPACE

Adventure. The story of the U.S.
government's attempts to further its
space program.

CAST
Col. Edward
  McCauley   William Lundigan
Mary McCauley, his
  wife   Joyce Taylor
Lt. Johnny Baker   Corey Allen
Capt. Harvey Sparkman   Kem Dibbs
Music: David Rose.

MEN INTO SPACE—30 minutes—
CBS—September 30, 1959 - September 7, 1960. 38 episodes. Syndicated.

MEN OF ANNAPOLIS

Anthology. Dramatizations based on
incidents in the training of men
attending Annapolis, the U.S. Naval
Academy. Filmed with the technical
assistance of the U.S. Naval Academy
and the Department of Defense. The
midshipmen of Annapolis perform in
all stories.
Included:

The Crucial Moment. Constantly
rejected by the Navy football team,
Paul Towner is suddenly given a
chance when the coach sees him play.
The story depicts his attempts to
prove his worthiness in an important
game.
Starring: Jack Diamond, Robert J.
  Stevenson, Mason Alan Dinehart,
  Keith Vincent.

Sink Or Swim. A sensitive nineteen-

year-old midshipman decides to assert
himself against his father's domination
and try out for the Academy's water-
polo team.
Starring: Mark Damon.

The Blue And Grey. Shortly before
the Army-Navy football game, three
midshipman conspire to perform a
long-coveted feat.

Starring: Darryl Hickman.

MEN OF ANNAPOLIS—30 minutes—
Syndicated 1957. 39 episodes.

MENSHA THE MAGNIFICENT

Comedy. The misadventures of
Mensha Shrunk, the manager of a
decrepit restaurant.

CAST
Mensha Shrunk   Himself
His employer,
  the owner of the
  restaurant   Jean Cleveland
Also   Vinton Hayworth
                      Danny Leane
Producer: Martin Goodman.
Director: Alan Newman.

MENSHA THE MAGNIFICENT—30
minutes—NBC 1950.

THE MEREDITH WILSON SHOW

Musical Variety.
Host: Meredith Wilson.
Orchestra: Meredith Wilson.

THE MEREDITH WILSON SHOW—
30 minutes—NBC—July 31, 1949 -
September 1949.

MESSING PRIZE PARTY

A game show, hosted by Bill Slater,
and featuring couples performing
stunts for prizes.

30 minutes—CBS 1949.

MERV GRIFFIN

Listed: The television programs of
singer-actor Merv Griffin.

**Song Snapshots On A Summer Holi-
day**—Musical Variety—15 minutes—
CBS 1954.

Host: Merv Griffin.
Hostess: Betty Ann Grove.
Featured: The Peter Birch Dancers.
Orchestra: Unidentified.

Play Your Hunch—Game—NBC—
1958. (See title.)

Keep Talking—Game—ABC—1959.
(See title.)

The Merv Griffin Show—Talk/Variety
—55 minutes (Daily)—NBC—
1962-1963.
Host: Merv Griffin.
Orchestra: Under direction of guest
  leaders.

Word For Word—Game—NBC—1963.
(See title.)

Hollywood Talent Scouts—Variety—
CBS—1963. (See title.)

The Merv Griffin Show—Talk/Variety
—90 minutes—Syndicated 1965.

Host: Merv Griffin.
Announcer: Arthur Treacher.
Orchestra: Mort Lindsey.

The Merv Griffin Show—Talk/Variety
(11:30 p.m.—1:00 a.m., EST)—CBS—
August 18, 1969 - February 11, 1972.
Host: Merv Griffin.
Announcer: Arthur Treacher.
Orchestra: Mort Lindsey.

The Merv Griffin Show—Talk/Variety
—90 minutes—Syndicated 1972.
Host: Merv Griffin.
Orchestra: Mort Lindsey.

M—G—M PARADE

Documentary. Metro—Goldwyn—
Mayer's first television venture. A
behind-the-scenes look at Hollywood,
its past and present (1955). Features:
Tours, interviews and guests from the
M—G—M Culver City lot sound stages,
and film sequences highlighting var-
ious Metro features.
Host: George Murphy.
Co-Host: Pete Smith.
Premiere guest: Dore Schary, the
  studio head.

M—G—M PARADE—30 minutes—

ABC—September 14, 1955 - May 2, 1956.

MIAMI UNDERCOVER

Crime Drama. Background: Miami Beach, Florida. Posing as a sophisticated man-about-town, Jeff Thompson, a troubleshooter hired by the Miami Hotel Owners Association, attempts to eliminate the sources of trouble that invade Florida.

CAST
Jeff Thompson — Lee Bowman
Rocky, his partner — Rocky Graziano

MIAMI UNDERCOVER—30 minutes —Syndicated 1961. 38 episodes.

MICHAEL SHAYNE, PRIVATE DETECTIVE

Crime Drama. Background: Miami Beach, Florida. The investigations of private detective Michael Shayne. Based on the character created by Brett Halliday.

CAST
Michael Shayne — Richard Denning
Lucy Hamilton, his secretary — Patricia Donahue
— Margie Regan
Tim Rourke, a photographer-reporter — Jerry Paris
Lieutenant Gentry, Florida Sheriff's Office — Herbert Rudley
Dick Hamilton, Lucy's kid brother — Gary Clark
Joe Demarest — Meade Martin
Richard Banke-McCord — Will Gentry

Music: Leslie Stevens.

MICHAEL SHAYNE, PRIVATE DETECTIVE—60 minutes—NBC— September 1960 - September 1961. Syndicated. 32 episodes.

THE MICHAELS IN AFRICA

Documentary. Various aspects of the people and animals of South Africa.

Hosts—Narrators: George and Marjorie Michaels (Mr. & Mrs.).

THE MICHAELS IN AFRICA—30 minutes—Syndicated 1958.

MICKEY

Comedy. Background: The Newport Arms Hotel in Newport Beach, Cali-

The Mickey Mouse Club. The Mouseketeers. © *Walt Disney Productions.*

fornia. The trials and tribulations of its owner-operators, the Gradys: Mickey, a retired businessman; his wife, Nora; and their children, Timmy and Buddy.

CAST
Mickey Grady — Mickey Rooney
Nora Grady — Emmaline Henry
Timmy Grady — Timmy Rooney
Buddy Grady — Brian Nash
Sammy Ling, the hotel's Chinese manager — Sammee Tong

MICKEY—30 minutes—ABC—September 16, 1964 - January 13, 1965. 17 episodes.

THE MICKEY MOUSE CLUB

Children. Background: The Mickey Mouse Club House. Music, songs dances, cartoons, guests, news features, and adventure serials.

Host: Jimmie Dodd.

Co-Host: Roy Williams ("The Big Mooseketeer").

Assistant: Bob Amsberry.

The Mouseketeers: Annette Funicello, Darlene Gillespie, Carl "Cubby" O'Brien, Karen Pendleton, Bobby Burgess, Tommy Cole, Cheryl Holdridge, Lynn Ready, Doreen Tracy, Linda Hughes, Lonnie Burr, Bonni Lynn Fields, Sharon Baird, Ronnie Young, Jay Jay Solari, Margene Storey, Nancy Abbate, Billie Jean Beanblossom, Mary Espinosa, Bonnie Lou Kern, Mary Lou Sartori, Bronson Scott, Dennis Day, Dickie Dodd, Michael Smith, Ronald Steiner, Mark Sutherland, Don Underhill, Sherry Allen, Paul Peterson, Judy Harriett, John Lee John-

son, Eileen Diamond, Charley Laney, Larry Larsen, Don Agrati (a.k.a. Don Grady).

Professor Wonderful: Julius Sumner Miller.

Music: The Disneyland Band, Joseph Dubin, Buddy Baker, William Lava, Joseph Mullendore, Franklin Marks.

Voice of the Animated Jiminy Cricket: Cliff Edwards.

Voice of Mickey Mouse: Jim Macdonald (for the TV series; Walt Disney's voice is heard as Mickey prior to 1949).

Narrator of the Mickey Mouse Newsreel: Hal Gibney.

Special News Correspondent: Dick Metzzi.

Director of the Mouseketeers: Sid Miller, Clyde Geronimi.

Executive Producer: Walt Disney.

Producer: Bill Walsh, Dick Darley.

Director: Jonathan Lucas, William Beaudine, Charles Haas, Lee Clark.

Choreography: Tom Mahoney.

Serials:

Adventures In Dairyland. Background: The McCandless Sunny Acres Dairy Farm in Wisconsin. Its operation as seen through the eyes of guests Annette Funicello and Sammy Ogg. Their efforts are complicated by Moochie, the McCandlesses' mischievous young son.

CAST
Annette Funicello: Herself; Sammy Ogg: Himself; Moochie McCandless: Kevin Corcoran; Mr. McCandless: Herb Newcombe; Mrs. McCandless: Mary Lu Delmonte; Jimmy McCandless, their son: Glen Garber; Pauli, the ranch hand: Fern Parsons.

The Adventures of Clint and Mac. Background: London, England. The story of two boys, Clint Rogers, an American, and his friend, Alastair "Mac" MacIntosh, as they attempt to solve a crime—the theft of the original manuscript of *Treasure Island.*

CAST:
Clint Rogers: Neil Wolfe; Alastair MacIntosh: Jonathan Bailey; Inspector MacIntosh, Mac's father: John Warwick; Mac's mother: Dorothy Smith; Clinton Rogers, Clint's father: Bill Nagy; Clint's mother: Mary Barclay; Pamela Stuart, Clint and Mac's friend: Sandra Michaels; John Stuart, Pam's father: Gordon Harris; Toby Jug, the criminal: George Woodbridge.

The Mickey Mouse Club. *Adventures in Dairyland.* Kevin Corcoran. © *Walt Disney Productions.*

The Mickey Mouse Club. *Annette.* Left to right: Sylvia Fields, Annette Funicello, Richard Deacon. © *Walt Disney Productions.*

The Mickey Mouse Club. *The Hardy Boys and the Mystery of Ghost Farm.* Left to right: Tim Considine, and Tommy Kirk. © *Walt Disney Productions.*

Annette. Background: The town of Ashford. The story of Annette McCleod, a country girl who comes to live with her relatives in the big city. The serial focuses on her attempts to adjust to a life she finds new and confusing and her efforts to win the friendship of Laura Rogan, a girl who takes an instant dislike to her.

CAST

Annette McCleod: Annette Funicello; Dr. Archie McCleod, her uncle: Richard Deacon; Lila McCleod, Archie's sister: Sylvia Fields; Katie, their housekeeper: Mary Wickes; Laura Rogan: Jymme Shore; Stephen Abernathy, Annette's friend: Tim Considine; Annette's friends: Val Abernathy: Doreen Tracy; Mike Martin: David Stollery; Jet Maypen: Judy Nugent; Moselle Corey: Shelley Fabares; Olmstead Ware: Ruby Lee; Kitty: Sharon Baird; Madge: Cheryl Holdridge.

Border Collie. Background: Hamilton County in Southern Illinois. The story of Rod Brown, a young boy and his attempts to train a Scottish Border Collie named Scamp for competition in a local dog show.

Starring: Bobby Evans as Rod Brown.

Also: Arthur Allen.

Narrator: Alvy Moore.

The Boys of the Western Sea. Background: Russia. The story of a teenage boy named Paul and his struggles to support his brother and sister, as a fisherman, after his father's untimely death. Filmed in Russia; dubbed in English. Credits are not given.

Corky and White Shadow. Background: The small Midwestern town of Beaumont. Assisted by her German Shepherd dog, White Shadow, a young girl, Corky Brady, attempts to capture the Durango Dude, an outlaw sought by her father, Sheriff Matt Brady.

CAST

Corky Brady: Darlene Gillespie; Matt Brady: Buddy Ebsen; Uncle Dan: Lloyd Corrigan; White Shadow: Chinook.

The Hardy Boys and the Mystery of the Applegate Treasure. Background: The town of Bayport. Amateur detectives, brothers Joe and Frank Hardy, attempt to solve the baffling theft of pirate treasure from the estate of Silas Applegate.

CAST

Joe Hardy: Tim Considine; Frank Hardy: Tommy Kirk; Iola Morton, Joe's girlfriend: Carole Ann Campbell; Fenton Hardy, the boys' father: Russ

The Mickey Mouse Club. *Corky and White Shadow.* Darlene Gillespie and her dog Chinook. © *Walt Disney Productions.*

Conway; Gertrude Hardy, Fenton's sister: Sarah Selby; Silas Applegate: Florenz Ames.

The Hardy Boys and the Mystery of Ghost Farm. Amateur sleuths Joe and Frank Hardy attempt to solve the baffling mystery of a farm supposedly haunted by a ghost. Cast listing is exactly the same as the above "Hardy Boys" mystery (which see).

Moochie of the Little League. Background: The Town of Winston. The comic escapades of Montgomery "Moochie" Morgan, Jr., as he struggles to succeed as a Little Leaguer with the Bobcats baseball team.

CAST

Moochie: Kevin Corcoran; Montgomery Morgan, Sr., Moochie's father: Russ Conway; Louise Morgan, Moochie's mother: Frances Rafferty; Marion Morgan, Moochie's sister: Dorothy Green; Bee Bee Preston, Moochie's friend: Annette Gorman; Fred Preston, Bee Bee's father: Alan Hale, Jr.; Andy Clinton, the manager: James L. Brown; Lou Rosen, the team owner: Stu Erwin; Cecil Bennett, a friend: Reginald Owen.

Moochie of Pop Warner Football. Sequel to the above serial. Moochie's experiences—and misadventures—as a member of the Pop Warner Football team, Pee Wee division. Cast is exactly the same as the above "Moochie" serial with the addition of Dennis Joel as Moochie's friend.

The Secret of Mystery Lake. Background: Real Foot Lake in Tennessee. The story concerns naturalist Bill

Richards as he attempts to uncover the wonders of Nature as it abounds in and around the lake.

CAST

Bill Richards: George Fenneman; Lanie Thorne, his pretty guide: Gloria Marshall.

Spin and Marty. Background: The Triple R Ranch in North Fork, a Summer boys camp. The experiences of two boys, Spin Evans and Marty Markham. The story itself concerns their efforts to train for competition in a local rodeo.

CAST

Spin Evans: Tim Considine; Marty Markham: David Stollery; Jim Logan, the ranch head: Roy Barcroft; Bill Burnett, the counselor: Harry Carey, Jr.; Perkins, Marty's guardian: J. Pat O'Malley; Sam, the cook: Sammee Tong. Campers: Ambitious: B.G. Norman; Joe: Sammy Ogg; George: Joe Wong; Speckle: Tim Hartnagel.

The Further Adventures of Spin and Marty. Continued events in the lives of Spin Evans and Marty Markham. The story concerns itself with the rivalry that ensues between Spin and Marty for the affections of Annette, a pretty young lady attending the Circle H Girls Camp.

CAST

Exactly the same as in "Spin and Marty" with these additions: Annette: Annette Funicello; Ollie, the wrangler: Dennis Moore; Moochie O'Hara, a camper: Kevin Corcoran.

The New Adventures of Spin and Marty. The story concerns Spin and Marty's attempts to stage a variety show to pay for damages caused by Marty's jalopy when it ran into the ranch house.

CAST

Exactly the same as in "Spin and Marty" with these additions: Annette: Annette Funicello; Darlene, Annette's friend: Darlene Gillespie; Moochie, a camper: Kevin Corcoran; Hank, the wrangler: Dennis Moore.

What I Want To Be. Background: Kansas City, Missouri. The training and study periods of two young hopefuls: Patricia Morrow, airline stewardess; and Duncan Richardson, pilot.

Starring: Patricia Morrow, Duncan Richardson, and, as the reporter: Alvy Moore.

THE MICKEY MOUSE CLUB—60 and 30 minute versions—ABC—October 3, 1955 - September 25, 1959. Syndicated. See also: "The New Mickey Mouse Club."

THE MICKEY ROONEY SHOW

See title: "Hey, Mulligan."

MICKEY ROONEY'S SMALL WORLD

Discussion. Eight children, aged four to eight, who vary from program to program, appear and are first questioned about themselves, then ask questions and discuss various matters with a guest celebrity.

Host: Mickey Rooney.

Music: Recorded open and close (theme: "It's A Small World").

Executive Producer: Mickey Rooney.

MICKEY ROONEY'S SMALL WORLD—30 minutes—Syndicated 1975.

MICKIE FINN'S

Musical Variety. Background: The Mickie Finn Nightclub, "America's number one speakeasy," in San Diego, California. The music, song, and dance of yesteryear—from the Gay Nineties to the Sensational Sixties.

Host: Fred Finn.

Hostess: Mickie Finn (Mrs.)

Regulars: Alex, the headwaiter; Hoot, the doorman; The Mickie Finn Waitresses.

Vocals: Mickie Finn and guests.

Choreographer: Alex Plasschaert.

Music: The Mickie Finn Band. Comprising: Fred Finn (piano); Mickie Finn (banjo); Spider Marillo (drums); Bobby Jensen (trumpet); Story Gormley (tuba); Owen Leinhard (trombone); Don Van Paulta, the Flying Dutchman (banjo).

MICKIE FINN'S—30 minutes—NBC—April 21, 1966 - September 1, 1966.

THE MIDNIGHT SPECIAL

Variety. Performances by Rock, Pop, and Soul personalities.

The Mickey Mouse Club. *The New Adventures of Spin and Marty.* Darlene Gillespie and Annette Funicello. © *Walt Disney Productions.*

Mickie Finn's. Fred Finn and Mickie Finn.

Hosting: Weekly guests.

Premiere Hostess: Helen Reddy.

Announcer: Wolfman Jack.

Music: Provided by guests.

Premiere Guests: Curtis Mayfield, Don McLean, Rare Earth, Sam Neely, Ike and Tina Turner. The Byrds, The Impressions.

THE MIDNIGHT SPECIAL—90 minutes—NBC (1:00 a.m. - 2:30 a.m., EST)—Premiered: February 2, 1973.

MIDWESTERN HAYRIDE

Musical Variety. Performances by Country and Western personalities.

Hosts: Paul Dixon, Dean Richards, Willie Thall, Bill Thall.

Regulars: Phyllis Brown, Bonnie Lou, Helen Scott, Billy Scott, Paul Arnold, Mary Jane Johnson, Clay Eager, Phyllis Holmes, Bill Holmes, Freddy Langdon, Tommy Watson, Zeeke Turner, Wally Praetor, Martha Hendricks, Barney Sefton, Jim Philpot, Ernie Lee, Judy Perkins, Kenny Roberts, Bob Shredi, The Pleasant Valley Boys, The Country Briar Hoppers, The Hometowners, The Kentucky Boys, The Midwesterners, The Lucky Pennies, The Trail Blazers, The Girls Of The Golden West, The Brown Ferry Four.

Announcer: Hal Woodward.

Music: The Pleasant Valley Rangers.

MIDWESTERN HAYRIDE—30 and 60 minutes versions—Syndicated— 1947-1967. Also appeared on ABC: June 29, 1957 - September 22, 1958.

THE MIGHTY HERCULES

Animated Cartoon. Background: The Learien Valley in Ancient Greece. The exploits of Hercules, the legendary hero of mythology.

Characters:

Hercules. Positioned on Mount Olymus, he receives his power by exposing his magic ring to lightning

Wilamene, the evil sea witch

Deadalius, the villainous wizard

Helena, the beautiful maiden

Newton, half human and half horse, a friend of Hercules

Tweet, half human and half horse, a friend of Hercules

THE MIGHTY HERCULES—05 minutes—Syndicated 1960. 130 episodes.

THE MIGHTY HEROES

An animated cartoon that details the exploits of Diaper Man, a daring avenger who, working out of a crib and with the aide of an incredible baby bottle, battles evil. 26 eight minute films; Syndicated 1966.

THE MIGHTY MOUSE PLAYHOUSE

Animated Cartoon. The exploits of Mighty Mouse, the courageous and daring defender of the weak and oppressed.

Voice of Mighty Mouse: Tom Morrison.

Narrator: Tom Morrison.

Music: Philip Scheib.

Producer: Bill Weiss.

Director: Eddie Donnelly, Manning Davis, Connie Rosinski.

THE MIGHTY MOUSE PLAYHOUSE—30 minutes (four six minute segments)—CBS—December 10, 1955 - September 2, 1967. 150 episodes. Syndicated.

MIKE AND BUFF

Celebrity Interview.

Host: Mike Wallace.

Hostess: Buff Cobb (Mrs.)

MIKE AND BUFF—45 minutes—CBS 1951.

THE MIKE DOUGLAS SHOW

Discussion-Variety.

Host: Mike Douglas.

Music: The Ellie Frankel Quartet; The Joe Harnell Sextet; The Frank Hunter Band. The Joe Massimino Band.

THE MIKE DOUGLAS SHOW—90 minutes—Syndicated 1966.

MIKE HAMMER, DETECTIVE

Crime Drama. Background: New York City. The investigations of Mike Hammer, a suave, sophisticated, quick-tempered, and rugged private detective. Based on the character created

by Mickey Spillane.

Starring: Darren McGavin as Mike Hammer.

Narrator: Darren McGavin.

Music: David Kahn, Melvyn Lenard.

MIKE HAMMER, DETECTIVE—30 minutes—NBC—1958 - 1959. Syndicated.

THE MIKE WALLACE INTERVIEW

Interview. Probing discussions on topical issues.

Host: Mike Wallace.

THE MIKE WALLACE INTERVIEW —30 minutes—Syndicated 1957. ABC run: April 28, 1957 - September 14, 1958.

THE MILLIONAIRE

Drama. Of the two billion four hundred million people populating the world in 1955, only nineteen of these were worth five hundred million dollars or more. One such man was John Beresford Tipton, manufacturer, bachelor, multibillionaire.

Residing at Silverstone, his sixty-thousand-acre estate, Tipton conducted his business activities and lived his life of treasured seclusion. Upon doctor's orders that he find a means of relaxation, he undertook a most unusual hobby.

Seated in the study, toying with one of his ivory chess figures, Tipton sends for his executive secretary and confidant, Michael Anthony.

Mike: "You sent for me sir?"

Tipton: "You know Mike, these chessmen were the first luxury I ever allowed myself....I...decided to make my hobby a chess game with human beings."

Mike: "Human beings sir?"

Tipton: "I'm going to choose a number of people for my chessmen and give them each a million dollars....The bank [Gotham City Trust and Savings] will issue the check....No one is ever to know that I'm the donor....I want a complete report on what happens to each person's life in writing...."

After his death, the will instructed Michael Anthony to reveal the files of people, selected by a means known only to Tipton, who were mysteriously presented with a tax-free cashier's check for one million dollars.

In flashback sequences, John Beresford Tipton's intrusion on fate is revealed as stories disclose whether the money helped or hindered lives.

CAST

Michael Anthony   Marvin Miller
John Beresford Tipton
(never fully seen), voiced
by   Paul Frees
Andrew V. McMahon, the
president of the
bank   Roy Gordon

Announcer: Ed Herlihy.

Music: Stanley Wilson; George Sharder.

Included:

The Susan Birchard Story. Receiving the check, a young woman attempts to recapture her past and returns to the home town of her youth to find the childhood sweetheart she never stopped loving.

CAST

Susan Birchard: Luana Patten; Tony Cassella: Brett Halsey; Susan as a girl: Reba Waters; Harvey: Leon Tyler; Nancy: Eve Brent.

The Peter Bartley Story. Separated from his two brothers many years ago after his parents were killed in an automobile accident, Peter Bartley, the recipient of the check, returns to the orphanage and begins a search to find them.

CAST

Peter Bartley: John Ericson; Sister Mary: Jeanette Nolan; Dora McKenna: Kay Elhardt; James Bartley: Roland Green; Peter as a boy: John Washbrook; James as a boy: Rene Karper; John as a boy: Mickey Morgan.

The Jerry Bell Story. Considering himself unattractive, writer Jerry Bell meets and falls in love with a blind girl named Myra. Suddenly wealthy, he arranges for her sight-restoring operation. Realizing that she may never love him after she sees him, he walks out on her. Returning to a favorite spot of theirs on the beach, he and Myra meet—and find their love unchanged.

CAST

Jerry Bell: Charles Bronson; Myra: Georgianna Johnson.

THE MILLIONAIRE—30 minutes—CBS—January 19, 1955 - September 1960. 188 episodes. Syndicated. Also known as "If You Had a Million."

MILTON BERLE

Listed: The television programs of comedian Milton Berle.

The Texaco Star Theatre—Variety (outlandish, slapstick comedy)—60 minutes—NBC—September 21, 1948 - June 9, 1953.

Host: Milton Berle, "Mr. Televison."

Regulars: Dolores Gray, Sid Stone (Milton's pitchman), Arnold Stang (as Francis, his stagehand), Bobby Clark, Ruth Gilbert (as Berle's secretary), Willie Field, the Merry Texaco Repairmen, The Balicana Ivanko Troupe, The Dunhills.

Commercial Spokesman: Jimmy Nelson, ventriloquist; his dummy: Danny O'Day.

Orchestra: Allen Roth.

The Milton Berle Show—Variety—60 minutes—NBC—September 29, 1953 - June 14, 1955.

Host: Milton Berle.

Regulars: Arnold Stang, Ruth Gilbert, Nancy Walker, Connie Russell, Charlie Applegate, Fred Clark, The Herb Rose Dancers.

Announcer: Jack Lescoulie.

Orchestra: Allen Roth.

The Milton Berle Show—Variety—60 minutes—NBC—September 27, 1955 - June·5, 1956.

Format: Varying, tailored to the talents of guests.

Host: Milton Berle.

Orchestra: Victor Young.

The Kraft Music Hall—Variety—30 minutes—NBC—October 8, 1958 - May 13, 1959. (See title.)

Jackpot Bowling—Contest—30 minutes—NBC—September 19, 1960 - March 13, 1961.

Host: Milton Berle.

Play-by-play call: Chick Hearn.

Format: Two competing players. Object: To score six strikes during a nine-frame game. If one bowler achieves it, he is awarded five thousand dollars; if neither player achieves it, the bowler with the most strikes receives one thousand dollars.

The Milton Berle Show—Variety—60 minutes—ABC—September 9, 1966 - January 6, 1967.

Host: Milton Berle.

Regulars: Irving Benson (as Shpritzer, the studio audience heckler), Bobby Rydell, Donna Loren, The Berle Girls, The Louis Da Pron Dancers.

Announcer: Dick Tufeld.

Orchestra: Mitchell Ayres.

MILTON THE MONSTER

Animated Cartoon. Background: Horrible Hill in Transylvania. The misadventures of Milton, "the world's most lovable monster." A Hal Seeger production.

Additional characters: Professor Wierdo, Kool, Flukey Luke, Foxy, Muggy Doo, Penny Penguin, Stuffy Derma.

Additional segment: "The Adventures of Fearless Fly." An insect's lone battle against evil.

Voices: Bob McFadden, Beverly Arnold.

Music: Winston Sharples.

MILTON THE MONSTER—30 minutes—ABC—October 9, 1965 - September 2, 1967. 26 episodes.

MIND YOUR MANNERS

Panel Discussion. Teenagers relate their feelings on various topical issues.

Moderator: Allen Ludden.

MIND YOUR MANNERS—30 minutes—NBC 1952.

MINDY CARSON SINGS

Musical Variety.

Hostess: Mindy Carson.

Announcer: Don Pardo.

Regulars: Florian ZaBach, Danny Horton.

Orchestra: Earl Sheldon; Norman Cloutier.

MINDY CARSON SINGS—30 minutes—NBC—1949 - 1951.

THE MISCHIEF MAKERS

Comedy. Original Hal Roach "Our Gang" theatrical silent films. See title: "The Little Rascals."

MISS SUSAN

Serial. Background: Ohio. The cases of Susan Peters, a lawyer handicapped through a spinal injury.

CAST

Susan Peters   Herself
Her nurse   Katherine Grill
Her housekeeper   Natalie Priest
Also: Robert McQueeny, John Lormer.

Producer: Ted Ashley.

Sponsor: The Colgate-Palmolive Company.

MISS SUSAN–15 minutes–NBC 1951.

MISSING LINKS

Game. First reading a story that contains specific blanks, a contestant then chooses one guest from a panel of three celebrities and bets points on his ability to fill in the missing words within a specified time limit. Winners, the highest scorers, receive merchandise prizes.

Host (NBC): Ed McMahon.

Host (ABC): Dick Clark.

MISSING LINKS–30 minutes. NBC–September 9, 1963 - March 27, 1964; ABC–March 30, 1964 - December 25, 1964.

MISSION: IMPOSSIBLE

Adventure. The cases of the I.M.F. (Impossible Missions Force), a top secret U.S. government organization that handles dangerous and highly sensitive international assignments. Stories depict the step-by-step planning and final execution of highly tense and complicated missions.

CAST

Jim Phelps, the head of the I.M.F.   Peter Graves
Dan Briggs, the original head of the I.M.F. (1966-1967)   Steven Hill
Cinnamon Carter, an I.M.F. agent whose specialty is distraction   Barbara Bain
Rollin Hand, an I.M.F. agent, a master of disguises   Martin Landau
Barney Collier, an I.M.F. agent, an electronics expert   Greg Morris

Mission: Impossible. Bottom, left: Peter Lupus, Greg Morris, Peter Graves. Top, left: Barbara Bain. Top right: Martin Landau.

Willy Armitage, an I.M.F. agent, the strongman   Peter Lupus
Paris (replaced Rollin Hand)   Leonard Nimoy
Dana (replaced Cinnamon)   Lesley Ann Warren
Casey (replaced Dana)   Lynda Day George
Mimi Davis, an occasional I.M.F. agent   Barbara Anderson
Doug, an occasional I.M.F. agent   Sam Elliot
The recorded voice which gives Jim his assignment   Bob Johnson

Girls used in the interim between Barbara Bain and Lesley Ann Warren:

Tracey   Lee Meriwether
Beth   Ann Howes
Lisa   Michele Carey
Monique   Julie Gregg
Nora   Antoinette Bower
Valerie   Jessica Walter

Also, various villanious roles: Sid Haig.

Music: Lalo Schifrin.

Additional Music: Richard Markowitz, Gerald Fried, Richard Haig, Robert Dransin, Jerry Fielding, Kenyon Hopkins, Benny Golson, Harry Geller, Robert Prince, Leith Stevens.

Executive Producer-Creator: Bruce Geller.

Producer: Stanley Kallis, Lee H. Katzin, Richard Benedict, Robert Thompson, John W. Rogers, Joseph Gantman, Robert F.

O'Neil, Laurence Heath, Bruce Lansbury.

Director: Richard Benedict, Leonard J. Horn, Lee H. Katzin, Michael O'Herlihy, Alexander Singer, Stuart Hagmann, Bruce Kessler, Reza S. Badiyi, Marvin Chomsky, Barry Crane, Murray Golden, George Fenady, Robert Butler, Robert Gist, John Moxey, Paul Stanley, Alf Kjellin, Lewis Allen, Marc Daniels, Robert Totten, Don Richardson, Sutton Roley, John Florea, Virgil W. Vogel, David Rich, Paul Krasny, Seymour Robbie, Gerald Mayer, Terry Becker, Allan Greedy.

MISSION: IMPOSSIBLE–60 minutes –CBS–September 17, 1966 - September 8, 1973. 171 episodes. Syndicated.

MISSION MAGIC

Animated Cartoon. Background: A classroom. The story of six students, Carol, Vinnie, Kim, Socks, Harvey, and Franklin; their teacher, Miss Tickle, and troubleshooter Rick Springfield, who comprise the Adventurers Club.

Pinpointing trouble in a magic fantasy land, Rick contacts Miss Tickle through the magic gramaphone. Miss Tickle then approaches the statue of Tut Tut the cat, and speaks the magic words: "Tut Tut, cat of ancient lore, it's time to draw the magic door." The cat comes to life and Miss Tickle draws a door on a blackboard. The door becomes real, opens and, engulfing them all, transports them to wherever Rick is. Incorporating her magic powers, Miss Tickle attempts to resolve difficulties. Completing their mission they are automatically transported back to the classroom.

Additional characters: Tolamy, Rick's pet owl; and Mr. Samuels, the principal.

Voices: Rick Springfield, Erica Scheimer, Howard Morris, Lane Scheimer, Lola Fisher.

Music: Yvette Blais, Jeff Michael.

MISSION MAGIC–30 minutes–ABC –September 8, 1973 - August 31, 1974. 13 episodes.

THE MISSUS GOES A SHOPPING

With host John Reed King and assistant Jimmy Brown, the show features women shoppers competing in stunt contests for prizes. 30 minutes–CBS 1946.

MIXED DOUBLES

Comedy Serial. Background: New York City. The trials and tribulations of young marrieds, two newlywed couples who live side by side in one-room apartments. The men are both underpaid copyrighters in the same ad agency, and the wives struggle to make ends meet on scanty paychecks.

CAST

The hypochondriac, aggressive husband	Billy Idelson
His serious wife	Ada Friedman
Their neighbor, the healthy go-getter	Eddy Firestone
His glamorous, frivolous wife	Rhoda Williams

Also: Calvin Thomas.

Producer-Director: Carleton E. Morse.

MIXED DOUBLES—30 minutes—NBC 1949.

MOBILE ONE

Drama. Background: California. The daily adventures of reporter Pete Campbell and his cameraman, Doug McKnight, newsmen employed by television station KONE, Channel 1. (Mobile One is the code name for their car.)

CAST

Pete Campbell	Jackie Cooper
Doug McKnight	Mark Wheeler
Maggie Spencer, their assignment editor	Julie Gregg
Bruce Daniels, a station employee	Gary Crosby

Music: Nelson Riddle.

Executive Producer: Jack Webb.

Producer: William Bowers.

Director: Don Taylor, Joseph Pevney, George Sherman.

MOBILE ONE—60 minutes—ABC—September 12, 1975 - December 29, 1975.

MOBY DICK AND THE MIGHTY MIGHTOR

Animated Cartoon. Background: The Prehistoric Era.

Moby Dick. The exploits of Moby Dick, the legendary white whale. Utilizing his tremendous speed, he struggles to protect his human foundlings, shipwrecked youngsters Tom and Tub, from danger.

The Mighty Mightor. The story of Tor, a young boy who possesses the power to change his meek self into the Mighty Mightor, a hero of unparalleled power. Episodes depict his battle against the evils of a savage era.

Characters' Voices

Tom	Bobby Resnick
Tub	Barry Balkin
Scooby, the seal	Don Messick
Mightor	Paul Stewart
Tor	Bobby Diamond
Sheera	Patsy Garrett
Pondo	John Stephenson
L'il Rock	Norma McMillan
Ork	John Stephenson
Tog	John Stephenson

Music: Hoyt Curtin.

MOBY DICK AND THE MIGHTY MIGHTOR— 30 minutes —CBS—September 9, 1967 - September 6, 1969. A Hanna-Barbera Production. 26 episodes.

MODERN ROMANCES

Serial. Dramatizations based on modern romance stories. Five chapters comprise each story; casts and authors change weekly.

Hostess-Narrator: Martha Scott.

Host-Narrator: Mel Brandt.

Producer: William Stark, Jerry Layton.

Sponsor: The Colgate-Palmolive Company.

MODERN ROMANCES—15 minutes NBC—October 4, 1954 - September 19, 1958.

THE MOD SQUAD

Crime Drama. Background: Los Angeles, California. Arrested on minor charges, three young adults, Pete Cochran (a joy ride in a stolen car), antiestablishment, the troubled reject of a wealthy family; Julie Barnes (no visible means of support), a poor white girl who wants no part of her mother's existence as a prostitute; and Linc Hayes (during a Watts raid), a tough ghetto Negro, are recruited by Adam Greer, the captain of the L.A.P.D. to form the Mod Squad, a special youth detail of undercover agents designed to infiltrate the organizations that are impenetrable by police. Stories focus on their investigations and their attempts to seek their own identities.

CAST

Pete Cochran	Michael Cole
Julie Barnes	Peggy Lipton
Linc Hayes	Clarence Williams III
Adam Greer	Tige Andrews

Music: Earle Hagen; Shorty Rogers; Billy May.

Executive Producer: Aaron Spelling, Danny Thomas.

Producer: Harve Bennett, Tony Barrett.

Moby Dick. Scooby the seal (left), Moby Dick, and Tom and Tubb. *Courtesy Hanna-Barbera Productions.*

Director: Gary Nelson, Robert M. Lewis, Earl Bellamy, Terry Becker, Don Taylor, Lee H. Katzin, Gene Nelson, Michael Caffrey.

THE MOD SQUAD—60 minutes—ABC—September 24, 1968 - August 23, 1973. 124 episodes. Syndicated.

THE MOHAWK SHOWROOM

Musical Variety.

Hostess: Roberta Quinlan.

Host: Morton Downey.

Regulars: Carmen Mastren, The Chieftains.

Announcer: Bob Slanton.

Music: The Harry Clark Trio.

Producer: George R. Nelson, Roger Muir.

Director: Dick Schneider, Clark Jones.

Sponsor: Mohawk Carpets.

THE MOHAWK SHOWROOM—15 minutes—NBC—1949.

MOMENT OF DECISION

Anthology. Retitled episodes of "Ford Theatre."

Included:

Sudden Silence. A small-town sheriff arrests a young man for murder. When he is sentenced to death, the man's father vows to get even. The story concerns the sheriff's efforts to safeguard himself and his family.

CAST
Barbara Stanwyck, Jeff Morrow, Trevor Bardette.

Stand By To Dive. The story concerns a young naval officer who is assigned to the command of his father—a man he has not seen since his parent's divorce.

CAST
Farley Granger, Onslow Stevens, William Leslie, Roger Smith.

Fear Has Many Faces. During the Korean War, a sergeant is forced to kill a soldier who makes a break for the rear. The story concerns the torment that ensues as a result of the act.

CAST
James Whitmore, June Lockhart, Don Haggerty.

MOMENT OF DECISION—30 minutes—ABC—July 3, 1957 - September 1957.

MOMENT OF FEAR

Anthology. Dramatizations depicting the plight of people suddenly confronted with unexpected, perilous situations.

Included:

Farewell Performance. A psychological tale of a ventriloquist who finds confidence in his dummy after his wife leaves him.

CAST
Nimbo: John Hoyt; Julie: Joan Shawlee; Inspector: Alan Napier; George: Leslie Bradley.

A Little White Lye. Moving into a house, the scene of a brutal murder, a young couple attempt to uncover the sources of ghostly sounds in the night.

CAST
Ellen Rogers: Dorothy Malone; Dick Rogers: Michael Pate.

The Earring. A man attempts to blackmail his former fiancée, now the wife of a successful attorney.

CAST
Lydia: Greer Garson; David: Edward Franz; Phil: Philip Reed; Johnny: Norman Lloyd.

MOMENT OF FEAR—30 minutes—NBC—July 1, 1960 - September 1960; July 1961 - September 1961; June 1962 - September 1962; July 1963 - September 1963; May 19, 1964 - September 15, 1964; June 1965 - September 1965.

MOMENT OF TRUTH

Serial. Background: A small college town in Canada. The dramatic story of Dr. Wallace Bennett, professor and practicing psychologist. Episodes relate the conflicts and tensions that arise from the interactions of the characters—his family, friends, and colleagues.

CAST
Dr. Wallace Bennett   Douglas Watson
Nancy Bennett   Louise King
Helen Gould   Lucy Warner
Jack   Steven Levy
Professor Hamilton   Bob Christie

Wilma Leeds	Lynne Gorman
Carol	Toby Tarnow
Barbara Wallace	Mira Pawluk
Vince Conway	Peter Donat
Shelia	Barbara Pierce
Dr. Russell Wingate	Ivor Barry
Lila	Sandra Scott
Steve	Tom Fielding
Monique	Fernande Giroux
Dexter	Chris Wiggins
Eric	John Horton
Mr. Leeds	Robert Goodier
Johnny Wallace	Michael Dodds
Diane	Anne Campbell
Linda	Anna Hagan
Gil Bennett	John Bethune

MOMENT OF TRUTH—30 minutes—NBC—January 4, 1965 - November 5, 1965.

MONA McCLUSKEY

Comedy. Background: Hollywood, California. The trials and tribulations of Mona McCluskey, a beautiful film actress who, earning five thousand dollars per week, lives in a moderately furnished two-room apartment away from the Affluent Society to please her husband, U.S. Air Force sergeant Mike McCluskey, who earns and insists they subside on his salary of five hundred dollars per month.

Incorporating methods that are a bit deceiving, Mona struggles to supplement the strained family budget without arousing Mike's suspicions.

CAST
Mona McCluskey
  (stage name: Mona
  Jackson)   Juliet Prowse
Mike McCluskey   Denny Miller

Mona McClusky. Juliet Prowse and Denny Miller.

General Crone,
Mike's commanding
officer — Herbert Rudley
Sgt. Stan Gruzewsky, Mike's
friend — Robert Strauss
Alice, Stan's romantic
interest — Elena Verdugo
General Somers — Frank Wilcox
Mr. Caldwell, the studio
producer — Bartlett Robinson

Music: Sonny Burke.

Theme: "Yes Sir, That's My Baby."

MONA McCLUSKEY—30 minutes—NBC—September 16, 1965 - April 14, 1966. 26 episodes.

THE MONEYCHANGERS

Drama. A four-part miniseries based on the novel by Arthur Hailey. A behind-the-scenes look at the world of banking—a world dominated by greed, corruption, sex, and power.

CAST
Alex Vandervoort — Kirk Douglas
Roscoe Heyward — Christopher Plummer
Miles Eastin — Timothy Bottoms
Margot Bracken — Susan Flannery
Edwina Dorsey — Anne Baxter
Avril Devereaux — Joan Collins
Nolan Wainwright — Percy Rodrigues
Jerome Patterson — Ralph Bellamy
Tony Bear — Robert Loggia
Beatrice Heyward — Jean Peters
Celia Vandervoort — Marisa Pavan
Lewis Dorsey — Hayden Rorke
Wizard Wong — James Shigeta
Harold Austin — Patrick O'Neal
George Quartermain — Lorne Greene
Dr. McCartney — Helen Hayes

Music: Henry Mancini.

Producer: Ross Hunter, Jacque Mapes.

Director: Boris Sagal.

THE MONEYCHANGERS—6 hrs., 30 minutes—NBC—December 4, 1976 - December 19, 1976.

THE MONEY MAZE

Game. Two married couples compete. One member of each team stands before a large maze that is constructed on stage level one. The other member of each team is situated on stage level two, where they compete for points. A category topic is revealed (e.g., "Girls in Movies") with two clues ("My Friend (Irma)" and "Hello (Dolly)"). One player (through a flip-of-coin decision) chooses one clue and challenges his opponent to answer it. If he can, he receives one point. A new clue appears and he now chal-lenges his opponent to answer one. Eight clues are played per category. A miss ends the round and awards points to the player with the last correct response.

The player with the highest score at the end of several rounds receives a chance to play the money maze. Five large boxes, which are constructed in the maze are lit. Each contains one figure of ten thousand dollars. The player on stage level two directs his partner who has to run through the maze, enter each of the five boxes, press a button to activate a light, and return to his or her point of destination to press a red button—all within a one-minute time limit. Cash awards are determined by the number of boxes that are activated and whether or not the player made it back to the starting point before time expired.

Host: Nick Clooney.

Announcer: Alan Caulfield.

Music: Score Productions.

THE MONEY MAZE—30 minutes—ABC—December 23, 1974 - July 4, 1975.

THE MONKEES

Comedy. The misadventures of The Monkees, a Rock and Roll quartet as they romp through various comic escapades. Slapstick situations are played within nonrealistic frameworks and encompass speed photography and photographic nonsense.

CAST
Davy Jones — Himself
Mike Nesmith (Wool Hat) — Himself
Mickey Dolenz — Himself
Peter Tork — Himself

Music: The Monkees.

Background Score: Stu Phillips.

Music Supervision: Don Kirshner.

Producer: Robert Rafelson, Ward Sylvester.

Director: Robert Rafelson, Bruce Kessler, Gerald Shepard, David Winters, Peter H. Torkleson, James Frawley.

THE MONKEES—30 minutes—NBC—September 12, 1966 - August 19, 1968. CBS—September 13, 1969 - September 2, 1972. ABC—September 9, 1972 - September 1, 1973. 58 episodes.

THE MONROES

Western. Background: Wyoming, 1875. Arriving in the Teton Mountain region, a family of pioneers, the Monroes (parents: Albert and Mary; and their children: Clayt, eighteen; Kathleen, sixteen; twins Fennimore and Jefferson, twelve; and Amy, six) seek an unknown valley wherein Albert laid claim to land ten years ago.

Crossing the treacherous Snake River, Albert and Mary are caught in its turbulent current and drowned. In a tragic moment, the children are orphaned. (Clayt, narrating:) "I was

The Monkees. Left to right: Mike Nesmith, Davy Jones, Mickey Dolenz, Peter Tork. © Screen Gems.

...the oldest...I kept wondering what Pa would do. We couldn't stay here, and we didn't have a farm anymore to go back to. And up ahead there was nothing but wilderness—and one valley Pa had marked with a pile of rocks. But I was the Pa now, and I had no choice, I had to find that valley for him. We moved out into cold, strange country. All I had to guide me was a map Pa made for me ten years before."

After several days, landmarks begin to appear and the countryside begins to fit the map. Entering the valley, Clayt finds the pile of rocks—and his father's belt buckle—placed there ten years before (Clayt:) "Now it was ours, to root down, to hold—if we could."

The struggles of the Monroe children as they attempt to establish their parent's dream—a homeland. "It's just as Pa said, if it were easy, it wouldn't be worth having."

CAST

Clayt Monroe   Michael Anderson, Jr.
Kathleen Monroe   Barbara Hershey
Amy Monroe   Tammy Locke
Jefferson Monroe
  (Big Twin)   Keith Schultz
Fennimore Monroe
  (Little Twin)   Kevin Schultz
Jim, a renegade Indian
  befriended by the
  Monroes   Ron Soble
Major Mapoy, the
  land baron opposed
  to the Monroes'
  settling   Liam Sullivan
Ruel Jaxon, the Major's
  aide   James Westmoreland
Mr. Buttermore, the Major's
  aide   John Doucette
Albert Monroe (first
  episode)   Russ Conway
Mary Monroe (first
  episode)   Marilyn Moe
Sleeve, an employee
  of Mapoy   Ben Johnson
John Bradford, Mapoy's
  trail scout   Buck Taylor

Music Supervision: Lionel Newman.

THE MONROES—60 minutes—ABC—September 7, 1966 - August 30, 1967. Syndicated. 26 episodes.

THE MONSTER SQUAD

Comedy. While working as a night watchman at Fred's Wax Museum, Walt, a young student attending a criminology college, activates his invention, a crime computer, and, through its oscillating vibrations, it brings to life three legendary monsters—Dracula, Frankenstein, and the Werewolf. Hoping to make up for their past misgivings (creatures feared for centuries), they join Walt, and working independently of police, attempt to solve crimes.

CAST

Walt   Fred Grandy
Dracula   Henry Polic II
Bruce W. Wolf
  (the werewolf)   Buck Kartalian
Frank N. Stein   Michael Lane
Officer McMac Mac   Paul Smith

Music: Richard LaSalle.

Executive Producer: William P. D'Angelo, Ray Allen, Harvey Bullock.

Producer: Michael McClean.

Director: Herman Hoffman, James Sheldon.

THE MONSTER SQUAD—30 minutes—NBC—Premiered: September 11, 1976.

THE MONTEFUSCOS

Comedy. Background: New Canaan, Connecticut. The trials and tribulations of three generations of a large Italian-American family, the Montefuscos. Created by Bill Persky and Sam Denoff.

CAST

Tony Montefusco, the
  father, a
  painter   Joe Sirola
Rose Montefusco, his
  wife   Naomi Stevens
Frankie Montefusco, their
  son, a
  dentist   Ron Carey
Joseph Montefusco,
  their son,
  a priest   John Aprea
Nunzio Montefusco, their
  son, an unemployed
  actor   Sal Viscuso
Angelina Cooney,
  their married
  daughter   Linda Dano
Jim Cooney, Angelina's
  husband   Bill Cort
Theresa Montefusco,
  Frankie's wife   Phoebe Dorin
Antonio Cooney,
  Angelina and
  Jim's son   Damon Raskin
Gina Montefusco, Frankie
  and Theresa's
  daughter   Dominique Pinassi
Jerome Montefusco,
  Frankie and Theresa's
  son   Jeff Palladini

Music: Jack Elliott, Allyn Ferguson.

Executive Producer: Bill Persky, Sam Denoff.

Producer: Tom VanAtta, Bill Idelson.

Director: Bill Persky, Don Richardson.

Creator: Bill Persky, Sam Denoff.

THE MONTEFUSCOS—30 minutes—NBC—September 4, 1975 - October 23, 1975.

MONTGOMERY'S SUMMER STOCK

Anthology. Original dramatic productions aired as a summer replacement for "Robert Montgomery Presents."

Stock Performers: Elizabeth Montgomery, Vaughn Taylor, John Newland, Judy Parrish, Margaret Hayes.

MONTGOMERY'S SUMMER STOCK—30 minutes—NBC—June 1953 - September 1953.

MONTY NASH

Spy Drama. The cases of Monty Nash, a U.S. government special investigator who handles top-secret White House affairs. Based on the spy yarns by Richard Jessup.

Starring: Harry Guardino as Monty Nash.

MONTY NASH—30 minutes—Syndicated 1971. 31 episodes.

MONTY PYTHON'S FLYING CIRCUS

Satire. An absolutely meaningless title; tasteless, uneven, and insane material; men in female drag; glamorous women in various stages of undress; language not normally heard in American television programs (e.g., "filthy bastard"); and sexually provocative animation—all of which is ingeniously interwoven into a highly intellectual and entertaining program.

Produced by the British Broadcasting Corporation, which first began airing it in 1969 as an answer to America's "Laugh-In," it is created by five men, all graduates of Oxford or Cambridge, who use live action and animation to achieve their comedic results. An American artist provides the extremely lifelike animation. Whether enjoyable or not rests solely with the individual.

Starring: Graham Chapman, John Cleese, Eric Idle, Terry Gilliam, Terry Jones, Michael Palin.

Regulars: Donna Reading, Carol Cleveland, Katy Wayech, Dick Vosburgh.

Animation: Terry Gilliam.

Music: Recorded.

MONTY PYTHON'S FLYING CIRCUS—30 minutes. Imported by the member stations of the Eastern Educational Network in 1974.

MOREY AMSTERDAM

Listed: The television programs of comedian Morey Amsterdam.

Stop Me If You've Heard This One—Comedy Game—30 minutes—NBC 1948. Originally aired locally in Los Angeles in 1945 before switching to a network. The first television series to be broadcast with a live studio audience.

Emcee: Ted Brown.

Panelists: Morey Amsterdam, Lew Lehr, Cal Tinney.

Format: The Emcee reads an incomplete joke that has been submitted by a home viewer. A panel of three than have to complete it with an original, funny punch line. The sender receives five dollars for submitting the joke, and an additional five dollars if the panel fails to complete it.

The Morey Amsterdam Show—Variety—30 minutes—CBS 1948. The humor is set against the background of the Silver Swan Cafe, wherein Morey developed his "shtick" (gimmick)—his ability to provide an appropriate joke for any topic asked of him.

Host: Morey Amsterdam.

Regulars: Art Carney (Newton, the Waiter), Rosemary Clooney, Francey Lane, Jacqueline Susann.

Orchestra: Ray McKinley.

The Morey Amsterdam Show—Variety—30 minutes—DuMont 1949.

Host: Morey Amsterdam.

Regulars: Vic Damone, Art Carney, Mary Raye and Naldi.

Announcer: Don Russell.

Orchestra: Johnny Guarnieri.

Broadway Open House—Variety—NBC—1950. (See title.)

Battle Of The Ages—Game—DuMont—1951. (See title.)

The Morey Amsterdam Show—Variety—Local New York, WNBT-TV (now WNBC)—45 minutes (11:15 p.m.-Midnight)—1953.

Host: Morey Amsterdam.

Regulars: Connie Russell, Jean Martin.

Orchestra: Milton DeLugg.

The Morey Amsterdam Show—Variety—Local New York, WABC-TV—60 minutes—1954.

Host: Morey Amsterdam.

Vocalist: Francey Lane.

Orchestra: Milton DeLugg.

Can You Top This?—Game—30 minutes—Syndicated 1970. (See title.)

MORNING COURT

Courtroom Drama. Reenactments based on actual metropolitan courtroom cases. Actors portray all of the involved.

Judges: William Gwinn, Georgiana Hardy.

MORNING COURT—30 minutes—ABC—October 10, 1960 - May 12, 1961.

THE MORNING SHOW

Information-Entertainment. The CBS competition for NBC's "Today Show."

Hosts: Walter Cronkite, Jack Paar, Will Rogers, Jr.

News Reporters: Walter Cronkite, Charles Collingwood.

Regulars: Edie Adams, Dick Van Dyke, The Bill and Cora Baird Puppets.

Music: Jose Melis.

Producer: Avarm Westin, James Calligan, John Cosgrove, Robert Northsheld, James Fleming.

THE MORNING SHOW—2 hours (7:00 a.m.-9:00 a.m., EST)—CBS—January 20, 1956 - April 5, 1957. Also known as "Good Morning." Premiered earlier, in some markets on March 15, 1954.

THE MORNING SHOW

Talk-Variety.

Host: Ed Nelson.

Semiregulars: Rona Barrett, Mr. Blackwell, Dr. Julius Sumner Miller.

THE MORNING SHOW—90 minutes Syndicated 1969. 130 tapes. Also known as: "The Ed Nelson Show."

MORNING STAR

Serial. "No matter how dark the night there is always a new dawn to come, the sun is but a Morning Star...." Background: New York City. The dramatic story of Kathy Elliot, a model caught in the intrigue and excitement of high fashion. Episodes relate her struggles, "facing today and looking forward to tomorrow's bright promise."

CAST

Kathy Elliot	Elizabeth Perry
Jan	Adrienne Ellis
Ed Elliot	Ed Prentiss
Ann Burton	Olive Dunbar
Aunt Milly	Sheila Bromley
George Ross	Burt Douglas
Joan Mitchell	Betty Lou Gerson
Bill Riley	Edward Mallory
Joan Mitchell	Betty Lou Gerson
Eve Blake	Floy Dean
Stan Manning	John Stephenson
Dr. Blake	William Arvin
Jerry	Michael Bell
Joe Bernie	Norman Burton
Marcus Stein	Michael Fox
Eric Manning	Ron Jackson
The Man	Vic Tayback
Mrs. Allison	Phyllis Hill

Creator: Ted Corday.

MORNING STAR—30 minutes—NBC—September 27, 1965 - July 1, 1966. 188 episodes.

THE MORTON DOWNEY SHOW

Musical Variety.

Host: Morton Downey.

Announcer: Bob Stanton.

Orchestra: Carmen Mastren.

THE MORTON DOWNEY SHOW—15 minutes—NBC 1949. Also known as "The Mohawk Showroom."

MOSES THE LAWGIVER

Drama. Background: Egypt during the thirteenth century B.C. A six-part series, drawn from the book of Exodus, that follows Moses as he defies the Egyptian empire to deliver the Jews from their enslavement and lead them to the promised land. Produced by England's Independent Television Corporation and Italy's RAI-TV.

CAST

Moses	Burt Lancaster
Moses, as a young man	Will Lancaster
Aaron	Anthony Quayle
Zipporah	Irene Papas
Miriam	Ingrid Thulin
Pharaoh	Laurent Teizieff
Dathan	Yousef Shiloah
Joshua	Aharon Ipale
Eliseba	Marina Berti
Pharaoh's wife	Melba Englander
Caleb	Michele Placido
Koreh	Antonio Piovonelli
Jethro	Shmuel Rodensky

Narrator: Richard Johnson.

Music: Ennio Morricone.

Additional Music and Songs: Dov Seltzer.

MOSES THE LAWGIVER—60 minutes—CBS—June 21, 1975 - August 7, 1975.

THE MOST DEADLY GAME

Crime Drama. Background: Los Angeles, California. The cases of master criminologist Ethan Arcane, and his protégés, Vanessa Smith, and Jonathan Croft. Stories relate their attempts to solve crimes of the most deadly nature—murder.

CAST

Ethan Arcane	Ralph Bellamy
Vanessa Smith	Yvette Mimieux
Jonathan Croft	George Maharis

Music Supervision: Lionel Newman.

The Most Deadly Game. Left to right: George Maharis, Ralph Bellamy, and Yvette Mimieux.

THE MOST DEADLY GAME—60 minutes—ABC—October 10, 1970 - January 16, 1971. 13 episodes.

THE MOST IMPORTANT PEOPLE

Musical Variety.

Host: Jimmy Carroll (accompanying himself on the piano).

Hostess: Rita Carroll (Mrs.)

THE MOST IMPORTANT PEOPLE—15 minutes—DuMont 1950.

THE MOST IN MUSIC

Musical Variety. Programs are tailored to the talents of guests. Produced in England.

Hosts: Weekly guests, including Barbara McNair, Vikki Carr, Johnny Mathis.

Featured: The Irving Davies Dancers, The Michael Sammes Singers.

Orchestra: Jack Parnell.

THE MOST IN MUSIC—60 minutes—Syndicated 1966.

M.V.P. (MOST VALUABLE PLAYER)

Interview. Interviews with sports figures and show-business personalities.

Host: Johnny Bench, Cincinnati Reds catcher.

Music: Recorded.

M.V.P.—30 minutes—Syndicated 1971.

MOST WANTED

Crime Drama. Background: Los Angeles, California. The investigations of the Most Wanted Unit, an elite law enforcement division of the L.A.P.D. designed to specialize in cases involving the most wanted criminals.

CAST

Captain Lincoln Evers	Robert Stack
Sgt. Charlie Nelson	Shelly Novack
Officer Kate Manners	Jo Ann Harris
The Mayor	Harry Rhodes

Music: Lalo Schifrin, Richard Markowitz.

Executive Producer: Quinn Martin, John Wilder, Paul King.

Producer: Harold Gast.

Director: Don Medford, Virgil W. Vogel, William Wiard, Corey Allen.

MOST WANTED—60 minutes—ABC—October 16, 1976 - April 4, 1977.

MOTHERS DAY

Game. Three mothers compete in various contests based on the operation of a household. Winners, those who successfully complete all tasks, are crowned. "Mother for a Day," and receive merchandise prizes.

Host: Dick Van Dyke.

Assistants: Betty Anders, Dotty Mack.

MOTHERS DAY—30 minutes—ABC—October 3, 1958 - January 2, 1959.

THE MOTHERS-IN-LAW

Comedy. Background: Hollywood, California. Residing at 1805 Ridgewood Drive are the Hubbards: Herb, an attorney; his wife, Eve; and their daughter Suzie. Living next door, at 1803 Ridgewood Drive are the Buells: Roger, a television script writer; his wife, Kaye; and their son, Jerry.

Raised and growing up together, Suzie and Jerry fall in love, and, after completing high school, marry and establish housekeeping in the converted Hubbard garage.

Stories depict: the struggles of young marrieds; and the trials and tribulations of their bickering mothers-in-law, who, wanting only the best for their children, continually meddle in their lives.

CAST

Eve Hubbard	Eve Arden
Herb Hubbard	Herbert Rudley
Kaye Buell	Kaye Ballard
Roger Buell	Roger C. Carmel
	Richard Deacon
Suzie Hubbard (Buell)	Deborah Walley
Jerry Buell	Jerry Fogel
Dr. Butler, Suzie's pediatrician	Herb Voland
Raphael del Gado, a friend, a Mexican Bull Fighter	Desi Arnaz

Music: Wilbur Hatch.

THE MOTHERS-IN-LAW—30 minutes—NBC—September 10, 1967 - September 7, 1969. 56 episodes. Syndicated.

THE MOTOROLA TV HOUR

An early anthology series of sixty-minute dramas sponsored by the

Magnavox Corporation. Produced by Herbert Brodkin.

MOTOR MOUSE

Animated Cartoon. A spin-off from "The Cattanooga Cats." A Hanna-Barbera production.

Segments:

Motor Mouse And Auto Cat. The story of Auto Cat's endless attempts to outrace Motor Mouse.

It's The Wolf. Mildew the wolf's pursuit of the poor defenseless lamb, Lambsy. Savior of the lamb is Bristol Hound—"Bristol Hound's my name, saving sheep's my game."

Segment Hosts: The Cattanooga Cats: Country Kitty Jo, Groovey, Chessie, Scoots.

Characters' Voices

Motor Mouse	Dick Curtis
Auto Cat	Marty Ingels
Mildew Wolf	Paul Lynde
Lambsy	Marty Ingels
Bristol Hound	Allan Melvin
Country	Bill Galloway
Groovey	Casey Kaseem
Scoots	Jim Begg
Kitty Jo	Julie Bennett
Chessie	Julie Bennett

Music: Hoyt Curtin.

MOTOR MOUSE—30 minutes—ABC—September 12, 1970 - September 4, 1971. 26 episodes. Syndicated.

THE MOUSE FACTORY

Children's Variety. Guest celebrities appear and relate various aspects of the world assisted by film clips from Walt Disney features.

Appearing: Annette Funicello, discussing the career of Mickey Mouse; Jonathan Winters, interplanetary travel; Joe Flynn, water sports; Wally Cox, dancing; Pat Paulsen, sports; Johnny Brown, aviation; Pat Buttram, bull fighting; Jo Anne Worley, women's lib; John Astin, the story of Pluto, the klutz canine.

Music Supervision: George Bruns.

THE MOUSE FACTORY—30 minutes—Syndicated 1972. 17 episodes.

THE MOVIE CLASSICS OF DAVID O. SELZNICK

Movies. A film tribute to director David O. Selznick.

THE MOVIE CLASSICS OF DAVID O. SELZNICK—90 minutes—ABC—June 22, 1972 - July 13, 1972.

THE MOVIE GAME

Game. Basis: Movie trivia—who did what and who played whom. Rounds are divided into "Screentests," worth twenty points; and "Closeups," which are played after each "Screentest" and worth five points each. Distinguished by two formats:

Format One:

Two competing teams, each composed of three members (two celebrities and one noncelebrity contestant). The Screentest Round: The contestant competes. The host asks a question and the first player to identify himself through a buzzer signal receives a chance to answer. If correct, points are awarded. The Closeup segment: two questions are directed to that contestant's celebrity partners. Correct answers award five points. The contestant scoring the highest is the winner and receives two hundred and fifty dollars.

Host: Sonny Fox.

Assistant: Army Archid.

Announcer: Johnny Gilbert.

Music: Recorded.

Format Two:

Six celebrity guests who comprise two three-member teams. The Screentest Round: the host states a question. The team first to identify themselves through a buzzer signal receives a chance to answer. If correct, the points are scored. The closeup Round, containing three questions, is directed to that team. Winners are the highest-scoring teams. Their preselected home viewer (via post card) receives two hundred and fifty dollars.

Host: Larry Blyden.

Assistant: Army Archid.

Announcer: Johnny Gilbert.

Music: Recorded.

Additional segments (both versions):
The Film Clip Round. Questions are based on the observation of film clips. Worth twenty points.
The Action Round. Specially prepared scenes are performed by the losing team. One member of the winning team has to identify its concealed name or title. Addi-

tional cash is awarded if successful.
Army Archid's Portrait of a Star. A specially prepared biography is read. The team who correctly identifies the personality receives fifty points.

THE MOVIE GAME—30 minutes—Syndicated 1969.

MOVIELAND QUIZ

Game. Set: A theatre front. Object: For a contestant to identify celluloid personalities, cast roles, or film titles. Cameras dolly up to and hold still shots of selected frames; questions are then asked regarding these. Cash is awarded with each correct response.

Host: Arthur Q. Bryan.

Assistant-Cashier: Patricia Bright.

Producer: Lester Lewis.

Director: Ralph Warren.

MOVIELAND QUIZ—30 minutes—ABC—August 12, 1948 - September 1948.

MOVIN' ON

Drama. Background: Various areas between Oregon, Utah, and Nevada. The experiences of two gypsy truck drivers: Sonny Pruitt, a tough, uneducated veteran; and his partner, Will Chandler, a rebellious, college-educated youth, who is seeking to discover how the other half lives.

CAST

Sonny Pruitt	Claude Akins
Will Chandler	Frank Converse
Myrna, Sonny's girlfriend	Janis Hansen
Betty, Will's girlfriend	Ann Coleman
Benjy, a gypsy truck driver	Rosey Grier
Moose, his partner	Art Metrano

Music: George Romanis.

Additional Music: Earle Hagen.

Theme: Merle Haggard.

Executive Producer: Barry Whitz, Philip D'Antoni.

Producer: Ernie Frankel.

Director: Bob Helljan, Lawrence Dobkin, Corey Allen, Michael Schultz, Leo Penn.

MOVIN' ON—60 minutes—NBC—September 12, 1974 - April 20, 1976; June 1, 1976 - September 14, 1976.

MR. ADAMS AND EVE

Comedy. Background: Hollywood, California. The home and working lives of Eve and Howard Adams, a husband-and-wife show business couple.

CAST

Howard Adams	Howard Duff
Eve Adams (stage name: Eve Drake)	Ida Lupino
J.B. Hafter, the studio producer	Alan Reed
Steve, the Adam's agent	Hayden Rorke
Elsie, the Adams's housekeeper	Olive Carey
The director	Larry Dobkin
The slate boy	Alan Wood
The assistant director	Paul Grant

Producer: William Webb, Warner Toub, Jr., Frederick de Cordova.

Director: Frederick de Cordova.

MR. ADAMS AND EVE—30 minutes —CBS—January 4, 1956 - September 23, 1958. 66 episodes. Syndicated.

MR. AND MRS. MYSTERY

Mystery. Background: New York City, 46 Perry Street, Apartment 3-C. The cases of criminologist John Gay and his wife, his self-proclaimed assistant, Barbara.

CAST

John Gay	Himself
Barbara Gay	Herself

MR. AND MRS. MYSTERY—15 minutes—CBS—1949 - 1950.

MR. AND MRS. NORTH

Mystery. Background: Greenwich Village in New York City, the residence of the Norths: Jerry, a former private detective turned publisher, and his attractive, level-headed wife, Pamela. Stories depict their investigations when Pam accidentally stumbles upon and involves Jerry in crimes. Based on the stories by Frances and Richard Lockridge.

CAST

Jerry North	Joseph Allen (1949)
	Richard Denning (1952-54)
Pamela North	Mary Lou Taylor (1949)
	Barbara Britton (1952-54)
Lieutenant Bill Weingand	Francis DeSales

Music: Charles Paul

Producer: John W. Loveton.

Director: Marc Daniels.

Sponsor: Colgate; Revlon.

MR. AND MRS. NORTH—30 minutes—NBC 1949; CBS—October 3, 1952 - September 25, 1953; NBC—January 26, 1954 - July 20, 1954. 57 episodes. Syndicated

MR. ARSENIC

Drama. True crime exposés.

Host: Burton Turkus, the author of *Murder Inc.*

MR. ARSENIC—30 minutes—ABC—May 8, 1952 - June 26, 1952.

MR. BLACK

Anthology. Mystery presentations.

Host: Anthony Christopher, as Mr. Black (situated in a cobweb, flickering light atmosphere).

MR. BLACK—30 minutes—ABC—September 19, 1949 - November 7, 1949.

MR. BROADWAY

Drama. Background: New York City. The exploits of Mike Bell, a sophisticated Broadway press agent.

CAST

Mike Bell	Craig Stevens
Hank McClure, his contact man	Horace McMahon
Toki, his girl friday	Lani Miyazaki

MR. BROADWAY—60 minutes—CBS —September 26, 1964 - December 26, 1964. 13 episodes.

MR. CITIZEN

Anthology. Dramatizations that detail the unselfish acts of heroism of ordinary people. The person whose story is selected receives the "Mister Citizen Award."

Host: Allyn Edwards.

Award Presenter: Senator Clifford Chase.

Organist: John Gart.

MR. CITIZEN—30 minutes—ABC—April 20, 1955 - July 20, 1955.

Mr. Deeds Goes To Town. Monte Markham (seated), and Pat Harrington. © *Screen Gems.*

MR. DEEDS GOES TO TOWN

Comedy. Background: New York City. The misadventures of Longfellow Deeds, a philosophical country gentleman who inherits the multimillion-dollar Deeds Enterprises after the death of his uncle Alonzo. Stories depict his attempts to adjust to life in the big city; and his efforts to run a corporation that he feels can easily take advantage of people.

CAST

Longfellow Deeds	Monte Markham
Tony Lawrence, Deeds's assistant	Pat Harrington, Jr.
Henry Masterson, the chairman of the board	Herbert Voland
George, Deeds's Butler	Ivor Barry

Deeds's dog: Sam.

Music: Warren Barker.

MR. DEEDS GOES TO TOWN—30 minutes—ABC—September 26, 1969 - January 16, 1970. 17 episodes.

MR. DISTRICT ATTORNEY

Crime Drama. Dramatizations based on the facts of crime from the files of the District Attorney's office.

CAST

Paul Garrett, Mr. District Attorney	Jay Jostyn
	David Brian
Edith Miller, his secretary	Vicki Vola

Harrington, his Irish
investigator   Len Doyle   Jackie Loughery

Voice of the Law: Jay Jostyn; David Brian.

Announcer: Fred Uttal.

Music: Peter Van Steeden.

Producer-Director: Edward Byron.

Sponsor: Bristol-Myers.

Program Open:

Announcer: Mr. District Attorney, champion of the people, defender of truth, guardian of our fundamental rights to life, liberty, and the pursuit of happiness.

D.A.: And it shall be my duty as District Attorney not only to prosecute to the limit of the law all persons accused of crimes perpetrated within the country but to defend with equal vigor the rights and privileges of all citizens.

MR. DISTRICT ATTORNEY—30 minutes—Syndicated 1951. 78 episodes. Based on the radio program of the same title.

MR. ED

Comedy. Background: Los Angeles, California. Settling into their first home, newlyweds Wilbur Post, architect, and his wife, Carol, discover a horse in the barn. Meeting Roger Addison, a neighbor, they discover that the horse is theirs, left to them by the previous owner. Unable to part with the animal, Wilbur persuades Carol to let him keep it.

Shortly after, while brushing the horse (named Mr. Ed), Wilbur discovers that he possesses the ability to talk and, because Wilbur is the only person he likes well enough to talk to, will speak only to him.

Stories depict the misadventures that befall Wilbur as he struggles to conceal the fact of his possession of a talking horse—"the playboy horse of Los Angeles."

CAST

Wilbur Post   Alan Young
Carol Post   Connie Hines
Roger Addison, their
neighbor   Larry Keating
Kay Addison, his
wife   Edna Skinner
Gordon Kirkwood, their
neighbor   Leon Ames
Winnie Kirkwood, his
wife   Florence MacMichael
Mr. Carlisle, Carol's

father   Barry Kelly
Voice of Mr.
Ed   Allan "Rocky" Lane
Paul Fenton, Kay's
brother   Jack Albertson
Dr. Bruce Gordon, the
psychiatrist   Richard Deacon

Music: Jay Livingston, Ray Evans; Raoul Kraushaar; Dave Kahn.

Executive Producer: Al Simon, Arthur Lubin.

Producer: Herbert W. Browar.

Director: Arthur Lubin.

The Posts Address: 1720 Valley Road.

MR. ED—30 minutes. Syndicated 1960-1961; CBS—October 1, 1961 - September 4, 1966. 143 episodes. Syndicated.

MR. GARLUND

Drama. The story of Frank Garlund, a youthful tycoon (thirty years of age), financial wizard, and mysterious industrial head, a key figure in national and international affairs. Raised by a wealthy Chinese gentleman, Po Chang, his ancestry remains a mystery. In flashback sequences, the lives of people who had come in contact with him during his struggle to reach the top of the financial ladder are dramatized.

CAST

Frank Garlund   Charles Quinlivan
Po Chang   Philip Ahn
Kam Chang, his foster
brother, the owner of
a pawn shop in San Francisco's
China Town   Kam Tong

MR. GARLUND—30 minutes—CBS—October 7, 1960 - January 13, 1961. Also known as: "The Garlund Touch."

MR. I MAGINATION

Children. Background: The mythical kingdom of Imagination Town, a place where children's dreams come true. Fantasy is coupled with education as vignettes dramatize legendary figures and events of past history.

Host: Paul Tripp, as Mr. I Magination.

Regulars: Johnny Stewart, Michael Petrie, Ruth Enders, Butch Cavell, Ted Tiller, Joe Silvan, David McKay, Donald Devlin,

Don Harris, Clifford Sales, Robin Morgan, Richard Trask.

Orchestra: Ray Carter.

Producer: Norman and Irving Pincus, Worthington Miner.

Director: Don Richardson.

Sponsor: Nestle.

MR. I MAGINATION—30 minutes—CBS—April 24, 1949 - June 28, 1952.

MR. LUCKY

Adventure. Background: Los Angeles, California. The story of Joe Adams, alias Mr. Lucky, gambler, the owner of the *Fortuna,* a fancy supper club and gambling yacht. Episodes depict his struggles to maintain an honest operation.

CAST

Mr. Lucky   John Vivyan
Andamo, his partner   Ross Martin
Maggie Shank, his girl-
friend   Pippa Scott
Lieutenant Rovacs,
L.A.P.D.   Tom Brown
The *Fortuna*
Maitre'd   Jed Scott

Music: Henry Mancini.

Producer: Blake Edwards, Gordon Oliver, Jack Arnold.

MR. LUCKY—30 minutes—CBS—October 24, 1959 - September 10, 1960. 34 episodes. Syndicated.

MR. MAGOO

Animated Cartoon. The misadventures of Quincy Magoo, a near-sighted gentleman.

Additional characters: Charlie, his Japanese houseboy; Waldo and Presley, his nephews.

Voice of Mr. Magoo: Jim Backus.

Music: Shorty Rogers.

MR. MAGOO—05 minutes—Syndicated 1963. 130 episodes.

MR. MAYOR

See title: "Captain Kangaroo."

MR. NOVAK

Drama. Background: Jefferson High School in Los Angeles, California. Stories depict the life of John Novak,

English professor, a tough-minded idealist; student-teacher relationships; and the struggles of beginners as they learn the ropes of the teaching profession.

CAST

John Novak	James Franciscus
Albert Vane, the principal	Dean Jagger
Martin Woodridge, an English instructor, the principal in the last thirteen episodes	Burgess Meredith
Miss Wilkinson	Phyllis Avery
Paul Webb	David Sheiner
Mr. Peeples	Stephen Brooks
Miss Scott	Marian Collier
Mr. Butler	Vince Howard
Miss Dorsey	Marjorie Corley
Mr. Parkson	Peter Hansen
Mrs. Vreeland	Anne Seymour
Miss Pagano	Jeanne Bal

Music: Lyn Murray.

Producer: William Froug, John T. Dugan, Jack E. Neuman.

MR. NOVAK—60 minutes—NBC—September 24, 1963 - August 31, 1965. 60 episodes. Syndicated.

MR. PEEPERS

Comedy. Background: Jefferson Junior High School in Jefferson City. The simple pleasures and trying times of Robinson J. Peepers, a timid and mild-mannered Biology instructor.

CAST

Robinson J. Peepers	Wally Cox
Harvey Weskitt, his friend, the English teacher	Joseph Foley
	Tony Randall
Nancy Remington, the school nurse, Robinson's girlfriend; married on May 23, 1954	Norma Crane
	Patricia Benoit
Marge Weskitt, Harvey's wife	Georgianna Johnson
Mrs. Gurney, a friend	Marion Lorne
Mr. Remington, Nancy's father	Ernest Truex
Mrs. Remington, Nancy's mother	Sylvia Field
Mr. Bascomb, the principal	George Clark
Also	David Tyrell

Orchestra: Bernie Green.

Producer: Fred Coe, Hal Keith.

Sponsor: Reynolds Metals.

MR. PEEPERS—30 minutes—NBC—July 3, 1952 - June 12, 1955.

MR. ROBERTS

Comedy-Drama. Background: The South Pacific during World War II. The story of Lieutenant Douglas Roberts, cargo officer of the *Reluctant,* a U.S. Navy cargo ship nicknamed "The Bucket" by its reluctant-to-serve crew. Feeling he is displaced, and longing to serve aboard a fighting vessel, he seeks to acquire a transfer, but, by shouldering the antics of his men, he encounters the hostility of the ship's commander, Captain John Morton, who, feeling that the morale of his men precedes Roberts's wants, refuses to forward his letters to the proper authorities. Through his continual efforts, a sentimental version of the war is seen.

CAST

Lt. J.G. Douglas Roberts	Roger Smith
Captain John Morton	Richard X. Slattery
Ensign Frank Pulver, the lazy, disorganized morale officer	Steve Harmon
Doc, the surgeon	George Ives
Seaman D'Angelo	Richard Sinatra
Seaman Mannion	Ronald Starr
Seaman Reber	Roy Reese

MR. ROBERTS—30 minutes—NBC—September 17, 1965 - September 2, 1966. 30 episodes.

MR. ROGERS' NEIGHBORHOOD

Educational. The program concerns the emotional development of children from three to eight years of age. Through actual demonstrations and guests who discuss topics, an attempt is made to help children cope with or overcome their problems.

Host: Fred Rogers.

Music: John Costa.

Neighbors: Betty Aberlin, Jewel Walker, Francois Clemmons, Joe Negri (as the handyman).

Executive Producer: Fred Rogers.

Producer: Bill Moates, Bob Walsh.

Director: David Fu-Yung Chen, Bill Moates, Bob Walsh.

MR. ROGERS' NEIGHBORHOOD—30 minutes. NET—October 1967 - October 1970. PBS—October 1970 - June 1975. Syndicated to PBS stations.

MR. SMITH GOES TO WASHINGTON

Comedy. Background: Washington, D.C. After the death of a senator, Eugene Smith, a country politician, is elected to replace him. Encompassing mature wisdom, boyish charm, warmth, and dignity, he struggles to adjust to the norms of Capitol life. Based on the movie.

CAST

Eugene Smith	Fess Parker
Patricia Smith, his wife	Sandra Warner
Cooter Smith, his uncle, a guitar-playing rural philosopher	Red Foley
Miss Kelly, his secretary	Rita Lynn
Arnie, his butler	Stan Irwin

MR. SMITH GOES TO WASHINGTON—30 minutes—ABC—September 29, 1963 - March 30, 1964.

MR. T AND TINA

Comedy. Background: Chicago. The trials and tribulations of Taro Takahashi, a widowed Japanese businessman who moves from Tokyo to Chicago with his family: his children, Sachi and Aki, his uncle Matsu, and his live-in sister-in-law, Michi. Stories focus on the complications that ensue following his hiring Tina Kelly, a dizzy young American woman, as governess for his children.

CAST

Taro Takahashi, executive v.p. of Moyati Industries	Pat Morita
Tina Kelly	Susan Blanchard
Sachi Takahashi	June Angela
Aki Tahahashi	Gene Profanata
Uncle Matsu	Jerry Hatsuo Fujikawa
Michi	Pat Suzuki
Miss Llewellyn, the manager of the apartment building	Miriam Byrd-Nethery
Harvard, the maintenance engineer	Ted Lange

Music: George Tipton.

Executive Producer-Creator: James Komak.

Producer: Madelyn Davis, Bob Carroll, Jr.

Director: James Sheldon, Rick Edlestein, James Komack, Dennis Steinmetz.

MR. T AND TINA—30 minutes—ABC
—September 26, 1976 - October 30,
1976. 5 episodes.

MR. TERRIFIC

Comedy. Background: Washington,
D.C. Experimenting with methods to
cure the common cold, a U.S government research scientist discovers a
power pill. Tested, it produces incredible strength in animals, but makes the
strongest of men quite ill. Faced with
a problem, Barton J. Reed, the Bureau
of Special Projects subchief, begins
the secret search—"to find the one
and only man."

After many months, their search
ends at Hal and Stanley's Gasoline
Station. Approached, Stanley
Beemish, the proprietor, "a weak and
droopy daffodil," is persuaded to test
the pill. Seconds after taking it, he is
transformed into the invincible Mr.
Terrific. Sworn in as an agent, Stanley
Beemish adopts a dual life: as a
private citizen; and as the U.S. government's secret weapon against crime.

Stories depict Stanley's investigations and the problems that befall the
costumed avenger: his inability to
locate assigned targets when airborne;
his struggles to adjust to a secret alias;
and his attempts to cope with the
predicaments that occur when the pill,
lasting only one hour in effectiveness,
wears off at crucial moments.

CAST

Stanley Beemish/Mr. Terrific	Stephen Strimpell
Hal, Stanley's partner	Dick Gautier
Barton J. Reed	John McGiver
Hanley Trent, Reed's assistant	Paul Smith

Music: Gerald Fried.

MR. TERRIFIC—30 minutes—CBS—
January 9, 1967 - August 28, 1967.

MR. WIZARD

Educational. The basics of various
scientific experiments.
Host-Instructor: Don Herbert (Mr.
    Wizard).
Assistants, including: Bruce Lindgren
    (as Willie Watson), Rita
    MacLaughlin, Alan Howard,
    Buzzy Podwell, Betty Sue
    Albert.

MR. WIZARD—30 minutes—NBC—
March 5, 1951 - September 5, 1965:
also: NBC—September 11, 1971 -
September 2, 1972.

MRS. G GOES TO COLLEGE

Comedy. Background: An unidentified college that resembles the University of Southern California. The
trials and tribulations of Sarah Green,
a middle-aged widow who enrolls in
the school to reach a long-sought
dream—her college education.

CAST

Sarah Green	Gertrude Berg
Professor Crayton, her advisor; a visiting instructor from England	Sir Cedric Hardwicke
Maxfield, her boarding-house land-lady	Mary Wickes
Joe Caldwell, a fresh-man	Skip Ward
Susan, Sarah's daughter	Marion Ross
Jerry Green, Sarah's son	Leo Penn
George Howell	Paul Smith
Irma Howell	Aneta Corsaut
Carol	Karyn Kubcinet

Music: Herschel Burke Gilbert.

MRS. G GOES TO COLLEGE—30
minutes—CBS—October 4, 1961 -
April 5, 1962. 26 episodes.

M SQUAD

Crime Drama. Background: Chicago.
The story of Lieutenant Frank
Ballinger, a special plainclothes detective with the M Squad division of the
Chicago Police Department. Episodes
depict his investigations into cases
that surpass the requirements of systematic law-enforcement procedure.

CAST

Lt. Frank Ballinger	Lee Marvin
Captain Grey	Paul Newlan

Narrator: Lee Marvin.
Music: Stanley Wilson.

M SQUAD—30 minutes—NBC—
September 20, 1957 - January 29,
1960. Syndicated. 117 episodes.

MUGGSY

Drama. Background: An unidentified
city that is representative of any city
where situations depicted on the program actually happen. The series explores life in the inner city as seen
through the eyes of Margaret "Muggsy" Malloy, a thirteen-year-old
orphan, and her older half-brother,
her guardian, Nick Malloy, a taxicab
driver. The program, though aimed at
children, is realistic and penetrating.
Taped in Bridgeport, Connecticut.

CAST

Margaret "Muggsy" Malloy	Sarah MacDonnell
Nick Malloy	Ben Masters
Gus, their friend	Paul Michael
Clytmnestra, Muggsy's friend	Star-Shemah
T.P., Clytmnestra's brother	Danny Cooper

Music Performed By: Blood, Sweat,
    and Tears.
Musical Coordinator: Robert
    Gessinger, Phebe Haas.
Executive Producer: George Heine-
    man.
Director: Bert Saltzman, J. Philip Mil-
    ler, Sidney Smith.

MUGGSY—30 minutes—NBC—September 11, 1976 - April 9, 1977.

MULLIGAN'S STEW

Drama. Background: Birchfield, California. The story of the Mulligan
family—Michael, a high school athletic
coach, his wife, Jane, the school
nurse, their three children, Mark, Melinda, and Jimmy, and their four
adopted children, Stevie, Adam, Polly,
and Kimmy—who became a part of
the family after Mike's sister and
husband perished in a plane crash. The
series focuses on the attempts of the
family members to accept and understand each other's differences.

CAST

Michael Mulligan	Lawrence Pressman
Jane Mulligan	Elinor Donahue
Mark Mulligan	Johnny Whitaker Johnny Doran
Melinda Mulligan	Julie Haddock
Jimmy Mulligan	K.C. Martel
Stevie Mulligan	Suzanne Crough
Adam "Moose" Mulligan	Christopher Ciampa
Polly Mulligan	Lory Kochheim
Kimmy Mulligan, an adopted Vietnamese orphan	Sunshine Lee

Music: George Tipton.
Producer: Joanna Lee.

MULLIGAN'S STEW—60 minutes—
NBC—Premiered: October 25, 1977.

The Munsters. Fred Gwynne (top), Yvonne DeCarlo (left), Beverly Owen, Al Lewis, and Butch Patrick (bottom).

THE MUNSTERS

Comedy. Background: Mockingbird Heights, 1313 Mockingbird Lane, the creepy, spider-web-covered residence of the Munsters, a family who resemble celluloid fiends of the 1930s: Herman (a Frankenstein-like creature), a funeral director at Gateman, Goodbury, and Graves; his wife, Lily (a female vampire); their ten-year-old son, Edward Wolfgang (a werewolf); Lily's father, Count Dracula (Grandpa), a 378-year-old mad scientist; and their "poor unfortunate" niece, Marilyn, young and beautiful, the black sheep of the family.

Living in their own world, and believing themselves to be normal, the family struggles to cope with the situations that foster their rejection by the outside world.

CAST
Herman Munster	Fred Gwynne
Lily Munster	Yvonne DeCarlo
Grandpa	Al Lewis
Marilyn Munster	Beverly Owen
	Pat Priest
Marilyn Munster (feature version, "Munster Go Home")	Debbie Watson
Edward Wolfgang Munster (Eddie)	Butch Patrick
Mr. Gateman, Herman's employer	John Carradine
Clyde Thornton, Herman's co-worker	Chet Stratton
Dr. Edward Dudley, the Munster family physician	Paul Lynde

Munster family pets: Spot, a prehistoric creature found by Grandpa while digging in the backyard; Igor the bat; and an unnamed raven who constantly speaks the immortal words of Edgar Alan Poe— "Nevermore."

Music: Jack Marshall.

Music Supervision: Stanley Wilson.

Producer: Joe Connelly, Bob Mosher.

Director: Seymour Burns, Joseph Pevney, Lawrence Dobkin, Earl Bellamy, David Alexander, Jerry Paris, Charles R. Rondeau, Gene Reynolds, Ezra Stone, Norman Abbott, Charles Barton.

Eddie's doll: Woff Woff (a werewolf).

THE MUNSTERS—30 minutes—CBS —September 24, 1964 - September 8, 1966. 70 episodes. Syndicated.

THE MUPPET SHOW

Variety. A adult oriented series wherein the Muppets (fanciful puppets created by Jim Henson) perform in sketches (with guests), sing, and dance.

Host: Kermit the Frog (manipulated and voiced by Jim Henson).

Voices: Frank Oz, Jim Henson, Jerry Nelson, Richard Hunt, Peter Friedman, John Loveday, Jane Henson.

Puppet Operators: Carolyn Wilcox, Mari Kaestyle, Dave Goelz, Larry Jameson, Richard Hunt, Frank Oz, Jim Henson.

Orchestra: Jack Parnell.

Music Conductor: Derek Scott.

Executive Producer: Jim Henson.

Producer: Jack Burns.

Director: Peter Harris.

THE MUPPET SHOW—30 minutes— Syndicated 1976.

MUSIC BINGO

Game. A musical adaptation of bingo. Two competing contestants. An instrumental selection is played by the orchestra. The player first to sound his buzzer receives a chance to identify the song title. If correct, a square is marked on a large electronic game board. Object: To complete the bingo board through the identification of song titles. Winners receive merchandise prizes.

Host: Johnny Gilbert.

Orchestra: Harry Salter.

MUSIC BINGO—30 minutes. NBC—June 5, 1958 - December 5, 1958; ABC—December 8, 1958 - January 1, 1960.

MUSICAL CHAIRS

Game. Three celebrity panelists who play for home viewers. A vocal group presents a musically oriented question. Panelists then have to answer it by impersonating its recording artist. One point is awarded for each correct impersonation and answer. Winners are the highest point scorers. Home viewers receive cash prizes.

Host: Bill Leyden.

Panelists: Bobby Troup, Johnny Mercer, Mel Blanc.

Vocalists: The Cheerleaders.

Orchestra: Bobby Troup.

MUSICAL CHAIRS—30 minutes— NBC—July 9, 1955 - September 17, 1955.

MUSICAL CHAIRS

Game. Four contestants compete. A song, either sung by the host or a guest, is stopped one line before its conclusion. Three possible last lines to the song appear on a board. Players then press a button and lock in their choice. The player who was first to press in receives a chance to select a line. If he is correct, he receives money. If not, the player who was second to press in receives a chance. In round one, three songs are played and each is worth fifty dollars. In round two, each of the three songs played is worth seventy-five dollars. Round three is the elimination round and at the end of each song, the player with the lowest score is defeated. Each song is worth one hundred dollars. The winner is the highest-scoring player.

Host: Adam Wade.

Announcer: Pat Hernan.

Music: The Musical Chairs Orchestra directed by Derek Smith.

MUSICAL CHAIRS—30 minutes— CBS—June 16, 1975 - October 31, 1975.

MUSICAL COMEDY TIME

Variety. Guest performers recreate great moments from hit Broadway plays.

Producer: Richard Berger, Bernard L. Schubert.

Director: William Corrigan, Richard Berger.

MUSICAL COMEDY TIME–30 minutes–NBC 1950.

MUSIC BOWL

A fifteen minute variety series, broadcast on CBS in 1950, and starring Danny O'Neil and Carolyn Gilbert.

MUSIC CITY U.S.A.

Musical Variety. Performances by Country and Western artists.
Hosts: Jerry Naylor; Teddy Bart.

MUSIC CITY U.S.A.–60 minutes–Syndicated 1968. 13 tapes.

MUSIC COUNTRY

See title: "Dean Martin Presents Music Country."

MUSIC '55

Musical Variety. An intimate party flavor is emphasized as all fields of music are explored.
Host: Stan Kenton.

Guests, representing selected fields: Jaye P. Morgan, Peggy Lee, Duke Ellington, Louis Armstrong, Ella Fitzgerald, Woody Herman, Lena Horne, Frankie Laine.
Announcer: Stu Metz.
Orchestra: Stan Kenton.

MUSIC '55–30 minutes–CBS–July 12, 1955 - September 1955.

MUSIC FOR A SPRING NIGHT

Musical Variety.
Host: Glenn Osser.
Vocalists: The Glenn Osser Chorus.
Orchestra: Glenn Osser.

MUSIC FOR A SPRING NIGHT–60 minutes–ABC–March 20, 1960 - May 11, 1960.

MUSIC FOR A SUMMER NIGHT

Musical Variety.
Host: Glenn Osser

Vocalists: The Glenn Osser Chorus.
Orchestra: Glenn Osser.

MUSIC FOR A SUMMER NIGHT–60 minutes–ABC–June 3, 1959 - September 21, 1959.

MUSIC FROM MEADOWBROOK

Musical Variety. Background: Frank Dailey's Meadowbrook in Cedar Grove, New Jersey.
Host: Jimmy Blaine.
Music: King Guron's Rhythm Orchestra; Ray McKinley's Band.

MUSIC FROM MEADOWBROOK–60 minutes–ABC–May 23, 1953 - September 26, 1953.

MUSIC HALL AMERICA

Musical Variety.
Hosts: Guests.
Regulars: Dean Rutherford, Sadi Burnett, The Even Dozen.
Orchestra: Bill Walker.
Choreography: Jean Sloan.
Vocal Backgrounds: L'Adidas.
Executive Producer: Lee Miller.
Director: Lee Bernhardi.

MUSIC HALL AMERICA–60 minutes–Syndicated 1976.

MUSIC ON ICE

Musical Variety. Background: An "ice capade."
Host: Johnny Desmond.
Regulars (skating personalities): Jacqueline du Bief; Skip Jacks, The Dancing Blades.
Orchestra: Bob Boucher.

MUSIC ON ICE–60 minutes–NBC–May 8, 1960 - September 1960.

THE MUSIC PLACE

Variety. Performances by Country and Western entertainers.
Host: Stu Phillips.
Regulars: Bob and Pat Geary.
Producer: Gary Brockhurst.

THE MUSIC PLACE–30 minutes–Syndicated 1975.

THE MUSIC SCENE

Musical Variety. A modern version of "Your Hit Parade." Performances by the top artists in various fields of music (Country and Western, Ballad, Rock, Folk, and Blues). Musical numbers are interwoven with comedy sketches.
Host; David Steinberg.
The Music Scene Troupe: Paul Reid Roman, Lilly Tomlin, Larry Hankin, Christopher Ross, Pat Williams.
Orchestra: Pat Williams.

THE MUSIC SCENE–45 minutes–ABC–September 22, 1969 - January 12, 1970. 13 episodes.

THE MUSIC SHOP

Musical Variety. Performances by the recording industry's top personalities.
Host: Buddy Bergman.
Orchestra: Buddy Bergman.

THE MUSIC SHOP–30 minutes–NBC–January 11, 1959 - March 8, 1959.

THE MUSIC SHOW

Musical Variety.
Host: Robert Trendler.
Regulars: Mike Douglas, Elena Warner, Jackie Van, Henri Noel.
Orchestra: Robert Trendler.

THE MUSIC SHOW–30 minutes–DuMont 1953.

MY FAVORITE HUSBAND

Comedy. Background: New York City. The trials and tribulations of the Coopers: George, a young bank executive, and his beautiful but scatterbrained wife, Liz.

CAST
Liz Cooper	Joan Caulfield
	Vanessa Brown
George Cooper	Barry Nelson
Gilmore Cobb, their neighbor, a peanut manufacturer	Bob Sweeney
Myra Cobb, his wife	Alexandra Talton

Orchestra: Lud Gluskin.
Producer: Norman Tokar.
Sponsor: International Silver

MY FAVORITE HUSBAND–30 minutes–CBS–September 12, 1953 - December 27, 1955.

MY FAVORITE MARTIAN

Comedy. Background: Los Angeles, California. Enroute to the office, *Los Angeles Sun* newspaper reporter Tim O'Hara, witnesses the crash landing of a damaged U.F.O. Investigating, he discovers and befriends its passenger, a professor of anthropology from Mars whose specialty is the primitive planet Earth. Tim takes the marooned professor back to his apartment where the Martian adopts the guise of Martin O'Hara, an uncle staying with Tim after a long journey.

Hindered by a lack of scarce items—which are presently unknown on Earth—Martin struggles to repair his crippled craft, conceal his identity, and adjust to the discomforts of a primitive, backward planet.

CAST

Martin O'Hara (Uncle Martin)	Ray Walston
Tim O'Hara	Bill Bixby
Lorelei Brown, Tim's landlady	Pamela Britton
Detective Bill Brennan, L.A.P.D., Martin's rival for Lorelei's affections	Alan Hewitt
Mr. Burns. Tim's employer	J. Pat O'Malley
The police captain	Roy Engle

Music: George Greeley.

MY FAVORITE MARTIAN—30 minutes—CBS—September 15, 1963 - September 4, 1966. 107 episodes. Syndicated. Spin-off series: "My Favorite Martians" (see title).

MY FAVORITE MARTIANS

Animated Cartoon. A spin-off from "My Favorite Martian." Background: Los Angeles, California. A damaged alien spacecraft lands on Earth. Its occupants, Uncle Martin, his nephew Andy, and their dog, Oakie Doakie, are befriended by the sole witnesses, newspaper reporter Tim O'Hara and his niece Katy.

Sheltering the stranded Martians, Tim arouses the suspicions of free-lance security officer Bill Brennan, who sets his goal to uncover Martin's true identity.

Plagued by the discomforts of primitive Earth, Martin struggles to conceal his and Andy's true identities and to make the repairs needed to return home to Mars.

Additional Characters: Lorelei Brown, Tim's landlady; Brad Brennan, Bill's son; and Chump, Brad's pet chimpanzee.

Voices: Jonathan Harris, Edward Morris, Jane Webb, Lane Scheimer.

Music: The Horta-Mahana Corporation.

MY FAVORITE MARTIANS—25 minutes—CBS—September 8, 1973 - August 30, 1975. 16 episodes.

MY FRIEND FLICKA

Adventure. Background: The Goose Bar Ranch in Coulee Springs, Wyoming during the early 1900s. The series, which details the experiences of the McLaughlins, a horse-ranching family, focuses on the adventures shared by their young son, Ken, and his horse, Flicka (Swedish for Little Girl), a once wild stallion given to him by his father in an attempt to help teach him responsibility. Based on the stories by Mary O'Hara.

CAST

Rob McLaughlin, the father	Gene Evans
Nell McLaughlin, his wife	Anita Louise
Ken McLaughlin	Johnny Washbrook
Gus Broeberg, their ranchhand	Frank Ferguson
Hildy Broeberg, Gus's niece	Pamela Beaird
Sheriff Walt Downey	Hugh Sanders
	Sydney Mason
The U.S. Marshal	Craig Duncan
Sgt. Tim O'Gara, Rob's friend	Tudor Owen
Flicka	Wahama

Music Supervision: Alec Compinsky.

Producer: Alan A. Armor, Peter Packer, Sam White, Herman Schlom.

Director: Robert Gordon, James Clark, Frederick Stephani, Nathan Juran, Albert S. Rogell.

MY FRIEND FLICKA—30 minutes. CBS—February 10, 1956 - September 1959; ABC—September 30, 1959 - December 31, 1963; CBS—September 30, 1961 - September 26, 1964. 39 episodes. Syndicated.

MY FRIEND IRMA

Comedy. Distinguished by two formats.

Format One: (1952-1953)
Background: New York City; Mrs. O'Reilly's Boarding House, 185 West

My Friend Irma. Marie Wilson.

73rd Street, Manhattan, Apartment 3-B, the residence of secretaries Irma Peterson, a beautiful but dumb blonde, and Jane Stacey, a level-headed girl who is constantly plagued by Irma's scatterbrained antics.

Stories depict their romantic heartaches: Irma and her boyfriend, the impoverished and jobless Al, a con artist who sees her, his "Chicken," as only a means by which to further his harebrained money-making ventures; and Jane and her boyfriend, her multi-millionaire employer, Richard Rhinelander III, an investment counselor whom she struggles to impress and hopefully one day marry.

Jane, aware of a studio and home audience, speaks directly to the camera and establishes scenes.

Format Two: (1953-1954)
Background: Same. In an opening curtain speech, Irma informs viewers of Jane's transfer to Panama; and of her acquiring a new roommate, news-paperwoman Kay Foster, by placing an ad in the classified section of the newspaper.

Stories continue to relate the life of a beautiful proverbially dumb blonde; and the trials and tribulations of her roommate, who becomes the recipient of her harebrained attempts to assist others.

CAST

Irma Peterson	Marie Wilson
Jane Stacey	Cathy Lewis
Kay Foster	Mary Shipp
Al	Sid Tomack
Richard Rhinelander III	Brooks West
Joe Vance, Irma's romantic interest (later episodes)	Hal March
Mrs. O'Reilly, Irma's landlady	Gloria Gordon
Mrs. Rhinelander, Richard's socialite	

mother   Margaret DuMont
Professor Kropotkin,
   the girl's downstairs
   neighbor, a violinist at
   The Paradise Burlesque
   Cafe   Sig Arno
Mr. Clyde, Irma's
   employer   Donald MacBride
Bobby Peterson, Irma's
   ten-year-old
   nephew   Richard Eyer
The neighbor   John Carradine
Also: Frances Mercer, Aileen Carlyle.

Orchestra: Lud Gluskin.

Announcer: Frank Bingham.

Producer: Richard Whorf, Cy Howard.

Creator: Cy Howard.

Sponsor: Camel Cigarettes.

MY FRIEND IRMA—30 minutes—
CBS—January 8, 1952 - June 25,
1954.

MY FRIEND TONY

Crime Drama. Background: Los
Angeles, California. The investigations
of John Woodruff, private detective
and criminologist professor at
U.C.L.A.; and his Italian partner,
Tony Novello, whom he befriended
while in service during World War II.

CAST

John Woodruff   James Whitmore
Tony Novello   Enzo Cerusico

MY FRIEND TONY—60 minutes—
NBC—January 5, 1969 - August 31,
1969. 16 episodes.

MY HERO

Comedy. Background: The Thackery
Realty Company in Los Angeles, California. The trials and tribulations of
Robert S. Beanblossom, a carefree and
easygoing salesman.

CAST

Robert S. Beanblossom Bob Cummings
Julie Marshall, the office
   secretary   Julie Bishop
Mr. Thackery, their
   employer   John Litel

Producer: Mort Green.

Sponsor: Dunhill Products.

MY HERO—30 minutes—NBC—
November 8, 1952 - September 12,
1953. Syndicated. Also known as
"The Robert Cummings Show."

My Little Margie. Gale Storm and Charles Farrell.

MY LITTLE MARGIE

Comedy. Background: New York
City; The Carlton Arms Hotel, Apartment 10-A, the residence of the
Albrights: Vernon, widower, vice-
president of the investment firm of
Honeywell and Todd; and his
beautiful twenty-one-year old
daughter, Margie.

Stories depict the problem that
each has, and their individual attempts
to solve it:

Vern's problem: Margie—"I've been
both mother and father to her since
she was born. She's grownup
now....When she was a little I could
spank her and make her mind me. I
had control over her....When she
disobeyed I took her roller skates
away for a week. What can you do
when a girl reaches this age? She's
completely out of hand. I've got a
problem, believe me, I've got a problem."

Margie's problem: Vern—"I've raised
him from...my childhood. He's
nearly fifty now and you'd think he'd
s e t t l e d o w n, w o u l d n' t
you?....Today, he looks better in
shorts on a tennis court than fellows
twenty-five. Girls wink at him and
what's worse he winks back at them. I
want a nice old comfortable father. I
try to look after him, but he just
won't settle down. I've got a problem,
believe me, I've got a problem."

Intervening in Vern's romantic life,
Margie attempts to achieve her goal;
and Vern, by threatening to deprive
Margie of her desires, struggles to
acquire an obedient, nonmeddling
daughter.

CAST

Margie Albright   Gale Storm
Vern Albright   Charles Farrell
Freddy Wilson, Margie's
   impoverished boy-
   friend   Don Hayden
George Honeywell, Vern's
   employer   Clarence Kolb
Roberta Townsend,
   Vern's romantic
   interest   Hillary Brooke
Mrs. Odettes, the Albrights'
   eighty-three-year-old
   neighbor   Gertrude Hoffman
Charlie, the elevator
   operator   Willie Best

Music: Lud Gluskin.

Producer: Hal Roach, Jr.

Director: Walter Strenge.

Sponsor: Philip Morris; Scott Paper.

MY LITTLE MARGIE—30 minutes—
CBS—June 16, 1952 - September 8,
1952; June 1, 1953 - July 30, 1953;
NBC—September 9, 1953 - August 24,
1955. 126 episodes. Syndicated.

MY LIVING DOLL

Comedy. Background: Los Angeles,
California. Completing United States
Space Project AF 709, a delicate,
intricate, and beautifully constructed
female robot, the ultimate in feminine
composition, Dr. Carl Miller assigns
her (Rhoda) to psychiatrist Dr. Bob
McDonald to mold her character.

Living with his sister, Irene, he
introduces Rhoda as a patient who
requires constant care and attention.
Encountering Irene's interference, and

My Living Doll. Julie Newmar and Bob Cummings.

the smooth techniques of his bachelor-playboy friend, Dr. Peter Robinson, who has fallen in love with her, Bob struggles to develop her mind and character for the benefit of science.

CAST

Rhoda	Julie Newmar
Bob McDonald	Bob Cummings
Irene McDonald	Doris Dowling
Peter Robinson	Jack Mullaney
Carl Miller	Henry Beckman

MY LIVING DOLL—30 minutes—CBS—September 27, 1964 - September 8, 1965. 26 episodes.

MY MOTHER THE CAR

Comedy. Background: Los Angeles, California. Planning to purchase a station wagon, lawyer Dave Crabtree is distracted when he becomes fascinated with a decrepit 1928 Porter. Inspecting it, he hears a feminine voice call his name. Finding that the voice emerges from the radio, he discovers that the car is his mother, the late Abigail Crabtree, reincarnated.

Purchasing her, he returns home and encounters the objections of his family, who want a station wagon. Hoping to change their minds, the car is overhauled in a custom body shop, and the exquisite Touring Mobile, license plate PZR 317, is still rejected by his family.

Concealing the fact of reincarnation, Dave struggles to defend his mother against a family who eagerly await a station wagon; and, from the devious attempts of Captain Bernard Mancini, an antique car collector who is determined to add the Porter to his collection.

CAST

Dave Crabtree	Jerry Van Dyke
Barbara Crabtree, his wife	Maggie Pierce
Mother's voice	Ann Sothern
Captain Bernard Mancini	Avery Schreiber
Cindy Crabtree, Dave and Barbara's daughter	Cindy Eilbacher
Randy Crabtree, Dave and Barbara's son	Randy Whipple

Music: Paul Hampton.

MY MOTHER THE CAR—30 minutes—NBC—September 14, 1965 - September 6, 1966. 30 episodes. Syndicated.

MY NAME'S McGOOLEY, WHAT'S YOURS?

Comedy. The bickering relationship between a scheming father and his obnoxious, beer-swilling son-in-law.

CAST

The father	Gordon Chates
His daughter	Judi Farr
The son-in-law	John Meillon

MY NAME'S McGOOLEY, WHAT'S YOURS?—30 minutes—Syndicated 1966.

MY PARTNER THE GHOST

Crime Drama. Background: London, England. While investigating a case, private detective Marty Hopkirk is killed. Returning as a ghost, he appears only to his former partner, Jeff Randall. Assisted by Jeff, he solves his murder, but violates an ancient rhyme ("Before the sun shall rise on you, each ghost unto his grave must go. Cursed the ghost who dares to stay and face the awful light of day") and is cursed to remain on Earth for one hundred years.

Spiritually assisting his wife, Jean, Marty assumes his former position as a private detective. Stories depict his and Jeff's case investigations.

CAST

Marty Hopkirk	Kenneth Cope
Jeff Randall	Mike Pratt
Jean Hopkirk, working as Jeff's secretary	Annette Andre
Police Inspector Large	Ivor Dean

Music: Edwin Astley.
Producer: Monty Berman.
Director: Cyril Frankel, Jeremy Summers.
Creator: Dennis Spooner.

MY PARTNER THE GHOST—60 minutes—Syndicated (U.S.) 1973. 26 episodes. An ITC Presentation.

MY SISTER EILEEN

Comedy. Background: Greenwich Village in New York City. The trials and tribulations of sisters Ruth and Eileen Sherwood: Ruth, a writer for *Manhattan* magazine; and Eileen, an actress. Based on the movie.

CAST

Ruth Sherwood	Elaine Stritch
Eileen Sherwood	Shirley Boone
Mr. Appopolous, the owner of the Appopolous Arms, an apartment house where the girls reside	Leon Belasco
Marty, Eileen's agent	Stubby Kaye
Robert Beaumont, Ruth's publisher	Raymond Bailey
Chick Adams, a newspaper reporter on the *Daily News*	Jack Weston / Linden Charles
Bertha Bronsky, a friend	Rose Marie
Galavan	Richard Deacon
Walters	Henry Hunter

MY SISTER EILEEN—30 minutes—

My Partner the Ghost. Left to right: Mike Pratt, Kenneth Cope, and Annette Andre. *Courtesy Independent Television Corp.; an ATV Company.*

CBS—October 5, 1960 - April 12, 1961. 26 episodes.

MY SON JEEP

Comedy. The story of Doc Allison and his attempts to reconstruct his life after the death of his wife. Episodes focus on the antics of Jeep, his mischievous young son.

CAST

Doc Allison	Jeffrey Lynn
Jeep Allison	Martin Houston
Peggy Allison, Jeep's sister	Betty Lou Keim
Barbara, Doc's receptionist	Anne Sargent
Mrs. Birby, the Allison housekeeper	Leona Powers

MY SON JEEP—30 minutes—ABC—June 1954 - September 1954.

MYSTERIES OF CHINATOWN

Crime Drama. Background: San Francisco's Chinatown. The investigations of Dr. Yat Fu, owner of a curio shop and amateur crime sleuth.

CAST

Dr. Yat Fu	Marvin Miller
Ah Toy, his niece	Gloria Saunders
Police Lieutenant Hargrove	Bill Eythe
Police Lieutenant Cummings	Richard Crane

Also: Robert Bice, Marya, Wong Artarno, Ed MacDonald.

MYSTERIES OF CHINATOWN—30 minutes—ABC—December 4, 1949 - October 2, 1950.

MYSTERY CHEF

Cooking. Step-by-step methods in the preparation of meals.
Host: John McPherson (when first televised the chef was not identified.)
MYSTERY CHEF—30 minutes—NBC—1949. Based on the radio program.

MYSTERY FILE

See title: "Q.E.D."

MYSTERY IS MY BUSINESS

See title: "Ellery Queen."

My Three Sons. Left to right: Tim Considine, Stanley Livingston, Fred Mac-Murray, William Frawley, Don Grady.

MY THREE SONS

Comedy. Background: The town of Bryant Park. The trials and tribulations of the Douglas family—Steve, widower, aeronautical engineer; his sons, Mike, Robbie, and Chip; and their grandfather, Michael Francis O'Casey, "Bub."

Changes:
1965: Charlie O'Casey, a retired sailor, replaces Bub. Mike, the elder son, marries Sally Ann Morrison. Leaving the family nest, they move east where Mike acquires a job as a psychology instructor. Shortly after, Chip, the youngest, befriends an orphaned boy, Ernie Thompson, whom Steve later adopts.

1967-1970: Transferred to North Hollywood, Steve and the family relocate. Attending college, Robbie, the middle child, meets, falls in love with, and marries Kathleen Miller; later, they are the parents of triplets: Steve Douglas, Jr., Charley Douglas, and Robbie Douglas II.

1970-1971: Attending high school, Ernie encounters difficulty with a new teacher, Barbara Harper, widow, and mother of a young daughter, Dodie. Attempting to resolve the difficulty, Steve meets, falls in love with, and marries Barbara. Shortly after, Chip, who is attending college, meets, falls in love with and marries Polly Thompson, a coed.

1972: Arriving from Scotland seeking a first lady, Laird (Lord) Fergus McBain Douglas betrothes Terri Dowling, a cocktail waitress working at the Blue Berry Bowling Alley as Lady Douglas.

Stories from 1967 - 1972 mirror the lives of the individual members of the Douglas family

CAST

Steve Douglas	Fred MacMurray
Michael Francis "Bub" O'Casey	William Frawley
Charley O'Casey (Uncle Charley)	William Demarest
Mike Douglas	Tim Considine
Robbie Douglas	Don Grady
Chip (Richard) Douglas	Stanley Livingston
Sally Ann Douglas (Morrison)	Meredith MacRae
Barbara Douglas (Harper)	Beverly Garland
Katie Douglas (Miller)	Tina Cole
Ernie Douglas (Thompson)	Barry Livingston
Polly Douglas (Thompson, unrelated to Ernie)	Ronnie Troup
Dodie Douglas (Harper)	Dawn Lyn
Steve Douglas, Jr.	Joseph Todd
Charley Douglas	Michael Todd
Robbie Douglas II	Daniel Todd
Terri Dowling	Anne Francis
Fergus McBain Douglas (enacted by)	Fred MacMurray
Fergus McBain Douglas (voiced by)	Alan Caillou
Bob Walters, Steve's employer	Russ Conway John Gallaudet
Sylvia Walters, his wife	Irene Hervey
Tom Williams, Polly's father*	Norman Alden
Margaret Williams, Polly's mother	Doris Singleton
Also	Jodie Foster

The Douglas Family Dog: Tramp.
Music: Frank DeVol.
Executive Producer: Don Fedderson.
Producer: Fred Henry, Edmund Hartmann, George Tibbles.
Director: Gene Reynolds, Frederick de Cordova, James V. Kern.

*For unknown reasons, Polly's last name was changed with the introduction of her parents.

MY THREE SONS—30 minutes—ABC—September 29, 1960 - September 9, 1965; CBS—September 16, 1965 - August 24, 1972. CBS Daytime rebroadcasts: December 20, 1971 - September 1, 1972. 369 episodes.

MY TRUE STORY

Anthology. Dramatic adaptations of stories appearing in *My True Story* magazine.

Announcer: Herbert Duncan.

Producer-Director: Charles Powers.

MY TRUE STORY–30 minutes– ABC–May 5, 1950 - September 22, 1950.

MY WORLD . . . AND WELCOME TO IT

Comedy. Background: Westport, Connecticut. The real life and dream world of John Monroe, a cartoonist for *Manhattanite* magazine. Discontented with his job; uneased over the smartness of children and the hostility of animals; intimidated by his loving wife, Ellen, and his precocious daughter, Lydia; and scared to death of life, he retreats to his secret world of imagination, wherein his cartoons become real, life becomes tolerable, and he is a king—irresistible to women and a tower of strength in the eyes of men. Animation is combined with live action to present life as seen through the eyes of John Monroe. Based on "drawings, stories, inspirational pieces, and things that go bump in the night" by James Thurber.

CAST
John Monroe	William Windom
Ellen Monroe	Joan Hotchkis
Lydia Monroe	Lisa Gerritsen
Hamilton Greeley, John's employer	Harold J. Stone
Phil Jensen, a magazine writer	Henry Morgan
Ruth Jenson, Phil's wife	Olive Dunbar

Monroe family dogs: Irving and Christabel.

Music: Warren Barker; Danny Arnold.

MY WORLD . . . AND WELCOME TO IT–30 minutes–NBC–September 15, 1969 - September 7, 1970. Rebroadcasts: CBS–May 25, 1972 - September 7, 1972. 26 episodes.

𝓃

NAKED CITY

Crime Drama. Background: New York City. The grueling day-to-day activities of the police detectives assigned to Manhattan's 65th precinct. Realistic police drama, filmed in the streets, on the sidewalks, and in the buildings of New York, The Naked City.

CAST–1958-1960
Detective Lieutenant Dan Muldoon	John McIntire
Detective Jim Halloran	James Franciscus
Janet Halloran, his wife	Suzanne Storrs

Music: Billy May, George Duning.

CAST–1960-1963
Detective Adam Flint	Paul Burke
Sergeant Frank Arcaro	Harry Bellaver
Detective Mike Parker	Horace McMahon
Libby, Adam's girlfriend	Nancy Malone

Also: Hal Gaetano, Max Klevin, stuntmen appearing in roles requiring daredevil action.

Music: Nelson Riddle.

NAKED CITY–30 minutes–ABC– September 30, 1958 - October 5, 1960; 60 minutes–ABC–October 12, 1960 - September 11, 1963. Syndicated. 39 half-hour, and 99 one hour episodes.

NAKIA

Crime Drama. Background: Davis County, New Mexico. The investigations of Deputy Nakia Parker, a Navajo Indian who sometimes finds his heritage and beliefs clashing with the law he has sworn to uphold.

CAST
Deputy Nakia Parker	Robert Forster
Sheriff Sam Jericho	Arthur Kennedy
Deputy Irene James	Gloria DeHaven
Deputy Hubbel Martin	Taylor Lacher
Half Cub	John Tenorio, Jr.
Ben Redearth	Victor Jory

Music: Leonard Rosenman.

NAKIA–60 minutes–ABC–September 21, 1974 - December 28, 1974. 15 episodes.

THE NAMEDROPPERS

Game. Involved: Three guest celebrities who comprise the panel; twenty selected studio audience contestants; and two Namedroppers (per show), people who are in some way related to the celebrities. One Namedropper appears and briefly tells how he is related to one of the celebrities, but not to which one. Each of the celebrities then relates a story concerning their relationship, but only one story is true. Two of the twenty studio audience members compete at a time. The eighteen remaining players each press a button and select the celebrity each believes is related to the Namedropper. The stage players then verbally divulge their choice. The celebrity identifies the Namedropper; and the studio audience votes are revealed. Each incorrect vote awards the correct player ten dollars; if neither is correct, the Namedropper receives the money. Two such rounds are played per game, enabling all twenty contestants to compete during a five-day period.

Hosts: Al Loman and Roger Barkley.

Announcer: Kenny Williams.

Music: Recorded.

THE NAMEDROPPERS–30 minutes –NBC–October 2, 1969 - March 27, 1970.

THE NAME OF THE GAME

Crime Drama. Background: Los Angeles, California; the offices of *Crime* magazine. The investigations of three men: Glenn Howard, its publisher, a man who built the defunct *People* magazine into a multi-million dollar empire; Dan Farrell, the senior editor, a former F.B.I. agent conducting a personal battle against the underworld (his wife and child were a victim of their bullets); and Jeff Dillon, the editor of the *People* segment of *Crime*. Their individual attempts to uncover story material are depicted on a rotational basis.

CAST
Glenn Howard	Gene Barry
Jeff Dillon	Tony Franciosa
Dan Farrell	Robert Stack
Peggy Maxwell, their girl friday	Susan Saint James
Joe Sample, a reporter	Ben Murphy
Andy Hill, a reporter	Cliff Potter
Ross Craig, a reporter	Mark Miller

Music: Dave Grusin; Stanley Wilson.

THE NAME OF THE GAME–90 minutes–NBC–September 20, 1968 - September 10, 1972. Syndicated.

THE NAME'S THE SAME

Game. Through question-and-answer probe rounds with John and/or Jane Does—people who possess famous names—a celebrity panel has to identify their famous birth names. Players receive cash prizes based on the number of probing questions asked of them by the panel. Ten questions is the limit; and twenty-five dollars is the amount that is awarded if the panel fails to identify the name.

Hosts: Robert Q. Lewis; Dennis James; Bob Elliott and Ray Goulding.

Panelists: Joan Alexander, Bess Myerson, Gene Rayburn, Arnold Stang, Abe Burrows, Meredith Wilson, Audrey Meadows, Laraine Day, Walter Slezak, Roger Price.

Announcers: John Reed King; Lee Vines.

Producer: Mark Goodson, Bill Todman.

Director: Jerome Schnur.

Sponsor: Swanson Foods; Ralston Purina Company.

THE NAME'S THE SAME—30 minutes—ABC—December 12, 1951 - October 7, 1955.

NAME THAT TUNE

Musical game. Distinguished by six formats.

Format One:

Name That Tune—30 minutes—NBC—1953-1957; CBS—1957-1960.

Two contestants stand approximately twenty feet from hung bells. A musical selection is played. Recognizing it, players run up to and ring the bell. The first player to sound his bell is permitted to identify the song title. If correct, he receives the tune and cash. Three such wins and he receives the opportunity to double his earnings via a mystery melody round, wherein he must idenitfy as many song titles as possible within a specified time limit.

Hosts: Red Benson; Bill Cullen; George de Witt.

Songstress: Vicki Mills.

Announcers: Johnny Olsen; Wayne Howell.

Orchestra: Harry Salter; Ted Rapf.

Format Two:

Name That Tune—30 minutes—NBC—Syndicated 1970.

Same as Format One.

Host: Richard Hayes.

Format Three:

Name That Tune—30 minutes—NBC—July 29, 1974 - January 3, 1975.

Two competing contestants.
Round One: A musical selection is played. Recognizing the tune, players run up to and ring a bell that is hung approximately ten feet away. The first player to sound his bell receives the chance to identify the song. If correct, he receives the tune. Five songs are played, and the contestant who identifies three receives ten points.

Round Two: Varies greatly in presentation; but the basic format is to identify three out of five tunes for ten points.

Round Three: The host relates clues to the identity of a song title. Players then bet as to the amount of notes (from seven down to one) it will take them to identify the tune. The lowest bidder receives the opportunity. The player who acquires three out of five tunes is the winner and receives twenty points.

The winner, the highest point scorer, receives a chance to earn money via "The Golden Melody." Object: To identify six song titles in one minute. Each correct response awards two hundred dollars.

Host: Dennis James.

Announcer: John Harlan.

Orchestra: Bob Alberti.

Format Four:

Name That Tune—30 minutes—Syndicated 1974.

Same as Format Three.

Host: Tom Kennedy.

Announcer: John Harlan.

Orchestra: Bob Alberti.

Format Five:

The $100,000 Name That Tune—30 minutes—Syndicated 1976. The game is played the same as format three, with the added bonus of allowing a player to win $100,000 by correctly identifying a very difficult mystery tune.

Host: Tom Kennedy.

Model: Geri Fiala.

Announcer: John Harlan.

Orchestra: Tommy Oliver.

$100,000 Pianist: Joe Harnell.

Executive Producer: Ralph Edwards.

Director: John Dorsey.

Format Six:

Name That Tune—30 minutes—NBC—January 3, 1977 - June 10, 1977. Played the same as format three. Credits are the same as format five with the exclusion of the $100,000 pianist.

NANCY

Comedy. Background: Center City, Iowa. Meeting and falling in love, Adam Hudson, veterinarian, and Nancy Smith, the daughter of the President of the United States, marry. Stories depict their romantic misadventures; and their struggles to adjust to a marriage wherein their lives are more public than private.

CAST

Nancy Hudson (Smith)	Renne Jarrett
Adam Hudson	John Fink
Abby Townsend, Nancy's guardian	Celeste Holm
Everett Hudson, Adam's uncle	Robert F. Simon
Willie Wilson, a newspaper reporter	Eddie Applegate
Secret Serviceman Turner	William H. Bassett
Secret Serviceman Rodriquez	Ernesto Macias

Music: Sid Ramin.

NANCY—30 minutes—NBC—September 17, 1970 - January 7, 1971. 13 episodes.

THE NANCY DREW MYSTERIES

Mystery. Background: The town of River Heights, New England. The adventures of Nancy Drew, the pretty, proficient teenage daughter of criminal attorney Carson Drew. Stories concern her investigations as she attempts to help her father solve baffling crimes. Based on the stories by Carolyn Keene. Alternates with "The Hardy Boys Mysteries."

CAST

Nancy Drew	Pamela Sue Martin
Carson Drew	William Schallert

The Nancy Drew Mysteries. Jean Rasey (left), and Pamela Sue Martin. *Courtesy of the Call-Chronicle Newspapers, Allentown, Pa.*

George Fayne, Nancy's
 girlfriend   Jean Rasey
Ned Nickerson, Carson's
 assistant   George O'Hanlon, Jr.
The Sheriff   Robert Karnes
Music: Stu Phillips, Glen A. Larson.
Executive Producer: Glen A. Larson.
Producer: Arlene Sidaris, B.W. Sande-
 fur.
Director: E.W. Swackhamer, Noel
 Black, Michael Caffrey, Alvin
 Ganzer, Jack Arnold, Andy Si-
 daris.

THE NANCY DREW MYSTERIES—
60 minutes—ABC—Premiered: February 6, 1977.

THE NANCY WALKER SHOW

Comedy. Background: Hollywood,
California. The misadventures of
Nancy Kitteridge, theatrical agent and
mother whose troubles stem not only
from her difficulties in handling clients, but in her inability to cope with
her family: her husband, Kenneth, a
retired Naval officer, and her neurotic
daughter, Lorraine.

CAST
Nancy Kitteridge   Nancy Walker
Kenneth Kitteridge   William Daniels
Lorraine   Beverly Archer
Terry Folsom, Nancy's
 assistant   Ken Olfson
Glen, Lorraine's
 husband   James Cromwell
Music: Marilyn Bergman, Alan Berg-
 man, Nancy Hamlisch.
Theme Vocal: Nancy Walker.
Executive Producer: Norman Lear.
Producer: Rod Parker.
Director: Hal Cooper, Alan Rafkin.
Creator: Norman Lear, Rod Parker.

THE NANCY WALKER SHOW—30

minutes—ABC—September 30, 1976 -
December 23, 1976. Returned with a
final first run episode on July 11,
1977.

THE NANETTE FABRAY SHOW

See title: "Yes Yes Nanette."

Nanny and the Professor. Juliet Mills.

NANNY AND THE PROFESSOR

Comedy. Background: 10327 Oak
Street, Los Angeles, California, the
residence of Professor Harold Everett,
widower, mathematics instructor at
Clinton College; his children, Hal,
Butch, and Prudence; and their beautiful, but mysterious housekeeper,
Phoebe Figalilly, "Nanny," a woman
who, when the professor needed assistance, mysteriously appeared and
acquired the position.
 Stories depict the events that befall
the Everett family—unexplainable, but
favorable situations that are seemingly
caused by Nanny, who is neither
magic nor a witch, but possesses the
ability to spread love and joy.

CAST
Phoebe Figalilly
 (Nanny)   Juliet Mills
Professor Harold
 Everett   Richard Long
Hal Everett   David Doremus
Bentley (Butch)
 Everett   Trent Lehman
Prudence Everett   Kim Richards
Francine Fowler, Hal's
 girlfriend   Eileen Baral
Florence Fowler, her
 mother   Patsy Garrett
Aunt Henrietta, Nanny's
 relative   Elsa Lanchester
Everett Family Pets: Waldo, a dog;
 Mertyl and Mike, guinea pigs;

Sebastian, a rooster; Jerome and
Geraldene, kids (baby-goats).
Music: George Greeley; Charles Fox.
Executive Producer: David Gerber.
Producer: Wes McAfee, Charles B.
 Fitzsimmons.

NANNY AND THE PROFESSOR—30
minutes—ABC—January 21, 1970 -
December 27, 1971. 65 episodes.
Syndicated.

NASH AIRFLYTE THEATRE

Anthology. Dramatic presentations.
Host: William Gaxton.
Producer-Director: Marc Daniels.
Sponsor: Nash.

NASH AIRFLYTE THEATRE—30
minutes—CBS—1950 - 1951.

NASHVILLE 99

Crime Drama. Background: Nashville,
Tennessee. The cases of Stonewall
"Stoney" Huff, and Trace Mayne, his
partner, police detectives attached to
the Nashville Metropolitan Police Department. (Nashville 99: Stoney's
badge number.)

CAST
Det. Lt. Stoney
 Huff   Claude Akins
Det. Trace Mayne   Jerry Reed
Birdie Huff, Stoney's
 mother   Lucille Benson
R.B., a deputy   Charlie Pride
Music: Earle Hagen.
Music Supervision: Lionel Newman.
Executive Producer: Ernie Frankel.
Director: Don McDougall, Lawrence
 Dobkin, George Sherman.

NASHVILLE 99—60 minutes—CBS—
April 1, 1977 - April 22, 1977. 3
episodes.

NASHVILLE NOW

See title: "The Ian Tyson Show."

NATIONAL GEOGRAPHIC

Documentary. Films exploring various
aspects of man's world.
Host-Narrator: Joseph Campanella.
Music: Walter Scharf.

NATIONAL GEOGRAPHIC—60 minutes—Syndicated 1971. Compiled from a CBS network series of specials.

NATIONAL VELVET

Drama. The story of a young girl, Velvet Brown, and her attempts to train her horse, King, for competition in the Grand National Steeplechase. Based on the motion picture.

CAST

Velvet Brown	Lori Martin
Herbert Brown, her father, the owner of a farm	Arthur Space
Martha Brown, her mother	Ann Doran
Edwina Brown, her older sister	Carole Wells
Donald Brown, her younger brother	Joey Scott
Mi Taylor, their handyman	James McCallion

Music: Robert Armbruster.

NATIONAL VELVET—30 minutes—NBC—September 18, 1960 - September 10, 1962. 58 episodes. Syndicated.

NATION AT WAR

Documentary. Films highlighting the major events of World War II from 1936 to 1946.

Host-Narrator: Budd Knapp.

NATION AT WAR—30 minutes—Syndicated 1961. 13 episodes.

THE NAT KING COLE SHOW

Musical Variety.

Host: Nat King Cole.

Regulars: The Randy Van Horne Singers, The Boataneers.

Orchestra: Gordon Jenkins; Nelson Riddle.

THE NAT KING COLE SHOW—30 minutes—NBC—November 5, 1956 - December 17, 1957.

NAVY LOG

Anthology. Dramatizations based on incidents in the lives of the men in service of the U.S. Navy.

Included:

Storm Within. A Navy psychiatrist attempts to cure a depressed chief quartermaster after an act of heroism.

CAST

Harry Bellaver, John Zaremba.

One If By Sea. Braving the hazards of a raging sea, a captain struggles to attend a meeting in North Africa.

CAST

Reed Hadley, John Hoyt, Leonard Penn.

Survive. After their ship is attacked by enemy fire, three men, adrift in the Atlantic, struggle for survival.

CAST

Scotty Beckett.

Phantom Of The Blue Angels. The story of a jet pilot's involvement with secretive, off-duty activities.

CAST

Paul Picerni, William Phipps, Edward Binns, Tony Rock, Morgan Jones.

NAVY LOG—30 minutes—CBS—September 20, 1955 - September 1956; CBS—October 17, 1956 - September 25, 1958. 102 episodes. Syndicated.

NBC ACTION PLAYHOUSE

Anthology. Rebroadcasts of dramas that were originally aired via "The Bob Hope Chrysler Theatre."

Host: Peter Marshall.

Included:

Verdict For Truth. Believing his brother was wrongly sentenced to the gas chamber, a lawyer attempts to uncover the truth.

CAST

Reynolds: Cliff Robertson; Cooper: Michael Sarrazin; Emily: Jo Ann Fleet.

Nightmare. Assisted by her sister's husband, a girl seeks to kill her crippled twin.

CAST

Isobel/Vicky: Julie Harris; Morgan: Farley Granger; Detective Ryan: Thomas Gomez.

The Crime. A vengeful prosecuting attorney attempts to pin a murder on the girl who jilted him.

CAST

Abe Perez: Jack Lord; Sarah Rodman:

Dana Wynter; DA Hightower: Pat O'Brien.

NBC ACTION PLAYHOUSE—60 minutes—NBC—June 24, 1971 - September 7, 1971; May 23, 1972 - September 5, 1972.

NBC ADVENTURE THEATRE

Anthology. Rebroadcasts of dramas that were originally aired via "The Bob Hope Chrysler Theatre."

Hosts: Art Fleming; Ed McMahon.

Included:

Echoes Of Evil. Through the testimony of a reformed gangster, a D.A. attempts to apprehend an underworld dope-ring leader.

CAST

Oscar Teckla: Barry Sullivan; Sara: Jane Wyatt; Martin Vesper: Nehemiah Persoff; Florence: Joan Hackett.

Corridor 400. A nightclub entertainer attempts to apprehend a narcotics kingpin for the F.B.I.

CAST

Anita King: Suzanne Pleshette; Ralph Travin: Theodore Bikel; Donald Guthrie: Andrew Duggan.

Deadlock. A woman's efforts to achieve revenge by planting a bomb in a police station.

CAST

Virginia: Lee Grant, Detective Baker: Jack Kelly; Detective Owens: Tige Andrews; Stacy Carter: Brooke Bundy.

NBC ADVENTURE THEATRE—60 minutes—NBC—July 24, 1971 - September 4, 1971; June 15, 1972 - August 31, 1972.

NBC BANDSTAND

See title: "Bandstand."

NBC BEST SELLERS

See title: "Best Sellers."

NBC COMEDY THEATRE

Anthology. Rebroadcasts of comedy episodes that were originally aired via "The Bob Hope Chrysler Theatre."

Host: Jack Kelly.

Included:

Dear Deductible. A songwriter and a socialite attempt to solve their tax problems by marrying and filing a joint return.

CAST

Mike Galway: Peter Falk; Virginia Ballard: Janet Leigh; Eddie: Norman Fell.

Holloway's Daughters. Unofficially assisted by his two teenage daughters, a detective attempts to solve a jewel theft.

CAST

George Holloway: David Wayne; Nick Holloway: Robert Young; Fleming Holloway: Brooke Bundy; Casey Holloway: Barbara Hershey; Martha Holloway: Marion Ross.

The Reason Nobody Hardly Ever Seen A Fat Outlaw In The Old West Is As Follows:. An outlaw, The Curly Kid, attempts to make a name for himself.

CAST

Curly: Don Knotts; Sheriff: Arthur Godfrey; Pauline: Mary-Robin Reed.

NBC COMEDY THEATRE—60 minutes—NBC—July 7, 1971 - August 30, 1971; July 8, 1972 - September 4, 1972.

NBC COMICS

See title: "The Telecomics."

THE NBC FOLLIES

Variety. A revue based on the music, song, dance, and comedy of vaudeville.

Host: Sammy Davis, Jr.

Regulars: Mickey Rooney, The Carl Jablonski Dancers.

Announcers: Colin Mayer, John Harlan.

Orchestra: Harper MacKay.

THE NBC FOLLIES—60 minutes—NBC—September 13, 1973 - December 27, 1973. 7 tapes.

THE NBC MOVIE OF THE WEEK

Movies. Theatrical features produced especially for television.

Announcer: Peggy Taylor, Donald Rickles.

Included:

How To Breakup a Happy Divorce. The story concerns a woman's attempts to win back her ex-husband from the woman who caused their marital breakup.

Cast: Ellen Dowling: Barbara Eden; Carter Dowling: Peter Bonerz; Jennifer: Liberty Williams; Tony: Hal Linden.

Flood. A disaster film wherein a small town is threatened by the imminent collapse of an earthen dam.

Cast: Steve Brannigan: Robert Culp; Paul Blake: Martin Milner; Abbie Adams: Carol Lynley; Mary: Barbara Hershey.

Night Terror. The story concerns a woman who, after witnessing a murder on a desert highway, suddenly finds her own life in jeopardy when she is stalked by the killer.

Cast: Carol Turney: Valerie Harper; Killer: Richard Romanus.

THE NBC MOVIE OF THE WEEK—90 minutes—NBC—Premiered: October 13, 1976.

NBC MOVIES

Movies. Theatrical releases.

Announcers: Don Rickles, Don Stanley, Frank Barton, Peggy Taylor, Eddie King.

Titles:

NBC SATURDAY NIGHT AT THE MOVIES—2 hours—NBC—Premiered: September 23, 1961.

NBC MONDAY NIGHT AT THE MOVIES—2 hours—NBC—Premiered: September 16, 1968.

NBC TUESDAY NIGHT AT THE MOVIES—2 hours—NBC—September 14, 1965 - September 7, 1971; January 1973 - September 1973; Returned: Premiered: September 9, 1974.

NBC WEDNESDAY NIGHT AT THE MOVIES—2 hours—NBC—1964-1965; January 1974 - September 3, 1974.

NBC MYSTERY MOVIE
NBC SUNDAY MYSTERY MOVIE

Crime Drama. The overall title for a series of nine rotating crime dramas.

The Series:

Amy Prentiss. Background: San Francisco, California. The story of Amy Prentiss, widow, the chief of detectives, a woman with style and intelligence who often finds her investigations compounded by resentment from her male colleagues.

CAST

Amy Prentiss	Jessica Walter
Sgt. Tony Russell	Steve Sandor
Detective Roy Pena	Art Metrano
Joan Carter, Amy's secretary	Gwenn Mitchell
Chief Demsey	M. Emmet Walsh
Jill Prentiss, Amy's daughter	Helen Hunt

Music: John Cacavas; Don Costa.

Columbo. Background: Los Angeles, California. The investigations of Lieutenant Columbo, an underpaid and untidy L.A.P.D. homicide detective. Slurred in speech and fumbling in exterior, his forceful nature and razor-sharp mind enable him to solve baffling acts of criminal injustice.

CAST

Lieutenant Columbo	Peter Falk
Captain Sampson	Bill Zuckert

Music: Bernard Segal, Jeff Alexander, Oliver Nelson, Dick De Benedictis, Billy Goldenberg.

Producer: Everett Chambers.

Director: Patrick McGoohan, Bernard Kowalski, Robert Douglas, Harvey Hart.

Hec Ramsey. Background: New Prospect, Oklahoma, 1901. The investigations of Deputy Hector (Hec) Ramsey, an ex-gunfighter turned law enforcer who attempts to solve crimes by means of scientific evaluation and deduction.

CAST

Deputy Hec Ramsey	Richard Boone
Sheriff Oliver B. Stamp	Rick Lenz
Amos B. Coogan, the town barber and doctor	Harry Morgan
Norma Muldoon, a widow, Hec's romantic interest	Sharon Acker
Andy Muldoon, her son	Brian Dewey

Narrator: Harry Morgan.

Music: Fred Steiner; Lee Holdridge.

Lanigan's Rabbi. Background: Cameron, California. The cases of Paul

Lanigan, the police chief, and his friend and sometimes assistant, David Small, a Rabbi who preaches at the Temple Beth Halell Synagogue.

CAST

Paul Lanigan	Art Carney
Rabbi David Small	Stuart Margolin (pilot)
	Bruce Solomon
Kate Lanigan, Paul's wife	Janis Paige
Miriam Small, David's wife	Janet Margolin
Lieutenant Osgood	Robert Doyle
Bobbi, the reporter	Barbara Carney
Hannah Prince, one of the Rabbi's perishoners	Reva Rose

Music: Don Costa.

Executive Producer: Leonard B. Stern.

Producer: David J. Connell.

Director: Leonard B. Stern, Joseph Pevney, Noel Black.

McCloud. Background: New York City. The investigations of Sam McCloud, a deputy marshall from Taos, New Mexico assigned to the Manhattan 27th precinct to study metropolitan crime-detection methods.

CAST

Deputy Sam McCloud	Dennis Weaver
Police Chief Peter B. Clifford	J.D. Cannon
Sergeant Joe Broadhurst	Terry Carter
Chris Coughlin, Sam's romantic interest	Diana Muldaur

Music: Richard Clements.

Additional Music: Stu Phillips.

Executive Producer: Glen A. Larson.

Director: E.W. Swackhamer, Lou Antonio, Noel Black, Bruce Kessler.

McCoy. Background: Los Angeles, California. The exploits of McCoy, an engaging con artist who, to pay off his gambling debts, first undertakes a criminal case, then, by incorporating his unique skills, seeks to solve the crime.

CAST

McCoy	Tony Curtis
Gideon Gibbs, his assistant	Roscoe Lee Browne

Music: Billy Goldenberg, Dick De Benedictis.

Producer: Roland Kibbee.

McMillan And Wife. Background: San Francisco, California. The saga of Sally McMillan, the pretty, but trouble-prone wife of police commissioner Stewart "Mac" McMillan. Stories depict their investigations into crimes Sally accidentally stumbles upon and in which she involves Mac.

CAST

Stewart McMillan	Rock Hudson
Sally McMillan	Susan Saint James
Sergeant Charles Enright	John Schuck
Mildred, the McMillan's housekeeper	Nancy Walker
Maggie, Mac's secretary	Gloria Stroock
Chief Paulson	Bill Quinn

Music: Jerry Fielding.

Executive Producer: Leonard B. Stern.

Producer: Jon Epstein.

Director: Lou Antonio, Harry Falk, Bob Finkel, James Sheldon, Lee H. Katzin.

McMillan. Revised title after the departure of Susan Saint James (her character, Sally, was killed in a plane crash) and Nancy Walker. Background: San Francisco, California. The cases of Stewart McMillan, the police commissioner.

CAST

Stewart McMillan	Rock Hudson
Agatha Thornton, his housekeeper	Martha Raye
Lt. Charles Enright	John Schuck
Sgt. Di'Maggio	Richard Gilliland
Maggie, Mac's secretary	Gloria Stroock
Chief Paulson	Bill Quinn

Music: Jerry Fielding.

Executive Producer: Leonard B. Stern.

Producer: Jon Epstein.

Director: Jackie Cooper, James Sheldon.

NBC Sunday Mystery Movie: McMillan and Wife. Susan Saint James and Rock Hudson.

Quincy, M.E. See title.

NBC MYSTERY MOVIE—90 minutes—NBC—September 15, 1971 - September 12, 1972; as "NBC Sunday Mystery Movie:" Premiered: September 17, 1972.

NBC's SATURDAY NIGHT

Variety. Musical acts coupled with topical comedy. Broadcast live from New York City (11:30 p.m.-1:00 a.m., E.S.T.)

Hosts: Guests, including George Carlin, Rob Reiner, Lily Tomlin, Robert Klein.

Regulars (billed as "The Not Ready For Prime Time Players"): Chevy Chase, Jim Henson and the Muppets, Danny Ackroyd, John Belushi, Jane Curtin, Garrett Morris, Laraine Newman, Gilda Radner.

Announcer: Don Pardo.

Orchestra: Howard Jones, Howard Shore.

Musical Director: Paul Shaffer.

Producer: Lorne Michaels.

Director: Dave Wilson.

NBC's SATURDAY NIGHT—90 minutes—NBC—Premiered: October 11, 1975.

NBC THURSDAY NIGHT AT THE MOVIES

Theatrical and made for television films. Listed are examples of the films produced especially for television. See "NBC Movies" for the additional network film series.

Who Is the Black Dahlia? (1975). A haunting film that details veteran police inspector Harry Hanson's investigation into the mysterious, bizarre death of Elizabeth Short, whose body, drained of blood and bisected at the waist, was found in a Los Angeles field on January 15, 1947. The case concerning Miss Short, who had a penchant for black clothing and a tattoo of a black dahlia, is still unsolved.

CAST

Elizabeth Short: Lucie Arnaz; Insp. Harry Hanson: Efrem Zimbalist, Jr.;

Also: Gloria DeHaven, June Lockhart, Ronny Cox, Macdonald Carey.

Ransom for Alice (1977). Background: Seattle during the 1890s. The story of two law officers— one male, the other female—as they attempt to find a girl kidnapped by a white slavery ring.

CAST

Deputy Jeannie Cullen: Yvette Mimieux; Deputy Kirk: Gil Gerrard; Marshal Pete Phelan: Charles Napier; Yankee Sullivan: Gavin MacLeod.

Snowbeast (1977). A thriller that centers on a Rocky Mountain resort that is terrorized by a killer beast similar to Bigfoot.

CAST

Ellen Seberg: Yvette Mimieux; Gar Seberg: Bo Svenson; Carrie Bill: Sylvia Sidney; Sheriff Paraday: Clint Walker.

NBC THURSDAY NIGHT AT THE MOVIES—2 hours—NBC—May 22, 1975 - August 28, 1975; Returned— January 15, 1976 - September 8, 1977.

NBC WEDNESDAY MYSTERY MOVIE

Crime Drama. The overall title for six rotating series: "Banacek"; "Cool Million"; "Faraday and Company"; "Madigan"; "The Snoop Sisters"; and "Tenafly."

Banacek. Background: Boston. The investigations of Thomas Banacek (pronounced: Ban-a-check), a self-employed insurance-company detective who recovers stolen merchandise for ten percent of its value.

CAST

Thomas Banacek   George Peppard
Felix Mulholland,
  his information man,
  the owner of a rare-book
  store   Murray Matheson
Jay Drury, his
  chauffeur   Ralph Manza
Carlie Kirkland, an agent
  for the Boston Insurance
  Company   Christine Belford
Music: Billy Goldenberg; Jack Elliot and Allyn Ferguson.

Cool Million. The investigations of Jefferson Keyes, a former U.S. government agent turned confidential private detective who charges one million dollars and guarantees results or re-

funds the money. Unable to afford a busy signal, he establishes a base in Lincoln, Nebraska (where telephone lines are always open), in the home of a woman named Elena. When his special telephone number, 30-30100, is dialed, Elena, the only person able to contact him, relays the message to him.

CAST

Jefferson Keyes   James Farentino
Tony Baylor,
  the pilot of his
  private jet   Ed Bernard
Elena   Adele Mara
Music: Billy Goldenberg.

Faraday And Company. Background: Los Angeles, California. Escaping from a Caribbean prison after twenty-eight years of internment on false charges, Frank Faraday returns to the States and, after exposing and apprehending the man responsible for his plight, assumes his former position as private detective with his son, Steve, a security consultant for industry. Stories relate the investigations of a 1940s-style private detective and the dated techniques he uses to apprehend the seventies generation of criminal.

CAST

Frank Faraday   Dan Dailey
Steve Faraday   James Naughton
Louise "Lou" Carson,
  Frank's former
  Secretary—and Steve's
  mother   Geraldine Brooks
Holly Barrett, their
  secretary   Sharon Gless
Music: Jerry Fielding.

Madigan. Background: New York City. The investigations of Sergeant Dan Madigan, an embittered plainclothes detective attached to the Manhattan tenth precinct.

Starring: Richard Widmark as Sgt. Dan Madigan.

Music: Jerry Fielding.

The Snoop Sisters. Background: New York City. The investigations of Ernesta and Gwen Snoop, sisters, eccentric fictitious mystery story writers who become involved with and solve crimes while seeking story material.

CAST

Ernesta Snoop   Helen Hayes
Gwen Snoop   Mildred Natwick
Lt. Steve Ostrowski,
  N.Y.P.D., their

nephew   Bert Convy
Barney, an ex-con
  hired by Steve to
  watch over his mis-
  chievous aunts   Lou Antonio
Music: Jerry Fielding.

Tenafly. Background: Los Angeles, California. The investigations of Harry Tenafly, a private detective employed by Hightower Investigations, Incorporated.

CAST

Harry Tenafly   James McEachin
Ruth Tenafly, his
  wife   Lillian Lehman
Lorrie, his
  secretary   Rosanna Huffman
Lt. Sam Church,
  L.A.P.D.   David Huddleston
Herb Tenafly,
  Harry and Ruth's
  son   Paul Jackson

Their other son, an infant, is not given credit.

Music: Gil Mellé.

NBC WEDNESDAY MYSTERY MOVIE—90 minutes—NBC—September 13, 1972 - January 9, 1974. As "NBC Tuesday Mystery Movie:" 90 minutes—NBC—January 15, 1974 - September 4, 1974.

NBC WORLD PREMIERE MOVIE

Movies. Feature films produced especially for television.
Included:

Once Upon A Dead Man. Through the efforts of his scatterbrained wife, a police commissioner becomes involved in a charity auction theft and murder. The pilot film for "McMillan and Wife."

CAST

Stewart McMillan: Rock Hudson; Sally McMillan: Susan Saint James.

Emergency. The exploits of Squad 51 of the Los Angeles County Fire Department. The pilot film for "Emergency."

CAST

Dr. Brackett: Robert Fuller; Nurse McCall: Julie London; Dr. Early: Bobby Troup; John Gage: Randolph Mantooth; Roy DeSoto: Kevin Tighe.

Ellery Queen: Don't Look Behind You. The famed gentleman detective attempts to apprehend a strangler.

CAST

Ellery Queen: Peter Lawford; Insp. Richard Queen: Harry Morgan; Celeste: Stefanie Powers.

NBC WORLD PREMIERE MOVIE—2 hours—NBC—September 17, 1971 - September 8, 1972.

NEEDLES AND PINS

Comedy. Background: New York City; 463 7th Avenue, Manhattan; the business address of Lorelei Fashions. Life in the aggravating world of the garment industry as seen through the experiences of Wendy Nelson, a struggling young apprentice fashion designer.

CAST

Wendy Nelson	Deirdre Lenihan
Nathan Davidson, the manufacturing head	Norman Fell
Harry Karp, Nathan's brother-in-law and partner	Louis Nye
Charlie Miller, the firm salesman	Bernie Kopell
Sonia Baker, the firm bookkeeper	Sandra Deel
Max, the material cutter	Larry Gelman
Myron Russo, the pattern maker	Alex Henteloff
Julius Singer, the competitor, the owner of Singer Sophisticates	Milton Selzer
Elliott, the waiter at the local restaruant	Joshua Shelley

Music: Mike Post and Pete Carpenter.

NEEDLES AND PINS—30 minutes—NBC—September 21, 1973 - December 28, 1973. 14 episodes.

Needles and Pins. Deirdre Lenihan and Norman Fell.

THE NEIGHBORS

Game. Five actual neighbors, all of whom are female, are involved. Two are selected as the players; the remaining three comprise the panel. A question, that refers to one of the two players, is read. Each player has to predict to whom the question refers—herself or her neighbor. The answers are based on a survey of the panel, and if the player's choice agrees with the panel's, she receives $25. Four such questions are played. Round two concerns the players' abilities to pinpoint which neighbor said something about her. A statement, made by one of the panelists, about one of the players, is read. Each panelist relates a story telling why she made the statement. Having heard all three stories, the player picks the one she feels actually made the statement. One hundred dollars is scored if she is correct. Four such situations are played. In round three, the host reads a statement about one of the two players that all three panelists agree with. Players have to determine to whom the statement refers. Four such questions are played, worth $50, $100, $200, and $500. The player with the highest cash score is the winner.

Host: Regis Philbin.

Model: Jane Nelson.

Announcer: Joe Sinan.

Music: Stan Worth.

Producer-Director: Bill Carruthers.

THE NEIGHBORS—30 minutes—ABC—December 29, 1975 - April 9, 1976.

NEVER TOO YOUNG

Serial. Background: Malibu Beach, California. The overall behavior and problems of eight young people: Alfie, the owner of "Alfie's Cafe," the local beach hangout; his girlfriend, Barbara; and teenagers: Joy, Susan, Jo Jo, Tad, Chet, and Tim.

CAST

Alfie	David Watson
Tad	Michael Blodgett
Joy	Robin Grace
Jo Jo	Tommy Rettig
Chet	Tony Dow
Susan	Cindy Carol
Barbara	Pat Connolly
Tim	Dack Rambo
Rhoda, Joy's mother	Patrice Wymore
Frank, Susan's father	John Lupton
Rhoda's sister	Merry Anders

Announcer: Roger Christian.

Music: Ray Martin.

NEVER TOO YOUNG—25 minutes—ABC—September 27, 1965 - June 24, 1966.

THE NEW ADVENTURES OF BATMAN

Animated Cartoon. The further crime fighting adventures of Batman, Robin, and Batgirl. See title "Batman" for storyline information.

Characters' Voices:

Batman	Adam West
Robin	Burt Ward
Batgirl	Melendy Britt
Batmite, the mouse	Lennie Weinrib.

Music: Yvette Blais, Jeff Michael.

Executive Producer: Lou Scheimer, Norm Prescott.

Producer: Don Christensen.

THE NEW ADVENTURES OF BATMAN—25 minutes—CBS—Premiered: February 12, 1977.

THE NEW ADVENTURES OF CHARLIE CHAN

Mystery. Background: Europe. The investigations of Charlie Chan, a courteous, shrewd, and philosophical Chinese detective. Based on the character created by Earl Derr Biggers.

CAST

Charlie Chan	J. Carrol Naish
Barry Chan, his Number One Son	James Hong
Inspector Duff	Rupert Davies
Inspector Carl Marlowe	Hugh Williams

Executive Producer: Leon Fromkess.

Producer: Rudolph Flothow, Sidney Marshall.

Director: Leslie Arliss, Charles Bennett, Jack Gage, Charles Haas, Don Chaffey, Leslie Goodwins, Alvin Rakoff.

THE NEW ADVENTURES OF CHARLIE CHAN—30 minutes—Syndicated 1957. 39 episodes.

THE NEW ADVENTURES OF GILLIGAN

Animated Cartoon. A spin-off from "Gilligan's Island." Background: A small uncharted island in the South

Pacific. Shipwrecked after their charter ship, the S.S. *Minnow*, is damaged in a tropical storm at sea, the five passengers and two crew members establish a community when all attempts to acquire help fail. Stories relate their struggle for survival; their attempt to understand nature; and compatibility with one's fellow human.

Characters' Voices

Jonas Grumby, the skipper	Alan Hale
Gilligan, his bumbling first mate	Bob Denver
Ginger Grant, a beautiful movie actress	Jane Webb
Thurston Howell III, a multimillionaire	Jim Backus
Lovey Howell III, his wife	Natalie Schafer
Roy Hinkly, a brilliant research scientist, the professor	Russell Johnson
Mary Ann Summers, a clerk from Kansas	Jane Edwards

Music: Yvette Blais, Jeff Michael.

THE NEW ADVENTURES OF GILLIGAN—30 minutes—ABC—Premiered: September 7, 1974.

THE NEW ADVENTURES OF HUCKLEBERRY FINN

Adventure. Adapted from the novel, *The Adventures of Huckleberry Finn,* by Mark Twain. Pursued by the vengeful Injun Joe, Huckleberry Finn, Becky Thatcher, and Tom Sawyer run into a cave where they are engulfed by a fierce, raging sea and transported to strange fantasy lands that are populated by cartoon characters. Assisting where needed, they seek to escape from Injun Joe and find the secret of the way back to their homes in Hannibal, Missouri, 1845. Live action is played against superimposed animated backgrounds.

CAST

Huckleberry Finn	Michael Shea
Becky Thatcher	Lu Ann Haslam
Tom Sawyer	Kevin Schultz
Injun Joe	Ted Cassidy

Voices: Hal Smith, Ted de Corsia, Peggy Webber, Jack Krusacher, Paul Stewart, Mike Road, Vic Perrin, Charles Lane, Julie Bennett, Paul Frees, Marvin Miller.

Music: Hoyt Curtin.

THE NEW ADVENTURES OF HUCKLEBERRY FINN—30 minutes—NBC—September 15, 1968 - September 7, 1969. 20 episodes.

THE NEW ADVENTURES OF MARTIN KANE

See title: "Martin Kane."

THE NEW ADVENTURES OF PERRY MASON

See title: "Perry Mason."

THE NEW ADVENTURES OF PINOCCHIO

Marionettes. The adventures of Pinocchio, the wooden boy who was brought to life to please the lonely old man Gipetto, and his friend, Jiminy Crickett. Filmed in Animagic (giving life to marionettes).

Music: Jules Bass.

THE NEW ADVENTURES OF PINOCCHIO—05 minutes—Syndicated 1961. 130 episodes.

THE NEW ADVENTURES OF SUPERMAN

See title: "The Adventures of Superman."

THE NEW ADVENTURES OF WONDER WOMAN

Adventure. A spin-off from "Wonder Woman," which see for background information. (Storyline begins where the original leaves off.) Having successfully aided America in its fight against the Nazis, Diana Prince, alias Wonder Woman, returns to Paradise Island following World War II in 1945.

Now, thirty-two years later (1977), as a plane carrying U.S. Government agents to a special meeting in Latin America passes through the Bermuda Triangle, an enemy saboteur, who is later caught, releases a gas that renders the crew and passengers unconscious. Caught in the magnetic field of the Triangle, the jet comes under the control of the inhabitants of the uncharted Paradise Island—a race of super women called Amazons. Entering the downed aircraft, the Princess Diana is startled to see whom she

The New Adventures of Wonder Woman. Lynda Carter and Lyle Waggoner. *Courtesy of the Call-Chronicle Newspapers, Allentown, Pa.*

believes is Major Steve Trevor, a mortal she aided during the 1940s. When brought to the medical center and treated, Diana learns that her Steve is now U.S. Government Security Agent Steve Trevor, Jr., son of the late Major General Steve Trevor.

Realizing that the world is still threatened by evil, Diana requests permission from her Queen Mother to become an emissary and assist the outside world in its battle for truth and justice. A special council meeting is held and Diana's request is granted. To protect her true identity as Wonder Woman, the Princess again adopts the guise of Diana Prince. Steve is then hypnotized and led to believe that Diana is his replacement assistant, whom he is to meet in Latin America.

From her Queen Mother, Diana receives the special wrist bracelets, made of feminum, to reflect bullets; the magic belt to maintain her strength and cunning away from Paradise Island; the magic lariat, which compels people to tell the truth; and the magic tiara, which contains a special ruby that enables Diana to contact her mother whenever the need arises. Diana then chooses a revealing red, white, and blue costume to signify her allegiance to freedom and democracy.

The passengers and crew, still unconscious, are placed back aboard the plane. Diana pilots it to twelve thousand feet, sets it on automatic, then plays a special musical tune to awaken those aboard. As they begin to regain consciousness, Diana leaves through an escape hatch and boards her invisible plane, which she uses to ensure the jet's safe arrival in Latin America.

At the scheduled meeting, Diana introduces herself to Steve—who, upon seeing her—accepts her as his assistant. (Later, when returning to Washington, D.C., Diana gains access to the government's computerized personnel files and programs her own employment record—the final step to again create Diana Prince—now assistant to Steve Trevor of the I.A.D.C. [Inter Agency Defense Command], and protect her true identity as Wonder Woman.)

Stories depict Diana's exploits as she battles for freedom and democracy throughout the world as the mysterious Wonder Woman. (By performing a twirling striptease, the attractive Diana Prince emerges into the gorgeous Wonder Woman.) Based on the characters created by Charles Moulton.

CAST

Diana Prince/ Wonder Woman	Lynda Carter
Steve Trevor, Jr.	Lyle Waggoner
Joe Atkinson, Steve's superior	Normann Burton
The Queen Mother	Beatrice Straight

Music: Artie Kane.

Theme: Charles Fox, Norman Gimbel.

Executive Producer: Douglas S. Cramer, Wilfred Baumes.

Producer: Charles B. Fitzsimons, Mark Rodgers.

Animation: Phill Norman.

THE NEW ADVENTURES OF WONDER WOMAN—60 minutes—CBS—Premiered: September 16, 1977.

THE NEW ANDY GRIFFITH SHOW

Comedy. Background: Greenwood, North Carolina. The trials and tribulations of Andy Sawyer, former sheriff and justice of the peace turned mayor.

The New Andy Griffith Show. Top: Andy Griffith, Marty McCall; bottom: Lori Ann Rutherford, Lee Ann Meriwether.

CAST

Andy Sawyer	Andy Griffith
Lee Sawyer, his wife	Lee Ann Meriwether
Lori Sawyer, their daughter	Lori Ann Rutherford
T.J. Sawyer, their son	Marty McCall
Nora, Lee's sister	Ann Morgan Guilbert
Buff MacKnight, the senior town councilman	Glen Ash

Music: Earle Hagen.

THE NEW ANDY GRIFFITH SHOW —30 minutes—CBS—January 8, 1972 - June 4, 1972. 13 episodes.

THE NEW ARCHIE/SABRINA HOUR

Animated Cartoon. Newly animated adventures of the Archie Gang—Archie, Veronica, Jughead, Valerie, Reggie, and Hot Dog; and Sabrina, the teenage witch. See also: "The Archie Show," and "Sabrina, the Teenage Witch."

Voices: Dallas McKennon, Jane Webb, Don Messick, John Erwin, Jose Flores, Howard Morris.

Music: Yvette Blais, Jeff Michael.

Executive Producer: Norm Prescott, Lou Scheimer.

Producer: Don Christensen.

THE NEW ARCHIE/SABRINA HOUR—60 minutes—NBC—Premiered: September 10, 1977.

THE NEW BILL COSBY SHOW

Variety. Various songs, dances, and comedy sketches that depict the world as seen through the eyes of comedian Bill Cosby.

Host: Bill Cosby.

Regulars: Susan Tolsky, Lola Falana, Foster Brooks, Oscar De Grury, Erin Fleming, The Donald McKayle Dancers.

Announcer: Lola Falana.

Orchestra: Quincy Jones; Bobby Bryant.

Featured Sketch: "The Wife of the Week." A domestic sketch wherein a guest actress portrays Bill's constantly nagging wife.

THE NEW BILL COSBY SHOW—60 minutes—CBS—September 11, 1972 - May 17, 1973.

THE NEW BREED

Crime Drama. Background: Los Angeles, California. The investigations of the Metropolitan Squad, a special L.A.P.D. detective force designed to disrupt the workings of organized crime.

CAST

Lieutenant Price Adams	Leslie Nielsen
Sergeant Vince Cavelli	John Beradino
Captain Keith Gregory	Byron Morrow
Officer Joe Huddleston	John Clark
Officer Pete Garcia	Greg Roman

THE NEW BREED—60 minutes—ABC—October 3, 1961 — September 15, 1962. 36 episodes. Syndicated.

THE NEW CANDID CAMERA

See title: "Candid Camera."

THE NEW CASPER CARTOON SHOW

See title: "Casper, the Friendly Ghost."

THE NEW CBS FRIDAY NIGHT MOVIE THE NEW CBS TUESDAY NIGHT MOVIE

Movies. Feature-length suspense thrillers produced especially for television.

Included:

The Cable Car Murder. A detective attempts to solve a contract murder committed in broad daylight.

CAST

Van Alsdale: Robert Hooks; Sgt. Cassidy: Jeremy Slate; Kathie Cooper: Carol Lynley; McBride: Robert Wagner.

Death Of Innocence. The ordeal of a mother as she witnesses her daughter's murder trial.

CAST

Elizabeth Cameron: Shelley Winters; Buffie Cameron: Tisha Sterling.

Black Noon. A minister's battle against an unseen power that is gripping a desert town in a strange hold of misfortune.

CAST

The Rev. Mr. Keyes: Roy Thinnes; Lorna Keyes: Lynn Loring; Deliverance: Yvette Mimieux.

She Waits. The story of a young bride stalked by the spirit of her husband's first wife.

CAST

Laura Wilson: Patty Duke; Mark Wilson: David McCallum; Sarah Wilson: Dorothy McGuire; Dr. Carpenter: Lew Ayres; Dave Brody: James Callahan.

THE NEW CBS FRIDAY NIGHT MOVIE–90 minutes–CBS–September 17, 1971 - September 8, 1972.

THE NEW CBS TUESDAY NIGHT MOVIE–90 minutes–CBS–September 12, 1972 - September 3, 1974.

THE NEW CHRISTY MINSTRELS SHOW

Musical Variety.

Starring: The New Christy Minstrels: Ann White. Paul Potash. Art Podell, Barry Kane, Karen Gunderson, Barry McGuire, Nick Woods, Clarence Treat, Larry Romos.

Regulars: Rowlf, the hound-dog muppet; The Chuck Casey Singers, The Doerr-Hutchinson Dancers.

Orchestra: Peter Matz.

THE NEW CHRISTY MINSTRELS SHOW–30 minutes–NBC–August 5, 1964 - September 2, 1964.

NEW COMEDY SHOWCASE

Pilot Films. Proposed comedy series for the 1960-1961 season.

Included:

Johnny Come Lately. The misadventures of television newscaster Johnny Martin.

CAST

Johnny Martin: Johnny Carson; Eddie: Dick Reeves; Miss Talbot: Marie Windsor.

They Went Thataway. Fancying himself as the meanest man in the West, Black Ace Burton begins his quest to acquire the title.

CAST

Black Ace Burton: James Westerfield; Poison Pete: Ron Haggerthy; Sam Cloggett: Wayne Morris.

The Trouble With Richard. The misad-

ventures of a good-natured bank teller.

CAST

Richard: Dick Van Dyke; Gramps Parker Fennelly.

You're Only Young Once. After their children are married, a middle-aged couple attempt to rediscover life.

CAST

Charles Tyler: George Murphy; Kit Tyler: Martha Scott; Lois: Sue Randall; Arthur: Roger Perry.

NEW COMEDY SHOWCASE–30 minutes–CBS–August 1, 1960 - September 19, 1960.

THE NEW DICK VAN DYKE SHOW

Comedy. Distinguished by two formats.

Format One:

The New Dick Van Dyke Show–30 minutes–CBS–September 18, 1971 - September 3, 1973.

Background: Carefree, Arizona. The trials and tribulations of Dick Preston, the host of "The Dick Preston Show," a ninety-minute talk-variety program produced by KXIU-TV, Channel 2, in Phoenix.

CAST

Dick Preston	Dick Van Dyke
Jenny Preston, his wife	Hope Lange
Bernie Davis, Dick's agent and business manager	Marty Brill
Carol Davis, Bernie's wife	Nancy Dussault
Michele (Mike) Preston, Dick's sister and secretary	Fannie Flagg
Annie Preston, Dick and Jenny's daughter	Angela Powell
Lucas Preston, Dick and Jenny's son	Michael Shea
Ted Atwater, Dick's boss, the president of the Compton Broadcasting Company	David Doyle

Music: Jack Elliott, Allyn Ferguson.

Format Two:

The New Dick Van Dyke Show–30 minutes–CBS–September 10, 1973 - September 2, 1974.

Background: 747 Bonnie Vista Road, Tarzana, California. Relocating after his show is cancelled, Dick acquires the role of Dr. Brad Fairmont, a surgeon at Pleasant Valley Hospital on the mythical daytime TV soap opera, "Those Who Care." Stories relate his home and working life.

CAST

Dick Preston	Dick Van Dyke
Jenny Preston	Hope Lange
Annie Preston	Angela Powell
Max Mathias, the program's producer	Dick Van Patten
Alex Montez, the director	Henry Darrow
Dennis Whitehead, the script writer	Barry Gordon
Richard Richardson; Dick's neighbor, the star of the mythical TV series "Harrigan's Holligans"	Richard Dawson
Connie Richardson, his wife	Chita Rivera
Margot Brighton, the serial lead, playing Dr. Susan Allison	Barbara Rush

Music: Jack Elliott, Allyn Ferguson.

THE NEW HOWDY DOODY SHOW

Children. A spin-off from "Howdy Doody" (which see for story line information). The updated version features puppets, guest performers, and sketches geared for children.

CAST

Buffalo Bob Smith, the host	Bob Smith
Clarabell Hornblow, the clown	Lou Anderson
Happy Harmony, the school-teacher	Marilyn Patch
Cornelius Cobb, the prop man	Bill LeCornec
Nicholson Muir, the mythical producer	Nick Nicholson
Jackie Davis, a singer	Himself

Puppets: Howdy Doody (voiced by Bob Smith), Phineas T. Bluster (voiced by Dayton Allen), Dilly Dally, The Flubadub, Outer Orbit, the flying saucer (voiced by Nick Nicholson).

Music: The Doodyville Doodlers, conducted by Jackie Davis.

Executive Producer: Nick Nicholson, E. Roger Muir.

Producer: Ronald Wayne.

Director: Errol Falcon.

THE NEW HOWDY DOODY SHOW
—30 minutes—Syndicated 1976.

THE NEW LAND

Drama. Background: Minnesota, 1858. The life and struggles of the Larsen family, Scandinavian immigrants attempting to carve a life and share in the American Dream.

CAST

Christian Larsen, the father	Scott Thomas
Ann Larsen, his wife	Bonnie Bedelia
Tuliff Larsen, their son	Todd Lookinland
Anneliese Larsen, their daughter	Debbie Lytton
Bo Larsen, Christian's brother	Kurt Russell
Mr. Lundstrom, their neighbor	Donald Moffat
Molly Lundstrom, his wife	Gwen Arner

Music: The Orphanage.

THE NEW LAND—60 minutes—ABC —September 14, 1974 - October 19, 1974. 4 episodes.

THE NEW MICKEY MOUSE CLUB

Children. An updated version of the 1950s "Mickey Mouse Club" (which see), featuring twelve new Mouseketeers in songs, dances, and sketches, and an array of never-before televised Disney cartoons and films.

The Mouseketeers: Kelly Parsons, Lisa Whelchel, Mindy Feldman, Nita (DiGiampaolo) Dee, Curtis Wong, Julie Piekarski, Scott Craig, Shawnte Northcutte, Allison Fonte, Todd Turquand, Angel Florez, William "Pop" Attmore.

Voice of Mickey Mouse: Wayne Allwine (for the series; Walt Disney's voice is heard in the cartoons prior to 1949).

Voice of Jiminy Cricket: Cliff Edwards.

Music: Buddy Baer, Robert F. Brunner, William Schaefer.

Executive Producer: Ron Miller.

Producer: Ed Ropolo, Mike Wuergler.

Director: John Tracy, Dick Amos, James Field, Dick Krown.

The New Mickey Mouse Club. The new Mouseketeers: bottom, left to right: Todd, Curtis, Julie, Nita, Lisa, Pop; top row, left to right: Allison, Scott, Mindy, Shaunte, Angel, Kelly. © *Walt Disney Productions.*

THE NEW MICKEY MOUSE CLUB— 30 minutes—Syndicated 1977. 130 tapes.

THE NEW NEWLYWED GAME

Game. A spin-off from "The Newlywed Game," which see for format.

Host: Bob Eubanks.

Announcer: Johnny Jacobs.

Music: Lee Ringuette.

Executive Producer: Chuck Barris.

Producer: Mike Metzger.

Director: John Dorsey.

Creator: Roger Muir.

THE NEW NEWLYWED GAME—30 minutes—Syndicated 1977.

THE NEW, ORIGINAL WONDER WOMAN

See title: "Wonder Woman."

THE NEW PEOPLE

Drama. Enroute from Southeast Asia to the mainland, a small inner island charter is caught in a fierce storm. Damaged, and unable to maintain a steady flight pattern, the plane crash lands on Buamo, a remote Pacific island once chosen as a hydrogen bomb test site by the Atomic Energy Commission, but abandoned due to a fear of contamination by the trade winds.

Of the fifty passengers, forty young adults, American college students on a cultural exchange program, survive. Stories depict: Their struggle for survival; and, having a completely provisioned city on the island, their attempts to establish a society un-

touched by the destruction of modern man.

CAST

Susan Bradley	Tiffany Bolling
Robert Lee	Zooey Hall
Eugene "Bones" Washington	David Moses
George Potter	Peter Ratray
Errol "Bull" Wilson	Lee Jay Lambert
Dexter	Kevin Michaels
Barbara	Brenda Sykes
Gloria	Nancy DeCarol
Stanley	Dennis Olivieri
	Kevin O'Neal
Ginny	Jill Jaress
Laura	Elizabeth Berger
Jack	Clive Clerk
Wendy	Donna Baccala
Dan Stoner	Carl Reindel

Music: Earle Hagen.

THE NEW PEOPLE—45 minutes— ABC—September 22, 1969 - January 12, 1970. 13 episodes.

NEWSSTAND THEATRE

A series of thirty minute dramas broadcast on ABC from January 23, 1952 - February 6, 1952.

THE NEW STU ERWIN SHOW

See title: "Trouble With Father."

THE NEW SUPER FRIENDS HOUR

Animated Cartoon. A spin-off from "Super Friends." Background: The Hall of Justice in Washington, D.C., an organization formed by the world's mightest super heroes to battle injustice. The series depicts their individual and/or joint ventures.

The Super Friends: Superman, Batman and Robin, Wonder Woman, Aquaman, Rima the Jungle Queen, The Black Vulcan, Samural the Apache Chief, and Space Twins Zan and Jana, and their space monkey Gleek.

Voices: Sherry Alberoni, Danny Dark, Casey Kaseem, Olan Soule, Ted Knight, John Stevenson, Franklin Rucker, Frank Welker, Shannon Farnon, Norman Alden.

Music: Hoyt Curtin, Paul DeKorte.

Executive Producer: William Hanna, Joseph Barbera.

Producer: Iwao Takamoto.

Director: William Hanna, Joseph Barbera.

THE NEW SUPER FRIENDS HOUR
—55 minutes—ABC—Premiered: September 10, 1977.

THE NEW TEMPERATURES RISING SHOW

See title: "Temperatures Rising."

THE NEW TREASURE HUNT

Game. A spin-off from "Treasure Hunt." Three contestants are chosen from the studio audience. Brought on stage, each selects one of three boxes. The contestant whose box contains a "Treasure Hunt" card receives the opportunity to seek $25,000 in cash. The player chooses one of thirty boxes that are displayed on stage. The box, which contains a cash amount (two hundred to two thousand dollars), is offered to the player to forfeit whatever the box contains. If the player refuses the money she receives the contents of the box—cash (five thousand to twenty-five thousand dollars), valuable merchandise (cars, airplanes, furniture), or a clunk (inexpensive prizes). Two such rounds are played on each program.

Host: Geoff Edwards.

Assistants: Jane Nelson, Joey Faye.

Announcer: Johnny Jacobs.

Music: Frank Jaffe; Lee Ringuette.

Check Guard: Emil Arture, a bonded security agent.

Model: Sivi Aberg.

Executive Producer: Chuck Barris.

Producer: Michael J. Metzger.

Director: John Dorsey.

Creator: Jan Murray.

THE NEW TREASURE HUNT—30 minutes—Syndicated 1973.

THE NEW TRUTH OR CONSEQUENCES

See title: "Truth Or Consequences."

NEW YORK CONFIDENTIAL

Crime Drama. Background: New York City. The investigations of newspaper reporter-columnist Lee Cochran. Based on the book by Lee Mortimer and Jack Lait.

Starring: Lee Tracy as Lee Cochran.

NEW YORK CONFIDENTIAL—30 minutes—Syndicated 1958. 39 episodes.

THE NEW ZOO REVUE

Educational. Background: A zoo. Various aspects of the world are related to children via songs, dances, sketches, and stories.

CAST

Doug	Doug Momary
Emmy Jo	Emily Peden
Charlie, the wise owl	Sharon Baird
Freddie, the frog	Yanco Inone Scutter McKay
Henrietta, the hippo	Thomas Carri Larri Thomas
Mr. Dingle, the general-store owner	Chuck Woolery

Voices for the costumed characters (Freddie, Charlie, and Henrietta): Bob Holt, Hazel Shermit, Joni Robbins, Bill Callaway.

Orchestra: Denny Vaughn; Milton Greene.

THE NEW ZOO REVUE—30 minutes—Syndicated 1972.

THE NEWLYWED GAME

Game. Four husband-and-wife couples compete. The husbands appear before camera; the wives are isolated backstage in a soundproof room. The host asks each husband three five-point questions. The couples are reunited and the questions are restated one at a time. If the wife matches her husband's answer, they receive the points. There is no penalty for an incorrect response.

The second half is played in reverse. The wives are asked three ten-point questions and one twenty-five point bonus question. The husbands have to match their wives' answers.

Winners, the highest point scorers, receive a specially selected merchandise prize.

Host: Bob Eubanks.

Announcer: Johnny Jacobs.

Music: Frank Jaffe; Lee Ringuette.

THE NEWLYWED GAME—30 minutes—ABC. Daytime version: July 11, 1966 - December 20, 1974. Evening version: January 7, 1967 - August 30, 1971.

NICHOLS

Western. Background: Nichols,

Arizona, 1914. Returning to his home town after an eighteen-year absence, Nichols finds that the town, homesteaded from his mother, no longer belongs to him. Drowning his sorrows at the Salter House bar, he begins talking to its beautiful barmaid, Ruth, and enrages her jealous boyfriend, Ketchum. A fight ensues, and Nichols is held responsible for three hundred dollars in damages. Unable to pay it, he is sentenced to six months duty as sheriff by Sara Ketchum, Ketchum's mother, the self-appointed law.

Stories depict his reluctant attempts to maintain law and order.

Last episode. Nichols, in an attempt to stop a barroom brawl, is killed. Several days following, his twin brother, Jim Nichols, arrives in town. After discovering what has happened, he apprehends his brother's killer. Refusing to accept the position of sheriff, he parts town, never to darken its path again.

Expected to have been renewed, "Nichols" was cancelled at the last minute after the aforedescribed episode evolved to establish a more courageous and forceful hero, Jim Nichols.

CAST

Nichols (not identified by a first name)	James Garner
Jim Nichols	James Garner
Mitchell, the deputy	Stuart Margolin
Sara Ketchum (Ma)	Neva Patterson
Ruth	Margot Kidder
Ketchum	John Beck
Salter, the owner of the bar	John Harding
Johnson, a con-artist	Paul Hampton
Bertha, the saloon keeper	Alice Ghostley
Judge Thatcher	Richard Bull
Gabe, the general-store owner	M. Emmett Walsh
Scully One, the owner of the town	John Quade
Scully Two, his brother	Jesse Wayne
Mitchell's dog: Slump.	

NICHOLS—60 minutes—NBC—September 16, 1971 - August 8, 1972. 29 episodes. Also known as: "James Garner As Nichols."

NIGHT COURT

Courtroom Drama. Dramatizations based on the files of New York and Los Angeles Night Court hearings.

Judge: Jay Jostyn.

Public Defenders: Sandy Spillman, Barney Biro.

NIGHT COURT—30 minutes—Syndicated 1965. 78 episodes.

NIGHT EDITOR

Anthology. Dramatizations depicting the struggles of newspapermen.

Host: Hal Burdick.

NIGHT EDITOR—30 minutes—DuMont 1949.

NIGHT LIFE

Variety. Celebrity guests and interviews.

Hosts: Les Crane, Nipsey Russell.

Announcer: Nipsey Russell.

Orhcestra: Elliot Lawrence.

NIGHT LIFE—1 hour, 45 minutes—ABC—March 4, 1965 - October 22, 1965.

NIGHT GALLERY

See title: "Four-In-One," *Night Gallery* segment.

NIGHTMARE

Anthology. Dramatizations depicting the plight of people suddenly involved in unexpected and perilous situations. Included:

Magic Formula. The story of an actress who finds herself trapped in a plane after a crash.

Starring: Claudette Colbert, Patric Knowles.

High Adventure. The story concerns a woman and her attempts to find help for her ill son after they are marooned in a mountain lodge.

Starring: Virginia Carroll, Gordon Gebert.

Turn Back The Clock. The story concerns a war verteran who is suffering from amnesia and his attempts to discover who he is.

Starring: Richard Carlson.

NIGHTMARE—30 minutes—Syndicated 1958.

THE NIGHT STALKER

Mystery. Background: Chicago. The investigations of Carl Kolchak, a reporter for the *Independent News Service* (I.N.S.). Stories relate his attempts to solve baffling, bizarre, and supernatural crimes.

CAST

Carl Kolchak	Darren McGavin
Tony Vincenzo, his editor	Simon Oakland
Ron Updyke, an I.N.S. reporter	Jack Grinnage
Monique Marmelstein, an I.N.S. reporter	Carol Ann Susi
Gordon Spangler (Gordy the Goul), the mortician	John Fiedler
Emily Cowles, the advice columnist	Ruth McDevitt

Narrator: Darren McGavin.

Music: Gil Mellé.

Executive Producer: Cy Chermak.

Producer: Paul Playdon.

Director: Seymour Robbie, Doug McDougall, Allen Baron, Alex Grassoff.

Creator: Jeff Rice.

THE NIGHT STALKER—60 minutes—ABC—September 13, 1974 - August 30, 1975. 20 episodes. Original title: "Kolchak: The Night Stalker."

THE NINE LIVES OF ELFEGO BACA

See title: "Walt Disney Presents," *The Nine Lives of Elfego Baca* segment.

NINETY BRISTOL COURT

Comedy. The overall title for three family comedies: "Harris Against the World"; "Karen"; and "Tom, Dick, and Mary."

Background: Ninety Bristol Court in Southern California, the address and name of a fashionable but fictitious apartment-motel. Through the eavesdropping of Cliff Murdock, the superintendant, segments are introduced and scenes are established.

Harris Against The World. The trials and tribulations of Alan Harris, a businessman struggling to survive the constant barrage of everyday problems.

CAST

Alan Harris	Jack Klugman

Ninety Bristol Court. Mary La Roche and Debbie Watson of "Karen."

Kate Harris, his wife	Patricia Barry
Billy Harris, their son	David Macklin
Dee Dee Harris, their daughter	Claire Wilcox
Cliff Murdock	Guy Raymond

Karen. The life of Karen Scott, a beautiful, delightful, and resourceful high-school girl; a carbonated teenager with an unquenchable thirst for life and an uncontrollable penchant for mischief.

CAST

Karen Scott	Debbie Watson
Steve Scott, her father, a lawyer	Richard Denning
Barbara Scott, her mother	Mary La Roche
Mimi Scott, Karen's sister	Gina Gillespie
Mrs. Rowe, the Scott housekeeper	Grace Albertson
Cliff Murdock	Guy Raymond

KAREN'S FRIENDS:

Candy	Trudi Ames
Janis	Bernadette Winters
Spider	Murray MacLeod
David	Richard Dreyfuss

Music: Jack Marshall.

Theme: "Karen" sung by the Beachboys.

Tom, Dick, And Mary. Unable to afford a flat at Ninety Bristol Court, intern Tom Gentry and his wife Mary solve their problem by arranging to share an apartment and expenses with their bachelor-intern friend, Dick Moran. Stories depict: Dick's endless romantic entanglements; and Tom and

Mary's attempts to regain their cherished privacy.

CAST

Tom Gentry	Don Galloway
Mary Gentry	Joyce Bulifant
Dick Moran	Steve Franken
Dr. Kievoy, their supervisor	John Hoyt
Cliff Murdock	Guy Raymond

NINETY BRISTOL COURT—90 minutes (thirty minutes per segment)—NBC—October 5, 1964 - January 4, 1965. Spin-off: "Karen"—30 minutes—NBC—January 11, 1965 - September 6, 1965.

NOAH'S ARK

Drama. The struggles of two dedicated veterinarians: Dr. Sam Rinehart, the wiser, ill and aging; and Dr. Noah McCann, the younger, eager and progressive.

CAST

Dr. Noah McCann	Paul Burke
Dr. Sam Rinehart	Vic Rodman
Liz Clark, a nurse	May Wynn
Glenn White	Russell Whitney
Agnes Marshall	Natalie Masters
Davey Marshall	Paul Engle

NOAH'S ARK—30 minutes—NBC—February 26, 1957 - September 1957. 23 episodes.

NO HIDING PLACE

A nine-episode crime series, produced in England, and starring Raymond Francis. Syndicated 1960.

NO—HONESTLY

Comedy. Background: London, England. A thirteen-part series that follows the courtship and early married life of the Danbys: Charles, an actor, and his scatterbrained wife, Clara, the author of "Ollie the Otter" childrens stories. Produced in England.

CAST

Charles Danby (C. D.)	John Alderton
Clara Danby	Pauline Collins
Lord Burrell, Clara's absent-minded father	James Berwick
Lady Burrell, Clara's mother	Franny Rowe
Royal, the Burrell's butler	Kenneth Benda

Music: Lynsey De Paul.

Producer: Humphrey Barclay.

Director: David Askey.

NO—HONESTLY—25 minutes—PBS —July 9, 1975 - September 3, 1975.

THE NOONDAY SHOW

Variety. Comedy skits, interviews, guests. Broadcast each day at 12:00 p.m., E.T.

Host: David Steinberg.

Regulars: Stan Cann, Jane Dulo, Caroline Grosky, Gaillard Sartaine.

Orchestra: David Foster.

Producer: Marty Pasetta.

Director: Eric Lieber.

THE NOONDAY SHOW—NBC—December 15, 1975 - December 19, 1975. 5 shows; three were 25 minutes; two were 55 minutes each.

N.O.P.D.

Crime Drama. Background: New Orleans, Louisiana. The investigations of Detectives Beaujac and Conroy, law enforcers attached to the New Orleans Police Department (N.O.P.D.).

CAST

Senior Detective Beaujac	Stacy Harris
Detective Conroy	Lou Sirgo

N.O.P.D.—30 minutes—Syndicated 1956. 39 episodes.

NORBY

Comedy. Background: Pearl River, New York. Events in the lives of the Norby family: Pearson, the vice-president of small loans at the First National Bank; his wife, Helen; and their children, Diane (age eleven) and Hank (six).

CAST

Pearson Norby	David Wayne
Helen Norby	Joan Lorring
Diane Norby	Susan Holloran
Hank Norby	Evan Elliott
Bobo, their friend and neighbor	Jack Warden
Maureen, his wife	Maxine Stuart
Wahleen Johnson, the bank telephone operator	Janice Mars
The bank president	Paul Ford

Also: Carol Vegazie; Ralph Dunn.

NORBY—30 minutes—NBC—January 5, 1955 - April 6, 1955.

NORMAN CORWIN PRESENTS

Anthology. Original dramatic presentations.

Host: Norman Corwin.

NORMAN CORWIN PRESENTS—30 minutes—Syndicated 1971.

NORTHWEST PASSAGE

Adventure. Background: New York State, 1754, during the era of the French and Indian War. The story of Major Robert Rogers, and his search for the fabled Northwest Passage, a waterway that supposedly links the East and West.

CAST

Major Robert Rogers	Keith Larsen
Sergeant Hunk Marriner, a master woodsman	Buddy Ebsen
Ensign Langdon Towne, a mapmaker	Don Burnett

NORTHWEST PASSAGE—30 minutes—NBC—September 14, 1958 - September 7, 1959. 26 episodes. Syndicated.

NOT FOR HIRE

Crime Drama. Background: Honolulu, Hawaii. The investigations of Sergeant Steve Dekker, U.S. Army Criminal Investigations Division, into crimes associated with the military: desertion, sabotage, and hijacking.

CAST

Sgt. Steve Dekker	Ralph Meeker
Sonica Zametoo, his WAC aide	Lizabeth Rush
Corporal Zimmerman, his aide	Ken Drake

Music: Joseph Hooven.

NOT FOR HIRE—30 minutes—Syndicated 1959. 39 episodes. Also known as: "Sgt. Steve Dekker."

NOT FOR PUBLICATION

Crime Drama. Background: New York City. The investigations of reporter Collins of the *New York Ledger.* Stories reveal the facts hidden behind headline-making stories.

Starring: Jerome Cowan as Collins.

NOT FOR PUBLICATION—30 minutes—DuMont 1951. Also known as "Reporter Collins."

NOT FOR WOMEN ONLY

Discussion. A panel of five guests discuss current topical issues.

Hostesses: Aline Saarinen, Barbara Walters, Polly Bergen, Lynn Redgrave.

Hosts: Hugh Downs, Frank Field.

Music: Recorded.

NOT FOR WOMEN ONLY—30 minutes—Syndicated 1972. Originally aired locally in New York (WNBC-TV, Ch. 4) under the title: "For Women Only."

NOTHING BUT THE BEST

A thirty-minute variety series, broadcast on NBC in 1953, and starring Eddie Albert.

NOTHING BUT THE TRUTH

Game. Three contestants appear, each laying claim to the same identity. The host reads a short biography concerning one of the contestants who is the person involved. Through a series of question-and-answer probe rounds with the contestants, a panel of three celebrities have to determine the purveyor of the truth.

Host: John Cameron Swayze.

Panel: Polly Bergen, Dick Van Dyke, Hildy Parks.

NOTHING BUT THE TRUTH—30 minutes—CBS—December 18, 1956 - December 25, 1956.

NO TIME FOR SERGEANTS

Comedy. Background: Andrews Air Force Base. The misadventures of Private Will Stockdale, a reluctant and naive Georgia farm boy who was drafted into the Air Force. Stories relate his attempts to adjust to military life, and the trials and tribulations of his superior officers who are plagued by his philosophy of kindness. Based on the movie.

CAST
Private Will
  Stockdale   Sammy Jackson
Sgt. Orville King, Will's
  superior   Harry Hickox
Captain Paul
  Martin   Paul Smith
Private Ben Whitledge,
  Will's friend   Kevin O'Neal
Millie Anderson, Will's
  romantic interest;
  operates the camp supply
  store   Laurie Sibbald
Grandpa Anderson,
  her grandfather, a
  farmer   Andy Clyde
Colonel Farnsworth   Hayden Rorke
Private Irving Blanchard,
  Will's nemesis   Greg Benedict
Private Jack
  Langdon   Michael McDonald
Private Neddick   Joey Tata
Pa Stockdale, Will's
  father   Frank Ferguson
Tilda Jay Stockdale,
  Will's sister   Stacey Maxwell
General Thomas   Bill Zuckert
Will's dog: Blue.

NO TIME FOR SERGEANTS—30 minutes—ABC—September 14, 1964 - September 6, 1965. 34 episodes. Syndicated.

NO WARNING

Anthology. Dramatic presentations that depict the plight of people whose lives are suddenly thrown into turmoil by an unexpected crisis.

Narrator: Westbrook Van Voorhis.

Included:

Fire Lookout Post. The story of a woman who is held prisoner by an arsonist amid the rages of a raging forest fire.

Starring: Ann Rutherford, Strother Martin, Wheaton Chambers.

Stranded. The story concerns a couple's attempts to find help after their car stalls, stranding them in the Mojave Desert.

Starring: Marsha Hunt, Walter Coy.

The Prisoner. A man, sentenced to life imprisonment, requests permission to see his dying wife, an inmate of a women's prison. When his request is refused, he vows to escape and free his wife so she will not die in the penitentiary.

Starring: Kenneth Tobey, Jaclynne Greene, Tim Powers, Vivi Janiss.

NO WARNING—30 minutes—NBC— April 6, 1958 - September 7, 1958.

THE NOW EXPLOSION

Variety. Prerecorded Rock music is coupled with the appearance of the actual performer. Visual and audio effects prevail in an attempt to televise a radio program.

Local station personalities serve as hosts, who, using the voice-over technique, conduct the show as if it were a radio program.

THE NOW EXPLOSION—7 hours, 30 minutes—Syndicated 1970.

NOW YOU SEE IT

A fifteen minute variety series that features performances by magaicians. *Host:* Andre Baruch. CBS 1949.

NOW YOU SEE IT

Game. Two competing teams each composed of two members.
Round One: The "Now You See It" board is displayed, which contains four vertical lines of run-on letters. The four vertical lines, which are numbered one to four, become the line; and the fourteen letters each line contains (numbered one to fourteen across the top) become the position. Teams compete one at a time. One player sits with his back to the board; the host reads a question; and the other player has to locate the answer on the board by calling the line (one, two, three, or four). If correct, his partner, seated on a swivel chair, faces the board and has to call the position of the answer (one to fourteen). Points are awarded according to the line and position total (e.g., line, 3; position 10; points: 13). The remaining team competes in the same manner. Winners are the highest point scorers.

Round Two: The members of the winning team compete against each other. One blank line containing fourteen spaces is displayed. After the host reads a question, two letters to the answer appear. The player first to sound his buzzer receives a chance to answer. If correct, the three- or four-letter answer appears on the board and the player receives one point. Another question is asked, and the last letter of the previous answer becomes the first letter of the new answer. The player first to acquire four points is the winner.

The Solo Round: The champion competes. The game follows the format of round one wherein the player has to locate ten answers within sixty seconds. One hundred dollars is awarded for each correct answer; five thousand dollars if locating all ten.

Host: Jack Narz.

Announcer: Johnny Olsen.

Music: Michael Malone.

NOW YOU SEE IT—30 minutes—CBS —Premiered: April 1, 1974.

NUMBER PLEASE

Game. A line of twenty spaces is placed before each player. After a clue is given, the host calls a number. Players then remove that number, which reveals a letter, and attempt to identify the concealed phrase that the line contains. The game continues until one player correctly identifies the message. Incorrect answers disqualify players from that particular round. Winners, the highest scorers (most correct identifications), receive merchandise prizes.

Host: Bud Collyer.

NUMBER PLEASE—30 minutes— ABC—January 30, 1961 - December 21, 1961.

THE NURSES
THE DOCTORS AND THE NURSES

Medical Drama. Background: Alden General Hospital in New York City. The personal and professional lives of nurses Liz Thorpe and Gail Lucas.

CAST

Nurse Liz Thorpe	Shirl Conway
Nurse Gail Lucas	Zina Bethune
Dr. Ted Steffen	Joseph Campanella
Dr. Alexander Tazinski	Michael Tolan
Nurse Ayres	Hilda Simms
Dr. Lowry	Stephen Brooks
Dr. Kiley	Edward Binns

Producer: Herbert Brodkin, Robert Costello, Arthur Lewis.

THE NURSES—CBS—September 27, 1962 - September 17, 1964. As "The Doctors and the Nurses"—60 minutes —CBS—September 22, 1964 - September 7, 1965. Syndicated. 103 episodes.

THE NURSES

Serial. A daily afternoon version based

The Nurses. Zina Bethune and Shirl Conway.

on the prime-time series. Background: Alden General Hospital. Continued events in the working lives of nurses Liz Thorpe and Gail Lucas.

CAST

Liz Thorpe	Mary Fickett
Gail Lucas	Melinda Plank
Brenda	Patricia Hyland
Nurse Dorothy Warner	Leonie Norton
Dr. John Crager	Nat Polen
Donna	Carol Gainer
Mrs. Grassberg	Polly Rowles
Mike	Darryl Wells
Hugh	Arthur Franz
Cora	Mauriel Kirkland
Paul	Paul Stevens
Martha	Joan Wetmore

Also: Alan Yorke, Nicholas Pryor, John Beal.

THE NURSES—30 minutes—ABC— September 27, 1965 - March 31, 1967.

N.Y.P.D.

Crime Drama. Background: New York City. The investigations of Mike Haines, Johnny Corso, and Jeff Ward, plainclothes police detectives attached to Manhattan's 27th precinct (N.Y.P.D.: New York Police Department).

CAST

Mike Haines	Jack Warden
Johnny Corso	Frank Converse
Jeff Ward	Robert Hooks

Music: Charles Gross.

Executive Producer: Daniel Melnick, Bob Markell.

Producer: Robert Butler.

Director: Daniel Petrie, Robert Butler, David Pressman, Joshua Shelley, Reza S. Badiyi, Robert Gist, Alex March, Lawrence Dobkin.

Creator: David Susskind, Arnold Perl.

N.Y.P.D.—30 minutes—ABC—September 5, 1967 - September 16, 1969. 49 episodes. Syndicated.

O

THE OBJECT IS

Game. Six players compete: three celebrity guests and three studio audience members. The format involves identifying personalities from object clues.

Host: Dick Clark.

THE OBJECT IS—30 minutes—ABC— December 30, 1963 - March 24, 1964.

OCCASIONAL WIFE

Comedy. Background: New York

City. Seeking an executive position with his company that is only available to a married man, Peter Christopher, a swinging young bachelor, solves his problem by proposing to a girlfriend, a beautiful hat check girl: "Greta, I want you to be my wife ... occasionally." The agreement: She will pose as his wife whenever the situation warrants; and he will pay for her rent and art lessons. Living in the same apartment house, and on different floors (he, the seventh; she, the ninth), stories depict the chaos that ensues as two unmarried people struggle to affect a normal, happy marriage.

CAST

Peter Christopher	Michael Callan
Greta Patterson	Patricia Harty
Mr. Brahms, Peter's employer, the owner of Brahm's Baby Foods Company	Jack Collins
Mrs. Brahms, his wife	Joan Tompkins
Mrs. Christopher, Peter's mother	Sara Seeger
The man-in-the-middle, residing in an apartment on the eighth floor	Bryan O'Byrne
Bernie, Greta's jealous boyfriend	Stuart Margolin
Wally	Jack Riley
Vera	Susan Silo

OCCASIONAL WIFE–30 minutes–NBC–September 13, 1966 - August 29, 1967. 30 episodes.

THE ODDBALL COUPLE

Animated Cartoon. The misadventures of two trouble-prone, free-lance magazine writers: Fleabag the dog, a natural-born slob; and Spiffy, a perfectionist cat. A spin-off from "The Odd Couple."

Characters' Voices

Fleabag	Paul Winchell
Spiffy	Frank Nelson
Goldie, their secretary	Joan Gerber

Additional Voices: Frank Welker, Sarah Kennedy, Joe Besser, Don Messick, Bob Holt, Ginny Tyler.

Music: Doug Goodwin.

THE ODDBALL COUPLE–30 minutes–ABC–Premiered: September 6, 1975.

THE ODD COUPLE

Comedy. Background: New York City; 1049 Park Avenue, Apartment 1102, the residence of two divorced men: Oscar Madison, sportswriter for the *New York Herald,* an irresponsible slob; and Felix Unger, a commercial photographer, an excessively neat perfectionist. Stories depict the chaos that ensues as they struggle to live together. Based on the play by Neil Simon.

CAST

Felix Unger	Tony Randall
Oscar Madison	Jack Klugman
Police Officer Murray Grechner, their friend	Al Molinaro
Speed, a poker-playing friend	Gary Walberg
Vinnie, a poker-playing friend	Larry Gelman
Roy, a poker-playing friend	Ryan MacDonald
Dr. Nancy Cunningham, Oscar's romantic interest	Joan Hotchkis
Cecily Pigeon, Felix and Oscar's upstairs neighbor	Monica Evans
Gwen Pigeon, her sister	Carole Shelley
Miriam Welby, Felix's romantic interest	Elinor Donahue
Myrna Turner, Oscar's secretary	Penny Marshall
Gloria Unger, Felix's ex-wife	Janis Hansen
Edna Unger, Felix's daughter	Pamelyn Ferdin Doney Oatman
Blanche Madison, Oscar's ex-wife	Brett Somers Klugman

Music: Neil Hefti; Kenyon Hopkins.

Music Supervision: Leith Stevens.

Executive Producer: Garry Marshall, Jerry Belson, Harvey Miller, Sheldon Keller.

Producer: Tony Marshall.

Director: Mel Ferber, Jerry Paris, Frank Buxton, Dan Dailey, Hal Cooper, Charles R. Rondeau, Jay Sandrich, Jack Winter, Garry Marshall, Jack Donohue, Harvey Miller, Jerry Belson.

Program Open:

Announcer: "On November thirteenth Felix Unger was asked to remove himself from his place of residence. That request came from his wife. Deep down he knew she was right. But he also knew that someday he would return to her. With no where else to go, he appeared at the home of his childhood friend, Oscar Madison. Sometime earlier, Madison's wife had thrown him out, requesting that he never return. Can two divorced men share an apartment without driving each other crazy?"

THE ODD COUPLE–30 minutes–ABC–September 24, 1970 - July 4, 1975.

ODYSSEY

Documentary. Dramatizations based on the events that shaped the world.

Host-Narrator: Charles Collingwoood.

ODYSSEY–30 minutes–CBS–January 6, 1957 - June 16, 1957.

OFFICIAL DETECTIVE

Anthology. Dramatizations based on stories that appear in *Official Detective* magazine.

Host-Narrator: Everett Sloane.

OFFICIAL DETECTIVE–30 minutes–Syndicated 1957. 39 episodes.

OFF THE RECORD

A comedy series starring Zero Mostel and Joey Faye. Producer: Martin Gosch; Director: Tony Kraber. 30 minutes–DuMont 1949.

OFF TO SEE THE WIZARD

Anthology. Adventure films geared for children.

Hosts: Animated "Wizard of Oz" characters: Dorothy, The Scarecrow, The Tin Woodman, The Cowardly Lion, and the Wizard.

Included:

Island of the Lost. Shipwrecked off an uncharted island, an anthropologist and his family struggle for survival.

CAST

Josh MacRae: Richard Green; Stu: Luke Halpin; Gabe: Mart Hulswit; Liz: Robin Mattson.

The Hellcats. An unsold pilot film. Coming to the aid of a beautiful woman, three pilots attempt to recover the money left to her by her father who lived on a remote South American island.

CAST

Melinda: Barbara Eden; Lee Ragdon: George Hamilton; El Primero:

Nehemiah Persoff; Bugs: John Craig; Ripple: Warren Berlinger.

Gypsy Colt. The story of a young girl's devotion to an orphaned colt.

CAST

Frank MacWarde: Ward Bond; Meg: Donna Corcoran; Em: Frances Dee.

Mike and the Mermaid. An unsold pilot film. Background: Florida. The complications that ensue when a young boy discovers a beautiful mermaid in a river.

CAST

The Mermaid: Jeri Lynn Fraser; Mike Malone: Kevin Brodie; Jim Malone: Ned Foley, Nellie Malone: Rachel Ames.

OFF TO SEE THE WIZARD—60 minutes—ABC—September 8, 1967 - September 20, 1968.

OF LIFE AND LOVE

Anthology. Rebroadcasts of dramas that were originally aired via other filmed anthology programs. Stories emphasize the struggles of man and nature.

OF LIFE AND LOVE—30 minutes—ABC 1960.

OH, BABY!

Baby Talk. The host talks with infants who respond via voice-over dubbing.

Host: Jack Barry.

OH, BABY!—05 minutes—Syndicated 1952.

OH, BOY!

Musical Variety. Performances by Country and Western artists.

Host: Tony Hall.

Regulars: Brenda Lee, Cherry Warner, Don Lang, Cudley Dudley Helsop, Dickie Pride, Lorie Mann, Mike Preston, Dene Webb, Red Price, Chris Andrews, Neville Taylor, The Cutters, Lord Rockingham's XI; The Vernons, Tony Sheridan, The Wreckers.

OH, BOY!—30 minutes—ABC—July 16, 1954 - September 3, 1959.

OH, KAY!

Variety. Music, songs, and interviews.

Hostess: Kay Westfall.
Regulars: Jim Dimitri, Ellen White.
Pianist: David le Winter.

OH, KAY!—30 minutes—ABC—February 24, 1951 - May 26, 1951.

OH! SUSANNA

See title: "The Gale Storm Show."

OH, THOSE BELLS!

Comedy. Background: The Hollywood Prop Shop, a theatrical warehouse in California. The misadventures of its financially insecure custodians, the Bell Brothers: Harry, Sylvester, and Herbert.

CAST

Herbert Bell	Herbert Wiere
Harry Bell	Harry Wiere
Sylvester Bell	Sylvester Wiere
Mr. Slocum, their employer	Henry Morgan
Kitty, his secretary	Carol Byron

OH! THOSE BELLS—30 minutes—CBS—March 8, 1962 - May 31, 1962. 13 episodes.

Oh, Those Bells! Left to right: Harry Wiere, Jessie White (guest), Herbert Wiere, and Sylvester Wiere.

O'HARA, UNITED STATES TREASURY

Crime Drama. Background: Washington, D.C. The investigations of James O'Hara, United States Treasury Department agent, into crimes perpetrated against customs, secret service, and internal revenue.

Starring: David Janssen as James O'Hara.

O'HARA, UNITED STATES TREASURY—60 minutes—CBS—September 17, 1971 - September 8, 1972. 22 episodes.

THE O'HENRY PLAYHOUSE

Anthology. Dramatizations based on the stories of William Sydney Porter, who, while in prison, wrote under the pen name of O'Henry.

Host-Narrator: Thomas Mitchell.

Included:

Hearts and Hands. The story of a safecracker who marries the girl who sent him to prison.

CAST

Marueen Stephenson, Lester Matthews, Frank Kreig.

Between Rounds. The story of a street cleaner who recounts heroic tales of General Custer and the Battle of Little Big Horn to an eight-year-old admirer.

CAST

Thomas Mitchell, Paul Engle.

Georgia's Ruling. The story of a U.S. land commissioner and his struggles to perform his job after the death of his young daughter.

CAST

Thomas Mitchell, Richard Arlen.

THE O'HENRY PLAYHOUSE—30 minutes—Syndicated 1957. 39 episodes.

OKAY MOTHER

Testimonial tributes to mothers of celebrities or mothers who have become famous on their own. With Dennis James as host, the series was first broadcast on DuMont in 1950.

O.K. CRACKERBY!

Comedy. Background: California. Settling in Palm Springs, O.K. Crackerby, a rough and ready Oklahoman, widower, father of three children, Cynthia, Hobart, and O.K., Jr., and the world's richest man, finds that he is not acceptable to the genteel society circle. Determined to change matters, he hires St. John Quincy, a penniless Harvard graduate, to tutor his children in the ways of society. Stories depict O.K.'s battle of wits against snobbery.

CAST

O.K. Crackerby	Burl Ives
St. John Quincy	Hal Buckley
Cynthia Crackerby	Brooke Adams
Hobart Crackerby	Joel Davison
O.K. Crackerby, Jr.	Brian Corcoran
The chauffeur	John Indrisano
Susan Wentworth, Quincy's girlfriend	Laraine Stephens
Slim, O.K.'s friend	Dick Foran

Creator: Abe Burrows, Cleveland Amory.

O.K. CRACKERBY!—30 minutes—ABC—September 16, 1965 - January 6, 1966. 17 episodes.

THE OLDSMOBILE MUSIC THEATRE

Anthology. Dramatizations interwoven with songs of the past and present.

Hosts: Florence Henderson, Bill Hayes.

Included:

The Almost Perfect Plan. Background: Japan. Adopting western ways, a young man attempts to court the niece of an old-fashioned businessman.

CAST

Jimmy Kimura: James Shigeton; Kinirme Sagoyan: Michi Kobi; Kasho Eguchi: Richard Loo.

Too Bad About Sheila Troy. After the death of her father, her guiding light, an actress attempts to adjust to life without him.

CAST

Sheila Troy: Carol Lawrence; Tom Walker: Roddy McDowall.

A Kiss Before Leaving. A lonely girl attempts to impress a visiting stranger she has become infatuated with.

CAST

Gabrielle: Florence Henderson; Nick Bill Hayes; Adrian: Ernest Truex.

THE OLDSMOBILE MUSIC THEATRE—30 minutes—NBC—March 26, 1959 - May 7, 1959.

THE OLSEN AND JOHNSON SHOW

Variety. Music, songs, dances, blackouts, and slapstick comedy.

Hosts: John "Ole" Olsen, Harold "Chic" Johnson.

Regulars: Marty May, June Johnson.

Orchestra: Milton DeLugg.

Producer: Ezra Stone.

Director: Frank Burns, Ezra Stone.

THE OLSEN AND JOHNSON SHOW —60 minutes—NBC Summer of 1949.

OMNIBUS

Educational. Programs devoted to people and "living ideas"; dramatic presentations; explanations, discussions, and demonstrations concerning music, dance, history, theatre, opera, ballet, and literature.

Host: Alistair Cooke.

Music: Merrill Slanton; Milton Weinstein.

OMNIBUS—60 minutes. CBS—November 9, 1952 - April 1, 1956; ABC—October 7, 1956 - March 3, 1957; NBC—October 20, 1957 - May 10, 1959.

ON BROADWAY TONIGHT

Variety. Performances by undiscovered professional talent.

Host: Rudy Vallee.

Orchestra: Harry Zimmerman; Harry Sosnick.

ON BROADWAY TONIGHT—60 minutes—CBS—July 8, 1964 - September 16, 1964.

ONCE UPON A CLASSIC

Children. Adaptations of classic children's stories.

Host: Bill Bixby.

Included:

Heidi. The heartwarming story of a lovable Swiss Orphan named Heidi.

CAST

Heidi: Emma Blake; Grandfather: Hans Meyer; Peter: Nicholas Lyndhurst.

The Prince and the Pauper. The story of two lookalike boys, Tom Canty, the impoverished son of a petty thief, and Edward, the Prince of Whales, and the chaos that results when they switch roles.

CAST

Tom/Edward: Nicholas Lyndhurst; Charles: Donald Eccles.

ONCE UPON A CLASSIC—30 minutes—PBS—Premiered: October 11, 1976.

ONCE AN EAGLE

See title: "Best Sellers."

ONCE UPON A TUNE

Variety.

Host: Phil Hanna.

Regulars: Sondra Lee, Holly Harris.

Pianist: Reggie Bean.

ONCE UPON A TUNE—30 minutes—DuMont 1950.

One Day at a Time. Pat Harrington and Bonnie Franklin.

ONE DAY AT A TIME

Comedy. Background: Indianapolis, Indiana. The story of Ann Romano, a thirty-four-year-old divorcee whose transition from wife to working mother is complicated by her two headstrong daughters, Julie and Barbara Cooper (Ann retains her maiden name).

CAST

Ann Romano	Bonnie Franklin
Julie Cooper	Mackenzie Phillips
Barbara Cooper	Valerie Bertinelli
Dwayne Schneider, the building super	Pat Harrington
David Kane, Ann's romantic interest	Richard Masur
Ginny Wrobliki, Ann's friend	Mary Louise Wilson

Ed Cooper, Ann's
    ex-husband   Joseph Campanella
Music: Jeff Barry, Nancy Barry.

Executive Producer: Norman Lear, Mort Lachman, Norman Paul, Jack Elinson.

Producer: Allan Manings.

Director: Hal Cooper, Don Richardson, Norman Campbell, Howard Morris, Sandy Kenyon, Herbert Kenwith.

Creator: Whitney Blake, Allan Manings.

ONE DAY AT A TIME—30 minutes—CBS—Premiered: December 16, 1975.

THE ONEDIN LINE

Drama. Background: Liverpool, England, 1860. The exploits of tradesman James Onedin, captain of the *Charlotte Rhodes,* a three-masted topsail schooner, as he seeks to maintain a cargo transporting business.

CAST

Captain James
    Onedin   Peter Gilmore
Anne Onedin, his
    wife   Anne Stallybrass
Robert Onedin, James's
    brother   Brian Rawlinson
Elizabeth Onedin, James's
    sister   Jessica Benton
Captain Joshua Webster,
    Anne's father   James Hayter
Sara Onedin, Robert's
    wife   Mary Webster
Albert Frazer, Elizabeth's
    romantic interest Philip Bond

Music: Anthony Isaac.

Producer: Peter Graham Scott.

THE ONEDIN LINE—60 minutes—Syndicated 1976. Produced in England.

ONE HAPPY FAMILY

Comedy Marrying, but unable to afford their own home, Dick and Penny Cooper move in with her parents, Barney and Mildred Hogan; and her grandparents, Charley and Lovey Hackett. Stories depict the trials and tribulations that befall the families as generations clash.

CAST

Dick Cooper   Dick Sargent
Penny Cooper   Jody Warner
Barney Hogan   Chick Chandler
Mildred Hogan Elizabeth Fraser
Charley Hackett Jack Kirkwood
Lovey Hackett Cheerio Meredith

ONE HAPPY FAMILY—30 minutes—NBC—January 13, 1961 - September 8, 1961.

ONE HUNDRED GRAND

Game. One contestant, possessing knowledge in at least one specific field, is placed opposite a panel of five professional authorities. The panelists then ask him questions. Each correct response awards a large amount of cash. The player is permitted to continue or quit and leave with his earnings at any time. One incorrect response and the player is defeated. If the player survives several of these knowledge battles, he then faces the final competition: to answer five questions compiled from questions sent in by home viewers. If he is successful, he receives $100,000; if he is incorrect, he is defeated and loses his earnings.

Host: Jack Clark.

ONE HUNDRED GRAND—30 minutes—ABC—September 15, 1963 - September 29, 1963.

THE $100,000 BIG SURPRISE

Game. Contestants first choose a subject category, then select one of two types of questions, the "easy" or the "difficult." Related questions are asked of the player, and each correct response awards a large amount of cash. The player is permitted to continue or depart after any question with his accumulated earnings. Players are defeated and lose their money if they incorrectly answer a question. Players vie for the opportunity to win $100,000 by answering increasingly difficult questions in their chosen subject category.

Hosts: Jack Barry; Mike Wallace.

Assistants: Sue Oakland, Mary Gardiner.

THE $100,000 BIG SURPRISE—30 minutes—CBS—September 18, 1956 - April 2, 1957.

THE $100,000 NAME THAT TUNE

See title: "Name That Tune."

THE $128,000 QUESTION

Game. An updated version of "The $64,000 Question." Players, who possess knowledge in at least one specific field, compete. Each is asked a series of questions ranging from $64 doubled to $64,000. The contestant, who risks loss of everything if, at any time he should give an incorrect response, can either continue playing or quit after answering a question. His decision determines his earnings, if any. For players who continue, the first plateau is reached when the $4,000 question is answered. A 1977 car becomes the player's prize—and he continues because he has nothing to lose. If a player successfully answers the $16,000 question he reaches the second plateau and again continues, as this money is his and he has nothing to lose. The next series of questions, if successfully answered, earns the player $64,000 and the opportunity to return at a later date and compete further with the object being to win another $64,000. Failure to correctly answer the $32,000 or $64,000 questions earns a player his second plateau winnings.

Host: Mike Darrow; Alex Trebek.

Models: Lauri Locks, Cindy Reynolds, Pattie Lee.

Announcer: Alan Calter.

Music: Recorded.

Security Director: Michael O'Rourke.

Executive Producer: Steve Carlin.

Producer: Willie Stein.

Director: Dick Schneider, George Choderker.

THE $128,000 QUESTION—30 minutes—Syndicated 1976.

THE O'NEILLS

Serial. The dramatic story of Peggy O'Neill, fashion designer.

CAST

Peggy O'Neill   Vera Allen
Bill O'Neill   Ian Martin
Mrs. Levy   Celia Budkin
Mr. Levy   Ben Fishbern
Also: Janice Gilbert, Michael Lawson, Jane West, Maurice Franklen.

Producer: Ed Wolf.

Director: Jack Rubin.

THE O'NEILLS—30 minutes—DuMont 1949.

ONE IN A MILLION

Game. Through a series of question-and-answer probe rounds, contestants have to discover the secrets shared by a panel of four guest celebrities. Winners, those who identify the most secrets, receive merchandise prizes.

Host: Danny O'Neil.

ONE IN A MILLION—30 minutes—ABC—April 3, 1967 - June 16, 1967.

ONE LIFE TO LIVE

Serial. Background: Philadelphia. The dramatic story of two families, each from different sides of the tracks: The Woleks, first generation Americans struggling for a position on top of the social ladder; and the Lords, an established family entrenched in the dominant social and economic milieu. Episodes present an insight into life in contemporary America, and the problems faced by the underprivileged, the uneducated, the nonwhite, and the non-Angelo Saxon Protestant.

CAST

Cathy Craig	Amey Levitt
	Dorrie Kavanaugh
	Jane Alice Brandon
	Jennifer Harmon
Dr. James Craig	Nat Polen
Victoria Lord	Erika Slezak
	Gillian Spencer
Dr. Mark Toland	Tom Lee Jones
Anna Wolek	Doris Belack
Meredith Lord Wolek	Lynn Benesch
	Trish Van Devere
Bert Skelly	Herb Davis
Stephen Burke	Bernard Grant
Dr. Larry Wolek	Michael Storm
Daniel Lord Wolek	Justin White
Vince Wolek	Anthony Ponzini
	Jordan Charney
Joe Riley	Lee Patterson
Eileen Riley	Patricia Roe
	Alice Hirson
Dave Siegal	Allan Miller
Julie Siegal	Lee Warrick
Carla Gray	Ellen Holly
Dr. Marcus Polk	Norman Rose
	Donald Moffat
Victor Lord	Ernest Graves
	Shepperd Strudwick
Dr. Joyce Brothers	Herself
Lt. Ed Hall	Al Freeman, Jr.
Sadie Gray	Lillian Hayman
Susan Barry	Lisa Richards
Jack Dawson	Jack Ryland
Wanda Webb	Marilyn Chris
Joshua West	Laurence Fishburne
	Todd Davis
Dr. Dorian Cramer	Nancy Pinkerton
	Claire Malis
Melinda Cramer	Patricia Pearcy
Rachel Wilson	Nancy Barrett
Karen Martin	Niki Flacks
Tom Edwards	Joe Gallison
Merry	Lynn Benish
Millie Parks	Millee Taggart
Dr. Price Trainor	Peter DeAnda
Jenny Siegal	Kathy Glass
Mario Dane	Gerald Anthony
Peggy Filmore	Valerie French
Timmie Siegal	Tom Berenger
Eileen Siegal	Alice Hirson
Julie Toland	Leonie Norton
Tony Lord	George Reinholt
John Douglas	Donald Madden
Sheila Rafferty	Christine Jones
Peter Blair	Peter Brouwer
Michiko	Lani Gerrie Miyazaki
Dr. Will Vernon	Farley Granger
	Bernie McInerney
Lana	Jackie Zeman
Also	Peggy Wood

Music: Aeolus Productions.

Music Theme: George Reinholt.

Producer: Doris Quinlan, Joseph Stuart.

Creator: Agnes Nixon.

ONE LIFE TO LIVE—30 minutes—ABC—July 15, 1968 - July 23, 1976. 45 minutes—ABC—Premiered: July 26, 1976.

ONE MAN'S EXPERIENCE

Serial. Human-interest accounts depicting the joys and sorrows of men. Guests appear in stories that run four days each.

ONE MAN'S EXPERIENCE—15 minutes—DuMont 1952 - 1953.

ONE MAN'S FAMILY

Serial. Background: The swank Sea Cliff section of Bay City in San Francisco, California. The dramatic story of the Barbour family: Henry, a stockbroker; his wife, Frances; and their children, Paul, Hazel, Clifford and Claudia (twins), and Jack. Episodes depict the life, sex values, and worthiness of the family. Created by Carlton E. Morse.

CAST

Henry Barbour	Bert Lytell
	Theodore Von Eltz
Frances (Fanny) Barbour	Marjorie Gateson
	Mary Adams
Hazel Barbour	Lilian Schaff
	Linda Reighton
Jack Barbour	Robert Wigginton
	Martin Dean
	Arthur Cassell
Claudia Barbour	Eva Marie Saint
	Anne Whitfield
Clifford Barbour	James Lee
Paul Barbour	Russell Thorson
Bob	Walter Brooke
John Roberts	Jack Edwards
Beth Holly	Susan Shaw
Mac	Tony Randall
Joe	Jim Boles
Teddy Barbour	Medaline Bugard

Also: Billy Idelson, Patricia Robbins, Nancy Franklin.

Announcer: Bob Sheppard.

Music: Paul Watson.

Producer: Carleton E. Morse, Richard Clemmer.

Director: Edgar Kahn.

Sponsor: Sweetheart Soap.

ONE MAN'S FAMILY—15 and 30 minute versions—NBC—November 4, 1949 - April 1, 1955.

ONE MAN SHOW

Variety. Performance by guest comedians. "Wherever laughter is king, it's One Man Show."

Hosts: Including Bob and Ray (Bob Elliott and Ray Goulding), Morey Amsterdam, Rip Torn, Groucho Marx.

ONE MAN SHOW—30 minutes—Syndicated 1969.

ONE MINUTE PLEASE

Game. Two teams, each composed of three members. The host states a topic (e.g., raccoon coats; the perfect woman; how to make glue); and each panelist then has to incorporate it in conversation for one minute without undue repetition, hesitation, or straying from the point. Winners are the wordiest talkers. Prizes are awarded to studio audience members who are represented by the individual players. Based on the B.B.C. radio and television program.

Host: John K. M. McCaffery.

Panel: Ernie Kovacs, Beatrice Straight, Hermione Ginggold, Alice Pearce, Cleveland Amory, Jimmy Cannon.

Announcer: Don Russell.

ONE MINUTE PLEASE—30 minutes—DuMont 1954.

ONE NIGHT STAND

A variety series featuring performances by musical groups. 24 minutes—Syndicated 1969.

ONE STEP BEYOND

Anthology. Dramatizations based on true events that are strange, frightening, and unexplainable in terms of normal human experience.

Host: John Newland, "Our guide into the world of the unknown."

Music: Harry Lubin.

Executive Producer: Larry Marcus.

Producer: Collier Young.

Included:

The Clown. Infatuated with Pippo, a deaf-mute clown, a young woman, Nonnie, follows him to his trailer. Found by her jealous husband, Tom, she is accidentally killed when he picks up a pair of scissors and attempts to stab Pippo. Found with the dead girl in his arms, Pippo is blamed for the murder. Police are summoned and he is locked in and guarded. Tom, though free, is haunted by visions of Pippo choking him. Standing by a small bridge overlooking a river, Tom falls in when he believes Pippo is choking him. Screaming for help, he is rescued and confesses to killing Nonnie. Back at the fair grounds, Pippo's trailer is unlocked, and Pippo, constantly under guard, is soaking wet. How?

CAST

Nonnie: Yvette Mimieux; Pippo: Mickey Shaughnessey; Tom: Christopher Dark.

The Hand. Background: New Orleans. When piano player Tom Brandt discovers that his girl friend, Alma, is no longer interested in him, he picks up a bottle, breaks it, and kills her by jabbing its sharp edges into her stomach. His hand, though uncut, continually bleeds. Unable to stop the bleeding, and driven to the point of hysteria, he confesses—and the bleeding stops.

CAST

Tom Brandt: Robert Loggia; Alma: Miriam Colon; Johnny: Pete Candall; Harmon: Joseph Sullivan.

Night of the Kill. Found safe and well after being lost in the woods for three days, a young boy relates the story of his being found and cared for by a huge, friendly beast. His parents and friends are disbelieving until the following day when huge footprints, a strange odor, and a sighting of the creature convinces them otherwise. Wanting only to visit his young friend, the creature, supposedly sixteen feet tall, is tracked and trapped in a box canyon. The canyon is set ablaze, but no trace has ever been found of the creature, who, according to the story,

escaped, still roams a backwoods area in America, and has been sighted since on several occasions.

CAST

Ann Morris: Ann McCrea; John Morris: Fred Beir; Danny Morris: Dennis Holmes.

Program Open:

Host: "Have you ever been certain the telephone would ring within the next ten seconds? Or have you ever walked down a street and had the feeling you knew what lay beyond the unturned corner? Yes? Then you've had a brief encounter with the world of the unknown. . a small step beyond. Now take a giant one."

ONE STEP BEYOND—30 minutes—Syndicated 1962. Originally broadcast as "Alcoa Presents"—30 minutes—ABC—January 26, 1959 - October 3, 1961. 94 episodes.

ONE, TWO THREE—GO!

Educational. Through filmed and taped explorations to places of interest, various aspects of the world are explained to children.

Host: Jack Lescoulie.

Assistant: Richard Thomas.

ONE, TWO THREE—GO!—30 minutes—NBC—October 8, 1961 - May 27, 1962.

ONE WOMAN'S EXPERIENCE

Serial. Human interest accounts depicting the joys and sorrows of women. Guests appear in stories that run four days each.

ONE WOMAN'S EXPERIENCE—15 minutes—DuMont—1952 - 1953.

ON OUR OWN

Comedy. Background: New York City. The story of two women in the creative department of the Madison Avenue Bedford Advertising Agency: Julia Peters, a copywriter, and Maria Bonino, an art director.

CAST

Julia Peters	Bess Armstrong
Maria Teresa Bonino	Lynnie Greene
Toni McBain, the head of the agency	Gretchen Wyler
April Baxter, a copywriter	Dixie Carter
Eddie Barnes, the producer	

of TV commericals	John Christopher Jones
Craig Boatwright, the agency's salesman	Dan Resin
Mrs. Oblenski, Julia and Maria's landlady	Sasha Van Scherler

Also: Flotsam the dog.

Executive Producer: David Susskind.

Producer: Sam Denoff.

Creator: Bob Randall.

ON OUR OWN—30 minutes—CBS—Premiered: October 9, 1977.

ON PARADE

Variety. The series consists of musical programs that were produced by the C.B.C. and first shown in Canada.

The Performers: Rosemary Clooney (7-17-64); Tony Bennett (7-24); Henry Mancini (7-31); Phil Ford and Mimi Hines (8-7); Juliet Prowse (8-14); Diahann Carroll (8-21); Julius La Rosa (8-28); Jane Morgan (9-4): The Limelighters (9-11); Steve Lawrence and Eydie Gormé (9-18).

ON PARADE—30 minutes—NBC—July 17, 1964 - September 18, 1964.

ON STAGE

Anthology. Stories written, produced, directed, and performed by Canadian actors.

ON STAGE—60 minutes—Syndicated 1962.

ON THE BOARDWALK

Musical Variety. Background: The Steel Pier in Atlantic City, New Jersey.

Host: Paul Whiteman.

Orchestra: Paul Whiteman.

ON THE BOARDWALK—30 minutes—ABC—May 30, 1954 - August 1, 1954.

ON THE GO

Variety. Guests, interviews, and visits to various areas around Los Angeles.

Host: Jack Linkletter.

Announcer: Johnny Jacobs.

ON THE GO—30 minutes—CBS—April 27, 1959 - July 8, 1960.

ON THE ROCKS

Comedy. Background: Alamesa State Prison. Life in a minimum security prison as seen through the eyes of convict Hector Fuentes, a streetwise and wisecracking petty thief. Based on the British television series "Porridge."

CAST

Hector Fuentes	Jose Perez
Mr. Gibson, a correctional officer	Mel Stewart
Mr. Sullivan, a correctional officer	Tom Poston
The Warden	Logan Ramsey
Dorothy Burgess, the warden's secretary	Cynthia Harris

The Convicts:

DeMott	Hal Williams
Cleaver	Rick Hurst
Nick Palik	Bobby Sandler
Gabby	Pat Cranshaw

Music: Jerry Fielding.
Producer: John Rich, H.R. Poindexter.
Director: John Rich, Dick Clement.

ON THE ROCKS—30 minutes—ABC—September 11, 1975 - May 17, 1976.

ON TRIAL

Anthology. Dramatizations based on actual courtroom trials.
Host-Occasional performer: Joseph Cotten.

Included:

The Case of the Jealous Bomber. After a businessman discovers that his partner is secretly seeing his wife, he plots to kill him.

CAST
Joseph Cotten, Audrey Totter, William Hopper.

The Case of the Abandoned Horse. An Indian girl, a lawyer, attempts to defend her people against government attempts to force her tribe off their land.

CAST
Eva Bartok, Hugh Marlowe.

Alibi for Murder. After three partners discover uranium, one is killed. The story relates police efforts to discover which partner is the murderer.

CAST
Macdonald Carey, Peggy Knudsen, John Vivyan, Morris Ankrum.

ON TRIAL—30 minutes—CBS—September 14, 1956 - September 13, 1957; July 6, 1959 - September 21, 1959. 27 episodes. Also known as "The Joseph Cotten Show."

ON YOUR ACCOUNT

Game. Contestants appear on stage and bear their sorrows. A panel then questions them to determine the seriousness of their individual situations. Each question asked deposits five dollars in a bank. After a specified time, the panel chooses the person they feel is the most desperate. The contestant receives the money that has been deposited in the bank.
Hosts: Eddie Albert; Win Elliot; Dennis James.
Producer: Bob Quigley.
Sponsor: Procter and Gamble.

ON YOUR ACCOUNT—30 minutes—CBS—June 1953 - September 1954.

ON YOUR MARK

Game. Children, aged from nine to thirteen, and who are pursuing the same career goal, compete. A series of question and answer rounds, based on the contestants career potential, follow, with the player scoring the highest being declared the winner.
Host: Sonny Fox.

ON YOUR MARK—30 minutes—CBS—September 23, 1961 - December 30, 1961.

ON YOUR WAY

Game. Selected studio-audience members compete. The host reads a general-knowledge type of question. The player who first identifies himself through a buzzer signal receives a chance to answer. If correct he is awarded points. The winner, the highest scorer, receives an all-expense-paid trip to his place of desire.
Hosts: Bud Collyer; John Reed King; Kathy Godfrey.
Producer: Larry White.
Sponsor: Welch's Wines.

ON YOUR WAY—30 minutes—DuMont 1953.

OPEN END

See title: "The David Susskind Show."

OPENING NIGHT

Anthology. Retitled episodes of "Ford Theatre."
Hostess: Arlene Dahl.

Included:

Strange Disappearance. After his wife leaves him, a man is accused of murdering her. The story depicts his attempts to find her and clear his name.

CAST
Stephen McNally, June Vincent, Peggy Knudsen.

Sometimes it Happens. Living in Manhattan with her aunt and uncle, a Welsh girl believes in the Old World legend that says that a love that proves itself three times will last forever. When she meets a man in a train, she is certain that she is in love with him, but they are separated before she can learn his name. The story concerns her frantic search to find him.

CAST
Dianne Foster, Guy Madison, Jeanne Cooper.

The Gentle Deceiver. The story of a hobo who is mistaken for an eccentric millionaire.

CAST
Keenan Wynn, Lucy Marlow, Lucien Littlefield.

OPENING NIGHT—30 minutes—NBC—June 14, 1958 - September 6, 1958.

OPERA CAMEOS

Music. Condensed versions of operas. Background information and anecdotes are presented before the actual performance.
Host: Giovanni Martinelli.

OPERA CAMEOS—30 minutes—DuMont—1953 - 1954.

OPERA VS. JAZZ

Musical Symposium. Discussions and demonstrations of opera and jazz.
Hostess: Nancy Kenyon.

Jazz Representative: Don Cornell.

Opera Representatives: Jan Peerce, Robert Merrill.

Regulars: Alan Dale, The Strawhatters.

Orchestra: Johnny Reo.

OPERA VS. JAZZ—30 minutes—ABC—May 25, 1953 - September 21, 1953.

OPERATION: ENTERTAINMENT

Variety. U.S.O.-type performances geared to American servicemen.

Host: Jim Lange.

Singers/Dancers: The Operation Entertainment Girls.

Music: The Terry Gibbs Quartet.

OPERATION: ENTERTAINMENT—60 minutes—ABC—January 5, 1968 - January 31, 1969. 39 tapes.

OPERATION: NEPTUNE

Adventure. Background: Nadiria, a kingdom thirty-two thousand feet beneath the surface of the sea. The battle against evil as undertaken by Commander Hollister, the skipper of a United States government submarine, who is known and feared as Captain Neptune.

CAST
Commander Hollister	Tod Griffin
Dink, his assistant	Humphrey Davis
Thirza, the empress of Nadiria	Margaret Stewart
Dick Saunders, his assistant	Richard Holland
Mersenus, a villain	Harold Conklin

OPERATION: NEPTUNE—30 minutes—NBC—June 28, 1953 - August 16, 1953. Also known as: "Captain Neptune."

OPERATION PETTICOAT

Comedy. Background: The South Pacific during World War II. The series revolves around the misadventures of the officers and crew of the jerry-built Navy submarine *USS Sea Tiger*—a pink* sub, captained by Matthew Sherman, whose crew includes five sexy Army Nurses (Edna Hayward, Ruth Colfax, Barbara Duran, Claire Reid, and Dolores Crandall), who, stranded on and rescued from a Pacific Island, are now trapped aboard the *Tiger* as it roams the seas.

CAST
Lt. Cmdr. Matthew Sherman	John Astin
Lt. Nick Holden, the supply officer	Richard Gilliland
Major Edna Hayward	Yvonne Wilder
Lt. Dolores Crandall	Melinda Naud
Lt. Barbara Duran	Jamie Lee Curtis
Lt. Ruth Colfax	Dorrie Thompson
Lt. Claire Reid	Bond Gideon
Yeoman Alvin Hunkle	Richard Brestoff
Ensign Stovall	Christopher J. Brown
Seaman Dooley	Kraig Cassity
Chief Herbert Molumphrey	Wayne Long
Seaman Gossett	Michael Mazes
Chief Tostin	Jack Murdock
Seaman Horwich	Peter Schuck
Lt. Watson	Raymond Singer
Seaman Broom	Jim Varney
Seaman Williams	Richard Marion

Narrator: John Astin.

Music: Artie Butler.

Executive Producer: Leonard B. Stern.

Producer: David J. O'Connell, Si Rose.

*Only a shocking pink undercoat was possible due to an enemy plane destroying the sub's supply of gray paint.

OPERATION PETTICOAT—30 minutes—ABC—Premiered: September 17, 1977. Based on the film of the same title.

THE ORCHID AWARD

Variety. Show business achievement awards. Selected personalities are first interviewed then perform their material.

Host: Bert Lytell.

Announcer: John Heistand.

Orchestra: Paul Weston.

Included award receivers: Rex Harrison, Lilli Palmer, Eddie Fisher, Teresa Brewer, Marguerite Piazza.

THE ORCHID AWARD—30 minutes—ABC—May 24, 1953 - January 24, 1954. Also broadcast under the title: "The Orchid Room."

THE OREGON TRAIL

Western. Era: 1842. The story follows the journey of a group of pioneers traveling by wagon train from Illinois to Oregon; people seeking the free land offered by the government to settlers willing to farm it.

CAST
Evan Thorpe, a widower, the wagon master	Rod Taylor
Andrew Thorpe, his son	Andrew Stevens
William Thorpe, his son	Tony Becker
Rachel Thorpe, his daughter	Gina Marie Smika
Margaret Devlin, a young pioneer	Darleen Carr
Luther Sprague, the trail scout	Charles Napier
Mr. Cutler, the captain	Ken Swofford

Music: Dick De Benedictis.

Theme Vocal: Danny Darst.

Executive Producer: Michael Gleason.

Producer: Richard Collins, Carl Vitale.

THE OREGON TRAIL—60 minutes—NBC—Premiered: September 21, 1977.

THE ORIENT EXPRESS

Anthology. Dramatizations set against the background of the Old East.

Included:

Portrait of a Lady. The effect of malicious gossip on a happily married couple.

CAST
Colette Marchand, Peter Walker, Roger Treville.

One in a Million. Suspecting her daughter-in-law is involved in a shoddy operation, a woman intervenes and attempts to find out.

CAST
Gertrude Flynn, Espanita Cortes.

Uppercut. The story of a boxing champion who loses everything when a combination of love, arrogance, and selfishness interferes with his rigid life as a prizefighter.

CAST
Steve Barclay.

Disaster. The Orient Express, on which a spoiled American is traveling to meet her husband, crashes between Rome and Florence. The story relates her discovery of her faults while awaiting rescue.

CAST
Patricia Roc, Philip Reed.

THE ORIENT EXPRESS—30 minutes—ABC—1953 - 1954. Syndicated.

ORSON WELLES' GREAT MYSTERIES

Anthology. Mystery presentations.

Host: Orson Welles.

Music: John Barry.

Included:

The Dinner Party. Having swindled a million dollars from his company, a man attempts to conceal the fact by attending a dinner party in which he is being considered for a promotion, and have his rude and vicious wife jeopardize all his chances of promotion out of the bookkeeping department.

CAST

Jane Blake: Joan Collins; Edmond Blake: Anton Rodgers.

The Ingenious Reporter. Posing as the sought murderer of young women, a newspaper reporter attempts to acquire an exclusive story on the mysterious killings.

CAST

David Birney, Peter Madden, Pam St. Clement, Geoffrey Blenden.

Ice Storm. The story of a woman who is trapped with a would-be thief who is posing as one of three experts invited to view a valuable manuscript collection.

CAST

Claire Bloom, Donald Eccles.

ORSON .WELLES' GREAT MYS-TERIES—30 minutes—Syndicated 1973. 26 episodes.

THE OSMONDS

Animated Cartoon. Appointed as goodwill ambassadors by the United States Music Committee, the Osmond Brothers Rock group begins a round-the-world concert tour to promote understanding between nations. Stories depict their various misadventures as they become involved in intrigues in foreign lands.

Characters' Voices

Allen Osmond	Himself
Jay Osmond	Himself
Jimmy Osmond	Himself
Donny Osmond	Himself
Merril Osmond	Himself
Wayne Osmond	Himself
Fugi, their dog	Paul Frees

Background Orchestrations: Maury Laws.

THE OSMONDS—30 minutes—ABC—September 9, 1972 - September 1, 1974.

O.S.S.

Adventure. Background: Europe during World War II. The behind-enemy-lines assignments of Frank Hawthorn, an agent for the United States Intelligence Office of Strategic Services (O.S.S.).

CAST

Frank Hawthorn	Ron Rondell
The O.S.S. chief	Lionel Murton

O.S.S.—30 minutes—ABC—September 20, 1957 - March 14, 1958. Syndicated.

OUR FIVE DAUGHTERS

Serial. The dramatic story of Jim and Helen Lee and their five daughters: Ann, Marjorie, Barbara, Jane, and Mary.

CAST

Jim Lee	Michael Keene
Helen Lee	Esther Ralston
Mary Lee Weldon	Wynne Miller
Barbara Lee	Patricia Allison
Jane Lee	Nuella Dierking
Marjorie Lee	Iris Joyce
Anne Lee	Jacqueline Courtney
Don Weldon	Ben Hayes
Uncle Charlie	Robert W. Stewart
Kyle Townsend	Randy Kraft
Dr. Briggs	Allen Nourse
Joe Tully	Earl Muron
Evvy	Susan Halloran
Thelma	Melinda Plank
Bob Purdon	Bill Tabbert
Mort Lucas	Duke Farley
Greta	Janis Young
Lucy	Ann Hillary
Ed Lawson	Michael Higgins
Mary Lawson	Kay Lyder
Bill Cannon	Alfred Sandor
Pat	Ed Griffith
Peter Stevens	Ronn Cummings
George Barr	Ralph Ellis
Cynthia Dodd	Joan Anderson
Randy	Carlton Coyler
Driscoll	Jon Cypher
Ginny	Suzanne Tripp
Mrs. Hess	Claudia Morgan
Mr. Hess	Douglas Gregory
Gil Morton	Alan Bergman

OUR FIVE DAUGHTERS—30 minutes—NBC—January 2, 1962 - September 28, 1962.

OUR MAN HIGGINS

Comedy. Background: New York State. Inheriting a rare and expensive silver service from a titled British relative, the MacRobertses, a middle-class American family, also inherit a high-tone English butler named Higgins whom they must retain to keep the silver service. Stories depict the problems that befall both Higgins and the MacRoberts family as they struggle to rearrange their lives and adjust to each other. Based on the radio program "It's Higgins, Sir."

CAST

Higgins	Stanley Holloway
Duncan MacRoberts, the father	Frank Maxwell
Alice MacRoberts, his wife	Audrey Totter
Tommy MacRoberts, their son	Rickey Kelman
Joanne MacRoberts, their daughter	Regina Groves
Dinghy MacRoberts, their son	K. C. Butts

OUR MAN HIGGINS—30 minutes—ABC—October 3, 1962 - September 11, 1963. 34 episodes.

OUR MISS BROOKS

Comedy. Distinguished by two formats.

Format One: 10-3-52 - 10-7-55.

Background: Madison High School in the town of Madison. The trials and tribulations of Connie Brooks, the English teacher. Stories depict her romantic misadventures as she struggles to impress Philip Boynton, the biology instructor; and her continual clash with Osgood Conklin, the principal.

CAST

Connie Brooks	Eve Arden
Osgood Conklin	Gale Gordon
Philip Boynton	Robert Rockwell
Walter Denton, the main problem student	Richard Crenna
Harriet Conklin, Osgood's daughter	Gloria McMillan
Mrs. Davis, Connie's landlady	Jane Morgan
Stretch Snodgrass, a student	Leonard Smith

Mrs. Davis's cat: Minerva.

Music: Lud Gluskin.

Orchestra: Wilbur Hatch.

Announcer: Bob Lemond.

Producer: Larry Berns.

Creator: Eddie Bracken.

Sponsor: General Foods.

Format Two: 10-14-55 - 9-21-56.

Background: The San Fernando Valley in California. Relocating after Madison High is demolished for a highway, Connie acquires a position as English teacher at Mrs. Nestor's Private Elementary School. Stories depict her continued clash with Osgood Conklin, who, also relocating, acquired the position of principal; and her romantic misadventures as she becomes involved with two suitors: Gene Talbot, the gym instructor, and Clint Albright, the athletic director.

CAST

Connie Brooks	Eve Arden
Osgood Conklin	Gale Gordon
Gene Talbot	Gene Barry
Clint Albright	William Ching
Angela Nestor, the owner of the school	Nana Bryant
	Jesslyn Fax
Oliver Munsey, Angela's eccentric brother	Bob Sweeney
Mrs. Nestor, Angela's sister	Isobel Randolph
Benny Romero, the ten-year-old problem child	Ricky Vera
Mrs. Davis, also relocating, Connie's landlady	Jane Morgan

Music: Lud Gluskin.

OUR MISS BROOKS–30 minutes–CBS–October 3, 1952 - September 21, 1956. 127 episodes. Based on the radio program.

OUR PLACE

Musical Variety.

Hosts: Jack Burns and Avery Schreiber.

Regulars: The Doodletown Pipers, Rowlf (the hound-dog muppet from "The Jimmy Dean Show").

Orchestra: George Wilkins.

OUR PLACE–60 minutes–CBS–July 2, 1967 - September 3, 1967.

OUR PRIVATE WORLD

Serial. A prime-time verison of the afternoon serial "As the World Turns." Background, from the previous Oakdale: New York City. The dramatic story of Lisa Hughes, a nurse struggling to readjust to life after a deeply affecting divorce.

CAST

Lisa Hughes	Eileen Fulton
Eve	Julienne Marie
Brad	Robert Drivas
Helen	Geraldine Fitzgerald
Dick	Ken Tobey
John	Nicholas Coster
Sandy	Sandra Scott
Tom	Sam Groom
Franny	Pamela Murphy
Tony	David O'Brien

Music: Charles Paul.

OUR PRIVATE WORLD–30 minutes–CBS–May 5, 1965 - September 10, 1965.

OUR STREET

Serial. Background: Our Street, an any street in an any city. A street filled with the hopes and the despairs of any family caught in the echos of slow-dying prejudice. The dramatic story of one such family, the Robinsons, a black family searching for dignity and respect.

CAST

Mae Robinson, the mother	Barbara Mealy
Bull Robinson, her husband	Gene Cole
	Clayton Corbin
Jet Robinson, their eldest son	Curt Stewart
Slick Robinson, the middle child	Darryl F. Hill
	Howard Rollins
Tony Robinson, the youngest son	Tyrone Jones
Kathy Robinson, their daughter	Sandra Sharp
J. T. Robinson, Mae's half brother	Arthur French
Grandma Robinson	Alfredine Parham
Cynthia, a friend	Janet League
Emily, a friend	Frances Foster
Mrs. Ryder, Grandma's friend	Birdie Hale
Pearlina, Slick's girlfriend	Pat Picketts

Music: Don Schwartz.

OUR STREET–30 minutes–PBS (not all markets)–October 4, 1971 - October 10, 1974.

THE OUTCASTS

Western. Background: The post-Civil War West. Bound to an alliance of survival, two outcasts, Earl Corey, an uprooted Virginian Aristocrat, and Jemal David, an ex-slave freed by the Proclamation, team and become bounty hunters. Stories depict their exploits, distrustful of each other because of their respected backgrounds, but standing together in times of duress. The overall series underlines the general feeling of prejudice and animosity toward blacks in the West of the 1860s.

CAST

Earl Corey	Don Murray
Jemal David	Otis Young

THE OUTCASTS–60 minutes–ABC –September 23, 1968 - September 15, 1969. 26 episodes.

THE OUTER LIMITS

Anthology. Science-fiction presentations.

Creator: Leslie Stevens.

Music: Dominic Frontiere; Harry Lubin.

The Control Voice: Vic Perrin.

Executive Producer: Joseph Stefano.

Producer: Sam White, Ben Brady.

Director: John Brahm, Gerd Oswald, Charles Haas, Byron Haskin, Laslo Benedek, Leon Benson, James Goldstone, Paul Stanley, Felix Feist, John Erman, Alan Crosland, Jr.

Included:

The Tumbleweeds. A couple's efforts to escape from tumbleweeds that seem to possess intelligence and seek to kill them.

CAST

Eddie Albert, June Havoc.

The Guests. Five people, mysteriously transported to a home where times stands still, attempt to escape.

CAST

Florida: Gloria Graham; Norton: Geoffrey Horne; Tess: Luana Anders.

The Chameleon. An intelligence agent attempts to infiltrate a party of creatures from another world.

CAST

Louis Mace: Rober Duvall; Chambers: Howard Caine; General - Crawford: Henry Brandon.

Fun and Games. Transported to a

distant planet and placed in a contest of death with creatures from another world, two Earthlings struggle to save the planet Earth from the destruction it will face if they should lose.

CAST

Nancy Malone, Nick Adams, Bill Hart.

The Galaxy Being. The disaster that results when a scientist invents three-dimensional television and contacts a creature from another galaxy.

CAST

Cliff Robertson, Jacqueline Scott.

Program Open: A distorted picture appears, followed by a control voice: "There is nothing wrong with your television set, do not attempt to adjust the picture. We are controlling transmission. . . . For the next hour sit quietly and we will control all that you see and hear. You are about to participate in a great adventure, you are about to experience the awe and mystery which reaches from the inner mind to the Outer Limits."

Program Close: The Control Voice: "We now return control of your television set to you, until next week at this same time when the Control Voice will take you to the Outer Limits."

THE OUTER LIMITS—60 minutes—ABC—September 16, 1963 - January 16, 1965. 49 episodes. Syndicated.

THE OUTLAWS

Western. Background: The Oklahoma Territory during the nineteenth century. The events surrounding the apprehension of wanted outlaws by U.S. Marshal Frank Caine and his deputies Will Foreman, Heck Martin, and Chalk Breeson.

CAST

Marshal Frank Caine	Barton MacLane
Deputy Heck Martin	Jack Gaynor
Deputy Marshal Will Foreman	Don Collier
Constance, Will's romantic interest	Judy Lewis
Deputy Chalk Breeson	Bruce Yarnell
Slim, a town character	Slim Pickens

Music: Joseph Hooven; Vic Mizzy.

THE OUTLAWS—60 minutes—NBC—September 29, 1960 - September 13, 1962. 50 episodes. Syndicated.

OUT OF THE INKWELL

Animated Cartoon. The antics of Koko the Clown and his friends, Kokonut, Mean Moe, and Kokete.

Voice characterizations: Larry Storch.

Creator: Max Fleischer.

OUT OF THE INKWELL—05 minutes—Syndicated 1961. 100 episodes.

OUTRAGEOUS OPINIONS

Discussion. Celebrity guests discuss various topical issues.

Hostess: Helen Gurley Brown.

Music: Recorded.

OUTRAGEOUS OPINIONS—30 minutes—Syndicated 1967.

THE OUTSIDER

Crime Drama. Background: Los Angeles, California. The investigations of David Ross, an embittered ex-con turned private detective.

Starring: Darren McGavin as David Ross.

Music: Stanley Wilson.

THE OUTSIDER—60 minutes—NBC—September 18, 1968 - September 10, 1969. 26 episodes.

OUT THERE

Anthology. Science-fiction presentations. Stories are culled from originals and pulp magazines.

Producer: John Haggatt.

Director: Byron Paul, Andrew McCullough.

OUT THERE—30 minutes—CBS—1951 - 1952.

OVERLAND TRAIL

Western. Era: The nineteenth century. The saga of the Overland Stage, the first complete coach line to run from Missouri to California and back.

CAST

Frederick Thomas Kelly, the superintendant	William Bendix
Frank "Flip" Flippen, his assistant	Doug McClure

OVERLAND TRAIL—30 minutes—Syndicated 1960. 17 episodes.

OVERSEAS ADVENTURE

See title: "Foreign Intrigue."

OWEN MARSHALL: COUNSELOR AT LAW

Crime Drama. Background: Santa Barbara, California. The cases and courtroom defenses of attorney Owen Marshall.

CAST

Owen Marshall (widower)	Arthur Hill
Jess Brandon, his assistant	Lee Majors
Melissa Marshall, Owen's daughter	Christine Matchett
Frieda Krause, Owen's secretary	Joan Darling
Danny Paterno, Owen's colleague	Reni Santoni
Ted Warrick, Owen's colleague	David Soul

Music: Elmer Bernstein; Richard Clements.

OWEN MARSHALL: COUNSELOR AT LAW—60 minutes—ABC—September 16, 1971 - August 24, 1974. 69 episodes.

OZARK JUBILEE

See title: "Jubilee U.S.A."

OZMOE

Children. Background: Studio Z, a storeroom in the sub-sub-basement of the ABC television center. The misadventures of electronically operated puppets: Ozmoe, a lighthearted monkey; Roderick Dhon't, the leprechaun; Horatio, the caterpillar; Misty Waters, a curvaceous mermaid; Poe the Crow; Sam the Clam; and Throckmorton the Sea Serpent.

Voices: Bradley Bolke, Jack Urbant, Elinor Russell, Alan Stapleton, Jan Kindler.

Producer: Henry Banks.

Director: Carl Shain, Richard Ward.

OZMOE—15 minutes—ABC—March 6, 1951 - April 12, 1951.

OZZIE AND HARRIET

See title: "The Adventures of Ozzie and Harriet."

OZZIE'S GIRLS

Comedy. A spin-off from "The Adventures of Ozzie and Harriet." Background: 822 Sycamore Street, Hillsdale, the residence of Ozzie and Harriet Nelson. With their children, Dave and Ricky, grown and married, Ozzie and Harriet rent the boys' room to two college girls, Susan Hamilton and Brenda MacKenzie. Stories depict the trials and tribulations of the four members of the Nelson household. (Ozzie's occupation, as in the original series, is not identified.)

CAST

Ozzie Nelson	Himself
Harriet Nelson	Herself
Susan Hamilton	Susan Sennett
Brenda MacKenzie (first introduced as Jennifer MacKenzie)	Brenda Sykes
Lenore Morrison, their neighbor	Lenore Stevens
Alice Morrison, her daughter	Joie Guercio
The mailman	Jim Begg
Professor McCutcheon, the girl's psychology instructor	David Doyle

Also, portraying various friends of Susan and Brenda: Mike Wagner, Gaye Nelson, Tom Harmon.

Music: Frank McKelvey.

OZZIE'S GIRLS—30 minutes—Syndicated 1973. 24 episodes.

THE PACKARD SHOWROOM

See title: "The Martha Wright Show."

PADDY THE PELICAN

Children. Background: Pelicanland. The misadventures of Paddy, the mischievous pelican. Stories unfold through comic-strip drawings.

Hostess: Mary Frances Desmond, as Pam, Paddy's assistant.

Paddy's voice and manipulation: Helen York.

The Artist and creator: Sam Singer.

Other character voices (puppets): Ray Suber.

PADDY THE PELICAN—15 minutes—ABC—1950 - 1951.

THE PALLISERS

Drama. Background: Victorian England. Based on the novels by Anthony Trollope, the series chronicles twenty-five years in the lives of Plantagenet Palliser, a respected member of Parliament, and his wife, Lady Glencora M'Clockie Palliser. Produced by the B.B.C.

CAST

Plantagenet Palliser	Philip Latham
Glencora Palliser	Susan Hampshire
The Duke of Omnium	Roland Culver
Alice	Caroline Mortimer
George	Gary Watson
Lady Dumbello	Rachel Herbert
John Gray	Bernard Brown
Burgo Fitzgerald	Barry Justice
Phineas Finn	Donal McCann
Slide	Clifford Rose
Laura Kennedy	Anna Massey
Lizzie Eustace	Sarah Badel
Mme. Max Goesler	Barbara Murphy

Music: Herbert Chappel, Wilfred Joseph.

Music Played By: The New Philharmonic Orchestra, conducted by Marcus Dods.

Producer: Martin Lisemore, Roland Wilson.

THE PALLISERS—60 minutes—PBS—January 31, 1977 - June 20, 1977. 22 episodes.

PALL MALL PLAYHOUSE

Anthology. Dramatic presentations.

Included:

Square Shootin'. An eastern city newspaper reporter attempts to adjust to life on the Western range.

CAST

Jim Caltin: John Newland; Polly Dorman: Marcia Patrick.

Reunion at Steepler's Hill. A reformed outlaw attempts to persuade his former partner in crime to surrender.

CAST

Billy Bob Jackson: John Ireland; Luke Powers: John Larch; Beth Powers: Dorothy Patrick.

No Compromise. A Texas Ranger struggles to face a difficult assignment: bring in his childhood friend who is now wanted for murder.

CAST

Pvt. Earl Webb: Stephen McNally; John Fenner: Robert Strauss; Judge Fenner: Fay Roope.

Prisoners in Town. A deputy sheriff attempts to defend a beautiful woman accused of murder.

CAST

June Sando: Carolyn Jones; Jim Regan: John Ireland; Cal York: Carleton Young.

PALL MALL PLAYHOUSE—30 minutes—ABC—July 20, 1955 - September 9, 1955.

PANHANDLE PETE AND JENNIFER

Children. Background: A ranch in Chickamoochie Country (the Old South). Incorporating a cartoon story format, yarns told by Johnny Coons, Jennifer Holt, and her life-size dummy, Panhandle Pete, are illustrated by an artist.

Starring: Jennifer Holt, Johnny Coons.

Cartoonist: Bill Newton.

Organist: Adele Scott.

PANHANDLE PETE AND JENNIFER—15 minutes—NBC 1950.

PANIC

Anthology. Suspense dramatizations. Stories of people confronted with sudden, unexpected, and perilous situations.

Host-Narrator: Westbrook Van Voorhis.

Included:

Airline Hostess. On an airline flight across America's Southwest, the pilot informs stewardess Janet Hunter of a radio message that a foreign agent, fleeing the country is aboard the plane and may attempt to divert the flight to Mexico. The story depicts Janet's attempts to discover the spy without alarming the passengers.

CAST

Janet Hunter: Carolyn Jones.

The Moth and the Flame. The story of

June Sullivan, a vaudeville dancer who is threatened by a maniacal knife-thrower, a man who believes that she is the reincarnation of his wife—a dancer he murdered years before and plans to kill again.

CAST

June Sullivan: June Havoc; the knife-thrower: Alan Napier; the stage manager: Norman Alden.

May Day. Trapped in his burning home, a paraplegic radio "ham" is unable to reach his transmitter set to summon help. The story depicts the worldwide short-wave rescue search.

CAST

Steve Bridges: Richard Jaeckel; Charlene: Kathy Garver; Honolulu: Keye Luke; Loretta: Florence Shaen; Tokyo: Dale Ishimoto.

Love Story. The time: December 24, 1957. Two lonely people, a discouraged boy and a desperate girl, meet by chance on a wharf where each had contemplated suicide. Being Christmas Eve, the couple agree to meet for a Yuletide celebration at her apartment in one hour. The story depicts the boy's frantic efforts to find the girl after he loses her address.

CAST

The boy: Darryl Hickman; the girl: Mary Webster; the storekeeper: Lila Lee.

PANIC—30 minutes—NBC—September 1957 - September 1958. 31 episodes.

PANTOMIME QUIZ

Game. Two competing teams, the Home and the Visiting, each composed of four members. The host presents one member of one team with a charade. The player than has to perform the charade, which has a two-minute time limit, to his team. The amount of time accumulated before the charade is identified is calculated. All remaining players compete in the same manner. Teams who accumulate the least amount of overall time are the winners. Home viewers, who submit charades, receive merchandise prizes if the team fails to identify their charade.

Host: Mike Stokey.

Regulars: Dorothy Hart, Angela Lansbury, Rocky Graziano, Carol Haney, Robert Clary, Hans Conried, Jackie Coogan, Milt

Kamen, Howard Morris, Carol Burnett, Stubby Kaye, Denise Darcell, Tom Poston, Vincent Price, Coleen Gray, Robert Stack, Sandra Spence, Dave Willock, Fred Clark, George O'Brien, George Macready, Frank DeVol, Beverly Tyler, Virginia Field.

Announcers: Ken Niles; Art Fleming; Ed Reimers.

Orchestra: Frank DeVol.

PANTOMIME QUIZ—30 minutes. CBS—October 4, 1949 - December 1954; ABC—January 22, 1955 - March 6, 1955; ABC—April 8, 1958 - October 4, 1959.

PAPA CELLINI

Comedy. Background: New York City. The trials and tribulations of the Cellinis, an Italian-American family.

CAST

Papa Cellini	Tito Virolo
	Carlo DeAngelo
Mama Cellini	Ada Ruggeri
Nita Cellini, their daughter	Carol Sinclair
Antino Cellini, their son	Aristide Sigismondi

PAPA CELLINI—30 minutes—ABC—September 28, 1952 - November 16, 1952.

PAPER MOON

Comedy. Background: The Midwest during the 1930s. The story of Moses "Moze" Pray, conartist, a fast-talking salesman for the Dixie Bible Company, and a precocious eleven-year-old-girl, Addie Pray, who believes, that because he looks like her, he is her father. Traveling in a 1931 roadster, they struggle to survive the Depression through imaginative swindles. Based on the motion picture.

CAST

Moze Pray	Christopher Connelly
Addie Pray	Jodie Foster

Music: Harold Arlen.

Theme: "Paper Moon."

PAPER MOON—30 minutes—ABC—September 12, 1974 - January 2, 1975. 13 episodes.

PARADISE BAY

Serial. Background: Paradise Bay, a small coastal community in Southern California. The impact of the new-world standards as experienced by the Morgan family: Jeff, a radio-station manager; his wife, Mary; and their teenage daughter, Kitty.

CAST

Jeff Morgan	Keith Andes
Mary Morgan	Marion Ross
Kitty Morgan	Heather North
Duke Spalding	Dennis Cole
Walter	Walter Brooke

Also: Barbara Boles, Paulie Clark, Steve Mines.

PARADISE BAY—30 minutes—NBC—September 27, 1965 - July 1, 1966.

PARAGON PLAYHOUSE

Anthology. Rebroadcasts of dramas that were originally aired via "Douglas Fairbanks, Jr., Presents."

Host: Walter Abel.

PARAGON PLAYHOUSE—30 minutes—CBS—June 1953 - September 1953.

THE PARENT GAME

Game. Three married couples compete. Object: To match their ideas in raising children with those of a child psychologist. The host reads a question relating to children and reveals four possible answers. Each couple chooses the answer it believes is correct. The correct answer is revealed and points are awarded accordingly (round one: five points per correct choice; round two: ten; round three: fifteen; the finale: thirty). Winners, the highest point scorers, receive a specially selected merchandise prize.

Host: Clark Race.

Announcer: Johnny Jacobs.

Music: Frank Jaffe.

THE PARENT GAME—30 minutes—Syndicated 1972.

PARENTS, PLEASE!

Information. Discussions on the problems faced by parents in the raising of children. A trio of performers enact a situation that is the incorrect approach to raising a child. Three studio-audience members appear on stage and suggest the proper techniques. After the approaches are discussed, the situation is reenacted in correct fashion.

Hostess: Mrs. Bess B. Lane, of the N.Y. State Board of Regents.

Father: Jim Daly.

Mother: Helen Mary.

Daughter: Patsy Cooper.

PARENTS, PLEASE!—30 minutes—DuMont 1947.

PARIS CAVALCADE OF FASHION

See title: "Faye Emerson."

PARIS PRECINCT

Crime Drama. Background: Paris, France. The investigations of Surete (French police department) Inspectors Bolbec and Beaumont.

CAST

Inspector Bolbec	Claude Dauphin
Inspector Beaumont	Louis Jourdan

PARIS PRECINCT—30 minutes—ABC—April 3, 1955 - June 20, 1955; September 25, 1955 — December 18, 1955. 26 episodes. Syndicated title: "World Crime Hunt."

PARIS 7000

Mystery. Background: The American Consulate in Paris, France. The investigations of Jack Brennan, a troubleshooter who aides distressed U.S. citizens. Paris 7000: the consulate telephone number.

CAST

Jack Brennan	George Hamilton
Jules Maurois, the Surete chief	Jacques Aubuchon
Robert Stevens, Brennan's assistant	Gene Raymond

Music Supervision: Lionel Newman.

PARIS 7000—60 minutes—ABC—January 22, 1970 - June 4, 1970. 10 episodes.

THE PARTNERS

Comedy. Background: Los Angeles, California. The fumbling investigations of inept Sergeant Lennie Crooke, and his level-headed partner, Sergeant George Robinson, plainclothes police detectives attached to the Los Angeles thirty-third precinct.

CAST

Sgt. Lennie Crooke	Don Adams
Sgt. George Robinson	Rupert Crosse
Captain Aaron William Andrews	John Doucette
Sergeant Nelson Higgenbottom	Dick Van Patten
Freddie Butler, the man with the compulsion to confess to every crime	Robert Karvelas

Music: Lalo Schifrin.

THE PARTNERS—30 minutes—NBC—September 18, 1971 - January 8, 1972. Rebroadcasts (NBC): July 28, 1972 - September 8, 1972. 20 episodes.

THE PARTRIDGE FAMILY

Comedy. Background: 698 Sycamore Road, San Pueblo, California, the residence of a show-business Rock group, the Partridge Family: Shirley, a widow; and her children: Keith, Laurie, Danny, Tracy, and Chris. Stories depict the home and working lives of an ordinary family who became prominent when Danny, their ten-year-old manager, organized the family into a Rock group, recorded a song, and talked agent Reuben Kinkade into hearing the demonstration tape, which lead to a recording contract and fame.

CAST

Shirley Partridge	Shirley Jones
Keith Partridge	David Cassidy
Laurie Partridge	Susan Dey
Danny Partridge	Danny Bonaduce
Tracy Partridge	Suzanne Crough
Chris Partridge	Jeremy Gelbwaks Brian Foster
Reuben Kinkade	Dave Madden
Alan Kinkade, his nephew	Alan Bursky
Ricky Stevens, the neighbor's four-year-old son	Ricky Segal
Walter Renfrew, Shirley's father	Ray Bolger Jackie Coogan
Amanda Renfrew, Shirley's mother	Rosemary DeCamp

Partridge Family dog: Simon.

Music: Hugo Montenegro.

Additional Music: Shorty Rogers, George Duning, Benny Golson.

Executive Producer: Bob Claver.

Producer: Larry Rosen, Mel Swope, Paul Junger Witt.

Director: Ralph Senesky, Lee Philips, E.W. Swackhamer, Russ Mayberry, Jerry London, Herb Wallerstein, Lou Antonio, Christopher Morgan, Bob Claver, Jerry

The Partridge Family. Bottom, left to right: Suzanne Crough, Shirley Jones, Susan Dey. Top, left to right: Brian Foster, David Cassidy, Danny Bonaduce. © *Screen Gems.*

Berstein, Claudio Guzman, Herbert Kenwith, Richard Kinon, Earl Bellamy, Peter Baldwin.

Creator: Bernard Slade.

Background voices (additional to Shirley Jones and David Cassidy) who comprise the Partridge Family: John Bahler, Tom Bahler, Jackie Ward, Ron Hicklin.

THE PARTRIDGE FAMILY—30 minutes—ABC—September 25, 1970 - September 7, 1974. 96 episodes. Syndicated. Spin-off series: "Partridge Family: 2200 A.D."

PARTRIDGE FAMILY: 2200 A.D.

Animated Cartoon. A spin-off from "The Partridge Family." Background: Earth, 2200 A.D. The misadventures of the traveling (to other planets) show-business Rock group, the Partridge Family: Shirley, Keith, Laurie, Danny, Tracy, and Chris.

Additional characters: Reuben Kinkade, their manager; and their friends: Judy, Beannie, and Marion.

Voices: Sherry Alberoni, Danny Bonaduce, Suzanne Crough, Susan Dey, Brian Foster, Joan Gerber, Dave Madden, Chuck McLennan, Julie McWhirter, Allan Melvin, Alan Oppenheimer, Mike Road, Hal Smith, John Stephenson, Lennie Weinrib, Franklin Welker.

Music: Hoyt Curtin.

PARTRIDGE FAMILY: 2200 A.D.–
25 minutes–CBS–September 7, 1974
- March 9, 1975. 16 episodes.

PARTY TIME AT CLUB ROMA

Variety. The series, filmed in San
Francisco, features performances by
guest artists.

Host: Ben Alexander.

Producer: Ben Alexander.

Sponsor: Roma Wines.

PARTY TIME AT CLUB ROMA–30
minutes–NBC 1950.

THE PASSING PARADE

Anthology. Reedited theatrical shorts.
Touching dramas revealing the lives of
people and events of the past.

Narrator: John Nesbitt.

Included:

The Immortal Blacksmith. The story
of blacksmith Tom Davenport and his
invention of the printing-press motor.

The Giant of Norway. The efforts of
statesman Fridtjof Nansen to assist
refugees as they return home after
World War II.

Magic on a Stick. John Walker's discovery of the safety match.

My Old Town. Life in a small
American town before the invention
of the automobile.

People on Paper. A history of the
comic strip, beginning with *"The Yellow Kid."*

Stairway to Light. French doctor
Philippe Pinel's efforts in the treatment of the mentally ill.

THE PASSING PARADE–15 minutes–Syndicated 1961.

PASSPORT 7

Travel. The filmed expeditions of
various explorers.

Host-Narrator: Bob Maxwell.

PASSPORT 7–30 minutes–Syndicated 1964.

PASSPORT TO DANGER

Adventure. The global assignments of
Steve McQuinn, a United States diplo-
matic courier, and the unwitting

decoy of the Hungarian Secret Police.

Starring: Cesar Romero as Steve
McQuinn.

PASSPORT TO DANGER–30 minutes–CBS 1956. 39 episodes.

PASSWORD

Game. Distinguished by four formats.

Format One:

Password–30 minutes–CBS–October
2, 1961 - September 15, 1967. Syndicated.

Two competing teams, each composed
of two members–one celebrity and
one noncelebrity contestant. Each
member of one team is handed a
concealed password (e.g., "discover").
The player then relates a one word
clue to his partner, who must identify
the password. If he is unable, their
opponents then receive a chance to
identify it. The word is played until it
is identified or until it is voided by
the use of ten clues. Words start at ten
points and diminish one point with
each additional clue. Winners are the
teams first to score twenty-five points.
The champions then compete in the
bonus "Lightning Round." Object: to
identify five words within sixty
seconds. Fifty dollars is awarded for
each correct identification.

Host: Allen Ludden.

Announcer: Jack Clark; John Harlan.

Music: Recorded.

Format Two:

Password–30 minutes–ABC–April 5,
1971 - November 15, 1974.

The same as format one.

Host: Allen Ludden.

Announcer: John Harlan.

Music: Recorded.

Format Three:

Password All Stars–30 minutes–ABC
–November 18, 1974 - February 21,
1975.

Six celebrities compete. Four at a
time play, divided into two teams of
two. One player on each team receives
a password and through one-word
clues has to relate its meaning to his
partner. Words start at ten points and
diminish one point with each clue to a
limit of five clues. The team first to
score twenty-five or more points is the

winner. Each member of the team
receives that amount of points and a
chance to double it via "20-20 Password." Within a twenty-second time
limit, each player has to identify one
word. The time one player uses is
deducted from the total time and
becomes the amount of time the
remaining player has.

To determine who will compete as
partners with each member of the
winning team, "The Qualifying
Game" is played. The four remaining
players compete. The two champions
rotate, each giving one word clues to
the identification of a password. The
player first to press a button and
sound a buzzer receives a chance to
answer. If correct, he scores one password. The first two players to score
two passwords each qualify. The first
player to qualify selects his partner
from the previous winning team. The
remaining two players, the champion
and the second to qualify, form the
opposing team.

The game plays as such, four days,
Monday through Thursday. The four
players with the highest point scores
compete in the fifth day tournament
segment wherein the highest scoring
player receives a silver master award
and five thousand dollars for purposes
of donation to a favorite charity.

Host: Allen Ludden.

Announcer: John Harlan.

Music: Recorded.

Format Four:

Password–30 minutes–ABC–February 24, 1975 - June 27, 1975.

The same as Format One.

Host: Allen Ludden.

Announcer: John Harlan.

Music: Recorded.

PAT BOONE

Listed: The television programs of
singer-actor Pat Boone.

The Pat Boone Show–Musical
Variety–30 minutes–ABC–October
3, 1957 - June 25, 1959 (1958 title:
"The Pat Boone Chevy Show").

Host: Pat Boone.

Regulars: The Artie Malvin Chorus,
The Jada Quartet, The McGuire
Sisters.

Orchestra: Mort Lindsey.

The Pat Boone Show–Musical Variety
(Daily)–30 minutes–NBC–October
17, 1966 - March 31, 1967.

Host: Pat Boone.

Pat Boone in Hollywood—Talk-Variety—90 minutes—Syndicated 1969.

Host: Pat Boone.

Announcer: Jay Stewart.

The Patchwork Family. Carol Corbett with Rags the puppet.

THE PATCHWORK FAMILY

Children. Songs, games, sketches, and related educational entertainment geared to children.

Hostess (Portraying Carol): Carol Corbett.

Voice of Rags the puppet: Cary Antebi.

Regulars: Joanna Pang, John Canemaker, Arlene Thomas, Elaine Lefkowits.

Music: Recorded.

Executive Producer: Linda Allen.

Producer-Director: Bill Bryan.

THE PATCHWORK FAMILY—60 minutes—Premiered: January 1, 1974. Broadcast on CBS owned and operated stations.

PAT PAULSEN'S HALF A COMEDY HOUR

Comedy. A satire of the contemporary scene.

Host: Pat Paulsen.

Regulars: Jean Byron, Sherry Miles, Bob Einstein, Peppe Brown, Vanetta Rogers, Pedro Regas (as Mrs. Buffalo Running Schwartz, an eighty-seven-year-old Indian).

Announcer: Billy Sands.

PAT PAULSEN'S HALF A COMEDY HOUR—30 minutes—ABC—January 22, 1970 - March 9, 1970. 13 tapes.

THE PATRICE MUNSEL SHOW

Musical Variety.

Hostess: Patrice Munsel.

Featured: The Martins Quartet.

Orchestra: Charles Sanford.

THE PATRICE MUNSEL SHOW—30 minutes—ABC—October 18, 1957 - July 18, 1958.

THE PATRICIA BOWAN SHOW

Musical Variety.

Hostess: Patricia Bowan.

Regulars: Paul Shelly, Maureen Cannon, The Pastels.

Music: The Norman Paris Trio.

THE PATRICIA BOWAN SHOW—15 minutes—CBS 1951.

PATROL CAR

Rebroadcasts of "Inspector Fabian of Scotland Yard" (which see).

PATTI PAGE

Listed: The television programs of singer-actress Patti Page.

The Scott Music Hall—Musical Revue—30 minutes—CBS—July 15, 1952 - September 25, 1952.

Hostess: Patti Page.

Regulars: Frank Fontaine, Mary Ellen Terry.

Orchestra: Carl Hoff.

The Patti Page Show—Musical Variety—15 minutes—NBC—July 3, 1955 - July 7, 1956.

Hostess: Patti Page.

Featured: The Page Five Singers.

Orchestra: Jack Rael.

The Patti Page Show—Musical Variety (summer replacement for "The Perry Como Show")—30 minutes—NBC—June 16, 1956 - July 16, 1956.

Hostess: Patti Page.

Featured: The Spellbinders.

Orchestra: Jack Rael.

The Patti Page Show—Musical Variety—15 minutes—CBS—February 9, 1957 - June 11, 1958.

Hostess: Patti Page.

Orchestra: Jack Rael.

The Big Record—Musical Variety—60 minutes—CBS—September 18, 1957 - June 11, 1958 (see title).

The Patti Page Show. Patti Page.

The Patti Page Show—Musical Variety—30 minutes—ABC—September 24, 1958 - March 16, 1959.

Hostess: Patti Page.

Regulars: The Jerry Packer Singers, The Matt Mattox Dancers.

Orchestra: Vic Schoen.

THE PATTY DUKE SHOW

Comedy. Background: Number Eight Remsen Drive, Brooklyn Heights, Brooklyn, New York, the residence of the Lane family: Martin, the managing editor of the *New York Chronicle;* his wife, Natalie; their daughter, Patty; their son, Ross; and their glamorous European cousin, Cathy Lane, who is residing with them until she completes her high school education and is able to rejoin her father, Kenneth Lane, a foreign correspondent for the *Chronicle.*

Stories depict the lives of two pretty high school girls, sixteen-year-old identical cousins, Patty and Cathy Lane. Patty, the average American girl, possesses an unquenchable thirst for life and the ability to complicate matters that are seemingly uncomplicatable; and Cathy, shy, warm, and sensitive, possesses a love for the arts, and, treasuring her European upbringing, sometimes encounters difficulty as she struggles to ·adjust to the American way of life.

CAST

Patty Lane	Patty Duke
Cathy Lane	Patty Duke
Martin Lane	William Schallert
Natalie Lane	Jean Byron
Ross Lane	Paul O'Keefe
Richard Harrison, Patty's boyfriend	Eddie Applegate

The Patty Duke Show. Patty Duke as Patty Lane.

The Patty Duke Show. Patty Duke as Cathy Lane, her European cousin.

Sue Ellen Turner,
Patty's rival for
Richard — Kitty Sullivan

Ted Brownley, Cathy's
boyfriend — Skip Hinnant

Gloria, Patty's rival
for Richard (later
episodes) — Kelly Wood

J.R. Castle, Martin's
employer — John McGiver

Nikki Lee Blake, Ross's
girlfriend — Susan Melvin

William Smithers, Martin's
employer (later
episodes) — Ralph Bell

Mr. Brewster, the
principal of Brooklyn
Heights High
School — Charles White

Sammy, the owner
of the Shake Shop,
the after-school
hangout — Sammy Smith

Jonathan Harrison, Richard's
father — David Doyle

Mrs. Harrison, Richard's
mother — Amzie Strictland

Kenneth Lane, Cathy's
father — William Schallert

T. J. Blodgett, the
publisher of the
Chronicle — Alan Bunce
Robert Carson
Jerry Hauser

Mrs. Marlow, Natalie's
friend — Natalie Masters

Miss Gordon, J.R.'s
secretary — Phyllis Coates

Louie, the waiter at
Leslie's Ice Cream
Parlor (the hangout
in later epi-
sodes) — Bobby Diamond

Monica Robinson, Patty's
friend — Laura Barton
Kathy Garver

Mrs. MacDonald, the Lane

housekeeper — Margaret Hamilton

Alice, Patty's
friend — Alice Rawlings

Rosiland, Patty's
friend — Robyn Millan

Alfred, Patty's
friend — Jeff Siggins

Patty Duke's stand-in: Rita McLaughlin (portraying Cathy when Miss Duke is portraying Patty; Patty when Miss Duke is portraying Cathy).

Lane family dog: Tiger.

Music: Sid Ramin; Harry Geller.

THE PATTY DUKE SHOW—30 minutes—ABC—September 18, 1963 - August 31, 1966. 104 episodes. Syndicated.

PAULA STONE'S TOY SHOP

Children. Music, comedy, and fantasy set against the background of a toy store.

Hostess: Paula Stone.

Regulars: Tim Herbert (as Freddie Fun) and dancers Howard and Marge as Pitter and Patter.

Producer-Director: Paula Stone.

PAULA STONE'S TOY SHOP—60 minutes—ABC 1955.

PAUL BERNARD—PSYCHIATRIST

Drama. Background: Canada, the office of psychiatrist Paul Bernard. The session between doctor and patient is dramatized. The patient relates her elements of distress; and, in the final moments of the program, Dr. Bernard analizes her seemingly un-

complicated and innocent thoughts. Produced with the cooperation of the Canadian Mental Health Association.

CAST

Paul Bernard,
Psychiatrist — Chris Wiggins

Regular Patients:

Mrs. Alice Talbot — Dawn Greenhalgh

Mrs. Howard — Tudi Wiggins

Mrs. Finley — Marcia Diamond

Miss Parker — Valerie-Jean Hume

Mrs. Connie Walker — Phyllis Maxwell

Mrs. Katie Conner — Nuala Fitzgerald

Mrs. Wilkins — Vivian Reis

Miss Barbara
Courtney — Sheley Sommers

Mrs. Bradshaw — Diane Polley

Mrs. Collins — Kay Hawtrey

Mrs. Donaldson — Gale Garnett

Mrs. Roberts — Paisley Maxwell

Mrs. Patterson — Josephine Barrington

Mrs. Johnson — Anna Commeron

Miss Michaels — Peggy Mahon

Mrs. Karen Lampton — Barbara Kyle

Mrs. Brookfield — Carol Lazare

Mrs. Jennifer Barlow — Micki Moore

Mrs. Vickie Lombard — Arlene Meadows

Music: Milani Kymlicka.

PAUL BERNARD—PSYCHIATRIST—30 minutes—Syndicated 1972. 195 tapes.

PAUL DIXON

Listed: The television programs of singer Paul Dixon.

The Paul Dixon Show—Variety—60 minutes—ABC—August 8, 1951 - November 15, 1951.

Host: Paul Dixon.

Regulars: Wanda Lewis, Dottie Mack, Lennie Gorrian.

The Paul Dixon Show—Variety—30 minutes—Syndicated 1974. Music, songs, and conversation geared to women.

Host: Paul Dixon ("Paul baby.")

Regulars: Coleen Sharp, Bonnie Lou ("Star of the now defunct Midwestern Hayride.")

Music: The Bruce Brownfield Band.

THE PAUL LYNDE SHOW

Comedy. Background: Ocean Grove, California, the residence of the Simms family: Paul, an attorney with the firm of McNish and Simms; his wife, Martha; and their children, Barbara (twenty-one), and Sally (fourteen).

Completing her studies at college, Barbara Simms and Howie Dickerson, a penniless former graduate studying for his Masters degree in oceanogrophy, elope, return to Ocean Grove from Las Vegas, and establish housekeeping in the Simms home, where Howie encounters Paul's objections—concerned over Barbara's welfare and Howie's inability to support her. Stories depict the bickering relationship between Paul and Howie; and Paul's desperate attempts to find Howie (a genius with an I.Q. of 185 who can't function properly in the business world) suitable employment. Based on the stage play, "Howie."

CAST

Paul Simms	Paul Lynde
Martha Simms	Elizabeth Allen
Barbara Dickerson (Simms)	Jane Actman
Howie Dickerson	John Calvin
Sally Simms	Pamelyn Ferdin
J.J. McNish, Paul's business partner	Herb Voland
Barney Dickerson, Howie's father, a butcher in Eagle Rock California	Jerry Stiller
Grace Dickerson, Howie's mother	Anne Meara
Alice, Paul's secretary	Allison McKay
Jimmy Fowler, Sally's boyfriend	Anson Williams
Jimmy Lyons, Sally's boyfriend	Stuart Getz

Music: Shorty Rogers.

THE PAUL LYNDE SHOW—30 minutes—ABC—September 13, 1972 - September 8, 1973. 26 episodes.

PAUL WHITEMAN'S SATURDAY NIGHT REVUE

Musical Variety.

Host: Paul Whiteman.

Regulars: Linda Romay, Eric Viola, Joe Young, Duffy Otel.

Orchestra: Paul Whiteman.

Choreographer: Frank Westbrook.

Producer: Tony Stanford, Ward Byron, Dick Eckler.

Director: William H. Brown.

Sponsor: Goodyear.

PAUL WHITEMAN'S SATURDAY NIGHT REVUE—30 minutes—ABC—November 6, 1949 - October 29, 1950. Also titled: "The Paul Whiteman Goodyear Revue."

PAUL WHITEMAN'S TEEN CLUB

Variety. Performances by teenage talent discoveries.

Host: Paul Whiteman.

Regulars: Nancy Lewis, June Keegan, Maureen Cannon, The Ray Porter Singers.

Orchestra: Paul Whiteman.

Producer: Jack Sleck, Skipper Dawes, Paul Whiteman.

Director: Herb Horton.

Sponsor: Griffin Shoe Polish.

PAUL WHITEMAN'S TEEN CLUB—60 minutes—ABC—April 2, 1949 - March 28, 1954.

PAUL WINCHELL AND JERRY MAHONEY

Listed: The television programs of ventriloquist Paul Winchell.

Winchell and Mahoney—Children—30 minutes—NBC 1947.

Background: Jerry Mahoney's Club House. Twenty Children from the studio audience compete in various games for prizes.

Host: Paul Winchell.

His Dummies: Jerry Mahoney, Knucklehead Smith.

Regulars: Dorothy Claire, Hilda Vaughn.

Orchestra: John Gart.

Dunninger and Winchell—Variety—30 minutes. NBC—October 14, 1948 - September 28, 1949; CBS—October 5, 1949 - December 28, 1949. Also known as "The Bigelow Show."

Format: Demonstrations on the art of mind reading.

Hosts: Paul Winchell, Jerry Mahoney.

Starring: Joseph Dunninger, the "master mentalist."

The Paul Winchell and Jerry Mahoney Speidel Show—Variety—30 minutes—NBC—1950 - 1953.

Hosts: Paul Winchell, Jerry Mahoney.

Regulars: Dorothy Claire, Hilda Vaughn, Jimmy Blaine, Patricia Bright, Sid Raymond.

Announcer: Ted Brown.

Orchestra: John Gart.

Paul Winchell and Jerry Mahoney's What's My Name—Game—30 minutes—NBC—January 1952 - May 22, 1954.

Format: Object: For players to identify the name of a famous person through clues provided by Paul and his dummies as they dramatize an incident in the subject's life. War bonds are awarded to winners.

Hosts: Paul Winchell, Jerry Mahoney.

Regulars: Maybin Hewe, Mary Ellen Terry.

The Paul Winchell and Jerry Mahoney Show. Paul Winchell and his dummy friend, Jerry Mahoney.

Orchestra: Milton DeLugg.

Toyland Express—Children—30 minutes—ABC—November 7, 1955 - December 12, 1955.

Hosts: Paul Winchell, Jerry Mahoney.

Orchestra: Ralph Herman.

Circus Time—Circus Variety Acts—60 minutes—ABC—October 4, 1956 - June 27, 1957.

Ringmasters: Paul Winchell, Jerry Mahoney.

Orchestra: Ralph Herman.

The Paul Winchell Show—Variety—30 minutes—ABC—September 29, 1957 - April 3, 1960.

Hosts: Paul Winchell, Jerry Mahoney.

Featured: Frank Fontaine.

Orchestra: Milton DeLugg.

The Paul Winchell Show—Variety—30 minutes—ABC—December 25, 1960 - April 16, 1961.

Hosts: Paul Winchell, Jerry Mahoney.

Music: Milton DeLugg.

Cartoonsville—Cartoons—30 minutes—ABC—April 6, 1963 - September 28, 1963.

Hosts: Paul Winchell, Jerry Mahoney, Knucklehead Smith.

Cartoons: "Sheriff Saddle Head"; "Goodie the Gremlin"; "Scatt Skit."

Winchell and Mahoney Time—Children—60 minutes—Syndicated 1965.

Background: Jerry's Club House. Selected members of the studio audience compete in games for prizes.

Hosts: Paul Winchell, Jerry Mahoney, Knucklehead Smith.

Runaround—Game—30 minutes—NBC—September 9, 1972 - September 1, 1973. See title.

PAY CARDS

Game. Three contestants compete in a game of poker. Twenty cards, which contain singles, pairs, and three and four of a kind, are displayed face down on an electronic board. By selecting the numbered cards (one to twenty) players have to build a five-card hand better than their opponents. Players begin by selecting three cards, then two on their next

turn. The player with the best hand is the winner.

Cash: a pair: ten dollars; three of a kind or a full house: thirty dollars; four of a kind: one hundred dollars.

Rounds Two and Three: "Joker's Wild." The format and the payoffs are the same as round one.

Round Four: "The Jackpot." The winner, the highest cash scorer, is shown the faces of twelve cards for twelve seconds. At the end of the time the cards are hidden by overlaying numbers. The host spins a wheel which when stopping pinpoints one of the twelve cards. If the player can guess the number that the card is hidden under, he wins a new car.

Host: Art James.

Announcer: Fred Collins.

PAY CARDS—30 minutes—Syndicated 1968. 260 tapes.

P.D.Q.
(PLEASE DRAW QUICKLY)

A game show, hosted by Ed Cooper, that features players competing in a drawing type of guessing game for prizes. 30 minutes—ABC 1950.

P.D.Q.

Game. Two competing teams, "The Home Team" and "The Challengers." The Home Team is composed of two celebrities; and the Challengers comprise one celebrity and one non-celebrity contestant. One member of each team is placed in a soundproof isolation booth. As the sound is turned off in one booth, the other team competes. Standing before a phrase that is spelled out in large plastic letters, the outside player has to place letters on a wall rack within six second intervals and induce his partner into identifying it. The amount of letters used until the phrase is guessed is calculated. The sound is turned on in the other booth and the team competes in the same manner with the same phrase. The team using the fewest letters is the winner of that round. If it is the contestant's team, she wins a merchandise prize. A two-out-of-three-game competition is played.

If the challengers accumulate the least amount of overall time, the contestant receives the opportunity to win five hundred dollars and a new car. The player is shown three letters of one word (e.g., WTR—— WATER) and has to identify ten words within

sixty seconds. For each correct identification she receives fifty dollars. If she guesses all ten she wins five hundred dollars and a new car. Should the contestant have scored lower than the Home Team, each correct identification awards twenty-five dollars.

Host: Dennis James.

Announcer: Kenny Williams.

P.D.Q.—30 minutes—Syndicated 1965-1970. Withdrawn. Revised as: "Baffle" (see title).

PEABODY'S IMPROBABLE HISTORY

See title: "Rocky and His Friends."

PEANUTS

Animated Cartoon. The misadventures of the Peanuts gang: eight children (Charlie Brown, Linus, Lucy, Schroeder, Pig Pen, Frieda, Peppermint Patty, and Sally), and one mischievous dog, Snoopy, who believes he is a World War I flying ace in battle with the Red Baron. Stories depict their attempts to solve problems without help from the adult world. Created by Charles Schultz.

Characters' Voices

Charlie Brown	Peter Robbins
	Chad Webber
	Duncan Watson
Snoopy	Bill Melendez
Lucy	Sally Dryer
	Tracy Stratford
	Pamelyn Ferdin
	Robin Kohn
Linus	Christopher Shea
	Stephen Shea
Pig Pen	Jeff Orstein
	Thomas A. Muller
Peppermint Patty	Gail De Faria
	Kip De Faria
	Maureen McCormick
	Donna Forman
Schroeder	Glenn Mendelson
	Danny Hjelm
	Brian Kayanjian
	Greg Felton
Sally	Kathy Steinberg
	Hilary Momberger
	Lynn Mortensen
Frieda	Ann Altieri

Music composed by: Vince Guaraldi.

Orchestra: John Scott Trotter.

Animation: Bill Melendez.

The Series:

A Charlie Brown Christmas. With the Christmas season approaching, Charlie, disillusioned by the commer-

Peanuts. The cast of "Peanuts." Created by Charles Schultz. © *United Features Syndicate, Inc.*

cialism of the holiday, attempts to relay his feelings to his friends who are eagerly awaiting the big day.

A Charlie Brown Thanksgiving. Charlie's efforts to organize a Thanksgiving feast.

Be My Valentine, Charlie Brown. The episode focuses on several characters: Sally, who thinks Linus's purchase of a box of candy is for her, when in reality it is for his homeroom teacher; Lucy, who seeks Schroeder's attention; and Charlie Brown, who begins a vigil by his mailbox, hoping for a valentine.

Charlie Brown's All Stars. With 999 straight losses, and 3000 runs given up by its pitcher, Charlie Brown, the All Stars baseball team, which is composed of five boys, three girls, and a dog, play—and lose—their thousandth game.

He's Your Dog, Charlie Brown. Charlie's efforts to curtail the antics of his mischievous dog, Snoopy.

It's a Mystery, Charlie Brown. Donning the guise of Sherlock Holmes, Snoopy attempts to solve the case of Woodstock's missing nest.

It's Arbor Day, Charlie Brown. The chaos that results when the students of the Birchwood School decide to observe Arbor Day and proceed to beautify the world.

It's The Easter Beagle, Charlie Brown. The story focuses on the Peanuts gang as they prepare for the Easter Beagle, a mythical dog who magically appears to hand out candy and decorate eggs on Easter Sunday Morning.

It's the Great Pumpkin, Charlie Brown. The saga of Linus's vigil in a pumpkin field where he eagerly awaits the arrival of the Great Pumpkin, a mythical being who is supposed to give toys to good girls and boys.

It Was a Short Summer, Charlie Brown. Charlie and the gang recall a summer at camp where the boys were pitted against the girls in various sports events.

Play it Again, Charlie Brown. Through Lucy's meddling, Schroeder, the gifted pianist, is booked to play his toy piano for the P.T.A. The story focuses on his efforts to please an audience who are expecting a rock concert from a boy who is strictly a Beethoven man.

There's No Time For Love, Charlie Brown. A hectic day in the lives of the Peanuts gang is recalled through essay tests, Peppermint Patty's crush on Charlie, and a misguided field trip.

You're a Good Sport, Charlie Brown. The story focuses on a cross-country race with the Peanuts characters as the main competitors.

You're Elected, Charlie Brown.

Charlie's disastrous campaign against Linus for the presidency of the sixth grade.

You're In Love, Charlie Brown. With only two days left before the end of the term, Charlie attempts to acquire the affections of the red-haired girl who sits in front of him.

PEANUTS—30 minutes—CBS. First broadcast as a series of specials during the 1965-1966 season.

THE PEARL BAILEY SHOW

Musical Variety.

Hostess: Pearl Bailey.

Announcer: Roger Carroll.

Orchestra: Louis Bellson.

THE PEARL BAILEY SHOW—60 minutes—ABC—January 23, 1971 - May 5, 1971. 13 episodes.

PEBBLES AND BAMM BAMM

See title: "The Flintstones."

PECK'S BAD GIRL

Comedy. The misadventures of twelve-year-old Torey Peck.

CAST

Torey Peck	Patty McCormack
Steve Peck, her father, a lawyer	Wendell Corey
Jennifer Peck, her mother	Marsha Hunt
Roger Peck, her seven-year-old brother	Roy Ferrell
Francesca, her girlfriend	Reba Waters

PECK'S BAD GIRL—30 minutes—CBS—May 5, 1959 - August 4, 1959. Rebroadcasts: CBS—June 28, 1960 - September 20, 1960.

THE PEE WEE KING SHOW

Musical Variety. Performances by Country and Western entertainers.

Host: Pee Wee King.

Regulars: Chuck Wiggins, Neal Burris, Redd Stuart, Ellen Long, The Cleveland Jamboree, The Golden West Cowboys.

Orchestra: Pee Wee King.

THE PEE WEE KING SHOW—30 minutes—ABC—May 23, 1955 - September 5, 1955.

THE PENDULUM

Anthology. Retitled episodes of "The Vise."

Host: John Bentley.
Producer: Bob Breckner.
Director: Dean Reed.

THE PENDULUM—30 minutes—Syndicated 1956. 65 episodes.

PENNY TO A MILLION

Game. Two competing teams, each composed of five members. Through general-knowledge question-and-answer rounds, eight of the ten players are eliminated. An incorrect response defeats a player. The remaining two players, one per team, compete in a spelling bee wherein they receive one penny doubled to a possible million ($10,000). The surviving player receives what money he has won, and returns the following week, competes again in the question-answer session, and if successful again, competes in the spelling bee to increase the money he has already won.

Host: Bill Goodwin.

PENNY TO A MILLION—30 minutes—ABC—June 1955 - September 1955.

PENTAGON CONFIDENTIAL

Drama. Background: Washington, D.C. Factual dramatizations based on the files of the United States Army Criminal Investigation Division.

CAST
The C.I.D. colonel   Addison Richards
The police detective   Gene Lyons
The army investigator   Edward Binns
The army investigator   Larry Fletcher

PENTAGON CONFIDENTIAL—30 minutes—CBS 1953.

PENTAGON U.S.A.

See title: "Pentagon Confidential." (One week after the premiere of "Pentagon Confidential," the title changed to "Pentagon U.S.A.".)

PENTHOUSE PARTY

Variety. Music, songs, and celebrity interviews.

Hostess: Betty Furness.
Vocalist: Don Cherry.
Music: The Buddy Weed Trio.
Producer: Lester Lewis.
Director: Alex Segal.
Sponsor: Best Foods.

PENTHOUSE PARTY—30 minutes—ABC—September 15,.1950 - June 8, 1951.

PENTHOUSE SONATA

Classical Music.

Hostess: June Browne.
Music: The Fine Arts Quartet (Leonard Sorkin, George Sopkin, Sheppard Lehnoff, Joseph Stepansky).

PENTHOUSE SONATA—30 minutes—ABC—June 19, 1949 - June 26, 1949.

PEOPLE ARE FUNNY

See title: "Art Linkletter."

THE PEOPLE'S CHOICE

Comedy. Background: New City, California. The trials and tribulations of Socrates "Sock" Miller, a Bureau of Fish and Wildlife Ornithologist studying to become a lawyer.

Stranded on a country road by an inoperative car, Amanda "Mandy" Peoples, the mayor's daughter, is assisted by Sock, who, after fixing the flat tire, befriends her. Feeling that he is the right man for a city-council vacancy, she delivers a television speech and urges a write-in vote for Miller. An overwhelming voter response elects Sock as a city-councilman and as the head of Barkerville, a housing development.

Following the format of a serial, episodes depict: Sock and Mandy's secret marriage—eloping after her father, John Peoples, refused to grant his permission (feeling Sock is not worthy, as yet, not a lawyer); their attempts to conceal their marriage, which after several months is discovered by John, who, though bitter, accepts Sock; the struggles of newlyweds; and Sock's attempts to promote Barkerville.

Through voice-over dubbing, the proceedings are observed and commented on by Cleo, Sock's bassethound dog.

CAST
Socrates "Sock"
  Miller   Jackie Cooper
Amanda "Mandy" Peoples
  (Miller)   Patricia Breslin
Mayor John Peoples   Paul Maxey
Augusta "Gus" Miller,
  Sock's aunt   Margaret Irving
Hex Hexley (Rollo), Sock's
  friend   Dick Wesson
Miss Larson, Sock's
  employer   Elvia Allman
Pierre, a penniless
  artist, a friend of
  Sock's   Leonid Kinskey
Cleo's Voice: Mary Jane Croft.
Music: Raven Kosakoff.

THE PEOPLE'S CHOICE—30 minutes—CBS—October 6, 1955 - September 25, 1958. Syndicated. 104 episodes.

THE PEOPLE'S COURT OF SMALL CLAIMS

Courtroom Drama. Dramatic reenactments of small-claims court hearings.

Judge: Orrin B. Evans.

THE PEOPLE'S COURT OF SMALL CLAIMS—30 minutes—Syndicated 1958.

PEOPLE WILL TALK

Game. Two competing contestants. The host reads a yes-or-no type of answerable question to a panel of fifteen selected studio audience members who lock in an answer of the corresponding type. Contestants, one at a time, choose a panelist and predict his or her answer. The panelist reveals his answer and if it is in accord with the contestant's, he receives one point. Winners, the highest scoring contestants, receive merchandise prizes.

Host: Dennis James.

PEOPLE WILL TALK—25 minutes—NBC—July 1, 1963 - December 27, 1963.

PEPSI-COLA PLAYHOUSE

Anthology. Dramatic presentations.
Hostesses: Anita Colby; Polly Bergen.

Included:

One Thing Leads to Another. The trials and tribulations of a young lawyer and his fiancée.

CAST
Patrick O'Neal, Bridgett Carr.

Adopted Son. A mother attempts to reconstruct her adopted, musically inclined son into the image of her deceased, athletic son.

CAST
Frances Gifford.

Bachelor's Week. The story of a bachelor's doubts about marriage.

CAST
Robert Paige.

Playmates. The life of a lonely girl whose world is dominated by invisible playmates.

CAST
Natalie Wood, Alan Napier.

PEPSI-COLA PLAYHOUSE—30 minutes—ABC—October 2, 1953 - June 26, 1955. Also titled: "Playhouse '54."

THE PERFECT MATCH

Game. Two three-member teams, the men and the women. Object: For the men to discover which female a computer has matched him with and vice versa.

Round One: The host presents a romantic situation to the men who then answer and attempt to solve it. Choosing any of the men, each woman is permitted to question him concerning his answers.

Round Two: The reverse of round one. The men are permitted to question the women concerning their responses to a romantic problem.

Round Three: Varies greatly in presentation, but the basic format is an exchange of questions and answers between the two teams to determine the romantic natures of each individual.

Finale: Each male chooses the girl he feels he is best suited for, and vice versa. Players who match receive fifty dollars. The computer choices, which are validated by the Computer Match Company, are revealed, and the couples who paired themselves as did the computer, have a perfect match and each receive two hundred dollars.

Host: Dick Enberg.

Music: Score Productions.

THE PERFECT MATCH—30 minutes —Syndicated 1967.

THE PERILS OF PENELOPE PITSTOP

Animated Cartoon. Becoming the legal guardian of Penelope Pitstop, a young and vulnerable female racer, Sylvester Sneekly dons the guise of the Hooded Claw and sets his goal to acquire her wealth by killing her. Traveling around the world in her car, the *Compact Pussycat,* Penelope and her protectors, the Ant Hill Mob, struggle to foil the Hooded Claw's sinister efforts. A Hanna-Barbera Production.

Characters' Voices

Penelope Pitstop	Janet Waldo
Sylvester Sneekly	Paul Lynde
Chugaboom	Mel Blanc
Yak Yak	Mel Blanc
The Bully Brothers	Mel Blanc

The Ant Hill Mob:

Clyde	Paul Winchell
Softly	Paul Winchell
Zippy	Don Messick
Pockets	Don Messick
Dum Dum	Don Messick
Snoozy	Don Messick

Narrator: Gary Owens.

Music: Hoyt Curtin.

Musical Director: Ted Nichols.

Producer-Director: William Hanna, Joseph Barbera.

THE PERILS OF PENELOPE PITSTOP—30 minutes—CBS—September 13, 1969 - September 4, 1971. 26 episodes. Syndicated.

PERRY COMO

Listed: The television programs of singer Perry Como.

The Chesterfield Supper Club—Musical Variety—15 minutes—NBC—December 24, 1948 - May 28, 1950.

Host: Perry Como.

Regulars: The Fontaine Sisters (Geri, Margie, and Bea), Martin Block.

Orchestra: Mitchell Ayres.

Sponsor: Chesterfield Cigarettes.

The Perry Como Show—Musical Variety—15 minutes—CBS—October 4, 1950 - June 24, 1955.

Host: Perry Como.

Regulars: The Ray Charles Singers, The Fontaine Sisters.

Announcer: Frank Gallop.

Orchestra: Mitchell Ayres.

The Perry Como Show—Musical Variety—60 minutes—CBS—September 17, 1955 - June 6, 1959.

Host: Perry Como.

Regulars: The Fontaine Sisters, Mindy Carson, Don Adams, Sandy Stewart, Joey Heatherton, Kaye Ballard, Milt Kamen, The Ray Charles Singers, The Louis Da Pron Dancers.

Announcer: Frank Gallop.

Orchestra: Mitchell Ayres.

PERRY MASON

Crime Drama. Background: Los Angeles, California. The cases and courtroom defenses of criminal attorney Perry Mason. Based on the character created by Erle Stanley Gardner.

Versions:

Perry Mason—60 minutes—CBS—September 21, 1957 - September 4, 1966. 271 episodes. Syndicated.

CAST

Perry Mason	Raymond Burr
Della Street, his secretary-Girl Friday	Barbara Hale
Paul Drake, a private investigator	William Hopper
Lieutenant Arthur Tragg, L.A.P.D.	Ray Collins
Hamilton Burger, the state prosecuting attorney	William Talman
Lieutenant Steve Drumm, L.A.P.D.	Richard Anderson
Gertie Lade, Mason's receptionist	Connie Cezon
Margo, Drake's secretary	Paula Courtland
Drake's operator	Lyn Guild
David Gideon, a law student, Mason's associate	Karl Heid
Anderson, Mason's associate	Wesley Lau
Sgt. Brice	Lee Miller
Clay	Dan Tobin

Music: Richard Shores, Fred Steiner.

Executive Producer: Gail Patrick Jackson, Arthur Marks.

Producer: Art Seid, Sam White, Ben Brady.

Director: Jerry Hopper, John Peyser, Arthur Marks, Christian Nyby, Gordon Webb, Francis D. Lyon, Anton Leader, Lalso Benedek, Ted Post.

The New Adventures Of Perry Mason

-60 minutes—CBS—September 16, 1973 - January 27, 1974. 15 episodes.

CAST

Perry Mason	Monte Markham
Della Street	Sharon Acker
Hamilton Burger	Harry Guardino
Paul Drake	Albert Stratton
Lt. Arthur Tragg	Dane Clark
Gertie Lade	Brett Somers

Music: Earle Hagen; Lionel Newman.

PERRY PRESENTS

Musical Variety. A summer replacement for "The Perry Como Show."

Hosts: Teresa Brewer, Jaye P. Morgan, Tony Bennett.

Regulars: Hans Conried, The Four Lads, The Modernaires, The Mel Pahl Chorus, The Louis Da Pron Dancers.

Orchestra: Mitchell Ayres; Jimmy Lytell.

PERRY PRESENTS—60 minutes—NBC—June 13, 1959 - September 5, 1959.

PERSON TO PERSON

Interview. Cameras are established in the home of a celebrity, a world leader, or a political figure. Seated in a studio-set living room, the host chats with prominent people who relate aspects of their private lives.

Hosts: Edward R. Murrow (10/2/53 - 7/2/59).
Charles Collingwood (6/23/61 - 9/16/61).

Announcer: Bob Dixon.

Producer: Jesse Zousmer, Robert Sammon, Charles Hill, John Aaron.

PERSON TO PERSON—30 minutes—CBS—October 2, 1953 - July 2, 1959; June 23, 1961 - September 16, 1961.

PERSONAL APPEARANCE

Anthology. Rebroadcasts of dramas that were originally aired via other filmed anthology programs.

Included:

The Brush Roper. An elderly cowpoke struggles to prove his tall tales are true.

Starring: Walter Brennan.

The Girl Who Scared Men Off. A hillbilly schoolmarm attempts to acquire the affections of her British exchange professor.

Starring: Phyllis Avery, Hans Conried.

Waiting House. The story of a young woman's fears about moving into a house with an accident reputation.

Starring: Phyllis Kirk, Paul Langton, Dorothy Green.

PERSONAL APPEARANCE—30 minutes—CBS—June 1958 - September 1958.

PERSONALITY

Game. Basis: The individual personalities of show business celebrities. Three celebrities appear, playing for members of the home audience (post card selection).

Round One: "Awareness." Celebrities have to determine how well they know each other. The host reads one question, which refers to one of the celebrities, and reveals three answers, only one of which is his. The remaining two players have to determine the correct response. A prerecorded video tape is played to reveal the answer. The manner of play is the same regarding the remaining two celebrities. Correct guesses score twenty-five dollars.

Round Two: "Self Public Image Awareness." Questions that were asked of a studio audience of three hundred regarding the celebrities, are restated, one at a time, with three possible answers, of which only one is correct. Celebrities have to determine the correct responses. Twenty-five dollars is scored for each correct guess.

Round Three: "Finale." A prominent personality is asked three questions (prerecorded on tape). The host reveals question one and three possible answers, one of which is correct. Celebrities have to determine the correct response. The tape is played to reveal the answers. Twenty-five dollars is scored for each correct guess.

The money each celebrity has accumulated is awarded to the home-audience players.

Host: Larry Blyden.

Announcer: Jack Clark.

PERSONALITY—30 minutes—NBC—July 3, 1967 - September 26, 1969. 500 tapes.

PERSONALITY PUZZLE

Game. Four competing contestants who comprise the panel. Seated with their backs to a celebrity guest, panelists are handed articles of clothing and tools of their guest's trade. Through their examination and indirect question and answer probe rounds, panelists have to establish the celebrity's identity. Correct identifications score points. Winners, who receive merchandise prizes, are the highest point scorers.

The Persuaders. Tony Curtis and Roger Moore. *Courtesy Independent Television Corporation; an ATV Company.*

Hosts: John Conte; Robert Alda.

PERSONALITY PUZZLE—30 minutes—ABC 1953.

PERSPECTIVE ON GREATNESS

Documentary. Through film clips and interviews, the lives of celebrated individuals are recalled (e.g., Babe Ruth, John Wayne, Barbara Stanwyck, Lee Marvin).

Host-Narrator: Pat O'Brien.

Music Score: Music for Films.

Producer-Director: Harry Rasky.

PERSPECTIVE ON GREATNESS—60 minutes—Syndicated 1961.

THE PERSUADERS

Adventure. Background: Europe. The hectic exploits of two handsome young playboys: Brett Sinclair, a wealthy and debonair British Lord; and Daniel Wilde, a self-made American millionaire from the Bronx. Tricked into becoming justice-seeking partners by a retired judge, Fulton, the two reluctant troubleshooters encounter beautiful women, misadventure, and trouble as they seek to uncover the facts behind the criminal cases that Judge Fulton feels warrant further investigation. Spiced with light humor. Produced in Europe by I.T.C.

CAST
Lord Brett Sinclair	Roger Moore
Daniel Wilde	Tony Curtis
Judge Fulton	Laurence Naismith

Music: John Barry.

THE PERSUADERS!—60 minutes—ABC—September 18, 1971 - June 14, 1972. 24 episodes. Syndicated.

PETE AND GLADYS

Comedy. Background: Los Angeles, California. The trials and tribulations of the Porters: Pete, an insurance salesman, and his beautiful but scatterbrained wife, Gladys. A spin-off from "December Bride." Portraying Gladys, Cara Williams became Pete's never-before-seen, but often-referred-to wife.

CAST
Gladys Porter	Cara Williams
Peter Porter	Harry Morgan
Hilda Crocker, their friend	Verna Felton
Peggy Briggs, the Porter's friend	Mina Kobb

Pete and Gladys. Harry Morgan and Cara Williams.

Ernie Briggs, her husband	Joe Mantell
Paul Porter, Pete's uncle	Gale Gordon
Howie, the Porters' friend	Alvy Moore
Alice, his wife	Barbara Stuart
Gladys's father	Ernest Truex
Bruce, Gladys's nephew, a college student who is residing with her	Bill Hinnait
Mr. Slocum, Pete's employer	Barry Kelly
Mrs. Slocum, his wife	Helen Kleeb
George Colton, a neighbor	Peter Leeds
Janet Colton, his wife	Shirley Mitchell

Music: Wilbur Hatch.

Producer: Devery Freeman, Parke Levy.

Director: James V. Kern.

PETE AND GLADYS—30 minutes—CBS—September 19, 1960 - September 10, 1962. Syndicated. 70 episodes.

PETE KELLY'S BLUES

Drama. Background: Kansas City during the 1920s. Events in the lawless era of prohibition and gangsterism as seen through the eyes of Pete Kelly, coronet player, and leader of "The Big Seven," a jazz band that steadily plays at 17 Cherry Street, a brownstone-turned-funeral-parlor-turned-speakeasy. Based on the motion picture.

CAST
Pete Kelly	William Reynolds
Savannah Brown, the band's songstress	Connee Boswell
George Lupo, the club owner	Phil Gordon
Police Officer Johnny Cassino	Anthony Eisley

The Band: Johnny Silver, Thann Wyenn, Fred Beems, Rickey Allen, Dick Cathcart.

Music for the club scenes: The Matty Matlock Combo.

Background Music: Frank Comstock.

Off-screen coronet player for Kelly: Dick Cathcart.

PETE KELLY'S BLUES—30 minutes—NBC—April 5, 1959 - September 4, 1959. 13 episodes. Syndicated.

PETE SMITH SPECIALTIES

Comedy. Theatrical shorts. Humorous glimpses depicting the problems that befall people in everyday life.

Narrator: Pete Smith.

CAST
Dave O'Brien, Don DeFore.

PETE SMITH SPECIALTIES—10 minutes—Syndicated 1968. 101 episodes.

THE PETER AND MARY SHOW

Comedy. A domestic comedy series that focuses on the misadventures of a man, his wife, and a friend who "sort of comes for dinner and stays on to become a perpetual scavenger."

CAST
Peter, the husband	Peter Lind Hayes
Mary, his wife	Mary Healy
The friend	Claude Stroud
Their housekeeper	Mary Wickes

Music: Bert Farber.

Producer: Allen Ducovny.

Director: Theodore Sills.

THE PETER AND MARY SHOW—30 minutes—NBC 1950.

PETER GUNN

Crime Drama. Background: Los Angeles, California. The investigations of private detective Peter Gunn.

CAST
Peter Gunn	Craig Stevens
Edie Hart, his girlfriend, a	

singer at Mother's
Night Club   Lola Albright
Lieutenant Jacoby   Herschel Bernardi
Mother, the nightclub
    owner   Hope Emerson
                     Minerva Urecal
Leslie   James Lamphier
Emmett   Bill 'Chadney

Gunn's hangout: Mother's, a waterfront nightclub.

Music: Henry Mancini.

Producer: Blake Edwards.

Gunn's Address: 351 Ellis Park Road.

PETER GUNN—30 minutes—NBC—
September 22, 1958 - September
1960. ABC—30 minutes—October 3,
1960 - September 21, 1961. 114
episodes. Syndicated.

THE PETER LIND HAYES SHOW

Musical Variety.

Host: Peter Lind Hayes.

Regulars: Mary Healy, Don Cherry,
    John Bubbles, The Four Voices,
    The Malagon Sisters.

Orchestra: Bert Farber.

THE PETER LIND HAYES SHOW—
60 minutes—ABC—October 31, 1958 -
April 10, 1959.

PETER LOVES MARY

Comedy. Background: Connecticut,
the residence of Peter and Mary
Lindsey, a show-business couple, and
their children Leslie and Steve. Stories
depict Peter and Mary's attempts to
divide their time between a career on
Broadway and a home life in the
country.

CAST
Peter Lindsey   Peter Lind Hayes
Mary Lindsey   Mary Healy
Leslie Lindsey   Merry Martin
Steve Lindsey   Gil Smith
Wilma, their
    housekeeper   Bea Benaderet
Happy Richman, their
    agent   Alan Reed
Charlie, Wilma's boy-
    friend   Arch Johnson

Music: Bert Farber.

PETER LOVES MARY—30 minutes
—NBC—October 12, 1960 - May 31,
1961. 32 episodes.

THE PETER MARSHALL VARIETY SHOW

Variety. Music, songs, interviews, and
comedy sketches.

Host: Peter Marshall.

Regulars: Rod Gist, Denny Evans, The
    Chapter 5.

Orchestra: Alan Copeland.

Choreographer: Kevin Carlisle.

Executive Producer: David Salzman.

Producer: Rocco Urbisci, Neil Mar-
    shall, Beth Uffner.

Director: Jeff Margolis.

THE PETER MARSHALL VARIETY
SHOW—90 minutes—Syndicated
1976.

PETER POTTER'S JUKE BOX JURY

Discussion. Guest Hollywood personalities judge and discuss the merits of
just and/or prereleased recordings;
"Will it be a hit (Bong!) or a miss
(Clunk!)."

Host: Peter Potter.

Producer: Peter Potter.

Sponsor: Hazel Bishop Cosmetics.

PETER POTTER'S JUKE BOX
JURY—30 minutes—ABC—September
6, 1953 - October 4, 1953. 42 episodes.

THE PETER POTAMUS SHOW

Animated Cartoon. The global adventures of Peter Potamus, the purple
hippo, and his assistant, So So the
monkey.

Character segments:
"Breezly," the polar bear; "Sneezly,"
the seal; and "Yippie, Yappie, and
Yahooey," three mischievous dogs.

Characters' Voices
Peter Potamus   Daws Butler
So So   Don Messick
Breezly   Howard Morris
Sneezly   Mel Blanc
The Colonel   John Stephenson
Yippie   Hal Smith
Yahooey   Daws Butler
The King   Hal Smith

Music Supervision: Hoyt Curtin.

THE PETER POTAMUS SHOW—30
minutes—Syndicated 1964. A Hanna-
Barbera Production.

PETROCELLI

Crime Drama. Background: San
Remo, a Southwestern cattle town.
The cases and courtroom defenses of
Tony Petrocelli, an Italian, Harvard-
educated attorney.

CAST
Tony Petrocelli   Barry Newman
Maggie Petrocelli, his
    wife   Susan Howard
Pete Toley, his
    investigator   Albert Salmi
Frank Kaiser, the assis-
    tant D.A.   Michael Bell
Lt. John Clifford   David Huddleston

Music: Lalo Schifrin.

Executive Producer: Thomas L. Mil-
    ler, Howard Milkis.

Producer: Leonard Katzman.

PETROCELLI—60 minutes—NBC—
September 11, 1974 - March 2, 1976.
48 episodes.

THE PET SET

Discussion. Discussions concerning pet
care, ecology, and wildlife preserva-
tion.

Hostess: Betty White.

Assistants: Ralph Helfer, of Africa,
    U.S.A. (Calif.); Dare Miller, a dog
    psychiatrist.

Announcer: Allen Ludden.

Appearing: Doris Day, Mary Tyler
    Moore, Barbara Bain, Amanda
    Blake, Barbara Eden, Barbara
    Feldon, Lorne Greene, Paul
    Lynde, Bob Barker, Eva Gabor,
    Michael Landon, Johnny Mathis,
    Shirley Jones, James Stewart,
    Peter Lawford.

Music: Recorded.

THE PET SET—30 minutes—Syndicated 1971. 39 tapes.

PETTICOAT JUNCTION

Comedy. Background: Hooterville, a
rural farm valley. A depiction of life
in a small American town as seen
through the activities of Kate Bradley,
widow, proprietress of the Shady Rest
Hotel; her three beautiful daughters,
Billie Jo, Bobbie Jo, and Betty Jo; and
their uncle, the hotel's self-proclaimed
manager, Joe Carson.

Recurring story line: Discovering a
long-abandoned, but still operational
railroad branch line in Hooterville,
Homer Bedlow, the vice president of
the C.F. & W. Railroad, sets his goal
to scrap the Cannonball (an 1890s

steam engine, coal car, and mail/passenger coach) and discharge its engineers, Charlie Pratt and Floyd Smoot. Though continually encountering Kate's objections, Bedlow deviously schemes to achieve his goal in hopes of becoming a company big shot.

Changes: After crash landing near the Shady Rest Hotel, pilot Steve Elliott is rescued and nursed back to health by the Bradley girls. Seemingly in love with Billie Jo, he finds an attraction to and later marries Betty Jo. Establishing housekeeping a short distance from the hotel, they are presented with a daughter, Kathy Jo.

Bea Benaderet's untimely death in 1968 ended the characterization of Kate Bradley. The need for an understanding and comforting mother figure evolved the character of Janet Craig, a doctor who assumes the practice of the valley's retiring physician, Barton Stuart.

Stories depict: the struggles of young marrieds; Janet's attempts to acquire the trust of people who are distrustful of women doctors; Joe's endless money-making ventures; and the romantic heartaches of Billie Jo and Bobbie Jo.

Petticoat Junction. The original Bradley girls: (left to right) Pat Woodell (Bobbie Jo), Jeannine Riley (Billie Jo), and Linda Kaye (Betty Jo).

CAST

Kate Bradley	Bea Benaderet
Joe Carson	Edgar Buchanan
Billie Jo Bradley	Jeannine Riley
	Gunilla Hutton
	Meredith MacRae
Bobbie Jo Bradley	Pat Woodell
	Lori Saunders
Betty Jo Bradley (Elliott)	Linda Kaye Henning
Charley Pratt	Smiley Burnette
Floyd Smoot	Rufe Davis
Sam Drucker, the general-store owner	Frank Cady
Steve Elliott	Mike Minor
Homer Bedlow	Charles Lane
Norman Curtis, the railroad president	Roy Roberts
Fred Ziffel, a pig farmer	Hank Patterson
Ben Miller, a farmer	Tom Fadden
Newt Kiley, a farmer	Kay E. Kuter
Dr. Janet Craig	June Lockhart
Dr. Barton Stuart	Regis Toomey
Wendell Gibbs, the Cannonball engineer (later episodes)	Byron Foulger
Orrin Pike, the game warden	Jonathan Daly
Doris Ziffel, Fred's wife	Barbara Pepper
Selma Plout, Kate's nemesis, the woman determined to snag Steve for her daughter	Elvia Allman
Henrietta Plout, her daughter	Lynette Winter
Kathy Jo Elliott	Elaine Daniele Hubbel
Herby Bates, a friend of the girls	Don Washbrook

Also appearing: the "Green Acres" regulars:

Oliver Douglas, a farmer	Eddie Albert
Lisa Douglas, his wife	Eva Gabor
Eb Dawson, their handyman	Tom Lester
Cousin Mae*	Shirley Mitchell
Aunt Helen*	Rosemary DeCamp

Bradley family dog: Boy.

Music: Curt Massey.

*Both actresses temporarily replaced Bea Benaderet during her illness.

PETTICOAT JUNCTION—30 minutes—CBS—September 24, 1963 - September 12, 1970. 148 episodes. Syndicated.

PEYTON PLACE

Serial. Background: The small New England town of Peyton Place. Dramatic incidents in the lives of its townspeople.

CAST

Dr. Michael Rossi	Ed Nelson
Constance MacKenzie	Dorothy Malone
	Lola Albright
Alison MacKenzie	Mia Farrow
Rodney Harrington	Ryan O'Neal
Matthew Swain	Warner Anderson
Leslie Harrington	Paul Langton
Laura Brooks	Patricia Breslin
Betty Anderson	Barbara Parkins
Rita Jacks Harrington	Patricia Morrow
Norman Harrington	Christopher Connelly
David Schuster	William Smithers
Doris Schuster	Gail Kobe
Clair	Mariette Hartley
Elliot Carson (Connie's husband)	Tim O'Connor
Dr. Morton	Kent Smith
Julie Anderson	Kasey Rogers
George Anderson	Henry Beckman
Paul Hanley	Richard Evans
Kim	Kimberly Beck
Sherwood Price	Roy Roberts
Fowler	John Kerr
Martin Peyton	George Macready
Hannah Cord	Ruth Warrick
Steven Cord	James Douglas
Eli Carson	Frank Ferguson
Miss Nolan	Penelope Gillette
Lee	Stephen Oliver
Sandy	Lana Wood

Chris	Gary Haynes
Susan Winter	Diana Hyland
Dr. Miles	Percy Rodriques
Marsha Russell	Barbara Rush
Lew Miles	Glynn Turmann
The Reverend	
Mr. Bedford	Ted Hartley
Alma Miles	Ruby Dee
Joanne Walker	Jeanne Buckley
Carolyn Russell	Elizabeth Walker
Jeff	John Findlater
Tom	Robert Hogan
Fred	Joe Maross
Maggie Riggs	Florida Friebus
Nurse Jennifer Ivers	Myrna Fahey
Atwell	Mario Alcalde
Vickie	Judy Pace
Nurse Choate	Erin O'Brien-Moore
The Judge	Michael Strong
	John Lormer
Sgt. Walker	Morris Buchanan
Ada Jacks	Evelyn Scott
Jill	Joyce Jillson
Joe	Michael Christian
Stella	Lee Grant
Richard	Don Gordon
Russ	David Canary
Adrienne	Gena Rowlands
Eddie	Dan Duryea
Ted	Patrick Whyte
Mrs. Dowell	Heather Angel
Mrs. Chernak	Anna Karen
Donna Franklin	Sharon Hugueny
Gus	Bruce Gordon
Marian	Joan Blackman
Rachel	Leigh Taylor-Young
Chandler	John Kellogg
Joe	Don Quine

Music: Arthur Morton; Lionel Newman.

Additional Music: Cyril Mockridge, Lee Holdridge.

Music Theme: Franz Waxman.

Executive Producer: Paul Monash.

Producer: Everett Chambers, Richard Goldstone, Felix Feist, Richard DeRoy.

Director: Walter Doniger, Ted Post.

PEYTON PLACE—30 minutes—ABC

—September 15, 1964 - June 2, 1969. 514 episodes. Syndicated. Spin-off series: "Return to Peyton Place" (see title).

PHILBIN'S PEOPLE

Discussion. Five guest panelists discuss controversial topical issues.
Host: Regis Philbin.
Music: Recorded.

PHILBIN'S PEOPLE—90 minutes (12:30 a.m. -2:00 a.m)—1969-1970. Aired over the R.K.O. General owned stations in New York and Los Angeles.

PHILCO TELEVISION PLAYHOUSE

Anthology. Dramatic presentations. Created by Fred Coe.
Producer: Fred Coe, Gordon Duff, Garry Simpson.
Director: Delbert Mann, Fred Coe, Garry Simpson.
Sponsor: Philco (also Goodyear when broadcast as "The Philco-Goodyear Playhouse").

Included:

A Room in Paris. The tender love affair between a young American girl and an ex-G.I. studying abroad.

CAST
Stan Kagen: John Cassavetes; Janet Wells: Kathleen Maguire; Buzz Shapion: Al Markin.

The Takers. A police chief struggles to break the city's numbers racket.
CAST
Bernard Zysski: Ed Begley; Walter Gregg: Martin Balson; Edna Zysski: Peggy Allenby.

Gretel. The difficulties that arise when the son of a socially prominent family marries a teenage refugee.
CAST
Gretel: Eva Stein; Alan Putnam: Geoffrey Horne.

Marty. Paddy Chayefsky's heartwarming story of a lonely Bronx butcher who is goaded by his mother and friends to find himself a girl.
CAST
Marty: Rod Steiger; Clara: Nancy Marchand.

The Rich Boy. An adaption of the F. Scott Fitzgerald novel. The story of a neurotic flapper during the 1920s.
CAST
Phyllis Kirk (her first televison appearance).

Friday the 13th. Of the three women involved in an automboile accident, one is killed. When their husbands are informed, the identity of the dead woman is not revealed. Arriving at the hospital, the husbands find numerous obstacles as they attempt to discover who the dead woman is.
CAST
Brett Somers, Julie Follansbee, Rebecca Sands, Mark Roberts.

PHILCO TELEVISION PLAYHOUSE—60 minutes—NBC—October 3, 1948 - October 2, 1955. Also known as "The Philco-Goodyear Playhouse."

THE PHIL DONAHUE SHOW

Discussion. Discussions on the contemporary issues that affect women in their daily lives. Representative guests appear.
Host: Phil Donahue.
Music: Recorded.

THE PHIL DONAHUE SHOW—60 and 30 minute versions (depending on the local station)—Syndicated 1969.

PHIL SILVERS

Listed: The television programs of comedian Phil Silvers.

Welcome Aboard—Musical Variety—30 minutes—NBC 1948.
Host: Phil Silvers.
Featured: The Four Step Brothers.
Orchestra: Russ Morgan.
Producer-Director: Vic McLeod.
Sponsor: Admiral.

The Phil Silvers Arrow Show—Variety—30 minutes—NBC 1949.
Host: Phil Silvers.
Regulars: Connie Sawyer, Jerry Hausner, Len Hale, Herbert Coleman, The Mack Triplets.
Orchestra: Harry Salter.
Producer: Wes McKeeb.
Director: Hal Keith.
Sponsor: Arrow Shirts.

You'll Never Get Rich—Comedy—30 minutes—CBS—1955-1959. (See title.)

The Phil Silvers Show—Comedy—30 minutes—CBS—1963 - 1964.

The story of Harry Grafton, a factory foreman for Brink Enterprises; a conartist who manipulates men and machines for the benefit of himself.

CAST
Harry Grafton	Phil Silvers
Mr. Brink, Harry's employer	Stafford Repp
Harry's co-workers, dupes for the master	

mind:

Waluska	Herbie Faye
Lester	Jim Shane
Roxy	Pat Renella
Scarpitta	Norman Grabowski
	Henry Scott
Starkey	Steve Mitchell
Audrey, Harry's sister	Elena Verdugo
Susan, Audrey's daughter	Sandy Descher
Andy, Audrey's son	Ronnie Dapo

Music: Harry Geller.

Producer: Nat Hiken, Rod Amateau.

Note: Harry is also known to be associated with Osborne Industries.

PHILIP MARLOWE

Crime Drama. The investigations of private detective Philip Marlowe. Based on the character created by Raymond Chandler.

Starring: Philip Carey as Philip Marlowe.

PHILIP MARLOWE—30 minutes— ABC—September 29, 1959 - March 29, 1960. 26 episodes.

THE PHILIP MORRIS PLAYHOUSE

Anthology. Dramatic presentations.

Host: Charles Martin.

Announcer: Joe King.

Music: Ray Bloch.

Producer: Charles Martin.

Sponsor: Philip Morris Cigarettes.

THE PHILIP MORRIS PLAYHOUSE —30 minutes—CBS 1953.

PHOTOPLAY TIME

A series of thirty minute anthology dramas, produced by Perry Lafferty, and first broadcast on ABC in 1949.

PHYLLIS

Comedy. A spin-off from "The Mary Tyler Moore Show." Following the death of her husband, Lars, Phyllis Lindstrom, a self-satisfied woman, leaves Minneapolis and relocates to San Francisco where she acquires a job as assistant to commercial photographer Julie Erskine, the owner of Erskine's Commercial Photography Studio.

Stories relate the misadventures of a glamorous widow as she struggles to begin a new life.

CAST

Phyllis Lindstrom	Cloris Leachman
Bess Lindstrom, her daughter	Lisa Gerritsen
Julie Erskine	Barbara Colby
	Liz Torres
Leo Heatherton, the photographer employed by Julie	Richard Schaal
Audrey Dexter, Lars's scatterbrained mother (recently remarried)	Jane Rose
Jonathan Dexter, her husband	Henry Jones
Sally Dexter, Jonathan's mother	Judith Lowry
Dan Valenti, Phyllis' employer, later episodes*	Carmine Caridi
Leonard Marsh, Dan's associate	John Lawlor
Harriet Hastings, Leonard's assistant	Garn Stephens
Mark Valenti, Dan's nephew, married Bess on 2-27-77	Craig Wasson
Arthur Lanson, married Mother Dexter on 12-13-76	Burt Mustin
Van Horn, the park wino, Phyllis' confidante	Jack Elam

Music: Dick De Benedictis.

Executive Producer-Creator: Ed Weinberger, Stan Daniels.

Director: Jay Sandrich, Joan Darling, James Burrows, Harry Mastrogeorge, Asaad Keleda.

Phyllis's Address: 4482 Bayview Drive.

*A cast change during the second season dropped the Julie Erskine role. Julie, who supposedly married, closed the studio, leaving Phyllis unemployed—temporarily, that is—until she found employment as administrative assistant to Dan Valenti, a supervisor for the San Francisco Board of Supervision.

PHYLLIS—30 minutes—CBS—Premiered: September 8, 1975.

THE PHYLLIS DILLER SHOW

See title: "The Pruitts of Southampton."

PICCADILLY PALACE

Musical Variety. Songs and comedy sketches set against the background of

London's Piccadilly Palace.

Hostess: Millicent Martin.

Regulars: Eric Morecambe, Ernie Wise, The Paddy Stone Dancers, The Michael Sammes Singers.

Orchestra: Jack Parnell.

PICCADILLY PALACE—60 minutes —ABC—May 26, 1967 - September 9, 1967.

PICTURE THIS

Game. Two competing teams, each composed of one celebrity and one noncelebrity contestant. One member of each team is presented with a phrase that is concealed from his partner. The player then directs his partner by telling him what clues to draw to its identity. The "artist" first to identify the phrase receives points for his team. The game is played to enable all players to share equally on directing and drawing. Winners, the highest scoring teams, receive cash.

Host: Jerry Van Dyke.

Announcer: Art Baker.

Premiere guests: Gretchen Wyler, Orson Bean.

PICTURE THIS—30 minutes—CBS— June 25, 1963 - September 17, 1963.

THE PINK PANTHER SHOW

Animated Cartoon. The misadventures of a nontalking, nondiscouraging Pink Panther.

Hosts: Lennie Schultz; The Ritts Puppets.

Puppeteers: Paul and Mark Ritts.

Voices: John Byner, Dave Barry, Paul Frees, Rich Little, Marvin Miller, Athena Forde.

Music: William Lava, Doug Goodwin, Walter Green.

The Pink Panther theme: Henry Mancini.

THE PINK PANTHER—30 minutes— NBC—Premiered: September 6, 1969.

THE PINKY LEE SHOW

Variety. Music, songs, circus variety acts, and burlesque comedy skits.

Host: Pinky Lee, vaudeville comedian.

Regulars: Roberta Shore, Jane Howard (as Lily Chrysanthemum), Mel Knootz, Jimmy

Brown.

Music: The Charlie Couch Trio.

THE PINKY LEE SHOW—30 minutes
—NBC—1950 - 1955.

THE PIONEERS

Western Anthology. Retitled episodes
of "Death Valley Days."

Host: Will Rogers, Jr.

Music: Marlen Skiles.

Included:

Man on the Run. Broke, a tenant
attempts to sneak out of town and
away from his landlady.

CAST
Billy Nelson, Mary Field.

Death and Taxes. A young deputy
attempts to collect taxes from a gang
of outlaws.

CAST
Wayne Mallory, Jean Lewis.

The Million Dollar Wedding. The story
of a miner who is offered a large sum
of money to marry a homely waitress.

CAST
James Best, Virginia Lee.

THE PIONEERS—30 minutes—Syndicated 1964. 104 episodes.

PIP THE PIPER

Children. Mythical adventures set
against the background of Pipertown,
a magic and musical city in the clouds.

CAST
Pip the Piper   Jack Spear
Miss Merrynote   Phyllis Spear
Mr. Leader, a pompous
  buffoon   Lucien Kaminsky

PIP THE PIPER—30 minutes—ABC—
December 5, 1960 - June 6, 1961.
NBC—30 minutes—July 7, 1961 - September 1962. 52 episodes. Syndicated.

PISTOLS 'N' PETTICOATS

Western Comedy. Background:
Wretched, Colorado, 1871. The saga
of the gun-carrying Hanks family:
Henrietta, a widow; her father,
Andrew; his wife, referred to as
Grandma; and, opposed to violence,
Henrietta's twenty-one-year-old

daughter, Lucy. Stories depict their
attempts to maintain law and order in
a restless territory.

CAST
Henrietta (Hank)
  Hanks   Ann Sheridan
Andrew Hanks   Douglas Fowley
Lucy Hanks   Carole Wells
Grandma Hanks   Ruth McDevitt
Harold Sikes, the
  town's inept
  sheriff   Gary Vinson
Bernard Courtney,
  a land baron seeking
  to acquire the Hanks
  ranch   Robert Lowery
Mark Hangman, his
  gunman   Morgan Woodward
Jed Timmins, a
  lawyer working for
  Courtney   Stanley Adams
Eagle Shadow, Chief of
  the Kiowa
  Indians   Lon Chaney, Jr.
Gray Hawk, his
  son   Mark Cavell
Great Bear, Chief of the
  Atona
  Indians   Jay Silverheels
Little Bear, his
  son   Alex Hentlehoff
Town Drunk   Gil Lamb
Mrs. Tinsley, a
  townsperson   Eleanor Audley
The W.C. Fields type of
  character who hangs
  out in the bar   Bill Oberlin
Cyrus Breech, the double-
  crossing gun
  smuggler   Leo Gordon

Hanks family dog: Bowzer.

Music: George Tibbles; Jack Elliott;
  Stanley Wilson.

Executive Producer: Joe Connelly.

Producer: Irving Paley.

Director: Joe Connelly, Lou Watts

PISTOLS 'N' PETTICOATS—30 minutes—CBS—September 17, 1966 -
August 26, 1967. 26 episodes.

PITCHING HORSESHOES

See title: "Billy Roses Playbill."

PITFALL

Anthology. Dramatizations depicting
the plight of people caught in a web
of concealed danger.

Included:

Agent From Scotland Yard. A British
agent attempts to capture a wanted

criminal in San Francisco's Chinatown.

CAST
Lynn Bari, Patric Knowles.

The Hot Welcome. The story of an
eccentric old woman who changes the
destinies of a beautiful girl and two
men.

CAST
Gale Storm, Richard Denning, Elizabeth Patterson.

Hit and Run. The story of a man and
his attempts to clear himself of a false
hit-and-run charge.

CAST
Robert Hutton, Bonita Granville.

PITFALL—30 minutes—Syndicated
1955.

PLACES PLEASE

Variety. The setting is the backstage
of a television studio where the performances of bit players and chronies
from Broadway shows and nightclubs
are featured.

Host: Barry Wood.

Producer: Barry Wood.

Director: Ralph Levy.

PLACES PLEASE—15 minutes—CBS
1948.

PLACE THE FACE

Game. Specially selected contestants
are placed opposite someone from
their past. Through clues that are
provided by the host, players have to
associate each other's faces. Prizes are
awarded to the player who is first to
make the association.

Hosts: Jack Smith; Jack Paar; Bill
  Cullen

PLACE THE FACE—30 minutes—
CBS—August 27, 1953 - August 26,
1954. NBC—30 minutes—June 28,
1955 - September 1955.

THE PLAINCLOTHESMAN

Crime Drama. Background: New York
City. The subjective camera method is
incorporated to detail the investigations of a never-seen police lieutenant.
By use of the subjective camera,
which enacts emotion and becomes
the eyes of the lieutenant, the viewer
hears the actor's voice and experiences

situations as if he were actually present.

CAST

The Unseen Lieutenant	Ken Lynch
Sergeant Brady, his assistant	Jack Orrison

Producer: John L. Clark, John Clarol.

Director: William Marclare, Charles Harrell.

Sponsor: Edgeworth.

THE PLAINCLOTHESMAN—30 minutes—DuMont—September 1950 - September 12, 1954.

PLANET OF THE APES

Science Fiction Adventure. Penetrating a radioactive turbulence area, a United States Air Force space capsule passes through the time barrier and is hurled from the present 1988 to Earth in the year 3085.

In the crash-landing, one of the three astronauts aboard the craft is killed. Discovering themselves in an era ruled by intellectual apes (humans, treated as a lesser species, serve as laborers), the survivors, Alan Virdon and Pete Burke, are captured and imprisoned due to a fear among the ape leaders that awareness of their presence may inaugurate a revolt among the other humans.

Intrigued by the intelligence of the astronauts, Galen, an intellectual ape, befriends them, seeking to absorb their knowledge. However, distrustful of the astronauts, Veska, one of the ape leaders, plans their demise.

Finding their cell door unlocked, Pete and Alan escape. Arriving to speak with the astronauts, Galen spots Veska in the bushes with a gun aimed at the front door of the prison. As Pete and Alan open the door, Galen yells, warns them, and in the attempt to thwart Veska's plan, accidentally kills him. The three, branded dangerous fugitives, are sought for murder.

Stories depict their struggle for survival; and Pete and Alan's attempts, assisted by Galen, to return to the Earth of the 1980s. Adapted from the motion picture.

CAST

Galen	Roddy McDowall
Alan Virdon	Ron Harper
Pete Burke	James Naughton
Zaius, the ape leader	Booth Colman
Urko, his assistant	Mark Lenard
Veska (first episode)	Woodrow Parfrey

Music: Lalo Schifrin; Lionel Newman.

Executive Producer: Herbert Hirschman.

Producer: Stan Hough.

PLANET OF THE APES—60 minutes—CBS—September 13, 1974 - December 27, 1974. 13 episodes.

PLANET PATROL

Marionette Adventure. Era: Twenty-first-century Earth. The work of the agents of the Galasphere Patrol, an interplanetary police force established to protect the planets of a united solar system.

Characters:
Colonel Raeburn, the Galasphere leader
Captain Larry Dart
Husky, the Martian
Slim, the Venusian
Berridge, an enemy

PLANET PATROL—30 minutes—Syndicated 1963.

PLAYBOY'S PENTHOUSE
PLAYBOY AFTER DARK

Variety. Background: The Chicago penthouse apartment of *Playboy* magazine publisher Hugh Hefner. Guests, conversation, and entertainment.

Playboy's Penthouse—60 minutes—Syndicated 1960.

Host: Hugh Hefner.

Hostesses: The Playboy Bunnies.

Music: The Marty Ruberstein Trio.

Playboy After Dark—60 minutes—Syndicated 1969.

Host: Hugh Hefner.

Hostesses: The Playboy Bunnies.

Music: Provided by guests.

PLAY YOUR HUNCH

Game. Two husband-and-wife couples compete. Object: To solve problems by instinct. Three sets that pertain to one subject are displayed (e.g., three sets of eyes, X, Y, and Z). Couples have to determine the factor that distinguishes one from the others (e.g, "Which eyes are Marilyn Monroe's?"). The couple first to score three correct identifications are the winners and receive merchandise prizes.

Hosts: Merv Griffin; Robert Q. Lewis.

Assistant: Liz Gardner.

Producer: Bob Rowe, Ira Skutch.

Director: Mike Gargiulo.

PLAY YOUR HUNCH—30 minutes—CBS—June 30, 1958 - June 17, 1962. NBC—30 minutes—June 20, 1962 - September 27, 1963. Evening run: NBC—April 15, 1960 - June 25, 1960.

PLAYHOUSE

Anthology. Dramatic presentations.

Included:

Tourists Overnight. The story revolves around two women travelers who stop at a tourist home only to find themselves held captive by a criminal.

CAST

Dorothy Lee: Barbara Hale; Aunt Ella: Norma Varden; Eddie: Donald Murphy; Mrs. Welkins: Frances Bavier.

Ambitious Cop. The story concerns a policeman's efforts to overcome the resentment that occurs after he kills an old friend turned mobster in a gun duel.

CAST

Joe Devlin: Gene Evans; Arthur Healy: Dayton Lummis; Dr. Gerski: John Stephenson.

PLAYHOUSE—30 minutes—NBC—May 13, 1958 - July 1, 1958.

PLAYHOUSE '54

See title: "Pepsi Cola Playhouse."

PLAYHOUSE 90

Anthology. Dramatic presentations.

Music: George Smith; Robert Allen.

Producer: Martin Manulis, John Houseman, Russell Stoneham, Fred Coe, Arthur Penn.

Included:

Seven Against the Wall. Chicago, 1928. Al Capone's revenge against the Bugs Moran gang when they begin to muscle in on his lucrative bootleg business. A recreation of the famed St. Valentine's Day Massacre.

CAST

Al Capone: Paul Lambert; Bugs

Moran: Dennis Patrick; Nick Serrello: Frank Silvera; Pete Gusenberg: Dennis Cross.

A Marriage of Strangers. The trials and tribulations of a newlywed couple. Adapted from the play by Reginald Rose.

CAST
Red Buttons, Diana Lynn.

The Helen Morgan Story. A biographical drama based on the life of torch singer Helen Morgan.

CAST
Helen Morgan: Polly Bergen.

Rumors of Evening. England, World War II. The story of U.S. Air Force Captain Neil Dameron and his attempts to impress a girl in a visiting U.S.O. show.

CAST
Capt. Neil Dameron: John Kerr; Sidney Cantrell: Barbara Bel Geddes; General Strayer: Robert F. Simon; Irma-Jean Deever: Pat Hitchcock; Major Woulman: Robert Loggia.

PLAYHOUSE 90—90 minutes—CBS— October 4, 1956 - September 19, 1961.

PLAYHOUSE OF MYSTERY

Anthology. Rebroadcasts of mystery dramas that were originally aired via "Schlitz Playhouse of Stars."

Included:

Vol Turio Investigates. The story of a suave jewel thief and his attempts to track down three accomplices after a jewel robery.

CAST
Basil Rathbone, Edward Ashley, Melville Cooper.

The Menace of Hasty Heights. The story of a woman who is held hostage in her home by an escaped criminal.

CAST
Jean Hagen, Steve Cochran, Kent Taylor.

The Quiet Stranger. When the new school teacher arrives in Three Forks, he discovers that the school has burned down and that the citizens have done nothing about it. The story relates his struggles to rebuild it.

CAST
George Montgomery, Forrest Tucker, Bobby Clark.

PLAYHOUSE OF MYSTERY—60 minutes—CBS—September 3, 1957 - September 24, 1957.

PLAYHOUSE OF STARS

Anthology. Dramatic presentations.

Hostess: Irene Dunne.

PLAYHOUSE OF STARS—30 minutes—CBS—May 30, 1952 - September 1952.

PLAYHOUSE OF STARS

Anthology. Rebroadcasts of dramas that were originally aired via other filmed anthology programs.

Included:

O'Connor and the Blue-Eyed Felon. The story of a man, alone in his fishing lodge, who is confronted by a girl intent on shooting him for a past grievance.

CAST
Diana Lynn, Chuck Connors, Bob Nichols.

The Breaking Point. The story of a man and wife, the owner-operators of a service-station café The husband is satisfied; the wife is not and constantly complains about the situation, hoping he'll sell the business so they can begin life elsewhere.

CAST
Carolyn Jones, Dane Clark, Doris Singleton, Philip Reed.

The Night They Won the Oscar. The story of a movie director and his attempts to save his rocky marriage.

CAST
Richard Carlson, June Lockhart, Hayden Rorke, Dorothy Green.

PLAYHOUSE OF STARS—30 minutes—NBC—June 1960 - September 1960.

PLAY OF THE WEEK

Anthology. Dramatic presentations.

Included:

Archy and Mehitabel. A musical fantasy. A pensive cockroach with a flair for free verse tries to reform his flamboyant friend, a cat with a penchant for free love.

CAST
Tammy Grimes, Eddie Bracken, Jules Munshin.

Mary Stuart. The dramatic story of Mary, the deposed Queen of Scotland.

CAST
Signe Hasso, Eva Le Gallienne, Staats Cotsworth.

The Grass Harp. The story of an old lady, a rebellious boy, and a Negro servant who, finding themselves badgered by the forces of order, take to a home in the trees.

CAST
Lillian Gish, Nick Hyams, Russell Collins, Georgia Burke.

PLAY OF THE WEEK—2 hours— Syndicated 1960.

PLAYWRIGHTS '55 ('56)

Anthology. Dramatic adaptations of stories by famous authors. Broadcast live from New York.

Producer: Fred Coe.

Director: Delbert Mann, Arthur Penn, Vincent Donehue.

Sponsor: Pontiac.

Included:

The Battler. The story concerns a young fighter's decision not to enter the ring after he meets a down-and-out former champ. Adapted from Ernest Hemmingway's story by A.E. Hockner and Sidney Carroll.

Starring: Paul Newman, Phyllis Kirk.

The Answer. During a nuclear-bomb test, an army general discovers that an angel has been shot down and mortally wounded. Feeling that the angel was bearing an important message, the story follows his efforts to find "The Answer." Adapted from Philip Wylie's story by Donald Davidson.

Starring: Paul Douglas, Nina Foch, Albert Dekker, Conrad Nagel.

PLAYWRIGHTS '55 ('56)—60 minutes—NBC—October 4, 1955 - June 19, 1956.

PLEASE DON'T EAT THE DAISIES

Comedy. Background: 228 Circle Avenue, Ridgemont, New York. The trials and tribulations of the Nash family: James, an English professor at Ridgemont College; his wife, Joan, a free-lance magazine writer (pen name: Joan Holliday); and their children: Kyle, Joel, and Trevor and Tracy (twins). Based on the book by Jean Kerr.

CAST

Joan Nash	Patricia Crowley
Jim Nash	Mark Miller
Kyle Nash	Kim Tyler
Joel Nash	Brian Nash
Tracy Nash	Joe Fithian
Trevor Nash	Jeff Fithian
Marge Thorton, their neighbor	Shirley Mitchell
Herb Thorton, her husband, a lawyer	King Donovan
Ed Hewley, the repairman	Dub Taylor
Gerald Carter, the college dean	Bill Quinn
Martha O'Reilly, the Nash maid	Ellen Corby
Ethel Carter, the dean's wife	Jean VanderPyl

Nash family dog: Lad (a sheep dog).

Music: Jeff Alexander.

Producer: Paul West.

Director: Peter Baldwin, David Alexander, Richard Whorf, Tay Garnett, Gary Nelson, John Erman, Alvin Ganzer.

PLEASE DON'T EAT THE DAISIES—30 minutes—NBC—September 14, 1965 - September 2, 1967. 58 episodes. Syndicated.

P.M. EAST . . . P.M. WEST

Talk-Variety. Specific topics of discussion (e.g., violence, Rock and Roll, jazz) are coupled with entertainment performances. Broadcast from both New York and San Francisco.

Hosts (New York): Mike Wallace, Joyce Davidson.

Host (San Francisco): Terrence O'Flaherty.

P.M. EAST . . . P.M. WEST—90 minutes—Syndicated—1960 - 1961. Withdrawn.

POLICE CALL

Anthology. Dramatizations based on the files of various law enforcement agencies throughout the country.

Included:

The Alleghanny County Story. The story of detective James McGinley and his attempts to track down a ring of blackmailers.

Starring: Russell Hardie.

The Dallas, Texas Story. The story of Sheriff Decker and his attempts to track down confidence men who are swindling elderly women.

Starring: Robert Emhardt.

Switzerland. Police efforts to track down a handsome ladies man who earns his living by swindling the women who fall for him.

Starring: Philip Reed, Adam Gannette, Anna Korda.

POLICE CALL—30 minutes—Syndicated 1955.

POLICE STORY

Anthology. Criminal case dramatizations based on the files of the Nashville, Tennessee Police Department.

Narrator: Norman Rose.

POLICE STORY—30 minutes—CBS 1952.

POLICE STORY

Anthology. Dramatizations depicting the day-to-day struggles of police officers. Based on the files of various law-enforcement agencies throughout the country.

Music: Jack Elliott, Allyn Ferguson, Jerry Goldsmith, Richard Markowitz.

Executive Producer: Stanley Kallis.

Producer: Liam O'Brien, David Gerber, Christopher Morgan.

Director: Corey Allen, Vince Edwards, Barry Shear, Gary Nelson, Seymour Robbie, Alex March, Lee H. Katzin, Arthur Kean, John Badham.

Creator: Joseph Wambaugh.

Included:

Collison Course. The problems of an experimental patrol are depicted as a male officer, Vincent LaSorda, and a beautiful police woman, June Culhane, are teamed.

CAST
Vincent LaSorda: Hugh O'Brian; June Culhane: Sue Ane Langdon.

Dangerous Games. Posing as a producer, a vice-squad detective attempts to apprehend the leader of a prostitution racket.

CAST
Charlie Czonka: James Farentino; Janette Johnson: Elizabeth Ashley; Snake McKay: Fred Williamson.

The Big Walk. A realistic portrayal of the complex pressures, harassment, and dangers of the cop on the neighborhood beat.

CAST
Jack Bonner: Don Murray; Harriet Bonner: Dorothy Provine; Hecker: Noah Beery; Angela Wilson: Lynda Day George.

The Gamble. Posing as a prostitute, vice-squad detective Lisa Beaumont attempts to infiltrate and expose the ranks of a gambling syndicate. The pilot film for "Police Woman."

CAST
Lisa Beaumont: Angie Dickinson; Carl Vitalle: Joseph Campanella; Sgt. William Crowley: Bert Convy.

POLICE STORY—60 minutes—NBC—Premiered: October 2, 1973.

POLICE SURGEON

Crime Drama. Background: Toronto, Canada. The cases of Simon Locke, a surgeon with the Emergency Medical Unit of the Metropolitan Police Department, a "doctor with the mind of a detective." A spin-off from "Dr. Simon Locke."

CAST

Dr. Simon Locke	Sam Groom
Lt. Dan Palmer	Len Birman
Lt. Jack Gordon	Larry Mann
Police radio dispatcher	Nerene Virgin
Tony, Locke's ambulance driver	Marc Hebet

Music: Lewis Helkman; Score Productions.

POLICE SURGEON—30 minutes—Syndicated 1972. 76 episodes.

POLICE WOMAN

Crime Drama. Background: Los Angeles, California. The cases of Sergeant Suzanne "Pepper" Anderson, divorcée, a sensual, brassy, compassionate, sincere, and beautiful undercover police woman with the Criminal

Police Woman. Left to right: Angie Dickinson, Ed Bernard, Earl Holliman, Charles Dierkop.

Conspiracy division of the Los Angeles Police Department.

Stories, which are adult and open minded about sex and marriage, realistically depict the life of a police woman. A spin-off from "Police Story," wherein the pilot episode, "The Gamble," aired.

CAST

Sgt. Suzanne "Pepper" Anderson	Angie Dickinson
Sgt. William Crowley	Earl Holliman
Sgt. Pete Royster	Charles Dierkop
Sgt. Joe Styles	Ed Bernard
Lt. Paul Marsh	Val Bisoglio
Cheryl, Pepper's sister, enrolled at the Austin School for the Handicapped	Nichole Kallis

Music: Jerry Goldsmith; Morton Stevens; Geroge Romanis; Pete Rugolo; Jeff Alexander.

Executive Producer: David Gerber.

Producer: Douglas Benton.

Director: Barry Shear, John Newland, Alf Kjellin, Corey Allen, Alvin Ganzer, Alexander Singer, Douglas Benton, Herschel Daugherty, Barry Crane, Robert Vaughn, David Moessinger.

Creator: Robert Collins.

Pepper's Address: 102 Crestview Drive.

Note: Pepper's first name is also known to be Lee Anne.

POLICE WOMAN—60 minutes—NBC —Premiered: September 13, 1974.

POLICE WOMAN DECOY

See title: "Decoy."

POLKA-GO-ROUND

Variety. Polka songs and dances.

Host: Bob Lewandowski.

Regulars: Carolyn De Zurick, Rusty Gill, Jimmy Hitchinson, Jack Cordaro, Lenny Druss, John Hunt, Lou Prout, Georgia Drake, The Polka Rounders, Tom Fouts, The Singing Waiters.

POLKA-GO-ROUND—60 minutes— ABC—June 23, 1958 - September 14, 1959.

POLKA PARTY

Variety. Polka songs and dances.

Host: Eddie Gronet.

Featured: Dolores Ann Duda.

Orchestra: Stan Jaworski; Al Siszeski.

POLKA PARTY—30 minutes—Syndicated 1958. Withdrawn.

POLKA TIME

Variety. Polka songs and dances.

Host: Bruno Junior Zienlinski.

Regulars: Carolyn De Zurik, The Polka Chips, The Kenal Siodmy Folk Dancers.

Music: Stan Wolowic's Seven Man Instrumental Group.

POLKA TIME—60 minutes—ABC— July 13, 1956 - August 31, 1956.

THE POLLY BERGEN SHOW

Musical Variety.

Hostess: Polly Bergen.

Orchestra: Luther Henderson, Jr.

Producer: Irving Mansfield.

THE POLLY BERGEN SHOW—30 minutes—NBC—September 21, 1957 - May 3, 1958.

PONDEROSA

See title: "Bonanza."

PONY EXPRESS

Western. Background: Sacramento, California, 1860s. The investigations of Brett Clark, a troubleshooter for the Central Overland Express Company, better know as the Pony Express.

CAST

Brett Clark	Grant Sullivan
Tom Clyde	Bill Cord
Donovan	Don Dorell

PONY EXPRESS—30 minutes—Syndicated 1960. 39 episodes.

POPEYE THE SAILOR

Animated Cartoon. The endless battle between love-hungry sailors Popeye and Bluto over the long-sought affections of Olive Oyl, a skinny, fickle woman. Their bickering usually begins verbally, then becomes violent as Popeye, the underdog, removes a can of spinach from his blouse, devours it, acquires incredible strength, and, as good triumphs over evil, deals justice

Popeye The Sailor. © *King Features Syndicate, Inc.*

to Bluto.

Characters' Voices

Popeye	Det Poppen
	Floyd Buckley
	Jack Mercer
Bluto	Jackson Beck
Olive Oyl	Olive La Moy
	Mae Questel
Wimpy, a friend, forever seeking hamburgers	Charles Lawrence
	Jack Mercer
Swee' pea, Olive's nephew	Mae Questel
Shorty, a sailor friend of Popeye's	Arnold Stang

Additional characters: Popeye's nephews: Pupeye, Peepeye, Poopeye, Pipeye; Popeye's father: Grandpappy; Popeye's dog: The visible/invisible Jeep.

Music: Winston Sharples.

Additional Music: Sam Lerner, Sammy Timberg, Bob Loymberg, Tot Seymour, Vee Lawnhurst.

Producer: Associated Artists Productions.

Director: Seymour Kenietel, I. Sparber, Dave Fleischer.

POPEYE THE SAILOR—06 minutes —Syndicated 1958. 200 Theatrical Cartoons, 1933-1954; 220 televison produced episodes, 1961-1963.

POP GOES THE COUNTRY

Musical Variety. Performances by Country and Western entertainers.

Host: Ralph Emery.

Music: Jim Malloy.

POP GOES THE COUNTRY—30 minutes—Syndicated 1974.

POPPI

Comedy. Background: New York City. The misadventures of Abraham Rodriquez, the Puerto Rican widower of two children, Abraham Junior and Luis, as he struggles to hold down several part time jobs and raise his mischievous sons.

CAST

Abraham Rodriquez	Hector Elizondo
Abraham Rodriquez, Jr.	Anthony Perez
Luis Rodriquez	Dennis Vasquez

Lupe, Abraham's girlfriend	Edith Diaz
Angelo Maggio, Abraham's friend	Lou Criscuolo

Music: George Del Barrio.

Executive Producer: Herbert B. Leonard, Arne Sultan.

Producer: Nick Anderson, A.J. Nelson.

Director: Hy Averback, Al Viola.

Creator: Tina and Lester Pine.

POPPI—30 minutes—CBS—January 20, 1976 - March 2, 1976; July 20, 1976 - August 24, 1976.

THE PORKY PIG SHOW

Animated Cartoon. The misadventures of the stuttering Porky Pig.

Additional segments: "Daffy Duck"; "Bugs Bunny"; "Sylvester and Tweety"; "Foghorn Leghorn"; "Pepe le Pew."

Voice characterizations: Mel Blanc.

Music: Carl Stalling; Milt Franklin.

THE PORKY PIG SHOW—30 minutes—ABC—1964 - 1965. Syndicated. Also known as "Porky Pig and His Friends."

THE PORTER WAGONER SHOW

Musical Variety. Background: The Wagon House. Performances by Country and Western entertainers.

Host: Porter Wagoner.

Regulars: Dolly Parton, Bruce Osborne, Barbara Lee, Spec Rose.

Announcer: Don Housner.

Music: The Wagon Masters.

THE PORTER WAGONER SHOW— 30 minutes—Syndicated 1960.

PORTIA FACES LIFE

Serial. The dramatic story of Portia Manning, attorney and mother, who struggles to divide her time between the demands of work and the necessities of a home and a family.

CAST

Portia Manning	Fran Carlon
	Frances Reid
Walter Manning, her husband	Karl Swenson
	Donald Woods
Shirley Manning, their daughter	Ginger McManus
	Renne Jarrett
Dick Manning, their son	Charles Taylor
Karl Manning, Walter's brother	Patrick O'Neal

Also: Elizabeth York, Richard Kendrick.

Music: Tony Mottola.

PORTIA FACES LIFE—15 minutes—

Portia Faces Life. Left to right: Charles Taylor, Fran Carlon, Ginger McManus, Karl Swenson.

CBS—April 4, 1954 - March 11, 1955.
Also known as: "The Inner Flame."

PORTRAIT

Celebrity Interview.

Host: Harry Reasoner.

PORTRAIT—30 minutes—CBS—January 30, 1963 - September 13, 1963.

THE PRACTICE

Comedy. Background: New York City. The trials and tribulations of Dr. Jules Bedford, a gruff but lovable West Side Manhattan physician. The series focuses on the running battle that exists between Jules, who practices on the Lower East Side, and his son, Dr. David Bedford, a Park Avenue physician, who objects to his father's methods and longs for him to join him on Park Avenue.

CAST
Dr. Jules Bedford   Danny Thomas
Dr. David Bedford   David Spielberg
Jenny Bedford, David's
  wife   Shelley Fabares
Molly Gibbons, Jule's
  nurse   Dena Dietrich
Helen, Jule's
  receptionist   Didi Conn
Paul Bedford, David and
  Jenny's son   Allen Price
Tony Bedford, David and
  Jenny's son   Damon Raskin
Nate, the hospital restaurant
  waiter   Sam Laws
Dr. Roland Caine, David's
  partner   John Byner
Lenny, an intern   Mike Evans
Dr. Byron Fisk   Barry Gordon

Music: David Shire, James DiPasquale.

Executive Producer: Danny Thomas, Paul Junger Witt.

Producer: Steve Gordon, Tony Thomas.

Director: Lee Philips, Noam Pitlik, Bill Persky, Tony Mordente, George Tyne.

Creator: Steve Gordon.

THE PRACTICE—30 minutes—NBC—January 30, 1976 - August 6, 1976; October 13, 1976 - January 20, 1977.

PREMIERE

Pilot Films. Proposed dramas for the 1968-1969 season.

Included:

Lassiter. A magazine writer's probe of corruption in a large Midwestern city.

CAST
Lassiter: Burt Reynolds; Stan Marchek: Cameron Mitchell; Joan Mears: Sharon Farrell; Russ Faine: James MacArthur.

The Search. Background: Switzerland. Probing a supposed accidental drowning, an American private detective attempts to prove that it was murder.

CAST
Paul Cannon: Mark Miller; Inspector Sheppard: Barry Foster; Molly: Julie Sommars.

Call to Danger. A federal troubleshooter's efforts to retrieve stolen Treasury Department currency plates. The pilot film for "Mission: Impossible." (Filmed in 1966.)

CAST
Jim Kingsley: Peter Graves; Paul Wilkins: James Gregory; John Hinderson: Dan Travanty; Andre Kellman: Albert Paulsen.

Crisis. A psychiatrist struggles to locate a man who phones him and threatens to commit suicide.

CAST
Frank Chandler: Carl Betz; Lisa Edwards: Susan Strasberg; Art Winters: Robert Drivas; June Fielding: Davey Davison.

PREMIERE—60 minutes—CBS—July 1, 1968 - September 9, 1968. Rebroadcast as "Suspense Theatre"—60 minutes—CBS—May 24, 1971 - July 5, 1971.

PREVIEW

Previews of forthcoming Broadway plays and films. Hosts: Tex McCrary, Jinx Falkenberg. 30 minutes—CBS 1949.

PREVIEW THEATRE

Pilot Films. Proposed comedy series for the 1961-1962 season.

Included:

I Married a Dog. Marrying Joyce Nicoll, Peter Chance suddenly finds his life hindered by Noah, her extremely jealous French poodle.

CAST
Peter Chance: Hal March; Joyce Nicoll: Marcia Henderson; Madge Kellogg: Mary Carver.

Five's a Family. The misadventures of Harry Canover, a retired detective who can't resist the urge to solve crimes.

CAST
Harry Canover: Joe E. Brown; Bill Hewitt: Dick Foran; Peg Hewitt: Hollis Irving; Bobby Hewitt: Michael Petit.

Picture Window. The trials and tribulations of a suburban couple.

CAST
Joe Saxon: Charles Stewart; Amy Saxon: Mary La Roche.

Innocent James. The misadventures of a footloose, free-lance magazine writer.

CAST
Innocent James: Chris Warfield; Prudence Brown: Merry Anders.

PREVIEW THEATRE—30 minutes—CBS—July 14, 1961 - September 1961.

PREVIEW TONIGHT

Pilot Films. Proposed series for the 1966-1967 season.

The Complete Series:

Somewhere in Italy, Company B. Comedy. Background: Italy, World War II. The misadventures of a foul-up squadron cut off from its battalion command.

CAST
Lt. John Leahy: Robert Reed; Sgt. Wilkie Krantz: Harold J. Stone; Paulo Pietri: Vassili Lambrinos; Selena: Barbara Shelly.

Roaring Camp. Western. Background: Roaring Camp, a mining town struck by gold fever. Teaming with a U.S. marshall, a gunslinger attempts to maintain law and order.

CAST
Marshall Walker: Richard Bradford; Cain: Jim McMullan; Rachel: Katherine Justice; Angus: Ian Hendry.

Great Bible Adventures. "Seven Rich Years...And Seven Lean." The dramatic story of Joseph, tracing his rise out of bondage to his reign as the pharaoh's minister.

CAST

Joseph: Hugh O'Brian; Pharaoh: Joseph Wiseman; Aton: Eduardo Ciannelli; Asenath: Katherine Ross.

Program Open:

Announcer: "Each year many of the new shows developed for television fail to make the network grade even though they are entertaining and well produced. Tonight's pilot film is one of these. We invite you behind the scenes to see what you think of [name of show] on Preview Tonight. . . ."

PREVIEW TONIGHT—60 minutes—ABC—August 14, 1966 - September 11, 1966.

THE PRICE IS RIGHT

Game. Four studio-audience members compete. The game varies greatly in presentaiton, but the basic format for each version and each segment is to price merchandise items exactly or as close as possible to the manufacturer's suggested retail selling price. Players who surpass the selling price forfeit their chance to win that particular item; the contestant whose bid comes closest to the selling price receives the item as her gift.

Versions:

The Price Is Right—30 minutes—NBC—September 1956 - September 9, 1963; ABC—30 minutes—September 18, 1963 - September 3, 1965.

Host: Bill Cullen, Jack Clark.

Assistants: Beverly Bently, Toni Wallace, June Ferguson.

The New Price Is Right—30 minutes—CBS—September 4, 1972 - October 31, 1975. 60 minutes—CBS—Premiered: November 3, 1975.

Host: Bob Barker.

Assistants: Nancy Myers, Pamela Parker.

Models: Anitra Ford, Holly Hallstrom, Janice Pennington, Dian Parkinson.

Announcer: Johnny Olsen.

Music: Ed Kalehoff.

The New Price Is Right—30 minutes—Syndicated 1972.

Host: Dennis James.

Assistants: Nancy Myers, Pamela Parker.

Models: Anitra Ford, Holly Hallstrom,

Janice Pennington, Dian Parkinson.

Announcer: Johnny Olsen.

Music: Ed Kalehoff.

PRIDE OF THE FAMILY

Comedy. The trials and tribulations of the Morrison family: Albie, the advertising head of a small-town newspaper; his wife, Catherine; their daughter, Ann; and their son, Albie, Jr.

CAST

Albie Morrison	Paul Hartman
Catherine Morrison	Fay Wray
Ann Morrison	Natalie Wood
Albie Morrison, Jr.	Bobby Hyatt

PRIDE OF THE FAMILY—30 minutes—ABC—October 9, 1953 - September 24, 1954. 40 episodes. Also known as "The Paul Hartman Show."

PRIMUS

Adventure. Background: Nassau. The cases of oceanographer Carter Primus, a global underwater troubleshooter.

His equipment: Big Kate, an underwater robot; the *Pegasus,* an exploration and photography vehicle; *Tegtight,* his operational base; *Dagat,* the mother ship; and the *Orka,* his patrol boat.

CAST

Carter Primus	Robert Brown
Toni Hyden, his assistant	Eva Renzi
Charlie Kingman, his assistant	Will Kuluva

Narrator: Robert Brown.

Music: Leonard Rosenman.

PRIMUS—30 minutes—Syndicated 1971. 26 episodes.

PRINCE DINOSAUR

A science fiction series, set on a prehistoric island in the South Pacific, that details the exploits of a jungle boy as he battles evil. 30 minutes—Syndicated 1967, 26 episodes.

PRINCE PLANET

Animated Cartoon. Background: Twenty-first-century Earth; the city of New Metropolis. The battle against evil as undertaken by Prince Planet, a youngster from the Universal Peace Corps of the planet Radion. Produced in Japan.

Characters:

Prince Planet, known as Bobby
Diana, his girlfriend, forever in distress
Haja Baba, a friend
Dynamo, a friend
Warlock, the evil Martian

PRINCE PLANET—30 minutes—Syndicated 1966. 52 episodes. Also known as "The Prince of Planets."

THE PRISONER

Adventure. Assigned to locate a missing scientist, secret agent John Drake* permits him to defect to Russia when he discovers the nature of the doctor's work: to complete a deadly mind transference device. Returning to England and reprimanded for his actions, Drake resigns, feeling it is a matter of principal.

Leaving the Ministry building, he is unknowingly followed by a mysterious black-clothed gentleman. Entering the hallway of the apartment, the gentleman places a nozzle in the keyhole and releases gas that knocks Drake unconscious.

Awakening, Drake finds himself in a strange room. He discovers that he is no longer a man, but a number—Number Six—and the prisoner of a self-contained community known as The Village, a flowery, courtyarded, fantasylike area boarded by mountains and ocean—a place from which there is no escape.

Continuing his probe, he enters the Green Dome and meets one of the leaders, Number Two. Though unable to discover who his captors are, or where The Village is, he learns the reason for his abduction: "It's a question of your resignation. . .a lot of people are curious about. . .why you suddenly left. . .the information in your head is priceless. . .a man like you is worth a great deal on the open market. . .it's my job to check your motives."

Stories depict his attempts to discover the identity of Number One and who his captors are; and his desperate attempts to escape from The Village.

Last episode. Proving himself extraordinary—unable to be broken by exhaustive mind-bending experiments—Drake, after defeating Number Two, is led to an area below The Village. There, he is presented to an assembly, recognized as an individual—a man superior to them—and

*The agent's name is not revealed, but is assumed to be John Drake as "The Prisoner" is a continuation from the last episode of "Secret Agent."

given a choice: leave or remain and lead the people of The Village. Undecided, he is taken to see Number One.

Met by his only friend, The Silent Butler, he is led through a heavily guarded hallway and to a room, containing highly complex machinery, that is designed to destroy him. Discovering that the room is a trap, he, The Silent Butler, and two system revolters, Number Two (imprisoned for failing to defeat Number Six), and Number Forty-eight join forces. Overpowering the guards, the machines are disengaged and reset to destruct. Boarding a truck, the four escape through an underground tunnel as the inner workings of The Village are destroyed.

Approaching London** the truck stops. Numbers Two and Forty-eight depart; Number Six, a free man, and The Silent Butler remain a team.

Intriguing, highly imaginative, and at times complex, "The Prisoner" requires one's full and uninterrupted attention to appreciate it.

CAST

Number Six	Patrick McGoohan
The Silent Butler	Angelo Muscat
Number Two	Colin Gordon
	Clifford Evans
	Mary Morris
	John Sharpe
	Peter Wyngarde
	Guy Doleman
	Leo McKern
Number Forty-eight	Alexis Kanner
The President	Kenneth Griffith

Orchestra: Albert Elms.

Prisoner Theme: Ron Grainer.

**Though not revealed, the location of The Village is assumed to be within fifty miles of London by the last episode. The series is filmed in North Wales.

THE PRISONER—60 minutes—CBS—June 1, 1968 - September 21, 1968. CBS—June 1969 - September 1969 (rebroadcasts). 17 episodes.

PRIVATE SECRETARY

Comedy. Background: New York City. The misadventures of Susie McNamara, private secretary to theatrical agent Peter Sands.

CAST

Susie McNamara	Ann Sothern
Peter Sands	Don Porter
Vi Praskins, the office receptionist	Ann Tyrrell
Cagey Calhoun, a rival talent agent	Jesse White
Sylvia, Susie's secretarial friend	Joan Banks
The drugstore boy	Joseph Nartocana

Producer: Jack Chertok.

Sponsor: American Tobacco.

PRIVATE SECRETARY—30 minutes—CBS—September 12, 1954 - September 10, 1957. 104 episodes. Syndicated title: "Susie.". Also known as "The Adventures of Susie."

PRIZE PERFORMANCE

Variety. Performances by undiscovered professional talent.

Hostess: Arlene Francis.

Regulars: Cedric Adams, Peter Donald.

PRIZE PERFORMANCE—30 minutes—CBS—July 3, 1950 - September 1950.

PRIZE STORY

Anthology. Dramatizations depicting the plight of people confronted with everyday emotional problems.

PRIZE STORY—30 minutes—NBC 1952.

PROBE

Discussion. In-depth discussions on worldly affairs.

Host: Dr. Albert E. Burke.

PROBE—30 minutes—Syndicated—1961 - 1964. Withdrawn.

PRODUCERS' CHOICE

Anthology. Dramatic presentations.

Included:

The Last Rodeo. The story concerns a girl who, after witnessing a fatal rodeo accident, attempts to convince her fiancé to give up his career as a rodeo performer.

Starring: Robert Horton, Nancy Olson, Stacy Harris, Claude Akins.

Battle for a Soul. The story of a man who plots revenge against his former fiancée for framing him for a jewel theft he never committed.

Starring: Ray Milland, Lisa Daniels.

Long Distance. Minutes before her husband's scheduled execution, a wife finds a letter that proves his innocence. The story concerns her hysteria as she tries to reach the governor.

Starring: Jessica Tandy, Isobel Elsom, Carl Benton Reid.

PRODUCERS' CHOICE—30 minutes—NBC—March 31, 1960 - September 22, 1960.

PRODUCERS' SHOWCASE

Anthology. Lavish adaptations of stories by noted authors.

Included:

Peter Pan. A musical adaptation of the Barrie fantasy. Peter Pan's battle against the evil Captain Hook.

CAST

Peter Pan: Mary Martin; Captain Hook: Cyril Ritchard.

Our Town. A musical adaptation of the Thornton Wilder play. The story of life in a small American town.

CAST

Eva Marie Saint, Paul Newman, Frank Sinatra.

Music: Sammy Cahn, James Van Heusen.

The Sleeping Beauty. An adaptation of the Sadler Wells Ballet. When a young girl is cursed to a lifetime of sleep, a handsome young prince is sought to awaken her.

CAST

Sleeping Beauty: Margot Fonteyn; Prince Charming: Michael Somes.

Jack and the Beanstalk. The story of a poor farm family and the problems that ensue when Jack, the son, trades their milk cow for some magic beans.

CAST

Joel Gray, Billy Gilbert, Celeste Holm, Peggy King, Cyril Ritchard, Dennis King.

PRODUCERS' SHOWCASE—60 and 90 minutes (depending on the production)—NBC—October 18, 1954 - June 24, 1957.

PROFESSIONAL FATHER

Comedy. The trials and tribulations of the Wilson family: Thomas, a child psychologist; his wife, Helen; and their two mischievous children, Kit and Twig.

CAST

Dr. Thomas Wilson	Steve Dunne
Helen Wilson	Barbara Billingsley
Kit Wilson	Beverly Washburn
Twig Wilson	Ted Marc
Nana, their house- keeper	Ann O'Neal
Fred, their neighbor	Joseph Kearns
Madge, his wife	Phyllis Coates
Mr. Boggs, the handyman	Arthur Q. Bryan

Also: Sammy Ogg, Harry Cheshire.

PROFESSIONAL FATHER–30 minutes–CBS–January 8, 1955 - September 1955. 13 episodes.

PROFILES IN COURAGE

Documentary. Dramatizations based on events in past American history. Stories stress the valor of political figures who risked their careers, reputations and even lives to undertake unpopular causes. Based on the book, *Profiles in Courage*, by John F. Kennedy.

Program open: an excerpt from the book's prologue.

Program close: the words that close the final chapter: "The stories of past courage can define that ingredient–they can teach, they can offer hope, they can provide inspiration. But they cannot supply courage itself. For this, each man must look into his own soul."

PROFILES IN COURAGE–60 minutes–NBC–November 8, 1964 - September 1965. Syndicated.

THE PROJECTION ROOM

Anthology. Mystery presentations.
Hostess: Ruth Gilbert.

THE PROJECTION ROOM–30 minutes–ABC–March 19, 1952 - March 26, 1952.

THE PROTECTORS

See title: "The Bold Ones," *The Protectors* segment.

THE PROTECTORS

Adventure. Background: London, England. The investigations of Harry Rule, American; Contessa Caroline di

The Protectors. Left to right: Robert Vaughn, Nyree Dawn Porter, Tony Anholt. *Courtesy Independent Television Corp.; an ATV Company.*

Contini, British; and Paul Buchet, French–private detectives, members of the Protectors, an international organization of the world's finest investigators united in the battle against crime in the capitols of Europe.

CAST

Harry Rule	Robert Vaughn
Contessa Caroline di Contini, widow of a wealthy Italian	Nyree Dawn Porter
Paul Buchet	Tony Anholt
Suki, Harry's Japanese housekeeper	Yasuko Nagazumi
Chino, a Protector	Anthony Chinn

Harry's dog: Gus.
Music: John Cameron.
Executive Producer: Sherwood Price.
Producer: Gerry Anderson, Reg Hill.

THE PROTECTORS–30 minutes–Syndicated 1972. 52 episodes.

PRUDENTIAL FAMILY THEATRE

Anthology. Dramatic presentations.
Producer: Donald Davis.
Sponsor: Prudential Life Insurance Company.
PRUDENTIAL FAMILY THEATRE –60 minutes–CBS–1950 - 1951.

THE PRUITTS OF SOUTHAMPTON

Comedy. Background: Southampton, Long Island, New York. Forced to drastically reduce her living standards when an Internal Revenue investigation discloses that she owes ten million dollars in back taxes, society matron Phyllis Pruitt struggles to maintain the appearance of wealth and social status, while at the same time attempting to adjust to the squalid life of a family, a home with eight rooms, one car, and a butler.

CAST

Phyllis Pruitt	Phyllis Diller
Ned Pruitt, her uncle	Reginald Gardiner
Stephanie Pruitt, her daughter	Pamela Freeman
Sturgis, the butler	Grady Sutton
Regina, Phyllis's social rival	Gypsy Rose Lee
Suzy, Regina's daughter	Lisa Loring
Internal Revenue Agent Baldwin	Richard Deacon
General Cannon, a friend of Phyllis's	John McGiver
Mr. Krump, the repairman	Marty Ingels
Vernon Bradley, the stuffy boarder	Billy DeWolfe
Rudy	John Astin
Maxwell	Charles Lane

Music: Vic Mizzy.

THE PRUITTS OF SOUTHAMPTON –30 minutes–ABC–September 6, 1966 - January 6, 1967. As "The Phyllis Diller Show"–30 minutes–ABC–January 13, 1967 - September 1, 1967. 30 episodes.

THE PSYCHIATRIST

See title: "Four-in-One," *The Psychiatrist* segment.

PUBLIC DEFENDER

Drama. The cases and courtroom defenses of Bart Matthews, a public defender of indigent people.

Starring: Reed Hadley as Bart Matthews.

PUBLIC DEFENDER—30 minutes—CBS—March 11, 1954 - June 23, 1955. 69 episodes.

PUBLICITY GIRL

A comedy series starring Jan Sterling as a publicity girl for a P.R. firm in Southern California. 30 minutes—Syndicated 1956.

THE PUBLIC LIFE OF CLIFF NORTON

Comedy. Capsule skits depicting one man's approaches and solutions to everday problems (e.g., "Table Manners"; "Police Your Bureau Drawer"; "Disposal of Your Christmas Tree"; "Building a Fruit Bowl").

Host-Demonstrator: Cliff Norton.

THE PUBLIC LIFE OF CLIFF NORTON—05 minutes—NBC—1950 - 1952.

PUBLIC PROSECUTER

Game. Three competing players who are designated detective-fiction experts. A fifteen-minute whodunit film is played and stopped prior to the denouement. Players have to determine who the culprit is. The film is played to reveal the answer. Winners receive a merchandise prize.

Host: John Howard.

Announcer: Bob Shepard.

Film Performers: John Howard, Anne Gwynne, Walter Sande.

PUBLIC PROSECUTER—30 minutes—DuMont 1947.

PUD'S PRIZE PARTY

Variety. Nonprofessional child entertainers perform and compete against each other for merchandise prizes and a title that names one individual the most talented child of the week.

Host: Todd Russell.

PUD'S PRIZE PARTY—30 minutes—ABC 1952.

PULSE OF THE CITY

Anthology. Dramatizations set against the background of New York City.

PULSE OF THE CITY—30 minutes—DuMont 1952.

PULITZER PRIZE PLAYHOUSE

Anthology. Dramatic adaptations of Pulitzer Prize-winning stories.

Producer: Edgar Peterson, Lawrence Carra.

Director: Charles S. Dubin, Alex Segal.

PULITZER PRIZE PLAYHOUSE—60 minutes—ABC—October 6, 1950 - June 29, 1951.

PUPPET PLAYHOUSE

See title: "Howdy Doody."

PURSUIT

Anthology. Dramatizations depicting the plight of people pursued by others.

Producer: Peter Kortner, Norman Felton, Charles Russell.

Included:

Tiger on a Bicycle. After his friend, a policeman, is killed while attempting to stop an armored-car robbery, a man sets out to find the murderers.

CAST

Matt Shaw: Dan Duryea; Kathy Nelson: Laraine Day; Mood: Chester Morris.

Kiss Me Again Stranger. Assisting the local sheriff, a lieutenant attempts to discover the murderer of a young airman.

CAST

Lt. Aaron Gibbs: Jeffrey Hunter; Mara: Margaret O'Brien; Skip: Mort Sahl; Evelyn: Mary Beth Hughes.

The Dark Cloud. Suspended from the force on false charges, a police detective attempts to uncover the facts behind a bookie's death and clear his name.

CAST

Det. Eddie Hackett: Gary Merrill; Sunny: Ann Sheridan; Det. Mike Robbins: Darryl Hickman; Andrea: Fay Spain.

PURSUIT—60 minutes—CBS—October 22, 1958 - January 14, 1959.

Q

Q.E.D.

Game. Object: For a celebrity panel to solve mystery stories that are submitted by members of the viewing audience. The facts are relayed by the host, and panelists each receive one guess. If mysteries remain unsolved, the sender receives a merchandise prize.

Host: Fred Uttal.

Panel: Nina Foch, Hy Brown, plus guests.

Q.E.D.—30 minutes—ABC—April 13, 1951 - September 1951. Also known as "Mystery File."

Q.T. HUSH

Animated Cartoon. The investigations of Q.T. Hush, a fumbling private detective.

His assistants: Shamus, his dog; and Quincy, his shadow, which is able to operate independently of him.

Q.T. HUSH—30 minutes—Syndicated 1960. 100 episodes.

QUADRANGLE

A comedy game show with Beverly Fite, Frank Stevens, Burt Taylor, Dean Campbell, Bob Burkhardt, Ray Kirschner, Claire Granville.

Producer-Director: Ralph Levy.

15 minutes—CBS 1949.

THE QUEEN AND I

Comedy. Background: New York Harbor. The story of master schemer Duffy, the first mate of the *Amsterdam Queen,* an old and decrepit ocean liner, and his attempts to save the ship, a floating paradise for his money-making schemes.

CAST

Mr. Duffy	Larry Storch
First Officer Nelson	Billy De Wolfe
Captain Washburn	Liam Dunn
Commodore Dodds, the ship's owner	Reginald Owen

Duffy's Crew:

Seaman Becker	Carl Ballantine
Wilma, Duffy's romantic interest	Barbara Stuart
Ozzie	Dave Willock
Max Kowalski	Dave Morick
Barney Cook	Pat Morita

THE QUEEN AND I–30 minutes–CBS–January 16, 1969 - May 1, 1969. 13 episodes.

QUEEN FOR A DAY

Contest. Four women appear and bare their souls, stating their single most needed object. Through electronic voting machines, the audience then selects the one woman they feel is the most needy. The woman is crowned "Queen For A Day," and receives, in addition to the requested gift, various merchandise prizes.

Versions:

Queen For A Day–30 minutes–NBC - April 28, 1955 - September 25, 1960; ABC–September 28, 1960 - October 2, 1964.

Host: Jack Bailey.

Fashion Commentator: Jeanne Cagney.

Announcer: Gene Baker.

Queen For A Day–30 minutes–Syndicated 1970.

Host: Dick Curtis.

Fashion Commentator: Nancy Myers.

QUENTIN DERGENS, M.P.

Drama. Background: London, England. The story of Quentin Dergens, a Member of Parliment (M.P.) who crusades against British government apathy and red tape.

Starring: Gordon Pinsent as Quentin Dergens.

QUENTIN DERGENS, M.P.–60 minutes–Syndicated 1966. 9 episodes.

THE QUEST

Western. Background: The Frontier during the last quarter of the 19th Century. Eight years after being captured and raised by the Cheyenne Indians who attacked the wagon train on which he was traveling, Morgan "Two Persons" Baudine is freed by the army. Shortly after, as he begins to search for his sister, Patricia, who is reputed to be living among the Cheyenne, he meets his long-lost brother, Quentin, a young medical student who, raised by an aunt in San Francisco, has also begun a search for Patricia. Reunited by a common goal, they begin a hazardous quest to find their sister. The series concerns their adventures as they travel throughout the rugged West following new leads.

CAST

Morgan Baudine	Kurt Russell
Quentin Baudine	Tim Matheson

Music: Richard Shores.

Executive Producer: David Gerber.

Producer: Mark Rogers, James H. Brown.

Director: Earl Bellamy, Michael O'Herlihy, Corey Allen, Bernard McEveety.

THE QUEST–60 minutes–NBC–September 22, 1976 - December 22, 1976.

QUEST FOR ADVENTURE

Travel. Excursions to various areas around the globe via the *Quest,* a sixty foot sailing vessel.

Host: Michael O'Toole.

QUEST FOR ADVENTURE–30 minutes–Syndicated 1966. 20 episodes.

QUICK AS A FLASH

Game. Two competing teams, each composed of one celebrity and one studio-audience contestant. A specially prepared film sequence, that describes a person, place, or event is played. The player first to identify himself by a flashing light signal (pressing a button), receives a chance to answer. If he identifies the subject, he receives one point; if he fails, he and his partner are disqualified from that particular round. The opposing team then views the entire film before hazarding a guess. Winners, the highest point scorers, receive merchandise prizes.

Host: Bobby Sherwood.

QUICK AS A FLASH–30 minutes–ABC–March 12, 1953 - September 10, 1953.

QUIET, PLEASE

Anthology. Mystery and adventure presentations.

Narrator: Ernest Chappel.

Announcer: Ed Michael.

Music: Albert Buhrmann.

Producer: Wyllis Cooper.

QUIET, PLEASE–30 minutes–ABC –June 16, 1949 - July 21, 1949.

QUICK DRAW McGRAW

Animated Cartoon. A spoof of the adult westerns of the 1950s. Background: The territory of New Mexico. The exploits of Marshal Quick Draw McGraw, a dim-witted horse who, assisted by Baba Looey, the Mexican burro, struggles to maintain law and order. A Hanna-Barbera production.

Additional segments:

"Snagglepuss." The misadventures of a trouble-prone lion.

"Snooper and Blabber." The antics of a mischievous cat and mouse.

"Augie Doggie and Doggie Daddy." The efforts of a father to control his potentially juvenile deliquent son.

Characters' Voices

Quick Draw McGraw	Daws Butler
Baba Looey	Daws Butler
Snooper	Daws Butler
Blabber	Daws Butler
Augie Doggie	Daws Butler
Doggie Daddy	Doug Young
Snagglepuss	Daws Butler

Music Supervision: Hoyt Curtin.

Quick Draw McGraw. Quick Draw McGraw.
Courtesy Hanna-Barbera Productions.

QUICK DRAW McGRAW—30 minutes—Syndicated 1959. 195 episodes.

QUICK ON THE DRAW

Game. Object: For contestants to identify phrases that are presented by a series of cartoon drawings.

Hostess: Eloise McElhone.

Artist: Bob Dunn.

QUICK ON THE DRAW—30 minutes —NBC 1950.

QUINCY, M.E.

Crime Drama. Background: Los Angeles, California. The story of Dr. Quincy, a medical examiner (M.E.) for the coroner's office, who prefers to probe as a detective rather than just working in a lab.

CAST

Dr. Quincy	Jack Klugman
Lee Potter, his girlfriend	Lynnette Mettey
Dr. Robert Astin, his superior	John S. Ragin
Dr. Sam Fugiyama, his assistant	Robert Ito
Lt. Frank Monahan, the homicide detective	Garry Walberg
Danny Tarvo, Quincy's friend, the owner of Danny's Place, a bar	Val Bisoglio

Music: Stu Phillips.

Theme: Glen A. Larson.

Executive Producer: Glen A. Larson.

Producer: Lou Shaw, Robert O'Neil, Michael Star.

Director: E.W. Swackhamer, Stephen Stern, Noel Black, Bruce Kessler, David Moessinger, Corey Allen, Ronald Stalof, Alvin Ganzer, Jackie Cooper.

QUINCY, M.E.—60 minutes—NBC— Premiered: February 4, 1977. Broadcast as part of "The NBC Sunday Mystery Movie" from October 3, 1976 to January 2, 1977.

THE QUIZ KIDS

Panel. Five exceptionally intelligent children attempt to answer difficult questions. Based on the radio program.

Host: Joe Kelly; Clifton Fadiman.

Producer: Louis G. Cowan, John Le-Wellen.

Director: Don Meler.

Sponsor: Alka Seltzer; Miles Labs; Cat's Paw.

THE QUIZ KIDS—30 minutes—CBS— November 13, 1952 - September 27, 1956.

QUIZZING THE NEWS

Game. Object: For a panel to identify news events through a series of three cartoon drawings.

Host: Allan Prescott.

Panel: Arthur Q. Bryan, Ray Joseph, Mary Hunter, Milton Coniff.

Artist: Albee Treider.

QUIZZING THE NEWS—30 minutes —ABC—August 16, 1948 - March 5, 1949.

R

RACKETS ARE MY RACKET

Drama. Dramatizations exposing confidence games—"The tricks of the tricky traders."

Host: Sgt. Audley Walsh, of the Ridgefield, New Jersey, Police Department.

RACKETS ARE MY RACKET—15 minutes—DuMont 1947.

RACKET SQUAD

Crime Drama. Background: San Francisco, California. Dramatizations exposing the confidence game and its organizers.

Detailing the investigations of Captain John Braddock of the San Francisco Racket Squad, the series presents the step-by-step methods taken to expose rackets.

Starring: Reed Hadley as Captain John Braddock.

Narrator: Reed Hadley.

Music: Joseph Mullendore.

Producer: Hal Roach, Jr., Carroll Chase.

Director: Frank McDonald.

Sponsor: Philip Morris Cigarettes.

Program open:

Capt. Braddock: "What you are about to see is a real life story taken from the files of police racket and bunco squads, business protective associations, and similar

sources all over the country. It is intended to expose the confidence game, the carefully worked out frauds by which confidence men take more money each year from the American public than all the bank robbers and thugs with their violence."

Program close:

Capt. Braddock: "I'm closing this case now, but they'll be others because that's the way the world is built. Remember there are people who can slap you on the back with one hand and pick your pocket with the other—and it could happen to you."

RACKET SQUAD—30 minutes. Syndicated 1950; CBS—June 7, 1951 - September 28, 1953. 98 episodes. Syndicated (again after the network run).

RAFFERTY

Medical Drama. Background: California. The story of Sid Rafferty, M.D., a former army doctor turned brilliant diagnostician in private practice; a doctor who, working part time in City General Hospital, "believes in healing people, not in setting himself up in a fancy business just to make money."

CAST

Dr. Sid Rafferty	Patrick McGoohan
Dr. Daniel Gentry, his associate	John Getz
Vera Wales, his office nurse	Millie Slavin
Beryl Keynes, the hospital admissions nurse	Joan Pringle

Music: Leonard Rosenman, Richard Clements.

Executive Producer: Jerry Thorpe

Producer: James Lee, Norman S. Powell.

Director: Jerry Thorpe, Barry Crane, Alexander Singer.

Creator: James Lee.

RAFFERTY—60 minutes—CBS—Premiered: September 5, 1977.

RAMAR OF THE JUNGLE

Adventure. Background: Nairobi, Africa. The experiences of Dr. Thomas Reynolds, a research scientist known as Ramar—White Witch Doctor.

CAST

Dr. Thomas Reynolds	Jon Hall

Professor Ogden, his
assistant   Ray Montgomery

RAMAR OF THE JUNGLE—30 minutes—Syndicated 1952. 52 episodes.

RANCH PARTY

Musical Variety. Performances by Country and Western entertainers.

Host: Tex Ritter.

Regulars: Jim Reeves, Bonnie Guitar.

RANCH PARTY—30 minutes—Syndicated 1957. 39 episodes.

THE RANGE RIDER

Western. Background: California, 1860s. The exploits of the Range Rider, a wandering defender of justice, and his sidekick, Dick West, "the all-American boy."

CAST
The Range Rider	Jock Mahoney
Dick West	Dick Jones

Program Open:
Song: "Home, home on the range, where the deer and the antelope play . . .

Announcer (over music): And who could be more at home on the range than the Range Rider, with his exciting experiences, rivaling those of Davy Crockett, Daniel Boone, Buffalo Bill, and other pioneers of this wonderful country of ours."

THE RANGE RIDER—30 minutes—Syndicated 1951. 76 episodes.

RANGO

Western Comedy. Background: Gopher Gulch, Texas, 1870s. The exploits of Rango, a fumbling, dim-witted Texas Ranger who struggles to successfully carry out his assignments and glorify the dignity of the Texas Rangers.

CAST
Rango	Tim Conway
Pink Cloud, his Indian assistant	Guy Marks
Captain Horton	Norman Alden

Music: Earle Hagen.

RANGO—30 minutes—ABC—January 13, 1967 - June 25, 1967.

THE RANSOM SHERMAN SHOW

Variety. Music, songs, and comedy sketches.

Host: Ransom Sherman.

Regulars: Johnny Bradford, Nancy Wright.

Music: The Art Damme Quintet.

THE RANSOM SHERMAN SHOW—30 minutes—NBC 1950.

THE RAT CATCHERS

Mystery. The global activities of a group of London based spies. Stories detail their battle against criminal masterminds.

CAST
Glyn Owen, Gerald Flood, Philip Stone.

THE RAT CATCHERS—50 minutes—Syndicated 1965. 13 episodes.

THE RAT PATROL

Adventure. Background: North Africa during World War II. The exploits of the Rat Patrol, a squadron of four desert allies assigned to harass and demoralize Rommel's Afrika Korps.

CAST
Sgt. Sam Troy	Christopher George
Sgt. Jack Moffitt	Gary Raymond
Pvt. Tully Pettigrew	Justin Tarr
Pvt. Mark Hitchcock	Larry Casey
Captain Hans Dietrich, their German nemesis	Hans Gudegast

Music: Dominic Frontiere.

Producer: Mark Weingart.

THE RAT PATROL—30 minutes—ABC—September 12, 1966 - September 16, 1968. 58 episodes. Syndicated.

RAWHIDE

Western. Era: The 1860s. The struggles and hardships faced by the men of the cattle drive from San Antonio, Texas, to Sedalia, Kansas.

CAST
Gil Favor, the trail boss	Eric Fleming
Rowdy Yates, the ramrod	Clint Eastwood
Pete Nolan, the trail scout	Sheb Wooley
Wishbone, the	

cook	Paul Brinegar
The Drovers:	
Mushy	James Murdock
Clay Forrester	Charles Gray
Joe Scarlett	Rock Shahan
Quince	Steve Raines
Hey Soos	Robert Cabal
Simon Blake	Raymond St. Jaques
Ian Cabot	David Watson

Music: Dimitri Tiomkin.

Theme: "Rawhide," by Ned Washington, Dimitri Tiomkin; Recorded by Frankie Laine.

Producer: Charles Warren, Endre Bohem, Vincent M. Fennelly.

Program Open:
Announcer (over music and scene of a cattle drive): "This is the landscape of Rawhide: desert, forest, mountain and plains; it is intense heat, bitter cold, torrential rain, blinding dust; men risking their lives, earning small reward—a life of challenge—Rawhide. It is men like trail scout Pete Nolan, the cantankerous Wishbone, Ramrod Rowdy Yates, good natured Mushy, and trail boss Gil Favor —these men are Rawhide!"

RAWHIDE—60 minutes—CBS—January 1, 1959 - January 4, 1966. 144 episodes. Syndicated.

RAY ANTHONY

Listed: The television programs of band leader Ray Anthony.

The Ray Anthony Show—Musical Variety—ABC—60 minutes—1949.

Host: Ray Anthony.

Regulars: Frank Leahy, The Four Freshman, The Belvaders.

Orchestra: Ray Anthony.

The Ray Anthony Show—Musical Variety—60 minutes—Syndicated 1956.

Host: Ray Anthony.

Regulars: The Four Freshman, The Bookends (singers, dancers), Don Durant, Med Flory, Frank Leahy.

Orchestra: Ray Anthony.

The Ray Anthony Show—Musical Variety—60 minutes—Syndicated 1962.

Host: Ray Anthony.

Regulars: Vikki Carr, Lisa Marne,

Kellie Greene, The Bookends.

Orchestra: Ray Anthony.

THE RAY BOLGER SHOW

See title: "Where's Raymond?"

THE RAY KNIGHT REVUE

Musical Variety.

Host: Ray Knight.

Regulars: Phyllis Gehrig, Don Weismuller, Jonathan Lucas, Harry Archer, Ernie Burtis, Tony Craig, Kaye Conner, Joan Fields, Adam Carroll, Frank Seporelli.

Orchestra: Ray Knight.

Producer: Michael Cramoy.

Director: Howard Cordery.

THE RAY KNIGHT REVUE—30 minutes—ABC—May 15, 1949 - September 1949.

THE RAY MILLAND SHOW

Comedy. Distinguished by two formats.

Format One:

Meet Mr. McNutly—30 minutes—CBS —September 17, 1953 - July 15, 1954. Also known as: "Meet Mr. McNutley."
Background: The town of Lynnhaven. The trials and tribulations of Ray McNutly (McNutley), a drama professor at Lynnhaven, an all-girl college.

CAST

Professor Ray McNutly	Ray Milland
Peggy McNutly, his wife	Phyllis Avery
Dean Bradley	Minerva Urecal
Pete Thompson, Ray's friend	Gordon Jones
Ruth Thompson, his wife	Jacqueline de Wit

Announcer: Del Sharbutt.

Format Two:

The Ray Milland Show—30 minutes—CBS—September 16, 1954 - September 30, 1955. Syndicated.
Background: Los Angeles, California. The trials and tribulations of Ray McNutly, a drama professor at Comstock, a coeducational college.

CAST

Professor Ray McNutly	Ray Milland
Peggy McNutly, his wife	Phyllis Avery

Dean Dodsworth   Lloyd Corrigan

Announcer: Del Sharbutt.

THE RAY STEVENS SHOW

Variety. Music, songs, and comedy sketches.

Host: Ray Stevens.

Regulars: Lulu, Dick Curtis, Steve Martin, Carol Robinson, Florian Carr, Billy Van, Max Elliott, Cass Elliott.

Orchestra: Jimmy Dale.

THE RAY STEVENS SHOW—60 minutes—NBC—July 1970 - September 1970. Original title: "Andy Williams Presents the Ray Stevens Show."

THE R.C.A. VICTOR SHOW

See title: "The Dennis Day Show."

REACH FOR THE STARS

A game show wherein contestants have to perform stunts in return for merchandise prizes. Hosted by Bill Mazer, the thirty minute series ran on NBC from January 3, 1967 to March 31, 1967.

THE REAL McCOYS

Comedy. Background: The San Fernando Valley in California. The struggles of a poor farm family, the McCoys: Grandpa Amos, widower, the head of the clan; Luke, his grandson; Kate, Luke's wife; and Hassie and Little Luke, Luke's sister and brother (their parents, deceased).

CAST

Amos McCoy	Walter Brennan
Luke McCoy	Richard Crenna
Kate McCoy ("Sugar Babe")	Kathleen Nolan
Hassie McCoy	Lydia Reed
Little Luke McCoy	Michael Winkleman
Pepino Garcia, their hired hand	Tony Martinez
George MacMichael, Amos's friend	Andy Clyde
Flora MacMichael, George's sister	Madge Blake
Mac Maginnis, Amos's friend	Willard Waterman
Lela Maginnis, Mac's wife	Shirley Mitchell
Mrs. Jensen, the McCoy housekeeper	Connie Gilchrist
Helga, replaced Mrs. Jensen	Eva Norde
Frank Grant, Helga's	

boyfriend	James Lydon
Louise Howard, the owner of the ranch next to the McCoys (CBS episodes)	Janet De Gore
Gregg Howard, her son	Butch Patrick
Frank, their handyman	John Qualen
Winifred Jordan, Louise's aunt	Joan Blondell
Hank Johnson, Amos's friend	Lloyd Corrigan
Harry Purvis, Amos's partner in the roadside egg business	Charles Lane
"Rightly" Ralph McCoy, Luke's uncle	Jack Oakie
Mr. Taggart, the Grand Pharoah of Amos's lodge	Frank Ferguson
Mrs. Purvis, Kate's mother	Lurene Tuttle

Music: Billy Loose; Ed Norton; Harry Ruby.

Executive Producer: Irving Pincus, Danny Thomas.

Producer: Danny Arnold, Norman Pincus, Charles Isaacs.

Director: Danny Arnold, David Alexander, Sidney Miller, Richard Crenna, Hy Averback, Sheldon Leonard.

Creator: Irving Pincus.

Note: Amos's fraternity: The Royal Order of the Mystic Nile Lodge; The McCoys car: Gertrude, a Model T Ford.

THE REAL McCOYS—30 minutes. ABC—October 3, 1957 - September 20, 1962. CBS—September 24, 1962 - September 22, 1963. 224 episodes. Syndicated.

THE REAL TOM KENNEDY SHOW

Talk-Variety.

Host: Tom Kennedy.

Regulars: Kelly Garrett, John McCormick, Foster Brooks.

Announcer: Tom Kennedy.

Orchestra: Dave Pell.

THE REAL TOM KENNEDY SHOW —60 minutes—Syndicated 1970. 45 tapes.

THE REBEL

Western. Era: The post-Civil War West. The exploits of Johnny Yuma, an embittered, leather-tough young Confederate who journeys West after the Civil War to seek self-identify.

Starring: Nick Adams as Johnny Yuma.

Music: Richard Markowitz.

Theme: "Johnny Yuma," sung by Johnny Cash.

THE REBEL—30 minutes—ABC—October 4, 1959 - September 24, 1961. 76 episodes. Syndicated.

THE REBUS GAME

Game. Two competing teams, each composed of two contestants. One member of each team receives a secret name or phrase. Each partner in turn then draws pictures on a board and attempts to relate its meaning. A player is only permitted to guess when his partner is drawing. Each correct identification scores one point. Winners, the highest scorers, receive merchandise prizes.

Host: Jack Linkletter.

THE REBUS GAME—30 minutes—ABC—March 29, 1965 - September 24, 1965.

RECKONING

Anthology. Rebroadcasts of dramas that were originally aired via "Climax," "Pursuit," and "Studio One."

Included:

Tongues of Angels. The story of a young man who pretends to be a deaf mute to get a job working on a farm.

CAST
Ben Adams: James MacArthur; Jenny Walker: Margaret O'Brien; Cyrus Walker: Leon Ames; Mrs. Walker: Frances Farmer.

The Vengeance. The story of a young man who is hounded by the father of a boy he accidentally crippled in his youth.

CAST
Richie Rogart: Sal Mineo; Harry Talback: Macdonald Carey; Elaine Hermann: Carol Lynley; Detective Fraelich: Stu Erwin.

A Leaf Out of the Book. The story of two women, one successful, the other ambitious.

CAST
Diana Lynn, Sylvia Sidney.

RECKONING—60 minutes—CBS—June 1959 - September 1959; June 1960 - September 1960; June 1961 - September 1961; June 1962 - September 1962; June 1963 - September 1963.

THE RED BUTTONS SHOW

Variety. Music, songs, dances, and comedy sketches.

Host: Red Buttons.

Regulars: Phyllis Kirk, Paul Lynde, Beverly Dennis, Jean Carson, Sara Seeger, Jimmy Little, Ralph Stanley, Sonny Birch, Dorothy Jolliffee, Howard Smith, Allan Walker, Bobby Sherwood, Joe Silver, Betty Ann Grove, The Ho Ho Kids (named after Red's hit recording, "The Ho Ho Song.")

Announcer: Nelson Case.

Producer: Don Appel, Ben Brady, Leo Morgan.

Sponsor: Pontiac; General Foods.

Orchestra: Elliott Lawrence.

Characters portrayed by Red: Keeglefarven, the knucklehead German; Rocky Buttons, the punch-drunk prizefighter; Buttons the bellboy; Razzberry Buttons; The Kupke Kid; The Sad Sack.

THE RED BUTTONS SHOW—60 minutes—CBS—October 14, 1952 - June 14, 1953.

THE REDD FOXX COMEDY HOUR

Variety. Basically, a series of comedy sketches spotlighting the talents of comedian Redd Foxx.

Host: Redd Foxx.

Regulars: Murray Langston, Deborah Pratt, Hal Smith, Dick Owens, Walt Hanna, Andrew Johnson.

Announcer: Roger Carroll.

Orchestra: Gerald Wilson.

Producer: Allyn Blye, Bob Einstein.

Director: Donald Davis.

Choreographer: Lester Wilson.

THE REDD FOXX COMEDY HOUR—60 minutes—ABC—Premiered: September 15, 1977.

THE RED HAND GANG

Children. The adventures of five preteen city children, members of the Red Hand Gang club, as they stumble upon and seek to solve crimes. Stories are episodic.

CAST
Frankie	Matthew La Borteaux
J. R.	J. R. Miller
Joannie	Jolie Neman
Lil Bill	Johnny Brogna
Doc	James Bond III

Music: Score Productions.

Executive Producer: William P. D'Angelo, Ray Allen, Harvey Bullock.

Producer-Director: William P. D'Angelo.

THE RED HAND GANG—30 minutes—NBC—Premiered: September 10, 1977.

REDIGO

Drama. Background: Mesa, New Mexico. The story of Jim Redigo, a rancher struggling to maintain a vast cattle spread. A spin-off from "Empire."

CAST
Jim Redigo	Richard Egan
Gerry, the assistant manager of the Gold Hotel	Elena Verdugo
Linda Franks, the ranch cook	Mina Martinez
Mike, a ranch hand	Roger Davis
Frank, a ranch hand	Rudy Solari

REDIGO—30 minutes—NBC—September 24, 1963 - December 31, 1963. 15 episodes.

RED RYDER

Western. Era: The nineteenth century. The exploits of Red Ryder and his Indian friend, Little Beaver, as they struggle to maintain law and order throughout the West.

CAST
Red Ryder	Rocky Lane
Little Beaver	Louis Letteri
The Dutchess	Elizabeth Slifer

RED RYDER—30 minutes—Syndicated 1956. 39 episodes. Withdrawn. Based on the radio program.

THE RED SKELTON SHOW

Variety. Music, songs, dances, and comedy sketches.

Host: Red Skelton.

Regulars: Chinan Hale, Sheila Rogers, Jan Arvin, Helen Funai, Lloyd Kino, Jan Davis, Billy Barty, Beverly Powers, Ida Moe McKenzie, Elaine Joyce, Jimmie Cross, Lester Mathews, Kathryn Cord, Stanley Adams, Peggy Rae, Mike Wagner, Dorothy Love, Bob Duggan, Adam Kaufman, Stuart Lee, Linda Sue Risk, The Tom Hanson Dancers, The Alan Copeland Singers, The Skeltones (Dancers); The Burgandy Street Singers.

Announcer: Art Gilmore.

Orchestra: David Rose.

Characters portrayed by Red: Freddie the Freeloader; Clem Kadiddlehopper (the farm boy); Sheriff Deadeye (the corrupt lawman); Junior, the Mean Widdle Kid; Cauliflower McPugg (the punchy boxer); George Appleby (the henpecked husband); San Fernando Red (the con artist); Ludwick von Humperdoo (the scientist); Bolivar Shagnasty; Willy Lump Lump (the drunk).

THE RED SKELTON SHOW—30 minutes—NBC—September 30, 1951 - June 1953; CBS—30 and 60 minute versions—September 22, 1953 - June 1970; NBC—30 minutes—September 14, 1971 - August 29, 1972. Also known as "The Red Skelton Hour."

THE REEL GAME

Game. Three competing contestants, each beginning with two hundred and fifty dollars bidding money.

The Film Clip Round: The host states a category topic (e.g., "comedy teams") and players wager any amount of their money on their ability to answer the forthcoming question. The question is then read (e.g., "For years the team of George Burns and Gracie Allen ended their comedy routine by George telling Gracie to do something. What?"). After players write their answers on a card, a film clip is shown that reveals the answer ("Say goodnight, Gracie."). Contestants whose answers are correct receive the wagered amount of money; if incorrect, it is deducted.

Each of the three film clip rounds are divided by a question-and-answer session wherein three questions are asked regarding the subject of the film clip round. Players first to sound a buzzer receive a chance to answer. Twenty-five dollars are either deducted from or added to a player's score.

The Grand Finale: The category question is stated. Each player secretly writes his answer and his wager on a card. A film clip reveals the correct answer. Winners, who receive their earnings, are the highest cash scorers.

Host: Jack Barry.

Announcer: Jack Clark.

THE REEL GAME—30 minutes—ABC—January 18, 1971 - May 3, 1971. 13 tapes.

THE REGIS PHILBIN SHOW

Talk-Variety.

Host: Regis Philbin.

Music: The Terry Gibbs Sextet.

THE REGIS PHILBIN SHOW—90 minutes—Syndicated 1964. 100 tapes.

REHEARSAL CALL

Variety. The series features music, songs, and a behind-the-scenes look, as "Rehearsal Call" takes viewers backstage at TV productions.

Hostess: Dee Parker.

Music: The Leonard Stanley Trio.

Producer: John Pival.

REHEARSAL CALL—15 minutes—ABC 1949.

THE RELUCTANT DRAGON AND MR. TOAD

Animated Cartoon. Based on the novel *The Wind in the Willows.*

The Reluctant Dragon. Background: The Willowmarsh Village in England. The story of Sir Malcolm and his struggles to protect Tobias, a four-hundred-year-old dragon cursed to breathing fire, from the little girl (not identified by a name) who delights in causing misery by presenting Tobias with daisies—which cause him to sneeze, breathe fire, and disrupt life in the village.

Mr. Toad. The adventures of a carefree, gadabout frog, Mr. Toad.

THE RELUCTANT DRAGON AND

MR. TOAD—30 minutes—ABC—September 12, 1970 - September 3, 1972. 52 episodes.

RENDEZVOUS

Drama. Background: The Chez Nikki, a sophisticated nightclub in Paris, France. The story of its proprietress, a beautiful woman who, supposedly engaged in underground activities during World War II, involves herself in and attempts to solve the problems of others.

Starring: Ilona Massey.

Music: Edward Vito.

RENDEZVOUS—30 minutes—ABC—February 13, 1952 - March 12, 1952.

RENDEZVOUS

Anthology. Dramatic presentations.

Host-Narrator: Charles Drake.

RENDEZVOUS—30 minutes—Syndicated 1958.

RENDEZVOUS WITH ADVENTURE

Adventure. Films revealing the hazardous expeditions of explorers.

Host-Narrator: Lee Green.

RENDEZVOUS WITH ADVENTURE—30 minutes—Syndicated 1963.

RENDEZVOUS WITH MUSIC

Musical Variety.

Hostess: Carol Reed.

Regulars: Rosemary Bangham, Andy McCann, Mary Jane Boone, Tommy Johnson, Teddy Katz.

Music: The Tony DeSimone Trio.

RENDEZVOUS WITH MUSIC—30 minutes—NBC 1950.

RENFREW OF THE ROYAL MOUNTED

Adventure. Background: Canada. The investigations of Douglas Renfrew, a Royal Canadian Mounted Policeman.

CAST
Douglas Renfrew — James Newell
Constable Kelly — Dave O'Brien
Carol Girard,

Renfrew's romantic
interest   Louise Stanley

RENFREW OF THE ROYAL
MOUNTED—30 minutes—Syndicated
1953. 13 episodes.

THE REPORTER

Drama. Background: Manhattan. The
investigations of Danny Taylor, a
newspaper reporter-columnist for the
New York Globe.

CAST

Danny Taylor   Harry Guardino
Lou Sheldon,
  the city
  editor   Gary Merrill
Artie Burns, a
  friend of
  Danny's   George O'Hanlon
Ike Dawson,
  the bartender,
  a friend of
  Danny's   Remo Pisani

Music: Kenyon Hopkins.

Executive Producer: Keefe Brasselle.
Producer: John Simon.

THE REPORTER—60 minutes—CBS
—September 25, 1964 - December 15,
1964. 15 episodes.

RESCUE 8

Drama. Background: California. The
experiences of Wes Cameron and Skip
Johnson, paramedics with the Rescue
8 Division of the Los Angeles County
Fire Department. Stories depict their
attempts to rescue people trapped in
unusual predicaments.

CAST

Wes Cameron   Jim Davis
Skip Johnson   Lang Jeffries
Patty Johnson, their
  dispatcher   Nancy Rennick
Producer: Herbert B. Leonard.

RESCUE 8—30 minutes—Syndicated
1958. 73 episodes.

THE RESTLESS GUN

Western. "I ride with the wind, my
eyes on the sun, and my hand on my
Restless Gun." Background: The West
of the 1860s. The exploits of Vint
Bonner, a wandering ex-gunfighter
("The Six Gun") who aides people in
distress.

Starring: John Payne as Vint Bonner.

Narrator: John Payne.
Bonner's horse: Scar.
Music: Stanley Wilson.
Producer: John Payne, David Dortort.

THE RESTLESS GUN—30 minutes.
NBC—September 1957 - September
14, 1959; ABC—October 12, 1959 -
September 30, 1960. 77 episodes.
Syndicated.

RETURN ENGAGEMENT

Anthology. Rebroadcasts of dramas
that were originally aired via other
filmed anthology programs.

RETURN ENGAGEMENT—30 min-
utes—ABC—June 1953 - September
1953.

RETURN TO PEYTON PLACE

Serial. A spin-off from "Peyton
Place." Background: The small New
England town of Peyton Place. Continued events in the turmoil-ridden
lives of its citizens.

CAST

Constance MacKenzie Carson,
  the owner of
  the town
  bookstore   Bettye Ackerman
Elliot Carson, her
  husband; the
  editor-publisher of the
  Peyton Place
  Clarion   Warren Stevens
Alison MacKenzie,
  their illegitimate
  daughter   Kathy Glass
Eli Carson,
  Elliot's father,
  the owner of
  the general
  store   Frank Ferguson
Rodney Harrington,
  the nephew of
  Martin Peyton, the
  founder of Peyton
  Place   Yale Summers
                      Lawrence Casey
Norman Harrington, Rodney's
  brother   Ron Russell
Betty Anderson
Harrington, Rodney's
  wife   Julie Parrish
                      Lynn Loring
Rita Jacks
Harrington, Norman's
  wife   Patricia Morrow
Leslie Harrington,
  the father of
  Rodney and
  Norman   Stacy Harris

Ada Jacks,
  Rita's mother,
  the owner of
  Ada Jack's Tavern,
  a waterfront
  bar   Evelyn Scott
Dr. Michael Rossi,
  the town
  physician   Guy Stockwell
Stephen Cord,
  the illegitimate son
  of Martin Peyton's
  daughter   Joe Gallison
Hannah Cord, one
  time mistress and
  housekeeper for
  Martin Peyton; raised
  Stephen Cord
  as her own
  son   Mary K. Wells
Benny Tate,
  a mysterious,
  menacing figure
  from Alison's
  past   Ben Andrews
Matthew Carson,
  the three-year-old
  son of Constance
  and Elliot   John Levin
Martin Peyton, the
  founder of Peyton
  Place   John Hoyt
Dr. Wells   Alex Nicol
Lt. Ed Riker   Chuck Daniel
Judge Foster   Anne Seymour
Seena Cross   Margaret Mason
Monica Bell, a
  waitress   Betty Ann Carr
The Attorney   Rudy Solari
Music: Linda Line.

RETURN TO PEYTON PLACE—30
minutes—NBC—April 3, 1972 - January 4, 1974.

RETURN TO THE PLANET OF
THE APES

Animated Cartoon. A spin-off from
"Planet of the Apes." Traveling
aboard the NASA space craft *Venture*,
three astronauts, Bill, Judy, and Jeff,
penetrate a time vortex and are hurled
from their present day Earth (1975)
to Earth in the year A.D. 3979—into a
world that is ruled by intellectual apes
(humans, treated as a lesser species,
serve as pets, servants, and sport for
hunters). Seeking shelter after their
ship crash lands, the astronauts find
refuge in the humanoid colony of
New City. As they learn what fate has
befallen the Earth, the colony is raided by an army of apes; Bill is captured
and brought to ape scientists Corneileus and Zera for experimentation
purposes. In his attempt to communicate with them, Bill speaks, shocking

Corneileus and Zera, who held a mis-belief that humans were incapable of speech.* Realizing that Bill will be killed by the ape leaders if they learn of his capability, Corneileus and Zera set him free.

Stories follow the astronauts adventures as they struggle for survival and seek a way to return to the Earth of their time.

Characters' Voices:

Bill	Tom Williams
Judy	Claudette Nevins
Jeff	Austin Stoker
Corneileus	Henry Corden
Dr. Zera	Phillipa Harris

Additional Voices: Richard Blackburn, Edwin Mills.

Music: Dean Elliot, Eric Rogers.

*The few elder ape leaders are the only ones who know that humans once ruled the planet Earth. Humanoid greed, folly, and lust for power caused him to destroy his civilization in a cataclysmic war. From his ruins, the ape society emerged. It is written that if the humanoids were to regain the intelligence of language, they would once again become the masters of the planet and would once again destroy it. Thus, the intelligence possessed by the humans has been kept secret from the ape population to prevent panic.

RETURN TO THE PLANET OF THE APES—30 minutes—NBC—September 6, 1975 - September 4, 1976.

REVLON MIRROR THEATRE

Anthology. Dramatic presentations.

Hostess—Commercial Spokeswoman: Robin Chandler.

REVLON MIRROR THEATRE—30 minutes—NBC—June 23, 1953 - September 1953.

RHEINGOLD THEATRE

Anthology. Dramatic presentations.

Hosts: Henry Fonda; Douglas Fairbanks, Jr.

Included:

Louise. Fearing to lose her daughter to a struggling young lawyer, a domineering mother attempts to prevent their marriage.

Starring: Judith Anderson.

The Norther. A sheriff attempts to track a gang of outlaws through a blistering heat wave ("Norther").

Starring: Stephen McNally.

End Of Flight. A fugitive's flight from justice.

Starring: Edmond O'Brien.

Honolulu. When the captain of a ship discovers that his first mate has fallen in love with his wife, he attempts to destroy him through voodoo.

Starring: Frank Lovejoy.

RHEINGOLD THEATRE—30 minutes—NBC—1955 - 1956.

RHODA

Comedy. A spin-off from "The Mary Tyler Moore Show," wherein the character of Rhoda Morganstern was portrayed as a plumpish brunette whose main challenges were to land an occasional date and, with some will power, slim down so as not to eat her heart out everytime she looked at her attractive friend, confidante, and neighbor, Mary Richards (Mary Tyler Moore).

Now, four years later, slim, glamorous, and single, Rhoda leaves Minneapolis for a two-week vacation and returns to home of her birth, New York City (born in the Bronx), where she moves in with her sister, Brenda, an overweight bank teller.

Preparing for a date her mother has arranged for her, Rhoda meets and falls in love with Joe Gerard, the head of the New York Wrecking Company, when he comes to the apartment to leave his ten-year-old son, Donny (by a former marriage which ended in divorce), with Brenda, his baby-sitter.

Cancelling her plans to return to Minneapolis, Rhoda secures employment as a store window dresser and, shortly after, accepts Joe's proposal of marriage.

Married, Rhoda and Joe establish housekeeping in the same apartment house as Brenda. Stories depict the trials and tribulations of newlyweds as they struggle to survive the trying first years in difficult times.

CAST

Rhoda Morganstern (Gerard)	Valerie Harper
Joe Gerard	David Groh
Brenda Morganstern	Julie Kavner
Ida Morganstern, Rhoda's mother	Nancy Walker
Martin Morganstern, Rhoda's father	Harold Gould
Voice of Carlton, the never seen, intoxicated doorman	Lorenzo Music
Mae, Joe's secretary-bookkeeper	Cara Williams
Justin Culp, Joe's partner	Scoey Mitchlll
Donny Gerard	Todd Turquand
Alice, Joe's secretary-bookkeeper (later episodes)	Candy Azzara
Sally Gallagher, Rhoda's friend	Anne Meara
Myrna Morganstein, Rhoda's friend	Barbara Sharma
Nick Lobo, Brenda's friend	Richard Masur
Lenny Fielder, Brenda's friend	Wes Stern

Music: Billy Goldenberg.

Executive Producer-Creator: James L. Brooks, Allan Burns.

Producer: Charlotte Brown, David Davis, Lorenzo Music.

Director: Robert Moore, Tony Mordente, Howard Storm, Jay Sandrich.

Program Open:

Rhoda: "My name is Rhoda Morganstern. I was born in the Bronx, New York in December of 1941. I've always felt responsible for World War II. The first thing that I remember liking that liked me back was food. I had a bad puberty, it lasted seventeen years. I'm a high school graduate. I went to art school—my entrance exam was on a book of matches. I decided to move out of the house when I was twenty-four. My mother still refers to this as the time I ran away from home. Eventually I ran to Minneapolis where it's cold, and I figured I'd keep better. Now I'm back in Manhattan. New York, this is your last chance."

RHODA—30 minutes—CBS—Premiered: September 9, 1974.

RHYME AND REASON

Game. Six celebrity guests and two contestants are involved. The host reads a rhyming phrase (e.g., "I did a double take when I first met Mae West..."). The contestants then write a word that rhymes with the last word of the phrase. One player selects a celebrity who must then make up a rhyme to complete the phrase. If he uses the same word as the contestant, the contestant scores two points; if the celebrity matches the opponent, the opponent scores one point. Three points are played per game and the first player to win two games is the champion and receives five hundred dollars.

Host: Bob Eubanks.

Announcers: Johnny Jacobs, Jack Clark.

Regular Panelist: Nipsey Russell.

Semiregular Panelists: Conny Van Dyke, Jaye P. Morgan, Charlie Brill, Mitzi McCall, Pat Harrington, Frank Gorshin, Jamie Farr.

Music: Recorded.

RHYME AND REASON—30 minutes—ABC—July 7, 1975 - July 9, 1976.

THE RICHARD BOONE SHOW

Anthology. Dramatic presentations. A regular cast of players appear in non-continuing roles.

Host-Performer: Richard Boone.

Repertory Company: Harry Morgan, Laura Devon, Robert Blake, June Harding, Warren Stevens, Bethel Leslie, Guy Stockwell, Lloyd Bochner, Jeanette Nolan, Ford Rainey.

Music: Vic Mizzy.

Producer: Mark Goodson, Bill Todman, Buck Houghton.

Included:

First Sermon. A priest's fears and doubts about his abilities to address his parishioners.

CAST

Guy Stockwell, Robert Blake, Richard Boone.

Where Did You Hide An Egg? Three unqualified safecrackers attempt a bank robbery.

CAST

Richard Boone, Harry Morgan, Robert Blake.

Don't Call Me Dirty Names. The struggles of an unwed mother to be.

CAST

June Harding, Lloyd Bochner.

Where's The Million Dollars? Pursuing an underworld character, federal authorities attempt to learn the whereabouts of a million dollars.

CAST

Guy Stockwell, Harry Morgan.

THE RICHARD BOONE SHOW—60 minutes—NBC—September 24, 1963 - September 15, 1964. 25 episodes.

RICHARD DIAMOND, PRIVATE DETECTIVE

Crime Drama. Distinguished by two formats.

Format One:

Background: New York City. The investigations of private detective Richard Diamond. Operating without police assistance, his life rests solely in the hands of a woman identified only as Sam, a beautiful, sexy-voiced telephone operator who is aware of his presence at all times and possesses the ability to sense endangering situations and summon help. Operating from a small room in Manhattan, Sam, who is never fully seen, is situated in a dimly lit atmosphere designed to display her shapely figure, notably her legs.

CAST

Richard Diamond	David Janssen
Sam	Mary Tyler Moore
	Roxanne Brooks

Music: Pete Rugolo; Richard Shores.

Format Two:

Background: Hollywood, California. The investigations of private detective Richard Diamond.

CAST

Richard Diamond	David Janssen
Karen Wells, his girlfriend	Barbara Bain
Lieutenant McGouh, L.A.P.D.	Regis Toomey
Lt. Pete Kile	Russ Conway
Sgt. Alden	Richard Devon

Music: Pete Rugolo; Richard Shores.

RICHARD DIAMOND, PRIVATE DETECTIVE—30 minutes—CBS—July 1, 1957 - September 30, 1957; December 2, 1958 - September 25, 1958; February 15, 1959 - September 20, 1959; NBC—October 5, 1959 - January 25, 1960. 51 episodes. Syndicated. Also known as "Call Mr. D."

THE RICHARD PRYOR SHOW

Variety. Basically, a series of comedy sketches spotlighting the talents of comedian Richard Pryor.

Host: Richard Pryor.

Regulars: Paula Kelly, Jeff Corey, Sam Laws, Juanita Moore, Charles Fleischer, Jimmy Martinez, The Chuck Davis Dance Company.

Orchestra: Johnny Pate.

Special Musical Material: Lenny La-Crox.

Executive Producer: Burt Sugarman.

Producer: Rocco Urbisci.

Director: John Moffitt.

Choreographer: Chuck Davis.

THE RICHARD PRYOR SHOW—60 minutes—NBC—September 13, 1977 - October 18, 1977.

RICHARD THE LION HEART

History. Background: Eleventh-century England. The life of King Richard the Lion Heart—from his participation in the Crusades, to his capture in Austria, to his final return to England.

Starring: Dermot Walsh as King Richard.

RICHARD THE LION HEART—30 minutes—Syndicated 1963. 39 episodes.

THE RICH LITTLE SHOW

Variety.

Host: Rich Little.

Regulars: Julie McWhirter (as "The Family Hour Fairy"), Charlotte Rae, Joe Baker, R.G. Brown, Mel Bishop.

Orchestra: Robert E. Hughes.

Executive Producer: Jerry Goldstein.

Producer: Al Rogers, Rick Eustis.

Director: Lee Bernhardi.

THE RICH LITTLE SHOW—60 minutes—NBC—February 2, 1976 - May 18, 1976.

RICH MAN, POOR MAN, BOOK I

Drama. A miniseries that follows the lives of the Jordache brothers: Rudy, the straight one who moves up the establishment ladder; and Tom, the troublemaker. The series also simultaneously covers the changes that occur in America from World War II through the mid-1960s. Based on the novel by Irwin Shaw.

CAST

Tom Jordache	Nick Nolte
Rudy Jordache	Peter Strauss
Julie Prescott	Susan Blakely
Axel Jordache	Edward Asner
Mary Jordache	Dorothy McGuire
Kate Jordache	Kay Lenz
Wesley Jordache	Willie Aames
	Michael Morgan
Sue Prescott	Gloria Grahame
Bill Falconetti	William Smith

Willie Abbott	Bill Bixby
Duncan Calderwood	Ray Milland
Virginia Calderwood	Kim Darby
Teddy Boylan	Robert Reed
Linda Quales	Lynda Day George
Brad Knight	Tim McIntire
Smitty	Norman Fell
Gloria	Jo Ann Harris
Marsh Goodwin	Van Johnson
Irene Goodwin	Dorothy Malone
Rod Dwyer	Herbert Jefferson, Jr.
Sid Gossett	Murray Hamilton
Colonel Bainbridge	Andrew Duggan
Bayard Nichols	Steve Allen
Teresa Santoro	Talia Shire

Muisc: Alex North.

Executive Producer: Harve Bennett.

Producer: Jon Epstein.

Director: David Greene, Boris Sagal.

RICH MAN, POOR MAN, BOOK I—12 hours—ABC—February 1, 1976 - March 15, 1976. Rebroadcasts: ABC—May 10, 1977 - June 21, 1977.

RICH MAN, POOR MAN, BOOK II

Drama. A continuation of the mini-series "Rich Man, Poor Man, Book I." Continued events in the life of Rudy Jordache, now a United States Senator. Serial-type episodes.

CAST

Rudy Jordache	Peter Strauss
Maggie Porter, his lawyer	Susan Sullivan
Wesley Jordache, Rudy's ward (Tom had been killed off)	Gregg Henry
Ramona Scott, Wesley's girlfriend	Penny Peyser
Billy Abbott, Rudy's stepson	James Carroll Jordan
Kate Jordache, Tom's widow	Kay Lenz
Bill Falconetti, the man seeking to destroy Rudy	William Smith
Diane Porter, Maggie's daughter	Kimberly Beck
Mr. Scott, Ramona's father	John Anderson
Charles Estep, the ruthless billionaire	Peter Haskell
Rod Dwyer, Wesley's friend	Herbert Jefferson, Jr.
Claire Estep, Charles's wife	Laraine Stephens
Marsh Goodwin	Van Johnson
Annie	Cassie Yates
Vickie St. John	Collen Camp

Music: Alex North, Michael Isaacson.

Music Supervision: Stanley Wilson.

Executive Producer: Michael Gleason.

Producer: Jon Epstein.

Director: Alex Segal, Bill Bixby, Karen Arthur, Paul Stanley.

RICH MAN, POOR MAN, BOOK II—60 minutes—ABC—September 21, 1976 - March 8, 1977.

THE RIFLEMAN

Western. Background: North Fork, New Mexico, 1888. The story of Lucas McCain, widower, "The Rifleman" (the fastest man with a .44-40 hair-trigger action rifle), and his young son, Mark, ranchers, and their struggles to maintain a small cattle spread.

CAST

Lucas McCain	Chuck Connors
Mark McCain	Johnny Crawford
Marshal Micah Torrance	Paul Fix
Hattie Denton, the owner of the general store (early episodes)	Hope Summers
Millie Scott, the owner of the general store (later episodes)	Joan Taylor
Eddie Holstead, the owner of the Madera House Hotel	Larry Perron
Lou Mallory, the owner of the Mallory House Hotel	Patricia Blair
Nils Svenson, the blacksmith	Joe Higgins
Sweeney, the Last Chance Saloon bartender	Bill Quinn
Jay Burrage, the town doctor	Edgar Buchanan Jack Kruschner Ralph Moody
Angus Evans, the gunsmith	Eddie Quinlan
Ruth, a hotel waitress	Amanda Ames
Betty Lind, a hotel waitress	Carol Leigh
John Hamilton, the banker	Harlan Warde
Aggie Hamilton, his wife	Sarah Selby

Music: Herschel Burke Gilbert.

THE RIFLEMAN—30 minutes—ABC—September 30, 1958 - July 1, 1963. Syndicated. 168 episodes.

RIN TIN TIN

See title: "The Adventures Of Rin Tin Tin."

The Rifleman. Left to right: Chuck Connors, Johnny Crawford, Joan Taylor.

RIPCORD

Adventure. The experiences of Jim Buckley and Ted McKeever, sky-diving instructors for Ripcord, Incorporated, a sky-diving school.

CAST

Jim Buckley	Ken Curtis
Ted McKeever	Larry Pennell

Program Open:

Announcer: "This is the most danger-packed show on television. Every aerial manuver is real, photographed just as it happened, without tricks or illusions. All that stands between a jumper and death is his Ripcord."

RIPCORD—30 minutes—Syndicated 1961. 76 episodes.

RIPTIDE

Adventure. Background: Bermuda. The experiences of Moss Andrews, the captain of the charter boat service Riptide, Incorporated.

CAST

Moss Andrews	Ty Hardin
His secretary	Jacki Hickmont

RIPTIDE—60 minutes—Syndicated 1965.

THE RIVALS OF SHERLOCK HOLMES

Anthology. Mystery presentations depicting incidents in the lives of fictional detectives who were popular in Europe at the time of Sherlock Holmes. Produced in England.

Music: Robert Sharples.

Executive Producer: Kim Mills, Lloyd Shirley.

Producer: Jonathan Alwyn, Robert Lane, Reginald Collen.

Director: Reginald Collen, Bill Bain.

THE RIVALS OF SHERLOCK HOLMES—60 minutes—PBS—1975 - 1976.

RIVERBOAT

Adventure. Background: Areas along the Mississippi and Missouri Rivers during the 1840s. The experiences of Grey Holden, the captain of the riverboat *Enterprise.*

CAST

Grey Holden	Darren McGavin
Ben Frazer, the pilot (early episodes)	Burt Reynolds
Bill Blake, the pilot (later episodes)	Noah Beery, Jr.
Brad Turner, the captain (later episodes)	Dan Duryea

The Crew:

Joshua	Jack Lambert
Chip	Mike McGreevy
Carney	Dick Wessell
Pickalong	John Mitchum
Terry Blake	Bart Patton

Music: Elmer Bernstein; Richard Sendry; Leo Shuken.

RIVERBOAT—60 minutes—NBC— September 13, 1959 - January 16, 1961. 44 episodes.

RIVIERA POLICE

A crime drama series, set on the French Riviera. 13 films. 60 minutes— Syndicated 1965.

R.J. AND COMPANY

Music. Borrowing its format from "American Bandstand," the show features teenagers dancing to popular music.

Host: Ron Joseph (R.J.).

Announcer: Jim Bacon, Mark Anthony, Gene Arnold.

Musical Director: Marty Morley, Glen Rosewald.

Executive Producer: Ron Joseph.

R.J. AND COMPANY—30 minutes—

Syndicated 1976. Originally, aired locally over WTAF-TV, Channel 29 in Philadelphia.

ROAD OF LIFE

Serial. Background: The town of Merimac. The dramatic story of Doctor Jim Brent and his wife, Joycelyn. Episodes relate the conflicts and tensions that befall three generations of two families: the Brents and the Overtons (Joycelyn's family). Based on the radio program.

CAST

Jim Brent	Don McLaughlin
Joycelyn Brent	Virginia Dwyer
Malcolm Overton	Harry Holcombe
Sybil Overton	Barbara Becker
Conrad Overton	Charles Dingle
Aunt Reggie	Dorothy Sands

Also: Bill Lipton, Elizabeth Lawrence, Michael Kane, Elspeth Eric, Hollis Irving, Jack Lemmon.

Narrator: Nelson Case.

ROAD OF LIFE—15 minutes—CBS —December 13, 1954 - June 24, 1955.

ROAD OF ROMANCE

Anthology Rebroadcasts of romantic dramas originally aired via other filmed anthology programs.

ROAD OF ROMANCE—30 minutes— ABC 1955.

THE ROAD RUNNER SHOW

Animated Cartoon. Background: The desert. Using defective Acme Warehouse products, Wile E. Coyote, a scavenger, endlessly attempts to catch himself a decent meal: a foxy, out-smarting bird, the Road Runner. Composed of both theatrical and made-for-television cartoons.

Voice characterizations: Mel Blanc.

Music: William Lava.

THE ROAD RUNNER SHOW—30 minutes—CBS—September 2, 1967 - September 7, 1968.

THE BUGS BUNNY/ROAD RUNNER HOUR—60 minutes—CBS —September 14, 1968 - September 4, 1971.

THE ROAD RUNNER SHOW—30 minutes—ABC—September 11, 1971 -

September 2, 1972. Syndicated. Theatrical shorts syndicated prior to the network run.

THE ROADS TO FREEDOM

Serial. Background: Europe. The collapse of pre-world War II France is dramatized as it is seen through the eyes of three people: Mathieu, an intellectual college professor; Daniel, a homosexual; and Brunet, a Communist—men unable to act or think definitively. Based on Jean Paul Sarte's *The Roads To Freedom* Trilogy: *The Age of Reason; Loss of Innocense;* and *The Awakening.* Produced by the B.B.C.

CAST

Mathieu De LaRue	Michael Bryant
Marcelle, his mistress	Rosemary Leach
Daniel	Daniel Massey
Lola Montero, a singer in a Paris night club	Georgia Brown
Boris, her romantic interest	Anthony Corlan
Ivich, his sister	Alison Fiske
Jacques De LaRue, Mathieu's brother	Clifford Rose
Odette De LaRue, his wife	Anna Fox
Sarah	Heather Canning
Rose	Bella Amberg
Brunet	Donald Burton
Andre Pinette	Donald Burnet
Emil	Tom Marshall
Chamberlain	Michael Goodlife
Hitler	Tenniel Edans
Phillipe	Simon Ward
The Mayor	George Roderick
Fiske	Dick Allison
Laytex	Peter Wyatt
Longin	John Carter
Nippert	Christian Rodska
Gomez	Andrew Faulds
Schoolmaster	Blake Butler
Clipot	Donald Webster
Post girl	Claire Sutcliffe
Sgt. Clossom	James Appleby
Blonde woman	Kate Brown

Dramatization: David Turner.

Music (theme only): "La Route Est Dure." Arranged by Richard Holmes; vocal (in French): Georgia Brown.

THE ROADS TO FREEDOM—45 minutes. Imported and presented to PBS stations in 1972 by WNET-TV, Channel 13, New York. Official title: "La Route Est Dure."

ROAD TO REALITY

Serial. The program dramatizes what happens at a group therapy session. With the help of a doctor, six people discuss their emotional problems.

CAST
Dr. Lewis	John Beal
Vic	Robert Drew
Rosalind	Robin Howard
Margaret	Eugena Rawls
Joan	Judith Braun
Lee	James Dimitri
Chris	Kay Doubleday

ROAD TO REALITY—30 minutes—ABC—October 17, 1960 - March 31, 1961.

THE ROAD WEST

Western. Background: Lawrence County, Kansas, 1860. The struggles of a family of homesteaders, the Prides, as they attempt to establish a new life.

CAST
Ben Pride, the father	Barry Sullivan
Elizabeth Pride, Ben's wife	Kathryn Hays
Tim Pride, Ben's son	Andrew Prine
Midge Pride, Ben's daughter	Brenda Scott
Chance Reynolds, Elizabeth's brother	Gleń Corbett
Christopher (Kip) Pride, Ben's son	Kelly Corcoran
Thomas Jefferson (Tom) Pride, Ben's father	Charles Seel

Music: Leonard Rosenman.

THE ROAD WEST—60 minutes—NBC—September 12, 1966 - September 4, 1967. 26 episodes.

THE ROARING TWENTIES

Drama. Background: Manhattan, 1920s. The investigations of Scott Norris and Pat Garrison, newspaper reporter-columnists for the *New York Record*. Assisted by Pinky Pinkham, a beautiful singer at The Charleston Club, they strive to acquire the headline-making stories by infiltrating the rackets and exposing the racketeers. Through rear-screen projection and intercutting of newsreel film of the era, an illusion of authenticity is presented.

The Roaring 20's. Guest Maxie Rosenbloom and star Dorothy Provine. Episode: "Asparagus Tips."

CAST
Pinky Pinkham	Dorothy Provine
Pat Garrison	Donald May
Scott Norris	Rex Reason
Chris Higbee, the copy boy	Gary Vinson
Jim Duke Williams, a reporter	John Dehner
McDonald, the city editor	Emile Meyer
Dixie, the hat check girl at The Charleston Club	Carolyn Komant
Chauncey Kowalski, the bartender at The Charleston Club	Wally Brown
Lt. Joe Switolski, N.Y.P.D.	Mike Road

Background Music: Sandy Courage.

Miss Provine's musical accompaniment: Pinky and Her Playboys—a re-created Syncopation Dance Orchestra composed of Pinky's Playboys (a cabaret band) and six squeaky-voiced chorus girls, "And the Girls."

THE ROARING TWENTIES—60 minutes—ABC—October 15, 1960 - September 2, 1962. 45 episodes. Syndicated.

ROAR OF THE RAILS

Model Railroads. Stories of railroading told via narration over scenes of model railroads in operation.

Hostess: Mimi Strangin.
Narrator: Rusty Slocum.

Producer: Ray Nelson.
Sponsor: A.C. Gilbert Electric Trains.

ROAR OF THE RAILS—15 minutes—CBS—1948-1949.

THE ROBBINS NEST

Variety. Various comedy sketches satirizing life.
Host: Fred Robbins.
Regulars: Nat Cantor, Fran Gregory.
Announcer: Cynthia Carlin.

THE ROBBINS NEST—15 minutes—ABC—September 29, 1950 - December 22, 1950.

THE ROBERT HERRIDGE THEATRE

Anthology. Dramatic presentations. Adaptations of short stories and plays by noted authors.
Host: Robert Herridge.

Included:

The World Of Irving Harmon. Screen comedian Irving Harmon enacts a series of sketches that tell about himself and the people he has encountered during his career.

CAST
Irving Harmon, Sandra Lee, Joe Silver, Lee Sherman.

The Tell-Tale Heart. A servant kills his master because he is haunted by the old man's pale blue eyes. Believing that he has committed the perfect murder, he allows police to search the room in which the body is hidden. Suddenly, the servant hears the old man's heart beat—louder and louder until it causes him to confess.

CAST
Michael Kane.

The Story of a Gunfighter. The story of a gunfighter who is hired to kill the town sheriff.

CAST
William Shatner, Philip Coolidge, Dennis Kohler.

THE ROBERT HERRIDGE THEATRE—30 minutes—CBS—July 7, 1960 - September 1960.

ROBERT MONTGOMERY PRESENTS

Anthology. Dramatic presentations.

Host-Narrator-Producer-Occasional Performer: Robert Montgomery.

Included:

Bella Fleace Gave a Party. Despising her heirs, a woman decides to spend her money on one last, lavish ball.

CAST

Bella Fleace: Fay Bainter; Riley: J. Pat O'Malley.

The Tall Dark Man. After witnessing a murder, a young girl, who is addicted to telling tall tales, struggles to prove her story truthful.

CAST

Sarah Grass: Robin Morgan; Mrs. Everett: Margaret Warwick; Mrs. Grass: Mary Jackson.

P.J. Martin and Son. Realizing that she can't run her family as she does her successful construction company, a woman struggles to regain their love.

CAST

Pauline Martin: Edna Brent; David Martin: Lin McCarthy; Tommy Martin: Jack Mullaney; Joan Martin: Gloria Strovck.

ROBERT MONTGOMERY PRESENTS—60 minutes—NBC—January 30, 1950 - June 24, 1957. Also known as "The Lucky Strike Theatre."

THE ROBERTA QUINLAN SHOW

Musical Variety.

Hostess: Roberta Quinlan.

Announcer: Bob Stanton.

Music: The Harry Clark Trio; The Tony Mottola Trio; The Elliott Lawrence Orchestra.

Versions:

THE ROBERTA QUINLAN SHOW— 15 minutes—NBC—May 3, 1949 - November 23, 1951. Also known as "Especially For You."

ROBERTA Q'S MATINEE—30 minutes—NBC—1952 - 1956.

THE ROBERT Q. LEWIS SHOW

Musical Variety.

Host: Robert Q. Lewis.

Regulars: Jaye P. Morgan, Rosemary

Clooney, Merv Griffin, Jan Ardan, Earl Wrightson, Jill Corey, Lois Hunt, Pat Lytell, Nat Cantor.

Orchestra: Ray Bloch; George Wright.

Producer: Rai Purdy, Lester Gottlieb.

Director: Jerome Schnur.

THE ROBERT Q. LEWIS SHOW—30 minutes—CBS—January 11, 1954 - May 25, 1956.

ROBERT YOUNG, FAMILY DOCTOR

See title: "Marcus Welby, M.D."

ROBIN HOOD

See title: "The Adventures of Robin Hood."

ROBINSON CRUSOE

Adventure Serial. Background: Somewhere off the coast of South America during the seventeenth century. Caught in a tropical storm at sea, a young Englishman, Robinson Crusoe, is shipwrecked on an uncharted island from which there is no escape. The thirteen-part dramatization depicts his first day of life on the island to his rescue twenty-eight years later. Based on the novel by Daniel Defoe.

Starring: Robert Hoffman as Robinson Crusoe.

ROBINSON CRUSOE—30 minutes—Syndicated 1964.

ROCKET ROBIN HOOD

Animated Cartoon. Background: New Sherwood Forest, A.D., 3000 a floating, solar-powered asteroid—the headquarters of Rocket Robin Hood and his band of Merry Men: Will Scarlet, Little John, Allen, Jiles, and Friar Tuck—the futuristic defenders of justice. Stories depict their battle against the forces of villainy throughout the universe, namely, the evils of the Sheriff of Knott.

Music: Winston Sharples.

ROCKET ROBIN HOOD—30 minutes—Syndicated 1967. 156 episodes.

THE ROCK FOLLIES

Musical Drama. Background: London,

England. A penetrating satire that follows the careers of "The Little Ladies" (Anna Wynd, Devonia "Dee" Rhoades, and Nancy "Q" Qunard), a three girl British Rock Group, as they struggle to succeed in the world of Pop music.

CAST

Anna Wynd	Charlotte Cornwell
Devonia "Dee" Rhoades	Julie Covington
Nancy "Q" Qunard	Rula Lenska
Derek Huggin, Q's romantic interest	Emlyn Price
Spike, Dee's romantic interest	Billy Murray
Jack, Anna's romantic interest	Stephen Moore
Gloria, a friend	Angela Bruce
Bob, a friend	Bob Stewart
Mrs. Wynd, Anna's mother	Vivienne Burgess

The Little Ladies Rock Band: Brian Chatton, Peter Hooke, Tony Stevens, Ray Russell.

Music: Andy Mackay.

Producer: Andrew Brown.

Director: Jon Scoffield, Brian Farnum.

THE ROCK FOLLIES—60 minutes— PBS—March 5, 1977 - March 10, 1977. 6 episodes. Produced in England.

THE ROCKFORD FILES

Crime Drama. Background: Los Angeles, California. The investigations of Jim Rockford, the chief operative of the Rockford Private Detective Agency, as he attempts to solve criminal cases that are considered unsolvable and labled inactive by police.

CAST

Jim Rockford	James Garner
Joseph (Rocky) Rockford, his father	Noah Beery
Beth Davenport, a lawyer	Gretchen Corbett
Sergeant Dennis Becker, L.A.P.D.	Joe Santos
Angel Martin, Jim's friend	Stuart Margolin
Peggy Becker, Dennis's wife	Pat Finley

Executive Producer: Meta Rosenberg, Stephen J. Cannell.

Producer: Charles Johnson, David Chase.

Creator: Roy Huggins, Stephen J. Cannell.

Music: Mike Post, Pete Carpenter.

THE ROCKFORD FILES—60 minutes—NBC—Premiered: September 13, 1974.

ROCKY AND HIS FRIENDS

Animated Cartoon. A battle against evil as seen through the activities of Rocky the flying squirrel and his simple-minded friend, Bullwinkle the moose. Stumbling upon the evils of Mr. Big, the midget, they struggle to thwart his plans by foiling the work of his agents, Boris Badenov, "International Bad Guy," and his aide, the deadly Natasha Fataly.

Additional segments:

Fractured Fairy Tales. Modern adaptations of childrens fables.

Aesop's Fables. The wise Aesop's efforts to explain the aspects of a changing world to his impressionable son.

Peabody's Improbable History. Through the use of their Way Back Machine, Mr. Peabody, the intelligent dog, and his friend, Sherman, a young boy, travel throughout history to help famous people achieve their fame.

Dudley Do-Right. The efforts of a simple-minded Mountie to apprehend the notorious Snively Whiplash.

Bullwinkle's Corner. Ninety seconds of nonsense poetry.

Characters' Voices
Rocky	June Foray
Bullwinkle	Bill Scott
Boris Badenov	Paul Frees
Natasha Fataly	June Foray
Snively Whiplash	Hans Conried
Peabody	Bill Scott
Sherman	June Foray
Aesop	Charlie Ruggles

Narrator of the Rocky and Bullwinkle Segment: Paul Frees.

Narrator of "Fractured Fairy Tales:" Edward Everett Horton.

Additional Voices: Bill Conrad, Walter Tetley, Skip Craig, Barbara Baldwin, Adrienne Diamond.

Music: Fred Steiner; Frank Comstock.

Producer: Jay Ward, Bill Scott.

Note: The character voiced by Hans Conried, is also known to be Snidely Whiplash.

ROCKY AND HIS FRIENDS—30 minutes—ABC—September 29, 1959 -

September 3, 1961. Syndicated. Spin-off series: "Bullwinkle"—30 minutes—NBC—September 1961 - September 1962; ABC—30 minutes—September 20, 1964 - September 2, 1973. Syndicated.

ROCKY JONES, SPACE RANGER

Adventure. Era: Twenty-first-century Earth. The battle against interplanetary evil as undertaken by Rocky Jones, chief of the Space Rangers, an organization of men and women established to protect the planets of a united solar system.

CAST
Rocky Jones	Richard Crane
Winky, his assistant	Scott Beckett
Vena Ray, his assistant	Sally Mansfield
Bobby, his junior assistant	Robert Lyden
Professor Newton	Maurice Cass
Yarra, the ruler of the planet Medina	Dian Fauntelle

Rocky's ship: The *Orbit Jet.*

Producer: Roland Reed.

Director: William Beaudine, Hollingsworth Morse.

ROCKY JONES, SPACE RANGER—30 minutes—NBC—1954 - 1955. 31 episodes. Syndicated.

ROCKY KING, DETECTIVE

Crime Drama. Background: New York City. The investigations of Rocky King, a plainclothes police detective with the Manhattan 24th precinct.

CAST
Rocky King	Roscoe Karns
Sergeant Hart	Todd Karns

Producer: Lawrence Menkin, Charles Speer, Jerry Layton.

Director: Dick Sandwick.

Sponsor: American Chicle.

ROCKY KING, DETECTIVE—30 minutes—DuMont—1950 - 1951. Original title: "Inside Detective."

ROD BROWN OF THE ROCKET RANGERS

Adventure. Era: Twenty-second-century Earth. The battle against inter-planetary evil as undertaken by the Rocket Rangers, a celestial defense organization established on Omega Base. Stories relate the work of Ranger Rod Brown as he explores the unknown realms of outer space.

CAST
Ranger Rod Brown	Cliff Robertson
Ranger Frank Boyle	Bruce Hall
Commander Swift	John Boruff
Ranger Wilbur Wormser (Wormsey)	Jack Weston
Also	Shirley Standlee

Rod's rocket ship: The *Beta.*

Program Open:

Announcer: "CBS Television presents Rod Brown of the Rocket Rangers. Surging with the power of the atom, gleaming like great silver bullets, the mighty Rocket Rangers space ships, stand by for blast-off. [Rockets are seen blasting off.] Up, up, rockets blazing with white hot fury, the man-made meteors ride through the atmosphere, breaking the gravity barrier, pushing up and out, faster and faster and then outer space and high adventure for the Rocket Rangers."

ROD BROWN OF THE ROCKET RANGERS—30 minutes—CBS—April 18, 1953 - May 29, 1954.

ROD ROCKET

A cartoon series, based on space travel, that details the adventures of Rod Rocket, his sidekick Joey, and Professor Argus. 130 five minute films, Syndicated 1962.

ROD SERLING'S NIGHT GALLERY

See title: "Four-In-One," *Night Gallery* segment.

THE ROGER MILLER SHOW

Musical Variety.

Host: Roger Miller.

Regulars: Arthur Godfrey, The Doodletown Pipers.

Orchestra: Eddie Karam.

THE ROGER MILLER SHOW—30 minutes—NBC—September 12, 1966 - January 3, 1967. 16 tapes.

ROGER RAMJET

Animated Cartoon. Experimenting,

scientist Roger Ramjet discovers a pill that, when taken, endows him with the power of twenty atom bombs for twenty seconds. Incorporating its power, he battles the sinister forces of evil.

ROGER RAMJET—05 minutes—Syndicated 1965. 150 episodes.

THE ROGUES

Drama. Background: London, England. The saga of the Fleming-St. Clairs, a family of con artists who devise ingenious schemes to steal treasures from those who can afford to be robbed, or deserve to be.

CAST

Alec Fleming, British, the head of the family	David Niven
Marcel St. Clair, the Suave French cousin	Charles Boyer
Tony Fleming, the American cousin	Gig Young
Timmy Fleming, an English cousin	Robert Coote
Margaret Fleming, an English cousin	Gladys Cooper
Scotland Yard Inspector Briscoe	John Williams.

Music: Nelson Riddle.

THE ROGUES—60 minutes—NBC—September 13, 1964 - September 5, 1965. 29 episodes. Syndicated.

The Rogues. Left to right: Gig Young, Charles Boyer, David Niven.

ROLL OUT!

Comedy. Background: World War II France (1944). The saga of the men assigned to the 5050th Quartermaster Trucking Company of the U.S. Third Army's Red Ball Express, the mostly black American trucking company designed to deliver supplies to the front lines, swing around, and return for more.

CAST

Cpl. Carter "Sweet" Williams, a smooth-talking, conniving draftee from Harlem	Stu Gilliam
Pfc. Jed Brooks, his sidekick, a Southern draftee, a country boy responsive to the system	Hilly Hicks
Sgt. B.J. Bryant	Mel Stewart
Captain Rocco Calvelli, the C.O.	Val Bisoglio
Lt. Robert Chapman	Ed Begley, Jr.
Madame Delacourt, the owner of the restaurant	Penny Santon
Wheels Dawson	Garrett Morris
High Strung	Theodore Wilson
Jersey Hampton	Darrow Igus
Phone Booth	Rod Gist
Focus	Jeff Burton
Sergeant Grease, the cook	Sam Laws

Music: Dave Grusin; Benny Golson.

ROLL OUT!—30 minutes—CBS—October 5, 1973 - January 4, 1974. 13 episodes.

ROLLIN' ON THE RIVER

Musical Variety. Background: The Mississippi River Boat, the *River Queen.*

Host: Kenny Rodgers.

Regulars: The First Edition: Mary Arnold, Terry Williams, Kin Vassey, Mickey Jones.

Musical Direction: Larry Cansler.

ROLLIN' ON THE RIVER—30 minutes—Syndicated 1971. 26 tapes. Also titled: "Rollin' with Kenny Rodgers and The First Edition."

ROMAN HOLIDAYS

Animated Cartoon. Twentieth-century life is depicted in Ancient Rome. Background: 4960 Terrace Drive, the Venus DiMillo Arms apartment house in Pastafasullo, Rome, A.D. 63—the residence of the Holidays: Gus, an engineer with the Forum Construction Company; his wife, Laurie; and their children Precocia and Happius. Stories depict the trials and tribulations of a family as they struggle to cope with the endless problems of a changing world. A Hanna-Barbera production.

Characters' Voices

Gus Holiday	Dave Willock
Laurie Holiday	Shirley Mitchell
Precocia Holiday	Pamelyn Ferdin
Happius Holiday (Happy)	Stanley Livingston
Mr. Evictus, the Landlord	Dom De Luise
Mr. Tycoonius, Gus's Employer	Hal Smith
Brutus, the Holiday pet lion	Daws Butler
Groovia, Happy's girlfriend	Judy Strangis
Herman, Gus's friend	Hal Peary
Henrietta, his wife	Janet Waldo

Music: Hoyt Curtin.

ROMAN HOLIDAYS—30 minutes—NBC—September 9, 1972 - September 1, 1973.

ROMANTIC INTERLUDE

Anthology. Rebroadcasts of dramas that were originally aired via other filmed anthology programs.

Included:

The Perfect Gentleman. The story of a self-made man who tries to make himself over to please his fiancée.
Starring: Bruce Cabot.

Angel. The story of a man who pretends to be the guardian angel of a little girl to escape from the police.
Starring: Steve Brodie.

The Return of Van Sickle. An elderly man tries to teach his vicious son-in-law the meaning of kindness.
Starring: Cliff Arquette.

ROMANTIC INTERLUDE—30 minutes—ABC 1955.

ROMPER ROOM

Educational. Entertainment geared to preschoolers. A basic format, which includes sets, games, songs, stories, and activities, is syndicated to local stations to allow the inclusion of their own instructresses.

Hostesses-Instructresses, including: Gloria Flood (WABC-TV, New York); Jean Mosley (WBAC-TV, Baltimore); Rosemary Rapp (WGN-TV, Chicago); Joan Thayer (WNEW-TV, New York); Connie Sullivan (WCDA-TV,

Albany, N.Y.); June Hurley (WLCY-TV, Tampa-St. Petersberg, Florida); Louise Redfield (WOR-TV, New York).

ROMPER ROOM—60 minutes—Syndicated 1953.

RONA BARRETT'S HOLLYWOOD

Hollywood Gossip Reports.

Hostess-Commentator: Rona Barrett.

RONA BARRETT'S HOLLYWOOD —2 minutes, 30 seconds (five times weekly)—Syndicated 1969.

THE ROOKIES

Crime Drama. Background: California. The investigations of William Gillis, Terry Webster, Michael Danko, and Chris Owens, Rookies attached to Station Number Seven of the Southern California Police Department. Reluctant to use firearms, they represent the new breed of law enforcer and the nonviolent approach to crime control.

CAST

Lieutenant Edward Ryker	Gerald S. O'Loughlin
Patrolman William Gillis	Michael Ontkean
Patrolman Terry Webster	Georg Stanford Brown
Patrolman Michael Danko	Sam Melville
Jill Danko, Mike's wife, a nurse	Kate Jackson
Patrolman Chris Owens	Bruce Fairbairn
The Police Radio Dispatcher	Darlyn Ann Lindley

Music: Elmer Bernstein; Lawrence Rosenthal; Pete Rugolo; Jack Elliott, Allyn Ferguson.

Executive Producer: Aaron Spelling, Leonard Goldberg.

Producer: Rick Husky, Skip Webster, William Blinn, Paul Junger Witt, Hal Sitowitz.

Director: E.W. Swackhamer, Phil Bondelli, Alvin Ganzer, Leonard Horn, Lee Philips, Gene Nelson, Harry Falk, Gerald S. O'Loughlin, Ralph Senesky, Jerry Jamison, Walter Claxton, Michael Caffrey, Ivan Dixon, Fernando Lamas.

Creator: Rita Lakin.

Note: Jill works at Memorial Hospital.

THE ROOKIES—60 minutes—ABC— September 11, 1972 - June 15, 1976. 68 episodes.

ROOM FOR ONE MOORE

Comedy. Background: Los Angeles, California. Incidents in the lives of the Rose family: George, an engineer; his wife, Anna; and their children, Laurie and Flip (their own); and Jeff and Mary (adopted). Stories depict Anna's fond love of children and her attempts to help the misplaced and lonely. Based on the film, "The Easy Way."

CAST

George Rose	Andrew Duggan
Anna Rose	Peggy McCay
Laurie Rose	Carol Nicholsen
Flip Rose	Ronnie Dapo
Jeff Rose	Timmy Rooney
Mary Rose	Anna Capri
Walter Burton, their neighbor	Jack Albertson
Ruth Burton, his wife	Marine Stuart
Elsie, Anna's friend	Sara Seeger

Rose Family Dog: Tramp.

Music: Paul Sawtell, Frank Perkins.

ROOM FOR ONE MORE—30 minutes—ABC—January 27, 1962 - September 22, 1962. 26 episodes. Syndicated.

ROOM 222

Comedy-Drama. Background: Walt Whitman High School in Los Angeles, California. Life in an integrated urban high school as seen through the eyes of Pete Dixon, a black American History instructor whose classes are held in Room 222.

CAST

Pete Dixon	Lloyd Haynes
Seymour Kaufman, the principal	Michael Constantine
Liz Macintyre, the guidance counselor, Pete's romantic interest	Denise Nicholas
Alice Johnson, a student teacher	Karen Valentine
Miss Evans	Hollis Irving
Miss Hogarth	Patsy Garret
Miss Portnoy	Carol Worthington
Students:	
Richie Lane	Howard Rice
Jason Allen	Heshimu
Larry	Eric Laneuville
Pamela	Ta Tanisha
Helen Loomis	Judy Strangis
Bernie	David Jolliffe
Laura	Pamela Peters

Music: Richard La Salle.

Additional Music: Jerry Goldsmith, Lionel Newman, Benny Golson.

Executive Producer: William P. D'Angelo.

Producer: Gene Reynolds, Jon Kubichan, Ronald Rubin.

Room 222. Left to right: Lloyd Haynes, Karen Valentine, Michael Constantine.

Director: Allen Baron, Seymour Robbie, Lee Philips, Hal Cooper, Herman Hoffman, James Sheldon, Leslie H. Martinson, Richard Michaels, Charles R. Rondeau, William Wiard, Gene Reynolds.

Creator: James L. Brooks.

ROOM 222–30 minutes–ABC–September 17, 1969 - January 11, 1974. Syndicated.

ROOTIE KAZOOTIE

Children. Puppet antics set against the background of the Rootie Kazootie Club.

Host: Todd Russell.

Assistant: John Schoepperle as Mr. Deetle Dootle.

Puppet characters: Rootie Kazootie, a freckle-faced little boy; Gala Poochie Pup, his wide-eyed dog; Polka Dottie, Rootie's girlfriend; El Squeako the mouse; Nipper, Catador, and Poison Sumac.

Producer: Steve Carlin.

Director: Dwight Hemion.

ROOTIE KAZOOTIE–30 minutes–ABC–January 3, 1952 - February 5, 1954. NBC run: October 13, 1951 - November 21, 1952.

ROOTS

Drama. An eight-part adaptation of the novel by Alex Haley, which dramatizes a century in Haley's family history–from his ancestors' life in 18th-century tribal Africa to their emancipation in the post-Civil War South.

CAST

Kunta Kinte	LeVar Burton
	John Amos
Binta, Kunta's mother	Cicely Tyson
Omoro, Kunta's father	Thalmus Rasulala
Capt. Thomas Davies	Edward Asner
Slater	Ralph Waite
Brima Cesay	Harry Rhodes
Fanta	Ren Woods
	Beverly Todd
Nyo Boto	Maya Angelou
Kintango	Moses Gunn
Reynolds	Lorne Greene
Fiddler	Louis Gossett, Jr.
Ames	Vic Morrow
Dr. William Reynolds	Robert Reed
Mrs. Reynolds	Lynda Day George
Kizzy	Leslie Uggams

Missy Anne Reynolds	Sandy Duncan
Mrs. Moore	Carolyn Jones
Noah	Lawrence-Hilton Jacobs
Tom Moore	Chuck Connors
Sam Bennett	Richard Roundtree
Kadi Touray	O.J. Simpson
Tom	Georg Stanford Brown
Chicken George	Ben Vereen
Irene	Lynne Moody
Evan Brent	Lloyd Bridges
Jeremy Brent	Doug McClure
Ol' George	Brad Davis
Virgil	Austin Stoker
Senator Justin	Burl Ives

Also: Todd Bridges, Robert Phalen, Macon McColman, Lillian Randolph, Wally Taylor, William Watson.

Music: Gerald Fried.

Executive Producer: David L. Wolper.

Producer: Stan Margulies.

Director: David Greene, John Erman, Gilbert Moses, Marvin Chomsky.

ROOTS–12 hours–ABC–January 23, 1977 - January 30, 1977.

ROSEMARY CLOONEY

Listed: The television programs of singer Rosemary Clooney.

The Rosemary Clooney Show– Musical Variety–30 minutes–Syndicated–1956 - 1957.

Hostess: Rosemary Clooney.

Vocalists: The Hi-Lo's.

Orchestra: Nelson Riddle.

The Rosemary Clooney Show– Musical Variety–30 minutes–NBC– September 26, 1957 - June 19, 1958.

Hostess: Rosemary Clooney.

Vocalists: Paul Kelly and The Modernaires.

Orchestra: Frank DeVol.

ROSETTI AND RYAN

Drama. Background: California. The cases of Joseph Rosetti and Frank Ryan, a playboy and an ex-cop, now freewheeling attorneys who incorporate unorthodox methods as they strive to seek justice for their clients.

CAST

Joseph Rosetti	Tony Roberts
Frank Ryan	Squire Fridell
Jessica Hornesby, the assistant D.A.	Jane Elliot

Rocky (originally Georgia), Joe's secretary	Randi Oakes
Rosa Rosetti, Joe's mother	Penny Santon

Music: Peter Matz, Gordon Jenkins.

Executive Producer: Leonard B. Stern.

Producer: Jerry Davis.

ROSETTI AND RYAN–60 minutes– NBC–Premiered: September 22, 1977.

THE ROSEY GRIER SHOW

Variety.

Host: Rosey Grier.

Featured: Charles Brown, columnist.

THE ROSEY GRIER SHOW–30 minutes–Syndicated 1969. 52 tapes.

THE ROUGH RIDERS

Western. Background: Various areas between the Great Smokies and the High Sierras during the 1860s. Following the surrender at Appomattox, two Union officers, Captain Jim Flagg and Sergeant Buck Sinclair, and one Confederate, Lieutenant Kirby, team and journey West to begin a new life. Seeking land on which to settle, they involve themselves in and attempt to solve the problems of others.

CAST

Captain Jim Flagg	Kent Taylor
Lieutenant Kirby	Jan Merlin
Sergeant Buck Sinclair	Peter Whitney

THE ROUGH RIDERS–30 minutes– ABC–October 2, 1958 - September 24, 1959. 39 episodes. Syndicated.

THE ROUNDERS

Comedy. Background: The J. L. Cattle Ranch. The saga of two dimwitted cowboys, hired hands, Ben Jones and Howdy Lewis.

CAST

Jim Ed Love, the ranch owner	Chill Wills
Ben Jones	Ron Hays
Howdy Lewis	Patrick Wayne
Sally, Ben's girlfriend	Janis Hansen
Ada, Howdy's girlfriend	Bobbi Jordan
Vince, Jim Ed's right-hand man	J. Pat O'Malley

Shorty Davis, a
  ranch hand   Jason Wingreen

Music: Jeff Alexander.

THE ROUNDERS–30 minutes–ABC
–September 6, 1966 - January 3,
1967. 17 episodes.

ROUTE 66

Adventure. Left penniless after the
death of his wealthy father, Tod
Stiles, and Buzz Murdock, an
employee of Tod's father, a poor boy
from New York's Hell's Kitchen, pool
their resources, purchase a 1960 Chevrolet, and begin an uncertain journey,
wandering along the highway of
Route 66.

Seeking work and eventually a
place to settle down, they involve
themselves in and attempt to solve the
problems of others.

CAST

Tod Stiles   Martin Milner
Buzz Murdock   George Maharis
Linc Case, a
  Vietnam war veteran,
  Tod's partner in
  later episodes   Glen Corbett

Music: Nelson Riddle.

Producer: Herbert B. Leonard, Jerry
  Thomas, Leonard Freeman, Sam
  Manners.

ROUTE 66–60 minutes–CBS–October 7, 1960 - September 18, 1964.
116 episodes. Syndicated.

Route 66. George Maharis and Martin
Milner. © *Screen Gems.*

THE ROWAN AND
MARTIN SHOW

Variety. Music, songs, and comedy
sketches.

Hosts: Dan Rowan, Dick Martin.

Regulars: Frankie Randall, Lainie
  Kazan, Judi Rolin, The Wisa
  D'Orso Dancers.

Orchestra: Les Brown.

THE ROWAN AND MARTIN SHOW
–60 minutes–NBC–June 16, 1966 -
September 8, 1966.

ROYAL CANADIAN
MOUNTED POLICE

Adventure. Background: Shamattawa,
Canada, a base of the Royal Canadian
Mounted Police. Stories depict the
investigations of three Canadian
policemen and the methods incorporated in the battle against crime.

CAST

Corporal Jacques
  Gagnier   Gilles Pelletier
Constable Scott   John Perkins
Constable Mitchell Don Francks

ROYAL CANADIAN MOUNTED
POLICE–30 minutes–Syndicated
1960. 39 episodes. Also known as
"R.C.M.P."

ROYAL PLAYHOUSE

Anthology. Retitled episodes of
dramas originally aired via "Fireside
Theatre" during its 1949 - 1950
season.

Producer: Bing Crosby Enterprises.

ROYAL PLAYHOUSE–30 minutes–
DuMont 1953. 32 episodes.

ROYAL SHOWCASE

Variety. Performances by an established or up and coming comic, movie
figure, or recording personality.

Host: George Abbott.

Announcer: Ben Grauer.

Orchestra: Gordon Jenkins.

ROYAL SHOWCASE–30 minutes–
NBC 1952.

THE ROY ROGERS AND
DALE EVANS SHOW

Musical Variety. Performances by
Country and Western entertainers.

Hosts: Roy Rogers and Dale Evans
  (Mrs.)

Regulars: Pat Brady, Cliff Arquette,
  The Sons of the Pioneers, and
  the Rogers's children: Dodie,
  Debbie, Dusty, and Sandy.

Orchestra: Ralph Carmichael.

Producer: Ralph Wonders, Bob Henry.

Director: Bob Henry.

THE ROY ROGERS AND DALE
EVANS SHOW–60 minutes–ABC–
September 29, 1962 - December 23,
1962.

THE ROY ROGERS SHOW

Modern Western. Background: The
Double R Bar Ranch in Mineral City.
The exploits of Roy Rogers and Dale
Evans, ranchers and the owners of a
diner, as they strive to maintain law
and order. Spiced with light comedy.

CAST

Roy Rogers,
  "King of the
  Cowboys"   Himself
Dale Evans,
  "Queen of the
  West"   Herself
Pat Brady, the
  diner cook   Himself
Mayor Ralph Cotton Harry Lauter
Sheriff Potter   Harry Harvey, Sr.

Also: The Sons of the Pioneers: Bob
  Nolan, Karl Farr, Lloyd
  Perryman, Hugh Farr.

Orchestra: Lou Bring.

Theme: "Happy Trails To You."

Producer: Jack Lacey, Bob Henry,
  Roy Rogers, Leslie H. Martinson.

Sponsor: General Foods.

Roy's horse: Trigger.

Dale's horse: Buttercup.

Pat's jeep: Nellybelle.

Roy's dog: Bullet.

Program Open:
Announcer: "The Roy Rogers Show,
  starring Roy Rogers, king of the
  cowboys; Trigger, his golden Palo-
  mino; and Dale Evans, queen of
  the West. With Pat Brady, his
  comical sidekick; and Roy's wonder dog, Bullet."

THE ROY ROGERS SHOW–30 minutes–CBS–October 4, 1951 - September 19, 1964. 100 episodes. Syndicated.

THE RUFF AND READY SHOW

Animated Cartoon. The adventures of Ruff the cat and Ready the dog as they unite to battle the sinister forces of evil. A Hanna-Barbera Production.

Host: Jimmy Blaine.

Characters' Voices

Ruff	Don Messick
Ready	Daws Butler

Additional characters: Professor Gismo, Captain Greedy, Killer and Diller, Salt Water Daffy, Harry Safari.

THE RUFF AND READY SHOW—30 minutes—NBC—December 14, 1957 - September 1964. Syndicated.

THE RUGGLES

Comedy. The trials and tribulations of the Ruggles family.

CAST

Charlie Ruggles	Himself
Mrs. Ruggles	Erin O'Brien Moore
	Ruth Tedrow
Sharon Ruggles, their daughter	Margaret Kerry

Also: Judy Nugent, Jimmy Hawkins, Tommy Bernard.

Music: Fred Howard

Producer: Robert Raisbeck.

Director: George M. Cahan.

THE RUGGLES—30 minutes—ABC—January 1, 1950 - April 1, 1950.

RUN, BUDDY, RUN

Comedy. Background: Los Angeles, California. In a clouded steam room, the unsuspecting meeting place of gangland hoods, Buddy Overstreet, a mild-mannered accountant, overhears their plotting of the killing of "The Man in Chicago," and the mysterious words, "Chicken Little." Spotted by Mr. Devere, the underworld boss, Buddy is chased, but escapes capture. Considered a threat to their plan of operation, Devere orders Buddy's apprehension. Endlessly pursued by the mob, Buddy struggles to avoid being captured and to resolve the differences between him and Devere.

CAST

Buddy Overstreet	Jack Sheldon
Mr. Devere	Bruce Gordon
Junior Devere	Jim Connell

Devere's Aides:

Harry	Gregg Palmer

Wendell	Nick Georgiade
Joseph	Dort Clark

RUN, BUDDY, RUN—30 minutes—CBS—September 12, 1966 - January 2, 1967. 16 episodes.

RUN FOR YOUR LIFE

Adventure. Discovering he has only a short time to live when a medical report reveals he is dying of an incurable disease, attorney Paul Bryan decides to cram a lifetime of living into his remaining one or two years. Clinging to the slim hope of a medical breakthrough, he travels around the world and involves himself in and attempts to solve the problems of others.

CAST

Paul Bryan	Ben Gazzara
The doctor (program opening)	John Hoyt

Music: Pete Rugolo.

RUN FOR YOUR LIFE—60 minutes—NBC—September 13, 1965 - September 11, 1968. 85 episodes. Syndicated.

RUN, JOE, RUN

Adventure. Distinguished by two formats.

Format One:

Falsely accused of attacking his master, Joe, a black and tan army trained German Shepherd dog, escapes before he is able to be destroyed. Declared an army fugitive, a two hundred dollar reward is posted for his capture. Able to prove his innocence, his master, Sergeant William Corey, begins a cross-country trek and, against numerous obstacles, attempts to capture Joe and clear his name.

Starring: Arch Whiting as Sgt. William Corey.

Music: Richard La Salle.

RUN, JOE, RUN—30 minutes—NBC—September 7, 1974 - August 30, 1975. Returned: NBC—December 6, 1975 - September 4, 1976.

Format Two:

Before he is able to prove Joe's innocence, Sgt. Corey is ordered back to active duty. Still wandering, Joe

meets and befriends Josh McCoy, a backpacker who is unaware of Joe's past. Stories depict their adventures as they travel across the country.

Starring: Chad States as Josh McCoy.

Music: Richard La Salle.

RUN, JOE, RUN—30 minutes—NBC—September 6, 1975 - November 29, 1975.

RUNAROUND

Game. Nine children compete. After the host reads a question, three answers appear on stage. On the word "go" the players run to the lane that they each believe is the correct answer. A light reveals the correct answer, and players standing on that particular lane receive one token. Other players are placed in a penalty box. The game continues until two players remain. Each is then asked a question. The player who correctly answers it is the winner and receives one additional token. The players are removed from the penalty box and a new game begins. Winners, the highest token accumulators, receive merchandise prizes.

Host: Paul Winchell.

Assistants: His dummy friends, Jerry Mahoney and Knucklehead Smith.

Announcer: Kenny Williams.

Music: Mort Garson.

RUNAROUND—30 minutes—NBC—September 9, 1972 - September 1, 1973.

THE RUSS MORGAN SHOW

Musical Variety.

Host: Russ Morgan.

Vocalist: Helen O'Connell.

Orchestra: Russ Morgan.

THE RUSS MORGAN SHOW—60 minutes—CBS—July 7, 1956 - September 1, 1956.

RUTHIE ON THE TELEPHONE

Comedy. Via a split-screen effect, which is accomplished through mirrors, a girl relentlessly pursues a guy, who'd rather be left alone, by telephone. Adapted from a sketch on the CBS radio program, "The Robert Q. Lewis Show."

CAST

Ruthie	Ruth Gilbert

The guy	Philip Reed

RUTHIE ON THE TELEPHONE–05 minutes–CBS 1948.

RUTH LYONS 50 CLUB

Variety. Music, songs, guests, interviews, and household tips.

Hostess: Ruth Lyons.

Regulars: Dick Noell, Bill Thall.

Orchestra: Bert Farber.

RUTH LYONS 50 CLUB–60 minutes–NBC 1951.

RYAN'S HOPE

Serial. Background: The upper West Side in New York City. The triumphs and tragedies of three generations of an Irish-American family, the Ryans.

CAST

John Ryan	Bernard Barrow
Mary Ryan	Kate Mulgrew
Maeve Ryan	Helen Gallagher
Frank Ryan	Michael Hawkins
	Andrew Robinson
Delia Ryan	Ilene Kristen
Dr. Pat Ryan	Malcolm Groome
Jack Fenelli	Michael Levin
Jillian Coleridge	Nanci Addison
Dr. Clem Moultrie	Hannibal Penney
Nell Baulac	Diana van der Vlis
Dr. Roger Coleridge	Ron Hale
Faith Coleridge	Faith Catlin
	Nancy Barrett
	Catherine Hicks
Ramona Gonzalez	Rosalinda Guerra
Dr. Edward Coleridge	Frank Latimore
Dr. Bucky Carter	Justin Deas
Bob Reid	Earl Hindman
Nick Szabo	Michael Fairman
Seneca Baulac	John Gabriel
Annie Burney	Jody Catlin
Tom Desmond	Tom MacGreevey
Alicia	Anita Ortiz
Father Richards	Bernie McInerney
Alex Webster	Ed Evanko

Music: Aelous Productions.

Music Supervision: Sybil Weinberger.

Additional Music: Carey Gold.

Producer: Robert Costello, Monroe Carroll.

Director: Lela Swift.

RYAN'S HOPE–30 minutes–ABC–Premiered: July 7, 1975.

S

SABER OF LONDON

See title: "Mark Saber."

SABRINA, THE TEEN-AGE WITCH

Animated Cartoon. Background: The town of Riverdale. The misadventures of Sabrina, a high school student and apprentice witch who struggles to conceal the existence of her powers. A spin-off from "The Archie Show."

Characters:
Sabrina, Aunt Hilda, Aunt Zelda, Archie Andrews, Jughead Jones, Reggie Mantle, Veronica Lodge, Valerie, Hot Dog (the Archie gang pet), Salem (Sabrina's cat), Harvey, Mr. Weatherby (the school principal), Miss Grundy (a teacher), Cousin Ambrose, The Groovie Goolies.

Voices: Larry Storch, Jane Webb, Dallas McKennon, John Erwin, Don Messick, Howard Morris.

Music: George Blais, Jeff Michael.

SABRINA, THE TEEN-AGE WITCH –30 minutes–CBS–September 11, 1971 - September 1, 1973. Originally broadcast as "Sabrina and the Groovie Goolies"–60 minutes–CBS–September 12, 1970 - September 4, 1971. 35 episodes.

SAFARILAND

Documentary. Film studies of the animals and people of Africa.

Host-Guide: Jim Stewart.

SAFARILAND–30 minutes–Syndicated 1963.

SAFARI TO ADVENTURE

Documentary. Films exploring the world of man and animal.

Host-Narrator: Bill Burrud.

SAFARI TO ADVENTURE–30 minutes–Syndicated 1971.

SAILOR OF FORTUNE

Adventure. Background: The Mediterranean. The assignments of Grant Mitchell, the captain of an American motor freighter.

CAST

Grant Mitchell	Lorne Greene
His assistant	Jack McGowran

SAILOR OF FORTUNE–30 minutes –Syndicated 1957.

THE SAINT

Adventure. The global exploits of Simon Templar, alias The Saint, a dashing dare-devil free-lance trouble-shooter. Wealthy, young, handsome, suave, and sophisticated, he possesses rich and fancy `tastes in wine and women; is cunning, ingenious, and a master among thieves; and, though considered criminal by police, assists them in his quest to aid people in distress. Created by Leslie Charteris. An I.T.C. Production.

CAST

Simon Templar, The Saint	Roger Moore
Claude Eustace Teal, the Chief Inspector of Scotland Yard	Winsley Pithey Norman Pitt Ivor Dean
Hoppy, Simon's houseboy	Percy Herbert

Music: Edwin Astley.

THE SAINT–60 minutes. Syndicated –1963 - 1966; NBC–May 21, 1967 - September 2, 1967; NBC–February 18, 1968 - September 14, 1968; NBC–April 11, 1969 - September 12, 1969. 114 episodes. Syndicated.

The Saint. Roger Moore. *Courtesy Independent Television Corporation; an ATV Company.*

SAINTS AND SINNERS

Drama. Background: Manhattan. The investigations of Nick Alexander, newspaper reporter-columnist for the *New York Record*. Stories present a behind-the-scenes insight into the world of newspaper men and women.

CAST

Nick Alexander	Nick Adams
Mark Grainger, the city editor	John Larkin
Dave Tobak, the copyeditor	Robert F. Simon
Staff photographer Klugie	Richard Erdman
Liz Hogan, the Washington correspondent	Barbara Rush

• SAINTS AND SINNERS—60 minutes —NBC—September 18, 1962 - January 28, 1963. 18 episodes.

SALE OF THE CENTURY

Game. Three competing contestants who each receive twenty-five dollars bidding cash.

Round One: The host reads a general-knowledge type of question. The first player to identify himself through a buzzer signal receives a chance to answer. If he is correct he scores five dollars; incorrect, the amount is deducted. After several questions an "Instant Bargain" (e.g., "For only $27.95 you can buy an $800 mink coat") appears. The player first to sound his buzzer receives the merchandise; the amount, rounded off to the nearest dollar, is deducted from his score.

Round Two: Played the same. Values or deductions are ten dollars per question.

Round Three: Played the same. Values or deductions are twenty-five dollars per question.

The highest cash scorer is the winner, and, brought downstage, he is shown five bargains (e.g., "A $2,400 car for $239"). He is permitted to purchase any one of the five, providing it is with money earned on the program. If an item is desired, but the money is lacking, he is permitted to compete further to earn the additional resources.

Host: Jack Kelly; Joe Garagiola.

Announcer: Bill Wendell.

Music: Al Howard, Irwin Bazelon.

SALE OF THE CENTURY—30 minutes—NBC—September 29, 1969 - July 13, 1973. Syndicated first run during the 1973-1974 season.

SALLY

Comedy. Distinguised by two formats:

Format One: September 15, 1957 - February 9, 1958.

The story concerns the global travels of Myrtle Banford, a rich, elderly widow, part owner of the Banford and Bascomb Department Store, and Sally Truesdale, her pretty, young traveling companion.

Format Two: February 16, 1958 - March 30, 1958.

The format change focuses on the misadventures of Sally as she begins work as a salesgirl in Mrs. Banford's store after returning to the U.S.

CAST

Sally Truesdale	Joan Caulfield
Myrtle Banford	Marion Lorne
Bascomb Bleacher, Sr., Sally's employer	Gale Gordon
Jim Kendall, Sally's romantic interest	Johnny Desmond
Junior Bleacher, Bascomb's son	Arte Johnson

Producer: Frank Ross.

SALLY—30 minutes—NBC—September 15, 1957 - March 30, 1958.

SALTY

Adventure. Background: The Cove Marina in Nassau. When their parents are killed by a hurricane in the Bahamas, Taylor Reed and his brother, Tim, are unofficially adopted by their rescuer, Clancy Ames a retired lawyer, now the owner of the marina. Stories depict the difficulties in operating a marina, and the adventures shared by Tim and his pet sea lion, Salty. Filmed in the Bahamas.

CAST

Clancy Ames	Julius Harris
Taylor Reed	Mark Slade
Tim Reed	Johnny Doran
Rod Porterfield, Tim's friend	Vincent Dale

Music: Samuel Matlovsky.

Executive Producer: Kobi Jaeger.

Producer: Monroe Carroll.

Director: Ricou Browning.

SALTY—30 minutes—Syndicated 1974. 26 episodes.

SAM BENEDICT

Crime Drama. Background: San Francisco, California. The cases and courtroom defenses of attorney Sam Benedict. Based on the files of criminal attorney Jacob Ehrlich.

CAST

Sam Benedict	Edmond O'Brien
Hank Tabor, his assistant	Richard Rust
Trudy Warner, his secretary	Joan Tompkins

Music: Nelson Riddle; Jeff Alexander.

SAM BENEDICT—60 minutes—NBC —September 15, 1962 - September 7, 1963. 28 episodes. Syndicated.

THE SAM LEVENSON SHOW

Discussion. Celebrities appear with their children and discuss the problems that exist between them.

Host: Sam Levenson.

Orchestra: Henry Sylvern.

Producer: Irving Mansfield.

Director: Byron Paul.

THE SAM LEVENSON SHOW—30 minutes—CBS—January 27, 1951 - June 30, 1951.

SAMMY AND COMPANY

Variety. Music, songs, dances, interviews, and comedy sketches.

Host: Sammy Davis, Jr.

Regulars: Avery Schreiber, Johnny Brown, Joyce Jillson, Kay Dingle.

Announcer: William B. Williams.

Orchestra: George Rhodes.

SAMMY AND COMPANY—90 minutes—Syndicated 1975.

THE SAMMY DAVIS, JR. SHOW

Musical Variety.

Host: Sammy Davis, Jr.

Featured: The Lester Wilson Dancers.

Orchestra: George Rhodes.

Premiere guests: Richard Burton, Elizabeth Taylor, Nancy Wilson, Corbett Monica, The Will Martin Trio.

THE SAMMY DAVIS, JR. SHOW—60 minutes—NBC—January 7, 1966 - May 1966.

SAMMY KAYE'S MUSIC FROM MANHATTAN

Musical Variety.

Host: Sammy Kaye.

Regulars: Ray Michaels, Hank Kanui, Larry O'Brien, Charles Roder, Johnny McAfee, Joe Mack, Teddy Auletto, Larry Ellis, Lynn Roberts, J. Blasingame Bond, Toby Wright, Joe Macchiaverna, Janice Jones, Harry Reser, Jack Jennings, Richard Dini, Johnny Amorosa, The Dixieland Quartet, The Kaydettes.

Orchestra: Sammy Kaye.

SAMMY KAYE'S MUSIC FROM MANHATTAN–30 minutes–ABC–September 20, 1958 - June 13, 1959.

SAMSON AND GOLIATH

Animated Cartoon. A battle against crime and corruption as undertaken by a young boy, Samson, and his dog, Goliath. Whenever trouble becomes evident, the boy raises his wrists, touches his bracelets, and utters, "I need Samson power." Instantly he is transformed into the mighty Samson, and his dog into the vicious lion, Goliath.

Characters' Voices
Samson   Tim Matthieson

Music: Hoyt Curtin.

SAMSON AND GOLIATH–30 minutes–NBC–September 9, 1967 - September 7, 1968. 26 episodes. Syndicated.

SAN FRANCISCO BEAT

See title: "Line-Up."

SAN FRANCISCO INTERNATIONAL AIRPORT

See title: "Four-In-One," *San Francisco International Airport* segment.

THE SAN PEDRO BEACH BUMS

Comedy. Background: San Pedro, California. The misadventures of five knockabout young men (Buddy, Boychick, Dancer, Stuf, and Moose), who live on the *Our Boat* (originally called the *Challenger*), an old fishing boat docked in the San Pedro harbor.

Samson and Goliath. The mighty Samson and his lion, Goliath. *Courtesy Hanna-Barbera Productions.*

CAST
Buddy Binder	Christopher Murney
Boychick	Jeff Druce
	Christopher DeRose
Edward "Dancer" McClory	John Mark Robinson
Stuf Danelli	Stuart Pankin
Moose	Darryl McCullough
Suzi Camelli, their friend, the operator of a sightseeing boat	Susan Mullen
Louise, the waitress at Tiny Teena's, the beach café	Louise Hoven
Marge, Moose's girlfriend, the lifeguard	Lisa Reeves
Julie, a friend	Nancy Morgan
Ralphie Walker, a friend	Christoff St. John

Music: Pete Rugolo, Mark Snow.

Executive Producer: Aaron Spelling, Douglas S. Cramer.

Producer: E. Duke Vincent, Earl Barret, Simon Munter.

Creator: E. Duke Vincent.

THE SAN PEDRO BEACH BUMS–60 minutes–ABC–Premiered: September 19, 1977. Originally titled "The San Pedro Bums."

THE SANDY DUNCAN SHOW

Comedy. Background: 130 North

Weatherly, the Royal Weatherly Hotel, Apartment 2-A, the residence of Sandy Stockton, a student teacher enrolled in U.C.L.A., and a part-time secretary employed with the advertising agency of Quinn and Cohen. Stories depict her misadventures as she struggles to divide her time between work, school, and studies. A spin-off from "Funny Face."

CAST
Sandy Stockton	Sandy Duncan
Bert Quinn, her employer	Tom Bosley
Kay Fox, Sandy's neighbor	Marian Mercer
Hilary, the agency receptionist	Pamela Zarit
Alex Lembert, Sandy's neighbor, a police officer	M. Emmet Walsh

The Sandy Duncan Show. Sandy Duncan.

Leonard Cohen, Bert's
partner   Alfie Wise
Ben Hampton,
the building
janitor   Eric Christmas

Music: Pat Williams.

THE SANDY DUNCAN SHOW—30
minutes—CBS—September 17, 1972 -
December 31, 1972. 13 episodes.

SANDY STRONG

A fifteen minute puppet show first
seen on ABC in 1950.

SANFORD AND SON

Comedy. Background: 9114 South
Central, Los Angeles, California, the
residence and business address of Fred
and Lamont Sanford, black junk
dealers. Fred, a sixty-five-year-old
widower who refuses to retire, is
satisfied with the business; Lamont,
his thirty-four-year-old son, a bachelor, is dissatisfied with existing conditions and wants to better himself by
beginning a new life on his own.
Fearing his life will be meaningless
without Lamont, Fred struggles to
keep him with him by feigning illness,
usually heart attacks, and calling on
his deceased wife—"Elizabeth, I'm
coming Elizabeth." Aware of his pre-
tense, Lamont remains, saving his
money, and hoping one day to establish a life of his own.

Stories depict their continual bickering and their misadventures as they
struggle to operate a junk business.
Based on the British series "Steptoe
and Son."

CAST

Fred Sanford   Redd Foxx
Lamont Sanford   Demond Wilson
Grady Wilson, Fred's
friend   Whitman Mayo
Aunt Esther, Elizabeth's
sister   LaWanda Page
Rollo Larson, Lamont's
friend   Nathaniel Taylor
Julio, the Sanfords'
neighbor   Gregory Sierra
Melvin, Fred's
friend   Slappy White
Officer Swanhauser,
L.A.P.D.   Norman Pitlik
Officer Smith (Smitty),
L.A.P.D.   Hal Williams
Officer Hoppy,
L.A.P.D.   Howard T. Platt
Bubba, Fred's
friend   Don Bexley
Donna Harris,
Fred's romantic
interest   Lynn Hamilton

Leroy, Fred's
friend   Leroy Daniels
May Hopkins, Hoppy's
mother   Nancy Kulp
Woody Anderson, Esther's
husband   Raymond Allen
Janet, Lamont's
girlfriend   Marlene Clark
Roger, Janet's son, from
a marriage that ended
in divorce   Edward Crawford
Frances Victor, Fred's
sister   Mary Alice
Rodney Victor, Frances's
husband   Allan Drake

Music: Quincy Jones.

Executive Producer: Norman Lear,
Bud Yorkin.

Producer: Bernie Orenstein, Saul Turteltaub.

Director: Norman Abbott, Chick
Liotta, Peter Baldwin, Russ
Petranto, Mike Warren, Alan
Rafkin.

British Cast ("Steptoe and Son"):
Albert Steptoe   Wilfred Bramwell

Harold Steptoe   Harry H. Corbett

SANFORD AND SON—30 minutes—
NBC—Premiered: January 14, 1972.

SANFORD ARMS

Comedy. A spin-off from "Sanford
and Son." Background: 9114 South
Central, Los Angeles, California, the
address of the Sanford Arms, a junkyard turned rooming house owned
and operated by Phil Wheeler, a
widower and retired Army man with
two children who purchased the residence from Fred Sanford as an investment to enable him to remain home
and raise his children, Angie and Nat.
The series focuses on his attempts to
cope with the numerous problems
associated with running a rooming
house.

CAST

Phil Wheeler   Theodore Wilson
Angie Wheeler   Tina Andrews
Nat Wheeler   John Earl
Esther Anderson, the
landlady   LaWanda Page
Woody Anderson, Esther's
husband   Raymond Allen
Jeannie, Phil's
girlfriend   Bebe Drake-Hooks
Grady Wilson, a
tenant   Whitman Mayo
Bubba, the handyman-
bellboy   Don Bexley

Music: Henry Mancini.

Executive Producer: Bud Yorkin, Saul
Turteltaub, Bernie Orenstein.

Producer: Woody Kling.

SANFORD ARMS—30 minutes—NBC
—Premiered: September 16, 1977.

Sara. Brenda Vaccaro.

SARA

Western Drama. Background: Independence, Colorado, 1870. The
story of Sara Yarnell, a pretty schoolteacher who leaves what she considers
to be a dull existence in Philadelphia
to teach school in the West. Episodes
revolve around her difficulties as she
struggles to educate the town of Independence.

CAST

Sara Yarnell   Brenda Vaccaro
Emmett Ferguson, her friend,
a rancher   Bert Kramer
Martin Pope, publisher of
the *Bulletin*, the town
newspaper   Albert Stratton
Julia Bailey, Sara's
friend   Mariclare Costello
George Bailey, Julia's
husband, the owner of
the bank   William Wintersole
Claude Barstow, the
mayor   William Phipps
Martha Higgins, the owner of
the boarding
house   Louise Latham
Emma Higgins, her
daughter   Hallie Morgan
Deborah Higgins, her
daughter   Debbie Leyton
Samuel Higgins, Martha's
husband   Al Henderson
Georgie Bailey, Julia's
son   Kraig Metzinger
Claranet, the Bailey's
housekeeper   Silva Soares
Frank Dixon, a
rancher   Jerry Hardin

Jimmy Waggins, a student of
Sara's   Stephen Manley

Music: Lee Holdridge.

Music Supervision: Hal Mooney.

Executive Producer: George Eckstein.

Director: Judd Taylor, Stuart Margolin, Gordon Hessler, Alf Kjellin, William F. Claxton, Michael Preece, William Wiard, Daniel Haller.

Creator: Richard Collins.

SARA—60 minutes—CBS—February 13, 1976 - July 30, 1976.

SARGE

Drama. Background: California. Shattered emotionally after his wife is killed by an assassin's bullet that was meant for him, veteran detective Sarge Swanson enters the priesthood. Three years later he is ordained Father Samuel Patrick Cavanaugh and assigned to the Saint Aloysius Parish in San Diego. Still referred to as "Sarge," and using unorthodox methods, he attempts to solve the problems of his urban community.

CAST

Father Samuel Patrick
Cavanaugh   George Kennedy
Valerie, his
secretary   Sallie Shockley
Lieutenant Barney
Verick   Ramon Bieri
Kenji Takichi,
the parish athletic
coach   Harold Sakata

SARGE—60 minutes—NBC—September 21, 1971 - January 11, 1972.

THE SATURDAY NIGHT DANCE PARTY

Variety. Music and comedy set against the background of a country club.

Host: Jerry Lester.

Music: Guest orchestra leaders, including: Ray Malone, Louis Prima, Billy May, Stan Kenton, Lionel Hampton, Ray Anthony.

THE SATURDAY NIGHT DANCE PARTY—60 minutes—NBC—June 7, 1952 - September 1952.

SATURDAY NIGHT LIVE WITH HOWARD COSELL

Variety. Appearances and/or performances by major stars, front-page news-makers, and celebrities from every continent. Broadcast live from the Ed Sullivan Theatre in New York City.

Host: Howard Cosell.

Regulars: The Peter Gennaro Dancers.

Announcer: John Bartholomew Tucker.

Orchestra: Elliott Lawrence.

Executive Producer: Roone Arledge.

Producer: Rubert Hitzig.

Director: Don Mischer.

SATURDAY NIGHT LIVE WITH HOWARD COSELL—60 minutes—ABC—September 20, 1975 - January 17, 1976.

THE SATURDAY NIGHT REVUE

Variety. Name bands, filmed European variety acts, and performances by show business personalities. Broadcast live from the Studebaker Theatre in Chicago, and the International Theatre on Columbus Circle in New York.

Host (Chicago): Jack Carter.

Host (New York): Sid Caesar.

Also hosting: Eddie Albert, Hoagy Carmichael, Alan Young, Ben Blue.

Regulars: Donald Richards, Jackie Lockridge, Susan Stewart, Misha Elman, Jackie Kannon, Betty Bruce, Anita Dorian, Andy Roberts, Hoctor and Byrd, Lou Wills, Jr., Pat Carroll, Hy Averback, The Bill Callahan Dance Troupe.

Orchestra: Lou Breese; Sauter-Finegan.

THE SATURDAY NIGHT REVUE—2 hours, 30 minutes—NBC—1950 - 1954.

SATURDAY PLAYHOUSE

Anthology. Retitled episodes of "Schlitz Playhouse of Stars."

SATURDAY PLAYHOUSE—30 minutes—CBS 1957.

THE SATURDAY SUPERSTAR MOVIE

Animated Cartoon Features. Subjects are drawn from real life, TV, literature, films, and comic strips. Included:

Nanny and the Professor. A spin-off from the series of the same name. After the Everett children find a microdot, Nanny struggles to prevent its theft until it is returned to the proper authorities.

Voices: Nanny: Juliet Mills; Professor Everett: Richard Long; Hal: David Doremus; Prudence: Kim Richards; Butch: Trent Lehman.

Gidget Makes the Wrong Connection. Gidget and her friends attempt to expose a ring of gold smugglers.

Voices: Gidget: Kathy Gori; Jud: David Lander; Steve: Denny Evans.

Lassie and the Secret of Thunder Mountain. Lassie's efforts to thwart plans to build an amusement park on sacred Indian Lands.

Voices: Father: Ted Knight; Mother: Jane Webb; Little Ben: Keith Allen.

THE SATURDAY SUPERSTAR MOVIE—60 minutes—ABC—September 9, 1972 - August 31, 1974.

SAY IT WITH ACTING

Game. Object: For contestants to identify charades that are performed on stage.

Hostess: Maggie McNellis.

Performers: Robert Alda, Bud Collyer.

SAY IT WITH ACTING—30 minutes—NBC 1951.

SAY WHEN

Game. Two competing contestants. A specific amount of money (up to two thousand dollars) is established, and various merchandise items are displayed on stage. Unaware of their selling prices, players have to select items that add up to, but do not surpass the established amount. When both players stop, the value of their items are totaled, and the player who has come the closest to the established amount is the winner and receives the merchandise items.

Host: Art James.

Producer: Ron Kweskin, Robert S. Rowe.

Director: Don Bohl.

SAY WHEN—30 minutes—NBC 1961.

THE SCARLET PIMPERNEL

Adventure. Background: England, 1792. The exploits of Sir Percy Blakeney, a man of wealth and social status who adopts the guise of the mysterious Scarlet Pimpernel (named after a small, red, star-shaped flower that is common to the English countryside). Appearing as the Scarlet Pimpernel whenever trouble is apparent, he battles injustice in his endeavor to aid the oppressed.

Starring: Marius Goring as Sir Percy Blakeney, The Scarlet Pimpernel.

Orchestra: Sidney Torch.

THE SCARLET PIMPERNEL—30 minutes—Syndicated 1954.

SCARLETT HILL

Serial. Background: The Russell Boarding House in Scarlett Hill, New York. The dramatic story of three people: Kate Russell, widow, its proprietress; Ginny Russell, her rebellious teenage daughter; and Janice Turner, a young girl residing at the inn.

CAST

Kate Russell	Beth Lockerbie
Ginny Russell	Lucy Warner
Janice Turner	Suzanne Bryant
David Black	Gordon Pinsent
Walter Pendleton	Ivor Barry
Harry Russell	Ed McNamara
Pearl	Cosette Lee
Tom Harvey	Marty Stetrop
Sidney	Alan Pearce
Sandy	Norman Ettlinger
Dr. Spangle	Tony Kramriether

SCARLETT HILL—30 minutes—Syndicated 1965. 260 tapes.

SCENE 70

Musical Variety. Performances by Rock Personalities.

Host: Jay Reynolds.

Featured: The Scene 70 Action Dancers.

Music: Recorded.

SCENE 70—60 minutes—Syndicated 1970.

THE SCHAEFER CENTURY THEATRE

Anthology. Dramatic presentations.

THE SCHAEFER CENTURY THEATRE—30 minutes—NBC 1950.

SCENES FROM A MARRIAGE

Drama. Background: Sweden. A penetrating study of the incidents that break up and lead to a couple divorcing after ten years of marriage. Produced in Sweden; expertly dubbed in English.

CAST

Marianne, the wife	Liv Ullman
Johan, the husband	Erland Josephson

Hostess: Liv Ullman.

Producer: Lars-Owe Carlberg.

Director: Ingmar Bergman.

English Version Producer: Paulette Rubinstein.

Director of Liv Ullman's Segments: John Marden.

Series Producer: David Griffiths.

SCENES FROM A MARRIAGE—60 minutes—PBS—March 9, 1977 - April 20, 1977. 6 episodes. Originally aired in Sweden in 1973. Broadcast on some PBS stations in both English and Swedish.

SCHLITZ PLAYHOUSE OF STARS

Anthology. Dramatic presentations.

Hostess: Irene Dunne.

Producer: Joseph T. Naar, William Self, Edward Lewis, Felix Jackson, Jules Bricker.

Director: Frank Telford, William H. Brown, Jr., Edward Lewis.

Sponsor: Schlitz Beer.

Included:

For Better or Worse. Accused of a hit-and-run accident, a woman, a pathological liar, attempts to prove her innocence.

CAST
Irene Wagner: Bette Davis; Van Wagner: John Williams.

The Restless Gun. The pilot film for the series of the same title. A wandering cowboy attempts to save an old friend from a ruthless bounty hunter.

CAST
Britt Pinsett (later changed to Vint Bonner): John Payne; Don Maler: William Hopper; Red Dawson: Andrew Duggan.

The Traveling Corpse. A criminologist professor attempts to solve the mysterious case of a vanishing corpse.

CAST
Prof. Stephen Bolt: Dennis O'Keefe; Doctor: John Baragrey; Mrs. Ditwiter: Leora Dana.

SCHLITZ PLAYHOUSE OF STARS —60 minutes—CBS—1951 - 1955.

SCIENCE FICTION THEATRE

Anthology. Though science fiction in nature, stories present an insight into the problems man faces as he ventures to unravel the mysteries of science and nature.

Host-Narrator: Truman Bradley.

Producer: Ivan Tors.

Director: Leigh Jason, Leon Benson, Jack Arnold.

Included:

Gravity Zero. The work of two scientists as they attempt to discover a method for neutralizing gravity.

CAST
Lisa Gaye, Percy Hilton.

The Legend of Carter Mountain. The story of a school teacher who is confronted with three pupils who possess the power to move objects by thought.

CAST
Marilyn Erskine.

The Miracle of Doctor Dove. A security officer attempts to locate three missing scientists.

CAST
Gene Lockhart.

The Sound of Murder. A scientist attempts to clear himself of a murder charge.

CAST
Howard Duff, Russell Collins.

The Dark Side. The story of an astronomer's efforts to construct a telescopic camera that is capable of photographing the dark side of the moon.

CAST
Skip Homeier.

SCIENCE FICTION THEATRE—30 minutes—Syndicated 1955-1957. 78 episodes.

SCHOOLHOUSE

Variety. Comedy, songs, and performances by undiscovered professional talent. Based on the vaudeville routine "School Days."

Host: Kenny Delmar.

Regulars: Arnold Stang, Maureen Cannon, Betty Ann Morgan, Wally Cox, Tommy Dix, Mary Ann Reeves.

SCHOOLHOUSE—30 minutes—DuMont 1947.

SCOOBY-DOO, WHERE ARE YOU?

Animated Cartoon. Traveling throughout the country in their car, the *Mystery Machine,* four teenagers, Freddy, Daphne, Velma, and Shaggy, and their Great Dane, Scooby-Doo, a dog who is afraid of his own shadow, all members of a mystery club, involve themselves in and attempt to solve supernatural-based mysteries. A Hanna-Barbera production.

Characters' Voices

Scooby-Doo	Don Messick
Freddy	Frank Welker
Daphne	Heather North
Shaggy	Casey Kaseem
Velma	Nichole Jaffe

Additional Voices: John Stephenson, Henry Cardin, Ann Jillian, Joan Gerber, Ted Knight, Olan Soule, Vincent Van Patten, Cindy Putman, Pat Harrington, Frances Halop, Jim McGeorge, Mike Road.

Music: Hoyt Curtin.

Musical Director: Ted Nichols.

Executive Producer: William Hanna, Joseph Barbera.

Director: Charles A. Nichols.

SCOOBY-DOO, WHERE ARE YOU? —30 minutes—CBS—September 13, 1969 - September 2, 1972; 60 minutes—CBS—September 9, 1972 - August 31, 1974.

THE SCOOBY-DOO/ DYNOMUTT HOUR

Animated Cartoon. Exactly the same story line, cast, and credits as the previous title, "Scooby-Doo, Where Are You?" (which see) with the only difference being a segment detailing the exploits of the Blue Falcon and his assistant, Dynomutt, a mechanical dog.

THE SCOOBY-DOO/DYNOMUTT HOUR—55 minutes—ABC—Premiered: September 11, 1976.

SCOOBY'S ALL STAR LAFF-A-LYMPICS

Animated Cartoon.

Segments:

The Laff-A-Lympics. Features three teams (The Yogi Yahooes; The Scooby Dooies; and The Really Rottens) competing in wild olympiclike games throughout the world.

Captain Caveman and the Teenangels. The story of a fumbling prehistoric caveman and his three female helpers, the Teenangels, as they battle crime.

Scooby Doo. The misadventures of a cowardly dog detective. See title: "Scooby Doo, Where Are You?" for information.

The Blue Falcon and Dynomutt. The adventures of super crime-fighter Blue Falcon (voiced by Gary Owens) and his robot dog, Dynomutt.

Announcer: Gary Owens.

Voices: Don Messick, Joan Gerber, Julie McWhirter, Pat Harrington, Daws Butler, John Stephenson, Alan Oppenheimer, Vic Perrin, Janet Waldo, Frank Welker, Nichole Jaffe, Heather North, Casey Kaseem, Jim MacGeorge, Mike Road.

Music: Hoyt Curtin, Paul DeKorte.

Executive Producer: William Hanna, Joseph Barbera.

Producer: Iwao Takamoto.

Director: Charles A. Nichols.

SCOOBY'S ALL STAR LAFF-A-LYMPICS—2 hours—ABC—Premiered: September 10, 1977. The first two-hour Saturday morning series.

Scooby-Doo, Where Are You? Left to right: Daphne Blake, Shaggy, Freddy, and Scooby-Doo. *Courtesy Hanna-Barbera Productions.*

SCOTLAND YARD

Crime Drama. Background: London, England. Dramatizations based on the files of Scotland Yard's Criminal Investigation Division.

CAST

Host-Narrator	Edgar Lustgarten
Inspector Duggan	Russell Napier
Inspector Ross	Ken Henry
Sergeant Mason	Arthur Mason

SCOTLAND YARD—30 minutes—Syndicated 1955. ABC run: November 17, 1957 - April 6, 1958. 39 episodes.

SCOTT ISLAND

See title: "Adventures at Scott Island."

SCOTT MUSIC HALL

See title: "Patti Page."

SCREEN DIRECTORS PLAYHOUSE

Anthology. Dramatic and comedic presentations.

Included:

Meet The Governor. The struggles of a mid-west lawyer as he attempts to become the governor of the state.

CAST
Clem Waters: Herb Shriner; June Walo: Barbara Hale; Sonny Waters: Bobby Clark.

The Life of Vernon Hathaway. The story of a meek watch repairman who daydreams himself into exciting adventure.

CAST
Ernest Stockhaffer: Alan Young; Irma: Cloris Leachman; Red Beecham: Douglas Dumbrille.

The Brush Roper. Prone to telling tall tales, an elderly cowpoke attempts to prove his stories true by roping a dangerous bull that is loose in the brush.

CAST
Grandpa Atkins: Walter Brennan; Grandma Jenny: Olive Carey; Cowhide: Lee Aaker; Royal: Edgar Buchanan.

SCREEN DIRECTORS PLAY-HOUSE—30 minutes—NBC—October 5, 1955 - September 26, 1956. 35 episodes.

SEA HUNT

Adventure. Background: The Pacific. The investigations of Mike Nelson, an ex-Navy frogman turned underwater troubleshooter. Underwater sequences filmed at Silver Springs, Florida; above-water sequences filmed at Marineland of the Pacific.

Starring: Lloyd Bridges as Mike Nelson.
Music: Ray Llewellyn.
SEA HUNT—30 minutes—Syndicated 1958. 155 episodes

SEALAB 2020

Animated Cartoon. Era: Earth A.D.

2020. The struggles of two hundred fifty men, women, and children, pioneers, as they attempt to maintain sealab 2020, a complex, scientific experimental city constructed beneath the ocean floor. A Hanna-Barbera production.

Characters' Voices

Captain Mike Murphy	John Stephenson
Dr. Paul Williams	Ross Martin
Hal, a diver	Jerry Dexter
Gail, a diver	Ann Jillian
Ed, a diver	Ron Pinckard
Bobby Murphy, the captain's nephew	Josh Albee
Salli Murphy, the captain's niece	Pamelyn Ferdin
Sparks, the radio dispatcher	Bill Callaway
Jamie	Gary Shapiro
Mrs. Thomas	Olga James

Gail's pet dolphin: Tuffy.
Music: Hoyt Curtin.

SEALAB 2020—30 minutes—NBC—September 9, 1972 - September 1, 1973. 24 episodes.

SEA WAR

Documentary. Films depicting Britian's naval battles during World War II.

Host-Narrator: Rear Admiral Ray Foster Brown.

Introductions: Admiral Sir Caspor John.
SEA WAR—30 minutes—Syndicated 1963. 13 episodes

SEARCH

Adventure. Background: World Security Corporation in Washington, D.C.—the headquarters of Probe, a supercomputerized detective agency. Stories relate the investigations of its three top operatives: Hugh Lockwood, Probe One; Nick Bianco, Omega Probe; and Christopher Grove. Standby Probe—agents who incorporate the ultimate in electronic wizardry: a super miniaturized two-way radio that is implanted in the ear; a ring that houses a miniaturized TV camera and a scanner; and delicate and highly sensitive body detectors (implanted under the skin) that enable where-abouts, heartbeat, and brainwaves to be transmitted to Probe Control, who monitor their agents at all times.

CAST
Hugh Lockwood	Hugh O'Brian
Nick Bianco	Tony Franciosa
Christopher R. Grove	Doug McClure
B.C. Cameron, the head of Probe	Burgess Meredith
Dr. Barnett, the senior director	Ford Rainey

Probe Control Agents:

Gloria Harding	Angel Tompkins
Kuroda	Byron Chung
Miss Keach	Ginny Golden
Miss James	Pamela Jones
Harris	Tom Hallick
Anna Mulligan	Ann Prentiss
Carlos	Ron Costro
Ramos	Tony DeCosta
Griffin	Albert Popwell
Amy	Cheryl Stoppelmoor

Music: Dominic Frontiere.

SEARCH—60 minutes—NBC—September 12, 1972 - August 29, 1973. 26 episodes.

SEARCH AND RESCUE: THE ALPHA TEAM

Adventure. Background: The Alpha Ranch in Canada. The exploits of the Ganelle family—Bob, a widower, and his teenage children, Katie and Jim, as they train wild animals for difficult rescue missions.

CAST
Bob Ganelle	Michael J. Reynolds
Katie Ganelle	Donann Cavin
Jim Ganelle	Michael Tough

Music: Lew Lehman.
Executive Producer: Seymour Berns, Will Lorin.
Producer: Lew Lehman.
Director: Peter Carter, Lawrence Dobkin.
Creator: Seymour Berns, Ray Freeman, Will Lorin.

SEARCH AND RESCUE: THE ALPHA TEAM—30 minutes—NBC—Premiered: September 10, 1977.

SEARCH FOR BEAUTY

Women. Beauty tips and advice.
Host: Ern Westmore.
Announcer: Dick Hageman.

SEARCH FOR BEAUTY—30 minutes—NBC 1955.

SEARCH FOR THE NILE

Documentary. Through on-location filming, old journals, and letters, the 1857 explorations of Sir Richard Francis Butler and John Hanning Speke, members of the Royal Geographical Society, are recounted as they attempt to uncover the source of the Nile River—the mysterious life source for Africa.

CAST

Sir Richard Butler	Kenneth Haigh
John Hanning Speke	John Quentin
David Livingston	Michael Gough
Henry Stanley	Keith Buckley
Isabel	Barbara Leigh-Hunt
James Grant	Ian McCulloch
Mutesa	Oliver Litondo
Samuel Baker	Norman Rosington
Florence	Catherine Schell

Narrator: James Mason.

Music: Joseph Horowitz.

SEARCH FOR THE NILE—60 minutes—NBC—January 25, 1972 - February 29, 1972. Syndicated.

SEARCH FOR TOMORROW

Serial. Background: The town of Henderson. The dramatic story of Joanne Barron.* Episodes depict the conflicts and tensions that arise from the interactions of the characters.

CAST

Joanne Barron	Mary Stuart
Victor Barron	Cliff Hall
Keith Barron	John Sylvester
Patty Barron	Lynn Loring
	Abigail Kellogg
	Patricia Harty
	Trish Van Devere
	Gretchen Walther
	Melissa Murphy
	Melinda Plank
	Leigh Lassen
	Tina Sloan
Irene Barron	Bess Johnson
Marge Bergman	Melba Raye
Henri Cartier	John LaGioia
Grace Boulton	Jill Clayburgh
Arthur Tate	Terry O'Sullivan
Susan Carter	Sharon Smyth
Ida Weston	Vera Allen
Andrea Whiting	Virginia Gilmore
	Joan Copeland
Dr. Wade Collins	John Cunningham
Stu Bergman	Larry Haines
Doug Martin	Ken Harvey
Dr. Dan Walton	Martin Brooks
	Philip Abbott
	Ron Husmann
Dr. Bob Rogers	Carl Low
Dr. Len Whiting	Dino Narizzano
	Jeff Pomerantz
Liz Walton	Denise Nickerson
Gary Walton	Tom Nordon
	John Driver
Scott Phillips	Peter Simon
Jim McCarren	Michael Shannon
Kathy Parker	Courtney Sherman
Carl Devlin	David Ford
Marcy	Jeanne Carson
Eunice Gardiner	Marion Brash
	Ann Williams
Lauri Phillips	Kelly Wood
Eric Lawson	Chris Lowe
Liza Walton	Kathy Beller
Emily Rogers Hunter	Kathryn Walker
Nick Hunter	Ken Kercheval
Helen	Sandy Duncan
Wilbur	Don Knotts
Dr. Murphy	Charles Siebert
Ross Cavanaugh	Keith Charles
Bruce Carson	Bobby Benson
	Garry Tomlin
Sam Reynolds	Robert Mandan
	George Gaynes
	Ray Shuman
Bill Lang	Tom Ewell
Dr. Tony Vincente	Anthony George
Chris	Daniel Leddy
Dr. Facciola	Conrad Bain
Rose Peabody	Lee Grant
	Constance Ford
	Nita Talbot
Dr. Wheeler	Roy Scheider
Dr. Joe Foster	Joe Morton
John Wyatt	Val Dufour
Stephanie Wilkins	Marie Cheatham
Dr. Walter Osmond	Byron Sanders
Miss Markham	Sharon Spellman
Ralph Hayward	James O'Sullivan
Harriet Kane	Chase Crosley
Monica Bergman	Barbara Baxley
Larry Carter	Hal Linden
Hazel	Mary Patton
Rex Twining	Laurence Hugo
Frank Gardiner	Eric Dressler
	Harry Holcombe
Mrs. Millie	Freida Allman
The social worker	Margaret Draper
Agnes Lake	Ann Revere
Fred Metcalf	David O'Brien
Janet Bergman	Ellen Spencer
	Sandy Robinson
	Fran Sharon
	Marian Hailey
	Millee Taggart
Tom Bergman	Peter Broderick
	Ray Bellaran
Nathan Walsh	George Petrie
Ellie Harper	Billie Lou Watt
Brette Moore	Martin Brooks
Allison Simmons	Ann Pearson
Harriet Baxter	Viki Viola
Budd Gardner	George Maharis
Kathy Merritt	Donna Theodore
Ed Minter	Richard Cox
Jennifer Phillips	Morgan Fairchild
Walter Pace	Tom Klunis
Gail Caldwell	Sherry Rooney
Greg Hartford	Robert Rockwell
Ralph Haywood	James O'Sullivan
Wendy Wilkins	Lisa Peluso
	Andrea McArdle
Sam Hunter	Stephen Joyce
Wade Collins	John Cunningham
Dave Wilkins	Dale Robinette
Clay Collins	Brett Halsey

Also: Ross Martin, Margaret Hamilton, Louise Larabee, Lenka Peterson, House Jameson, Sara Anderson, Martin Rudy, Robert Gentry, Audra Lindly, Jan Miner, Ken Rabat.

Announcer: Dwight Weist.

Organists: Chester Kingsbury; Ashley Miller.

SEARCH FOR TOMORROW—15 and 30 minute versions—CBS—Premiered: September 3, 1951.

*Originally Joanne Barron. After her husband, Keith, is killed in an automobile accident, she secures employment in Henderson Hospital where she meets, falls in love with, and marries Arthur Tate. After Arthur's death years later, she marries Dr. Tony Vincente. Her daughter, Patty, also marries a physician, Dr. Len Whiting.

SEAWAY

Adventure. Background: Montreal, Canada. The investigations of Nick King, an agent for the Ship Owners Association, an organization responsible for security along the Saint Lawrence Seaway.

CAST

Nick King	Stephen Young
Admiral Fox, the head of the Ship Owners Association	Austin Willis

Music: Edwin Astley.

SEAWAY—60 minutes—Syndicated (United States) 1969. Produced in Canada in 1965. 30 episodes.

SECOND CHANCE

Game. Three contestants compete. After a question is read, each player writes his answer on a card, which he places before him. Three possible answers to the question are now revealed and players receive a second chance with which to change their original answers if they wish to. The correct answer is then revealed and points are scored accordingly: three points for an original answer; one point for a second chance answer. Three such questions are played. The number of points earned are now used by the players for spins on a large, electronic prize board (which is divided into a series of small squares containing cash amounts, merchandise prizes, and devils). The machine, which is characterized by flashing lights (to indicate individual boxes) is started. When a player pushes a button, the machine stops and the lights pinpoint one box. Cash or merchandise prizes are added to the players score; a devil erases all earnings up to that point. The second half of the game is played in the same manner and the player who scores the highest cash value is the winner.

Host: Jim Peck.

Announcer: Joe Sider, Jay Stewart, Jack Clark.

Music: Score Productions.

Executive Producer: Bill Carruthers.

Producer: Joel Stein.

Director: Chris Darley.

SECOND CHANCE—30 minutes—ABC—March 7, 1977 - July 15, 1977.

SECOND CITY TELEVISION

Comedy. Background: The ficticious Second City Television Station, Channel 109, in Canada. The program satirizes life at a "typical" television station by spoofing, via short sketches, the programs broadcast throughout the day.

Starring: Andrea Martin, Dave Thomas, John Candy, Catherine O'Hara, Joe Flaherty, Eugene. Levy, Harold Ramis.

Music: Recorded.

Producer: Bernard Sahlins, Miland Bessada.

Director: Miland Bessada.

SECOND CITY TELEVISION—30 minutes—Syndicated 1977.

THE SECOND HUNDRED YEARS

Comedy. Alaska, 1900. Prospecting for gold, Luke Carpenter, thirty-three years of age, is buried and frozen alive when caught in an avalanche.

Series background: Woodland Oaks, California, 1967. Summoned to the office of Air Force Colonel Garroway,

The Second Hundred Years. Arthur O'Connell and Monte Markham. © *Screen Gems.*

Edwin Carpenter, sixty-seven years of age, widower and retired businessman, is informed of a recent avalanche in Alaska and of a find—his father, alive, and, though chronologically one hundred years old, physically and mentally unchanged since 1900.

Remaining top secret, the concern of cryogenicists (scientists involved with the study of deep cold), he is released to his son, Edwin, and, returning home, Luke meets his thirty-three-year-old grandson, Ken, his exact double. Stories depict the struggles of a turn-of-the-century prospector to adjust to life in the late 1960s.

CAST
Luke Carpenter	Monte Markham
Ken Carpenter	Monte Markham
Edwin Carpenter	Arthur O'Connell
Colonel Garroway	Frank Maxwell
Erica, Ken's girlfriend	Kay Reynolds
Mr. Tolliver, Ken's employer	Don Beddoe

THE SECOND HUNDRED YEARS—30 minutes—ABC—September 6, 1967 - September 19, 1968. 26 episodes.

SECRET AGENT

Adventure. The investigations of British Intelligence agent John Drake into situations that endanger world security. A spin-off from "Danger Man."

Starring: Patrick McGoohan as John Drake.

Music: Edwin Astley.

SECRET AGENT—60 minutes—CBS—April 1965 - September 11, 1965; December 4, 1965 - September 10, 1966. 45 episodes. Syndicated.

SECRET FILE, U.S.A.

Adventure. The investigations of American espionage agent Major Bill Morgan and his female assistant Colonel Custer into situations that threaten U.S. security.

CAST
Major Bill Morgan	Robert Alda
Colonel Custer	Lois Hensen
Mrs. Morgan	Kay Callard

Narrator: Frank Gallop.

Music: Ella Sacco.

Producer-Director: Arthur Dreifuss.

SECRET FILE, U.S.A.—30 minutes—Syndicated 1954. 26 episodes.

THE SECRET FILES OF CAPTAIN VIDEO

See title: "Captain Video and His Video Rangers."

THE SECRET LIVES OF WALDO KITTY

Animated Cartoon. The program begins to establish three live-action animals: Waldo, a cat; Felicia, a cat, his girlfriend; and Tyrone, their nemesis, a mean bulldog. When Tyrone becomes a threat to Felicia's safety, Waldo, who is a coward at heart, imagines himself as her heroic savior. The program then becomes animated and each week features Waldo as a different hero struggling to protect Felicia from harm.

Characters' Voices

Waldo Kitty	Howard Morris
Felicia	Jane Webb
Tyrone	Allan Melvin

Music: Yvette Blais, Jeff Michael.

THE SECRET LIVES OF WALDO KITTY—30 minutes—NBC—Premiered: September 6, 1975.

THE SECRETS OF ISIS

CBS's Fall 1977 title for "Isis," which see for information.

SECRETS OF THE DEEP

Documentary. Films exploring mans final frontier—the oceans and seas of the world.

Host-Narrator: Scott Carpenter.

Music: Ugo Calise, Danielle Palucchi.

SECRETS OF THE DEEP—30 minutes—Syndicated 1974.

SECRET SQUIRREL

See title: "The Atom Ant/Secret Squirrel Show."

THE SECRET STORM

Serial. Background: The town of Woodridge. Dramatic incidents in the lives of the Ames family.

CAST

Peter Ames	Peter Hobbs
	Cec Linder
	Ward Costello
Amy Ames	Jada Rowland
	Lynn Adams
Susan Ames	Jean Mowry
	Judy Lewis
Jerry Ames	Warren Berlinger
	Wayne Tippert
Pauline Rysdale	Haila Stoddard
Mr. Tyrell	Russell Hicks
Hugh Clayborn	Peter MacLean
Dan Kincaid	Bernard Barrow
Mickey Potter	Larry Block
Valerie Northcote	Lori March
Jill Stevens	Barbara Rodell
Kevin Kincaid	David Ackroyd
Belle Clements	Marla Adams
Nancy Vallin	Iris Braun
Ursula Winthrope	Jacqueline Brooks
Paul Britton	Nick Coster
	Linden Chiles
Ken Stevens	Joel Crothers
Lisa Britton	Judy Safran
	Diane Dell
	Terri Falis
Kitty Styles	Diane Ladd
Jonathan Styles	Scott Mefford
Peter Dunbar	Donnie Melvin
Grace Tyrell	Marjorie Gateson
	Eleanor Phelps
Dr. Ian Northcote	Gordon Rigsby
	Alexander Scourby
Doug Winthrope	Bruce Sherwood
Tom Gregory	Richard Venture
Aggie Parsons	Jane Rose
Reilly	Joe Ponazecki
Laurie Stevens	Stephanie Braxton
Polly	Susan Oakes
Phil Forrestor	Patrick Fox
Mike	Devin Goldenberg
Alden	Cliff de'Young
Martha Ann Ashley	Audre Johnson
Freddy	Roberta Royce
Charlotte	Susan Sudert
Mulholland	Mike Galloway
Andrea	Roberta Rickett
Keefer	Troy Donahue
Kip Ripdale	Don Galloway
Ann Wicker	Diana Muldaur
Bob Hill	Roy Scheider
Tim Brannigan	Anthony Herrera
	Nicholas Lewis
The Assistant D.A.	Gary Campbell
Irene Simms	Jennifer Darling
Cecilia	Kathleen Cody
Herbie Vail	Noel Craig
Nola Hollister	Rosemary Murphy
	Mary K. Wells
Myra Lake	Joan Hotchkis
	June Graham
Alan Dunbar	Liam Sullivan
	James Vicary
Frank Carver	Jack Ryland
	Robert Loggia
	Laurence Luckinbill
Cassie	Mildred Clinton
Mark Reddin	David Gale
Dr. Brian Neeves	Jeff Pomerantz
	Keith Charles
Clay Stevens	Jamie Grover
Jason Ferris	Robert Alda
Robert Landers	Dan Hamilton
Monsignor Quinn	Sidney Walker
Joanna Morrison	Audrey Landers
	Ellen Barber

Also: Virginia Dwyer, Robin Strasser, Charles Baxter.

Announcer: Ken Roberts.

Music: Carey Gould.

THE SECRET STORM—30 minutes—CBS—February 1, 1954 - February 15, 1974.

SEE IT NOW

Documentary. An in-depth analysis of news-making stories. The program led television news out of infancy and into maturity.

Host: Edward R. Murrow.

Also: Eric Sevaried, Howard K. Smith.

Producer: Edward R. Murrow, Fred W. Friendly, Palmer Williams.

Director: Don Hewitt.

Sponsor: Alco.

SEE IT NOW—30 minutes—CBS—December 2, 1951 - July 7, 1958.

THE SEEKING HEART

Serial. The dramatic story of John Adams, general practitioner and criminologist.

CAST

John Adams	Scott Forbes
Grace Adams	Dorothy Lovett
Dr. McKay	Flora Campbell

Producer: Minerva Ellis.

Sponsor: Procter and Gamble.

THE SEEKING HEART—15 minutes—CBS—July 5, 1954 - December 10, 1954.

THE SENATOR

See title: "The Bold Ones," *The Senator* segment.

SENSE AND NONSENSE

Game. Two competing teams, each composed of three members. Basis: The testing of the five senses (sight, hearing, taste, touch, and smell). Players each compete in rounds that are designed to test one sense without the assist of the others. Points are awarded for each problem that is solved by each sense. Winners, the highest scorers, receive merchandise prizes.

Versions:

Sense and Nonsense—30 minutes—NBC 1952.

Host: Bob Kennedy.

Assistant: Vivian Farrar.

Sense and Nonsense Junior–30 minutes–NBC 1952. A children's version of the adult game.

Host: Ralph Paul.

Assistant: Vivian Farrar.

THE SENTIMENTAL AGENT

Adventure. The global investigations of Carlos Borella, an agent-troubleshooter for an import-export company.

Starring: Carlos Thompson as Carlos Borella.

THE SENTIMENTAL AGENT–60 minutes–Syndicated 1962.

SERGEANT BILKO

See title: "You'll Never Get Rich."

SERGEANT PRESTON OF THE YUKON

Adventure. Era: The 1890s. Completing his college studies, William Preston receives word from the Yukon of his father's death. So as to have the legal authority to apprehend his father's murderer, he journeys to Alaska and joins the ranks of the Northwest Mounted Police. After months of hardships and deprivation, his search ends when the culprit, Spike Wilson, is apprehended.

Shortly after, Constable Preston intervenes in a lynx attack and rescues a husky puppy that had been raised by a female wolf. Naming the dog Yukon King, he teaches it to command a team, respect good men, and hate evil ones.

Months following, after Spike Wilson escapes from prison, Preston is again assigned to capture him. Succeeding, he is promoted to Sergeant.

Stories depict Sergeant Preston's attempts to maintain law and order in the early Gold Rush days of the Yukon.

Starring: Richard Simmons as Sergeant William Preston.

Preston's horse: Rex.

Program Open:

Announcer: "Sergeant Preston of the Northwest Mounted Police, with Yukon King, swiftest and strong-est lead dog, breaking the trail in the relentless pursuit of lawbreakers in the wild days of the Yukon."

SERGEANT PRESTON OF THE YUKON–30 minutes–Syndicated 1955. 78 episodes.

SERGEANT STEVE DEKKER

See title: "Not For Hire."

SERPICO

Crime Drama. Background: New York City. The investigations of Frank Serpico, a daring undercover patrolman with the 22nd Police Precinct.

CAST

Frank Serpico (Badge No. 21049)	David Birney
Lt. Sullivan, his superior	Tom Atkins

Music: Robert Dransin, Elmer Bernstein.

Executive Producer: Emmet G. Larvey, Jr.

Producer: Don Ingalls, Barry Oringer.

Director: Reza S. Badiyi, Michael Caffrey, Art Fisher, Sigmund Neufeld, Jr., Robert Markowitz, Alex March, Paul Stanley.

SERPICO–60 minutes–NBC–September 24, 1976 - January 28, 1977.

SESAME STREET

Educational. Entertainment geared to preschoolers. Background: Sesame Street–an anywhere street of learning in an anywhere city or town. Live action is coupled with cartoons, puppets, stories, and songs to help children solve problems, reinforce their reading skills, and assist them as they attempt to learn the alphabet and count from one to twenty.

Starring: Jim Henson's Muppets, Bob McGrath, Matt Robinson, Loretta Long, Will Lee, Charlotte Rae, Elmo Delgado, Roscoe Orman, Alaina Reed, Clarice Taylor, Anne Revere, Paul B. Brice, Raul Julia, Larry Block, Northern J. Calloway.

Music: Joe Raposo.

Musical Director: Sam Pottle.

Executive Producer: Jon Stone.

Producer: Dulcy Singer.

Director: Robert Myhrum.

SESAME STREET–60 minutes. NET–November 10, 1969 - November 6, 1970; PBS–Premiered: November 9, 1970.

SEVEN AT ELEVEN

Variety. Broadcast on an alternating basis with "Broadway Open House."

Host: George de Witt.

Regulars: Sid Gould, Denise Lor, Betty Luster, Jack Stanton.

Orchestra: Milton DeLugg.

Producer: Hal Friedman.

Director: Douglas Rodgers.

SEVEN AT ELEVEN–60 minutes–NBC–May 28, 1951 - August 1951. Broadcast from 11:00 p.m.-12:00 a.m.

SEVEN KEYS

Game. Two competing contestants. A picture, which represents a person, place, event, or object, is flashed on a screen. The player who is first to identify himself via a buzzer signal, receives a chance to answer. If correct, one point is scored. Winners, the highest scorers, receive merchandise prizes and one key. If the player is successful and wins seven straight games, he acquires seven keys and is awarded a merchandise showcase.

Host: Jack Narz.

SEVEN KEYS–30 minutes–ABC–April 3, 1961 - March 27, 1964.

SEVEN LEAGUE BOOTS

Travel. Films depicting the life styles and customs of people around the world.

Host-Narrator: Jack Douglas.

SEVEN LEAGUE BOOTS–30 minutes–Syndicated 1959. 38 episodes.

THE SEVEN LIVELY ARTS

Anthology. Dramatizations based on literary works and events of past and present history.

Host: John Crosby.

Orchestra: Alfredo Antonino.

Producer: Jud Kinberg, Robert Herridge, Robert Goldman.

THE SEVEN LIVELY ARTS—60 minutes—CBS—November 3, 1957 - February 16, 1958.

SEVENTH AVENUE

See title: "Best Sellers."

77 SUNSET STRIP

Mystery. Background: Hollywood, California. The investigations of Stuart Bailey and Jeff Spencer, private detectives operating from plush offices at 77 Sunset Strip.

CAST

Stuart Bailey	Efrem Zimablist, Jr.
Jeff Spencer	Roger Smith
Gerald Lloyd Kookson III (Kookie), their parking-lot attendant; later a detective	Edward Byrnes
Detective Rex Randolph	Richard Long
Suzanne Fabray, their switchboard operator	Jacqueline Beer
Roscoe, their junior partner, an ex-Broadway horse player	Louis Quinn
Lieutenant Gilmore, Hollywood Police Department	Byron Keith
J. R. Hale, the parking lot attendant at Dino's, the bar next to 77 Sunset Strip	Robert Logan
Hannah, Stu's secretary	Joan Staley

Music: Warren Barker; Frank Ortega; Frank Perkins; Paul Sawtell; Jay Livingston, Ray Evans.

Producer: William T. Orr, Roy Huggins, William Conrad, Howie Horwitz, Fenton Earnshaw.

77 SUNSET STRIP—60 minutes—ABC—October 10, 1958 - February 26, 1964. 205 episodes. Syndicated (excluding twenty 1961 episodes with star Efrem Zimbalist, Jr. and Joan Staley; available for export use only).

79 PARK AVENUE

Drama. A three-part miniseries based on the novel by Harold Robbins. The story, which spans thirteen years beginning in New York in August 1935, focuses on the life of Marja Fludjicki, a high-priced call girl, and the two men who love her: Ross Savitch, the rich son of a syndicate boss; and Mike Koshko, a poor, hard-working young man. (The series title is derived from the address of a modeling agency that fronts for high-priced call girls.)

CAST

Marja Fludjicki	Lesley Ann Warren
Ross Savitch	Marc Singer
Mike Koshko	David Dukes
Kaati Fludjicki, Marja's mother	Barbara Barrie
Ben Savitch, Ross's father	Michael Constantine
Myrna Savitch, Ross's mother	Margaret Fairchild
Peter Markevich, Marja's step-father	Albert Salmi
Paulie Fludjicki, Marja's brother	Scott Jacoby
Vera Keppler, the madam	Polly Bergen
Harry Vito	John Saxon
Armond Perfido	Raymond Burr
Joker	Jack Weston
Brian Whitfield	Peter Marshall

Music: Nelson Riddle.

Executive Producer: George Eckstein.

Producer-Director: Paul Wendkos.

79 PARK AVENUE—6 hours (total)—NBC—October 16, 1977 - October 18, 1977.

SHADDER BOY

An animated series that follows the exploits of Shadder Boy, a daring crusader for justice. 286 five minute films, Syndicated 1968.

SHADOW OF THE CLOAK

Spy Drama. A private detective's battle against espionage rings.

Starring: Helmut Dantine as the private detective.

SHADOW OF THE CLOAK—30 minutes—DuMont 1951.

SHAFT

Crime Drama. Background: New York City. The investigations of John Shaft, a hip black private detective who strives to solve complex and baffling crimes. Based on the movie of the same title with sex and violence curtailed for television.

CAST

John Shaft	Richard Roundtree
Lt. Al Rossi, N.Y.P.D.	Ed Barth

Music: Johnny Pate.

Theme: Isaac Hayes.

SHAFT—90 minutes—CBS—October 9, 1973 - September 3, 1974. 8 episodes.

SHA NA NA

Variety. Musical numbers, blackouts, and comedy sketches set against the background of a city neighborhood in the 1950s.

Starring: Sha Na Na, a ten-member Rock group.

Regulars: Avery Schreiber, Kenneth Mars, Pamela Myers, Jane Dulo, Phil Roth, Jack Wohl.

Announcer: Pamela Myers.

Musical Director: Ray Charles.

Executive Producer: Pierre Cossette.

Producer: Bernard Rothman, Jack Wohl.

Director: Walter Miller.

Choreography: Walter Painter.

Additional Music/Choreography: Sha Na Na.

SHA NA NA—30 minutes—Syndicated 1977.

SHANE

Western. Background: Wyoming, 1900. The story of Shane, a mysterious wandering ex-gunman who, for reasons that are unknown, sides with homesteaders against cattlemen in the bloodthirsty quest for land. Hooking on as a rancher for the Starrett family —Marian, a widow who is drawn to the stranger; Joey, her young son who idolizes him; and Tom, the boy's grandfather—Shane strives to peacefully resolve the difficulties that arise over cattle baron Rufe Ryker's attempts to acquire land.

CAST

Shane	David Carradine
Marian Starrett	Jill Ireland
Tom Starrett	Tom Tully
Joey Starrett	Christopher Shea
Rufe Ryker	Bert Freed
Grafton, Ryker's assistant	Sam Gilman

SHANE—60 minutes—ABC—September 10, 1966 - December 31, 1966. 17 episodes.

SHANNON

Adventure. The cases of Joe Shannon, an insurance investigator for the Transport Bonding and Surety Company.

CAST
Joe Shannon — George Nader
Bill Cochran, his employer — Regis Toomey

SHANNON–30 minutes–Syndicated 1961. 36 episodes.

SHARI LEWIS

Listed: The television programs of ventriloquist Shari Lewis.

Facts 'N' Fun–Children–15 minutes–Local New York (WNBT-TV)–1953. Also known as "The Shari Lewis Show."

Hostess: Shari Lewis.

Shari and Her Friends–Children–30 minutes–Local New York (WPIX-TV)–1954. Also known as "Kartoon Kapers."

Hostess: Shari Lewis.

Puppets: Lamb Chop, Charlie Horse, Hush Puppy.

Format: Songs, stories, and sketches geared to children.

Shariland–Children–30 minutes–NBC–1957.

Hostess: Shari Lewis.

Puppets: Lamb Chop, Charlie Horse, Hush Puppy.

Format: Songs, stories, and sketches geared to children.

Hi Mom–Information-Variety–60 minutes–NBC–1957-1959. See title.

The Shari Lewis Show–Children–30 minutes–NBC–October 1, 1960 - September 28, 1963.

Hostess: Shari Lewis.

Her Assistant: Ronald Radd as Mr. Goodfellow.
Shari's puppets and format are the same as "Shariland."

The Shari Lewis Show–Children–10 minutes to one hour–B.B.C.-TV, London, England–1967-Present.

Hostess: Shari Lewis.

The puppets and format are the same as "Shariland."

The Shari Show–Children–30 minutes–NBC–Premiered: October 7, 1975. Broadcast as a series of monthly specials on NBC's five owned and operated stations.

Background: The Bearly Broadcasting Company, a television station that is run by twenty-five animal puppets. The series, which features Shari Lewis as the human assistant station manager, deals with people and how they relate to one another; how they create problems, and how they resolve them.

Starring: Shari Lewis.

Shari's Partner: Ron Martin.

Puppeteers: Shari Lewis, Mallory Tarcher, Bill Jackson, Nancy Wettler.

Musical Director: Bob Alberti.

Voices: Shari Lewis.

SHAZAM!

Adventure. Selected by the immortal elders — Solomon, Mercury, Zeus, Achilles, and Atlas–Billy Batson, a radio station broadcaster, is endowed with the ability to transform himself into Captain Marvel, a daring crusader for justice.

Stories relate Billy's battle against evil as the mysterious crime fighter, Captain Marvel. (When Billy utters the word "Shazam!" he is transformed into Captain Marvel.) Based on the comic strip, "Shazam!"

CAST
Billy Batson — Michael Gray
Mentor, his assistant — Les Tremayne
Captain Marvel — Jackson Bostwick
 — John Davey

Music: Yvette Blais, Jeff Michael.

Executive Producer: Norm Prescott, Lou Scheimer, Dick Rosenbloom.

Producer: Arthur H. Nadel, Robert Chenault.

Director: Hollingsworth Morse, Robert Chenault, Harry Lange, Jr., Arnold Laven, Arthur H. Nadel.

SHAZAM!–30 minutes–CBS–Premiered: September 7, 1974.

THE SHAZAM!–ISIS HOUR

See individual titles: "Shazam!" and "Isis."

SHAZZAN!

Animated Cartoon. Finding two ring halves, twins Nancy and Chuck place them together, completing the word "Shazzan." Instantly they are transported from America to the age of the Arabian Knights, where they command the powerful sixty-foot genie, Shazzan. Stories depict their battle against evil. A Hanna-Barbera production.

Characters' Voices
Shazzan — Barney Phillips
Nancy — Janet Waldo
Chuck — Jerry Dexter

Music: Hoyt Curtin.

SHAZZAN!–30 minutes–CBS–September 9, 1967 - September 6, 1969. 26 episodes.

SHEENA, QUEEN OF THE JUNGLE

Adventure. Background: Africa. Having survived a plane crash as a child, and growing up in the savage continent, Sheena, a beautiful and courageous white jungle goddess, struggles to protect her adopted homeland from the forces of evil. Filmed on location in Mexico.

CAST
Sheena — Irish McCalla
Bob, her friend, a white trader — Christian Drake

Sheena's assistant: Chim (a chimpanzee).

Irish McCalla's stand-in: Raul Gaona, a Mexican acrobat. Unable to find a woman tall enough, a man, dressed in tiger skin and wig, was selected to perform the stunts that are unable to be performed

Shazzan! The genie Shazzan and his masters Nancy and Chuck. *Courtesy Hanna-Barbera Productions.*

by Irish McCalla (seventy-three-inches tall).

SHEENA, QUEEN OF THE JUNGLE —30 minutes—Syndicated 1955. 26 episodes.

THE SHEILA GRAHAM SHOW

Celebrity Interview.

Hostess: Sheila Graham, Hollywood gossip columnist.

THE SHEILA GRAHAM SHOW—15 minutes—NBC 1951.

THE SHEILA MacRAE SHOW

Interview. Interviews with guests on topical issues.

Hostess: Sheila MacRae.

Co-Hostesses: Meredith MacRae and Heather MacRae (her daughters).

THE SHEILA MacRAE SHOW—30 minutes—Syndicated 1971.

SHENANAGANS

Game. Two children compete. Background: A three-dimensional game board. Players' moves are determined by the roll of two dice. Players move space by space and perform whatever is printed on the square on which they fall (either answer a question or perform a stunt). Each correct answer or performance awards Shenanagans play money. The first player to complete the board is the winner and is permitted to trade his play money for merchandise prizes.

Host: Stubby Kaye.

Announcer: Kenny Williams.

SHENANAGANS—30 minutes—ABC —September 26, 1964 - September 1965.

THE SHERIFF OF COCHISE U.S. MARSHAL

Western. Background: Cochise, Arizona. Law enforcer Frank Morgan's battle against the modern-day breed of criminal. In 1956, under the title "Sheriff of Cochise," as sheriff; and in 1958, under the title "U.S. Marshal," as marshal.

CAST
Sheriff, then Marshal Frank Morgan	John Bromfield
Rafe Patterson, his deputy	Stan Jones

THE SHERIFF OF COCHISE—30 minutes—Syndicated 1956 - 1958.

U.S. MARSHAL—30 minutes—Syndicated 1958.

SHERLOCK HOLMES

Mystery. Background: 221-B Baker Street, London, England, the residence of Sherlock Hólmes, a consulting detective (a man who intervenes in baffling police matters), and his roommate, Dr. John H. Watson. Stories depict their investigations into and attempts to solve baffling acts of criminal injustice through deductive reasoning and scientific evaluation. Based on the character created by Sir Arthur Conan Doyle.

CAST
Sherlock Holmes	Ronald Howard
Dr. John H. Watson	H. Marion Crawford
Inspector Lestrade	Archie Duncan

Music: Claude Durant.

SHERLOCK HOLMES—30 minutes—Syndicated 1954. 39 episodes.

SHIELDS AND YARNELL

Variety. Music, comedy, songs, dances, and mime.

Hosts: Robert Shields, Lorene Yarnell.

Regulars: Ted Zeigler, Joanna Cassidy

Orchestra: Norman Mamey.

Executive Producer: Steve Binder.

Director: Steve Binder.

SHIELDS AND YARNELL—30 minutes—CBS—June 13, 1977 - July 25, 1977.

SHINDIG

Musical Variety. Performances by Rock, Folk, and Country and Western entertainers.

Host: Jimmy O'Neal.

Regulars: Bobby Sherman, Ray Pohlman, The Blossoms, The Shindig Dancers, The Shindogs.

Music: The Shin-Diggers.

SHINDIG—60 minutes—ABC—September 16, 1964 - January 5, 1966.

THE SHIRLEY MacLAINE SHOW

See title: "Shirley's World."

SHIRLEY TEMPLE'S STORYBOOK

Anthology. Musical adaptations of fairytales.

Hostess-Frequent Performer: Shirley Temple.

Music: Vic Mizzy; Vic Schoen; Mack David; Walter Scharf.

Included:

Land of Oz. A sequel to L. Frank Baum's *The Wizard of Oz.* The evil Lord Nikidik's efforts to control the kingdom of Oz.

CAST
Princess Ozma: Shirley Temple; Mombi the Witch: Agnes Moorehead; Lord Nikidik: Jonathan Winters; Scarecrow: Ben Blue; Pumpkinhead: Sterling Holloway; Tin Woodman: Gil Lamb; Glinda: Frances Berger.

Kim. Background: India. The adventures of Rudyard Kipling's young hero, Kim O'Hara.

CAST
Captain Creighton: Michael Rennie; Kim: Tony Haig; White Suit: Arnold Moss.

Tom and Huck. Mark Twain's classic of life along the Mississippi River. The story of Tom Sawyer and his friend Huckleberry Finn and their involvement with Muff, the gravedigger.

CAST
Tom Sawyer: David Ladd; Huck Finn: Teddy Rooney; Aunt Polly: Janet Blair; Muff: Dan Duryea; Becky Thatcher: Ruthie Robinson; Injun Joe: Paul Stevens.

Little Men. An adaptation of the story by Ed James and Louisa May Alcott. Background: The Plumfield School for Boys in New England. The story of Professor Fritz Bhaer and his wife Jo as they attempt to solve the problem of a new arrival, Dan Baker, a lad who has a habit of running away from home.

CAST
Professor Bhaer: Fernando Lamas; Jo Bhaer: Shirley Temple; Dan Baker: Bobby Crawford.

SHIRLEY TEMPLE'S STORYBOOK —60 minutes. NBC—January 12, 1958 - September 12, 1958; ABC—January 12, 1959 - June 8, 1959; NBC—September 18, 1960 - September 10, 1961. 27 episodes. Syndicated.

SHIRLEY'S WORLD

Shirley's World. Shirley MacLaine. *Courtesy Independent Television Corporation; an ATV Company.*

Comedy. Background: London, England, the offices of *World Illustrated* magazine. The assignments of Shirley Logan, a beautiful, wanderlust photojournalist who possesses an insatiable curiosity and a warm-hearted nature that involves her with other people's problems.

CAST

Shirley Logan	Shirley MacLaine
Dennis Croft, her editor	John Gregson

Music: John Barry.

Executive Producer: Sheldon Leonard, Ronald Rubin.

Producer: Barry Delmaine, Ray Austin.

SHIRLEY'S WORLD—30 minutes—ABC—September 15, 1971 - January 5, 1972. 17 episodes.

SHIVAREE

Musical Variety. Performances by Rock personalities.

Host: Gene Weed.

Featured: The Shivaree Dancers.

Music: Recorded.

SHIVAREE—30 minutes—Syndicated 1965. 26 tapes.

SHOOT FOR THE STARS

Game. Two teams compete, each composed of one celebrity and one non-celebrity contestant. Each team begins with $100. From a board that con- tains twenty-four numbered boxes, a player chooses one. A phrase is revealed (e.g., "Cleaver as a lash") and has to be unscrambled as follows: the contestant has to give the first half ("Smart as") and the celebrity the second half (a whip"). Each phrase is worth money and is added to a player's score only if both halves of the phrase are correctly answered. Turns alternate back and forth between the teams and the first team to score $1500 is the winner.

Host: Geoff Edwards.

Announcer: Bob Clayton.

Music: Bob Cobert.

Executive Producer: Bob Stewart.

Producer: Bruce Burmester.

Director: Mike Gargiulo.

SHOOT FOR THE STARS—30 minutes—NBC—Premiered: January 3, 1977.

SHORT STORY DRAMA

Anthology. Dramatic presentations.

Hostess: Ruth Woods.

Producer: Bernard Prockter.

Sponsor: Pepsi Cola.

SHORT STORY DRAMA—15 minutes—NBC 1952.

SHORT STORY THEATRE

Anthology. Dramatic presentations.

Hostess: Mary Kay.

Producer: Ted Mills.

Director: Dave Brown.

SHORT STORY THEATRE—15 minutes—ABC 1952.

SHOTGUN SLADE

Western. Background: The Frontier, 1860s. The exploits of Shotgun Slade, a wandering detective who, possessing a unique two-in-one shotgun, struggles to enforce justice.

CAST

Shotgun Slade	Scott Brady
Monica, his romantic interest	Monica Lewis

SHOTGUN SLADE—30 minutes—Syndicated 1959. 78 episodes.

SHOW BUSINESS INCORPORATED

Variety. Highlights of past Broadway shows are spotlighted with performances by the original cast members.

Host: Danton Walker.

Producer: Martin Jones.

Director: Ralph Nelson.

SHOW BUSINESS INCORPORATED—30 minutes—NBC 1949.

SHOWCASE '68

Variety. Performances by undiscovered professional talent. Taped on various college campuses throughout the country.

Host: Lloyd Thaxton.

SHOWCASE '68—60 minutes—NBC—June 11, 1968 - September 10, 1968.

SHOWDOWN

A game show wherein two three member teams compete in a series of question and answer rounds.

Host: Joe Pyne.

Music: The Bantams.

30 minutes—NBC—July 4, 1966 - October 4, 1966.

SHOWER OF STARS

Musical Variety. Broadcast once a month in place of "Climax."

Host: Jack Barry.

Orchestra: David Rose.

Premiere Guests: Betty Grable, Harry James, Mario Lanza.

SHOWER OF STARS—60 minutes—CBS—1954 - 1955.

THE SHOW GOES ON

Variety. Undiscovered professional talent acts perform with the hope of receiving bookings from talent buyers who are present.

Host: Robert Q. Lewis.

Producer: Lester Gottlieb, Lou Melamed.

Director: Alexander Leftwich.

Sponsor: American Safety Razor; Columbia Records.

THE SHOW GOES ON—60 minutes—CBS 1950.

Showoffs. Left to right: Studio contestant, host Bobby Van and guests Dick Gautier, Sally Struthers, Ron Masak, and Joyce Bulifant.

SHOWOFFS

Game. Two teams, each composed of two celebrities and one noncelebrity contestant, compete. One team is placed in a sound-proof isolation booth while the other team is at play. One player is made the guesser; the other two the actors. The object is for the actors to pantomime as many words as possible during a sixty-second time limit. Each word that is identified by the guesser scores one point. At the end of the round the other team is brought out and the game is played in the same manner. The team with the highest score is the winner of round one. A two-out-of-three match competition is played (the roles of actor and guesser alternate). The winner receives a thousand dollars in merchandise prizes.

Host: Bobby Van.

Announcer: Gene Wood.

Music: Recorded.

Executive Producer: Mark Goodson, Bill Todman.

Producer: Howard Flesher.

Director: Paul Alter.

SHOWOFFS—30 minutes—ABC—June 30, 1975 - December 26, 1975.

SHOWROOM

Variety. Interviews and entertainment acts.

Host: Cesar Romero.

SHOWROOM—30 minutes—ABC—1953 - 1954.

SHOW STREET

Variety. Performances by undiscovered professional talent.

Hostess: Phyllis Diller.

SHOW STREET—30 minutes—Syndicated 1964.

SHOWTIME

Musical Variety. Produced in England.

Hosts: American guests including Juliet Prowse, Bill Dana, Liberace.

Regulars: The Mike Sammes Singers, The London Line Dancers.

Orchestra: Jack Parnell.

SHOWTIME—60 minutes—CBS—June 11, 1968 - September 17, 1968. 12 tapes. Syndicated.

SHOWTIME AT THE APOLLO

Variety. Celebrity performances set against the background of the Apollo Theatre.

Host: Willie Bryant.

Appearing: Nat King Cole, Count Basie, Dinah Washington, Cab Calloway, Sarah Vaughn, Herb Jeffries, Martha Davis, Bill Bailey, Amos Millburn, Nipsey Russell, Mildred Melvin, The Larks.

SHOWTIME AT THE APOLLO—30 minutes—Syndicated 1954.

SHOWTIME, U.S.A.

Musical Variety. Scenes from Broadway plays are presented and performed by the original cast members.

Hosts: Henry Fonda; Vinton Freedly.

Announcer: Tom Gilbert.

Orchestra: Nathan Kroll.

SHOWTIME, U.S.A.—30 minutes—ABC 1951.

SHOW WAGON

Variety. The series spotlights entertainment figures who received their first break on Horace Heidt's talent programs of the past. The program also travels from state to state to showcase native talent.

Host: Horace Heidt.

Orchestra: Fran DeVol.

SHOW WAGON—30 minutes—NBC—January 8, 1955 - October 1, 1955.

SID CAESAR

Listed: The television programs of comedian Sid Caesar.

The Admiral Broadway Revue—Variety—60 minutes—NBC—January 28, 1949 - June 17, 1949.

Host: Sid Caesar.

Regulars: Imogene Coca, Mary McCarthy, Marge and Gower Champion, Roy Atwill, Bobby Van, Coren Welch.

Choreography: James Starbuch.

Orchestra: Charles Sanford.

Sponsor: Admiral.

Your Show of Shows—Variety—90 minutes—NBC—February 25, 1950 - June 5, 1954.

Host: Sid Caesar.

Regulars: Imogene Coca, Carl Reiner, Howard Morris, Judy Johnson, Cliff Norton, Robert Merrill, Marguerite Piazza, Bill Hayes, Nellie Fisher, Bambi Linn, Rod Alexander, The Bob Hamilton Trio, the Billy Williams Quartet, The Chandra Kaly Dancers.

Announcer: Vaughn Monroe.

Orchestra: Charles Sanford; Tony Romano.

Creator: Pat Weaver.

Producer: Max Liebman.

The Saturday Night Revue—Variety—NBC—1950. See title.

Caesar's Hour—Variety—60 minutes—NBC—September 27, 1954 - May 25, 1957.

Host: Sid Caesar.

Regulars: Carl Reiner, Howard Morris, Nanette Fabray, Janet Blair, Ellen Parker, Earl Wild, William Lewis, Sondra Dell, Cliff Norton, Virginia Curtis, Shirl Conway. The Ted Cappy Dancers.

Announcer: Vaughn Monroe; Joe De Santis.

Orchestra: Bernie Green.

The Sid Caesar Show—Comedy—30 minutes—ABC—January 20, 1958 - May 25, 1958.

Host: Sid Caesar.

Regulars: Imogene Coca, Carl Reiner, Howard Morris, Jeanne Bal, Paul Reed, Milt Kamen, The Kirby Stone Four.

Orchestra: Paul Weston.

The Sid Caesar Show—Comedy—30 minutes—ABC—September 19, 1963 - March 14, 1964.

Host: Sid Caesar.

Regulars: Gisele MacKenzie, Joey Forman.

Orchestra: Peter Matz.

SID CAESAR PRESENTS COMEDY PREVIEW

Comedy. The summer replacement for "Caesar's Hour.."

Hosts: Phil Foster, Bobby Sherwood.

Regulars: Barbara Nichols, Cliff Norton, Sid Gould, The Ted Cappy Dancers.

Music: Bill Hayes, Judy Tyler.

SID CAESAR PRESENTS COMEDY PREVIEW—60 minutes—NBC—July 4, 1955 - September 1955.

SIERRA

Drama. Background: Sierra National Park (fictional). The rescue operations of the park rangers—men and women dedicating their lives to protecting people from nature—and nature from people.

CAST

Ranger Tim Cassidy	James C. Richardson
Ranger Matt Harper	Ernest Thompson
Ranger Julie Beck	Susan Foster
Ranger P.J. Lewis	Mike Warren
Chief Ranger Jack Moore	Jack Hogan

Music: Lee Holdridge.

SIERRA—60 minutes—NBC—September 12, 1974 - December 12, 1974. 13 episodes.

SIGMUND AND THE SEA MONSTERS

Comedy. Background: 1730 Ocean Drive, Cyprus Beach, California, the residence of brothers Johnny and Scott Stuart and their pet sea monster, Sigmund, who, when disowned by his family for his inability to scare humans, was found and befriended by Johnny and Scott, taken home, and concealed in their club house. Stories depict Johnny and Scott's attempts to conceal Sigmund's presence and protect him from the devious efforts of his family, who seek to retrieve him when emergencies arise that require his presence at home (a cave at Dead Man's Point).

CAST

Sigmund Ooz	Billy Barty
Johnny Stuart	Johnny Whitaker
Scott Stuart	Scott Kolden
Zelda Marshall, their housekeeper; caring for Scott and Johnny whilst their parents are away on business	Mary Wickes
Sheriff Chuck Bevins, Zelda's boyfriend	Joe Higgins
Sheldon, the Sea Genie	Rip Torn
Miss Eddels, the Stuart's nosey neighbor	Margaret Hamilton
Shelby, Sheldon's nephew	Sparky Marcus
Gertrude Gouch, the housekeeper, later episodes	Fran Ryan

Also: Sharon Baird, Van Snowden, Paul Gale, Walter Edmonds, Larry Larson.

Additional characters (not given screen credit): Big Daddy, Sigmund's father; Sweet Mama, Sigmund's mother; Blurp Ooz, Sigmund's brother; Slurp Ooz, Sigmund's brother.

Ooz family pet: Prince (a barking lobster).

Characters: The Sid and Marty Krofft Puppets.

Music: Jimmie Haskell, Wes Farrell. *Additional Music:* Michael Lloyd.

Producer: Sid and Marty Krofft.

Director: Dick Darley, Murray Golden.

SIGMUND AND THE SEA MONSTERS—30 minutes—NBC—September 8, 1973 - October 18, 1975.

The Silent Force. Left to right: Ed Nelson, Percy Rodrigues, Lynda Day.

THE SILENT FORCE

Crime Drama. Background: Washington, D.C. The investigations of Amelia Cole, Jason Hart, and Ward Fuller, undercover agents for the Federal government who comprise The Silent Force, a secret organization designed to corrupt the inner workings of organized crime.

CAST

Amelia Cole	Lynda Day
Jason Hart	Percy Rodrigues
Ward Fuller	Ed Nelson

THE SILENT FORCE—30 minutes—ABC—September 21, 1970 - January 11, 1971. 13 episodes.

THE SILENT SERVICE

Anthology. Backgrounds: World War II; and the Korean War. Dramatizations based on incidents in the lives of the officers and men of the submarine division of the U.S. Navy.

Host-Narrator: Rear Admiral Thomas Dykers, U.S.N.

Included:

The Ugly Duckling. Ridiculed because their sub, the USS *Nautilus,* is oversized and ungainly, its crew bet a month's pay that she'll score the biggest hit on her first patrol. The story follows the maiden voyage of the atomic-powered submarine.

CAST

Carl Betz, Peter Hansen.

The Unsuccessful Patrol. The story of the maiden voyage of the S-34, which runs aground on her first patrol.

CAST

Richard Carlyle, Robert Knapp.

The Sculpin Story. The story of a submarine captain who elects to go down with his ship rather than to fall into enemy hands.

CAST

Ray Montgomery, Leon Sullivan.

THE SILENT SERVICE—30 minutes—Syndicated 1957. 78 episodes.

THE SILENT YEARS

Movies. Silent film classics.

Host-Narrator: Orson Welles.

THE SILENT YEARS—90 minutes—PBS—July 6, 1971 - September 24, 1971.

SILENTS PLEASE

Documentary. A history of the silent era of motion pictures—"The great stars, the excitement, the thrills, the laughter, and the heartbreak of Hollywood's Golden Era."

Host: Ernie Kovacs.

SILENTS PLEASE—30 minutes—ABC—August 4, 1960 - October 13, 1960; March 23, 1961 - October 5, 1961. Syndicated. 40 episodes.

SILVER THEATRE

See title: "Conrad Nagel."

SING ALONG

Musical Variety. The lyrics of familiar songs are rolled across the bottom of the screen to enable home viewers to participate.

Host: Jim Lowe.

Regulars: Florence Henderson, Tina Robin, June Roselle, Somethin' Smith and the Red Heads.

Orchestra: Harry Sosnick.

Featured Segment: "The Money Song." A limerick melody is played. Home audience members whose lyrics (which are sent to the program) best fit the music, receive merchandise prizes.

SING ALONG—30 minutes—CBS—June 4, 1958 - September 1958.

SING ALONG WITH MITCH

Musical Variety. The lyrics of familiar songs are rolled across the bottom of the screen to enable home viewers to sing along.

Host: Mitch Miller.

Regulars: Gloria Lambert, Louise O'Brien, Victor Griffin, Paul Friesen, Keith Booth, Gloria Chu, Bill Ventura, Phil Okon, Leslie Uggams, Frank Raye, Len Stokes, Bob McGrath, Mary Lou Rhyal, Hubie Hendrie, Tommy Nordon, Stan Carlson, Diana Trask, Jack Brown, Rita McLaughlin.

Musical Director: Jimmy Carroll.

SING ALONG WITH MITCH—60 minutes—NBC—September 28, 1962 - September 21, 1964. Rebroadcasts: NBC—May 1966 - September 1966. Several episodes (holiday broadcasts) are syndicated.

SING IT AGAIN

Musical Quiz. Object: For contestants to identify mystery song titles after hearing only several notes. Prizes are awarded to those who score the most correct identifications.

Home audience segment: "The Phantom Voice." The host places four telephone calls during one program and if recipients are able to identify a famous but unknown voice, they are awarded a fifty-dollar bond.

Hosts: Dan Seymour (1950); Jan Murray(1951).

Regulars: Alan Dale, Judy Lynn, Jack Stanton, Larry Douglas, Betty Luster, Bob Howard, The Riddlers.

Orchestra: Ray Bloch.

Producer: Lester Gottlieb, Louis Cowan, Herb Moss.

Director: Bob Bleyer.

SING IT AGAIN—60 minutes—CBS—1950 - 1951.

THE SINGING LADY

Children. Music, songs, stories, and marionette sketches.

Hostess: Irene Wicker, The Singing Lady.

Puppets: The Suzarri Marionettes.

Announcer: Walter Herlihy.

Orchestra: Allen Gart.

Producer: Blair Wallister.

Sponsor: Kellogg's.

THE SINGING LADY—30 minutes—ABC—August 12, 1948 - January 26, 1949.

SIR FRANCIS DRAKE

Adventure. Background: Sixteenth-century England. The exploits of Sir Francis Drake, an admiral of the Queen's Navy, as he defends the crown against warring marauders.

CAST
Sir Francis Drake	Terrence Morgan
Queen Elizabeth I	Jean Kent
Mindoza	Roger Delgado
Trevelyan	Patrick McLaughlen
John Drake	Michael Crawford

Drake's ship: the *Golden Hind.*

SIR FRANCIS DRAKE—30 minutes—NBC—June 24, 1962 - September 1962. 23 episodes.

SIROTA'S COURT

Comedy. Background: An unidentified American City. A comical look at life in a night court as seen through the hectic experiences of Matthew J. Sirota, a compassionate judge.

CAST
Judge Matthew Sirota	Michael Constantine
Maureen O'Connor, the court clerk	Cynthia Harris
Gail Goodman, the public defender	Kathleen Miller
Sawyer Dabney, the private attorney	Ted Ross
Bud Nugent, the assistant D.A.	Fred Willard
John Belson, the U.S. Marshal	Owen Bush

Music: David Shire.

Theme Vocal: Ted Ross.

Producer: Harvey Miller, Peter Engel.

Director: Mel Ferber, Tom Trobrich.

SIROTA'S COURT—30 minutes—NBC—December 1, 1976 - January 26, 1977.

THE SIX MILLION DOLLAR MAN

Adventure. Seriously injured after crashing in an Air Force research jet that malfunctioned, civilian astronaut Steve Austin becomes the immediate concern of the Office of Strategic Operations, a U.S. government organization that requires an extraordinary agent and spends six million dollars to reconstruct Austin to their specifications.

Through biotic and cybernetic surgery, both of Austin's legs, one arm and one eye are replaced with synthetic, nuclear-powered mechanisms that produce superhuman abilities and make him something that has never before existed: a cyborg (cybernetic organism), part human and part machine.

Stories detail Austin's attempts on behalf of the O.S.O. to resolve situations that pose a threat to humanity.

CAST
Steve Austin	Lee Majors
Dr. Rudy Wells, the aeromedical surgeon	Alan Oppenheimer Martin E. Brooks
Oscar Goldman, Austin's superior	Richard Anderson
Jaime Sommers, the Bionic Woman (recurring role)	Lindsay Wagner
Janet Callahan, Oscar's	

The Six Million Dollar Man. Richard Anderson (left) and Lee Majors.

secretary   Jennifer Darling
Miss Johnson, Oscar's
secretary   Susan Keller

Music: Stu Phillips; Gil Mellé.

Additional Music: J.J. Johnson, Richard Clements.

Executive Producer: Harve Bennett.

Producer: Kenneth Johnson, Lionel E. Siegel.

Director: Richard Moder, Jerry London, Alan Crosland, Barry Crane, Richard Doner, John Lucas, Cliff Bole, Phil Bondelli, James Lydon, Arnold Laven, Lawrence Dohney.

Note: In later episodes, the organization Steve works for, had become the O.S.I. (Office of Scientific Intelligence).

Vocal: "The Six Million Dollar Man" sung by Dusty Springfield.

THE SIX MILLION DOLLAR MAN —90 and 60 minute versions—ABC— Premiered: October 20, 1973.

THE SIXTH SENSE

Suspense Drama. Background: Los Angeles, California. The investigations of Michael Rhodes, professor of parapsychology at the University School, as he attempts to aid people threatened by "ghosts" and solve crimes that are linked to supernatural occurrences.

CAST
Michael Rhodes   Gary Collins
Nancy Murphy, his
   assistant   Catherine Farrar

Music: Billy Goldenberg.

THE SIXTH SENSE—60 minutes— ABC—January 15, 1972 - December 30, 1972. 25 episodes.

THE $64,000 QUESTION

Game. One contestant competes at a time. The player begins by selecting one category from a list. The host then asks him a question for one dollar. If he responds correctly, he receives the money. Each succeeding question doubles the previous amount of money if the player successfully answers it. Incorrect answers defeat a player, and players are permitted to leave at any established amount of money.

After ten questions are asked, the player reaches the first plateau of $512. The money is frozen and remains his.

The player continues for he has nothing to lose. He is then asked the one thousand dollar question. If he decides to continue, the two thousand dollar question is stated. Should the player decide to try to double the previous amount, the second plateau is reached if he correctly answers the four thousand dollar question. Once again, the money remains frozen and his, and he continues because he has nothing to lose.

For the eight thousand dollar question, he is placed in the Revlon Isolation Booth. The question is stated and the player receives thirty seconds with which to answer. If correct, he is then asked the sixteen thousand dollar question. Should he win the money he is given one week to decide if he wishes to continue or quit.

If he continues, he is again placed in the booth. The player selects one of two question that are held by the host. The question is read, and the player, if correct, wins $32,000. The player then receives another week to decide if he wants to quit or gamble it on a chance to answer the $64,000 question. Should he decide to continue, he is permitted to bring an expert in his category field into the booth with him. However, should both fail to correctly answer the question, the player receives his second plateau earnings.

Host: Hal March.

Assistant: Lynn Dollar.

Announcer: Wayne Howell.

Judge: Dr. Bergen Evans.

Music: Norman Leyden.

Question Guard: Mr. Harrington, of the Bankers Trust Co. in N.Y. who assures "no one has had previous access to questions."

Producer: Merrill Heatter, Mert Hoplin.

Sponsor: Revlon.

Note: During one stage of the series, a 1955 Cadillac was also the consolation prize.

THE $64,000 QUESTION—30 minutes—CBS—June 7, 1955 - November 2, 1958.

THE $64,000 CHALLENGE

Game. A spin-off from "The $64,000 Question." Three contestants compete, one "$64,000 Question" champion and two challengers. Each has to answer questions based on the subject chosen by the champion. Each is placed in a separate isolation booth, and all three players are asked the same question, one at a time (the sound is turned off in two when one is in use). Incorrect answers defeat a player, and money doubles in the same manner as "The $64,000 Question." If successful, previous champions can win as much as $128,000. Players who are defeated receive a Cadillac as a consolation prize.

Hosts: Sonny Fox; Ralph Story.

Announcer: Bill Rogers.

Music: Norman Leyden.

THE $64,000 CHALLENGE—30 minutes—CBS—April 8, 1956 - September 14, 1958.

THE SIX WIVES
OF HENRY VIII

Historical Drama. Chronicled: The life and six marriages of Henry VIII (1491-1547), the ruler of England during the fifteenth century.

CAST
Henry VIII   Keith Michell
Princess Catherine of
   Aragon, his first
   wife   Annette Crosbie
Anne Boleyn,
   his second
   wife   Dorothy Tutin
Jane Seymour,
   his third
   wife   Anne Stallybrass
Anne of Cleves,
   his fourth
   wife   Elvi Hale
Catherine Howard,
   his fifth
   wife   Angela Pleasence
Catherine Parr,
   his sixth
   wife   Rosalie Crutchley
Wolsey   John Baskcomb
Maria   Margaret Ford
The Duke of
   Norfork   Patrick Troughton

Chapuys	Edward Atienza
Princess Mary	Verina Greenlaw
Thomas Seymour	John Ronane
Lady Rochford	Shelia Burrell
Cromwell	Wolfe Morris
Archbishop Cranmer	Bernard Hepton
Mark Smeaton	Michael Osborne
Bishop Gardiner	Basil Dignam
Lord Hertford	Daniel Moynihan
Thomas Wriothesley	Patrick Godfrey
Francis Dereham	Simon Prebble
Dowager, Dutchess of Norfolk	Catherine Lacey

Narrator: Anthony Quayle.

Music: David Munrow.

THE SIX WIVES OF HENRY VIII–90 minutes–CBS–August 1, 1971 - September 5, 1971. Syndicated. Produced by the B.B.C.

THE SKATEBIRDS

Children. A series of cartoons hosted by three roller skating birds–Sach, Knock Knock, and Scooter.

Animated Segments:
The Robonic Stooges. A take-off on the 1940s "Three Stooges" wherein a Space Age Moe, Larry, and Curly, constructed from the finest parts available, battle evil throughout the universe.

Wonder Wheels. The story of Wheelie, the owner of a decrepit motorcycle, which, when the need arises, he transforms into Wonder Wheels to battle evil. His girlfriend: Doolie.

Woofer and Wimper. The misadventures of detective dogs Woofer and Wimper and their human masters, the teenage members of the Clue Club, a professional investigative organization. See title "Clue Club" for further information.

Live Action Segment:
Mystery Island. Retreating to an uncharted island, the evil Dr. Strenge establishes a base where he constructs his diobolical machines to control the world. His device, however, is incomplete and needs the aide of Paups, a sophisticated computer robot to fully activate it. Discovering that the robot is being transported, Dr. Strenge forces the plane carrying Paups to crash land on his island, marooning scientists Chuck Kelly, Sue Corwin, her brother, Sandy–and Paups. Stories concern Chuck, Sue, and Sandy's attempts to safeguard Paups from Dr. Strenge and escape from the island.

Music: Hoyt Curtin.

Executive Producer: William Hanna, Joseph Barbera.

Producer (of "Mystery Island"): Terry Morse, Jr.

Film Director: Hollinsworth Morse, Sidney Miller.

Animation Director: Charles A. Nichols.

Skatebirds Director: Sidney Miller.

THE SKATEBIRDS–55 minutes–CBS–Premiered: September 10, 1977.

THE SKIP FARRELL SHOW

Variety.

Host: Skip Farrell.

Featured: The Honeydreamers Quintet.

Announcer: Jack Lester.

Music: The George Baines Trio.

THE SKIP FARRELL SHOW–15 minutes–ABC–January 17, 1949 - August 28, 1949.

SKIPPY, THE BUSH KANGAROO

Adventure. Background: The Waratah National Park in Australia. Crossing the path of an injured and orphaned baby kangaroo, Sonny Hammond, the son of the chief park ranger, takes her home, cares for her, and, adopting her, names her Skippy. Stories depict the efforts of park rangers to maintain a game reserve; and the adventures shared by a young boy and his tame and intelligent pet kangaroo.

CAST

Matt Hammond, the chief ranger, Sonny's father	Ed Devereaux
Sonny Hammond	Garry Pankhurst
Mark Hammond, Sonny's brother, the river-patrol ranger	Ken James
Jerry King, the flight ranger	Tony Bonner
Clarissa (Clancy) Merrick, a pretty teenager residing with Hammonds while her parents are away on a business trip	Liza Goddard
Dr. Alexander Stark	Frank Thring

SKIPPY, THE BUSH KANGAROO–30 minutes–Syndicated 1969. 91 episodes.

SKYERS 5

The animated exploits of a quintet of crime fighters. 30 minutes–Syndicated 1967. 39 episodes.

SKYHAWKS

Animated Cartoon. The assignments of Skyhawks, Incorporated, a daredevil air transport and rescue service owned and operated by the Wilson family.

Characters: The Wilson family: Mike Wilson, widower, former Air Force colonel; his children: Steve, and Carolyn; his father: Patty Wilson, a World War I air ace; and his foster children: Red Hughes and Little Cindy.

Music: Jack Fascinato.

SKYHAWKS–30 minutes–ABC–September 6, 1969 - September 2, 1971.

SKY KING

Adventure. Background: The Flying Crown Ranch in Grover City. The exploits of rancher Sky King, a former World War II naval aviator who struggles to maintain law and order in the California ranch country.

CAST

Sky King	Kirby Grant
Penny King, his niece	Gloria Winters
Clipper King, his nephew	Ron Hagerthy
The sheriff	Ewing Mitchell

Producer: Jack Chertok.

Sponsor: Derby Foods; Nabisco.

Sky's plane: The *Songbird.*

SKY KING–30 minutes–CBS–September 1952 - September 3, 1966. 72 episodes. Syndicated.

THE SKY'S THE LIMIT

Game. Selected studio-audience members compete in various contests, both question-and-answer and stunt rounds. Prizes are awarded to players in accord with their ability to complete tasks.

Host: Gene Rayburn.

Assistants: Hope Lange, Marilyn Cantor.

THE SKY'S THE LIMIT–15 minutes–NBC–November 1, 1954 - August 19, 1955; 30 minutes–NBC–August 22, 1955 - June 1, 1956.

Slattery's People. Richard Crenna.

SLATTERY'S PEOPLE

Drama. The story of James Slattery, politician, lawyer, and minority leader in the state legislature who crusades against the injustices of government.

CAST

James Slattery	Richard Crenna
B. J. Clawson	Maxine Stuart
Bert Metcaff	Tol Avery
Mike Valera	Alejandro Rey
Wendy Wendkoski	Francine York
Liz Andrews	Kathie Brown
Frank Radcliffe	Edward Asner
Johnny Ramos	Paul Geary

Program Open:

Announcer: "Democracy is a very bad form of government, but I ask you never to forget it, all the others are so much worse."

SLATTERY'S PEOPLE—60 minutes—CBS—September 21, 1964 - November 26, 1965. 30 episodes.

THE SMALL FRY CLUB

Children. Stories, game contests, audience participation, magic tricks and other related entertainment for children.

Host: Bob Emery.

Producer: Bob Emery, Kay Emery.

Sponsor: General Foods.

THE SMALL FRY CLUB—60 and 30 minute versions—DuMont—1948-1951.

SMILIN' ED'S GANG

See title: "Andy's Gang."

THE SMITH FAMILY

Comedy-Drama. Background: 219 Primrose Lane, the residence of the Smith family: Chad, a twenty-five-year veteran detective sergeant, L.A.P.D.; his wife, Betty; and their children: Cindy, Bob, and Brian. Stories depict: the home and working life of a law enforcer; and the conflicts and crises that face a family in everyday life.

CAST

Chad Smith	Henry Fonda
Betty Smith	Janet Blair
Cindy Smith	Darleen Carr
Bob Smith	Ronny Howard
Brian Smith	Michael-James Wixted
Ray Martin, Chad's partner	John Carter
Captain Hughes	Charles McGraw

Music: Frank DeVol.

THE SMITH FAMILY—30 minutes—ABC—January 20, 1971 - September 8, 1971; April 12, 1972 - June 14, 1972. 39 episodes.

THE SMOKEY THE BEAR SHOW

Animated Cartoon. The adventures of Smokey the Bear, as both a bear and cub, as he struggles to protect the forests and their creatures from fire. Stories are conservative in nature and relate the careful use of fire and the importance of nature's woodlands to children.

Music: Maury Laws.

THE SMOKEY THE BEAR SHOW—30 minutes—ABC—September 6, 1969 - September 12, 1971. 17 episodes.

THE SMOTHERS BROTHERS

Listed: The television programs of comedians Tom and Dick Smothers.

The Smothers Brothers Show—Comedy—30 minutes—CBS—September 17, 1965 - September 9, 1966.
   Background: Los Angeles, California. Drowned at sea many years ago, Tom Smothers returns to Earth as an apprentice angel and takes up residence in the bachelor apartment of his brother, Dick. Inept, and ordered to assist people in distress, Tom, reluctantly assisted by Dick, struggles to complete his assignments and acquire the status needed to become a full-fledged angel.

CAST

Dick Smothers	Himself
Tommy Smothers	Himself
Leonard J. Costello, Dick's boss	Roland Winters
Diane Costello, his daughter	Marilyn Scott
Mrs. Costello, his wife	Harriet MacGibbon
Janet, Dick's girlfriend	Ann Elder

Music: Alfred Perry; Perry Botkin, Jr.

The Smothers Brothers Comedy Hour—Variety—60 minutes—CBS—February 5, 1967 - June 8, 1969.

Format: Controversial humor, satire, songs, and topical sketches.

Hosts: Tom and Dick Smothers.

Regulars: Pat Paulsen, John Hartford, Jennifer Warren, Murray Romas, Leigh French, Mason Williams, Bob Einstein (as Officer Judy), Don Wyatt, Carl Gottlieb, Cathy Cahill, Jessica Myerson, The Jimmy Joyce Singers, The Anita Kerr Singers, The Ron Poindexter Dancers, The Louis Da Pron Dancers.

Announcer: Roger Carroll.

Orchestra: Nelson Riddle.

The Smothers Brothers Comedy Hour—Variety—60 minutes—ABC—July 15, 1970 - September 16, 1970.

Format: Same as the CBS sixty minute version.

Hosts: Tom and Dick Smothers.

Regulars: Sally Struthers, Spencer Quinn.

Announcer: Roger Carroll.

Orchestra: Denny Vaughn.

The Smothers Organic Prime Time Space Ride—Variety—30 minutes—Syndicated 1971.
Format: Offbeat, controversial comedy. The Space Ride: Performances by new talent finds.

Host: Tom Smothers.

Occasional co-host: Dick Smothers.

The Smothers Brothers Show—Variety—60 minutes—NBC—January 13, 1975 - May 26, 1975.

Hosts: Tom and Dick Smothers.

Regulars: Pat Paulsen, Don Novello, Pete Smith, Betty Aberlain, Evelyn Russell.

Orchestra: Marty Paich.

SNAP JUDGEMENT

Game. Two competing two-member teams. One member of each team is presented with a concealed word. The player then relates a one-word clue to his partner, who must identify the word. If he is unable, their opponents then receive a chance to identify it. The word is played until it is identified or until it is voided by the use of ten clues. Words start at ten points and diminish one point with each clue. Winners, the highest scoring teams, receive both cash and merchandise prizes.

Hosts: Ed McMahon; Gene Rayburn.

Announcer: Johnny Olsen.

Music: Recorded.

SNAP JUDGEMENT—30 minutes—NBC—April 3, 1967 - March 28, 1969.

SNEAK PREVIEW

Pilot Films. Proposed comedy series for the 1956 - 1957 season.

Included:

Calling Terry Conway. The misadventures of Terry Conway, a public relations director in a glamorous Las Vegas Hotel.

CAST
Terry Conway: Ann Sheridan; Pearl McGrath: Una Merkel; Stan: Philip Ober.

Carolyn. Named the guardian of three children after their parents' death, an actress struggles to win their affection.

CAST
Carolyn: Celeste Holm; Mrs. Little: Jeanette Nolan; Smattering: Parley Baer.

Real George. The misadventures of George Gidley, a junior salesman in a department store.

CAST
George Gidley: George O'Hanlon; Mr. Tutwiter: Ray Collins; Janet: Gloria Henry.

Just Plain Folks. The misadventures of a Hollywood couple who are type cast as an actress and writer.

CAST
Zsa Zsa Gabor, Cy Howard.

SNEAK PREVIEW—30 minutes—NBC—July 3, 1956 - August 24, 1956.

THE SNOOKY LANSON SHOW

Musical Variety.

Host: Snooky Lanson.

Vocalists: The Mellow-Larks.

THE SNOOKY LANSON SHOW—15 minutes—NBC—July 17, 1956 - September 26, 1956.

THE SNOOP SISTERS

See title: "NBC Wednesday Mystery Movie," *Snoop Sisters* segment.

SOAP

Satire. Background: Dunn's River, Connecticut. Spoofing afternoon soap operas, the series focuses on the lives of two sisters: the wealthy Jessica Tate, and the not-so-rich Mary Campbell, and the outlandish activities of their families—who live on opposite sides of the town. The stories, which are adult, are episodic.

CAST
Jessica Tate	Cathryn Damon
Mary Campbell	Katherine Helmond
Chester Tate, Jessica's husband	Robert Mandan
Corinne Tate, Jessica's daughter	Diana Canova
Eunice Tate, Jessica's daughter	Jennifer Salt
Billy Tate, Jessica's son	Jimmy Baio
Burt Campbell, Mary's husband	Richard Mulligan
Jodie Campbell, Mary's son	Billy Crystal
Danny Campbell, Mary's son	Ted Wass
Benson, the Tate's butler	Robert Guillaume
The Major, Jessica's crazed father (believes he is living World War II)	Arthur Peterson
Peter, Jessica's lover; Corinne's boyfriend	Robert Urich
Godfather, the head of the local Mafia in which Danny is involved	Richard Libertini

Announcer-Narrator: Rod Roddy.

Music: George Tipton.

Executive Producer: Paul Junger Witt, Tony Thomas.

Producer: Susan Harris.

Director: Jay Sandrich.

Creator: Susan Harris.

SOAP—30 minutes—ABC—Premiered: September 13, 1977.

SOLDIER PARADE

Variety. Performances by army talent. Broadcast from military bases throughout the country.

Hostesses: Arlene Francis; Martha Wright.

Co-Emcee: Pfc. Richard Hayes.

Soap. From far left: Diana Canova (seated), Robert Mandan (next to Diana), Katherine Helmond (seated on arm of chair); top, left: Arthur Peterson (in military uniform), Jennifer Salt (behind Miss Helmond), and Robert Guillaume (center). Right side: Cathryn Damon (seated); standing, left to right: Ted Wass, Richard Mulligan, Robert Urich, Billy Crystal. *Courtesy of the Call-Chronicle Newspapers, Allentown, Pa.*

Vocalists: The Ford Dix Chorus.
Music: The Ford Dix Band.

SOLDIER PARADE—30 minutes—
ABC—1949 - 1955.

THE SOLDIERS

Comedy. The misadventures of two reluctant G.I.s: Hal March and Tom D'Andrea—soldiers conducting a private battle with the U.S. army.

CAST

Private Hal March	Himself
Private Tom D'Andrea	Himself
The captain	John Dehner
The sergeant	Red Pearson

THE SOLDIERS—30 minutes—NBC—June 25, 1955 - September 3, 1955.

SOLDIERS OF FORTUNE

Adventure. The exploits of American globetrotters Tim Kelly and Toubo Smith as they battle the forces of injustice throughout the world.

CAST

Tim Kelly	John Russell
Toubo Smith	Chick Chandler

SOLDIERS OF FORTUNE—30 minutes—Syndicated 1955. 52 episodes.

SOMERSET

Serial. A spin-off from "Another World." Background: The town of Somerset. The dramatic story of three families: the Lucases, the Grants, and the Delaneys. Episodes depict the conflicts and tensions that arise from the interactions of the characters.

CAST

Sam Lucas	Jordan Charney
Lahoma Lucas	Ann Wedgeworth
Missy Lucas	Carol Roux
Robert Delaney	Nicholas Coster
Laura Cooper	Dorothy Stinnette
Randy Buchanan	Gary Sandy
Ben Grant	Ed Kemmer
Jill Grant	Susan McDonald
David Grant	Ron Martin
Peter Delaney	Len Gochman
Marsha Davis	Alice Hirson
Ellen Grant	Georgann Johnson
Gerald Davis	Walter Matthews
Jessica Buchanan	Wynn Miller
India Delaney	Marie Wallace
Rex Cooper	Paul Sparer
Tom Cooper	Ernest Thompson
Chuck Hillman	Ed Winter
Dr. Stan Kurtz	Michael Lipton
Ginger Kurtz	Meg Winter
	Fawne Harriman
	Renne Jarrett
Leo Kurtz	Gene Fanning
Eve Lawrence	Bibi Besch
Julian Cannel	Joel Crothers
Dr. Terri Martin	Gloria Hoy
Frieda Lang	Polly Rowles
Becky Winkle	Jane Rose
Doris Hiller	Gretchen Wyler
Mark Mercer	Stanley Grover
Edith Mercer	Judy Searle
Tony Cooper	Barry Jenner
	Doug Chapin
Mrs. Benson	Eleanor Phelps
Greg Mercer	Gary Swanson
Pamela Davis	Pamela Toll
Crystal Ames	Diahn Williams
Danny Catsworth	Melinda Plank
Mitch Farmer	Dick Shoberg
Bill Greeley	Bill Hunt
Andrea Moore	Harriet Hall
Emily Moore	Lois Kibbee
Phil	Bob Gabriel
Kenny	Ed Bryce
Philip Matson	Frank Scofield
Dana Moore	Chris Pennock
Karen MacMillan	Nancy Pinkerton
Jasper Delaney	Ralph Clanton
Zoe Cannel	Lois Smith
Rafe Carter	Phil Sterling
Carter Matson	Jay Gregory
Virgil Paris	Marc Alaimo
Heather Lawrence	Audrey Landers
Luke MacKenzie	Robert Burr
Lai Ling	Helen Funai
Bobby Hanson	Matthew Greene
Joey Cooper	Sean Wood
Buffy	Roxanne Gregory
Carrie Wheeler	Jobeth Williams
Chip Williams	Roger Rathbun
Heather Kane	Audrey Landers
Kate Cannell	Tina Sloan
Jerry Kane	James O'Sullivan
Lena Andrews	Abby Lewis

Music: Chet Kingsbury.

Additional Music: Charles Paul.

Announcer: Bill Wolff.

Executive Producer: Lyle B. Hill, Sid Sirulnik.

Director: Jack Coffey, Bruce Minnix.

SOMERSET—30 minutes—NBC—March 30, 1970 - December 31, 1976. Original title: "Another World in Somerset."

THE SOMERSET MAUGHAM THEATRE

See title: "Teller of Tales."

SOMETHING ELSE

Musical Variety. Performances by the recording industry's top artists.

Host: John Byner.

Featured: The Action Faction Dancers.

SOMETHING ELSE—30 minutes—Syndicated 1969. 68 tapes.

SOMETHING SPECIAL

Musical Variety.

Hosts, monthly guests: Barbara McNair, Patti Page, Peggy Lee, The New Christy Minstrels, Pearl Bailey, Allan Sherman, Julie London, The Young Americans, Ethel Waters.

Orchestra: Marty Paich.

SOMETHING SPECIAL—60 minutes—Syndicated 1966. 10 tapes.

SONG SNAPSHOTS ON A SUMMER HOLIDAY

See title: "Merv Griffin."

SONGS FOR SALE

Variety. The material of four songwriters (per show) is performed, then judged and evaluated by professional authorities.

Hosts: Jan Murray; Steve Allen.

Vocalists: Margaret Whiting, Rosemary Clooney, Richard Hayes, Toni Arden, Betty Clooney, Bob Carroll, Martha Stewart, Don Cherry, Eileen Burton, Helen Forrest, Joan Edwards, Johnny Johnston, Jack Robbins, Tony Bennett, Dorothy Field, The Four Aces, The Ink Spots, Richard Himber.

Judges: Mitch Miller, Morey Amsterdam, Bob Hillard, Martin Block, Duke Ellington, Dorothy Loudon.

Orchestra: Ray Bloch.

Producer: Al Span, Herb Morse, Bob Bleyer.

Director: John Morse.

SONGS FOR SALE—30 minutes—CBS 1951.

THE SONNY AND CHER SHOW

Variety. Music, songs, dances, and comedy sketches.

The Sonny and Cher Show. Cher (left) and Sonny.

Hosts: Sonny and Cher (Salvatore Bono and his wife Cher—Cheryl La Piere).

Regulars: Chastity Bono (their daughter), Peter Cullen, Clive Clerk, Murray Riff, Teri Garr, Freeman King, Steve Parker, Ted Zeigler, Ted Bickle, Tom Filari, Ralph Morrow, Billy Van, Murray Langston, The Jaime Rogers Dancers, The Tony Mordente Dancers, The Earl Brown Singers.

Announcer: Peter Cullen.

Orchestra: Jimmy Dale; Marty Paich.

THE SONNY AND CHER SHOW—60 minutes—CBS—August 1, 1971 - September 5, 1971; December 27, 1971 - May 29, 1974. Also titled: "The Sonny and Cher Comedy Hour." Spin-offs: "Cher" and "The Sonny Comedy Revue."

THE SONNY AND CHER SHOW

Variety. Music, songs, dances, and comedy sketches.

Hosts: Sonny and Cher.

Regulars: Ted Zeigler, Billy Van, Peter Cullen, Jack Harnell, Richard Lewis, Felix Silla.

Orchestra: Harold Battiste.

Special Musical Material: Billy Barnes, Earl Brown.

Choreographer: Jaime Rogers.

Producer: Nick Vanoff.

Director: Tim Kiley.

THE SONNY AND CHER SHOW—60 minutes—CBS—February 1, 1976 - March 18, 1977.

THE SONNY COMEDY REVUE

Variety. Music, songs, dances, and comedy sketches.

Host: Sonny Bono.

Regulars: Teri Garr, Freeman King, Ted Zeigler, Peter Cullen, Billy Van, Murray Langston.

Announcer: Peter Cullen.

Orchestra: Lex DeAzevedo.

THE SONNY COMEDY REVUE—60 minutes—ABC—September 22, 1974 - December 29, 1974.

SONS AND DAUGHTERS

Drama. Background: Stockton, California, 1956. A depiction of the last innocence of American youth as seen through the eyes of Anita Cramer and Jeff Reed, Southwest High School seniors who are steadily dating and struggling to cope with difficult family readjustments: Jeff, to his father's recent passing; and Anita, to her mother's decision to live with another man.

CAST

Anita Cramer	Glynnis O'Connor
Jeff Reed	Gary Frank
Lucille Reed, Jeff's mother	Jay W. Macintosh
Walter Cramer, Anita's father	John S. Ragin
Ruth Cramer, Anita's mother	Jan Shutan
Danny Reed, Jeff's brother	Michael Morgan

Jeff and Anita's friends:

Murray "Moose" Kerner	Barry Livingston
Stash	Scott Colomby
Charlie	Lionel Johnston
Evie Martinson	Debralee Scott
Mary Anne	Laura Siegel

Music: James Di Pasquale.

SONS AND DAUGHTERS—60 minutes—CBS—September 12, 1974 - November 6, 1974.

SOS FREQUENCY 17

A six-episode series of fifty-two-minute mystery films first syndicated to the U.S. in 1968.

SO THIS IS HOLLYWOOD

Comedy. Background: The LaPaloma Courts, the residence of Kim Tracy, an aspiring actress, and her roommate, Queenie Dugan, a stunt girl. The hopes and heartaches of two young show business hopefuls are seen through the eyes of Kim Tracy as she and Queenie struggle to make their mark on the movie capital.

CAST

Queenie Dugan	Mitzi Green
Kim Tracy	Virginia Gibson
Hubie Dodd, Queenie's boyfriend	Gordon Jones
Andy Boone, Kim's agent	James Lydon
April Adams, Kim's friend, an actress	Peggy Knudsen
Mr. Snead, their landlord	Charles Lane

Narrator: Virginia Gibson.

Mitzi Green's stand-in: Shirley Lucas.

SO THIS IS HOLLYWOOD—30 minutes—NBC—January 1, 1955 - August 19, 1955. 24 episodes. Syndicated.

SOUL TRAIN

Musical Variety. Performances by Soul personalities.

Host: Don Corneileus.

Announcer: Don Cobb.

Music: Recorded.

SOUL TRAIN—60 minutes—Syndicated 1971.

SOUND OFF TIME

Variety. Music, songs, performances by guests, and comedy sketches.

Hosts, on an alternating basis: Bob Hope, Fred Allen, Jerry Lester.

Announcer: Hy Averback.

Orchestra: Les Brown.

Producer: Doug Coulter, Monroe Hack.

Director: Warren Jacober, Ezra Stone.

Sponsor: Chesterfield Cigarettes.

SOUND OFF TIME—30 minutes—NBC—1951 - 1952.

THE SOUNDS OF SUMMER

See title: "Steve Allen."

SOUPY SALES

Listed: The television programs of comedian Soupy Sales.

Program background: Soupy's house.

Characters: White Fang (represented by a white paw), "The biggest and meanest dog in the United

States"; Black Tooth (a brown paw), "The kindest dog in the United States."

Puppets: Pookie, the whistling lion; Hippie, the silent hippopotamus; Herman, the flea; Willie, the worm.

Other characters: Marilyn Monwolf, a curvaceous friend of White Fang and Black Tooth; Peaches, Soupy's flirtatious friend; and salesmen and irate neighbors who are seen only by their hands and arms as they talk from the side of the house near an open door.

Programs:

Soupy's On—Children—30 minutes—Local Detroit—1953.

Host: Soupy Sales.

Assistant: Clyde Adler.

The Soupy Sales Show—Children—30 minutes—ABC—July 4, 1955 - August 26, 1955.

Host: Soupy Sales.

Assistant: Clyde Adler.

The Soupy Sales Show—Children—30 minutes—ABC—October 3, 1959 - June 25, 1960. Based on his local Los Angeles show which is aired over KABC-TV, Ch. 7.

Host: Soupy Sales.

Assistant: Clyde Adler.

The Soupy Sales Show—Children—30 minutes—Syndicated—1966 - 1968. Originally a local New York program aired over WNEW-TV, Ch. 5.

Host: Soupy Sales.

Assistant: Clyde Adler.

Sketch: "The Adventures of Philo Kvetch." A cliff-hanger type of serial wherein private detective Philo Kvetch (Soupy) attempts to apprehend the notorious Mask and his henchman, Onions Oregano (Clyde).

SO YOU WANT TO LEAD A BAND

Variety. Music, comedy vignettes, and songs.

Quiz segment: Four members of the studio audience are selected to lead the orchestra. Studio audience applause determines the winner (the best conductor), who receives a merchandise prize.

Host: Sammy Kaye.

Regulars: Jeffrey Clay, Barbara Benson, Tony Alamo, The Kaydettes, The Kay Choir.

Orchestra: Sammy Kaye.

The Band Boy (brings the baton to the contestant): Chubby Silvers.

Producer: Jim Lichtman, Vic McLeod.

Director: Vic McLeod.

Sponsor: Brillo.

SO YOU WANT TO LEAD A BAND —30 minutes. CBS—1951 - 1954; ABC—1954.

SPACE ACADEMY

Science Fiction Adventure. Era: Earth in the year 3732. The story of the Nova Blue Team, a group of young cadets assigned to the man-made planetoid Space Academy for training. Their experiences, as they patrol, protect, and explore the universe are dramatized.

CAST

Commander Gampu	Jonathan Harris
Cadet Laura Gentry	Pamelyn Ferdin
Captain Chris Gentry	Ric Carrott
Adrian, a cadet	Maggie Cooper
Lt. Paul Jerome	Ty Henderson
Tee Gar Sume, a cadet	Brian Tochi
Loki, the alien	Eric Greene

The Robot: Peepo.

Music: Yvette Blais, Jeff Michael.

Executive Producer: Norm Prescott, Lou Scheimer.

Producer: Arthur H. Nadel.

Director: Jeffrey Hayden, George Tyne.

SPACE ACADEMY—25 minutes—CBS—Premiered: September 10, 1977.

SPACE ACE

Science fiction blended with animation as a superboy from outer space assists Earth in its battle against evil. 30 minutes—Syndicated 1968. 39 episodes.

SPACE ANGEL

Animated Cartoon. The exploits of Scott McCloud, Interplanetary Space Force agent, as he protects the planets of a united solar system from the sinister forces of evil.

Music: Paul Horn.

SPACE ANGEL—05 minutes—Syndicated 1964. 260 episodes.

SPACE GHOST

Animated Cartoon. The exploits of Space Ghost, an interplanetary crime fighter. (Through the use of a magic belt he receives the gift of invisibility.)

Additional characters: Jan and Jayce, his teenage wards; and Blip, their pet space monkey.

Additional segment: "Dino Boy."

Characters' Voices

Space Ghost	Gary Owens
Jan	Ginny Tyler
Jayce	Tim Matthieson
Dino Boy (Tod)	Johnny Carson
Ugh	Mike Road

Music: Hoyt Curtin.

Musical Director: Ted Nichols.

Producer-Director: William Hanna, Joseph Barbera.

SPACE GHOST—30 minutes—CBS—September 10, 1966 - September 7, 1968. 48 episodes. A Hanna-Barbera production.

SPACE GIANTS

Science Fiction Adventure. Background: Tokyo, Japan. Seeking to control the planet Earth, Rodak, an evil, alien scientist, appears to Tomoko Mura, a newspaper reporter, and relates the details of his plans. The published story brings Matuslah, an old, white-bearded alien scientist to Earth. Seeking and finding Tomoko, Matuslah tells him about the evils of Rodak and of his own battle to destroy him. To assist the Earth in its soon to ensue war against Rodak, Matuslah constructs Goldar, a fifty-foot golden robot; Silva, his fifty-foot silver robot wife, and their gold son, Gam.

The series depicts Earth's battle against Rodak, who, by establishing a base in an orbiting spaceship with an advanced laboratory, manufactures and sends to Earth giant, prehistoric type monsters to carry out his plan of domination. Produced in Japan; dubbed in English.

CAST

Tomoko	Mayako Yashiro
Mikko, his wife	Toshio Egi
Itomura	Masumi Okada
Gam	Hideki Ninomiya

Music: Naozumi Yamamoto.

Producer: Kazuo Kamuima.

Writer: Osamu Tezuka.

Program Open:

Announcer: "From the far reaches of outer space comes a threat to planet Earth. Mankind faces its most powerful enemy—the mastermind Rodak. The Space Giants."

SPACE GIANTS—30 minutes—Syndicated 1969. 52 episodes.

SPACE G-MEN

A futuristic space drama about an interplanetary protection organization. 30 minutes—Syndicated 1963. 13 episodes.

SPACE KIDDETTES

Animated Cartoon. The battle against celestial evil as undertaken by the Space Kiddettes, a group of space-age youngsters. A Hanna-Barbera production.

Characters' Voices

Scooter	Chris Allen
Snoopy	Lucille Bliss
Countdown	Don Messick
Jenny	Janet Waldo
Captain Sykhook	Daws Butler
Pupstar	Don Messick

Music: Hoyt Curtin.

SPACE KIDDETTES—30 minutes—NBC—September 10, 1966 - September 2, 1967.

SPACE: 1999

Science Fiction Adventure. Establishing an early warning system on the

Space: 1999. Left to right: Barbara Bain, Catherine Schell, Martin Landau.

Moon to repel invaders, three hundred men and women, from all nations on Earth, are assigned to man it. Accidentally blasted out of its orbit due to a radioactive chain reaction, the Moon begins to wander in space, seeking a new planet on which to afix itself. Considered the invaders by the inhabitants of other planets, the marooned Earthlings struggle to combat the life forms of distant worlds, the elements of outer space, and sustain life on their new world as it wanders on its unexpected odyssey across the universe. An I.T.C. production.

CAST

Commander John Koenig	Martin Landau
Dr. Helena Russell	Barbara Bain
Professor Victor Bergman	Barry Morse
Maya, the beautiful alien, a metamor* from the planet Psychon	Catherine Schell
Tony Verdeschi, the security officer	Tony Anholt
Captain Alan Carter	Nick Tate
Sandra Benes, a communications officer (a.k.a. San)	Zienia Merton
Yasko, a communications officer	Yasuko Nagazumi
Dr. Bob Mathias	Anton Phillips
Dr. Ben Vincent	Jeffrey Kisson
Bill Fraser	John Hug
Peter Irving	Michael Culver
Dr. Ed Spencer	Sam Destor
Nurse	Hazel McBride
David Kano	Clifton Jones
Paul Morrow	Prentis Hancock
Commissioner Simmonds	Roy Dotrice

Opening Narration: Barbara Bain.

Music: Barry Gray, Vic Elms, Derek Wadsworth.

Executive Producer: Gerry Anderson.

Producer: Sylvia Anderson, F. Sherwin Greene, Fred Freiberger.

Director: Lee H. Katzin, Val Guest, Robert Lynn, Kevin Connor, Tom Clegg, Bob Brooks, Peter Medak, David Tomblin, Ray Austen, Bob Kellett, Charles Crichton.

SPACE: 1999—60 minutes—Syndicated 1975.

* A woman who is capable of transforming herself into any form on which she concentrates.

SPACE PATROL

Adventure. Era: Twenty-first-century Earth. The battle against celestial dangers as seen through the assignments of Buzz Corey, the commander

-in-chief of the Space Patrol, an Earth-based organization responsible for the safety of the United Planets (Earth, Mars, Venus, Jupiter, and Mercury).

CAST

Commander Buzz Corey	Ed Kemmer
Cadet Happy, his co-pilot	Lyn Osborn
Carol Karlyle, the daughter of the Secretary General of the United Planets	Virginia Hewitt
Dr. Von Meter, a Space Patrol scientist	Rudolph Anders
Tonga, a Space Patrol ally	Nina Bara

Also: Jack Narz.

Corey's Rocket Ship: The *X-R-Z.*

Producer: Mike Mosser, Mike Devery, Helen Mosser.

Director: Dick Darley.

Sponsor: Nestle; Ralston.

Program Open:

Announcer: "High adventure in the wild vast regions of space. Missions of daring in the name of interplanetary justice. Travel into the future with Buzz Corey, commander-in-chief of the Space Patrol."

SPACE. PATROL—30 minutes—ABC—September 11, 1950 - December 29, 1956.

SPARRING PARTNERS

Game. Background: A simulated boxing ring. Contestants, who are drawn from business arts and professions, comprise two three member teams—the men vs. the women. The basis is a question and answer game with the team scoring the most correct answers being declared the winner.

Host: Walter Kiernan.

SPARRING PARTNERS—30 minutes—ABC 1949.

SPEAKEASY

Interview. Performances by and interviews with Rock personalities.

Host: Chip Monck.

SPEAKEASY—60 minutes—Syndicated 1973.

SPECIAL AGENT 7

Drama. The investigations of Treasury Agent Conroy as he probes the elements behind crimes perpetrated against the U.S. Department of Internal Revenue. Based on official files.

Starring: Lloyd Nolan as Treasury Agent Conroy.

SPECIAL AGENT 7–30 minutes–Syndicated 1958. 26 episodes.

SPECIAL BRANCH

Crime Drama. Background: London, England. The cases of the Special Branch, an elite team of Scotland Yard undercover agents. Produced in London by Thames TV.

CAST
Chief Inspector Craven	George Sewell
Chief Inspector Tom Haggerty	Patrick Mower
Chief Inspector Strand	Paul Eddington
Commander Fletcher	Frederick Jaeger

Music: Robert Earley.

Executive Producer: George Taylor.

Producer: Ted Childs.

SPECIAL BRANCH–60 minutes–Syndicated 1976.

SPECIAL EDITION

Documentary. Filmed versions of magazine stories.

Hostess: Barbara Feldon.

Music: Richard LaSalle.

Producer: Alan Sloan.

Director: Steve Kattin.

SPECIAL EDITION–30 minutes–Syndicated 1977.

SPECIAL FOR WOMEN

Anthology. Sympathetic dramatizations based on the problems faced by women. Following the drama, brief discussions are held with guest doctors and pyschiatrists.

Hostess: Pauline Fredericks.

Producer: George Lefferts.

Sponsor: Purex.

SPECIAL FOR WOMEN–60 minutes –NBC–October 14, 1960 - August 29, 1961.

SPEED BUGGY

Animated Cartoon. Traveling throughout the country in their car, *Speed Buggy,* which possesses a Saint Bernard-like personality, teenagers Debbie, Tinker, and Mark, involve themselves in and attempt to solve the problems of others.

Voices: Chris Allen, Arlene Golonka, Mel Blanc (as *Speed Buggy*), Phil Luther, Jr., Hal Smith, Michele Road, Sid Miller, Ron Feinberg, Virginia Gregg, John Stephenson, Ira Paran.

Music: Hoyt Curtin, Paul DeKorte.

SPEED BUGGY–30 minutes–CBS–September 8, 1973 - August 31, 1974.

SPEED RACER

Animated Cartoon. The exploits of Speed Racer, a daring young racing-car driver. Produced in Japan; dubbed in English.

Characters:

Speed Racer.
Trixie, his girlfriend.
Spridal, Speed's kid brother.
Chim Chim, Spridal's pet monkey.

Speed's car: The *Special Formula Mark Five.*

SPEED RACER–30 minutes–Syndicated 1967. 52 episodes.

SPENCER'S PILOTS

Adventure. Background: California. The exploits of Cass Garrett and Stan Lewis, charter pilots for Spencer Aviation, an organization that undertakes hazardous assignments.

CAST
Cass Garrett	Christopher Stone
Stan Lewis	Todd Susman
Spencer Parish, their employer	Gene Evans
Linda Dann, Spencer's secretary	Margaret Impert
Wig Wiggins, the mechanic	Britt Leach

Music: Bruce Broughton, Morton Stevens, Jerrold Immel.

Executive Producer: Bob Sweeney, Edward H. Feldman.

Producer: Larry Rosen.

Director: Bill Bixby, Marc Daniels, Don Weis, Ernest Pintoff, Bruce Bilson, Gordon Hessler.

SPENCER'S PILOTS–60 minutes–CBS–September 17, 1976 - November 19, 1976.

SPIDER-MAN

Animated Cartoon. Background: New York City. Completing his notes following a demonstration on radioactivity, Central High School student Peter Parker is bitten by a spider that has been exposed to the deadly effects of the demonstration.

Returning home, he realizes that the spider's venom has become a part of his bloodstream and that he has absorbed the proportionate power and ability of a living spider.

Experimenting, he develops his webbed feeler (a liquid that enables him to spin a web) and the costume of Spider-Man to conceal his real identity.

Acquiring a position as reporter for the *New York Daily Bugle,* he institutes a battle against crime, dispensing justice as the mysterious Spider-Man.

Characters' Voices
Peter Parker/ Spider-Man	Bernard Cowan Paul Sols
Betty Brandt, a reporter	Peg Dixon
J. Jonah Jameson, the editor	Paul Kligman

Music: Ray Ellis.

Theme: Bob Harris, Paul Francis Webster.

Executive Producer: Robert L. Lawrence, Ralph Bakshi.

Producer: Ray Patterson.

Director: Ralph Bakshi.

Note: On September 14, 1977, CBS presented a ninety-minute live action pilot film, titled "Spider-Man," with Nicholas Hammond in the title role and David White as J.J. Jameson.

SPIDER-MAN–30 minutes–ABC–September 9, 1967 - August 30, 1969; March 22, 1970 - September 6, 1970. 52 episodes. Syndicated.

SPIKE JONES

Listed: The television programs of comic Spike Jones.

The Spike Jones Show–Variety–60 minutes–NBC 1951.

Host: Spike Jones.

Regulars: Helen Grayco, Jan Peerce, The Wayne Marlin Trio.

Orchestra: The City Slickers.

The Spike Jones Show—Variety—60 minutes—NBC—January 2, 1954 - May 8, 1954.

Host: Spike Jones.

Regulars: Helen Grayco, George Rock, Freddie Morgan, Sir Frederick Gar.

Orchestra: The City Slickers.

The Spike Jones Show—Variety—30 minutes—CBS—April 2, 1957 - June 25, 1957.

Host: Spike Jones.

Regulars: Helen Grayco, Billy Barty, The Dixie Pixies, The Polka Dots, The Clypso Kings, The Rock 'N' Rollers.

Orchestra: The City Slickers.

Club Oasis—Variety—30 minutes—ABC—June 1958-September 6, 1958.

Host: Spike Jones.

Regulars: Helen Grayco, Joyce Jameson, Billy Barty, Georgia Rock, Gil Bernard, Carl Fortina, Joel Paul.

Orchestra: The City Slickers.

The Spike Jones Show—Variety—60 minutes—CBS—August 1, 1960 - September 19, 1960; July 17, 1961 - September 1961.

Host: Spike Jones.

Vocalist: Helen Grayco.

Orchestra: The City Slickers.

SPIN-OFF

Game. Before each of the two husband-and-wife teams that compete are five wheels that each contain numbers (1 to 6) and spin at the rate of seventeen numbers per second. The game begins when the host reads a question. The team that is first to identify themselves through a buzzer signal receives a chance to answer. If correct, they receive a chance to play the spinning wheels. One player activates the wheels by pressing a green plunger. The other player presses a red plunger to stop one of the wheels. A number is then revealed. Since scoring follows the rules of poker, they can either keep it or spin it off and try for a different number (only three spins are permitted per wheel). Once the decision is made, another question is asked and the game follows in the same manner (five questions are

played per game). The team that scores the highest number values (as in cards) wins the game and the money associated with the numbers (1 pair: $50; 2 pair: $75; 3 of a kind: $100; straight: $125; full house: $150; 5 of a kind: $200).

Host: Jim Lange.

Music: Recorded.

SPIN-OFF—30 minutes—CBS—June 16, 1975 - September 5, 1975.

SPIN THE PICTURE

Game. Object: For players to identify photographs of famous celebrities. A rapidly spun picture is flashed on a screen and is accompanied by a verbal clue. A telephone call is then placed to a home viewer. If the home viewer can identify the picture, he receives the merchandise prizes that have been accumulated to date. If not, an additional prize is added to the jackpot and the player receives a consolation prize.

Hostess: Kathi Norris.

Assistant: Eddie Dunn.

SPIN THE PICTURE—60 minutes—DuMont 1949.

SPLIT PERSONALITY

Game. Two competing contestants. Two sets of clues, each depicting one facet of a celebrity's life, are related by the host. The player who is first to identify the represented personality is the winner of that round and receives points. Winners, the highest point scorers, receive merchandise prizes.

Host: Tom Poston.

Producer: Mark Goodson, Bill Todman, Robert Rowe.

SPLIT PERSONALITY—30 minutes—NBC—September 28, 1959 - February 5, 1960.

SPLIT SECOND

Game. Three competing contestants.

Round One: Three topics are displayed (e.g., *Mad* magazine, *Playboy* magazine, and *World* magazine). The host then reads a question that refers to the topic. ("Pick one of these current magazines and tell me did it begin publishing before or after 1960.") Players each sound a bell and receive a chance to answer as they are

recognized. Each player chooses one of the three topics and states his answer. If all three responses are correct, the players each receive five dollars; if only two are correct, these players receive ten dollars each; should only one player correctly respond, he receives twenty-five dollars. (Answers: *Mad* and *Playboy*, before 1960; *World*, after 1960.)

Round Two: Played in the same manner with larger cash amounts: one correct response, fifty dollars; two correct answers, twenty-five dollars; three correct, ten dollars each.

Round Three: Each player is assigned a specific number of questions to answer. The highest cash scorer has to answer three questions; the second-place contestant, four questions; and the lowest scorer, five questions. The topics are displayed followed by their questions. The first player to be recognized is permitted to answer one or all parts of the question. The player who is first to answer all his questions is the winner. Losers receive their accumulated earnings.

The champion is brought downstage and placed opposite five new automobiles—only one of which will start. He selects one, and turns the ignition key. If the car starts he wins it; if not, he is permitted to return and compete again.

Host: Tom Kennedy.

Announcer: Jack Clark.

SPLIT SECOND—30 minutes—ABC—March 20, 1972 - June 27, 1975.

SPORTS CHALLENGE

Game. Two competing teams, each composed of three sports personalities. Basis: Sports-related question-and-answer rounds.

Rounds One and Two: "Break the Record." A film clip is shown, followed by a question that relates to it. The team that is first to identify itself through a buzzer signal receives a chance to answer. If correct, twenty-five points are scored.

Round Three: "Unforgettable Moments." Same format as above; sixty points are scored for correct answers.

Finale: "The Biography Round." The biography of a prominent sports figure is read. The team that correctly identifies the personality receives sixty points.

Winners, the highest point scorers, receive AMF sports equipment for purposes of donation to worthy causes.

Host: Dick Enberg.

Announcer: Johnny Gilbert.

SPORTS CHALLENGE–30 minutes –Syndicated 1971.

SPOTLIGHT

A daily dramatic series that adopts stories from all fields including plays and novels. Each play stars three actors, one of whom narrates, and uses no sets and few props. The use of music, rear-screen projection and sound-effects, coupled with the viewer's imagination, provides the setting. 30 minutes–Syndicated 1954.

SPOTLIGHT

Variety. Produced in England. Guest celebrities host.

Regulars: The Lionel Blair Dancers.

Orchestra: Jack Parnell.

Producer-Director: Ian Scofield.

SPOTLIGHT–60 minutes–CBS–July 4, 1967 - August 29, 1967.

SPOTLIGHT ON THE STARS

Anthology. Rebroadcasts of dramas originally aired via other filmed anthology programs.

SPOTLIGHT ON THE STARS–30 minutes–CBS–June 1958 - September 1958.

SPOTLIGHT PLAYHOUSE

Anthology. Rebroadcasts of dramas originally aired via other filmed anthology programs.

Included:

The Net Draws Tight. The story of a roadside diner owner who suspects and attempts to discover if his teenage helper is robbing him.

CAST
Edmond O'Brien, Skip Homeier, Paul Bryar.

Something Wonderful. The story of an actress who decides to take one final fling at a stage career before marrying and settling down.

CAST
Marcia Patrick, Claude Dauphin, John Bryat.

The Long Trail. The struggles faced by a Texas Ranger as he attempts to bring a murder suspect to Oregon.

CAST
Anthony Quinn, Robert Armstrong, Maxine Cooper, John Bryat.

SPOTLIGHT PLAYHOUSE–30 minutes–CBS–June 21, 1955 - September 21, 1955.

SPOTLIGHT PLAYHOUSE

Anthology. Retitled episodes of "Ford Theatre."

Included:

Four Things He'd Do. Background: The Old West. When ridiculed by the townspeople for his inability to find gold, a young Irishman becomes even more determined to find gold and show them he's a man to be reckoned with.

CAST
Michael O'Shea.

Model Wife. The story of a model who struggles to acquire the attentions of a photographer who couldn't care less about her.

CAST
Ralph Bellamy, Felica Farr, Emlen Davis, Pat Conway.

The Man Across the Hall. Discovering that a friend of her mother's is coming to visit, a young woman, who is not a successful television star and lives in a run-down apartment, acquires the keys to the glamorous apartment of the man who lives across the hall and attempts to impress the friend by saying that she lives there. Complications ensue when the man, who cut his weekend short, returns home.

CAST
Robert Sterling, Vera-Ellen, Marga Deighton.

SPOTLIGHT PLAYHOUSE–30 minutes–CBS–July 2, 1957 - September 1957.

SPOTLIGHT PLAYHOUSE

Anthology. Retitled episodes of "The Loretta Young Theatre." Selected dramas do not star Loretta Young.

Hostess: Anita Louise.

Music: Harry Lubin.

Included:

Power Play. The story of a coach who believes his lifelong dream has been fulfilled when he is asked to coach a college football team.

CAST
Anita Louise, James Daly.

Man On A String. A wife's difficulties as she struggles to understand her husband, a writer, and his preoccupation with work.

CAST
Laraine Day, Kim Spaulding.

The Defense. Accepting the case of a delinquent, an attorney attempts to prevent him from making the same mistakes that he made as a youth.

CAST
Mark Stevens, Addison Richards.

SPOTLIGHT PLAYHOUSE–30 minutes–CBS–July 1, 1958 - September 1958.

SPOTLIGHT PLAYHOUSE

Anthology. Rebroadcasts of dramas originally aired via other filmed anthology programs.

Hostess: Julia Meade.

Host: Zachary Scott.

Included:

The Dead Are Silent. Infatuated with a young admirer, a woman, the beautiful wife of a tyrannical man, plots to leave her husband.

CAST
Susan Hobson: Glynis Johns; Aaron Hobson: Robert Middleton; Mary Lee: Sandy Descher.

That's The Man. The effect of a false robbery charge accusation on the life of an innocent man.

CAST
Russell Kent: Ray Milland; Evelyn Kent: Nancy Davis.

Tunnel Eight. Era: The 1860s. The obstacles that plague railroad officials as they attempt to lay track.

CAST
Preston Foster.

A Question Of Survival. Surrounded by Commanche Indians, a cavalry captain faces a difficult decision: to let the doctor, a man he despises, operate on the chief's fatally injured son, which would mean his certain death, but an escape for his men; or risk the lives of his squad in one inevitable battle.

CAST
Capt. John Arnette: Ronald Reagan; Dr. Towne: Kevin McCarthy; Charlie Taney: Arthur Space.

SPOTLIGHT PLAYHOUSE—30 minutes—CBS—June 1959 - September 1959.

SPREAD OF THE EAGLE

Anthology. Dramatizations based on the Roman plays of William Shakespeare: *Anthony and Cleopatra*, *Coriolanus* and *Julius Caesar*. Produced by the B.B.C.

Performers: Paul Eddington, Barry Jones, Peter Cushing, Keith Michell, Mary Morris, David Williams, Jerome Willis.

SPREAD OF THE EAGLE—60 minutes—Syndicated 1964. 9 episodes.

SPUNKY AND TADPOLE

Animated Cartoon. The adventures of Spunky, a young boy, and his come-to-life teddy bear, Tadpole, as they battle evil.

Voices: Joan Gardner.

SPUNKY AND TADPOLE—05 minutes—Syndicated 1960. 150 episodes.

THE SQUARE WORLD OF ED BUTLER

Discussion. Discussions with concerned guests on topical issues.

Host: Ed Butler.
Music: Recorded.

THE SQUARE WORLD OF ED BUTLER—30 minutes—Syndicated 1970.

S.R.O. PLAYHOUSE

Anthology. Retitled episodes of "Schlitz Playhouse of Stars."

Included:

Two Bit Gangster. Traveling to a small town to cover what appears to be a routine robbery, a reporter discovers that a master thief has killed an ex-con who interfered with the getaway. The story depicts the reporter's attempts to find the murderer and the reason why the ex-con risked his life to foil the robbery.

CAST
Keenan Wynn, Robert Wilke, Addison Richards.

Moment Of Triumph. The story of a college professor who is unjustly discharged because he refuses to give a wealthy man's son the passing grade he does not deserve.

CAST
Kevin McCarthy, Eduard Franz, Angela Greene.

Foolproof. After an accident, a woman awakens in a hospital bed. Her eyes are covered with bandages and, unknown to her, she has been kidnapped and is being held hostage. The story relates the attempts of the kidnappers to fool her long enough to collect the ransom.

CAST
Claire Trevor, Walter Coy, Christopher Dark.

S.R.O. PLAYHOUSE—60 minutes—CBS—May 11, 1957 - September 1957.

THE S.S. HOLIDAY

Musical Variety.
Host: Phil Hanna.
Regulars: Ralph Stanley, Marya, Joe Curtis, Hollis Harris.
Musical Interlude: Reginald Beane, pianist.

THE S.S. HOLIDAY—30 minutes—DuMont 1950.

THE S.S. TELE CRUISER

Variety. Musical numbers played against photographic backgrounds.
Host: Jack Steck.
Regulars: Eddie Roecker, Carol Wynne, Bon Bon, The Thomas Cannon Ballet, The Crewman.
Music: The Dave Appel Trio.

THE S.S. TELE CRUISER—2 hours—ABC—April 28, 1951 - September 1951.

STAGECOACH WEST

Western. Background: Areas between California and Missouri during the 1860s. The experiences of Luke Perry and Simon Kane, drivers for the Overland Stage Coach Lines.

CAST
Luke Perry — Wayne Rogers
Simon Kane (a widower) — Robert Bray
David Kane, Simon's son — Richard Eyer

STAGECOACH WEST—60 minutes—ABC—October 4, 1960 - September 26, 1961. Syndicated. 38 episodes.

STAGE DOOR

A dramatic series that focuses on show-business life. Starring Louise Albritton and Scott McKay. 30 minutes—CBS 1950.

STAGE ENTRANCE

Variety. Performances by undiscovered professional talent.
Host: Earl Wilson.

STAGE ENTRANCE—15 minutes—DuMont 1951.

STAGE 7

Anthology. Dramatic presentations.

Included:

Appointment In Highbridge. The romance between a British army captain and an American nurse is recalled when the two meet ten years later in New York City.
Starring: Dan O'Herlihy.

The Legacy. After her grandmother's death, a young woman, who had unselfishly cared for her for three years, struggles to claim her share of the inheritance from a greedy cousin who wants it all.
Starring: Vanessa Brown, Elizabeth Patterson, George Nader.

Debt Of Honor. The difficult assignment of a detective: the man he is ordered to bring in is the man who

saved his daughter's life.
Starring: Edmond O'Brien.

The Deceiving Eye. Incorporating unorthodox methods, a criminology professor attempts to prove that the eye never accurately records what it sees.
Starring: Frank Lovejoy.

STAGE 7—30 minutes—CBS—January 30, 1955 - September 25, 1955.

STAGE SHOW

Musical Variety.
Hosts: Tommy and Jimmy Dorsey.
Featured: The June Taylor Dancers.
Music: The Dorsey Orchestra.

STAGE SHOW—60 minutes—CBS—July 2, 1954 - September 18, 1954; March 12, 1955 - March 19, 1955; 30 minutes—October 1, 1955 - September 26, 1956.

STAGE 13

A thirty-minute anthology series, produced and directed by Wyllis Cooper, that, geared to children, was first broadcast by CBS in 1950.

STAGE TWO REVUE

Musical Revue.
Hostess: Georgia Lee.
Regulars: Arlene Harris, Bob Harris.
Orchestra: Buzz Adlam.

STAGE TWO REVUE—60 minutes—ABC—1949 - 1951.

STAND UP AND BE COUNTED

Advice. Basis: The solving of problems. Participants, who are selected via letters, appear on stage and state the specific problems that confront them. Selected studio-audience members then suggest solutions. Through an audience vote, the most feasible advice is tried by the participants. At a later date, he returns and states the results of the advice.
Host: Bob Russell.

STAND UP AND BE COUNTED—30 minutes—CBS 1956.

STAND UP AND CHEER

See title: "Johnny Mann's Stand Up and Cheer."

STANLEY

Comedy. Background: New York City. The misadventures of Stanley, the sloppy, nonaggressive proprietor of a hotel-lobby newsstand.

CAST

Stanley	Buddy Hackett
Celia, his girlfriend	Carol Burnett
Mr. Phillips, the hotel manager	Frederic Tozere
Jane, Celia's girlfriend	Jane Connell

STANLEY—30 minutes—NBC—September 24, 1956 - March 11, 1957.

STAR ATTRACTION

Anthology. Rebroadcasts of dramas originally aired via other filmed anthology programs.

STAR ATTRACTION—30 minutes—ABC—June 1958 - September 1958.

STAR FOR TODAY

Anthology. Retitled episodes of "Telephone Time."
Hosts: John Nesbitt, Dr. Frank Baxter.

Included:

Campaign For Marriage. The story of a young woman who plots to acquire the proposal of her employer, the attorney general of Montana.

CAST
Robert Sterling, Anne Jeffreys.

She Sette Her Little Foote. The story of a group of women from London sent to become the wives of Virginia colonists.

CAST
Barbara Baxley, Ron Randall.

Smith of Ecuador. A dramatization recounting the disastrous 1949 earthquake that struck Ecuador.

CAST
Harold J. Stone.

STAR FOR TODAY—30 minutes—Syndicated 1963.

THE STARLAND VOCAL BAND

Musical Variety.
Starring: The Starland Vocal Band: Bill Danoff, Taffy Danoff, Margot Chapman, Jon Carroll.
Regulars: Mark Russell, David Letterman.
Announcer: David Letterman.
Musical Director: Eddie Karam.
Executive Producer: Jerry Weintraub.
Producer: Al Rogers.
Director: Rick Bennewitz.

THE STARLAND VOCAL BAND—30 minutes—CBS—July 31, 1977 - September 2, 1977. 6 tapes.

STARLIT TIME

Musical Revue.
Host: Phil Hanna.
Regulars: Bill Williams, Gordon Dilworth, Holly Harris, Alan Prescott, Ed Holmes, Bibi Osterwald, The Reggie Beane Dancers.
Music: The Reggie Beane Trio.

STARLIT TIME—45 minutes—DuMont 1950.

THE STARLOST

Science Fiction. Era: Earth, A.D. 2790. Unable to marry Rachel, the girl he loves, because he is the son of a poor farmer, Devon defies the law and speaks in protest. Deemed unsuitable by the elders, he is sentenced to death. Escaping their grasp, he enters a forbidden cave wherein the Earth Ship Ark lies. Approaching a control board, he accidentally activates a computer and learns of the fate of Earth from Mulander One Sixty-Five, a recorded image: "In the year A.D. 2285, a catastrophe...threatened all Earth life with extinction...so the Committee of Scientists...set about selecting desireable elements of Earth life to seed other planets...to do this, the committee between Earth and the Moon had to build Earth Ship Ark...an organic cluster of environmental domes called biospheres, looped to each other through tubular corridors for life support power and communication. In the biospheres we have representative segments of Earth's population, three million souls in all. Whole, separate ecologies sealed from each other and isolated to preserve their characteristics...Earth Ship

Ark was launched...to seek out and find a solar system of a class six star...Earth Ship Ark traveled for one hundred years before...there was an accident...Earth Ship Ark locked in collision course with class G solar star, an unidentified sun...no further data recorded."

Returning to his home in Cypress Corners, Devon seeks Rachel, but when returning to the ship, they are followed by Garth, the man who is pledged to marry her. Unable to persuade Rachel to return with him, Garth remains, determined to protect Rachel from Devon.

Drifting in space for eight hundred years and containing the sole survivors of the dead planet Earth—beings locked in separate worlds—Devon Rachel, and Garth begin their exploration of the various biospheres seeking to find someone or something to explain the mystery of the great catastrophe and save the remains of Earth life by locating a class six star. The Starlost. Produced in Canada.

CAST

Devon	Keir Dullea
Rachel	Gay Rowan
Garth	Robin Ward
Mulander One	
Sixty-five, the	
computer host	William Osler

Music: Score Productions.

THE STARLOST—60 minutes—Syndicated 1973. 16 episodes.

STAR MAIDENS

Science Fiction Adventure. Faraway, in the solar system Proxsema Centauri, there exists the planet Medusa—a world of advanced, humanlike life in which women are the rulers and men subservient. For one thousand orbits the populace enjoyed a life of peace and serenity. Then suddenly, the great comet Dioneses, with its awesome force, passes over the planet; Medusa's orbit is altered and the planet is slowly dragged toward the frozen regions of outer space. Before its final destination—a planet of ice—the Medusians plan and construct a new world beneath the surface.

Now, frozen, and having drifted for generations, the planet locks itself onto a solar system in which another life supporting planet—Earth—is discovered. The Earth, however, contradicts the Medusians programmed society and is declared out of bounds to all its citizens.

As with all laws, it, too, is violated, when two Medusian men, Adam and Shem, escape to Earth and thus open the doorway for the inhabitants of the two worlds to meet. The series depicts incidents in the lives of the Earthlings and Medusians as they meet and interact for the first time.

CAST

Fulvia, a Medusian leader	Sally Geeson
Octavia, a Medusian leader	Christiane Kruger
Liz, the Earth scientist	Lisa Harrow
Adam, Fulvia's servant	Pierre Brice
Shem, the mechanic, Adam's friend	Gareth Thomas
The Medusian Announcer	Penelope Horner
Evans	Derek Farr
Kate Moss	Jenny Morgan
Rudi	Christian Quadflieg

Music: Patrick Aulton.

Producer-Director: James Gatward.

Creator: Eric Paice.

STAR MAIDENS—30 minutes—Syndicated 1977. Produced in England.

STAR OF THE FAMILY

Variety. Music and songs coupled with performances by selected members of American families (preselected by letters that are written to the program by members of the individual's family).

Host: Morton Downey.

Regulars: Peter Lind Hayes, Mary Healy, The Beatrice Kroft Dancers.

Announcer: Frank Waldeeker.

Orchestra: Carl Hoff.

Producer: Perry Lafferty, Coby Ruskin, Newt Stammer.

Director: John Wray.

Sponsor: Ronson Lighters; Kelvinator.

STAR OF THE FAMILY—60 minutes—CBS 1952.

STAR ROUTE

Musical Variety. Performances by possessors of gold records in Country and Western music.

Host: Rod Cameron.

Regulars: Glenn Campbell, Lorrie Collins, The Collins Kids.

Orchestra: Gene Davis.

STAR ROUTE—30 minutes—Syndicated 1964. 26 tapes.

STARRING BORIS KARLOFF

Anthology. Mystery presentations.

Host-Performer: Boris Karloff.

Announcer: George Gunn.

Organist: George Henniger.

STARRING BORIS KARLOFF—30 minutes—ABC 1949.

Starsky and Hutch. David Soul (left) and Paul Michael Glaser.

STARSKY AND HUTCH

Crime Drama. The investigations of Dave Starsky and Ken "Hutch" Hutchinson, plainclothes police detectives.

CAST

Dave Starsky	Paul Michael Glaser
Ken "Hutch" Hutchinson	David Soul
Captain Dobey, their superior	Bernie Hamilton
Huggy Bear, their information man	Antonio Fargas

Music: Lalo Schifrin, Tom Scott, Jack Elliott, Allyn Ferguson.

Executive Producer: Aaron Spelling, Leonard Goldberg.

Producer: Joseph T. Naar.

Creator: William Blinn.

STARSKY AND HUTCH—60 minutes—ABC—Premiered: September 10, 1975.

STAR SPANGLED REVUE

A series of lavish variety hours produced by Max Liebman and directed by Hal Keith. First broadcast on NBC in 1950, the series would later emerge into television's first specials series, "Max Liebman Presents," which see for information.

STAR STAGE

Anthology. Dramatic presentations.
STAR STAGE–30 minutes–NBC–
September 9, 1955 - September 7,
1956.

STAR THEATRE

Anthology. Rebroadcasts of dramas
that were originally aired via other
filmed anthology programs.

Included:

Passport To Life. The story of a
Russian commissar who reverts to
slave practices in a small Hungarian
town.
Starring: William Campbell.

Fortunatus. A French immigrant's
search for gold in California.
Starring: Jacques Sernas.

Recipe For Success. The story of
Henri Charpentier, the creator of the
crêpe suzette.
Starring: Walter Slezak.

The Hole in the Wall. Era: World War
II Germany. Trapped in a farmhouse
occupied by a German patrol, two
members of the Italian underground
desperately attempt to escape un-
noticed.
Starring: Paul J. Cessari, Joseph
Vitale.

Away Boarders. A redramatization of
the capture of a German submarine
that was captured by boarding in
1944.
Starring: Arthur Space, Robert
Brubaker.

Program Open:
Announcer: "From the world's most
exotic cities, from Paris, London,
Shanghai, New York, stories of
the people who give these cities
life on Star Theatre."

STAR THEATRE–30 minutes–Syndicated 1963.

STARTIME

Musical Variety.
Hosts: Frances Langford, Don
Ameche.

Regulars: Lew Parker, Ben Blue, Phil
Regan, Kathryn Lee, The Benny
Goodman Sextet, The Don
Liberti Chorus.
Orchestra: Artego.
Producer: Hubbell Robinson, Robert
Wright.
Director: George Forbes, Robert
Wright.

STARTIME–60 minutes–DuMont–
1950 - 1951.

STAR TIME PLAYHOUSE

Anthology. Dramatic presentations.

STAR TIME PLAYHOUSE–30 minutes–CBS 1954.

STAR TONIGHT

Anthology. Dramatic presentations.
Scripts are suited to the talents of
young performers.

Included:

Giants' Star. A sheriff's efforts to
locate a missing woman's husband
during the rages of a rain storm.
Starring: Bruce Gordon.

You Need Me. The fears of a reformed
alcoholic as he prepares tó meet his
wife's family for the first time.
Starring: Jacqueline Holt, Kevin
McCarthy, Joanna Ross, Fred
Stewart.

Uppercut. The influence of a beautiful
woman on the rigid life of a prizefighter.
Starring: Steve Barclay.

STAR TONIGHT–30 minutes–ABC
–February 3, 1955 - August 9, 1956.

STAR TREK

Science Fiction Adventure. Era: The
twenty-second century. The voyages
of the starship U.S.S. *Enterprise,*
representing the United Federation of
Planets, as it explores the endless
universe, seeking new life, new worlds,
and new civilizations. Created by
Gene Roddenberry.

CAST

Captain James Kirk,
    commander of the

Star Trek. Nichelle Nichols (top, left),
DeForest Kelley (top, right), Leonard
Nimoy (bottom left), William Shatner
(bottom right).

Enterprise	William Shatner

Science Officer Spock,
  half Earthling,
  half Vulcan
	Leonard Nimoy

Dr. Leonard McCoy
  ("Bones"), the
  chief medical
  officer
	DeForest Kelley

Lieutenant Uhura, the
  communications
  officer
	Nichelle Nichols

Lt. Commander
  Montgomery Scott
  ("Scotty"), the
  chief engineer
	James Doohan

Yeoman Janice Rand	Grace Lee Whitney
Nurse Christine Chapel, McCoy's assistant	Majel Barrett
Mr. Sulu, a navigator	George Takei
Ensign Paval Chekov, a navigator	Walter Koenig
Mr. Farrell, a navigator	Jim Goodwin
Lt. Starnes	James Wellman

Narrator: William Shatner.
Music: Alexander Courage; Fred
Steiner; Gerald Fried; Wilbur
Hatch; George Duning; Sol
Kaplan.
Executive Producer: Gene Rodden-
berry.
Producer: John Meredyth Lucas, Gene
L. Coon, Fred Freiberger.
Director: Marc Daniels, Herschel
Daugherty, Ralph Senesky, Har-
vey Hart, James Komack, John
Meredyth Lucas, John Newland,
Joseph Pevney, Jud Taylor,
Robert Sparr, Michael O'Herlihy,
Herb Wallerstein, Murray Gold-

en, David Alexander, Marvin Chomsky, Joseph Sargent, Herbert Kenwith, Don McDougall, Gerd Oswald, Robert Gist, James Goldstone, Vincent McEveety, Tony Leader, Lawrence Dobkin, Leo Penn.

The Enterprise identification number: NCC 1701.

STAR TREK—60 minutes—NBC—September 8, 1966 - April 4, 1969. Rebroadcasts: NBC—June 3, 1969 - September 9, 1969. 78 episodes. Syndicated.

Animated Version:

STAR TREK. The further explorations of the starship *Enterprise.*

Characters' Voices

Captain James Kirk	William Shatner
Science Officer Spock	Leonard Nimoy
Dr. Leonard McCoy	DeForest Kelley
Lieutenant Uhura	Nichelle Nichols
Mr. Sulu	George Takei
Chief Engineer Montgomery Scott	James Doohan
Ensign Paval Chekov	Walter Koenig
Nurse Christine Chapel	Majel Barrett

Music: Yvette Blais, Jeff Michael.

Producer: Norm Prescott, Lou Scheimer.

Director: Hal Sutherland.

STAR TREK—30 minutes—NBC—September 8, 1973 - August 30, 1975.

STARS OVER HOLLYWOOD

Anthology. Dramatic presentations.

STARS OVER HOLLYWOOD—30 minutes—NBC 1950.

STATE TROOPER

Crime Drama. Background: Nevada. The investigations of Rod Blake, chief of the Nevada State Troopers.

Starring: Rod Cameron as Rod Blake.

Music: Stanley Wilson; Maury Leaf.

STATE TROOPER—30 minutes—Syndicated 1957. 104 episodes.

STEP THIS WAY

Dance Contest. Selected studio-audi-

ence couples compete in two phases of a dance contest: their own specialty dances and "The Dance of the Week Selection." Couples are judged and the winners receive merchandise gifts.

Versions:

Step This Way—30 minutes—ABC—July 25, 1955 - April 14, 1956.

Host: Bobby Sherwood.

Judges: Zedan and Carol, professional dancers.

Orchestra: Nat Brandywyne; Buddy Weed.

Step This Way—30 minutes—Syndicated 1966.

Hostess: Gretchen Wyler.

Announcer: Jim Lucas.

Judges: Guest celebrities (three per show).

Orchestra: Warren, Covington.

STEVE ALLEN

Listed: The television programs of author-comedian-composer-pianist Steve Allen.

Songs For Sale—Variety—30 minutes—CBS—1951. See title.

Talent Patrol—Variety—30 minutes—ABC—1953.

Format: Performances by servicemen.

Host: Steve Allen.

Hostess: Arlene Francis.

The Tonight Show—Variety—40 minutes (11:20 p.m.-12:00 a.m.)—Local New York (WNBT-TV, Ch. 4)—July 27, 1953 - September 24, 1954.

Host: Steve Allen.

Regulars: Steve Lawrence, Helen Dixon, Pat Kirby.

Announcer: Gene Rayburn.

Orchestra: Bobby Byrne.

The Tonight Show—Variety—90 minutes—NBC—September 27, 1954 - January 25, 1957 (Steve's appearance as the host).

Host: Steve Allen.

Regulars: Steve Lawrence, Eydie Gormé, Pat Marshall, Helen Dixon, Andy Williams, Don Knotts, Tom Poston, Louis Nye.

Announcer: Gene Rayburn.

Orchestra: Skitch Henderson.

The Steve Allen Show—Variety—60

minutes—NBC—June 24, 1956 - May 3, 1959.

Host: Steve Allen.

Regulars: Don Knotts (as The Nervous Chap), Louis Nye (as Gordon Hathaway), Tom Poston (as The Perennial Amnesiac), Skitch Henderson (The Man from the Bronx), Dayton Allen (as The Why Not Man), Gabe Dell, Pat Harrington, Jr., Bill Dana (as Jose Jiménez).

Announcer: Gene Rayburn.

Orchestra: Skitch Henderson.

Commercial Spokesman: John Cameron Swayze; Erin O'Brian.

The New Steve Allen Show—Variety—60 minutes—NBC—1959 - 1960.

Host: Steve Allen.

Regulars: Louis Nye, Don Knotts, Dayton Allen, Gabe Dell, Pat Harrington, Jr.

Orchestra: Les Brown.

The New Steve Allen Show—Variety—60 minutes—ABC—September 27, 1961 - December 27, 1961.

Host: Steve Allen.

Regulars: Louis Nye, Pat Harrington, Jr., Joey Forman, Bill Dana, The Smothers Brothers (Tom and Dick), Tim Conway.

Orchestra: Les Brown.

The Steve Allen Show—Variety—90 minutes—Syndicated 1963.

Host: Steve Allen.

Announcer: Johnny Jacobs.

Orchestra: Donn Trenner.

I've Got a Secret—Game—30 minutes—CBS—1964 - 1967. See title.

The Steve Allen Comedy Hour—Comedy—60 minutes—CBS—July 1967 - September 1967.

Host: Steve Allen.

Regulars: Jayne Meadows, Ruth Briggs, Louis Nye, The David Winters Dancers.

Music: The Terry Gibbs Band.

The Steve Allen Show—Variety—90 and 60-minute versions (pending local stations)—Syndicated 1968. Also known as "The Allen Show" and "The New Steve Allen Show."

Host: Steve Allen.

Orchestra: Paul Smith.

The Sounds of Summer—Music—2 hours—NET—June 1, 1969 - August 1969.

Format: Jazz, Folk, and Symphonic concerts.

Host: Steve Allen.

Music: Provided by guest performers.

I've Got a Secret—Game—30 minutes —Syndicated 1972. See title.

Steve Allen's Laugh-Back—Variety— 90 minutes—Syndicated 1976. The series combines new material with clips from Steve's previous series.

Host: Steve Allen.

Regulars: Jayne Meadows, Louis Nye, Bill Dana, Martha Raye, Don Knotts, Skitch Henderson, Pat Harrington.

Music: The Terry Gibbs Sextet.

Executive Producer: Jerry Harrison.

Producer: Rogers Ailes.

Director: John Rumbaugh.

Meeting of the Minds—History—60 minutes—PBS—January 15, 1977 - February 19, 1977. In an intimate party setting, several historical figures meet to discuss their lives, careers and the world situation.

Host: Steve Allen.

Featured: Jayne Meadows.

Music: Steve Allen.

Creator-Writer: Steve Allen.

Producer: Perry Rosemond.

STEVE CANYON

Adventure. Background: Big Thunder Air Force base. The investigations of Lieutenant Colonel Stevenson B. Canyon, pilot-troubleshooter, as he probes the elements behind crimes perpetrated against the U.S. government. Based on the comic strip by Milton Coniff.

CAST

Lt. Col. Steve Canyon	Dean Fredericks
Major Willie Williston, his superior	Jerry Paris

Music: Walter Schumann, Nathan Scott.

STEVE CANYON—30 minutes—NBC —September 13, 1958 - September 7, 1959.

WESTERN MARSHAL

Western. Background: The Frontier

during the latter nineteenth century. The exploits of U.S. Marshal Steve Donovan and his deputy, Rusty Lee, as they attempt to maintain law and order.

CAST

Steve Donovan	Douglas Kennedy
Rusty Lee	Eddy Waller

STEVE DONOVAN, WESTERN MARSHAL—30 minutes—Syndicated 1955. 39 episodes.

THE STEVE LAWRENCE AND EYDIE GORMÉ SHOW

Musical Variety.

Hosts: Steve Lawrence, Eydie Gormé.

Vocalists: The Artie Malvin Singers.

Announcer: Gene Rayburn.

Orchestra: Jack Kane.

THE STEVE LAWRENCE AND EYDIE GORMÉ SHOW—60 minutes —NBC—July 13, 1958 - September 1958.

THE STEVE LAWRENCE SHOW

Musical Variety.

Host: Steve Lawrence.

Regulars: Charles Nelson Reilly, Donna Mills, Betty Walker, The Pussycat Dancers.

Orchestra: Joe Guercio.

THE STEVE LAWRENCE SHOW—60 minutes—CBS—September 13, 1965 - December 13, 1965.

STINGRAY

Marionette Adventure. Era: Earth, A.D. 2000. The battle against the destructive forces of evil as undertaken by the World Aquanaut Security Patrol, an international organization established on the ocean floor. Filmed in Supermarionation. An I.T.C. presentation.

Characters' Voices

Troy Tempest, the captain of the submarine *Stingray*	Don Mason
Atlanta, the Earth girl	Lois Maxwell
Sam Shore, the commander of the Marineville base	Ray Barrett
Phones, the hydrophonic operator	Robert Easton
X-20	Robert Easton
Titan	Ray Barrett

Additional characters: Marina, the enchanting girl from the sea (nonspeaking).

Music: Barry Gray.

STINGRAY—30 minutes—Syndicated 1965. 39 episodes.

STONEY BURKE

Adventure. The experiences of Stoney Burke, a champion rodeo rider, as he travels from rodeo to rodeo seeking to secure "The Gold Buckle," the trophy that is awarded to the world's best saddle bronco buster.

CAST

Stoney Burke	Jack Lord
E.J. Stocker, a rodeo performer	Bruce Dern
Wes Paineter, a rodeo performer	Warren Oates
Cody Bristal, a rodeo performer	Robert Dowdell

Music: Dominic Frontiere.

STONEY BURKE—60 minutes—ABC —October 1, 1962 - September 2, 1963. 32 episodes. Syndicated.

STOP THE MUSIC

Musical Game. As the orchestra plays a song, three girls place telephone calls. When a call is completed, she yells "Stop the Music." Taking the phone, the host asks the viewer to identify the song that was just played. If the participant is able, he receives the prizes that have been accumulated to date; if not, another prize is added to the jackpot, and he receives a home appliance as a consolation prize.

Studio Audience Competition:

Selected members have to identify song titles. Each correct identification awards fifty dollars, to a maximum of four hundred dollars. Players are defeated by incorrect responses.

Hosts: Bert Parks; Jimmy Blaine.

Regulars: Jaye P. Morgan, Jack Haskell, Betty Ann Grove, Jimmy Blaine, Estelle Loring, Sonya and Courtney Van Horne, Don Little, Wayne Lamb, Martin Croft, Maureen Palmer, Ruth Ostrander, Harriet Roeder, Charles Luchsinger, Kay Armen.

Announcer: Jack Haskell.

Orchestra: Harry Sosnick.

Producer: Louis Cowan, Steve Carlin,

Joe Cates, Mark Goodson.

Director: Ralph Warren.

Sponsor: Admiral; Old Golds; Exquisite Form Bras.

STOP THE MUSIC—60 minutes—ABC—May 5, 1949 - June 14, 1956.

STOP ME IF YOU'VE HEARD THIS ONE

Game. The emcee reads an incomplete joke that has been submitted by a home viewer. A panel of four comics then have to complete it with an original, funny punch line. The sender receives five dollars for submitting the joke, and an additional five dollars if the panel fails to complete it.

Emcee: Leon Janney.

Panelists: Mae Questel, Cal Tinney, Benny Rubin, George Givot.

STOP ME IF YOU'VE HEARD THIS ONE—30 minutes—NBC 1949.

THE STOREFRONT LAWYERS

Crime Drama. Background: The Neighborhood Legal Services in Century City (downtown Los Angeles, California). The cases and courtroom defenses of attorneys David Hansen, Deborah Sullivan, and Gabriel Kay, representatives of indigent clients.

CAST

David Hansen	Robert Foxworth
Deborah Sullivan	Sheila Larken
Gabriel Kay	David Arkin
Attorney Roberto Barelli	A. Martinez
Mr. Thatcher, the defense attorney	Gerald S. O'Loughlin
Rachel, the N.L.S. secretary	Royce Wallace

THE STOREFRONT LAWYERS—60 minutes—CBS—September 16, 1970 - January 13, 1971. 13 episodes. Spin-off series: "Men At Law" (see title).

STORIES OF THE CENTURY

Western. Era: The 1890s. The investigations of Matt Clark and his female assistant, Frankie Adams, detectives for the Southwestern Railroad. Based on official newspaper files and records.

CAST

Matt Clark	Jim Davis
Frankie Adams	Mary Castle

Jonsey Jones, his female assistant in later episodes — Kristine Miller

STORIES OF THE CENTURY—30 minutes—Syndicated 1956. 39 episodes. Also known as "The Fast Guns."

THE STORK CLUB

Interview. Celebrity interviews are conducted against the background of the Stork Club.

Host: Sherman Billingsley.

Hostesses: Virginia Peine, Betty Ann Grove.

Announcer: George Byran.

Producer: Irving Mansfield, Mike Dutton.

Director: Fred Rickey.

Sponsor: Fatima Cigarettes.

THE STORK CLUB—CBS—1950 - 1953; ABC—30 minutes—1953.

THE STORYBOOK SQUARES

Game. A spin-off from "The Hollywood Squares." Two children compete, designated as Player X and Player O. Nine guest celebrities, who each occupy one of the squares on a huge Tic Tac Toe board, are attired in costumes representing children's literary characters. Object: To win two out of three Tic Tac Toe games.

The first player begins by choosing one of the characters who is then asked a question by the host. The player must determine whether the answer is correct or a bluff, i.e., agree or disagree. If the player is correct, the appropriate letter is lit on the board; incorrect, the opponent receives the square. Exception: Should the square complete a Tic Tac Toe game for the opponent, he does not receive it. Players have to earn essential squares by themselves. Winners, those who acquire three squares in a row, up and down or diagonally, receive cash and prizes.

Host: Peter Marshall.

Announcer (Town Crier): Kenny Williams.

Music: Recorded.

THE STORYBOOK SQUARES—30 minutes—NBC—January 1968 - August 31, 1968.

STORY FOR AMERICANS

Anthology. Dramatic delineations of America's past.

Performers: Carmen Andrews and Eugene Lee.

STORY FOR AMERICANS—30 minutes—CBS—June 1952 - September 1952.

THE STORY OF—

Anthology. Dramatizations depicting the events that spark the lives of interesting individuals.

Host-Narrator: John Willis.

THE STORY OF— —30 minutes—Syndicated 1962.

STORY THEATRE

Fables. Stories, based on tales by Aesop and The Brothers Grimm, are dramatized against the background of an improvosational theater with performers speaking their lines in narrative, as if reading from a book, and providing their own narration.

CAST

Paul Sills Broadway Repertoire Company: Bob Dishy, Mina Kolb, Peter Bonerz, Judy Graubart, Richard Libertini, Melinda Dillon, Paul Sand, Hamid Hamilton Camp, Ann Sweeny, Severn Darden, Peter Bones, Dick Schall, Eugene Troabnick, Mickey LaGare, Heath Lambertal, Jeff Brownstein.

STORY THEATRE—30 minutes—Syndicated 1971. 26 episodes.

STRAIGHTAWAY

Adventure. The experiences of Scott Ross and Clipper Hamilton, the owners and operators of the Straightaway Garage, as they become involved with professional drivers and races.

CAST

Scott Ross	Brian Kelly
Clipper Hamilton	John Ashley

STRAIGHTAWAY—30 minutes—ABC—October 6, 1961 - July 4, 1962. 26 episodes. Original title: "The Racers."

STRANGE PARADISE

Serial. Background: The forbidding Caribbean island of Maljardin (French for "Garden of Evil"). Once thriving on rare wine, exotic food, and beautiful women, Jean Paul Desmond, after meeting the beautiful Erica Kerr, retreats to the island after they are married.

After one year, Erica is stricken with an unknown disease and mysteriously dies. Unable to accept her death, and determined to bring her back to life, he places her body in a metal casing and preserves her through the process of cryogenics.

Hoping to achieve his goal by summoning the powers of darkness, he breaks the ancient spell that has ruled the island and cursed his family when he conjures up the spirit of Jacques Eloi De Monde, an ancestor who, three hundred years before, also lost his wife. To conceal and protect himself, the spirit takes refuge in a portrait of Jacques that hangs over a fireplace. Discovering Jean Paul's act, Raxil, priestess and Desmond family servant, vows to return Jacques to hell.

As the powers of evil work to restore Erica's life, seven people arrive on the island—each to meet bizarre destinies: Alison Kerr, Erica's sister; Dan Forest, Jean Paul's business manager; Tim Stanton, an artist hired by Alison to paint Erica's portrait; Holly Marshall, a beautiful young heiress; Elizabeth Marshall, her mother; and Reverend Matthew Dawson, a friend of the Marshalls'.

Alive, but evil and deadly, Erica, to exist, must kill all visitors to the island, pierce Holly's heart with a silver pin, then possess her body.

Through Jacques's possession of Jean Paul, the murders are committed: Vangie (a medium incorporated by Raxil to help rid Jacques); Tim, Reverend Dawson, Dan, and Alison.

A fire, started by Jacques in the boathouse, leaves Elizabeth, Holly, and Erica alone in the mansion, while Jean Paul, Raxil and Quito, her assistant, battle the blaze.

Overtaken by her will, Holly stands before Erica, who with a large silver pin, is about to pierce her heart. Spotting the two, Elizabeth pushes Holly aside—and is herself killed when stabbed. Entering the house, and in possession of his own will, Jean Paul awakens Holly, who is taken to safety by Raxil and, approaching Jacques's portrait, sets it on fire. Spreading, the flames engulf the house, wherein Erica perishes.

Safely outside, Jean Paul looks back and hears the final words of Jacques echoing the atmosphere: "Whether you live or die Jean Paul Desmond, wherever you choose to run, your curse will follow you, and life will be for you always a Strange Paradise. Aha ha ha ha ha ha ha."

CAST

Jean Paul Desmond	Colin Fox
Jacques Eloi De Monde	Colin Fox
Holly Marshall	Sylvia Feigel
Erica Desmond	Tudi Wiggins
Alison Kerr	Dawn Greenhalgh
Raxil	Cosette Lee
Quito	Kurt Schiegl
Elizabeth Marshall	Paisley Maxwell
Vangie	Angela Roland
Reverend Matthew Dawson	Dan McDonald
Tim Stanton	Bruce Gray
Dan Forrest	John Granik

Also: Patricia Collins, Trudy Young.

Music: Score Productions.

STRANGE PARADISE—30 minutes—Syndicated 1969. 195 episodes. Produced in Canada.

STRANGE PLACES

Documentary. Films exploring various remote regions of the world.

Host-Narrator: Peter Graves.

Music: Gerherd Trede.

STRANGE PLACES—30 minutes—Syndicated 1973. Produced by the B.B.C. Also known as "Other People, Other Places."

THE STRANGE REPORT

Mystery. Background: London, England. The investigations of criminologist Adam Strange as he intervenes in domestic and international crises and attempts to solve ingenious criminal acts of injustice.

CAST

Adam Strange	Anthony Quayle
Evelyn McLane, his assistant	Anneke Wells
Ham Gynt, his assistant	Kaz Garas

Music: Edwin Astley.

THE STRANGE REPORT—60 minutes—NBC—January 8, 1971 - September 12, 1971. 16 episodes.

THE STRANGER

Drama. The story of The Stranger, an unknown man who, whenever innocent people are threatened by unscrupulous individuals, mysteriously appears, assists, and when completing his task, vanishes, accepting no fees for his services.

Starring: Robert Carroll as The Stranger.

Producer: Frank Telford.

THE STRANGER—30 minutes—DuMont—June 25, 1954 - September 1954.

THE STRAUSS FAMILY

Biography. A seven-part dramatization depicting the lives of composers Johann Strauss and his son, Johann Strauss, Jr., "The Waltz Kings of the nineteenth century."

CAST

Johann Strauss	Eric Woolfe
Anna Strauss	Anne Stallybrass
Johann Strauss, Jr.	Stuart Wilson
Josef Lanner	Derek Jacobi
Emilie Trampusch	Barbara Ferris
Olga	Ania Marson
Madamee Smirnitska	Jill Balcon
Hirsh	David de Keyser
Dommayer	Christopher Benjamin
Lucari	Sonia Dresdel
Hetti	Margaret Whiting
Edi	Tony Anholt
Josef Strauss	Nikolas Simmonds
Lili	Georgina Hale
Annele	Hilary Hardiman
Theresa	Amanda Walker
Max Steiner	William Dexter
Adele	Lynn Farleigh

Music: The London Symphony Orchestra.

Conductor: Cyril Ornadel.

THE STRAUSS FAMILY—60 minutes—ABC—May 5, 1973 - June 16, 1973.

STRAWHAT MATINEE

Women. Music, songs, variety acts, and fashion shows.

Host: Mel Martin.

Music: Ernie Lee's Hillbilly Band.

STRAWHAT MATINEE—30 minutes—NBC 1951.

THE STRAWHATTERS

Musical Variety. Background: Palisades Amusement Park, Palisades New Jersey. Performances by: Country and Western bands, guest vocalists, and acrobats.

Host: Johnny Olsen.

THE STRAWHATTERS—30 minutes —DuMont—May 27, 1953 - September 1953.

STRAWHAT THEATRE

Musical Variety. Performances by Country and Western artists.

Hosts: Mel Martin, Rosemary Olberding.

Regulars: June Pickens, Marian Spellman, Lee Jones, Dick and Pat, The Log Jammers, The Pine Mountain Boys.

Orchestra: Ernie Lee.

STRAWHAT THEATRE—60 minutes —NBC 1951.

STRAWHAT THEATRE

Anthology. Dramatic presentations.

STRAWHAT THEATRE—30 minutes —ABC—July 5, 1953 - September 20, 1953.

STREETS OF DANGER

See title: "The Lone Wolf."

THE STREETS OF SAN FRANCISCO

Crime Drama. Background: San Francisco, California. The investigations of Lieutenant Mike Stone, "a street smart homicide detective," and his impulsive, college-trained partner, Steve Keller.

CAST

Lt. Mike Stone	Karl Malden
Detective Steve Keller	Michael Douglas
Lt. Lessing	Lee Harris
Officer Haseejian	Vic Tayback
Inspector Dan Robbins	Richard Hatch
Jean Stone, Mike's daughter	Darleen Carr
Sgt. Sekulovich	Art Passarella

Music: John Elizade; Pat Williams.

Executive Producer: Quinn Martin.

Producer: John Wilder, Cliff Gould, William Yates.

Director: Virgil W. Vogel, Walter Grauman, William Wiard, Barry Crane, Robert Day, John Badham, Paul Stanley, Harry Falk, George McCowan, Kenneth Gilbert, William Hale.

THE STREETS OF SAN FRANCISCO—60 minutes—ABC— September 16, 1972 - June 23, 1977.

STRICTLY SKITCH

See title: "Faye Emerson."

STRIKE IT RICH

Game. Contestants stand before the studio audience and relate their hard-luck stories, stating their single most needed possession. Home viewers are then permitted to call the program and donate money. The saddest storytellers, as determined by the studio audience, receive the program's "heartline," a cash bonanza.

Host: Warren Hull.

Substitute Host: Monty Hall.

Assistant: Jack Carson.

Commercial Spokeswoman: Virginia Graham.

Announcer: Ralph Paul.

Producer: Walt Framer.

Director: Matthew Harlib.

Sponsor: The Colgate-Palmolive Company.

STRIKE IT RICH—30 minutes—CBS —May 7, 1951 - January 3, 1958.

STRYKER OF SCOTLAND YARD

Crime Drama. Background: London, England. The investigations of Robert Stryker, the chief inspector of Scotland Yard, into cases wherein innocent people have become the pawns of master criminals.

Starring: Clifford Evans as Inspector Robert Stryker.

STRYKER OF SCOTLAND YARD— 30 minutes—NBC 1957. 39 episodes.

THE STU ERWIN SHOW

See title: "Trouble with Father."

STUDIO '57

Anthology. Dramatic presentations.

Included:

The Haven Technique. A skilled surgeon attempts to perform a difficult and revolutionary type of operation on the son of a former sweetheart.

CAST

Dr. Glenn Haven: Brian Keith; Helen Blaine: Sallie Brophy; Ann Randall: Irene Hervey.

The Bitter Rival. A wife's efforts to end her husband's unfounded jealousy.

CAST

Beryl Miller: Margaret Field; Harry Miller: Larry Dobkin; Joe Perry: Don Haggerty; Margaret Perry: Ann Robinson.

The Engagement Ring. When an heiress hears a rumor that her fiancé is marrying her for her money, she begins an investigation to uncover the truth.

CAST

Hugh O'Brian, K.T. Stevens, Lili Fontaine.

Hazel Crane. Believing his wife is a murderess, a lawyer begins an investigation to uncover her past.

CAST

Hazel Crane: Eleonara Tanin; Ben Crane: Walter Reed.

STUDIO '57—60 minutes—DuMont— 1954 - 1956.

STUDIO ONE

Anthology. Dramatic presentations.

Producer: Worthington Miner, Fletcher Markle, Felix Jackson, Norman Felton, Gordon Duff, William Brown, Paul Nickell, Franklin Schaffner, Charles Schultz.

Director: John Peyser, Paul Nickell, Charles Schultz, Worthington Miner.

Sponsor: Old Golds; Westinghouse.

Included:

Signal Thirty-Two. The story of a rookie policeman's misuse of his position as he succumbs to the temptations of bribes.

CAST

Joe Maross, Gene Lyons.

The Walsh Girls. A psychological study of the relationship between two sisters.

CAST
Jane Wyatt.

The Trial of John Titler Zenger. The true story of John Zenger, a printer who was imprisoned for publishing the truth about the corrupt administration of a colonial government.

CAST
Eddie Albert, Marian Selder.

The Incredible World of Horace Ford. The story of a man who escapes the pressures of business by daydreaming himself into adventures.

CAST
Art Carney, Leora Dana.

STUDIO ONE—60 minutes—CBS— November 17, 1948 - September 16, 1957. Also known as "Studio One in Hollywood" (from September 23, 1957 to September 29, 1958).

STUD'S PLACE

Comedy. Background: Stud's Place, a restaurant-bar in Chicago. The misadventures of its owner-operator, Studs Terkel, as he becomes involved with staff and clientele difficulties.

CAST
Studs Terkel	Himself
The waitress	Beverly Younger
The Folk-singing handyman	Win Strackle
The blues-singing pianist	Chet Robel

Music: Chet Robel.

Producer: Biggie Levin, Norman Felton, Dan Petrie, Ben Paric.

Director: Dick Locke, Norman Felton.

STUD'S PLACE—30 minutes—ABC 1950.

STUMPERS

Game. Two teams compete, each composed of one celebrity captain and one noncelebrity contestant. A stumper, which contains three clues to the identity of a person, place, or thing, is revealed to one member of one team. That player then relates one of the clues to one member of the opposing team. If the player identifies the stumper he scores fifteen points. If, within five seconds, he is stumped, a second clue is given (worth ten points) and finally a third clue (worth five points). If he is still stumped, the team at play is given a chance to solve it and win fifteen points. Each player receives two turns at giving and guessing stumpers per round. Two such rounds are played, the second being the double up round (points are 30, 15, and 10). The winner is the highest scoring team.

Host: Allen Ludden.

Music: Alan Thicke.

Executive Producer: Lin Bolen.

Producer: Walt Case, Noreen Colen.

Director: Marty Pasetta, Jeff Goldstein.

STUMPERS—30 minutes—NBC—October 4, 1976 - December 31, 1976.

STUMP THE STARS

Game. Two competing teams, the Regulars and the Visitors, each composed of four Hollywood celebrities. Object: The performance of charades. One member of one team is handed a charade. Within a two-minute time limit, he has to perform it and relay its meaning to his teammates. The amount of time consumed until it is identified is calculated. Each player competes in the same manner. The team accumulating the least amount of overall time is the winner. Prizes are awarded to home viewers whose charades are selected to be played.

Versions:

S t u m p   T h e   S t a r s — 3 0 minutes—CBS—September 17, 1962 - September 16, 1963. Syndicated. Withdrawn (due to poor audio and video quality).

Host: Mike Stokey.

Regulars: Beverly Garland, Ross Martin, Diana Dors, Sebastian Cabot, Ruta Lee, Hans Conried.

S t u m p   T h e   S t a r s — 3 0 minutes—Syndicated 1969.

Host: Mike Stokey.

Regulars: Vera Miles, Deanna Lund, Roger C. Carmel, Dick Patterson.

SUCCESS STORY

Interview. Interviews with people who have struggled for and achieved success.

Hostess: Betty Furness.

SUCCESS STORY—15 minutes—ABC 1951.

SUGARFOOT

Western. Background: The Frontier during the 1860s. The exploits of Tom Brewster, Sugarfoot,* student of law, and wanderer who encounters and reluctantly aids people in distress.

Starring: Will Hutchins as Tom Brewster.

Music: Paul Sawtell.

*A cowboy designated one grade lower than a tenderfoot.

SUGARFOOT—60 minutes—ABC— September 17, 1957 - September 13, 1960. Syndicated.

SUGAR TIME

Comedy. Background: Los Angeles, California. The heartaches, loves, struggles, and misadventures of Maxx, Diane, and Maggie, three starry-eyed Rock singers, who comprise the act "Sugar," hoping to make the big time.

CAST
Maxx Douglas	Barbi Benton
Diane Zukerman	Didi Carr
Maggie Barton	Marianne Black
Al Marks, the owner of the Tryout Room Night Club	Wynn Irwin
Paul Landson, Diane's boyfriend	Mark Winkworth
Lightning Jack Rappaport, a performer at the Tryout Room	Charles Fleischer

Musical Director: David Garland.

Musical Supervision: Paul Williams.

Executive Producer-Creator: James Komack.

Producer: Hank Bradford, Martin Cohan.

Director: Bill Hobin, Howard Storm.

Choreography: Helen Funai.

SUGAR TIME—30 minutes—ABC— August 13, 1977 - September 3, 1977. 4 episodes.

THE SUMMER SMOTHERS BROTHERS SHOW

Musical Variety. The summer replacement for "The Smothers Brothers Comedy Hour."

Host: Glen Campbell.

Regulars: Sally Struthers, Pat Paulsen, Jack Burns, John Hartford.

Announcer: Roger Carroll.

Orchestra: Nelson Riddle.

THE SUMMER SMOTHERS BROTHERS SHOW—60 minutes—CBS—June 23, 1968 - September 8, 1968. 13 tapes. Spin-off series: "The Glen Campbell Goodtime Hour."

SUMMER FUN

Pilot Films. Proposed comedy series for the 1966-1967 season.

Included:

McNab's Lab. The misadventures of Andrew McNab, small town druggist and amateur inventor.

CAST
Andrew McNab: Cliff Arquette; Harvey Barter: Paul Smith; Ellen McNab: Sherry Alberoni; Timmy McNab: David Bailey.

Little Leatherneck. Fascinated by her father, a marine drill sergeant, a young girl decides to follow in his footsteps—and become a leatherneck.

CAST
Cindy Fenton: Donna Butterworth; Sgt. Mike Fenton: Scott Brady; Dolores: Sue Ane Langdon; Mess Sgt.: Ned Glass.

Meet Me in Saint Louis. Background: Saint Louis, 1903. The misadventures of Esther Smith, a beautiful young debutante from New York.

CAST
Esther Smith: Shelley Fabares; Anne Smith: Celeste Holm; Glenn Smith: Larry Merrill.

The Pirates of Flounder Bay. Era: The 1800s. The effort of the son of the infamous Captain Kidd, Barnaby Kidd, to achieve fame.

CAST
Capt. Barnaby Kidd: William Cort; Governor: Basil Rathbone; Capt. Jack Slash: Keenan Wynn; Mayor Abner Bunker: Harold Peary; Molly Bunker: Bridget Hanley; Sidney: Jack Soo.

Thompson's ·Ghost. The misadventures of Henry Thompson, a four-thousand, seven-hundred-year-old ghost who is conjured up by a ten-year-old girl.

CAST
Henry Thompsonn: Bert Lahr; Annabel Thompson: Pamela Dapo; Milly Thompson: Phyllis Coates; Sam

Thompson: Robert Rockwell.

SUMMER FUN—30 minutes—ABC— July 22, 1966 - September 2, 1966.

SUMMER IN THE CITY

Variety. The summer replacement for "Faye Emerson's Wonderful Town."

CAST
Bob Sweeney, Hal March, Nancy Kelly, Gladys Swarthout, Virginia Conwell, Bobby Scheer.

SUMMER IN THE CITY—30 minutes—CBS—August 18, 1951 - August 25, 1951.

SUMMERTIME U.S.A.

Musical Variety.

Hosts: Teresa Brewer, Mel Tormé.

Featured: The Honeydreamers.

Orchestra: Ray Bloch.

SUMMERTIME U.S.A.—15 minutes—CBS—July 9, 1953 - September 1, 1953.

SUNDAY AT THE BRONX ZOO

Educational. Background: The Bronx (New York) Zoological Garden. Visits to and facts about the various exhibits.

Host: William Bridges.

Announcer: Durwood Kirby.

Producer: Louis Cowan.

Director: Gail Compton.

SUNDAY AT THE BRONX ZOO—30 minutes—ABC 1950.

SUNDAY DATE

Musical Variety.

Hostess: Helen Lee.

Regulars: Dick Style, Paulette Seslan, Shirley Levitt, Joe E. Marks.

Music: The Cavalier Trio.

SUNDAY DATE—15 minutes—NBC 1949.

SUNDAY MYSTERY

Anthology. Mystery presentations.

Host: Walter Slezak.

Included:

Dead Man's Walk. An amnesiac's search for his past.

CAST
Abel: Robert Culp; Karen Prescott: Abby Dalton; Lt. Spear: Bruce Gordon; Florence: Barbara Stuart.

Trial By Fury. A woman attempts to prove that her daughter's fiancé is her husband's murderer.

CAST
Elizabeth Marshall: Agnes Moorehead; Jim Powell: Warren Stevens; Joanna Marshall: Louise Carroll.

Femme Fatale. Police efforts to prove that a famous movie queen is responsible for the deaths of two of her husbands.

CAST
Lisa Townsend: Janet Blair; Claire Bradford: Tracey Roberts; Daniel Otis: Joe DeSantis.

Murder Me Nicely. Detesting a student, a teacher sets out to destroy the young man's career.

CAST
Alfred Emerson: Everett Sloane; Peter: Mark Goddard; Carolyn: Yvonne Craig.

SUNDAY MYSTERY—60 minutes— NBC—July 2, 1961 - September 17, 1961.

SUNSHINE

Comedy-Drama. Background: Van Couver, California. The story of Sam Hayden, a happy-go-lucky musician who is left in charge of his young daughter, Jill, after the death of his wife. Episodes focus on his attempts to fill the maternal void left in Jill's life.

CAST

Sam Hayden	Cliff De Young
Jill Hayden	Elizabeth Cheshire
Nora, Sam's girlfriend	Meg Foster
Weaver, Sam's friend, a musician	Bill Mumy
Corey Givits, Sam's friend, a musician	Corey Fischer
Ms. Cox, Jill's teacher	Barbara Bosson

Music: Hal Mooney.

SUNSHINE—30 minutes—NBC— March 6, 1975 - June 19, 1975. 13 episodes.

THE SUPER

Comedy. Background: A less-than-fashionable apartment building in New York City. The trials and tribulations of Joe Girelli, its two-hundred-and-forty-pound Italian-American superintendant. Plagued by tenant complaints, building condemnation threats, and a family "which ain't got no respect," he struggles to solve problems, survive the daily tensions of city living, and enjoy what simple pleasure life affords him.

CAST

Joe Girelli	Richard S. Castellano
Francesca Girelli, his wife	Ardell Sheridan
Joanne Girelli, their daughter	Margaret E. Castellano
Anthony Girelli, their son	B. Kirby Jr.
Frankie Girelli, Joe's brother, studying to become a lawyer	Phil Mishkin
Officer Clark, a tenant	Ed Peck
Dottie Clark, his wife	Virginia Vincent
Sylvia Stein, a tenant	Janet Brandt
Janice Stein, her daughter	Penny Marshall
Pizuti, Joe's friend, owner of a neighborhood bar	Vic Tayback
Fritz, Joe's friend	John Lawrence
Herbie, Joe's friend	Wynn Irwin
Louie, Joe's friend	Louis Basile

Music: Larry Grossman.

THE SUPER—30 minutes—ABC—June 21, 1972 - August 23, 1972. 13 episodes.

SUPERCAR

Marionette Adventure. The battle against crime as undertaken by Supercar, Incorporated, an international anti-crime organization.

Characters:

Mike Mercury, the pilot of *Supercar*, an indestructible automobile
Dr. Beeker.
Professor Popkiss.
Jimmy, Mike's ward.
Mitch, Jimmy's pet monkey.
Masterspy, a criminal.
Zorin, a criminal.

Voices: Paul Maxwell, David Graham, John Bluthal, Sylvia Anderson.

Music: Barry Gray.

SUPERCAR—30 minutes—Syndicated 1962. 39 episodes.

SUPER CIRCUS

Circus Variety Acts.

Ringmasters: Claude Kirchner; Jerry Colonna.

Regulars: Mary Hartline ("Queen of the Super Circus"), Cliff Soubier, Bordie Patton, Nick Francis, C. D. Charlie, Sandy Wirth, Will "Blooper" Able, Otto Griebling.

Clowns: Nicky, Scampy, and Cliffy.

Orchestra: Bruce Case.

Producer: Jack Gibney, Phil Patton, Morton Stone.

Director: Ed Skotch.

Sponsor: Kellogg's; Mars Candies.

SUPER CIRCUS—60 minutes—ABC—January 16, 1949 - June 3, 1956.

SUPER FRIENDS

Animated Cartoon. Background: The Hall of Justice in Washington, D.C.—the headquarters of the Super Friends: Batman and Robin, Superman, Wonder Woman, Aquaman, Marvin, Wendy, and Wonder Dog—indestructible crusaders who've united to form the Justice League of America. Stories depict their battle against the sinister forces of evil.

Character evolvement:

Batman and Robin: See title: "Batman."

Aquaman: See title: "Aquaman."

Superman: See title: "The Adventures of Superman."

Wonder Woman: See title: "Wonder Woman."

Marvin, Wendy and Wonder Dog: Details not related.

Voices: Sherry Alberoni, Danny Dark, Casey Kaseem, Olan Soule, Ted Knight, John Stephenson, Franklin Rucker, Frank Welker, Shannon Farnon, Norman Alden.

Music: Hoyt Curtin, Paul DeKorte.

SUPER FRIENDS—55 minutes—ABC—September 8, 1973 - August 30, 1975.

SUPERMAN

See title: "The Adventures of Superman."

SUPERMARKET SWEEP

Game. Three competing husband-and-wife couples. Background: A supermarket. Couples, each with shopping carts, stand before a white line. A specific amount of time is established, and on the word "go," players run up and down the aisles, cramming grocery items into their carts. At the end of the time, the items are totaled, and the couple with the largest cash amount are the winners and receive the items and the opportunity to compete again.

Host: Bill Malone.

SUPERMARKET SWEEP—30 minutes—ABC—December 20, 1965 - July 17, 1967.

SUPER PRESIDENT

Animated Cartoon. Background: Washington, D.C. The exploits of James Norcross, Chief Justice of the United States, possessing unique powers as the result of a cosmic storm, as he battles the sinister forces of evil.

Additional segment:

Spy Shadow. The crime-battling exploits of private detective Richard Vance and, able to operate independently of himself, his shadow.

SUPER PRESIDENT—30 minutes—NBC—September 16, 1967 - September 14, 1968. 15 episodes.

THE SUPER SIX

Animated Cartoon. The exploits of the Super Six, futuristic crime fighters.

Characters: Super Bwoing; The Super Services Incorporated; and The Brothers Matzoriley.

THE SUPER SIX—30 minutes—NBC—September 10, 1966 - September 6, 1969. 26 episodes.

SUPERSONIC

Music. Performances by Rock Personalities. The program does not include a host, announcer, regulars, or a studio orchestra (guests provide their own music). Produced in England.

Producer-Director: Mike Mansfield.

SUPERSONIC–30 minutes--Syndicated 1976.

SUPER WITCH

Animated Cartoon. Background: The town of Riverdale. The misadventures of Sabrina, a beautiful, but mischievous teenage witch. See also: "Sabrina, the Teenage Witch."

Additional Characters: The Archies (Archie, Jughead, Betty, Veronica, Reggie, and Hot Dog) and The Groovie Goolies.

Voice of Sabrina: Jane Webb.

Additional Voices: Dallas McKennon, Don Messick, John Erwin, Jose Flores, Howard Morris.

Music: Yvette Blais, Jeff Michael.

Executive Producer: Lou Scheimer, Norm Prescott.

Producer: Don Christensen.

SUPER WITCH–30 minutes–NBC– Premiered: November 11, 1977.

SURE AS FATE

Anthology. Dramatic presentations.

SURE AS FATE–30 minutes–CBS– 1950 - 1951.

SURFSIDE SIX

Mystery. Background: Miami Beach, Florida. The investigations of private detectives Dave Thorne, Ken Madison, and Sandy Winfield, into society-based crimes. (Surfside Six: The address of their houseboat.)

CAST

Dave Thorne	Lee Patterson
Ken Madison	Van Williams
Sandy Winfield	Troy Donahue
Daphne DeWitt Dutton, their girlfriend	Diane McBain
Cha Cha O'Brien, a friend, a nightclub singer	Margarita Sierra
Lieutenant Snediger	Donald Barry
Lieutenant Plehn	Richard Crane

Music: Frank Ortega; Frank Perkins; Paul Sawtell; Mack David, Jerry Livingston.

SURFSIDE SIX–60 minutes–ABC– October 3, 1960 - September 24, 1962. 74 episodes. Syndicated.

SURF'S UP

Documentary. Backgrounds: Hawaii and California. Films depicting the lives and world of surfers.

Host: Stan Richards.

SURF'S UP–30 minutes–Syndicated 1965.

SURVIVAL

Documentary. Filmed coverage of both natural and human-caused disasters.

Host-Narrator: James Whitmore.

SURVIVAL–30 minutes–Syndicated 1964. 38 episodes.

THE SURVIVORS

Serial. Background: New York City. The struggles and emotional problems of the rich as seen through the activities of the wealthy Carlyle family, the owners of a Wall Street banking empire. Created by Harold Robbins.

CAST

Baylor Carlyle, the head of the empire	Ralph Bellamy
Tracy Carlyle Hastings, his daughter	Lana Turner
Philip Hastings, her greedy husband	Kevin McCarthy
Duncan Carlyle, Baylor's son	George Hamilton
Jeffrey Carlyle, Tracy's illegimite son	Jan-Michael Vincent
Jonathan	Louis Hayward
Belle	Diana Muldaur
Jean Vale	Louise Sorel
Riakos	Rossano Brazzi
Miguel Santerra	Robert Viharo
Marguerita	Donna Baccalor
Sheila	Kathy Cannon
Tom	Robert Lipton
Rosemary	Pamela Tiffin
Corbett	Michael Bell

THE SURVIVORS–60 minutes– ABC–September 22, 1969 - September 17, 1970. 15 episodes.

SUSAN'S SHOW

Children. An imaginative program that features songs, stories, and "Popeye" cartoons.

Hostess: Susan Heinkel (twelve years old).

Characters: Rusty, her terrier; a magic flying stool from her mother's kitchen; and Mr. Pegasus, a talk-

The Survivors. Louise Sorel and Kevin McCarthy.

ing table.

Producer: Paul Frumkin, Frank Atlass.

SUSAN'S SHOW–30 minutes–CBS– May 4, 1957 - January 18, 1958.

SUSIE

See title: "Private Secretary."

SUSPENSE

Anthology. "Well-calculated tales to keep you in Suspense." Based on the radio classic.

Included:

I, Christopher Bell. Despite a recent heart attack, a man attempts to prove that he is capable of living a strenuous life.

CAST

Christopher Bell: Charles Bickford; Anna: Lila Skala; Betty: Kathleen McGuire.

I, Bradford Charles. After an alligator kills his father, a seventeen-year-old boy begins to hunt for it, determined to kill it.

CAST

Bradford Charles: Andrew Prine; Sheriff: Victor Jory; Reporter: Norman Fell; Brad's mother: Doreen Long.

Web of Circumstance. Embezzling pennies for years, a bank teller plots to escape from his shrewd wife and retreat to a South Seas paradise. Complications ensue when a shortage is discovered.

CAST

Carl Smith: Thomas Mitchell; Elva Smith: Jeanette Nolan; Tom Sutton: Hugh Beaumont; Fred Carlson: Lyle Talbot.

Witness to Condemn. Witnessing a murder and psychologically losing her sight as the result of an attack by the killer, a young woman struggles to overcome the fear that is blocking her sight.

CAST

Laurie Savage: Teresa Wright; Peter Jordan: Warren Stevens.

Fast Break. Once jailed for accepting a bribe, a former basketball player struggles to settle down and end his life of running, despite his constant fear of his record catching up with him.

CAST

Bill Harlow: Jackie Cooper; Lois Harlow: Betty Lynn; Joey Harlow: Michael Winkleman; Pastor

Thompson: Hayden Rorke.

Versions:

Suspense–30 minutes–CBS–March 1, 1949 - August 17, 1954.

Voice of Suspense (Narrator): Paul Frees.

Music: Wilbur Hatch.

Producer: Robert Stevens, Martin Manulis.

Director: Robert Stevens.

Sponsor: Auto-Lite.

Suspense–30 minutes–CBS–March 25, 1964 - September 9, 1964.

Host: Sebastian Cabot.

Producer: Fred Hendrickson.

SUSPENSE PLAYHOUSE

Pilot films. Rebroadcasts of series projects originally aired via "Premiere" (see title).

SUSPENSE PLAYHOUSE–60 minutes–CBS–May 24, 1971 - July 5, 1971.

SUSPENSE THEATRE

Anthology. Retitled episodes of "The Bob Hope Chrysler Theatre" and "The Kraft Suspense Theatre" (see titles for examples of the type of dramas presented).

SUSPENSE THEATRE–60 minutes–Syndicated 1969.

SUSPICION

Anthology. Suspense mysteries.

Hosts: Dennis O'Keefe; Walter Abel.

Producer: Mort Abrams, Robert Fashko, Mark Smith, Frank Rosenberg, Richard Lewis, William Frye, Allan Miller.

Included:

The Other Side of the Curtain. A psychiatrist attempts to discover the reason behind a woman's recurring dream of a dark hallway, a curtain, and the unsuspecting fear that lurks behind it.

CAST

Donna Reed, Herbert Anderson, Jeff Richards, Ainsile Pryor.

Hand in Glove. Aiding a Scotland Yard inspector, a woman attempts to find the man who framed her nephew for murder.

CAST

Ramskill: Burgess Meredith; Aunty B.: Cathleen Nesbitt; Hughie: Fred Gwynne.

The Story of Margery Reardon. Returning home from an evening party, a young woman is attacked by a psycopath. Developing a strong distrust of men, she moves to the city to begin a new life. The story revolves around her struggles to overcome her fears when she meets a handsome young man.

CAST

Margery: Margaret O'Brien; Jim: Rod Taylor: Dick: Henry Silva.

Diary of Death. Journeying to New York City, a young man attempts to avenge the death of his sister.

CAST

Jeremiah Taylor: Macdonald Carey; Ralph Storkey: Everett Sloane.

SUSPICION–60 minutes–NBC–September 30, 1957 - September 6, 1959. 21 episodes available for syndication.

SWAMP FOX

See title: "Walt Disney Presents, *Swamp Fox* segment.

S.W.A.T.

Crime Drama. Background: California. The cases of the Special Weapons and Tactics Unit (S.W.A.T.) of the West California Police Department, a group of five men who assist police who are in trouble.

CAST

Lieutenant Hondo Harrelson	Steve Forrest
Sergeant Deacon Kay	Rod Perry
Officer James Street	Robert Urich
Officer T. J. McCabe	James Coleman
Officer Dominic Luca	Mark Shera

Music: Barry De Vorzon; John Parker.

Executive Producer: Aaron Spelling, Leonard Goldberg.

Producer: Robert Hamner, Barry Shear, Gene Levitt.

Director: George McCowan, Richard Benedict, Earl Bellamy, William Crane, Bruce Bilson, Harry Falk, Dick Moder, Reza S. Badiyi.

Creator: Robert Hamner.

S.W.A.T.–60 minutes–ABC–February 24, 1975 - June 26, 1976.

THE SWEENEY

Crime Drama. Background: London, England. The cases of the Flying Squad, an elite team of specially trained Scotland Yard police detectives.

CAST

Inspector Jack Regan	John Thaw
Sergeant Carter	Dennis Waterman
Chief Inspector Haskins	Garfield Morgan

Music: Harry South.

Executive Producer: Lloyd Shirley, George Tayler.

Producer: Ted Childs.

THE SWEENEY–60 minutes–Syndicated 1976.

THE SWIFT SHOW

Variety. Music, songs, fashion, cooking, and interviews.

Host: Tex McCrary.

Hostess: Jinx Falkenberg.

Music: The Swift Foods Orchestra.

Additional Music: The Johnny Guarnieri Quintet.

Vocalists: Helen Carroll and the Escorts.

Announcer: Dan Seymour.

Producer: Lee Cooley.

Sponsor: Swift Foods.

THE SWIFT SHOW—30 minutes—NBC 1946. Also known as "The Tex and Jinx Swift Show." In 1948, Lanny Ross became the host (see title "The Lanny Ross Show").

THE SWIFT SHOW WAGON WITH HORACE HEIDT AND THE AMERICAN WAY

Musical Variety. Musical salutes to the cities and states that comprise the United States.

Host: Horace Heidt.

Orchestra: Horace Heidt.

THE SWIFT SHOW WAGON WITH HORACE HEIDT AND THE AMERICAN WAY—30 minutes—CBS—1954 - 1955.

SWINGING COUNTRY

Musical Variety. Performances by Country and Western entertainers.

Host: Roy Clark.

Substitute Host: Minnie Pearl.

Regulars: Molly Bee, Rusty Draper, The Swinging Countrymen, The Hometown Singers.

SWINGING COUNTRY—25 minutes —NBC—July 4, 1966 - December 30, 1966.

SWISS FAMILY ROBINSON

Adventure. Era: The nineteenth century. The series follows the adventures of the Robinson family, shipwrecked on an almost deserted tropical island, as they struggle for survival and seek a way to escape. Based on the story by Johann Wyss.

CAST

Karl Robinson, the father	Martin Milner
Lotte Robinson, his wife	Pat Delany
Fred Robinson, their son	Willie Aames
Ernie Robinson, their son	Eric Olson
Jeremiah Worth, a marooned, loud-mouthed sea dog	Cameron Mitchell
Helga Wagner, the Robinson's adopted daughter	Helen Hunt

Music: Lionel Newman, Richard La Salle.

Producer: Irwin Allen.

Director: Harry Harris, Leslie H. Martinson, George Fenady.

SWISS FAMILY ROBINSON—60 minutes—ABC—September 14, 1975 - April 11, 1976. 26 episodes.

THE SWISS FAMILY ROBINSON

Adventure. Background: An uncharted island in the year 1881. The series follows the adventures of the Robinsons, a Swiss family who were shipwrecked on a deserted island, which they name New Switzerland, after their ship was destroyed during a tropical storm at sea. Closely follows the novel by Johann Wyss; more so than the previous title. Produced in Canada.

CAST

Johann Robinson, the father	Chris Wiggins
Elizabeth Robinson, his wife	Diana Leblanc
Marie Robinson, their daughter	Heather Graham
Franz Robinson, their son	Micky O'Neill
Ernest Robinson, their son	Michael Duhig

Narrator: Chris Wiggins.

Music: Score Productions.

Music Supervision: Lewis Lehman.

Producer: Gerald Mayer.

Director: Peter Carter, Gerald Mayer, Don Haldane.

THE SWISS FAMILY ROBINSON—30 minutes—Syndicated 1976.

SWITCH

Crime Drama. Background: Los Angeles, California. The story of Frank MacBride, a tough, retired bunco cop; and Pete Ryan, his partner, a soft-soap ex-con, the owner-operators of the Ryan-MacBride Private Detective Organization. Episodes relate their investigations as they attempt to beat swindlers at their own game.

CAST

Frank MacBride	Eddie Albert
Pete Ryan	Robert Wagner
Maggie, their secretary	Sharon Gless
Malcolm, their con-artist friend	Charlie Callas
Revel, the waitress at Malcolm's bar	Mindi Miller
Lt. Schiller	William Bryant

Music: Stu Phillips, Glen A. Larson.

Executive Producer: Glen A. Larson, Matthew Rapf.

Producer: Leigh Vance, Jack Laird, John Guss, Paul Playdon, John Peyser.

Director: Noel Black, Bruce Kessler, John Peyser, Sutton Roley, Leo Penn, Sigmund Neufeld, Jr., Bruce Evans, Glen A. Larson, E.W. Swackhamer, Walter Doniger.

SWITCH—60 minutes—CBS—Premiered: September 9, 1975.

THE SWORD OF FREEDOM

Adventure. Background: Florence, Italy, during the Renaissance period of the fifteenth century. The exploits of Marco del Monte, swordsman, painter, and lover, as he attempts to defend the Free Republic against the iron-hand rule of the Medicis.

Starring: Edmund Purdom as Marco del Monte.

THE SWORD OF FREEDOM—30 minutes—Syndicated 1957. 39 episodes.

SYLVESTER AND TWEETY

Animated Cartoon. The series, composed of various Warner Brothers theatrical cartoons, most often features the antics of Sylvester and Tweety—a cat (Sylvester) who relentlessly pursues one goal—to catch himself a decent meal, that being Tweety, the foxy bird.

Voice Characterizations: Mel Blanc.

Music: William Lava, Milt Franklin, John Seely, Carl W. Stalling.

Director: Robert McKimson, Friz Freeling, Chuck Jones.

SYLVESTER AND TWEETY—30 minutes—CBS—Premiered: September 11, 1976.

SZYSZNYK

Comedy. Background: Washington, D.C. The story of Nick Szysznyk (pronounced Ziznik), an ex-Marine sergeant turned playground supervisor, as he attempts to salvage the financially troubled Northeast Community Center.

CAST

Nick Szysznyk   Ned Beatty
Ms. Harrison, the district
    supervisor   Olivia Cole
Sandi Chandler, Nick's
    assistant   Susan Lanier
Leonard Kriegler, the
    assistant to the
    director; in charge of
    sports equip.   Leonard Barr
Ray Gun, one of the teen-
    agers at the
    center   Thomas Carter
Ralph, same as
    Ray   Jarrod Johnson
Tony, same as
    Ray   Scott Colomby
Fortwengler, same as
    Ray   Barry Miller

Music: Doug Gilmore.
Theme Vocal: Sonny Curtis.
Executive Producer: Jerry Weintraub.
Producer: Rich Eustis, Michael Elias.
Director: Peter Bonerz.
Creator: Jim Mulligan, Ron Landry.

SZYSZNYK—30 minutes—CBS—August 1, 1977 - August 29, 1977. 5 episodes.

J

THE TAB HUNTER SHOW

Comedy. Background: Malibu Beach, California. The romantic misadventures of Paul Morgan, playboy, and creator-artist of the comic strip "Bachelor at Large."

CAST

Paul Morgan   Tab Hunter
Peter Fairfield III,
    his friend   Richard Erdman
John Larsen, the publisher
    of *Comics Incorporated,*
    Paul's employer   Jerome Cowan

Music: Pete Rugolo.

THE TAB HUNTER SHOW—30 minutes—NBC—September 20, 1960 - September 10, 1961. 32 episodes.

TABITHA

Comedy. A spin-off from "Bewitched." Background: Los Angeles, California. Events in the life of Tabitha Stevens, a witch (the daughter of Samantha and Darrin Stevens), now a beautiful young woman employed by ABC affiliated station KXLA-TV; a young woman who frequently resorts to bits of conjured magic to achieve her goal.

CAST

Tabitha Stevens   Lisa Hartman
Adam Stevens, her
    brother   David Ankrum
Paul Thurston, the star of
    his own program
    on KXLA   Robert Urich
Marv, Paul's
    producer   Mel Stewart
Minerva, Tabitha's
    aunt   Karen Morrow
Dr. Bombay, the war-
    lock doctor   Bernard Fox

Music: Dick De Benedictis.
Executive Producer: Jerry Mayer.
Producer: George Yanok.
Director: Charles S. Dubin.
Creator: Jerry Mayer.

TABITHA—30 minutes—ABC—Premiered: September 10, 1977. Broadcast on an irregular basis throughout the 1977-1978 season.

TAG THE GAG

Game. Selected members of the studio audience compete. A group of actors pantomime a joke on stage and stop prior to its punch line. The player who is able to verbally complete it is the winner of that round. Cash prizes are awarded to players who most often tag the gag.

Host: Hal Block.
Producer: Ray Buffum.
Director: Jack Hein.

TAG THE GAG—30 minutes—NBC—August 20, 1951 - September 1951.

TAKE A CHANCE

Game. A player, who is given five dollars, is either able to leave with it or risk it in an attempt to answer a question. If choosing the latter, he is asked a general-knowledge type of question. A correct response awards the player a gift and a choice: to continue or leave. A maximum of four questions are asked and prizes range

from gags to costly items. An incorrect answer defeats a player, who then loses his money and prizes.

Host: Don Ameche.
Producer: Dick Lewis.
Sponsor: Nestle.

TAKE A CHANCE—30 minutes—ABC 1950.

TAKE A GIANT STEP

Discussion. Teenagers (thirteen to fifteen years of age) discuss personal and social matters. The program attempts to help children between the ages of seven and fourteen develop their own sense of judgment.

Revised title and format "Talk to a Giant."

Teenagers discuss various aspects of the world with celebrities—giants in their respected fields.

Hosts (chosen from a group of twenty-five teenagers): Andrea Mays, Nancy Melendez, Nancy Wemmer, John Rucker, Bill Bliss, Linda Lloyd da Silva, Heather Thomas, Chip Portocarrero, Scott Falloner, Rinky Favor, Linda Lagisola, David Kollack, Sherry Shapiro.

Music: Recorded.

TAKE A GIANT STEP—60 minutes—NBC—September 11, 1971 - August 26, 1972.

TALK WITH A GIANT—30 minutes—NBC—September 9, 1972 - September 1, 1973.

TAKE A GOOD LOOK

Game. Distinguished by two formats.

Format One:

Three contestants compete. Object: To identify prominent news figures from film clips and sound recordings.

Format Two:

A celebrity panel of three compete. A cast performs a dramatic sketch on stage that relates clues to a mystery guest. The panelist who first associates the clues and identifies the celebrity guest is the winner of that round. Winners are the highest-scoring players. Prizes are awarded to home viewers who are represented by panelists.

Host: Ernie Kovacs.

Panelists: Edie Adams, Cesar Romero, Carl Reiner.

Dramatic Cast: Ernie Kovacs, Peggy Connelly, Bob Lauher.

TAKE A GOOD LOOK—30 minutes —ABC—October 22, 1959 - July 21, 1960; October 27, 1960 - March 16, 1961.

TAKE A GUESS

Game. Selected members of the studio audience compete. Through question-and-answer probe rounds with a celebrity panel, players have to uncover a mystery phrase that is known only to the host and panel. Players start with $150. Each "yes" answer by a panelist deducts five dollars from that player's total. The round continues until a player, who receives four guesses, identifies the phrase. The player then receives the total amount of money deducted from all the scores added to his total. The winner, the highest cash scorer, receives his accumulated earnings as a prize.

Host: John K. M. McCaffery.

Panelists: Ernie Kovacs, John Crawford, Dorothy Hart, Margaret Lindsey.

TAKE A GUESS—30 minutes—CBS—June 18, 1953 - September 1953.

TAKE ANOTHER LOOK

Game. Contestants compete in a fashion quiz for prizes.

Host: Sonny Mars.

Vocalist: Peggy Taylor.

Music: The Bill Otto Band.

TAKE ANOTHER LOOK—60 minutes—CBS 1950.

TAKE FIVE WITH STILLER AND MEARA

Comedy. A series of humorous blackout type skits satirizing various aspects of everyday life.

Starring: Jerry Stiller and Anne Meara.

Music: Recorded.

Executive Producer: John Davis.

Producer: William Watts.

Director: Ivan Curry.

TAKE FIVE WITH STILLER AND MEARA—05 minutes—Syndicated 1977.

TAKE IT FROM ME

Comedy. Background: The Bronx, New York. The life of the average American housewife as interpreted by comedienne Jean Carroll.

CAST

The housewife	Jean Carroll
Her husband	Alan Carney
Their daughter	Lynn Loring
Their neighbor	Alice Pearce

Orchestra: Bernie Greene.

TAKE IT FROM ME—30 minutes—ABC—November 4, 1953 - January 13, 1954. Also known as: "The Jean Carroll Show."

TAKE MY ADVICE

Discussion. Four celebrity guests discuss and suggest answers to problems sent in by viewers.

Hostess: Kelly Lange.

Announcer: Bill Armstrong.

Music: Score Productions.

Executive Producer: Burt Sugarman.

Producer: Mark Massari, Ken Salter.

Director: Hank Behar.

Creator: Armand Grant.

TAKE MY ADVICE—25 minutes—NBC—January 5, 1976 - June 11, 1976.

TAKE TWO

Game. Four celebrity guests, divided into two teams of two. Four pictures are flashed on a screen (e.g., Marilyn Monroe, Amy Vanderbilt, Jayne Mansfield, and a cat). The team that is first to identify themselves receives a chance to answer. If they are able to identify two pictures related to one set (Monroe and Mansfield, actresses), they receive points. Winners are the highest scorers. Selected members of the studio audience, who are represented by the celebrities, receive merchandise prizes.

Host: Don McNeil.

TAKE TWO—30 minutes—ABC—May 5, 1963 - August 11, 1963.

TALENT PATROL

See Title: "Steve Allen."

TALENT VARIETIES

Musical Variety. Performances by Country and Western entertainers.

Host: Slim Wilson.

Announcer: Chuck Hesington.

Music: The Tall Timber Trio; The Country Rhythm Boys.

TALENT VARIETIES—30 minutes—ABC—June 28, 1955 - September 6, 1955.

TALES OF THE BLACK CAT

Anthology. Horror, suspense, and mystery presentations.

Host: James Monks.

Assisting: Thanatopsis, his black siamese cat.

TALES OF THE BLACK CAT—30 minutes—CBS 1950.

TALES OF THE CITY

Anthology. Dramatizations set against the background of New York City.

Host: Ben Hect.

Included:

Miracle In The Rain. The tender and heartwarming story of a lonely girl who keeps a spiritual vigil for her sweetheart who was killed in the war.

CAST
William Prince, Phyllis Thaxter.

Blackie Gagin. The story of Blackie Gagin, one of the dumbiest crooks who ever lived, is told via song and story by Burl Ives.

CAST
Blackie Gagin: Dane Clark.

TALES OF THE CITY—30 minutes—CBS—June 25, 1953 - September 16, 1953.

TALES OF MYSTERY

A thirty-minute anthology series, first syndicated in 1954, that delves into the world of the supernatural.

TALES OF THE 77th BENGAL LANCERS

Adventure. Background: India. The saga of the British forces, 77th Bengal

Lancers, as they battle the constant Afrid uprisings.

CAST

Lieutenant Rhodes	Philip Carey
Lieutenant Storm	Warren Stevens
Colonel Standish	Pat Whyte
Captain Scott Ellis	John Hubbard
Captain Clary	Sean McClory

TALES OF THE 77th BENGAL LANCERS—30 minutes—NBC—October 21, 1956 - June 2, 1957. 26 episodes. Syndicated.

TALES OF THE TEXAS RANGERS

Western. Background: Texas. Dramatizations based on the files of the Texas Rangers, North America's oldest law-enforcement organization. Stories detail the investigations of Rangers Jace Pearson and Clay Morgan, and the time-honored methods of crime control from the 1830s to the 1950s.

CAST

Ranger Jace Pearson	Willard Parker
Ranger Clay Morgan	Harry Lauter

Producer: Colbert Clark, Jonal Seinfield, Harry Ackerman.

TALES OF THE TEXAS RANGERS—30 minutes—ABC—September 21, 1957 - May 25, 1959. 52 episodes. Syndicated.

TALES OF THE UNEXPECTED

Anthology. Suspense and mystery presentations.

Host-Narrator: William Conrad.

Music: Richard Markowitz, David Shire.

Executive Producer: Quinn Martin.

Producer: John Wilder.

Included:

The Mark of Adonis. The story concerns an aging producer who relies on the mysterious rejuvenation process of a doctor to maintain the appearance of a young man.

CAST

Alexander Cole: Robert Foxworth; Viviana: Marlyn Mason; Gerry: Linda Kelsey; Davidion: Victor Jory.

Devil Pack. The story of a small, isolated community terrorized by fearce wild dogs.

CAST

Jerry Colby: Ronny Cox; Ann Colby: Christine Belford; Sheriff: Van Johnson.

The Final Chapter. The story of Frank Harris—a crusading newspaper reporter who has himself placed on death row in an attempt to write about capital punishment. The unexpected occurs when he is scheduled for execution and cannot convince anyone of his masquerade.

CAST

Frank Harris: Roy Thinnes; Warden Greer: Ramon Bieri; Chaplain: Brendon Dillon.

TALES OF THE UNEXPECTED—60 minutes—NBC—February 2, 1977 - March 9, 1977.

TALES OF THE UNKNOWN

Anthology. Science fiction tales enacted by a single actor or actress.

TALES OF THE UNKNOWN—30 minutes—Syndicated 1954.

TALES OF THE VIKINGS

Adventure. Background: Scandinavia, A.D. 1000. Episodes of conflict and conquest in the lives of Leif Ericson and his sea raiders, the Vikings.

CAST

Leif Ericson	Jerome Courtland
Finn	Walter Barnes
Firebeard	Stefan Schnabel
Haldar	Peter Bull
Jessica	June Thorburn

TALES OF THE VIKINGS—30 minutes—Syndicated 1960. 39 episodes.

TALES OF TOMORROW

Anthology. Stories of the supernatural.

Music: Bobby Christian.

Producer: Mort Abrams.

Director: Leonard Valenta.

Sponsor: Kreisler Products.

Included:

Ahead of His Time. The story of an ordinary man who becomes extraordinary when he invents a time machine.

Starring: Paul Tripp.

Discovered Heart. The story of a young girl who makes a playmate of a visitor from outer space.

Starring: Susan Holloran.

Dark Angel. The story of a woman who never grows old.

Starring: Meg Mundy, Sidney Blackmer.

TALES OF TOMORROW—30 minutes—ABC—August 3, 1951 - September 18, 1953.

THE TALES OF WELLS FARGO

Western. Background: The Frontier during the 1860s. The investigations of Jim Hardie, agent-troubleshooter for Wells Fargo, Incorporated, gold transporters.

Revised Format:
Background: San Francisco, California. The series focuses on both Jim Hardie's home life, now the owner of a ranch, and his experiences as a Wells Fargo Troubleshooter.

CAST

Jim Hardie	Dale Robertson
Jeb Gane, the foreman	William Demarest
Beau McCloud, Hardie's assistant	Jack Ging
Widow Ovie, Jim's neighbor	Virginia Christine
Mary Gee, Ovie's daughter	Mary Jane Saunders
Tina, Ovie's daughter	Lory Patrick

Narrator: Dale Robertson.

Music: Stanley Wilson; Melvyn Lenard; Morton Stevens.

Producer: Nat Holt, Earl Lyon.

THE TALES OF WELLS FARGO—30 minutes (first format)—NBC—March 18, 1957 - August 28, 1961. 60 minutes (revised format)—NBC—September 30, 1961 - September 8, 1962. 167 episodes. Syndicated.

TALES OF THE WIZARD OF OZ

An animated series, produced in Canada, that follows the further adventures of L. Frank Baum's memorable "Wizard of Oz" characters. 130 five minute films, syndicated 1961.

TALK TO A GIANT

See title: "Take A Giant Step."

TALLAHASSEE 7000

Crime Drama. Background: Miami Beach, Florida. The investigations of Lex Rogers, special agent-trouble-shooter for the Florida Sheriff's Bureau. (Tallahasse 7000: The Florida Sheriff's Bureau telephone number.)

Starring: Walter Matthau as Lex Rogers.

Narrator: Walter Matthau.

Music: Irving Friedman.

TALLAHASSEE 7000–30 minutes–Syndicated 1961. 39 episodes.

THE TALL MAN

Western. Background: Lincoln County, territory of New Mexico, 1879. The relationship between a law enforcer, Sheriff Pat Garrett, and his captor, William Bonney, alias Billy the Kid, now released in the custody of an English rancher. Stories detail Garrett's attempts, helped and hindered by Billy, to maintain law and order.

CAST

Sheriff Pat Garrett	Barry Sullivan
William Bonney	Clu Gulager

Music: Esquivel.

THE TALL MAN–30 minutes–NBC –September 10, 1960 - September 1, 1962. 75 episodes. Syndicated.

TAMMY

Comedy. Background: Louisiana. Raised in the desolate Bayou country by her grandfather after her parents' death, Tammy Tarleton, a young and lonely riverboat girl, enrolls as a student in a secretarial school after completing special educational courses at nearby Seminola College.

Completing the course, she applies for a position as secretary to John Brent, a wealthy widower.

Shortly after, while milking her goat, Nan, a telegram arrives at the *Ellen B,* her houseboat, informing her of an appointment for an interview with Mr. Brent at Brentwood Hall.

Interviewed and impressing Mr. Brent with her ability to type approximately two hundred words a minute, she is hired as his secretary-receptionist. Immediately, she encounters the wrath of Lavinia Tate, an attractive widow who had hoped to acquire the position for her daughter, Gloria, and further her own plans to acquire John's long-sought proposal of marriage. With her chances ruined, Lavinia sets her goal to acquire the secretarial position for Gloria by disgracing Tammy in the hope that it will either cause her to quit or be dismissed.

Having lived a sheltered life, and conveying a philosophy of love and understanding, Tammy struggles to overcome the situations that arise as

Tammy. Left to right: Frank McGrath, Denver Pyle, Debbie Watson.

Lavinia deceitfully attempts to achieve her goal. Based on the motion pictures *Tammy and the Bachelor,* which stars Debbie Reynolds, and *Tammy Tell Me True* which stars Sandra Dee.

CAST

Tammy Tarleton	Debbie Watson
Mortecai Tarleton, her grandfather	Denver Pyle
Lucius Tarleton, her uncle	Frank McGrath
John Brent	Donald Woods
Lavinia Tate	Dorothy Green
Gloria Tate	Linda Marshall
Dwayne Witt, John's associate	George Furth
Peter Tate, Lavinia's son	David Macklin
Stephen Brent, John's son	Jay Sheffield
Cletus Tarleton, Tammy's cousin	Dennis Robertson

Theme: "Tammy," composed by Jay Livingston and Ray Evans.

Background music composed by: Frank Skinner.

Series music supervision: Stanley Wilson.

Series Music: Jack Marshall.

Producer: Dick Wesson.

Director: Ezra Stone, Sidney Miller, Harry Keller, Leslie Goodwins.

TAMMY–30 minutes–ABC–September 17, 1965 - July 15, 1966. 26 episodes. Theatrical version culled from the series: "Tammy and the Millionaire."

THE TAMMY GRIMES SHOW

Comedy. Background: New York City. The story of Tammy Ward, a young heiress who is restricted to a tight budget by her stingy Uncle Simon, and who is unable to claim her multi-million dollar inheritance because she has not yet reached the age of thirty. Episodes depict her misadventures as she struggles to

Tallahassee 7000. Walter Matthau. © Screen Gems.

The Tammy Grimes Show. Tammy Grimes.

finance her expensive tastes through elaborate schemes.

CAST

Tammy Ward	Tammy Grimes
Simon Ward	Hiram Sherman
Terence Ward, Tammy's brother	Dick Sargent

THE TAMMY GRIMES SHOW—30 minutes—ABC—September 8, 1966 - September 29, 1966. 10 episodes (only four of which aired).

TARGET

Anthology. High-tension, impact dramas that depict the conflicting forces that drive men and women.

Host: Adolphe Menjou.

Included:

The Last Stop. The story focuses on the desperation of two kidnappers as they flee from a police agent.

Starring: Neville Brand.

Backfire. The story of a nurse who is kidnapped and forced to treat a wounded criminal.

Starring: Pat O'Brien.

Unreasonable Doubt. The story of a man and his attempts to clear himself of a false murder charge.

Starring: Macdonald Carey.

Fateful Decision. The story of a man and his attempts to kill his wife's supposed lover.

Starring: Marshall Thompson.

TARGET—30 minutes—Syndicated 1951. 38 episodes.

TARGET: THE CORRUPTORS

Crime Drama. The investigations of Paul Marino, a racket reporter, and Jach Flood, a federal undercover agent, as they attempt to infiltrate the rackets and expose the methods of organized crime through the power of the press.

CAST

Paul Marino	Stephen McNally
Jach Flood	Robert Harland

Music: Herschel Burke Gilbert; Rudy Schrager.

TARGET: THE CORRUPTORS—60 minutes—ABC—September 29, 1961 - September 20, 1962. 34 episodes. Syndicated.

TARO, GIANT OF THE JUNGLE

An animated series about Taro, a jungle boy who, to battle evil, acquires his powers from a radioactive tree. 30 minutes—Syndicated 1969. 39 episodes.

TARZAN

Adventure. Background: Africa. Put ashore by the mutinous crew of a ship bound for England, Lord John Greystoke and his wife Alice, left with tools and firearms, construct a small shack near the coast when all attempts to escape fail. One year later, a son is born to them.

Shortly after, the cabin is attacked by a tribe of bull apes. John and Alice are savagely slaughtered, and little Lord Greystoke is taken by Kalah, a young female. ape, who raises him as Tarzan, Lord of the Jungle.

Twenty years later, after a safari is marooned on the island, Tarzan befriends a Frenchman who, teaching him to speak English, persuades him to return to England. Educated in the finest finishing schools, but unable to adjust to civilized life, he returns to the land of his birth.*

Stories relate Tarzan's attempts to protect his beloved homeland from the sinister forces of evil. His female companion, Jane,** and his poor English are deleted from the story and character created by Edgar Rice Burroughs.

CAST

Tarzan	Ron Ely
Jai, an orphaned jungle boy	Manuel Padilla, Jr.
Jason Flood, Jai's tutor	Alan Caillou
Rao, the village veterinarian	Rockne Tarkington
Tall Boy, his assistant	Stewart Rafill

Music: Walter Greene, Nelson Riddle.

Producer: Maurice Unger.

Tarzan's chimpanzee: Cheetah.

TARZAN—60 minutes—NBC—September 8, 1966 - September 13, 1968. CBS (rebroadcasts): June 4, 1969 - September 10, 1969. 57 episodes. Syndicated.

*One of two versions relating Tarzan's education.
**Separated from a safari, Jane Parker is suddenly propelled amid a web of pending death: a rampaging elephant and savage Pygmies. Rescued by Tarzan, she befriends him and teaches him to talk. The "Me Tarzan, you Jane" type of dialogue prevails through many of the features.

TARZAN: LORD OF THE JUNGLE

Animated Cartoon. Background: Africa. The further adventures of Tarzan as he battles the evils of man and beast.

Tarzan's assistant: Nakima, the monkey.

Voices: Bob Ridgley, Linda Gray, Joan Gerber, Ted Cassidy, Barry Gordon, Alan Oppenheimer, Jane Webb.

Music: Yvette Blais, Jeff Michael.

Executive Producer: Norm Prescott, Lou Scheimer.

Director: Don Christensen.

TARZAN: LORD OF THE JUNGLE —25 minutes—CBS—Premiered: September 11, 1976.

TATE

Western. Background: The Frontier during the 1870s. The saga of Tate, a wandering one-armed (the left, smashed during the Civil War is preserved in a black leather casing) exgunfighter who sides with justice against criminal elements.

Starring: David McLean as Tate.

TATE—30 minutes—NBC—June 8, 1960 - September 28, 1960.

TATTLETALES

Game. Three celebrity couples compete, each representing one third of the studio audience.

Round One: The husbands are isolated offstage; the wives are before camera. The host reads a question (e.g., "It happened on vacation"). The player who first sounds her buzzer receives a chance to answer. She then relates a situation that concerns her marriage and a one- or two-word clue that summarizes the answer. The host then presses a button and airs the husbands, who appear on monitors placed before each of their mates. The question is restated and the one- or two-word clue is given. The husband who believes it is his wife's response sounds a bell. He then has to relate a similar story. If correct, one hundred dollars is scored.

Round Two: The reverse of round one: wives have to recognize and match what their husbands have said regarding their marriage. One hundred dollars is scored for each correct association.

Winners are the highest scoring teams. The program adds one thousand dollars to the total and it is then divided between the studio audience members who are represented by that celebrity couple.

Host: Bert Convy.

Announcer: Jack Clark.

Music: Recorded.

TATTLETALES—30 minutes—CBS—Premiered: February 18, 1974.

TED MACK

Listed: The television programs of Ted Mack.

Ted Mack And The Original Amateur Hour—Variety—30 minutes. NBC—October 4, 1949 - September 11, 1954; ABC—October 30, 1955 - June 23, 1957; NBC—September 1957 - October 4, 1958; CBS—October 1958 - September 1971.

Host: Ted Mack.

Announcers: Dennis James; Roy Greece.

Orchestra: Lloyd Marx.

Format: Performances by undiscovered professional talent.

Ted Mack's Family Hour—Variety—30 minutes—ABC—January 7, 1951 - November 25, 1954.

Host: Ted Mack.

Vocalist: Andy Roberts.

Announcer: Dennis James.

Orchestra: Lloyd Marx.

Format: Performances by professional entertainers.

Ted Mack's Matinee—Variety—30 minutes—NBC—1954 - 1955.

Host: Ted Mack.

Regulars: Elsie Rhodes, Dick Lee and the Honeydreamers.

Orchestra: Lloyd Marx.

Format: Performances by professional entertainers.

THE TED STEELE SHOW

Musical Variety.

Host: Ted Steele.

Regulars: Helen Wood, Michael Rich, Nola Day, Mardi Bryant, Charles Danford.

Orchestra: Ted Steele.

THE TED STEELE SHOW—30 minutes—DuMont 1949.

THE TELECOMICS

Animated Cartoon. The overall title for four rotating series: "Danny March"; "Johnny and Mr. Do-Right"; "Kid Champion"; and "Space Barton." The first cartoons made especially for television. Character credits are not given.

Danny March. Background: Metro City. Shortly after his parents are killed in an automobile accident, young Danny March is sent to live with his uncle, a shady character who soon meets with a violent end. Sent to an orphanage, he grows up as one of the toughest kids in town.

But instead of turning to a life of crime, he decides to devote his life to combatting crime. Rejected by the Metro City police force when he falls short of height requirements, he becomes a private detective and soon afterward, because of his heroic exploits, is appointed as the mayor's personal detective. Stories depict his investigations.

Johnny And Mr. Do-Right. The adventures shared by a young boy and his dog.

Kid Champion. Dreaming of becoming a musician, Eddie Hale relinquishes his desire and begins to train as a prizefighter to please his father, a once-

famous boxer who has only one year to live.

Passing a gas station, and witnessing a robbery, Eddie, in an attempt to save the attendant, accidentally knocks him to the ground. Fearing to have killed the man, he flees, drops his real name and adopts the alias of Kid Champion. Sometime later, when crossing the path of Lucky Skinner, a manager, he is persuaded to further his career as a boxer. Stories depict his attempts to become a champion.

Space Barton. Fascinated by space, Horace Barton, Jr., sets his goal to become the world's greatest pilot. His ambition, which is reflected in everything he does, earns him the nickname of "Space."

After three years of college, and just prior to World War II, he joins the army air corps. Assigned to test the first U.S. jet, he receives his first experience with outer space. Stories relate his attempts to achieve a dream.

THE TELECOMICS—15 minutes—NBC—1950-1951. CBS—15 minutes—1951. Syndicated. Withdrawn. Also known as "The NBC Comics."

TELEDRAMA

Anthology. Dramatizations based on stories by leading playwrights. Included:

Pier 23. The story of a San Francisco storekeeper who turns detective to track down two murderers.

CAST
Richard Travis, Hugh Beaumont, Ann Savage.

Traffic In Crime. A police spy attempts to break up two gambling syndicates that are operating in a small town.

CAST
Kane Richmond, Ruth Terry, Adele Mara.

Tales Of Robin Hood. A video adaptation of the classic folk tale. The story of Robin Hood, an outlaw who stole from the rich to give to the poor.

CAST
Robert Clark.

TELEDRAMA—30 minutes—CBS 1953.

TELEPHONE TIME

Anthology. Dramatizations depicting the events that spark the lives of ordinary people.

Hosts: John Nesbitt, Frank Baxter.

Included:

The Golden Junkman. The story of a junkman with an amazing ability to make money.

CAST

Lon Chaney, Jr.

Harry In Search Of Himself. The story of the founder of the American Society for the Prevention of Cruelty to Animals.

CAST

Edgar Buchanan, Frances Reid, Philip Bourneuf.

Time Bomb. The true story of the manager of a Shanghai textile factory and his diabetic wife who are trapped in the city by the Japanese occupation at the beginning of World War II.

CAST

Steven Geary, Terie Shimada, Osa Massen, Keye Luke.

TELEPHONE TIME—30 minutes—CBS—1956 - 1958.

TELE PUN

Game. Standing before the studio audience, a player has to perform a pun, which represents geographical locations, songs, people, proverbs, or titles, through charades to their satisfaction. If he is successful (rarely) he receives a prize. However, should he make a mistake, he is charged with "punning in public places" and arrested. Taking on the atmosphere of a courtroom hearing, the player is then comically defended by an attorney. When the judge dismisses the case, the player receives a consolation prize and the crime, "the errant pun" is performed in the correct manner.

Home participation segment: "The Tele Pun of the Week." A pun is enacted during the course of the program. Left unanswered, it is offered for solution to home viewers who respond via post cards. Answers are judged and prizes are awarded accordingly.

Host-Judge: Johnny Bradford.

Announcer-Attorney: Ray Michael.

TELE PUN—30 minutes—NBC 1948.

TELL IT TO THE CAMERA

Comedy. A spin-off from "Candid Camera." People, who are aware of a camera, speak directly into it and reveal their thoughts concerning personal and/or wordly problems. Created by Allen Funt.

Host: Red Rowe.

Music: Sid Ramin.

TELL IT TO THE CAMERA—30 minutes—CBS—January 11, 1962 - May 24, 1962.

TELL IT TO GROUCHO

Interview-Quiz. Two contestants are first comically interviewed by the host, then compete in a quiz wherein they attempt to identify persons, places, or objects from pictures that are rapidly flashed on a screen. Players earnings, which are divided, are based on the number of correct identifications. A spin-off from "You Bet Your Life."

Host: Groucho Marx.

Assistants: Patty Harmon, Jack Wheels.

Announcer: George Fenneman.

Orchestra: Jerry Fielding.

TELL IT TO GROUCHO—30 minutes—CBS 1962.

TELL US MORE

Documentary. The careers of famous celebrities are recalled through film clips, photographs, letters, and newspaper clippings. Two biographies of similar personalities are presented on each program.

Host-Narrator: Conrad Nagel.

Included Biographies: Marilyn Monroe, Elizabeth Taylor; Bing Crosby, Bob Hope; Spencer Tracy, Pat O'Brien; Joan Fontaine, Olivia De Havilland; Grace Kelly, Audrey Hepburn; Bud Abbott and Lou Costello, Stan Laurel and Oliver Hardy; Kate Smith, Marian Anderson; Johnny Weissmuller, Buster Crabbe; Lon Chaney, Boris Karloff; Jackie Robinson, Joe Dimaggio.

TELL US MORE—30 minutes—NBC —September 9, 1963 - March 16, 1964.

TELLER OF TALES

Anthology. Dramatizations based on stories by author William Somerset Maugham.

Host: William Somerset Maugham.

Producer: John Gibbs, Anne Marlowe, Martin Ritt.

Director: David Alexander, Martin Ritt.

Sponsor: Tintair

TELLER OF TALES—30 minutes—CBS—1950 - 1951. Also known as "The Somerset Maugham Theatre."

THE TELLTALE CLUE

Crime Drama. Background: New York City. The investigations of Detective Captain Richard Hale, of the Metropolitan Homicide Squad, as he attempts to solve crimes through one seemingly insignificant piece of evidence: The Telltale Clue.

Starring: Anthony Ross as Richard Hale.

THE TELLTALE CLUE—30 minutes —CBS—July 15, 1954 - September 23, 1954.

TEMPERATURES RISING

Comedy. Distinguished by two formats.

Format One:

Background: Capitol General Hospital in Washington, D.C. A comical portrait of life in a hospital as seen through the eyes—and antics—of Dr. Jerry Noland, a gambling-inclined intern who, with his cohorts, Nurses Ann Carlisle, Mildred MacInerney, and Ellen Turner, struggles to aid patients who are in need of financial assistance.

Upsetting normal hospital routines by his endless attempts to raise money, he encounters the wrath of Dr. Vincent Campanelli, the chief of surgery, who attempts, but fails to keep him in line, and struggles to return the hospital to normalcy.

CAST

Dr. Vincent Campanelli	James Whitmore
Dr. Jerry Noland	Cleavon Little
Nurse Ann Carlisle	Joan Van Ark
Nurse Mildred MacInerney	Reva Rose
Nurse Ellen Turner	Nancy Fox
Miss Liewellen, Dr. Campanelli's secretary	Olive Dunbar

Music: Shorty Rogers.

TEMPERATURES RISING—30 minutes—ABC—September 12, 1972 - September 4, 1973.

Format Two:

Background: Capitol General Hospital in Washington, D.C. The harassed life of Paul Mercy, its administrator, a nonpracticing doctor who struggles to solve endless patient and staff difficulties.

CAST

Dr. Paul Mercy	Paul Lynde
Wendy Winchester, R.N.	Jennifer Darling
Miss Tillis, the admissions nurse	Barbara Cason
Dr. Jerry Noland	Cleavon Little
Dr. Charles Claver	John Dehner
Dr. Lloyd Axton	Jeff Morrow
Edwina Mercy, Paul's sister	Alice Ghostley
Agatha Mercy, Paul's mother	Sudie Bond
Nurse Kelly	Barbara Rucker
Haskell, the orderly	Jerry Houser

Music: Vic Mizzy.

THE NEW TEMPERATURES RISING SHOW—30 minutes—ABC—September 25, 1973 - January 8, 1974. Returned (ABC): July 28, 1974 - August 30, 1974.

TEMPLE HOUSTON

Western. Background: The post-Civil War Southwest. The cases of Temple Houston, a circuit-riding attorney, and his partner, an ex-gunslinger turned law enforcer, George Taggert, as they attempt to defend unjustly accused people before circuit-riding judges.

CAST

Temple Houston	Jeffrey Hunter
George Taggert	Jack Elam

TEMPLE HOUSTON—60 minutes—NBC—September 19, 1963 - September 17, 1964. 26 episodes.

TEMPTATION

Game. Three female contestants compete. Each player chooses one of three merchandise showcases, the contents of which are unknown, that are displayed on stage. Object: For the player to identify the contents of their selection. A general-knowledge type of question is asked. The player who is first to identify herself by a buzzer signal receives a chance to

answer. If correct, she is permitted to ask the host a question regarding the contents of the showcase. To sway players from the showcase, tempting and expensive merchandise items are offered to them after every several questions. If a player chooses to have the article, she forfeits her chances at the showcase. The game continues until one player correctly identifies the showcase, which is then awarded to her.

Host: Art James.

TEMPTATION—30 minutes—ABC—December 4, 1967 - July 2, 1968.

TENAFLY

See title "NBC Wednesday Mystery Movie," *Tenafly* segment.

TENNESSEE ERNIE FORD

Listed: The television programs of singer Tennessee Ernie Ford.

The Kollege Of Musical Knowledge—Variety-Quiz—30 minutes—NBC 1954. See title: "Kay Kyser's Kollege of Musical Knowledge."

The Tennessee Ernie Ford Show—Musical Variety—30 minutes—NBC—January 3, 1955 - June 28, 1957.

Host: Tennessee Ernie Ford.

Regulars: Molly Bee, Doris Drew, Reginald Gardiner, The Voices of Walter Schumann.

Announcer: Skip Farrell.

Orchestra: Walter Schumann.

The Tennessee Ernie Ford Show—Musical Variety—30 minutes—NBC—1958 - 1960.

Host: Tennessee Ernie Ford.

Announcer: Jack Narz.

Orchestra: Harry Geller.

The Tennessee Ernie Ford Show—Musical Variety—30 minutes—ABC—April 2, 1961 - March 26, 1965.

Host: Tennessee Ernie Ford.

Regulars: Dick Noel, Anita Gordon, Billy Strange.

Announcer: Jim Lange.

Orchestra: Jack Fascinato.

TENNESSEE TUXEDO AND HIS TALES

Animated Cartoon. Background: The Megopolis Zoo. The misadventures of

Tennessee Tuxedo, a penguin, and his friend, Chumley, the walrus, as they struggle to improve living conditions against the objections of Stanley Livingstone, the curator.

Additional characters: Mr. Whoopie, a friend of Tennessee's, a professor who teaches him and Chumley to apply scientific principles in everyday life; and Flunkey, Stanley's assistant.

Additional segments:

Tutor The Turtle. Background: The Great Forest. The story of Tutor, a turtle who becomes whatever he wishes through the magic of Mr. Wizard, the lizard.

The World Of Commander McBragg. A retired naval officer's tall tales concerning his experiences while in the service.

The Hunter. A Beagle detective's relentless pursuit of the cunning criminal, the Fox.

Voices: Don Adams (Tennessee), Jackson Beck, Bradley Bolke, Larry Storch, Ben Stone, Allen Swift, Delo Stokes, Norman Rose, Mort Marshall, Kenny Delmar, George S. Irving.

Music: Not credited.

TENNESSEE TUXEDO AND HIS TALES—30 minutes—Syndicated 1963. 70 episodes.

THE $10,000 PYRAMID

Game. Two competing teams, each composed of one celebrity and one noncelebrity contestant. One team chooses one subject from six categories that are displayed on a board (e.g., "Keep Going"). A question is then read that states its purpose ("Describe things that go from one place to another."). One player has a small monitor before him on which the key words appear, one at a time.

Through one-word clues, he has to relate the meaning to his partner. One point is scored for each correct identification. Rounds are limited to thirty seconds each, and each team competes in three games. The highest scoring team is the winner, and the contestant receives the opportunity to win ten thousand dollars.

The contestant and his partner are escorted to the Winner's Circle. One player sits with his back to a large pyramid that contains six subject categories, each designated by a cash value—fifty to two hundred dollars. The player who is facing the pyramid relates clues to the identity of each of the subjects. If the player guesses all six within one minute, he receives ten thousand dollars. If not, he receives what money is represented by the subjects he correctly identifies.

Host: Dick Clark.

Announcer: Bob Clayton.

Music: Recorded.

Executive Producer: Bob Stewart.

Producer: Anne Marie Schmitt.

Director: Mike Gargiulo.

THE $10,000 PYRAMID—30 minutes—CBS—March 26, 1973 - March 29, 1974. ABC—30 minutes—May 6, 1974 - January 16, 1976. On January 19, 1976, the title changed to "The $20,000 Pyramid," which is played in the same manner and permits players to win $20,000 instead of ten.

TEN WHO DARED

Documentary. A ten-episode series that re-creates the explorations of ten explorers: Christopher Columbus (portrayed by Carlos Ballesteros), Francisco Pizarro (Francisco Cordova), James Cook (Dennis Burgess), Alexander von Humboldt (Matthias Fuchs), Jebediah Smith (Richard Clark), Robert Burke and William Wills (Martin Shaw and John Bell), Henry Morton Stanley (Sean Lynch), Charles Doughty (Paul Chapman), Mary Kingsley (Penelope Lee), and Roald Amundsen (Per Theodor Haugen).

Host-Narrator: Anthony Quinn.

Producer: The B.B.C, Michael Latham.

Sponsor: Mobil Oil.

Note: European title: "The Explorers" (narrated by David Attenborough).

TEN WHO DARED—60 minutes—Syndicated 1977.

TERROR

A thirty-minute anthology series, based on the world of the supernatural, which was first syndicated in 1952.

TERRY AND THE PIRATES

Adventure. Inheriting an abandoned gold mine from his grandfather, Terry Lee, a colonel in the U.S. Air Force, journeys to the Orient, where he begins his search for it. Captured by a sinister band of cutthroats, he is taken to a secret mountain hideaway. Standing at the end of a long line of prisoners, he meets his evil Eurasian captor, Lai Choi San, alias The Dragon Lady, who plans to enslave him.

Resisting, and escaping her bounds, he remains in the Orient, where, while searching for the gold mine, he attempts to battle the evils of The Dragon Lady.

CAST

Terry Lee	John Baer
Lai Choi San, The Dragon Lady	Gloria Saunders
Burma	Sandra Spence
Hot Shot Charlie	Walter Tracy
Chopstick Joe	Jack Reitzen

TERRY AND THE PIRATES—30 minutes—DuMont—1952 - 1953.

TESTIMONY OF TWO MEN

Drama. A six-hour, three-part adaptation of Taylor Caldwell's novel. Background: Hamilton, Pennsylvania. The story, which begins with the end of the Civil War and ends at the turn of the century, focuses on the lives of the Ferrier brothers: Jonathan, a crusading physician, and Harald, who seeks an easy life and ready money. This is the first series to be produced by Operation Prime Time, a project that allows independent stations to pool their resources and purchase excellent quality, first-run programs.

CAST

Jonathan Ferrier	David Birney
Harald Ferrier	David Huffman
Mavis Ferrier, Jonathan's wife	Linda Purl
Dr. Martin Eaton	Steve Forrest
Marjorie Ferrier	Barbara Parkins
Hilda	Barbara Parkins
Adrian Ferrier	William Shatner
Flora Eaton	Margaret O'Brien
Louis Hedler	Tom Bosley

Narrator: Tom Bosley.

Music: Leonard Rosenman, Gerald Fried.

Producer: Jack Laird.

Director: Leo Penn.

TESTIMONY OF TWO MEN—6 hours—Operation Prime Time—1977.

TEXACO STAR THEATRE

See Title: "Milton Berle."

THE TEXAN

Western. Background: Texas during the 1870s. The exploits of Bill Longley, a wandering ex-gunfighter who aides people in distress.

Starring: Rory Calhoun as Bill Longley.

Narrator: Rory Calhoun.

THE TEXAN—30 minutes. CBS—September 29, 1958 - September 1959; ABC—October 3, 1960 - January 6, 1961; September 4, 1961; - May 12, 1962. Syndicated.

THE TEX AND JINX SHOW

See title: "The Swift Show."

TEXAS JOHN SLAUGHTER

See title: "Walt Disney Presents," *Texas John Slaughter* segment.

The Texas Wheelers. From bottom, then left to right: Tony Becker, Mark Hamill, Jack Elam, Gary Busey, Karen Oberdiear.

THE TEXAS WHEELERS

Comedy. Background: Lamont, Texas. Deserting his family after the death of his wife, Zack Wheeler, a lazy good for nothing, returns to his children eight months later, intent on sponging off them. Disliked by his elder offspring, Truckie, twenty-four, a general contractor, and Doobie, seventeen; and loved by the younger, Boo, twelve, and T. J., ten, he struggles to revert to his previous, shiftless life, and solve the problems that ensue from four independent children who can't wait to grow up.

CAST

Zack Wheeler	Jack Elam
Truckie Wheeler	Gary Busey

Doobie Wheeler	Mark Hamill
Boo Wheeler	Karen Oberdiear
T. J. Wheeler	Tony Becker
The Sheriff	Noble Willingham

Music: Mike Post, Pete Carpenter.

THE TEXAS WHEELERS—30 minutes—ABC—September 13, 1974 - October 4, 1974. Returned: ABC—June 26, 1975 - July 24, 1975.

THAT GIRL

Comedy. Background: New York City. Talented, young, and beautiful, and hoping to embark on a career as an actress, Ann Marie leaves her home in Brewster, New York and moves to Manhattan, where she acquires Apartment 4-D at 344 West 78th Street.*

Stories tenderly depict her world of joys and sorrows as she struggles to further a dream, supporting herself by taking various part-time jobs, cope with parents who don't understand her, and share the interests of her boyfriend, Don Hollinger, a reporter for *Newsview* magazine.

CAST

Ann Marie	Marlo Thomas
Don Hollinger	Ted Bessell
Lou Marie, Ann's father, the owner of the Le Parisienne restaurant	Lew Parker
Helen Marie, Ann's mother	Rosemary DeCamp
Jules Benedict, Ann's drama coach	Billy De Wolfe
Judy Bessimer, Ann's neighbor	Bonnie Scott
Leon Bessimer, Judy's husband, a doctor	Dabney Coleman
Jerry Myer, Don's co-worker, Ann's neighbor (early episodes)	Bernie Kopell
Jerry Bauman, Don's co-worker (later episodes)	Bernie Kopell
Margie Myer, Jerry's wife (early episodes)	Arlene Golonka
Ruth Bauman, Jerry's wife (later episodes)	Carolyn Daniels Alice Borden
Marcy, Ann's friend	Reva Rose

*Her address in early episodes. In later episodes; 627 East 54th Street.

That Girl. Ted Bessell and Marlo Thomas.

Pete, Ann's friend	Ruth Buzzi
Gloria, Ann's telephone answering service girl	Bobo Lewis
Jonathan Adams, the publisher of *Newsview*	Forrest Compton James Gregory
Agnes Adams, his wife	Phyllis Hill
Bert Hollinger, Don's father	Frank Faylen
Mildred Hollinger, Bert's wife	Mabel Albertson
Nino, the owner of the Italian restaurant frequented by Ann and Don	Gino Conforti
Mr. Brantano, Ann's landlord	Frank Puglia
Mrs. Brantano, his wife	Renata Vanni

Ann's agents (the Gilliam & Norris Theatrical Agency):

Seymour Schwimmer	Don Penny
Harvey Peck	Ronnie Schell
Sandy Stone	Morty Gunty
George Lester	George Carlin

Music: Walter Scharf; Earle Hagen; Warren Barker; Harry Geller.

Executive Producer-Creator: Bill Persky and Sam Denoff.

Producer: Bernie Orenstein, Saul Turteltaub, Jerry Davis.

Director: Jay Sandrich, Homer Powell, James Sheldon, Danny Arnold, Alan Rafkin, Bob Sweeney, Sidney Miller, David MacDearmon, Jeff Hayden, Ted Bessell, John Rich, Roger Dochaway, Bill Persky, Saul Turteltaub, Russ Mayberry, Hal Cooper, Harry Falk, John Erman, James Frawley, Jerry Davis.

THAT GIRL—30 minutes—ABC—September 8, 1966 - September 10, 1971. 136 episodes. Syndicated.

THAT GOOD OLD NASHVILLE MUSIC

A thirty-minute Country and Western variety series, hosted by Dave Dudley, and first syndicated in 1975.

THAT SHOW

Talk-Variety.

Hostess: Joan Rivers.

Announcer: Jim Perry.

Music: Recorded.

THAT SHOW—30 minutes—Syndicated 1968. 260 tapes. Also known as "That Show Starring Joan Rivers."

THAT REMINDS ME

Game. Through a series of question-and-answer probe rounds, a celebrity panel has to uncover the identity of celebrity guests who appear in elaborate disguises.

Hostess: Arlene Francis.

Panelists: Nina Foch, Roger Price, Robert Coates.

THAT REMINDS ME—30 minutes—NBC 1952.

THAT'S HOLLYWOOD!

Documentary. Various aspects of films produced by 20th Century-Fox—from leading ladies, to westerns, to disaster epics—are showcased with on camera performances and behind-the-scenes preparations.

Narrator: Tom Bosley.

Music: Ruby Raksin.

Executive Producer: Jack Haley, Jr.

Producer: Lawrence Einhorn, Phillip Savenick.

Associate Producer: Eytan Keller, Draper Lewis.

Executive In Charge Of Production: David Lawrence.

THAT'S HOLLYWOOD!—30 minutes—Syndicated 1977.

THAT'S LIFE

Musical Comedy. Background: New York. Combining the format of a serial, and the Broadway paced blend of romance, music, comedy, song, and dance, the series depicts the meeting and courtship of Robert Dickson, a junior executive with a chalk company, and Gloria Quigley, and their later marriage, struggle as newlyweds, and attempts to adjust to parenthood when presented with a son, Robert Dickson, Jr.

CAST
Robert Dickson — Robert Morse
Gloria Quigley
 (Dickson) — E. J. (Edra Jeanne) Peaker
Mr. Quigley, Gloria's
 father — Shelly Berman
Mrs. Quigley, Gloria's
 mother — Kay Medford

Choreography: Tony Mordente; The Tony Mordente Dancers.

Orchestra: Elliott Lawrence.

THAT'S LIFE—60 minutes—ABC—September 24, 1968 - May 19, 1969. 26 tapes.

THAT'S MY BOY

Comedy. Background: Rossmore, Ohio, the residence of the Jackson family: "Jarrin" Jack, businessman, ex-college athlete; his wife, Alice, a former Olympic swimming champion; and their son, Jack Junior, a nearsighted bookworm who is prone to hayfever and sinus attacks.

Stories depict the elder's attempts to relive his college youth through Junior by instilling him with the sports spirit and broadening his character; and Junior's attempts to pursue his own goals as he enters his freshman year at Rossmore College. Based on the motion picture.

CAST
Jack Jackson, Sr. — Eddie Mayehoff
Alice Jackson — Rochelle Hudson
Jack Jackson, Jr. — Gil Stratton, Jr.
Henrietta Patterson,
 Jack's employer's
 wife — Mabel Albertson

Sam Baker, their
 neighbor — Larry Blake

Announcer: Bill Baldwin.

Producer: Cy Howard.

Sponsor: The Chrysler Corporation, Plymouth Division.

THAT'S MY BOY—30 minutes—CBS—April 10, 1954 - January 1, 1955.

Rebroadcasts: CBS—30 minutes—June 1959 - September 1959.

THAT'S MY MAMA

Comedy. Background: Oscar's Barber Shop in Washington, D.C. Events in the lives of the Curtis family as seen through the eyes of Clifton Curtis, the eldest child, a twenty-five-year-old bachelor who, while attempting to operate his late father's business and live his own life, constantly finds his life being run by his meddling, well-meaning mother, Eloise.

CAST
Clifton Curtis — Clifton Davis
Eloise "Mama"
 Curtis — Theresa Merritt
Tracy Taylor,
 her married
 daughter — Lynne Moody
  — Joan Pringle
Leonard Taylor, Tracy's
 husband — Illunga Adell
Earl Chambers,
 their friend, the
 postman — Ed Bernard
  — Theodore Wilson
Wildcat, a
 friend of the
 family — Jester Hairston
Junior,
 a friend of
 Clifton's — Ted Lange
Josh, a
 friend of the
 family — DeForest Covan

Music: Jack Eskew.

Additional Music: Lamont Dozier.

Producer: David Pollock.

Director: Herbert Kenwith, Mort Lachman, Arnold Margolin.

Address of Oscar's Barber Shop: 14th and Grant Street.

THAT'S MY MAMA—30 minutes—ABC—September 4, 1974 - December 24, 1975.

THAT WAS THE WEEK THAT WAS

Satire. Utilizing the format of a news program, sketches, blackouts, and commentary are used to satirize the news events of the week preceding the broadcast. Unlike its sophisticated parent show, the British "That Was the Week That Was," the American version suffers from an uneven flow of material and a constant degrading of major political parties.

American Version:

Host: Elliott Reid.

TW3 Girl: Nancy Ames (introducing each broadcast with a musical commentary of the preceding week's events).

CAST
Henry Morgan, Phyllis Newman, Pat Englund, David Frost, Doro Merande, Buck Henry, Burr Tillstrom, Bob Dishy.

THAT WAS THE WEEK THAT WAS—30 minutes—NBC—September 29, 1964 - May 4, 1965. Also known as "TW3."

British Version:

Host: David Frost.

TW3 Girl: Millicent Martin.

CAST
Lance Percival, Roy Kinnear, William Rushton, Kenneth Cope, David Kernan, Ned Sheriin.

Orchestra: Dave Lee.

THAT WAS THE WEEK THAT WAS—30 minutes—B.B.C. TV 1963.

THAT WONDERFUL GUY

Comedy. Background: New York City. The romantic and business misadventures of Harold, a would-be actor who is employed by a sophisticated drama critic.

CAST
Harold — Jack Lemmon
The drama critic — Neil Hamilton
Harold's girlfriend — Cynthia Stone

Orchestra: Bernard Green.

Producer: Charles Irving.

Director: Babette Henry.

THAT WONDERFUL GUY—30 minutes—ABC 1950.

THEATRE '58

Anthology. Rebroadcasts of dramas that were originally aired via other filmed anthology programs.

Included:

Always The Best Man. The story of a man who falls in love with his friend's ex-fiancee.

CAST
Angie Dickinson, Don Taylor, Adam Kennedy, Greta Tyssen.

The House That Jackson Built. Fed up with manhunting, a career girl purchases a house and decides to settle down to a life as a spinster. The story relates the changes that occur in her life when she falls in love with the designer of the house.

CAST

Diana Lynn, Arthur Franz, Jean Carson.

A Mule For Santa Fe. Because he is short one mule, a man finds that he cannot join a wagon train destined for Santa Fe. The story relates his desperate attempts to secure the money he needs to buy one.

CAST

Will Rogers, Jr., Stephen Woolton.

THEATRE '58–30 minutes–CBS– June 18, 1958 - September 1958.

THEATRE '59

Anthology. Rebroadcasts of dramas that were originally aired via other filmed anthology programs.

Included:

A Very Fine Deal. The problems that arise when a New York City transit walker discovers a diamond mine beneath Central Park.
Starring: Bert Lahr.

Markheim. A lawyer's defense of a man who is accused of committing murder.
Starring: Charles Drake.

Too Early Spring. The story of two young lovers confused by the complications of the adult world.
Starring: Burt Brinckerhoff, Jan Norris.

The Wonderful Ice Cream Suit. Pooling their resources, six men purchase a white suit. The story depicts the changes in their lives as each takes a turn wearing it.
Starring: Mike Kellin, Lou Nova.

Alone. The fear that grips a woman who lives alone in a house in a neighborhood where police are searching for an escaped murderer.
Starring: Laraine Day, Joseph Wiseman.

THEATRE '59–30 minutes–Syndicated 1959.

THE THEATRE HOUR

Anthology. Dramatic presentations.

THE THEATRE HOUR–60 minutes –CBS 1949.

THEATRE '60

Anthology. Varying dramatic and musical presentations that feature guest hosts and performers.

Music: The CBS Symphonic Orchestra, conducted by Alfredo Antonini.

Included:

The Treasure. The story of an eccentric French nobleman who prefers his friend's treasured wine celler to that of his beautiful wife.

CAST

Charles Drake, Francios Christophe.

Cotch's Catch. The story of a young American actor who, in order to get a good part in an English film, agrees to a marriage of convenience.

CAST

Charles Drake, Dora Bryan.

An Early Winter. The trials and tribulations of a young bride and groom.

CAST

Kim Hunter, Pat Hingle.

THEATRE '60–60 minutes–CBS 1960.

THEATRE TIME

Anthology. Retitled episodes of "Fireside Theatre" and "The General Electric Theatre."
Hostess: Anita Louise.

Included:

Father Happe. The story of a spinster who finds a new lease on life when a priest encourages her to take up painting.

CAST

Mercedes McCambridge, Rommey Brent.

Louise. The story of a woman who struggles to aid European children following World War II.

CAST

Viveca Lindfors, Herbert Marshall, Norma Varden.

A Shadow Believes. The story of a psychiatrist who seeks to discover whether a patient of his, an amnesiac, is the former fiance' of the woman he loves.

CAST

Marjorie Lord, Stephen McNally, Mary Sinclair.

THEATRE TIME–30 minutes–ABC– July 25, 1957 - September 26, 1957.

T.H.E. CAT

Adventure. Background: A contemporary metropolis. The cases of Thomas Hewitt Edward (T.H.E.) Cat, aerialist turned cat burglar turned professional bodyguard.

CAST

Thomas Hewitt Edward Cat	Robert Loggia
Pepe, the owner of the Casa de Gate cafe	Robert Carricart
William McAllister, the police captain	R.G. Armstrong
Maria, Cat's romantic interest	Norma Bengell

T.H.E. CAT–30 minutes–NBC–September 16, 1966 - September 8, 1967. 26 episodes. Syndicated.

THEN CAME BRONSON

Adventure. Disillusioned after his friend commits suicide, Jim Bronson, a newspaper reporter, resigns, and, inheriting his friend's motorcycle, begins his travels across the United States to discover the meaning of life. Stories depict his involvement with the people he meets and the effect in their lives as the result of his intervention.
Starring: Michael Parks as Jim Bronson.
Music: George Duning.

THEN CAME BRONSON–60 minutes–NBC–September 17, 1969 - September 9, 1970. 26 episodes. Syndicated.

THERE'S ONE IN EVERY FAMILY

Variety. The series spotlights members of a family who are outstandingly different. Several such people appear on each telecast to relate their stories (why they are different) to the studio audience. The audience then votes on each subject by applauding, which is registered on a meter. The person whose score registers the highest is judged the winner and receives the opportunity to win prizes for his family by competing in a question-and-answer session.
Host: John Reed King.

THERE'S ONE IN EVERY FAMILY–30 minutes–CBS–September 29, 1952 - June 18, 1953.

THESE ARE MY CHILDREN

Serial. The struggles of a mother as

she attempts to raise her fatherless children.

CAST

The Mother	Alma Platto

Her children: Jane Brooksmith, George Kluge, Martha McCain, Joan Alt, Eloise Kunner.

THESE ARE MY CHILDREN—15 minutes—NBC 1949.

These Are the Days. Left to right: Martha, Cathy, Jeff (center), Ben, and Danny. © *Hanna-Barbera Productions.*

THESE ARE THE DAYS

Animated Cartoon. Background: The town of Elmsville during the early 1900s. Life in America at the turn of the century as seen through the experiences of the Day family: Martha, a widow; her children, Ben, Cathy, and Danny; and their grandfather, Jeff Day, the owner of the Day General Store.

Characters' Voices

Martha Day	June Lockhart
Cathy Day	Pamelyn Ferdin
Danny Day	Jackie Haley
Ben Day	Andrew Parks
Jeff Day	Henry Jones
Homer, Jeff's friend	Frank Cady

Music: Hoyt Curtin.

Executive Producer: William Hanna, Joseph Barbera.

Director: Charles A. Nichols.

THESE ARE THE DAYS—30 minutes—ABC—September 7, 1974 - September 5, 1976.

THEY STAND ACCUSED

Courtroom Drama. Dramatizations based on actual court records.

Judge: Charles Johnson.

Announcer: Harry Creighton.

Lawyers and Defenders: Guest actors.

Jurists: The studio audience.

Producer: William Wines, Richard Albrecht.

Director: Sheldon Cooper.

Sponsor: Crawford Clothes.

THEY STAND ACCUSED—60 minutes—DuMont 1948.

THEY WENT THAT'A WAY

Documentary. The role of the western film on American cultural history is explained and illustrated through the use of film clips.

Hosts: Ruane Hull, Jon Tuska.

THEY WENT THAT'A WAY—30 minutes—PBS—February 16, 1971 - April 20, 1971.

THICKER THAN WATER

Comedy. Aging, and critically ill for the past ten years, Jonas Paine, the founder of Paine's Pure Pickles, stipulates that for his children (Nellie, a forty-year-old spinster, and Ernie, a thirty-four-year-old penniless playboy, who dislike each other) to receive an inheritance, they must live together in the family residence for a period of five years and operate the family pickle factory.

Stories depict: the impatient wait of two feuding siblings as they struggle to live together, operate the business, and care for a father who just won't kick the bucket. Based on the British TV series, "Nearest and Dearest."

CAST

Nellie Paine	Julie Harris
Ernie Paine	Richard Long
Jonas Paine	Malcolm Atterbury
Lily Paine, a cousin	Jessica Myerson
Walter Paine, Lily's husband	Lou Fant
Bert Taylor, the factory foreman	Pat Cranshaw
Lyle Woodstock, Jonas's lawyer	Jim Connell
Agnes Dorsell, a factory employee	Dolores Albin

Music: Michael Melvoin.

THICKER THAN WATER—30 minutes—ABC—June 13, 1973 - August 8, 1973. 13 episodes.

THINK FAST

Game. Object: For celebrity panelists to reach a throne by out-talking each other on topics that are relayed by the host (or hostess). Winners are the wordiest talkers.

Host (1949): Mason Gross.

Hostess (1950): Gypsy Rose Lee.

Panelists: Lois Wilson, Leon Janney, Eloise McElhone, Vivian della Chiesa, David Broekman.

Orchestra: David Broekman.

THINK FAST—30 minutes—ABC—March 26, 1949 - October 8, 1950.

THE THIN MAN

Mystery. Background: Greenwich Village in New York City, the residence of the Charleses: Nick, a former private detective turned mystery editor for a publishing house; and his beautiful, trouble-prone wife, Nora. Stories depict their investigations when Nora accidentally stumbles upon and involves Nick in crimes. Based on the characters created by Dashiell Hammett.

CAST

Nick Charles	Peter Lawford
Nora Charles	Phyllis Kirk
Beatrice Dean, alias Blondie Collins, a beautiful con-artist and friend of Nick's who arouses Nora's jealous streak	Nita Talbot
Lt. Jack Evans, N.Y.P.D.	Jack Albertson
Mrs. Durkem, the Charles's neighbor	Blanche Sweet

The Charles dog: Asta.

Music: Pete Rugolo.

THE THIN MAN—30 minutes—NBC—September 20, 1957 - June 26, 1959. 72 episodes. Syndicated.

THE THIRD MAN

Mystery. Background: London, England. The exploits of Harry Lime, business tycoon, troubleshooter, and private detective, as he aides people in distress.

CAST

Harry Lime	Michael Rennie
Bradford Webster, his assistant	Jonathan Harris

The Thin Man. Peter Lawford and Phyllis Kirk (holding Asta).

THE THIRD MAN—30 minutes—Syndicated 1960. 77 episodes.

THIS COULD BE YOU

Game. Three married couples compete. Couples are first interviewed, then in return for prizes, each reenacts a personal situation in their lives that was brought about as the result of a popular song.

Host: Bill Gwinn.

THIS COULD BE YOU—30 minutes —ABC 1951.

THIS IS ALICE

Comedy. The misadventures of nine-year-old Alice Holliday.

CAST
Alice Holliday	Patty Ann Gerrity
Mr. Holliday, her father	Tommy Farrell
Mrs. Holliday, her mother	Phyllis Coates
Also	Stephen Woolton

THIS IS ALICE—30 minutes—Syndicated 1958. 39 episodes.

THIS IS CHARLES LAUGHTON

Readings. Selections from the Bible and classical and modern stories are read.

Host: Charles Laughton, "The man of many moods."

THIS IS CHARLES LAUGHTON—60 minutes—Syndicated 1952.

THIS IS GALEN DRAKE

Variety. Music, songs, and celebrity interviews.

Host: Galen Drake.

Regulars: Rita Ellis, Stuart Foster.

THIS IS GALEN DRAKE—30 minutes—ABC—January 12, 1957 - May 11, 1957.

THIS IS MUSIC

Musical Variety.

Hostess: Alexandra Gray.

Host: Colin Male.

Regulars: Jacqueline James, Bruce Foote, Jackie Van, Bill Snarz.

Orchestra: Robert Trendler.

THIS IS MUSIC—30 minutes—ABC— June 6, 1958 - May 21, 1959.

THIS IS SHOW BUSINESS

Variety. Guest celebrities entertain then air their problems to a panel, who in turn offer advice.

Host: Clifton Fadiman.

Panelists: Sam Levenson, George S. Kaufman, Abe Burrows.

Regulars: Toni Arden, Jack E. Leonard, Lou Willis, Jr., Russell Arms, Dorothy Collins.

Orchestra: Ray Bloch, Hank Sylvern.

Producer: Irving Mansfield.

Director: Alexander Leftwich, Paul Byron.

Sponsor: American Tobacco Company.

THIS IS SHOW BUSINESS—30 minutes—CBS—July 15, 1949 - September 11, 1956. Also known as "This Is Broadway."

THIS IS TOM JONES

Musical Variety.

Host: Tom Jones.

Regulars: Big Jim Sullivan, The Norman Maen Dancers, The Mike Sammes Singers.

Orchestra: Jack Parnell; Johnnie Spence.

THIS IS TOM JONES—60 minutes— ABC—February 7, 1969 - January 1971. 27 tapes. Syndicated.

THIS IS YOUR LIFE

Variety-Interview. A semidocumentary-style presentation wherein the lives of show-business personalities, who appear as guests, are relived through the testimonies of friends and family.

Appearing: Marilyn Monroe, Jayne Mansfield, Stan Laurel, Jack Benny, Hugh O'Brian, Andy Griffith, Barbara Eden, Carol Channing, Ruth Gordon, Irene Ryan, Jackie Cooper, Pearl Bailey, Shirley Jones, Florence Henderson, Pat Boone, Nanette Fabray, Bette Davis, Johnny Cash, Ann-Margret, Bob Hope, Cliff Robertson, Totie Fields.

Versions:

This Is Your Life—30 minutes—NBC —October 2, 1952 - September 10, 1961.

Host: Ralph Edwards.

Announcer: Bob Warren.

Orchestra: Von Dexter.

This Is Your Life—30 minutes—Syndicated 1971.

Host: Ralph Edwards.

Announcer: Bob Warren.

Orchestra: Nelson Riddle.

THIS IS YOUR MUSIC

Musical Variety.

CAST

Byron Palmer, Joan Weldon, David Lechine, Jana Ecklund, Rita Walsh, Betty Wand, Suzie Baree, Mary Margaret Gelden, The Pied Pipers.

Choreography: David Lechine.

Orchestra: Nelson Riddle.

THIS IS YOUR MUSIC—30 minutes —Syndicated 1955.

THIS MAN DAWSON

Crime Drama. Background: A large unidentified urban community. The methods incorporated in the battle against crime as seen through the investigations of Colonel Frank Dawson, the police chief.

Starring: Keith Andes as Colonel Frank Dawson.

THIS MAN DAWSON—30 minutes— Syndicated 1959. 39 episodes.

THOSE ENDURING YOUNG CHARMS

Comedy. The trials and tribulations of the Charms, an American family.

CAST

The father	Maurice Copeland
His wife	Betty Arnold
Their daughter	Pat Matthews
Their son	Gerald Garvey
The uncle	Clarence Hartzell
The delivery boy	Norm Gottschalk

Also: Everett Clark, Helen Barrett.

THOSE ENDURING YOUNG CHARMS—30 minutes—NBC—1951 - 1952.

THOSE TWO

Variety. Music, songs, dances, and vaudeville routines.

Host: Pinky Lee.

Co-hostesses: Martha Stuart, Vivian Blaine.

Orchestra: Harry Lubin.

Producer: Olive Barbour, Walter Craig.

Director: William Slate.

Sponsor: Procter and Gamble.

THOSE TWO—15 minutes—NBC— November 20, 1951 - April 24, 1953.

Those Whiting Girls. Margaret (top) and Barbara Whiting.

THOSE WHITING GIRLS

Comedy. Background: Hollywood, California. The romantic misadventures of the Whiting sisters: Barbara, an actress; and Margaret, a songstress.

CAST

Barbara Whiting	Herself
Margaret Whiting	Herself
Mrs. Whiting, their mother	Mabel Albertson
Artie, Margaret's accompanist	Jerry Paris
Daisy Dunbar, Barbara's friend	Beverly Long

Orchestra: Eliot Daniel.

THOSE WHITING GIRLS—30 minutes—CBS—July 4, 1955 - September 26, 1955.

THREE FOR THE MONEY

Game. Two three-member teams, each composed of one celebrity captain and two noncelebrity contestants, compete for five days, Monday through Friday. Three categories, each containing three questions, are revealed. One team, as determined by the flip of a coin, receives a chance at play. The captain either selects himself or his teammates, to compete against the opposing team. If he chooses to match one player from his team against one opponent, the question is worth $100; should he choose to play one against two, the question value is $200; if one player is pitted against three, the question is worth $300 for the team at play. A question, chosen from one of the categories, is then read by the host and clues to its answer appear on an electronic board. The player who is first to sound a buzzer signal stops the clues from progressing and receives a chance to answer. If the question is correctly answered by the member of the team at play, the money is scored accordingly; however, should the opposing team respond first, or supply a correct answer for an incorrect response on the part of the team at play, they score $100. The remaining categories are played in the same manner. The game itself continues in this same manner with a final two round contest played on the Friday program. The team whose accumulative five day score is the highest is the winner (the money is divided between the two contestants).

Host: Dick Enberg.

Announcer: Jack Clark.

Model: Jane Nelson.

Executive Producer: Stefan Hatos, Monty Hall.

Producer: Stu Billett.

Director: Hank Behar.

THREE FOR THE MONEY—25 minutes—NBC—September 29, 1975 - November 28, 1975.

THREE FOR THE ROAD

Drama. The assignments of photographer Pete Karras, a widower who roams the country in his motor home, the *Zebec,* with his two sons John and Endy.

CAST

Pete Karras	Alex Rocco
John Karras	Vincent Van Patten
Endy Karras	Leif Garrett

Music: James Di Pasquale, David Shire.

THREE FOR THE ROAD—60 minutes—CBS—September 14, 1975 - November 30, 1975.

THREE GIRLS

A live situation comedy series that features the misadventures of three beautiful career girls (played by Janis Carter, Barbara Gayelord, and Jeannie Johnson). Broadcast on ABC in 1955.

3 GIRLS 3

Variety. A musical comedy series that spotlights the talents of three unknown "but terribly talented girls doing a variety series about three unknown but terribly talented girls."

Starring: Mimi Kennedy, Ellen Foley, Debbie Allen.

Regulars: Oliver Clark, Richard Byrd.

Orchestra: Marvin Laird.

Executive Producer: Gary Smith, Dwight Hemion.

Producer: Kenny Solms, Gail Parent.

Director: Tony Mordente, Tim Kiley.

Choreography: Alan Johnson.

3 GIRLS 3–60 minutes–June 15, 1977 - June 29, 1977. One episode was previously seen on March 30, 1977. 3 tapes.

THE THREE MUSKETEERS

Adventure. Background: Paris during the 1620s. The exploits of the Three Musketeers, D'Artagnan, Porthos, and Aromas, as they struggle to protect the thrown of France from the machinations of the evil Prime Minister Richelieu. Based on the story by Alexandre Dumas.

CAST

D'Artagnan	Jeffrey Stone
Porthos	Peter Trent
Aromas	Paul Campbell
Jacqueline	Marina Berti
The Count of Brisemont	Sebastian Cabot
Sasquinet	Alan Furlan
Captain De Treville	George Conneaur

THE THREE MUSKETEERS–30 minutes–Syndicated 1956. 26 episodes.

THREE ON A MATCH

Game. Three competing contestants. Three topic categories are revealed. Players each press a button and lock in the number of questions they wish to answer (one to four). Their choices are revealed, and each bet scores ten dollars, which becomes the money that is available for that round. If each player has chosen a different amount of questions, the highest bidder chooses one of the categories. He is then asked true-and-false type of questions. If he correctly answers his bet amount of questions, he wins the money and a new round begins. If he fails to answer correctly, the second highest player chooses one of the remaining categories. Should he fail, the lowest bidder receives a chance to win the money. Exception: Should all players bid the same amount, they cancel each other out and rebid; if two bid the same amount, they cancel each other out and the remaining player automatically receives a chance to win the money.

When a player scores at least one hundred and fifty dollars, he is permitted to play "Three On a Match." A large game board is displayed. The board is composed of twelve squares that are divided into three horizontal rows of four vertical squares each. Each horizontal row is marked by a color: red, green, yellow, or blue; the vertical rows represent the cash values of each square: twenty, thirty, or forty dollars. The player purchases a square by naming a color and an amount. A merchandise prize or a cash value is revealed. If the player is able to match the first square with two identical squares, he receives the prize that is represented, becomes the champion, and faces two new challengers. If he is unsuccessful, the game continues and follows the previous format until one player matches three squares (the prizes change position with each player's gamble).

Host: Bill Cullen.

Announcers: Roger Tuttle; Don Pardo.

Music: Bob Cobert.

THREE ON A MATCH–30 minutes–NBC–August 2, 1971 - June 28, 1974.

THREE PASSPORTS TO ADVENTURE

Travel. Films depicting the global travels of the Hinker Family.

Hosts-Narrators: Hal Halla, and David Hinker.

THREE PASSPORTS TO ADVENTURE–30 minutes–Syndicated 1970. 39 tapes.

THREE STEPS TO HEAVEN

Serial. Background: New York City. The dramatic story of Poco Thurman, a young model frought with romantic heartaches.

CAST

Poco Thurman	Phyllis Hill
	Kathleen McGuire
Bill Morgan	Mark Roberts
	Walter Brooks
Mike	Joe Brown, Jr.
Jennifer	Lori March
Alice	Laurie Vendig
Angela	Ginger McManus
Mrs. Doane	Doris Rich
Barry Thurmond	Roger Sullivan
Laura	Inge Adams
Uncle Frank	Frank Twedell
Pigeon Malloy	Eata Linden
Walter Jones	Earl George
Charlotte Doane	Mona Burns
Jason Cleve	Lauren Gilbert
Nan	Beth Douglas
Vince Bannister	John Marley
Alice	Laurie Ann Vendig
Alan Anderson	Dort Clark

Also: Diana Douglas, Mercer McCloud, Irving Taylor.

Producer: Caroline Burke.

Creator: Irving Vendig.

Sponsor: Miles Laboratories.

THREE STEPS TO HEAVEN–15 minutes–NBC–July 31, 1953 - December 31, 1954.

The Three Stooges. Bottom to top: Larry Fine, Moe Howard, Curly Howard. © *Screen Gems.*

THE THREE STOOGES

Comedy. The misadventures of Moe Howard, Larry Fine, and Curly Howard, three misfits plagued by life's abounding obstacles.

CAST

Moe Howard	Himself
Larry Fine	Himself
Curly Howard	Himself
Shemp Howard (replaced Curly)	Himself
Joe De Rita (replaced Shemp)	Himself

Also: Joe Besser, who replaced Joe DeRita during the 1950s.

Producer-Director: Jules White.

THE THREE STOOGES—20 minutes (approximately)—Syndicated 1959. 190 episodes.

THREE'S COMPANY

Musical Variety.

Host: Cy Walters.

Regulars: Stan Freeman, Judy Lynn.

THREE'S COMPANY—30 minutes—CBS 1950.

THREE'S COMPANY

Comedy. Background: Los Angeles, California. Finding that the high cost of apartment rent is preventing them from living comfortably, working girls Janet Wood and Chrissy Snow resolve their problem by taking in a male roommate—Jack Tripper, a culinary student whom they find sleeping in their bathtub after a wild party. The series focuses on the misadventures that occur in such a situation as Janet, Chrissy, and Jack struggle to live their own lives while attempting to maintain a strictly platonic relationship.

CAST

Janet Wood, runs a flower shop	Joyce DeWitt
Chrissy Snow, a typist	Suzanne Somers
Jack Tripper	John Ritter
Stanley Roper, the landlord	Norman Fell
Helen Roper, his wife	Audra Lindley

Music: Joe Raposo.

Producer: Don Nicholl, Bernie West, Michael Ross.

Director: Bill Hobin.

Three's Company. Left to right: Joyce DeWitt, Suzanne Somers, John Ritter. *Courtesy of the Call-Chronicle Newspapers, Allentown, Pa.*

THREE'S COMPANY—30 minutes—ABC—March 15, 1977 - April 21, 1977. Returned: ABC—Premiered: August 11, 1977.

British Version, upon which "Three's Company" is based:

Man About The House. Background: London, England. The story of two working girls, Jo and Chrissy, and their ensuing misadventures when they decide to share a flat with Robin Tripp, a male catering student, in an attempt to resolve the housing problem.

CAST

Jo	Sally Thomsett
Chrissy	Paula Wilcox
Robin Tripp	Richard O'Sullivan
George Roper, the landlord	Brian Murphy
Mrs. Roper, his wife	Yotta Joyce

Producer-Director: Peter Jones.

THRILL HUNTERS

Adventure. Films depicting the perilous occupations of people (e.g., mountain climbers, racers, test pilots).

Host-Narrator: Bill Burrud.

THRILL HUNTERS—30 minutes—Syndicated 1966.

THRILL SEEKERS

Adventure. Films examining the perilous occupations of people.

Host-Narrator: Chuck Connors.

Music: David Davis.

THRILL SEEKERS—30 minutes—Syndicated 1973.

THRILLER

Anthology. Mystery and suspense presentations. Twisted tales of people who are suddenly trapped in unexpected situations that are fostered through emotion, greed, or the threat of crime.

Host-Occasional Performer: Boris Karloff.

Music: Pete Rugolo; Jerry Goldsmith.

Musical Supervision: Stanley Wilson.

Executive Producer: Hubbell Robinson.

Producer: Fletcher Markle, William Frye.

Director: Ida Lupino, Herschel Daugherty, John Brahm, Arthur Hiller.

Included:

Mr. George. The story of a young heiress who is protected from harm by a friendly spirit (Mr. George).

CAST

Priscilla: Gina Gillespie; Edna: Virginia Gregg; Laura: Joan Tompkins; Jarrad: Howard Freeman.

Parasite Mansion. Knocked unconscious during a minor automobile accident, a woman is taken prisoner by the owners of a decrepit mansion. Attempting to escape, she learns of a spirit that holds the family in a grip of fear. The story revolves around her attempts to expose it.

CAST

Marcia: Pippa Scott; Harrod: James Griffith; Lollie: Beverly Washburn; Granny (the spirit): Jeannette Nolan.

The Finger Of Fate. A detective's efforts to apprehend a psychopathic child killer.

CAST

Nehemiah Persoff, Robert Middleton, Kevin Hagen.

The Fatal Impulse. The frantic police search for a woman who, unbeknown to her, carries a live and ticking bomb in her pocketbook.

CAST

Rome: Robert Lansing; Jane: Whitney Blake; Mary: Mary Tyler Moore; Secretary: Cynthia Pepper; Elser: Elisha Cook.

THRILLER—60 minutes—NBC—September 10, 1960 - July 9, 1962. 67 episodes. Syndicated.

THRILLER

Anthology. Mystery and suspense presentations. Out-of-the-ordinary stories about chilling and eerie events that could happen to anyone. An ATV/I.T.C. production (British).

Producer: John Sichel.

Director: Peter Jeffries, John Sichel, Bill Hayes, John Cooper, Robert Tronson, Shaun O'Riordan, Alan Gibson.

Included:

Possession. Turning to the occult, a

Thriller. Polly Bergen and Paul Burke in "An Echo of Theresa." *Courtesy of Independent Television Corp.; an ATV Company.*

terrified young woman attempts to combat a sinister spirit that has possessed her husband.

CAST

John Carson, Joanna Dunham, Hilary Hardiman.

An Echo Of Theresa. Honeymooning in London, an American couple is suddenly plunged into a nightmare world when Brad, the husband, witnesses an event that triggers memories hidden deeply in the recesses of his mind. Imagining himself as someone else, and married to a woman named Theresa, he believes his wife, Suzy, is an enemy and plots to kill her. The story depicts the conflict that ensues when the past and present merge into one.

CAST

Brad Hunter: Paul Burke; Suzy Hunter: Polly Bergen; Earp: Dinsdale Landen; Trasker: William Job.

File It Under Fear. An amateur detective attempts to solve the baffling murders of several young women.

CAST

Liz: Maureen Lipman; George: Richard O'Callaghan; Superintendent: James Grout.

Lady Killer. A husband's careful planning and attempts to murder his wife.

CAST

Barbara Feldon, Robert Powell, Linda Thorson, T. P. McKenna, Mary Wimbush, Jessie Evans.

THRILLER—66/68 minutes (actual running time, less commercials)—Syndicated 1973. Telecast in the United States via "ABC Wide World of Entertainment."

THROUGH THE CRYSTAL BALL

A variety series, hosted by Anita Alvarez, and first broadcast by CBS in 1949.

THROUGH WENDY'S WINDOW

Interview.

Hostess: Wendy Barrie.

THROUGH WENDY'S WINDOW—15 minutes—NBC—December 22, 1949 - February 16, 1950.

THUNDER

Adventure. The story of a semiwild black stallion named Thunder and the adventures of the young girl, Cindy Prescott, who befriends him.

CAST

Bill Prescott, Cindy's
   father   Clint Ritchie
Ann Prescott, Cindy's
   mother   Melissa Converse
Cindy Prescott   Melora Hardin
Willie Williams, Cindy's
   friend   Justin Randi

Also: Cupcake the mule.
Music: Ray Ellis.

Producer-Creator: Irving Cummings, Charles Marion.

Director: Sigmund Neufeld, Jr., William Beaudine, Jr.

THUNDER—30 minutes—NBC—Premiered: September 10, 1977.

THUNDERBIRDS

Marionette Adventure. Background: A remote island in the Pacific, the headquarters of International Rescue (I.R.), a global organization of highly complex machinery, the Thunderbirds, and skillfully trained men who are dedicated to rescuing people trapped in unusual predicaments. Stories depict I.R.'s rescue operations. Filmed in Supermarionation. An I.T.C. presentation.

Characters' Voices

Jeff Tracy, the head
   of I.R.   Peter Dyneley
Scott Tracy,
   his son,
   the pilot of
   Thunderbird I   Shane Rimmer
Virgil Tracy,
   his son,
   the pilot of
   Thunderbird II   David Holliday
Alan Tracy,
   his son,
   the pilot of
   Thunderbird III   Matt Zimmerman
Gordon Tracy,
   his son,
   the pilot of Aquanaut
   Thunderbird IV   David Graham
John Tracy,
   his son,
   the pilot of
   Space Monitor
   Thunderbird V   Ray Barrett
Lady Penelope Creighton-
   Ward, the London
   agent   Sylvia Anderson
Professor Brains, an I.R.
   scientist .   David Graham
Kyrano, Jeff's
   servant   David Graham
Tin Tin Kyrano,
   his daughter   Christine Finn
The Hood,
   a diabolical fiend
   bent on acquiring
   I.R.'s secrets   Ray Barrett
Parker, Lady Penelope's
   chauffeur   David Graham

Music: Barry Gray.

THUNDERBIRDS—60 and 30 minute versions—Syndicated 1968. Episodes are available complete in one hour, or in two thirty minute cliff-hanger installments.

Thunderbirds. A Supermarionation series. The figures are electronic marionettes, members of International Rescue.

TIC TAC DOUGH

Game. Two competing contestants, Player X and Player O; basis: the game of Tic Tac Toe. A general-knowledge type of question is read. The player who first identifies himself through a buzzer signal receives a chance to answer. If correct, he is permitted to choose one square on a Tic Tac Toe board that is displayed on stage. The game continues until one player wins by acquiring three squares in a row, up and down, or diagonally. Cash prizes are awarded.

Hosts: Jay Jackson; Jack Barry.

Organist: Paul Taubman.

Producer: Stan Greene, Hudson Faussett, Robert Noah, Howard Flesher.

TIC TAC DOUGH—30 minutes—NBC —July 30, 1956 - October 30, 1959.

TIGHTROPE

Crime Drama. The investigations of Nick Stone, undercover police agent, as he attempts to infiltrate the underworld and expose the ranks of organized crime.

Starring: Mike Connors as Nick Stone.

Music: George Duning.

Producer: Clarence Greene, Russell Rouse.

Note: The character portrayed by Mike Connors is not identified by a name in some sources; he is referred to as "The Unnamed Agent" or "The Undercover Agent."

TIGHTROPE—60 minutes—CBS— September 8, 1959 - September 13, 1960. 37 episodes. Syndicated.

TIM CONWAY

Listed: The television programs of comedian Tim Conway.

RANGO—Comedy—30 minutes— ABC—1967. See title.

THE TIM CONWAY SHOW—Comedy —30 minutes—CBS—January 30, 1970 - June 19, 1970.

Background: Crawford Airport in Los Angeles, California, the business and operations base of Timothy "Spud" Barrett, pilot, and Herbert Kenworth, executive officer, the owners of the *Lucky Linda,* a decrepit plane that comprises Triple A Airlines. Unable to pay creditors, and threatened by eviction, they struggle to acquire passengers, relieve monetary burdens and maintain an airline.

CAST

Timothy "Spud" Barrett	Tim Conway
Herbert Kenworth	Joe Flynn
Mrs. Crawford, the owner of the airport	Anne Seymour
Ronnie Crawford, her son	Johnnie Collins III
Becky, the Crawford Airlines reservationist, Spud's girlfriend	Emily Banks
Sherman, the radio-control-tower operator	Dennis Robertson
Harry, the owner of the airport coffee shop	Fabian Dean

THE TIM CONWAY COMEDY HOUR—Variety—60 minutes—CBS— September 20, 1970 - December 28, 1970.

Tightrope. Mike Connors as Nick Stone, police agent, demonstrating his special gun draw. © *Screen Gems.*

Host: Tim Conway.

Regulars: Sally Struthers, McLean Stevenson, Art Metrano, Bonnie Boland, Belland and Somerville, The Tom Hanson Dancers.

Orchestra: Nelson Riddle.

TIME FOR BEANIE

See title: "The Beanie and Cecil Show."

TIME TO REMEMBER

Documentary. Through re-creations and available material (film, newspaper files, stills, and drawings) events that sparked the world from 1895-1945 are recalled.

Narrators: Guest actors.

TIME TO REMEMBER—30 minutes —Syndicated 1963. 39 episodes.

A TIME FOR US

Serial. The dramatic story of two sisters, Linda and Jane Driscoll. Breaking her engagement to Steve Reynolds, Linda Leaves home and travels to New York City, where she hopes to further her acting career. Jane, who is secretly in love with Steve, remains behind, hoping to one day marry her sister's fiancé.

CAST

Linda Driscoll	Joanna Miles
Jane Driscoll	Beverly Hayes
Steve Reynolds	Gordon Gray
Martha	Lenka Peterson
Al	Roy Poole
Jason	Walter Coy
Chris	Richard Thomas
Kate Austen	Kathleen Maguire
Elizabeth	Nancy Franklin
Roxanne Reynolds	Maggie Hayes
Ted	John McMartin
Linda Skerba	Jane Elliot
Paul	Conrad Fowkes
Nick	Jon Stone
Louise	Josephine Nichols
Tony Grey	Morgan Sterne
Flora	Jacqueline Brooks
Dave	Terrence Logan
Craig Reynolds	Frank Schofield
Sue Michaels	Jill O'Hara
Jane Skerba	Margaret Ladd
Leslie Farrell	Rita Lloyd
Fran	Elaine Hymas
Gillespie	Robert Hogan
Doug	Ira Berger
Nancy	Lynn Rogers

A TIME FOR US—30 minutes— ABC—June 28, 1965 - December 16, 1966. Original title: "Flame In the Wind.

A TIME TO LIVE

Serial. Background: A small Midwestern town. The dramatic story of Julie Byron, newspaper proofreader and occasional reporter.

CAST

Julie Byron	Patricia Sully
Don Riker, a reporter	Larry Kerr
Madge Byron	Viola Berwick
Chic	Len Wayland
Carl Sherman	Jack Lester
Justin	John Devoe
Lenore	Barbara Foley
Lucy	Nell Clark
Miles Dow	Dort Clark
Daphne	Toni Gilman
Ann	Rosemary Kelly
Rudy	Zachary Charles
Patricia	Beverly Younger
Dr. Clay	Dana Elcar

Executive Producer-Creator: Adrian Samish.

Producer-Director: Alan Beaumont.

A TIME TO LIVE—15 minutes— NBC—July 5, 1954 - December 31, 1954.

THE TIME TUNNEL

Science Fiction Adventure. Background: Tic Toc Base, a concealed underground lab, the secret location of the Time Tunnel, a seven and one half billion dollar U.S. government project concerned with time displacement.

Discovering that government officials, who are considering scrapping the project, are dissatisfied with their inability to send a man through time, scientist Tony Newman takes matters into his own hands and enters the Time Tunnel's psychedelic portal chamber. Within seconds he disappears and is sent into time—"yesterday, today, tomorrow, or a million years from now."

Because Tony has previously taken a radioactive bath, engineers are able to pinpoint his whereabouts and receive his voice and image through the Tunnel's recorders. However, their ability to control his destiny or return him to the present (1968) has not been mastered.

When discovering that Tony has been sent back in time to April 14, 1912, as an unregistered passenger on the disaster bound *Titanic,* scientist Doug Phillips enters the Time Tunnel in an attempt to save Tony who, though of the present, is effected by events of the past—or future.

Meeting with Tony, the two are frozen by Tunnel engineers, removed from danger, and sent into time.

Stories depict the experiences of scientists Tony Newman and Doug Phillips, travelers lost in time.

CAST

Tony Newman	James Darren

The Time Tunnel. Left to right: James Darren, Robert Colbert, and guest Victor Jory. Episode: "Pirates of· Deadman's Island."

Doug Phillips	Robert Colbert
General Heywood Kirk, the Time Tunnel's supervisor	Whit Bissell
Dr. Ann McGregor, a Time Tunnel engineer	Lee Meriwether
Dr. Raymond Swain, a scientist	John Zaremba
Sergeant Jiggs, the security guard	Wesley Lau
Jerry, a Time Tunnel engineer	Sam Groom

Music: Lionel Newman.

Additional Music: Joseph Mullendore, Lyn Murray, Robert Dransin, Johnny Williams, George Duning.

Producer-Creator: Irwin Allen.

Director: Herschel Daugherty, Harry Harris, William Hale, Sobey Martin, Murray Golden, Nathan Juran, Paul Stanley.

Program Open:

Announcer: "Two American scientists are lost in the swirling maze of past and future ages during the first experiments on America's greatest and most secret project—The Time Tunnel. Tony Newman and Doug Phillips now tumble helplessly toward a new fantastic adventure somewhere along the infinite corridors of time."

THE TIME TUNNEL—60 minutes—ABC—September 9, 1966 - September 1, 1967. 30 episodes. Syndicated.

TIMES SQUARE PLAYHOUSE

Anthology. Rebroadcasts of dramas that were originally aired via other filmed anthology programs.

Host-Narrator: Herbert Marshall.

Included:

His Name Is Jason. The story of a woman's unselfish devotion to her alcoholic husband.

CAST
John Warburton, Gertrude Michael.

The Hitchhiker Was A Lady. After picking up a woman hitchhiker, a truck driver is accused of attempting to murder her. The story concerns his efforts to prove his innocence.

CAST
Jane Nigh, John Kellogg.

Call Me Irving. By changing his name an actor attempts to acquire a part in a play.

CAST
Johnny Johnston, Jean Byron.

The Biggest Little Theatre. The story of a counterfeiter who uses a theater as a front for his illegal undertaking.

CAST
Paul Bryar.

TIMES SQUARE PLAYHOUSE—30 minutes—Syndicated 1963. 39 episodes.

TIMMIE AND LASSIE

See title: "Lassie."

TIN PAN ALLEY TV

Musical Variety.

Host: Johnny Desmond.

Orchestra: Gloria Van.

TIN PAN ALLEY TV—30 minutes—ABC 1950.

TIN TIN

Animated Cartoon. The adventures of Tin Tin, a twelve-year-old boy, and his dog, Snowy, as they become involved with and attempt to solve crimes. Based on the European comic strip, *The Adventures of Tin Tin.* Voices, music, and announcer credits are not given screen or verbal credit.

Additional characters: The Thompson Brothers, detectives; Professor Calculis; and Captain Haddock, the skipper of the ship, *Karaboudjan.*

TIN TIN—30 minutes—Syndicated 1961. Also known as: "Herge's Adventures of Tin Tin" and "The Adventures of Tin Tin."

TOAST OF THE TOWN

See title: "The Ed Sullivan Show."

TODAY IS OURS

Serial. Background: The town of Bolton. The dramatic story of Laura Manning, assistant principal at Bolton Central High School. Episodes depict her conflicts and tensions: divorced, the mother of a young son, and romantically involved with a married man, architect Glenn Turner.

CAST
Laura Manning	Patricia Benoit
Nick Manning	Peter Lazer
Glenn Turner	Patrick O'Neal
Laura Turner	Joyce Lear

Also: Ernest Graves, Tom Carlin, Nancy Sheridan, Chase Crosley, Joanna Roos, Martin Blaine, Eugene Roos, John McGovern, Nelson Olmstead, Barry Thompson, Eugenia Raivis.

TODAY IS OURS—30 minutes—NBC—August 30, 1958 - January 27, 1959.

THE TODAY SHOW

Information. News, weather, sports, politics, fashion, and entertainment.

Host: Dave Garroway (1952-1961); John Chancellor (1961-1962); Hugh Downs (1962-1971); Frank McGee (1971-1974); Jim Hartz (1974-1976); Lloyd Dobbins (7-19-76 – 8-27-76); Tom Brokaw (8-30-76).

Hostess: Barbara Walters; Jane Pauley

Substitute Host: Jim Backus.

Regulars: Charles Van Doren, Betsy Palmer, Robin Chandler, Judith Crist, Frank Blair, Louise O'Brien, Bob Elliott, Ray Goulding, Margaret O'Sullivan, Estelle Parsons, Helen O'Connell, Barbara Walters, Pat Fontaine, Martin Agronsky, Joe Garagiola, Paul Cunningham, Florence Henderson, Anita Colby, Robbin Bain, Lee Ann Meriwether, Gene Shalit, Beryl Pfizer, James Fleming, Jack Lescoulie, Lew Wood, The Muppets, J. Fred Muggs (a chimpanzee), Roberta MacDonald.

Music Theme: "This Is Today" by Ray Ellis.

THE TODAY SHOW—2 hours (7:00 a.m.-9:00 a.m., E.S.T.)—NBC—Premiered: January 14, 1952.

TODAY WITH MRS. ROOSEVELT

Interview. Guests are first interviewed then asked to answer questions that were submitted by home viewers.

Hostess: Elinor Roosevelt.

TODAY WITH MRS. ROOSEVELT—30 minutes—NBC—1950 - 1955. Also known as: "Mrs. Roosevelt Meets the Public."

TOMA

Crime Drama. Background: Newark, New Jersey. The investigations of Dave Toma, undercover police agent, and master of disguise, as he attempts to infiltrate and expose the "Organization," which is responsible for numerous illegal rackets. Based on the real-life exploits of David Toma, Newark detective.

CAST

Dave Toma	Tony Musante
Patty Toma, his wife	Susan Strasberg
Inspector Spooner	Simon Oakland
Donna Toma, their daughter	Michele Livingston
Jimmy Toma, their son	Sean Mannering
Also, various parts	David Toma

Music: Mike Post, Pete Carpenter.

TOMA—60 minutes—ABC—October 4, 1973 - September 6, 1974.

TOMAHAWK

Adventure. Background: America's Northwest during the seventeenth century. The exploits of Pierre Radisson and his partner, Medard, as they assist pioneers in their attempts to settle in new and unexplored territory.

CAST

Pierre Radisson	Jacques Godin
Medard	Rene Caron

TOMAHAWK—30 minutes—Syndicated 1957. 26 episodes.

TOM AND JERRY

Animated Cartoon. The misadventures of two non-talking animals: Tom the cat, and Jerry the mouse.

Vocal Effects: June Foray, Mel Blanc.

Music: Scott Bradley, Eugene Poddany.

Producer: Fred Quimby.

Director: William Hanna, Joseph Barbera, Chuck Jones.

TOM AND JERRY—30 minutes—CBS—September 1965 - September 17, 1972.

THE TOM AND JERRY/ GRAPE APE SHOW

Cartoon. The overall title for two

Tom and Jerry. Tom the cat and Jerry the mouse.

animated series: "Tom and Jerry" and "The Grape Ape."

Tom and Jerry. The misadventures of the mischievous cat and mouse team of Tom and Jerry. The main characters are nonspeaking.

The Grape Ape. The misadventures of the Grape Ape, a forty-foot purple gorilla, and his fast-talking friend, Beagle the dog.

Characters' Voices

Beagle	Marty Ingels
The Grape Ape	Daws Butler

Additional Voices: Henry Corden, Joan Gerber, Bob Holt, Bob Hastings, Virginia Gregg, Cathy Gori, Don Messick, Alan Oppenheimer, Allan Melvin, Hal Smith, Joe E. Ross, John Stevenson, Jean VanderPyl, Janet Waldo, Lurene Tuttle, Paul Winchell, Frank Welker, Lennie Weinrib.

Music: Hoyt Curtin, Paul DeKorte.

THE TOM AND JERRY/GRAPE APE SHOW—55 minutes—ABC—Premiered: September 6, 1975.

TOMBSTONE TERRITORY

Western. Background: Tombstone, Arizona, 1880s. The exploits of Harris Clayton, editor of the *Tombstone Epitaph* as he attempts to establish peace through the power of the press in "the town too tough to die."

CAST

Harris Clayton	Richard Eastham
Sheriff Clay Hollister	Pat Conway
Deputy Charlie Riggs	Gil Ranken

Producer: Andy White, Frank Pittman.

Program Open:

Clayton: "An actual account from the pages of my newspaper, the *Tombstone Epitaph.* This is the way it happened in the town too tough to die."

TOMBSTONE TERRITORY—30 minutes—ABC—October 16, 1957 - October 9, 1959. 91 episodes. Syndicated.

TOM CORBETT, SPACE CADET

Adventure. Era: Earth, A.D. 2350. The exploits of Tom Corbett, a Space Cadet at Space Academy, U.S.A., an Earth-based West Point wherein young men and women train to become Solar Guards, the agents of a celestial police force established to protect Earth, Mars, Venus, and Jupiter, the planets that comprise a universal council of peace known as the Solar Alliance.

CAST

Tom Corbett	Frankie Thomas
Cadet Roger Manning	Jan Merlin
Astro, the Venusian	Al Markhim
Captain Larry Strong	Michael Harvey
Dr. Joan Dale,	

a Space Academy
instructress   Patricia Ferris
                      Margaret Garland
Cadet T. J. Fissell   Jack Grimes
Commander Arkwright,
  the head of Space
  Academy   Carter Blake
Betty, a teacher   Beryl Berney
Gloria, a teacher   Marian Brash

Announcer: Jackson Beck.

Producer: Al Ducovny, Leonard Carlton.

Director: George Gould.

Sponsor: Kellogg's; Kraft.

Corbett's rocket ship: the *Polaris.*

Program Open:

Announcer: "Space Academy, U.S.A., in the world beyond tomorrow. Here the Space Cadets train for duty on distant planets. In roaring rockets they blast through the millions of miles from Earth to far-flung stars and brave the dangers of cosmic frontiers, protecting the liberties of the planets, safeguarding the cause of universal peace in the age of the conquest of space."

TOM CORBETT, SPACE CADET—15 and 30 minute versions—NBC—1950 - 1956.

TOM, DICK AND MARY

See title: "Ninety Bristol Court," *Tom, Dick and Mary* segment.

THE TOM EWELL SHOW

Comedy. Background: Los Angeles, California. The trials and tribulations of the Potter family: Tom, a real-estate salesman; his wife, Frances; their daughters, Debbie, Carol, and Cissy; and Tom's mother-in-law, Irene Brady.

CAST
Tom Potter   Tom Ewell
Frances Potter   Marilyn Erskine
Debbie Potter   Sherry Alberoni
Carol Potter   Cindy Robbins
Cissy Potter   Eileen Chesis
Irene Brady   Mabel Albertson

Music: Jerry Fielding.

THE TOM EWELL SHOW—30 minutes—CBS—September 27, 1960 - September 1961. Syndicated. Also known as "The Trouble with Tom."

TOMFOOLERY

Animated Cartoon. Sketches, songs, and poetry based on children's literature.

Characters: The Youngie Bungi Bow (a creature whose head is bigger than his body), The Scroovy Snake, The Umbrageous Umbrella Maker, Fastidious Fish, and The Enthusiastic Elephant.

TOMFOOLERY—30 minutes—NBC—September 12, 1970 - September 4, 1971. 17 episodes.

THE TOMMY HUNTER SHOW

Musical Variety. Performances by Country and Western entertainers.

Host: Tommy Hunter.

Regulars: The Rhythm Pals, The Allen Sisters.

Orchestra: Bert Niosi.

THE TOMMY HUNTER SHOW—60 minutes—Syndicated 1966. 125 tapes. Produced in Canada.

TOMORROW

Discussion. Interviews with people rarely seen on television and for the most part nonshow business, who have a story to tell.

Host: Tom Snyder.

Announcers: Frank Barton: Bill Wendell.

Music: Recorded.

TOMORROW—60 minutes—NBC—Premiered: October 15, 1973. Broadcast from 1:00 a.m.-2:00 a.m., E.S.T.

TOM TERRIFIC

A cartoon series that details the adventures of a small boy named Tom Terrific. 130 four minute films, syndicated in the early 1960s.

TONIGHT ON BROADWAY

Variety. Condensed versions of Broadway plays are presented.

Host: Martin Gosch.

TONIGHT ON BROADWAY—30 minutes—CBS 1949.

THE TONIGHT SHOW

Talk-Variety. Television's first late-night entertainment series. The series first began as "Broadway Open House," then continued as "Seven At Eleven" and "The Left Over Revue" (see titles) before becoming "The Tonight Show."

Versions:

The Tonight Show—40 minutes—Local New York (WNBT-TV, Channel 4)—July 27, 1953 - September 24, 1954. Broadcast from 11:20 p.m. - 12:00 a.m.

Host: Steve Allen.

Regulars: Steve Lawrence, Helen Dixon, Pat Kirby.

Announcer: Gene Rayburn.

Orchestra: Bobby Byrne.

The Tonight Show—105 minutes—NBC—September 27, 1954 - January 25, 1957.

Host: Steve Allen.

Regulars: Steve Lawrence, Edyie Gormé, Pat Marshall, Helen Dixon, Andy Williams.

Announcer: Gene Rayburn.

Orchestra: Skitch Henderson.

The Tonight Show—105 minutes—NBC—October 1, 1956 - January 22, 1957. Broadcast twice a week for a period of four months, preempting version two (above) on Monday and Tuesday evenings.

Host: Ernie Kovacs.

Vocalists: Maureen Arthur, Pete Hanley.

Announcer: Bill Wendell.

Orchestra: Leroy Holmes.

Tonight! America After Dark—News-Entertainment—NBC—105 minutes—January 28, 1957 - July 26, 1957.

Format: Live interviews coupled with on-the-spot news coverage.

Hosts: Jack Lescoulie; Al "Jazzbo" Collins.

Vocalist: Judy Johnson.

Newsmen: Hy Gardner, Bob Considine, Earl Wilson (New York); Irv Kupcinet (Chicago); Vernon Scott, Paul Coates, Lee Giroux (Los Angeles).

Music: The Lou Stein Trio (January -March); The Mort Lindsey Quartet (March-June); The Johnny Guarnieri Quartet.

The Tonight Show—105 minutes—NBC—July 29, 1957 - March 30, 1962.

Host: Jack Paar.

Regulars: Cliff Arquette (as Charlie Weaver); Pat Harrington, Jr. (as Guido Panzini), Peggy Cass, Alexander King, Mary Margaret McBride, Dodie Goodman, Betty Johnson, Elsa Maxwell, Tedi Thurman (the weather girl), The Bil and Cora Baird Puppets.

Announcers: Hugh Downs; Art James.

Orchestra: Jose Melis.

The Tonight Show (Interim)—105 minutes—NBC—April 2, 1962 - September 28, 1962.

Hosts: Guests, including Bob Cummings, Jan Murray, Jack Carter, Peter Lind Hayes, Art Linkletter, Joey Bishop, Merv Griffin, Steve Lawrence, Jerry Lewis, Arlene Francis, Jimmy Dean, Jack E. Leonard, Hal March, Groucho Marx, Soupy Sales, Mort Sahl.

Announcers: Hugh Downs; Ed Herlihy.

Orchestra: Skitch Henderson.

The Tonight Show—105 and 90 minute versions—NBC—Premiered: October 1, 1962.

Host: Johnny Carson.

Announcers: Jack Haskell; Durwood Kirby; Ed McMahon.

Featured in sketches: Carol Wayne (as "The Tea Time Movie Girl").

Orchestra: Skitch Henderson; Milton DeLugg; Doc Severinsen.

Substitute Orchestra Leader: Tommy Newson.

THE TONY BENNETT SHOW

Musical Variety.

Host: Tony Bennett.

Regulars: The Spellbinders, The Frank Lewis Dancers.

Premiere Guests: June Valli, Ben Blue, and George Reeves (as a singer-guitarist).

THE TONY BENNETT SHOW—60 minutes—NBC—August 11, 1956 - September 8, 1956.

THE TONY MARTIN SHOW

Musical Variety.

Host: Tony Martin.

Vocalists: The Interludes.

Orchestra: Hal Bourne; David Rose.

THE TONY MARTIN SHOW—15 minutes—NBC—April 26, 1954 - February 26, 1956.

TONY ORLANDO AND DAWN

Variety. Various comedy sketches and musical numbers.

Hosts: Tony Orlando and Dawn (a singing duo comprising Joyce Vincent Wilson and Telma Hopkins).

Regulars: Steve Franken, Susan Tolsky, George Carlin, Bob Holt.

Featured: The Jerry Jackson Singers.

Announcer: Roger Carroll, Dick Tufeld.

Orchestra: Bob Rozario.

TONY ORLANDO AND DAWN—60 minutes—CBS—July 3, 1974 - July 24, 1974. Returned: CBS—December 4, 1974 - December 28, 1976. Also titled: "The Tony Orlando and Dawn Rainbow Hour."

THE TONY RANDALL SHOW

Comedy. Background: Philadelphia. The home and working life of widower Walter Franklin, a less-than-magisterial judge of the Court of Common Pleas.

CAST

Judge Walter O. Franklin	Tony Randall
Roberta "Bobby" Franklin, his daughter	Devon Scott
	Penny Peyser
Oliver Franklin, Jr., his son	Brad Savage
Janet Reubner, his secretary	Allyn Ann McLerie
Mrs. McClellan, his housekeeper	Rachel Roberts
Judy Trowbridge, his law clerk	Brooke Adams
Jack Terwilliger, the court stenographer	Barney Martin
Mr. Franklin, Walter's father	Hans Conried

Music: Patrick Williams.

Producer-Creator: Tom Patchett, Jay Tarses.

Director: Jay Sandrich, James Burrows, Hugh Wilson.

THE TONY RANDALL SHOW—30

minutes—ABC—September 23, 1976 - March 10, 1977. Returned: CBS—Premiered: September 1977.

TOOTSIE HIPPODROME

Variety. Entertainment geared to children: circus variety acts and telephone quizzes (a prize is awarded to the child who is able to answer a question correctly).

Host: John Reed King.

Producer: Vernon Becker, Eli Broidy, Whitey Carson, Milton Stanson.

Sponsor: Sweets Company.

TOOTSIE HIPPODROME—15 minutes—ABC—February 3, 1952 - August 19, 1953.

TOO YOUNG TO GO STEADY

Comedy. The innocent romantic misadventures of fifteen-year-old Pamela Blake, a tomboy who suddenly discovers the opposite sex and is endowed with an urge to date.

CAST

Pamela Blake	Brigid Bazlen
Tom Blake, her father, a lawyer	Don Ameche
Mary Blake, her mother	Joan Bennett
John Blake, her older brother	Martin Huston

TOO YOUNG TO GO STEADY—30 minutes—NBC—May 14, 1959 - June 25, 1959.

TOP CAT

Animated Cartoon. A spin-off from the Phil Silvers character, Sgt. Bilco (see title: "You'll Never Get Rich"). Background: The alley way of the 13th police precinct in New York City, the residence of Top Cat, a master conartist, and his feline dupes: Choo Choo, Benny the Ball, Spook, The Brain, Fancy Fancy, Pierre, and Goldie. Stories depict their attempts to enjoy a carefree, easy life despite the constant threats of eviction and arrest by Officer Dibble, the cop upon whose beat Top Cat enacts his ingenious money-making ventures.

Characters' Voices

Top Cat (T.C.)	Arnold Stang
Choo Choo	Marvin Kaplan

Top Cat. Top Cat and his gang. *Courtesy Hanna-Barbera Productions.*

Benny the Ball	Maurice Gosfield
Spook	Leo de Lyon
The Brain	Leo de Lyon
Officer Dibble	Allen Jenkins
Goldie	Jean VanderPyl
Fancy Fancy	John Stephenson
Pierre	John Stephenson

Additional Voices: Paul Frees.

Music: Hoyt Curtin.

TOP CAT—30 minutes—ABC—September 27, 1961 - March 30, 1962. 30 episodes. Syndicated.

TOP DOLLAR

Game. Three competing contestants. Object: To form words. A line that contains blank spaces is displayed. Clues to the identity of a word (eight letters or more) are relayed by the host. Players then contribute three letters each to its formation. For each additional letter that a player contributes that is correct, he receives one hundred dollars. Players suggest letters in turn and are disqualified if they complete the unknown word by supplying the last letter. The first player to identify the word is the winner of that round. The highest cash scorer is the overall champion and competes until he is defeated.

Home participation segment: The first eight letters that are created by players are matched with the digits on a telephone dial. The number that appears represents serial numbers and are flashed on a screen. Home viewers who possess matching dollar bills receive one hundred dollars if they submit them to the program.

Host: Toby Reed.

Judge: Dr. Bergen Evans.

TOP DOLLAR—30 minutes—CBS—

March 29, 1958 - August 30, 1958 (evening run); September 1, 1958 - October 23, 1959 (daytime run).

TOPPER

Comedy. Background: New York City. Purchasing a home, Cosmo Topper, the henpecked vice-president of the National Security Bank, inherits three ghosts: George and Marian Kirby, its previous owners, man and wife, who were killed while skiing in Switzerland, and a liquor-consuming Saint Bernard dog, Neil, who was also the victim of the avalanche. Stories depict Topper's attempts to cope with the situations that result as three ghosts, who appear and only talk to him, interfere in his personal and business life. Based on the motion picture.

CAST

Cosmo Topper	Leo G. Carroll
Marian Kirby	Anne Jeffreys
George Kirby	Robert Sterling
Henrietta Topper, Cosmo's wife	Lee Patrick
Mr. Schuyler, the bank president	Thurston Hall
Katie, the Topper's maid	Kathleen Freeman
Maggie, the Topper's housekeeper, later episodes	Edna Skinner
Thelma Gibney, Henrietta's friend	Mary Field
Buck	Neil

Music: Charles Koff.

Producer: John W. Loveton, Bernard L. Schubert.

Director: Leslie Goodwins, Lew Landers, Philip Rapp, James V. Kern, Richard L. Bare.

Sponsor: R.J. Reynolds.

Topper's Address: 101 Maple Drive.

Note: Throughout the run of the series Topper is also known to be associated with these additional banks: City Bank, Gotham Trust Company, City Trust and Savings Bank.

Program Open:

Announcer: "Anne Jeffreys as Marian Kirby, the ghostess with the mostess; Robert Sterling as George Kirby, that most sporting spirit; and Leo G. Carroll, host to said ghosts as Topper."

TOPPER—30 minutes. NBC—October 9, 1953 - September 30, 1955. ABC—October 3, 1955 - September 17, 1956. 78 episodes. Syndicated.

TOP OF THE MONTH

Variety. Highlights of the months of the year are saluted through songs, sketches, and dances.

Host: Tony Randall.

Co-hostess: E. J. (Edra Jeanne) Peaker.

Regulars: Anson Williams, Tina Andrews, The Anita Mann Dancers, The Alan Copeland Singers.

Orchestra: Alan Copeland.

TOP OF THE MONTH—30 minutes—Syndicated 1972.

TOP PLAYS OF 1954

Anthology. Rebroadcasts of outstanding dramas that were originally aired via other filmed anthology programs.

Included:

A Season To Love. The story of a plain-looking girl who falls in love with a disreputable vagrant.

CAST
Ida Lupino, Howard Duff, Sara Hoden.

Wonderful Day For A Wedding. The story of a bride who changes her mind at the last minute and refuses to make the march to the altar.

CAST
Scott Brady, Joan Leslie, Spring Byington.

Keep It In The Family. An episode in the hectic life of the Warren family. The story centers on the chaos that results when teenage daughter Peggy announces that she has been discovered by a talent agent and will star on Broadway.

CAST
Robert Young, Ellen Drew, Sally Foster, Tina Thompson.

TOP PLAYS OF 1954—30 minutes—June 1954 - August 24, 1954.

TOP SECRET

Adventure. The exploits of Peter Dallas, a British agent of law and order in South America.

Starring: William Franklyn as Peter Dallas.

TOP SECRET—30 minutes—Syndicated 1961.

TOP SECRET U.S.A.

Drama. The work of United States government undercover agents in conjunction with the Bureau of Scientific Information (B.S.I.).

CAST

Professor Brand	Paul Stewart
Powell, his assistant	Gena Rowlands

TOP SECRET U.S.A.–30 minutes–Syndicated 1954.

TO ROME WITH LOVE

Comedy. Background: Rome, Italy. Hired to teach at the American School in Europe, Professor Michael Endicott, widower, and his three daughters, Alison, Penny, and Mary Jane (Pokey), leave Iowa and, relocating in the Eternal City, take up residence at Mama Vitale's Boarding House.

Stories depict the trials and tribulations of an American family as they struggle to adjust to a new homeland.

CAST

Michael Endicott	John Forsythe
Alison Endicott	Joyce Menges
Penny Endicott	Susan Neher
Pokey Endicott	Melanie Fullerton
Andy Pruitt, the girls' grandfather	Walter Brennan
Harriet Endicott, Mike's sister	Kay Medford
Gino Mancini, their friend, a cab driver	Vito Scotti
Mama Vitale, their landlady	Peggy Mondo
Nico, a friend of Penny's	Gerald Michenaud
Margot, a friend	Brioni Farrell
Tina, a friend of Alison's	Brenda Benet

Music: Frank DeVol.

TO ROME WITH LOVE–30 minutes–CBS–September 28, 1969 - September 1, 1971. 48 episodes.

TO SAY THE LEAST

Game. Two teams, each composed of three players–two celebrities and one noncelebrity contestant–compete. Two players from each team are placed backstage and isolated so as not to be able to see or hear. A phrase is then shown to the on stage players (e.g., "Dutch girls clop around in them"); on an alternating basis, the players eliminate words from it. At any time, the contestant at play can challenge or take out a word. When a challenge is made, the opposing team must attempt to identify the meaning of the phrase. The backstage players are brought out and the challenged player's teammates are shown the remaining words to the phrase. If they can identify it ("Wooden shoes" for the given example) they score one point; if not, the opposing team scores the point. If a challenge is not made the game continues until only two words remain. At this point, the contestant at play has to either challenge or take out a word. If he takes out a word then his teammates have to attempt to answer; if not, then the challenge is made and the opposing team has to guess it. The first team to score two points is the winner and the noncelebrity player receives merchandise prizes.

Host: Tom Kennedy.

Announcer: Kenny Williams.

Producer: Merrill Heatter, Bob Quigley.

TO SAY THE LEAST–30 minutes–NBC–Premiered: October 3, 1977.

TO TELL THE TRUTH

Game. Three people appear, each laying claim to the same identity. Through question-and-answer probe rounds, a celebrity panel of four have to determine which person is telling the truth. Cash prizes are awarded to players depending on the number of incorrect guesses on the part of the panel.

Versions:

To Tell The Truth–30 minutes–CBS–January 1, 1957 - May 22, 1967 (evening run); June 18, 1962 - September 6, 1968 (daytime run).

Moderator: Bud Collyer.

Regular Panelists: Phyllis Newman, Peggy Cass, Sally Ann Howes, Tom Poston, Orson Bean, Kitty Carlisle, Milt Kamen, Bess Myerson, Joan Fontaine, Sam Levenson, Barry Nelson, Dr. Joyce Brothers, Polly Bergen, Dick Van Dyke, John Cameron Swayze, Hildy Parks.

Announcer: Johnny Olsen.

To Tell The Truth–30 minutes–Syndicated 1969.

Moderator: Garry Moore.

Regular Panelists: Orson Bean, Bill Cullen, Kitty Carlisle, Peggy Cass.

Announcers: Johnny Olsen; Bill Wendell.

Music: Score Productions.

TOUCHE TURTLE

Animated Cartoon. The exploits of Touche Turtle, a fumbling modern-day knight who assists the distressed. A Hanna-Barbera production.

Characters' Voices

Touche Turtle	Bill Thompson
Dum Dum, his assistant	Alan Reed

Music: Hoyt Curtin.

TOUCHE TURTLE–05 minutes–Syndicated 1962. 52 episodes.

A TOUCH OF GRACE

Comedy. Background: Oakland, California. The story of Grace Sherwood, a sixty-five-year-old widow struggling to make a life for herself at the home of her married daughter, Myra Bradley, a beautician, and her husband, Walter Bradley, the manager of the produce department of the Penny Mart Supermarket.

One day, while tending her husband's grave, Grace meets and falls in love with the grave digger, a widower, Herbert Morrison.

Believing Herbert is not a gentleman, Myra disapproves of him. A family crisis ensues when Grace, feeling her life is unfulfilled because Myra and Walter are childless, states her intent to continue seeing him.

Serial-type episodes relate Grace and Herbert's courtship, Myra's final acceptance of Herbert when she realizes her mother's feelings, and Herbert's proposal to Grace. Based on the British television series, "For the Love of Ada."

CAST

Grace Sherwood (also known as Grace Simpson)	Shirley Booth
Herbert Morrison	J. Pat O'Malley
Myra Bradley	Marian Mercer
Walter Bradley	Warren Berlinger

Music: Pete Rugolo.

A TOUCH OF GRACE–30 minutes–ABC–January 20, 1973 - June 16, 1973.

TOYLAND EXPRESS

See title: "Paul Winchell and Jerry Mahoney."

THE TOY THAT GREW UP

Documentary. The history of the silent era of motion pictures.

Host: Don Ferris.

THE TOY THAT GREW UP–60 minutes. NET–1965 - 1970; PBS–1970 - 1972.

TRACER

Mystery. The investigations of Police Inspector Regan as he attempts to solve baffling acts of criminal injustice.

Starring: James Chandler as Inspector Regan.

TRACER–30 minutes–Syndicated 1957.

TRACKDOWN

Western. Background: The Frontier during the 1870s. The cases of Hoby Gilman, Texas Ranger, as he attempts to apprehend wanted offenders.

Starring: Robert Culp as Hoby Gilman.

TRACKDOWN–30 minutes–CBS–October 4, 1957 - September 23, 1959. 71 episodes. Syndicated.

TRAFFIC COURT

Courtroom Drama. Dramatizations based on official traffic-court files.

Judge: Edgar Allan Jones, Jr.

Defendants and Lawyers: Guest actors.

TRAFFIC COURT–30 minutes–ABC–June 18, 1958 - September 24, 1958.

TRAILS TO ADVENTURE

Travel. Historical landmarks are explored and, through dramatizations, incidents in its past are re-created.

Host-Narrator: Jack Smith.

Performers: Guest actors.

TRAILS TO ADVENTURE–30 minutes–Syndicated 1968.

TRAILS WEST

Anthology. Retitled episodes of western dramas that were originally aired via "Death Valley Days."

Host: Ray Milland.

Music: Marlen Skiles.

Included:

The Little Dressmaker Of Bodie. The story of Tiger Lil, dancehall queen of Virginia City, as she struggles to begin a new life.

CAST
Tracey Roberts, Arthur Space, Myron Healy.

The Diamond Babe. The story of a dancehall queen who is scorned by the townspeople.

CAST
Ann Savage.

Solomon In All His Glory. An ex-newspaperman, who has become the town drunk, struggles to reform in time for the arrival of his younger sister.

CAST
James Griffith, Gloria Winters.

A Woman's Rights. The story of the first woman judge and her fight against corruption.

CAST
Bethel Leslie, Dean Harens.

TRAILS WEST–30 minutes–Syndicated 1958. 104 episodes.

THE TRAP

Anthology. Dramatizations depicting the plight of people suddenly confronted with uncertain situations.

Host: John Bentley.

Producer: Franklin Heller.

Director: Byron Paul.

Included:

Lonely Boy. The story of a chance meeting between two lonely people.

Starring: Cara Williams, Dorothy Sands, Larry Fletcher, Howard Wierum, John Hudson.

The Secret Place. The story of a rich but neglected wife and her attempts to make her husband jealous by letting him believe that she has a secret love.

Starring: Margaret Rawlings.

THE TRAP–30 minutes–CBS 1950.

TRAVEL WITH DON AND BETTINA

See title: "Faces and Places."

The Travels of Jaimie McPheeters. Dan O'Herlihy and Kurt Russell.

THE TRAVELS OF JAIMIE McPHEETERS

Western. Era: 1849. The hardships encountered by the Beaver Patrol, a wagon train of settlers destined for California. Stories depict their experiences as seen through the eyes of twelve-year-old Jaimie McPheeters.

CAST

Doc Sardius McPheeters, Jaimie's father	Dan O'Herlihy
Jaimie McPheeters	Kurt Russell
Buck Coulter, the wagonmaster	Michael Witney

Settlers:

Dick McBride	John Chandler
Matt Kissel	Mark Allen
Mrs. Kissel	Meg Wyllie
The Kissel Children	The Osmond Brothers
Othello	Vernett Allen III
Murdock	Charles Bronson
Jenny	Jean Engstrom
	Donna Anderson
Shep Bogott	Sandy Kenyon
Hard Luck Slater	Robert Carriort
John Munlett	James Westerfield

Producer: Robert Thompson, Robert Sparks, Don Ingalls.

THE TRAVELS OF JAIMIE

McPHEETERS—60 minutes—ABC—September 17, 1963 - March 15, 1964. 26 episodes.

TREASURE

Documentary. Films relating the search for fabled treasures. Legends, strange facts, and histories concerning the particular treasures are also related.

Host-Narrator: Bill Burrud.

TREASURE—30 minutes—Syndicated 1960.

TREASURE HUNT

Game. Two competing players, a male and female. A question, which is based on a specific topic, is related by the host. The player who first identifies himself through a buzzer signal receives a chance to answer. If correct, he receives one point. The winner, the highest point scorer, receives the opportunity to win up to $25,000 in cash.

He or she is escorted to a wall that contains thirty treasure chests. The player chooses one, and its contents—from a head of cabbage to valuable merchandise prizes to large sums of cash—are his or her prize.

Host: Jan Murray.

Pirate Girl (his assistant): Marian Stafford.

TREASURE HUNT—30 minutes. ABC—September 17, 1956 - August 23, 1957; NBC—August 12, 1957 - December 4, 1959.

TREASURE ISLE

Game. Background: A specially constructed island in Florida. Three married couples compete. Object: To seek buried treasure.

Round One: A large pile of styrofoam puzzle pieces are placed opposite the players. In fifteen second intervals, individual players run up to the pile, take one piece at a time, and place it in its appropriate place on a large board. Each piece that is properly fitted awards that team one point. When the puzzle is completed it relates a rhyming clue. The team who correctly decifers it receives additional points.

Round Two: Various stunt contests that award the best performers points.

Round Three: Players, situated on one island, have to cross to another island (about twenty-five yards distant). Each team receives an inflatable raft. The husbands lie face down so as to use their hands as oars; the wives are seated at the opposite side of the raft and direct their husband's rowing. The team that is first to reach the island receives points.

The team with the highest point score is the winner and receives the opportunity to hunt for buried treasure chests. Time limit: three minutes. The host reads clues, one at a time, to the location of buried chests. The couple has to unscramble the clue and dig in the sand until a chest is found. They then return to the position of the host and receive another clue. Players receive what prizes, usually merchandise, that the chests contain (written on cards).

Host: John Bartholemew Tucker.

Models (Pirate Girls): Bonnie Maudsley, Renee Hampton.

TREASURE ISLE—30 minutes—ABC—December 18, 1967 - March 28, 1968.

TREASURE QUEST

See title: "Bon Voyage."

TREASURY MEN IN ACTION

Crime Drama. Dramatizations based on the files of the United States Customs and Treasury departments.

Starring: Walter Greaza as The Chief (introducing stories).

Announcer: Durwood Kirby.

Music: Murray Golden.

Producer: Everett Rosenthal, Robert Sloane, Bernard Prockter.

Director: David Pressman.

Sponsor: Borden; Chevrolet.

TREASURY MEN IN ACTION—30 minutes. ABC—September 11, 1950 - December 4, 1950; NBC—April 5, 1951 - September 30, 1955. Syndicated title: "Federal Men." 39 episodes available for syndication.

THE TRIALS OF O'BRIEN

Drama. Background: New York City. The cases and courtroom defenses of Daniel J. O'Brien, an untidy and disorganized criminal attorney. Spiced with light humor.

CAST

Daniel J. O'Brien	Peter Falk
Katie O'Brien, his ex-wife, whom he seeks to remarry	Joanna Barnes
The Great McGonigle, a conartist, a friend of O'Brien's	David Burns
Margaret, Katie's mother	Ilka Chase
Mrs. G., O'Brien's secretary	Elaine Stritch
Lieutenant Garrison, N.Y.P.D.	Dolph Sweet

Music: Sid Ramin.

THE TRIALS OF O'BRIEN—60 minutes—CBS—September 18, 1965 - May 27, 1966. 20 episodes.

TROPIC HOLIDAY

Musical Variety. Set against a South of the Border motif, a merchant sailor reminisces about his experiences in various South American countries. Through the performances of guest personalities, the music, song, and dance of foreign lands are seen.

Host-Narrator: Sandy Buckert (as the merchant sailor).

Orchestra: Esy Morales.

TROPIC HOLIDAY—30 minutes—NBC 1949.

THE TROUBLESHOOTERS

Adventure. The experiences of Kodiak and Dugan, construction supervisors who intervene in construction-site difficulties and attempt to return the job to normality.

CAST

Kodiak	Keenan Wynn
Dugan	Bob Mathias

Troubleshooter Team:

Loft	Eddie Firestone
Scotty	Bob Fortier
Skinner	Cary Loftin

Producer: Frank Rosenberg, John Gibbs, Richard Steenberg.

THE TROUBLESHOOTERS—30 minutes—NBC—September 11, 1959 - June 17, 1960. 26 episodes.

TROUBLE WITH FATHER

Comedy. Background: The town of

Hamilton. The trials and tribulations of the Erwin family: Stu, the principal of Hamilton High School; his wife, June; and their daughters, Joyce and Jackie.

CAST

Stu Erwin	Himself
June Erwin	June Collyer
Joyce Erwin	Ann Todd
	Merry Anders
Jackie Erwin	Sheila James
Marty Clark, Joyce's boyfriend	Martin Milner
Willie, the handyman	Willie Best

Producer: Roland Reed, Hal Roach, Jr.

Sponsor: General Mills.

TROUBLE WITH FATHER—30 minutes—ABC—October 21, 1950 - April 13, 1955. 130 episodes. Syndicated. Original title: "Life With the Erwins" also known as "The Stu Erwin Show" and "The New Stu Erwin Show."

THE TROUBLE WITH TRACY

Comedy. Background: Toronto, Canada. The trials and tribulations of the Youngs: Douglas, an executive with the advertising firm of Hutton, Dutton, Sutton, and Norris; and his well-meaning but scatterbrained wife, Tracy. Produced in Canada.

CAST

Tracy Young	Diane Nyland
Douglas Young	Steve Weston
Sally Anderson, Doug's secretary	Bonnie Brooks
Paul Sherwood, Tracy's unemployed brother	Franz Russell
Jonathan Norris, Doug's employer	Ben Lennick
Margaret Norris, his wife	Sandra Scott

THE TROUBLE WITH TRACY—30 minutes—Syndicated 1971.

TRUE

See title: "General Electric True."

TRUE ADVENTURE

Travel. Films relating the journeys of various explorers.

Host: Bill Burrud.

TRUE ADVENTURE—30 minutes—Syndicated 1960. 78 episodes.

TRUE STORY

Anthology. Dramatic presentations.

Hostess: Kathi Norris.

Included:

The Imperfect Secretary. The trials and tribulations of a trouble-prone male secretary.

Starring: Dick Van Dyke.

Say A Few Words. The complications that ensue when a college coed impersonates a Polish immigrant to attend a handsome English teacher's lectures.

Starring: Phyllis Newman.

Aunt Eppy. An advertising executive's efforts to cope with the antics of his eccentric aunt.

Starring: Barney Martin, Nancy Pollock.

The Accused. A lawyer's efforts to prove his wife is innocent of a murder charge.

Starring: Lorne Greene, Jim Boles, Fred J. Scollay.

TRUE STORY—30 minutes—NBC—March 16, 1957 - December 20, 1958.

TRUTH OR CONSEQUENCES

Game. Selected contestants (numbers vary) are first briefly interviewed, then asked to answer a nonsense riddle. If they are unable to answer it before Beulah the Buzzer sounds, they have to pay the consequences and perform stunts. Prizes are awarded in accord with the success of their performances. Based on the radio program.

Versions:

Truth Or Consequences—30 minutes—NBC—July 5, 1950 - September 25, 1965.

Hosts: Ralph Edwards; Jack Bailey; Bob Barker.

Announcer: Ken Carpenter.

Music: Buddy Cole; Jack Fascinato.

Truth Or Consequences—30 minutes—Syndicated 1967.

Host: Bob Barker.

Announcer: Charles Lyon.

Music: Dave Bacoll.

The New Truth Or Consequences—30 minutes—Syndicated 1977.

Host: Bob Hilton.

Announcer: John Harlan.

Music: Bruce Belland, Gary Edwards.

Executive Producer: Jon Ross.

Producer: Ralph Edwards, Bruce Belland.

Director: Richard Gottlieb.

TRY AND DO IT

Game. Background: A picnic grounds. Object: For contestants to perform stunts. Prizes are awarded to players in accord with the success of their performances.

Host: Jack Bright.

Orchestra: Thomas Lender.

TRY AND DO IT—30 minutes—NBC 1948.

TUESDAY MYSTERY OF THE WEEK

Anthology. Mystery and suspense presentations.

Included:

Nick and Nora. Though technically retired, former private detective Nick Charles and his wealthy wife, Nora, attempt to solve the case of a corpse they find floating in a swimming pool.

CAST
Nick Charles: Craig Stevens; Nora Charles: Jo Ann Pflug; Sgt. Steinmetz: Jack Kruschen.

Mr. and Ms. and the Magic Studio Mystery. The story of a young lawyer and his wife and their attempts to solve the puzzling mystery of a woman who was murdered when she stepped into a magician's trick iron maiden.

CAST
David Robbins: John Rubinstein; Mandy Robbins: Lee Kroeger; Lt. Ben Robbins: Milton Selzer; Barbara: Udana Power.

Mr. and Ms. and the Bandstand Mystery. Lawyer David Robbins and his wife Mandy (Mr. and Ms.) attempt to solve the baffling murder of a British Rock star.

CAST
David Robbins: John Rubinstein;

Mandy Robbins: Lee Kroeger; Lt. Ben Robbins: Milton Selzer; Dottie: Lezlie Dalton.

TUESDAY MYSTERY OF THE WEEK—90 minutes—ABC—Premiered: January 13, 1976. Broadcast from 11:30 p.m. to 1:00 a.m., E.T.

TUESDAY NIGHT PILOT FILM

Pilot Films. Proposed comedy series for the 1976 - 1977 season.

Included:

Three Times Daley. The misadventures of Bob Daley, a newspaper columnist.

CAST
Bob Daley: Don Adams; Mr. Daley: Liam Dunn; Wes Daley: Jerry Houser.

Maureen. The life of Maureen Langaree, a middle-aged department store saleswoman.

CAST
Maureen: Joyce Van Patten; Ruth: Sylvia Sidney; Alice: Karen Morrow; Trudy: Leigh French.

This Better Be It. The episode focuses on incidents in the lives of two newlyweds—each of whom has a grown child from a previous marriage that ended in divorce.

CAST
Annie: Anne Meara; Harry: Alex Rocco; Diana: Ballie Gerstein; Paul: David Pollock.

TUESDAY NIGHT PILOT FILM—30 minutes—CBS—July 27, 1976 - September 7, 1976.

TUGBOAT ANNIE

Comedy. Background: The Pacific Northwest. The misadventures of Annie Brennan, the middle-aged, sympathetic, often troubled skipper of the tugboat *Narcissus.* Based on the stories by Norman Reilly Raine.

CAST

"Tugboat" Annie Brennan	Minerva Urecal
Horatio Bullwinkle, Annie's employer	Walter Sande
Murdoch McArdle, the owner of the *Narcissus*	Stan Francis

TUGBOAT ANNIE—30 minutes—Syndicated 1957. 39 episodes. Also known as "The Adventures of Tugboat Annie."

THE TURNING POINT

Anthology. Dramatizations depicting the plight of people suddenly faced with unexpected situations.

Included:

Saddle Tramp. A drifter's search for the murderer of a friend.
Starring: William Joyce.

Borrow My Car. A young man's efforts to prove he is not guilty of stealing a car that he borrowed for a date.
Starring: Lola Albright, Allan Dexter.

The Little Pig Cried. A woman's second thoughts about divorcing her husband.
Starring: Frances Rafferty, Robert Rockwell.

THE TURNING POINT—30 minutes—ABC 1953.

TURNING POINT

Anthology. Dramatic presentations.

Included:

Once Upon a Crime. The story revolves around a thief who steals a money box from an amusement park then attaches himself to a group of children to avoid capture.
Starring: Peter Lawford, Rudy Lee, Roy Farrell, Wendy Winkelman.

This Land Is Mine. A western drama depicting the plight of homesteaders vs. gunmen for control of land.
Starring: John Ireland, Joy Page.

Heroes Never Grow Up. The story of an acclaimed hero whose heroism is put to the test in a second emergency.
Starring: Dane Clark, Alex Nicol, Barbara Turner.

TURNING POINT—30 minutes—NBC—April 12, 1958 - September 20, 1958.

TURN OF FATE

Anthology. Dramatizations depicting the plight of people who are suddenly involved in unexpected and perilous situations.

Regular performers: Robert Ryan, Jane Powell, Jack Lemmon, David Niven, Charles Boyer.

Included:

Voices In The Fog. Background: London, England. Waiting for a train, an American doctor overhears a plot to murder a man. Boarding the train, he discovers that he is the victim. Previously unable to see the murderers' faces because of a thick fog, and pretending to be unaware of their plans, he attempts to discover who they are and the reason why.

CAST
Dr. Cameron: Jack Lemmon; Cynthia: Joan Banks; Conductor: John Rogers.

Circumstantial. Getting himself arrested, an attorney attempts to prove, through his own defense, that circumstantial evidence can lead to a conviction.

CAST
Mark Garron: David Niven; Mrs. Garim: Angie Dickinson.

Silhouette Of A Killer. An amnesiac, mistaken for a killer, struggles to prove his innocence.

CAST
Man: Robert Ryan; Ellen: Beverly Garland.

TURN OF FATE—30 minutes—NBC—1957-1958. 38 episodes.

TURN ON

Variety. Visual, fast-paced comedy combined with electronic distortion and stop-action photography.

Because gags were said to contain underlying factors* and pictures were said to represent ideas other than presented, the program was cancelled the same night it premiered.

Host (Guest): Tim Conway.

Regulars: Chuck McCann, Bonnie Boland, Hamilton Camp, Teresa Graves, Maura McGiveney, Debbie Macomber, Carlos Manteca, Bob Staats, Mel Stuart, Cecil Ozorio, Ken Greenwald,

*For example: A scene from the opening. A beautiful woman is standing before a firing squad. The squad leader, instead of saying the customary, "Do you have any last requests?" remarks: "I know this may seem a little unusual miss, but in this case the firing squad has one last request."

Alma Murphy, Maxine Green, Alice MaVega.

Announcer: Chuck McCann.

Music: Computerized.

TURN ON—30 minutes—ABC—Premiered/Ended: February 5, 1969.

TURN TO A FRIEND

Game. Contestants appear and bear their souls, stating their single most needed possession. The studio audience then selects the person with the saddest story. The player receives her plea, and additional help from the program in terms of prizes.

Host: Dennis James.

TURN TO A FRIEND—30 minutes—ABC—1953 - 1954.

TV AUCTION

Game. Various merchandise items are displayed on stage. The limit price of each item is stated. Via wire or mail, and on a first-come-first-served basis, the items are sold to the home viewers whose bids are found acceptable.

Host (Auctioneer): Sid Stone.

TV AUCTION—30 minutes—ABC—June 1954 - September 1954.

TV GENERAL STORE

Game. Various merchandise items are displayed on stage. The limit price of each item is stated. Via wire or mail home viewers participate. The viewer whose bid is the highest on a particular item is able to purchase it. Arrangements for the actual purchase are made after buyers are selected and off the air.

Host: Dave Clark.

Hostess: Judy Clark.

TV GENERAL STORE—60 minutes—ABC—June 23, 1953 - September 6, 1953.

TV READERS DIGEST

Anthology. Dramatizations based on stories appearing in *Readers Digest* magazine.

Host: Hugh Riley.

Included:

The Last Of The Old Time Shooting Sheriffs. Background: Arizona. A retired sheriff attempts to aid the citizens of a town plagued by a series of bank robberies.

Starring: Russ Simpson.

Master Counterfeiters. Master detective William J. Burns attempts to crack a counterfeiting case.

Starring: Roy Roberts.

The Trigger-Finger Clue. The police search for a criminal who, after robbing a bank president, killed him and his two sons.

Starring: Elisha Cook.

The Manufactured Clue. Police efforts to track a criminal who leaves a trail of false clues.

Starring: Paul Stewart.

TV READERS DIGEST—30 minutes—ABC—January 17, 1955 - July 9, 1956. 65 episodes. Syndicated.

TV SHOPPER

Women. Shopping hints, fashion tips, marketing advice, and consumer values.

Hostess: Kathi Norris.

TV SHOPPER—15 minutes—DuMont 1949.

TV SOUND STAGE

Anthology. Dramatic presentations.

Included:

Innocent Til Proved Guilty. A husband's efforts to end his wife's constant habit of jumping to conclusions.

Starring: Leora Dana, Paul McGrath.

One Small Guy. The story of a man who misuses his talent to make people like him.

Starring: Jack Lemmon, Georgiann Johnson, Doro Merande, Bruce Gordon.

Deception. Returning to his home town, a young man seeks revenge for the wrongs done to him.

Starring: Martin Brookes, Howard Freeman.

TV SOUND STAGE—30 minutes—NBC—July 10, 1953 - September 1953.

TV'S TOP TUNES

Musical Variety. Renditions of popular songs.

Versions:

TV's Top Tunes—15 minutes—CBS—July 4, 1951 - August 26, 1951.

Hosts: Peggy Lee, Mel Tormé.

Vocalists: The Skylarks.

Orchestra: Mitchell Ayres.

TV's Top Tunes—30 minutes—CBS—June 28, 1954 - September 3, 1955.

Host: Julius La Rosa.

Regulars: Helen O'Connell, Bob Eberly, Tommy Mercer, Marcie Miller, Lee Roy, The Ray Anthony Chorus.

Announcer: Tony Marvin.

Orchestra: Ray Anthony.

THE 20th CENTURY

Documentary. Historical films recounting the events of the twentieth century.

Host-Narrator: Walter Cronkite.

Music: Kenyon Hopkins; Laurence Rosenthal.

Producer: Burton Benjamin, Albert Wasserman, Isaac Kleinerman, Peter Poor, Marshall Flaum.

THE 20th CENTURY—30 minutes—CBS—October 20, 1957 - August 28, 1966. Syndicated. Spin-off series: "The 21st Century" (see title).

TWELVE O'CLOCK HIGH

Drama. Background: England during World War II. The experiences of the men and officers of the American 918th B-17 Bomber Squadron.

CAST

Brigadier General Frank Savage	Robert Lansing
Major General Wiley Crowe	John Larkin
Major Harvey Stovall	Frank Overton
Major Joseph Cobb	Lew Gallo
Major Doc Kaiser	Barney Philips
Colonel Joe Gallagher	Paul Burke
T/Sgt. Sandy Komansky	Chris Robinson
Brigadier General Edward Britt	Andrew Duggan

Music: Dominic Frontiere.

TWELVE O'CLOCK HIGH—60 minutes—ABC—September 18, 1964 - January 13, 1967. 78 episodes. Syndicated.

THE 20th CENTURY FOX HOUR

Anthology. Dramatic presentations.

Host: Joseph Cotten, Robert Sterling.

Director: Lewis Allen, John Brahm, Gerd Oswald, Robert Stevenson, Ted Post, Peter Godfrey, William Seiter, James V. Kern, Jules Bricken, Jerry Thorpe, Albert S. Rogell, Devery Freeman, William Russell.

Included:

Miracle On 34th Street. The heartwarming story of a man who believes he is the real Santa Claus.
Starring: Thomas Mitchell, Teresa Wright, Macdonald Carey.

Child Of The Regiment. The story of an army captain and his wife and their attempts to adopt a Japanese war orphan.
Starring: Teresa Wright.

Men Against Speed. A female photographer struggles to reunite her two feuding brothers in time for an important Italian car race.
Starring: Farley Granger, Mona Freeman.

Men In Her Life. When she discovers that a former student of her's is now running for governor, a teacher recalls the past and the trouble caused by the former problem student.
Starring: Phyllis Kirk, Kendell Scott, Beverly Washburn, Ann Doran.

THE 20th CENTURY FOX HOUR—60 minutes—CBS—October 5, 1955 - September 18, 1957.

TWENTIETH CENTURY TALES

Anthology. Rebroadcasts of dramas that were originally aired via other filmed anthology programs.

Included:

Rock Against The Sea. A girl who is afraid of the sea falls in love with a handsome sea captain.
Starring: Marjorie Bennett.

My Rival Is A Fiddle. A woman struggles to snatch the attentions of a man whose love is his fiddle.
Starring: Hans Conried, Maria Palmer.

TWENTIETH CENTURY TALES—30 minutes—ABC—June 1953 - September 1953.

THE 21st CENTURY

Documentary. Films relating the scientific and medical advances that will mark the twenty-first century.
Host: Walter Cronkite.

THE 21st CENTURY—30 minutes—CBS—January 20, 1967 - September 28, 1969.

THE $25,000 PYRAMID

Game. Two competing teams, each composed of two members: one celebrity and one noncelebrity contestant. One team chooses one subject from six categories that are displayed on a board (e.g., "Sleepy Head"). A question is then read that relates its purpose ("Describe things that are associated with sleep"). One player has a small monitor before him in which the key words appear, one at a time. Through one-word clues, he has to relate the meaning to his partner. One point is scored for each correct identification. Rounds are limited to thirty seconds and each team competes in three games. The highest scoring team is the winner and the contestant receives the opportunity to win ten thousand dollars.

Appearing in the winner's circle, one player sits with his back to a large pyramid that contains six categories, worth from one hundred to three hundred dollars each. The player who is facing the pyramid relates clues to their identification. If the player identifies all six within one minute, he wins ten thousand dollars, and the opportunity to compete in another game. Should he win again, he returns to the winner's circle and competes for twenty-five thousand dollars by identifying six subjects in one minute. Should he fail, he receives what money he has accumulated by identifying individual subjects. A spin-off from "The $10,000 Pyramid."

Host: Bill Cullen.
Announcer: Bob Clayton.
Executive Producer: Bob Stewart.
Producer: Anne Marie Schmitt.
Director: Mike Gargiulo.

THE $25,000 PYRAMID—30 minutes—Syndicated 1974.

TWENTY-ONE

Game. Two competing players. Object: To score twenty-one points by answering questions. Players are situated in separate isolation booths. Questions, which are selected from categories over which players have no control, are numbered from one to eleven. The number represents the point value of questions, the higher it is, the more difficult it is. Questions are asked of players as they are chosen, one per time. The first player to score twenty-one is the winner and receives five hundred dollars per point difference between his score and his opponent's score. Players compete until defeated.

Host: Jack Barry.
Announcer: Bill McCord.
Orchestra: Paul Taubman.

TWENTY-ONE—30 minutes—NBC—September 12, 1956 - October 16, 1958.

21 BEACON STREET

Mystery. Background: Boston, Mass. The cases of David Chase, a private detective who incorporates scientific deduction and electronic wizardry as he and his associates attempt to solve baffling crimes. (21 Beacon Street: The address of the David Chase Detective Agency).

CAST
David Chase	Dennis Morgan
Lola, his Girl Friday	Joanna Barnes
Brian, their assistant, a law student	Brian Kelly
Jim, their assistant, a master of disguise	James Maloney

21 BEACON STREET—30 minutes—NBC—July 2, 1959 - September 24, 1959.

TWENTY QUESTIONS

Game. Four players: three regular panelists and one studio-audience contestant. A subject, which is either animal, vegetable, or mineral, is revealed. Players have to identify it by asking questions, twenty being the maximum. If the contestant can identify the subject before the panel he receives a prize.

Hosts: Bill Slater; Jay Jackson.

Announcers: John Gregson; Frank Woldecker.

Panelists: Fred Von Deventer, Florence Rinard, Bobby McGuire, Herb Palesie, Johnny McFee.

Producer: George Elbes, Gary Stevens.

Director: Roger Bower, Dick Sondwick.

Sponsor: Ronson Lighters; Mennen; Luden's; Florida Citrus Growers.

TWENTY QUESTIONS—30 minutes —ABC—March 31, 1950 - June 22, 1951; July 6, 1954 - May 3, 1955.

26 MEN

Western. Background: The Arizona Territory, 1903. Dramatizations based on the files of the Arizona Rangers—men, limited by law to twenty-six, dispensing justice in the final days of the Old West.

CAST

Captain Tom Rynning   Tris Coffin
Ranger Clint Travis   Kelo Henderson
Music: Hal Hopper.

26 MEN—30 minutes—Syndicated 1958. 78 episodes.

THE $20,000 PYRAMID

See title: "The $10, 000 Pyramid."

TWILIGHT THEATRE

Anthology. Retitled episodes of dramas that were originally aired via other filmed anthology programs.

Included:

The Roustabaut. The story of a drifter who is forced into the middle of a fight between ranchers and storekeepers.
Starring: Scott Brady.

That Time In Boston. The story of a married couple and a sophisticated woman who spend a not very tranquil New Year's Eve together.
Starring: Hillary Brooke.

The Black Sleep's Daughter. The story of a wealthy playboy and his attempts to persuade his wife to grant him a divorce.
Starring: Carolyn Jones, Philip Ober,

Marcia Patrick.

TWILIGHT THEATRE—30 minutes— ABC—July 1958 - October 8, 1958.

THE TWILIGHT ZONE

Anthology. Tales of people confronted with the mysterious unexplored regions of the fifth dimension—the area that is everywhere, yet nowhere; the ground between all that is known and what is beyond understanding—an area called "The Twilight Zone."

Host-Narrator: Rod Serling.

Music: Leith Stevens; Bernard Herrmann; Jerry Goldsmith; William Lava.

Additional Music: Fred Steiner, Nathan Scott, Van Cleave, Leonard Rosenman, Tommy Morgan.

Executive Producer-Creator: Rod Serling.

Producer: Buck Houghton, William Froug, Herbert Hirschman.

Director: Robert Stevens, Justis Addiss, Douglas Heyes, John Brahm, Ronald Winston, William Claxton, Montgomery Pittman, James Sheldon, Mitchell Leisen, Jack Smight, Robert Sparr, Ida Lupino, Don Medford, Buzz Kulik, Richard L. Bare, John Rich, Elliott Silverstein, Boris Sagal, Anton Leader, Lamont Johnson, Christian Nyby, Robert Enrico (for the French film "An Occurance At Owl Creek Bridge" which was telecast on 2-28-64 and 9-11-64).

Included:

Jess-Belle. The story of a backwoods girl who uses a love potion on her old beau.

CAST

Jess-Belle: Anne Francis; Granny Hart: Jeanette Nolan.

A Most Unusual Camera. The story of a couple who, after their latest heist, acquire a camera that takes pictures of the future.

CAST

Chester: Fred Clark; Paula: Jean Carson; Woodward: Adam Williams.

The Night of the Meek. A heartwarming Christmas story about a department store santa who, after being fired for drinking, discovers that he is

the real Santa Claus.

CAST

Henry Corwin: Art Carney; Mr. Dundee: John Fiedler; Officer Flaherty: Robert P. Lieb; Burt: Burt Mustin.

Queen of the Nile. The story of a beautiful movie queen who seems never to age.

CAST

Pamela: Ann Blyth; Jordon: Lee Philips; Mrs. Draper: Ceila Lousky.

Program opening (one of several):

Host: "There is a fifth dimension beyond that which is known to man. It is a dimension as vast as space and as timeless as infinity. It is the middle ground between light and shadow, between science and superstition and it lies between the pit of man's fears and the summit of his knowledge. It is an area which we call The Twilight Zone."

THE TWILIGHT ZONE—30 minutes —CBS—October 2, 1959 - September 14, 1962. Syndicated. 60 minutes— CBS—January 3, 1963 - September 27, 1963. Rebroadcasts (CBS): June 1964 - September 18, 1964; May 1965 - September 1965. Syndicated. 134 half-hour episodes; 17 one-hour episodes.

TWIN TIME

Variety. Performances by undiscovered professional talent.
Host: Jack Lemmon.

Regulars: Arlene and Ardell Terry (the singing teenage twins), Jim Kirkwood, Lee Goodwin, Jack Kriza, Ann Koesun.

Producer: Sherman Marks.

Sponsor: Toni.

TWIN TIME—30 minutes—CBS 1950.

TWO FACES WEST

Western. Background: The town of Gunnison during the 1860s. The efforts of twin brothers Ben January, the marshal, and Rick January, a doctor, to maintain law and order.

CAST

Rick January   Charles Bateman
Ben January   Charles Bateman
Deputy Johnny Evans   Paul Comi
Music: Joe Weiss; Irving Friedman.

TWO FACES WEST—30 minutes—Syndicated 1961. 39 episodes.

TWO FOR THE MONEY

Game. Three competing contestants.

Round One: A general-knowledge type of question is read. The player who is first to identify himself through a buzzer signal receives a chance to answer. If correct, he receives money. The game continues until one player, the highest cash scorer, is declared the winner.

Round Two: The champion competes. Within a fifteen-second time limit, a rapid-fire question-and-answer session is conducted. For each correct answer the player gives, he receives the amount of money he won in the first round.

Round Three: Follows the format of round two. For each correct response the player gives, he receives the total earnings of rounds one and two.

Hosts: Herb Shriner; Sam Levenson.

Announcer: Dennis James.

Orchestra: Milton DeLugg.

Answer Judge: Dr. Mason Gross.

TWO FOR THE MONEY—30 minutes—CBS—August 15, 1953 - June 17, 1956.

TWO GIRLS NAMED SMITH

Comedy. Background: New York City. The misadventures of two small-town girls, aspiring models, sisters Babs and Peggy Smith, as they attempt to further their careers.

CAST
Babs Smith	Peggy Ann Garner
	Marcia Henderson
Peggy Smith	Peggy French
Babs' boyfriend	Richard Hayes
Peggy's boyfriend	Joseph Buloff
The girl's landlady	Aledardi Klein

Also: Jane Dulo, Scott Tennysa, Arthur Walsh.

Producer: Richard Lewis.

Director: Charles S. Dubin.

TWO GIRLS NAMED SMITH—30 minutes—ABC—January 20, 1951 - October 31, 1951.

TWO IN LOVE

Game. Newly married or engaged couples compete. Object: To build a nest egg. Friends and family of the individual couples appear on stage. Each time a personal question is answered by a friend or relative, that couple receives money. After a nest egg has been built for each couple, the couples then compete in a quiz. Before a question is asked, players have to state the amount of time, in seconds, it will require them to answer it. The question is asked and the couple who comes closest to their prediction wins the nest egg.

Host: Bert Parks.

TWO IN LOVE—30 minutes—NBC 1954.

THE TYCOON

Comedy. Background: Thunder Holding Corporation in Los Angeles, California. The story of Walter Andrews, industrialist, millionaire, and board chairman, a sixty-five-year-old widower who, facing objections from younger corporate executives, struggles to operate his company in accord with his established standards.

CAST
Walter Andrews	Walter Brennan
Herbert Wilson, the corporation president	Jerome Cowan
Pat Burns, Walter's aide	Van Williams
Betty Franklin, Walter's secretary	Janet Lake
Martha Keane, Walter's granddaughter	Patricia McNulty
Una Fields, Walter's housekeeper	Monty Margetts
Louise Wilson, Herbert's wife	Grace Albertson
Tom Keane, Martha's husband	George Lindsay

THE TYCOON—30 minutes—ABC—September 15, 1964 - September 6, 1965. 32 episodes.

𝒰

U.F.O.

Science Fiction Adventure. Background: London, England, 1980. As Unidentified Flying Objects (U.F.O.s) become established and believed to be a threat to the safety of Earth, world governments unite and sponsor the construction of S.H.A.D.O. (Supreme Headquarters, Alien Defense Organization), which is closely guarded under a veil of deep secrecy and housed beneath the Harlington-Straker film studios.

Establishing bases on both the Earth and the Moon, and incorporating highly complex defense equipment, S.H.A.D.O.'s battle of secrecy* against alien invaders is dramatized as it attempts to discover who they are, where they come from and what they want. An I.T.C. presentation.

*Public awareness of U.F.O.s is feared to cause worldwide panic.

U.F.O. Ed Bishop. *Courtesy Independent Television Corp.; an ATV Company.*

CAST

Edward Straker,
the commander of
S.H.A.D.O.   Ed Bishop
Colonel Alec Freeman, his
assistant   George Sewell
Lt. Gay Ellis,
the commander of
Moon Base   Gabrielle Drake
Colonel Paul Foster, Straker's
assistant   Michael Billington
Lt. Nina Barry, a
space tracker   Dolores Mantez
Lt. Joan Harrington, a
space tracker   Antoni Ellis
Colonel Virginia Lake   Wanda Ventham
Captain Peter Karlin   Peter Gordeno
Miss Eland, Straker's
secretary   Norma Roland
Douglas Jackson, the
psychiatrist   Valdek Sheybol
Lt. Keith Ford   Keith Alexander
Skydiver operator   Georganna Moon
Skydiver navigator   Jeremy Wilkin
Skydiver engineer   Jon Kelly
Skydiver captain   David Warbeck
Moon Base operator   Andrea Allan
Third Mobile officer   Hugh Armstrong
General James Henderson, Straker's
superior   Grant Taylor
S.H.A.D.O. operative   Penny Spencer
S.H.A.D.O. operative   Ayshea
Tunner, the radio
operator   Patrick Allen
Lew Waterman, an
Interceptor pilot   Garry Myers
Mark Bradley, an
Interceptor pilot   Harry Baird
Miss Scott, Henderson's
secretary   Louise Pajd
Interceptor pilot   Mark Hawkins
Miss Holland, Straker's
secretary (later
episodes)   Lois Maxwell
The radar technician   Michael Ferrand

Music: Barry Gray.

Producer: Reg Hill, Gerry Anderson.

Director: Ken Turner, David Bell,
Alan Perry, David Lane, Jeremy
Summers, Gerry Anderson,
David Tomblin, Cyril Frankel.

U.F.O.—60 minutes—Syndicated
1972. 26 episodes.

THE UGLIEST GIRL
IN TOWN

Comedy. Heartbroken after actress
Julie Renfield returns to London
following her completion of a movie,
Hollywood talent scout Tim Blair is
approached by his photographer-

The Ugliest Girl in Town. Peter Kastner as
Timmie Blair. © *Screen Gems.*

brother, Gene, who, requiring hippie
pictures, persuades him to pose as a
girl. The photographs, which manage
to find their way to a London ad
agency, impress its head, Mr.
Courtney, who commissions Gene to
shoot a layout using the girl who,
unknown to him, is a man.

Discovering a way to be with Julie,
Tim retains his disguise and adopts the
secret alias of Timmie Blair. Sharing
each other's company, Tim finds himself deeply in love with Julie and
unable to leave London. As the ad
campaign nears completion, Gene
loses eleven thousand pounds in a
gambling casino—money that has to
be paid "or else." Discovering Gene's
plight, Tim voluntarily agrees to continue with the masquerade to assist in
paying the debt.

Girlish, modeling by day; and
boyish, dating his starlet, Julie, by
night, Tim Blair struggles to conceal
the fact of, and maintain, two separate existances.

CAST

Tim Blair   Peter Kastner
Timmie Blair   Peter Kastner
Julie Renfield   Patricia Brake
Gene Blair   Gary Marshall
Mr. Courtney   Nicholas Parsons

Music: Howard Greenfield.

THE UGLIEST GIRL IN TOWN—30
minutes—ABC—September 26, 1968 -
January 30, 1969. 20 episodes.

UKULELE IKE

Variety. Music, songs, and comedy
sketches.

Host: Cliff Edwards, Ukulele Ike.

Vocalist: Beverly Fite.

Music: The Slim Jackson Quartet.

UKULELE IKE—15 minutes—CBS
1950.

ULTRAMAN

Science Fiction Adventure. Background: Twenty-first-century Japan.
As two Unidentified Flying Objects
approach Earth they collide; one veers
off course and crashes in a lake; the
other strikes a Scientific Patrol Headquarters exploratory ship and kills its
pilot, Iota. Emerging from the
grounded alien craft, a mysterious
being, from the Nebula M-78 in the
fortieth galaxy, appears and to repay
Iota for the wrong done to him, gives
him his life and a special capsule:
"...you and I will become one and we
will fight as one for the peace of Earth
for all time to come. You will remain
in your present form, Iota. Whenever
you are in trouble use the Beta Capsule and you, Iota, will become Ultraman."

Stories depict the exploits of Iota, a
member of the Scientific Patrol, as he,
in his secret alias as Ultraman, battles
dangerous and monstrous alien phenomena. Produced in Japan; dubbed in
English. Characters are not given
screen credit. Created by Eiji
Tsuburaya.

ULTRAMAN—30 minutes—Syndicated 1967. 39 episodes.

THE UNCLE AL SHOW

Children. Music, songs, stories, and
puppet acts.

CAST

Uncle Al (Host)   Al Lewis
Cinderella   Janet Green
Captain Windy   Wanda Lewis

Also: Larry Smith and his puppets.

THE UNCLE AL SHOW—60 minutes
—ABC—October 18, 1958 - September
19, 1959.

UNCLE CROC'S BLOCK

Children. A spoof of children's television programs. The series itself, set
in a television studio, focuses on the
misadventures that befall Uncle Croc,
the costumed (as a crocodile) host of
"Croc's Block" a kids show he detests
doing. Live action segments are
coupled with short cartoons.

CAST

Uncle Croc	Charles Nelson Reilly
Basil Bitterbottom, the director	Jonathan Harris
Rabbit Ears, Croc's assistant	Johnny Silver
	Alfie Wise
The $6.95 Man	Bob Ridgley

Voices (for the cartoon segments): Allan Melvin, Kenneth Mars, Alan Oppenheimer, Bob Ridgley, Lennie Weinrib.

Music: Yvette Blais, Jeff Michael.

Cartoon Segments:

Fraidy Cat. The misadventures of a cat who, having lost eight of his nine lives, struggles to protect his last remaining life.

The Mush Puppies. The hectic exploits of MUSH (Mangy Unwanted Shabby Heroes), Northwest Mounted Canadian Police dogs.

Wacky and Packy. The story concerns the misadventures of a caveman named Packy and his pet elephant, Wacky, who were caught in an earthquake and transported to modern times.

UNCLE CROC'S BLOCK—55 minutes—ABC—September 6, 1975 - October 18, 1975; 30 minutes— October 25, 1975 - February 14, 1976.

THE UNCLE FLOYD SHOW

Children. Set against the background of a boarding house, the program features music, songs, and comedy sketches that revolve around the antics of the strange characters who inhabit the mythical premises. Ingenious puppets (also roomers), coupled with fan club news, birthday announcements, visual displays of viewer drawings, and contests for prizes heightens the program's mystique.

The Uncle Floyd Show. Floyd Vivino and his puppet Oogie.

Host-Producer-Creator: Floyd Vivino (as Uncle Floyd).

Regulars: Pat Cupo, Scott Gordon, Marc Nathan, Tony Petrillo.

Announcer: John Pichitino.

Director: Ralph Van Kuiken, Marc Nathan.

Among the characters portrayed by Floyd Vivino:

Rocky Rock 'N' Roll; Briscoe T. Fardell, a con-artist; Don Ho-Hum, the Hawaiian Singer; Don Goomba, a Godfather type character; Flojo, the TV clown; Strongzini; Cowboy Charlie, the off-key singer; Vinnie, the carpenter; The Storyman; Fatso Popasso, the glutton; Senor La Basura, the entrepreneur.

Main Puppets: Oogie, the mischievous boy; Poogie the dog; Donkey Oatie, Senor's cohort; Mr. Jones, the intoxicated singer; Old Hutch the sea captain; Mr. Bones, the dancing skeleton.

THE UNCLE FLOYD SHOW—30 minutes—Premiered: September 30, 1975. Though aired basically in New York and New Jersey (over WBTB-TV, Ch. 68), the program is known in many areas of the country and as faraway as Greece.

UNCLE JOHNNY COONS

Children. Stories, silent films, and sketches that relate good habits to children.

Host: Johnny Coons, ventriloquist.

His dummy: George.

Announcer: Bruce Roberts.

Producer: James Green.

Sponsor: Lever Brothers.

UNCLE JOHNNY COONS—30 minutes—CBS 1954.

UNCLE MISTELTOE AND HIS ADVENTURES

Children. Background: Wonderland. The series focuses on the lives of the magic little people (puppets) who live on Candy Cane Lane, a magic street where dreams come true.

Puppets: Uncle Misteltoe, the jovial story teller; Olio, Molio, and Rolio; Aunt Judy; Skippy Monkey; Obediah Pig; Tony Pony; Humphrey Mouse.

Voices-Puppeteers: The Marshall Field Marionette Company.

UNCLE MISTELTOE AND HIS AD-

VENTURES—15 minutes—ABC 1950.

UNCOVERED

See title: "Mark Saber."

UNDERCURRENT

Anthology. Retitled episodes of dramas that were originally aired via "The Web."

Included:

Trapmates. The story of a near victim who turns the tables on a would-be burglar by blackmailing him as a partner in an attempted holdup.

Starring: Hugh Beaumont.

The Old Lady's Tears. The story of a private detective, assigned to find the missing grandson of a wealthy old woman, who suddenly finds himself involved in two murders.

Starring: Lex Barker, Jean Byron, Lurene Tuttle.

Integrity. The story of a police informer who poses as a gambler to track down thieves in North Africa.

Starring: Jean Pierre Aumont, Jay Novello, Leon Asken.

UNDERCURRENT—30 minutes— CBS—June 1955 - September 1955.

UNDERDOG

Animated Cartoon. Background: Washington, D.C. The exploits of a lovable, humble dog, Shoeshine Boy, alias Underdog, a dauntless and fearless crusader for justice.

Additional Characters: Sweet Polly Purebred, ace television reporter; Sinister Bar Sinister, an evil scientist; and Cad, his aide.

Characters' Voices

Underdog	Wally Cox
Sweet Polly Purebred	Norma McMillan

Additional Voices: Sandy Becker, Allen Swift, Dello Stokes, Mort Marshall, Kenny Delmar, George S. Irving, Ben Stone.

UNDERDOG—30 minutes. NBC— October 3, 1964 - September 3, 1966; CBS—September 10, 1966 - September 2, 1967; NBC—September 7, 1968 - September 1, 1973. 125 episodes.

THE UNDERSEA WORLD OF JACQUES COUSTEAU

Documentary. Films relating the undersea explorations of Jacques Cousteau and the men of his ship, *Calypso*.
Narrators: Jacques Cousteau; Rod Serling; Joseph Campanella.
Music: Lyn Murray.

THE UNDERSEA WORLD OF JACQUES COUSTEAU—60 minutes —ABC—Premiered: January 8, 1968. Broadcast as a series of specials.

THE UNEXPECTED

Anthology. Dramatizations depicting the plight of people trapped in sudden, unexpected situations.
Host: Herbert Marshall.

THE UNEXPECTED—30 minutes— NBC 1952.

UNICORN TALES

Children. Twentieth-century adaptations of classic fairy tales.
Music: Jack Feldman.
Executive Producer: Nick DeNoia.

Producer: William P. Milling.

UNICORN TALES—30 minutes—Syndicated 1977.

UNION PACIFIC

Western. Background: Dale, Wyoming, 1880s. The saga of the final linking between East and West (Omaha to Cheyenne) of the Union Pacific Railroad.

CAST
Bart McClelland,
the operations
head   Jeff Morrow
Bill Kinkaid, the
chief surveyor   Judd Pratt
Georgia, the owner
of the local
dancehall   Susan Cummings

UNION PACIFIC—30 minutes—Syndicated 1958. 39 episodes.

UNIVERSAL STAR TIME

Anthology. Retitled episodes of dramas originally aired via "The Bob Hope Chrysler Theatre."

Included:

A Small Rebellion. A playwright attempts to persuade a famous actress to star in a play that he has written and believes will be a success.

CAST
Sara Lescaut: Simone Signoret; Michael Kolinos: George Maharis; Noel Greb: Sam Leven.

Escape Into Jeopardy. Working with authorities, a convicted counterfeiter escapes from prison to assist in exposing a counterfeiting ring.

CAST
Larry Martin: James Franciscus.

Two Is The Number. Police efforts to prove that a woman is responsible for the death of a hoodlum.

CAST
Jenny Dworak: Shelley Winters; Dave Breslau: Martin Balsam.

The Fifth Passenger. A British Intelligence officer attempts to discover if a naval hero is leaking top-secret information to the Soviets.

CAST
Peter Carrington: Mel Ferrer; Jane Day: Dana Wynter.

UNIVERSAL STAR TIME—60 minutes—Syndicated 1971. 30 episodes.

UNK AND ANDY

Children. Aimed at preschoolers, the program attempts to relate facts about nature's wildlife through the use of alphabet animals (i.e., letters of the alphabet are drawn to resemble animals—from Andy Auk to Zachary Zebra).

Host-Cartoonist: Jack Kenaston as Uncle Jack.
Assistant: Andy Auk, an animated character voiced by Jack Kenaston.
Producer-Director: Jack Kenaston.

UNK AND ANDY—15 minutes—Syndicated 1950. 25 episodes.

THE UNTAMED WORLD

Documentary. Films exploring the people and animals of the remote regions of the world.
Narrator: Philip Carey.

Music: Mort Garson.

THE UNTAMED WORLD—30 minutes—NBC—January 11, 1969 August 30, 1969. Syndicated.

THE UNTOUCHABLES

Crime Drama. Background: Chicago during the 1930s, the era of Prohibition and gangland rule. The exploits of the Federal Special Squad, an elite team of U.S. Treasury Department agents known as the Untouchables, as they, under the leadership of Eliot Ness, battle the forces of underworld corruption. A realistic and penetrating look at the violence and corruption that shook America's past.

CAST
Eliot Ness   Robert Stack
Agent Martin
Flaherty   Jerry Paris
Agent William
Longfellow   Abel Fernandez
Agent Jack Rossman   Steve London
Agent Enrico
Rossi   Nicholas Georgiade
Agent Cam Allison   Anthony George
Agent Lee Hobson   Paul Picerni
Mobster Frank
Nitti   Bruce Gordon
Mobster Al Capone   Neville Brand
Narrator: Walter Winchell.

Music: Wilbur Hatch; Nelson Riddle.
Executive Producer: Jerry Thorpe, Leonard Freeman.
Producer: Howard Hoffman, Alan A. Armer, Alvin Cooperman, Lloyd Richards, Fred Freiberger, Charles Russell.
Director: John Peyser, Stewart Rosenberg, Robert Butler, Walter Grauman, Ida Lupino.

THE UNTOUCHABLES—60 minutes —ABC—October 15, 1959 - September 10, 1963. 114 episodes. Syndicated.

UPBEAT

Musical Variety. The top songs, dances, and recording personalities of the day.

Versions:
Upbeat—15 minutes—CBS—July 15, 1955 - September 2, 1955.
Hosts: Guests of the week including: Mindy Carson, Teresa Brewer, Georgia Gibbs, The Four Lads, Don Cornell.
Dancers: The Tommy Morton Troupe.
Orchestra: Russ Case.

Upbeat—60 minutes—Syndicated 1966.

Host: Don Webster.

Featured: The Upbeat Dancers.

Music; Provided by guests.

UPSTAIRS, DOWNSTAIRS

See title: "Masterpiece Theatre."

UP TO PAAR

See title: "Jack Paar."

UPTOWN JUBILEE

Variety. Performances by black entertainers.

Host: Willie Bryant.

Producer: Barry Wood.

Director: John Wray.

UPTOWN JUBILEE—60 minutes—CBS 1949.

U.S. BORDER PATROL

Drama. The work of federal agents in conjunction with the U.S. Border Patrol.

Starring: Richard Webb as Don Jagger, deputy chief of the U.S. Border Patrol.

U.S. BORDER PATROL—30 minutes—Syndicated 1958. 39 episodes.

U.S. MARSHAL

See title: "The Sheriff of Cochise."

THE U.S. STEEL HOUR

Anthology. Dramatic and comedic productions.

Producer: Norman Felton, David Alexander, George Kondolf.

Sponsor: U.S. Steel.

Included:

The Bogey Man. Fearing to lose his mother's love, a young boy attempts to thwart her plans to remarry.

CAST
Madge Collins: Celeste Holm; Jack Roberts: Robert Preston; Tony Collins: Darryl Richard.

No Time For Sergeants. The misadventures of Will Stockdale, a naive Georgia farmboy who is drafted into the Air Force. Later made into a feature film.

CAST
Will Stockdale: Andy Griffith; Sgt. King: Harry Clark; Ben Whitledge: Eddie LeRoy; Captain: Alexander Clark.

Freighter. After twenty-five years as the skipper of the freighter *Singapore,* a captain discovers it is to end its operation. The story relates his attempts to adjust to the prospect of losing his beloved job.

CAST
Captain: Henry Hull; Scotty: Thomas Mitchell; Clay: James Daly.

Wish On The Moon. The story of two girls: Frances Barclay, who is determined to become an actress; and Olivia Beech, a carefree art student.

CAST
First version 1953: Frances Barclay: Eva Marie Saint; Olivia Beech: Phyllis Kirk.

Second version 1959: Frances Barclay: Peggy Ann Garner; Olivia Beech: Erin O'Brien.

THE U.S. STEEL HOUR—60 minutes —CBS—October 27, 1953 - June 11, 1963.

U

VAGABOND

Travel. Visits to interesting and unusual places.

Host-Narrator: Don Hobart.

Music: George Wasch.

VAGABOND—30 minutes—Syndicated 1959. 39 episodes.

VACATION PLAYHOUSE

Pilot Films. Proposed comedy series.

Included:

The Hoofer. The misadventures of two small-town vaudevillians in Chicago as they struggle to make the big time.

CAST
Donald Dugan: Donald O'Connor; Freddy Brady: Soupy Sales; Brainsley Gordon: Jerome Cowan.

Ivy League. The misadventures of Bull Mitchell, a retired marine who enrolls as a college freshman.

CAST
Bull: William Bendix; Timmy: Tim Hovey.

The Two Of Us. The story of a young boy who prefers the world of fantasy he has created from his mother's book illustrations to that of making real friends.

CAST
Elizabeth: Patricia Crowley; Chris: Bill Mumy; Captain Gibson: Barry Livingston; Helen: Mary Jane Croft.

Off We Go. The misadventures of a sixteen-year-old boy who enlists with the U.S. Army air corps.

CAST
Rod Ryan: Michael Burns; Jefferson Dale: Dick Foran; Lt. Sue Chamberlain: Nancy Kovack; Debbie Trowbridge: Anne Jilliann.

Mickey And The Contessa. The complications that arise when a football coach applies for a housekeeper and acquires a beautiful Hungarian contessa.

CAST
Mickey Brennan: Mickey Shaughnessey; Contessa Czigonia: Eva Gabor; Argey Tanner: John Fiedler; Sissy Brennan: Ann Marshall.

VACATION PLAYHOUSE—30 minutes—CBS—June 1963 - September 1963; June 1964 - September 1964; June 1965 - September 1965; June 1966 - September 1966. 27 episodes.

THE VAL DOONICAN SHOW

Musical Variety.

Host: Val Doonican.

Regulars: Bob Todd, Bernard Cribbins, The Norman Maen Dancers, The Mike Sammes Singers.

Announcer: Paul Griffith.

Orchestra: Jack Parnell; Kenny Woods.

THE VAL DOONICAN SHOW—60 minutes—ABC—June 5, 1971 - August

14, 1971.

British Version (upon which the above British produced American telecast version is based):

The Val Doonican Show—60 minutes —B.B.C.-1 from London—1967.

Host: Val Doonican.

Regulars: Nana Mouskouri, Daniel Remey, The Pattersons, The Gayos, The Adam Singers.

Orchestra: Peter Knight.

VALENTINE'S DAY

Comedy. Background: New York City. The life and times of playboy Valentine Farrow, the nonfiction editor for a Park Avenue publishing house.

CAST

Valentine Farrow	Tony Franciosa
Rocky Sin, his valet, a Chinese-American con merchant	Jack Soo
Libby, his secretary	Janet Waldo
Mr. Dunstall, his employer	Jerry Hausner
Fipple, the neighborhood handyman	Eddie Quillan

Music: Jeff Alexander.

VALENTINE'S DAY—30 minutes— ABC—September 18, 1964 - September 10, 1965. 34 episodes.

VALIANT LADY

Serial. The dramatic story of Helen Emerson, a woman who, despite financial strain, struggles to raise her three children.

CAST

Helen Emerson	Nancy Coleman Flora Campbell
Her husband	Jerome Cowan
Her son, nineteen years of age	James Kirkwood
Her daughter, seventeen years of age	Anne Pearson
Her daughter, nine years of age	Lydia Reed
Margo, a friend	Dolores Sutton

Also: Betty Oakes, Marc Cramer, Abby Lewis, Earl Hammon.

Organist: John Gart.

Producer: Carl Green, Leonard Blair.

Sponsor: Toni; General Mills.

Program Open:

Announcer: "Valiant Lady, the story of a brave woman and her brilliant but unstable husband; the story of her struggle to keep his feet planted firmly on the pathway to success."

VALIANT LADY—15 minutes—CBS —October 9, 1953 - August 16, 1957.

VALLEY OF THE DINOSAURS

Animated Cartoon. Exploring an uncharted river canyon in the Amazon, a twentieth-century family, the Butlers, are engulfed by a whirlpool, propelled through an underground cavern and transported to a time past, the prehistoric era, where they befriend a cave family parallel to them. Stories depict their struggles for survival. Scientific principles are illustrated as both families assist and learn from one another.

Characters:

The Modern Family:

John Butler, the father, a science instructor; Kim Butler, his wife; Katie Butler, their daughter; Greg Butler, their son; and Digger, their pet dog.

The Cave Family:

Gorak, the father; Gera, his wife; Tana, their daughter; Lock, their son; and Glomb, their pet stegasaurus.

Characters' Voices

John Butler	Mike Road
Kim Butler	Shannon Farnon
Katie Butler	Margene Fudenna
Greg Butler	Jackie Haley
Gorak	Alan Oppenheimer

Valley of the Dinosaurs. Left to right: Greg, Kim, Katie, and John (offering a hand to) Gorak. Behind Gorak: Gera (left) and Tana. Bottom right: Lock (holding Glomb's tail) and Digger the dog.© *Hanna-Barbera Productions.*

Gera	Joan Gardner
Lock	Steacy Bertheau
Tana	Melanie Baker

Music: Hoyt Curtin.

Executive Producer: William Hanna, Joseph Barbera.

Director: Charles A. Nichols.

VALLEY OF THE DINOSAURS—25 minutes—CBS—September 7, 1974 - September 4, 1976. 16 episodes. Syndicated.

VAN DYKE AND COMPANY

Variety. Music, songs, and comedy sketches.

Host: Dick Van Dyke.

Regulars: Lois January, Marilyn Soko, Mickey Rose, Pat Proft, Andy Kaufman, Al Bloomfield, Bob Einstein, Chuck McCann, The Los Angeles Mime Company.

Ochestra: Lex De Avezedo.

Musical Coordinator: D'Vaughn Pershing.

Choreography: Lester Wilson.

Executive Producer: Byron Paul.

Producer: Allan Blye, Bob Einstein.

Director: John Moffitt.

VAN DYKE AND COMPANY—60 minutes—NBC—September 20, 1976 - December 30, 1976.

VANITY FAIR

Women. Interviews, guests, beauty tips, and advice.

Hostess: Robin Chandler.

Co-hostess: Dorothy Doan.

Announcer: Tony Marvin.

Orchestra: Johnny Green.

Producer: John Cazabon, Gil Fates, Frances Buss.

Director: Frances Buss.

Sponsor: Maiden Form Bras; Airwick Air Freshner.

VANITY FAIR—30 and 45 minute versions—CBS—1948 - 1951.

VAUDEVILLE

Variety. Performances by Vaudeville comedians and re-creations of its associated comedy by new talent discoveries.

Guest Hosts: Milton Berle, Steve Allen

and Jayne Meadows, Edgar Bergen, Eddie Foy, Jr., Rudy Vallee, Jack Carter, Red Buttons.

The Card Girl: Donna Jean Young.

Orchestra: George Wyle.

Executive Producer: Burt Rosen.

Producer: Mort Green.

Director: Jack Scott.

VAUDEVILLE—60 minutes—Syndicated 1975.

VAUGHN MONROE

Listed: The television programs of singer-bandleader Vaughn Monroe.

The Vaughn Monroe Show—Musical Variety—30 minutes—CBS—October 10, 1950 - July 3, 1951.

Host: Vaughn Monroe.

Regulars: Shayne Cogan, Ada Lynne, Ziggy Latent, Henry Davis, Olga Suarey, The Moon Maidens.

Orchestra: Vaughn Monroe.

The Vaughn Monroe Show—Musical Variety—15 minutes—NBC—August 31, 1954 - September 28, 1954.

Host: Vaughn Monroe.

Regulars: McCaffrey and Susan; The Satisfiers.

Orchestra: Richard Hayman.

The Vaughn Monroe Show—Musical Variety—15 minutes—NBC—August 31, 1954 - September 28, 1954.

Host: Vaughn Monroe.

Vocalists: The Tunestones.

Orchestra: Richard Maltby.

THE VEIL

Anthology. Dramatizations based on incredible but true phenomena.

Host-Performer: Boris Karloff.

THE VEIL—30 minutes—Syndicated 1958.

THE VERDICT IS YOURS

Courtroom Drama. Dramatizations based on actual court records. The studio audience comprises the jury, which relates the verdict at the end of the trial.

Judges, Witness, Plaintiffs: Guest actors.

Defense Council: Practicing attorneys.

Court Reporters: Jim McKay; Bill Stout.

THE VERDICT IS YOURS—30 minutes—CBS—July 3, 1958 - September 28, 1962.

British Version:

The Verdict Is Yours—30 minutes—Granada TV from Manchester—1958.

CAST

Martin Benson, Simon Kester, David Ensor, John McGregor.

VERSATILE VARIETIES

A variety series, broadcast on NBC in 1949 with host George Givat, and Jerry Terune and his Orchestra.

VERSATILE VARIETIES

Variety. Performances by undiscovered professional talent.

Hosts: Bob Russell; Harold Barry.

Regulars: Janis Paige, Leonardo & Zola, The Delmars, The Youman Brothers & Frances.

Orchestra: Jerry Jerome.

VERSATILE VARIETIES—30 minutes—NBC 1950.

VERSATILE VARIETIES

Musical Variety.

Hostess: Lady Iris Mountbatten.

Orchestra: Mark Towers; Bernie Sands.

Commercial Spokeswoman: Anne Francis.

Producer: Charles Basch, Frances Scott.

Director: Mark Hawley.

Sponsor: Bonafide Mills.

VERSATILE VARIETIES—30 minutes—CBS 1951. Also known as "The Bonny Maid Versatile Varieties Program."

VIC DAMONE

Listed: The television programs of singer-actor Vic Damone.

The Vic Damone Show—Musical Variety—CBS—30 minutes—July 2, 1956 - September 1956.

Host: Vic Damone.

Announcer: Rex Marshall.

Orchestra: Tutti Carmarata.

The Vic Damone Show—Musical Variety—30 minutes—CBS—July 3, 1957 - September 1957.

Host: Vic Damone.

Regulars: Peggy King, The Spellbinders.

Announcer: Johnny Olsen.

Orchestra: Bert Farber.

The Lively Ones—Musical Variety—30 minutes—NBC—1962; 1963. See title.

Dean Martin Presents The Vic Damone Show—Musical Variety—60 minutes—NBC—July 1967 - September 1967. Rebroadcasts: NBC—60 minutes—July 8, 1971 - August 19, 1971.
August 19, 1971.

Host: Vic Damone.

Regulars: Carol Lawrence, Gail Martin.

Orchestra: Les Brown.

THE VICTOR BORGE SHOW

Variety.

Host: Victor Borge.

Orchestra: Phil Ingallis.

THE VICTOR BORGE SHOW—30 minutes—NBC 1951.

VICTORY AT SEA

Documentary. Films detailing the United States Naval operations during World War II.

Narrator: Leonard Graves.

Music: The NBC Symphony Orchestra, conducted by Robert Russell Bennett.

Symphonic Score (13 hours): Richard Rodgers.

VICTORY AT SEA—30 minutes—NBC—October 16, 1952 - April 19, 1953. 26 episodes. Syndicated.

VIDEO CHEF

Cooking. The preparation and making of foreign and American meals.

Host: Jean Holt.

VIDEO CHEF—15 minutes—ABC 1952.

VIDEO VILLAGE

Game. Background: Video Village, a huge game board composed of three lanes of squares, each of which are marked as in a game (e.g., "Lose one turn"; "Move ahead two spaces"; "Go to jail"). Two competing players. Players move up and down the lanes via the roll of two dice (chuck-a-luck). The player who is first to reach the finish line is the winner and receives merchandise prizes.

Host (The Mayor): Jack Narz; Monty Hall.

Assistants: Eileen Barton; Joanna Copeland.

Announcer (The Town Crier): Kenny Williams.

Versions:

VIDEO VILLAGE—30 minutes—CBS —July 11, 1960 - June 11, 1962.

VIDEO VILLAGE JUNIOR (a children's version of the adult game)—30 minutes—September 1960 - June 16, 1962.

THE VIM TALENT SEARCH

Variety. Performances by aspiring entertainers. Highlight of the program was its search to find "Miss U.S. Television." Being new, the medium prompted many local stations to sponsor a "Miss Television Contest," wherein local beauties competed for titles such as "Miss Chicago TV," "Miss New York TV," etc. Girls, at least eighteen years of age, married or single, attractive, and possessing several talents, were eligible. Most notable of the winners was Edythe Adams, the local New York winner who was crowned "Miss U.S. Television of 1950." Today known as Edie Adams, she received prizes and awards valued at $10,000 plus a contract for TV performances.

Host: Dick Kollmar (1949); Skitch Henderson (1950).

Sponsor: Vim.

THE VIM TALENT SEARCH—30 minutes—NBC—1949-1950.

THE VIN SCULLY SHOW

Variety. Guests, music, and celebrity interviews.

Host: Vin Scully.

Announcer: Harry Blackstone Jr.

Orchestra: H.B. Barnum.

THE VIN SCULLY SHOW—30 min-utes—CBS—January 15, 1973 - March 23, 1973.

THE VINCENT LOPEZ SHOW

Musical Variety.

Host: Vincent Lopez.

Regulars: Judy Lynn, Teddy Norman, Eddie O'Connor, Johnny Messner, Johnny Amorosa, Danny Davis.

THE VINCENT LOPEZ SHOW—30 minutes—CBS—October 13, 1956 - April 27, 1957.

V.I.P.

Biography. Through films, photographs, and interviews, the lives of Very Important People are recalled.

V.I.P.—15 minutes—Syndicated 1963.

THE VIRGINIA GRAHAM SHOW

Talk-Variety.

Hostess: Virginia Graham.

Music: The Ellie Frankel Quintet; The Jimmy Rowles Quartet.

THE VIRGINIA GRAHAM SHOW —60 and 30 minute versions (depending on the local station)—Syndicated 1970.

THE VIRGINIAN

Western. Background: The Shiloh Ranch in Medicine Bow, Wyoming, 1880s. Events in the shaping of Wyoming as seen through the experiences of a mysterious drifter, the man everybody respects, but nobody really knows, The Virginian, foreman of the Shiloh Ranch.

CAST

The Virginian (referred to as Jim in several episodes)	James Drury
Judge Henry Garth, the first owner of the Shiloh Ranch	Lee J. Cobb
Trampas, the assistant foreman	Doug McClure
Molly Wood, the newspaper publisher	Pippa Scott
Betsy Garth, the judge's daughter	Roberta Shore
Steve Hill, a ranch hand	Gary Clarke
Emmett Ryker, the deputy sheriff	Clu Gulager
Randy Garth, the judge's son	Randy Boone
Belden, a ranch hand	L. Q. Jones
Jennifer Garth, the judge's orphaned niece	Diane Roter
Morgan Starr, the temporary owner of the Shiloh Ranch	John Dehner
Sheriff Mark Abbott	Ross Elliot
John Grainger, the second owner of the Shiloh Ranch	Charles Bickford
Elizabeth Grainger, his niece	Sara Lane
Stacy Grainger, his grandson	Don Quine
Clay Grainger, the third owner of the Shiloh Ranch	John McIntire
Holly Grainger, his wife	Jeanette Nolan
David Sutton, a ranch hand	David Hartman
Jim Horn, a ranch hand	Tim Matheson
Sheriff Brannon	Harlan Warde
Gene, a ranch hand	Jean Peloquin
The town bartenders	The Irish Rovers

Music: Leonard Rosenman; Percy Faith; Hans Salter; Leo Shuken.

Producer: Roy Huggins, Jules Schermer, Richard Irving, Winston Miller, Frank Price.

THE VIRGINIAN—90 minutes—NBC —September 19, 1962 - September 9, 1970. 225 episodes. Syndicated.

Revised format: "The Men From Shiloh."

Background: The Shiloh Ranch in Medicine Bow, Wyoming, 1890s. The exploits of four men: Colonel Alan MacKenzie, Englishman, the owner of the ranch; The Virginian, the foreman; and hired hands Trampas and Roy Tate, as they attempt to maintain law and order.

CAST

The Virginian	James Drury
Colonel Alan MacKenzie	Stewart Granger
Trampas	Doug McClure
Roy Tate	Lee Majors

Music: Leonard Rosenman.

THE MEN FROM SHILOH—90 minutes—NBC—September 16, 1970 - September 8, 1971. 24 episodes.

THE VISE

Anthology. Dramatizations depicting the plight of people who are caught in a web of their own misdeeds.

Host: Ron Rondell.

Included:

Set Of Murder. Facing financial ruin, a wealthy businessman plots to save himself by murdering an inventor and cashing in on his invention.

CAST
Clifford Evans, Honor Blackman, Martin Baddley.

The Secret Place. Finding some old love letters, a neglected wife plots to test her husband's jealousy.

CAST
Margaret Rawlings, John Stewart.

The Eavsdropper. The story of an older woman's romance with a younger man.

CAST
Milda Parley, Frederick Leister.

Let Murder Be Done. Seeking to marry a younger woman, a man plots to murder his rich but older wife.

CAST
Dennis Price, Avis Scott.

THE VISE—30 minutes—ABC—October 1, 1954 - June 27, 1957. Produced in England.

VISION ON

Educational. Through total visual entertainment (cartoons, sketches, and songs) aspects of the adult world are related to children with impaired hearing. Produced in England.

Host: Tony Hart.
Hostess: Patricia Keysell.
Regulars: Wilfred Lunn, Ben Benison, David Cleveland, Humphrey Umbrage.

Music: Recorded.

VISION ON—30 minutes—Syndicated 1973.

VISIONS

Anthology. Dramatizations of American plays written especially for television.

Music: Mark Snow.
Music Theme: Joe Raposo.
Producer: Barbara Schultz.
Director: Paul Bogart.

Included:

The War Widow. The story centers on the love between two young women: Amy, a lonely girl living with her mother while her husband is serving overseas during W.W. I; and Jenny, an independent woman struggling to succeed as a photographer.

CAST
Amy: Pamela Bellwood; Jenny: Frances Lee McCain; Sarah: Katherine Bard; Emily: Maxine Stuart; Kate: Barbara Cason; Annie: Nan Martin.

Liza's Pioneer Diary. A drama that chronicles the journeys of a young pioneer woman through Oregon in 1848.

CAST
Liza Stedman: Ayn Ruymen; Eben Stedman: Dennis Redfield; Aunt Sara: Katherine Helmond.

VISIONS—60 minutes—PBS—October 21, 1976 - February 10, 1977.

VISUAL GIRL

Advice. Geared to teenage girls. Background: The Visual Workshop. Ideas and suggestions concerning exercise, makeup, and skin care are presented.

Host: Ron Russell.
Model Expert: Lois Rose.
Music: Recorded.

VISUAL GIRL—30 minutes—Syndicated 1971.

VIVA VALDEZ

Comedy. Background: East Los Angeles, California. The trials and tribulations of the Valdezes, a Mexican-American family, as they strive to maintain their traditional values in a rapidly changing world.

CAST
Sophie Valdez, the mother	Carmen Zapata
Luis Valdez, the father, a plumber	Rodolfo Hoyos
Victor Valdez, their son	James Victor
Connie Valdez, their daughter	Lisa Mordente
Ernesto Valdez, their son	Nelson D. Cuevas
Pepe Valdez, their son	Claudio Martinez
Jerry Ramerez, their cousin	Jorge Cervera, Jr.

Music: Shorty Rogers.
Executive Producer: Stan Jacobson, Bernard Rothman, Jack Wohl.
Director: Alan Rafkin.
The Valdez Address: 3632½ La Hamber Street.

VIVA VALDEZ—30 minutes—ABC—May 31, 1976 - September 6, 1976.

VOICE OF FIRESTONE

Music. Classical and semiclassical concerts.

Host-Narrator: John Daly.
Vocalists: The Howard Barlow Chorus.
Announcer: Hugh James.
Orchestra: Howard Barlow.
Producer: Charles Polachek, Herbert Swope, Jr., Frederick Heider.
Director: Clark Jones.
Sponsor: Firestone.

VOICE OF FIRESTONE—60 minutes—NBC—September 5, 1949 - June 1, 1959. Premiered as a special: NBC: March 22, 1948.

VOYAGE TO THE BOTTOM OF THE SEA

Adventure. Era: 1983. The experiences of the men and officers of the atomic-powered submarine *Seaview*, as they explore and battle the sinister elements of the ocean floor on behalf the U.S. government's attempts to further scientific research.

CAST
Admiral Harriman Nelson	Richard Basehart
Cdr. Lee Crane	David Hedison
Chief Petty Officer Curley Jones	Henry Kulky
Chief Francis Sharkey	Terry Becker
Commander Chip Morton	Bob Dowdell
Crewman Kowalski ("Ski")	Del Moore

Crewman Sparks, the radar technician	Arch Whiting
Doc, the medical officer	Richard Bull
	Wright King
	Wayne Heffley
Crewman Patterson	Paul Trinka
Crewman Stu Riley	Allan Hunt
Crewman Malone	Mark Slade

Music: Paul Sawtell, Harry Geller, Lionel Newman, Leith Stevens, Jerry Goldsmith, Nelson Riddle.

Producer: Irwin Allen.

Director: Harry Harris, Charles R. Rondeau, Alan Crosland, Jr., Sobey Martin, Sutton Roley, Gerald Mayer, Josef Leytes, Felix Feist, James Goldstone, Alex March, Tom Gries, Justis Addiss, Robert Sparr, Jerry Hopper, Harmon Jones, James Clark, Nathan Juran, Irwin Allen.

VOYAGE TO THE BOTTOM OF THE SEA–60 minutes–ABC–September 14, 1964 - September 15, 1968. 110 episodes. Syndicated.

ω

THE WACKIEST SHIP IN THE ARMY

Adventure. Background: The South Pacific during World War II. The story of the *USS Kiwi,* a leaky, two-masted 1871 schooner incorporated by U.S. Army Intelligence to assist in winning the war. Posing as neutral Swedish sailors, its crew attempts to observe Japanese movements, assist allies, and inform officials of enemy strategy. Spiced with light comedy. Based on the motion picture.

CAST

Major Simon Butcher	Jack Warden
Lt. Richard "Rip" Riddle	Gary Collins
Chief Miller	Mike Kellin
Trivers	Fred Smoot
Tyler	Don Penny
Finch	Duke Hobbie
Nagurski	Rudy Solari
Hollis	Mark Slade
General Cross	Bill Zuckert
Admiral Beckett	Charles Irving

THE WACKIEST SHIP IN THE ARMY–60 minutes–NBC–September 19, 1965 - September 4, 1966. 29 episodes. Syndicated.

WACKO

Children's Variety. Background: The Wacko Clubhouse. A series of unrelated, outlandish comedy and musical skits geared to children.

Starring: Julie McWhirter, Bo Kaprall, Charles Fleischer.

Regulars: Millicent Crisp, Doug Cox,

Bob Comfort, Rick Kellard.

Music: Stu Gardner.

Executive Producer: Chris Bearde, Bob Wood.

Producer: Coslough Johnson, Richard Adamson.

Director: Stanley Dorfman.

Animation: John Wilson.

WACKO–25 minutes–CBS–Premiered: September 17, 1977.

THE WACKY RACES

Animated Cartoon. The saga of a cross-country automobile race. Episodes depict the endless and devious efforts of the evil Dick Dastardly to secure the winning prize, the title "The World's Wackiest Racer."

Competitors: Pat Pending, the ingenious inventor, who drives the Convert-A-Car; Rufus Ruftut and Sawtooth, drivers of the Buzz Wagon; Penelope Pitstop, "the glamour gal of the gas pedal," who drives the Compact Pussycat; The Slag Brothers, Rock and Gravel, drivers of the Boulder Mobile; The Ant Hill Mob, drivers of the Bulletproof Bomb; The Red Max, pilot of the Crimson Haybailer; The Gruesome Twosome, drivers of the Creepy Coupe; Luke and Blubber Bear, drivers of the Arkansas Chugabug; and Dick Dastardly and his aide Mutley (a snickering dog), who command

The Wackiest Ship in the Army. The *Kiwi.* © *Screen Gems.*

Wagon Train. Left to right: Frank McGrath, John McIntire, Terry Wilson, Robert Fuller.

the Mean Machine.

Voices: Paul Winchell, Janet Waldo, Mel Blanc, Don Messick.

Narrator: Dave Willock.

Music: Hoyt Curtin.

THE WACKY RACES—30 minutes—CBS—September 14, 1968 - September 5, 1970.

THE WACKY WORLD OF JONATHAN WINTERS

See title: "Jonathan Winters."

WAGON TRAIN

Western. Era: The 1880s. The saga of a wagon train's journey from the midwest to California. Episodes focus on the lives of individuals who have booked passage—people, both the troubled and carefree, who are alive in the dream of promise that awaits them at their journey's end.

CAST

Seth Adams, the wagonmaster (1957-1961)	Ward Bond
Chris Hale, the wagonmaster (1961-1965)	John McIntire
Flint McCullough, the trail scout	Robert Horton
Charlie Wooster, the cook	Frank McGrath
Bill Hawks, a trail scout	Terry Wilson
Cooper Smith, a trail scout	Robert Fuller
Duke Shannon, a trail scout	Denny Miller
Barnaby West, a teenager who, under Hale's care, is riding with the train	Michael Burns
Kate Crowley, Hale's romantic interest (semiregular role)	Barbara Stanwyck

Music: Melvyn Lenard; Jerome Moross; Hans Salter; Richard Sendry.

WAGON TRAIN—60 minutes—NBC—September 18, 1957 - September 12, 1962; ABC—60 and 90 minute versions—September 19, 1962 - September 5, 1965. Syndicated. Rebroadcasts, under the title, "Major Adams, Trailmaster"—60 minutes—ABC—January 6, 1963 - September 18, 1963. 442 episodes. Also known as: "Trailmaster."

WAIT TIL YOUR FATHER GETS HOME

Animated Cartoon. Background: Los Angeles, California. The trials and tribulations that befall Harry Boyle, president of the Boyle Restaurant Supply Company, as he, an old-fashioned father, struggles to bridge the generation gap that exists between him and his progressive children.

Characters' Voices

Harry Boyle	Tom Bosley
Irma Boyle, his wife	Joan Gerber
Alice Boyle, their daughter	Kristina Holland
Chet Boyle, their son	David Hayward
Jaimie Boyle, their son	Jackie Haley
Ralph, their neighbor	Jack Burns

Additional voices: Pat Harrington, Jr., Gil Herman.

Boyle family dog: Julius.

Music: Richard Bowden.

WAIT TIL YOUR FATHER GETS HOME—30 minutes—Syndicated 1972.

WALLY GATOR

Animated Cartoon. The misadventures of Wally Gator, a bon vivant man-about-town. A Hanna-Barbera production.

Characters' Voices

Wally Gator	Daws Butler
Twiddles, his friend	Don Messick

Music: Hoyt Curtin.

WALLY GATOR—05 minutes—Syndicated 1962. 52 episodes.

WALLY WESTERN

Children. Re-edited western feature films presented in cliff-hanger installments.

Hosts: Wally Western and his pal Skeets (animated cartoon characters).

Featuring: Ken Maynard, Hoot Gibson, Tex Ritter, Bob Steele.

WALLY WESTERN—15 minutes—Syndicated 1960.

WALLY'S WORKSHOP

Advice. Home repair instruction, tips, and advice.

Host: Wally Bruner.

Assistant: Natalie Bruner (Mrs.)

Announcer: Johnny Olsen.

Music: Recorded.

WALLY'S WORKSHOP—30 minutes—Syndicated 1972.

WALT DISNEY PRESENTS

Anthology. Various presentations.

Included Miniseries:

Daniel Boone. The exploits of Frontiersman-scout Daniel Boone.

CAST

Daniel Boone	Dewey Martin
Rebecca Boone	Mala Powers
Squire Boone	Richard Banke
John Finley	Eddy Waller

The Nine Lives of Elfego Baca. Western. Background: Socorro County, New Mexico, late 1800s. The true story of Elfego Baca, "the man who couldn't be killed."

CAST

Elfego Baca	Robert Loggia
Sheriff Morgan	Robert Simon
Zangano, Baca's friend	Leonard Strong

Music: William Lava.

Swamp Fox. Adventure. Era: The American Revolutionary War. The exploits of Francis Marion, the Swamp Fox, an American general who

Walt Disney Presents. *The Nine Lives of Elfego Baca.* Left to right: Leonard Strong, Robert Simon, Robert Loggia. © *Walt Disney Productions.*

attempts to thwart British advances in the South by attacking silently from the glen.

CAST

General Francis Marion,
The Swamp Fox   Leslie Nielsen
Captain Richardson   James Seay
Sergeant O'Reilly   J. Pat O'Malley
Mary, Marion's romantic
interest   Barbara Eiler
Ezra   Arthur Hunnicutt

Music: Buddy Baker.

Texas John Slaughter. Western. Background: Friotorian, Texas, 1880s. The exploits of John Slaughter, Texas Ranger, as he attempts to maintain law and order. Stories are based on actual incidents in the life of John Slaughter, Civil War officer, trailblazer, cattleman, and law enforcer.

CAST

John Slaughter   Tom Tryon
Ranger Ben
Jenkins   Harry Carey, Jr.
Norma Moore   Adeline Harris
Viola   Betty Lynn
Willie   Brian Corcoran
Addie   Annette Gorman

WALT DISNEY PRESENTS—60 minutes—ABC—September 12, 1958 - June 17, 1959.

WALT DISNEY'S WONDERFUL WORLD OF COLOR

Anthology. Excursions into the realm of reality and fantasy. Various types of presentations, including: cartoon,

Walt Disney Presents. *Swamp Fox.* Leslie Nielsen (right) and Barbara Eiler (standing beside him). © *Walt Disney Productions.*

Walt Disney Presents. *Texas John Slaughter.* Tom Tryon as John Slaughter. © *Walt Disney Productions.*

drama, mystery, action-adventure, educational, comedy, and nature and science studies.

Host: Walt Disney.

Included:

Summer Magic. The heartwarming story of a penniless Boston family and their struggles to survive during the pre-World War I era.

CAST

Hayley Mills, Burl Ives, Dorothy McGuire, Deborah Walley.

The Monkey's Uncle. By perfecting man-powered flight, a college genius struggles to acquire a ten-million-dollar grant for his school.

CAST

Merlin Jones: Tommy Kirk; Jennifer: Annette Funicello; Judge Holmsby: Leon Ames; Dearborn: Frank Faylen.

Inside Outer Space. A discussion on the problems to be faced by man as he begins his exploration of space.

Host-Narrator: Professor Ludwig Von Drake (an animated cartoon character).

Those Calloways. Background: New England. The story of a backwoodsman and his son, and their attempts to provide a sanctuary for migrating wild geese.

CAST

Cam Calloway: Brian Keith; Liddy Calloway: Vera Miles; Bucky Calloway: Brandon de Wilde; Alf Simes: Walter Brennan; Ed Parker: Ed Wynn; Bridie Mellott: Linda Evans.

WALT DISNEY'S WONDERFUL WORLD OF COLOR—60 minutes—NBC—Premiered: September 17, 1961.

ABC titles and running dates (all 60 minutes):

DISNEYLAND—October 27, 1954 - September 3, 1958.

WALT DISNEY PRESENTS—September 12, 1958 - June 17, 1959.

WALT DISNEY'S ADVENTURE TIME—September 30, 1958 - September 24, 1959.

WALT DISNEY'S WORLD—October 1, 1959 - September 10, 1961. Moved to NBC the following week, which is stated above.

WALTER WINCHELL

Listed: The television programs of newspaper columnist-reporter Walter Winchell.

The Walter Winchell Show—News Commentary—15 minutes—ABC—

October 5, 1952 - June 26, 1955.

Host: Walter Winchell. "Good evening Mr. and Mrs. North America and all the ships at sea..." (his opening).

The Walter Winchell Show—Variety—30 minutes—NBC—October 5, 1956 - December 28, 1956.

Format: Performances by undiscovered professional talent.

Host: Walter Winchell.

Orchestra: Carl Hoff.

The Walter Winchell File—Crime Drama—30 minutes—ABC—October 2, 1957 - March 28, 1958. Syndicated.
   Background: New York City. Dramatizations based on official newspaper files. Appearing as himself, Walter Winchell, newspaper reporter for the *Daily Mirror*, recounts stories and interviews the people involved.

The Walter Winchell Show—Variety—30 minutes—ABC—October 2, 1960 - November 6, 1960.

Host: Walter Winchell.

THE WALTER WOLFE KING SHOW

Variety.
Host: Walter Wolfe King.

THE WALTER WOLFE KING SHOW —15 minutes—DuMont 1954.

THE WALTONS

Drama. Background: Jefferson County, Virginia, 1930s. Events in the lives of a poor, rural family, the Waltons, the operators of a sawmill, as seen through the sentimental eyes of the eldest son, John Boy, a high school (later college) student who hopes to become a writer. John Boy's fond recollections of his youth and his family's struggles to survive during the Depression extol the simple virtues of chastity, honesty, thrift, family unity, and love.

CAST

John Walton, the father	Ralph Waite
Olivia Walton, his wife	Miss Michael Learned
Zeb (Grandpa) Walton, John's father	Will Geer
Esther (Grandma) Walton, John's mother	Ellen Corby

The seven Walton children:

John Boy Walton   Richard Thomas

The Waltons. Left: Jon Walmsley (with guitar), Judy Norton (standing); center: Richard Thomas (on piano bench) and Kami Cotler (on Richard's knee). Right side, from bottom to top: David Harper, Mary McDonough, and Eric Scott (behind Thomas).

Mary Ellen Walton	Judy Norton
Jim-Bob Walton	David S. Harper
Elizabeth Walton	Kami Cotler
Jason Walton	Jon Walmsley
Erin Walton	Mary Elizabeth McDonough
Ben Walton	Eric Scott
Ike Godsey, the owner of the general store	Joe Conley
Corabeth Godsey, Ike's wife	Ronnie Claire Edwards
Aimee Godsey, their adopted daughter	Rachel Longaker
Dr. Curtis Willard, married Mary Ellen Walton on 11-14-76	Tom Bower
Mamie Baldwin, a friend of the Waltons	Helen Kleeb
Emily Baldwin, Mamie's sister	Mary Jackson
Reverend Matthew Fordwick	John Ritter
Rosemary Fordwick, Matthew's wife*	Mariclare Costello
Sheriff Ep Bridges	John Crawford
Yancy Tucker, a friend of the Waltons	Robert Donner
Flossie Brimmer, the owner of the rooming house	Norma Marlowe
Maude Gromley, a friend of Esther's	Merie Earle
Patsy Brimmer, Flossie's niece	Eileen McDonough
Professor Parks, John Boy's	

*Originally Rosemary Hunter, the schoolteacher. In 1975 she married Reverend Fordwick.

English Instructor at Boatright University	Paul Jenkins
Nora, the county nurse	Kaiulani Lee
Clarence Johnson, publisher of the *Jefferson County Times*	Walter Brooke
Fannie Tatum, Erin's employer at the phone company	Sheila Allen
Thelma, the owner of the Dew Drop Inn, the cafe-bar where Jason works	Dorothy Shay

Walton family dog: Reckless.

Narrator: Earl Hamner, Jr. (the series' creator, upon whose childhood the series is based).

Music: Jerry Goldsmith; Arthur Morton, Alexander Courage.

Executive Producer: Lee Rich, Earl Hamner, Jr.

Producer: Robert Jacks, Andy White.

Director: Harry Harris, Ralph Senesky, Harvey Laidman, Ralph Waite, Lawrence Dobkin, Richard Bennett, Ivan Dixon, Philip Leacock, Lee Philips, Vincent Sherman, Robert Butler.

THE WALTONS—60 minutes—CBS— Premiered: September 14, 1972.

WANDERLUST

Travel. Visits to interesting and unusual places.

Host-Narrator: Bill Burrud.

WANDERLUST—30 minutes—Syndicated 1957. 113 episodes.

WANTED

Documentary. Dramatizations based on incidents in the lives of criminals wanted by the F.B.I. Programs recap their lives and update viewers as to their offenses. Interviews are conducted with friends and family of those involved, and viewers who possess information regarding the subject are urged, under confidential protection, to inform police or F.B.I. officials.

Host-Narrator-Reporter: Walter McGraw.

WANTED—30 minutes—CBS—October 20, 1955 - January 12, 1956.

WANTED: DEAD OR ALIVE

Western. Background: The Frontier during the 1870s. The exploits of Josh Randall, bounty hunter, a man who, though tracking wanted men and women for their offered rewards, often finds himself in the position as protector, struggling to safeguard his prisoners from the less scrupulous bounty hunters.

CAST

Josh Randall	Steve McQueen
Jason Nichols, his partner	Wright King

Also, various parts: Gloria Talbot, Warren Oates.

Randall's gun: His "Mare's Laig," a .30-40 caliber sawed-off carbine rifle.

Jason's dog: an unnamed mutt referred to as "Hey, dog!"

Music: Harry King; Rudy Schrager; Herschel Burke Gilbert.

Producer: John Robinson, Ed Adamson, Harry Harris.

Director: Richard Donner, Thomas Carr, Murray Golden, Ed Adamson, Gene Reynolds, George Blair.

WANTED: DEAD OR ALIVE—30 minutes—CBS—September 6, 1958 - September 1961. 94 episodes. Syndicated.

WAR AND PEACE

Historical Serial. An adaptation of the Leo Tolstoy classic. Background: Moscow. A tableau of Russian society during the turbulent era of the Napoleonic Wars (1805-1820). Produced by the B.B.C.

CAST

Natasha	Morag Hood
Prince Andre Balkonsky	Alan Dobie
Prince Nikolai Bolkonsky	Anthony Jacobs
Maria Bolkonsky	Angela Down
Anatole Kuragin	Colin Baker
Napoleon Bonaparte	David Swift
Prince Vasili Kuragin	Basil Henson
Helene Kuragin	Fiona Gaunt
Pierre Bezuhov	Anthony Hopkins
Dolohov	Donald Burton
Count Ilya Rostov	Rupert Davies
Countess Natalia Rostov	Faith Brook
Sonya	Joanna David
Nicolai Rostov	Sylvester Morand
Denisov	Gary Watson
Boris Drubetskoy	Neil Stacy
Tzar Alexander I	Donald Douglas
Kutuzov	Frank Middleman

Producer: David Conroy.

Director: John Davies.

WAR AND PEACE—PBS—November 20, 1973 - January 15, 1974. Broadcast in seven ninety-minute and two two-hour installments. Originally broadcast in England in twenty forty-five-minute episodes (seventeen hours).

WAR IN THE AIR

Documentary. Films recounting the history of the Royal Air Force during World War II. Produced by the B.B.C.

Host-Narrator: Robert Harris.

Music: The London Philharmonic Orchestra, conducted by Muir Mathieson.

WAR IN THE AIR—30 minutes—Syndicated 1956.

WARNER BROTHERS PRESENTS

Drama. The overall title for four rotating series: "Casablanca"; "Cheyenne"; "Conflict"; and "King's Row."

Host: Gig Young.

Music: David Buttolph.

Producer: Roy Huggins, Richard L. Bare, John Peyser, Jerome Robinson, E. St. Joseph, Paul Stewart.

Casablanca. Mystery. Background: The Café American in Casablanca. The story of Rick Jason, its owner, an American who assists people in distress by offering his establishment as a place of refuge.

CAST

Rick Jason	Charles McGraw
Sam, the piano player	Clarence Muse

Cheyenne. Western. Background: The Frontier, 1870s. The exploits of wanderers Cheyenne Bodie and his friend Smitty, a mapmaker, as they assist people in distress.

CAST

Cheyenne Bodie	Clint Walker
Smitty	L. Q. Jones

Conflict. Anthology. Dramatizations depicting the plight of people whose lives are suddenly changed by unexpected and unfavorable circumstances.

Included(three examples listed):

Capital Punishment. The story of a man, tried and sentenced to death for a murder he did not commit, who struggles to prove his innocence.

CAST
Will Hutchins, Rex Reason, Barbara Eiler.

Anything For Money. The story of a private detective who is secretly hired as a bodyguard to a yachtsman on a pleasure cruise to Havana.

CAST
Efrem Zimbalist, Jr., Barton MacLane, Margaret Hayes.

Shock Wave. The story of a test pilot who takes a plane up before a safety device is perfected.

CAST
Scott Brady, Ted de Corsia, Kenneth Tobey.

King's Row. Drama. Background: The town of King's Row. The work of psychiatrist Parris Mitchell as he attempts to aid people caught in the turmoil of human emotion.

CAST

Dr. Parris Mitchell	Jack Kelly
Randy	Nan Leslie
Drake	Robert Horton
Eloise	Peggy Webber
Dr. Tower	Victor Jory

WARNER BROTHERS PRESENTS—60 minutes—ABC—September 13, 1955 - September 11, 1956 (for "Casablanca," "Cheyenne," and "King's Row"); September 18, 1956 - September 10, 1957 (for "Cheyenne" and "Conflict").

WASHINGTON: BEHIND CLOSED DOORS

Drama. A six part miniseries loosely based on John Ehrlichman's political novel, *The Company*. Background: Washington, D.C. The complex story, which centers on the rise to power and life of Richard Monckton from senator to President of the United States, exposes the public and intimate lives of the people who control our nation—lives filled with greed, lust, and corruption.

CAST

Richard Monckton — Jason Robards
William Martin, the
  C.I.A. director — Cliff Robertson
Linda Martin, William's
  wife — Lois Nettleton
Sally Whalen, the
  spy — Stefanie Powers
Frank Flaherty, the
  Chief of
  Staff — Robert Vaughn
Esker Anderson, the
  retiring
  President — Andy Griffith
Bob Bailey, the Press
  Secretary — Barry Nelson
Carl Tessler, the
  Foreign Affairs
  Advisor — Harold Gould
Adam Gardiner, the
  young idealist — Tony Bill

Also: David Selby (as Roger Castle), Nicholas Pryor (Hank Ferris), Diana Ewing (Kathy Ferris), Meg Foster (Jennie Jameson), Thayer David (Elmer Morse), John Randolph (Bennett Lowman), John Lehne (Tucker Tallford), Lara Parker (Wanda Elliott), John Houseman (Myron Dunn), Frances Lee McCain (Paula Gardiner), Alan Oppenheimer (Simon Cappell), Linden Chiles (Jack Atherton), Frank Marth (Lawrence Allison), June Dayton (Mrs. Monckton), Skip Homeier (Lars Haglund), Mary La Roche (Anne Lowman).

Music: Dominic Frontiere.
Executive Producer: Stanley Kallis.
Producer: Norman S. Powell.
Director: Gary Nelson.

WASHINGTON: BEHIND CLOSED DOORS—12 hours (total)—ABC—September 6, 1977 - September 11, 1977.

WASHINGTON SQUARE

Variety. Music, songs, dances, and comedy sketches set against the background of New York's Greenwich Village.

Host: Ray Bolger.
Regulars (the people of the square): Elaine Stritch, Rusty Draper, Kay Armen, Arnold Stang, Daniza Ilistsch, Threa Flames, The Bil and Cora Baird Puppets, The Danny Daniels Singers.
Orchestra: Charles Sanford.

WASHINGTON SQUARE—60 minutes—NBC—October 2, 1956 - June 13, 1957.

WATERFRONT

Adventure. Background: The San Pedro Harbor in Los Angeles, California. The experiences of John Herrick, captain of the tugboat *Cheryl Ann.*

CAST

Captain John Herrick — Preston Foster
May Herrick, his
  wife — Lois Moran
Carl Herrick, their
  son — Douglas Dick
Tip Hubbard,
  the captain's
  friend — Pinky Tomlin
Dan Cord,
  the captain of
  the tugboat
  Isabel — Ramon Vallo

Also: Willie Best, Eddie Waller.
Music: Alexander Laszlo.

WATERFRONT—30 minutes—Syndicated. 1954. 78 episodes.

WAY OF THE WORLD

Serial. Adaptations of stories appearing in leading women's magazines. Vignettes are allotted the time needed, in days, to run without any interference to the original content.

Hostess: Gloria Louis, appearing as Linda Porter.

WAY OF THE WORLD—15 minutes—NBC 1955.

WAY OUT

Anthology. Tales of the supernatural.
Host: Roald Dahl.

Included:

Dissolve To Black. The story of a television actress trapped in a deserted studio by a killer.

CAST
Bonnie Draco: Kathleen Widdoes.

Death Wish. Annoyed by his wife's constant habit of relentlessly talking about the television programs she watches, a husband plots her murder —as she describes a crime show she saw.

CAST
The wife: Charlotte Rae.

Hush Hush. Experimenting with sound waves, a professor attempts to develop a state of perfect tranquility.

CAST
Professor Ernest Lydecker: Philip Coolidge; Bernice Lydecker: Rosemary Murphy; William Rogers: Woodrow Parfrey.

WAY OUT—30 minutes—CBS—June 1961 - July 14, 1961.

WAY OUT GAMES

Game. Two three-member teams of junior high school students compete in various contests of skill with the object being to complete stunts in the least amount of time. Points are awarded after each of the three rounds and the team scoring the highest receives the opportunity to compete in the quarter finals—a tournament for prizes.

Host: Sonny Fox.
Assistant: Mark Smith.
Executive Producer: Jack Barry, Dan Enright.
Director: Richard S. Kline.

WAY OUT GAMES—25 minutes—CBS—Premiered: September 11, 1976.

WAYNE AND SHUSTER TAKE AN AFFECTIONATE LOOK AT . . .

Documentary. Through film and commentary, the comic movie trends of the past and the lives of individual comedians are recalled.

Hosts: Johnny Wayne and Frank Shuster.

WAYNE AND SHUSTER TAKE AN AFFECTIONATE LOOK AT . . .—60 minutes—CBS—June 17, 1966 - July 29, 1966. 13 episodes.

THE WAYNE KING SHOW

Musical Variety.
Host: Wayne King.
Regulars: Jackie Jones, Harry Hull, Barbara Becker, The Don Large Chorus.
Orchestra: Gloria Van.
Producer: Ken Craig, Andy Christian.
Director: Bill Hobin, Dave Brown.

THE WAYNE KING SHOW—30 minutes—NBC 1950; DuMont 1951.

THE WEAKER (?) SEX

Discussion. Women from various fields of business appear and discuss the controversial issues that affect women in their daily lives.

Hostess: Pamela Mason.

Music: Recorded.

THE WEAKER (?) SEX–30 minutes- Syndicated 1968. 260 tapes.

THE WEB

Anthology. Dramatizations depicting the plight of people trapped in sudden, perilous situations.

Host-Narrator: Jonathan Drake.

Producer: Franklin Heller, Mark Goodson, Bill Todman.

Director: Franklin Heller.

Sponsor: Embassy Cigarettes.

Included:

End Of The Line. A mobster's wife attempts to double-cross her husband.

Starring: Jayne Meadows.

Last Chance. A thief attempts to save the life of a young girl who is contemplating suicide.

Starring: John Larch, Rebecca Wells.

Hurricane Coming. Planning to run away with another man, a woman attempts to dispose of her husband by leaving him stranded on an island due to be hit by a hurricane.

Starring: Beverly Garland, Mark Roberts.

Kill And Run. Having borrowed his employer's car without permission, a young man attempts to prove that he is innocent of a hit-and-run killing.

Starring: James Darren.

THE WEB–30 minutes–CBS–July 4, 1950 - September 26, 1954.

WEDDING DAY

Wedding Performances. Actual ceremonies performed on TV.

Hostess: Patricia Vance.

Assistant: Vin Gottschalk.

WEDDING DAY–60 minutes–ABC 1950.

THE WEDDING GAME

Game. Three married couples play. The wives are isolated back-stage; the husbands appear before camera. The husbands each select three similar prizes from a group of merchandise items displayed on the stage. The husbands are then isolated offstage, and the wives, before camera, are permitted to choose three items also. The couples are then reunited. If the husband and wife have both independently chosen the same item or items, they receive it as their gift.

Host: Al Hamel.

THE WEDDING GAME–30 minutes –ABC–April 1, 1968 - July 12, 1968. Also known as "Wedding Party."

WEEKEND WORKSHOP

Advice. Home-repair instruction, tips, and advice.

Host: Bob Hamilton.

Assistant: Kay Westerfield.

WEEKEND WORKSHOP–30 minutes–NBC–1954 - 1955.

WELCOME ABOARD

See title: "Phil Silvers.."

WELCOME BACK, KOTTER

Comedy. Background: James Buchanan High School in Bensonhurst, Brooklyn, New York. The trials and tribulations of Gabe Kotter, a former graduate who returns to his school ten years later to teach Special Guidance Remedial Academics to a class of incorrigible students known as Sweat Hogs, teenagers who are much like the way he was when he was attending the same school.

CAST

Gabe Kotter	Gabriel Kaplan
Julie Kotter, his wife	Marcia Strassman
Michael Woodman, the vice-principal	John Sylvester White
Voice of the principal	James Komack
Judy Borden, a student	Helaine Lembeck

The Sweat Hogs:

Vinnie Barbarino	John Travolta
Juan Epstein	Robert Hegyes
Fredrick "Boom Boom" Washington	Lawrence-Hilton Jacobs
Arnold Horshack	Ron Palillo
Rosalie "Hotsie" Totzi	Debralee Scott
Vernajean Williams	Vernee Watson

Music: John B. Sebastian.

Executive Producer: James Komack.

Producer: Eric Cohen, Alan Sacs.

Director: James Komack, Bob LaHendro.

WELCOME BACK, KOTTER–30 minutes–ABC–Premiered: September 9, 1975.

WELCOME TRAVELERS

Interview. Travelers, met at bus, railroad, and plane terminals, are invited to a studio where, in exchange for gifts, they relate their experiences and impressions of Chicago.

Host: Tom Bartlett; Bob Cunningham.

Announcer: William T. Lazar.

Producer: Tom Hicks, Charles Powers, Tom O'Connor.

Director: Don Meier, Charles Powers.

Sponsor: Procter and Gamble.

WELCOME TRAVELERS–30 minutes–NBC–September 8, 1952 - October 10, 1955. Based on the radio program.

Welcome Back, Kotter. Left to right: Marcia Strassman, Gabriel Kaplan, and Lawrence-Hilton Jacobs. Center, left to right: John Travolta, Ron Palillo, Robert Hegyes. (The actress with Travolta is not credited).

WE'LL GET BY

Comedy. Background: Suburban New Jersey. Events in the lives of the Platt family: George, a lawyer, his wife, Liz, and their three bright and saucy children, Muff, Andrea, and Kenny. Created by Alan Alda.

CAST

George Platt	Paul Sorvino
Liz Platt	Mitzi Hoag

Michael "Muff"
Platt   Jerry Houser
Andrea Platt   Devon Scott
Kenny Platt   Willie Aames

Music: Joe Raposo, Sheldon Harnick.

Producer-Creator: Alan Alda.

Director: Jack Shea, Jay Sandrich.

WE'LL GET BY–30 minutes–CBS–March 6, 1975 - May 30, 1975.

Wendy and Me. George Burns and Connie Stevens.

WENDY AND ME

Comedy. Background: Los Angeles, California. The marital misadventures of the Conways: Jeff, an airline pilot; and his beautiful but scatterbrained wife, Wendy.

The program has the imprint of "The George Burns and Gracie Allen Show." Appearing as the Conway's landlord, George Burns speaks directly to the audience, establishes scenes, relates monologues, and, as in the past, further complicates what Wendy, as Gracie, has already complicated.

CAST

George Burns   Himself
Wendy Conway   Connie Stevens
Jeff Conway   Ron Harper
Danny Adams, their
  neighbor, Jeff's
  co-pilot   James Callahan
Mr. Bundy, the
  janitor   J. Pat O'Malley
Mr. Norton, Jeff's
  employer   Bartlett Robinson
Mrs. Norton, his
  wife   Jane Morgan
Catherine, Wendy's
  friend   Robyn Grace

Music: Ervin Drake.

WENDY AND ME–30 minutes–ABC –September 14, 1964 - September 6, 1965. 34 episodes. Syndicated.

THE WENDY BARRIE SHOW

See title: "Through Wendy's Window."

WESLEY

Comedy. The misadventures of Wesley, a mischievous twelve-year-old boy.

CAST

Wesley   Donald Devlin
His father   Frankie Thomas, Sr.
His mother   Mona Thomas
His teenage
  sister   Joy Reese
Her suitor   Jack Ayres
Wesley's friend   Billy Nevard
Wesley's grandfather   Joe Sweeney

Producer: Worthington Miner.

Director: Franklin Schaffner.

WESLEY–30 minutes CBS 1949.

THE WESTERNER

Western. Background: Various areas along the Mexican Border during the 1890s. The exploits of Dave Blasingame, a wandering cowboy who aids people in distress.

CAST

Dave Blasingame   Brian Keith
Burgundy Smith, his
  friend   John Dehner

Dave's dog: Brown.

Music: Herschel Burke Gilbert.

THE WESTERNER–30 minutes–NBC–September 30, 1960 - December 30, 1960. 13 episodes.

THE WESTERNERS

Anthology. Rebroadcasts of western dramas that were originally aired via: "Black Saddle"; "Dick Powell's Zane Grey Theatre'; "Johnny Ringo"; and "The Law of the Plainsman." See individual titles for program information.

Host: Keenan Wynn.

THE WESTERNERS–30 minutes–Syndicated 1965. 125 episodes.

WESTERN HOUR

Anthology. Rebroadcasts of western dramas that were originally aired via: "The Rifleman" and "Dick Powell's Zane Grey Theatre." See individual titles for program information.

Host: Chuck Connors.

WESTERN HOUR–60 minutes–Syndicated 1963. 312 episodes.

WESTERN STAR THEATRE

Anthology. Rebroadcasts of western dramas that were originally aired via "Death Valley Days." See either of the following titles for program information: "Death Valley Days"; "The Pioneers"; or "Trails West."

Host: Rory Calhoun.

WESTERN STAR THEATRE–30 minutes–Syndicated 1963. 67 episodes.

WESTERN THEATRE

Anthology. Rebroadcasts of western dramas that were originally aired via "Dick Powell's Zane Grey Theatre."

Included:

The Thousand Dollar Gun. Background: The town of Broken Lance. The story of a gunfighter and his attempts to end the reign of a gang of outlaws.

CAST

George Montgomery, John Agar, Chuck Connors, Jean Allison.

The Castaway. The story of a wagonmaster and his attempts to avert an Indian attack on the train.

CAST

Ronald Reagan, Jeanette Nolan, Dick Crockett.

The Easygoing Man. An easygoing rancher attempts to control a rebellious teenage boy.

CAST

Lee Marvin, Virginia Grey, Danny Richards, Robert Rockwell, Alan Lee.

WESTERN THEATRE–30 minutes–NBC–July 3, 1959 - September 4, 1959.

WESTINGHOUSE SUMMER THEATRE

A series of thirty-minute anthology

dramas broadcast on CBS during the summer of 1951. Produced by Montgomery Ford and sponsored by Westinghouse.

WEST POINT

Anthology. Dramatizations based on incidents in the training periods of West Point Academy cadets.

Host: Donald May, appearing as Cadet Charles C. Thompson.

Semiregular: Clint Eastwood.

Producer: James Sheldon, Leon Benson, Henry Kessler, Maurice Unger.

Included:

Contact. Though lacking physical ability, a cadet attempts to compete with his classmates.

CAST

George Nelson: Steve Terrell; Tim Tobin: Del Erickson.

Flareup. The story of a cadet's struggles to control his explosive temper.

CAST

Peter Baldwin, Jerry Charlebous, Rad Fulton.

Cold Peril. When the Hudson River freezes over, a young cadet decides to walk across it to the village to meet his girlfriend. Discovering that an ice breaker is touring the river, three of his friends desperately struggle to get to him before he is stranded.

CAST

Bob Matson: Larry Pennell; Steve Pauley: Brett Halsey; Tom Kennedy: Leonard Nimoy.

WEST POINT—30 minutes—ABC—October 8, 1957 - July 1, 1958. Syndicated.

WEST SIDE COMEDY

See title: "East Side Comedy."

WESTSIDE MEDICAL

Medical Drama. Background: California. The personal and professional lives of Doctors Sam Lanagan, Janet Cottrell, and Phil Parker, staff physicians at Westside Memorial Hospital.

CAST

Dr. Sam Lanagan	James Sloyan
Dr. Janet Cottrell	Linda Carlson
Dr. Phil Parker	Ernest Thompson
Carrie, the woman who assists them in the clinic	Alice Nunn

Music: Billy Goldenberg.

Executive Producer: Martin Starger.

Producer: Alan A. Armer.

Director: Ralph Senesky, Gerald Mayer, Larry Elikann, Vincent Sherman, Paul Stanley.

Creator: Barry Oringer.

WESTSIDE MEDICAL—60 minutes—ABC—March 15, 1977 - April 14, 1977.

THE WESTWIND

Adventure. Background: Hawaii. The adventures of the Andrews family—Steve, an underwater photographer, his wife Kate, a marine biologist, and their teenage children Robin and Tom—as they travel through the various islands seeking to further man's knowledge of the sea.

CAST

Steve Andrews	Van Williams
Kate Andrews	Niki Dantıne
Robin Andrews	Kimberly Beck
Tom Andrews	Steve Burns

Their yacht: The *Westwind.*

Music: Richard La Salle.

THE WESTWIND—30 minutes—NBC—September 6, 1975 - September 4, 1976.

WE TAKE YOUR WORD

Game. Object: For a celebrity panel to relate definitions and derivations of words submitted by home viewers. Words that stump the panel award the senders cash prizes.

Hosts: John Daly; John K. M. McCaffrey.

Panelists: Al Capp, Cornelia Otis Skinner, Abe Burrows.

WE TAKE YOUR WORD—30 minutes—CBS—1950 - 1951.

WE, THE PEOPLE

Celebrity Interview.

Host: Dan Seymour.

Orchestra: Oscar Bradley.

Producer: Dan Seymour, James Sheldon, Rod Erickson.

Sponsor: Gulf Oil.

WE, THE PEOPLE—30 minutes—CBS 1948.

WE'VE GOT EACH OTHER

Comedy. Background: California. The story centers on the chaotic misadventures of the Hibbards: Judy, a not-so-attractive, lanky photographer's assistant, and her husband, Stuart, who works at home as a copywriter for bizarre devices advertised in the Herman Gutman Mail Order Catalogue.

CAST

Judy Hibbard	Beverly Archer
Stuart Hibbard	Oliver Clark
Damon Jerome, Judy's employer	Tom Poston
Dee Dee, Damon's top model	Joan Van Ark
Donna, Damon's secretary	Ren Woods
Ken Redford, the Hibbard's neighbor	Martin Kove

Music and Theme Vocal: Nino Candido.

Executive Producer: Tom Patchett, Jay Tarses.

Producer: Jack Burns.

WE'VE GOT EACH OTHER—30 minutes—CBS—Premiered: October 1, 1977.

WHAT DO YOU HAVE IN COMMON?

Game. Three specially selected contestants, who each possess something in common, but are unknown to each other, compete. Within a three-minute time limit, and through a cross-examination session, each has to discover what the common denominator is. Clues are provided by an unseen fourth party (e.g., the same doctor; the same real estate salesman). The player who is first to identify the common bond is the winner and receives merchandise prizes.

Host: Ralph Story.

WHAT DO YOU HAVE IN COMMON?—30 minutes—CBS 1954.

WHAT EVERY WOMAN WANTS TO KNOW

Discussion. Informative discussions on topics of current concern.

Hostess: Bess Myerson.

Music: Recorded.

WHAT EVERY WOMAN WANTS TO KNOW—30 minutes—Syndicated 1972.

WHAT HAPPENED?

Game. An individual, who performed some unique act for which he received newspaper coverage, appears on the program. A panel of four celebrities then question him with the object being to determine what he did. If they fail, the contestant receives a prize.

Host: Ben Grauer.

Panel: Roger Price, Lisa Ferraday, Maureen Stapleton, Frank Gallop.

Announcer: Frank Gallop.

WHAT HAPPENED?—30 minutes—NBC 1952.

WHAT HAVE YOU GOT TO LOSE?

Game. Four competing contestants. Through question-and-andwer probe rounds with the host, players have to identify white-elephant objects that have been submitted by home viewers. If one of the panelists identifies the mystery article, he receives a prize; if not, the sender receives a prize.

Host: John Reed King.

WHAT HAVE YOU GOT TO LOSE? —30 minutes—ABC—May 25, 1953 - August 7, 1953.

WHAT REALLY HAPPENED TO THE CLASS OF '65?

Anthology. Dramatizations that update the lives of the 1965 graduating class of the fictional Bret Hart High School in Los Angeles. Stories open with the commentary of Sam Ashley, a '65 grad and now a teacher at Bret Hart High, as he recalls his fellow classmates; the program then chronicles the life of a particular grad from 1965 to 1977. Based on the book by Michael Medved and David Wallechinsky.

Starring: Tony Bill as Sam Ashley.

Music: Don Costa.

Executive Producer-Producer: Richard Irving.

WHAT REALLY HAPPENED TO

THE CLASS OF '65?—60 minutes—NBC—Premiered: December 8, 1977.

WHAT'S GOING ON?

Game. Two three-member teams compete: The Insiders and The Outsiders. The Outsiders are brought to a remote location and asked to perform certain activities. Through ·remote pickup, their activities are displayed on a large screen behind each of The Insiders. Through a series of question and answer probe rounds with the host, The Insiders have to discover where The Outsiders are and what they are doing. Prizes are awarded accordingly: to The Insiders if they correctly identify the situation and activities; to The Outsiders if The Insiders fail.

Host: Lee Bowman.

Players (rotating team assignments): Kitty Carlisle, Hy Gardner, Jayne Meadows, Cliff Norton, Susan Oakland, Gene Raymond.

Announcer: Jimmy Blaine.

WHAT'S GOING ON?—30 minutes—CBS—July 22, 1954 - September 1954.

WHAT'S HAPPENING!!

Comedy. Background: Southern California. An inane series that follows the antics of three black teenagers: Roger Thomas, Dwayne Clemens, and Freddie Stubbs, nicknamed "Rerun" for his constant habit of repeating in summer school what he should have learned in the fall.

CAST

Roger Thomas	Ernest Thomas
Dwayne Clemens	Haywood Nelson
Rerun	Fred Berry
Mabel Thomas, Roger's mother	Mabel King
Dee Thomas, Roger's sister	Danielle Spencer
Shirley, the waitress at the local soda shop, Robert's Place	Shirley Hemphill
Bill Thomas, Roger's father	Thalmus Rasulala

Music: Henry Mancini.

Executive Producer: Saul Turteltaub, Bernie Orenstein, Bud Yorkin.

Director: Dennis Steinmetz, Bud Yorkin, Jack Shea, Mark Warren, Dick Harwood, Alan Rafkin, Hal Alexander.

WHAT'S HAPPENING!!—30 min-

utes—ABC—August 5, 1976 - August 26, 1976; Returned: Premiered: November 13, 1976.

WHAT'S IN A WORD?

Game. A contestant, selected from the studio audience, presents a single rhyme to the host (e.g., "Pink Mink."). Through one word clues provided by the host, a celebrity panel has to identify the rhyme. For each clue used before the panel identifies it, the contestant receives five dollars.

Hosts: Mike Wallace; Clifton Fadiman.

Panelists: Faye Emerson, Audrey Meadows, Carl Reiner, Jim Moran.

WHAT'S IN A WORD?—30 minutes—ABC—1954 - 1955.

WHAT'S IT ALL ABOUT WORLD?

Variety. An attempt, through the satirization of everyday life, to explain our troubled world—a world that finds it difficult to make light of its faults.

Host: Dean Jones.

Regulars: Dick Clair, Jenna McMahon, Alex Dreier, Geri Granger, Scoey Mitchlll, Dennis Allen, Ron Price, Maureen Arthur, Byan Johnson (Happy Hollywood), The Kevin Carlisle Three.

Orchestra: Denny Vaughn.

Announcer: Roger Carroll.

WHAT'S IT ALL ABOUT WORLD?— 60 minutes—ABC—February 6, 1969 - May 1, 1969. 13 episodes.

WHAT'S IT FOR?

Game. Inventors or their descendants appear with actual working models of thingamajigs patented by the U.S. Patent Office since 1800. Through a series of question-and-answer probe rounds, a panel of four have to identify it and its purpose. Guests receive cash for each question asked by the panel before it is identified.

Host: Hal March.

Panelists: Hans Conried, Betsy Palmer, Abe Burrows, Cornelia Otis Skinner.

WHAT'S IT FOR?—30 minutes—NBC —October 12, 1957 - January 4, 1958.

WHAT'S IT WORTH?

Human Interest. Owners of paintings

and objets d'art are the subjects of the program. Each person appears with and tells how he acquired his treasure. A panel of experts then appraise the object and quote its actual value. As the experts give their opinion, cameras reveal the human emotions of the owner.

Host: Gil Fates.

Permanent Panelist: Sigmund Rothschild.

Producer-Director: Frances Buss.

WHAT'S IT WORTH?—30 minutes—CBS 1948.

WHAT'S MY LINE?

Game. Through a series of question-and-answer probe rounds with a guest, a celebrity panel of four has to uncover his or her occupation. Three such rounds are played per broadcast, one involving a mystery guest celebrity (panelists are blindfolded during the questioning). Guests receive merchandise prizes.

Versions:

What's My Line?—30 minutes—CBS—February 2, 1950 - September 3, 1967.

Host: John Daly.

Panelists: Arlene Francis, Dorothy Kilgallen, Bennett Cerf, Fred Allen, Steve Allen, Hal Block, Louis Untermeyer, Harold Hoffman.

Announcers: John Briggs; Johnny Olsen.

Music: Milton DeLugg.

What's My Line?—30 minutes—Syndicated 1968.

Hosts: Wally Bruner; Larry Blyden.

Panelists: Arlene Francis, Soupy Sales, Jack Cassidy, Kaye Ballard, Anita Gillette, Gene Rayburn, Alan Alda, Nancy Dussault, Joanna Barnes, Bennett Cerf, Bert Convy.

Announcers: Johnny Olsen; Chet Gould.

Music: Score Productions.

WHAT'S MY LINE? (British)—30 minutes—B.B.C.-TV—1951.

Host: Eamonn Andrews.

Panelists: Chislaine Alexander, Elizabeth Allen, Jerry Desmonde, Gilbert Harding.

WHAT'S NEW MR. MAGOO

Animated Cartoon. Newly animated adventures of the nearsighted Quincy Magoo and his equally nearsighted dog, McBarker. See also: "The Famous Adventures of Mr. Magoo," and "Mr. Magoo."

Characters' Voices

Quincy Magoo	Jim Backus
McBarker	Frank Welker

Additional Voices: Hal Smith.

Music: Doug Goodwin, Eric Rodgers, Dean Elliott.

Producer: David DePatie, Friz Freleng.

Director: Sid Marcus, Bob McKimson, Spencer Peel.

WHAT'S NEW MR. MAGOO—30 minutes—NBC—Premiered: September 10, 1977.

WHAT'S THIS SONG?

Game. Two competing teams, each composed of two members: one celebrity captain and one noncelebrity contestant. A song is played. The team who is first to identify itself through a buzzer signal receives a chance to answer. If the team identifies the song title it receives points and the opportunity to score additional points by singing the four opening bars. If the opposing team believes the lyrics are incorrect it is permitted to challenge. If correct, it wins the points if one member can sing the correct lyrics; if incorrect in assuming the lyrics are wrong, the points are deducted from the team's score and awarded to the other team. Winners are the highest-scoring teams. The contestant receives merchandise prizes.

Host: Wink Martindale.

Premiere Guests: Beverly Garland, Lorne Greene.

WHAT'S THIS SONG?—25 minutes—NBC—October 26, 1964 - September 24, 1965.

WHAT'S THE STORY?

Game. Through dramatizations performed on stage, a panel of four contestants have to identify news events. Prizes are awarded to the individual player who scores the most correct identifications.

Host: Walter Raney.

Producer: David Lowe, Gil Fates.

Sponsor: DuMont Labs.

WHAT'S THE STORY?—30 minutes—DuMont 1951.

WHAT WILL THEY THINK OF NEXT?

Humor. Inventors of clever gadgets (e.g., a music writing typewriter) appear and demonstrate their invention to a panel of three comedians who, in turn, appraise it. A gift is awarded to the inventor who appears with the hope of interesting a manufacturer in his product.

Host: Ed Herlihy.

Panel: Arthur Q. Bryan, Janet Graham, Harry Hirsh.

Producer-Director: Lawrence Schwab.

WHAT WILL THEY THINK OF NEXT?—30 minutes—NBC 1948.

WHAT'S YOUR BID?

Game. A merchandise item is offered for bid. With their own money, studio-audience members bid for it. The highest bidder receives it and donates it to charity. For his generosity, the program awards him a duplicate item plus additional gifts for his kindness.

Hosts: Robert Alda; Leonard Rosen.

Announcers: John Reed King; Dick Shepard.

WHAT'S YOUR BID?—30 minutes—ABC 1953.

Wheelie and the Chopper Bunch. Left to right: Rota, Wheelie, and the Chopper Bunch. © *Hanna-Barbera Productions.*

WHEELIE AND THE CHOPPER BUNCH

Animated Cartoon. The adventures of Wheelie, and almost human Volkswagon, the world's greatest stunt-racing car, as he, and his girlfriend, Rota Ree, also a V.W., struggle to overcome the evils of the Chopper

Bunch, diabolical motorcycles led by Chopper, who seeks and plots to acquire Rota's affections.

Characters' Voices

Wheelie	Frank Welker
Rota	Judy Strangis
Chopper	Frank Welker
Revs	Paul Winchell
Hi Riser	Lennie Weinrib

Music: Hoyt Curtin.

Executive Producer: William Hanna, Joseph Barbera.

Director: Charles A. Nichols.

WHEELIE AND THE CHOPPER BUNCH—30 minutes—NBC—September 7, 1974 - August 30, 1975.

WHEEL OF FORTUNE

Testimonial. Good samaritans are honored and awarded prizes for their unselfish acts of kindness to other people. Both individuals appear and relate the circumstances surrounding the good deed.

Host: Todd Russell.

WHEEL OF FORTUNE—30 minutes —CBS—October 3, 1952 - December 25, 1953.

WHEEL OF FORTUNE

Game. Three competing contestants. Involved: a large spinning wheel that contains varying amounts of cash and several columns that assist or hinder players: "Lose one turn"; "One free spin"; and "Bankruptcy." The final category, bankruptcy, erases all a player's earnings if the wheel pinpoints it when it stops.

A line of spaces, which represents the number of letters in a famous name, place, or event is displayed. One player spins the wheel. If it stops on a cash amount, the player suggests a letter. If it is contained in the name, it appears in its appropriate place on the board. The player then receives that amount of money. He continues to spin the wheel until he suggests an incorrect letter or lands on "Bankruptcy" or "Lose one turn." The next player then receives his turn. The player who is first to identify the mystery name is the winner, receives what money he has accumulated, and is permitted to shop for merchandise items—which are offered at their retail selling prices. Any money that the player has that remains is put into an account wherein it can only be spent if he wins another game. The player with the highest cash score (merchan-

dise purchases included) is the winner and returns to compete again.

Host: Chuck Woolery.

Hostess: Susan Stafford.

Announcer: Charlie O'Donnell.

First Champion: Ginny Hubert.

WHEEL OF FORTUNE—30 minutes —NBC—Premiered: January 6, 1975.

WHEN TELEVISION WAS LIVE

Nostalgia. Through the use of kinescopes, the television careers of Peter Lind Hayes and Mary Healy are recalled.

Hosts: Peter Lind Hayes and Mary Healy.

Producer: Peter Lind Hayes.

Director: Debra Gangnebin.

WHEN TELEVISION WAS LIVE—30 minutes—PBS—August 6, 1975 - September 17, 1975. 7 episodes.

WHEN THINGS WERE ROTTEN

Comedy. A satire based on the legend of Robin Hood. Background: Twelfth-century England. The series depicts Robin Hood, the man who stole from the rich to give to the poor, as a birdbrain; his Merry Men, free-born Englishmen loyal to the king, as bumbling klutzes; and Maid Marian, Robin's romantic interest, as a sexy dingbat. The story: When Prince John usurps the throne from his brother, Richard the Lionhearted, he provokes hatred between Normans and Saxons by imposing a tax on the Saxons. When Sir Robin of Locksley, a Saxon, opposes this, he is declared the wanted criminal Robin Hood. Retreating to Sherwood Forest, he establishes a base near the Gallows Oak with his Merry Men (Alan-A-Dale, Friar Tuck, Renaldo, and Little John). Episodes depict Robin's efforts to return the throne to its rightful king, protect the weak, avenge the oppressed, and foil the evils of the Sheriff of Nottingham, who acts on behalf of Prince John. Created by Mel Brooks.

CAST

Robin Hood	Dick Gautier
Maid Marian	Misty Rowe
Alan-A-Dale	Bernie Kopell
Friar Tuck	Dick Van Patten
Renaldo	Richard Dimitri
Little John	David Sabin
Lord Hubert, the Sheriff of	

Nottingham	Henry Polic II
Bertram, the sheriff's aide	Richard Dimitri
Prince John	Ron Rifkin
Sylvester, a peasant	Jimmy Martinez

Music: Artie Butler.

Executive Producer-Creator: Mel Brooks.

Producer: Norman Steinberg.

Director: Jerry Paris, Joshua Shelley, Marty Feldman, Peter H. Hunt, Bruce Bilson.

WHEN THINGS WERE ROTTEN—30 minutes—ABC—September 10, 1975 - December 24, 1975.

WHERE'S HUDDLES

Animated Cartoon. The misadventures of Ed Huddles and Bubba McCoy, quarterback and team center for the Rhinos, a disorganized professional football team. A Hanna-Barbera production.

Characters' Voices

Ed Huddles	Cliff Norton
Bubba McCoy	Mel Blanc
Marge Huddles, Ed's wife	Jean VanderPyl
Penny McCoy, Bubba's wife	Marie Wilson
Claude Pertwee, their perfectionist neighbor	Paul Lynde
The Coach	Alan Reed
Freight Train, a team member	Herb Jeffries

Additional characters: Fumbles, the Huddles's dog; and Beverly, Claude's cat.

Announcer: Dick Enberg.

Music: Hoyt Curtin.

WHERE'S HUDDLES—30 minutes— CBS—July 1, 1970 - September 10, 1971. Rebroadcasts: CBS—July 11, 1971 - September 5, 1971. 17 episodes.

WHERE'S RAYMOND

Musical Comedy. Background: The community of Pelham, New York. The misadventures of Raymond Wallace, a professional song-and-dance man.

CAST

Raymond Wallace	Ray Bolger
Susan, his girlfriend	Margie Millar
Peter Morrisey, his	

partner	Richard Erdman
Farley, his	
understudy	Charles Smith
Ruth Farley, his	
wife	Gloria Winters
Ruth's mother	Verna Felton
Katie, a	
friend	Chris Nelson

Also: Sylvia Lewis, Allyn Joslyn, Betty Lynn, Rise Stevens, Betty Kean.

Orchestra: Al Goodwin; Herbert Spencer, Earle Hagen.

WHERE'S RAYMOND—30 minutes—ABC—October 8, 1953 - June 10, 1955. 59 episodes. Also titled: "The Ray Bolger Show."

WHERE THE ACTION IS

Variety. Performances by Rock personalities.

Host: Dick Clark.

Regulars: Linda Scott, Steve Alaimo, Paul Revere and the Raiders.

Music: Provided by guests.

WHERE THE ACTION IS—30 minutes—ABC—July 5, 1965 - April 14, 1967.

WHERE THE HEART IS

Serial. Background: Nothcross, Connecticut. The conflicts, tensions, and drives of the close-knit Hathaway family.

CAST
Julian Hathaway	James Mitchell
Mary Hathaway	Diana Walker
Michael Hathaway	Greg Abels
Vicky Hathaway	Lisa Richards
Kate Prescott	Diana Van der Vlis
Alison Jessup	Louise Shaffer
Dr. Hugh Jessup	David Cryer
Dr. Joe Prescott	Bill Post, Jr.
Nancy Prescott	Katherine Meshill
Ed Lucas	Joe Mascolo
Stella O'Brien	Bibi Osterwald
Christine Cameron	Delphi Harrington
Loretta Jorden	Alice Drummond
Peter Jorden	Mike Bersell
Carol Gault	Janet League
Elizabeth Harris	
Rainey	Tracy Brooks Swope
John Rainey	Peter MacLean
Dr. Adrienne Harris	Priscilla Pointer
Lt. Hayward	Philip Sterling
Amy Snowden	Clarice Blackburn
Dr. Jim Hudson	Ruben Greene
Terry Stevens	Ted La Platt
Will Watts	Robert Symonds
Detective Munford	Gil Rogers
Lt. Fenelli	Ted Beniodes
Dr. Homes Rayburn	Alan Manson

Margaret Jordas	Rue McClanahan
	Barbara Baxley
Daniel Hathaway	Joseph Dolen
Ellie Jordas	Zohra Lampert
Mrs. Harrison	Caroline Coates
Lois Snowden	Jeanne Ruskin
The judge	William Prince
Ben Jessup	Daniel Keyes
Steve Prescott	Laurence Luckinbill
	Ron Harper
Terry Prescott	Ted Leplat
Mrs. Pangborn	Paula Truman
Bill Conway	Barton Hayman
Dave, the	
bartender	Charles Dobson
Judge Halstad	Mason Adams
Baby Katina	Kara Fleming

Music: Eddie Layton.

WHERE THE HEART IS—30 minutes—CBS—September 8, 1969 - March 23, 1973.

WHERE WAS I?

Game. Through a series of question-and-answer probe rounds with the host, a panel of four celebrities have to locate objects depicted in photographs.

Host: Dan Seymour.

Panelists: Peter Donald, Nancy Guild, David Ross, Bill Cullen.

Announcer: Bob Williams.

WHERE WAS I?—30 minutes—NBC 1952.

WHIPLASH

Adventure. Background: Australia during the 1850s. The story of Chris Cobb, the American owner of the Cobb and Company Stage Coach Lines, as he struggles to maintain the country's first stage route.

CAST
Chris Cobb	Peter Graves
Dan, his	
partner	Anthony Wickert

WHIPLASH—30 minutes—Syndicated 1961. 39 episodes. Filmed in Australia.

WHIRLPOOL

Anthology. Rebroadcasts of dramas that were originally aired via other filmed anthology programs.

Included:

Beneath The Surface. The struggles

that face a woman as she attempts to escape her past.

Starring: Ida Lupino.

The Contest. A detective attempts to clear his brother and his fiancée of a murder charge.

Starring: Dick Powell.

The Stranger. The story of a young woman who finds aid from a stranger just after her husband escapes from prison.

Starring: Charles Boyer, Beverly Garland.

WHIRLPOOL—30 minutes—Syndicated 1959.

THE WHIRLYBIRDS

Adventure. Background: California. The experiences of Chuck Miller and P. T. Moore, pilots for Whirlybirds, Incorporated, a helicopter charter service.

CAST
Chuck Miller	Ken Tobey
P. T. Moore	Craig Hill
Chuck's girlfriend	Nancy Hale
P. T.'s girlfriend	Sandra Spence

Copter pilot (stand-in for Ken Tobey): Robert Gilbreath.

Stuntman (stand-in for Craig Hill): Earl Parker.

THE WHIRLYBIRDS—30 minutes—Syndicated 1957. 39 episodes. Also known as "Copter Patrol."

WHISPERING SMITH

Crime Drama. Background: The Denver Police Department during the 1870s. The investigations of Detectives Tom "Whispering" Smith and his partner, George Romack.

CAST
Tom "Whispering"	
Smith	Audie Murphy
George Romack	Guy Mitchell
John Richards,	
the police	
chief	Sam Buffington

Music: Richard Shores; Leo Shuken.

WHISPERING SMITH—30 minutes—NBC—May 18, 1961 - September 18, 1961. 25 episodes.

THE WHISTLER

Anthology. Mystery presentations. Stories of people who are suddenly caught in a destructive web of their own misdeeds. The Whistler, who is identified by the mournful whistling of the theme music, is never seen. His observations concerning the actions of the individuals prevail throughout each drama.

The Whistler (Narrator): Bill Forman.

Orchestra: Wilbur Hatch.

Theme: "The Whistler," whistled by Dorothy Roberts. Wilbur Hatch is the composer.

Included:

Dark Hour. The story of a man who believes he's committed a murder during a mental blackout.

Starring: Robert Hutton, Nancy Gates.

Windfall. The story of a man who stumbles upon a corpse with a one-hundred-thousand-dollar bank account and the ensuing difficulties when he tries to claim the money.

Starring: Charles McGraw, Dorothy Green.

Fatal Fraud. The story of a larcenous blonde who uses her feminine wiles to convince a clever impersonator to master the voice of a wealthy importer. Her intent: to divert a valuable shipment.

Starring: Marie Windsor.

Backfire. Suspicious of his wife's actions, a man follows her to a nightclub. When he discovers that she is planning to double cross him, he decides to put his own plan into effect.

Starring: Lon Chaney, Jr., Dorothy Green.

Program Opening:

The Whistler: "I am The Whistler. And I know many things, for I walk by night. I know many strange tales hidden in the hearts of men and women who have stepped into the shadows. Yes, I know the nameless terrors of which they dare not speak."

THE WHISTLER—30 minutes—Syndicated 1954. 39 episodes. Based on the radio program.

THE WHISTLING WIZARD

Puppet Adventure. Looking into an enchanted well, J. P., an inquisitive child, loses his balance, falls in, and reappears in the fantasy kingdom of the Land of Beyond. Stories relate his adventures in the bewitched kingdom.

Characters:

J. P., distinguished by four toes on each foot.

Dooley, the Whistling Wizard, an Irish elf who rules the Land of Beyond.

Heathcliff, J.P.'s horse.

Thimble, assistant ruler of the kingdom.

Davey Jones, the guardian of treasures at the bottom of the sea.

King Rutabaga, the ruler of the neighboring kingdom, Nagard.

Spider Lady, a villainess who seeks control of the Land of Beyond.

Character movement and voices: Bil and Cora Baird.

THE WHISTLING WIZARD—15 minutes—CBS 1952.

WHITE HUNTER

Adventure. Background: Africa. Dramatizations based on the experiences of John A. Hunter, game hunter and trapper.

CAST

John Hunter	Rhodes Reason
The Game Commissioner	Tim Turner

WHITE HUNTER—30 minutes—Syndicated 1958. 39 episodes.

WHO DO YOU TRUST?

See title: "Do You Trust Your Wife?"

WHO PAYS?

Game. Through the cross-examination of two of his or her employees, a celebrity panel of three have to identify mystery-guest personalities. The star's employees receive one hundred dollars each if the panel fails to uncover their employer's identity.

Host: Mike Wallace.

Panelists: Sir Cedric Hardwicke, Celeste Holm, Gene Klavan.

Premiere Guests: Carol Channing, Red Buttons.

WHO PAYS?—30 minutes—CBS—July 2, 1959 - September 1959.

WHO SAID THAT?

Game. Quotations taken from news stories are related to a celebrity panel. The panel must then identify the news story from which the quotation was taken. Failure to do so adds, each time, five dollars to a jackpot. At the program's end, a question, submitted by a home viewer, is read to the panel. If they fail to answer it, the viewer receives a $50 savings bond plus the money that has been accumulated in the jackpot.

Host: Robert Trout.

Regular Panelist: John Cameron Swayze.

Announcer: Peter Roberts.

Producer: Fred W. Friendly, Anne Gillis, Herb Leder.

Director: Mark Hawley, Garry Simpson.

WHO SAID THAT?—30 minutes—NBC—December 9, 1948 - July 19, 1954; ABC—30 minutes—February 2, 1955 - July 26, 1955.

WHO'S TALKING?

A game show, hosted by Frann Weigle, in which contestants have to identify celebrities from masked photos and recordings of their voice. Broadcast on CBS for fifteen minutes in 1951.

WHO'S THE BOSS?

Game. Through question-and-answer probe rounds with their secretaries, a celebrity panel of four have to identify their prominent employers. Secretaries receive one hundred dollars each if the panel fails to uncover their employer's identity.

Host: Walter Kiernan.

Panelists: Polly Rowles, Dick Kollman, Sylvia Lyons, Horace Sutton.

WHO'S THE BOSS?—30 minutes—ABC 1954.

WHO'S THERE?

Game. Through props, personal items, and apparel clues, a celebrity panel of three has to identify mystery-guest personalities.

Hostess: Arlene Francis.

Panelists: Bill Cullen, Paula Stone, Robert Coote.

Announcer: Rex Marshall.

WHO'S THERE?—30 minutes—CBS—July 14, 1952 - September 1952.

THE WHO, WHAT OR WHERE GAME

Game. Three competing contestants who each receive one hundred and twenty-five dollars bidding cash. A category topic is revealed, followed by three questions—each characterized by three parts: The Who (even money), the What (two to one), and the Where (three to one). Players then press a button and secretly lock in a "W" of their choice and a cash wager (fifty dollars minimum). Choices are then revealed. If all three have chosen differently, the highest wagerer receives the "W" question. Correct answers award the player his bet amount of money; incorrect responses deduct the amount. If two players have chosen the same "W" a verbal auction is held. The highest cash wagerer receives the question. If all three have bid on the same "W" it is an automatic cancellation and a new category is introduced. Winners, the highest cash scorers, receive the money as their prize.

Host: Art James.

Announcer: Mike Darrow.

Music: George David Weiss.

THE WHO, WHAT OR WHERE GAME—25 minutes—NBC—December 29, 1969 - January 4, 1974.

WHO'S WHO

Documentary. A magazine-type program that reveals the human side of public figures through in-depth interviews.

Host: Dan Rather.

Co-Hosts: Charles Kuralt, Barbara Howar.

Producer: Don Hewitt.

WHO'S WHO—60 minutes—CBS—January 4, 1977 - May 10, 1977; June 5, 1977 - June 26, 1977.

WHO'S WHOSE?

Game. One woman and three men, who each claim to be her husband, appear opposite a panel of four celebrities (three regulars and one guest). Through a series of question-and-answer probe rounds, first with the woman, then with the men, the panel has to identify her spouse. Players

receive money for participating.

Host: Phil Barker.

Panelists: Basil Rathbone, Robin Chandler, Art Ford.

Announcer (as identified): "Gunga."

WHO'S WHOSE?—30 minutes—CBS—June 25, 1951 - September 1951.

WHY?

Game. Involved: The five W's—Who, What, When, Where, and Why. The host states the first four W's of a situation; through a series of question and answer probe rounds, a contestant panel has to determine the Why. Prizes are awarded to the panelist with the most correct answers.

Host: John Reed King.

Question Man: Bill Cullen.

WHY?—30 minutes—ABC—July 29, 1952 - September 1952.

WICHITA TOWN

Western. Background: Wichita Town, Kansas, 1870s. The story of Marshall Mike Dunbar and his efforts to maintain law and order.

CAST
Marshall Mike Dunbar	Joel McCrea
Deputy Ben Matheson	Jody McCrea

Music: Hans Salter.

WICHITA TOWN—30 minutes—NBC—September 30, 1959 - April 4, 1960.

WIDE COUNTRY

Adventure. Background: The rodeo circuit between Texas and California. The experiences of Mitch Guthrie, a champion rodeo rider, as he travels from rodeo to rodeo seeking to secure the Gold Buckle, the trophy that is awarded to the world's best bronco buster.

CAST
Mitch Guthrie	Earl Holliman
Andy Guthrie, his brother	Andrew Prine

Music: Stanley Wilson.

WIDE COUNTRY—60 minutes—NBC—September 20, 1962 - September 12, 1963. 28 episodes. Syndicated.

WIDE WIDE WORLD

See title: "Dave Garroway."

THE WILBURN BROTHERS SHOW

Musical Variety. Performances by Country and Western entertainers.

Hosts: Ted and Doyle Wilburn.

Vocalist: Loretta Lynn.

Music: The Nashville Tennessians.

THE WILBURN BROTHERS SHOW—30 minutes—Syndicated 1963. 52 tapes.

Wild Bill Hickok. Guy Madison.

WILD BILL HICKOK

Western. Background: The Frontier, 1870s. The exploits of James Butler (Wild Bill) Hickok, U.S. Marshall, and his partner, Jingles, as they battle injustice throughout the West.

CAST
Wild Bill Hickok	Guy Madison
Jingles	Andy Devine

Announcer: John Cannon.

Producer: William F. Brady, Wesley Barry.

Sponsor: Kellogg's.

Wild Bill's Horse: Buckshot.

Jingles P. Jones's Horse: Joker.

WILD BILL HICKOK—30 minutes—Syndicated 1952. Also appeared on ABC—30 minutes—October 2, 1957 - September 24, 1958. 113 episodes.

WILD CARGO

Documentary. Films depicting the

capture of wild animals for zoos.

Host-Narrator: Arthur Jones.

WILD CARGO—30 minutes—Syndicated 1963.

WILD KINGDOM

Documentary. Films detailing the life and struggles of animals.

Hosts: Marlin Perkins, Jim Fowler, Stan Brock, Tom Allen.

Narrator: Joe Slattery.

Music: James Bourgeois.

WILD KINGDOM—30 minutes—NBC —January 6, 1963 - September 5, 1973. Syndicated.

THE WILD, WILD WEST

Western. Background: The Frontier, 1870s. The investigations of James T. West and Artemus Gordon, United States government underground intelligence agents, as they incorporate ingenious scientific weapons to battle diabolical villains.

CAST

James T. West	Robert Conrad
Artemus Gordon	Ross Martin
President Ulysses S. Grant, their superior	James Gregory
	Roy Engle
Dr. Miguelito Lovelace, an enemy agent	Michael Dunn
Jeremy Pike, West's assistant for a short period	Charles Aidman
Count Manzeppi, the evil magician	Victor Buono

Music: Richard Shores; Richard Markowitz; Morton Stevens.

Executive Producer: Philip Leacock, Michael Garrison.

Producer: Richard Landau, Leonard Katzman, Fred Freiberger, Collier Young, John Mantley, Gene L. Coon, Bruce Lansbury.

Director: Bill Witney, Richard Sarafian, Bernard Kowalsky, Don Taylor, Irving Moore, Harvey Hart, Alvin Ganzer, Justis Addiss, Alan Crosland, Paul Wendkos, Richard Whorf, Lee H. Katzin, Mark Rydell, Ed Dein, Ralph Senesky, Richard Donner, Robert Sparr, Sherman Marks, Jesse Hibbs, Charles R. Rondeau, Leon Benson, Gunnar Hellstrom, James B. Clark, Marvin Chomsky, Alex Nichol, Mike Moder, Lawrence Dobkin, Michael Caffrey, Vincent McEveety, Paul Stanley, Bernard McEveety, Herb Wallerstein.

Creator: Michael Garrison.

THE WILD, WILD WEST—60 minutes—CBS—September 17, 1965 - September 19, 1969. Rebroadcasts: CBS—June 1970 - September 1970. 104 episodes. Syndicated.

WILD, WILD WORLD OF ANIMALS

Documentary. Films depicting the animal struggle for survival.

Narrator: William Conrad.

Additional Narrative: Hugh Faulk, Mary Batten.

Music: Gerherd Trede, Beatrice Witkin.

WILD, WILD WORLD OF ANIMALS —30 minutes—Syndicated 1973.

WILLIE WONDERFUL

A puppet series for children dealing with the adventures of Willie Wonderful, a young boy who travels with a circus. Voices for the thirty-eight puppet characters are provided by Stan Freberg and Eddie Bracken. The series, composed of 195 thirty-minute episodes, was first broadcast over ABC in 1959.

WILL THE REAL JERRY LEWIS PLEASE SIT DOWN

Animated Cartoon. The misadventures of Jerry Lewis, a fumbling janitor with the Odd Job Employment Agency. The series incorporates the celluloid creations of Jerry Lewis (e.g., The Playboy, The Nutty Professor, The Errand Boy) as it depicts his fruitless attempts to successfully complete his assigned tasks. Created by Jerry Lewis.

Additional characters: Geraldine, Jerry's sister; Mr. Blunderpuss, Jerry's employer; Rhonda, Jerry's girlfriend; and Spot, Geraldine's pet frog.

WILL THE REAL JERRY LEWIS PLEASE SIT DOWN—30 minutes— ABC—September 12, 1970 - September 2, 1972.

WILLY

Comedy. Distinguished by two formats.

Format One: September 18, 1954 - March 31, 1955.

Background: Renfrew, New Hampshire. The misadventures of Willy Dodger, an attorney, as she struggles to practice law in a town where people are distrustful of female barristers.

CAST

Willy Dodger	June Havoc
Mr. Dodger, her father	Wheaton Chambers Lloyd Corrigan
Charlie Bush, her boyfriend, the town veterinarian	Whitfield Connar
Emily, her widowed sister	Mary Treen
Franklin Sanders, her nephew	Danny Richards, Jr.

Willy's dog: Rags.

Format Two: April 7, 1955 - July 7, 1955.

Background: New York City. The cases of Willy Dodger, legal council for the Bannister Vaudeville Company.

CAST

Willy Dodger	June Havoc
Perry Bannister, her employer	Hal Peary
Harvey Evelyn, her friend, the owner of a stock company	Sterling Holloway

WILLY—30 minutes—CBS—September 18, 1954 - July 7, 1955. Syndicated; withdrawn.

WIN WITH A WINNER

Game. Five competing players, each of whom stands before a numbered post (as in a horse race). Object: For players to reach the finish line by answering questions. Players each select their own questions by point values—the higher the point value, the more difficult the question. If the player correctly answers the question he moves forward in accord with its value. Incorrect answers halt a player until his next turn. The winner receives merchandise prizes.

Host: Sandy Becker.

Assistant: Marilyn Toomey.

Announcer: Bill Wendell.

WIN WITH A WINNER—30 minutes —NBC—June 24, 1958 - September 9, 1958.

WIN WITH THE STARS

Game. Involved: Two celebrity guests and four noncelebrity contestants. Object: the identification of song titles.

Round One: Two of the four contestants compete, each paired with one of the celebrities to form two teams of two. One team at a time competes. A musical selection is played. As soon as the title is recognized, the player presses a button to stop a ticking clock (set for forty-five seconds). If a correct title is given, the team scores two points and receives the opportunity to earn additional points by singing the first two lines of the song. Each correct lyric awards one point. The game continues until the forty-five-second time limit has elapsed. Team two then competes in the same manner with the object being to beat their opponents' score. The winner is the highest scoring team.

Round Two: The remaining two contestants compete in the same manner.

Round Three: The two highest scorers of rounds one and two compete in a final segment, which is played in the same manner. The winner, the highest scorer, receives his points transferred into dollars.

Host: Allen Ludden.

Announcer: Jay Stewart.

Orchestra: Bobby Hammock.

Appearing: Judy Carne, Jaye P. Morgan, Steve Allen, Jayne Meadows, Ruta Lee, Barbara McNair, Paul Lynde, Abby Dalton, Betty White, Bill Dana, Mel Tormé, Rose Marie, Roddy McDowall, Bob Crane.

WIN WITH THE STARS—30 minutes —Syndicated 1968. 26 tapes.

WINDOW ON MAIN STREET

Comedy-Drama. Background: The town of Millsburg. Life in a small American town as seen through the eyes of Cameron Garrett Brooks, a novelist who, after the death of his wife and son, returns to his home town to write about its people.

CAST

Cameron Brooks	Robert Young
Lloyd Ramsey, the newspaper editor	Ford Rainey
Chris Logan, a widow, his assistant	Constance Moore
Wally Evans, the owner of the Majestic Hotel	James Byron
Peggy Evans, his wife	Carol Byron
Henry McGill, the hotel desk clerk	Warner Jones
Arnie Logan, Chris's young son	Brad Berwick

WINDOW ON MAIN STREET—30 minutes—CBS—October 2, 1961 - September 12, 1962. 36 episodes.

WINDOWS

Anthology. Dramatic presentations.

Included:

The World Out There. Through the efforts of her educated younger cousin, an illiterate woman attempts to learn how to read and write.

CAST

Cora: Mary Perry; Benji: Anthony Perkins; Tom: Joseph Perkins.

Rose's Boy. A one-character play. A woman's struggles to face the difficult task of telling a young boy the circumstances surrounding his mother's death.

CAST

The woman: Judith Evelyn.

The Calliope Tree. Through the worship of a young boy, an ex-circus clown attempts to relive the glories of his past.

CAST

The Clown: Henry Hull; The boy: Van Dyke Parks.

Domestic Dilemma. The effect of a woman alcoholic on her family.

CAST

The woman: Geraldine Page.

WINDOWS—30 minutes—CBS—July 8, 1955 - August 26, 1955.

WINDOW SHOPPING

Game. Three competing contestants. A photograph is briefly flashed on a screen. Each player then relates the items that he believes were depicted in the photograph. For each correct identification he receives one point. Several such rounds are played. The player with the highest point total is the winner and receives the opportunity to window shop. His point total is transferred into seconds and for that amount of time, a stage window, which contains numerous merchandise items, is displayed. The items he is then able to describe become his gifts.

Host: Bob Kennedy.

Judge: Professor William Wood, Columbia School of Journalism.

WINDOW SHOPPING—30 minutes— ABC—April 2, 1962 - June 29, 1962.

WINDY CITY JAMBOREE

Musical Variety. Background: Chicago.

Host: Danny O'Neal.

Orchestra: Gloria Van.

WINDY CITY JAMBOREE—30 minutes—DuMont 1950.

WINGO

Game. Two competing players, a champion and a challenger. Basis: Very difficult question-and-answer rounds. The host reads a question. The player who is first to identify himself through a buzzer signal receives a chance to answer. If correct he receives one point; if incorrect the point is deducted from his score. The winner, the highest scorer, receives one thousand dollars. Players compete until defeated vying for the top prize of $250,000.

Host: Bob Kennedy.

WINGO—30 minutes—NBC—April 1, 1958 - May 13, 1958.

WINKY DINK AND YOU

Children. Children participate at home via inexpensive Winky Dink kits. A magic transparent screen is placed over the television screen. The host relates the adventures of Winky Dink, an animated cartoon boy, and his friend Woofer, the animated dog. The events unfold through a series of cartoon drawings that enable children to assist the characters when they are in trouble by drawing the life-saving essentials on their screen with a wax crayon. For example: As Woofer faces a life and death situation, Winky Dink speaks: "Oh boys and girls, we've got to save our pal Woofer. Please draw that special part of the machine...Oh thanks, just in time, Woofer is saved. Quick gang, erase your drawing with your magic cloth while we figure out what to do next." Incidents are also related by the host.

Host: Jack Barry.

Assistant: Mike McBean.

Orchestra: John Gart.

WINKY DINK AND YOU—30 minutes—CBS—October 10, 1953 - April 27, 1957. A five-minute animated version appeared via syndication in 1969.

WINNER TAKE ALL

Game. Two competing contestants, a challenger and the previous champion. Object: To answer questions based on sketches that are performed on stage. The player with the most correct answers is the winner and receives merchandise prizes.

Host: Bill Cullen.

Assistant: Sheila Connolly.

Performers: Barry Gray, Betty Jones Watson, Jerry Austen, Howard Malone.

Orchestra: Bernard Leighton.

Producer: Mark Goodson, Bill Todman, Gil Fates.

Director: Frances Buss, Roland Gillette.

Sponsor: Chevrolet; Gillette.

WINNER TAKE ALL—45 minutes—CBS—July 1, 1948 - April 20, 1951.

WINNING STREAK

Game. Two competing contestants. Sixteen letters of the alphabet, each representing a different point value, are displayed on a large board. One player chooses a letter, which reveals its point value. If the player seeks to earn the points, he is asked a question that corresponds to that letter (e.g., If letter I is chosen, the answer will begin with the letter I). If the player answers correctly he receives the points. The opponent then receives his selection. Should the player pass the question, the opponent automatically has to answer it, and the next selection reverts back to the original player. The first player to reach the

goal (varies from 250-350 points) is the winner.

The present champion is placed opposite the previous winner. A board that contains eighteen numbers, numbered as such from one to eighteen, is displayed. The present champion then chooses one number from one to six. A cash amount of money is then revealed, which becomes the cash value of each number from seven to eighteen. The champion then selects one number. A letter of the alphabet is revealed and the player has to give a word using that letter. When he does, the money is placed in a jackpot. The opponent then selects a number and has to give a word using the two letters that are now displayed. The money is again added to the jackpot. The game continues in this manner; for each additional number that is selected the player has to give a word using all the exposed letters. When a player is stumped or gives an incorrect word he is defeated. The other player becomes the champion and receives whatever money has been accumulated in the jackpot. The player remains to face the winner of the qualifying round.

Host: Bill Cullen.

Announcer: Don Pardo.

Music: Recorded.

First champion: Jean Sheridan.

WINNING STREAK—30 minutes—NBC—July 1, 1974 - January 3, 1975.

WINSTON CHURCHILL

Documentary. Through films, interviews, and stills, the life of Sir Winston Churchill is recalled. The series focuses on his career as a statesman during World War II.

Narrator: Gary Merrill.

Reading Churchill's works: Richard Burton.

Music: Richard Rodgers.

WINSTON CHURCHILL—30 minutes—ABC—September 30, 1962 - April 5, 1963. Broadcast under the title "The Valiant Years"—ABC—November 27, 1960 - June 11, 1961.

WIRE SERVICE

Adventure. The global investigations of Dean Evans, Katherine Wells, and Dan Miller, wire-service reporters for *Trans Globe News.* Stories depict their experiences on a rotational basis.

CAST

Dean Evans	George Brent
Katherine Wells	Mercedes McCambridge
Dan Miller	Dane Clark

Program Open (related by the star of the particular episode):

"Nothing travels faster than news. An electronic impulse splinters distance at one hundred and eighty-six thousand miles per second. From Tokyo, from London, from Rio, from New York. An age of speed and curiosity, the news probes and the probe is truth."

WIRE SERVICE—60 minutes—ABC—September 1956 - September 1957. 39 episodes. Syndicated.

WISDOM OF THE AGES

Discussion. Children and adults, from ten to eighty years of age, discuss and suggest possible solutions to problems that have been submitted by home viewers.

Host: Jack Barry.

WISDOM OF THE AGES—30 minutes—DuMont 1953.

WITH THIS RING

Discussion. Two engaged couples, selected from the lists of applicants for marriage licenses, appear. A marital problem, which has been submitted by a home viewer, is read then discussed by the couples who relate their thoughts concerning possible solutions.

Host: Bill Slater.

WITH THIS RING—30 minutes—DuMont 1951.

WITNESS

Crime Drama. People who have witnessed or become innocently involved in crimes appear and through the questioning of a panel of defense attorneys relate their experiences. The program attempts to expose rackets and criminals by making people aware of confidence games.

Panel: William Geoghan, Richard Steele, Benedict Ginsberg, Charles Hayden.

WITNESS—30 minutes—CBS—September 29, 1960 - February 2, 1961.

THE WIZARD OF ODDS

Game. Selected studio-audience members compete in greatly varying contests designed to test their knowledge of national odds and averages and bring forth a "Wizard's Champion."

Regular segments:

"The Elimination Round." Three contestants appear on stage. The host reveals clues to the identity of a mystery celebrity one at a time to a limit of five clues. The player who is first to correctly identify the personality is the winner and receives a valuable merchandise prize.

"The Odds and Averages Board." Two players compete. Three items are displayed on a board, one of which is the odd item. The player who is first to shout the odd item receives one point. Should he give the wrong item his opponent receives the point. The first player to score three points receives a valuable merchandise item.

Before the final round is played the names of all the players who have competed are placed on a large spinning wheel. The player whose name is selected by the wheel when it stops receives the opportunity to play "Wizard's Wheel of Fortune."

One figure is displayed on the top of a large board. Below it are seven questions, each of which is answerable by a number, but only four of which will total just below the established figure. If the player can select the four correct questions (or items as they are also referred to), he receives a new car. If he fails he receives merchandise prizes according to his correct number of selections.

Host: Alex Trebek.

Assistant: Mary Pom.

Announcers: Owen Spam; Charlie O'Donnell.

Music: Stan Worth.

THE WIZARD OF ODDS—30 minutes—NBC—June 17, 1973 - June 28, 1974.

WODEHOUSE PLAYHOUSE

Comedy. A series of humorous stories based on the prolific pen of P.G. Wodehouse.

Introduced By: P.G. Wodehouse.

Regular Performers: John Alderton, Pauline Collins.

Music: Raymond Jones.

Producer: Michael Mills.

WODEHOUSE PLAYHOUSE—30 minutes—Syndicated 1977.

THE WOLFMAN JACK SHOW

Variety. A mixture of music, songs, and comedy sketches.

Host: Wolfman Jack.

Regulars: Peter Cullen, Murray Langston, John Harris, The Incredible Puppets, and Vivian, the talking mule.

Executive Producer: Don Kelley.

Producer: Rif Markowitz.

Director: Mark Warren.

THE WOLFMAN JACK SHOW—30 minutes—Syndicated 1977.

WOMAN

Discussion. Discussions on topics of interest that concern women in their daily lives.

Hostess: Sherrye Henry.

Music: Recorded.

WOMAN—30 minutes—Syndicated 1971.

A WOMAN TO REMEMBER

Serial. Background: An AM radio station in New York City where a daily serial originates. An unknown woman, hired to replace the lead on the program, is disliked by the other members of the cast. Through rehearsal proceedings, the program dramatizes her attempts to overcome existing hostilities and tensions.

Though considered by many to be television's first serial, extensive research disproved this, revealing "Faraway Hill" (1946) the medium's inaugural serialized endeavor.

CAST
The Serial Star	Patricia Wheel
The Replacement	Joan Castle
The Director	John Raby
The Sound Man	Frankie Thomas

A WOMAN TO REMEMBER—15 minutes—DuMont—1947-1949.

WOMAN WITH A PAST

Serial. The dramatic story of Lynn Sherwood, fashion designer.

CAST
Lynn Sherwood	Constance Ford
Her daughter	Barbara Myers
Peggy Sherwood, her sister	Ann Hegira
Gwen	Jean Stapleton

WOMAN WITH A PAST—15 minutes—CBS—February 1, 1954 - July 2, 1954.

WONDERAMA

Children. Cartoons, game contests for prizes, and performances by top-name guests.

Hosts: Sandy Becker; Herb Sheldon; Sonny Fox; Bob McAllister.

Music: Recorded.

WONDERAMA—3 hours—1955 Present. Broadcast on Metromedia stations around the country. Original title: "Let's Have Fun."

WONDERBUG

See title: "The Krofft Supershow," *Wonderbug* segment.

WONDERFUL JOHN ACTION

Comedy. Background: The Ohio River Valley, 1919. Events in the lives of the Actions, an Irish-American family.

CAST
John Action, the father, a court clerk and the owner of the general store	Harry Holcombe
Julia Action, his wife	Virginia Dwyer
Kevin Action, their son	Ronnie Walker
Terrence Action, John's brother, the manager of the general store	Ian Martain
Peter Bodkin, Jr., John's employer at the court	Pat Harrington
Bessie Action, John's sister	Jane Rose

Also: Lou Gilbert, Robert Sullivan.

Orchestra: John Gart.

WONDERFUL JOHN ACTION—30 minutes—ABC—July 13, 1953 - September 1953.

Wonder Woman. Lynda Carter.

WONDER WOMAN

Adventure. In the year circa 200 B.C., when the rival gods Mars and Aphrodite ruled the Earth, Aphrodite, who was unable to defeat Mars, organized a group of superwomen called Amazons and retreated to Paradise Island, an uncharted land mass within the Bermuda Triangle. There, she selected Hippolyte as her queen and presented her with the magic girdle, a gold belt that produces superhuman strength. However, still determined to defeat his adversary, Mars retreated to skullduggery and used love, Hippolyte's own weapon against her, to snatch the magic girdle. Though displeased, Hippolyte received forgiveness from Aphrodite but had to, as all Amazons, wear special wrist bracelets made of feminum to remind them always of the dangers of submitting to men's domination. To further show her sorrow, Hippolyte fashioned a small statue that, when offered to Aphrodite, was brought to life as the baby Diana.

The time: now that of World War II. Crash landing on Paradise Island when his plane is hit by enemy gun fire, U.S. Fighter Pilot Steve Trevor is found by Diana and nursed back to health. An olympic games competition is held and Diana, who proves herself superior, is chosen to escort Steve back to civilization and to assist America in the war effort.

From the Queen Mother, Diana receives the gold belt (to maintain her cunning and strength away from Paradise Island) and the magic lariat, which compels people to tell the truth. Diana then chooses a revealing red, white, and blue costume to signify her allegiance to freedom and democracy. With the final words of her mother, "In the words of ordinary mortals you are a Wonder Woman," Diana incorporates her invisible plane to fly Steve back to Washington, D.C.

(Prior to their departure, Steve had been given a special drug from the Hybernia Tree to erase all memory of Paradise Island.)

In order to be at Steve's side, Diana adopts the guise of Diana Prince and, after achieving remarkably high scores on army aptitude tests, she is made Yeoman First Class and assigned to the U.S. War Department as Major Trevor's secretary. Stories depict Diana's crusade, as Wonder Woman, against Nazi activities in America. (By doing a twirling striptease, the plain-looking Diana emerges into the beautiful Wonder Woman.)

CAST

Diana Prince/Wonder Woman	Lynda Carter
Major Steve Trevor	Lyle Waggoner
General Phillip Blankenship	Richard Eastham
Yeoman Etta Candy, the general's secretary	Beatrice Colen
Drusilla/Wonder Girl, Diana's sister	Debra Winger
The Queen Mother	Cloris Leachman Carolyn Jones
Magda, an Amazon	Pamela Shoop
Dalma, an Amazon	Erica Hagen

Music: Artie Kane, Charles Fox.

Theme: "Wonder Woman" by Norman Gimbel, Charles Fox.

Executive Producer: Douglas S. Cramer.

Producer: Wilfred Baumes.

Director: Stuart Margolin, Bruce Bilson, Herb Wallerstein, Charles R. Rondeau, Richard Kinon, Leonard Horn, Alan Crosland, Barry Crane.

WONDER WOMAN—60 minutes—ABC—Premiered: March 31, 1976. Original title: "The New, Original Wonder Woman."

The character of "Wonder Woman," created by Charles Moulton, was first seen in 1973 as part of the animated series "Super Friends" (which see). On March 12, 1974, ABC presented an unsold pilot film entitled "Wonder Woman," with Cathy Lee Crosby as Diana and Kaz Garas as Steve, in an updated, modern version of the 1940s character that failed to become a series.

THE WOODY WOODBURY SHOW

Talk-Variety.

Host: Woody Woodbury.

Music: The Michael Melvoin Combo.

THE WOODY WOODBURY SHOW—

90 minutes—Syndicated 1967.

THE WOODY WOODPECKER SHOW

Animated Cartoon. The misadventures of Woody Woodpecker, the world's most beloved bird.

Additional segments: "Andy Panda"; "Space Mouse"; "Charley Beary"; "Gabby Gator."

Host: Walter Lantz, Woody's creator.

Woody's voice: Grace Lantz (Mrs.).

Additional Voices: Paul Frees, June Foray, Walter Tetley, Daws Butler.

Music: Charles Wheeler, Walter Greene.

Producer: Walter Lantz.

Director: Paul Smith, Alex Lovey, Sid Marcus.

THE WOODY WOODPECKER SHOW—30 minutes—ABC—1957 - 1958. Syndicated. NBC—30 minutes—September 12, 1970 - September 2, 1972. 52 episodes.

WORD FOR WORD

Game. Two competing players. Object: To form as many three- and four-letter words from larger words (e.g., "Make as many words as you can from aspidistra"). Players receive one point for each acceptable word. The player with the highest score is the winner and receives that score transferred into seconds, which he uses against the Electronic Word-O-Meter. Object: To unscramble a jumbled word before the machine. His cash prize depends on the number of words he successfully unscrambles before the machine and before his time runs out.

Host: Merv Griffin.

Announcer: Frank Sims.

WORD FOR WORD—30 minutes—NBC—September 30, 1963 - October 23, 1964.

WORDS AND MUSIC

Musical Variety.

Hostess: Barbara Marshall.

Music: The Jerry Jerome Trio.

Producer-Director: Duane McKinney.

WORDS AND MUSIC—15 minutes—NBC 1949.

WORDS AND MUSIC

Game. Three contestants compete. A large board that contains sixteen squares (numbered from one to sixteen) is displayed cn stage. Each square contains a clue that is associated with a particular word in a particular song. One player (through a flip of coin decision) chooses one number. The host reads the clue (e.g., "The very yeast"), and a song is sung ("The Sound of Music."). The player who is first to associate the clue with the word in the song presses a button to identify himself. If he gives a correct answer ("Rise"–"Of the wings of the birds that rise"), he receives cash. The person with the last correct response selects the next clue. The player with the highest cash score is the winner. The player vies to win three straight games and a new car.

Cash at stake: Round one: twenty dollars; round two: forty dollars; round three: sixty dollars; and round four: eighty dollars for each correct association. Four clues are played per round.

Host: Wink Martindale.

Announcer: Johnny Gilbert.

Vocalists: Peggy Connelly, Bob Marlo, Katie Grant, Don Minter, Pat Henderson.

WORDS AND MUSIC–30 minutes–NBC–September 28, 1970 - February 12, 1971.

WORLD ADVENTURES

Travel. Films depicting the people, music, and life styles of countries throughout the world.

Host: Gunther Less.

Music: Recorded.

WORLD ADVENTURES–30 minutes–Syndicated 1965. Also aired under the title: "Journey to Adventure."

A WORLD APART

Serial. The dramatic story of Betty Kahlam, a serial writer and the unwed mother of two children, Patrice and Chris. Against a plaguing generation gap, she struggles to achieve their love and foster a sense of family unity and togetherness.

CAST

Patrice Kahlam	Susan Sarandon
Betty Kahlam	Augusta Dabney
Chris Kahlam	Matthew Cowles
Dr. John Karr	Robert Gentry
T.D. Drinkard	Tom Logan
Matilda	Rosetta La Noire
Nancy Condon	Susan Sullivan
	Judith Barcroft
Linda Peters	Heather MacRae
Russell Barry	William Prince
Sara Sims	Kathy Parker
Dr. Edward Sims	James Noble
Thomas Walsh	Roy Shuman

Also: M'el Dowd, Elizabeth Lawrence.

A WORLD APART–30 minutes–ABC–March 30, 1970 - June 25, 1971.

THE WORLD AT WAR

Documentary. The history of World War II is traced through film–from the rise of Hitler to Allied victory.

Narrator: Sir Laurence Olivier.

Music: Carl Davis.

THE WORLD AT WAR–60 minutes–Syndicated 1973. Produced in England.

WORLD CRIME HUNT

See title: "Paris Precinct."

THE WORLD OF GIANTS

Adventure. The investigations of Mel Hunter and Bill Winters, American counterespionage agents reduced, through scientific experimention, to six inches in height. Stories relate their attempts to infiltrate and expose criminal organizations.

CAST

Mel Hunter	Marshall Thompson
Bill Winters	Arthur Franz

THE WORLD OF GIANTS–30 minutes–Syndicated 1961. 13 episodes.

THE WORLD OF LOWELL THOMAS

Travel. Films exploring remote regions of the world.

Host-Narrator: Lowell Thomas.

THE WORLD OF LOWELL THOMAS–30 minutes–Syndicated 1966.

THE WORLD OF MISTER SWEENY

Comedy. Background: The town of Mapleton. The lighthearted misadventures of Cicero P. Sweeny, a general-store owner who involves himself in and attempts to solve the problems of others.

CAST

Cicero P. Sweeny	Charlie Ruggles
Kippie Sweeny, his grandson	Gene Walker
Marge Sweeny, his daughter	Helen Wagner
Tom Millikan, a friend	Harry Gresham
Abigail Millikan, his wife	Betty Garde
Henrietta, Marge's friend	Janet Fox
Molly, the town spinster	Jane Cleveland
Little Eva, the refugee girl	Lydia Reed

THE WORLD OF MISTER SWEENY–15 minutes (Daily)–NBC–June 30, 1954 - December 30, 1955.

THE WORLD OF SURVIVAL

Documentary. Films depicting the animal struggle for survival.

Host-Narrator: John Forsythe.

Music: Howard Blake.

THE WORLD OF SURVIVAL–30 minutes–Syndicated 1972.

WORLD WAR I

Documentary. Films recalling the events leading up to and the key battles and campaigns of World War I.

Narrator: Robert Ryan.

Music: Morton Gould.

WORLD WAR I–30 minutes–CBS–September 22, 1964 - January 1965. 26 episodes.

WRANGLER

Western. Background: The Frontier during the 1880s. The exploits of Pitcarin, a wandering, two-fisted cowboy who aids people in distress.

Starring: Jason Evers as Pitcarin.

WRANGLER–30 minutes–NBC–August 4, 1960 - September 15, 1960.

WREN'S NEST

Comedy. Background: Suburban New York. The trials and tribulations of marrieds Sam and Virginia Wren.

CAST

Sam Wren	Himself
Virginia Wren	Herself

Producer: Sherling Oliver.

Director: Tom DeHuff.

WREN'S NEST–15 minutes–ABC 1949.

WYATT EARP

See title: "The Life and Legend of Wyatt Earp."

X

THE XAVIER CUGAT SHOW

Musical Variety. The Continental sound.

Host: Xavier Cugat.

Vocalist: Abbe Lane.

Orchestra: Xavier Cugat.

THE XAVIER CUGAT SHOW–15 minutes–NBC–February 27, 1957 - May 24, 1957.

Y

YADAMAN

An animated series about a lovable, slightly mischievous monster. 30 minutes–Syndicated 1966. 26 films.

YANCY DERRINGER

Adventure. Background: New Orleans, Louisiana, 1880s. The exploits of Yancy Derringer, a roguish riverboat gambler, as he and his Indian friend, Pahoo, under city administrator John

Colton, struggle to institute a system of law and order in a city overrun with corruption.

CAST

Yancy Derringer	Jock Mahoney
Pahoo-Ka-Ta-Wha	X Brands
John Colton	Kevin Hagen
Mme. Francine, Yancy's romantic interest	Frances Bergen

Music: Don Quinn, Henry Russell.

YANCY DERRINGER–30 minutes–CBS–October 2, 1958 - September 24, 1959. 34 episodes. Syndicated.

A YEAR AT THE TOP

Comedy. Background: Hollywood, California. The story of Greg and Paul, two unknown songwriters offered musical stardom by prominent backer Frederick J. Hanover (of Paragon Records)–the Devil's son–who, on behalf of his father, grants them one year at the top in return for their souls.

CAST

Mickey Durbin, Greg and Paul's uncle	Mickey Rooney
Greg	Greg Evigan
Paul	Paul Shaffer
Frederick J. Hanover	Gabriel Dell
Linda, Greg's girlfriend	Priscilla Lopez
Miss Worley, Hanover's secretary	Priscilla Morrill
Grandma Bell Durbin, Mickey's mother	Nedra Volz
Trish, a friend of Greg and Paul	Julie Cobb

Music Supervision: Don Kirshner.

Executive Producer: Norman Lear.

Producer: Darryl Hickman, Patricia Fass Palmer.

Director: Alan Rafkin, Marlena Laird.

Creator: Woody Kling.

A YEAR AT THE TOP–30 minutes–CBS–August 5, 1977 - September 4, 1977. 5 episodes.

Originally, the series was scheduled to air beginning January 19, 1977, but was cancelled at the last moment, then revised, supposedly to improve it. Following are the cast and credits to the original version, dealing with the Rock group top (Cliff, Studly, and Lillian), which never aired.

CAST

Mickey:	Mickey Rooney; Lillian: Vivian Blaine; Cliff: Robert Alda; Studly: Phil Leeds; Young Cliff: Greg Evigan; Young Studly: Paul Shaffer; Young Lillian: Judith Cohen; Dee Dee: Kelly Bishop; Stage Manager: Kay Dingle.

Credits:

Music Supervision: Don Kirshner.

Musical Coordinator: Jay Siegel.

Special Musical Material: Earl Brown.

Musical Staging: Kevin Carlisle.

Executive Producer: Norman Lear.

Producer: Darryl Hickman.

Director: Jim Drake, Alan Myerson.

Creator: Woody Kling, Don Kirshner.

YES, YES NANETTE

Comedy. Background: Los Angeles, California. Events in the lives of the McGovern family: Dan, a Hollywood writer; Nanette, his wife, a former Broadway actress; and their children: Nancy and Buddy. Stories are based on real-life incidents drawn from the lives of Nanette Fabray and her husband, writer Ranald MacDougall.

CAST

Nanette McGovern	Nanette Fabray
Dan McGovern	Wendell Corey
Nancy McGovern	Jacklyn O'Donnell
Buddy McGovern	Bobby Diamond
Mrs. Harper, their housekeeper	Doris Kemper

YES, YES NANETTE–30 minutes–NBC–January 6, 1961 - July 7, 1961. 26 episodes. Also known as "The Nanette Fabray Show."

YOGA FOR HEALTH

Health. The principal and practical applications of yoga exercises.

Host: Richard Hittleman.

Assistant: Diane Hittleman (Mrs.)

Music: Richard Hittleman, Mike Batt.

YOGA FOR HEALTH–30 minutes–Syndicated 1968.

YOGI BEAR

Animated Cartoon. Background: Jellystone National Park. The misadventures of Yogi Bear, who, despite

Yogi Bear. Yogi Bear. *Courtesy Hanna-Barbera Productions.*

warnings from the park ranger, ingeniously schemes to acquire picnickers' lunch baskets. A Hanna-Barbera production.

Additional segments: "Snagglepuss" and "Yakky Doodle Duck."

Characters' Voices

Yogi Bear	Daws Butler
Boo Boo Bear, his innocent accomplice	Don Messick
John Smith, the ranger	Don Messick
Snagglepuss	Daws Butler
Yakky Doodle	Jimmy Weldon
Chopper	Vance Colvig

Music Supervision: Hoyt Curtin.

YOGI BEAR—30 minutes—Syndicated 1958. 123 episodes.

YOGI'S GANG

Animated Cartoon. As living conditions become intolerable, Yogi Bear and his friends decide to do something about it and commission inventor Noah Smith to construct a flying ark. Beginning a crusade to protect the environment, they travel throughout the country and attempt to battle the enemies of man and nature.

Characters' Voices

Yogi Bear	Daws Butler
Boo Boo Bear	Don Messick
Paw Ruggs	Henry Corden
Doggie Daddy	John Stephenson
Huckleberry Hound	Daws Butler
Snagglepuss	Daws Butler
Quick Draw McGraw	Daws Butler
Peter Potomus	Daws Butler
Augie Doggie	Daws Butler
Wally Gator	Daws Butler
Touche Turtle	Don Messick
Squiddly Diddly	Don Messick
Ranger Smith	Don Messick
Magilla Gorilla	Allan Melvin
Atom Ant	Don Messick

Music: Hoyt Curtin.

Executive Producer: William Hanna, Joseph Barbera.

Director: Charles A. Nichols.

YOGI'S GANG—30 minutes—ABC—September 8, 1973 - August 30, 1975.

YOU ARE THERE

Anthology. Historical dramatizations. Through reenactments and present-day interviews, America's past is brought to life. The people and events that contributed to its founding and growth are seen through eyewitness accounts.

Host: Walter Cronkite.

Reporters-Interviewers: CBS news correspondents.

Music: Glenn Paxton.

Included:

The Mystery Of Amelia Earhart. The mysterious disappearance of the aviatrix on a 1937 flight across the Pacific is chronicled.

CAST

Amelia Earhart: Geraldine Brooks; Fred Noonan: Thomas Connelly.

The Record Ride For The Pony Express. Bob Haslam's thirty-six-hour ride through three hundred and eighty miles of hostile Indian territory is recalled.

CAST

Bob Haslam: John Glover; Baumer: Gerald Matthews; McCool: John Coe; Tolliman: Ronny Cox.

Ordeal Of A President. The events that caused President Wilson's decision to involve America in World War I are recounted.

CAST

Wilson: G. Wood; Senator Lodge: William Prince.

Paul Revere's Ride. The famed ride of April 18, 1775, is re-created.

CAST

Paul Revere: Richard Branda; Sam Adams: E. G. Marshall.

The Siege Of The Alamo. Santa Anna's final assault and defeat of the Alamo, (March 5, 1836) the Texas stronghold for independence, is dramatized.

CAST

Davy Crockett: Fred Gwynne; Sam Houston: Philip Bosco; Jim Bowie: Bernard Kates; Santa Anna: Manuel Sebastian.

Yogi's Gang. Left to right: Yakky Doodle Duck (on top of piano), Snagglepuss, Boo Boo Bear, and Yogi Bear. © *Hanna-Barbera Productions.*

Program open:

Announcer: "The time...; the place... All things are as they were then except YOU ARE THERE."

Program close:

Host: "What kind of day was it? A day like all days, filled with those unexpected events which alter our lives—and you were there."

Versions:

YOU ARE THERE—30 minutes—CBS—November 4, 1953 - October 13, 1957. 65 episodes.

YOU ARE THERE—30 minutes—CBS—September 11, 1971 - September 2, 1972.

YOU ASKED FOR IT

Variety. Through films, viewers requests—unusual sights or entertainment acts—are presented.

Program Open:

Announcer: "Whatever it is, wherever it is, at home or around the world, you see it here, You Asked For It."

Versions:

You Asked For It—30 minutes—ABC—December 10, 1951 - September 2, 1959.

Hosts: Art Baker; Jack Smith.

You Asked For It—30 minutes—Syndicated 1972.

Host: Jack Smith.

YOU BET YOUR LIFE

Game. Before the proceedings begin, a stuffed duck is lowered to reveal a secret word that, if said during the course of the program, awards players an extra hundred dollars. Two players who work jointly as a team are first introduced, then comically interviewed by the host. Following the interview they compete in a game segment that is distinguished by two formats.

Format One:

The couple, having previously selected one category from a list of twenty subjects, receives one hundred dollars betting money. Players then select a question by cash value—from ten to one hundred dollars. If it is correctly

answered the money is added to their total; if not, they lose half of their one hundred dollars. Four questions are played; each correct answer adds money; each incorrect answer cuts the previous total in half. Of the two, sometimes three couples, the highest cash winners receive a chance to answer the bonus question, which starts at $500 and increases by this amount each time one couple fails to answer it. The question is read and players receive fifteen seconds with which to answer. A correct answer awards the money; an incorrect answer allows them to keep their original earnings, which are divided between them.

Format Two:

Players are asked questions based on the categories they have chosen. Four correct answers in a row awards players one thousand dollars; two misses in a row disqualifies them. The couples who have won a thousand dollars are permitted to risk it in an attempt to win ten thousand dollars. A large spinning wheel with numbers ranging from one to ten is displayed. Couples select two numbers: one for ten thousand dollars and one for five thousand dollars. The wheel is spun. If it stops on one of the two numbers that have been selected, the question is worth that amount of money; if it doesn't, the question is worth two thousand dollars. The question is asked and players receive fifteen seconds with which to answer. If an incorrect answer is given they lose half of their thousand dollars; the five hundred dollars is then divided between them.

Host: Groucho Marx.

Announcer: George Fenneman.

The Secret Word Girl (appearing at times in place of the duck): Marilyn Burtis.

Orchestra: Jack Meakin.

Producer: John Guedel.

Director: Robert Dawn, Bernie Smith.

Sponsor: De Soto Plymouth Dealers.

YOU BET YOUR LIFE—30 minutes—NBC—October 5, 1950 - September 21, 1961. Syndicated title: "The Best of Groucho."

YOU CAN'T SEE AROUND CORNERS

Drama. Background: Australia. The stresses of today's youth as seen through the eyes of Frankie McCoy, a young, proud, distrustful, and independent Australian adult.

CAST
Frankie McCoy   Ken Shorter
His girlfriend   Rowena Wallace

YOU CAN'T SEE AROUND CORNERS—30 minutes—Syndicated 1967.

YOU DON'T SAY

Game. Two teams, each composed of one celebrity captain and one non-celebrity contestant, compete. One player on each team receives the name of a famous person or place. The player then makes up and relates a sentence to his partner wherein he leaves the last word, which sounds like a part of the name, blank (what you don't say). His partner then receives five seconds to identify the name. If he is able, the team scores one point; if he is unable, his opponent receives a turn. The round continues until the name is identified or five clues have been used. A two-out-of-three match competition is played. The team that is first to score three points is the winner and the contestant receives one hundred dollars and the opportunity to play the bonus round, wherein he can win three hundred dollars by identifying a famous name in one clue. Players compete until they are defeated by losing two games.

Host: Tom Kennedy.

Announcer: John Harlan.

Music: Recorded.

Producer: Bill Yagemann, Ralph Andrews

YOU DON'T SAY—30 minutes—NBC—April 1, 1963 - September 26, 1969.

Revised Version: YOU DON'T SAY.

Four guest celebrities and two contestants are involved. The celebrities are each given the name of a famous person or place. One contestant chooses a celebrity who must then give him a clue by making up a sentence and leaving the last word, which sounds like a part of the name, blank. If the player identifies the name within five seconds he scores two hundred dollars. If not, his opponent receives a chance and a correct identification is worth one hundred and fifty dollars. Two additional clues are played, worth one hundred and finally fifty dollars. If the name is not identified on the fourth clue, it is disqualified and a new round begins. The first player to score six hundred dollars is the winner and receives the opportunity to play the bonus round. The object is for the player to relate clues to the celebrities. If the celebrities identify four names in five clues he wins five thousand dollars. Players compete until defeated by two losses.

Host: Tom Kennedy.

Announcer: John Harlan.

Music: Stan Worth.

Executive Producer: Bill Carruthers.

Producer: John Harlan, Mike Henry.

Director: Tom Cole.

YOU DON'T SAY—30 minutes—ABC —July 7, 1975 - November 26, 1975.

YOU'LL NEVER GET RICH

Comedy. Background: The Camp Freemont army base at Fort Baxter in Roseville, Kansas. The life of Master Sergeant Ernest Bilko, Company B, 24th Division, a master conartist in charge of the motor pool. Totally dedicated to acquiring money, he ingeniously schemes to bamboozle the system and manipulate the U.S. Army for his own personal benefit. A classic television series satirizing army life. Created by Nat Hiken.

CAST

Sgt. Ernie Bilko	Phil Silvers
Colonel John T. Hall, Commanding Officer (also refered to as Jack Hall)	Paul Ford
Master Sgt. Joan Hogan, WAC, Bilko's girlfriend	Elizabeth Fraser
Private Duane Doberman	Maurice Gosfield
Corporal Henshaw	Allan Melvin
Private Dino Paparelli	Billy Sands
Private Fender	Herbie Faye
Private Zimmerman	Mickey Freeman
Corporal Rocco Barbella	Harvey Lembeck
Mess Sgt. Rupbert Ritzik	Joe E. Ross
Sgt. Francis Grover	Jimmy Little
Private Mullin	Jack Healy
Private Lester Mendelsohn	Gerald Hiken
Private Greg Chickeriny	Bruce Kirby
Captain Hodges	Nelson Olmsted
The Chaplin	John Gilson
Nell Hall, the Colonel's wife	Hope Sansberry
Edna, a nurse	Barbara Barry
Emma Ritzik, Rupbert's wife	Beatrice Pons
Major Lewken	Edward Andrews

Also: Tige Andrews, Walter Cartier, Skippy Colby, Bill Hickey, Jack Davis.

Announcer: Bern Bennett.

Music: John Strauss.

Executive Producer: Edward J. Montagne.

Producer: Aaron Ruben.

Director: Al De Caprio.

YOU'LL NEVER GET RICH—30 minutes—CBS—September 20, 1955 - September 1959. 138 episodes. Syndicated title: "Sgt. Bilko." Also known as "The Phil Silvers Show."

YOUNG AND GAY

Comedy. Background: Greenwich Village, New York during the 1920s. The misadventures of Beth Skinner and Mary Kimbrough, young women struggling to make their way in the business world.

CAST

Beth Skinner	Bethel Leslie
Mary Kimbrough	Mary Malone

Also: Kenneth Forbes, Harry Bannister, Agnes Young, Alexander Ivo, John Campbell.

Producer: Carol Irwin.

Director: David Rich.

YOUNG AND GAY—30 minutes—CBS 1950.

THE YOUNG AND THE RESTLESS

Serial. Background: Genoa City. The story of the new morality as seen through the lives of several young, upper-middle-class adults, people seeking to find themselves and love in a contemporary world.

CAST

Brad Eliot	Tom Hallick
Stuart Brooks	Robert Colbert
Jennifer Brooks	Dorothy Green
Leslie Brooks	Janice Lynde
Chris Brooks	Trish Stewart
Peggy Brooks	Pamela Peters
	Pamela Solow
Liz Foster	Julianna McCarthy
Bill "Snapper" Foster	William Gray Espy
	David Hasselhoff
Greg Foster	James Houghton
	Brian Kerwin
Jill Foster	Brenda Dickson
Pierre Rolland	Robert Clary

Sally McGuire	Lee Crawford
Barbara Anderson	Deidre Hall
Marianne	Lilyan Chauvan
Gwen Sherman	Jennifer Leak
Philip Chancelor	Donnelly Rhodes
Kaye Chancelor	Jeanne Cooper
Jed Andrews	Tom Sellick
Laurlee Brooks	Jaime Lyn Bauer
Brock Reynolds	Beau Kayzer
Sam Powers	Barry Cahill
Bruce Henderson	Paul Stevens
Mark Henderson	Steve Carlson
Jed Andrews	Tom Sellick
Lance Prentiss	John McCook
Vanessa Prentiss	K.T. Stevens
Cynthia Harris	Lori Saunders

Music: David McGinnis, J. Wood, B. Todd.

THE YOUNG AND THE RESTLESS —30 minutes—CBS—Premiered: March 26, 1973.

YOUNG DAN'L BOONE

Adventure. Background: Kentucky during the 19th century. The story concerns itself with the exploits of Dan'l Boone, the frontiersman-pioneer, as a young man (aged 25), before he became a legend. See also: "Daniel Boone," and "Walt Disney Presents," *Daniel Boone* segment.

CAST

Dan'l Boone	Rick Moses
Rebecca Bryan, his girlfriend	Devon Ericson
Peter Dawes, the young boy who tags along with Dan'l	John Joseph Thomas
Hawk, the ex-slave	Ji-Tu Cumbuka

Music: Earle Hagen.

Music Supervision: Lionel Newman.

Theme Vocal: The Mike Curb Congregation.

Executive Producer: Ernie Frankel.

Producer: Jimmy Sangster.

Creator: Ernie Frankel.

YOUNG DAN'L BOONE—60 minutes—CBS—Premiered: September 12, 1977.

YOUNG DOCTOR KILDARE

Medical Drama. A spin-off from "Dr. Kildare." Background: Blair General Hospital. The experiences, defeats, and victories of James Kildare, a young resident intern.

CAST

Dr. James Kildare	Mark Jenkins

Dr. Leonard Gillespie,
his mentor — Gary Merrill
Nurse Marsha
Lord — Marsha Mason
Nurse Ferris — Dixie Marquis
Nurse Newell — Olga James
The orderly — Dennis Robinson

Music: Harry W. Lojewski; Score Productions.

YOUNG DOCTOR KILDARE—30 minutes—Syndicated 1972.

YOUNG DOCTOR MALONE

Serial. Background: Valley Hospital. The dramatic story of the Malone family: Jerry, a doctor, the head of the hospital; his wife, Tracy; and their children, Jill and David, also a doctor.

CAST

Dr. Jerry Malone — William Prince
Tracy Malone — Augusta Dabney
Dr. David Malone — John Donnell
Jill Malone — Freda Holloway
— Sarah Hardy
Emory Bannister — Judson Laire
Lisa Steele — Michele Tuttle
Claire Bannister — Lesley Woods
Miss Fisher — Betty Sinclair
Lionel Steele — Martin Blaine
Stefan — Michael Ingram
Ted Powell — Peter Brandon
Faye Bannister — Lenka Patterson
Natalie — Joan Wetmore
Fran Merrill — Patricia Bosworth
Paul Brown — David Stewart
— Edmond Ryan
Eileen Seaton — Emily McLaughlin
Phyllis Brooks — Barbara O'Neill
Ernest Cooper — Bob Drivas
— Nicholas Pryor
Peter Brooks — Robert Lansing
Carla — Joyce Van Patten
Claire Bannister — Leslie Woods
Dierdre Bannister — Margot Anders
Opal — Ruth Hammond
Gail Prentiss — Joan Hackett
Dorothy Ferris — Liz Gardner
— Florence Mitchell
Cranston — William Post
Miss Fisher — Betty Sinclair
Peter Ferris — Luke Halpin
Lisha — Zina Bethune
— Michelle Tuttle
— Susan Hallaran
Amanda — Ruth McDevitt
Larry Renfrew — Dick Van Patten
Lester — Scott McKay
Marge Wagner — Terri Keane

Creator-Producer: Carol Irwin.

Producer: Doris Quinlan.

Director: Jim Young.

YOUNG DOCTOR MALONE—30 minutes—NBC—December 29, 1958 - December 29, 1961.

THE YOUNG MARRIEDS

Serial. Background: Suburban New York. The dramatic story of three couples: Dan and Peggy Garrett; Ann and Walter Reynolds; and Roy and Lena Gilroy. Episodes depict their relationships within the family and with their friends.

CAST

Susan Garrett — Peggy McCay
Dan Garrett — Paul Picerni
Ann Reynolds — Susan Brown
— Lee Meriwether
Walter Reynolds — Michael Mikler
Lena Gilroy — Norma Connolly
Roy Gilroy — Barry Russo
Paul — Michael Stefani
Jerry — Pat Rossen
Jimmy — Ken Metcalf
Carol — Susan Seaforth
King — Dort Clark
Jill McComb — Betty Conner
— Brenda Benet
Matt Crane — Scott Graham
— Charles Grodin
Liz Forsythe — Floy Dean
Buzz — Les Brown, Jr.
Aunt Alice — Irene Tedrow
Mr. Coleman — Frank Marvel
Mandy — Maria Palmer
Theo — Don Randolph
Mr. Korman — Frank Maxwell
Mrs. Korman — Maxine Stuart

THE YOUNG MARRIEDS—30 minutes—ABC—October 5, 1964 - March 25, 1966.

YOUNG MR. BOBBIN

Comedy. The misadventures of Alexander Bobbin, a determined but trouble-prone young businessman.

CAST

Alexander Bobbin — Jackie Kelk
Nancy, his
girlfriend — Pat Holsey
Susie Bobbin, his
sister — Laura Webber
Aunt Bridie — Jane Seymour
His other aunt — Nydia Westman

Also: Cameron Prud'Homme.

Announcer: Tex Antoine.

Producer: Jack Scibetta.

Director: Norman Tokar.

Sponsor: General Foods.

YOUNG MR. BOBBIN—30 minutes—NBC—August 26, 1951 - May 18, 1952.

THE YOUNG LAWYERS

Drama. Background: The Neighbor-

hood Law Office (N.L.O.), a legal-aid service in Boston, Massachusetts. The cases and courtroom defenses of its three staff members: David Barrett, Aaron Silverman, and Pat Walters, Bercol University law students.

CAST

David Barrett — Lee J. Cobb
Aaron Silverman — Zalman King
Pat Walters — Judy Pace

Music: Lalo Schifrin; Leith Stevens.

THE YOUNG LAWYERS—60 minutes—ABC—September 21, 1970 - May 5, 1971. 26 episodes.

YOUNG PEOPLE'S CONCERTS

Music. Explanations and demonstrations of various musical categories.

Hosts: Leonard Bernstein; Michael Tilson Thomas.

Narrators: Leonard Bernstein; Peter Ustinov; Michael Tilson Thomas.

Music: The New York Philharmonic Orchestra.

Conductors: Leonard Bernstein; Michael Tilson Thomas.

YOUNG PEOPLE'S CONCERTS—60 minutes—CBS—Premiered: 1958. Broadcast as a series of specials.

THE YOUNG REBELS

Adventure. Background: Chester, Pennsylvania, 1777. The story of the Yankee Doodle Society, a secret organization composed of four people: Jeremy Larken, a man who is regarded as the town fool; Henry Abington, a chemist and explosives expert; Isak Poole, a blacksmith; and Elizabeth Coates, their one-woman auxiliary. Pretending to be indifferent to the American cause, and achieving a front thought of as worthless, they struggle to foil British advances on the Colonies.

CAST

Jeremy Larken — Rick Ely
Isak Poole — Lou Gossett
Henry Abington — Alex Henteloff
Elizabeth Coates — Hilarie Thompson
General Lafayette, their
ally — Philippe Forquet

Music Supervision: Lionel Newman.

THE YOUNG REBELS—60 minutes—ABC—September 20, 1970 - January 15, 1971. 13 episodes.

The Young Rebels. Left to right: Alex Henteloff, Lou Gossett, Rick Ely. © *Screen Gems.*

THE YOUNG SENTINELS

Animated Science Fiction Adventure. At a time when the Earth was young, Sentinel One, an intelligent life force from another galaxy, carefully selected three young people for training on his planet. Granting them astounding powers and eternal youth, the three Earthlings—Hercules, with the strength of one hundred men; Astria, the beautiful woman capable of assuming any life form; and Mercury, able to move with the speed of light—were returned to their native planet to watch over the human race and help the good survive and flourish. Now, with the guiding influence of Sentinel One and his maintenance robot, Mo, the series details the exploits of the Young Sentinels as they battle evil on Earth.

Characters' Voices

Hercules	George DiCenzo
Astria	Dee Timberlake
Mercury	Evan Kim
Sentinel One	George DiCenzo
Mo	Evan Kim

Music: Yvette Blais, Jeff Michael.

Executive Producer: Norm Prescott, Lou Scheimer.

Producer: Don Christensen.

Director: Hal Sutherland.

THE YOUNG SENTINELS—30 minutes—NBC—Premiered: September 10, 1977.

THE YOUNG SET

Discussion. Celebrity guests discuss topical issues.

Hostess: Phyllis Kirk.

Premiere Guest: Peter Lawford.

Music (recorded open and close):

"The Young Set," composed by Ray Martin.

THE YOUNG SET—60 minutes—ABC—September 6, 1965 - December 17, 1965.

YOUR ALL AMERICAN COLLEGE SHOW

Variety. Performances by college entertainment acts (four per telecast). Winners, determined by three celebrity guest judges, receive one thousand dollars.

Hosts: Dennis James; Rich Little; Arthur Godfrey.

YOUR ALL AMERICAN COLLEGE SHOW—30 minutes—Syndicated 1968.

YOUR BIG MOMENT

A human-interest type of program wherein host Melvyn Douglas arranges blind dates for people who have written ten letters requesting a certain type of companion. First broadcast on DuMont in 1953.

YOU'RE IN THE PICTURE

Game. Four competing contestants. Players are situated behind large picture scenes (such as those found in amusement parks) with their heads through appropriate cut outs. Through clues that are related by the host, players have to identify their particular situation. Winners receive merchandise prizes.

Host: Jackie Gleason.

YOU'RE IN THE PICTURE—30 minutes—CBS—January 20, 1961 - March 24, 1961.

YOU'RE INVITED

A thirty minute variety series hosted by Ralph Vincent. Broadcast on ABC in 1949.

YOU'RE ON YOUR OWN

Game. Three competing contestants. The host reads a general-knowledge type of question. The player who is first to identify himself through a buzzer signal receives a chance to answer. If he gives a correct response he scores one point. If he is incorrect he has to pay a penalty by performing a humiliating stunt. Players receive prizes in accord with the number of questions they answer.

Host: Steve Dunne.

Orchestra: Paul Taubman.

YOU'RE ON YOUR OWN—30 minutes—CBS—December 22, 1956 - March 16, 1957.

YOU'RE PUTTING ME ON

Game. Three two-member celebrity teams compete. One member of each team reveals a different name plate and assumes his or her identity. The host states a category (e.g., "The pool room") and a question ("As the person you are now pretending to be, if you were anything or anybody in a pool room, who or what would you be?"). The pretender then relates the person or object that fits the description of the personality he is pretending to be to his partner. The host then reveals four name possibilities. Each team partner has to select the one he believes is being put on by his partner. If correct, one point is scored. Three such rounds are played. Rounds two and three consist of two category questions and a choice of five personalities. Winners are the highest point scorers. Selected studio audience members, who are represented by the celebrities, receive merchandise prizes.

Hosts: Bill Cullen; Larry Blyden.

Announcer: Jack Clark.

Regular Panelists: Larry Blyden (before hosting), Peggy Cass, Bill Cullen, Anne Meara.

YOU'RE PUTTING ME ON—30 minutes—NBC—July 1969 - December 26, 1969.

YOUR FIRST IMPRESSION

Game. Through a series of question-and-answer probe rounds with the host, a panel of three celebrities have to identify a mystery guest celebrity from a list of five possibilities.

Host: Bill Leyden.

Panel: Dennis James, George Kirby, plus one guest celebrity.

YOUR FIRST IMPRESSION—30 minutes—NBC—January 2, 1962 - April 27, 1964.

YOUR FUNNY FUNNY FILMS

Comedy. Amateur-made home movies are showcased. The photographer appears and narrates his films, which have been professionaly reedited for laughs.

Host: George Fenneman.

YOUR FUNNY FUNNY FILMS—30 minutes—ABC—July 8, 1963 - - September 9, 1963.

YOUR HIT PARADE

Variety. America's taste in popular music is dramatized. The top songs of the day, which are played from number twelve to "the song that's number one all over America," are determined by surveys of the best sellers, sheet music, phonograph-record sales, jukebox selections, and songs played over the radio.

Version One:

Your Hit Parade—60 and 30 minute

Your Hit Parade. Clockwise from upper right: Tommy Leonetti, Jill Corey, Alan Copeland, Virginia Gibson (CBS 1958).

productions—NBC—July 10, 1950 - June 17, 1958.

CAST
Eileen Wilson, June Valli, Dorothy Collins, Snooky Lanson, Russell Arms, Giselle MacKenzie, Tommy Leonetti, Jill Corey, Alan Copeland, Virginia Gibson, Niles & Fosse (dancers), The Hit Paraders (singers), The Hit Parade Dancers.

Choreography: Tony Charmoli; Ernest Flatt; Peter Gennaro.

Announcers: Andre Baruch; John Laing.

Orchestra: Raymond Scott; Peter Van Steeden; Dick Jacobs; Harry Sosnick.

Verstion Two:

Your Hit Parade—30 minutes—CBS—October 10, 1958 - April 14, 1959.

CAST
Dorothy Collins, Johnny Desmond, The Hit Parade Singers and Dancers.

Orchestra: Harry Sosnick.

Version Three:

Your Hit Parade—30 minutes—CBS—August 2, 1974 - August 30, 1974.

CAST
Kelly Garrett, Sheralee, Chuck Woolery, The Tom Hanson Dancers (who are referred to as The Hit Parade Dancers).

Announcer: Art Gilmore.

Orchestra: Milton DeLugg.

YOUR LUNCHEON DATE

Musical Variety.

Host: Hugh Downs.

Vocalist: Nancy Wright.

Music: The Art Van Damme Quintet.

YOUR LUNCHEON DATE—30 minutes—DuMont—1951 - 1952.

YOUR LUCKY CLUE

Game. Two competing two-member teams. A dramatic sketch, which outlines the facts of a criminal case, is enacted on stage. The teams then receive time with which to discuss the facts between them. The team that correctly solves the case is the winner and receives prizes.

Host: Basil Rathbone.

Announcer: Andre Baruch.

YOUR LUCKY CLUE—30 minutes—CBS—July 13, 1952 - September 1952.

YOUR PLAY TIME

Anthology. Dramatic presentations.

Included:

The Loner. The story of a young boy who, neglected by his parents, retreats to a world of fantasy to find happiness.

CAST
Peter Votrian, Ann Lee, Hayden Rorke.

The House Nobody Wanted. The fears that grip a young couple as they move into a house that is believed to be haunted.

CAST
Marilyn Erskine, Craig Stevens, Sheila Bromley, Jack Paine.

Wait For Me Downstairs. A young man's efforts to find his fiancée, who disappeared on the eve of their wedding.

CAST
John Hudson, Allene Roberts.

YOUR PLAY TIME—30 minutes—CBS—June 13, 1954 - September 3, 1955.

YOURS FOR A SONG

Game. Two competing players. The lyrics to a popular song, which contain certain word omissions, are flashed on a screen. The player who is first to identify himself through a buzzer signal receives a chance to answer. For each correct word that he is able to fill in he receives twenty dollars. Winners, who receive their earnings, are the highest cash scorers. Broad clues are provided by the host, and the studio audience is led in sing-a-longs of chorus segments.

Host: Bert Parks.

Orchestra: Ted Raph.

Announcer: Johnny Gilbert.

Model: Michaelina Martel.

Producer: Harry Salter.

YOURS FOR A SONG—30 minutes—ABC. Daytime: December 4, 1961 - March 29, 1963; Evening: November 14, 1961 - September 18, 1963.

YOUR SHOW OF SHOWS

See title: "Sid Caesar."

YOUR STAR SHOWCASE

Anthology. Retitled episodes of "The General Electric Theatre."

Host: Edward Arnold.

YOUR STAR SHOWCASE—30 minutes—Syndicated 1953.

YOUR SURPRISE PACKAGE

Game. Three competing contestants. A large box, which contains merchandise items, is displayed on stage. The host reveals their value but not their identity. A general-knowledge type of question is then read. The player who is first to identify himself through a buzzer signal receives a chance to answer. If correct, he receives cash. After each question, the player with the last correct response is permitted to purchase buying time with which to question the host concerning the contents of the surprise package. The game continues until one player wins it by identifying its contents.

Host: George Fenneman.

YOUR SURPRISE PACKAGE—30 minutes—CBS—March 13, 1961 - February 23, 1962.

YOUR SURPRISE STORE

Game. Selected studio-audience members compete in a series of question-and-answer rounds or by performing various stunts. The person with the highest quiz score, the most correct answers, or the player who is the most successful at completing stunts, receives the opportunity to select valuable merchandise items from a surprise store constructed on stage.

Host: Lew Parker.

Assistant: Jacqueline Susann.

Announcer: Bern Bennett.

YOUR SURPRISE STORE—30 minutes—CBS—May 11, 1952 - June 27, 1952.

YOUTH TAKES A STAND

Discussion. Four high-school and/or junior-college students discuss world affairs with guest newsmen.

Host: Marc Cramer.

YOUTH TAKES A STAND—30 minutes—CBS 1953.

3

ZERO ONE

Adventure. Background: London, England. The cases of an international-airline crime-detection team.

CAST

Alan Garrett, the head of Airline Security International	Nigel Patrick
Jimmy Delaney, his assistant	Bill Smith
Maya, their secretary-assistant	Katya Douglas

ZERO ONE—30 minutes—Syndicated 1964. 39 episodes.

THE ZOO GANG

Crime Drama. Background: Europe. The story of four World War II resistance fighters known as The Zoo Gang who reunite twenty-eight years later to battle crime in Europe.

CAST

Steven Halliday, an antique dealer; code name: The Fox	Brian Keith
Manouche Roget, the owner of the Les Pecheurs Bar in France; code name: The Leopard	Lilli Palmer
Tom Devon, a jeweler; code name: The Elephant	John Mills
Alec Marlowe, a mechanic; code name: The Tiger	Barry Morse
Police Lt. Georges Roget, Manouche's son	Michael Petrovitch
Jill Barton, Tom's niece	Seretta Wilson

Music Theme: Paul and Linda McCartney.

Music Score: Ken Thorne.

Producer: Herbert Hirschman.

Director: Sidney Hayers, John Hough.

THE ZOO GANG—60 minutes—NBC—July 16, 1975 - August 6, 1975.

ZOO PARADE

Educational. Background: The Chicago Zoo. Visits to specific areas of interest.

Host: Marlin Perkins.

Assistant: Jim Hurlbut.

Producer: Don Meier, Reinald Warrenrath.

Sponsor: Quaker Oats.

ZOO PARADE—30 minutes—NBC—1950 - September 1, 1957. Originally broadcast as a local program in Chicago from 1946-1950.

ZOOM

Educational. Nonprofessional preteen children relate stories, songs, dances, games, and jokes either written by themselves or submitted by home viewers. The program represents a television framework for the creative efforts of children.

Hosts (seven per telecast; identified by a first name only): Nancy, Maura, David, Ann, Kenny, Tracy, Jay, Bernadette, Luiz, Edith, Tommy, Jon, Lori, Danny, Neil, Nina, Donna, Mike,

Leon, Timmy.

Orchestra: Newton Wayland.

ZOOM—30 minutes—PBS—Premiered: January 9, 1972.

ZOORAMA

Educational. Background: The San Diego Zoo. Visits to specific areas of interest.

Host: Bob Dale.

ZOORAMA—30 minutes—Syndicated 1968.

ZORAN, SPACE BOY

A ninety-six episode series that focuses on the exploits of Zoran, a space boy who, with his pet space squirrel, journeys to Earth to find his lost sister. 30 minutes—Syndicated 1966.

ZORRO

Adventure. Background: Monterey, California, 1820. Arriving in Monterey at the request of his late father to assist in ending the reign of Monastano, an evil Spanish commandant who has established himself as ruler, Don Diego de la Vega adopts the guise of the mysterious masked rider, Zorro, a defender of the weak and oppressed.

Revealing his dual identity only to Bernardo, his father's deaf mute serv-

Zorro. Guy Williams, as Zorro, atop his stallion Phantom. © *Walt Disney Productions.*

ant, he poses as a wealthy but lazy man-about-town to protect his secret alias. Appearing whenever the need arises, Don Diego, as the mysterious Spanish nobleman, Zorro, crusades against injustice and attempts to end Monastano's reign.

CAST

Don Diego de la Vega	Guy Williams
Zorro	Guy Williams
Bernardo	Gene Sheldon
Captain Monastano	Britt Lomond
Sergeant Garcia, his bumbling aide	Henry Calvin
Torres, an escaped political prisoner	Jan Arvan
Elena Torres, his daughter	Eugenia Paul
Anita Cabrillo, a friend of Don Diego's	Annette Funicello
Ricardo Del Amo, a friend of Don Diego's	Richard Anderson
Anna Maria, a friend of Don Diego's	Jolene Brand

Zorro's white stallion: Phantom.

Zorro's black stallion: Tornado.

Music: George Bruns.

Producer: Walt Disney, William H. Anderson.

Theme: "Zorro."
    Words: Norman Foster.
    Music: George Bruns.
    © Copyright 1957 by Walt Disney Music Company. Reprinted by permission.

Out of the night when the full moon is bright
Comes the horseman known as Zorro.
This bold renegade carves a Z with his blade,
A Z that stands for Zorro.
Zorro, the fox of cunning and free,
Zorro, who makes the sign of the Z.
Zorro, Zorro, Zorro, Zorro.

ZORRO—30 minutes—ABC—September 19, 1957 - September 24, 1959. Syndicated.

Program Addendum

Network and syndicated series broadcast from January 28, 1978 through January 1, 1979.

A. E. S. HUDSON STREET

Comedy. Spoofing medical series, the program focuses on the hectic goings-on in a poorly-equipped adult emergency service (A. E. S.) hospital on Hudson Street on the lower East Side of Manhattan in New York City.

CAST

Dr. Tony Menzies	Gregory Sierra
Nurse Rose Santiago	Rosana Soto
Nurse Rhonda Todd	Julienne Wells
Foshko, the ambulance driver	Susan Peretz
Stawky, her assistant	Ralph Manza
Nurse Newton	Ray Stewart
Carbow, the administrator	Stefan Gierasch
Dr. Jerry Meckler	Bill Cort
Dr. Glick	Allan Miller

Music: Jack Elliott, Allyn Ferguson.

Executive Producer: Danny Arnold.

Producer: Roland Kibbee.

Director: Noam Pitlik.

Creator: Danny Arnold, Tony Sheenan, Chris Hayward.

A. E. S. HUDSON STREET—30 minutes—ABC—March 16, 1978 - April 20, 1978. 5 episodes.

THE AMAZING SPIDER-MAN

Adventure. Following a demonstration on radioactivity, Peter Parker, a graduate student at Empire State University, is bitten by a spider that had been exposed to the deadly effects of the demonstration. Shortly after, Peter realizes that the spider's venom has become a part of his bloodstream and he has absorbed the proportionate power and ability of a living spider. Developing a special costume to conceal his true identity, and to be able to learn of crimes immediately, Parker acquires a position as a part-time photographer for the *New York Daily Bugle.* The series depicts Parker's battle against crime as the mysterious Spider-Man.

CAST

Peter Parker/ Spider-Man	Nicholas Hammond
Spider-Man (stunt sequences)	Fred Waugh
J. Jonah Jameson, editor of the *Bugle*	Robert F. Simon
Police Captain Barbera	Michael Pataki
Rita Conway, Jonah's secretary	Chip Fields
Julie Masters, a rival freelance photographer	Ellen Bry

Music: Stu Phillips, Dana Kaproff.

Executive Producer: Charles Fries, Daniel R. Goodman.

Producer: Robert Janes, Ron Satlof, Lionel E. Siegel.

Director: Ron Satlof, Fernando Lamas, Dennis Donnelly, Cliff Bole, Larry Stewart, Tom Blank.

THE AMAZING SPIDER-MAN—60 minutes—CBS—April 5, 1978 - May 3, 1978; September 5, 1978 - September 12, 1978. 7 episodes.

AMERICA ALIVE!

Variety. A daily series of interviews, music, and news events.

Host: Jack Linkletter.

Co-hosts: Janet Langhart, Bruce Jenner, Pat Mitchell.

Regulars: David Horowitz, Virginia Graham, David Sheehan.

Music Theme: Don Costa.

Music: Elliott Lawrence.

Executive Producer: Woody Fraser.

Producer: Susan Winston, Kenny Price.

Senior Director: Don King.

AMERICA ALIVE!—60 minutes—NBC—July 24, 1978 - January 5, 1979. 104 episodes.

THE AMERICAN GIRLS

Drama. The story of Rebecca Tomkins and Amy Waddell, two beautiful, roving, female reporter-researchers for "The American Report," a TV newsmagazine series.

CAST

Rebecca Tomkins	Priscilla Barnes
Amy Waddell	Debra Clinger
Francis X. Casey, their producer	David Spielberg
Jason Cook, the host of "The American Report"	William Prince

Music: Jerrold Immel.

Executive Producer: Harve Bennett, Harris Katleman.

Producer: Simon Muntner, George Lehr.

Director: Rod Holcomb, Alvin Ganzer, James D. Parriott, John Peyser, Lee Philips.

Creator: Lane Slate, Mike Lloyd Ross, Lee Philips.

THE AMERICAN GIRLS—60 minutes—CBS—September 23, 1978 - November 10, 1978. 6 episodes.

AMERICA 2-NIGHT

Satire. A spin-off from "Fernwood 2-Night." Unable to raise the necessary funds to continue his local talk show in Ohio, Barth Gimble relocates to fictional Alta Coma, California, "the unfinished furniture capitol of the world," where he becomes the host of "America 2-Night" over the U.B.S. (United Broadcasting System) Network ("The network that puts U before the B.S."). The series, which spoofs talk-variety programs, presents interviews with well-known celebrities as well as the most grotesque people imaginable.

Host: Martin Mull as the conceited Barth Gimble.

Announcer: Fred Willard as the dimwitted Jerry Hubbard.

Music: Frank DeVol (as Happy Kyne) and his Orchestra (the Mirth Makers).

Regulars: Michelle and Tanya Della Fave, Kenneth Mars (as William W.B. "Bud" Prize, the talent scout), Jim Varney (as Virgil Simms, a mobile home daredevil), Bill Kirchenbauer (as Tony Roletti, the lounge singer).

Producer: Alan Thicke.

Director: Jim Drake, Jerry Leshay, Marvin Kupfer, Randy Winburn, James Field, Dick Weinberg.

Creator: Norman Lear.

AMERICA 2-NIGHT—30 minutes—Syndicated 1978. 65 episodes.

ANOTHER DAY

Comedy. Background: Los Angeles, California. Events in the lives of Don and Ginny Gardner, a married couple whose lives are complicated by their jobs, their children, and Don's outspoken mother.

CAST

Don Gardner	David Groh
Ginny Gardner	Joan Hackett
Kelly Gardner, their daughter	Lisa Lindgren
Mark Gardner, their son	Al Eisenmann
Olive Gardner, Don's mother	Hope Summers

Music: Paul Williams.

Executive Producer: James Komack.

Producer: Paul Mason, George Kirgo.

Director: James Komack, Gary Shimokawa, Nick Havinga, Burt Brinckerhoff.

Creator: James Komack.

ANOTHER DAY—30 minutes—CBS—April 8, 1978 - April 29, 1978. 4 episodes.

APPLE PIE

Comedy. Background: Kansas City, Missouri, 1933. The series depicts the antics of the Hollyhocks, a group of strangers who became a family through the efforts of Ginger-Nell Hollyhock, a lonely woman who acquired them by placing ads in the local newspaper.

CAST

Ginger-Nell Hollyhock, the mother	Rue McClanahan
"Fast" Eddie Barnes, the father	Dabney Coleman
Grandpa	Jack Gilford
Anna Marie, the daughter	Caitlin O'Heaney
Junior, the son	Derrel Maury

Producer: Charlie Hauck.

Associate Producer: Rita Dillon.

Director: Peter Bonerz.

APPLE PIE—30 minutes—ABC—September 23, 1978 - October 7, 1978. 7 episodes produced; 3 aired.

THE AWAKENING LAND

Western Drama. A three part miniseries based on the novels by Conrad Richter. Background: The Ohio Territory from 1790 - 1817. The series follows the life of Sayward Luckett and her triumphant struggles over the hardships of pioneer life.

CAST

Sayward Luckett	Elizabeth Montgomery
Genny Luckett, her sister	Jane Seymour
Achsa Luckett, her sister	Derin Altay
Sulie Luckett, her sister (as a young girl)	Michelle Stacy
Sulie Luckett (older)	Theresa Landreth
Worth Luckett, Sayward's father	Tony Mockus
Jary Luckett, Worth's wife	Louise Latham
Portius Wheeler, the lawyer; later Sayward's husband	Hal Holbrook
Resolve Wheeler, their son	Sean Frye
Resolve (as an adult)	Martin Scanlan
Huldah Wheeler, their daughter	Pia Romans
Huldah (as an adult)	Devon Ericson
Kinzie Wheeler, their son	Johnny Timko
Kinzie (as an adult)	Paul Swanson

Narrator: Elizabeth Montgomery.

Music: Fred Karlin.

Executive Producer: Harry Bernsen, Tom Kuhn.

Producer: Robert E. Relyea.

Director: Boris Sagal.

THE AWAKENING LAND—7 hours (total)—NBC—February 19, 1978 - February 21, 1978.

BABY, I'M BACK!

Comedy. Background: Washington, D.C. Unable to cope with the responsibilities of raising a family, Ray Ellis departs, leaving his wife Olivia and children Angie and Jordan to fend for themselves. The series follows Ray's misadventures when, returning seven years later, he tries to win back Olivia's affections and prove that he can be a good husband.

CAST

Ray Ellis	Demond Wilson
Olivia Ellis	Denise Nicholas
Luzelle Carter, Olivia's mother	Helen Martin
Angie Ellis	Kim Fields
Jordan Ellis	Tony Holmes
Col. Wallace Dickey, Olivia's employer at the Pentagon	Ed Hall

Music: Jeff Berry.

Executive Producer: Charles Fries, Sandy Krinski.

Producer: Lila Garrett.

Director: Dick Harwood, Nick Havinga, Asaad Keleda, Mark Warren.

Creator: Lila Garrett, Mort Lachman.

BABY, I'M BACK!—30 minutes—CBS—January 30, 1978 - August 12, 1978. 12 episodes.

BATTLE OF THE PLANETS

Animated Cartoon. Era: Earth in the year 2020. The series depicts the exploits of G-Force, five fearless young orphans, members of Center Neptune (an Earth-based defense organization established beneath the sea. They oppose evil beings from other planets, such as Zoltar, the leader of the planet Spectre, with his power-mad attempts to destroy our world.

Characters' Voices

7-Zark-7, the head of Center Neptune	Alan Young
Zoltar	Keye Luke

G-Force:

Mark	Casey Kaseem
Princess	Janet Waldo
Keop	Ronnie Schell
Jason	Ronnie Schell
Tiny	Alan Dinehart

Music: Hoyt Curtin.

Executive Producer: Jameson Brewer.

Producer-Director: David Hanson.

BATTLE OF THE PLANETS—30 minutes—Syndicated 1978. 85 episodes.

BATTLESTAR GALACTICA

Science Fiction Adventure. In the seventh millenium of time, in a galaxy far beyond that of our own, a thousand-year-old war rages: that of mankind versus the Cylons, a mechanical race of beings bent on destroying the human race because they pose a threat to their existence. When a last-ditch effort on the part of mankind to effect peace fails, and their twelve-colony planets are destroyed, the surviving members, representing every known colony in the galaxy, band together (in spaceships) and follow the *Galactica,* a gigantic battlestar spaceship, in an attempt to rebuild their lives on their thirteenth colony—a distant and unknown planet called Earth. The series follows their perilous journey—warding off alien creatures and battling the Cylon robots who are now determined to thwart their plans—as they seek the planet Earth.

CAST

Commander Adama	Lorne Greene
Captain Apollo, his son	Richard Hatch
Athena, his daughter	Maren Jensen
Lieutenant Starbuck	Dirk Benedict
Colonel Tigh	Terry Carter
Boomer, a member of Galactica	Herb Jefferson, Jr.
Boxey, Apollo's son	Noah Hathaway
Cassiopea, a member of Galactica	Laurette Spang
Jolly, a member of Galactica	Tony Swartz
Baltar, the Cylon leader	John Colicos
Regal, a member of Galactica	Sarah Rush
Girl Warrior, a member of Galactica	Jennifer Joseph
Cylon	Bruce Wright
Cylon	Paul Coufos

Music: Stu Phillips.

Music Played By: The Los Angeles Symphonic Orchestra.

Executive Producer: Glen A. Larson.

Supervising Producer: Leslie Stevens.

Producer: John Dykstra, Don Belisario, Paul Playdon, David J. O'Connell.

Director: Richard Colla, Christian Nyby, Rod Holcomb, Vince Edwards.

BATTLESTAR GALACTICA—60 minutes—ABC—Premiered: September 17, 1978.

BONKERS!

Variety. A series of music, songs, and outlandish comedy.

Hosts: Bill, Mark, and Brett Hudson.

Regulars: Bob Monkhouse, Jack Burns, Linda Cunningham, The Bonkettes Chorus.

Music: Jack Parnell.

Executive Producer: Thomas M. Battista.

Producer: Jack Burns.

Director: Peter Harris.

BONKERS!—30 minutes—Syndicated 1978. 26 episodes.

CELEBRITY CHALLENGE OF THE SEXES

Game. The series pits male and female TV personalities against one another in various athletic contests.

Host: Tom Brookshire.

Male Team Coach: McLean Stevenson.

Female Team Coach: Barbara Rhoades.

Judge: Jim Tunney.

Music: Peter Matz.

Executive Producer: Howard Katz.

Producer: Mel Ferber.

Director: Bernie Hoffman.

CELEBRITY CHALLENGE OF THE SEXES—30 minutes—CBS—January 31, 1978 - February 28, 1978. 5 programs.

THE CHEAP SHOW

Game. A spoof of game and quiz shows. Two contestants appear with a friend or relative. One member of each team is placed in the punishment pit. A question based on a ridiculous category (e.g. "Underwater Nostalgia"), is read to two guest celebrities—each of whom gives a response, but only one of which is correct. By a flip-of-the-coin decision, one of the two outside-the-pit players chooses the celebrity he feels has the correct answer. If he chooses the right one, he wins a cheap prize (nothing over $16.00) and his opponent's loved one gets "punished" (hit with foods that are harmless). If the player is wrong, the prize is awarded to the opponent and his loved one is punished. Two such rounds are played, each worth one point. Round two consists of one twenty-point question that determines the winner.

The winning team now plays "The Super Collossal Prize Sweepstakes Finale." A large spinning-wheel board with twelve holes is displayed. Oscar the Wonder Rodent (a white rat) is placed on the board. Oscar runs briefly about the board and into one of the holes. The contestants win a prize corresponding to the number of the hole Oscar chooses to enter. A decent and expensive merchandise prize is awarded to the team.

Host: Dick Martin.

Wanda, the Hostess: Janelle Price.

Polly, the Prize Lady: Shirl Bernheim.

Oscar, the Wonder Rodent: Himself..

Roger, Oscar's Security Guard: Roger Chapline.

The Perveyors of Punishment: Joe Baker, Billy Beck.

Announcer: Charlie O'Donnell.

Music: John "J.C." Phillips.

Executive Producer: Chris Bearde, Bob Wood.

Producer: Terry Kyne, Kathy Connolly.

Director: Terry Kyne.

THE CHEAP SHOW—30 minute
Syndicated 1978.

THE CHUCK BARRIS RAH-RAH SHOW

Variety. Performances by professional
and amateur talent.

Host: Chuck Barris.

Regulars: Jaye P. Morgan, The Unknown Comic, Gene Gene, The
Dancing Machine.

Announcer: Johnny Jacobs.

Orchestra: Milton DeLugg.

Executive Producer: Chuck Barris.

Producer: Gene Banks.

Director: John Dorsey.

THE CHUCK BARRIS RAH-RAH
SHOW—60 minutes—NBC—February
28, 1978 - April 11, 1978. 6 tapes.

THE COMEDY SHOP

Comedy. Performances by guest comedians: name celebrities and new
and upcoming performers.

Host: Norm Crosby.

Music: Jack Elliott, Allyn Ferguson.

Executive Producer: Paul Roth.

Producer: Joe Siegman, Perry Rosemond.

Director: Perry Rosemond.

THE COMEDY SHOP—30 minutes—
Syndicated 1978.

DALLAS

Drama. Background: Dallas, Texas.
The story concerns itself with a feud
that exists between two families: the
Ewings and the Barnes; a feud started
when Jock Ewing, an oil-and-cattle
baron, supposedly cheated his neighbor, Digger Barnes in earlier days
when they were partners drilling for
oil. The feud intensified when Jock's
youngest son, Bobby, married Digger's
beautiful daughter, Pamela. (The
Ewings own the Southfork Ranch.)

CAST

Jock Ewing, the oil-and-cattle baron	Jim Davis
Eleanor Ewing, his wife	Barbara BelGeddes
J.R. Ewing, their eldest son	Larry Hagman
Bobby Ewing, their younger son	Patrick Duffy
Sue Ellen Ewing, J.R.'s wife	Linda Gray
Lucy Ewing, Jock's granddaughter	Charlene Tilton
Willard "Digger" Barnes, Jock's neighbor	David Wayne
Pamela Barnes Ewing, Digger's daughter; Bobby's wife	Victoria Principal
Cliff Barnes, Digger's son	Ken Kercheval
Ray Krebbs, the Ewing ranch foreman	Steve Kanaly
Julie, J.R.'s secretary	Tina Louise

Music: Jerrold Immel, John Parker.

Executive Producer: Lee Rich, Philip
Capice.

Producer: Leonard Katzman.

Director: Robert Day, Irving J.
Moore, Alexander March, Barry
Crane, Vincent McEveety.

Creator: David Jacobs.

DALLAS—60 minutes—CBS—April 2,
1978 - April 30, 1978. 5 episodes. Returned: CBS—60 minutes—Premiered:
September 23, 1978.

DAVID CASSIDY— MAN UNDERCOVER

Crime Drama. Background: Los An-
geles, California. The cases of Officer
Dan Shay, an undercover man for the
L.A.P.D.

CAST

Officer Dan Shay	David Cassidy
Joanne Shay, his wife	Wendy Rastatter
Cindy Shay, their daughter	Elizabeth Reddin
Sgt. Walt Abrams, Shay's superior	Simon Oakland

Music: Harold Bettes.

Theme Vocal: David Cassidy.

Executive Producer: David Gerber.

Producer: Mark Rodgers, Mel Swope.

Director: Bernard McEveety, Vincent
Edwards, Sam Wanamaker, Alvin
Ganzer.

Creator: Richard Fielder.

DAVID CASSIDY—MAN UNDER-
COVER—60 minutes—NBC—Pre-
miered: November 2, 1978.

DICK CLARK'S LIVE WEDNESDAY

Variety. A live Wednesday-evening variety hour (8 p.m., E.T.) that features
top show business performers as well
as reunions and tributes to screen
idols (a prerecorded segment).

Host: Dick Clark.

Orchestra: Lenny Stack.

Executive Producer: Dick Clark.

Producer: Bill Lee.

Director: John Moffitt.

Location Producer-Director: Perry
Rosemond.

DICK CLARK'S LIVE WEDNES-
DAY—60 minutes—NBC—Premiered:
September 20, 1978.

DIFF'RENT STROKES

Comedy. Background: New York
City. The story of Phillip Drummond,
a Park Avenue millionaire who adopts
two Harlem orphans, Arnold and Willis Jackson, the sons of his late housekeeper.

CAST

Phillip Drummond	Conrad Bain
Arnold Jackson	Gary Coleman
Willis Jackson	Todd Bridges
Kimberly Drummond, Phillip's daughter	Dana Plato
Mrs. Garrett, Phillip's housekeeper	Charlotte Rae

Music: Alan Thicke, Al Burton, Gloria
Loring.

Executive Producer: Budd Grossman.

Producer: Howard Leeds, Herbert
Kenwith.

Director: Herbert Kenwith.

DIFF'RENT STROKES—30 min-
utes—NBC—Premiered: November 3,
1978.

THE $1.98 BEAUTY SHOW

Contest. A spoof of beauty pageants
wherein six females compete in contests of beauty, poise, talent, and
swimwear for the title "The Dollar
Ninety-eight Beauty of the Week" and
the top prize—$1.98—in cash. It is a
mythical search to find the most
beautiful girl in the world.

Host: Rip Taylor.

Announcer: Johnny Jacobs.

Music: Milton DeLugg.

Executive Producer-Creator: Chuck
Barris.

Producer: Gene Banks.

Director: John Dorsey.

THE $1.98 BEAUTY SHOW—30 min-
utes—Syndicated 1978.

THE DONNA FARGO SHOW

Variety. Comedy skits coupled with performances by Country and Western entertainers.

Hostess: Donna Fargo.

Regular: Tom Biener.

Announcer: Harrison Henderson.

Music: Bob Rozario.

Executive Producer: The Osmond Brothers.

Producer: Tom Biener.

Director: Rick Bennewitz.

THE DONNA FARGO SHOW—30 minutes—Syndicated 1978.

THE EDDIE CAPRA MYSTERIES

Mystery. Background: Los Angeles, California. The story of Eddie Capra, an attorney with the firm of Devlin, Linkman, and O'Brien, who has an uncanny knack for solving complex crimes. The series gimmick is to challenge viewers to guess the identity of the culprit before Capra does. As in the 1975 version of "Ellery Queen," nothing is withheld from the viewer, and nothing extra is given to Capra.

CAST

Eddie Capra	Vincent Baggetta
Lacey Brown, his secretary	Wendy Phillips
J.J. Devlin, senior partner of the law firm	Ken Swofford
Harvey Mitchell, Capra's legman	Michael Horton
Jennie Brown, Lacey's daughter	Seven Ann McDonald
Devlin's secretary	Lynn Topping

Music: John Addison, John Cacavas.

Executive Producer: Peter S. Fischer.

Producer: James McAdams.

Director: James Frawley, Ronald Satlof, James Benson, Nicholas Sgarro, Edward Abroms, Sigmund Neufeld, Jr.

Creator: Peter S. Fischer.

THE EDDIE CAPRA MYSTERIES—60 minutes—NBC—Premiered: September 22, 1978.

EVERYDAY

Comedy-Variety. A daily series of music, songs, interviews, and comedy.

Hosts: Stephanie Edwards, John Bennett Perry.

Regulars: Tom Chapin, Murray Langston, Anne Bloom, Judy Gibson, Robert Corff, Emily Levine.

Executive Producer: David Salzman.

Producer: Viva Knight.

Director: Louis J. Horvitz.

EVERYDAY—60 minutes—Syndicated 1978.

FANTASY ISLAND

Anthology. A series of interwoven vignettes set against the background of Fantasy Island, a mysterious tropical resort where, for an unspecified price, dreams are granted. Stories open with guests arriving on the island, followed by their meeting with Mr. Roarke, the man who arranges for people to act out their wildest fantasies. The individual's fantasy is then dramatized with the program showing how that person's life changes as a result of the experience.

CAST

Mr. Roarke	Ricardo Montalban
Tattoo, his assistant	Herve Villechaize

Music Theme: Laurence Rosenthal.

Music: Elliot Kaplan, Laurence Rosenthal, Charles Albertine.

Executive Producer: Aaron Spelling, Leonard Goldberg.

Producer: Michael Fisher.

Director: Cliff Bole, John Newland, Phil Bondelli, Earl Bellamy, George McCowan.

Creator: Gene Levitt.

FANTASY ISLAND—60 minutes—ABC—Premiered: January 28, 1978.

FLYING HIGH

Comedy-Drama. The story of Pam Bellagio, Marcy Bower, and Lisa Benton, three beautiful stewardesses for Sun West Airlines.

CAST

Pam Bellagio	Kathryn Witt
Marcy Bower	Pat Klous
Lisa Benton	Connie Sellecca
Capt. Douglas Robert March, a pilot for Sun West	Howard Platt

Music Theme: David Shire.

Music: Robert Prince.

Executive Producer: Mark Carliner.

Producer: Robert Van Scoyk, Marty Cohan.

Director: Peter Hunt, Nicholas Sgarro, Alan Myerson, William Jurgenson, James Sheldon.

FLYING HIGH—60 minutes—CBS—Premiered: September 29, 1978.

FREE COUNTRY

Comedy. Background: Manhattan (New York City). The series focuses on the lives of Joseph and Anna Bresner, Lithuanian immigrants, from 1909 to 1978. The program opens with Joseph at 89 years of age, as he talks about his life. Flashback sequences are used to highlight the events of both his and Anna's arrival and struggles in a new land.

CAST

Joseph Bresner	Rob Reiner
Anna Bresner	Judy Kahan
Ida Gevertsman, their friend	Renee Lippin
Sidney Gevertsman, Ida's husband	Fred McCarren
Leo, their friend	Larry Gelman

Music: Jack Elliott, Allyn Ferguson.

Executive Producer-Creator: Rob Reiner, Phil Mishkin.

Producer: Gareth Davies.

Director: Hal Cooper, James Burrows.

FREE COUNTRY—30 minutes—ABC—June 24, 1978 - July 22, 1978. 5 episodes.

GRANDPA GOES TO WASHINGTON

Comedy-Drama. Forced to retire at age sixty-six, Joe Kelley, an honest and outspoken professor of political science in California, is persuaded to run for the U.S. Senate following a political scandal. Winning the election, Kelley, now a senator, moves to Washington, D.C., where his adventures, as he tries to practice what he taught—honest government—are dramatized.

CAST

Joe Kelley	Jack Albertson
Gen. Kevin Kelley, his son	Larry Linville
Rosie Kelley, Kevin's wife	Sue Ane Langdon
Cathleen Kelley, their daughter	Michele Tobin
Kevin Kelley, Jr., their son	Sparky Marcus
Madge, Joe's secretary	Madge Sinclair
The President	Richard Eastham
Tony DuVall, Joe's friend and advisor	Tom Mason

Music: Artie Butler.

Executive Producer: Richard P. Rosetti.

Producer: Robert Stambler.

Director: Richard Crenna, Herbert Kenwith, Larry Elikann, Paul Stanley, George Tyne.

GRANDPA GOES TO WASHINGTON—60 minutes—NBC—Premiered: September 20, 1978.

THE HANNA-BARBERA HAPPY HOUR

Variety.

Hosts: Honey and Sis (two life-sized puppets).

Honey and Sis Voices: Udana Power, Wendy McKenzie.

Musical Material: Mitzie Welch, Ken Welch.

Musical Director: Billy Byers.

Executive Producer: Joseph Barbera.

Producer: Ken Welch, Joe Layton, Mitzie Welch.

Director: Jim Washburn, Joe Layton.

Puppeteers: Jerry Vogel, J. Paul Higgins, Greg Dendler.

Honey and Sis Segment Director: Bob Mackie.

THE HANNA-BARBERA HAPPY HOUR—60 minutes—NBC—April 13, 1978 - May 4, 1978. 4 programs.

THE HARVEY KORMAN SHOW

Comedy. Background: Hollywood, California. The misadventures of Harvey A. Kavanaugh, an actor with a small career, as he attempts to find work in a world that he feels is passing him by.

CAST

Harvey A. Kavanaugh	Harvey Korman
Maggie Kavanaugh, his daughter	Christine Lahti
Jake, his agent	Milton Selzer
Stuart Stafford, Maggie's boyfriend	Barry Van Dyke

Music: Peter Matz.

Executive Producer: Hal Dresner.

Producer: Don Van Atta.

Director: Alan Myerson, Jeff Bleckner.

THE HARVEY KORMAN SHOW—30 minutes—ABC—March 4, 1978 - April 18, 1978; July 15, 1978 - August 4, 1978. 6 episodes.

HEADLINERS WITH DAVID FROST

Interview. Live and taped segments are used to interview headliners.

Host: David Frost.

Regulars: Liz Smith, Kelly Garrett.

Music: Elliott Lawrence.

Executive Producer: David Frost.

Producer: John Gilroy.

Director: Bruce Gowers.

HEADLINERS WITH DAVID FROST—60 minutes—NBC—May 31, 1978 - July 5, 1978. 6 programs.

THE HEE HAW HONEYS

Comedy. The story of the Honey family, the owner-operators of a country music night club in Nashville, Tennessee (the home of the TV series "Hee Haw," of which the series is an extension and presents songs by guests).

CAST

Kenny Honey, the father	Kenny Price
Lulu Honey, his wife	Lulu Roman
Kathy Lee Honey, their daughter	Kathy Lee Johnson
Misty Honey, their daughter	Misty Rowe
Willy Billy Honey, their son	Gailard Sartain

Music: Charlie McCoy.

Executive Producer: Sam Louvello.

Producer: Barry Adelman.

Director: Bob Boatman.

THE HEE HAW HONEYS—30 minutes—Syndicated 1978.

The original concept of the series, which was dropped in favor of the above format, was to have been as follows:

The Hee Haw Honeys—The series follows the misadventures of Chrissy, Lee Anne, and Toby, three former bit-players from the "Hee Haw" TV series, struggling to achieve success as the singing trio, The Hee Haw Honeys.

Starring: Kathy Lee Johnson as Chrissy, Catherine Hickland as Toby, Muffy Durham as Lee Anne, and Kenny Price as Kenny, their mobile home driver.

Music: Charlie McCoy.

Director: Ron Kantor.

HIGH HOPES

Serial. Background: The fictional town of Cambridge. The dramatic story of Dr. Neal Chapman, a family counselor.

CAST

Dr. Neal Chapman	Bruce Gray
Jessie Chapman	Miranne McIsaac
Paula Myles	Nuala Fitzgerald
Trudy Bowen	Barbara Kyle
Walter Telford	Colin Fox
Meg Chapman	Doris Petrie
Amy Sperry	Gena Dick
Louise Bates	Jayne Eastwood
Michael Stewart, Sr.	Michael Tait
Michael Stewart, Jr.	Gordon Thompson
Georgia Morgan	Gerry Salsberg
Carol Tauss	Dorothy Malone
Victor Tauss	Nehemiah Persoff
Dr. Dan Gerard	Jan Muszynski

Music: Aeolus Productions.

Music Supervision: Teri Smith.

Executive Producer: Dick Cox.

Director: Bruce Minnix, Patrick Corbett, Barry Cranston.

HIGH HOPES—30 minutes—Syndicated 1978.

HOT CITY

Disco Music.

Host: Shadoe Stevens; David Jones.

Regulars: The Jeff Kutect Dancers.

Music Theme: Vernee White, Robert Wright, Gary Goetzman.

Executive Producer: Marc Robertson, Ed Warren.

Producer-Director: Kip Walton.

HOT CITY—60 minutes—Syndicated 1978.

HUSBANDS, WIVES, AND LOVERS

Comedy. Background: The San Fernando Valley in California. The series focuses on the hassles, foibles, and frivolities of five suburban couples, each with diverse backgrounds.

CAST

Ron Willis, a dentist	Ron Rifkin
Helene Willis, his wife	Jesse Welles
Harry Bellini, a garbage tycoon	Eddie Barth
Joy Bellini, his wife	Lynne Marie Stewart
Lennie Bellini, Harry's	

brother, the part
owner of a boutique
shop   Mark Lonow
Rita DeLatorre, Lennie's
partner; the girl
with whom he
lives   Randee Heller
Dixon Fielding, a
lawyer   Charles Siebert
Courtney Fielding, Dixon's
wife   Claudette Nevins
Murray Zuckerman, a
salesman   Stephen Pearlman
Paula Zuckerman, Murray's
wife   Cynthia Harris

Music: Jack Elliott, Allyn Ferguson.

Theme: Ken Welch, Mitzie Welch.

Executive Producer: Hal Dresner.

Producer: Don Van Atta.

Director: Marc Daniels, Alan Myerson, James Burrows.

Creator: Joan Rivers, Hal Dresner.

HUSBANDS, WIVES, AND LOVERS—60 minutes—CBS—March 10, 1978 - June 30, 1978. 9 episodes.

IN THE BEGINNING

Comedy. The story of Father Dan Cleary, an uptight, conservative priest, and Sister Agnes, a free-spirited, street-wise nun, and the bickering that ensues when the two join forces to open a mission amid the hookers, drunks, runaways, and teenage gangs in the neighborhood. Their inability to agree on issues concerning the welfare of the mission or its people is the focal point of the series.

CAST
Father Dan Cleary McLean Stevenson
Sister Agnes   Priscilla Lopez
Monsignor Frank Barlow,
Dan's superior   Jack Dodson
Sister Lillian, Agnes's
superior   Priscilla Morrill
Willie, one of the
street-wise kids
of the
mission   Olivia Barash
Jerome Rockefeller, same
as Willie   Bobby Ellerbee
Tony, same as
Willie   Cosie Costa
Bad Lincoln, same as
Willie   Michael Anthony
Frank, same as
Willie   Fred Lehne
Music: Barry DeVorzon.

Executive Producer: Mort Lachman, Norman Steinberg.

Producer: Jim Mulligan, Rita Dillon.

Director: Jack Shea, Doug Rogers, Randy Winburn.

Creator: Jack Shea, Jim Mulligan; developed by Norman Lear.

IN THE BEGINNING—30 minutes—CBS—September 20, 1978 - November 1, 1978. 6 episodes.

THE INCREDIBLE HULK

Science Fiction Adventure. Scientist Dr. David Bruce Banner and his assistant, Elaina Marks, undertake a research program in an attempt to determine how certain people can tap hidden resources of strength under stress situations. During one such experiment, Banner is exposed to an extreme overdose of gamma radiation, which causes a change in his body's DNA chemistry. Whenever he becomes angry or enraged, a startling metamorphosis takes place: the mild Banner is transformed into the green Hulk, a creature of incredible strength. During one such fit of rage, the Hulk destroy's Banner's car. Intrigued by the enormous footprints found at the scene, *National Register* reporter Jack McGee traces the creature to the lab where Banner and Elaina (who previously witnessed the transformation and has agreed to help David find a cure) are planning an experiment. While speaking with Banner outside, a leaking chemical solution triggers an explosion in the lab. McGee and Banner are thrown by its force. Banner, still conscious, becomes enraged when the flames prevent him from entering the building to help Elaina. Banner, now transformed into the Hulk, rescues Elaina, who dies shortly after. Regaining his senses, McGee sees the Hulk with Elaina and assumes that he killed her. Unable to find Banner, McGee theorizes that he perished in the flames, in a fire he mistakenly believes was caused by the Hulk.

Now, believed to be dead, Banner wanders across the country, seeking a way to control the creature and hopefully find a means by which to reverse the process. His efforts are hindered, however, by McGee, who has vowed to bring the creature to justice. (Though the creature is innocent, David can't prove it—he has little or no recollection when he transforms back to Banner—so he keeps moving until he can stop the occurences.)

CAST
Dr. David Banner   Bill Bixby
The Hulk   Lou Ferrigno
Jack McGee   Jack Colvin
Elaina Marks (pilot

episode)   Susan Sullivan
Music: Joseph Harnell.

Executive Producer: Kenneth Johnson.

Producer: James D. Parriott, Chuck Bowman, Nicholas Corea, James G. Hirsch.

Director: Alan J. Levi, Kenneth Gilbert, Larry Stewart, Sigmund Neufeld, Jr., Jeffrey Hayden, Harvey Laidman, Reza S. Badiyi, Frank Orsatti, Joseph Pevney, Ray Danton.

THE INCREDIBLE HULK—60 minutes—CBS—March 10, 1978 - June 30, 1978. 12 episodes. Returned: CBS—60 minutes—Premiered: August 11, 1978.

THE JIM NABORS SHOW

Discussion-Variety.

Host: Jim Nabors.

Regulars: Susan Ford, Ronnie Schell.

Orchestra: Fred Werner.

Executive Producer: Carol Raskin.

Producer: Ken Harris.

Director: Barry Glazer.

THE JIM NABORS SHOW—60 minutes—Syndicated 1978.

JOE AND VALERIE

Comedy. Background: Brooklyn, New York. The romantic misadventures of Joe Pizo, an apprentice plumber, and Valerie Sweetzer, a cosmetics salesgirl. The series, which is partly a takeoff of the film, *Saturday Night Fever,* has its stories centered around a disco.

CAST
Joe Pizo   Paul Regina
Valerie Sweetzer   Char Fontane
Frank Boganski, Joe's
friend   Bill Beyers
Paulie Veroni, Joe's
friend   David Elliott
Stella Sweetzer, Valerie's
mother   Pat Benson
Thelma, Valerie's
friend   Donna Ponterotto
Vincent Pizo, Joe's
father   Robert Costanzo
Music: Jack Elliott, Allyn Ferguson.

Theme Vocal: Char Fontane, Randy Winburn.

Executive Producer: Linda Hope.

Producer: Bernie Kahn.

Director: Bill Persky.

Creator: Bernie Kahn, Ronald Rubin.

Choreography: Anita Mann.

JOE AND VALERIE—30 minutes—NBC—April 24, 1978 - May 10, 1978. 4 episodes.

JULIE FARR, M.D.

Medical Drama. The story of Julie Farr, an obstetrician in a large Los Angeles hospital. Several stories, not only those dealing with pregnancy, are interwoven into each episode. Originally titled "Having Babies," the series lent itself to dealing with the joys and traumas of childbirth.

CAST

Julie Farr	Susan Sullivan
Dr. Blake Simmons	Mitchell Ryan
Kelly, Julie's receptionist	Beverly Todd
Intern Ron Daniels	Dennis Todd

Music: Lee Holdridge.

Theme Vocal: Marilyn McCoo.

Executive Producer: B. W. Sandefur, Gerald I. Isenberg.

Producer: James Heinz.

Director: Mel Damski, Edward Parone, Bob Kelljan.

Creator: Peggy Elliott, Ann Marcus.

JULIE FARR, M.D.—60 minutes—ABC—March 28, 1978 - April 18, 1978. 2 episodes. As "Having Babies"—60 minutes—ABC—March 7, 1978 - March 21, 1978. 3 episodes.

KAZ

Drama. Background: Los Angeles, California. The story of Martin "Kaz" Kazinski, an ex-con turned attorney who studied for the bar while serving a six-year prison term. Now working with a prestigious law firm, Kaz's cases are dramatized as he attempts to help people in deep trouble.

CAST

Martin Kazinski	Ron Leibman
Samuel Bennett, senior partner in the law firm	Patrick O'Neal
Mary Parnell, the owner of the Starting Gate Nightclub, above which Kaz lives	Gloria LeRoy
Malloy, the bartender	Dick O'Neill
Katie McKenna, the court reporter; Kaz's girlfriend	Linda Carlson
Peter Colcourt, Bennett's partner	Mark Withers
Mrs. Fogel, Bennett's secretary	Edith Atwater
Frank Revko, the D.A.	George Wyner

Music: Fred Karlin.

Executive Producer: Lee Rich, Marc Merson.

Producer: Peter Katz, Sam Rolfe.

Director: Russ Mayberry, Bob Kelljan, Bernard McEveety, David Moessinger.

KAZ—60 minutes—CBS—Premiered: September 24, 1978.

LIFELINE

Profile. An unusual television series that, using no actors or scripts, follows the day-to-day lives of various doctors on and off the job.

Narrator: Jackson Beck.

Music: Theo Mocero.

Executive Producer: Thomas W. Moore.

Producer: Nancy Smith, E. Fuisz, M.D.

Director: Alfred Kelman, Robert Elfstrom.

LIFELINE—60 minutes—NBC—Premiered: October 8, 1978.

THE LOVE EXPERTS

Advice. A panel of four celebrities offer advice to real people with problems of living and loving in today's world.

Host: Bill Cullen.

Regular Panelist: Geoff Edwards.

Announcer: Jack Clark.

Executive Producer: Bob Stewart.

Producer: Anne Marie Schmitt.

Director: Bruce Burmester.

THE LOVE EXPERTS—30 minutes—Syndicated 1978.

THE MADHOUSE BRIGADE

Comedy. A series of blackouts and sketches that satirize politics and culture.

Starring: J. J. Lewis, Karen Rushmore, Alexander Marshall, Frank Nastasi, Joe Piscopo, Dan Resin, Carlos Carrasco, Rocket Ryan, Nola Fairbanks.

Music: Tony Monte.

Executive Producer: Jim Larkin.

Producer: Dale Keidel, Alexander Marshall.

Director: Dale Keidel.

THE MADHOUSE BRIGADE—30 minutes—Syndicated 1978.

MARY

Variety. A comedy-accented series that spotlights the many talents of Mary Tyler Moore.

Hostess: Mary Tyler Moore.

Regulars: Dick Shawn, Judy Kahan, James Hampton, Swoosie Kurtz, Michael Keaton, David Letterman, Leonard Barr, Jack O'Leary.

Orchestra: Alf Clausen.

Executive Producer: Tom Patchett, Jay Tarses.

Director: Rob Iscove.

Choreographer: Tony Stevens.

MARY—60 minutes—CBS—September 24, 1978 - October 8, 1978. 11 episodes produced; 3 aired.

MEL AND SUSAN TOGETHER

Musical Variety.

Hosts: Mel Tillis, Susan Anton.

Music: Bob Rozario.

Executive Producers: The Osmond Brothers.

Producer: Jerry McPhie, Toby Martin.

Director: Jack Regas.

MEL AND SUSAN TOGETHER—30 minutes—ABC—April 22, 1978 - May 13, 1978. 4 tapes.

MORK AND MINDY

Comedy. Dispatched from the planet Ork to study life on primitive Earth, Mork, an alien, lands in Boulder, Colorado, where he meets and befriends Mindy McConnell, a pretty twenty-one-year-old girl who becomes taken aback by his peculiar manner. When Mork tells Mindy that he is an alien and has been assigned to study Earthlings, she agrees to help him learn our ways and keep his secret. The series focuses on Mork's attempts to adjust to and learn about life on Earth.

CAST

Mork	Robin Williams
Mindy McConnell	Pam Dawber
Frederick McConnell, Mindy's father	Conrad Janis
Cora Hudson, Mindy's grandmother	Elizabeth Kerr

Eugene, a friend
of the above
regulars   Jeffrey Jacquet
Exidor, the religious
fanatic befriended by
Mork (recurring
role)   Robert Donner
Orson, Mork's superior
on Ork   Ralph James

Music: Perry Botkin, Jr.

Executive Producer: Garry K. Marshall, Tony Marshall.

Producer: Dale McRaven, Bruce Johnson.

Director: Howard Storm, Joel Zwick.

MORK AND MINDY—30 minutes—ABC—Premiered: September 14, 1978.

THE NEW AVENGERS

Adventure. A revised and updated version of "The Avengers," which see for original storyline information. The new version, set in England, continues to depict the exploits of John Steed, a debonair British Government Agent, and his new assistants, Purdy, a beautiful and courageous woman, and the daring Mike Gambit.

CAST
John Steed   Patrick Macnee
Purdy   Joanna Lumley
Mike Gambit   Gareth Hunt

Music: Laurie Johnson.

Producer: Albert Fennell, Brian Clemens.

Director: Desmond Davis, Ernest Day, Graeme Clifford, James Hill, Don Thompson, John Hough, Sidney Hayers.

THE NEW AVENGERS—75 minutes—CBS—Premiered: September 15, 1978.

THE NEW OPERATION PETTICOAT

Comedy. A revised and updated version of "Operation Petticoat," which see for information. After most of the original crew of the *Sea Tiger* transfers due to the anxiety problems caused with being stationed on a pink submarine, the *Sea Tiger* is reassigned to duty as a sea-going ambulance and outfitted with a new crew, including three beautiful nurses. The series follows the misadventures of the crew of the *Sea Tiger* as it roams the South Pacific during the early years of W.W. II (1942).

CAST
Captain Haller   Robert Hogan
Lt. Michael
Bender   Randolph Mantooth
Lt. Dolores Crandall   Melinda Naud
Lt. Catherine O'Hara   Jo Ann Pflug
Lt. Betty Wheeler   Hilary Thompson
Chief Mechanic Stanley
Dobritch   Warren Berlinger
Yeoman Hunkle   Richard Brestoff
Lt. Travis Kern   Sam Chew, Jr.

Music: Peter Matz.

Executive Producer: Jeff Harris, Bernie Kukoff.

Producer: Michael Rhodes.

Director: Hollingsworth Morse, Gene Nelson.

THE NEW OPERATION PETTICOAT—30 minutes—ABC—September 25, 1978 - October 19, 1978. 4 episodes.

THE NEXT STEP BEYOND

Anthology. A revised and updated version of "One Step Beyond." True stories of psychic happenings.

Host-Narrator: John Newland.

Theme: Mark Snow.

Music: Ron Ramin.

Executive Producer: Collier Young.

Producer: Alan Jay Factor.

Director: John Newland.

Creator: Merwin Gerard.

THE NEXT STEP BEYOND—30 minutes—Syndicated 1978.

OPERATION: RUNAWAY

Drama. Background: Los Angeles, California. The story of David McKay, a former vice squad police officer turned private-practice psychologist, who specializes in tracking down runaways. (McKay also teaches psychology at Westwood University.)

CAST
Dr. David McKay   Robert Reed
Karen Wingate, the
dean of women at
the college   Karen Machon
Mark Johnson, David's
assistant   Michael Biehn

Music: Richard Markowitz.

Executive Producer: William Robert Yates.

Producer: Mark Rodgers.

Director: William Waird, Michael Preece, Walter Grauman.

OPERATION: RUNAWAY—60 minutes—NBC—April 27, 1978 - May 18, 1978. 4 episodes. Rebroadcasts: NBC: August 10, 1978 - August 31, 1978.

THE PAPER CHASE

Drama. Background: A prestigious Northeastern university. The series follows the joys and frustrations of first-year law students; in particular, those of James Hart, an earnest, likeable Minnesota farm boy on a paper chase (seeking a diploma that says he graduated from law school). The program focuses also on the relationship between Hart and Professor Charles Kingsfield, a brilliant contract law instructor feared for his classroom tyranny, who will either make or break him. Based on the movie of the same title.

CAST
Professor Charles
Kingsfield   John Houseman
Students:
James T. Hart   James Stephens
Franklin Ford   Tom Fitzsimmons
Elizabeth Logan   Francine Tacker
Linda O'Connor   Katherine Dunfee
Willis Bell   James Keane
Jonathan Brooks   Jonathan Segal
Thomas Anderson   Robert Ginty

Also:

Asheley Brooks, Jonathan's
wife   Deka Beaudine
Mrs. Nottingham, Kingsfield's secretary   Betty Harford
Ernie, the owner of
the tavern where
Hart works   Charles Hallahan

Music: Charles Fox, Stephen Seretan, Richard Shores, Lionel Newman.

Executive Producer: Robert C. Thompson.

Producer: Robert Lewin.

Director: Joseph Hardy, Philip Leacock, Gwen Arner, Harvey Laidman, Alex March, William Hale, Robert C. Thompson, Seymour Robbie.

THE PAPER CHASE—60 minutes—CBS—Premiered: September 19, 1978.

PEOPLE

Variety Magazine. An adaptation of *People* magazine to television: celebrity profiles and interviews.

Hostess: Phyllis George.

Music: Tony Romeo.

Executive Producer: David Susskind.

Producer: Charlotte Schiff Jones.

Segment Producers: Clay Cole, Dolores Danska, Sue Solomon.

Director: Merrill Mazuer.

PEOPLE—30 minutes—CBS—September 18, 1978 - November 6, 1978. 6 episodes.

PLEASE STAND BY

Comedy. Discontent with his job in Los Angeles, Frank Lambert, a business executive, moves to the small town of DeQueen, New Mexico with his wife Carol, and their children Susan, David, and Rocky. He is hired to run KRDA, the world's smallest television station, from the family garage. The series focuses on the problems Frank and Carol face as they attempt to run the station.

CAST
Frank Lambert	Richard Schaal
Carol Lambert	Elinor Donahue
Susan Lambert	Darian Mathias
David Lambert	Stephen M. Schwartz
Rocky Lambert	Bryan Scott
Vicki Janes, works at the station	Marcie Barkin
Crash, works at the station	Danny Mora

Music: Phil Cody.

Theme Vocal: Stephen M. Schwartz.

Executive Producer: Bob Banner.

Producer: William Bickley, Michael Warren.

Director: Howard Storm, Alan Myerson, Jim Drake.

Creator: William Bickley, Michael Warren.

PLEASE STAND BY—30 minutes—Syndicated 1978.

PROJECT U.F.O.

Science Fiction Drama. Dramatizations of incidents as seen through the investigations of USAF Major Jake Gatlin and his assistant, Sgt. Harry Fitz, of reported sightings of U.F.O.s (Unidentified Flying Objects). Based on the official records of the U.S. Air Force's Project Bluebook, the Federal Government's record of U.F.O. reports and investigations.

CAST
Major Jake Gatlin	William Jordan
Staff Sgt. Harry Fitz	Caskey Swaim
Libby, their secretary	Aldine King
Capt. Ben Ryan (replaced Gatlin)	Edward Winter

Narrator: Jack Webb.

Music: Nelson Riddle.

Executive Producer: Jack Webb.

Producer: Robert Leeds, Colonel W. Coleman, USAF, ret., Gene Levitt, Robert Blees.

Director: Richard Quine, Robert Leeds, Dennis Donnelly, Sigmund Neufeld, Jr., John Patterson.

PROJECT U.F.O.—60 minutes—NBC—Premiered: February 19, 1978.

QUARK

Science Fiction Comedy. Era: 2226 A.D. The voyages of an interplanetary garbage scow whose mission, on behalf of the U.G.S.P. (United Galaxy Sanitation Patrol) is to clean up the Milky Way.

CAST
Captain Adam Quark	Richard Benjamin
Betty I, the co-pilot	Tricia Barnstable
Betty II, her clone, the co-pilot	Cyb Barnstable
Ficus, the Vegeton, a plant, the emotionless science officer	Richard Kelton
Gene/Jean, the transmute, the chief engineer	Tim Thomerson
Andy, the cowardly robot	Bobby Porter
The Head, the head of U.G.S.P.	Allan Caillou
Otto Palindrome, the chief architect of Space Station Perma One, the base for U.G.S.P.	Conrad Janis

Music: Perry Botkin, Jr.

Executive Producer: David Gerber.

Producer: Bruce Johnson.

Director: Hy Averback, Bruce Bilson, Peter H. Hunt.

Creator: Buck Henry.

QUARK—30 minutes—NBC—February 24, 1978 - April 14, 1978. 8 episodes.

THE RETURN OF CAPTAIN NEMO

Adventure. During routine war games, Tom Franklin and Jim Porter, U.S. Naval underwater intelligence agents, find trapped in a coral reef beneath the sea the fabled submarine *Nautilus*. Upon boarding the ship, they meet its captain, Nemo, and learn what has happened. On March 16, 1877, while searching for Atlantis, the *Nautilus* wedged itself under a coral reef and stuck. After dispensing the crew, Nemo, in the hope that one day help would come, suspended himself in a crystalline cylinder, from which, due to the depth charges, he has emerged. The constant barrage also sets the *Nautilus* free and brings Nemo in contact with Miller, the Naval Intelligence head, who agrees to repair the damaged sub in return for Nemo's help in performing certain hazardous missions for the government. The series depicts Nemo's adventures as he aids the U.S. Government while seeking the fabled Lost Continent of Atlantis. Based on the story by Jules Verne.

CAST
Captain Nemo	Jose Ferrer
Cmdr. Tom Franklin	Tom Hallick
Lt. Jim Porter	Burr DeBenning
Dr. Kate Melton, Nemo's aide	Lynda Day George
Prof. Waldo Cunningham, the evil, modern-day scientist; Nemo's nemesis	Burgess Meredith
Mr. Miller	Warren Stevens

Music: Richard La Salle.

Producer: Irwin Allen.

Director: Alex March.

THE RETURN OF CAPTAIN NEMO—60 minutes—CBS—March 8, 1978 - May 5, 1978. 3 episodes.

RICHIE BROCKELMAN, PRIVATE EYE

Crime Drama. Background: Los Angeles, California. The story of Richie Brockelman, a twenty-three-year-old young man who, despite scrapes with the law, is determined to make his way as a private detective.

CAST
Richie Brockelman	Dennis Dugan
Sharon, his secretary	Barbara Bosson
Sgt. Coopersmith	Robert Hogan
Richie's father	John Randolph

Music: Mike Post and Pete Carpenter.

Executive Producer: Stephen J. Cannell, Steve Bochco.

Supervising Producer: Alex Beaton.

Producer: Peter S. Fischer.

Director: Arnold Laven.

RICHIE BROCKELMAN, PRIVATE EYE—60 minutes—NBC—March 17, 1978 - April 14, 1978. 5 episodes.

THE ROLLERGIRLS

Comedy. Background: Pittsburgh, Pennsylvania. The on-and-off-the-rink antics of the Pittsburgh Pitts, a five woman roller-derby team.

CAST

Don Mitchell, the team owner	Terry Kiser

The Pittsburgh Pitts:

Mongo Sue Lampert	Rhonda Bates
Books Cassidy	Joanna Cassidy
Honeybee Novak	Marcy Hanson
Shana "Pipeline" Akira	Marilyn Tokuda
J. B. Johnson	Candy Ann Brown

Also:

Howard Divine, the rink announcer	James Murtaugh

Music: Tony Asher, John Bahler, Kevin Clark.

Theme Vocal: Shari Saba.

Executive Producer: James Komack, Stan Cutler, George Tricker.

Producer: Tom Cherones.

Director: Burt Brinckerhoff, James Komack, Gary Shimokawa.

Creator: James Komack.

THE ROLLERGIRLS—30 minutes—NBC—April 24, 1978 - May 10, 1978. 4 episodes.

SAM

Crime Drama. Background: Los Angeles, California. The series follows the cases of Officer Mike Breen and his partner, Sam, a yellow Labrador retriever specially trained for police work.

CAST

Officer Mike Breen	Mark Harmon
Captain Tom Clagett	Len Wayland

Music: Billy May.

Executive Producer: Jack Webb.

Producer: Leonard B. Kaufman.

Director: Robert Leeds, Richard Moder, John Florea, Robert Wynn.

Creator: Jack Webb, Dan Noble.

SAM—30 minutes—CBS—March 14, 1978 - April 18, 1978. 6 episodes.

SWORD OF JUSTICE

Adventure. Jack Cole, a wealthy playboy, is framed and imprisoned for a crime he did not commit (embezzling two and a half million dollars from his father's company). Bitter for the wrong done to him, Cole vows to get even with the crooks who framed him. He begins by learning the tricks of the criminal's trade from his fellow prisoners. Released from prison two years short of his five year sentence for good behavior, Cole teams with his cellmate, Hector Ramirez, and together they reveal the people responsible for the frame. Instilled with a goal to seek justice, Cole continues in his dual capacity—a New York playboy by day and an anonymous crime fighter by night, helping the federal authorities get the goods on white-collar thieves.

CAST

Jack Cole	Dack Rambo
Hector Ramierz	Bert Rosario
Arthur Woods, the federal agent Cole helps	Alex Courtney

Music: John Andrew Tartaglia.

Executive Producer: Glen A. Larson.

Supervising Producer: Michael Sloan.

Producer: Joe Boston, Herman Groves.

SWORD OF JUSTICE—60 minutes—NBC—Premiered: October 7, 1978.

TAXI

Comedy. Background: New York City. The series focuses on the trials and tribulations of the drivers and garage crew of the Sunshine Cab Company.

CAST

Alex Reiger, a cabbie	Judd Hirsch
Elaine Nardo, a cabbie	Marilu Henner
Bobby Wheeler, a cabbie	Jeff Conaway
Tony Banta, a cabbie	Tony Danza
Louie DePalmer, the nasty dispatcher	Danny DeVito
Latka Gravas, the mechanic	Andy Kaufman
John Burns, a cabbie	Randall Carver

Music: Bob James.

Executive Producer-Creator: James L. Brooks, Stan Daniels, Ed Weinberger, David Davis.

Producer: Glen Charles, Les Charles.

Director: James Burrows.

TAXI—30 minutes—ABC—Premiered: September 12, 1978.

THE TED KNIGHT SHOW

Comedy. Background: New York City. The misadventures of Roger Dennis, the owner of the Mr. Dennis Escort Service.

CAST

Roger Dennis	Ted Knight
Dottie, his obnoxious secretary	Iris Adrian
Bert Dennis, his brother	Norman Burton
Winston Dennis, Roger's son	Thomas Leopold

The Escort Service Girls:

Graziella	Cissy Colpitts
Honey	Fawne Harriman
Irma	Ellen Regan
Cheryl	Janice Kent
Phil	Tanya Boyd
Joy	Debbie Harmon

Music: Michael Leonard.

Executive Producer: Mark Rothman, Lowell Ganz.

Producer: Martin Cohan.

Director: Joel Zwick, Howard Storm, Martin Cohan.

THE TED KNIGHT SHOW—30 minutes—CBS—April 8, 1978 - May 13, 1978.

TWIGGY'S JUKE BOX

Music. Performances by Rock musicians.

Hostess: Twiggy (the model turned singer).

Music: Recorded and/or provided by guests.

Executive Producer: Malcolm Gold.

Producer-Director: Mike Mansfield.

TWIGGY'S JUKE BOX—30 minutes—Syndicated 1978.

VEGA$

Crime Drama. Background: Las Vegas,

Nevada. The cases of Dan Tana, a macho private detective with an eye for finding and helping beautiful women in trouble.

CAST

Dan Tana	Robert Urich
Angie, his secretary	Judy Landers
Beatrice, a showgirl, Dan's friend	Phyllis Elizabeth Davis
Binzer, Dan's inept legman	Bart Braverman
Philip "Slick" Roth, the casino owner	Tony Curtis
Sgt. Bella Archer, the policewoman who supplies Dan with info	Naomi Stevens
Eli Two Leaf, an Indian, Dan's legman	Will Sampson
Beverly, work's in Roth's casino	Barbara McNair

Music: Dominic Frontiere.

Executive Producer: Aaron Spelling, Douglas S. Cramer.

Supervising Producer: E. Duke Vincent.

Producer: Alan Godfrey.

Director: Harry Falk, Sutton Roley, Bernard McEveety, Don Chaffey, Marc Daniels, Lawrence Doheny, Lawrence Dobkin, Paul Stanley.

Creator: Michael Mann.

VEGA$—60 minutes— ABC—Premiered: September 20, 1978.

THE WAVERLY WONDERS

Comedy. The series concerns itself with the misadventures of Joe Casey, a washed-up professional basketball player who now coaches basketball, as well as teaching history, at Waverly High School.

CAST

Joe Casey (originally Harry Casey)	Joe Namath
Linda Harris, the principal	Gwynne Gilford
George Benton, a teacher	Ben Piazza

Students comprising the Waverly Wonders Basketball Team:

Connie Rafkin	Kim Lankford
Tony Faguzzi	Joshua Grentock
Hasty	Tierre Turner
John Pate	Charles Bloom

Music: Fred Karlin.

Executive Producer: Lee Rich, Marc Merson.

Producer: Bruce Kane, Steve Zacharias.

Director: Bill Persky, Dick Martin.

THE WAVERLY WONDERS—30 minutes—NBC—September 22, 1978 - October 6, 1978. 4 episodes.

W.E.B.

Drama. Background: New York City. A behind-the-scenes look at the world of television as seen through the experiences of Ellen Cunningham, an up-and-coming programming executive with the Trans-Atlantic Broadcasting Company (TAB).

CAST

Ellen Cunningham	Pamela Bellwood
Jack Kiley, the programming chief	Alex Cord
Dan Costello, the sales executive	Andrew Prine
Gus Dunlap, the news director	Richard Basehart
Walter Matthews, the director of operations	Howard Witt
Harvey Pearlstein, the head of research	Lee Wilkof
Harry Brooks, the board chairman	Stephen McNally
Christine Nichols, Ellen's secretary	Tish Raye
Kevin, Ellen's assistant	Peter Coffield

Music: Jerry Fielding, David Rose, Morton Stevens.

Music Supervision: Lionel Newman.

Executive Producer: Lin Bolen.

Producer: Christopher Morgan.

Director: Harvey Hart, Alex March.

Creator: David Karp.

W.E.B.—60 minutes—NBC—September 13, 1978 - October 5, 1978. 5 episodes.

THE WHITE SHADOW

Drama. Background: Carver High School in Los Angeles, California. The story of Ken Reeves, a former pro-basketball player (washed up when he injured his knee) turned coach for a losing and unruly ghetto high school basketball team. (The title is derived from Reeves remark after his team's first win—he'll be behind them like a White Shadow.)

CAST

Ken Reeves	Ken Howard
Jim Willis, the principal	Jason Bernard
Sybil Buchanan, the vice principal	Joan Pringle
Katie, Ken's sister	Robin Rose
Bill, Katie's husband	Jerry Fogel

Music: Mike Post, Pete Carpenter.

Executive Producer: Bruce Paltrow.

Producer: Mark C. Tinker.

THE WHITE SHADOW—60 minutes—CBS—Premiered: November 27, 1978.

WHO'S WATCHING THE KIDS?

Comedy. Background: Las Vegas, Nevada. The story focuses on the misadventures of Stacy Turner and Angie Vitola, two luscious showgirls at the seedy Club Sand Pile. The girls share an apartment with Frankie, Angie's mischievous sixteen-year-old brother, and Melissa, Stacy's know-it-all nine-year-old sister. The series title is derived from the problem the girls have: who can watch their kids when they're working? Their solution: Larry Parnell, a KVGS TV Newscaster, and Burt Gunkel, his cameraman, neighbors who, to impress Angie and Stacy, babysit when they are able.

CAST

Stacy Turner	Caren Kaye
Angie Vitola	Lynda Goodfriend
Frankie Vitola	Scott Baio
Melissa Turner	Tammy Lauren
Larry Parnell	Larry Breeding
Burt Gunkel	James Belushi
Mitzi Logan, the apartment-house manager	Marcia Lewis
Memphis, a showgirl	Lorrie Mahaffey
Cochise, a showgirl	Shirley Kirkes
Bridget, a showgirl	Elaine Bolton

Music: Charles Bernstein.

Executive Producer: Garry Marshall, Tony Marshall, Don Silverman.

Producer: Martin Nadler, Gary Menteer.

Director: John Thomas Lenox, Ray DeVally, Jr., David Ketchum.

WHO'S WATCHING THE KIDS?—30 minutes—NBC—Premiered: September 22, 1978.

WKRP IN CINCINATTI

Comedy. The series focuses on the antics of the management and staff of WKRP, a 50,000 watt, hard-rock format radio station in Cincinatti, Ohio.

CAST

Andy Travis, the program

director   Gary Sandy
Arthur Carlson, the
    station manager   Gordon Jump
Jennifer Marlowe, Carlson's
    secretary   Loni Anderson
Herb Tarlek, the
    sales manager   Frank Bonner
Johnny Caravella, the
    d.j. who works
    as Dr. Johnny
    Fever   Howard Hessemen
Bailey Quarters, Andy's
    assistant   Jan Smithers
Les Nesman, the news
    director   Richard Sanders
Venus Flytrap, the
    night man   Tim Reid

Music: Tom Wells.

Producer: Hugh Wilson.

Director: Jay Sandrich, Michael Zinberg, Asaad Keleda.

WKRP IN CINCINATTI—30 minutes—CBS—September 17, 1978 - November 6, 1978. 13 episodes produced; 8 aired.

THE YOUNG PIONEERS

Western Drama. Background: The Dakota Territory during the 1870s. The series follows the enduring hardships of Molly and David Beaton, young newlyweds struggling to establish a life for themselves on the hostile frontier.

CAST

Molly Beaton   Linda Purl
David Beaton   Roger Kern
Dan Gray, their
    neighbor   Robert Hays
Mr. Peters, their
    neighbor, a
    widower   Robert Donner
Nettie Peters, his
    daughter   Shelly Juttner
                        Mare Winningham
Flora Peters, his
    daughter   Michelle Stacy
Charlie Peters, his
    son   Jeff Cotler

Narrator: Linda Purl.

Music: Dominic Frontiere.

Executive Producer: Earl Hamner, Lee Rich.

Producer: Robert L. Jacks.

Director: Harry Harris, Alf Kjellin, Irving J. Moore.

THE YOUNG PIONEERS—60 minutes—ABC—April 2, 1978 - April 16, 1978. 3 episodes. Pilot aired January 9, 1977 and January 16, 1977 (a 2-part story).

Index